Norwood Ravenswood

Giving People a Chance in Life

C000176858

Norwood Ravenswood is Europe's largest Jewish family services charity, working with over 6,000 children, young people and adults, people of all ages with learning disabilities and their families every year.

...at the heart of

We aim to offer one stop, easily accessible and high quality services. Many of our services are entirely reliant on charitable donations.

the community

- Social Work and Counselling
- Residential homes in the community
- Ravenswood Village
- Binoh - special education needs
- Fostering and Adoption
- Respite Care
- Day Services
- Family Centres
- Vocational Training
- Family Information Link
- Unity - integrated youth club for children
- Links - recreation for adults with learning disabilities
- Association for Jewish Youth
- Annie Lawson School

For more information please contact

Norwood Ravenswood
80-82 The Broadway, Stanmore HA74HB
Phone 0181 954 4555
norwoodravenswood@nwrw.org
www.nwrw.org

Norwood Ravenswood is a company limited by guarantee registered in England under the number 3263519. Reg.Charity.No. 1059050

THE JEWISH YEAR BOOK
2000

Yehudi Menuhin, 1916–1999
(*by courtesy of Sym Music Company Limited;
photographer Klaus Schmidt*)

The Jewish Year Book

Published in association with
the Jewish Chronicle, London

Founded 1896

2000
5760–5761

Edited by
STEPHEN W. MASSIL

VALLENTINE MITCHELL
LONDON • PORTLAND, OR

Published in 2000 in Great Britain by
VALLENTINE MITCHELL
Newbury House, 900 Eastern Avenue,
London IG2 7HH

and in the United States of America by
VALLENTINE MITCHELL
c/o ISBS, 5804 N.E. Hassalo Street,
Portland, Oregon, 97213-3644

Website: www.vmbooks.com

ISBN 0 85303 381 1
ISSN 0075 3769

Printed in Great Britain by
Bookcraft (Bath) Ltd., Midsomer Norton, Somerset

Contents

Preface   [7]
    In Memoriam: Lord Jakobovits; David Kessler
Essays
    Scottish Jewry   *John A. Cosgrove*   [12]
    The Jews in Wales   *Hal Weitzman and*
                                                             David Weitzman   [24]
    Christian–Jewish Relations   *Jonathan Gorsky*   [32]
    Education and the Future of Anglo-Jewry   *Robin and*
                                                             Nitza Spiro   [42]
    Anglo-Jewish Attitudes and Minhag
      Anglia   *William Frankel*   [45]
    The Shoah   *Simone Veil*   [51]
    Sir John Foster and the Jews   *Miriam Rothschild*   [56]
    Reflections   *Lotte Kramer*   [69]
    Four Positions in Anglo-Jewry   *Louis Jacobs*   [76]
    Yehudi Menuhin, 1916–1999: An
      Appreciation   *Alexander Goehr*   [82]
Abbreviations Used   [88]
Anglo-Jewish Institutions
    Representative Organisations   1
    Jewish Press, Radio and Information Services   5
    Religious Organisations   7
    Welfare Organisations   14
    Refugee Organisations   17
    Organisations Concerned with
      the Jews of Eastern Europe   19
    Zionist Organisations   20
    Other Organisations Concerned with Israel   24
    Educational and Cultural Organisations   35
    University Centres and Organisations   42
    Organisations Concerned with Jewish Youth   46
    Libraries, Museums and Exhibitions   54
    Professional Organisations   60
    Miscellaneous Organisations   61
International Organisations   66
Local Organisations
    London
      Synagogues   76
      Religious Organisations   88

Memorials, Cemeteries 89
Educational Organisations 90
Welfare Organisations 94
Clubs and Cultural Societies 98
Miscellaneous Organisations 101
The Regions
England 103
Wales 131
Scotland 132
Northern Ireland 135
Isle of Man 135
Channel Islands 135
Ireland 135
Other Countries 137
Jewish Statistics 194
Historical Note on British Jewry 200
United Kingdom Legislation Concerning Jews 203
Listed Synagogues and Other Jewish Sites in the UK 207
Privy Counsellors, Peers, MPs, etc. 209
Who's Who 213
Obituaries 1998–1999 313
Events of 1999 315
Publications of 1998–1999 and Booksellers 317
Principal Festivals and Fasts 324
The Jewish Calendar 325
The Jewish Year 326
Abridged Calendar for 2000 327
Abridged Calendar for 2001 328
Hebrew and English Calendar 329
Evening and Twilight Variations for Regions 343
Sidrot and Haftarot for 2001 344
Marriage Regulations 346
Jewish Calendar for 30 years 348
Index 362

Preface

General Elections were held in Israel in May 1999 which meant that the 14th Knesset had lasted for only three years. While the balance of power shifted to the benefit of the smaller parties and both the Labour Alliance and Likud lost significant numbers of seats, Ehud Barak in winning a substantial personal majority brought in a Labour-led government with prospects of reviving and promoting the peace process which had languished during Mr Netanyahu's administration. The death of King Hussein early in the year was the occasion for reflection on the state of the Middle East, where the will for peace is clearly holding ground despite the occasions for fighting in Lebanon and the predictable spate of bombs accompanying the renewed steps towards peace-making between Israel and the Palestinians, for which talks are even now under way. *Détente* with Syria, wished for and faltering, remains in the balance. Mr Barak has paid visits to Washington and London establishing his credentials and making contacts, followed up at Foreign Office level with positive diplomatic prospects. More than ever over the coming twelve months Israel will be the focus of world attention with the Christian millennial celebrations, which may yet bring the Pope to Jerusalem.

At home, the opening of the devolved Parliament in Edinburgh saw the Jewish community formally represented in the proceedings despite the fact that there were no Jewish candidates in the elections, and the community has established its new Council of Scottish Communities to ensure a voice in devolved affairs where the Board of Deputies no longer has a place. The Conservative electoral revival saw David Sumberg displace Eddie Newman as the sole Jewish MEP in Britain. The vote in favour of the monarchy in the Australian referendum on establishing a Republic defers for a time a review of a critical question of Australian-Jewish identity.

There were communal thanks and relief (and some element of apprehension) that Jewish targets were not included under the bombing campaign that hit Brixton, Brick Lane and Soho in the summer. The proposals to institute a Holocaust Memorial Day (on the Auschwitz anniversary), the War-Crime Trial of Sowaniuk (when the jury went off to Belarus to view the scenes of the crime), proposals for the Manchester Holocaust Museum and approval of designs by Liebeskind for this, and the imminent opening of the Holocaust Exhibit at the Imperial War Museum along with the country-wide circulation of the Anne Frank exhibition have ensured steady attention to holocaust memory throughout the year. That the film *Life is Beautiful* won an Oscar is also significant. All these deepen the sense of historical resonance which came through vividly when the Kosova Appeal was raised in April and Jewish support proved immediate and substantial. Tributes on the deaths of a galaxy of gentiles instrumental in rescue operations of 60 and more years ago – Lesley Marber, Veronica Gillespie, Lieutenant-Colonel Tony Simonds, Pierre-Marcel Wiltzer, Elinor Singer, Yvonne Kapp and others here and in France – do not go unnoticed in this context and Frank Foley was honoured at Yad Vashem.

The question of women's roles in formal and ceremonial Judaism continued to make the news with headlines in Masorti circles and at Belsize Square. The stepping up of action on behalf of the Agunot – there was, for instance, a fast on International Women's Day – and interventions by personalities such as Rabbi Moshe Morgenstern have ensured that pressure on the rabbinate to resolve the condition of the agunah will be sustained.

The United Synagogue did not evade the limelight in a year when its elections for a President to succeed Elkan Levy were postponed. It resolved its case against the former Dayan Caplin over the theft of books from the Beth Din Library but compounded that dereliction by selling manuscripts and books at Christie's in June. The Christie's sale of Anglo-Judaica is becoming an annual event. While Christie's are to be thanked for the production of a handsome catalogue of the collection, this catalogue constitutes a tombstone of Anglo-Jewry; Rabbi Rabinowicz in an article in the *TLS* called the sale a Hillul HaShem and it certainly looks like a sacrifice to Esau in terms of the Midrash. That the sale yielded over £2.5 million is impressive but that sum divided among the 63 synagogues will not stretch very far, and the contempt for scholarship will surely redound over the years. In December there is to be a further sale of silver.

The authorities at the Spanish and Portuguese Synagogue also made attempts to disencumber themselves from responsibilities at the Montefiore sites at Ramsgate, where plans for development of the neighbourhood of the synagogue and tomb of the Montefiores have brought obloquy and considerable public attention. Local pressure groups have formed and perhaps bringing the question to open attention will serve to achieve a better resolution. The 'silly season' topic of the reburial of Sir Moses in Jerusalem had another airing but also a proper, firm repudiation from the authorities. The closure of the Adelaide Road Synagogue in Dublin when, after a notable service of deconsecration, the building was demolished without ado made another dismal story.

I dwell on these things because of my article last year which concerned the fate of our books, heritage and institutions such as Jews' College and the continuity these represent. In this respect, there has also been good news this year: the proper disposition of the Harry S. Ward Zangwill Collection at Southampton and the Tuck Silver of the Jewish Historical Society at the Jewish Museum, following due professional and communal requirements; the promise of cultural developments for housing the Ben Uri Collection gradually coming to fruition; the highlighting of several years of patient work at the London Metropolitan Archives bringing the deposit of London-based communal records into proper focus; the steady work of the Survey of the Jewish Built Heritage which we encapsulate on pages 207–8. The publication of books on David Rodinsky coincides with the renewed profile of the Heritage Centre at Princelet Street under the guidance of its new secretary. The London School of Jewish Studies has secured a new platform for itself within the University of London in its formal association with the School of Oriental and African Studies. It held its degree ceremony at the University of London Senate House for the first time. The Joe Loss Lectureship transferred from City University to SOAS along with the Rosencweig Library.

Of the events that I like to note as being indicative of the standing of Anglo-Jewry, I would cite this year the attendance of the Chief Rabbi at the funeral of Cardinal Hume and the establishment of an Associate Presidency for the Reform community at the Council of Christians and Jews. Stefan Reif gave his inaugural lecture this afternoon. The formal naming of the Parkes Building at the University of Southampton also entrenches our bastions. The Board of Deputies debated and approved the proposed inclusion of a 'religious question' in the forthcoming census questionnary of 2001. The public debate was strenuous and taxing but the outcome ensures communal standing at a critical juncture in our demography.

I would also like to record the success of one of last year's efforts by the Jewish Music Heritage Trust (newly renamed the Jewish Music Institute) whose marathon shofar exercise on the South Bank last November must have had some resonance at the National Theatre where, probably for the first time other than as a prop, a shofar featured among the instruments deployed at a theatre production (in *Troilus and Cressida* no less).

C.P. Taylor's modern classic *Good* received a new production at the Donmar and there was a Yiddish Queen Lear in Hampstead; Arthur Miller's *Broken Glass* is currently on tour as I write; the L'Khaim Company performed Sholem Asch's *God of Vengeance* at the Hackney Empire. Gersher Theatre performed Isaak Babel's Odessa stories in Ivrit at the Barbican and Isaac Bashevis Singer's *Demons and Dybbuks* had another tour this year. Henry Goodman appeared as Shylock at the Cottesloe while at the Almeida a production of *The Jew of Malta* exhibited the cartoon quality of the rival playwright's less-performed classic. A Greek actress performed as Rose in Martin Sherman's new play of that title. A revised version of the ill-famed *Perdition* was finally performed under protest.

Paintings and drawings from Israel by Avigdor Arikha were exhibited in Edinburgh; in Oxford the Pasternak Trust opened its doors to the public on a regular basis; while at the Ashmolean portraits by Leonid Pasternak went on show to coincide with the publication of a *catalogue raisonné* of his Russian works. Poussain's 'Destruction of the Temple of Jerusalem' was acquired by the Israel Museum through grants in memory of Sir Isaiah

Berlin, whose first juvenile and valedictory final essays have been published together by Granta on the anniversary of his death. The winter exhibition at the Jewish Museum is devoted to Israel Zangwill, 'the Jewish Dickens', and the Wanderers of Kilburn, a *fin de siècle* reflection of the era 100 years ago whose leading figures – Bentwich, Myers, Wolf, Schechter, Solomon, and Zangwill himself, along with Joseph Jacobs, first editor of this Year Book – shaped our modern heritage. Forthcoming for 2000 is an exhibition on the Jews of Devon and Cornwall organised by the Hidden Legacy Foundation.

Books of note this year include: a biography of Frank Foley and the story of the Lost Jews of Cornwall, intended to dispel some myths and wishful thinking; Hyam Maccoby's *Ritual and Morality*, Israel Finestein's *Anglo-Jewry in Changing Times*, Louis Jacobs' *Beyond Reasonable Doubt*. Dalya Bilu won the Jewish Book Week prize for her translation of A.B. Yehoshua's *Open Heart*. The seventieth anniversary of Habonim is memorialised in a new publication and the long-awaited history of the Jews of Zambia has also come out. The *Jewish Quarterly* has incorporated *Jewish Book News & Reviews* in its pages. Kathleen Nott, author of *Mile End* (1938), has died.

The death of Yehudi Menuhin in full harness on a concert tour in Berlin (he had agreed to write one of my essays for the century only a few weeks beforehand) was perhaps the most poignant of the year. Widespread mourning for Lord Jakobovits solemnises these remarks as we go to press and crystallises a momentary harmony across the community; the *Jewish Chronicle* published a posthumous memorial by Chaim Bermant, his biographer, on the occasion. He was buried in Jerusalem. Other deaths of note have included a team of cartoonists: Harry Blacker, Ralph Sallon and Saul Steinberg. Leicester community lost two noted leaders, Neville Felstein and Monty Henig. George Black, custodian of Merthyr cemetery, died; also Joan Lipson, Trades Union leader; and architects Elizabeth Benjamin, Walter Bor and Otto Koenigsberger; in Israel, Yosef Burg and former Ambassador Gideon Rafael; in Germany, Ignatz Bubis on whom lay great hopes for European Jewry; Guido Pontecorvo, doyen of the Jewish members of the Royal Society, Professor David Daube, Geoffrey Wigoder, Lord Beloff and Monty Dobkin of the veterans, and David Englander of a much younger generation among the historians; the death of the revered Eli Cashdan came late last year.

Recent announcements have included the departures of Professors Geoffrey Alderman and David-Hillel Ruben to serve American universities, and along with the election of Peter Sheldon as the new President of the United Synagogue, Jewish Care, the UJIA and the Jewish Literary Trust have announced new chairmen and directors.

It would appear that none of the Jewish hereditary peers has secured a foothold in the interim arrangements for the reformed House of Lords but

Alex Carlile returns to Parliament in the recent creations of political Life Peers. Mrs Ruth Dreifuss took up office as President of Switzerland, the first woman and first Jewish incumbent. Zvi Gabay was succeeded by Mark Sofer as Israel's Ambassador to Ireland.

The Essays this year form two groups and an appendix. The first covers topical issues and I am grateful to John Cosgrove, the Weitzmans, father and son, and Jonathan Gorsky for their efforts. The second attempts a record of significant aspects of the century now drawing to its close, the voices of veterans selecting their own themes. My invitations were widely distributed so the mosaic is fortuitous but carries its own momentum. Lord Menuhin died at the outset so I am grateful to Professor Goehr for his memoir and to the Menuhin family and Agents for the use of a photograph. These mark the closing year of the century. The contribution by Robin and Nitza Spiro will form the preamble to my scheme for the 2001 volume, in which I hope to focus contributors on the theme of Anglo-Jewry and Jewish education for the new century as the significant issue of the immediate future. Also in 2001 will fall the tercentenary of Bevis Marks and I shall be taking the opportunity to highlight this event.

As well as thanks to the contributors of essays, I am pleased to record extensive assistance from the large number of people who make regular contributions to the updating of this volume. This year I record particular thanks for advice and information to Professor Edward Ullendorff, Lt.-Colonel Mordaunt Cohen of the Communal Enquiry Desk whose knowledge of the changing fabric of our organisations I always seek to emulate, Marion Cohen, Barry Hyman and Michael Burman, and, as ever, John Fischer who has charge of the calendar. As correspondents to the *Jewish Chronicle* have been keen to point out, 5760, which takes Pesach and the High Holydays to almost their very latest dates by the common calendar, apparently ushers in an extreme conjunction which will not fall again until the twenty-second century.

Cambridge & London   SWM
11.11.1999, 2 Kislev 5760

Postscript
The death of David Kessler at the age of 93 marks a division in the history of *The Jewish Year Book*, of the publisher Vallentine Mitchell, and of the Anglo-Jewish press in the twentieth century. I take the opportunity of a last-minute insertion to add the following tribute to the record, for it would be inappropriate to hold it over until the next edition, as also the brief obituary of Lord Jakobovits, whose place in the record of this century is assured.

30 November/21 Kislev   SWM

IN MEMORIAM

LORD JAKOBOVITS, Baron of Regent's Park,
8 February 1921–31 October 1999

Ha-Rav Lord Jakobovits proved a distinguished Chief Rabbi
and religious leader, and a remarkable public personality,
staunchly orthodox and independent in practice and public
life. His public pronouncements, like those of Hugo Gryn,
kept him in the forefront over many years and he endured considerable
public opprobrium for his stance on some aspects of Israeli affairs. Born in
Königsberg, the son of a Rabbi, and educated at the Adath, he came to
England under duress of the Nazi threat, where he completed his
education at Jews' College and Etz Chaim Yeshivah. He had hoped to
study the sciences and his London PhD was a thesis on medical ethics
(subsequently published by Bloch, 1969), but he entered the rabbinate in
1941 as a very young recruit, serving at Brondesbury Park and then New
Cross. He became rabbi to the remnant of the Great Synagogue at Aldgate
and then Chief Rabbi of Ireland in 1948, where he stayed for ten years. In
1958 he went to New York to inaugurate the Fifth Avenue Synagogue.

He returned again to London as Chief Rabbi in 1966, as successor to
Israel Brodie, when the position was fraught. His installation preceded the
Six Day War by a couple of months and that he was able at the critical
moment to voice communal concern at the public meeting held at the
Albert Hall secured his authority and sense of the moment. 'He showed
himself to be not quite as rigid as some feared, not as amenable as some
hoped, and far more dynamic than anyone could have imagined' is how
Chaim Bermant characterised his incumbency. That he was knighted
during his term of office and subsequently also ennobled is the mark of
public esteem and a domination of the religious sphere which was
recognised by the governments of the day. In the Lords he spoke on
medical ethics and also in the war-crimes debates.

He published on halakhah, medical ethics, zionism and modern
dilemmas, and was honoured in a volume (*Tradition and Transition*, Jews'
College, 1986), edited by Jonathan Sacks, on his twentieth anniversary as
Chief Rabbi. He lectured to the Jewish Historical Society. He had Chaim
Bermant as his biographer (*Lord Jakobovits*, Weidenfeld & Nicolson, 1990)
and the *Jewish Chronicle* published Bermant's last unpublished essay in
appreciation among the general obituaries. The general public response to
his death shows how completely he gained the hearts of the community, for
all his outspoken opinions on modern affairs and the conduct of Israeli
politics. He endeared himself as a pastoral rabbi in Ireland and New York;
he was scholarly, well-loved and of imposing presence. He was a complete
man of the diaspora and is buried in Jerusalem.

DAVID FRANCIS KESSLER, OBE,
6 June 1906–24 November 1999

The life of David Kessler spans almost a century. He was born in South Africa, educated in England and, as a businessman, was active in Paris, Aden and Palestine, acquiring skills in management, deployed later in his capacity as publisher and proprietor to monumental effect. His father, a mining engineer, acquired an interest in the *Jewish Chronicle* in 1907 and the paper, having survived its Victorian beginnings and through the editorships of Asher Myers and Leopold Greenberg, had kept abreast of the intellectual thrust of the fully burgeoning community of the emancipation years, facing the project of anglicisation of the immigrant generations, the nurturing of Zionism and the travail of the First World War under the Kessler family management.

David Kessler came into the newspaper in 1936 and over an unparalleled span (interrupted only by war service in the Royal Artillery, and in Iraq and Greece as the war ended) he secured the financial strength of the paper and its independence. Geoffrey Paul has written of his strategy for the management of the *JC* and the full account is given in David Cesarani's history of the newspaper (Cambridge University Press, 1994). He was the great exponent of proprietorial relations; he offered a clear vision for a 'proud, tolerant, outward-looking and adventuresome' enterprise as the *JC* in its recent editorial rousingly identified. He secured the *JC* as an institution, giving it an identity independent of narrow party interest.

Publishing is one of Anglo-Jewry's fields of success. David Kessler as founder of Vallentine Mitchell was one of the community's greatest benefactors and *The Jewish Year Book*, which marked its own centenary recently, and the *Jewish Travel Guide*, which was one of his initiatives, are only peaks of his encouragement and support over countless ventures and many years. He managed Vallentine Mitchell until his retirement in 1971, when the company was acquired by Frank Cass, who continues to publish in the tradition established by David Kessler.

Geoffrey Paul has called him the 'Squire of Furnival Street'. The accolade links his city life with that of the country, in particular the Buckinghamshire countryside, where he had his home in the purlieus of Hughenden and Rothschild territory in the vale of Aylesbury; it is also suggestive of an assuredly unquixotic series of involvements in public-spirited interests (within and outside the Jewish community) which reflect the character of the man. He failed in the battle to secure the retention of the Wiener Archives in London; he was active on behalf of the Falasha of Ethiopia and published authoritatively on their history; he was a founder-member of the Minority Rights Group; and was active also across a broad range of local endeavours on his home ground.

His ninetieth birthday was marked recently in a volume edited by Alan Crown, *Noblesse Oblige* (Vallentine Mitchell, 1998), in which his friends and surviving associates celebrated his career. He was a complete man of his many worlds.

Scottish Jewry

John Cosgrove

On the first of July 1999, immediately before the official opening of the new Scottish Parliament in Edinburgh, a historic service was held in Saint Giles Cathedral in the presence of the Queen and the Duke of Edinburgh and all the members of the new Parliament. In the congregation were Cardinal Thomas Winning of the Roman Catholic Church, the Primus of the Scottish Episcopal Church and Rabbi David Sedley, Minister of Edinburgh Hebrew Congregation. The Minister of the Cathedral, Reverend Gillesbuig Macmillan, began his sermon by quoting from the writings of Professor David Daiches on his father Rabbi Salis Daiches, a distinguished predecessor of Rabbi Sedley. Considering that, to the best of my knowledge, there were no Jewish candidates in the recent elections to the Scottish Parliament and that the number of Jews in Scotland represents less than 0.2 per cent of the general population, it is remarkable that any mention whatever was made of Jews.

Kenneth Collins in his recent guide to the history and community of the Jews in Scotland, entitled *Scotland's Jews*, concludes that Scottish Jewry is in essence 'a tale of two cities'. He was, of course, referring to the fact that Scotland's Jews are to be found mainly in Edinburgh and Glasgow with only a small number in Aberdeen (20), Dundee (4), and Argyll and Bute (12). The goodwill towards the Jewish community in Scotland probably stems from the traditional respect that Scots feel for the 'People of the Book', which manifested itself as early as 1691 when the minutes of the Edinburgh Town Council record the application of David Brown, a professing Jew, to reside and trade in the city. The minute (beautifully handwritten in copperplate old English) records that 'William Patoun, old dean of Guild, protested that noe person whatsomever that denies the basis or foundamentalls of our Christian religion can have any priviledge within the city of Edinburgh or suburbs. As the said David Brown does not deny he being a profest Jew.' In the course of a stirring rebuttal Hugh Blair, old Thesaurer, answered:

Jewes as such are not to be considered or treated as other infidels. They being the ancient people of God of the seed of Abraham ... The

John Cosgrove was brought up and educated in Glasgow where his late father, Reverend Dr I. K. Cosgrove, was the minister of Garnethill Synagogue, Glasgow's oldest synagogue. He has lived for over 30 years in Edinburgh and is closely associated with the Edinburgh Hebrew Congregation.

Jewish Church in their best estate had the love and affections of a sister to the future gentle Church then pagan and though now in their rejected state they are enemies to the gospell for our sake yet as touching the election they are beloved for their fathers sake upon which and several other acompts it is that they are allowed the libertie of trade in places of greatest trade wher the reformed religione is professed.

Hugh Blair carried the majority of the Council with him and Abraham Levy remarks in his 'Origins of Scottish Jewry', 'This minute may be regarded as a Charter of Liberty for the Jews of Seventeenth Century Edinburgh'.

ORIGINS

The first Jew to buy a burying place in Edinburgh was a dentist called Herman Lion. He came to Edinburgh from Germany in 1788 and described himself as a Dentist and Corn Operator. Lest it be thought that the term 'corn operator' has an agricultural significance, Levy notes that Lion was a chiropodist who wrote a remarkable book about corns of the foot. When Lion was 43 he went to Edinburgh University to study medicine but, although he passed his examinations, he was refused permission to graduate and there is the suggestion that this was because his conduct as a dentist and corn operator was more businesslike than professional. In addition, he was an alien and the country was at war. There is certainly no suggestion of anti-Semitism and we know that 15 years earlier, in 1779, Dr Joseph Hart Myers, who was born in New York in 1758, graduated as a Doctor of Medicine at Edinburgh University. He moved to London and became President of the Talmud Torah of the Great Synagogue, which developed into the Jews' Free School. Herman Lion is noteworthy because on 6 May 1795 he petitioned Edinburgh Town Council to purchase a plot of land on the Calton Hill for a burying place for himself and his family. It is marked on the Ordnance Survey Map of 1852 as 'Jew's Burial Vault' but the site was never properly identified until recently, when it was discovered by a Canadian pot-holer.

The first synagogue in Scotland was established in 1816 in Edinburgh, in a lane off Nicolson Street. There were 20 Jewish families and the minister was Reverend Moses Joel who remained in office for 46 years and died in 1862. In 1867, Ross House, in Park Place near George Square, was bought by the Edinburgh Hebrew Congregation and converted into use as a synagogue. The first Jewish cemetery was acquired in 1820 in Braid Place at Causewayside where the Hebrew inscriptions are quite visible to this day. This small burial place proved adequate for the needs of the Congregation until 1867 when the Jewish section of Echobank cemetery in Dalkeith Road was acquired. The present Jewish cemetery in Piershill has been in use since 1914.

It is not until 1812 that there is a record of a Jewish settler in Glasgow. In that year Isaac Cohen, a hatter, was admitted a Freeman of the City. He is said to have introduced the silk hat to Scotland. In 1823, the first synagogue in Glasgow was established, in two rooms in a first floor flat at 43 High Street, near Trongate. The first minister was Moses Liesenheim who, like his colleague Moses Joel in Edinburgh, also acted as shochet. The first Jewish burial ground in Glasgow was not established until 1831, and formed a small but picturesque part of the Glasgow Necropolis, the vast cemetery to the east of Glasgow Cathedral. This served the Jewish community until 1853 when additional burial space was purchased at Janefield Cemetery in the Gallowgate.

Dr Asher Asher, who was born in Glasgow in 1837, graduated in Medicine at Glasgow University, became Honorary Secretary to the Glasgow Hebrew Congregation and in 1862 moved to London, where he was instrumental in setting up the United Synagogue and served as its first secretary until his death in 1889. The Asher Asher Gold Medal for Medicine commemorates his name in Glasgow University.

GROWTH

It is always difficult to estimate the size of the Jewish population. A. Levy quotes Cecil Roth's *The Rise of Provincial Jewry* and notes the estimates of the Jewish populations of Edinburgh and Glasgow as reported in connection with the vote for the Chief Rabbinate in 1844. Edinburgh had 107, with 128 in Glasgow – numbers large enough to mark out the Scottish cities as fairly important centres of contemporary Jewish settlement.

A major expansion in the Scottish Jewish communities took place in the 1880s and 1890s with the flood of emigration from eastern Europe and from Lithuania in particular. The small Jewish population of Scotland was soon outnumbered by the influx of Yiddish-speaking Jews. Many arrived at Leith and Dundee from the Baltic ports and some had been duped by unscrupulous captains into believing that they had arrived in the United States. Many did move on to America but Glasgow attracted many more of the immigrants than Edinburgh because of its leading position as the centre of industry and commerce. Even before the massive immigration, the increase in number and degree of prosperity of the Jews in Glasgow was reflected in the opening of the impressive and imposing synagogue at Garnethill in 1879. It was opened as the Glasgow Hebrew Congregation and was consecrated by the son of the Chief Rabbi, Reverend Dr Herman Adler, who subsequently succeeded his father. The minister of the synagogue was Reverend E.P. Phillips who served the community with distinction for the next 50 years. The new immigrants must have found Garnethill to be rather 'English'. They settled mainly in the Gorbals, to the south of the River Clyde, where they established new synagogues. The Chevra Kadisha Congregation was opened in Buchan Street in 1897, followed in 1899 by the Great Synagogue in South Portland Street, seating 1,000 people, and the Beth Medrash Hagadol in Oxford Street in 1901. At first, Reverend Phillips and Garnethill looked after the affairs of the Gorbals community but by 1898 the Glasgow United Synagogue Council was set up, giving individual congregations autonomy. By 1902, the estimated Jewish population of Glasgow was about 7,000 and about 1,000 in Edinburgh; by 1914 there were some 12,000 Jews in Glasgow.

EDINBURGH

In 1880 a group of Jews arrived in the Dalry district of Edinburgh to work in the waterproof clothing industry for the Caledonian Rubber Company and established the Dalry Hebrew Congregation near Haymarket. The main Edinburgh Hebrew Congregation moved from Park Place to a converted chapel in Graham Street near Lauriston Place in 1898 and Chief Rabbi Herman Adler conducted the opening ceremony with a congregation of over 500 people. From 1879 to 1918, the minister of the Edinburgh Hebrew Congregation was Reverend Jacob Furst. In 1888, Mr Furst founded the Edinburgh Jewish Literary Society, which is still thriving and is the oldest surviving Jewish literary society in the United Kingdom. His son, Elias H. Furst, JP, had the distinction of being Chairman of Heart of Midlothian Football Club and President of the Edinburgh Board of Shechita at the same time. The *Jewish Year Book* of 1910 estimates the Edinburgh Jewish population at 1,800 and lists four synagogues – Graham Street, Dalry, Richmond Street and the Central Synagogue (with no address).

In 1918, Rabbi Dr Salis Daiches succeeded Mr Furst. Salis Daiches' achievements in the 27 years of his ministry included the unification of the Edinburgh Jewish Community into a single cohesive unit and at the same time acting as spokesman for the Jews in Scotland during the troubled inter-war years. As a tribute to him, a street in Edinburgh was named Daiches Brae. He had two sons, Lionel, who died in November 1999 aged 88 and in his prime was Scotland's leading QC specialising in criminal cases, and David, who has written over 40 books, has produced distinguished literary and critical histories, and is an acknowledged expert on Scotch whisky. His autobiography, *Two Worlds*, describing his childhood and his father is still in print and worth reading. He is a member of the Edinburgh Synagogue. This synagogue, in Salisbury Place, was built in 1932 to seat 1,000 people and is a monument to Rabbi Daiches' leadership. Salis Daiches died in 1945.

Since then there has been a gradual decline in the Jewish population, from about 2,000 in the 1930s to some 300 in 1999. To cope with this decline, the synagogue was reconstructed in 1980 when the floor of the synagogue was raised to the level of the ladies gallery, which provided space for a community centre with kitchen, halls, classrooms and a more compact but nevertheless spacious synagogue. Being an important academic centre, with three universities, Edinburgh has an active University Jewish Society which hosts an annual 'Rabbi Burns Supper' to which Jewish students come from all over Britain to celebrate the life of Robert Burns. There is also an ultra-modern Hillel House adjacent to the campus. Although numerically small, Edinburgh has many of the organisations found in larger centres, including a local branch of the Council of Christians and Jews, a Friendship Club and a Luncheon Club for senior citizens, a branch of Maccabi and a Future Generations Committee, as well as the Literary Society mentioned earlier.

GLASGOW

At the beginning of the twentieth century the Glasgow Jewish Community was numerically strongest in the Gorbals and, although some Jews moved to the west end of the city, where Garnethill maintained its leading position for many years, new synagogues were founded in a gradual movement southwards from the Gorbals. The 'new' synagogues were Queens Park (1906), Langside (1915), Pollokshields (1929), Crosshill (1932), Giffnock and Newlands (1934), Netherlee and Clarkston (1940) and Newton Mearns (1954). All these were orthodox. A Reform Synagogue was opened in 1931 in Pollokshields and this subsequently moved to Newton Mearns where there is the largest concentration of Jews. Today there are no Jewish facilities in the Gorbals and the Pollokshields and Crosshill synagogues have closed, leaving a total of seven synagogues in the Glasgow area. Giffnock and Newlands Synagogue is now the largest in Scotland, with a variety of communal organisations, including youth groups, housed in the Jewish Community Centre on its premises.

A glance at the current Annual Year Book of the Glasgow Jewish Representative Council shows the huge investment Glasgow Jewry has placed in Jewish education, support for Israel and welfare. The Jewish Primary School at Calderwood Lodge became a state school in 1982 and has been particularly successful in providing a sound Jewish and secular education. There are 12 youth organisations brought together in a Jewish Youth Forum run by the Community Youth Worker. Glasgow Jews have traditionally been great supporters of Israel and, despite a declining community, there are ten Zionist organisations.

In the last few years, the Jewish welfare organisations have been transformed from their origins in the Hebrew Philanthropic Society, founded by 1858. The direct successor is Jewish Care Scotland which co-ordinates welfare in a highly professional way. There is, in addition, the Jewish Housing Association, providing sheltered housing and augmented care for the elderly, and Cosgrove Care which looks after Jewish people with learning difficulties and provides residential accommodation for them. Newark Care is responsible for the Jewish Old Age Home, which includes a nursing home, and is currently building two new residential facilities in Newton Mearns.

PEOPLE

Some Rabbis
Like most Jewish communities in the United Kingdom, the population in Scotland is on the decline. There is no doubt that the twentieth century will be remembered as the time when Scottish Jews had most influence. It is interesting to speculate whether Rabbi Samuel Hillman, who was appointed Communal Rabbi in Glasgow in 1908, ever met Dr Isaac Eban, a schoolmaster at Fettes College Edinburgh where the Eban family lived, as did Chatzie Rifkind who arrived in Scotland exactly 100 years ago. Could they have possibly imagined that Hillman's grandson Chaim Herzog would become President of a State of Israel that was then a dream, that Eban's stepson Abba would marry Chaim Herzog's sister-in-law and be Israel's Foreign Minister, or that Chatzie Rifkind's grandson, Malcolm, would become Her Majesty's Secretary of State for Foreign Affairs?

Chatzie Rifkind, a Talmud scholar, would certainly have known the Yiddish-speaking Rabbi of Richmond Street Synagogue in Edinburgh, Rabbi Jacob Rabinowitz, who was a staunch Zionist and attended the fourth Zionist Congress in London as the Edinburgh delegate. His son, Rabbi Dr Louis Rabinowitz, born in Edinburgh, was to become Chief Rabbi of South Africa and later Deputy Mayor of Jerusalem. Glasgow also produced the present Chief Rabbi of South Africa, Rabbi Cyril Harris. The Scottish Jewish communities chose their clergy well. Reverend Dr I. K. Cosgrove was appointed to Garnethill in 1935 and until his death in 1973 continued the policy pursued by his predecessor, Reverend E.P. Phillips, in maintaining close links with the Christian and civic leaders, over and above his deep commitment to Jewish education and the welfare of the less fortunate members of the community. He was a regular broadcaster on the BBC and his sermons at Garnethill were reported in the *Glasgow Herald*, leading to him being widely referred to as the 'Chief Rabbi of Glasgow'. When Reverend Phillips was the Minister of Garnethill, the Cantor was the Reverend I. Levine and one of his sons was the Reverend Ephraim Levine who succeeded Reverend Simeon Singer of Prayer Book fame to become th equally celebrated Minister/Preacher at the New West End Synagogue in London.

In the 1940s and 1950s, Queens Park Synagogue regarded itself as the 'premier Shool' and, during the Second World War, they appointed Rabbi Dr Kopul Rosen who went on to found Carmel College, the first Jewish public school. One of those who applied unsuccessfully for the position at Queen's Park to succeed Kopul Rosen was the young Immanuel Jakobovits, which shows how highly regarded Queens Park was by up and coming Rabbis and demonstrates that lay leaders do make mistakes! Commenting on Jakobovits's rejection by Queens Park, Chaim Bermant wrote that it was because he was too young, too foreign and too frum. They later appointed Rabbi Dr Wolf Gottlieb, who also took over the leadership of the Glasgow Beth Din. His daughter, Aviva Gottlieb-Zornberg, is a distinguished teacher of Bible in Jerusalem.

Several Rabbis had their first pulpits in Glasgow. Rabbi Dr Jeffrey Cohen, now the minister of Stanmore in London, was the minister of Newton Mearns and combined this with being Director of Jewish Education and lecturer in Hebrew at Glasgow University. Rabbi Jeremy Rosen was minister of Giffnock immediately before his appointment as Principal of Carmel College. In Edinburgh, Salis Daiches was succeeded by Dr Isaac Cohen who left to become Chief Rabbi of Ireland. He was succeeded by Rabbi Dr Jacob Weinberg who was the minister of Oxford Hebrew Congregation during the Second World War. Another distinguished minister in Edinburgh was Daniel Sinclair who later became Principal of Jews' College in London. Rabbi Alan Plancey, who was born in Edinburgh and brought up in Glasgow, is the minister of one of London's largest congregations (Borehamwood).

Some Doctors

Noah Morris was the first Jew to be appointed to a Regius Chair at a Scottish University when he became Professor of Materia Medica at Glasgow University in 1937. It is said that as a student he augmented his income by teaching at the Garnethill Hebrew classes. Another prominent member of Garnethill, Sir Abraham Goldberg, was Regius Professor of Medicine at Glasgow University and was chairman of the important national Committee on the Safety of Medicines. Dr Jack Miller, an Honorary Vice-President of Garnethill, was for many years National

Treasurer of the British Medical Association. Henry Tankel in Glasgow and Phillip Harris in Edinburgh are well-respected surgeons.

Some Lawyers
Sheriff Gerald Gordon (a former Honorary Secretary of the Edinburgh Hebrew Congregation) was Professor of Scots Law and Dean of the Law Faculty at Edinburgh University. He wrote the standard textbook on criminal law in Scotland and is a temporary High Court Judge. The late Lord Kissen (Manuel Kissen) was the first Jewish Judge of the Court of Session (the Supreme Court) and Lord Caplan (Philip Caplan) is currently one of the most senior judges. Lady Cosgrove (Hazel Cosgrove) was the first woman, and at present the only woman, on the Court of Session bench.

Some Politicians
Scotland's first Jewish Councillor and Bailie was Michael Simons who was elected to Glasgow Town Council in 1883. Despite a distinguished career in public service (which included declining the office of Lord Provost of Glasgow), the 'Bailie' (as he was affectionately known) found time to be Secretary of the Glasgow (Garnethill) Hebrew Congregation. The first Jewish MP in Scotland was Emanuel Shinwell (Lord Shinwell) who was elected MP for Linlithgow in 1923 and was Minister of Defence in the Attlee government. Myer Galpern (Lord Galpern) was a member of Glasgow Corporation for 28 years, becoming the city's first and only Jewish Lord Provost. He entered Parliament on the Labour side in 1959 and became a Deputy Speaker of the House. Sir Malcolm Rifkind also started his political career in local politics in Edinburgh and was elected as a Conservative MP in 1974 for Edinburgh Pentlands. As a young backbencher he was Honorary Secretary of the Conservative Friends of Israel and wrote a regular column for the *Jewish Chronicle*. He was, successively, Secretary of State for Scotland, Secretary of State for Transport, Secretary of State for Defence and Foreign Secretary. Dr Maurice Miller was a Labour MP in Glasgow from 1964 until 1987 and served as Honorary Secretary of Labour Friends of Israel. Lord Greenhill (Labour) was a City Treasurer in Glasgow and Harold Oppenheim (Conservative) held the same position in Edinburgh Town Council and was President of the Synagogue.

Some Academics and other Notables
Professor Stefan Reif who was born and brought up in Edinburgh under the influence of Rabbi Isaac Cohen is responsible for the Taylor-Schechter Geniza Collection at Cambridge University. The President of the Oxford Centre for Hebrew and Jewish Studies, Professor Bernard Wasserstein, was

brought up and educated in Glasgow where his father, Abraham Wasserstein, was the Professor of Greek. Professor Sir Ian Heilbron (1882–1959), the son of one of the founders of Garnethill Synagogue, was an adviser to the British government in scientific matters and distinguished himself in the army during the First World War. Sir Jeremy Isaacs and Sir Horace Phillips both attended Garnethill Synagogue as young lads with their respective families. Sir Jeremy, one of the founding fathers of Channel Four, became General Director of the Royal Opera House, Covent Garden, and Sir Horace had a brilliant career as a diplomat, becoming British Ambassador to Turkey (1973–77). From the south side of Glasgow, Sir Monty Finniston distinguished himself as Chairman of the British Steel Corporation (1973–76).

Some Businessmen
Successful Scottish businessmen have included Sir Maurice Bloch, Sir Isaac Wolfson, Ephraim and Melach Goldberg, Louis and Isaac Jesner, and Isadore Walton (all deceased), who all contributed substantially to the welfare of the Glasgow Jewish community. Nowadays their work is being continued by a new generation of businessmen and others through the Jewish Community Trust, which is concerned with education and welfare. In the Zionist world, two Glaswegians are prominent in the National UJIA. David M. Cohen is the current chairman and Geoffrey Ognall is a former vice-chairman and treasurer.

A Sculptor, a Writer and a Boxer
The late Benno Schotz came from Estonia and lived and worked in Glasgow and made busts of leaders of Israel such as Golda Meir and David Ben Gurion. He became Sculptor in Ordinary to the Queen. Although she denies her Jewishness, Dame Muriel Spark, who is regarded by many as Scotland's greatest living author, is a daughter of the Edinburgh Jewish Community. Her son Robin Spark, a talented artist and a regular worshipper at Edinburgh Synagogue, has shown this conclusively in a recent article in the *Edinburgh Star*. And in the world of sport, Gary Jacobs from Glasgow won the IBF inter-continental welterweight championship in 1996 by knocking out Edwin Murillo in the fifth round.

THE SCOTTISH PARLIAMENT

The opening of the new Scottish Parliament in 1999 has presented the Jewish community with a new challenge. Historically, the Board of Deputies in London dealt with matters concerning 'Jewish' legislation even when the subject was purely Scottish. Thus, as far back as 1854, Sir Moses

Montefiore, then President of the Board, accompanied by the Board's secretary and legal adviser, met the Scottish Lord Advocate when the Scotch Birth Register Bill was being debated in Parliament. Kenneth Collins, referring to the *Diaries of Sir Moses and Lady Montefiore*, edited by Louis Loewe (1983), notes that, 'Following the submission of the Board, the Lord Advocate agreed that the wishes of the Jewish communities in Scotland would be complied with'.

Professor Philip Schlesinger, Professor of Film and Media Studies at Stirling University and Director of the Stirling Media Research Institute, is a member of the Glasgow Jewish Community and is presently researching the development of political communications around the Scottish Parliament. He is one of those advising the Jewish community on the momentous consequences of the new legislation. In a series of talks to the Glasgow Jewish Representative Council and other organisations, he argued for the need to reconstitute Jewish representation to present a coherent voice that represents the complex, multifold character of Scotland's Jews in a time of change. He saw the existing Scottish Jewish Standing Committee, representing the communities of Glasgow, Edinburgh, Dundee, Aberdeen, Argyll and Bute – which met annually to discuss matters of mutual concern, as being 'backward looking in its image and vocabulary' and proposed that the body be renamed the 'Scottish Council of Jewish Communities'. This was adopted after minimal discussion and the council is now under the chairmanship of Dr Kenneth Collins, with Ephraim Borowski, former convenor of the Standing Committee, playing a leading role. Schlesinger argued for a major reorientation of focus to recognise that most of the national legislative agenda in future would be enacted in Scotland and that this would include education, health, housing, social work and, in fact, everything except those matters which are specifically 'reserved' for the Westminster Parliament, such as foreign policy, defence and social security. He noted that the devolved parliament, unlike Westminster, would have a single chamber and, because of the lack of a scrutinising second chamber, the Committee system would be important and that a pro-active approach in dealing with matters being discussed by the Committees was essential. He also argued for the need to invest in lobbying and to recognise that the Board of Deputies, as an 'English' organisation, would have no standing in Edinburgh to lobby on behalf of Scottish Jewry. The Church of Scotland and the Roman Catholic Church had already appointed full-time lobbyists.

In February 1999, the Board of Deputies announced that its Honorary Officers had met with representatives of the Scottish Council in order to explore the way forward and that 'whilst continuing to be the voice for the entire Jewish Community in the United Kingdom, the Board will assist the Scottish Council in developing arrangements for liaison with the new

Scottish Parliament'. Later in the year the Board made an initial contribution of £5,000 to the work of the Scottish Council and agreed that the Communal Levy of £20 per member be divided equally between the Board and the Scottish Council. The appointment of Henry Lovat as Parliamentary and Public Affairs Officer with office accommodation in both Edinburgh and Glasgow has been announced.

By July 1999, the Scottish Council had made its first submission to the new Parliament, seeking an amendment to the proposed family law bill. The Scottish consultation paper proposed an amendment similar to the recent revision of English law, empowering judges to withhold a civil divorce until the completion of religious procedures, such as the granting of a *get* (a Jewish bill of divorce). Section 9(3) of the (English) Family Law Act provides that 'where a couple were married according to certain religious usages, the court *may*, on application of either party, require a declaration that they have taken such steps as are required to dissolve the marriage in accordance with these usages' (my italics). The Scottish Council seeks to improve upon this and for the Scottish version to read, 'the court *shall* require a declaration that they have taken such steps as are required to dissolve the marriage in accordance with these usages' (my italics). In other words, the Scottish Courts would refuse to administer a divorce which does not enable both parties to remarry under Scottish or Jewish law.

CONCLUSION

The late Chaim Bermant, a brilliant writer and the author of many books, came as a small boy from Eastern Europe to Glasgow where his father was a Rabbi. His articles about Scottish Jews were always penetratingly witty and peppered with a touch of humour which did not affect the serious message he sought to convey. He wrote this ten years ago:

I doubt if there is a country in the world where Jews have been more readily accepted and more happily integrated, than in Scotland. This may be due to the fact that as the Scots themselves have a wanderlust, they have strong sympathies with other wanderers. A more likely cause is a common devotion – even among the non-religious – to the Old Testament and its mores, so that the Jew is regarded as a sort of aboriginal Presbyterian. But whatever the causes, the hospitable environment has given Scottish Jews a confidence and self-assurance not always evident in other Jewish communities.

Hugh Blair said much the same in 1691.

BIBLIOGRAPHY

Bermant, Chaim, 'Jews who Fled from Fear and Found a Brave New Face in Scotland', *Observer Scotland*, 12 February 1989.

Collins, Kenneth, *Go and Learn: The International Story of Jews and Medicine in Scotland 1739–1945* (Aberdeen University Press, 1988).

—— *Second City Jewry: The Jews of Glasgow in the Age of Expansion, 1790–1919*, (Scottish Jewish Archives, 1990).

—— (ed.), *Aspects of Scottish Jewry* (Glasgow Jewish Representative Council, 1987).

—— *Scotland's Jews: A Guide to the History and Community of the Jews in Scotland* (Scottish Jewish Archives Centre, 1999).

Cosgrove, I.K., 'Fear Drove Them to Refuge in a Free Land – The Story of the Jews who Found a Haven in Scotland', *Weekly Scotsman*, 19 September 1956.

Daiches, David, *Two Worlds: An Edinburgh Jewish Childhood* (Canongate Classics, 1997).

—— *Was, A Pastime from Time Past* (London, 1975).

—— 'Jews in Scotland', in *Patterns and Images of Jewish Immigration in Scotland*, tenth anniversary magazine (Scottish Jewish Archives Centre, 1997)

Levy, Abraham, 'The Origins of Scottish Jewry', paper read to the Jewish Historical Society of England, 1958.

—— *The Origins of Glasgow Jewry 1812–1895* (Glasgow, 1949).

Phillips, Abel, *A History of the Origins of the First Jewish Community in Scotland – Edinburgh 1816* (Edinburgh, 1979).

Schlesinger, Philip, 'The Jewish Community and the Scottish Parliament', *Edinburgh Star*, No. 33 (July 1999).

Spark, Robin, 'Life with the Cambergs', *Edinburgh Star*, No. 32 (February 1999).

The Jews in Wales

Hal Weitzman and David Weitzman

Llandudno, Merthyr Tydfil, Tredegar... Names from the past but, for many Jews spread far and wide, names that rekindle memories and reawaken cultural identity. We were free men in Wales, they will recall, and their sojourn in that country and subsequent exodus may join the other folklore tales they will wish to pass on to their descendants.

The story of the Jews in Wales reads like a cameo of the larger history of world Jewry and of its dynamic ebb and flow. It is a tale of immigration to a strange land with a strange language, adventure, the quest for a modest living with growing ambition for betterment, the establishment of vibrant communities, encounter with anti-Semitic violence, growth, prosperity, consolidation and, finally, departure and decline. The Jewish community in Wales has, in general, been the subject of its adopted country's history, rather than its shaper. That Wales' Jews have always been more concentrated in the industrial south than in the more rural north and centre indicates that they came to the principality primarily in order to reap the benefits of the former's key position in industrial revolution-era Britain. As South Wales' heavy industry boomed, in coal, steel and shipping, so did the Jewish community. Conversely, as it has waned ever since, so has the number of Jews who have remained in the region.

Jews did not settle in Wales until relatively late in the industrial revolution, since Welsh ports were not on the traditional Jewish emigration route from Russia and Poland to America. The oldest known Jewish community in Wales sprang up in what was then the flourishing sea-port of Swansea in the mid-eighteenth century and comprised East European Ashkenazim. The community in Wales' capital city, Cardiff, was founded in 1813, and the valley town of Merthyr Tydfil opened its synagogue in 1848. At about the same time, the first Jewish community in North Wales was established in Bangor. A small number of Sephardi Jews, mostly refugees from the break-up of the Ottoman Empire in the Versailles settlement, also found their way to North Wales, and helped in the establishment of communities in Rhyl and Llandudno after 1918.

Hal Weitzman grew up in Cardiff and now lives in London, where he is the Deputy Foreign Editor of the *Jewish Chronicle*.

David Weitzman has lived in Cardiff for over 20 years and been active in Jewish communal affairs. A former professor of biochemistry, he now works as a consultant in higher education.

These early settlements followed a trend which was to endure, that of small and scattered Jewish communities. Welsh Jewry has always been, even in those early days when Orthodoxy was hegemonic, in a very real sense a 'community of communities'. The growth of these early Jewish settlements, as in the provinces across Britain, was aided by the development of the railways into the region. However, the Jewish population in Wales remained smaller than either the large Jewish provincial centres in England or the other immigrant communities in the area, especially the Irish and the Chinese, but was as well, if not better accepted than other minorities. Perhaps this was because Welsh Nonconformist Christianity had produced a more religiously pluralistic society than in England, or perhaps because Jews were not really seen as competitors for employment.

To say that the Jewish population grew in parallel with Wales' heavy industry is not to imply that most Jews were directly involved in that industry. In Cardiff, they made a significant contribution to the shipping industry, and there are records of a few Jewish miners in the valleys. In general, however, as the most authoritative chroniclers of South Wales Jewry have noted, Jews tended to remain outside the main industrial complex (Henriques, 1993). More popular fields of employment were the clothing trade, such as the occupation of 'credit draper', which predominated in North and South Wales alike, and pawnbroking. In 1894, 75 per cent of the Tredegar Jews in commerce were pawnbrokers. Consequently, great fortunes were not generally made among the Jews of Wales, as they were in London and elsewhere.

For every generalisation given thus far there were exceptions. Therefore, our central statement that Jews have not shaped Wales' history must be qualified by saying that there were incidents involving the Jewish community which are certainly worthy of inclusion in a general history of Wales. One such event was the so-called 'Jewess Abduction Case' in 1869. The eponymous Jewess was 16-year-old Esther Lyons from Cardiff, who ran away from her family, was initially given refuge at the house of a local Baptist Minister, and eventually went to live with a Mrs Thomas in London. Her father, Barnett Lyons, eventually received a letter from his daughter – months later – in which she said she had left home voluntarily and had embraced Christianity. Unconvinced by its strange tone, and contending that Esther had been enticed away from him and brainwashed by proselytising Christians, he successfully sued the Thomases, although the judgement was later overturned. The case captured the attention of the local and national press, but did not provoke expression of popular anti-Semitic sentiments, and the coverage was generally unfavourable in its view of the defendants.

A rather more sombre chapter in Welsh Jewish history centres on the Tredegar riots of 1911, the most serious anti-Semitic incident ever experienced in the principality. A 200-strong mob attacked and looted shops owned by 'rent-grabbing Jews', and several families were attacked. Anti-Jewish violence soon spread to nine nearby towns. Representation was made to Lord Rothschild, Anglo-Jewry's lay leader, in the hope that he might secure Government support for the maintenance of public order. But Rothschild is reputed to have said of the Jews of South Wales: 'They are a bad lot and probably deserve what they are getting'. Finally, it was Winston Churchill, the Home Secretary, who sent in troops to quell the rioters. A subsequent Home Office inquiry and press reports suggested that rumoured Jewish rack-renting by a Joseph Cohen had sparked the rampage. However, the riots' indiscriminate violence served as a stark reminder, if one were needed, that the Jews were viewed collectively as outsiders.

South Wales Jewry was among the earliest and most fervent hotbeds of Zionist activity in Britain – branches of Chovevei Zion were established in Cardiff, Newport, Swansea, Aberdare and Pontypridd – and in 1895 Theodore Herzl visited Cardiff to discuss his plans for a Jewish state with the prominent newcomer to the community, Colonel A.E.W. Goldsmid.

Up to this point in our historical sketch, the smaller communities in the South Wales valleys had thrived, their populations reaching a peak in the first few decades of the twentieth century. From then on, however, Jews began to drift away from the valleys, to the Jewish centres in Manchester, London and Cardiff, and, by the mid-1940s, most of the valley communities had disappeared. In one sense, this tore the heart out of Welsh Jewry. The romantic image of Jewish pedlars tramping the valleys of Glamorganshire and Monmouthshire now belonged to history, or to the cinema, as in the case of the recent film *Solomon and Gaenor*. This tells the story of the romance between the son of an Orthodox Jewish shopkeeper and the daughter of a devout Christian mining family at the turn of the century, a story made all the more exotic for the cinema-going public by the apparent incongruity of observant Jews in a traditional Welsh setting.

However, a number of developments indicated that there was much Jewish life left. One was the last major Jewish immigration to Wales, consisting of refugees from Nazi Germany, in the 1930s. Anthony Glaser has shown how the Home Office 'persuaded' these refugees to set up manufacturing plants in the Treforest Industrial Estate in South Wales and records that, by 1939, there were 49 Jewish-owned factories in the area (Henriques, 1993). These enterprises played and, in many cases, continue to play a significant role in providing much needed employment in the region. During the war, Jewish numbers in North Wales, notably in

Colwyn Bay, were also swelled by evacuees fleeing the bombing of London, Liverpool and Manchester, but the Allied invasion of Europe saw most of them return to their home cities.

The Jewish communities of Wales briefly became the victims of anti-Semitism again in August 1947. Sparked by the gruesome hanging of two British officers by the Irgun in Palestine, there were a number of unpleasant incidents in South Wales. In Swansea, a young man was arrested after he was found with a gun and was heard saying he was on his way 'to kill Abe Freedman', then Chairman of Swansea Town Football Club. In Cardiff, windows were smashed and graffiti daubed on Jewish property, including one marking on the back door of the town's *Jewish Chronicle* correspondent which read 'Jews – good old Hitler'.

Another development which raised the Jewish flag in Wales in this period was the foundation of a Reform community in Cardiff in 1948 and the consecration of the principality's only Reform synagogue in 1952. Relations between Reform and Orthodox were poor for much of the post-war era. This was, in large measure, due to the forceful personalities who offered rabbinic guidance to the two communities. On one side stood Ber Rogosnitzky, a product of the classical East European Telz yeshivah, whose zealous commitment to Orthodoxy was only outdone by his vehement opposition to Reform, whom he condemned as 'new assimilationists, one of whose objects it was to legalise intermarriage' (Liss, 1977). On the other side stood the imposing figure of Gerhard Graf, a German graduate of the Hochschule für die Wissenschaft des Judentums, who valued decorum and 'dignity' above what he saw as the unnecessarily ritualistic and all-too-frequently raucous Orthodox services. This personality clash was, with hindsight, inevitable, given the opposite ends of the Jewish immigrant spectrum from which the two rabbis came – the poor and rural shtetls of the East and the wealthy, urban, integrated Jewry of central Europe. Over the years, and in the post-Rogosnitzky–Graf era, the politics of theology and culture within Welsh Jewry necessarily gave way to the politics of survival, resulting in much improved relations between the two congregations. Indeed, as the century closes, the two enjoy an unprecedented degree of harmony and co-operation, and a mutual respect advanced by the courteous and friendly relations between their respective rabbis.

The apparently upbeat developments were to have no lasting effect on the decline of Welsh Jewry which, in the post-war era, was marked by the death of the vast majority of its communities. The Tredegar synagogue finally closed its doors in 1955; North Wales Jewry lost three of its four communities – Rhyl, Colwyn Bay and Bangor – in the 1970s, and Jewish life expired in the South Wales towns of Aberdare, Brynmawr, Llanelli and

Pontypridd. The Merthyr Tydfil synagogue was sold in the 1980s, and the last services in Llandudno were held in 1997. What was once a landscape dotted with small but vibrant communities (18 synagogues at one time) became barren, with only Cardiff, Swansea and Newport surviving. There are no formal records of the emigrants' destinations, but many left for London, Manchester, Liverpool and Bournemouth, while others ventured further afield to Israel, Canada and Australia.

As genuinely terrible as incidents such as the Tredegar riots had been, the positive contributions made by Welsh Jews to the principality's history, and to the UK as a whole, were far more significant. As far back as the last decade of the nineteenth century, there are records of Jews becoming active in Cardiff politics on behalf of the two main parties, a tradition which has continued to this day. Among Welsh Jewry's many political offspring are the celebrated Labour MP Leo Abse and the Conservative Home Secretary Michael Howard, as well as the two (father and son) Lords Janner. Several Jews have served as councillors and mayors, and one was Lord Mayor of Cardiff. However, there are very few Welsh speakers among the Jewish community, and Jews have generally not been attracted to Plaid Cymru, the Welsh Nationalist Party. As elsewhere, Jews had good reason to fear nationalism – even the relatively benign cultural kind for which Plaid Cymru is known. For, despite its rhetoric, there has always been an element of exclusion in the party's understanding of Welshness which has made Jewish participation problematic.

Perhaps it is for this reason that Jewry played no significant role in setting up the new Welsh Assembly in 1999. Perhaps it was merely that the Jewish community's struggle for its own survival and the inevitability of its demise deterred its involvement. Then again, it may simply be a reflection of a wider trend. The main Jewish community remaining in Wales is in Cardiff, home of the new Assembly, and yet, ironically, a city which voted against its establishment. For whatever reason, Jews now stand somewhat apart from the excitement which has surrounded the small measure of autonomy devolution has accorded the principality.

Despite the fact that the Assembly enjoys cross-party support, the role of minorities in the 'new Wales' is unclear. Alun Michael, the Assembly's First Secretary, addressed the Jewish community shortly after its work began and stressed his commitment to an inclusive approach. The challenge to the Assembly, however, will be its ability to translate this commitment into action and to show the Jewish community that it recognises and values its contribution.

Significant contributions by Jews have been made in other fields. They have been successful in the areas of law, medicine and academia, even producing a Nobel Prize-winning physicist. They have succeeded as musicians, writers and journalists, and their contribution is indicated by the fact that a slim volume of local poetry and prose, *A Cardiff Anthology* (Stephens, 1987) features a number of selections by two Jewish writers – Bernice Rubens and Dannie Abse – on distinctly Jewish themes. In sport, Jews acquired just a little of the Welsh enthusiasm by producing (the highest accolade in Wales) a Rugby International. Other stars have included a Welsh table tennis champion, a Glamorgan County cricketer, county and international athletes and swimmers, a Chairman of the Welsh Games Council and a President of the Welsh Hockey Association. In commerce, the boost they gave to South Wales industry has already been noted, and there are many other examples of successful businesses established in the region. The Sherman brothers, Harry and Abe, prospered from their football pools initiative, and their generous philanthropy through the Sherman Trust not only rescued Cardiff's synagogue from financial disaster but also contributed handsomely to the city of Cardiff, to other parts of Britain and to various institutions and organisations in Israel. Also noteworthy is the Wartski family who, before becoming jewellers to the Royal Family, were simply Jews from Llandudno.

Perhaps surprisingly, Wales has also produced a disproportionate crop of rabbis and ministers, including nationally known Rabbis Isaac Cohen, Chaim Feldman, Yisroel Fine and Norman Solomon, and Reverend Leslie Hardman. Llanelli was a particularly fertile breeding ground, and when a location was sought for the establishment of a major British yeshivah, the choice was between Llanelli and Gateshead. In the end, Gateshead won, but how different this essay might have been had the decision gone the other way.

As time progressed, achievement in all fields was sought elsewhere (few of those described above remained permanently in Wales) and, in this sense, Welsh Jewry became a victim of its own success. So where are we now, as we prepare to enter the twenty-first century? Cardiff's combined Jewish community numbers around 1,000, Swansea's around 100 and Newport's around 20. Otherwise, the occasional lone Jew or Jewish family is dotted around the principality, and an Orthodox Jewish sheep farmer is still to be found in mid-Wales. But the decline is inexorable. Newport's synagogue was sold in 1997, and Swansea seeks to sell its synagogue and move into smaller premises. Cardiff's Orthodox community, on the other hand, is seriously contemplating building a new synagogue, motivated either by an inexplicable optimism that decline can be reversed or by the wish to spend the community's twilight years in greater comfort. Looking ahead, perhaps 20 to 30 years, it seems probable that Newport will have disappeared completely from the Jewish scene and that Swansea will be reduced to negligible numbers. Cardiff's Orthodox and Reform communities will both have shrunk further, and it is likely that neither will be able to sustain a full-time rabbi or even a robust minyan. Perhaps, then, some more formal accommodation between the two communities may have to be attempted in order to sustain a viable measure of religious and communal life.

For the moment, however, Jewish life, particularly in Cardiff, is remarkably active. True, the community lacks some of the infrastructure of larger centres, for example a Jewish day school and a mikveh (demolished to make way for the new millennium stadium and not yet replaced). Where, not so long ago, several kosher butchers served the community, now none exists and the supply of meat and other kosher provisions is maintained by the weekly visits of a van-shop from Birmingham. But the Orthodox and Reform synagogues function well. Both have viable Shabbat and Festival minyanim, and the former maintains a daily morning and evening minyan as well. Both synagogues employ a rabbi, and both run cheder classes and some form of adult education. A programme of visiting speakers is open to all, and a range of societies and groups caters for a broad spectrum of interests – Zionist, cultural, social and fundraising – and frequently brings together the Cardiff, Swansea and Newport communities. Cardiff's excellent home for the elderly has been in existence for over 50 years, initially catering for the Jewish aged of South Wales and the West of England, but now welcoming applicants from any part of Britain. 'The Home', as it is affectionately known, occupies a central place in the community and is a real focus for much communal activity, all of which has created an environment which is the envy of other (non-Jewish) homes in the region. The community also sustains a high quality magazine which won the Jewish Community Magazine of the Year award in 1996 and 1997.

One cannot attend a simchah in Wales, or even one in England which involves Welsh participants, without becoming acutely aware of the strong sense of Welsh identity which living in the principality confers. To be present on such an occasion and to hear a resounding rendition of 'Mae hen wlad fy nhadau yn annwyl i mi...' (the Welsh national anthem) is to realise how feeble, by comparison, is the enthusiasm for 'God Save the Queen' (maybe also for 'Hatikvah') and to understand that Welsh Jews treasure both their Welshness and Jewishness. This extra pride of being a minority within a minority is retained in the consciousness of those who leave, and even in the descendants of those who once lived in Wales. 'My grandparents were Welsh' ranks alongside 'My family are Litvaks' in the Jew's constant quest for roots and a sense of belonging.

Yet with all this, anxiety and concern about the future are widespread. Unless there is a significant influx of newcomers, no community can survive without trans-generational continuity. As elsewhere, South Wales suffers the haemorrhage of child-loss that deprives it of the life-blood of that continuity. The large-scale take-up of higher education beyond school, coupled with the British predilection for studying away from home, combine to promote the transfer of young Jewish men and women to England. There, after graduating, they may find greater career opportunities and/or be attracted to life in the larger Jewish communities. In due course, parents back in Wales find themselves remote from children and grandchildren, and the temptation to migrate nearer to their family may prove irresistible. As a consequence, the community loses members of two consecutive generations. In other cases, alternative personal and individual reasons underlie the outward migration. For Cardiff in particular, there is an irony in the juxtaposition of continuing emigration alongside the city's exciting growth, booming economy, and full range of commercial, educational and cultural opportunities. In this sense, it is a strange time to be leaving, when the conditions and lifestyle exceed the wildest dreams of the earlier settlers.

But any attempt to identify some grand, overarching explanation for the demise of Welsh Jewry is ultimately futile. There is no blame to be apportioned for this condition, and probably no cure to be administered. There have been as many good reasons for leaving as for staying, and, consequently, while the cause of the Jewish exodus from Wales remains something of a mystery for the few who have remained, it is self-evident for the many who have drifted away. As the millennium closes, it seems likely that we are in end-game phase, playing out the final stages of a two-century episode. In the grand historical sweep of Jewish wanderings, this Welsh interlude will surely be reckoned among Anglo-Jewry's happiest periods and will have earned a secure place within its collective experience.

BIBLIOGRAPHY

U.R.Q. Henriques (ed.), *The Jews of South Wales* (Cardiff: University of Wales Press, 1993).
A.S. Liss, 'A Short History of Reform Judaism in South Wales, 1947–1970', thesis presented to the University of Wales (1977).
M. Stephens (ed.), *A Cardiff Anthology* (Bridgend: Seren Books, 1987).

Christian–Jewish Relations

Jonathan Gorsky

In 1934, James Parkes, one of the great pioneers of modern Christian–Jewish relations, encapsulated Christian perceptions of Jews in stark terms:

> The Christian public as a whole, the great overwhelming majority of the hundreds of millions of nominal Christians in the world, still believe that the Jews killed Jesus, that they are a people rejected by their God and all the beauty of the Bible belongs to the Christian Church and not to those by whom it was written; and if on this ground, so carefully prepared, modern anti-Semites have reared a structure of racial and economic propaganda, the final responsibility still rests with those who prepared this soil and created the deformation of the people.[1]

Seven years later when W.W. Simpson, a Methodist minister who was to be the first general secretary of the Council of Christians and Jews (CCJ), broadcast a warning about the evils of anti-Semitism to BBC listeners, he received letters of protest from Christians reminding him of Jewish responsibility for Christ's death. In 1942, Simpson was instrumental in establishing the CCJ, but he later reflected that in promoting Christian sympathy for Judaism, it was well ahead of its time.[2]

Even Archbishop of Canterbury William Temple, who held the CCJ together in its early days, told James Parkes in April 1942 that his interest in Christian–Jewish friendship in no way precluded an equal interest in 'attempting to convert Jews', which, given a choice between the two, 'would take precedence of the other'. He clearly believed that, while anti-Semitism was abhorrent, Judaism as a religion had been superseded by Christianity, and a missionary agenda was therefore entirely justified.[3]

But the relationship of Christians and Jews in Britain was more variegated and subtly nuanced than these negative perspectives would lead us to believe. By the 1930s close contacts had been established between Christian and Jewish refugee organisations at Bloomsbury House, the refugee organisations' headquarters, and W.W. Simpson felt that 'it was out of the close, friendly and fruitful co-operation that had developed in the

Jonathan Gorsky is Educational Adviser to the Council of Christians and Jews.

Bloomsbury House experience that the Council of Christians and Jews was born'.⁴ Throughout the 1930s and the war years, Church leaders of all denominations condemned the Nazi persecution of Jews and they were clearly moved by the plight of the Jewish communities of Europe: Methodists, Quakers and Christadelphians were all prominent in offering asylum to Jewish refugees from Nazi oppression. While some of the Catholic press was strongly tinged with anti-Jewish prejudice, Cardinal Hinsley condemned the 'brutal persecution of the Jews' and the *Tablet* believed that 'nothing like the horrors now going on in Eastern Europe has been seen before'.⁵

The wartime experience of Jewish children evacuated to largely Christian rural communities was likewise varied, with more negative experiences sometimes being attributed to the stresses of war and general mismanagement, rather than traditional prejudices, and positive and heart-warming accounts should not be overlooked. But only a minority of families concerned encouraged the children to remain steadfastly Jewish, and many who eschewed blatant proselytism nevertheless hoped that their kindness would attract the children to the Christian faith.⁶

It is important in assessing the relations of Christians and Jews in the 1930s and 1940s to bear in mind George Orwell's comment, made in 1944, doubting that anti-Semitism could be religious in origin on the grounds that twentieth-century Europeans did not care enough about their faith to attack people who did not share it. Orwell was drawing attention to the secularisation that accompanied the development of modern industrial societies, diminishing religious involvement and profoundly altering European consciousness.⁷

While it has been argued that ancient stereotypes simply reappeared in secular form and medieval characterisations retained their power, alternative theoretical perspectives are more illuminating. Bryan Cheyette's study of anti-Semitism in the literature of the period has shown a variety of negative images, all of modern secular provenance, being projected onto Jews in a complex set of cultural developments.⁸ The medieval stereotype thesis is difficult to sustain from the evidence cited, and does not explain, for example, why Jewish evacuees were treated with greater hostility in seaside resorts than elsewhere. Above all, it is important to compare the Jewish experience with the prejudice and racism that commonwealth immigrants were to encounter a few decades later: the Jewish experience was by no means unique and is sometimes intelligible in terms of xenophobic reactions that are still visible at the end of the century when numbers of asylum seekers show unusual increase.

In the 1930s and 1940s Jews were the only numerically substantial immigrant minority in this country. Both government and Jewish leaders were aware of popular anti-Semitism and responses to the Holocaust were arguably inhibited by fears of unpleasant social consequences if too many refugees were admitted. The Board of Deputies urged German-Jewish refugees to avoid making themselves unduly conspicuous and conformity to cultural norms was very important – Jews who assimilated successfully did not encounter undue hostility in British society, but there was a sense of structural fragility underlying the whole enterprise. A *Jewish Chronicle* columnist, writing in 1938, was disturbed by the prospect of an influx of 'Kaftaned Jews' from Poland, who would not realise the importance of 'discarding their traditional attire' when settling in this country.[9] Similarly, Helen Bentwich, the honorary secretary of an organisation looking after German-Jewish children, was anxious to spread the children as widely over the British Isles as possible, explaining to *Jewish Chronicle* readers that 'we do not want too great numbers of them in any one place'.[10] Communal leaders clearly did not wish to upset the delicate social balance upon which the well-being of Anglo-Jewry depended. Jews were still an immigrant community, the majority of relatively recent origin, and social prejudice had to be carefully managed.

The Christian component of this situation is difficult to pin down. Christians believed that Judaism had been superseded by Christianity. Jews were regarded by many as having a collective responsibility for the crucifixion, but the fundamental hope was they would see the light and recognise their redeemer. Philosemitism – derived from an affinity with the Old Testament – was eccentric but, nevertheless, had a long history and inspired some noble reactions to Jewish suffering. Christians did not believe that their faith was responsible for anti-Semitism and James Parkes' argument to the contrary, which he published in 1934, made little impression on the prevailing paradigm; his reception in theological colleges was highly sceptical, albeit more friendly than that accorded to C.G. Montefiore's voluminous attempt to illustrate the Jewishness of Christian ethical teaching. Jesus the Jew would not be acceptable for several generations and, despite the publication in English of some outstanding rabbinical scholarship, images of the Pharisees, derived from New Testament stereotypes, remained firmly entrenched, finding reflection in both common usage and the Oxford Dictionary.[11]

Nevertheless, when the Council of Christians and Jews was founded in 1942, Christians did not see it as an act of penitence. They were horrified by events on the continent, and aware of anti-Semitism in this country, but they were at war with the Nazi perpetrators and did not view English anti-Semitism as a derivative of their Christian religion. William Temple saw Nazi anti-Semitism as 'part of a general and comprehensive attack on Christianity ... and on the ethical principles common to both religions'.

The first aims of the Council contained no specific reference to anti-Semitism, because Temple emphasised that, albeit manifestly evil, it was not the ultimate evil but rather a symptom of deeper disorders in society, which Jews and Christians alike were obliged by their ethical heritage to expose and eradicate. The final aim was to combat all forms of religious prejudice, but first it was necessary to establish mutual understanding and respect between Christians and Jews, so that further advances might be made. This global perspective continues to inspire the CCJ mission statement, but in 1942 Jews were understandably less far-sighted, and joined the new organisation solely to combat the various prejudices that were levelled against them.[12]

No one at this stage anticipated inter-faith dialogue, or 'Christian–Jewish relations', least of all the Chief Rabbi, who departed with considerable alacrity when joint educational ventures were proposed, caricaturing the new council as a 'Society for the Promotion of Spiritual Intermarriage'. He returned when the executive retreated but boundaries had clearly been set, and the Council's remit was to be very limited indeed.[13] In 1927, the newly founded and more academically inclined London Society of Jews and Christians had encountered vehement opposition from both communities, and the CCJ only survived by carefully avoiding the pit-falls of religious engagement. (The London Society continues to offer an annual programme of lectures but, unlike the CCJ, it has not sought to make a popular impact.)

Despite CCJ's lack of impact during the war years, retrospectively its founding was a remarkable development. Relations between the religious communities had hitherto been distant, and their leaders' endeavour to influence popular prejudice at grass-roots level was highly novel. Christian leaders rarely appeared together – the World Council of Churches was founded only in 1948 – and joining forces with the Chief Rabbi had not previously been high on their agenda. Many Christians had profoundly negative views of Judaism, even if they sympathised with Jews, and Jewish images of Christianity were coloured by tragic memories, theological animus and the horrors being perpetrated on the continent. The notion of inter-faith dialogue and the prospect of a multi-cultural Britain were beyond the imaginings of British people in the 1940s and Christians in particular thought of other faith communities purely in terms of mission and prospective conversion. The CCJ's non-missionary agenda was a theological novum, as dubious for Christians as it was for Jews, albeit for radically different reasons. Christians had no grounds for accepting it, and Jews did not believe it was genuine, suspecting that in reality little had changed.

In the decades that followed the war, the fragility of the CCJ clearly emerged. Its remit remained very narrow, and major issues that divided the communities were deemed too sensitive to discuss. Missionary activity was periodically addressed by a select committee, but until the 1990s no progress was made. Jews were fiercely opposed, but Christians were fundamentally obliged to make disciples and propagate their faith. In practice, CCJ Christians such as W.W. Simpson made pragmatic adjustments, but there was no theological compromise. CCJ was rarely the scene of missionary activity and, contrary to popular Jewish imagery, most Christians do not spend their time proselytising, but some certainly do, and they were sufficient to foster a continuing sense of distance between the two communities, particularly on the Jewish side. The impasse meant that this thorny problem had to be side-stepped if the Council was to survive.

The fragilities of the new Council in its early decades can be ascribed to several sources. The Roman Catholic Church withdrew in 1954, returning only in the early 1960s. The reasons for the withdrawal are instructive: Cardinal Griffin, in his letter of resignation, noted that in the early days CCJ's main concern had been to counter anti-Semitism and encourage practical co-operation, but the emphasis seemed to have shifted to the educational field where the 'promotion of mutual understanding' was being conducted 'in a way likely to produce religious indifferentism'. There was only one true faith, and CCJ's involvement in education might mislead people into thinking the contrary. The Catholics overcame this suspicion, and returned to the fold in the early 1960s, but Cardinal Heenan continued to believe that conversion of the Jews was the only proper aim of Christian–Jewish relationship.[14]

The boundaries of the relationship were thus closely circumscribed; even educational activity was deemed dubious in an age when Religious Education (RE) was defined solely in terms of transmitting the Christian faith. Inter-faith dialogue was seen as both novel and threatening, and mission was the only proper objective. Countering anti-Semitism and practical co-operation were acceptable, but further development was effectively restrained.

Jewish doubts had been given fierce expression by the Chief Rabbi as early as 1942, when CCJ began, and concern about mission was only allayed in the 1990s. Many Jews felt that the CCJ had ulterior motives, and this ensured a continuing sense of distance. There were, however, further difficulties. CCJ branches sprang up all over the country and by the 1980s there were more than 60. The branches took it upon themselves to promote mutual understanding, and initial formality often gave way to genuine friendship, but it took a very long time. Jews, many of whom had encountered anti-Semitic prejudice in their formative years, were gradually coming to terms with the enormity of the Holocaust. They rarely identified as Jews in the public realm, where they wanted only to be as everyone else, and the new venture called upon them to step into the unknown. Christians had their own internal images of Jews and Judaism, which likewise created obstacles to further progress. For Jews, anti-Semitism was not merely one prejudice among many, but a dark and terrible shadow that fell upon themselves and their children. Both Christians and Jews were primarily concerned to overcome the horrors that had been disclosed by the war, but formalities were retained, for it was only thus that they were able to share each other's company.

The CCJ did not move towards William Temple's vision of a social crusade; Temple had greatly underestimated the difficulties of overcoming the barriers that separated the two communities and had not understood the depth of Jewish trauma. Christians who joined the organisation were primarily moved by the narrative of the war years and, like their Jewish colleagues, focused exclusively on anti-Semitism. Griffin's observation that, by 1954, the CCJ had changed its focus seems, in retrospect, quite correct. None of the founders anticipated that CCJ would be concerned with either religion or education, but this was precisely what was to happen. Christians often had – or developed – an interest in the faith that had provided the matrix of their scriptural narrative, and they did not necessarily share Temple's commitment to social action. Jews were preoccupied with the fragility of their situation, and memories of the past returned to the fore whenever anti-Semitic incidents were recorded in the press.

From the beginning of their endeavour, Christians and Jews had different perceptions of what they had set out to achieve. In 1942, anti-Semitism was the shared focus, but Temple had a viewpoint that was very different from the perception of his Jewish colleagues. As time passed, the Jewish community continued to see Christian–Jewish relations in terms of their battle against anti-Semitism and supported CCJ on those grounds, whereas some Christians gradually became more interested in their Jewish neighbours. The different interests occasionally caused misunderstanding but they did provide a basis for an on-going relationship.

The most significant development for Christian–Jewish relations in the second half of the twentieth century was a gradual transformation of Christian paradigms that had governed perceptions of the Jewish people for nearly two millennia. The landmark document is the Roman Catholic declaration 'Nostra Aetate' (In Our Time) issued by the Second Vatican Council in October 1965. This document rejected the charge of deicide and, recognising the greatness of the spiritual patrimony common to both faiths, sought to 'foster and recommend that mutual understanding and respect which is the fruit, above all, of Biblical and theological studies as well as fraternal dialogues'. 'Nostra Aetate' decried 'hatred, persecutions [and] displays of anti-Semitism, directed against Jews at any time and by anyone', reminding Catholics, albeit somewhat ambiguously, that 'God holds the Jews most dear for the sake of their Fathers'.

Future Vatican guidelines, issued in 1975 and 1985, were to be far more forthcoming, rebutting in detail the full range of anti-Jewish prejudices that had defined Christian perceptions down the generations, but the importance of 'Nostra Aetate' should not be under-estimated, despite its highly traditional setting. Notions of 'fraternal dialogue' and 'mutual understanding and respect' were entirely new, and no previous Church statement had spoken of Jewish–Christian relations in these terms. Unlike the remainder of the document, these phrases were not buttressed by a proof-text, for the simple reason that none existed. Jews rightly noted that the declaration made no mention of the Holocaust – or the State of Israel – and offered no acknowledgement of Christian responsibility for the tragedies of the past; these were to come only in the last decades of the twentieth century. But Nostra Aetate' transformed a regnant and powerful paradigm, and the first steps were bound to be both hesitant and halting.[15]

Roman Catholic progress was to be reflected in other major churches, but it was not until 1988 that similar discussion took place in the Anglican Communion, whose Bishops meet at Lambeth every ten years. The relevant document does not have the same significance as its Catholic counterpart, but it acutely reflects the tensions that Christian–Jewish relations can evoke for Church of England and Anglican leaders in the wider world.[16] The document as it finally emerged was entitled 'Jews, Christians and Muslims: The Way of Dialogue'. While the paper affirms that, for Christians, Judaism 'can never be one religion among others', as it has a 'special bond and affinity with Christianity', it was evidently felt that the statement could not be confined to Christians and Jews. The paper contains an eloquent description of dialogue and vigorously rebuts remnant Christian prejudices, but there is an unresolved tension between dialogue and mission.

The 1988 document records a three-way split on matters of mission to the Jewish people. There were those who supported such mission, others who believed that the Jewish way to God was eternally valid, and a third group whose perceptions had been changed by the Holocaust; despite affirming the theology of the first group, they believed that Christians could not bear true witness to Jews in the light of the horrors that had taken place in the heart of Christian Europe. All groups alike rejected aggressive or manipulative attempts at proselytism, and even the missionary group noted the spiritual riches of the Jewish faith, believing,

CHRISTIAN–JEWISH RELATIONS [39]

however, that such riches would not be compromised if Jews were to discover what Christians would later term Messianic Judaism.

At the end of the twentieth century, missionary activity continued to irritate relations between Christians and Jews. CCJ finally produced a definitive code of practice in 1997 that outlawed proselytism. Christians signed up to it because they, too, did not support the aggressive incursions that Jews found so objectionable and the *Jewish Chronicle* welcomed the initiative in fulsome terms, noting that deeply rooted suspicions in the community had at last been allayed.[17] Reports of unwanted missionary activity continued to appear periodically in the Jewish press, but those responsible were usually fringe groups rather than representatives of the major churches. When Dr George Carey became Archbishop of Canterbury he relinquished the patronage of the Church Mission to the Jews that went with his new post, on the grounds that it was incompatible with Christian–Jewish understanding.

As the millennium dawns, the salient contours of Christian–Jewish relations are very different from the landscape of the mid-twentieth century. Anglo-Jewry has integrated into multi-cultural British society, and anti-Semitism is no longer high on the communal agenda. Although concern about prospective urban terrorism from the Middle East or indigenous neo-fascists continues to dictate a high level of security, this has no connection with Christian–Jewish relations.

Educational development is very important. Most Jewish young people outside the very traditional orthodox communities attend state secondary schools, where they study Christianity and other faiths as part of their curriculum, in a wholly objective non-confessional context. The days of Jewish children being 'withdrawn' from assembly and (Christian) RE have long gone. State schools, particularly in Greater London, reflect a multi-cultural background which pupils take for granted, and Christian children and those from other faith communities receive at least a basic understanding of Jewish life.

At the end of the century, CCJ's development appears both striking and extraordinary. The organisation's Israel programmes, introducing students to a wide range of Israelis and Palestinians, moderates and extremists, are courageous, innovative and much appreciated by hundreds of participants for whom the tours have been an educational landmark. The fundamental concern is with reconciliation, and participants are expected to hear and understand a wide range of views, some of which will inevitably be unpalatable; the skills involved are essential, if they are to be conciliators in their own communities. Christian participants encounter a vibrant Jewish society, often for the first time: as many will become preachers, teachers and opinion-formers, the experience is clearly significant and helpful for the development of Christian–Jewish relations in the future.

CCJ is also involved in reconciliation work in Northern Ireland, where the local branch includes leading representatives of Christian and Jewish communities. CCJ Young Adults, working with a local educational group, have helped bring together schools in very conservative areas, across the communal divides, for day conferences. More than 1,000 Northern Ireland pupils have so far been involved, and the results are very heartening.

CCJ is in the forefront of Holocaust Education, and the organisation has specialised in promoting discussions of theological and ethical issues, primarily at sixth-form level. Its work is widely recognised, and a CCJ publication, sponsored by the Holocaust Education Trust, appeared in 1999 and broke new ground in Holocaust teaching.

The fragilities of the early decades have largely disappeared and CCJ has focused on innovative approaches to reconciliation in very different fields. In a multi-cultural society, it is vital for the diverse communities to learn to relate to each other across boundaries of faith and ethnicity, and CCJ's many branches are pathfinders for a process that is still in its infancy. In so many European countries, right-wing and neo-fascist groups are winning disturbingly large numbers of adherents and CCJ branches are in the forefront of endeavours to create a very different society, where people learn to care for and value each other across communal divides, standing over and against the resurgent forces of racism and xenophobia. At the end of the twentieth century, the future of Christian–Jewish relations looks bright. CCJ can turn for support and inspiration to new and important academic centres in Cambridge and Southampton, which are themselves reflections of the quiet revolution that has taken place in the past half-century, reversing the tragedy and conflict of nearly two millennia, and creating a new paradigm of Christian–Jewish friendship and reconciliation.

NOTES

1. J. Parkes, *The Conflict of the Church and Synagogue* (New York, 1961), p. 376.
2. *Jewish Chronicle*, 17 December 1941. W.W. Simpson, December 1984 to A. Kushner, cited in A. Kushner, 'Ambivalence or anti-Semitism? Christian Attitudes and Responses in Britain to the Crisis of European Jewry during the Second World War', *Holocaust and Genocide Studies*, Vol. 5, No. 2, p. 184.
3. Temple to Parkes, 19 April 1942, cited in Kushner, ibid., p. 186.
4. W.W. Simpson, 'History of the International Council of Christians and Jews' (unpublished manuscript, Simpson Papers), cited in Kushner, ibid., p. 180.
5. *Catholic Herald*, 18 September, 24 December 1942; *Tablet*, 26 December 1942, cited in Kushner, ibid., p. 179.

6. A. Kushner, *The Persistence of Prejudice: Anti-Semitism in British Society during the Second World War* (Manchester, 1989), pp. 48–77.

7. *Observer*, 30 January 1944, cited in Kushner, 'Ambivalence of Anti-Semitism', p. 186.

8. B. Cheyette, *Construction of 'The Jew' in English Literature and Society – 1875–1945* (Cambridge, 1995).

9. *Jewish Chronicle*, 28 October 1938, cited by L. London, 'Jewish Refugees and British Government Policy 1930–40' in D. Cesarani (ed.), *The Making of Modern Anglo-Jewry* (Blackwell, 1990).

10. *Jewish Chronicle*, 19 December 1938, cited by L. London, ibid., p. 128.

11. J. Parkes, *Voyages of Discoveries* (London, 1969), p. 128.

12. W.W. Simpson and G. Wigoder, *The International Council of Christians and Jews* (ICCJ, 1988), p. 21.

13. Chief Rabbi to Brodetsky, 26 May 1942, cited in Kushner, *Persistence of Prejudice*, p. 184.

14. Cardinal Griffin's letter is cited in M. Braybrooke, *Children of One God: A History of the Council of Christians and Jews* (Vallentine Mitchell, 1991), p. 33.

15. The Vatican documents are printed in G. Wigoder, *Jewish–Christian Relations Since the Second World War* (Manchester, 1945), pp. 143–58.

16. 'Jews, Christians and Muslims: The Way of Dialogue', printed in *The Truth Shall Make You Free* (Lambeth Conference, 1988), Appendix 6.

17. *Jewish Chronicle*, 9 August 1997.

Education and the Future of Anglo-Jewry

Robin and Nitza Spiro

When we look at Jewish education in this country today, the teaching of Jewish history, literature, philosophy, art, music, drama, the use of films are all accepted as legitimate and desirable elements in the teaching process. But, 20 years ago, when we embarked upon our educational journey, these subjects, as key tools to encourage Jewish identity, were often overlooked. In fact, a number of organisations refused to include such subjects in their curriculum, actually questioning their validity.

Today, the name Spiro, both in this country and beyond, represents success in Jewish education. This has been achieved through an innovative approach, imaginative ideas, cultural exploration and the courage to be self-critical and even to fail! But how and why did we do it?

Robin Spiro can best be described as a mixture of the conventional and the unconventional. The war years were spent in America, then back to England, Harrow School and the Cricket 1st XI, Oxford University and a Law degree, then a Chartered Accountancy qualification, followed by a National Service Commission in the 8th Queen's Royal Irish Hussars – it could have been the background for a political career in the Tory party!

Now for the unconventional: midstream in a successful business career Robin decided to return to Oxford, where he spent the next five years studying Jewish history for an M.Phil. degree. Previously lacking a strong anchor in Jewish religious or communal life – notwithstanding a United Synagogue background – yet feeling the need to try and understand his Jewish identity before losing it, Robin now became addicted to Jewish history and, in a somewhat mystical way, his place in it. He also began to realise the tremendous potential for including the subjects of Jewish history and culture in Jewish education.

Robin had discovered that the miracle of Jewish history enabled the learner both to become a participant in the Jewish experience and to be provided with a number of new paths to Jewish identity, hitherto not even considered. And, most important of all, he was convinced that this learning process could attract and affect the student whether he or she was a committed Jew, a marginal Jew, a fractional Jew or even an interested non-Jew.

Robin Spiro founded the Spiro Institute in 1978 and, together with Nitza Spiro, established the Spiro Ark (see page 41 of this volume), at the campus of Middlesex University, in 1998.

Thus it was that some 20 years ago Robin, then the father of a large family and controlling a flourishing property business (his company had just completed the redevelopment of the St Christopher's Place complex off London's Oxford Street), decided to change direction – to share his knowledge of Jewish history with others, especially those Jewish youth who were receiving a totally non-Jewish education. Devoting time and effort, not to mention much of the family wealth to the project, Robin embarked on his 'mission' with a passion. Before setting up and running the Spiro Institute he had single-handedly obtained approval from the Oxford and Cambridge Schools Examination Board for an A/O level examination in modern Jewish history (1780–1980). Although he had never taught before, Robin was soon teaching the subject in a number of public schools – Eton, Harrow, University College School, City of London, South Hampstead – to all creeds and none, as an integral part of the school programme. The examination results were excellent, statistically topping the UK averages, which encouraged more schools to include the subject in their curriculum.

Single-handedly, too, he obtained the enthusiastic support of the Hebrew University, which helped to train the first group of teachers. Many graduates of Robin Spiro's programmes have become leading Jewish history teachers and heads of Jewish organisations, both in the UK and abroad, influencing more than one generation of hitherto lapsed Jews, both Ashkenazi and Sephardi.

While these developments were taking place, Nitza, who had taken the same M.Phil. degree at Oxford, had been given a university lectureship in Hebrew and Hebrew literature. After a few years, however, Nitza decided to leave the 'ivory towers' of Oxford and join Robin in what was clearly becoming an exciting and groundbreaking venture. To the new organisation Nitza brought her familiarity with effective methods of adult education. She also brought her love of and skills in language and literature teaching to enable Jewish education to be opened up to an inter-disciplinary approach. But, above all, she brought her unique ability to inspire both teachers and students.

The combination of Nitza's and Robin's abilities, helped by an enthusiastic and ever-growing teacher cadre and student following, converted old-fashioned attitudes and apathy. Even the sceptics had to acknowledge that the Spiros' activities were important and effective. What was also vital was their success in attracting new and inspiring teachers, many of who had had little or no previous teaching experience.

All of this evolved over two decades of great effort, combined with slow but increasing support from many different sources. However, what was new and forward-thinking 20 years ago is not necessarily so today. At the threshold of the millennium there are new and even greater problems facing Jewish education and, therefore, Jewish survival. These problems are much talked about but little acted upon. Nitza and Robin, and their loyal and long-standing team at the Spiro Ark, believe that they have the power, the passion and the proof to take the lead in this struggle; for we have reached a true watershed in Jewish history.

Each new demographic survey produced anticipates the disappearance of the majority of the Jewish people within two generations – through inter-marriage, secular education and assimilation. Each new religious survey produced confirms the growing non-attendance at many synagogues. However, while a great falling away is undoubtedly taking place, it is important to recognise that the rejection of the synagogue does not mean a rejection by the individual of their 'Jewishness' or even their sense of Jewish responsibility. Nevertheless, unless such people are encouraged to learn, then, at least as far as the majority is concerned, we may as well say goodbye, thus making a mockery of Jewish history.

Facing this situation and knowing how effective their work has always been, Nitza and Robin Spiro have once again taken up the challenge. They have established the Spiro Ark where their ideas and talents will again be allowed to flourish. Today, of course, the basic problem is that, despite being highly educated (perhaps for the first time in Jewish history), the majority of Jews are 'Jewishly' ignorant; and without knowledge there can be little understanding or hope. What they must learn is who they are, where they came from and, as a result, the miracle of the very existence of Jews and what this realisation brings in its train.

Nitza and Robin Spiro chose the Ark as a symbol for two reasons. First, because the Ark was the means of surviving the flood – today the deluge is disintegration, which is threatening to sweep away the majority of the Jewish people. And connected with the Ark are the dove and the rainbow, symbols of peace and continuity so essential in today's fractured and warring Jewish world, where so many traditional values have lost their meaning. Second, there is the Ark of the Covenant, representing both Jewish spirituality and learning. The logo of the Spiro Ark is that of a star and a spark, alluding to the cabalistic yearning for light and enlightenment. In the Ark of the flood all were welcome, and so it is with the Spiro Ark.

Anglo-Jewish Attitudes and Minhag Anglia

William Frankel

'Wie es Christelt sich, so Judelt es sich', declared Heinrich Heine – and he may have been influenced by his 1827 stay in London where the Jewish religious scene accurately reflected this maxim. Mainstream Britain was, then as now, relaxed on matters of religion – one conformed but did not take it too seriously. Sir Roger de Coverley, the archetypal English gentleman created by Addison and Steele in the eighteenth-century *Spectator*, conscientiously attended church on Sundays – and slept during the proceedings.

Until the second half of the twentieth century, the Anglo-Jewish religious establishment of the two Chief Rabbis Adler and of J. H. Hertz continued to be guided by the spirit of what has been called 'minhag Anglia', which was, essentially, the application of the same easy and tolerant attitude towards religious matters that was the distinguishing mark of the Church of England. The United Synagogue, under the patronage of the Rothschilds, set the tone by creating the Chief Rabbinate in emulation of the ecclesiastical hierarchy of the established church. It also resisted extremes and insisted upon decorum in all aspects.

Minhag Anglia was the creation of the United Synagogue. In the 1930s, its Beth Din, with which Chief Rabbi Hertz was only marginally involved, took its tone from the Senior Dayan, Asher Feldman, a cultivated gentleman with a doctorate from London University. With him was Dayan Gollop, the Senior Jewish Chaplain to the Forces, also very much the English gentleman, and the minister of Hampstead Synagogue which had a mixed choir. All of them could occasionally be seen without head coverings, all wore clerical collars, while the Chief Rabbi sported gaiters on formal occasions, following the sartorial code of top Church of England clerics. The rigidity of the present Beth Din, happy clappy services and the demonstrative piety of contemporary orthodoxy are the antithesis of minhag Anglia.

By the time I occupied the editorial chair of *The Jewish Chronicle* (*JC*) in 1957 (the definite article in its title was then capitalised), Anglo-Jewry was experiencing the first intimations of the fundamental changes which

William Frankel, CBE, is Director of Jewish Chronicle Ltd and a former editor (1958–77) of the *Jewish Chronicle*. He is a vice-president of IJPR.

have transformed Jewish life and attitudes since the end of the Second World War. Although 12 years had passed since the defeat of Hitler and nine since the establishment of the state of Israel, these historic events had, as yet, made little impact on the community. The sturdily traditional, as distinct from orthodox, Anglo-Jewry took rather longer than most other Jewish communities to reconsider its ideas and institutions.

By that time, the two most significant organisations in the community had discarded the leadership of what the late Chaim Bermant characterised as 'the cousinhood', the inter-related Anglo-Jewry gentry. The Board of Deputies had been thoroughly Zionised during the war to ensure its support for the Biltmore programme calling for a Jewish state, and Professor Brodetsky, an East End Jew, had been elected its president in succession to a long line of acculturated eminencies. The United Synagogue, too, had replaced the patrician Sir Robert Waley-Cohen with the far more observant and first-generation Briton Sir Isaac Wolfson and, more importantly, had appointed Rabbi Israel Brodie as the successor to Hertz as Chief Rabbi. That appointment coincided with the growing strength and assertiveness of the more orthodox element in the United Synagogue and the incumbency of Rabbi Brodie became notable for its subordination to the right-wing.

This was the organisational scene on which it became my duty to comment. I had spent much time during the previous decade in observing Jewish life in the United States. When in 1947 I made the first of what became almost annual visits to the 'goldene medina' and travelled from coast to coast, I saw a huge Jewish community, consisting at that time of more than half the total world Jewish population. It was divided socially, economically and religiously but, none the less, was capable of acting in unity and with great effectiveness in the protection of Jewish interests both at home and abroad.

Not only in New York, in and around which about half of the Jewish population lived, but throughout the country, a social division existed at that period between German and East European Jews resembling that between the notable Anglo-Jewish families and the recent immigrants. There were, of course, exceptions, but the two groups generally did not mix socially. What was called the 'five o'clock shadow' (which fell between Jews and non-Jews and when the day's work was done) applied almost equally to the relationship between the German Jews and *Ostjuden*. Since almost all American country clubs did not admit them to membership, Jews created their own – and there were two kinds, to provide for that social division.

The American Jewish Communities (AJC), founded in 1906 by German Jews, is the oldest organisation devoted to the protection of Jewish rights.

At the end of the Second World War, when as a fledgling barrister I welcomed some regular income, I had been appointed its British correspondent. The following year, the AJC, together with the Anglo-Jewish Association (AJA) and the Alliance Israélite Universelle, convened the London Conference of Jewish Organisations. The Board of Deputies was represented but, irked by the sponsorship of the AJA, took only a cursory part in the proceedings.

It was the first occasion that representatives of the decimated European communities could meet each other, as well as Jews from lands which had been spared the Holocaust, and, although the invitation made it clear that its sole purpose was the exchange of views and information, some practical actions did result. One relevant to these observations was the formation of the United Jewish Educational and Cultural Organisation, whose work was eventually taken over by the Joint Distribution Committee. I became closely involved with that organisation and my experience as its honorary secretary led directly to the emphasis I placed on Jewish education and culture during my tenure at the *JC*.

A few years after the war ended, the American Jewish Committee ceased to be a German-Jewish organisation and its most effective president after Judge Proskauer, the last German Jew to hold that office, was Jacob Blaustein whose antecedents were Russian. The AJC was transformed from a non-Zionist organisation into one that was respected and courted by the Israeli leadership. There was no Board of Deputies purporting to represent the entire American Jewish community, nor was there a Chief Rabbi (and this remains the case), yet, and perhaps for that reason, Jewish communal and religious life was vigorous, highly argumentative but at the same time productive and innovative.

This, therefore, was some of the baggage I carried with me on undertaking the editorship of the journal which justifiably described itself as 'The Organ of Anglo-Jewry', a function it had been performing for almost 120 years. It recorded the actions of the community and reflected its attitudes with the placidity which typified Anglo-Jewry at the end of the first decade after the war. The excitement of the creation of Israel had subsided, the first flush of horror and mourning after the Holocaust had receded, there was no search for new and contemporarily relevant meaning in Judaism; the institutions for religious education were moribund and the only activity which generated any enthusiasm at all was fund-raising, in the main for Israel.

Little had been done to assess the composition and nature of the Anglo-Jewish population and the most reliable sources for this information in my early years in Furnival Street were the readership surveys commissioned by George (known to us all as Tony) Mandelson, our exuberant and talented advertisement manager. Intended to serve commercial purposes, these surveys also provided valuable information about the social structure and interests of the community.

The surveys revealed that this was an affluent group. In London, where many Jews lived, they had moved out of the East End slums and the great migration to the north-west was in full swing, with similar patterns being displayed in the provinces. There were, of course, still some poor Jews but the great majority owned cars and other costly consumer durables, enjoyed expensive holidays and a standard of living above the national average. Most expressed their communal loyalty through nominal synagogue membership, in most cases prompted far more by concern to ensure their burial rights than by religious fervour.

It was during this period that a young writer named Brian Glanville published a novel, *The Bankrupts*, set in the environment of a comfortable and philistine group of Jews in north-west London. Many Jews thought it a reprehensible caricature and the book generated a good deal of controversy in the community. Brian Glanville was one of a number of young Jews in Britain who, in the 1950s, were making names for themselves in the literary world but had little, if any, connection with the Jewish community; I asked Brian to interview a half dozen of them to ascertain their views.

Wolf Mankowitz told him, 'I don't play any part in communal affairs ... I don't know what the Anglo-Jewish community is doing'. Peter Shaffer was even more forceful, 'when people talk about Judaism they're simply thinking about yiddishkeit ... I'm sick and tired of yiddishkeit, it's to me the most boring thing in the world.' Arnold Wesker, Bernard Kops, Alexander Baron and Dannie Abse expressed similar sentiments.

The communal reaction came as something of a revelation to me. The *Jewish Chronicle* was assailed for having given space to the expression of these views which, in the opinion of the critics, were unfair, wrong and ill-informed. I, on the other hand, considered that I was rendering a service in publicising the attitudes towards their faith of some of the most articulate representatives of the rising generation of Anglo-Jewry. 'To deplore the attitude of this generation is not enough; we must endeavour to change it' was the comment of a leading article in the paper. But the communal leadership was more concerned with throwing bricks at the red light rather than drawing the warning signal to the attention of rabbis, teachers and parents.

The Brian Glanville controversy was a mild precursor to the Jacobs affairs (there were two) which pitted the *Jewish Chronicle* against the established orthodox religious leadership. The position taken by the Chief Rabbi and those who were now setting the standards of orthodoxy for the

Anglo-Jewish community was akin to that of the Christian fundamentalists. It was a reaction against the evolution of Judaism in this secular age and against the tolerance towards dissent which had until then characterised this community. Rabbi Louis Jacobs, a scholar and a meticulously observant Jew, was denounced as a heretic because he had stated that no educated individual could possibly deny, that there is a human element in the Scriptures. His exclusion from the orthodox community by fiat of the Chief Rabbi was vigorously challenged by the *JC*. I saw it as not merely an attack on one man but as a demonstration that the religious leadership, dominated by the die-hards, was determined to turn the clock back and, because a zealous minority can always defeat an indifferent majority, could achieve at least temporary success.

The *Jewish Chronicle* during that period was demonised by the right-wing activists as though this was a departure from its traditional position. The contrary was the case. A leading article in the issue of 5 March 1886, which seems to have aroused little controversy at the time, commented on the then current argument between Mr Gladstone and Professor Huxley on the new theology which denied that every word of the Bible was of direct divine origin. It concluded, 'For if the religious and ethical ideas of the Jews are wonderful when regarded as the outcome of a direct communication from God to Man, they become still more marvellous viewed as the result of, so to speak, a partnership between the Divine and mortals'. That identical issue was at the centre of the Jacobs' affairs and, in supporting his position, the *JC* had not changed its editorial stance.

I believe that these events marked a significant, and eventually positive, turn in Anglo-Jewish attitudes. A theological issue had divided the community; it had been 'a controversy for the sake of heaven' rather than another of the arid and trivial rows which had regularly blown up in the past. The fact that it was fully reported in the international and national press, as well as being extensively covered in the *JC*, had encouraged many young British Jews to think about Jewish beliefs and their Jewish identity.

The establishment of the Masorti movement was a direct consequence of the Jacobs affairs, as was a revival of interest in Jewish studies. That, in turn, encouraged the emergence of a number of popular adult educational institutions like the Spiro Institute, Yakar and the annual Limmud gathering. At the same time, Hebrew and Jewish studies were either introduced or expanded at several universities, the establishment of the Oxford Centre for Postgraduate Hebrew Studies being the outstanding innovation.

Communal institutions have also changed during the last three decades of this century. The United Synagogue is in decline. This is usually attributed to indifferent management and the ineptitude of its religious leadership. These have certainly contributed to its current impoverishment but it appears to me that, at the root of its problems, is the fact that it lives in a religious cloud-cuckoo land. While being driven by its governance in a rigid orthodox direction, most of its members are either as unobservant as they always were or care so little about belief that it does not matter to them which synagogue they do not attend. Future historians of Anglo-Jewry may well conclude that the beginning of the United Synagogue's descent from the heights it had once enjoyed was the role it had played in the Jacobs controversy.

However, if the major and central synagogal body is deteriorating, this has to be balanced against the revival in other aspects of communal life. In the religious area, the recent tendency has been towards polarisation. Obscurantist orthodoxy is increasing in assertiveness if not in numbers, while Masorti and reform groups make steady progress. The middle-of-the-roaders are drifting to one side or the other or out of the community altogether, largely as a consequence of intermarriage. Support for Israel continues to be a cohesive force in Anglo-Jewish life although, at the time of writing, there is a perceptible swing towards fund-raising for domestic concerns – which cannot but be of benefit to the community.

In his book *Diaspora* published in 1985, Howard Sachar quotes Chaim Bermant as prophesying that 'as a community [the Jews of England] seem on the way to extinction'. I doubt he would hold that opinion today. Yes, the numbers have declined and are declining, but there is encouraging evidence to suggest that a smaller Anglo-Jewry, now fewer than 300,000 from over half a million after the Second World War, may well be finding its way towards an effective formula for its survival in the new millennium.

The Shoah

Simone Veil
Translated by David Newman

At the end of this century, which is also the end of a millennium, we are all tempted to take stock, if only to draw some lessons for the future. Many people have confidently asserted that ours has been the most horrific century ever. Apart from the tens of millions of deaths caused by the two world wars, there have been even more deaths caused by other types of large-scale barbarity, including genocide, massacres of whole populations, concentration camps, gulags, 'disappearances' and torture. For Europeans, convinced of the superiority of their values, it is particularly painful to realise that it was they who initiated or were involved in many of these criminal activities.

The most revealing example of how barbarous this century has been is the extermination of six million Jews, and the name of Auschwitz, where more than one million were gassed or died of maltreatment by starvation or exhaustion, will remain its symbol in all our memories. Whether paradoxically or as history's revenge, it occurred at a time when, because of their integration into the countries of which they were citizens, the Jews felt safe from persecution. Yet they became the victims of this unprecedented genocide, and it is not surprising that for its survivors, of whom I am one, the place of the Shoah in the history of humanity is almost an obsession.

It is impossible to have lived through the effect of the camps on one's heart and on one's flesh without afterwards trying to come to terms with it. The extermination of the Jews by the Nazis amid the indifference of the rest of the world reminded those who had separated themselves from the Community that they were still part of it, in the same way as the pogroms had reminded their ancestors.

I was born into a family where my ancestors had become French citizens as a result of the French Revolution. My parents and, indeed, my grandparents had been totally assimilated for several generations and were French Jews, republican and patriotic. My parents, like many others whose Judaism was without any religious element and was nothing more than cultural loyalty, could not imagine that they were in any real danger. Only

Simone Veil is a former French government minister and was president of the European Parliament from 1979 to 1982.

in 1943, when German troops occupied Nice where we lived, did they become aware of a threat. In the spring of 1944 the whole family was arrested and deported – my father and brother to Lithuania, where they were undoubtedly shot, my mother, my sister and me to Auschwitz. My mother died in Bergen-Belsen a few weeks before the Liberation.

There is no point in recalling the suffering and humiliation of living in the camps: many stories and films bear witness to this. What does seem important to me to emphasise here, however, as I have done whenever I had an opportunity, is how premeditated was the fate of the Jews, deportation being only one short stage in the systematic process of their extermination which had been determined by the Wannsee conference in 1942. The deported Jews were constantly reminded of this fact.

Minutes after we arrived at Auschwitz, when we had just climbed or been pushed out of the cattle-trucks, amid the insults of the SS and the attacks of snarling, terrifying dogs, we were put into rows to be subjected to rigorous selection procedures. Normally, Dr Mengele himself authorised who was permitted to live and who was condemned to death. Twins of whatever age were always admitted into the camp as guinea-pigs for his experiments, which would continue until they were both dead. According only to their physical fitness, greater or smaller numbers of people were taken into the camp as they came off the trains. All the others – parents, grandparents, brothers, sisters or friends – were sent off to lorries, without even being able to kiss or say goodbye. Suspecting nothing, those sent into the camp soon became worried about their relations: what had happened to them? The only answer they received was to be shown the chimneys of the crematoria and the smoke which was coming out of them. Until the day that France was liberated, they lived in perpetual fear of hearing that other friends and relatives had been arrested or had arrived at the camp.

We were haunted by the selection process which took place every Sunday: we checked each other for any trace of scabies, boils, insect bites or signs of deficiencies that would have been enough to sentence us to the gas chambers. We also became aware of the realities of extermination when we saw trains arriving from all over Europe. Throughout the months of May and June 1944, train followed train from Budapest with amazing frequency, leaving on the platforms thousands of human beings who would be nothing more than smoke a few hours later. At that time, for a period of about ten days, I was put to work on an embankment near one of the crematoria. When we arrived each morning, we could see lying on the grass, which was dotted with pansies, clothes and toys and sometimes a child's pushchair or even crutches – the belongings of those who had arrived during the night ...

When we came back home, our stories seemed so unbelievable or intolerable to hear that no one would listen, and we soon chose to remain silent rather than face such indifference. Time had to pass before a new generation would want to know what their parents and grandparents had lived through, and before their attitudes could change. Survivors have now been persuaded to give testimony to learned institutions and to record their accounts for future generations. Irrespective of the local differences in each country, however, the former concentration camp inmates all came up against similar problems in making themselves heard and in putting across the message they felt they were carrying.

The rejection which our testimony caused did not surprise us. Primo Levi's *If This Is A Man*, written shortly after he returned, is still the most lucid and revealing account. He reported this same fear, which we all had, of the incredulity of people who found what we had lived through unimaginable. In the United States both the historian Raoul Hilberg and, more recently, Ruth Klüger in her remarkable *Testimony Refused* referred to the impossibility of talking about the Holocaust before the 1970s. Even in Israel, it was only the shock caused by the Eichmann trial that allowed the survivors to emerge from their silence. Some dared, and do still dare, to talk of the repressed guilt felt by the survivors at having survived. In fact, they are actually expressing the feelings projected onto them, more or less consciously, by those who were not directly involved.

However, this desire to prevent the past from being eclipsed by silence and oblivion but, on the contrary, to bear witness and to fight for the lessons of Auschwitz to be preserved has not prevented the appearance elsewhere of counter-reactions with political overtones. By condemning the Sabra and Chatila massacres as incidences of genocide of similar importance to Auschwitz, Hiroshima and Dresden, those who aim to diminish the tragic scale of the Holocaust have found insidious ways of rendering normal what happened there, and of trying to show that all countries bear a responsibility similar to that of the Nazis when they carried out their plans to exterminate the Jews and the Gypsies. After every such comparison, the use that could be made of it became apparent: if everyone is guilty, then no one is. If every group is a potential victim, there are no more victims; we are all targets, condemned in advance by our affiliation or our birth. Both the 'Final Solution' and the culpability of its creators and its perpetrators could now be viewed as only relatively horrific.

Going beyond this normalisation or dilution of the truth, some have dared to use their denial of the existence of the gas chambers as a way to deny the very reality of the Shoah itself. It seems all too easy to answer this acceptance of lies, coming as it does from the far right or sometimes even from the far left, and driven by anti-Semitism or by anti-Zionism, or even by both. However, when I have to respond to it, I feel humiliated and silenced, as I remember all the people I saw with my own eyes disappear into those brick buildings whose chimneys never ceased belching out stinking smoke, long columns of men, women and children who never came out again. The historians can deal with these Holocaust deniers, but I am not worried by them for the overwhelming proof of the dreadful reality of the Shoah is all around us.

The history that future generations will remember is being written today. As well as presenting a picture of the past, it should provide examples and lessons for us, and this is a fundamental reason for not allowing it to be falsified or to be presented so as not to be understood or to be misconstrued. In no way would I deny the horror of bombing civilian populations, used to deliver reprisals or to intimidate. Yet its purpose then was to put pressure on an enemy who themselves used fearful weapons against civilians: this was the price of victory over the Nazis.

More serious, because it has become the most common way of normalising horrors, is the failure to distinguish between these different situations, hateful or unacceptable though they may be. This uses the idea that all assaults on the rights of man, even though they are different through their historical context, should be equally condemned because of the universality of those rights.

Like many people who escaped the Shoah, I have involved myself in the fight against violations of the rights of man without bothering about the politics of the various regimes involved. I believe I have served this cause with some success and produced some concrete results, particularly when, as minister or president of the European Parliament, I was able to intervene on behalf of oppressed people whose rights were being violated or whose lives were being threatened. I regard this fight to defend human rights against oppression and intolerance as a duty. None the less, I do not believe that it is possible to compare the violence exerted by so many countries against their opponents with the genocide of the Jews and the Gypsies. Similarly, without distorting history, I do not believe it is possible to equate the 'ethnic cleansing' in the former Yugoslavia with the extermination which will for ever stigmatise the name of Auschwitz. Without question, it is totally hateful and unacceptable that the Serbs and others who use this method to take control of territory commit crimes and violence of every sort to terrorise the local populations, to force them to flee their homes and to leave behind all their possessions in order to ensure that their conquered territories become 'ethnically pure'. Yet the whole object of the 'Final Solution' was the extermination of a race; whole communities, including the elderly and babies, were hunted down – from the Greek islands to the villages of the Alps – in order to bring them to Auschwitz to be murdered. Europe had to be cleared of Jews (*judenfrei*) or cleansed of Jews (*judenrein*), without giving them any possibility of getting away to another continent.

To say that the Shoah was exceptional is not to minimise the horror of all the other genocides, crimes and ethnic cleansings committed in the most varied and cruellest ways over the last 50 years. However, apart from the murder of each individual victim, the importance of the whole ideology of hate and death and of the process which it set in train to achieve the 'Final Solution' should not be underestimated: this was the premeditated, planned and scientifically organised extermination of five to six million Jews – men, women, the old, the young – taken from every part of Nazi-dominated Europe.

It was not only because of its massive scale but also because of its methods that the extermination of the Jews, picked out on the basis of their religion or of that of their close or distant forebears, remains a catastrophe unprecedented in the history of humanity and one which should not have been possible in the twentieth century. This is what lies behind the questioning of the metaphysical and moral order which these facts have provoked and why people have seen Auschwitz as an abyss in the history of humanity.

No more than the Shoah should the genocides committed in Cambodia and in Rwanda be forgotten, and nor should the atrocities being committed in Bosnia or in Kosovo now. The Jews, knowing what mankind is capable of, for so long persecuted and caught in a spiral of violence and hate, feel more obliged than others to become involved in struggles against the extremism, totalitarianism, racism and intolerance which pervade our species. The individual character of each of these events should not be ignored despite any apparent similarities. The horrors of daily life and the consequences for the victims in each one are no less enormous for every individual involved, but we must take account of the historical and political context in which each has occurred. In this way we can attempt in the most appropriate way to stop them recurring, to fight against them and to vilify them.

In expressing myself in this way, I believe I am keeping faith with the women and men in the camp that I saw die in complete despair and wretchedness. In the hope that Auschwitz could not happen again, they had only one thought, which was that some should survive so that people would know how 'ordinary men', as American historian Robert Browning put it, could coldly murder other human beings simply because they were born Jews or Gypsies. That is why the Shoah will remain inscribed in history as a symbol of inhumanity.

Sir John Foster and the Jews

Miriam Rothschild

Isaiah Berlin both privately and publicly explained why he felt the necessity for a Jewish state. No matter where they lived in the world, no matter whether they were rich or poor, a success or a failure, Jews of the Diaspora inevitably felt 'different'; only in Israel did they lose this uncomfortable self-conscious characteristic.

John Foster's own great friendship and liking for Jewish people may have sprung from the fact that his lonely, confused and homeless childhood also resulted in a subtle sense of 'difference', a subconscious affiliation with a persecuted minority. As a boy, John's justifiable disapproval of his ruthless mother may have attracted him to anybody or anything which he knew she openly disliked. Mrs Foster was outspokenly anti-Semitic: in an apocryphal tale, she was stopped by the Bishop of Oxford while pushing John in his pram along the High Street. 'Oh my dear lady', he exclaimed, 'what a wonderfully beautiful child! He looks like a Renaissance picture of the Infant Jesus.' 'Don't insult my son', cried Mrs Foster, 'by suggesting he looks like a Jew!'

Be that as it may, John was genuinely and positively drawn to Jewish people. He sought out individuals who manifested an international, classless outlook, vitality and intelligence. He admired those with drive and multiple interests and, especially among Jews, the humour and jokes born of the trials and tribulations of an oppressed minority. He also liked people who maintained an informal, easy-going life-style, lacking in conventional snobbish good manners and official behaviour.

John appreciated Jewish ritual and attended Seder evenings in any country where he happened to be at the appropriate time, frequently noting errors in the Hebrew service which he knew better than most of his Jewish hosts. We were told a story about him, aged 16, concerning a distinguished Rabbi about to deliver an important address in the presence of the British ambassador. Shaking hands politely, John brushed against the lapel of his coat and exclaimed, 'Oh Rabbi! I see you are wearing schatnes!' The poor

Miriam Rothschild, CBE, FRS, is a zoologist and farmer. She gave the Romanes Lectures in 1985. She has published a biography of the 2nd Lord Rothschild, *The Butterfly Gardener, Animals and Man*, works on the Rothschild gardens and the Rothschild reserves, and an autobiography, *Butterfly Cooing like a Dove*. More recently she has published a memoir of Sir Isaiah Berlin as a student, for the John Foster Memorial Trust, and an appreciation of Tadeus Reichstein for the Royal Society. 'Sir John Foster and the Jews' was originally produced for the John Foster Memorial Trust in 1998.

man was horribly embarrassed. As a school boy, Foster had already read the Talmud, and could not resist a little mischievous exhibitionism.

Conscious of his sense of affinity with Jewish people, John had searched in vain for a trace of Semitic ancestry in his family history but, regretfully, found none. A rumour that he was in some way related to the Rothschilds was always cropping up but was without foundation.

John had dealt with the trauma and wounds of his unhappy childhood by totally eliminating memory of the past – his father's death, his mother's desertion and his homelessness – and any possible emotive perturbations in the present. This led Isaiah Berlin to describe him as 'the strangest man I ever encountered', but such an unusual quality also emphasised his unique gift of augmenting and gilding the actual moment. This prompted both Berlin and myself independently to describe John as the greatest life-enhancer we had ever met.

In 1939 Foster was in Washington when the Second World War was declared. He was immediately snapped up by the British Embassy and as First Secretary successfully negotiated the lend/lease of the Liberty Ships from the neutral United States to England.

Earlier that summer we had discussed the probability of an invasion of the British Isles by Germany and it was assumed that should their army obtain even a temporary foothold in this country, the Jewish civilians would be massacred. Three of my friends had most courageously offered to hide me: Theresa Clay provided a false birth certificate and passport, Mrs E. W. Sexton, a gifted marine biologist, suggested that I worked as her assistant from her flat in Plymouth on the genetics of *Gammarus*, and John offered me a roof and employment as a domestic servant. 'Remember', he remarked cheerfully, 'I'm not very brave.'

After D-Day, following his spell at the British Embassy, Foster became legal adviser to General Eisenhower and, at the end of the war, returned from occupied Germany with the rank of brigadier. Asked by a newspaper reporter how it happened that he had left the UK as a private citizen and returned at the end of hostilities as a brigadier in the British army, Foster replied amiably: 'One must start somewhere!'

In 1947 he started to rebuild his practice at the Bar – astonished and immensely touched by the fact that one of his Jewish acquaintances immediately offered to provide him with the necessary capital and sent a cheque without waiting for a reply. Foster shortly afterwards became a QC and head of Chambers at 2 Hare Court (the two previous incumbents had been Donald Somerville, Attorney General, and Hubert Parker, at that time Lord Chief Justice). Eventually he had two Jewish pupils, Mark Littman (presently a distinguished QC) and Peter Benenson (founder of Amnesty), but he also arranged room in his Chambers for a displaced Palestine lawyer, who subsequently became Chief Justice of Jordan. This was characteristic of John who was deeply benevolent, fundamentally egalitarian, uncritical and almost over-objective. Mark Littman described him as 'a very glamorous figure, a tall handsome man, a Fellow of All Souls, M.P. for Northwich and Recorder of Oxford ... At work he was extremely innovative and imaginative.' Foster also had a great sense of public values – international public values – and was a dedicated upholder of human and civil rights. The only contemporaries he actively disliked were people who were cruel or cynical or liable to cause pain in any way to others. In his opinion, blackmail was a terrible crime. Above all, he loathed injustice.

The end of hostilities did not terminate the misery and desolation of the few Central European Jews who had miraculously survived the Nazi holocaust or brutal forced labour. There were two categories of misfortune in which John Foster took special interest.

The first was the case of Jews still living in Germany, frequently the sole survivors of their family, homeless, without financial support and generally in poor health, who wanted to leave Germany and find a home elsewhere. These included the wretched, ill-treated Jewish survivors in so-called displaced persons camps in Germany, Hungary and Romania. The second was the pitiful fate of the survivors of concentration camps after their liberation by well-meaning, conquering Allied troops.

In 1946 arrangements drawn up by the Paris Agreement and, subsequently, the accounting rules prepared by the Inter-Allied Reparations Agency (IARA) came into force and allowed victims of oppression and persecution to claim their assets in the custody of the UK and the Allies generally. Certain conditions had to be satisfied. Thus applicants had to prove:

1. They had suffered deprivation of liberty under discriminatory legislation.
2. They had not enjoyed full rights of German citizenship since 1 September 1939.
3. They had emigrated or proposed to emigrate from Germany.
4. They did not act against the Allied cause during the war.
5. Their case merited favourable consideration.

John Foster believed that these rules were harshly and unjustly interpreted by the Custodian of Enemy Property in the UK and that many genuine victims of persecution were thus deprived of their assets here, and hence their means of beginning a new life. He submitted a Memorandum (see Appendix) to the department concerned and to various individuals, such as the Archbishop of Canterbury. In this he wrote that 'the practice followed by the Department gives no effect to the letter, much less to the spirit, of the Resolution'. He placed particular stress on the unfair interpretation of the words, 'deprivation of liberty'. Foster pointed out that to go underground to avoid arrest, which would have been followed inevitably by death in a camp such as Auschwitz, should also be accepted as deprivation of liberty. We agreed that I would send copies of his Memorandum, with an explanatory note, to friends, asking for their support, especially if the subject was eventually raised either in the House of Commons or in the Lords.

I approached the following: Sir William Aitken*, Viscount Bracken*, Rt Hon. Clement Davies*, Lord Drogheda, Lord Hinchingbrooke*, Lord Hore-Belisha*, Lord Jowitt, Viscount Margesson, Lord Harmar-Nicholls*, the Marquess of Reading, Lord Renton*, the Earl of Rosebery, the Marquess of Salisbury, Lord Shawcross, Lord Sherfield, Lord Thornycroft*, Lord Walker*, Lord Winterbottom*. (Asterisks denote all those who were, at the time, Members of Parliament.)

When John returned from his interview with Sir Henry Gregory (the Custodian of Enemy Property), with whom he had discussed the contents of his Memorandum, he was deeply troubled. 'We will get nowhere', he said, 'Gregory is himself a purposeful anti-semite.'

After Foster died in 1982 I had hoped to be able to write a short paper describing his efforts to help the unfortunate and unfairly treated survivors of the Hitler regime, but I was refused access to his papers by the various departments concerned. When I pointed out that I thought the 30-year period of restraint had elapsed, I was told that they had the right to withhold certain papers without explanation. Some years later permission was granted. One of the first files requested was that dealing with the mind-boggling case of the Shanghai Ghetto (see Appendix, section 2b). On opening this file, it was found to be empty, with a note reporting that the contents had been destroyed by the Public Record office (PRO). One hoped that the late Sir Henry Gregory may have experienced some moments of shame and even perhaps remorse, and a guilty conscience accounted for the mysterious destruction of these records. A note by him referring to Foster's Memorandum merely commented that Foster appeared to be a friend of the Jews.

One point stressed by John was that the IARA Rules had been more generously interpreted by the US than by the UK, particularly with regard to the meaning of the words 'deprivation of liberty'. (Reading through Sir Henry Gregory's notes in the files at the PRO, one is appalled at his attempts to destroy Foster's arguments – by scoring points, like winning or losing a game!) Thus Sir Henry ordered a search for the interpretation of the IARA Rules by the other Allied countries and it was discovered, to his obvious satisfaction, that France and Belgium had interpreted them even more harshly than Britain. Fine! The UK came midway between them and the more generous United States and we could therefore stand as we were … Gregory was trying hard to see that Foster's 'friends' would not get their savings and the melancholy fact is that he succeeded all too well. Thus, for example, Baron Ullmann, a Hungarian banker who had been hidden for eight months by his Christian barber in a windowless cupboard in an attic, had forfeited his savings – £4,000 in the UK – since he had 'not been deprived of personal liberty', for in order to escape deportation to a death camp he had 'voluntarily' gone into hiding in his barber's attic. Baron Ullmann was on his way to the US to meet his own son, who had also escaped the Holocaust, and he had hoped to find the money for his ticket in his savings deposit at a bank in the UK. We were standing in the hall at Claridge's Hotel waiting for a taxi, when an unknown visitor stepped forward and held out an envelope. 'I heard your story', he said, 'while you were having tea with your friend. I heard you describe what it was like to see the sky after eight months in the dark cupboard. I am bitterly ashamed of the way this country is behaving, but here is a cheque for the amount you mentioned and your ticket for the States', and he turned on his heel and walked out through the swing doors.

This gesture was by no means an isolated indication of sympathy among people in the UK. The attitude of the man-in-the-street was often in sharp contrast to that in government departments. Under the Baldwin Scheme a number of Jewish children were received and cared for in England before war was declared. In 1998, at long last, in response to Lord Lester's initiative and determination, the government decided to set aside an initial sum of £2 million to compensate Nazi victims who were still alive, or their heirs, for their savings unjustly confiscated at the termination of the war.

Lord Lester, in his impressive and apposite speech, pointed out that almost 50 years ago Sir John Foster gave examples of 'manifest absurdity, harshness and unfairness in the treatment of these cases and made concrete proposals to ensure that no real injustice would occur in any particular case. His representations fell on deaf ears.' How highly delighted John would have been that a man from his Chambers had at long last been heard to such good effect, and had after half a century 'opened the ears of men'.

Baron Ullmann was one of Foster's so-called failures, for he could not recover his assets, but two of the successes, curiously enough, concerned members of my mother's family. My aunt, Johanna de Wertheimstein, an

Austrian woman, 65 years old, was arrested by the police in Budapest in 1944 and together with a number of other Jewish women was imprisoned in a so-called 'Jewish house', to await deportation to a death camp. They were forced to wear a yellow star but were allowed to walk outside each day for an hour's exercise, although not after 5pm. My aunt was able to get a message to the Dutch Embassy. She staged a suicide by leaving some of her clothes and the yellow star, with a note, on the bank of the Danube and was picked up by a car from the Dutch Embassy. She was then concealed in the cellar of a house 'somewhere in the country'. The only furniture provided was a single wooden chair on which she had to sleep at night. She was liberated by the Russian army about eight months later, and was then temporarily housed with other refugees – not all Jewish – in an empty barn, fortunately with straw on the floor. My aunt had no family left alive in Hungary except perhaps a brother-in-law whom she heard had been arrested. Her father and younger brother had both died in a concentration camp. While she and her fellow refugees were living in the barn a small band of drunken Russian soldiers arrived and decided to kill the inmates. Men and women were lined up against the wall and shot one by one. A soldier, speaking quite good Hungarian, said to my aunt, 'Your turn next, old Granny'. At that moment a Russian officer arrived with a small troop and stopped the carnage. He held a court martial on the spot and the drunken soldiers were arrested and sentenced to banishment in Siberia.

My aunt was completely penniless and homeless, but it was not until 1957 that Foster, together with his solicitor, Philip Frere, after years of negotiation, was able to cut through the cocoon of red tape and send her some money via the Hungarian Bank, of which Ullmann had once been the chairman. That year I was able to meet her in Zurich and offer her a home in England with us. Her only worldly possessions when she arrived were her wedding ring and the potential share of a small settlement made by my mother in favour of her brothers and sisters. This, however, had been confiscated by the Custodian of Enemy Property on the grounds that Madam de Wertheimstein had never been deprived of her personal liberty – incarceration in a Jewish house awaiting deportation did not qualify as a prison or concentration camp.

In 1956 the president of the Board of Trade informed me that the so-called Ghetto cases had been reviewed. John Foster then made exhaustive enquiries about the exact construction of the so-called Jewish house in Budapest which, in the meantime, had been totally destroyed by bombing. He eventually discovered it had been surrounded by a wall – it therefore now qualified according to the Board of Trade as a ghetto. My aunt confessed she did not clearly remember the wall, but fortunately John found two independent witnesses who did. It was consequently conceded that my aunt had, after all, been deprived of her liberty and could now claim a share of my mother's settlement.

Meanwhile, my mother's sole surviving brother (now an elderly, skeletal man over six foot tall, weighing only five stones and with a serious heart condition) had been liberated, by the Russians, from a concentration camp in Hungary. He was also a potential beneficiary under the same settlement. In this case there could be no question of his deprivation of liberty but the Custodian found other grounds for confiscating his share of the settlement. In the IARA Rules agreed by the Allied, it was stipulated that no national who had remained in enemy territory during hostilities could claim, after the war ended, his property deposited in the United Kingdom. Since the concentration camp in which my uncle was forcibly incarcerated was located in Hungary, he had no option but to remain there. But that did not matter according to the Custodian's interpretation of the Rules. Once again, John Foster, Philip Frere and I (as one of the trustees of the settlement in question) began a long-drawn-out battle with the Custodian which Foster ultimately won. By then my uncle was also living with us in my home near Oxford, with a Visitor's Twelve Month Visa! Pressed by Foster and the Rothschild bank, the Custodian eventually agreed to surrender £6,000 of interest in addition to my uncle's share of the capital.

During these negotiations it became known that one of the beneficiaries of the settlement, my mother's eldest sister, had been deported to Germany from Hungary. At that time she was over 80 years old and blind. On arrival at Auschwitz she was dragged from the train and beaten to death on the railway line by guards wielding meat hooks. To my amazement a cheque for £2,000 was suddenly sent to me as her heir, which the Custodian for some reason had failed to confiscate. Possibly the fact that her death had occurred outside Hungary absolved her from the sin of remaining – however unwillingly – in an enemy country during hostilities.

Today it is difficult to imagine the practical difficulties which beset us in trying to assist the survivors of the persecution and the Holocaust. First of all when the war ended there was great confusion in Europe generally, and in the UK everyone had their own serious problems to contend with – not least of all in the various government departments. Communication with Hungary, for example, involved enormous delays since the bombing of cities had resulted in the loss of official papers on a massive scale. Thus the proof of nationality, birth, occupation, affiliations, imprisonment, and the like, now demanded from refugees, were impossible to find, especially by penniless, homeless people, usually in extremely poor health, who knew nothing about the regulations. A single case often entailed files of correspondence, even at our end. Nor did the work diminish in 1949 when the assets of German Jewish refugees were finally distributed to those

British subjects who had lost their assets in Germany during the hostilities. Foster was chairing an all-party meeting at the House of Commons as late as 10 July 1956 to consider the question of the assets of Hungarian and Romanian Nazi victims. The assets of Austrian victims had to be considered separately.

Unfortunately, when John Foster died in 1982, all his bulky papers dealing with the refugee problems were considered by his executor of no possible interest and were destroyed. This was inexcusable since the case of the Shanghai Ghetto and the papers on the liberation of the death camps of Auschwitz and Dachau were of great historical interest.

An example of the post-war difficulties with which Foster had to contend is well illustrated by his successful 'rescue' of the mother of the editor of *Paris Match*. This French lady, who had been in hiding in Germany for months, was most anxious to leave enemy territory to conform with the IARA Rules and join her son in France where she also had some financial savings of her own. Both the English and French authorities decided that after 31 December 1949 no German nationals would be recognised as refugees under the IARA Rules if they had not left the country by that date, and consequently no claim for their property or money would be recognised. However, this lady had been refused an exit visa from Germany – for no apparent reason. It was one of the serious problems – a catch-22 situation – bedevilling a number of the refugees John was attempting to help. Fortunately, in this case he was successful and Madam Mathias left Germany only half an hour before the deadline. The editor of *Paris Match* came over to England to tell us how profoundly grateful he was. I was glad he did so because, for obvious dreary reasons, such negotiations were generally thankless tasks and Foster worked tirelessly and without reward to redress what he believed was the phenomenal injustice of his countrymen, and an injustice moreover against the spirit of the IARA Rules.

Fifty years later it may seem incredible to us – almost surreal even – that the German authorities in 1949 were maliciously refusing exit visas to Jews who wished to leave Germany. But an extraordinary stroke of fate threw a little light on this for me. A Jewish boy, born in Frankfurt, was one of the refugee children I had looked after in my home at Ashton before the war. As a young man he had joined the American army and was selected for the secret service owing to his linguistic talent and high IQ. He rose to the rank of colonel and was put in charge of the aeroplane carrying the German High Command to prison in Spandau. On the flight Göring asked him where he had learned such excellent German. He ignored the question. The colonel told me he had returned with the invading army to the street in Frankfurt where he had been born. 'Unfortunately', he said, 'the whole of Germany is still run by indoctrinated Nazis. You cannot blame the Allies. Ignorance of the situation is of course rife, but the country has got to be run by Germans who know the job and they are all Nazis now, as they were then. Believe me, it is a depressing situation, but inevitable.' In due course the colonel was demobilized and I visited him in Chicago where he had become Professor of German Literature in the university. His family eventually emigrated to Israel.

The situation which developed when the conquering Allied forces swept across Germany was a macabre and tragic one. The death camps such as Auschwitz and Dachau were liberated by the army; the gates were thrown open and those inmates who were still alive were freed. However, word came to us that, starving and destitute, these doomed souls soon died after liberation. We decided that the only hopeful course would be to take food, clothing and medical care to the camps immediately, under the supervision of the Red Cross, and to delay the liberation of the survivors.

Of the various people to whom I wrote explaining that this unexpected but desperate situation had arisen, two Labour members of Parliament, Richard Crossman and Patrick Gordon Walker, offered advice and concrete help. We soon realised that the situation was too difficult and too complicated for us to tackle effectively. A direct appeal to Churchill was the only hope. John Foster agreed to pursue this line: as Legal Adviser to General Eisenhower in occupied Germany, he was able to have several meetings and discussions with Churchill.

Foster had many unusual characteristics and one of them was a genuine lack of interest in his own successes. Once a job was done, he appeared to forget it. For all I know he may well have discussed legal cases in detail with other lawyers, but as far as I was concerned he would remark casually, 'I won my case', and then change the subject. (He was Counsel in more than 160 post-war cases in the House of Lords.) All he said about the 'direct approach' to Churchill was that, fortunately, it had been a success and random freeing of concentration camps by a sympathetic army was now over, thanks to Churchill's intervention. I accepted this without further questioning, and merely said, 'Well, you have saved a great many lives'.

It is now 50 years since this conversation took place and I may only remember the good news and have forgotten the rest, but I do recall that, unlike John, I was terribly, terribly tired and emotionally drained, and I experienced an unworthy surge of relief that I need do nothing more about this particular and unexpected horror. Foster was apparently never tired and found three hours' sleep a night quite sufficient. I asked him how he remembered all the details about the number of refugees he was trying to assist. 'I don't *remember* conversations', he explained. 'I merely store them – anything I've heard – but I can fish them out if the facts are needed.'

Isaiah Berlin recalled that while in Washington during the war, Foster invited at least a dozen acquaintances to dinner every night. The meal was always identical: asparagus, chicken and ice-cream. If I asked who was coming that evening, Foster would shake his head and reply, 'I will remember when they come'. Berlin said that in Washington Foster was 'very, very popular and never had less than two or three hundred friends', adding, 'He was exceedingly kind to me at a difficult period of my life'.

This, then, was Berlin's 'strange', enigmatical but 'exhilarating' character, John Foster, who, unquestionably, was the Jews' best protagonist of our time.

APPENDIX

Memorandum on the practice in regard to *ex gratia* releases of property in the UK of victims of discriminatory laws in enemy territories.

1. The Administration of Enemy Property Department in a circular letter dated 18th May 1949 has laid down certain rules under which claims for the release of the property in the United Kingdom of victims of racial oppression will be recognised. These rules correspond on the whole to the terms of the Resolution taken by the General Assembly of the Inter-Allied Reparation Agency on the 21st November 1947.

It is submitted that the practice followed by the Department gives no effect to the letter, *much less to the spirit, of the Resolution* of the General Assembly, and the general impression gained from a great number of cases is that the practice of the Department whittles down the purpose of the Resolution so that very many claimants lose the benefit of the Inter-Allied Agreement.

2. The most important criticism to be made is directed against the interpretation of the words 'deprivation of liberty' constantly applied by the Department. Although the Department has so far refrained from issuing an official ruling as to the meaning of these words and even refusing in individual cases to specify the reasons for its decisions, a practice which is contrary to the principles of natural justice, it has become abundantly clear by the practice of the Department that the Department will accept nothing less than evidence of actual and lengthy incarceration in a prison or concentration camp for what the Department considers a 'substantial' period. Under this practice all those persons persecuted on racial or other grounds who were lucky enough to escape extermination by going underground cannot qualify for a release of their property. In fact few of those who were incarcerated in a concentration camp for a substantial period have survived.

It is submitted that the construction employed by the Department is not only incompatible with the obvious spirit of the Inter-Allied Agreement, but also with the strict interpretation of the words 'deprivation of liberty' according to their meaning in English law. The narrowest possible construction of the words would be that applied to false imprisonment. To quote Salmond's definition of that tort it is sufficient that 'the plaintiff has been in any manner wrongfully deprived of his personal liberty' and that 'any act whereby a man is unlawfully prevented from leaving the place in which he is' amounts to false imprisonment. The same authority expressly states that there need not even be actual incarceration.

The following cases selected from a considerable number may illustrate the way in which the Department interprets the words 'deprivation of liberty'.

a. A was arrested and detained in a prison cell for three days in order to make him sign away certain property rights. After suffering grave injuries he was released on giving his signature in accordance with the wishes of his gaolers. The Department holds that the period of three days detention is too short to constitute a 'deprivation of liberty'.

b. At Shanghai the Japanese created a ghetto, where the Jews were compelled to live under appalling conditions for a period of no less than two years, i.e. from 15th May 1943 to the liberation in 1945. The camp was under the command of two Japanese officers who were acting in co-operation with and under the instructions of the Gestapo. B was compelled to live in this ghetto from 1943 to 1945. This, according to the Department, was not a 'deprivation of liberty'.

c. C, a Roumanian Jew, fled from the State Police which tried to arrest him, in order to bring him into a concentration camp. He sought and found refuge in the house of the consul of a foreign power where he stayed for a number of months, being unable to leave the house. This too is according to the Department not a 'deprivation of liberty'.

d. In numerous cases the Department has stated that mere detention in a labour camp, even though this was intended solely for Jews, political opponents of the regime etc., was not sufficient to constitute a deprivation of liberty, if the conditions in the camp were not known to have been extremely bad.

It is not unfair to sum up the interpretation of the term 'deprivation of liberty' by the Department as restricting the application of the *ex gratia* release to the few persons hardy enough to survive lengthy confinement in an actual death camp.

3. The Department has, however, further reduced the number of those whose property is being released by the stringency with which it considers evidence on the question whether the deprivation was due to discriminatory reasons. Where Jews were arrested, whether by the police, the army authorities, the Iron Guards or their equivalents, they were not as a rule supplied with a statement – written or oral – of the reasons for their arrests. If in exceptional cases reasons were stated, they were often faked. Offences of all kinds, such as non-payment of fictitious debts to the revenue, failure to report to the labour service, etc. were intended to justify imprisonment. The Administration has seen fit to demand that the applicants should prove that these faked reasons were in fact non-existent, thus throwing upon the applicant the burden of proving what the motives for his arrest were. It is small wonder that in all too many cases this constitutes a *probatio diabolica*.

4. Notwithstanding the fact that the circular letter does not contain any stipulation as to the time when the deprivation must have taken place, the Administration now requires evidence that it took place during the period during which the applicant's country was at war with this country. This is done although in a number of cases, as e.g. in that of Roumania, the restrictions under the Trading with the Enemy Act 1939 existed in respect of the applicant's country already, several months before the outbreak of the war. Thus where an applicant had been interned and well nigh beaten to death in a concentration camp, his application was rejected on the ground that he had been released from the internment camp shortly before the entry of his country into the war. The fact that his health had been permanently undermined and that this was the ground for the release was ignored.

5. The circular letter requires that the applicant should have left the enemy country. This is interpreted to mean that he must have taken up permanent residence in a non-enemy country. This interpretation is in clear contradiction to the wording and the spirit of the circular letter, where it is stated that the mere intention to leave the applicant's country is sufficient to justify the application. The Department has indicated that a Roumanian who has left Roumania and had settled in Austria was not entitled to apply and the same applied to a Roumanian now settled in Paris, as long as the Paris authorities had not granted to him the right of permanently residing in Paris.

6. The term 'property of living enemy nationals or estates' is interpreted by the Department to mean that only property directly owned by the applicant and his heirs may be released. Thus applications for the release of the property of a partnership have been rejected although all its partners complied with all the requirements of the circular letter. Property of companies whose shares are entirely owned by victims complying with all requirements is treated in the same way. Where a partnership account existed in this country in addition to private accounts by the partners, the Department has gone so far as to demand evidence that the money on the private accounts of the partners did not in fact constitute money of the partnership or was not devoted to partnership purposes.

7. In many cases victims invested their money in the name of other persons. Thus Jewish Bulgarians invested their money in the name of a Roumanian non-Jewish friend or residents of Hungary invested their money in the name of persons they were at the time convinced would emigrate earlier than they themselves. In such cases the Administration now demands that evidence on the beneficial ownership should be contemporaneous with the investment. Affidavits by all persons concerned, if not made at the time of the investment, are declared to be insufficient. Contemporaneous evidence is, of course, never available. It was of the very nature of the investment that it should appear to be that of the person in whose name it was made and not that of the victim residing in enemy territory. The demand for this evidence can therefore never be met and is equivalent to rejecting the claim. Among the persons whose last savings are thus forfeited are parents,

incapable of escaping from enemy territory, who invested money in this country in order to secure the future of their children, who have succeeded to escape.

8. In respect of the estate of deceased persons the circular letter contains a most curious rule, which is not contained in the Resolution of the Inter-Allied Reparation Agency. According to this rule release may be granted only if the death occurred before the end of active hostilities in the enemy country of residence. Thus an application was rejected where the deceased was in a concentration camp at the time of the liberation and died a few days afterwards. It would have been granted had he died a few days earlier. Similarly release is refused where the deceased succeeded to escape into a non-enemy country and died there, even if the death took place before the end of hostilities. It is not understood why the Department has included this incomprehensible rule in its circular letter.

9. In its administration of the rules contained in the circular letter, the Department has admittedly been largely motivated by considerations which are incompatible with a judicial interpretation of its terms. Thus responsible officials have pointed out in conference that the Department must not interpret the terms of the letter so widely that the majority of the funds of Jews from occupied territories have to be released. It would appear to be most desirable indeed that the Department should cease to be judges in their own case and that the jurisdiction in cases of this type, many of which involve difficult legal problems, should be transferred to an independent administrative tribunal, presided over by a qualified lawyer.

10. The policy of the department in cases of this type compares most unfavourably with the attitude of the authorities of the United States of America, which is much more generous. There are numerous cases where applications for the release from custodian control have been granted by the U.S.A. authorities to the same person who has met with a rejection in this country. The comparison has naturally led to a particularly bitter feeling among those concerned.

11. The period within which applications had to be made was originally to end on 30th June. As it appeared that many more cases were gradually coming to light, it was extended to 1st October, 1949. This extention is quite insufficient. Correspondence with people living behind the iron curtain is so difficult and slow that many cases have not yet become known. There are numerous cases where the enforced delay of emigration from iron curtain countries renders it impossible for victims to make their applications in time. Part of the extention period coincided with the vacation period of the legal advisors of the applicants.

A complete revision of the ungenerous attitude of the Department to a group of persons which has suffered from Nazism and its allied ideologies more than any other group would appear to be highly desirable. May it not be forgotten that these persons invested their property in this country in confidence on the British sense of justice and fairness.

Reflections

Lotte Kramer

I was born in Mainz, in the Rhineland, a member of a large Jewish community in the Liberal tradition. Jews had been living in the city and other Rhineland centres for centuries; one of the earliest gravestones in the Jewish cemetery dates from the year 900. We were integrated, part of the city. As I grew up I had to learn to accept a certain uprootedness, especially after leaving for England with the Kindertransport in 1939. During the war I was an enemy alien.

In 1943 I got married to a schoolfriend from Mainz and in 1947 our son was born. Soon after we became British citizens. The official asked my husband at the interview how he felt at the thought that his son had been a British subject before him! After living for many years in the London area, with a cosmopolitan circle of friends, my husband's work took us to Peterborough, a cathedral city in a provincial environment. Again, the 'unbelonging' came to the fore, more so than ever. This is when I began to write poetry and poured out much of the earlier experiences which I had suppressed.

I have come to terms now with homelessness, and am ever grateful for being able to identify with a wider outlook on life. I am proud of my history as a Rhineland Jew who has been transplanted into the English countryside and culture which I appreciate. I am also eternally grateful to have encountered wonderful people among the Quakers who financed my early months in England; the good German Christians who were faithful friends in spite of the danger to themselves in the Nazi time and who kept things for me from my parents; the people in England who took me in as part of their family, who were of Christian faith.

My own experience has made me realise that understanding between religions is vital and I have been a longstanding member of the Council of Christians and Jews, and also of the local Interfaith Group. I want to promote mutual tolerance and appreciation wherever possible, both here and also in Germany. There some young people have shown great determination in the attempt at reconciliation without forgetting.

My eternal grief is the loss of my parents and many members of my family in the death camps; my Jewishness is my constant homesickness. I regret not having had a formal English education, for which there was no money in wartime and also I was called up for war work. But I am grateful

for the wonderful teacher of Jewish origin who also came out of Germany
with the help of the Quakers. In spite of her own unhappiness and
uprootedness when she was well into her sixties, she tried to instil in us the
lasting values of the spirit, the arts, music and literature. I later went to
evening classes, while doing all kinds of work by day, studying art and the
history of art. Eventually I came to transmute experience into literature,
my poems.[1]

From *Equation*, published in *Passport 1* (1990).[2]

1. 10 November 1938 – Mainz/Rhine, Germany

'Don't come to school today, it is burning. Tell your father to go out, they
are taking our men away to concentration camps.' He left at once.

This early telephone warning from my cousin who lives opposite the
Synagogue. In carefully hidden language; our phones are tapped. The
Jewish school had been housed in the large Liberal Synagogue building
since its inception in 1934, and had been functioning very well until then,
giving us security.

My friend, Evi, arrives. Unaware of events she actually tried to go to
school but has been turned away from the burning site.

Soon we realise that hordes of youths are ransacking Jewish homes,
beating up our people. We hear them howling down our street. Fearing the
attack, my mother, Evi and I go up to our attic under the roof to hide
among all the stored things.

Crouching below the window, we listen to the commotion outside as
the gang smash their way through a Jewish widow's house opposite. There
is shouting, breaking of glass, and we tremble, we wait.

Then – a miracle – a man's voice: the headmaster of a nearby boys'
grammar school has stepped into the road, yells at them to stop: 'Der
Führer will das Treiben nicht!' (The Führer does not want this behaviour!)

He is a very courageous man. Now all is silent. After a while we go
downstairs and my mother cooks some food. Then Evi insists on leaving
for home, we worry about her, walking through town, and also wait
anxiously for a word from my father.

It is afternoon and another schoolfriend, Elsbeth, arrives. She suggests
we go to the Stadtpark suburb to see if Dr S., the teacher that everyone
likes, is all right. We walk along the Rhine, where it is empty and peaceful.
But as we approach our teacher's house we see him coming towards us,

grey and shattered. He has just been to the nearby home of our Headmaster, Dr M., and found both him and his wife dead. They had gassed themselves.

We hear that former gentile pupils of his, from the grammar school where he taught science, had broken in and devastated the place, insulting and humiliating him. Cruel and disastrous. We are stunned.

We ask Dr S. about himself. 'They only smashed my records ... not much else.'

We return home and wait for my father. He comes back safely after dark. He had been hiding in woods.

Some careful telephone messages filter through about relatives in other cities. Cousins and uncles have been taken away. In my father's native village one uncle has been beaten up badly and dragged through the streets on a lead. Some aunts, in fear, have swallowed pieces of jewellery.

Friends call, lots of whispering and f e a r...

That night, and for quite a while afterwards, I slept with my parents in my mother's bed. Fearful of the knock at dawn.

2. May 1940 – Berkhamsted, England

I arrived in England in the summer of 1939 with a Kindertransport and came to live in a large house in Hertfordshire with four other girls and a teacher.

Money was scarce. We had to earn something and I was sent as an apprentice to the local laundry. That also counted as war work. In a long, low building.

I kept on telling myself that all of it was good experience, that I had to be grateful for having escaped Nazi persecution and London bombing, even if I ached all over from long hours of standing at the steamy mangle, catching hot sheets as they slipped through, listening to the unfamiliar, fruity language of the other girls.

I was fifteen years old, homesick, worried about my parents left behind in Nazi germany. No chance to go to school, no money for further study or a more suitable career.

'Hard work doesn't do any harm' – that slogan had been drummed into me from an early age. The typical German work ethic morality.

The war was going badly in France. Dunkirk became a glorious retreat – a new concept of defeat for me. I felt at one with local anguish, also a hint of double fear at the thought of Nazi invasion.

Out of the blue one morning after I have clocked in, a hostile group of women turns on me, tears running down their faces. A telegram had arrived to say that the husband of a newly married girl had been killed in France.

For the mourners I am 'The German' – 'The Enemy' – I am responsible.

From *Selected and New Poems, 1980–1997* (Rockingham Press, 1997).[3]

EQUATION

As a child I began
To fear the word 'Jew'.
Ears were too sensitive.
That heritage was
Almost a burden.

Then broke the years of war
In a strange country.
This time they sneered at me
'German' as a blemish,
And sealed a balance.

HOMESICK

Still the same search for home.
Not a return,
Nor familiarity,
But the once-known
Threshold of otherness.

Years wipe away
Your fingermarks. Your chair
Is too clean; too
Much light waits in this room;
These curtains fall

Together pointlessly.
Other voices
Carpet the stairs, picture
A wall, a nail
Curls against their colours,

Breaks inside me.
I must look for a place
Without echoes:
Hope will breed in a bed
Of hopelessness.

From *A Lifelong House* (Hippopotamus Press, 1983).[4]

NEVER TREE

Never quite here
Where the water flaps
Wings of soft waves;

Never quite there
Where the river flows
Faster than foam;

Never to be
A part or complete
With waiting days;

Never to know
The length of a street
As vacant grows

The Never Tree
With a hollow trunk
The bitter taste.

From *Earthquake and Other Poems* (Rockingham Press, 1994).

JOURNEY

Around us
The earth of my bones
Knowing me
Better than any other;
Sand in my blood
Edging the Rhine's centuries,
My life's river
Kneeling at the town's cobbles,
Watering
The reddening sins,
The sprouting
Memories of snakes
Licking away fire
With their quick tongues.

JUDGMENT

You, who have not walked
Through the blurred edge of my Hades,
Who have never been dwarfed
By insisting clinkers of spent flames,
Who look not for a name
In anonymous ashes –
Do not encapsulate
A judgment or eavesdrop on pain,
But learn to move
In the flux of a stranger's veins
Over mountains
And from room to room.

THE SOUND OF ROOTS

You remember more each day
Of language, people and town.
You have returned, a long way
From the burdened child to this sound

Of the whispering roots: "Come near,"
They say, "shed your fear, turn your
Janus head and see how far
And deep we can stretch through the years,

Through the centuries in this soil.
We moved with the Rhine, knew the Roman
Yoke, the crusaders' cruel toil.
Yet we harbour here where wine

Grows strong, where we still belong,
Do you hear?" Yes, you listen
And let the blindfold fall from
Your stranger's eyes and you mourn.

From *The Desecration of Trees* (Hippotamus Press, 1994).

AT BURGHLEY HOUSE

We walk here
Where each tree and shrub
Is a planned cypher
In Capability Brown's charter;
Where Englishness
And Tudor stone surround us
And pale sun whitens
Our footprints in the grass.
Your questions
Curl with American vowels
As they should after all those years
Since we walked along the Rhine
On a November day
Bright with dread and ashes
When flame had taken

Our holiest places.
Overnight
We had learnt the language
Of terror, but still could walk
Carelessly, as children will,
By that river that shone.

NOTES

1. Lotte Kramer's works include:

    Scrolls: A Poem, drawing by Trevor Covey (Keepsake Press, 1979)
    Ice-Break, with illustrations by Edith Covey (Annakinn, 1980)
    Family Arrivals: A Collection of Seventeen Poems and a Dedication (Poet &
    Printer, 1981)
    A Lifelong House (Hippopotamus Press, 1983)
    The Shoemaker's Wife: And Other Poems (Sutton, 1987)
    Family Arrivals, 2nd rev. ed. (Poet & Printer, 1992)
    The Desecration of Trees (Hippopotamus Press, 1994)
    Earthquake and Other Poems (Rockingham Press, 1994)
    Selected and New Poems, 1980–1997 (Rockingham Press, in association with
    the European Jewish Publication Society, 1997).

    Her latest publication is *Heimweh, Homesick, Poems*, a bilingual German–
    English edition, edited and translated by Beate Hörr (Brandes & Apsel, 1999).
2. Quotation from *Equation* magazine is acknowledged courtesy of Mike Gerrard
    and Thomas McCarthy.
3. Quotations from Rockingham Press are acknowledged courtesy of David
    Perman.
4. Quotations from Hippopotamus Press are acknowledged courtesy of Roland
    John.

Four Rabbinic Positions in Anglo-Jewry

Louis Jacobs

Like most Rabbis serving in this country, I have experienced at first-hand in my career what used to be called minhag anglia, a characteristic English way of approaching things Jewish, subtly different from that of, say, an Israeli or a Russian Jew or even an American Jew, common language notwithstanding. You do not have to be born in England to follow minhag anglia. My Rebbe, who hailed from Russia, was observed, during the semi-jubilee celebrations of the reign of King George V and Queen Mary, precariously balanced on the roof of the Yeshivah in order proudly to place there a Union Jack. When his pupils expressed their surprise at this seemingly unbecoming display of patriotism, he said: 'Kinderlech! If you had experienced, as I have, life under the Tsar or the Communist Regime you would understand my love for this free and tolerant country.' The minhag anglia element was present in varying degrees of emphasis in the four congregations I have had the privilege of serving and of which I here try briefly to give my impressions in turn.

The 'English' experience, so far as my own ancestry is concerned, began more than 130 years ago, when my Zaide emigrated from Telz in Lithuania to settle for a short while in Canterbury (of all places), where there was a small Jewish community and a synagogue at that time. My father used to regale me with stories he had heard of dignitaries from the cathedral paying visits to my Zaide's sukkah to learn from an observant Jew something about Jewish rites and ceremonies. Some months ago, when I was invited, as the Lord Mayor of Westminster's Chaplain, to preach at the civic service in Westminster Abbey, I could not help thinking it was not too far a cry from the rudimentary Jewish–Christian dialogue of my Zaide and his cathedral friends.

'MUNK'S'

My first position was that of assistant Rabbi of the Golders Green Beth Hamidrash, a semi-independent, strictly Orthodox congregation, loosely

Rabbi Dr Louis Jacobs, CBE, has been rabbi at the New London Synagogue since 1964 and is spiritual leader of the Assembly of Masorti Synagogues. His publications include: *We Have Reason to Believe*; *Principles of Jewish Faith*; *Religion and the Individual*; *The Jewish Religion: A Companion*; and *On Reason and Belief*.

affiliated to Adas Israel, consisting largely of Jews of German origin, headed by Rabbi Eli Munk and still called 'Munk's' after him. Before I came to this remarkable congregation I knew a little of the religious philosophy of Samson Raphael Hirsch, the great exponent of Torah and Derekh Eretz, representing an attempt to merge the ideals of Orthodox Judaism and Western thought and civilisation. At 'Munk's' I learned how the theory was coherently put into practice. Among the congregants were renowned lawyers, university teachers, scientists, writers and other well-educated Jews who yielded to none in their scrupulous adherence to Jewish law. Rabbi Munk had obtained a PhD in Germany on Wordsworth, thus providing a link with Englishness, which, for obvious reasons, he was glad to foster after the Holocaust. In many ways Dr Munk would have qualified as a Modern Orthodox Rabbi, in the sense of one who accepts that European literature, art and music are good in themselves, although in function and to some extent in outlook he belonged to Haredism, otherwise known as ultra-Orthodoxy.

The services at 'Munk's' were conducted with Western decorum. Heaven help anyone who dared to engage in conversation during the services. Only one mourner at a time was allowed to recite kaddish (in front of the Ark) in obedience to the Talmudic dictum: 'two different voices cannot be heard at the same time.' A favourite word for the congregation was discipline. Everything had to be carried out in the precise manner required by the sources. On the festivals not a single piyut was omitted. The men wore hats, never a yarmulke in sight. Only the Rav was allowed to wear his tallit over his head. For a congregant to do so would have been considered an ostentatious show of piety. This meticulousness, however, was redeemed from Teutonic thoroughness by the ability of the members to laugh at themselves. They loved to tell of a visit to Frankfurt by Rabbi Meir Shapiro of Lublin in Poland who was shown round the various institutions of that very frum city, eventually coming to an ice-cream factory which had the legend: 'All our products are frozen under the supervision of the Rabbinate.' 'That is true', wryly remarked Rabbi Shapiro, 'of the whole of their Yiddishkeit.' If at 'Munk's' there was a winning blend of European culture and Anglo-Jewish attitudes, in my next congregation there existed a different but happy combination of Lithuanian and English Jewish temperament.

THE CENTRAL SHUL, MANCHESTER

The Manchester Great Synagogue, where my parents were married by Rabbi Dr Salamon, a graduate of the Orthodox but westernised Seminary in Berlin, was known as the English Shul and was the epitome of Anglo-Jewish Orthodoxy, albeit in a blunt, northern manner. Quite different was the Central Shul in Heywood Street. The congregation at the Central were, in the main, immigrants from Lithuania and their offspring. After serving at 'Munk's' for nearly three years, I was appointed Rabbi of the Central in 1947. Rabbi J. Yoffe, my predecessor, a Rabbi of the old school and a great preacher in Yiddish (though he tried to address the Bar Mitzvah boys in English), sought to preserve Judaism in the best Litvitcher traditions. He died before the Second World War so that I was obliged, after a long gap, to step into his shoes with a determined effort on the part of the congregation to follow his Rabbinic outlook while, at the same time, catering to the needs of the younger members. My task was to preach in English, except for the Yiddish Derashah delivered on the Sabbaths before Pesach and Yom Kippur, and to conduct a nightly Talmud Shiur in Yiddish to oldsters who had been attending Rabbi Yoffe's class many years before. This class was conducted in the Bet Hamidrash equipped with long tables and surrounded by weighty tomes, exactly as in pre-war Lithuania. A London Jew on a visit, seeing a Rabbi with a beard teaching Talmud in Yiddish, remarked that he could only believe that he was not in Manchester at all but in a heimisher shtetl. Unlike my predecessor, however, I was expected to wear canonicals as did the Chazan and the Chazan Sheni. Even the choirboys wore short gowns and black, felt caps. Chazanut was highly prized at the Central. On the second night of Pesach hundreds of Manchester Jews descended on the synagogue to listen to Chazan Moshe Price's melodious rendering of the Ribbono shel Olam for the counting of the Omer. Although in my pastoral functions I was an English Minister, no one in the congregation ever dreamed of describing me, young though I was, as anything but the 'Rov'. From time to time I would even pasken shaalos, pious women bringing me chickens wrapped in newspaper which, after examining the innards, I had to pronounce either kosher or trief.

The members of the Central, with few exceptions, belonged to the lower-middle or working class. Like my father, uncles and cousins, they earned their living through various occupations in the waterproof and raincoat factories owned by Jews who released their Jewish employees from having to work on the Sabbath. It is not generally realised that there existed in Manchester a religious working class, the members of which, while admiring the wealthier Jews who managed to get on, were proud to be working men and women and who usually, like their counterparts in Lancashire nonconformism, saw no contradiction to religion in their stance. They may have blessed the squire and his relations, if they had known of such, but would only have accepted reluctantly their 'proper' station and would never have requested God to keep them in it. In my time, a splendid building was erected by the members of the Central and this was adequately maintained. How could a largely working-class congregation afford such luxury? The answer is that, in addition to the standard membership, there were hundreds of families in the city who, for sixpence a week, belonged to the Synagogue's Burial Society which entitled them to burial in the Shul's cemetery but not to actual membership. The revenues from the burial scheme made the Central rich as a congregation, though poor as individuals.

To what extent was the Central an Anglo-Jewish synagogue? The wearing of canonicals and sermons in English have already been mentioned. In addition, the affairs of the congregation were not conducted, as they were in Lithuania, solely by a few autocrats but by a democratically elected council operating not very differently from the Manchester City Council, with motions proposed and seconded, and regular cries of 'On a point of order'. At one of the meetings someone used the term *ipso facto*, and this became a catchword of the 'Boys', as the younger members were called. The members of the Central, like Manchester Jewry in general, kept kosher homes and were regular in their attendance at services, certainly on the Sabbath and, for many, at the twice-daily minyan during the week as well. They were all proud to speak English with a Manchester accent, and with a regular admixture of Yiddish words such as chutzpah, mazaldik and kenenhora.

THE NEW WEST END SYNAGOGUE

In 1954 I left Manchester for London to take up the position of Minister-Preacher in what was probably the most highly Anglicised Orthodox congregation in this country, counting among its membership peers of the realm, knights and their ladies, members of Parliament and others active in politics and social work. The first Minister of the New West End Synagogue was the Reverend Simeon Singer of Prayer Book fame and my immediate predecessor was the Reverend Ephraim Levine, who had just retired after almost 40 years of distinguished service. Both these men sought to preserve intact the older Victorian mores, but change was in the air, especially in the swing to the right that has now become the norm.

The New West End was 'Orthodox' in a peculiar, non-dogmatic use of that term. There was separate seating for men and women, the latter proudly occupying the ladies gallery, apparently without any need to see this as being politically incorrect. Rightly or wrongly, egalitarianism in Judaism would have been seen as a somewhat bizarre notion. And yet, with typical Anglo-Jewish compromise, not to say inconsistency, the synagogue had a mixed choir and the prayers for the restoration of the sacrificial system were either omitted or recited silently. The cultural shock involved in my transformation from Rov to Minister was not too severe, especially when I witnessed on my first Rosh Hashanah service the whole congregation carrying out with complete devotion the traditional kneeling during the Alenu prayer. In my induction address I declared how honoured I was to have been appointed to a congregation so successful in merging Orthodoxy with modernity, which led Ephraim Levine to observe, at the Kiddush, that it was a good job that this buttering up of the congregation did not take place after a meat meal.

It is hardly appropriate to rehearse here the 'Jacobs' Affair', except to say that the willingness of the New West End to reappoint me as Minister, after I had left for a position at Jews' College, was frustrated by a veto exercised by the Chief Rabbi because of my allegedly untraditional view. The members of the New West End become torn between two characteristic Anglo-Jewish loyalties, to the Chief Rabbi and to religious tolerance and the freedom of the pulpit. My supporters founded the New London Synagogue in 1964, purchasing the building, a fine example of late-Victorian architecture, from the St John's Wood Synagogue, belonging to the United Synagogue. We changed the name to the New London Synagogue, *bayit chadash* ('New House') in Hebrew.

THE NEW LONDON SYNAGOGUE

At the New London, the aim was to return in some way to the older Anglo-Jewish tradition, albeit with certain reservations. There was no mixed seating but we still have a mixed choir and we do not pray for the restoration of sacrifices. A departure from tradition took place in the election of a woman as chairman of the congregation in the belief that, whatever the great sage Maimonides had said 800 years ago, it was a move in full accordance with the spirit of the times. In its constitution the New London Synagogue is described as an Orthodox congregation but we are all aware that the problem of when to go along with the Zeitgeist and when to reject it is acute, as it is in every Anglo-Jewish congregation which claims to be modern.

ST JOHN'S WOOD

It is just coincidental, of course, but our congregation is situated in St John's Wood, a district long at the geographical centre of Anglo-Jewish affairs. At the time of the election of Judge Finestein, a resident of St John's Wood, to the presidency of the Board of Deputies, the other candidate was Eric Moonman of the nearby Belsize Square Synagogue. Some of the major congregations in Anglo-Jewry are situated in or adjacent to St John's Wood: the United Synagogue in Grove End Road; the Sephardi Synagogue in Maida Vale; the Liberal Synagogue in St John's Wood Road; Hampstead Synagogue in Dennington Park Road; and the Reform Synagogue in Upper Berkeley Street. The Saatchi Synagogue has recently been established in the neighbourhood. All that is missing is a Chasidic stiebel. The Israeli ambassador's official residence is only a few streets away. We know that Abraham Ibn Ezra stayed for a short while in London. He refers in his writings to a 'wood' near London. I am no historian of Anglo-Jewry but don't tell me that it was not in our neck of the Wood in which the mediaeval sage sojourned for a while.

There are signs that minhag Anglia is fast disappearing. Good riddance, some now say. More of us will hope that reports of its passing are grossly exaggerated.

Yehudi Menuhin, 1916–1999: An Appreciation

Alexander Goehr

The principle events of Menuhin's life and career have been so often recorded that it is hardly necessary here to do more than mention their outlines: born in San Francisco of Jewish émigré parents; early recognition of outstanding gifts leading to public appearances from 1924 onwards, first in the United States and then in Europe; recording, most famously in this country with Elgar in 1932; further study with Enesco, the great Romanian composer and violinist, and Adolf Busch (the leader of the legendary Busch Quartet). Even on the evidence of those early recordings, it is easy to understand why from the outset Menuhin was regarded as among the very best of prodigies and, very soon, of mature virtuosi of the violin. We hear there not only a flexibility and sweetness of tone and an expressivity of melodic performance, quite apart from the customary facility and fireworks, which immediately puts him among the legendary (Heifetz, Kreisler, Szigeti, Oistrakh), but also a refinement, elegance and stylishness, not always the attributes of the showman in the great performer. But nothing about this seemingly effortless progress to international fame prepares for what happened in the later life of this remarkable man. His sudden death, characteristically while on tour, was noticed by a public much greater and more general than any that had appreciated his musical pre-eminence. It 'made' the first item of the television news, a distinction reserved for world leaders or pop stars, and though interred under a tree in the Surrey grounds of the school he founded (at Stoke d'Abernon in 1962), his Service of Thanksgiving in Westminster Abbey was conducted by clergy of various denominations and was attended by a glittering and strangely assorted group of royals, spiritual and temporal leaders from the whole world as well as the many musicians and artists, great and humble, with whom he had collaborated at one time or another and most of whom owed him debts for kindnesses, small thoughtfulnesses and, above all, for the inspiration of his seemingly inexhaustible vitality and generosity.

While the list of distinctions accorded him takes up an entire page of the Westminster programme – he became a Lord and was awarded the Order of Merit in this country at one extreme, and the Buber-Rosenzweig Medaille from

Alexander Goehr, composer, was until 1999 Professor of Music at the University of Cambridge. He wrote a Trio for the Menuhin, Menuhin, Gendron Ensemble in the 1960s. His most recent work, the opera *Kantan and Damask Drum*, was premiered in Germany in September 1999.

the Gesellschaft Für Christlich-Jüdische Zusammenarbeit perhaps at the other, along with a great list of doctorates, honorary professorships and fellowships – and suggest what is normally called an 'establishment figure', many to be observed in the congregation at the Abbey brought to mind the numerous radical causes and enterprises with which he had become associated and had often initiated. These, too, might be listed. But to do so would be less useful than to try and explain the way in which the three essential, but seemingly contradictory aspects of his life – the musical genius, the social distinction and the radical enterprises – relate and are all aspects of a single personality. I should say that although I personally had the honour to know Menuhin, to write a piece for him and to be the recipient of his kindness from time to time, I have no close knowledge that could lend any authority to what I write, which is based on no more than impression, observation and affection, as well as on his own testimony.

Reading the article on Menuhin by Kinloch Anderson in *Grove*,[1] I was struck by the change of tone and emphasis which occurs halfway through it. In the second paragraph of the article, which mentions his wartime services ('he gave over 500 concerts for American and Allied troops in many theatres of war'), reference is made to criticism which he incurred by being the first Jewish artist to perform in Berlin after the overthrow of the Nazi regime – with Furtwängler, who had remained as conductor of the Berlin Orchestra throughout the war – as well to 'at times a loss of spontaneity and technical reliability'. The writer says, 'Menuhin has indeed made no secret of the fact that he had gone through periods during which he has had to rethink the whole basis of his approach to violin technique'. 'Rethinking the whole basis' is a restrained way of saying personal crisis. That there was a personal crisis of some sort is supported by a comparison between this reported statement and another, which Sir Ernst Gombrich recalls (in his introduction to *The Letters of Adolf Busch*[2]). It was Busch who told with pleasure how, when asked by a 'gushing admirer' how he could play so wonderfully with his little fingers, the boy Menuhin had answered 'I put them in the right position'. Reading this, I was reminded of a later remark of an older Menuhin (made while walking in the grounds of the Menuhin School), when he said to me: 'anyone can learn to play difficult passages on the violin [perhaps he did not say 'anyone']; the problem is how to hold the instrument'.

'Rethinking the whole basis' of a once child prodigy's art is a fascinating but, it would seem to me, potentially hazardous undertaking. If, indeed, other and comparable performers have undertaken analogous rethinkings, they have, as far as I am aware, remained part of their private developments. Menuhin, it would appear, was unique in this respect and the implications of this 'rethinking' seem to have altered not only the way he has been publicly perceived by others but, far more importantly, the way he has seen himself.

The implication of the Anderson entry in *Grove* (and it should be remembered that Anderson is a distinguished musician himself and was close to Menuhin) is that the life divides neatly into two: first, the brilliant international acclaim justly accorded to an outstanding prodigy and, second, the equally recognised life of a great musician who espouses all kinds of causes, some musical, some not, runs festivals, conducts, becomes chairman of the IMC (a committee of UNESCO) and creates a school for gifted children – and a great deal more. The link between the two is the period of rethinking.

To some extent Menuhin's own testimony in his remarkable *Unfinished Journey*[3] supports this view of the chronology of his own life. When he came to play to Enesco with a view to lessons, he remembers he 'played more or less as a bird sings, instinctively, uncalculatingly, unthinkingly ... and neither he nor I gave much thought to theory'. But later this blissful condition is remembered differently:

> I know I did not know how I did it, and not being by nature fraudulent, was later embarrassed to assert on forms demanding my occupation that I was a 'Violinist'. That I played the violin was a fact safely embalmed each day in the past, that I should be able to play it tomorrow a claim savouring of recklessness in my woeful ignorance of what 'playing the violin' signified.

An incident dating back to his tenth or eleventh year is used to exemplify his attitude. (Menuhin is, of course, writing in the later part of his life.) He asks a violinist named Pisatro in the San Francisco Orchestra how he did his *staccato*. 'I do this', he said, 'and this', and played it; and Menuhin remarks, 'he did not explain for the simple reason that he could not'.

Things seem to come to a head in the early 1950s (that is, when Menuhin was in his mid-thirties). Now, he writes, 'my worries reached a peak: ... having left my violins in their cases for some weeks, I found on unpacking them again that I could not be sure of promptly re-establishing intimacy. One day my fingers had their old reassurance, another they fumbled.' He continues, 'beneath surface mastery lay quicksands of doubt'. The relevant, if painful paragraph ends: 'intuition was no longer to be relied on, the intellect would have to replace it'.

The pages throughout the book modestly and objectively describe a most painful and courageous development which seems to have been brought to a head by Menuhin's study of yoga. A study of the philosophy of Constantin Brauner and, in India, experience with Iyengar helped him to come to terms with his difficulties, and the long process of relearning not only sets the tone for his own way of life from that time onwards, but suggests a link between personal experience and the many enterprises he later undertook. 'I am thankful to have been obliged to discover and assimilate so much, for the experience has given me something of value to impart to others.'

Two connected preoccupations reappear throughout the second part of

Menuhin's life, and both of them may be described as having to do with the relationship of mind and body. 'I was, for all my celebrity, another Western body knotted through and through.' India in general and Hatha Yoga in particular seem to have contributed to his peace of mind but 'first and foremost, of course, yoga made its contribution to my quest to understand consciously the mechanics of violin playing, a quest which by 1951 had long been one of the themes of my life'. How this was worked out is described in considerable detail, both philosophically ('Elegant management of the body is among the qualities civilization denies us, and too often the violin, inviting surrender, only makes rigidity more rigid') and practically in the description of how he prepared himself for practice ('Violin practice starts with me on my back on the floor, exploring the laws governing the working of the human anatomy').

But the discoveries he made must have contributed directly to an attitude towards people, cultures and wisdoms far away from his own. He writes a great deal about his own Russian-Jewish family, non-kosher, non-religious without wanting to offend the community, *chalutzim* austerely moralistic in stance. Having prodigy children (his sisters, Hephzibah and Yaltah, were also outstanding performers) took its toll on the parents' lives, which seem to have been devoted to the children. Menuhin's childhood is described by him as by and large a happy one, but here and there darkness creeps through the prevailing sunshine. 'We lived by daylight. Perhaps as a consequence I hated working after the sun went down ... like many children I was afraid of the dark', and 'goodness knows why I should have been haunted by disaster ... I think mine was a worrying nature'. But he appears to have contained such feelings, although at one point he does suggest a potential for, even a joy in, confrontation. 'Well-behaved all my life, at least in public, I had long been thwarting two desires. One was, precisely, to pull a train's emergency cord; the other was to abandon myself to anger without compunction, like Toscanini wreaking destruction on the telephone but preferably with greater cause.' There is no evidence that he succeeded in the first, but he certainly managed to upset various regimes, such as those of South Africa under apartheid and Israel. Nothing offends Israeli nationalists so much as the refusal of the anti-nationalist, liberal Jew to support policies which they justify as necessary for mere survival.

For Menuhin, Judaism seemed to represent not only a deep commitment to European culture, but also some kind of connection with Asia and Asian modes of thought. He observed parallels between Jews and Brahmins and thought that the Japanese and Chinese were in fact 'taking over' from earlier Jewish pre-eminence in violin playing. Never a Zionist, he did, however, believe in and was profoundly attached to the idea of a *Yishuv*, a Jewish homeland, and somehow subscribed to the sense of a special mission for the Jewish people which, if 'good Israelis' prevailed, ought to produce some kind of 'good' state. It was such a belief that led him the more to fear 'the ephemeral character of power, of property and even of nationhood'. His use of the term 'good Israeli', echoing as it does 'good German', speaks volumes.

Menuhin's attitude to the Soviet Union was as complex as was his view of Israel. Visiting it in the post-war Stalinist and post-Stalinist eras, he was acutely aware of the fact that it was from Russia that his family had come. He spoke neither the Hebrew nor Russian languages, but felt that both were somehow in his system. But in whatever language, he always spoke out, insofar as he felt this would not be counter-productive. One thing that the Soviet Union directly contributed to Menuhin was the idea for what became the Yehudi Menuhin School at Stoke d'Abernon in Surrey. He had visited the Central School of Music in Moscow in 1945 and from time to time afterwards and considered it 'the one corner in Russia where I could myself have found a place'. He admired both the methods and the philosophy of the teaching. 'Remarkably, Russia produces almost no child prodigies – not by default, but by deliberate strategy. I was told pupils did not play complete concerti until they were sixteen, but only passages or single movements.' This meant that they were prepared for four-year courses at the Conservatoire and did not emerge into public life until they were 25 or so.

However, when it was started in 1972, the Menuhin School was not intended to be a copy of Moscow. The primary difference at Stoke d'Abernon seems to have been the emphasis on chamber music – making music together – rather than on solo work. Analogously, there was great attention paid to the students' general education. One of the results was that graduates of the Menuhin School are good sight-readers. Although many, in fact, have achieved careers as soloists, more important probably is the type of musician the school produces, at the same time professional and idealistic.

Writing of Menuhin in 'Not a Preface ...' to *Unfinished Journey*, George Steiner observes: 'to find genius and happiness united is nearly a scandal'. The genius, yes, but is it happiness that characterises the man? I would suggest that the quality which really emerges from Menuhin is gratitude rather than happiness. His own vigorously honest and often painful development takes place against a background of continuous and well-earned love and admiration. He is grateful to his parents, to his sisters, to his teachers, to countless friends and acquaintances, great and humble, and, above all, to his wife. But even more than to all these is the feeling of gratitude for his gift and an awareness of the responsibility it imposed upon him.

If the conscious motives which impelled me to found a school – a sense of obligation to past, present and future, the conviction I had something to say, the searching for Utopia – concealed a subconscious urge, it was surely to prove that I was not a freak in playing the violin well in childhood.

Menuhin played beautifully – listen to the Bach Chaconne, the Bach A minor Concerto and the Double Concerto with Enesco and you can still hear the beauty, elegance and inwardness of the interpretation, now more than half a century old. But taking nothing of all this for granted, almost putting it aside, Menuhin has to be remembered as a questing and enquiring thinker and doer. His pre-eminence as a violinist seems to have been the necessary condition for achieving and sometimes failing to achieve everything he attempted. His is a remarkable and original story.

NOTES

1. *Grove's Dictionary of Music and Musicians* (Macmillan, 1981).
2. *The Letters of Adolf Busch* (Marlboro, Vermont).
3. *Unfinished Journey*, Y. Menuhin (Methuen, 1996).

Abbreviations Used

Ad. – Address
Admin. – Administrative; administration; administrator; administer
Adv. – Advisory; adviser
AJA – Anglo-Jewish Association
Ajex. – Association of Jewish Ex-Servicemen and Women
AJY – Association for Jewish Youth
Amer. – America; American
Assn. – Association
Asst. – Assistant
Auth. – Authority; author

B. – Born
Bd. – Board
BMA – British Medical Association
BoD – Board of Deputies
Br. – Branch
Brit. – British; Britain

C. – Council
CBF-WJR – Central British Fund for World Jewish Relief
CCJ – Council of Christians and Jews
C of E – Council of Europe
Cllr. – Councillor
Coll. – College
Com. – Communal; community; commission(er)
Comp. – Company
Cttee. – Committee

Dep. – Deputy
Dept. – Department
Dir. – Director
Distr. – District

Eccl. – Ecclesiastical
Edr. – Editor, Editorial
Educ. – Education; educationist; educational
Emer. – Emeritus
Exec. – Executive

Fdr. – Founder
Fed. – Federation; federal
Fel. – Fellow; Fellowship
Fin. – Finance; financial
Fom. – Former; formerly
Fr. – Friends

Gen. – General
Gov. – Governor; governing
Govt. – Government

H. – Honorary
Hist. – History; historical; historian
HM – Headmaster
HT – Head Teacher

IJPR– Institute for Jewish Policy Research
Instit. – Institute; institution(al)
Internat. – International

JBS – Jewish Blind Society
JEDT – Jewish Educational Development Trust
JIA – Joint Israel Appeal
JMC – Jewish Memorial Council

JNF – Jewish National Fund
JWB – Jewish Welfare Board

Lab. – Labour; laboratory
Lect. – Lecturer; lecture(ship)
Libr. – Librarian; library
Lit. – Literature
Lond. – London

M. – Minister
Man. – Manager; management; managing
Med – Medical; medicine
Min. – Ministry; ministerial
MEP – Member of European Parliament
MP – Member of Parliament

Nat. – National; nationalist; nation(s)

Off. – Officer; office
Org. – Organiser
ORT – Organisation for Resources and Technical Training

Parl. – Parliament; parliamentary
Pol. – Political; policy
Princ. – Principal
Prof. – Professor
Publ. – Publication; public; publicity; publishing

R. – Reader
Reg. – Registrar; Register(ed); region(al)
Rel. – Religion; religious; relation; relief
Rep. – Representative
Res. – Research; Residence
Ret. – Retired
RSGB – Reform Synagogues of Great Britain

Sch. – School; Scholar(ship)
SDP – Social Democratic Party
Sec. – Secretary
Soc. – Society; social; sociology
Sr. – Senior
Supt. – Superintendent
Syn. – Synagogue

T. – Treasurer
TAC – Trades Advisoy Council
Tech. – Technical; technology, -ical
Tr. – Trustee; trust

ULPS – Union of Liberal and Progressive Synagogues
Univ. – University
UK – United Kingdom
US – United Synagogue

V. – Vice
Vis. – Visitation; visitor; visiting
Vol. – Voluntary; volunteer; volume

W. – Warden
WIZO – Women's International Organisation
WJC – World Jewish Congress
WZO – World Zionist Organisation

Z. – Zionist; Zionism

ANGLO-JEWISH INSTITUTIONS

REPRESENTATIVE ORGANISATIONS

BOARD OF DEPUTIES OF BRITISH JEWS
5th Floor, Commonwealth House, 1–19 New Oxford Street, London WC1A 1NF.
☎ 020-7543 5400. Fax 020-7543 0010. E-mail info@bod.org.uk
Board of Deputies Charitable Foundation (Reg. Charity No.1058107)
Founded in 1760 as a joint committee of the Sephardi and Ashkenazi communities in London, the Board of Deputies of British Jews has flourished in its role as the elected representative body of the British Jewish community. It has taken part in all movements affecting the political and civil rights of British Jewry and in many cases at times of crisis in affairs overseas. It conveys the views of the community to Government and other public bodies on political and legislative matters which affect British Jewry, and provides information about the Jewish community and Israel to the non-Jewish world. The Board examines legislative proposals in Britain and the European Union which may affect Jews, and ensures the political defence of the community. It collects statistical and demographic information and undertakes research on and for the community. It maintains contact with and provides support for Jewish communities around the world and promotes solidarity with Israel. It counters bias in the media and ensures that Jews enjoy the full rights of all British citizens.
  The Board plays a co-ordinating role in key issues affecting the Jewish community, and promotes co-operation among different groups within the community. The basis of the Board's representation is primarily synagogal, although the body itself has no religious affiliations. All properly constituted synagogues in Great Britain are entitled to representation, as are other significant communal organisations, such as the Regional Representative Councils, youth organisations and other communal bodies, including major charities. The Board meets most months in London, but holds one meeting a year in a provincial community. It also holds an annual conference open to the community.
  President Eldred Tabachnik, Q.C.; *Senior Vice-President* Jo Wagerman, OBE; *V. Presidents* Henry Grunwald, Q.C., Eric Moonman, OBE; *Tr.* Flo Kaufmann, JP; *Dir. Gen.* Neville Nagler.

The work of the Board is channelled through four new Divisional Boards, each chaired by an Honorary Officer and supported by a professional Director.

External Issues: *Chairman* Eric Moonman, OBE; *V. Chairman* June Jacobs; *Dir.* Jon Sacker.
Community Issues: *Chairman* Henry Grunwald Q.C.; *V. Chairman* Robert Owen; *Dir.* Marlene Schmool.
Finance and Administration: *Chairman* Flo Kaufmann, JP; *V. Chairman* John Webber; *Dir.* Sandra Clarke.
Defence Policy and Group Relations: *Chairman* Jo Wagerman, OBE; *V. Chairman* Eleanor Lind, QC; *Dir.* Mike Whine, Jon Sacker.
Regional Council: *Chairman* Judith Tankel.
Community Research Unit: (Est. 1965) Compiles statistical data on various aspects of the community and prepares interpretative studies of trends. *Dir.* Marlena Schmool.
Yad Vashem Committee: *Chairman* Ben Helfgott.
Trades Advisory Council: Affiliated to the Board of Deputies, the Council seeks to

combat causes of friction in industry, trade and commerce, and discrimination in the workplace, where these threaten good relations in which Jews are concerned. The TAC offers arbitration and conciliation facilities in business disputes and advice to employees who consider that they have suffered discrimination.

Central Enquiry Desk, Communal Diary, JCI: (Under the auspices of the Board of Deputies). Operated entirely by volunteers, the CED provides factual information on all aspects of Jewish home and community life and indicates access to the appropriate authorities to members of the public requiring expert advice. The Desk provides the public access point for the community database created by Jewish Community Information (JCI). The Communal Diary is designed to avoid difficulties which often arise when dates and times of important meetings and functions clash. *H. Dir.* Lt.Col. M. Cohen, TD, DL. ☎ 020-7543 5421/5422.

All Aboard Shops Limited: (Est. 1988) To manage charity shops raising income for the Board and all British Jewish charities (see p.101). ☎ 020-7543 5404/05/15; *Officers* Stella Lucas, Monique Landau, Jeffrey Pinnick; *Admin.* Carol Marks.

JEWISH REPRESENTATIVE COUNCILS

Berkshire Jewish Representative Council (Est. 1995). *Chairman* J. Foreman, c/o 2(B) Tilehurst Road, Reading, Berks RG1 7TN. ☎ 0118-9571167. Fax 0118-9510740.

Representative Council of Birmingham & Midland Jewry (Est. 1937). *President* Roland Diamond, 35 Hunstanton Avenue, B17 8SX. ☎ 0121-554 2234; *Chairman* Sir Bernard Zissman. *Hon. S.* Leonard Jacobs. ☎ 0121-2306 1801; *Admin.Sec.* Mrs R. Jacobs, Singers Hill, Blucher St., B1 1QL. ☎/Fax 0121-643 2688. E-mail bjrepco@brijnet.co Website: www.brijnet.org//birmingham.

Bournemouth Jewish Representative Council. *President* Mrs. H. Greene, 32 Alyth Rd., Talbot Woods, BH3 7DG, ☎ 01202 762101, Fax 01202-763203; *H. Sec.* Mrs. M. Perry. ☎ 01202-300 089. (The Southampton and adjacent area is also represented).

Brighton & Hove Jewish Representative Council. *Chairman* Dr. H. Sless. ☎ 01273-735632; *H.Sec.* Mrs. D. Levinson and Aubrey Milstein, P.O.B 2001, Hove, BN3 4RY. ☎ 01273 558559.

Bristol Representative Council. *Chairman* Leonard Glynn, 42 Vicarage Rd., BS3 1PD. ☎ 0117-923 1835. *Sec.* Mrs K. Balint-Kurti, 6 Ashgrove Rd., BS6 6LY. ☎ 0117-973 1150. Email: bjlc@fishpond.demon.co.uk.

Cardiff Jewish Representative Council. *President* Prof. David Weitzman, 41 Hollybush Rd., Cardiff CF2 6SY; *H. Sec.* Mrs. J. Cotsen, 71 Cyncoed Road, Cyncoed, Cardiff, CF2 6AB. ☎ 02920 484999.

Glasgow Jewish Representative Council. 222, Fenwick Rd., Giffnock, Glasgow G46 6UE. ☎ 0141-577 8200. Fax 0141-577 8202. E-mail glasgow@j-scot.org. http://www.j.scot.org/glasgow. *President* Mrs D. Wolfson; *H. Sec.* S.I. Kliner; *Admin.* Mrs D. Zellman.

Hull Jewish Representative Council. *President* Prof. J. Friend, 9 Allanhall Way, Kirkella, Hull HU10 7QU, ☎ 01482 658930; *H. Sec.* Mrs. A. Segelman, 251 Beverley Road, Kirkella, Hull HU10 7AG. ☎ 01482 650288.

Leeds Jewish Representative Council. *President* Dr Kenneth Shenderey, 151 Shadwell La., LS17 8DW. ☎ 0113 2697520. Fax: 0113 2370851; *Hon. Sec.* Mrs S. Dorsey; *Exec. Off.* Dr D.A. Friedman.

Jewish Representative Council of Greater Manchester & Region. *President* Bella Ansell, Jewish Cultural Centre, Bury Old Road, M8 6FY. ☎ 0161-720 8721 (office). 0161-773 2540(home). *H. Secs* A.J. Cohen, E. Bolchover. *Publ.* Year Book.

Merseyside Jewish Representative Council. *President* D.A. Coleman. *H. Sec.* B. Levene, 433 Smithdown Road, L15 3JL. ☎ 0151-733 2292. Fax 0151-734 0212. *Publ.* Year Book.

Representative Council of North East Jewry. *President* David Franks; *V. Presidents* H. Ross, J. Gellert; *H. Sec.* Martin Levinson, 39 Kenton Rd., Newcastle upon Tyne

NE3 4NH. ☎ 0191-284 4647. Fax 01429 274796. Email tillylaw@enterprise.net.
Nottingham Representative Council. *Chairman* D. Lipman; *Sec.* Mrs A. Lewis, 42
Weardale Rd., Sherwood, NG5 1DD. ☎ 01159-606 121.
Redbridge & District Jewish Community Council. *Chairman* Mrs Angela Levene,
Sinclair House, Woodford Bridge Road, Ilford, Essex, IG4 5LN. ☎ 020-8551 0017.
Sheffield Jewish Representative Council. *President* Selwyn M. Burchhardt; *H. Sec.*
Tony Kay, 105 Bents Road, Sheffield S11 9RH. ☎ 0114 236 0970.
Southend & District Jewish Representative Council. *Chairman* Derek Baum, MBE;
☎ 01702 343789; *H. Sec.* J. Barcan, 22 2nd Avenue, Westcliff-on-Sea, Essex SS0
8HY. ☎ 01702-343192.
Southport Jewish Representative Council. *President* Mrs S. Abrahamson ☎ 01704
540704; *H. Sec.* I. Galkoff, Flat 16, Argyle Court, 3 Argyle Road, Hesketh Park,
Southport PR9 9LQ. ☎ 01704 538119.

ANGLO-JEWISH ASSOCIATION
Commonwealth House, 1-19 New Oxford Street, London W1A 1NF.
☎ 020-7404-2111. Fax 020-7404 2611.
The Anglo-Jewish Association was founded in 1871. Membership of the
Association is open to all British Jews who accept as their guiding principle loyalty to their faith and their country. Its aims are: To promote the education of Jews
in the United Kingdom and elsewhere; to instruct in Jewish affairs and matters
relating to the Jewish religion or race; to collect and publish information relating
to the religious and social conditions of Jews throughout the world; to encourage
Jews in the UK to support Jewish charitable organisations by personal service and
financial assistance; to join or promote any charitable society or body in the UK or
elsewhere, in order to further any of its objects and people; to use its education cultural and political experience for the promotion of good will towards Israel.
President David Loewe; *T.* Robin Stewart, FCA, FCCA; *Gen. Sec.* Cynthia Steuer,
MICM. *Publ.* AJA Review.

ASSOCIATION OF JEWISH FRIENDSHIP CLUBS
26 Enford Street, London W1H 2DD.
☎ 020-7724 8100. Fax 020-7724 8203.
(Est. 1948. Reg. Charity No. 211013) An umbrella organisation for a network of 70
social clubs throughout London and the country for men and women in the sixty-plus
age group, providing friendship with social and cultural activities. *Nat. Chairman* Mrs
Anita Daniels; *Hon. Chaplain* Rev. Dr N. Gale. Full details from the Association.

ASSOCIATION OF JEWISH WOMEN'S ORGANISATIONS IN THE UNITED KINGDOM
4th Floor, 24–32 Stephenson Way, London NW1 2JW.
☎ 020-7387 7688. Fax 020-7387 2110.
(Est. 1965.) To further communal understanding; to promote the achievement of
unity among Jewish women of differing shades of opinion, belonging to
autonomous organisations with different aims. *Member orgs.*: Assn. of US Women;
B'nai B'rith Women; British Emunah; Brit. ORT Women's Div.; Fed. of Women
Zionists (Brit Wizo); Frs. of the Hebrew Univ.; Jewish Women's Aid; Jewish
Women's Network; League of Jewish Women; Reform Syn. Guilds; Sephardi
Women's Assn.; 35's Women's Campaign for Soviet Jewry; UJIA Women's Div.;
ULPS; *H. President* V. Braynis; *Chairman* I. Gee; *V. Chairmen* S. Harris, L.
Freedman; *H. Sec.* S. Webber; *H. T.* J. Rose.

COUNCIL OF CHRISTIANS AND JEWS
Patron: Her Majesty the Queen.
Drayton House, 30 Gordon Street, London WC1H 0AN.

☎ 020-7388 3322. Fax 020-7388 3305. E-mail ccjuk@aol.com
(Est. 1942. Reg. Charity No. 238005.) The Council brings together the Christian and Jewish Communities in a common effort to fight the evils of prejudice, intolerance and discrimination between people of different religions, races and colours, and to work for the betterment of human relations, based on mutual respect, understanding and goodwill. It is neither a missionary nor a political organisation. *Presidents* The Archbishop of Canterbury; The Cardinal Archbishop of Westminster; The Archbishop of Thyateira and Gt. Brit.; The Moderator of the Church of Scotland; The Chief Rabbi; *Chairman, Exec. Cttee.* The Rt. Revd. R. Harries; *V. Chairmen* The Rt. Revd. C. Henderson, V.G., K.C.H.S., R.S. Rubin; *Jt. H. Ts.* Sir Michael Latham, D.L., M.A.; Roderick Wright, B.Sc., F.C.A.; *Jt. H. Secs.* Revd. Eric Allen, B.D. Rosalind Preston, O.B.E.; *Dir.* Sr. Margaret Shepherd nds, B.A., M.Th.; *Educ. Adv.* The Revd Jonathan Gorsky, M.A.; *Educ. Off.* Jane Clements, M.A., B.D. *Publ.* Common Ground.
There are 60 local Branches. A list of these is obtainable from the central office.

LEAGUE OF JEWISH WOMEN
24-32 Stephenson Way, London NW1 2JW.
☎ 020-7387 7688. Fax 020-7387 2110.
(Est. 1943. Reg. Charity No. 261199) Vol. Service Org. to unite Jewish women of every shade of opinion who are resident in the United Kingdom to intensify in each Jewish woman her Jewish consciousness and her sense of responsibility to the Jewish community and the community generally: to stimulate her personal sense of civic duty and to encourage her to express it by increased service to the country. *President* Corinne Van Colle; *H. Sec.* Mrs. B. Wilkinson.
Groups operate in the following centres:

London
Barnet; Bushey Heath; Chigwell & Hainault; Clissold; Coombe & District; Ealing; Finchley; Hampstead Garden Suburb; Harrow & Kenton; Hendon; Ilford; Kingston & Wimbledon; Loughton; Muswell Hill & Highgate; New Era; Newbury Park; North and East London; North West End; Northwood; Oakwood & Winchmore Hill; Outer Limits; Pinner; Potters Bar & Brookman's Park; Radlett; Richmond Park; Ruislip & Ickenham; Southgate; Stanmore; Streatham; Watford; Wembley; Young Herts & Middlesex; and Sefer Tov (Book Club).

Outside London
Brighton & Hove; Cardiff; Glasgow; Leicester; Maidenhead; Surrey; Thanet.

North West Region (centred at Manchester)
Bowdon & Hale; Brantwood; Broadway; Bury; Cheadle & Gatley; Didsbury; Fylde; Heaton Pk.; Higher Broughton & Polefield; Kingsway; Northenden; Park; Prestwich; Sale & Altrincham; Southport; Whitefield & Ringley; Windsor & Sunningdale.

League Associate Division (Men)

ORT HOUSE CONFERENCE CENTRE
126 Albert Street, London NW1 1NF.
☎ 020-7446 8509. Fax 020-7446 8651. Email pavilion@ort.org. Website www.pavpub.com
(Est. 1996) A Jewish conference centre with milk kitchen. Capacity 120. Suitable for business, community or social events. *Conference Centre Man.* Debbie Lodington.

THE THREE FAITHS FORUM
The Sternberg Centre, 80 East End Road, London N3 2SY.

☎ 020-7485 2538. Fax 020-7485 4512. E-mail: strnberg@netcomuk.co.uk (Est. 1997) To encourage friendship, goodwill and understanding amongst people of the 3 monotheistic faiths in the UK and elsewhere (Muslim, Christian and Jewish). Basis of equality and exploring and enjoying those differences where appropriate. *Co-Chairmen* Sir Sigmund Sternberg; Sheikh Dr Zaki M.A. Badawi; *Coord.* Sidney L. Shipton.

WORKING PARTY ON JEWISH ARCHIVES IN THE UK AND IRELAND

Department of History, The University, Southampton SO7 1BJ.
☎ 02380 592211.
The working party was set up in 1988 to create awareness inside and outside the Jewish community of the need to locate, preserve and make available the records of British Jewry. It has the specific aim of carrying out a comprehensive survey of Jewish archive material in the UK.
Chairman Dr. Tony Kushner; Representatives from Society of Archivists (Richard Potts); British Records Association (Peter Barber); British Library (Diana Rowland-Smith); Board of Deputies of British Jews (Sandra Chippeck); Anglo-Jewish Archives (Brian Diamond); *Historians* Tony Kushner, David Cesarani, Bill Williams, Geoffrey Alderman; JHSE (Edgar Samuel).

WORKING PARTY ON JEWISH MONUMENTS IN THE UK & IRELAND

c/o Jewish Memorial Council, 25 Enford Street, London W1H 2DD.
(Est. Dec. 1991. Reg. Charity No. 206565) For the preservation and documenta-tion of Jewish Monuments of architectural and historical importance. (See listings p.207.) **Project: Survey of the Jewish Built Heritage.** Supported by the Heritage Lottery Fund.
Chairman E. Jamilly (☎ 020-7839 5455); *Project Dir.* Dr Sharman Kadish ☎ 020-7724 7778, Fax 020-7706 1710; E-mail sharman.kadish@man.ac.uk. Website www.art.man.ac.uk/reltheol/jewish/heritage; *T.* Mr. A. Rosenzweig; *Sec.* Mrs K. B. Green. Steering Group: *Chairman* Mr R. Hook (English Heritage); *Fieldworkers* B. Bowman, A. Petersen.

JEWISH PRESS, RADIO AND INFORMATION SERVICES

The following is a selection of the major national publications. The Representative Councils of Leeds, Manchester, Merseyside and the North East all publish year-books. Many synagogues and communal organisations also publish newsletters and magazines.

BRITISH-JEWISH PRESS

AJR Information, 1 Hampstead Gate, 1A Frognal, London NW3 6AL. ☎ 020-7431 6161. Fax 020-7431 8454. Monthly. *Edr.* Richard Grunberger.
BIMAH: The Platform of Welsh Jewry (Est. 1994), 23 Solva Avenue, Llanishen, Cardiff CF14 0NP. ☎ 02920 750990. Quarterly. *Ed.* Alan Schwartz. *Ch.* Hanuš Weisl.
Edinburgh Star, 9 Warriston Crescent, Edinburgh EH3 5LA. Est. 1989. 3 issues a year. *Edr.* Michael Adler; *Ch.* John Cosgrove, 14 Gordon Terrace, Edinburgh, EH16 5QR.
European Judaism, Leo Baeck College, 80 East End Rd., London N3 2SY. ☎ 020-8349 4525. Fax 020-8343 2558. E-mail Leo-BaeckCollege@mailbox.ulcc.ac.uk. Website www.lb-college.demon.co.uk. Est. 1966. Two issues a year. *Edr.* Rabbi Dr A. H. Friedlander, Rabbi Professor J. Magonet.
Hamaor, Federation of Synagogues, 65 Watford Way, London NW4 3AQ. Est. 1962. Three issues a year. *Edr.* Sarah M. Ansbacher.
Jewish Book News and Reviews, now incorporated in the Jewish Quarterly.

Jewish Chronicle, 25 Furnival St., London EC4A 1JT. ☎ 020-7415 1500. Fax: 020-7405-9040. Est. 1841. Weekly. *Chairman*: Lionel Gordon; *Edr.* Ned. Temko.

Jewish Community Pages (incorporating the Jewish Business Directory), Forum Publications Ltd., 2300 Northolt Rd., Harrow, Middx HA2 8DU. ☎ 020-8422 7086. Fax 020-8422 9175. *Edr.* B. King.

Jewish Journal of Sociology, 187 Gloucester Place, London NW1 6BW. ☎ 020-7262 8939. Fd. 1959. Published by Maurice Freedman Research Trust (Reg. Charity No. 326077). Semi-annual. *Edr.* Judith Freedman.

Jewish Quarterly, incorporating Jewish Book News and Reviews, P.O. Box 2078, London W1A 1JR. ☎ 020-7629 5004. Fax: 020-7629 5110. E-mail jewish.quarterly@ort.org. Est. 1953. (Reg. Charity No. 268589.) *Edr.* Matthew Reisz.

Jewish Review, Mizrachi-Hapoel Hamizrachi Fed. of Great Britain & Ireland: the voice of Religious Zionism; 2b Golders Green Rd., London NW11 8LH. ☎ 020-8455 2243. Fax 020-8455-2244. Est. 1946. Quarterly. *Edr.* A. L. Handler.

Jewish Socialist: magazine of the Jewish Socialists' Group, BM3725, London WC1N 3XX. E-mail jsg@bardrose.dircon.co.uk. Est. 1985. Quarterly. Edr. Cttee.

Jewish Telegraph, 11 Park Hill, Bury Old Rd., Prestwich, Manchester M25 0HH. ☎ 0161-740 9321. Fax: 0161-740-9325. E-mail telegraph@jaytel-demon.co.uk. Est. 1950. Weekly. (Also in Leeds, Liverpool and Glasgow). *Edr.* P. Harris.

Jewish Travel Guide, Vallentine Mitchell, Newbury House, 890-900 Eastern Avenue, Ilford, Essex IG2 7HH. ☎ 020-8599-8866. Fax: 020-8599-0984. E-mail jtg@vmbooks.com. (Est. 1956. Formerly published by the Jewish Chronicle). Annual. *Edr.* M. P. Zaidner.

Jewish Tribune, 97 Stamford Hill, London N16 5DN. ☎ 020-8800 6688. Fax 020-8800 5000. E-mail.: jtdcharedim@demon.co.uk. English & Yiddish. Est. 1962. Weekly. *Edr.* J. Bentov (Agudas Yisroel of Great Britain).

Jewish Year Book, Vallentine Mitchell, Newbury House, 890-900 Eastern Avenue, Newbury Park, Ilford, Essex IG2 7HH. ☎ 020-8599-8866. Fax 020-8599-0984. E-mail jyb@vmbooks.com. (Est. 1896. Formerly published by the Jewish Chronicle). Annual. *Edr.* S. W. Massil.

Journal of Progressive Judaism, Two issues a year. *Edr.* Rabbi Dr S. D. Kunin, 46 Ebers Grove, Nottingham NG3 5EA.

Judaism Today: an Independent Journal of Jewish Thought, P.O. Box 16096, London N3 3WG. ☎ 020-8346 1668. Fax 020-8346 1776. E-mail colsh@ jto-day.u-net.com. Est. 1995. *Edr.* Dr Colin Shindler.

Le'ela: a journal of Judaism today, London School of Jewish Studies, Albert Rd., London NW4 2SJ. ☎ 020-8203 6427, Fax: 020-8203 6420. Est. 1975. Two issues a year. *Edr.* Rachel Schenker.

London Jewish News (incorporating **New Moon**, Jewish arts and listings monthly), 50 Colindeep Lane, Colindale, London NW9 6HB. ☎ 020-8358 6500, Fax 020-8205 9121.

Manna, Sternberg Centre for Judaism, 80 East End Rd., London N3 2SY. ☎ 020-8346 2288/349 4731. Fax 020-8343-0901. E-mail admin@ refsyn.org.uk. Quarterly. *Edr.* Rabbi Tony Bayfield.

Mazel & Brocho, 168 Stamford Hill, 2nd Floor, N16 6QX. ☎ 020-8211-7876, Fax: 020-8211-7874. *Edr.* Sarah Schleimer.

Menorah: a magazine for Jewish members of H.M. Forces and Small Communities, 25/26 Enford St., London W1H 2DD. ☎ 020-7724 7778. Fax 020-7706 1710. Semi-Ann. *Edr.* Rev. M. Weisman.

Recorder, The Birmingham Jewish, 29 Salisbury Cl., Birmingham B13 8JX. ☎ 0121-449 0362. Monthly. Est. 1935. *Edr.* A. Chesses.

The Scribe: journal of Babylonian Jewry, 20 Queen's Gate Terrace, London SW7 5PF. Est. 1971. Two issues a year. *Edr.* N.E. Dangoor.

Wessex Jewish News, P.O. Box 2624, Poole, BH13 6ZE.

JEWISH RADIO PROGRAMMES

Greater London Radio: Contact: 'Jewish London', 35c Marylebone High St., W1A 4LG. Programmes at 19.00 hours, every Sunday evening on GLR 94.9FM. *Ed.* Gloria Abramoff ☎ 020-7224 2424, 020-7935 1026; *Prod.* Roma Felstein ☎ 020-7224 2424, 020-8446 0927 (home); *Res.* Osa Fowler ☎ 020-7224 2424, 020-7935 1696; *Presenter* Wendy Robbins ☎ 0717-224 2424.
Jewish Spectrum Radio, 204-6 Queenstown Road, Battersea, London SW8 3NR. *Presenter* Richard Ford. A daily two-hour programme of news, views and discussion. Weekly features include Rabbi Shmuel Boteach, Chazanut, Israeli sports, Jewish music, live report from Israel, theatre, art and the Sedra. Broadcasts Sun. 12 noon-2 pm; Mon.-Fri. 1 pm-3.00 pm, 558 AM. ☎ 020-7627 4433. Phone-In: 020-7627 8383. Fax: 020-7627 3409. E-mail: spectrum@spectrum558am.co.uk
'It's Kosher': Produced by Basil Herwald. Broadcast every Thursday evening at 8.05pm-8.30pm. On G.M.R 95.1 and 104.6 FM. ☎ 0161 244-3050/3058. Write to 'It's Kosher', c/o BBC GMR, PO Box 951, New Broadcasting House, Oxford Road, Manchester M60 1SD.

INFORMATION SERVICES

Brijnet
11, The Lindens, Prospect Hill, Waltham Forest, London E17 3EJ.
☎ 0181 520 3531. Email: rafi@brijnet.org
Provider of UK Jewish communal internet services. Creates awareness of the use and benefits of the Internet in the community through training and assistance with all Internet tools. Creates and maintains a useful quality communal electronic information database. Published electronic listings including: brij-announce, daf-hashavua, ujs-update. Websites: http://www.shamash.org/ejin/brijnet/; http://www.brijnet.org *Dir.* Rafael Salasnik.

Jewish Community Information, Board of Deputies, Commonwealth House, 1–19 New Oxford Street, London WC1A 1NF. ☎ 020-7543 5423. Fax: 020-7543 0010. Email: jci@bod.org.uk. *Prof. Off.* Frances Cohen. (Est. 1996.) JCI is an on-going, in-depth information service of Jewish activities and resources. It is available to communal organisations. For general enquiries, contact the Central Enquiry Desk (p.2). ☎ 020-7543 5421/2.

RELIGIOUS ORGANISATIONS

THE CHIEF RABBINATE
The Chief Rabbinate of Britain has developed from the position of the Rabbi of the Great Syn., London. From the early years of the 18th century until recently, he was acknowledged as the spiritual leader of the London Ashkenazi Com. and this recognition was also accepted in the provinces and overseas. Jonathan Sacks was inducted into office in 1991. Previous holders of the office were: Aaron Hart (1709–1756); Hart Lyon (1756–1764); David Tevele Schiff (1765–1792); Solomon Herschell (1802–1842); Nathan Marcus Adler (1845–1890); Hermann Adler (1891–1911); Joseph Herman Hertz (1913–1946); Israel Brodie (1948–1965); Immanuel Jakobovits (1967–1991).
To conform with the constitutional practice, the official designation (1845–1953) was 'Chief Rabbi of the United Hebrew Congregations of the British Commonwealth of Nations' and subsequently 'Chief Rabbi of the United Hebrew Congregations of the Commonwealth'.
Chief Rabbi Rabbi Dr. Jonathan Sacks, M.A.(Cantab), Ph.D. Office of the Chief Rabbi: Adler House, 735 High Road, London N12 0US. ☎ 020-8343 6301. Fax 020-8343 6310. *Exec. Dir.*: Syma Weinberg.

8 RELIGIOUS ORGANISATIONS

Chief **Rabbinate** Council: *Chairman* Peter Sheldon; *Chief Exec.* *Publ.*: Le'ela (see p.6).

BETH DIN (COURT OF THE CHIEF RABBI)
Adler House, 735 High Road, London N12 0US. ☎ 020-8343 6270. Fax 020-8343 6257.
Dayanim Rabbis Chanoch Ehrentreu, Menachem Gelley, Ivan Binstock, BSc. *Asst. Registrar; Marriage Authorisations* Rabbi J. Shindler. ☎ 020-8343 6313.

The Beth Din fulfils the following functions for the orthodox community: (i) dispute arbitration and mediation, (ii) supervision of Jewish religious divorces, adoptions and conversions, (iii) certification of religious status; (iv) supervision of shechita and kashrut.

General enquiries may be made from 9.00 a.m. to 5.00 p.m. (Monday to Thursday). Enquiries on kashrut should be made to the Kashrut Division (see below). Visitors may attend the Beth Din by appointment only. Messages left on the answerphone will be dealt with as soon as possible.

Kashrut Division. ☎ 020-8343 6255. Fax 020-8343 6257. http://www.kosher.org.uk. *Dir.* Rabbi J. Conway, B.A.; *Marketing Dir.* D. Steinhof, B.Sc; *Kashrut Admin.* N. Lauer. *Publ.:* The Really Jewish Food Guide, Snack 'n' Sweet Guide, Passover Supplement.

UNITED SYNAGOGUE
While the Act of Parliament under which it was created bears the date July 14, 1870, the United Synagogue had its origin much earlier in the history of London Jewry. Of the five Constituent Synagogues which joined to form the United Synagogue, the oldest – the Great Synagogue – had a history of more than 280 years; the Hambro dated from 1707 while the New Synagogue was founded in 1761. The Constituent Synagogues now number 44, and the Affiliated Synagogues 19, providing religious facilities for over 38,000 families (about 100,000 people). From the outset, the US has also taken a large share in the social and philanthropic work of the Community.

The **Youth and Community Service Committee** arranges Services for youths and children on Sabbaths and Festivals where required, and is directly concerned with the religious and cultural needs of Jewish youth, appointing Officers to administer such work in Clubs. The US, together with the League of Jewish Women, is a sponsoring body of the Association of Jewish Friendship Clubs (see p.3).

The **Visitation Committee**, which is administered by the US, includes representatives not only of the US but of the Federation of Syns., the RSGB, the Union of Liberal and Progressive Synagogues, the Spanish and Portuguese Syn., the West London Syn., and the Western Syn. Its activities include: Visitation of Jewish inmates of hospitals, prisons, and other public institutions, visitation and religious welfare of deprived, maladjusted and educationally subnormal children in the care of local Councils and Education Authorities, and children committed to Approved Schools and Remand Homes; aftercare of Jewish adult and young prisoners and assistance in the care of Borstal and probation cases (see p.102).

The work of the **Bequests and Trusts Committee** includes marriage portions, New Year, winter and Passover cash gifts, clothing, blankets, Commodity Cards and other necessities. In addition grants are made for the purpose of assisting persons not necessarily members of the US, to obtain a livelihood, or as temporary relief in cases of distress usually in consultation and in conjunction with Jewish Care. The Mutual Aid Fund, which is also under this Cttee., derives its income entirely from the voluntary contributions of seatholders.

The **Conjoint Passover Flour Committee**, which consists of reps. of the US, the Spanish and Portuguese Syn., the Federation of Syns. and the Regional Communities, is responsible for the distribution of Matzot to the needy and to the Jewish inmates of hospitals and other public institutions (see p.9).

The US bears the financial responsibility for the **Beth Din** (Court of the Chief Rabbi), whose duties include not only the determination of civil disputes, but also supervision of Kashrut, licensing of Shochetim and the granting of Jewish religious divorce (Get) (see p.8).

The US is the main contributor to the maintainance of the Chief Rabbinate of the United Hebrew Congregation (see p.7).

The US plays a large part in the work of the **Jewish Committee for H.M. Forces,** which provides facilities for Jewish members of H.M. Forces to maintain the practices of their faith (e.g. by the provision of religious services etc.), arranges for the appointment of Jewish ministers as Chaplains and Officiating Chaplains and for the provision of Jewish literature of a religious and devotional character (see below).

President Peter Sheldon; *Ts.* Geoffrey Hartnell, Brian Wolkind, Jeremy Jacobs; *Chief Exec.* George Willman. (Reg. Charity no. 242552.)

Head Office: Adler House, 735 High Road, London N12 0US. ☎ 020-8343 8989. Fax: 020-8343 6262.

Constituent, Affiliated & Assoc. Synagogues are listed on pp.76–9.
Burial Society, *Sexton* R. I. Ezekiel.

CONJOINT PASSOVER FLOUR COMMITTEE
Adler House, 735 High Road, N12 0US. ☎ 020-8343 8989.

INITIATION SOCIETY
President Aaron Winegarten. *Medical Off.* Dr. M. Sifman, 47 The Ridgeway, NW11 8QP. ☎ 020-8455 2008. Fax 020-8731 6276; *Sec.* A. Minn, 15 Sunny Hill Ct., Sunningfields Cres. NW4 4RB. ☎/Fax: 020-8203 1352. (Est. 1745; Reg. Charity No. 207404) To train Mohalim and to supply Mohalim in cases where required. For a list of Mohalim practising in the British Isles and registered with the Society, apply to the Secretary.

JEWISH COMMITTEE FOR H.M. FORCES
25 Enford Street, W1H 2DD.
☎ 020-7724 7778 Fax 020-7706 1710. E-mail jmcouncil@btinternet.com
The Cttee. officially recognised by the Min. of Defence to appoint Jewish chaplains and to provide for the religious needs of Jewish members of H.M. Forces.

Chairman Lt.Col. Peter Davis, DSC, RM; *T.* Alfred Dunitz, J.P., C.C.; *Sen. Jewish Chaplain to H.M. Forces* Rev. Malcolm Weisman, M.A. (Oxon.); *Sec.* Miss S. Brest. *Publ.:* Menorah.

JEWISH MEMORIAL COUNCIL
25 Enford St., W1H 2DD.
☎ 020-7724 7778 Fax 020-7706 1710. E-mail jmcouncil@btinternet.com
(Est. 1919.) To commemorate the services rendered by Jews in the UK and British Empire in the war of 1914-18 by establishing an organisation which will carry on Jewish tradition as a permanent ennobling force in the lives of Jews in this country. *Chairman* E. Astaire; *Admin.* J. Zaltzman; *President* Edmund L. de Rothschild, T.D.; *V. President* Chief Rabbi; *H. Sec.* T. M. Simon; *H. T.* A. Rosenzweig. *Sec.* Miss L. Wolpert.

Public Schools Committee (which provides facilities for religious education for Jewish boarders in public schools). *Chairman* E. Astaire.

Jewish Memorial Council Pensions Fund. A superannuation fund administered by the JMC, membership of which is open to all communal officials. *Chairman* A. Rosenzweig; *Admin.* J. Zaltzman.

Scholarships. The following scholarships are admin. by the Council:

Alfred Louis Cohen Fund: For students of the J.F.S. Comprehensive School.

Higher Education Awards: For students of British nationality resident in the UK and studying at a UK univ. or equivalent academic institution.

Sir Robert Waley Cohen Memorial Scholarship. To provide Jewish Ministers holding appointments in any part of the British Commonwealth with Travelling Scholarships to pursue Jewish studies.

Provincial Hebrew Classes Committee. Promotes Jewish religious education by inspecting provincial classes and advising on methods and organisation. *Chairman* E. Astaire; *Educ. Adv.* D. Band.

JMC Bookshop. Admin. by the JMC to provide books and educational material to the Jewish community in the UK and overseas. Mail order service available.

Small Communities Committee (Est. 1919). Admins. the funds for the Rev. Malcolm Weisman and his colleagues as visiting Mins. to the Small Communities and isolated families. The Cttee. organises regular conferences in the various regions. *Chairman* Edgar Astaire.

NATIONAL COUNCIL OF SHECHITA BOARDS
P.O. Box 579, Adastra Suite, 401 Nether Street, N3 1YR
☎ 020-8349 9153. Fax 020-8346 2209.
To centralise information on all matters relating to the performance and administration of shechita, and to act as liaison between all the shechita boards and the various Ministries and orgs. affecting shechita and the kosher meat and poultry industry, throughout the UK and abroad.

The National Council registered a trade mark in 1955 and re-registered in 1955 a warranty of Kashrus testifying that the holder of this trade mark was a purveyor of kosher meat and/or poultry and is licensed by a recognised Shechita Board affiliated to the Council and under the supervision of a Rabbinical Authority. *President* N.C. Oster; *Jt V. Presidents* A. Schwalbe, Roy Stern; *Jt Ts.* I.R. Singer, S.D. Winegarten; *Exec. Dir.* M.T. Kester.

RABBINICAL COMMISSION FOR THE LICENSING OF SHOCHETIM
Est. under Schedule 12 of Statutory Instrument 731 of 1995 in respect of Welfare of Animals Regulations (1995), which provides for the shechita of animals and poultry by a shochet duly licensed for the purpose by the Rabbinical Com., and constitutes the Rabbinical Com. as follows: The Chief Rabbi, who shall be the permanent Chairman; one member appointed by the Spanish and Portuguese Syn. (London), who shall be a Vice-Chairman, three members appointed by the Beth Din (London); two members appointed by the Federation of Synagogues (London); one member appointed by the Union of Orthodox Hebrew Congregations (London); two members appointed by the President of the BoD to represent regional congregations. *Chairman* The Chief Rabbi. *H.Sec.* Alan Greenbat, Adler House, 735 High Rd., London N12 0US ☎ 020-8343 6301.

SINGER'S PRAYER BOOK PUBLICATION COMMITTEE
Administered by the United Syn. (☎ 020-8343 8989). *Chairman* E. D. Levy. The purpose of Singer's Prayer Book, first published in 1890, is 'to place within the reach of the Community at large a complete daily prayer Book in Hebrew and English, equally suitable for use in syns. families, and schools.' 1st edn., 1890; 26 imp., 1891-1961; 2nd revd. edn., 6 imp., 1962-1988; 3rd revd. centenary edn., 1990; enlarged centenary edn., 1992; revd. 1998.

SPANISH AND PORTUGUESE JEWS' CONGREGATION
The Community of Spanish and Portuguese Jews in London was founded by Marranos in the middle of the seventeenth century. The congregation 'Sahar Asamaim', worshipped in Creechurch Lane (where a tablet records the site) from 1657 to 1701, when the Bevis Marks Synagogue was built. It is the oldest extant syn. building in Britain except for the long-forgotten medieval syn. of Lincoln. The first branch syn. of the congregation in the West End was est. in Wigmore St. in

1853, and in 1861 removed to Bryanston Street; in 1896 the existing building in Lauderdale Road, Maida Vale was opened. In 1977 another branch of the S. & P. Jews' Cong. was opened in Wembley. The cong. is run by a Board of Elders as well as a Mahamad (five members) who act as Executive. An assessment (Finta) is levied on the Yehidim and congregational affairs are regulated by laws, termed Ascamot, the first code of which was drawn up in 1663.

The congregation maintains the Medrash of Heshaim (founded in 1664). Hebrew religious instruction is given at the Communal Centre, Ashworth Road, W9 as well as in Wembley.

A brotherhood Mikveh Israel (Lavadores), est. 1678, and a Burial Society, Hebrat Guemilut Hassadim (1665), attend to the last rites to the dead. A number of charitable and educational trusts exist for the benefit of Sephardim.

For the history of the Sephardi community in London see A. M. Hyamson: The Sephardim of England (reprinted 1991), L. D. Barnett: Bevis Marks Records Part I (1940), El Libro de los Acuerdos (1931); For genealogical records see Bevis Marks Records [Part II and III (marriages), IV (circumcisions), V (births), VI (burials)]. Available from the Synagogue offices. Other publications include: Treasures of a London Temple (1952), edr. R. D. Barnett, Laws and Charities of the Spanish and Portuguese Congregation, by Neville J. Laski, The Mitsvot of the Spanish & Portuguese Jews' Congregation, by G. H. Whitehill.

(Reg. Charity no. 212517.)

President of Elders L. Gubbay; *V. President of Elders* C. Sacerdoti; *Chief Exec.* Howard Miller; *Sec., London Sephardi Trust.* Office: 2 Ashworth Road, W9 1JY. ☎ 020-7289 2573. Fax: 020-7289 2709. Email howard@sandpsyn.demon.co.uk.

Dayan Dr P. Toledano, Ab Beth Din exercising his position as Ab Beth Din of the Congregation, Rabbi Dr. A. Levy, Communal Rabbi, exercising his position as Spiritual Head of the Congregation.

Synagogues and organisations are listed on pp.84–85.

FEDERATION OF SYNAGOGUES
65 Watford Way, NW4 3AQ.
☎ 020-8202 2263. Fax 020-8203 0610.

The Federation of Synagogues, then embodying 16 small syns. in the eastern districts of London, was est. in 1887. It now comprises 10 Constituent syns. and 16 affiliated congregations situated in most parts of Greater London. The objects of the Federation include:

To provide the services of Orthodox rabbis, ministers and dayanim; the provision of a Burial Society; to assist syns. in the erection, reconstruction or redecoration of their Houses of Worship, to assist in the maintenance of Orthodox religious instruction in Talmud Torahs and Yeshivot; to obtain and maintain Kashrut; to support charitable and philanthropic works; to further the progress of Eretz Yisrael.

President A. J. Cohen, F.C.A.; *V. Presidents* J. Gitlin, J. Winegarten; *Ts.* G. Halibard, A. Finlay; *Hon. Off.* B. Mire; *Admin.* G.D. Coleman.

Associated Bodies
Emer. Rav Rashi: Dayan M. Fisher.

Beth Din of the Federation of Synagogues. Dayan Yisroel Yaakov Lichtenstein Rosh Beth Din, Dayan Berel Berkovits, LL.B., Dayan M. D. Elzas *Dayan Emer.* Dayan Z. J. Alony; *Clerk* Rabbi S.A. Zaidan.

London Kashrus Board. *Kashrus Dir.* Dayan M. D. Elzas; *Chairman* A.J. Cohen.

Federation Burial Society. ☎ 020-8202 3903. Fax 020-8203 0610. *Admin.* M.L. Stuart; *Sexton* N. Kahler; *Ts.* H. Dony, N. Bruckheimer.

Constituent and affiliated synagogues are listed on pp.79–81.

UNION OF ORTHODOX HEBREW CONGREGATIONS
140 Stamford Hill, N16 6QT.☎ 020-8802 6226. Fax 020-8809-7092. (Reg. Charity No. 249892.)

The Union of Orthodox Hebrew Congregations was est. 1926 by the late Rabbi Dr. V. Schonfeld to protect traditional Judaism. The constituents consist of bodies affiliated to the Adath Yisroel Burial Society and others desirous of co-operating in the work of protecting Orthodoxy. Membership of the Union is stated to be more than 6,000.
Rabbinate Rabbi Henoch B. Padwa (Princ. Rab. Authority), Rabbi J. Dunner (Rabbi of the Union), Dayan A. D. Dunner, Dayan S. Friedman, Dayan D. Grynhaus, Rabbi E. Halpern, Rabbi P. Roberts, Rabbi H. I. Feldman (for Kashrus Ctte.); *President* D. Frand; *Registrar* J. R. Conrad.

Associated Bodies
Kashrus Committee-Kedassia, address as above. ☎ 020-8800 6833. Fax 020-8809 7092. *Chairman* E. M. Hochhauser; *Admin.* I. Feldman.
Central Mikvaoth Board, address as above. ☎ 020-8802 6226.
Adath Yisroel Burial Society, 40 Queen Elizabeth's Walk, N16 0HH. ☎ 020-8802 6262/3. Fax 020-8800 8764. *Sec.* A. Barnett. Cemeteries: Carterhatch Lane, Enfield. ☎ 020-8363 3384. Silver Street, Cheshunt Herts. ☎ 01707-874220.
Constituent and affiliated synagogues are listed on pp.81–3.

MASORTI
ASSEMBLY OF MASORTI SYNAGOGUES
1097 Finchley Road, NW11 0PU. ☎ 020-8201 8772. Fax 020-8201 8917. Email: office@masorti.org.uk   Website www.masorti.org.uk.
(Reg. Charity no. 801846). *Vice Presidents* Jaclyn Chernett, Ivor Jacobs, Michael Rose; *Chairman* Paul Shrank; *H. T.* Lionel Halpern; *Dir.* Harry Freedman.
Constituent synagogues are listed on p.83.

REFORM SYNAGOGUES OF GREAT BRITAIN
The Sternberg Centre for Judaism, 80 East End Road, N3 2SY.
☎ 020-8349 4731. Fax 020-8343 0901. E-mail admin@refsyn.org.uk Website http://www.refsyn.org.uk
Founded to co-ordinate a group of synagogues, the first of which – the West London Synagogue – was est. in 1840. Objects: to promote a living Judaism, to interpret the Torah in accordance with the spirit and needs of the present generation and, through its positive, constructive, and progressive view of Jewish tradition, raise and maintain a high standard of Jewish religious life throughout the country.
President Sir S. Sternberg; *Movement Chairman* S. Licht; *Vice Chairmen* J. Epstein, A. Gilbert; *Vice Chairwoman* A. Hallé; *T. J.* Samson; *Chief Exec.* Rabbi T. Bayfield; *Deputy Chief Exec.* M. Frankl; *Partnership and Programmes Dir.* D. Jacobs; *Human Resources Dir.* N. Landau; *Youth & Students Dir.* J. Boyd; *Publ.:* Manna (quarterly), Reform Judaism (quarterly).

Constituent Synagogues: Metropolitan: Synagogues are listed on pp.86–7.
   Regions: Cambridge Beth Shalom Syn.; Blackpool Ref. Jewish Cong.; Bournemouth Ref. Syn.; Bradford Syn.; Brighton & Hove New Syn.; Cardiff New Syn.; Glasgow New Syn.; Hull Reform Syn.; Maidenhead Ref. Syn.; Manchester Ref Syn.; Menorah Syn., Cheshire; Milton Keynes Ref. Syn.; Newcastle Ref Syn.; Sinai Syn., Leeds; Sha'arei Shalom N. Manchester Reform Cong.; South Hampshire Ref. Jewish Com.; Southend & Distr. Reform Syn.; Southport New Syn.; Thanet & Distr. Ref. Jewish Com.
   Associated Communities: Beit Klal Yisrael (North Kensington Ref. Syn); Coventry Jewish Ref. Syn; Darlington Hebrew Cong.; Sheffield & Distr. Ref. Jewish Syn.; Swindon Jewish Com.; Beth Shalom (Munich).
   Assembly of Rabbis: *Chairman* Rabbi D. Smith. ☎ 020-8958 9782; *H. Sec.* Rabbi C. Eimer. ☎ 020-8882 6828.
   Rabbinical Court: (Beit Din). ☎ 020-8349 2568. *Convenor* Rabbi Rodney Mariner.
   RSY-Netzer (RSGB's Youth & Students); *Shaliach* Yonatan Alter; *Northern*

Shlicha Sharon Topper-Amitay; *Mazkir* David Lemer; *Student Activities Co-Ord.:* Ruth Kay (see p.48).
Reform Foundation Trust: *Chairman* Jeffery Rose; *Appeals Co-ord.* M. Wohl.

THE STERNBERG CENTRE FOR JUDAISM
80 East End Road, N3 2SY.
☎ 020-8346 2288. Fax: 020-8343-0901.
(Est. 1982. Reg. Charity No. 283083) A major national centre for the promotion of Jewish religious, educational, intellectual and cultural matters. The Centre includes a Holocaust Memorial Garden and a Biblical garden and a mikveh; it houses the Akiva School, Centre for Jewish Education; C. of Reform & Liberal Rabbis; Manor House Soc.; Jewish Museum, Finchley; Leo Baeck Coll.; Michael Goulston Educ. Foundation; Manor House Books; Pro-Zion; Reform and Liberal Association of Mohalim; RSGB; and the Masorti New North London Synagogue.
   Chairman of Trs. Sir Sigmund Sternberg, KCSG., J.P.; *T.* H. Cohen; *Dir.* Rabbi Tony Bayfield, M.A. *Publ.:* Manna (quarterly).

UNION OF LIBERAL AND PROGRESSIVE SYNAGOGUES
(Jewish Religious Union) 21 Maple St., London W1P 6DS. ☎ 020-7580 1663. Fax 020-7436-4184. Email: montagu@ulps.org
Est. 1902 for the advancement of Liberal Judaism and to establish and organise Congregations, Groups and Religion Schools on Liberal Jewish principles.
   Hon. Life President Rabbi John Rayner, C.B.E.; *Senior V. President* Rabbi Dr Sidney Brichto, M.A., D.D; *Chairman* Jeromé Freedman; *Exec. Dir.* Rabbi Dr Charles H. Middleburgh; *Admin. Dir.* Michael Burman.
   Constituents: Barkingside Progressive Syn.; Birmingham Progressive Syn.; Brighton & Hove Progressive Syn.; Bristol & West Progressive Jewish Cong.; Bedfordshire Progressive Syn.; Crawley Jewish Com; Dublin Jewish Progressive Cong.; Ealing L. Syn.; East Anglia Progressive Jewish Com; Finchley Progressive Syn.; Harrow & Wembley Progressive Syn.; Hertsmere Progressive Syn.; Kent L. Jewish Community; Kingston L. Syn.; Leicester Progressive Jewish Cong.; The Liberal Jewish Syn., London; Lincoln Jewish Community; Liverpool Progressive Syn.; North London Progressive Syn.; Northwood & Pinner L. Syn.; Nottingham Progressive Syn.; Peterborough Liberal Jewish Com; South Bucks (Amersham) Liberal Jewish Com.; Southgate Progressive Syn.; South London L. Syn.; Thames Valley (Reading) Progressive Jewish Com.; West Central L. Syn. (Lond.); Woodford Progressive L. Jewish Syn.
   Rabbinic Conference: *Chair* Rabbi Danny Rich.
   Associate Communities: Hereford Jewish Community; Leamington & Distr. Progressive Jewish Group; Oxford; Welshpool; Or Hadash Liberal Jewish Community, Luxembourg.
   ULPS Youth Dept/ULPSNYC Netzer. *Dir.* Gideon Lyons; *Admin.* Sandra Levene. For further information see under the respective headings.

ASSOCIATION OF REFORM AND LIBERAL MOHALIM
The Sternberg Centre for Judaism, 80 East End Road, London N3 2SY. ☎ 020-8349-4731; Fax. 020-8343-0901.
(Est. 1988.) A full list of practitioners may be obtained from constituent synagogues, from RSGB (020-8349 4731), ULPS (020-7580 1663) or by writing to the Association at the Sternberg Centre.

COUNCIL OF REFORM AND LIBERAL RABBIS
The Sternberg Centre, Manor House, 80 East End Road, N3 2SY. ☎ 020-8349 4731.
Body est. to represent Progressive Rabbinate (RSGB & ULPS) in Britain. *Chairman* Rabbi W. Wolff.

WELFARE ORGANISATIONS

BRITISH ORT
The British branch of World ORT Union (Est. 1880)
126 Albert Street, London NW1 7NE.
☎ 020-7446 8520. Fax: 020-7446 8654. Email british.ort@ort.org Website: www.ort.org/britort
(Est. 1920. Reg. Charity No. 225975) Vocational training and technical education for Jews throughout the world. *Patron* M. Naughton; *President* The Hon. Sir David Sieff; *Co. Chairs* R. Bieber, A. Stern; *Chief Exec.* J. Benjamin; *Admin. Dir.* Mrs Peggy Ann King.

BRITISH TAY-SACHS FOUNDATION
Now under the administration of Jewish Care (see p.96). ☎ 020-8922 2222.

CHAI-LIFELINE
Norwood House, Harmony Way, off Victoria Road, London NW4 2BZ. ☎ Office: 020-8202-2211. Helpline: 020-8202-4567. Fax 020-8202-2111. E-mail info@chai-lifelineorg.uk Website www.chai-lifeline.org.uk
(Reg. Charity no. 1000171). Provides emotional, spiritual and physical support to cancer patients, their families and friends. Telephone help-line, weekly support groups, educational lectures, resource library. Professional counselling available where required. WellWoman and WellMan Screening Clinics. Complementary Therapy Clinics offering aromatherapy, reflexology, healing, reiki, laughter therapy, and a Homeopathic Clinic; legal and financial advice; genetic counselling. For more information or appointments contact Ruth Baum. *Co-chairmen* Susan Shipman and Frances Winegarten.

CHILDREN'S AID COMMITTEE CHARITABLE FUND
c/o 121 Whitehouse Avenue, Borehamwood, Herts WD6 1HB.
☎/Fax 020-8386 2346. Email: bandli21@aol.com
Chair Michael Green; *Vice-Chair* Lira Winston; *T.* Ian Marcusfield; *Sec.* Beverley Hoffman.

FINNART HOUSE SCHOOL TRUST
707 High Road, London N12 0BT.
☎ 020-8445 1670. Fax: 020-8446 7370. Email: finnart@ort.org
(Est. 1901. Reg. Charity No. 220917). A charitable trust, the object of which is to relieve children of the Jewish faith who are delinquent, deprived, sick, neglected and in need of care or education. *Chairman of Trustees* Dr Louis Marks; *Clerk* Peter Shaw.

GET
GET (*Religious Divorce*) *Advisory Service*, 23 Ravenshurst Avenue, London NW4 4EE. ☎ 020-8203-6314. Trained negotiators to help people who have problems in obtaining a Get.

JEWISH AIDS TRUST
Head Office: Colindale Hospital, Colindale Avenue, London NW9 5HG. ☎ 020-8200 0369. Fax 020-8200 1345. E-mail jat@ort.org Website: www.jat.ort.org
(Est. 1988. Reg. Charity No. 327936). The Jewish AIDS Trust works across the entire Jewish community. Its aims are to raise awareness of HIV/AIDS; to provide educational programmes tailored to the needs of each community group; to provide counselling for those in need; and where appropriate to give financial support to people with an AIDS diagnosis.
Patrons Professor Michael Adler, CBE, Mrs. Veronica Cohen, Lady Morris of Kenwood, The Hon. Miriam Rothschild; *Chairman of Tr.* Andrea Kelmanson; *Dir.* Rosalind Collin.

JEWISH ASSOCIATION FOR THE MENTALLY ILL
16a North End Rd, Golders Green, London NW11 7PH.
☎ 020-8458 2223. Fax 020-8458 1117.
(Reg. Charity No. 1003345). JAMI provides guidance, support and advice for sufferers and carers. Principal objectives are: recognition and support for the mentally ill through education and training; to ensure the provision of efficient and effective Jewish social and welfare services.

JAMI operates day-care facilities and a social club for the mentally ill at JAMI House, 131 Golders Green Road, London NW11,☎ 020-8731 7319. A new residential home for 15 sufferers is planned to open in Golders Green early in 2001.

JEWISH CHILD'S DAY
707 High Road, North Finchley, London N12 0BT
☎ 020-8446 8804. Fax: 020-8446 7370. Email: jcd@ort.org. http://www.jewish childsday.co.uk
(Est. 1947, Reg. Charity no. 209266) Raises funds to distribute to agencies providing services to Jewish children in need of special care throughout the world. Provides equipment of all kinds and supports specific projects for children who are blind, deaf, mentally, physically or multi-handicapped, orphaned, neglected, deprived, abused, refugee or in need of medical care. *Life President* Mrs. J. Jacobs; *Chairman* Mrs. J. Moss; T. S. Moss, O.B.E.; *Exec. Dir.* Peter Shaw.

JEWISH LESBIAN AND GAY HELPLINE
BM Jewish Helpline, London WC1N 3XX
☎ 020-7706 3123.
(Est. 1987; Reg. Charity No. 1008035.) An information, support and confidential counselling service for Jewish lesbians, gay men, bisexuals, those unsure about their sexuality, and their family and friends.

It also provides a programme of outreach, educating individuals and organisations to be more aware of the needs and experiences of Jewish lesbians, gay men and bisexuals. The phone line is open every Monday and Thursday 7.00 p.m. to 10.00 p.m. (except festivals and Bank Holidays).

Patrons Leo Abse; Rabbi A. M. Bayfield; Rabbi Lionel Blue; Prof. Sir Herman Bondi, K.C.B., F.R.S; Maria Charles; Dr. Wendy Greengross; Miriam Margolyes; Rabbi Julia Neuberger; Claire Rayner; *Co-ord.* Jack Gilbert; *Sec.* Sally Wexler.

JEWISH MARRIAGE COUNCIL
23 Ravenshurst Avenue, NW4 4EE.
☎ 020-8203 6311. Fax: 020-8203 8727.
(Est. 1946) The Council provides the following services: a counselling service for individual, marital and family problems; it assists anyone with a relationship problem whether they are single, married, divorced or separated (020-8203 6311); preventative counselling in the form of groups for engaged couples, newly-weds, adolescents as well as assertiveness and social skills courses; it provides a mediation service (Dialogue), a Get (religious divorce) Advisory Service (020-8203 6314) (see p.14), Connect Marriage Bureau (020-8203 5207) and Miyad the Nationwide Jewish Crisis Helpline (0345-581 999).

Dir. Jeffery Blumenfeld, B.A. (Hons.);

JMC Manchester: Levi House, Bury Old Road, Manchester M8 6FX. ☎ 0161-795 1240. Appointments 0161-740 5764; 0345 585159.

JEWISH WOMEN'S AID (JWA)
JWA, PO Box 2670, London N12 9ZE.
☎ Admin: 020-8445 8060. Fax: 020-8445 0305; Helpline: 0800-591203.
(Est. 1992. Reg. Charity No. 1047045) JWA aims to break the silence surrounding

domestic violence through education and awareness-raising programmes. JWA operates a freephone confidential national helpline and the first Refuge in Europe for Jewish women and their children fleeing domestic violence is now open. An informal Drop-In group meets weekly and counselling, support and befriending services are available. *H. President* Judith Usiskin; *Chair* Tanya Novick.

THE MANOR HOUSE CENTRE FOR PSYCHOTHERAPY AND COUNSELLING
The Sternberg Centre, 80 East End Road, N3 2SY.
☎ 020-8371 0180. Fax: 020-8343 2558.
The Manor House Centre for Psychotherapy and Counselling provides counselling and psychotherapy skills for voluntary and professional workers in the community. *Course Dirs. & enquiries* Judith Dell, Tina Simmonds.

MAZAL TOV: THE PROGRESSIVE JEWISH MARRIAGE BUREAU
c/o 28 St Johns Wood Rd, London NW8 7HA. ☎ 020-7289 8591. E-mail mazaltov@ulps.org
(Est. 1995. Reg. Charity no. 236590) Non-profit making marriage bureau under aegis of the Union of Liberal and Progressive Synagogues. *Chairperson Management Team* Rita Adler; *Admin* Ruth Green.

NATHAN AND ADOLPHE HAENDLER CHARITY
c/o World Jewish Relief, Drayton House, 30 Gordon Street, London WC1H 0AN. ☎ 020-7387 4747. Fax: 020-7383 4810. Email: wjri@wjr.org.uk
This charity is governed by a scheme which was approved by the Royal Courts of Justice in 1928, whereby the income of the Fund is applicable by the Trustees for the purpose of assisting poor Jews who, in consequence of religious persecution or other misfortune, have come or shall come to take refuge in England. Trustees now World Jewish Relief.

NATIONAL NETWORK OF JEWISH SOCIAL HOUSING
c/o Harmony Close, Princes Park Avenue, London NW11 0JJ. ☎ 020-8381 4901. Fax 020-8458 1772.
Co-ordinates the work of Jewish housing associations, enabling them to share information and assess the housing needs in the Jewish community. *President* Fred Worms, OBE; *Chairman* Robert Manning.

NATIONAL TAY-SACHS AND BIOCHEMICAL GENETICS CENTRE
Research Centre, Royal Manchester Children's Hospital, Pendlebury, Manchester, M27 4HA. ☎ 0161-794 4696 Ext. 2384.
(Reg. Charity No. 326403). Screening and counselling services for Tay-Sachs, Gauchers, Nieman-Pick etc. Community screening sessions in the North of England. Postal screening UK and Europe. Informative literature for students and families. Tay-Sachs Coordinator, any morning, or leave message on 24-hour answerphone. No fixed charge. Donations welcome. Medical enquiries to Dr. Sybil Simon (Research Centre).

OTTO SCHIFF HOUSING ASSOCIATION (OSHA)
The Bishop's Avenue, N2 0BG.
☎ 020-8209 0022. Fax: 020-8201 8089.
(Reg. Charity No.: 210396). (Est. 1934.) For over 60 years OSHA has been the specialist provider of residential, nursing care and sheltered housing in the UK to Jewish refugees from Nazi persecution. Accommodates over 300 people; services include short-term respite care, daycare and specialist care for people with dementia. *Admission inquiries* Jo Mindel Woolf. ☎ 020-8458 7792; *Council* Frank Harding (*H.T.*), Peter Held (*H.Sec*), Andrew Kaufman, Harry Kleeman, C.B.E.,

Rosemary Lewis, Paul Meyer and Ashley Mitchell; *Chief Exec.* Tony Shepherd; *General Mgr.* David Lightburn; *Financial Services Mgr.* David Lovell; *Personnel and Training* Esther Mayerson; *Campaign Mgr.* Leanda Walters.

TAY-SACHS SCREENING CENTRE
Genetics Centre, Guy's & St. Thomas' Hospital Trust, 8th Floor, Guy's Tower, Guy's Hospital, St. Thomas Street, London SE1 9RT.
☎ 020-7955 4648. Fax 020-7955 2550.
Provides information, carrier testing and genetic counselling for Tay-Sachs disease.
Sec. Mrs R. Demant.

WORLD JEWISH RELIEF
Drayton House, 30 Gordon Street, WC1H 0AN. ☎ 020-7387 3925. Fax: 020-7383 4810. Email: wjri@wjr.org.uk
(Est. 1933.) To advise and assist Jewish refugees in the UK who have fled from racial and religious persecution in any part of the world; to help Jews and Jewish communities in need outside the UK with their social, religious, cultural and development activities.
Presidents The Chief Rabbi, Communal Rabbi of Spanish & Portuguese Jews' Cong., Chairman, C. of Reform & Liberal Rabbis; K. D. Rubens; H. Kleeman, C.B.E; Sir Claus Moser, K.C.B., C.B.E., F.B.A.; Dame Simone Prendergast, D.B.E., D.L., J.P.; Lord Janner, Q.C.; D. Cope-Thompson; Lady Jakobovits; D. Lewis; Lord Nathan; Edmond de Rothschild; *Chairman* J. Joseph; *Exec. Dir.* Vivienne Lewis.
   Allocations (JTC Funds) Committee, est. 1953 to administer and make grants from funds received from the Jewish Trust Corporation for the benefit of former victims of Nazi oppression. *Chairman* Jonathan Joseph.
   Jewish Refugees Committee (est. 1933). ☎ 020-7387 4747. Case-working cttee. to assist and advise Jewish Refugees in the UK. *Chairman* Mrs. J. Cohen, J.P.
   British Association of Ethiopian Jewry (Est. 1967). All aid for Ethiopian Jewry is now directed towards their resettlement in Israel.

REFUGEE ORGANISATIONS

45 AID SOCIETY HOLOCAUST SURVIVORS
46 Amery Road, Harrow, Middx HA1 3UQ.
☎ 020-8422 1512.
(Est. 1963) The Society consists mainly of survivors who came to England in 1945/6 and others who have immigrated subsequently. It maintains close links with members who have emigrated to Israel, USA, Canada and other countries. The Society is active in the community, helps members as well as others in need. It furthers Holocaust education and other charitable causes.
President Sir Martin Gilbert; *Chairman* Ben Helfgott; *V. Chairman* Harry Balsam; *T.* Krvlik Wilder; *Sec.* Mick Zwirek.

ACJR (Association of Children of Jewish Refugees)
☎ 020-8579 9906. E-mail acjr@tiara.demon.co.uk
Cultural and social group for people whose parents were victims of or who fled from Nazi persecution in the 1930s and 1940s.
Chair Oliver Walter.

AJR CHARITABLE TRUST (Association of Jewish Refugees in Great Britain)
1 Hampstead Gate, 1A Frognal, London NW3 6AL.
☎ 020-7431 6161. Fax: 020-7431 8454.

(Reg. Charity No. 211239). The Trust's aim is to assist Jewish refugees from Nazi oppression and their families, primarily from Central Europe, by providing a wide range of services. These include regular financial support for the needy, weekly advice sessions on benefit and pension problems, the operation of a popular Day Centre, sheltered accommodation, financial aid for a number of residential homes for the aged, a meals-on-wheels service, a team of full-time social workers, volunteers, and a widely-read journal. *Chief Exec.* Michael Radbil. *Publ.* A.J.R. Information (monthly).

ANNE FRANK EDUCATIONAL TRUST
4th Floor, 43 Portland Place, London W1N 3AG.
☎ 020-8340 9077.
Touring exhibitions and resources on Anne Frank and the holocaust. *Contact* Gillian Walnes.

ASSOCIATION OF JEWISH EX-BERLINERS (AJEB)
33 Church Hill, London N21 1LN.
☎ 020-8882 1638.
(Est. 1990.) To exchange shared experiences of the most traumatic period of Jewish European history at social gatherings as well as record them in writings, individually and collectively.
Chairman P. H. Sinclair. ☎ 020-8882 1638; *T.* Manfred Alweiss, 22 Middleton Rd., London NW11 7NS. ☎ 020-8455 0115. *Publ.* 'So What's New?' (monthly).

CLUB 1943: ANGLO-GERMAN CULTURAL FORUM
51 Belsize Square, NW3 (Synagogue)
☎ 01442-54360.
The Society's aim and purpose was to preserve and develop their cultural standard attained in the country they had to leave. *Chairman* Hans Seelig, 27 Wood End Lane, Hemel Hempstead. ☎ 01442-54360; *Sec.* Julia Schwartz. ☎ 020-8209 0318. *Public Rel.* C. Krysler, 97 Hodford Road, NW11 8EH. ☎ 020-8455 8321.

COMMITTEE FOR THE WELFARE OF IRANIAN JEWS IN GT. BRITAIN
17 Arden Road, N3 3AB
☎ 020-8346 3121.
(Est. 1981.) To act as a co-ordinating and referral agency for Iranian Jews requiring any form of assistance, and to act as a co-ordinating committee for those organisations or individuals who can provide for their needs, and to work closely with the BoD as to their welfare and interests. *President* Lord Clinton Davis, LL.B; *Chairman*

COUNCIL OF JEWS FROM GERMANY
1 Hampstead Gate, 1A Frognal, London NW3 6AL.
☎ 020-7431 6161. Fax: 020-7431 8454.
To protect the rights and interests of Jews who emigrated from Germany.
Founder Organisations: Association of Jewish Refugees in Great Britain, London; American Federation of Jews from Central Europe, Inc., New York; Irgun Oley Merkaz Europa, Tel Aviv.
  Affiliated Organisations Almost all associations of former German Jews in their respective countries of resettlement. *Co-Chairmen* F. Estreicher (Tel Aviv), F. E. Falk (London), C. C. Silberman (New York); *H. Sec.* W. D. Rothenberg (London).

HOLOCAUST SURVIVORS' CENTRE
Corner of Parson Street/Church Road, London NW4 1QA.
☎ 020-8202 9844. Fax: 020-8202 5534.
To provide a centre for survivors of Nazi persecution.
  Jointly founded by WJR and Jewish Care and administered by Jewish Care. Runs courses on public speaking for survivors, retirement workshops, art exhibitions and

other courses of interest to survivors. *Co-ordinator* Rachelle Cohen.

POLISH JEWISH EX-SERVICEMEN'S ASSOCIATION
12 Antrim Grove, London NW3 4XR.
(Est. 1945.) To aid and protect Polish-Jewish ex-Servicemen in the UK, look after the interests of Polish-Jewish refugees, perpetuate the memory of Jewish martyrs of Nazi persecution. *Chairman* L. Kurzer; *V. Chairman* L. Feit; *H. Sec.* L. Kleiner. *H. T. J.* Tigner.

POLISH JEWISH REFUGEE FUND
143 Brondesbury Pk., NW2 5JL ☎ 020-8451 3425.
Chairman W. Schindler; *H. Sec.* Mrs. R. Gluckstein.

SOCIETY OF FRIENDS OF JEWISH REFUGEES
Reg. Charity No.: 227889.
Balfour House, 741 High Road, Finchley N12 0BQ.
☎ 020-8446 1477. Fax: 020-8446 1180.
Chairman G. Ognall; *H. Sec.* I. Connick; *Jt. H. Ts.* P. C. Leach, W. Sharron; *Fin. Sec.* E. H. Kraines.

ORGANISATIONS CONCERNED WITH THE JEWS OF EASTERN EUROPE

BRITISH COUNCIL FOR JEWS IN EASTERN EUROPE
Salisbury Hall, Park Road, Hull HU3 1TD.
☎ 01482 326848 (office), 01482 353981 (private). Fax 01482 568756.
(Est. 1990.) Support for Jewish revival in Eastern Europe. *Publ.* Working for a Cause.
(Belarus office: Apt. 19, 69a Pervomayskaya Str, Mogilev 212030. ☎ +7 1222 25 39 34 (Igor Ilyin)).

THE EAST EUROPEAN JEWISH HERITAGE PROJECT
Jarn, Old Boars Hill, Oxford, OX1 5JQ.
☎/Fax 01865 326578. Fax 01865 326922. E-mail: EEJHP@compuserve.com
(Reg. Charity No. 1061629.) The East European Jewish Heritage Project is a humanitarian, educational and research organization. It is dedicated to perpetuating East European Jewish Culture while improving the lives of Holocaust survivors. The EEJHP sends expeditions to East Europe to locate the last Shtetl Jews. Interviews conducted in Yiddish about pre-war life are tape-recorded and, along with a photographic record of architectural and other remains, are archived at the Taylorian Library of Oxford University. Courses in Yiddish and East European Jewish Studies are conducted in cooperation with East European Universities and other institutions. The East European Jewish Heritage Project also provides medical and other material and assistance to Holocaust survivors and their families. *Contact:* Frank Swartz.

EXODUS 2000
Sternberg Centre for Judaism, 80 East End Road, London N3 2SY.
☎ 020-8349 4731. Fax 020-8343 0901. E-mail admin:refsyn.org.uk
Reform Synagogues of Great Britain and ULPS Campaign for Progressive Judaism in Eastern Europe. Exodus has a national exec. and grps. in many Reform Syns. Its major areas of work are: (i) supporting the growth of Progressive Judaism in the former Soviet Union; (ii) twinning with new Eastern European Progressive Congregations; (iii) sending Rabbis and lay educators to teach. Exodus 2000 works closely with the World Union of Progressive Judaism, and the European Board in London. *Chairman* Rabbi David Soetendorp; *Admin* Linda Kann; *T.* Alan Langleben.

JEWISH RELIEF AND EDUCATION TRUST (JRET)
75 Abbotts Gardens, London N2.
☎ 020-8883 7006.
(Est. 1991. Reg. Charity no. 1007025.) The support of Jewish student and youth activities in the former Soviet Union. *Chairman* Adam Rose.

NATIONAL COUNCIL FOR JEWS IN THE FORMER SOVIET UNION
Contact: Board of Deputies.
☎ 020-7543 5400.
(Est. 1975) Initiates and coordinates activities on behalf of Jews in the FSU including safeguarding and promoting their human, civic, religious and cultural rights. It acts as the umbrella org. for all bodies in Britain with similar objects. The Council is the voice of the community to Government and other bodies in the UK & internationally on FSU Jewish issues. *President* E. Tabachnik Q.C.; *Acting Chairman* Jonathan Arkush.

WOMEN'S CAMPAIGN FOR SOVIET JEWRY (The 35's)
Pannell House, 779/781 Finchley Road, NW11 8DN.
☎ 020-8458 7148/9. Fax 020-8458 9971.
An activist organisation which helps disadvantaged families after they arrive in Israel. The campaign publicises the situation in the former Soviet Union and in Israel through a regular newsletter and through contacts with the media and professional and religious associations. Support is given to ex-Refuseniks, to children in need and to the new Olim in Israel with the organisation of the annual ONE TO ONE sponsored treks in Israel, First Cheque 2000 and the One to One Children's Fund. *Co-Chairmen* Mrs Rita Eker, MBE, Mrs Margaret Rigal.

ZIONIST ORGANISATIONS

BRITISH ALIYA MOVEMENT
Balfour House, 741 High Road, Finchley, London N12 0BQ.
☎ 020-8446 2266. Fax: 020-8446 4419. E-mail bam@jazouk.org
A support organisation providing practical information for future Olim and promoting Aliya. Local groups around Britain meet regularly with guest speakers and Shlichim in attendance on Israel-related topics. Fact finding tours to Israel organised for potential Olim.

BRITISH EMUNAH (Child Resettlement Fund)
Norwood House, Harmony Way, off Victoria Rd, London NW4 2DR.
☎ 020-8203 6066. Fax 020-8203 6668. Email Britishemunah@btinternet.com
(Est. 1933. Reg. Charity No. 215398) A charity organisation with 37 groups throughout the country working to support 27 projects in Israel for underprivileged children, children with learning difficulties, teenagers at risk, victims of violence in the family, programmes for social welfare, new immigrants and senior citizens. *H. L. President* The Lady Jakobovits; *H. President* Mrs Elaine Sacks; *Founder President* Mrs Gertie Landy; *Exec. President* Mrs Guggy Grahame; *Exec. Vice President* Mrs Vera Garbacz; *Co-Chairmen* Mrs Lilian Brodie, Mrs Daphne Kaufman.

BRITISH OLIM RELATIVES ASSOCIATION (BORA)
Balfour House, 741 High Road, Finchley, N12 0BQ
☎ 020-8343 9756/446 1477. Fax: 020-8446 0639.
(Est. 1984.) To maintain closer links between Brit. immigrants in Israel and their relatives in UK by providing services and concessions whenever possible, including reduced air fare, an emergency phone or fax link with Israel and monthly meetings. *President* Mrs. E. Imber-Lithman; *Chairman* J. Daniels.

BRITISH WIZO
(Federation of Women Zionists of Great Britain and Ireland)
105/107 Gloucester Place, London W1H 4BY.
☎ 020-7486 2691. Fax: 020-7486 7521. Finance Fax 020-7486 2691. Email central@britishwizo.org.uk
(Est. 1918) WIZO (FWZ) is the British Branch of World WIZO and a constituent of the Zionist Fed. of Great Brit. & Ireland and is non-party and apolitical. It has some 180 affiliated societies with over 11,000 members. *President* Mrs. R. Sotnick; *Chairman* Mrs. Sarah Glyn; *H. Sec.* Mrs L. Warren; *Co-Ts.* Mrs R. Gelbert, Mrs B. Harding. *Publ.* Vision Magazine (2 issues a year).

GENERAL ZIONIST ORGANISATION OF GREAT BRITAIN
c/o Balfour House, 741 High Road, N12 0BQ.
Chairman A. Stanton; *T. J.* Chart; *H. Sec.* Mrs. Y. M. Stanton.

ISRAEL EMBASSY: 2 Palace Green, Kensington, W8 4QB. ☎ 020-7957 9500.
Fax: 020-7957 9555. Email: info1@israel-embassy.org.uk. Opening Hours: Mon.-Thur. 09.00-17.30 and Fri. 09.00-13.30. Defence Sec. 2A Palace Green, Kensington, W8 4QB; ☎ 020-7957 9548. Consular Sec. 15A Old Court Place, Kensington, W8 4QB. ☎ 020-7957 9516; *Ambassador* H. E. Dror Zeigerman-Eden; *Min. Plenipotentiary* Amiram Magid; *Min.-Cllr.* E. Yerushalmi (Public Aff.); M. Harari (Political Aff.); Ahuva Oren (Cultural Aff.); D. Schneeweiss (Press); Dov Lev (2nd Sec); Gidon Siterman (Economic Aff.); Amos Wohl (Comm. Aff.); Prof A. Shimshoni (Agricultural Aff.); A. Lipzin (Tourism); Menashe Bar-On (Consular Aff.); G. Lahad (Admin.); *Att.* Miss Iris Shoshani, Nissim Bracha, Moshe Aharonov. **Travel Information:** Internet site: http://www.israel-embassy.org.uk/london

JEWISH AGENCY FOR ISRAEL
London office: 741 High Road, Finchley, N12 0BQ.
☎ 020-8446 1144. Fax: 020-8446 8296. E-mail general@jazouk.org
The reconstituted Jewish Agency, consisting of representatives of the World Zionist Organisation and of bodies raising funds on behalf of Israel, has assumed the following responsibilities: absorption of immigrants in Israel; social welfare services for immigrants; education in Israel; higher learning and research in Israel; youth care and training; agricultural settlement; immigrant housing. Project Renewal. *Chairman of the Exec.* Salai Meridor; *Hd. UK Delegation and Tr. for Europe* Dubi Bergman.

JEWISH NATIONAL FUND FOR ISRAEL
Head Office: 58-70 Edgware Way, Edgware, Middx HA8 8GQ.
☎ 020-8421 7600 (JNF); 020-8421 7601 (KKL Wills & Bequests); 020-8421 7602 (KKL Charity Accounts); 020-8421 7603 (Education). Fax 020-8905 4299. E-mail jnf@brijnet.org
President Gail Seal; *Jt. Vice-Presidents* Stanley Lovatt, Jeffrey Zinkin, F.C.A.; *H. T.* David Kibel, F.C.A.; *Chief Exec.* Simon Winters, M.IDM, M.IOD.
JNF Charitable Trust: *Chairman* Gail Seal; *Company Sec.* Harvey Bratt, LL.B.
KKL Executor & Trustee Co. Ltd.: *Chairman* Jeffrey Zinkin; *Company Sec.* Harvey Bratt, LL.B. Objects: Bequests, advisory and covenant services for charity.
Education Department: *Chairman* Helen Rosen; *Educ. Shaliach* Robert Berl, Cert. Ed. Supplies JNF/Israel educational resources to schools, nurseries, religion classes, youth movements and others. Arranges Bar/Bat Mitzvah ceremonies in Israel. Organises events in London and Provinces.
Young JNF: *Chairman:* Adam Caplin; *Co-ord.* Joel Rose.
Bloomsbury Advertising Agency Ltd.: *Company Sec.* Harvey Bratt, LL.B.

LIKUD-HERUT MOVEMENT OF GREAT BRITAIN
143-145 Brondesbury Park, NW2 5JL.
☎ 020-8451 0003. Fax 020-8459 8766.
(Est. 1970) To promote the Zionist ideology as conceived by Ze'ev Jabotinsky. Member of Likud Haolami and affiliated to National Zionist Council of Gt. Britain and a member of the Board of Deputies. *Life President* E. Graus; *Life Vice-Presidents* M. Benjamin, J. Gellert; *Chairman* R. Jacobs; *V. Chairmen* B. Gordon, LL.B., M. Kahtan; *H. T. G.* Avis; *H. Secs.* M. Malinsky, Dr C. Leci; *Memb. Sec.* M. Kayne.

Affiliated Organisations: Young Likud Herut; (Brit Nashim Herut Women's League); Betar-Tagar, Brit Hashmonayim.

MAPAM/MERETZ FOR A PROGRESSIVE ISRAEL
Hashomer House, 37A Broadhurst Gardens, NW6 3BN.
☎ 020-7328 5451. Fax 020-7624 6748.
(Reg. Charity No. 269903) An Anglo-Jewish organisation which identifies with Mapam's world outlook and strives to vitalise Anglo-Jewry in the spirit of Jewish humanism and democracy. It seeks to promote Socialist Zionism, the unity of the Jewish people, aliya, social justice in Israel; Jewish educ. and culture and peace as a vital element of Zionism, complete political, social and economic equality for all Israeli citizens, with religion left to the conscience of each individual. Affiliated to: World Union of Mapam; Z. Fed.; BoD; Monthly Newsletter. *Ch.* Pauline Levis; *Vice-Ch.* Michael Plight; *Sec.* Prof. Gertrude Falk. *Youth Org.* Hashomer Hatzair; Student Org. Kidmah.

MIZRACHI-HAPOEL HAMIZRACHI FEDERATION OF GREAT BRITAIN AND IRELAND
2b Golders Green Road, NW11 8LH.
☎ 020-8455 2243. Fax 020-8455 2244.
(Est. 1918) *President* A. L. Handler; *V. Presidents* Dayan M. Fisher, Dayan P. Toledano, Rabbi P. Greenberg, MA, MPhil, Sir Sidney S. Hamburger, CBE, JP, Dr E. Jaffe, ChB, K. Meyer, Rabbi E. Mirvis, BA, J. Reid; *V. Chairman* I. Rubin; *Jt. H.Ts* B.A. Berman, FCA, N. Cohen, BA, FCA; *Jt. H. Secs.* J.M. Goldblum, MA, S. Taylor. *Publ.*: Jewish Review.
Constituent Orgs.: Emunah: Child Resettlement, Bachad; Bnei Akiva.
Affiliated Orgs.: National Zionist Council, Yavneh Olami.
Mifal Hatorah: Central Foundation for Yeshivot in Israel and Med. Aid Fund.
Education Committee: *Chairman* M.M. Wreschner, FCA.
Public Relations Committee: *Chairman* Rev. R. Turner.
Midreshet Eretz Yisrael: *President* A.L. Handler; *Chairman* M. M. Wreschner.

NATIONAL ZIONIST COUNCIL
2b Golders Green Road, NW11 8LH.
☎ 020-8455 2243/4. Fax 020-8455 2244.
(Est. 1983.) Zionist rep. body for all Z. movements and individuals in Gt. Brit. & Ireland who subscribe to Zionist aims as defined in the Jerusalem programme. To work in particular in the fields of aliya, pub rel., information and economic activities and give maximum support to the J.I.A. It is affiliated with the Mizrachi Fed. *Co-Chairmen* A.L. Handler (Mizrachi), E. Graus (Herut); *V. Chairman* A. Stanton (Gen. Z. Org.).

POALE ZION—LABOUR ZIONIST MOVEMENT
(Affiliated to the British Labour Party.)
82 De Beauvoir Rd., N1 5AT.

Poale Zion, the Brit. section of the World Labour Z. Movement, is the sister party of the Israel Labour Party. It encourages aliya and demands effective internat. guarantees for the civil and political rights of Jews in the diaspora. It is affiliated to the BoD, the Z. Fed. and United Nations Assn. *Chairman* Lawrie Nerva; *Regional V. Chairman* Louise Ellman, M.P.; *H. T. E.* Strauss; *H. Sec.* Henry Smith.

PRO-ZION: PROGRESSIVE RELIGIOUS ZIONISTS
The Sternberg Centre for Judaism, 80 East End Road, N3 2SY.
☎ 020-8349 4731.
(Est. 1978) To work for full legal and rel. rights for Progressive Judaism in Israel, to affirm the centrality in Jewish life of the State of Israel. *Chairman* Estelle Gilston; *H. Sec.* M. Elliott; *H. T. B.* Noah.

UJIA (United Jewish Israel Appeal)
(former Joint Israel Appeal and Jewish Continuity)
Balfour House, 741 High Road, Finchley N12 0BQ.
☎ 020-8446 1477. Fax 020-8446 1180. E-mail: central@ujia.org.
The UJIA's mission is to secure the future of the Jewish People. We pursue this mission by mobilising the UK Jewish community's support for: the rescue of Jews in need throughout the world, and their absorption into Israel; the renewal of Jewish life in Britain, and of our partnership with Israel.
   The majority of the work for which the UJIA is known is carried out by its associated charity, the Joint Jewish Charitable Trust (Charity Reg. No. 1060078), a company limited by guarantee (registered in England, No. 3295115). *Hon. Presidents* Chief Rabbi Dr Jonathan Sacks, The Lord Sieff of Brimpton, O.B.E., M.A.; *President* Sir Trevor Chinn, C.V.O.; *Vice-Presidents* Stanley Cohen, Alan Fox, Ronald Preston, Stephen Rubin; *Chairman* Brian Kerner; *Vice-Chairmen* Geoffrey Ognall, Michael Sinclair, Michael Ziff; *H. T.* Howard Stanton, F.C.C.A.; *Chief Exec.* Jonathan Kestenbaum; *Finance Dir.* Eldred Kraines, C.A. (S.A.).

UNITED ZIONISTS OF GREAT BRITAIN & IRELAND
(affiliated to the World Confederation of United Zionists)
Balfour House, 741 High Road, London N12 0BQ.
☎ 020-8455 0987. Fax 020-8455 0987.
(Est. 1899) A founder of the World Confederation of General Zionists (originally the British Zionist Federation was affiliated to the World Confederation until the 1980s). The United Zionists are the British and Irish constituents of The World Confederation of United Zionists, the only Zionist faction within the WZO which is not affiliated to or associated with any Israeli political party. The United Zionists believe in a Zionism which takes a general approach to all issues. *Chairman* Sidney L. Shipton, LL.B MBA; *H. T.* Steven Elstein, M.Chem.; *H. Sec.* Judith Shipton.

WORLD ZIONIST ORGANISATION
741 High Road, Finchley, N12 0BQ.
☎ 020-8343 9756. Fax 020-8446 0639. Email zion-fed@dircon.co.uk. *UK Dir.* Alan Aziz.
The WZO was established by the first Zionist Congress, which met in Basle on August 29, 1897. The aim of the Org., as defined in the programme adopted by the Basle Congress, was to secure for the Jewish people a home in Palestine guaranteed by public law. At the Congress a constitution providing for a self-governing World Organisation, with the Zionist Congress as the supreme body, was adopted.
   In 1908 the Z.O. embarked upon the work of practical settlement and development in Palestine. When the Z.O. was recognised in 1922 as the Jewish Agency under the Palestine Mandate, it was already responsible for a wide field of

development and settlement activities and it commanded the support of important Jewish groups throughout the world.

The aims of Zionism, as enunciated in the 'New Jerusalem Programme' adopted by the 27th World Zionist Congress in June, 1968, are:
The unity of the Jewish People and the centrality of Israel in Jewish Life;
The ingathering of the Jewish people in its historic homeland, Eretz Israel, through Aliya from all countries;
The strengthening of the State of Israel which is based on the prophetic vision of justice and peace;
The preservation of the identity of the Jewish people through the fostering of Jewish and Hebrew education and of Jewish spiritual and cultural values.

ZIONIST FEDERATION OF GT. BRITAIN AND IRELAND
Balfour House, 741 High Road, N12 0BQ.
☎ 020-8343 9756. Fax 020-8446 0639. E-mail: zion-fed@dircon.co.uk
(Est. 1899) The Zionist Federation is an umbrella organisation encompassing most of the Zionist organisations and individuals in the country and, as such, represents the Zionist Movement in the United Kingdom. Its function is to support, co-ordinate and facilitate the work of all its affiliates nationwide. The Zionist Federation aims to encourage the participation of Jews in Zionist activities including education, culture, Hebrew language and Israel information, underpinned by our belief that the main goal of Zionism is Aliyah.
Chairman Ralph Stern; *V. Chairmen* Ian Myers, Mrs Estelle Gilston; *H. Sec.* Adam Quint; *H.T.* Steven Elstein; *Exec. Dir.* Alan Aziz; *Admin.* Mrs Miriam Shahar.
Committees: Constitution - *Chairman* S. Shipton; Finance - *Chairman* Steven Elstein; Israel Conference - *Chairman* Mrs Estelle Gilston; Moadon Ivri - *Chairman* Mark Novick; Yom Ha'atzmaut 51 - *Chairman* Lawrence Bentley.

OTHER ORGANISATIONS CONCERNED WITH ISRAEL AND ISRAELI ORGANISATIONS

ACADEMIC STUDY GROUP ON ISRAEL AND THE MIDDLE EAST
25 Lyndale Avenue, NW2 2QB.
☎ 020-7435 6803. Fax 020-7794 0291. E-mail: foiasg@foiasg.free-online.co.uk.
(Reg. Charity No. 801772) An academic org. which aims at forging and expanding contacts between academics in this country and their colleagues in Israel and develop among them an interest in their corresponding fields in Israel. Organises study missions to Israel and lectures and meetings on campuses throughout Britain.
President Sir Walter Bodmer, Hertford College, Oxon; *Chairman* Prof. J. Friend, Hull Univ.; *V. Chairman* Prof. Graham Zellick, University of London; *T.* Aviva Petrie, Eastman Dental Institute; *Dir.* J. D. A. Levy.

AKIM
(Est. 1964. Reg. Charity No.: 241458) To assist with the rehabilitation of mentally handicapped children in Israel. *President* Sir S. W. Samuelson C.B.E. *V. President* L. Gamsa. *Chairman* D. Marlowe; *H. T. W.* Raychbart. Corresp. to: 45 Brampton Grove, NW4 4AH. ☎ 020-8202 4022. Fax 020-8202 4747. Akim N.W.: D. Marlowe, 7 Faber Gardens, NW4. ☎ 020-8202 7481. Stanmore Akim: M. Marston, 35 Laburnum Ct., Dennis La., Stanmore, Middx. HA7 4JP. ☎ 020-8954 0543. Younger Akim: H. Turgel, 15 Longcroft Road, Canons Pk., Edgware, Middx. HA8 6RR. ☎ 020-8952 1586.

ANGLO-ISRAEL ARCHAEOLOGICAL SOCIETY
126 Albert St., London NW1E 7NE.
☎ 020-7286 1176.

(Reg. Charity No. 220367) Lectures on recent archaeological discoveries in Israel, publication of annual research bulletin and award of grants to students to participate in excavations in Israel. *Chairman* Prof. H. G. M. Williamson, Oriental Instit., Pusey Lane, Oxford; *Admin.* Mrs. C. A. Maraney.

ANGLO-ISRAEL ASSOCIATION
9 Bentinck Street, W1M 5RP.
☎ 020-7486 2300/935 9505. Fax 020-7935 4690. E-mail: aia@dircon.co.uk
(Reg. Charity No. 313523) The Assn. exists to inform and educ. the Brit. public about Israel's achievements. It holds a unique position among orgs. in Brit. which support Israel. It was est. in 1949 by influential non-Jews who were convinced that others than Jews must support Israel and its membership consists of Jews and non-Jews in all walks of life. This joint support is its great strength. The Assn promotes Israel by org. lectures, meetings and study tours of Israel and Anglo-Israel colloquia, by publishing and commissioning literature about Israel, by awarding scholarships and making grants. Fdr. The late Sir Wyndham Deedes, C.M.G., D.S.O.; *H. President* The Israeli Ambassador; *President* The Lord Peter Shore; *Chairman of C.* The Hon. David Sieff; *Chairman, Exec. Cttee.* John L. Marshall; *H. T. G. R.* Pinto; *Dir.* David Sumberg.

THE BALFOUR DIAMOND JUBILEE TRUST
3rd Floor, 26 Enford Street, London W1H 2DD.
☎ 020-7258 0008. Fax 020-7258 0344. E-mail: admin@bdjt.win-uk.net
(Est. 1977. Reg. Charity No. 276353) To consolidate and strengthen cultural relations between the UK and Israel. Provides the community with a diverse programme of topical activities throughout the year – in literature and the arts. Makes financial support available to individuals and small organisations – both in the UK and Israel – whose work will make an enduring cultural contribution.

The Lord Goodman Fellowship Award, a joint venture with the British Council and the Foreign & Commonwealth Office, encourages the annual exchange of distinguished scholars between the UK and Israel by awarding scholarships for up to a full year of study or research in a field related to the Environment (see http://www.britcoun.org/israel/isrgoodmantm). *Exec. Sec.* Sasha Treuherz.

BANK LEUMI (UK) plc.
London Office: 4/7 Woodstock Street, W1A 2AF.
☎ 020-7629 1205.
(One office in London; Northern branch in Manchester; subsidiary in Jersey, C.I., Bank Leumi Overseas Trust Corporation, Jersey, Ltd. incorporated in 1959 as a subsidiary of Bank Leumi Le-Israel B.M., which was originally established in London in 1902 as the financial instrument of the Zionist Movement under the name of Jewish Colonial Tr. *Chairman* E. Raff; *Dep. Chairman* B. D. Schreier; *Dir. & Gen. Man.* U. Galili; *Hd. Corp. Banking* C. Cumberland.

BEN GURION UNIVERSITY FOUNDATION
1st Fl., Bouverie House, 154 Fleet St., London EC4A 2JD.
☎ 020-7353 1395. Fax 020-7353 1396. Email bgv@paisner.co.uk
(Est. 1974. Reg. Charity No. 276203). To promote Ben-Gurion University of the Negev in Beer-Sheva, Israel, as an international centre for academic excellence and advanced research in medicine, science and desert agriculture – by donations, books, equipment and subscriptions. *Presidents* The Lord Weidenfeld; The Countess of Avon, Hyman Kreitman; *V. President* Suzanne Zlotowski; *Chairman* Harold Paisner; *V. Chairman* Dr Samuel S. Lawson.

BRITAIN-ISRAEL PUBLIC AFFAIRS CENTRE
Drayton House, 30 Gordon Street, London WC1H 0AN.
☎ 020-7387 5444. Fax 020-7387 5535.
(Est. 1976) Bipac provides an information service on all aspects of Israel and Middle East politics. Maintains a photo-library, film catalogue, news and features service and information centre, and provides professional assistance in public relations to pro-Israel orgs. *Chairman* Sir Trevor Chinn; *Dir.* Helen Davis; *Admin.* Angela Silverman.

BRITISH & EUROPEAN MACHAL ASSOCIATION
6 Broadlands Close, London N6 4AF.
☎/Fax 020-8348 8695.
MACHAL (Mitnadvei Chutz L'Aretz). Volunteers from abroad in the 1948 Israel War of Independence. To collect stories and memorabilia appertaining to Machal's crucial contribution for a new historical museum in Israel. To publicise Machal's endeavour and sacrifice. *Co-ordinator* Stanley Medicks. *Sec.* Sidney Lightman.

BRITISH COMMITTEE OF BNEI BRAK HOSPITAL
273 Green Lanes, N4 2EX.
☎ 020-8800 2996
European Off. 21D Devonshire Place, W1. Est. 1979 as part of communal efforts in many countries to build an Orthodox hosp. with a special cardiac dept. in Bnei Brak. Maternity and other wards are open. *Chairman* Dr. L. Freedman; *V. Chairmen* Dayan M. Fisher, V. Lucas, F.S.V.A.; *H. T. B.* Freshwater; *Med. Dir.-Gen.* Dr. M. Rothschild.

BRITISH COMMITTEE OF KEREN YALDENU
(Est. 1955.) To protect Jewish children in Israel through the opening of special centres and institutions from missionary activities and influences alien to Judaism. *Chairman* Mrs. A. Finn, 4 Cheyne Walk, NW4 3W ☎ 020-8202 9689.

BRITISH COUNCIL OF THE SHAARE ZEDEK MEDICAL CENTRE
766 Finchley Road, NW11 7TH.
☎ 020-8201 8933. Fax 020-8201 8935. Email office@shaare-zedek.demon.co.uk.
http://www.szmc.org.il
(Hospital est. Jerusalem 1902.) (Reg. Charity No. 262870) Raising funds by way of donations and legacies to support the hospital's med. care, research and nursing educ. programmes. *President* Lord Mishcon DL; *Chairman* Mrs. M. Rothem; *H.T.* Alfred Frei, F.C.A.; *Exec. Dir.* Miss Angela Margolis, B.A.

BRITISH FRIENDS OF THE ART MUSEUMS OF ISRAEL
Accurist House, 44 Baker Street, P.O. Box 2283, London W1A 1NP.
☎ 020-7935 3954. Fax 020-7224 0744.
(Est. 1948. Reg. Charity No. 313008) BFAMI raises funds to help maintain museums in Israel, acquire works of art and antiquities for them, sponsor exhibitions and youth-art educational programmes. *Patrons* H.E. The Ambassador of Israel, Avigdor Arikha, Sir Anthony Caro, CBE, the Duke of Devonshire, Walter Griessmann, Anish Kapoor, Sir Timothy Sainsbury P.C., Mrs V. Duffield, CBE.; *Chairman* Edward Lee; *Exec. Dir.* Sheila Myers.

BRITISH FRIENDS OF THE ASSAF HAROFEH MEDICAL CENTRE
PO Box 158, Borehamwood, Herts WD6 1ZH.
(Reg. Charity No. 281754) Provides assistance to the Assaf Harofeh Medical Centre, an 800-bed teaching hospital, affiliated with Tel Aviv University. The Assaf Hospital serves the whole spectrum of Israeli society – kibbutzim, moshavim, religious towns, secular cities, Jews, Arabs, a continuous flow of new immigrants and a major army

base. It provides a full range of medical services encompassing every speciality in modern medicine. *President* David Elias, BEM, MWI, FINO; *Chairman* Helen French; *H.T.* Leon Simon MA, CA; *H. Sec.* Ann Silverman.

BRITISH FRIENDS OF HAIFA UNIVERSITY
26 Enford St., London W1H 2DD.
☎ 020-7724 3777.
(Reg. Charity No. 270733) To further the interests and development of Haifa Univ. by donations, books, equipment and subscriptions. The Brit. Frs. are represented at the Bd. of Govs. of Haifa Univ. *Chairman* Victor Conway, F.C.A.; Lord Jacobs (Chairman of Board of Govs); *Dir.* Dr Joseph Shub.

BRITISH FRIENDS OF THE ISRAEL FREE LOAN ASSOCIATION
c/o Mrs. Audrey Druce, 30 Greyhound Hill, London NW4 4JP.
☎ 020-8203 7196. Fax 020-8203 3394.
(Reg. Charity No. 1009568). Provides interest free loans to Russian and Ethiopian immigrants in Israel and other needy Israelis, including small business loans, emergency housing, medical loans, and loans to families with handicapped children.
    Established in Jerusalem, 1990, and in 1992 in London.
    Chairman Dr. Joshua Saper, 1 High Sheldon, Sheldon Avenue, London N6 4NJ; *H. T.* Mrs. A. Druce; *Patrons* Chief Rabbi Dr Jonathan Sacks, Lady Jakobovits.

THE BRITISH FRIENDS OF THE ISRAEL PHILHARMONIC ORCHESTRA FOUNDATION
15 Portland Place, London W1N 3AA.
☎ 020-7872-6300. Fax 020-7872 8999.
(Reg. Charity No. 291129) *Contact* Ronald Cohen.

BRITISH FRIENDS OF ISRAEL WAR DISABLED
23 Bentinck St., W1M 5RL.
☎ 020-7935 5541.
(Est. 1974. Reg. Charity No. 269269) To organise rehabilitation holidays in the UK for groups of Israeli disabled soldiers injured whilst in service; staying in private homes on a community basis. Closely associated with Zahal Disabled Veterans Organisation in Israel. Finance raised in connection with the annual groups and for acquisition of specialised medical equipment. 7 local committees (London, Manchester, Birmingham, Bournemouth, Brighton etc.) *Chairman/Hon. Sol.* Brian B. Harris; *V.Chairman* Harold Newman; *Sec.* Mrs M. Cooper; *T.* David Stetson; *H. Pres.* Irwyn Prentis.

BRITISH FRIENDS OF RAMBAM MEDICAL CENTRE
51 The Vale, London NW11 8SE.
☎ 020-8458 0024. Fax 020-8455 3797.
(Reg. Charity No. 028061) Voluntary organisation raising funds for the purchase of medical equipment for all hospital departments. Current projects include refurbishment of a day-care centre for cancer patients. *Dir.* Anita Alexander-Passe.

BRITISH FRIENDS OF SARAH HERZOG MEMORIAL HOSPITAL (EZRATH NASHIM), JERUSALEM
609 Nelson House, Dolphin Square, London SW1V 3NZ.
☎/Fax 020-7798 5628.
(Reg. Charity No. 1024814) 300-bed teaching hospital affiliated with Hebrew Univ, Hadassah Med Sch, provides 210 geriatric beds and day hosp for health care and rehabilitation, plus 90 psychiatric beds. Community out-patient clinic has over

15,000 visits a year, gives comprehensive family and child counselling. In-depth research into Alzheimer's, Parkinson's diseases. Celebrated in 1995, 100 years service to Jerusalem area. *President* Lady Jakobovits; *V. President* Mrs Elaine Sacks, BA; *Chairman* J. Lehrer; *Admin.* Marion Press.

BRITISH ISRAEL ARTS FOUNDATION
98 Belsize Lane, London NW3 5BB
☎ 020-7435 9878. Fax 020-7435 9879.
(Est. 1985) To promote all forms of bilateral culture between Britain and Israel. The Foundation organises concerts theatre, dance and literary events and exhibitions. Arts Liaison Group est. to coordinate Israeli culture activities in UK. *President* Lilian Hochhauser; *V. President* Norman Hyams; *Chairman* S. Soffair; *Dir.* Ruth Kohn-Corman.

BRITISH-ISRAEL CHAMBER OF COMMERCE
Accurist House, P.O. Box 2281, 44, Baker St., London W1A 1NN.
☎ 020-7486 2371. Fax 020-7224 1783. Email mail@b-ice.org.uk.www.b-ice.org.uk
(Est. 1950) To study and promote trade and econ. relations between the UK and Israel. *Chairman* B. Morris; *V. Chairmen* A. Fox, R. Glatter, F.C.A.; *Chief Exec.* B. Cohen.
   North-West Branch *Regional Dir.* Gideon Klaus, ☎ 0161-929 8916. Fax 0161-929 6277. **North-East Branch** *Regional Dir.* Jane Clynes, ☎ 0113-393 0200.
   Publ. Trading-Up, Ed. Citroen Wolf Communications, 2 Holford Yard, Cruikshank St., London WC1X 9HD. ☎ 020-7713 5555.

BRITISH ISRAEL FORUM
c/o 9 Farm Avenue, London, NW2 2EG.
☎ 020-8452 5236. Fax 020-8452 7988.
(Est 1988. Reg. Charity No. 1042631) Non-political personal links with Israel and throughout Diaspora. Israel Forum 1983. North American Jewish Forum 1983. European Israel Forum 1983. In Britain 1988. *Chairman* Henry Grunwald; *Sec.* Marlena Schmool.

BRITISH-ISRAEL PARLIAMENTARY GROUP
House of Commons, SW1A 0AA. ☎ 020-7222 5853.
H. Sec. Stuart Bell, MP; *T.* Rev. Martin Smyth, MP.

BRITISH OVERSEAS TRADE GROUP FOR ISRAEL
P.O. Box 2283, Accurist House, 44 Baker Street, London W1A 1NP.
☎ 020-7935 4351. Fax 020-7268 2629. Email: amanda@botgi.easynet.co.uk
(Est. 1965) To promote British exports to Israel. BOTGI is an 'Area Advisory Group' to the Brit. Overseas Trade Bd. (DTI) and organises British Trade delegations and exhibitions to Israel. *Chairman* Dr S. Lanyado; *Exec. Dir.* Dr. G. Harris.

BRITISH TECHNION SOCIETY
62 Grosvenor Street, W1X 9DA.
☎ 020-7495 6824. Fax 020-7355 1525.
(Est. 1951. Reg. Charity No. 206922) To further the development of the Israel Institute of Technology (the Technion) at Haifa. *H. President* Lord Mishcon Q.C, Hon. D.L.; *Chairman* Sidney Corob CBE; *V. Chairman* M. Heller; *Ts.* Lois Peltz, A.M. Sorkin; *Sec.* Suzanne Posner. Social Cttees. in London & Regions.

CONSERVATIVE FRIENDS OF ISRAEL
45b Westbourne Terrace, W2 3UR.
☎ 020-7262 2493. Fax 020-7224 8941. Email admin@cfoi.co.uk
CFI is committed to the Conservative Party and to the welfare of the State of Israel and dedicated to establishing close links between GB and Israel. CFI distributes balanced and accurate information on events in the Middle East and through visits to Israel, gives MPs and candidates a greater understanding and insight into the Middle East. *President* Rt. Hon. Sir Timothy Sainsbury; *Chairman* Rt. Hon. Gillian Shepherd, MP; *Jt. V. Chairmen* Jeremy Galbraith, Mrs Betty Geller, John Taylor, CBE; *T. and Deputy Chairman* David Meller; *H. Secs.* Stanley Cohen, Michael Heller. **Parliamentary Group:** *Chairman* Rt. Hon. Gillian Shepherd; *V. Chairmen* John Butterfill, James Clappison; *T.* Nick Hawkins; *H. Sec.* David Amess; *Dir.* Stuart Polak.

FEDERATION OF JEWISH RELIEF ORGANISATIONS
143 Brondesbury Pk., NW2 5JL.
☎ 020-8451 3425. Fax 020-8459 8059.
(Reg. Charity No. 250006) *President* The Chief Rabbi; *Chairman* W. Schindler; *H. Sec.* Mrs. R. Gluckstein.

FRIENDS OF ALYN
(Est. 1962. Reg. Charity No. 232689) To assist the work of the Alyn Orthopaedic Hospital for physically handicapped children in Jerusalem, and provide free medical, surgical and educational aid for needy children. Mrs. Iris Landau, 1 Harford Walk, N2 0JB. ☎ 020-8883 3926.

FRIENDS OF BAR-ILAN UNIVERSITY
2B Golders Green Rd., London NW11 8LH.
☎ 020-8455 2243.
(Est. 1957. Reg. Charity No. 314139) To assist the development of the Bar-Ilan University at Ramat Gan. *Contact* C. Morris.

FRIENDS OF THE BIKUR CHOLIM HOSPITAL, JERUSALEM & BRITISH AID COMMITTEE
3A Princes Parade, Golders Green Road, NW11 9PS.
☎/Fax020-8458 8649.
Bikur Cholim, Jerusalem's oldest hosp. is now the largest med. centre in the heart of the city. *President* Lady Jakobovits; *V. President* Mrs. N. Freshwater; *Chairman* J. Cohen, B.A.; British Aid Committee: *Chairman* David Godfrey, M.A.; *V. Chairman* Morley Franks; *Jt. H. Ts.* B. S. E. Freshwater, P. Englard.

FRIENDS OF BOYS TOWN JERUSALEM
Heather House, Heather Gardens, NW11 9HS.
☎ 020-8731 9550. Fax 020-8731 9599.
(Est. 1963. Reg. Charity No. 227895) To organise support for secondary education and technical training for 1,500 residential students at Boys Town Jerusalem (Kiryat Noar, Bayit Vegan). *Chairman* E. Tabachnik, Q.C.; *T.* J. Pinnick, F.C.A.; *Exec. Dir.* J. Gastwirth.

FRIENDS OF THE HEBREW UNIVERSITY OF JERUSALEM
126 Albert St., London NW1 7NE.
☎ 020-7691 1500. Fax 020-7691 1501
(Est. 1926. Reg. Charity No. 209691) To promote the interests and development of the Hebrew University of Jerusalem through lectures, dinners, specialised events, student courses and donations.

President John Sacher C.B.E.; *Chairman* Michael Gee; *V. Chairman* Barry Townsley; *Exec Dir.* Stephen Goldman.
The Brit. & Irish Friends are represented on the Hebrew Univ. Bd. of Govs.
Groups:Young Friends/Alumni; Womens' Groups; The Jewish & National University Library Group; British Friends of YISSUM (commercialisation of HU research); Jerusalem Botanical Gardens Group; Legal; Medical; and 10 regional groups.

FRIENDS OF THE ISRAEL AGED (RE'UTH)
51 Woodlands, London NW11 9QS.
☎ 020-8455 1450.
To assist the work of the Women's Social Service (Re'uth) in maintaining sheltered housing, old age homes and the Re'uth Medical Centre in Israel.
Est. in Israel 50 years ago. (Reg. Charity No. 278505).
President Arieh L. Handler; *V. President* Anthony Rau; *H. Sec.* Carmel Gradenwitz; *H. T.* David Toledano.

FRIENDS OF THE ISRAEL CANCER ASSOCIATION
2 Serjeants' Inn, Fleet Street, London, EC4Y 1LT.
☎ 020-7583 5353. Fax 020-7353 3683.
(Reg. Charity No. 260710) The Charity is the UK fund raising arm of the Israel Cancer Association. The ICA, founded over 40 years ago, plays a prominent part in the fields of detection, research, treatment and education, supporting oncological institutes nationwide screening, patient care and information services. *President* Mrs. H. Gestetner, O.B.E.; *V. Presidents* Ruth Lady Wolfson, Mrs. V. Duffield, C.B.E., Stephan Wingate, Lady Alliance; *H. T.* Charles Corman; *Committee Chairman* Mrs V. Aaron.

FRIENDS OF ISRAEL EDUCATIONAL TRUST
25 Lyndale Avenue, NW2 2QB.
☎ 020-7435 6803. Fax 020-7794 0291. E-mail foiasg@foiasg.free-online.co.uk
(Reg. Charity No. 271983) To promote and advance the education of the public in the knowledge of the country of Israel and its citizens. F.O.I.E.T. undertakes an extensive UK education programme and sponsors a variety of young adult and professional scholarships in Israel. *Bd.:* Peter Levy (co-chair), Jeremy Manuel, The Lord Morris, Hon. Gerard Noel, Peter Oppenheimer, Rev. Dr. Isaac Levy, O.B.E., Harold Berwin, David Kaye, The Hon. Adrianne Marks (co-chair); *Dir.* J. D. A. Levy.

FRIENDS OF THE JERUSALEM COLLEGE OF TECHNOLOGY
P.O. Box 9700, London NW6 1WF.
☎/Fax 020-7435 5501.
(Est. 1971. Reg. Charity No. 263003) To promote the interests of the College and to support its charitable work. To endow and contribute towards campus projects and to further the work of development and research. *Chairman* R. Sherrington; T. H. Kramer.

FRIENDS OF JERUSALEM RUBIN ACADEMY OF MUSIC AND DANCE
11 Radnor Mews, W2 2SA.
☎ 020-7402 3167. Fax 020-7706 3045.
To provide scholarships for talented children and to help in providing musical instruments, publications, etc. *Jt. Chairmen* Manja Leigh, Lilian Hochhauser.

FRIENDS OF MAGEN DAVID ADOM IN GREAT BRITAIN
Pearl House, 746 Finchley Road, NW11 7TH.
☎/Fax 020-8381 4849. Fax 020-8381 4898. Email info@mda-uk.freeserve.co.uk
(Reg. Charity No. 210770) To assist the work of Israel's voluntary emergency medical and national ambulance services which are responsible for supplying and maintaining first-aid posts and casualty stations, national blood services, medical wing of Israel Civil Defence, medical care of immigrants, missing persons bureaux, beach rescue stations, national responsibility for First-Aid training and all the other services usually supplied by a Red Cross Society.
Nat. Chairman Prof G. Westbury; *V. Chairman* Alan Michaelson; *H. T.* Nicholas Posnansky, F.C.A.; *Exec. Dir.* Eli Benson.
Groups in many districts of London and the Regions.

FRIENDS OF THE MIDRASHIA
79 Princes Park Avenue, London NW11 0JS.
☎ 020-7515 9355. Fax 020-7987 8719.
(Reg. Charity No. 285047) The British Commonwealth and Eire Cttee. was est. in 1952 to aid the Midrashia, the boys' boarding schools at Pardess Hana and Kfar Saba with over 1,000 pupils. *Founder* The late Dr J. Braude; *Chairman* A. J. Braude.

FRIENDS OF PROGRESSIVE JUDAISM IN ISRAEL AND EUROPE
The Sternberg Centre, 80 East End Road, London N3 2SY.
☎ 020-8349 3779. Fax 020-8343 0901. Email EuropeanRegion@directmail.org
(Reg. Charity No. 241337) *Admin.* Neil Drapkin.

FRIENDS OF YAD SARAH
(Reg. Charity No. 294801) Yad Sarah, a volunteer-operated home care organization, lends free, regular and hi-tech medical rehabilitative equipment and provides a spectrum of home care supportive services. Services available to tourists. Head offices, Jerusalem; 77 branches in Israel. *Trustee* D.S. Davis, c/o Cohen Arnold & Co., 13–17 New Burlington Place, London W1X 2JP. ☎ 020-7734 1362. Fax 020-7434 1117.

FRIENDS OF YESHIVAT DVAR YERUSHALAYIM
(Jat: The Jerusalem Academy Trust)
Office: 1007 Finchley Road, London NW11 7HB.
☎/Fax 020-8458 8563.
(Reg. Charity No. 262716) London Cttee: *Jt. Chairmen* A. Maslo, B.Com.; F.C.A., and M. A. Sprei, M.A.(Cantab), M.Sc.; *V. Chairman* M. A. Toperoff; *H. Sec.* C. Cohen, B.A.; *Patrons* Chief Rabbi Dr Jonathan Sacks, Chief Rabbi Emeritus Lord I. Jakobovits, B.A., Ph.D., Rabbi J. Dunner, Dayan M. Fisher; *Principal* Rabbi B. Horovitz, M.A.; *V. Principal* Rabbi Aryeh Carmell, B.Sc.; *Exec. Dir.* Dov Horovitz.

HADASSAH MEDICAL RELIEF ASSOCIATION UK
26 Enford Street, London W1H 2DD.
☎ 020-7723 1144. Fax 020-7723 1222.
(Est. 1986. Reg. Charity No. 1040848) Committed to fund-raising and promoting the work of the Hadassah medical organisation, Hebrew Univ. Med. Centre at Ein Kerem and the Hadassah Univ. Hosp. on Mt. Scopus in Jerusalem. *H.President* Lady Wolfson; *Chairman* Juliet Dalwood; *H. Sec.* Ruth David; *H.T.* Jonathan Prevezer; *Exec. Dir.* Norman Brodie.

HOLYLAND PHILATELIC SOCIETY
(form. British Association of Palestine Israel Philatelists)
(Est. 1952.) For the study and encouragement of all branches of the philately of Palestine and the State of Israel, and of other countries connected with the postal

history of the territory form. known as Palestine. *H. Mem. Sec.* A. Tyler, 9 Ashcombe Avenue, Surbiton, Surrey KT6 6PX.

ISRAEL DISCOUNT BANK LTD.
ISRAEL DISCOUNT BANK OF NEW YORK
(UK Representative Office) Suite 9, 22 Grosvenor Square, W1X 0DY.
☎ 020-7499 1444. Fax 020-7499 1414.
Israel Discount Bank Ltd. (est. 1935) is one of the three largest banks in Israel. The Bank offers, in Israel, a complete range of domestic and international banking services.
   Israel Discount Bank of New York is the largest Israeli-owned bank operating overseas. It offers a full range of domestic and international banking services. *UK Rep.* Ilan Hadani.

ISRAEL GOVERNMENT TOURIST OFFICE
UK House, 180 Oxford Street, London W1N 9DJ.
☎ 020-7299 1111. Fax 020-7299 1112. Email igto-uk@dircon.co.uk
(Est. 1954) *Dir.* Amnon Lipzin.
The office provides information about Israel as a tourist destination.

ISRAEL–JUDAICA STAMP CLUB
(formerly Judaica Philatelic Society)
☎ 020-8886 9331. Fax 020-8886 5116.
A committee of the JNF and a ZF affiliate. Services collectors of the Jewish theme in philately; promotes KKL/JNF labels, Jewish education through philately, commemorative covers, and production of the Journal, the Israel-Judaica Collector, including an alphabetical listing of Jews and their achievements honoured on stamps world wide. Also illustrated lectures on this theme. *Patron* Sir Martin Gilbert; *President* M. Persoff, M.A., F.R.S.A.; *Chairman* C. H. Rosen, F.B.C.O.; *V. Chairman* A. Field; *Sec.* S. Kosky; *T.* E. Pollard. *Publ.* The Israel–Judaica Collector: F. Knoller, E. Sugerman (jt. eds).

ISRAEL PHILATELIC AGENCY IN GREAT BRITAIN
P.O. Box 5, Watford, Herts. WD2 5SW.
☎ 01923-475555. Fax 01923-475556.
Official Agents of the Philatelic Service, Israel Postal Authority, Tel Aviv-Yafo, Israel, for the distribution and promotion of postage stamps and related products of Israel (in the United Kingdom).
   Agency Man. Mrs Emma Hourihan on behalf of Harry Allen (International Philatelic Agencies).

THE JERUSALEM FOUNDATION
44A New Cavendish Street, London W1M 7LG.
☎ 020-7224 5185. Fax 020-7224 6328.
(Est. 1969. Reg. Charity No. 258306) To support charitable projects in the city of Jerusalem embracing (*inter alia*) education, social welfare, the arts and preservation of its historic heritage. *President* Alex Bernstein; *Chairman* Martin Paisner; *UK Dir.* Jane Biran.

JEWISH BLIND IN ISRAEL ASSOCIATION
c/o K. C. Keller F.C.A., Lynwood House, 373/375 Station Road, Harrow, Middx. HA1 2AW.
☎ 020-8357 2727. Fax 020-8357 2027.
(Reg. Charity No. 1006756) Provides financial support and equipment to the Jewish registered blind in Israel. *Adv:* Prof. Lutza Yanko & Prof. Eliezer D. Jaffe, Dr Ben-Zion Silverstone (Jerusalem), Joseph S. Conway, F.R.C.S. (London). *Chairman* Dr J. Saper.

LABOUR FRIENDS OF ISRAEL
BM LFI, London, WC1N 3XX.
☎ 020-7222 4323. Fax 020-7222 4324.
To present the facts of the Middle East situation; to build bridges of understanding between the British and Israeli Labour Movements; to encourage study groups and visits to Israel; to welcome Israeli Labour representatives to the UK; to forge strong links between the Jewish community and the British Labour Party.
Chairman Stephen Twigg, MP; *Dep. Chair* Mike Gapes, MP; *V. Chairs* Ivor Caplin, MP, Ivan Lewis, MP, Jim Murphy, MP; *Dir.* Nick Cosgrove.

LIBERAL DEMOCRAT FRIENDS OF ISRAEL
c/o 318 Whitchurch Lane, Canons Park, Edgware, Middlesex. ☎ 020-8952 8987.
or 31 The Vale, London NW11 8SE. ☎ 020-8455 5140.
Open to all supporters of the Liberal Democrats in UK who recognise the right of Israel to a free, independent, permanent and prosperous existence as a member state of the United Nations. The Assoc. exists to foster good relations and understanding between Britain and state of Israel.
President Lord Jacobs; *V. Presidents* Alan Beith, MP, The Lord Carlile, QC; *Chairman* Monroe Palmer, O.B.E.; *Sec.* David Lerner.

LIFELINE FOR THE OLD
6 Charlton Lodge, Temple Fortune Lane, NW11 7TY.
☎ 020-8455 9059.
(Reg. Charity No. 232084) To assist the work of Lifeline for the Old in Jerusalem, which aims to relieve poverty among the aged in Israel by providing training in occupational skills, and improve the welfare and quality of life of Jerusalem's elderly and disabled. *President* Mrs N. Winton; *H. Sec.* Miss J. Mitzman. *Leeds Branch*: *Chairman* Mrs A. Ziff.

MEDICAL AID COMMITTEE FOR ISRAEL
MAC-I: Reg. Charity No. 258697.
c/o 69 Hampstead Way, London NW11 7LG.
(Est. May 1969.) To provide med. and lab. equipment and offer techn. and prof. advice. To admin. Lewis Fellowships Fund (LFF) for post grad. study & exper. in Brit. hosp. & in the community. To assist and promote health and welfare projects in Israel. Applications from the Director Inter. Relations, Israel Min. of Health, 2 Ben Tabai Street, Jerusalem 93591. Dr. Lionel P. Balfour-Lynn, M.A., M.D., D.C.H.(Camb.).

NEW ISRAEL FUND
26 Enford St., W1H 2DD.
☎ 020-7724 2266. Fax 020-7724 2299. Email nif@cerbernet.co.uk
(Est. 1992. Reg. Charity No. 1060081) The New Israel Fund is an international collaboration with the aim of strengthening democracy and social justice in Israel. The Fund supports charitable projects in Israel which work to safeguard civil and human rights, promote Jewish–Arab co-existence, foster tolerance and religious pluralism, advance the status of women, bridge social and economic gaps, and assist citizen efforts to protect the environment. Through SHATIL, its capacity-building centre for social-change organisations, NIF also promotes action by coalitions of like-minded organisations. *Chair* Lady Dahrendorf; *Chief Exec.* Anna Josse.

OPERATION WHEELCHAIRS COMMITTEE
51 The Vale, London NW11 8SE.
☎ 020-8458 0024. Fax 020-8455 3797.
(Est. 1970. Reg. Charity No. 263089) Voluntary organisation providing rehabilitation and general medical equipment and handmaster units to hospitals in Israel

treating wounded soldiers. *Founder* Mrs. Lily Perry; *Chairman* Mrs. Anita Alexander-Passe.

POALE AGUDAT ISRAEL
Unites Orthodox religious workers to build up Eretz Yisrael in the spirit of the Torah. **World Central Off.:** 64 Frishman Street, Tel Aviv. *President* Rabbi A. Werdiger. **European Office and Great Britain:** P.A.I. Ho., 2A Alba Gardens, NW11 9NR. ☎/Fax 020-8458 5372. *Chairman* F. Wolkenfeld; *Corr.* D. Winter. *Publ.:* PAI Views.

RSGB ISRAEL ACTION
Sternberg Centre for Judaism, Manor House, 80 East End Road, London N3 2SY. ☎ 020-8349 4731 Ext. 228. Fax 020-8343 0901. E-mail refsyn.syn.org.uk (Est. 1989) Aims to create knowledge and love of Israel through theology, education and Israel action by raising Israel consciousness within the Reform Movement and by building links with IMPJ (Israel Movement Progressive Judaism) and its constituent communities. *Co-Chairmen* Paul Langsford, Paul Usiskin.

STATE OF ISRAEL BONDS
Development Company for Israel (UK) Ltd.
1–19 New Oxford Street, London WC1A 1NF. Email israel.bonds@talk21.com ☎ 020-7405 6222. Fax 020-7404 3434. Email israelbonds@brijnet.org (Est. 1981.) Promotes and sells State of Israel Bonds (Israel's gilt-edged securities). *Managing Dir.* Moshe Levy; *Sales Dir. & Comp. Sec. UK* Dr H. Stellman.

TEHILLA
Balfour House, 741 High Road, North Finchley, N12 0BQ. ☎ 020-8446 1477 Ext 2273. Fax 020-8446 4419. Tehilla is a non-political voluntary organisation dedicated to encouraging Aliyah and providing the support services needed by religious Jews coming to live in Israel. *U.K. Rep.* Mrs F. Berl.

TEL AVIV UNIVERSITY TRUST
1 Bentinck Street, W1M 5RN. ☎ 020-7487 5280. Fax 020-7224 3908. (Reg. Charity No. 314179) The principal aim of the Trust is to raise funds to promote the work of Tel Aviv University and to encourage support for academic projects, scholarships and campus development. The Trust also advises those who may wish to study at the University. *H. Presidents* Lord and Lady Wolfson, Sir Leslie and Dame Shirley Porter; *Chairman* Paul Norman.

TRADE UNION FRIENDS OF ISRAEL
BM LFI, London, WC1N 3XX. ☎ 020-7222 4323. Fax 020-7222 4324. To create and foster fraternal links between the Histadrut and the British Trade Union Movement; to educate and promote within the British Trade Union Movement the State of Israel and the Histadrut; to encourage study groups and delegations to visit Israel; to initiate dialogue between British Trade Union Movements and their Israeli counterparts. *H. Chairman* Gavid Laird; *Dir.*; *Admin.* Suzanne Weiniger.

UK SOCIETY FOR THE PROTECTION OF NATURE IN ISRAEL
(Reg. Charity No. 327268)
25 Lyndale Avenue, London NW2 2QB. ☎ 020-7435 6803. Fax 020-7794 0291. Email foiasg@foiasg.free-online.co.uk (Est. 1986.) To generate interest in the beauty of Israel's natural landscapes; muster support for the conservation lobby in Israel. *Trs.* Godfrey Bradman, Edward

Goldsmith, Zak Goldsmith, Arnold Kransdorff, John D. A. Levy, Bob Lewin, Bill Oddie.

UNITED MIZRAHI BANK LTD.
Finsbury House, 23 Finsbury Circus, EC2M 7UB.
☎ 020-7360 3800. Fax 020-7360 3810.
Br. of United Mizrahi Bank in Israel. *Gen. Man.* David Halperin.

WEIZMANN INSTITUTE FOUNDATION
Accurist House, 44 Baker St., P.O. Box 2282, London W1A 1NW.
☎ 020-7486 3954. Fax 020-7268 2629. E-mail 106042, 55@compuserve.com
(Est. 1956. Reg. Charity No. 232666) To stimulate financial, scientific and cultural support in the UK for the Weizmann Institute of Science in Rehovot. *Chairman of Exec. Cttee.* Hon. David Sieff; *Vice Chairman* Mrs V. Duffield, C.B.E.; *H. Sec.* J. O'Neill; *H.T.* Robert Glatter; *Chief Exec. Off.* Stuart Rogers.

YOUTH ALIYAH-CHILD RESCUE
Britannia House, 960 High Road, North Finchley, London N12 9YA.
☎ 020-8446 4321. Fax 020-8343 7383.
(Est. 1933. Reg. Charity No. 274512) Object: We offer a last-chance haven for under-privileged and deprived refugee, immigrant and native Israeli children. Our 5 Youth Villages offer an enriching environment through residential community care. *Jt. Chairman* Gerald Gaffin, Adrienne Sussman; *V. Chairman* Alan Diamond; *H. T.* Peter Rodney; *H. Sec.* Shiela Diamond; *H. Dir. Israel* Nanette Sacki; *Exec. Dir.* Kate Goldberg. *Publ.* Youth Aliyah-Child Rescue.

EDUCATIONAL AND CULTURAL ORGANISATIONS

Hebrew and Religion Classes are attached to most synagogues listed.
For University Centres and Institutions see pp.42–6.

AGENCY FOR JEWISH EDUCATION
Beit Meir, 44a Albert Road, NW4 2SJ.
☎ 020-8457 9700. Fax 020-8457 9707. Email aje@brijnet.org
Training, resourcing and servicing full and part-time education organisations for the Jewish community in Britain. Also organises Jewish Youth Study Group activities for teenagers through local and Israel based programmes. *Chief Exec.* Simon Goulden; *Dir. Education.* Jeffrey Leader; *Chairman of Gov.* David Rose.

ASSOCIATION OF JEWISH TEACHERS
c/o Education Dept., Board of Deputies, Commonwealth House, 1–19 New Oxford St., London WC1A 1NF.
☎ 020-7543 5400. Fax 020-7543 0010.
(Est. 1986) To promote, enhance and support the welfare and professional development of Jewish teachers in schools. *Chairman* Mrs Marilyn Nathan; *V. Chairman* Mrs D. Singer; *Publ.:* The Guide to Jewish Educational Resources.

BETH SHALOM HOLOCAUST MEMORIAL CENTRE
Laxton, Newark, Notts NG22 0PA.
☎ 01623-836627. Fax 01623-836647.
(Est. 1978 (as Beth Shalom Ltd.) Reg. Charity No. 509022). Holocaust education and commemoration. *Dir.* Stephen D. Smith, James M. Smith, Mrs Marina H. Smith.

CENTRE FOR JEWISH EDUCATION (CJE)
Sternberg Centre for Judaism, 80 East End Road, Finchley N3 2SY.
☎ 020-8343 4303. Fax 020-8349 0694. E-mail cjeuk@compuserve.com
URL http://www.knowledge.co.uk/cje
The central Education Agency for the Progressive Movements offering teacher training, community/family education, Hebrew programming, book service, offering a purchasing service for text books for schools, and three Resource Centres. Consultants are available to visit communities and offer programmes around the country. Established in 1987, amalgamating the RSGB Dept. of Education, ULPS Dept. of Education and Leo Baeck College Teacher Training Dept. *Dir.* Rabbi Dr Michael J. Shire; *Deputy Dir.* Helena Miller, M.A.; *Admin.* Suzanne Ophir; *Chairman of Tr.* Tony Sacker. **Branches:** Sternberg Centre Resource Centre, 80 East End Road, Finchley N3 2SY. ☎ 020-8343 4303. Fax: 020-8349 0694; Peggy Lang Resource Centre & Book Service, Montagu Centre, 21 Maple Street, W1P 6DS. ☎ 020-7580 0214. Fax 020-7436 4184; Sandra Vigon Resource & Learning Centre, Jackson's Row, Manchester M2 5WD. ☎ 0161-831 7092. Fax 0161-839 4865.

DAVAR, The Jewish Institute in Bristol and the South West
1-3 Percival Road, Clifton, Bristol, BS8 3LF.
☎/Fax 0117-970 6594.
Email: davar@telecall.co.uk   URL:http://www.telecall.co.uk/~davar/davar.html
(Est. 1995) DAVAR, the Jewish Institute in Bristol and the South West, is based at The Percival Centre, a specialist education centre in Clifton, Bristol. DAVAR provides a wide programme of cultural, educational and social activities for the Jewish community in Bristol and the South-West. A regular free newsletter is available, and Jewish groups in the area advertise their own events via the DAVAR mailing list. *Chairman* Martin Vegoda; *Admin.* Vena Bunker.

DVAR YERUSHALAYIM (London Jewish Academy)
24 Templars Avenue, NW11 0NS.
☎/Fax 020-8455 8631.
(Est. 1978. Reg. Charity No. 284740) To provide full- and part-time courses in adult education to enable men and women of limited Jewish knowledge and background to further their understanding of Jewish thought and practice. *Princ.* Rabbi J. Freilich, Ph.C.

EVENING INSTITUTE OF ULPS
The Montagu Centre, 21 Maple Street, W1P 6DS.
☎ 020-7580 1663. Fax 020-7436 4184. E-mail montagu@ulps.demon.co.uk
The ULPS Evening Institute has been affirming the importance of continuing Jewish education for 35 years by providing people, whatever their age and background, with the opportunity to study Judaism and Hebrew at all levels. Courses are held on Mondays during the academic year and include the annual Rabbi Dr. David Goldstein Lecture. *Principal* Rabbi Stephen Howard.

HOLOCAUST EDUCATIONAL TRUST
BCM Box 7892, London WC1N 3XX.
☎ 020-7222 6822/5853.
(Est. 1988) To promote research into the Holocaust and the collection of archival materials and artifacts of the Holocaust period and the production of written and audio-visual materials. Also to promote teaching of the Holocaust in schools and assist individuals and orgs. involved in Holocaust educ. *Patrons* Prof. Elie Wiesel, The Lord Jakobovits, His Grace the Duke of Norfolk, The Rt. Rev. Lord Runcie; *President* Lord Sainsbury; *Chairman* The Lord Janner, Q.C.; *Sec.* Sir Ivan Lawrence Q.C.; *Ts.* The Rt. Hon. Lord Merlyn Rees, David

Sumberg; *Jt. Ts.* Martin Paisner; *Bd. of Man.* David Gryn, Kitty Hart, Ben Helfgott, Jonathan Kestenbaum, Paul Phillips and Martin Savitt; *Dir.* Janice Lopatkin; *Assoc. Dir.* Stephen Ward; *Admin. Dir.* Jayne Ford.
British Video Archive for Holocaust Testimonies: *Admin:* Alberta Strage.

ISRAEL FOLK DANCE INSTITUTE
Balfour House, 741 High Road, London N12 0BQ.
Daytime ☎/fax 020-8446 6427. Evening ☎/fax 020-8445 6765.
(Reg Charity No. 279801) The Institute is an educational charity whose main work is in promoting Jewish and Israeli Cultural Heritage through the medium of song and dance. Recipient of the 13th Annual Award of the All-Party Parliamentary Committee for Soviet Jewry and the Chief Rabbi's Award for Excellence, 1995. The Institute has produced materials in both English and Russian, holds training seminars and runs classes for children, youth and adults. It is totally independent and has no political affiliation. *Chairman and Hon. Director:* Maurice Stone.

ISRAEL ZANGWILL MEMORIAL FUND
c/o Manor House Tr., Sternberg Centre For Judaism, 80 East End Road, N3 2SY.
☎ 020-8346-2288. E-mail admin@refsyn.org.uk
(Est. 1929) To assist poor Jews engaged in literary, artistic, dramatic and scientific work.

JEWISH BOOK COUNCIL
P.O. Box 20513, London NW8 6ZS.
☎ 020-7722-7925. Fax 020-7483 2029. Email info@jewishbookweek.org.uk
(Est. 1947. Reg. Charity No. 293800) To stimulate and encourage the reading of books on Judaism and on every aspect of Jewish thought, life, history and literature; organizes annual Jewish Book Week, now Europe's largest Jewish bookfair, and associated events. Administers a triennial prize for Hebrew translation. *President* Mrs M. R. Lehrer, M.A.(Oxon); *Chairman* Mrs M. J. Cohen, M.Phil.; *H. T.* E. Grodzinski F.C.A.; *H. Sec.* R. Tager, Q.C. *Admin:* Mrs R. Goldstein.

JEWISH CHRONICLE
25 Furnival Street, London EC4A 1JT.
☎ 020-7415 1500. Fax 020-7405 9040. Website: www.jchron.co.uk
(Est. 1841.) The world's oldest independent Jewish weekly newspaper. *Chairman* Lionel Gordon; *Edr.* Mr. Ned Temko.

JEWISH COMMUNITY DAY SCHOOL ADVISORY BOARD
c/o Centre for Jewish Education, Sternberg Centre, 80 East End Road, London N3 2SY.
☎ 020-8343 4303. Fax 020-8349 0694. Email cjeuk@compuserve.com
(Est. 1998) Jewish promotion and development of cross-community primary day schools throughout the UK. *Chairman* Peter L. Levy; *Educational Consultant* Judy Keiner.

JEWISH COMMUNITY THEATRE
157 Denmark Hill, London SE5 8EH.
☎/Fax 020-7737 4361.
(Reg. Charity No. 1000187) To advance, develop and maintain public education and awareness of the history of British Jews by the presentation at theatres and other suitable venues of plays reflecting the cultural identity of Anglo-Jewry. Est. 1990. *Chair* Jennifer Sclaire, 11 Glenwood Ct., Woodford Rd., South Woodford, London E18 2EU. *T.* Susan Kaye, 418 Addison House, Grove End Rd., London NW8 9EL.

JEWISH EDUCATION AID SOCIETY
(Est. 1896.) To investigate and advise on cases of highly talented students and in certain circumstances to provide interest-free loans to enable them to train for professions or the pursuit of art. Now under the administration of Anglo-Jewish Association (see p.3).

JEWISH EDUCATIONAL DEVELOPMENT TRUST
44 Albert Road, NW4 2SJ.
☎ 020-8203 6427. Fax 020-8203 6420.
(Est. 1971) To promote Jewish educ., teacher training and the development of the day school network relating to all sections of the com. *President* The Chief Rabbi; *V. President* Sir Trevor Chinn, C.V.O.; *Chairman* Michael Phillips; *T.* Ronald Metzger.

JEWISH FILM FOUNDATION
c/o 46a Minster Road, London NW2 3RD.
The Jewish Film Foundation is an educational charity whose aim is to promote the exhibition, distribution, production and study of Jewish cinema, television and video programmes. It initiates and co-ordinates education and cultural activities involving film and video and advises those who make and use programmes on Jewish themes. Organises an annual Jewish Film Festival in London. *Bd. of Dir.* Michael Green, Dorothy Berwin, Jonathan Davis, Dominique Green, Jeremy Isaacs, Verity Lambert, Michael May, Louis Marks, Alan Yentob; *Prog. Dir.* Sam Maser.

JEWISH GENEALOGICAL SOCIETY OF GREAT BRITAIN
Membership: 2 Milton Close, London N2 0QH.
Genealogical enquiries: 14 St Helens Road, Alverstoke, Gosport, Hants, PO12 2RN.
(Est. 1992. Reg. Charity No. 1022738) To promote and encourage the study of Jewish genealogy on a secular basis. The Society organises lectures, seminars and family history workshops (including those at The London Museum of Jewish Life, Sternberg Centre); publishes *Shemot*, a quarterly journal; promotes research; and is building up a library. *V. Presidents* Dr Anthony Joseph, David Jacobs; *Chairman* George Anticoni; *Sec. and Membership* Anthony Winner; *T.* David Weingott; *Northern Groups* Janina Hochland; *Scottish Group* Harvey Kaplan; *South West Group* Alan Tobias; *South Coast Group* Geoffrey Keene.

JEWISH HISTORICAL SOCIETY OF ENGLAND
33 Seymour Place, W1H 5AP.
☎/Fax 020-7723 5852. E-mail jhse@dircon.co.uk
(Est. 1893. Reg. Charity No. 217331) *President* Dr Gerry Black; *H. T.* Raphael Langham; *H. Sec.* Cyril Drukker; *Admin.* Jeanette Cannon. **Branches: Birmingham:** *Chairman* Dr Anthony Joseph, 25 Westbourne Road, Edgbaston, Birmingham B15 3TX; **Leeds:** *President* Judge Arthur Myerson QC, 20 Sandmoor Lane, LS17 7EA; **Liverpool:** *Chairman* Arnold Lewis, 61 Menlove Ave., L18 2EH; **Manchester:** *Chairman* Frank Baigel, 25 Ravensway, Bury Old Rd., Prestwich M25 0EU.

JEWISH MUSIC HERITAGE TRUST
PO Box 232, Harrow, Middx, HA1 2NN.
☎ 020-8909 2445. Fax 020-8909 1030. Email: jewishmusic@jmht.org
http://www.jmht.org
(Reg. Charity No. 328228) The Jewish Music Heritage Trust promotes study and performance of Jewish music to preserve this great heritage and teach it to successive generations.

Activities include:
London International Jewish Music Festival: a biennial, month-long festival featuring concerts, recitals, workshops, masterclasses, lectures, Yiddish theatre and comedy; in major concert halls in London and around the country.
Commissioning of new Jewish Music.
Jewish Music Heritage Centre: supplies information and resources including recordings and sheet music, as well as related books, videos and other items to the media, educational establishments and general public.
Joe Loss Lectureship in Jewish Music at School of Oriental and African Studies, University of London.
Jewish Music Distribution: Specialists in Jewish music, CDs, etc. and printed music from around the world.
Gregori Schechter's Klezmer Festival Band: Founding and promotion of band for concerts and functions.
Klezmer Classes: Teaching sessions for youth and adults.
Trust and Festival Dir. Mrs Geraldine Auerbach

KESHER – THE LEARNING CONNECTION
28 St Albans Lane, London NW11 7QE.
☎ 020-8455 2515. Fax 020-8455 6656. E-mail rsimon@kesher.org.uk
(Est. 1997. Reg Charity no. 1061689) Jewish Education and Outreach to singles and young couples. Reconnecting Jews of all backgrounds with their heritage. *Dir.* Rabbi Rashi Simon, M.A.

LIMMUD
1 Dennington Park Road, London NW6 1AX.
☎ 171-431 9444. Fax 020-7431 9555. E-mail limmud@bigfoot.com
(Reg. Charity No. 327111) Limmud is a cross-communal, adult educational organisation. The main event Limmud organises is its annual five-day residential conference in December. In addition, Limmud organises themed education events and regional Limmud days throughout the year. *Co-Chairs* Natan Tiefenbrun, Judy Trotter; *Exec. Dir.* Clive A. Lawton; *Admin.* Zahavit Shalev.

LITTMAN LIBRARY OF JEWISH CIVILIZATION
PO Box 645, Oxford OX2 6AS. ☎/Fax 01235-868104.
(Est. 1965. Reg. Charity No. 1000784) Established for the purpose of publishing scholarly works aimed at disseminating an understanding of the Jewish heritage and Jewish history and making Jewish religious thought and literary creativity accessible to the English-speaking world. *Dirs.* Mrs. C. C. Littman, R. J. Littman. *Contacts:* Connie Webber (Editorial); Ludo Craddock (Marketing & Admin.).

LONDON ACADEMY OF JEWISH STUDIES
2–4 Highfield Avenue, NW11 9ET.
☎ 020-8455 5938; 020-8458 1264.
Instit. for Rabbinics est. in 1975 to assist post-Yeshiva students to further their Jewish educ. and engage in advanced Talmudic res. Graduates are expected to take up rabbinical and teaching posts in the com. The Kolel also serves as a Torah-study centre for laymen. Its specialised library is open to the gen. public throughout the year incl. Shabbat and Yom Tov. *H. Princ.* Rabbi G. Hager.

MANOR HOUSE MEDIA
c/o Old School, High Street, Elstree, Herts WD6 3BY.
☎ 020-8386 9461/020-8343 4303. Fax 020-8386 9462.

(Est. 1980) MHM specialises in work for the Jewish Community using slides, audio and video media and cd-rom from its studio and two editing suites. Tenders for project design and production. *Contact* J. M. Black.

MASORTI ACADEMY
1097 Finchley Rd., NW11 0PU.
☎ 020-8201 8772. Fax 020-8201 8917. E-mail Masorti.uk@ort.org
Provides adult education in a number of different formats, offering seminars, evening classes, distance learning courses, residential study events and lectures, all within the Masorti context of open-minded enquiry within a spirit of authentic traditional Judaism. *Dir.* Harry Freedman.

MICHAEL GOULSTON EDUCATIONAL FOUNDATION
Sternberg Centre for Judaism, Manor House, 80 East End Road, N3 2SY.
☎ 020-8343 4303. Fax 020-8349 0694.
Established 1972 in memory of Rabbi Michael Goulston to pub. Jewish educ. materials, including books, audio visuals and study programmes. *Dir.* Rabbi Dr Michael J. Shire.

POLACK'S HOUSE, CLIFTON COLLEGE
1 Percival Road, Bristol BS8 3LF.
☎ 0117 9737634.
(Reg. Charity No. 1040218) Polack's House at Clifton College has provided boarding facilities and Jewish education since 1878. Now reconstituted as the Polack's House Educational Trust it houses Jewish boys aged 13–18 within the House, and provides Jewish education and kosher meals for Jewish boys and girls aged 8–18, fully integrated into Clifton College. *Housemaster* Jonathan Greenbury; *Dir.* David Prashker.

PROJECT SEED EUROPE
Middlesex House, 29-45 High Street, Edgware, Middx, HA8 7UU.
☎ 020-8381 1555. Fax 020-8381 1666.
London contact Bobby Hill. Edgware Community Centre contact Rabbi Y. Roll. Regions Rabbi A. Hassan.
(Est. 1980. Reg. Charity No. 281307) To provide Jewish adult educ. on a one-to-one teacher-student basis in communal study hall and regular weekend seminars for families and singles in January, May, August and December. *Dir.* Rabbi J. Grunfeld.
   Weekly study sessions in Greater London: Men & Women in the following areas: Barnet, Edgware, Finchley/HGS, Golders Green, Kenton, Maida Vale, Marble Arch, Mill Hill, Pinner, Ilford, Southgate, Stamford Hill/Tottenham, Westcliff. Men only: Belmont, Chigwell, Kingsbury, Wembley. Women only: Bushey, Hendon.
   Weekly study sessions in the Regions: Men & Women in the following areas: Bury, Prestwich, Whitefield, Fallowfield, Glasgow, Leeds, Liverpool, Newcastle. Men only: Sunderland.

SCOPUS JEWISH EDUCATIONAL TRUST (formerly ZFET)
Balfour House, 741 High Road, N12 0BQ.
☎ 020-8343 9228. Fax 020-8343 7309.
(Est. 1953. Reg. Charity No. 313154) To raise funds by way of endowment, legacy, bequest, gift or donation in order to provide a first-class education in Jewish Studies and Hebrew throughout its national network of 15 day schools, all of which have a Zionist ethos and emphasize the centrality of Israel in Jewish life. *H. President* Stanley S. Cohen; *Chairman* Peter Ohrenstein F.C.A; *H.T.* Philip Goodman, B.A., A.C.A.; *H. Sec.* Brenda Hyman. Schools: **London:** Harry & Abe Sherman Rosh Pinah School, Sebba Rosh Pinah Nursery, Mathilda Marks-Kennedy School, Ella & Ernst Frankel Kindergarten, Simon Marks School, Simon Marks Sherman Nursery;

Birmingham: King David Primary School; **Bournemouth:** Jewish Day School; **Glasgow:** Calderwood Lodge School; **Leeds:** Brodetsky Primary and Nursery School; Deborah Taylor Playgroup; **Liverpool:** King David Kindergarten, King David Primary School, King David High School; **Manchester:** North Cheshire Primary School.

THE SEPHARDI CENTRE
2 Ashworth Road, Maida Vale, London W9 1JY.
☎ 020-7266 3682. Fax 01781-289 5957.
(Reg. Charity No. 1039937) The Sephardi Centre was opened in 1994. The Centre's aim is to promote Sephardi culture. Courses focus on Religion, History, Music, Art and Cuisine. Courses are open to all age. A library and reading room specialising in Sephardi Literature is open to the public (see p.60). *Dir.* Rabbi S. Djanogly.

SOCIETY FOR JEWISH STUDY
(Est. 1946. Reg. Charity No. 283732) *Chairman*; *Sec.* Rosemary Goldstein, 1A Church Mount, London N2 0RW. The Society's objectives are the furtherance of learning and research through regular public lectures and support for the 'Journal of Jewish Studies'.

THE SPIRO ARK
Middlesex University, The Burroughs, Hendon NW4 4HE.
☎ 020-8201 7172. Fax 020-8201 7173.
The Spiro Ark has been established to meet the urgent problems facing the Jewish people in the twenty-first century by using innovative teaching methods in order to encourage a learning community. 'My People are destroyed through lack of knowledge' (Hosea, IV, 6). Hebrew and Yiddish are taught at all levels, together with Jewish history and other related subjects; outstanding cultural events (i.e., theatre, music, current events, films, book launches, etc.); the Spiro Ark Café to be a cultural meeting place in the heart of the West End for the young; tours of Jewish interest in London, the UK and abroad. Courses and activities weekdays, day and evening, and weekends. *Founders* Nitza and Robin Spiro.

THE SPIRO INSTITUTE FOR STUDY OF JEWISH HISTORY & CULTURE
The Old House, c/o King's College, Kidderpore Avenue, NW3 7SZ.
☎ 020-7431 0345. Fax 020-7431 0361. E-mail admin@spiro.demon.co.uk
(Est. 1978. Reg. Charity No. 1013594) To promote Jewish identity and self-awareness, the Institute engages in widespread teaching of Jewish history and culture including: literature, films, art, drama, Hebrew and Yiddish to adult classes; courses taught in secondary schools, and to others by correspondence; Holocaust education in schools and for LEAs including creation of teaching pack and accompanying video 'Lessons of the Holocaust' (with Holocaust Educational Trust and Rex Bloomstein); teacher training, preparation for GCSE and A-level in modern Hebrew; Jewish documentary and feature film archive; public lectures and cultural events, international tours of Jewish interest. *Founder* Robin Spiro; *Dirs. Adult Educ.* Trudy Gold, LLB, Anthony Hammond, MA; *Dir. Admin.* Diana Mocatta.

SPRINGBOARD EDUCATION TRUST
32 Foscote Road, London NW4 3SD.
☎ 020-8202 7147. Fax 020-8905 4901.
(Est. 1979. Reg. Charity No. 277946) Whilst specialising in reminiscence and stimulation programmes for senior citizens, Springboard has extended its range of audio-visual and video productions to cover Jewish and Zionist history, synagogue and home traditions, inter-faith projects.
Springboard also produces low-cost audio-visual/video programmes for other

orgs. and provides seminars for teachers and welfare workers in the use of its programmes with substantial back-up materials.
Dirs. Aumie and Michael Shapiro.

YAKAR STUDY CENTRE
2 Egerton Gardens, London NW4 4BA.
☎ 020-8202 5551/2. Fax 020-8202 9653. E-mail yakar@yakar.demon.co.uk
Website http://www.yakar.demon.co.uk
Founded by Rabbi Dr Michael Rosen in 1978, YAKAR is an independent study centre devoted to exploring Jewish religious texts, and philosophical and spiritual issues. YAKAR is open and non-judgemental and welcomes students from any position or background. YAKAR offers lectures, classes and tutorials for men and women throughout the week and religious services on Sabbaths and Festivals. The YAKAR community is informal, experimental and welcoming. *Dir.* Jeremy Rosen; *Admin.* Rosemary Genn.

UNIVERSITY CENTRES AND ORGANISATIONS
(See also Organisations concerned with Jewish students on p.52, and Libraries on pp.54–60).

BRITISH ASSOCIATION FOR JEWISH STUDIES
(Est. 1975.) Membership is open to scholars concerned with the academic pursuit of Jewish studies in the British Isles. The Assoc. promotes and defends the scholarly study of Jewish culture in all its aspects and organizes an annual conference. *President* (2000) Dr A. Shivtiel, Dept. of Modern Arabic Studies, University of Leeds, Leeds LS2 9JT; *Sec.* (2000) Dr Jonathan G. Campbell, Department of Theology & Religious Studies, University of Bristol, Bristol BS8 1TB; *T.* (2000) Dr Charlotte Hempel, Lucy Cavendish College, Cambridge CB3 0BU.

CENTRE FOR GERMAN-JEWISH STUDIES
University of Sussex, Falmer, Brighton BN1 9QN. ☎ 01273-678495
Dir. Professor Edward Timms; *London Liaison Off.* Diana Franklin. ☎ 020-8455 4785. Fax 020-8381 4721.

CENTRE FOR JEWISH–CHRISTIAN RELATIONS
Wesley House, Jesus Lane, Cambridge CB5 8BJ.
☎ 01223 462668. Fax 01223 462668. E-mail wesley-cjcr@lists.cam.ac.uk
(Est. 1997. Reg. Charity No. 1059772) The Centre for Jewish–Christian Relations is an independent Centre dedicated to the study and teaching of all aspects of the Jewish–Christian encounter throughout the ages. It is offering the first MA in Jewish–Christian Relations in the UK. Courses are available on a full- or part-time basis aimed primarily at graduate students. *Exec. Dir.* Edward Kessler; *Marketing & Admin. Man.* Deborah Patterson Jones; *Dir. of Studies* Melanie Wright.

CENTRE FOR JEWISH STUDIES (University of Leeds)
Leeds LS2 9JT.
☎ 0113-233 5197. Fax 0113-245 1977. E-mail e.frojmovic@leeds.ac.uk
(Est. 1995) Teaching of Jewish Studies: taught MA in Modern Jewish Studies and supervision of research degrees. *Dir.* Dr Eva Frojmović.

CENTRE FOR JEWISH STUDIES (University of London)
School of Oriental and African Studies, Thornhaugh Street, Russell Square, London WC1H 0XG. ☎ 020-7637 2388
Dir. Dr T. Parfitt.

CENTRE FOR MODERN HEBREW STUDIES
Faculty of Oriental Studies, Sidgwick Avenue, Cambridge CB3 9DA.
☎ 01223-335117. Fax 01223-335110.
A centre established within the University of Cambridge for the study and promotion of modern Hebrew language, literature and culture.
H. Dir. Dr R. Domb.

INSTITUTE OF JEWISH STUDIES
University College London, Gower Street, WC1E 6BT.
☎ 020-7380 7171. Fax 020-7209 1026. Email: uclhvtm@ucl.ac.uk
http://www.ucl.ac.uk/hebrew-jewish/htm
Established in 1953 (Reg. Charity No. 213114) by the late Prof. Alexander Altmann, located within the Dept. of Hebrew and Jewish Studies at Univ. College, London, while retaining its autonomous status. Funded by the private sector. Programme of activities dedicated to the academic study of all branches of Jewish history and civilisation, including series of public lectures, seminars, symposia, major internat. conferences, research projects and publs., especially of its conference proceedings. It brings together scholars, students, academic instits. from all sections inside and outside the Univ. of London and the scholarly scene in and outside the UK, worldwide. It equally reaches the community at large and acts as a unifying force between the Jewish and non-Jewish academic and lay public. The Institute celebrated its 40th anniversary in 1994. The 1999 conference was 'Officina Magica'. The 2000 conference will be on 'Nationalism, Zionism and Ethnic Mobilisation'. List of publications and programme mailings available on request.
Patrons The Lord Mishcon, Sir Claus Moser, The Rt. Hon. The Lord Woolf; Bd. of Govs: *Chairman; V. Chairman* Philip L. Morgenstern, B.A.; *H. Ts.* David J. Lewis, BSc., F.R.I.C.S., Edward M.Lee, BSc (Econ), Daniel Peltz, BA, Elliot E. Philipp, M.A., F.R.C.S., F.R.C.O.G., Nick Ritblat, MA; *Dir.* Prof. Mark J. Geller; *H. Sec.* J. Caplan, F.C.A.
The Trustees of the Institute of Jewish Studies, a non-profit making company limited by guarantee, registered in England No. 2598783.

JOE LOSS LECTURESHIP IN JEWISH MUSIC
Music Department, School of Oriental and African Studies, University of London, Thornhaugh St., Russell Sq., WC1H 0XG.
☎ 020-7691 3410. Fax 020-7637 6182. Email ak42@soas.ac.uk.
(Est. 1991) Incorporates Jewish Music Resource Centre, and the Harry Rosencweig Collection of Jewish Music (see p.55). Sponsored by the Jewish Music Heritage Trust (see p.38). Research, lecturing, teaching, consultancy. Studies cover the liturgical, semi-religious, folk, popular and art music of Ashkenazi, Sephardi and Oriental ethnic groups, in the context of Jewish culture, society, history, geography, language, psychology, religion and tradition (within wider Christian and Islamic environments). Specialized resources comprise extensive collections of books and audio-visual materials.
Lect. Alexander Knapp.

LEO BAECK COLLEGE
The Sternberg Centre for Judaism, 80 East End Road, N3 2SY.
☎ 020-8349 4525. Fax: 020-8343 2558.
E-mail Leo.Baeck.College@mailbox.ulcc.ac.uk
Website www.lb_college.demon.co.uk
(Est. 1956. Reg. Charity No. 209777) Established for the study of Judaism and the training of rabbis and teachers. Under the joint auspices of the Reform Syns. of Gt. Britain and the Union of Liberal and Progressive Syns.

President Prof. J. B. Segal; *V. Presidents* Rabbi Dr. A. H. Friedlander, Rabbi John Rayner; *Chairman* Gordon Smith; *Princ.* Rabbi Prof. J. Magonet; *Dean* Rabbi Dr. A. H. Friedlander; *Registrar* J. Olbrich.

A five-year programme leads to Rabbinic Ordination; the College offers full-time and part-time B.A. (Hons.) in Jewish Studies, a one-year M.A., as well as Open Univ. M. Phil and D. Phil degrees.

Chairman of Acad. B. Rabbi Prof. J. Magonet; *Lecturers* Rabbi L. Blue, Dr P. van Boxel, Rabbi C. Eimer, S. Gold, Rabbi Dr A. H. Friedlander, Dr A. Kershen, Rabbi J. Rayner, Rabbi E. Sarah, Dr J. Schonfield, Dr E. Seidel, Rabbi S. Sheridan, Rabbi M. Solomon, Rabbi S. Shulman, Dr J. Weinberg, Rabbi A. Wright.

LEO BAECK INSTITUTE
4 Devonshire Street, W1N 2BH.
☎ 020-7580 3493. Email ap@lbilon.demon.co.uk
Established in 1955 (Reg. Charity No. 235163) for research and publications on history of Central European German-speaking Jewry. Organises conferences and seminars. *Chairman* Prof. Peter Pulzer; *Dir.* Dr A. Paucker. *Publ.:* Year Book (*Edr.* Prof. J. A. S. Grenville), symposia, monographs, etc.

LONDON SCHOOL OF JEWISH STUDIES (formerly Jews' College)
Schaller House, Albert Road, Hendon NW4 2SJ.
☎ 020-8203 6427. Fax 020-8203 6420. E-mail LSJS@mailbox.ulcc.ac.uk
http://www.brijnet.org/lsjs
(Est. 1855) Educates the future teachers and leaders of the Jewish community through its BA, MA and PhD courses in Hebrew and Jewish Studies, and its rabbinical ordination and training programmes. It also houses one of the most extensive Judaica libraries in Europe which is visited regularly by scholars from around the world. The College hosts international conferences and evening lectures open to the public.
Governing Body: *President* The Chief Rabbi Dr Jonathan Sacks, MA (Cantab); *Deputy President* Rabbi Abraham Levy, BA, PhD; *Chairman* Alan Grant, BA, Clive Marks, FCA, ATII, Hon FLCM; *Ts.* Bernard Waiman, MA; *Hon. Sec.* Rabbi E. Mirvis, BA.
Dir.; *Registrar* Clive Fierstone, MA; *Admin.* Esther Miller; *Librarian* Esra Kahn. *Faculty:* Rabbi Michael Newman, MPhil; Daniel Rynhold, BA, MA; Rabbi Dr Sacha Stern, MA, DPhil (Oxon); Dr Tamra Wright, MA, PhD; Fiona Blumfield, MA. *Publ:* Le'ela (twice yearly).

OXFORD CENTRE FOR HEBREW AND JEWISH STUDIES
Yarnton Manor, Yarnton, Oxford, OX5 1PY.
☎ 01865 377946. Fax 01865 375079. Email: ochjs@sable.oxford.ac.uk
URL: http://associnst.ox.ac.uk/ochjs/shavuon
Teaching Centre: 45 St Giles, Oxford OX1 3LP.
☎ 01865 511869/311961. Fax 01865 311791.
(Est. 1972) The Centre is one of Europe's leading teaching and research institutions in the area of Hebrew and Jewish studies. Its work includes Jewish history and literature, ancient, medieval and modern; Talmudic studies; Jewish/Islamic and Jewish/Christian relationships at all periods; Hebrew and Yiddish language; anthropology; sociology; law; and theology. It provides instruction in Jewish studies towards the Oxford University B.A., M.St., M.Phil, M.Litt and D.Phil degrees. The Centre's one-year Graduate Diploma in Jewish Studies attracts students from many countries.
The Centre has its own faculty of 14 Fellows, the majority of whom are also Fellows of Oxford colleges and hold posts at the University. Some 20 visiting scholars come from all parts of the world each year.
Publications: Journal of Jewish Studies (half-yearly); the Jewish Law Annual; and

numerous books and articles by Fellows past and present. The Programme of Activities, the Annual Report of the Centre and Mercaz (newsletter) are available on request. *President* Prof. Peter Oppenheimer; *Chairman Bd. Gov.* Sir Richard Greenbury. (The Centre also houses the Leopold Muller Memorial Library, see p.58).

OXFORD INSTITUTE FOR YIDDISH STUDIES
Golden Cross Court, 4 Cornmarket, Oxford, OX1 3EX.
☎ 01865-798989. Fax 01865-798987. E-mail yiddishstudies@oxf-inst.demon.co.uk
Website http://www.oxf-inst.demon.co.uk
(Est. 1994) The Institute is one of the world's leading centres for teaching, research and publishing in the field of Yiddish language, literature and culture. The research and publishing programmes of the Institute have been incorporated into the University of Oxford's European Humanities Research Centre.
   In 1996, a joint programme was initiated with the University of London to provide courses in Yiddish in the School of Oriental and African Studies (see below). The annual Mendel Friedman conference on Yiddish issues is held at Christ Church, and the annual summer programme is held in July-August.
   In July 1998 the New York Yiddish newspaper, *The Forwards*, established in 1897, opened its European Bureau at the Institute. The Institute incorporates the Yonia Fain Collection of over 100 paintings. Full-time academic staff: Gennady Estraikh, Mikhail Krutikov, Dafna Clifford. *Dir. of Projects* Marie Wright.

QMW PROGRAMME FOR YIDDISH AND ASHKENAZIC STUDIES
Queen Mary & Westfield College, University of London, Kidderpore Avenue, London NW3 7ST.
☎ 020-7453 7141.
The Programme was primarily formed for the teaching of Yiddish language and literature towards the BA and MA degrees of London University. The Programme has expanded into the field of Ashkenazic Studies generally, including research into the history of Ashkenazic women. It hosts the weekly QMW Birnbaum Seminar, houses the Lisky Archive of East End Yiddish and has recently established its own publication series *(Editors* Dr. David Cesarani, Dr. Lewis Glinert, Dr. Devra Kay, Magdalena Pirozynska, Heather Valencia); *Dir. of Studies* Dr. Devra Kay.

SCHOOL OF ORIENTAL AND AFRICAN STUDIES (SOAS)
Dept. of the Languages and Cultures of the Near and Middle East, Thornhaugh Street, Russell Square, London WC1H OXG.
☎ 020-7637 2388. Fax 020-7691 3424. Website http://www.soas.ac.uk
SOAS is one of the world's greatest concentrations of expertise on Africa and Asia. The Near & Middle East Department offers a B.A. in Hebrew & Israeli Studies and degrees combining Hebrew with Law, Economics, Management, Arabic and with many other subjects – all affording a year's study at the Hebrew University of Jerusalem. A major new development is a Yiddish language and literature programme designed for both degree students and occasional students and including MA studies. The one-year Diploma in Jewish Studies caters for postgraduates from around the world seeking an entrée into the field. These programmes have the benefit of one of the largest open-stack Jewish Studies libraries in Europe.
   Also based at SOAS is the Centre for Jewish Studies, which hosts lecture series and symposia on a wide range of issues (see p.59).

STANLEY BURTON CENTRE FOR HOLOCAUST STUDIES
Dept. of History, University of Leicester, Leicester LE1 7RH.
☎ 0116-2522800 Fax 0116-2523986
To promote the study of and research into the Holocaust. *Dir.* Steve G. Paulsson; *H. Assoc. Dir.* Aubrey Newman; *H. Res. Fellow* Dr. J. Scott.

UNIVERSITY COLLEGE LONDON
Department of Hebrew and Jewish Studies, Gower Street, WC1E 6BT.
☎ 020-7380 7171. Fax 020-7209 1026.
The largest univ. dept. in the UK and Europe for obtaining honours degrees (B.A., M.A., M.Phil and PhD.) in Hebrew, medieval and modern Jewish history, Biblical Hebrew and Ancient Egyptian. The fields of teaching and research include: Ancient Near East, Hellenistic Jewish History; Jewish Mysticism; 18th and 19th century Hasidism; the ancient versions of the Hebrew Bible; Modern Jewish History; History of Jewry in Central and Eastern Europe, Jews in Islamic societies, Medieval Hebrew Literature; the History of the Jews in England; Medieval Jewry under Islam; Jewish Spirituality; modern Hebrew language and literature; Yiddish language and literature; History of Antisemitism; Holocaust Studies; Politics of the State of Israel.
The dept. hosts regular visitors from the Hebrew Univ. and offers all students the opportunity to spend one year in Israel.
The dept. comprises eight full-time members of staff and six part-time, with over 80 undergraduate and 40 postgraduate students.
The dept. houses the Instit. of Jewish Studies (see p.57). *Head* Professor John D. Klier.

ORGANISATIONS CONCERNED WITH JEWISH YOUTH

ASSOCIATION FOR JEWISH YOUTH
(Part of Norwood Ravenswood)
Norwood House, Harmony Way, London NW4 2BZ.
☎ 020-8203 3030. Fax: 020-8202 2030. E-mail: ajy@ort.org
Association for Jewish Youth Northern Office, 27 Bury Old Road, Prestwich, Manchester M25 0EY.
☎ 0161-740 6168. Fax 0161-740 6169. Email: north.ajy@ort.org
(Est. 1899. Now part of Norwood Ravenswood, see p.97).
AJY, working with Jewish youth workers, looks at the issues affecting young people today, which include eating disorders, drug abuse, Jewish identity and adolescent problems. AJY works in four main areas: an ongoing programme dealing with issues affecting the lives of young Jewish people; developing new and existing youth provisions; providing the best professional training available; offering the highest quality of information advice and resources to those involved in Jewish youth work.
Publ. Jewish Youth Work (quarterly).
Chairman Jon Barron, FCA; *Head of AJY* Eric Finestone.

B'NAI B'RITH YOUTH ORGANISATION
1–2 Endsleigh Street, WC1H 0DS.
☎ 020-7387 3115. Fax 020-7387 8014. E-mail bbyo@ort.org
BBYO is a unique, peer-led Zionist youth organisation. It promotes Zionism, Judaism, leadership, welfare and social awareness in a pluralist, open and totally youth-led environment. There are weekly meetings in 12 chapters, national events, Israel summer tour, 'Atid' Leadership tour and a one-year programme in Israel.
Contact names: *Youth Co-ord.* Carol Gould; *Shaliach* Shai Pinto.

EDUCATION AND YOUTH COMMITTEE, BOARD OF DEPUTIES
(See p.1).

JEWISH GUIDE ADVISORY COUNCIL
J.G.A.C. furthers the Guide movement in the Jewish Com. *Nat. Chairman* Mrs L. Myers, 13 Napier Drive, Bushey, Watford WD2 2JH. ☎ 01923 463199; *T.* Mrs R. Davis, 19 Gibbs Green, Edgware, HA8 9RS.

JEWISH LADS' AND GIRLS' BRIGADE

H.Q.: Camperdown, 3 Beechcroft Road, South Woodford, E18 1LA.
☎ 020-8989 8990. Fax: 020-8518 8832.
(Est. 1895. Reg. Charity No. 286950) The JLGB is the longest-established Jewish youth movement in the UK. It serves young people, both through its *Uniformed groups and bands* and also in Jewish schools, clubs, chedarim and in the smaller communities, through its *Outreach Kiruv Project*, for those not wishing to join a uniformed organisation. There are groups throughout the country.

The wide range of activities include sports, crafts & hobbies, drama, camping, outdoor and adventure activities, public service (first aid, life saving, sign language etc), public speaking, discos and weekends away. It is the only Jewish Operating Authority for the *Duke of Edinburgh's Award*. The JLGB also offers its own *Challenge Award for Jewish Youth*, which includes sections on Jewish Heritage and Israel and the annual Sir Peter E. Lazarus Public Speaking Competition.

Members are encouraged to develop an awareness of the needs of others, through its voluntary service projects, and through its 'Hand in Hand' Project has established partnerships with Ravenswood/Unity and Jewish Care to set up volunteer groups around the UK.

President Edmund L. de Rothschild, C.B.E., T.D.; *Commandant* Dame Simone Prendergast, DBE, JP, DL; *Chairman* E. C. Greenbury F.C.A.; *Chaplain-Emeritus* Rev. Saul Amias MBE; *Chaplain* Rev Stanley Cohen; *Brigade Sec.* R. S. Weber.

JEWISH LEARNING EXCHANGE

Lincoln Gate, 152–154 Golders Green Road, London NW11 8HE.
☎ 020-8458 4588. Fax 020-8458 4587. Email: 10626.1535@compuserv.com
A service of Ohr Somayach Institutions. Organises educational events for schools, universities, youth groups and young adults, and Jewish Learning programmes in Israel. *Dir.* Rabbi D. Kirsch, 29 The Drive, London NW11 9SX. ☎ 020-8458 4391. Fax 020-8458 5694.

JEWISH SCOUT ADVISORY COUNCIL

Furthers scouting in the Jewish com. *H. Sec.* P. Russell, 9 Graham Lodge, Graham Road, London NW4 3DG. ☎ 020-8202 8613.

JEWISH YOUTH FUND

707 High Road, North Finchley, London N12 0BT.
☎ 020-8445 1670. Fax 020-8446 7370. E-mail jyf@ort.org
(Est. 1937. Reg. Charity No. 251902) Provides funds to promote the social education of Jewish young people through the provision of leisure time facilities to clubs, movements and other Jewish youth organisations in the United Kingdom. *Chairman of Adv. Cttee* Jonathan Gestetner; *Ts.* Peter Levy, O.B.E. and Miss Wendy Pollecoff; *Tr.* Jonathan Gestetner, Lady Morris of Kenwood, Peter Levy, O.B.E., Miss Wendy Pollecoff; *Sec.* Peter Shaw.

JEWISH YOUTH ORCHESTRA OF GREAT BRITAIN

Rehearsals: Hillel House, 1-2 Endsleigh Street, WC1H 0DS.
(Est. 1970. Reg. Charity No. 294994) For young musicians (aged 13–20, Grade V and above) to give regular concerts in London and other cities. Occasional summer courses. Rehearsals Sunday mornings during term-time. *Co-founder and conductor* Sydney Fixman; *Chairman* Dr J. W. Frank, P.O. Box 24006, London NW4 4ZF, ☎ 0958 434999; *T.* S. Admoni.

JEWISH YOUTH STUDY GROUPS

(Agency for Jewish Education)
Beit Meir, 44a Albert Rd., London NW4 2SJ.
☎ 020-8457 9709. Fax 020-8457 9707. Email jysg-aje@brijnet.org

Holds weekly Sunday meetings for 13–18 age group on a variety of Jewish and secular topics in 13 areas around London and in the Regions as well as annual summer and winter schools, a post-GCSE Israel Tour and pre-university Year in Israel. This programme combines social events, intensive study and leadership training and discussion on a variety of Jewish issues. *Contact* Melanie Shutz.

JNF YOUTH & EDUCATION DEPT.
58-70 Edgware Way, Edgware, Middx HA8 8GQ.
☎ 020-8421 7603. Fax 020-8905 4299. Email jnf@brijnet.org
Provides educational resources and speakers to nurseries, schools, religion classes, youth movements, youth clubs and university campuses, in the areas of Israel partnership, land reclamation and ecological issues. Assists in co-ordinating and arranging Bar/Bat Mitzvahs in Israel.

MAKOR (formerly JPMP)
Balfour House, 741 High Road, London N12 0BQ.
☎ 020-8446 8020. Fax 020-8343 9037. Email makor@ujia.org
Makor is the educational resource centre for Jewish-Israel informal education and training for youth, student and young adult leadership. It also offers planning and evaluation services. It is cross-communal and its users include Movement Workers, Youth Leaders, Madrichim, Schools Contacts, Shlichim and other community professionals and leaders. The centre has specialist units for Jewish Education (The Texts and Values Project) and Leadership Training (The Hadracha Institute) and also specialises in all aspects of Israel/Zionist Education. The centre has a large collection of books, videos, equipment and other resources covering Judaism, Israel and general Jewish culture. Makor is able to draw upon the resources of the Jewish Agency, including its staff of Israeli Shlichim in Britain. It works with partner centres in Glasgow, Leeds, Manchester, Liverpool and Redbridge. It is a partnership project of the UJIA and the Jewish Agency. *Dir.* Roy Graham, LLB, MA.

NOAM (NOAR MASORTI)
97 Leeside Crescent, London NW11 0JL.
☎ 020-8201 8773. Fax 020-8458 4027. E-mail noam@ort.org
(Est. 1985. Reg. Charity No. 801846) NOAM is the Masorti Zionist youth movement. We run a wide variety of educational and social activities including clubs, weekends, summer camps and Israel tours for 8-16 year olds. NOAM also runs the MELTAM leadership course accredited by the University of Oxford delegacy of local examinations. Other activities include: Noam Israel Tour (post-GCSE); Drachim – year-in-Israel including Machon, kibbutz, volunteer work and Jewish learning; summer camps in Britain and France; weekly clubs; weekends away; social action and charity projects; and contact with Masorti youth in Israel, Europe and America. *Mazkir* Jonny Whine; *Activities Co-ord.* Michal Itzkovitch; *Shaliah* Doron Rubin. *Publ.* Hadashot Noam (termly news-letter); Norma (bi-annual magazine).

R.S.Y.-NETZER/RSGB YOUTH, STUDENTS AND YOUNG ADULTS DEPARTMENT
Manor House, 80 East End Road, N3 2SY.
☎ 020-8349 4731. Fax 020-8343 4972.
E-mail: rsy.refsyn.org.uk; students@refsyn.org.uk
Northern Office Northern Resource & Learning Centre, Jacksons Row, Albert Square, Manchester M2 5WD.
To educate young people towards a love of Reform Judaism and Reform Zionism and to offer them Jewish life options within an equal opportunity perspective.
    RSY-Netzer is the autonomous reform Zionist youth movement of the Reform

Movement and part of the worldwide Netzer youth movement. There are 26 anafim (branches) with weekly meetings around the country and a full calendar of residential activities, seminars and training courses for the four age groups – Garinim (10–12 yrs), Shtilim (13–16 yrs), Ilanot (16–18 yrs) and Bogrim (18+) Summer camps are run in England, Israel and Europe and a ten-month leadership training programme (Shnat Netzer) in Israel.

The Department offers youth work development and training to RSGB communities as well as developing innovative models of youth work practice and provides programmes, activities and support for Reform Jewish students.

SIR MAX BONN MEMORIAL JEWISH YOUTH CENTRE
Leigh House, 63 Ethelbert Road, Cliftonville, Kent.
(Est. 1947) To provide a holiday centre for young people and adolescents, conferences and discussion groups among clubs and institutions.

Contact Mrs. Doris Cohen, 2 Priory Court, Sparrows Herne, Bushey, Herts WD2 1EF. ☎ 020-8950 5141.

ULPS YOUTH DEPARTMENT/ULPSNYC - NETZER
The Montagu Centre, 21 Maple Street, W1P 6DS.
☎ 020-7631 0584. Fax 020-7436 4184. E-mail ulpsnyc.netzer.yd@ort.org
To informally educate young Jewish people towards a strong identity within a progressive Jewish and Zionist framework.

There is a network of youth clubs within the 28 ULPS synagogues which host monthly club sessions. The Youth Department in partnership with ULPSNYC Netzer offers residential activities, training in youth leadership and teaching. Summer camps are held in Britain and we offer tours to Israel, Europe and the USA. The Youth Dept. offers training, new models of youth work. Mind the Gap is the young adult group (21–35 age group) and offers social events and projects. We support and work with RSGB on student issues. *Dir. for Young People* Gideon Lyons; *Admin.* Sandra Levene; *Mazkir* Gideon Lyons; *Fieldworker* Zoe Leigh, Abigail Wharton.

UNION OF MACCABI ASSOCIATIONS IN GREAT BRITAIN AND IRELAND
Prestige House, Station Road, Borehamwood, Herts WD5 1DF.
☎ 020-8207 0700. Fax 020-8207 1707.
To promote the active participation in sports and education of young Jewish men and women, in order to enhance their Jewish identity, values and commitment to the community.
Chairman H. Minkoff; *Nat. Dir.* M. Herman; *H. Sec.* J. Barnett; *Hon. Sports Dir.* H. Moss; *Admin.* Mrs C. Green.

Affiliated clubs in the London area: Belmont; Brady; Bushey; Catford; Chigwell & Hainault; E.D.R.S.; Ivri; Kadimah/Victoria, Kenton; Kinnor; Launchpad; Luton; Maccabi Assn. London; Southend-on-Sea.

Affiliated clubs in the regions: Brighton and Hove; Cardiff; Dublin; Edinburgh; Glasgow; Liverpool; Leeds; Leicester; Manchester and South Manchester; Newcastle; Sheffield.

The following groups are associated with the Zionist Movement.

BACHAD FELLOWSHIP
Friends of Bnei Akiva, Alexander Margulies Youth Centre, 2 Halleswelle Road, London NW11 0DJ.
☎ 020-8458 9370. Fax 020-8209 0107.
(Est. 1942. Reg. Charity No. 227509) To promote Jewish religious education and provide agricultural and vocational training for Jewish youth. Establishes and maintains Youth Centres in London, Leeds, Manchester, Glasgow and Dublin. *Hon.*

Presidents Chief Rabbi Dr. Jonathan Sacks, The Rt. Hon. the Lord Jakobovits, Rabbi Cyril Harris, Chief Rabbi of South Africa; *V. President* Sir Sidney Hamburger, C.B.E., J.P.; *Chairman* Arieh L. Handler; *V. Chairman* Jack Lass; *H. Ts.* Harry T. Klahr, Michael Wreschner; *H. Sec* Mrs. Susan Sperber; *Admin.* Mrs Tania Fraenkel. Bnei Akiva Scholarship Institute (BASI) arranges for senior members to spend one or two years in Israel working and studying to prepare for ultimate settlement in the country after returning here to act as youth leaders for a period.

BETAR-TAGAR
143–145 Brondesbury Park, London NW2 5JL.
☎ 020-8451 0002. Fax 020-8459 8766. E-mail betar.tagar@ort.org
(Reg. Charity No. 290571) Betar-Tagar Zionist students movement educates Jewish students and youth towards Zionism by stressing Aliya, the value of Jewish tradition and concern for Jewish people everywhere, self-defence and Jewish identity.

BNEI AKIVA
2 Halleswelle Road, London NW11 0DJ.
☎ 020-8209 1319. Fax 020-8209 0107. E-mail bnei.akiva@ort.org
(Est. 1940) Aims to educate young people, aged between 7 and 25 years, in ideals of Religious Zionism and Torah Ve-Avodah. More than 40 groups in UK meeting on Shabbat afternoons. Regular weekend and summer seminars are run throughout the year. Bnei Akiva runs a highly successful year scheme in Israel known as Hachshara which has two tracks – one yeshiva-based and the other kibbutz-based. Bnei Akiva is the largest religious Zionist youth organisation in the world.
Mazkir David Zackon; *Admin.* Rosemary Davidson.
Publ.: Monthly education booklets, termly movement magazines, weekly Sidrah sheet. Supports Aliya to the State of Israel as the movement objective.
Regional centres: 72 Singleton Road, Salford M7 4LU.
☎ 0161-740 1621. Fax 0161-740 8018. Email: bnei.akiva.north@ort.org.

EZRA YOUTH MOVEMENT
British and European Off.: 2a Alba Gardens, London, NW11 9NR.
☎/Fax 020-8458 5372.
Associated with Poale Agudat Israel.
Orthodox Jewish movement based in London with a branch in Manchester and branches in Israel and other parts of the world.

FEDERATION OF ZIONIST YOUTH
25a Oakleigh Road North, London N20 9HE.
☎ 020-8445 6222. Fax 020-8445 6332. E-mail fzy@ort.org
FZY is an active and vibrant Zionist youth movement with societies throughout Britain. We are a pluralist movement, which means our members are drawn from all religious streams and are of all political colours. The movement aims to educate its members around Jewish and Zionist themes with the aim of fulfilling the four aims of FZY, namely: Aliya, Tarbut (promoting Jewish culture), Tzedaka and Magen (defence of Jewish rights).

FZY has weekly meetings all over the country organised around these aims which, when combined with weekend seminars for 14 to 18 year olds, our Winter Camp Shachar, our annual conference, our summer camp Kesher and our summer programmes in Israel, plus numerous other local and national events, create a dynamic and creative environment for Jewish Youth to express their heritage, culture and identity.

FZY Year Course is a prime example of our commitment to Israel. An exciting, stimulating and academic-year programme, with very strong leadership elements, Year Course allows FZYniks to explore and understand Israel and themselves, and encourages them to return as leaders in the community.
President Paul Lenga; *Hon. President* Abba Eban; *Mazkir* Andrew Levene; *Oved*

Chinuch Simon Cohen; *Camps Org.* Deborah Kaye; *Org. Secs.* Louise Jacobs, Vivienne Stone; *Northern Fieldworker* Debbie Elstein. *Publ.* 'The Young Zionist' (quarterly) and 'The Bulletin' (monthly).

HABONIM–DROR
523 Finchley Road, London NW3 7BD.
☎ 020-7435 9033/4. Fax 020-7431 4503.
Habonim-Dror was created in 1979 when Habonim and Dror merged, and is part of the international Habonim-Dror movement.

It is a radical Zionist Youth Movement which educates Jewish Youth towards a realisation of their Jewish heritage, both traditional and historical. In particular, it educates at a later age towards chalutzic (pioneering) self-realisation in Israel, and the value of a more equal caring society.

Activities are run once or twice weekly covering drama, arts and crafts, educational games, and social events. There are Winter and Summer Camps for all ages, from 9 to 23, including adventure camps for 14-year-olds.

European Camp, including a Holocaust seminar, for 15-year-olds and Israel Camp for 16-year-olds.

A central feature of Habonim-Dror's programme is its well-established Year Course in Israel: Shnat Hachsharah. This involves living on Kibbutz, Youth Leadership training, tours of the country and a full educational programme about Judaism and Israel.

Habonim-Dror groups are to be found in most Jewish com. in Great Britain. *President* Lady Morris of Kenwood; *Admin.* David Arram; *Nat. Sec.* Mandy Wilkins.
   Youth Centres
   London: North West & Central Office, 523 Finchley Road, London NW3 7BD (☎ 020-7435 9033. Fax 020-7431 4503. E-mail habonim@ort.org); Elstree & Borehamwood: c/o Central Office; Glasgow; Leeds: Fir Tree Lane, Leeds LS17 (☎ 01132 682055); Manchester: North, South Hale Barns, 11 Upper Park Road, Salford M7 0HY (☎ 0161-795 9447); Birmingham: 26 Somerset Road, Birmingham B15 2QD (☎ Central Office); Oxford: Jewish Centre, Oxford (☎ Central Office); Bristol: c/o Central Office; Ilford: Sinclair House, Woodford Bridge Road, Ilford, Essex (☎ 020-8551 0017); all other coms.: inquire 523 Finchley Road, NW3 7BD; (☎ 020-7435 9033).
   Publ.: Koleinu.

HANOAR HATZIONI
The Youth Centre, 31 Tetherdown, Muswell Hill, London N10 1ND.
☎ 020-88831022/3. Fax 020-8365 2272. E-mail hanoar@ort.org
Website http://www.ort.org/anjy/orgtions/hh/hh home.htm
Hanoar Hatzioni are a non-political Zionist Youth Movement catering for people between the ages of 7 and 23. Groups are run all over the country. Annual events include Summer and Winter Camps, Israel Tours for 16 year olds, outings, educational and social programmes. Hanoar Hatzioni also run the Shnat Sherut Year Scheme and the Gesher 6 months Scheme in Israel.
Mazkir Robert Anders; *Rosh Chinuch* Jon Kay; *Racaz Paylut* Damian Tash; *Shlicha* Noga Levtzion Nadan.

HASHOMER HATZAIR
Hashomer House, 37A Broadhurst Gardens, NW6 3BN.
☎ 020-7328 5451.
(Est. 1940) The British constituent of a world movement to educate its members in Socialist Zionist ideals as a basis for life in Israel especially kibbutz. *Sec.* D. Sacks.
Shlicha Sheva Friedman.
   Youth Centre as above.

JNF FUTURE
58-70 Edgware Way, Edgware, Middx HA8 8GG.
☎ 020-8421 7693. Fax 020-8905 4299. E-mail jnf@brijnet.org.
(Est. 1958) To support the work of the JNF in Israel in afforestation, land reclamation, environmental and ecological issues by fund-raising events organised
through young committees (18-30) nationwide.

KIBBUTZ REPRESENTATIVES
1A Accommodation Road, London NW11 8ED.
☎ 020-8458 9235. Fax 020-8455 7930. E-mail enquiries@kibbutz.org.uk
(Reg. Charity No. 294564) Representing all the Kibbutz movements in Israel.
The organisation arranges Working Visits on Kibbutz for persons aged 18–32;
Kibbutz Ulpan for persons aged 18-28, including the 'Oren' enrichment programme; and a 2-month short Summer Ulpan, for persons aged 18-26. Religious
Kibbutz options are available, and all applicants must be in good physical and mental health.

KIDMAH
c/o Hashomer House, 37a Broadhurst Gdns, London NW6 3BN.
☎ 020-7328 5451.
Left-Zionist student organisation promoting Jewish-Arab recognisation, religious
pluralism, anti-racism. Educational, social, political activities; provides lecturers to
Jewish and non-Jewish groups. *Fieldworker* Daniel Marcus.

YOUNG MAPAM
Hashomer House, 37A Broadhurst Gardens, London NW6 3BN.
☎ 020-7328 5451.
Anglo-Jewish youth and student group, ages 18–35, with a Socialist-Zionist outlook.
Social, cultural, educ. and political programme stressing humanistic values of
Judaism and progressive Zionist elements. Aliya of members encouraged. *Chairman*
Marc Bernstein.

The following organisations are concerned with Jewish students

ASSOCIATION OF JEWISH SIXTH FORMERS
1–2 Endsleigh Street, London WC1H 0DS.
☎ 020-7387 3384. Fax 020-7387 3392. E-mail aj6.hq@ort.org http://
www.come.to/aj6
(Est. 1977. Reg. Charity No. 1019445) Jewish youth organisation for fifth and
sixth formers (membership 600, service outreach 1,200). Aims to educate and promote a positive Jewish identity. Five main objectives: preparation for the challenges
of school and university campus life, outreach to unaffiliated youth, meaningful
and lasting Jewish education, hadracha and leadership training, and shared responsibility (arevut). Services include campus visits, interview techniques, university and
career information, regional weekly meetings, national weekends, shabbatons,
social events and summer tours to Israel and Europe. *Nat. Dir.* Mark Saunderson;
Educt. Dev. Worker Alexandra Benjamin; *Sec./ Admin* Anne Cutter.
   Publ. AJ6 Guide to Jewish Student Life – info on Campus, University J-Socs,
Hillel Houses, Chaplaincy; AJ6 Guide to Year Schemes in Israel; Sixth Sense
(quarterly magazine); monthly mailings.

B'NAI B'RITH HILLEL FOUNDATION
Hillel House, 1–2 Endsleigh Street, London WC1H 0DS.
☎ 020-7388 0801. Fax 020-7916 3973. E-mail hillel@ort.org
(Reg. Charity No. 313503) Jewish Student Centre, devoted to social and educational activities among Jewish students at colleges and universities. Facilities include

meeting rooms, common room, Kosher Restaurant. Closed Shabbat and Festivals, other than by arrangement.
President Fred S. Worms, O.B.E.; *Chairman* Dr Alan Webber; *Dep. Chairman* Jeffrey Green; *H.T.* Martin Korn; *Exec. Dir.* Gerry Lucas.
   Residential and social facilities available at Hillel Houses in the following locations (contact person named for further details):
   Birmingham: Frank Linden, ☎ 0121-4545042. **Bournemouth:** Marilyn Dexter ☎ 01202-304252, **Brighton:** Annabelle Lee, ☎ 01273 880596. **Bristol:** Sheila Tobias, ☎ 01454 412831. **Cardiff:** Paula Freed, ☎ 02920 758614. **Edinburgh:** Myrna Kaplan, ☎ 0131-399 8201. **Glasgow:** Linda Lovat, ☎ 0141-639 7741. **Hull:** Ian Dysch, ☎ 01482 54947. **Leeds:** Dr Roger Pollard, ☎ 0113 332080. **Leicester:** Melissa Morrison, ☎ 01162 70-5771. **Liverpool:** Carol Lewis, ☎ 0151-722 5021. **London:** (J. C. Gilbert House) Herman Greenbourne, ☎ 020-8998 7865, (Harold Godfrey House) Evelyn Bacharach, ☎ 020-7722 01420, (Mapesbury Rd, N.W.) Jackie Barnett, ☎ 020-7723 4735. **Manchester:** Dr Sydney Baigel, ☎ 0161-740 2521. **Newcastle:** Geoffrey Lurie, ☎ 0191-285 7928. **Nottingham:** Sandra Flitterman, ☎ 01152 937 5403. **Reading:** Richard Sassoon, ☎ 01734 613367. **Sheffield:** Elaine Jacob, ☎ 01142 308688. **Southampton:** Irene Weintroub ☎ 01202-527527; **York:** Phil Prosser ☎ 01904-423164.

NATIONAL JEWISH CHAPLAINCY BOARD
21 Gloucester Gardens, London NW11 9AB
☎ 020-8731 7471. Fax 020-8209 0927. Email njcb@brijnet.org
(Reg. Charity no. 261324) Appointment of full-time chaplains to serve all Jewish students at universities in the United Kingdom, in conjunction with local boards. For local contacts, apply to administrator. Chaplains available for personal counselling, practical support, as an educational resource and for spiritual guidance.
President: The Chief Rabbi; *V. Presidents* Anthony Cowen, Michael Weinstein; *Chairman* Dr Simon Woldman; *T.* Ben Lazarus; *Admin.* Ruth Marriott.

REFORM STUDENTS
The Sternberg Centre for Judaism, 80 East End Road, Finchley, London N3 2SY.
☎ 020-8349 4731 Ext. 107. Fax 020-8343 4972. E-mail students@refsyn.org.uk
Website http://www.refsyn.org.uk/students/
Reform Students offer: campus study, with National Chaplain Rabbi Deborah Myers-Weinstein; pastoral support; weekends away; e-mail bulletins; subsidies for European Jewish events; support for cross-communal events in UJS and Hillel. Contact: *Student Co-ord.* Ruth Kay.

UNION OF JEWISH STUDENTS
of the United Kingdom and Ireland
(formerly: Inter-University Jewish Federation of Gt. Britain and Ireland).
Hillel House, 1/2 Endsleigh Street, WC1H 0DS.
☎ 020-7387 4644/380 0111. Fax 020-7383 0390. E-mail ujs@brijnet.org
Co-ordinates the activities of the Jewish societies in the universities and colleges of the UK and Ireland. It stimulates an interest among Jewish students in Judaism, Zionism, Jewish history and education, and in Jewish thought. It encourages members to play their part in the religious and social life of the community. (Est. 1919.)
Chair Ruth Bookatz; *Admin.* Shirley Goldwater.
   Jewish student societies are attached to many universities and colleges. See under separate towns.
   London Region, Hillel House, 1/2 Endsleigh Street, WC1H 0DS.
☎ 020-7388 4919. There is a full cultural and social programme at the Centre in Hillel House and at Jewish Socs. in the regions.

WINGATE YOUTH TRUST

(Est. 1975. Reg. Charity No. 269678) To provide facilities for youth, for recreation and leisure. *Chairman* B. Myers; T. M. Rebak, 58 Southwood Park, Southwood Lawn Road, N6 5SQ. ☎ 020-8340 1287; *Sec.* Malcolm Davis.

LIBRARIES, MUSEUMS AND EXHIBITIONS

Anglo-Jewish Archives. An independent Registered Charity under the auspices of the Jewish Historical Society of England. The genealogical collections have been deposited at the Society of Genealogists and the main archive collection has been deposited with the Hartley Library, University of Southampton (see p.56). *H. Sec.* Cyril Drukker, (JHSE), 33 Seymour Place, London W1H 5AP. ☎/Fax 020-7723 5852.

Hebraica Libraries Group, c/o Library, Oriental Faculty, Sidgwick Ave., Cambridge CB3 9DR. ☎ 01223-335112. Email swm@ula.cam.ac.uk websites: http:// www.bodley.ox.ac.uk/users/gae/NCOLR/NCOLRWEB.htm and http://www. lib.cam/ac.uk/~jb127/
(Est. 1979) The Group brings together representatives of all the major Judaica and Hebraica collections in Great Britain and Ireland (as listed below) together with other academic libraries with an interest in the field. It holds an annual meeting and is affiliated to both the British Association of Jewish Studies and the European Association of Jewish Studies, and to the National Council on Orientalist Library Resources (NCOLR). It offers expertise in all aspects of Hebraica collections, preservation, security, conservation, cataloguing, computer systems and collection development. *Convenor* S.W. Massil.

AJEX Military Museum, AJEX House, East Bank, Stamford Hill, London N16 5RT. ☎ 020-8800 2844. Fax: 020-8880 1117.
A display of books, photographs and memorabilia from the reign of George III to the present. *Archivist:* H. Morris.

Ben Uri Art Society and Gallery, 126 Albert Street, London NW1 7NE. ☎ 020-7482 1234. Fax 020-7482 1414. E-mail benuri@ort.org. (Reg. Charity No. 280389) Open Mon.-Thurs., 10-5, Sun. 2-5 during exhibitions. Closed Jewish Holy-days, Bank holidays. The aim of the Society, which is a registered charity founded in 1915, is to promote Jewish Art as part of the Jewish cultural heritage. The Gallery provides a showcase for exhibitions of contemporary art as well as for the Society's own permanent collection of over 800 works by Jewish artists. A full programme of activities is provided for members of the Society including lectures, visits to other galleries and the popular annual picture fair.
Chairman Leslie Michaels; *V. Chairmen* Mrs Lois Peltz, Lewis Goodman, O.B.E.; *Hon. Sec.* Gerald Rothman; *H.T.* Andrew Coleman; *Chairman of Art Cttee.* David Glasser; *Dir.* Mrs Jo Velleman.

Bodleian Library, Broad Street, Oxford OX1 3BG. ☎ 01865 277000. *Bodley's Librarian:* Mr R. Carr. The Hebrew and Yiddish collections comprise 3,000 man-uscript volumes and 60,000 printed books, including many incunabula, fragments from the Cairo Genizah and the Oppenheimer library, the finest collection of Hebrew books and manuscripts ever assembled. Intending readers should always contact the Admissions Office in advance. Open to holders of a reader's ticket Mon. to Fri. 9-7, Sat. 9-1. *Hebrew Specialist Libr.* R. C. Judd, M.A., M.Phil. Email rjc@bodley.ox.ac.uk

The British Library, Oriental and India Office Collections, 96 Euston Road, London NW1 2DB. ☎ 020-7412 7657/7646. Fax 020-7412 7641. Email oioc-enquiries@

bl.uk. The Hebrew collection comprises over 3,000 manuscript volumes and 10,000 fragments (incl. Moses Gaster's collection and many fragments from the Cairo Genizah); Hebrew printed books, about 70,000 titles, incl. some 100 incunabula, rabbinic and modern Hebrew literature; Yiddish, Ladino, Judeo-Arabic and Judeo-Persian books; some 1,000 Hebrew and Yiddish periodicals and newspapers. Oriental Reading Room open to holders of readers' passes. (Hours of opening may be subject to revision at any time. Normal opening: Mon. 10.00–5.00; Tues.-Sat. 9.30–5.00). Some Hebrew manuscripts are on permanent display in the British Library Exhibition Galleries, open (free of charge): Mon., Wed. to Fri. 9.30–6.00, Tues. 9.30–8.00, Sat. 9.30–5.00, Sun. 11.00–5.00.

Brotherton Library, University of Leeds, Leeds LS2 9JT. ☎ 01132 335501. Fax: 01132 335561. *Librarian* Lynne Brindley. Holdings include substantial materials for Hebrew and Jewish studies and the Travers Herford Collection on Judaism and Talmudic studies. The primary Judaica collection is the Roth Collection comprising the manuscripts and printed books from the library of Cecil Roth, including 350 mss., 900 printed books (pre-1850) 6,000 modern books and other archival material. Available to bona fide scholars who should write to the Librarian in the first instance enclosing an appropriate recommendation. *Asst. Libr. (Semitic)* M. C. Davis. *Publ.* Selig Brodetsky lecture series.

Cambridge University Library, West Rd, Cambridge CB3 9DR. ☎ 01223 333000. Fax 01223 333160. E-mail library@ula.cam.ac.uk Websitehttp://www.lib.cam.ac.uk *Dir.* Mr P. K. Fox. The Hebraica and Judaica collections comprise c. 140,000 Cairo Genizah fragments (being catalogued in the Genizah Series, CUP); 1,000 complete Hebrew codices (see S.C. Reif, Hebrew Manuscripts at Cambridge University Library, CUP 1997); approximately 40,000 printed books. Available to members of the University and bona fide scholars by application, preferably in writing in advance, to the Admissions Officer. Reading rooms open 9.30–6.45; Admissions Office: 9.30–12.30, 2.00–4.15. *Dir. Genizah Res. Unit and Oriental Div.* Professor S. C. Reif; *Hebraica Libr.* Mrs J. Butterworth.

Czech Memorial Scrolls Centre (Memorial Scrolls Trust), Kent House, Rutland Gardens, London SW7 1BX. ☎ 020-7584 3741. (Reg. Charity No. 278900) This permanent exhibition tells the unique story of the rescue from Prague, in 1964, of 1,564 Torah Scrolls and of their restoration and distribution on permanent loan to communities throughout the world. The exhibits include some of the scrolls, a remarkable display of Torah binders, some dating from the 18th century, and other moving reminders of the vanished communities of Bohemia and Moravia. The centre is open on Tuesdays and Thursdays from 10am to 4pm. *Jt. Chairmen* Mrs R. Shaffer, Miss C. Stuart.

Harry Rosencweig Collection of Jewish Music, School of Oriental & African Studies, University of London. Printed sheet music includes 17th–20th century European, American and Israeli liturgical and art music, and various anthologies of folk music. Text books on Jewish music and dance. A few LPs. Many rare items. *Libr.*

The Hartley Library, University of Southampton, Highfield, Southampton SO17 1BJ. Holdings of the Special Collections Division include (i) the **Parkes Library**, founded by the late Revd. Dr. James Parkes in 1935 to promote the study of relations between the Jewish and the non-Jewish worlds, now containing 14,000 books and periodicals; (ii) extensive collections of manuscripts relating to Anglo-Jewry (containing many of the collections of **Anglo-Jewish Archives**) and encompassing the papers of the Council of Christians and Jews, the Anglo-Jewish Association, the papers of Rabbi Solomon Schonfeld and the Chief Rabbi's Religious Emergency Fund, archives of the Union of Jewish Women, private papers of Chief Rabbi Hertz, early records of the Board of Shechita, archives of the Federation of Jewish Relief Organisations, Zangwill family papers, and the papers of the Jewish Board of Guardians and of the Jewish Blind Society. A catalogue of the archives was published by the library in 1992. Open Mon., Tue., Thur. and Fri., 0900-1700; Wed. 1000-1700; by appointment. ☎ 0238 593335 (Parkes); 0238 592721 (MSS); Fax: 0238 593007. E-mail: library@soton.ac.uk (for Parkes); archives@soton.ac.uk (for MSS) Website http://www.soton.ac.uk/~papers1/collections/wwwintro.html. *Archivist* Dr. C. M. Woolgar.

The Hidden Legacy Foundation, Kent House, Rutland Gardens, London SW7 1BX. ☎ 020-7584 2754. Fax 020-7584 6896.
(Est. 1988. Reg. Charity no. 326032) Devoted to promoting the awareness of provincial (English) and rural (German) Jewish history as seen through buildings and artefacts, and has become particularly identified with German Genizot. It organises exhibitions: Genizah (1992), Mappot (1997), The Jews of Devon and Cornwall (2000), and, having been active in Germany, is now working in England cataloguing Judaica. Library, slide and photo archives on rural German Jewry. *Exec. Dir.* Evelyn Friedlander. *Publ.* Newsletter.

Imperial War Museum Holocaust Exhibition, Lambeth Road, London SE1 6HZ. *Project Office* ☎ 020-7416 5204/5285. Fax 020-7416 5278. *Project Dir.* Suzanne Bardgett; *Patrons* The Lord Bramall, Sir Martin Gilbert, Ben Helfgott, Sir Claus Moser, Lord Rothschild, Lord Weidenfeld, Lord Wolfson of Marylebone, Stephen Rubin; *Advisory Bd.* Professor D. Cesarani, Sir Martin Gilbert, Ben Helfgott, Antony Lerman, Martin Smith. *Publ.* Report (Edr. Maurice Samuelson).

Institute of Contemporary History and Wiener Library, Ltd., 4 Devonshire Street, W1N 2BH. Reg. Charity No. 313015. ☎ 020-7636 7247. Fax: 020-7436 6428. Email: lib@wl.u-net.com; http://www.geocities.com/athens/forum/3766
Founded by Dr. A. Wiener in Amsterdam, 1933, and since 1939 in London. Research Library and Institute on contemporary European and Jewish history, especially the rise and fall of the Third Reich; survival and revival of Nazi and fascist movements; antisemitism; racialism; the Middle East; post-war Germany. Holds Britain's largest collection of documents, testimonies, books and videos on the Holocaust. Active educ. programme of lectures, seminars and conferences. *Chairman of Exec. Cttee.* Ernst Fraenkel; *Dir.* Prof. David Cesarani.

Institute for Jewish Policy Research Library, 79 Wimpole Street, London W1M 7DD. ☎ 020-7935 8266. Fax: 020-7935 3252. E-mail JPR@ort.org.
The Edgar M. Bronfman library is open to JPR members and postgraduate researchers by appointment. Books and press cuttings collections include material on past and present Jewish issues: antisemitism, the Holocaust, Jewish–Christian relations, world Jewry, Israel and inter-faith relations. *Libr.* Patricia Schotten, B.A.

Jewish Community Exhibition Centre, c/o David Turner, 1 Village Close, Belsize Lane, London NW3. ☎ 020-7794 1542. (Est. 1985.) To provide exhibition material on subjects of Jewish interest. The central exhibition under the responsibility of the Education Dept. of the BoD is 'The Jewish Way of Life' which has travelled to many venues in the UK. Other exhibitions include 'The Anschluss', 'Sir Moses Montefiore', 'Shalosh Regalim', the three Foot Festivals and 'The Anglo Jewish Experience 1066-1990', the history of the Jews in England.
Co-Chairmen David Turner and Mrs. Ruth Winston Fox, MBE, J.P.

The Jewish Museum - London's Museum of Jewish Life
Website: http://www.jewmusm.ort.org
(Est. 1932. Reg. Charity No. 10098819) The Jewish Museum aims to recover, preserve and exhibit material relating to the roots and heritage of Jewish people in
Britain, and to illustrate and explain Jewish religious practice with objects of rari-
ty and beauty. It seeks to increase knowledge and understanding about Jewish life
and history through its programme of education and exhibitions, and also has a
programme of holocaust education. The Friends of the Jewish Museum has been
established to suport the work of the museum. Publ. include: Research Papers,
Education Resources, Map of the Jewish East End, *Living up West – Jewish Life in
London's West End, The Jews of Aden, What about the Children – 200 Years of
Norwood Child Care, The Portuguese Jewish Community in London (1656–1830);
Immigrant Furniture Workers in London, 1881–1939, Yiddish Theatre in London,
Child's Play – Jewish Children's Books & Games from the Past, The Last Goodbye
– An Education Resource on the Kindertransport.*
Dir. Rickie Burman, MA, MPhil; *Chairman* Kenneth Rubens, OBE, FRSA; *Dep.
Chairman* Robert Craig, LLM; *Friends Admin.* Sidney Berg and Sidney Budd.

The Jewish Museum – Camden Town
The museum has been awarded Designated status by the Museums and Galleries
Commission in recognition of its outstanding collections. History and
Ceremonial Art Galleries, audio-visual programmes and a Temporary
Exhibitions Gallery with changing exhibitions. Educational programmes avail-
able. Open: Sun–Thurs, 10 am–4 pm. Closed Jewish Festivals and Public
Holidays. Address: Raymond Burton House, 129–131 Albert Street, NW1 7NB.
☎ 020-7284 1997. Fax: 020-7267 9008.

The Jewish Museum – Finchley
Displays relating to the history of Jewish immigration and settlement in
London, including reconstructions of East End tailoring and furniture work-
shops. Holocaust Education Gallery with a moving exhibition on London-born
Holocaust survivor, Leon Greenman. Travelling Exhibitions, Educational
Programmes and Resources and Walking Tours of Jewish London. Open: Sun.
10.30 am–4.30 pm, Mon–Thurs, 10.30 am–5 pm. Closed Jewish Festivals,
Public Holidays, on Sundays in August and Bank Holiday weekends. Address:
80 East End Road, N3 2SY. ☎ 020-8349 1143. Fax 020-8343 2162.

Jewish Studies Library (Incorporating the Library of the Jewish Historical Society
of England), University College London, Gower Street, WC1E 6BT. ☎ 020-7387
7050 (ext. 2598). Fax 020-7380 7373. E-mail: library@ucl.ac.uk.; Website:
www.ucl.ac.uk/library
All collections are housed together in the Arnold Mishcon Reading Room. These
are the Mocatta Library, the Brodie Library, the Altmann Library, the Abramsky
Library, the William Margulies Yiddish Library, in addition to books and periodicals acquired for the support of teaching and research by the College's Department
of Hebrew and Jewish Studies. The Jewish Studies Library serves the academic
community of UCL and affiliates and is open for reference purposes to the general public engaged in research. The Arnold Mishcon Reading Room is part of the
Main Library. Contact the library to obtain current opening hours and admissions
procedure. Genealogical enquiries are referred to a professional genealogist unless
specifically related to collections in the Library. *Libr.* Dr P. Ayris.

John Rylands University Library of Manchester, Oxford Road, Manchester M13
9PP. The Special Collections Repository, 150 Deansgate, Manchester M3 3EH.
☎ 0161-834 5343. Fax 0161-834 5574. The Hebraica and Judaica comprise over

10,500 fragments from the Cairo Genizah; manuscripts and codices from the Crawford and Gaster collections; Samaritan manuscripts from the Gaster collection; 6,600 items of printed Hebraica and Talmudic literature in the Marmorstein collection; 1,000 volumes of the Haskalah collection; the Moses Gaster collection; and some 5,000 volumes in the Near Eastern collection in the main library dealing with Hebrew language and literature. Although primarily serving the staff and students of the University, other readers may obtain reference only access to the library on application (letter of introduction and evidence of identity required). A fee is charged to external readers requiring regular access to the main library. *Head of Special Collections* Dr P. McNiven.

Keren Hatorah Library, 97 Stamford Hill, London N16 5DN. ☎ 020-8800 6688. A comprehensive collection of Torah literature for the whole family. Operates as a lending library. Open Sun., Tues., Thurs., 10.30–12.30am. *Libr.* Mrs Grossnass.

Keren Hatorah Tape Library, 97 Stamford Hill, London N16. ☎ 020-8802 6388. Over ten thousand cassette recordings of Shiurim, lectures and conventions. The collection includes the complete Talmud in either English or Yiddish. Other subjects: Jewish History, Holocaust, the Festivals, Nach, Siddur, Hashkafa and Halacha. Open Sun 10.30–1.00, Mon to Thurs 11.00–4.00. *Libr.* A. Lauer.

Leo Baeck College Library, 80 East End Road, N3 2SY. ☎ 020-8345 4525 (ext. 400). Fax 020-8343 2558. Email Library@lbc.ac.uk. Est. 1956 to provide a library for Jewish Studies and research. Holdings: 35,000 vols; 75 current periodicals; 5,000 pamphlets with a special collection on Zionism; 15,000 sound records (shiurim and public lectures); 170 rabbinic and MA theses. Range: Bible, rabbinic literature, codes, liturgy, education, literature, history, holocaust and post-holocaust studies, Israel and Zionism. Open to members and occasional readers from Mon.–Thurs. 9.00–5.00, Fri. 9.00–1.00. Closed on Jewish Festivals, bank holidays and during the last week of December. During July and August, visits can be made only by appointment with the librarian. For regular access to the library a yearly contribution of £10 is to be made. For borrowing rights a further £10 will be charged. *Hd. Libr.* Dr P.W. van Boxel; *Ass. Libr.* César Merchán Hamann, MA.

Leopold Muller Memorial Library, Oxford Centre for Hebrew & Jewish Studies, Yarnton Manor, Yarnton, Oxford OX5 1PY. ☎ 01865-377946. Fax 01865-375079. (Reg. Charity No. 309720) The Oxford Centre houses the Leopold Muller Memorial Library whose main constituents are the Kressel and Elkoshi collections comprising some 35,000 volumes in Hebrew and over 7,000 volumes in western languages. The collections cover the full range of Hebrew and Jewish studies, with special focus on Hebrew literature of the 19th and 20th centuries, Haskalah, modern Jewish history, Zionism, Israel and Hebrew bibliography. The Kressel Collection includes a biographical and historical archive of some 500 box files of Hebrew newspaper and periodical cuttings on 12,000 Jewish pesonalities and on the early Yishuv in Palestine, as well as representative samples of the Hebrew and Yiddish press. *Libr.* Brad Sabin Hill.

London Metropolitan Archives, 40 Northampton Road, London EC1R 0HB. ☎ 020-7332 3820. Fax 020-7833 9136. Email ask.lma@ms.corpoflondon.gov.uk LMA has 2,000 sqare feet of archives deposited by major Jewish organisations. Open Mon.–Fri. 9.30am–4.45pm (Tues. and Thurs. until 7.30pm). See www.cityoflondon.gov.uk/lma for leaflet and gallery.

The London School of Jewish Studies (formerly Jews' College) **Library,** Schaller House, Albert Road, London NW4 2SJ. ☎ 020-8203 6427. Fax 020-8203 6420.

(Est. 1855. Reg. Charity no. 310023) Open Mon–Thurs 10am–4pm. Closed Jewish holidays and fast days. One of the most extensive Judaica libraries in Europe, the library contains 80,000 volumes, 20,000 pamphlets and 700 manuscripts. *Hd. Libr.* Esra Kahn.

Lubavitch Lending Library, 107–115 Stamford Hill, N16 5RP. ☎ 020-8800 5823. Established in 1972 to help the Jewish public study traditional Jewish culture and aid scholarship. The library contains 15,000 volumes in Hebrew, English and Yiddish. Services include a reference libr., a children's libr. and postal lending. Lectures and displays org. anywhere. Open Sun., 10am–12.30pm, 4pm–8pm; Mon.–Fri., 10am–4pm. Some weekday evgs. Other times available by appointment. *Libr.* Z. Rabin, A.L.A.

National Life Story Collection, at the British Library National Sound Archive, 96 Euston Road, London, NW1 2DB. ☎ 020-7412 7404. Fax 020-7412 7441. Email nsa-nlsc@bl.uk. Est. 1987, Reg. Charity No. 327571, to 'record first-hand experiences of as wide a cross-section of present-day society as possible'. As an independent charitable trust within the Oral History Section of the British Library's National Sound Archive, NLSC's key focus and expertise has been oral history fieldwork.
  Living memory of the Jewish Community is a major collection with a primary focus on pre-Second World War Jewish refugees to Britain, those fleeing from Nazi persecution during the Second World War and Holocaust survivors. The collection has recently expanded to include interviews with children of survivors. The collection complements other National Sound Archive material on Jewish life, notably the Holocaust Survivors' Centre interviews (C830), Central British Fund Kindertransport interviews (C526), Testimony: Video Interviews with British Holocaust Survivors (C533) and London Museum of Jewish Life oral history interviews (C525).

Porton Collection, Central Library, Municipal Buildings, Leeds LS1 3AB. ☎ 0113 2478282. Fax 0113 2478426. Comprises 3,700 items covering all aspects of the religion and culture of the Jewish people in English, Hebrew and Yiddish. Available for reference use only.

School of Oriental and African Studies (Univ. of London), Thornhaugh Street, Russell Square, London WC1H 0XG. ☎ 020-7323 6098. Fax 020-7636 2834. E-mail ps4@soas.ac.uk.
Ancient Near East, Semitics and Judaica Section of SOAS Library. *Section Head* P. S. Salinger. The Semitics and Judaica collections comprise about 15,000 Hebrew items covering the fields of modern Hebrew language and literature (one of the finest collections in Europe), biblical and intertestamental studies, Judaism, the Jewish people, and the land of Israel. There are also a considerable number of books in Western languages covering the above mentioned fields. In addition, largely owing to the acquisition of the Stencl and Leftwich collections in 1983 and some books from the Whitechapel collection in 1984, there are about 3000 books on Yiddish language and literature. Periodicals, of which the Library holds about 200 Hebrew titles, are shelved separately. The transfer of the Joe Loss Lectureship in Jewish Music from the City University to SOAS has brought also the Harry Rosencweig Collection of Jewish Music to the library (see p.55). For details of services, please refer to the Library Guide.

Spanish & Portuguese Jews' Congregation, 2 Ashworth Road, W9 1JY. ☎ 020-7289 2573. Fax: 020-7289 2709. **Archives:** The archives of the Spanish & Portuguese Jews' Congregation, London, and its institutions, which date from the mid-17th century, include Minute and Account Books, Registers of Births, Circumcisions,

Marriages and Burials. Most of the Registers have now been published and copies may be purchased from the Congregation's offices. The archives are not open to the public. Queries and requests by bona fide researchers should be submitted in writing to the Hon. Archivist. Advice and help will be given to general enquirers wherever possible. A search fee may be charged. *Hon. Archivist*: Miriam Rodrigues-Pereira. **Shasha Library** (Est 1936.) Designed to contain books on Jewish history, religion, literature and kindred interest from the Sephardi standpoint. The Library is intended for the use of members of the congregation. It contains over 1,200 books. These collections have been brought into the new Sephardi Centre opened at the end of 1994 (see p.41). *Libr.* Jack Epstein.

PROFESSIONAL ORGANISATIONS

AGUDAS HARABBONIM (ASSOCIATION OF RABBIS OF GREAT BRITAIN) (in association with the Agudas Israel World Rabbinical Council) 273 Green Lanes, London N4 2EX. ☎ 020-8802 1544. (Est. 1929) *Chairman Princ.* Rabbi H. Padwa, Av Beth Din, U.O.H.C.; *H. Dir.* Rabbi Ben Zion Blau; *H. Gen. Sec.* vacant.

AGUDATH HASHOCHTIM V'HASHOMRIM OF GREAT BRITAIN
Cattle Section: *H. Sec.* S. B. Spitzer, 33 Elm Park Avenue, N15 6AR.
Poultry Section: *H. Sec.* S. Leaman, 25 Rostrevor Road, N.15.

ASSOCIATION OF JEWISH COMMUNAL PROFESSIONALS
PO Box 73, Bushey, WD2 8XD. ☎/Fax: 020-8386 1857. The aims of the Association are to enhance the standing of the communal professional, represent their needs and interests, improve professional practice, provide a forum for professionals to discuss common issues and give mutual support, and to be a resource of relevant information. The Association publishes a Code of Practice which gives guidelines to Jewish communal organisations. *Chair* David Goldberg; *V. Chair* Alan Curtis, Angela Margolis; *H. Sec.* Rhoda Goodman; *H.T.* Maurice Ross.

ASSOCIATION OF MINISTERS (CHAZANIM) OF GREAT BRITAIN
Chairman Rev. S. I. Brickman, 9 Marlborough Mansions, Cannon Hill, London NW6 1JP. ☎ 020-7431 0575. *V. Chairman* Rev. A. Levin. ☎ 020-8554 0499. *Sec.* Rabbi D. A. Katanka; *T.* Rev. M. Haschel. ☎ 020-7483 1017.

ASSOCIATION OF ORTHODOX JEWISH PROFESSIONALS OF GREAT BRITAIN
53 Wentworth Road, NW11 0RT.
(Est. 1962) To promote research in matters of common interest, and the general acceptance of Torah and Halacha as relevant and decisive in all aspects of modern life and thought. *President* Prof C. Domb; *Chairman* H. J. Adler.

GUILD OF JEWISH JOURNALISTS
Affiliated to the World Federation of Jewish Journalists. *L. President* The Lord Janner; *V. Presidents* G. M. Smith, G. Tessler; *Chairman* J. Finklestone; *H.T.* Freda Riseman, 2 Holmdale Gardens, Hendon NW4 2LX. ☎ 020-8203 2540.

JEWISH NURSES & MIDWIVES ASSOCIATION
3 Cavendish Drive, Edgware, Middx.
☎ 020-8952 0711. Fax 020-7493 4895. E-mail sara.barnett@lineone.net
(Est. 1993) A social, educational and support group for all Jewish nurses, midwives and members of allied professions. *Chair* Sara Barnett.

RABBINIC CONFERENCE OF THE UNION OF LIBERAL & PROGRESSIVE SYNAGOGUES
The Montagu Centre, 21 Maple Street, W1P 6DS.
☎ 020-7588 1663. Fax 020-7436 4184. E-mail montagu@ulps.demon.co.uk
Rabbinic Chairperson: Rabbi Danny Rich.

RABBINICAL COUNCIL OF EAST LONDON AND WEST ESSEX
8 The Lindens, Prospect Hill, Waltham Forest, E17 3EJ.
☎ 020-85201759.
(Est. 1981) To co-ordinate and enhance Jewish com. and educ. facilities within the East London and West Essex area. *Patron* The Chief Rabbi; *Chairman* Rabbi E. Salasnik; *V. Chairman* Rev. S. Black; *Sec.* Rev. S. Kreiman.

RABBINICAL COUNCIL OF THE PROVINCES
c/o 71 Upper Park Road, Salford M7.
☎ 0161-773 1978. Fax 0161-773 7015
President Chief Rabbi Dr Jonathan Sacks; *Chairman* Rabbi Mordechai S. Ginsbury; *V. Chairman* Rabbi Ian Goodhardt; *H. T.* Rabbi Yoinosson Golomb; *H. Sec.* Rabbi Adam S. Hill, 163 Bristol Road, Birmingham B5 7UA. Email srni@heharim.sofnet.co.uk

RABBINICAL COUNCIL OF THE UNITED SYNAGOGUE
Adler House, 735 High Road, London N12 0US.
☎ 020-8343 6313. Fax 020-8343 6310.
Chairman Rabbi Ephraim Mirvis, BA, 69 Lichfield Grove, London N3 2JJ; *V. Chairmen* Rabbi Emanuel Levy, BA (Hons), Rabbi Z.M. Salasnik, BA (Hons), FJC; *Exec. Dir.* Rabbi Dr J. Shindler, MSc; *H.T.* Rabbi S. Coten, BSc Econ (Hons), MA, PGCE; *H. Sec.* Rabbi M. Van Den Bergh, BEd.

SOUTH LONDON COMMUNAL COUNCIL
c/o 40 York Road, Cheam, Surrey, SM2 6HH.
☎/Fax 020-8643 3228.
A grouping of Orthodox Synagogues in South London, meeting regularly to discuss matters of common concern in the fields of social, educational and other communal endeavours, also as a means of arranging joint activities where appropriate. *Correspondent* Michael Harris, 40 York Road, Cheam, Surrey, SM2 6HH. Communities involved include: Catford and Bromley, Croydon, Kingston and Surbiton, Richmond, South London, Staines, Sutton and Chabad House (Wimbledon).

UNITED SYNAGOGUE SECRETARIES' ASSOCIATION
☎ 020-8346 8551/020-7286 3838.
Jt. Chair Mrs B. Fireman, Finchley Synagogue, Kinloss Gardens, London N3 3DU; Mrs L. Young, St Johns Wood Synagogue, Grove End Road, London NW8 1AP.

MISCELLANEOUS ORGANISATIONS

ADVISORY COMMITTEE FOR THE ADMISSION OF JEWISH ECCLESIASTICAL OFFICERS
1-2 Endsleigh Street, WC1H 0DS. ☎/Fax 020-7387 7447.
(Est. 1932) To advise the Home Office in connection with applications for the admission of eccl. officers, including rabbis, ministers, readers, Talmudical students, etc. The Cttee. comprises nominees from the major synagogal and religious orgs. in the UK. Its work is conducted from the Jews' Temporary Shelter Offices. *H. Sec.*

ASSOCIATION OF JEWISH EX-SERVICEMEN AND WOMEN (AJEX)
Ajex House, East Bank, Stamford Hill, N16 5RT.
☎ 020-8800 2844. Fax 020-8880 1117.
(Est. 1923) *Nat. Chairman* Gabriel Kaufman; *Gen. Sec.* J. Weisser; *Hon. Secs.*
Richard Urban, David van Loen; *H. Chaplain* Rev. Malcolm Weisman, OBE. A list
of London and Regional Branches can be obtained from the Secretary. For the
Military Museum contact H. Morris, *Archivist.*

ASSOCIATION OF JEWISH GOLF CLUBS & SOCIETIES
Officers: *President* Gerald N. Tankel, Flat 9 Darnhills, Watford Road, Radlett,
Herts, WD7 8LQ; *Sec.* Martin S. Caller, 2 Sergeants Lane, Whitefield, Manchester,
M45 7TS; *Tournament Sec.* Mervyn Berg; *Assist Tournament Sec.* Stanley Fingret.

ASSOCIATION OF JEWISH HUMANISTS
12 Woodland Court, Woodlands, NW11 9QQ.
☎ 020-8455 2393.
(Est. 1983) Humanistic Jews believe each Jew has the right to create a meaningful
Jewish lifestyle free from supernatural authority and imposed tradition.
 Humanistic Jews believe the goal of life is personal dignity and self-esteem.
Humanist Jews believe the secular roots of Jewish life are as important as the reli-
gious ones, and the survival of the Jewish people needs a reconciliation between
science, personal autonomy and Jewish loyalty.
 The Association of Jewish Humanists is a constituent member of the
International Institute for Secular Humanistic Judaism (Jerusalem); an Associate of
the Society for Humanistic Judaism, Farmington Hills, MI, USA; an Affiliate of the
British Humanist Association, London WC1R 4RH.
 H. Jt. Chairmen M. Miller, 12 Woodland Court, Woodlands, NW11 9QQ, D.
Wilkes, 7 Ashley Close, Hendon, NW4; *H. Sec.* M. Miller, 12 Woodland Court,
Woodlands, NW11 9QQ; *H. T.* J. Hulman, 60 Morley Crescent East, Stanmore,
Middlesex.

CAMPAIGN FOR THE PROTECTION OF SHECHITA
66 Townshend Court, Townshend Road, Regents Park, London NW8 6LE.
☎ 020-7722 8523.
(Est. 1985) To protect the freedom of Jews to perform Shechita; to make representations to Government on proposed legislation or other measures which may
affect the proper performance of Shechita. *Nat. Co-ord. and Hon. Solicitors* Neville
Kesselman; *Reg. Coord.* Chanoch Kesselman, London; *Rabbinical Adv.* Rabbi
Benjamin Vorst and Rabbi Dr David Miller, MA, MSc, DPhil (Oxon).

CELEBRITIES GUILD OF GREAT BRITAIN
Knight House, 29-31 East Barnet Road, New Barnet, Herts EN4 8RN.
☎ 020-8449 1234, 020-8449 1515, weekdays 10.00–4.00.
(Est. 1977. Reg. Charity No. 282298) A social and fund-raising Guild of promi-
nent people in British Jewry who organise events to raise funds to provide equip-
ment for disabled and handicapped people. *H. Exec. Guilder* Mrs Ella Glazer,
M.B.E.; *H. Life President*: Stanley Black, O.B.E.; *Master Guilders* Ronnie Wolfe and
Leonard Fenton.

CONNECT – THE JEWISH MARRIAGE BUREAU
23 Ravenshurst Avenue, NW4 4EE.
☎ 020-8203 5207.
See Jewish Marriage Council, p.15.

HIGH SEAS SAILING CLUB
6a Langford Place, London NW8 0LL.
☎ 020-7624 0201.
(Est. 1989.) The UK's only sailing club for people with a 'Jewish affinity or friendship'. Dinghy and motorboat sections also. Membership of 200 from throughout UK and overseas. The club holds coastal sailing meets throughout the summer months. During the winter there is an active programme of lectures, sail training and social activities in the NW London area. Crewing Register maintained. Monthly newsletters. *Publ.* Wavelength (annual). *Club Commodore* Gillian Woodbridge; *V. Commodore* Alex Adamson-Leigh; *Rear Commodore* Michael Doctors; *T.* Laurence Factor; *Sec.* Uta Gosling.

INSTITUTE OF COMMUNITY RELATIONS
101 Dunsmure Road, London N16 5HT.
☎ 020-8800 8612.
(Est. 1975) Objects: To promote racial equality and good community relations in particular between Orthodox Jews and other ethnic groups. It seeks to promote marriage and the family, human rights and moral values, and to foster Franco-British friendship. Activities: Running a number of projects including campaigns for racial equality in education and television, a campaign for single sex health services, a campaign to support marriage and the family, an information project and a project to relieve poverty. *Dir.* Rabbi Henri Brand, *H.T.* Rabbi C. Pinter; *H. Sec.* I. Kraus.

JEWISH ASSOCIATION FOR BUSINESS ETHICS
P.O. Box 3840, The Hyde, Colindale, NW9 6LG
☎ 020-8200 8007 Fax 020-8200 8061. Email: jabe@brijnet.org
(Reg. Charity No. 1038453) To encourage the highest standards of integrity in business and professional conduct by promoting the Jewish ethical approach to business. *Chairman:* Stephen Rubin; *Exec. Dir.* Lorraine Spector.

JEWISH ASSOCIATION OF SPIRITUAL HEALERS
24 Greenacres, Hendon Lane, Finchley, London N3 3SF.
☎ 020-8349 1544.
(Est. 1966. Reg. Charity No. 275081) Aims: (1) To attempt to relieve sickness and suffering; (2) To demonstrate that Spiritual Healing is in keeping with the teachings of Judaism. *Chairman* Steve Sharpe, 22 Boldmere Road, Pinner HA5 1PS; *Sec.* Audrey Cane, 24 Greenacres, Hendon Lane, Finchley, London N3 3SF; *Healing Centre* Ruth Green, West London Synagogue, 33 Seymour Place, London W1.

THE JEWISH COUNCIL FOR RACIAL EQUALITY
33 Seymour Place, London W1H 6AT.
☎ 020-8455 0896. Fax 020-8458 4700. E-mail jcore@btinternet.com
(Est. 1976. Reg. Charity No. 281236) To improve race relations in Britain, encourage awareness in the Jewish community of responsibilities of a multi-racial society and join other organisations to combat racism. *Chairman* Dr. R. Stone; *V. Chairman* Mrs June Jacobs; *H.T.* Dr Lea MacDonald; *Dir.* Dr Edie Friedman.
   Projects: Developing Jewish anti-racist educational materials for schools, cheders and youth clubs; training for teachers and youth leaders on the use of anti-racist materials; the setting-up of a resource centre for youth leaders, teachers and community workers; additional campaigning on refugee and immigration issues, practical involvement with refugees and divided families; seminars with other Jewish organisations; extending cooperation with other minority groups to combat racism; establishing a campaigning role, working in solidarity with other minority organisations.

JEWISH FEMINIST GROUP
Box 39, Sisterwrite, 190 Upper Street, London N1.
(Est. 1979) To raise consciousness among Jewish women about their position in society, both as Jews and as women, and strive to improve both and combat antisemitism.
Publ.: Quarterly newsletter.

JEWISH FRIENDLY SOCIETIES
Grand Order of Israel and Shield of David. *Grand Sec.* R. Salasnik
11 The Lindens, Prospect Hill, Waltham Forest, London E17 3EJ.
☎ 020-8520 3531. E-mail goisd@brijnet.org.
(Est. 1896.) The membership is contained in five Lodges in the Metropolitan area and one in Birmingham.

JEWISH GAY AND LESBIAN GROUP
BM-JGLG, London WC1N 3XX
☎/Fax 020-8905 3531. E-mail jglg@jewishmail.com
(Est. 1972) Social group for Jewish gay men, lesbians and bisexuals of all ages.
President Richard Morris.

JEWISH SOCIALISTS' GROUP
BM 3725, London WC1N 3XX.
E-mail jsg@bardrose.dircon.co.uk
(Est. 1974) Political, cultural and campaigning organisation committed to socialism, diasporism and secularism, aiming to unite the Jewish community with other oppressed/persecuted minorities. Active on local, national and international issues.
National Committee (collective leadership).

THE MAIMONIDES FOUNDATION
38 Great Smith Street, London SW1P 3BU.
☎ 020-7222 1992. Fax 020-7233 0161. Email info@maimonides.org.uk
(Est. 1995. Reg. Charity No. 1044028) To foster understanding and promote and facilitate dialogue, interaction and co-operation between Jews and peoples of different faiths – especially between Jews and Muslims – and to build alliances between them based on mutual respect and trust. To strengthen the cultural, spiritual and intellectual ties between Jews and Muslims as the basis of a peaceful and meaningful co-existence. *President* Lord Janner, QC; *Chairman* Dr David Khalili; *T.* Dr Richard Stone; *Exec. Cttee* Sydney S. Assor, Michael Bradfield, Denise Catton, Robin Fisher, Naomi Gryn, Ivor Levene, Freddy Salem, Robert Yentob; *Exec. Dir.* Douglas Krikler; *Admin.* Joanna Ryam.

MONTAGU JEWISH COMMUNITY TRUST
c/o 16 Harrow Fields Gardens, Middx HA1 3SN.
☎ 020-8423 5840.
(Est. 1893 as West Central Club and Settlement.) A Trust concerned with the allocation of grants for community activities principally in the field of training and education.

NOAH PROJECT
PO Box 1828, London W10 5RT. ☎ 020-8994 5988.
Email environmentally.sound@virgin.net
(Est. 1997) Through 'Jewish Education, Celebration and Action for the Earth', the Noah Peoject promotes awareness of environmental issues throughout the community, and demonstrates how Jewish teachings provide guidance for greener living. Its quarterly newsletter, regular seminars and outdoor events also provide support and advice for Jews already concerned about the effect of modern living on the sustainability of the planet. It also provides a Jewish voice to secular and multi-

faith environmental movements. *Admin.* Vicky Joseph; *Educ. Co-ord.* Vivienne Cato; *Newsletter Ed.* John Schlackman. Groups in Birmingham and Manchester. Please contact the London number for details.

OPERATION JUDAISM
95 Willows Road, Birmingham B12 9QF.
☎ 0121-440 6673 (24 hrs ansaphone) Fax 0121-446-4199.
(Est. 1986) Operation Judaism is the community's defence against missionary attack. It operates nationally an information and counselling service. Information and support for those involved with cults. Man. Cttee. consists of representatives from: Office of the C. Rabbi, Board of Deputies and Lubavitch Foundation.

ROYAL BRITISH LEGION (MONASH BRANCH)
(Est. 1936. Reg. Charity No. 219279) *Chairman* W. M. Fisher, F.C.A.; *H. Sec.* A. Lawson, 21 Woronzow Road, London NW8 6BA. ☎ 020-7722 5404. Fax 020-7483 2592.

SHATNEZ CENTRE TRUST
22 Bell Lane, Hendon, London NW4 2AD
☎ 020-8202 4005.
(Est. 1990. Reg. Charity No. 1013840) To provide Shatnez checking at the Shatnez Centre and promote Shatnez observance in the community. *Ts.* A. E. Bude, David Rabson.

SUPPORT GROUP FOR PARENTS OF JEWISH GAYS AND LESBIANS
BM JGLG, London WC1N 3XX.
☎ 020-8958 4827. Fax 020-8905 3479. E-mail kenmowbray@aol.com
(Est. 1996) To give support and help to parents of Jewish gays and lesbians. *H. Sec.* Kenneth Morris.

TZEDEK
(Jewish Action for a Just World)
Steven Derby, Development Officer, 61 Pine Road, London NW2 6SB.
☎ 020-8452 5146. Email: tzedekuk@aol.com
(Est. 1990. Reg. Charity No. 1016767.) To provide direct support to the developing world working towards the relief and elimination of poverty regardless of race or religion; to educate people, particularly in the Jewish community, as to the causes and effects of poverty and the Jewish obligation to respond.
Programmes: support for development projects through a grant-making programme targeted at self-help, sustainable developments in Africa, Asia and South America; providing educational workshops on the themes of aid, development and Jewish values to schools, youth clubs and adult groups; Overseas Volunteer Programme – in which Jewish volunteers have the opportunity to work during the summer at development projects in the developing world; fundraising activities.

UNITED KINGDOM JEWISH AID AND INTERNATIONAL DEVELOPMENT
33 Seymour Place, W1H 6AT.
☎ 020-7723 3442. Fax 020-7723 3445. Email ukjaid@ort.org
(Est. 1989.) UKJAID is a Jewish humanitarian organisation which responds to international disasters and promotes sustainable development, aimed at reducing deprivation and suffering, irrespective of ethnicity, gender or religion. UKJAID has recently led the Jewish emergency aid coalitition's initiatives for Kosovan refugees, in Kosova, Macedonia and Albania. *Patrons* The Chief Rabbi, Communal Rabbi of the Spanish & Portugese Jews' Cong., Chairman of the Council of Reform and Liberal Rabbis, President of the Masorti Rabbinic Liaison Committee, President of the Board of Deputies of British Jews, The Lord Mishcon Q.C. Hon. D.L., The Lord Janner Q.C.; *Chairman* Ansel Harris; *H. Consultant.* Dr T. Scarlett Epstein.

INTERNATIONAL ORGANISATIONS

JEWISH ORGANISATIONS HAVING CONSULTATIVE STATUS WITH THE ECONOMIC AND SOCIAL COUNCIL OF THE UNITED NATIONS
Agudas Israel World Org.; Coordinating Bd. of Jewish Orgs. (comprising the British BoD, the South African BoD, and the B'nai B'rith); Consultative Council of Jewish Orgs. (comprising the Anglo-Jewish Assn., the Alliance Israélite Universelle, and the Canadian Friends of the Alliance); W.J.C. Internat. Council on Jewish Social and Welfare Services (comprising American Joint Distribution Committee, World Jewish Relief, Jewish Colonization Assn., European Council of Jewish Community Services, United Hias Service, World ORT Union); Internat. Council of Jewish Women.

AGUDAS ISRAEL WORLD ORGANISATIONS
The organisation was founded in Kattowitz in 1912. Its programme was defined as being 'the solution – in the spirit of the Torah – of problems which periodically confront the Jewish people in Eretz Yisroel and the Diaspora'. This object was to be fulfilled 'by coordination of Orthodox Jewish effort throughout the world ... by the representation and protection of the interests of Torah-true Jewish communities. The programme was formulated by our ancestors for the unconditional acceptance by all Jewish generations of the Biblical injunction 'And ye shall be unto Me a kingdom of priests and a holy nation.' The organisation seeks to implement this injunction by its endeavours. It opposes assimilation and different interpretations of Jewish nationhood. Consult. status with United Nations, New York and Geneva, and Unesco in Paris.

Agudas Israel of Gt. Britain. *Presidium:* Rabbi J. H. Dunner, Rabbi Y. H. Rosenbaum, 95-99 Stamford Hill, N16 5DN. ☎ 020-8800 6688. Fax 020-8800-5000.
Publ.: Jewish Tribune (weekly).

Zeire Agudas Israel (Reg. Charity No. 253513.), 95 Stamford Hill, N16; 35a Northumberland Street, Salford, 7. *Chairman* J. Schleider. *Sec. Gen.*

Agudas Israel Community Services, (Reg. Charity No. 287367), 97 Stamford Hill, N16 5DN. ☎ 020-8800 6688 & 802 6627. Est. 1980 to help find suitable employment for observant Jews, including immigrants and Yiddish speakers, and other social services. *Dirs.* J. Davis, M.M. Posen.

Beth Jacob Council of Great Britain, 97 Stamford Hill, N16 5DN. The following institutions are under the auspices of the Council: Teachers' Training Seminar, 69 Allerton Road, N16. *Princ.* Rabbi J. H. Dunner. *Menahel:* Rabbi B. Dunner, Beth Jacob Classes and Groups, 65 Amhurst Pk., N16 5ND. Gateshead Training Colleges for Teachers. (See p.110)

Jewish Rescue and Relief Cttee. (Reg. Charity No. X99706ES), 215 Golders Green Rd., NW11 9BY. ☎ 020-8458 1710. *Chairman* A. Strom.

Keren Hatorah Cttee. (Reg. Charity No. 281384). (For the relief of religious, educational and social institutions, a division of Agudas Yisroel in Great Britain), 97 Stamford Hill, N16 5DN. ☎ 020-8800 6688, 020-8800 5000. *Exec. Dir.* Rabbi C. Y. Davis.

Russian Immigrant Aid Fund, for the material and spiritual rehabilitation of Russian immigrants in Israel; 97 Stamford Hill, N16 5DN. ☎ 020-8800 6688. *Chairman* I. M. Cymerman.

Society of Friends of the Torah (Reg. Charity No. 238230), 97 Stamford Hill, N16

5DN, and, 215 Golders Green Rd., NW11 9BY. ☎ 020-8800 6687, 020-8458 9988. Fax 020-8800 5000. *Dir.* Rabbi C.Y. Davis.

ALLIANCE ISRAELITE UNIVERSELLE
45 rue La Bruyère, F 75425 Paris Cedex 09.
☎ (01)53 328855. Fax (01) 48 745133. E:mail aiu@imaginet.fr; http://www.aiu.org
(Est. 1860.) This educative and cultural-oriented organisation essentially works through a network of schools which affects today more than 20,000 pupils and its century-old defence of human rights before governmental and international institutions all over the world. Has two quarterly publs: Les Cahiers de L'Alliance Israélite Universelle and Les Cahiers du Judaïsme and a centre for pedagogical publs: Créer-Didactique, and NADIR. Its library with more than 120,000 books in the field of Hebraica-Judaica and its College des Etudes juives make it one of the most important Jewish centres in Europe. Today the Alliance operates in Belgium, Canada, France, Iran, Israel, Morocco, Spain. *President* Prof. A. Steg; *Dir.* Jean-Jacques Wahl.

ASIA PACIFIC JEWISH ASSOCIATION
306 Hawthorn Rd., South Caulfield, Victoria 3162.
☎ (03) 9272 5585. Fax (03) 9272 5589. E:mail aija@ozemail.com.au
The Assn. is the regional rep. org. for the Jewish coms. in Australia, Fiji, Hawaii, Hong Kong, India, Japan, Korea, New Caledonia, New Zealand, Papua New Guinea, Philippines, Singapore, Sri Lanka, Tahiti, Taiwan and Thailand. *Contact* Charla Smith.

ASSOCIATION OF EUROPEAN MASORTI COMMUNITIES
1097 Finchley Rd., London NW11 0PU.
☎ 020-8201 8772. Fax 020-8201 8917. Email office@masorti.org.uk.
(Est. March 1999). Umbrella and co-ordinating body for Masorti communities in Europe.

B'NAI B'RITH
B'nai B'rith is the world's largest international Jewish membership service organisation, bringing together Jews from all backgrounds to serve the communities they live in. With its head office in Washington, almost half a million members in 56 countries, an office at the European Union in Brussels and Non-Governmental Organisation status at the United Nations in New York, it is the most active Jewish membership body in the world and also one of the oldest, having celebrated 155 years in 1998.
The Core Objectives of B'nai B'rith in Great Britain and Ireland are:
• to foster friendship through social, cultural and recreational programmes;
• to support the State of Israel and World Jewry;
• to work for charitable endeavours;
• to initiate and develop community projects;
• to strengthen B'nai B'rith links across Europe.
B'nai B'rith has been instrumental in setting up and supporting:
• the B'nai B'rith Hillel Foundation (p.52);
• the B'nai B'rith Housing Association (p.94);
• the B'nai B'rith Jewish Music Festival (p.39);
• BBYO (p.46);
• Jewish Community Information (p.7).
Our latest development is the London Bureau of International Affairs which is designed to inform and act as a resource centre and serve as a major activity and lobbying facility where Jewish interests world wide are affected, working closely with the Centre for Public Policy at B'nai B'rith International in Washington DC, USA and at B'nai B'rith's offices at the European Union in Brussels.
B'nai B'rith has Lodges around the country and all are welcome to join. B'nai

B'rith in the UK is planning to merge with European B'nai B'rith with the target of holding the first joint convention in November 1999 in Amsterdam.

International HQ, 1640 Rhode Island Avenue, N.W. Washington, DC 20036, USA. ☎ 202 857 6600. Fax 202 857 1099. Website: http://www.bnaibrith.org

B'nai B'rith District 15 of Great Britain and Ireland, B'nai B'rith Hillel House, 1/2 Endsleigh Street, London WC1H 0DS. ☎ 020-7387 5278. Fax 020-8387 8014. Email bnaib@ort.org Website: http://www.ort.org/communit/bnai/ *Nat. President* Seymour G. Saideman; *V. Presidents* Valerie Bello, Dr M. Bliss; *Nat. T.* Graham Weinberg; *Nat. Sec.* Jack Finkler; *District Man.* Ela Trent.

London Bureau of International Affairs, *Chairman* Dr Michael Bliss; *Bureau Chief* Mark Marcus, B'nai B'rith Hillel House, 1/2 Endsleigh Street, London WC1H 0DS. ☎ 020-7383 0442. Fax 020-7387 8014. Email lbia@ort.org

Lodges
Abraham Lewin (Enfield) Unity; BB4T Yovel (Stanmore) Unity; Birmingham Joint; Bournemouth Unity; Cheshire Unity; Ealing (Selig Brodetsky) Joint; Edgware Women; Finchley Joint; First Lodge of England; First Unity; Ilford (Golda Meir) Unity; Jerusalem (Wembley & District); Kentgate Joint; Lees Unity; Leo Baeck Men's; Leo Baeck Women's; Manchester; North Manchester; Pegasus Unity; Raoul Wallenberg Unity; Shlomo Argov Unity; Southend & District Unity; Southgate (Ben Gurion) Joint; Surrey Joint; Thames; Thanet Montefiore Unity; West Riding Shalom; Yad B'Yad Unity; Yitzchak Rabin.

THE COMMITTEE FOR THE PRESERVATION OF JEWISH CEMETERIES IN EUROPE
66 Fairholt Rd., London N16 5EN.
☎ 020-8806 1696. Fax 020-8806-5911.
(Est 1991. Reg. Charity No. 1073225) Preservation of Jewish burial sites in Europe to ensure that they are maintained according to Jewish law and tradition. *Chairman* M.E. Stern; *Sec.* A. Ginsburg; *H.T.* A. Goldman.

COMMONWEALTH JEWISH COUNCIL AND TRUST
BCM Box 6871, London WC1N 3XX.
☎ 020-7222 2120. Fax 020-7222 1781. Internet: www.cjc.org.uk.
(Est. 1982.) To provide links between Commonwealth Jewish communities; to provide a central representative voice for Commonwealth Jewish communities and to help preserve their religious and cultural heritage; to seek ways to strengthen Commonwealth Jewish communities in accordance with their individual needs and wishes and provide mutual help and cooperation. *President* The Lord Janner, Q.C.; *Vice Presidents* Jonathan Metliss, Paul Secher, Jeff Durkin; *Sec.* J. Galaun, F.C.A.; *H. T.* H.B. Lipsith; *Dir.* Maureen Gold; *Contact* Suzi Israel.
   There are 38 members including those in Antigua, Australia, Bahamas, Barbados, Belize, Bermuda, Botswana, Canada, Cayman Is., Cyprus, Fiji, Gibraltar, Guernsey, India, Isle of Man, Jamaica, Jersey, Kenya, Mauritius, Namibia, New Zealand, Singapore, Sri Lanka, Trinidad & Tobago, Turks & Caicos Is., United Kingdom, Zambia and Zimbabwe.

Commonwealth Jewish Trust. (Reg. Charity No. 287564). *Trs.* Edward Bronfman, Harvey Lipsith, Dorothy Reitman, Jack Galaun, Sir Jack Zunz.
   The Trust undertakes charitable projects in Jewish communities throughout the Commonwealth, with special emphasis on smaller communities.

CONFERENCE OF EUROPEAN RABBIS
735 High Road, N12 0US.
☎ 020-8343 8989.
President; *V. Presidents* Grand Rabbin, J. Sitruk, Chief Rabbi of France; *Dir. Community Relations* Cllr A. Dunner. ☎ 020-8731 9025. Fax 020-8209 1565; *Dir.* Rabbi M. Rose, P.O.B. 5324, Jerusalem, Israel ☎ (02) 5812859.
Est. 1957, to provide a medium for co-operation on matters of common concern to rabbis of European communities.

CONFERENCE ON JEWISH MATERIAL CLAIMS AGAINST GERMANY, Inc.
15 East 26th Street, New York, N.Y. 10010.
☎ 212-696 4944. Fax 212-679 2126.
President Rabbi I. Miller. *Sec.* S. Kagan; *Tr.* A. Lewinsky. (Est 1951.) Has admin. funds received from the Federal German Republic for relief, rehabilitation and resettlement of victims of Nazi persecution residing outside Israel. Residual funds are now used for com. leaders of destroyed Jewish coms. or their widows, and for needy non-Jews who saved Jewish life at the risk of their own. Now also admin. Hardship Fund intended primarily for Jewish victims of Nazi persecution who left Eastern Europe after 1965. Since January, 1993 also administers Article 2 Fund for the benefit of severely perse-cuted Nazi victims. The Fdr President was the late Dr Nahum Goldmann.

CONSULTATIVE COUNCIL OF JEWISH ORGANISATIONS
420 Lexington Avenue, New York City, N.Y. 10170.
☎ (212) 808-5437. Fax (212) 983-0094.
Est. 1946 for the purpose of cooperating with the U.N. and other intergovern-mental orgs. and agencies in the advancement of human rights and the safeguard-ing of Jewish interests. Constituent Orgs.: Alliance Israelite Universelle, AJA, Canadian Frs. A.I.U. *Chairmen* Prof. Ady Steg, Clemens Nathan, Gary Waxman; *Sec. Gen.* Warren Green.

EUROPEAN ASSOCIATION FOR JEWISH STUDIES
Secretariat: Oxford Centre for Hebrew and Jewish Studies, Yarnton Manor, Yarnton, Oxon OX5 1PY. ☎ 01865 374010.
Publ. Newsletter; Directory of Jewish Studies in Europe.

EUROPEAN COUNCIL OF JEWISH COMMUNITIES
74 Gloucester Place, London W1H 3HN.
☎ 020-7224-3445. Fax 020-7224-3446. Email: ecjc@ort.org. Home page: JEWL-Jewish Euro Web Link: http://www.ort.org/ecjc/
Est. 1968 as the European Council of Jewish Community Services. The mission of the ECJC is to provide a forum for inter-European planning and co-operation in the areas of social welfare, formal and informal Jewish education, leadership train-ing and culture. Projects and activities include: MA'AYAN – The European Conference on Jewish Education; CARELINK – The European Jewish Welfare Fund; The European Centre for Jewish Leadership–LE'ATID EUROPE; Social Commission; Jewish Partnership for Europe.
A wide range of activities are organised in the framework of four ECJC region-al co-operation projects: Central European Co-operation Region; Mediterranean Co-operation Region; Nordic Co-operation Region; Southeastern European Co-operation Region.
Publ.: FAX-LINK The European Bulletin Board, Current Trends in European Jewry.
Fifty member organisations in 35 European countries. *President* David J. Lewis; *Chair* Ruth Zilkha; *Exec. Dir.* Michael May; *European Network Off.* Alexander Goldberg.

EUROPEAN ISRAELI FORUM
c/o 30 Bentley Way, Stanmore, Middx HA7 3RP.
☎ 020-8954 7440. Fax 020-8385 7221. Website: www.carmel.cz/eif/.
(Est. 1989) Development of individual personal links between European Jewish community and Israel. *Chairman* Claude Benoliel (France); *Vice Chair* Muriel Cardozo (Netherlands), Andrej Ernyei (Czech Rep.); *Sec.* Thelma Epstein (G.B.).

EUROPEAN JEWISH CONGRESS
78 Avenue des Champs-Elysées, 75008 Paris.
☎ (33)1 43 59 94 63. Fax (33)1 42 25 45 28. Email: jewcong@imaginet.fr
(Est. 1986, previously the European Branch of the World Jewish Congress) Federates and coordinates the initiatives of 37 communities in Europe and acts as their spokesman. Has consultative status with the Council of Europe, European Commission and Parliament. Current concerns are the democratic development of Eastern Europe and the problems of racism and antisemitism throughout Europe. *Sec. Gen.* Serge Cwajgenbaum.

EUROPEAN JEWISH PUBLICATION SOCIETY
6 Camden High St., London NW1 0JH.
☎ 020-8346 1668. Fax 020-8346 1776. Email cs@ejps.org.uk; http://www.ejps.org.uk.
(Est. 1994. Reg. Charity No. 3002158) A registered charity which makes grants to assist in the publication, translation and distribution of books relating to Jewish literature, history, religion, philosophy, politics, poetry and culture. *Chairman* Frederick Worms; *Dir.* Colin Shindler.

EUROPEAN UNION OF JEWISH STUDENTS
89 Chaussée de Vleurgat, B-1050, Brussels, Belgium.
☎ 010-32-2-647 72 79. Fax 010-32-2-6482431. Email: 106211.2511@compuserve.com. Website: http://www-students.unisg.ch/eujs/
Est. 1978 for co-ordination purposes between nat. unions in 32 countries. It represents more than 170,000 European Jewish students in international Jewish and non-Jewish forums dealing with cultural and political matters and opposes all forms of racism and fascism. The E.U.J.S. is also a 'service org.' for students. It helps with courses abroad, supplies material on different subjects for univ. students and organises visits and seminars. *H. Presidents* Mrs Simone Veil, Maram Stern; *H. Mems.* The Lord Janner, Q.C., David Susskind (Belgium), Suzy Jurysta (B.), Laslov Kadelburg (Yu.); *President* Ariane Platt.
   Member unions in: Austria, Belgium, Belorus, Britain, Bulgaria, Czech, Croatia, Denmark, Estonia, Finland, France, Germany, Gibraltar, Greece, Holland, Hungary, Ireland, Italy, Latvia, Lithuania, Luxembourg, Norway, Poland, Portugal, Russia, Serbia, Slovakia, Spain, Sweden, Switzerland, Turkey, Ukraine.

FRIENDSHIP WITH ISRAEL (European Parliament)
51 Tavistock Court, Tavistock Square, WC1H 9HG.
☎ 020-7387 4925.
(Est. 1979.) All-Party Group in European Parl. with more than 120 MEPs. Aims at promoting friendship and co-operation between the European Com. and Israel. Provides up-to-date inf. on Israeli matters and a balanced view of Middle East events. Holds regular meetings in Strasbourg at Palais de l'Europe when the Euro-Parl. sits. Recognised as an official 'Inter-Parl. Group'. *H. Patron* Mrs. Simone Veil MEP, past President, Euro-Parl.; *Chairman* Tom Normanton, MEP (UK); *V. Chairmen* Erik Blumenfeld, MEP, Hans-Joachim Seeler, MEP (West Germany), Hans Nord, MEP (Holland), John Tomlinson, MEP (UK); *H. Sec.* John Marshall, MEP (UK); *Dir.* Mrs. Sylvia Sheff, J.P., B.A.

HEBREWARE® USER GROUP
46 Norfolk Avenue, N15 6JX.
☎ 020-8802 6143. Fax 020-8802 1130
HEBREWARE® is the leading User Group for Hebrew computer software users in Europe.
Contact: Mr Menasche Scharf. Branches: USA, Belgium, Israel.

HEIMLER INTERNATIONAL
(Formerly The Heimler Foundation)
Peter Hudson, 47 Rosebery Road, SW2 4DQ
☎ 020-8674 6999.
(Est. 1972.) Heimler International was set up to facilitate the work and ideas of Prof. Eugene Heimler. Its aims are: 1. to provide counselling and therapy for individuals and groups, using the Heimler approach; 2. to provide basic and advanced training in the Heimler Method; 3. to recognise advanced practitioners and lecturers in the Heimler Method; 4. to sanction and collect bona fide research, act as a focal point, publish books/tapes describing the Heimler Method.
There are Branches in several different countries in Europe, Canada, USA.

HIAS
333 7th Avenue, New York, N.Y. 1000, U.S.A.
European H.Q.: 75 rue de Lyon 1211, Geneva 13, Switzerland.
Est. August, 1954, through merger of the Hebrew Sheltering and Immigrant Aid Society (HIAS), United Service for New Americans (USNA) and the migration service of the American Joint Distribution Committee (AJDC).
HIAS, the Hebrew Immigrant Aid Society, has been the internat. migration agency of the organised Amer. Jewish com. since its founding in 1880. It assists Jewish migrants and refugees to countries of freedom and security, arranges reception on arrival, helps newcomers become integrated in their new coms. Works with Govt. agencies and other orgs. to promote increased immigration opportunities.
President Ben Zion Leuchter.

INSTITUTE FOR JEWISH POLICY RESEARCH
79 Wimpole Street, W1M 7DD.
☎ 020-7935 8266. Fax 020-7935 3252. Email: jpr@jpr.org.uk. Website: http://www.jpr.org.uk
President The Lord Rothschild; *V. President* William Frankel CBE; *Chairman* Peter L. Levy OBE; *Dep. Chairman* The Lord Haskel; *Jt. T.* Larry Levine, Milton Z. Levine; *Int. Adv. Bd.*, The Lord Weidenfeld; *Res. Bd.* Peter M. Oppenheimer; *Exec. Director* Antony Lerman; *Res. Dir.* Prof. Barry Kosmin; *Dir. Pub. Activities* Lena Stanley-Clamp.
JPR is an independent think-tank which informs and influences policy, opinion and decision-making on issues affecting Jewish life worldwide by conducting and commissioning research, developing and disseminating policy proposals and promoting public debate. JPR's public activities include lectures, policy seminars and conferences.
Publications: Antisemitism World Report (annual survey on website); Patterns of Prejudice (quarterly); JPR Reports and Policy Papers; JPR News.

INTERNATIONAL ASSOCIATION OF JEWISH LAWYERS & JURISTS
4 Brick Court, Temple, London EC4Y 9AD
☎ 020-7583 8455. Fax 020-7353 1699.
(Est. 1990) The objectives of the Association are: to contribute, alone or in co-operation with other international or national organisations, towards the establishment of an international legal order based on the Rule of Law in relations between all nations and states; to promote human rights and the principles of equality of men

and the right of all states and peoples to live in peace; to act against racism and anti-semitism, whether openly expressed or covertly exercised, *inter alia,* where necessary, by legal proceedings; to promote the study of legal problems affecting the world's Jewish communities in the context of national and international law; to promote, in consultation with the legal profession within the State of Israel and its agencies, the study of legal problems of particular concern to the State of Israel; to promote the study of Jewish law in comparison with other laws and facilitate the exchange of any information resulting from research thereto among member groups; to collect and disseminate information concerning the *de facto* and *de jure* status of the Jewish communities and other minority ethnic and religious groups throughout the world and where the occasion arises, to give help and support pursuant to human rights treaties; to promote and support co-operation and communication between the Association's member groups; to concern itself with any other matter of legal interest considered of relevance by any of the member groups.

President Lord Woolf; *V. Presidents* His Honour Israel Finestein QC, Jonathan Goldberg QC; *Chairman* Her Honour Myrella Cohen QC; *V. Chairman* Mr Jonathan Lewis; *Sec.* Mrs Patricia May; *T.* Michael Caplan.

INTERNATIONAL COUNCIL OF CHRISTIANS AND JEWS
Martin Buber Haus, Werlestrasse 2, Postfach 1129, D-64629, Heppenheim, Germany. ☎ (0 62 52) 5041. Fax (0 62 52) 68331. Email iccj-buberhouse@t-online.dc *President* Rabbi Prof. D. Rosen; *Gen. Sec.* Rev. Friedhelm Pieper; *Patron* Sir Sigmund Sternberg; *Consultant* Ruth Weyl, Northwood, Middx HA6 3NG. Est. 1974 to strengthen Jewish-Christian understanding on an international basis and to co-ordinate and initiate programmes and activities for this purpose.

INTERNATIONAL COUNCIL OF JEWISH WOMEN
24-32 Stephenson Way, London NW1 2JW, UK. ☎ 020-7388 8311. Fax 020-7387 2110. Email hq@icjw.demon.co.uk. Website http://www.icijw.org.uk
ICJW is made up of 52 Jewish women's organisations in 47 countries, covering between them almost the whole spectrum of the Jewish world. For most of them the main focus of their work is the services they offer to the community. The core purpose of ICJW is to bring together Jewish women from all walks of life in order to create a driving force for social justic for all races and creeds. ICJW has consultative status with the United Nations and is represented on many international organisations. Headquarters currently in London. *President* June Jacobs.

INTERNATIONAL COUNCIL ON JEWISH SOCIAL AND WELFARE SERVICES
Drayton House, 30 Gordon Street, London WC1H 0AN. ☎ 020-7387 3925. Fax 020-7383 4810. Email wjri@wjr.org.uk
Est. 1961. Member Organisations: Amer. Jt. Distribution Cttee.; WJR.; European Council of Jewish Com. Services; HIAS; World ORT Union. *Exec. Sec.* V. Lewis.

INTERNATIONAL JEWISH GENEALOGICAL RESOURCES [IJGR(UK)]
25 Westbourne Road, Edgbaston, Birmingham B15 3TX. ☎ 0121-454 0408. Fax 0121-454 9758.
(Est. 1988). Provides guidance on Jewish genealogy; has a library including material on Anglo-Jewry/Anglo-Australasian Jewry; microfilm of Jewish Chronicle, etc. Research undertaken. *Org.* Dr Anthony P. Joseph and Mrs Judith Joseph.

INTERNATIONAL JEWISH VEGETARIAN SOCIETY
Bet Teva, 853/855 Finchley Road, NW11 8LX. ☎ 020-8455 0692. Fax 020-8455 0692. Email jvs@ivu.org. http://www.ivu.org/jvs/ (Est. 1965. Reg. Charity No. 258581.) Affiliated to the International Vegetarian Union. Branches: N. and S. America, S. Africa, Israel, Australia. *H. Sec.* S. Labelda.

IRANIAN JEWISH CENTRE
Sceptre House, 169/173 Regent Street, London W1R 7FB.
☎ 020-7414 0069. Fax 020-7287 0986.
(Est. 1981. Reg. Charity No. 287256). Fundraising to support Iranian Jewish communities in Britain, Iran and the USA. Promotion of Iranian/Jewish heritage and culture. *Chairman* Hamid Sabi.

JCA CHARITABLE FOUNDATION
Victoria Palace Theatre, Victoria St., SW1E 5EA.
☎ 020-7828 0600. Fax 020-7828 6882.
(Reg. Charity No. 207031) Charitable company est. in 1891 by Baron Maurice de Hirsch to assist poor and needy Jews. The JCA was instrumental in promoting the emigration from Russia of thousands of Jews who were settled in farm 'colonies' in North and South America, Palestine/Israel and elsewhere.
   Today JCA's main efforts are in Israel in rural areas where it supports schs., insts. of higher learning, agricultural research and helps to promote the subsistence of needy Jews. *President* Sir Stephen Waley-Cohen, Bt.; *Manager* Y. Lothan.

JEWISH RECONSTRUCTIONIST FEDERATION (JRF, formerly FRCH)
7804 Montgomery Ave., St. #9, Elkins Park, PA 19027, USA.
☎ (215) 782-8500. Fax (215) 782-8805. Email info@jrf.org.
(Est. 1955) JRF is the congrgational arm of the Reconstructionist movement, representing over eighty affiliates in North America. Dedicated to the concept of Judaism as an evolving religious civilisation, JRF provides outreach, consulting, programmatic and educational support to its congregations and havurot. JRF is the publisher of a variety of books, magazines and the *Kol Haneshamah* prayerbook series.

JEWS OF ZAMBIA PROJECT
34 John Street, London WC1N 2EU, and Dr Michael Bush, PO Box 30020, Lusaka, Zambia.
☎ 020-7831 0551. Fax 020-7405 3280.
(Est. 1989.) To record the history of the Jews in Zambia. The project was completed in 1999 with the publication of 'Zion in Africa: The Jews of Zambia' (I.B. Tauris). *Committee* Edwin Wulfsohn, Michael Galaun, Malcolm J. Gee, F.C.A., Michael Bush; *Jt. Authors* Frank Shapiro, M.A. and Hugh Macmillan.

MACCABI WORLD UNION
Kfar Maccabiah, Ramat Gan 52105, Israel.
The Union (est. 1921) is a coordinating body for the promotion and advancement of sports, educational and cultural activities among Jewish communities worldwide. *President* R. Bakalarz; *Chairman* Uzi Netanel; *Chairman, European Maccabi Confederation* Michel Grun; *Exec. Dir.* E. Tiberger. See Maccabi Assns., p.49.

MEMORIAL FOUNDATION FOR JEWISH CULTURE
1703, 15 East 26th Street, New York N.Y. 10010.
☎ 212 679-4074.
(Est. 1964.) Supports Jewish cultural and educational programmes all over the world in co-operation with educational research and scholarly organisationss, and provides scholarship and fellowship grants.
   President Rabbi Alexander M. Schindler; *Chairman of Exec. Cttee.* Dr Josef Burg; *Exec. V. President* Dr J. Hochbaum.

SIMON WIESENTHAL CENTRE, EUROPEAN OFFICE
64 Avenue Marceau, 75008 Paris, France.
☎ (331) 4723-7637. Fax (331) 4720-8401.
London office: Simon Wiesenthal Centre UK, 27 Old Gloucester Street, WC1N

3XX (Reg. Charity no. 1030966). *Chairman* Graham Morris.
☎ 020-7419 5014. Fax 020-7831 9489. Email: csweurope@compuserve.com.
(Est. Los Angeles, 1979). To study the contemporary Jewish and general social condition in Europe by drawing lessons from the Holocaust experience. To monitor, combat and educate against Anti-Semitism, Racism and Prejudice. *Int. Dir.* Rabbi Marvin Hier; *Chairman, Board of Trustees* Samuel Belzberg; *Dir. for Int. Affairs* Dr Shimon Samuels. 400,000 members. Headquarters: Los Angeles. Offices in: New York, Chicago, Washington D.C., Miami, Toronto, Jerusalem, Paris, Buenos Aires.

WORLD COUNCIL OF CONSERVATIVE/MASORTI SYNAGOGUES
155 Fifth Avenue, New York, N.Y. 10010.
☎ 212-533 7800 (Ext 2014); Fax 212-353 9439.
Email worldcouncil@compuserve. com
2 Agron St., PO Box 7456, Jerusalem 91073.
☎ 02-256 386.
(Est. 1957.) To foster the growth of Conservative Judaism in more than 30 countries in which it operates and to coordinate the activities of its autonomous orgs. and regions. Its constituents include the Utd. Syn. of Conservative Judaism, Rabbinical Assembly, Women's League for Conservative Judaism, Nat. Fed. of Jewish Men's Clubs, Jewish Educators Assembly, Israeli Masorti Movement, British Masorti Assembly of Synagogues, Utd. Syn. of India, and the Seminario Rabinico Latinamericano, Buenos Aires. *President* Rabbi Marc N. Liebhaber; *Co-President* Rabbi Benjamin Z. Kreitman; *Chairman of Exec. Cttee.* Rabbi Alan Silverstein; *Chairman of Bd.* Rabbi Jack Topal.

WORLD JEWISH CONGRESS
(a) To co-ordinate the efforts of its affliated orgs., in respect of the political, economic, social, religious and cultural problems of the Jewish people; (b) to secure the rights, status and interests of Jews and Jewish communities and to defend them wherever they are denied, violated or imperilled; (c) to encourage and assist the creative development of Jewish social, religious and cultural life throughout the world; (d) to represent and act on behalf of its affiliated orgs. before governmental, intergovernmental and other international authorities in respect of matters which concern the Jewish people as a whole. *Fdr President* Late Dr N. Goldmann; *Emer. President* P. M. Klutznick; *President* Edgar M. Bronfman; *Sec. Gen.* Israel Singer; *Chairman, Gov. Bd.* Mendel Kaplan; *Co-Chairman Gov. Bd.* Isi J. Leibler, A.O., C.B.E.; *Chairmen of Regions:* North America, Prof Irwin Cotler, Mrs Evelyn Sommer; Latin America, Dr David Goldberg, Dr Benno Milnitzky; Europe, Jean Kahn, Judge Israel Finestein, Q.C.; Israel, Matityahu Droblas, Yehiel Leket; Russia, Dr Michael Chlenov, Roman Spektor.
Principal Offices: New York, 501 Madison Avenue, 17th Fl., NY 10022. ☎ 755 5770; Geneva, 1 rue de Varembe. ☎ 734-13-25; Paris, 78 Av. des Champs Elysées. ☎ 4359 9463, Fax 4225 4528; Buenos Aires, Casilla 20, Suc. 53. ☎ 962-5028; Jerusalem, P.O.B. 4293, Jerusalem 91042, Rehov Jabotinsky 21. ☎ 635 261/4.
Publ.: Report W.J.C. (monthly), Boletin de Información O.J.I. (Spanish) (fortnightly), Gesher (Hebrew) (quarterly), Batfutzot (Hebrew).

WORLD ORT UNION
1 Rue de Varembé, Geneva, Switzerland.
☎ (022) 73414 34. Fax (022) 734 1096.
(Est. 1880.) Organisation for educational Resources and Technological training. Over three and a half million students have been trained since 1880, and currently 260,000 students are being trained in 60 countries in different parts of the world.
Operational Headquarters in U.K.: World ORT Trust, 126 Albert St., London NW1 7NE. ☎ 020-7446 8500.

WORLD UNION FOR PROGRESSIVE JUDAISM
13 King David Street, 94101 Jerusalem. ☎ 972 26203 447. Fax 262 203 446
(Est. 1926.) To foster the international growth and practice of Progressive Judaism, and to coordinate the activities of its autonomous constituent organisations. *President* Austin Beutel; *Exec. Dir.* Rabbi R. Block.
European Office: *Hon. Sec.* Oliver Kurer, The Montagu Centre, 21 Maple Street, London, WIP 6DS. ☎ 020-8349 3779. Fax 020-8343 0901. Email europeanregion@directmail.org.

WORLD UNION OF JEWISH STUDENTS
P.O. Box 7914, Jerusalem 91077, Israel.
☎ 025610133. Fax 025610741.
Est. 1924 to fight antisemitism and to act as an umbrella organisation for national Jewish students' bodies; organises educational programmes, leadership training seminars, Am Echad project, Project Areivim, Kol Isha – women's seminar, J.A.D.E. which is a service programme for Diaspora communities; divided into six regions; Congress every two years; members: 51 national unions representing over 700,000 students; NGO member of UNESCO; Youth affiliate of the World Jewish Congress; member organisation of the World Zionist Organisation. *First President* Prof. Albert Einstein; *Chairperson* Ilanit Sasson Melchior. *Publs.* Heritage & History, WUJS Reports, WUJS Leads, the Jewish student activist handbook, supplement to the Pesach Haggada, MASUA – monthly educational material, etc.

ZIONIST COUNCIL OF EUROPE
741 High Road, London N2 0BQ
☎ 020-8343 9756. Fax 020-8446 0639. Email zion-fed@dircon.co.uk
(Est. 1980) An umbrella organisation, consisting of the Zionist Federations from around Europe, with the aim of co-ordinating Zionist activities and developing young leadership on the continent. *Chairman* Howard Schaverien; *Dir.* Alan Aziz.

LONDON (196,000)

SYNAGOGUES

(D) where shown indicates regular daily services are held.

Ashkenazi

United Synagogue

Constituent and Affiliated Synagogues of the United Synagogue, Adler House, 735 High Road, N12 0US. *Chief Exec.* George Willman. ☎ 020-8343 8989. Fax 020-8343 6262. Email utdsyg@brijnet.org

MEMBER SYNAGOGUES

Belmont Synagogue, 101 Vernon Dr, Stanmore, Middx. HA7 2BW. *M.* Rabbi D. Roselaar; *Admin.* Mrs C. Fletcher. ☎ 020-8426 0104 Fax 020-8427 2046. (D)
Borehamwood & Elstree Synagogue, P.O. Box 47, Croxdale Road, Borehamwood, Herts. WD6 4QF. ☎ 020-8386 5227. Fax 020-8386 3303. Email: admin@bwoodshul.demon.co.uk (Est. 1955.) *M.* Rabbi A. Plancey; *Admin.* B. Winterman. (D)
Bushey & District Synagogue, 177/189 Sparrows Herne, Bushey, Herts. WD2 1AJ. ☎ 020-8950 7340. Fax 020-8421 8267, *M.* Rabbi Z. M. Salasnik, B.A., F.J.C.; *Admin.* Mrs M. Chambers. (D)
Central Synagogue, (Great Portland St.), 36-40 Hallam St., W1N 6NN. ☎ 020-7580 1355. Fax 020-7636 3831. (Consecrated 1870, destroyed by enemy action May, 1941, rebuilt 1958.) Admin.'s Office 36 Hallam Street, W1N 6NN; *M.* Rabbi B. Marcus; *R.* J. Murgraff; *Admin.* Mrs C. Jowell.
Chigwell and Hainault Synagogue, Limes Ave., Chigwell, Essex IG7 5NT. ☎ 020-8500 2451. *M.* Rabbi B. Davis; *Admin.* W. Land. (D)
Clayhall Synagogue, Sinclair Hse., Woodford Bridge Rd., Ilford, Essex IG4 5LN. ☎ 020-8551 6533. Fax 020-8551 9803. *M.* Rabbi J. Kleiman; *Admin.* Mrs M. Mervish.
Cockfosters & N. Southgate Synagogue, Old Farm Av., Southgate, N14 5QR. ☎ 020-8886 8225. Fax 020-8886 8234. (Est. 1948. Consecrated Dec., 1954.) *M.* Rabbi Y. Fine, B.A.; *R.* Rev. D. Speier; *Admin.* Mrs L. Brandon.
Cricklewood Synagogue, 131 Walm Lane, NW2 3AU. ☎ 020-8452 1739. (Consecrated 1931.) *M.* Rev. G. Glausiusz; *Admin.* K. N. Gamse. (D)
Dollis Hill Synagogue, Parkside, Dollis Hill Lane, NW2 6RJ. ☎ 020-8958 6777. *M.* Rev. M. Fine; *Admin.* W. Land.
Ealing Synagogue, 15 Grange Road, Ealing, W5 5QN. ☎ 020-8579 4894. *M.* Rabbi H. Vogel, M.A.; *Admin.* Mrs S. Hayman.
Edgware Synagogue, Parnell Close, Edgware Way, Edgware, Middx. HA8 8YE. ☎ 020-8958 7508. Fax 020-8905 4449. *M.* Rabbi B. Rabinowitz, B.A., M.Phil.; *R.*; *Admin.* L. J. Ford. (D)
Finchley Synagogue, Kinloss Gdns., N3 3DU. ☎ 020-8346 8551. Fax 020-8349 1579. (Consecrated 1935.) *M.* Rabbi E. Mirvis; *Admin.* Mrs B. Fireman. (D)
Finsbury Park Synagogue, 220 Green Lanes, N4 2NT. ☎ 020-8800 3526. *M.* Rabbi A. Cohn; *R.* Rev. E. Krausher; *Admin.* H. Mather.
Golders Green Synagogue, 41 Dunstan Road, NW11 8AE. ☎ 020-8455 2460. (Consecrated 1922.) *M.* Rabbi D. Katanka, M.A.; *Admin.* Mrs S. Alexander. (D)
Hackney & East London Synagogue, Brenthouse Road, Mare Street, E9 6QG. ☎ 020-8985 4600. Fax 020-8986 9507. (Consecrated 1897; enlarged and reconsecrated 1936, amalgamated 1993.) *M.* Rev. N. Tiefenbrun; *Admin.* Mrs B. Heumann.
Hammersmith and West Kensington Synagogue, 71 Brook Green, Hammersmith,

W6 7BE. ☎ 020-7602 1405. (Consecrated 1890.) *M.* Rabbi. Alex Chapper; *Admin.* S. Williams.

Hampstead Garden Suburb Synagogue, Norrice Lea, N2 0RE. ☎ 020-8455 8126. Fax 020-8201 9247. (Consecrated 1934). *M.* Rabbi R. Livingstone; *R.* Chazan A. Freilich; *Admin.* Mrs M. S. Wolff. (D)

Hampstead Synagogue, Dennington Park Road, West Hampstead, NW6 1AX. ☎ 020-7435 1518. Fax 020-7431 8369. (Consecrated 1892). *M.* Rabbi M.J. Harris; *R.* S. Brickman; *Admin.* I. Nadel. (D)

Hendon Synagogue, 18 Raleigh Close, Wykeham Road, NW4 2TA. ☎ 020-8202 6924. Fax 020-8202 1720 (Consecrated 1935.) *M.* Rabbi M. Ginsburg; *Emer. M.* Rev. L. Hardman, M.A.; *R.* Rabbi S. Neuman; *Exec. Sec.* J. Benson. (D)

Highgate Synagogue (Est. 1929.) Grimshaw Close, 57 North Road, Highgate, N6 4BJ. ☎ 020-8340 7655. *M.* Rabbi I.H. Sufrin, ☎ 020-8341 1714; *Admin.* Mrs J. Rubin.

Ilford Synagogue, 22 Beehive Lane, Ilford, Essex IG1 3RT. ☎ 020-8554 5969. Fax 020-8554 4543. Email ilfsyn@breathemail.net. (Est. 1936.) *M.* Rabbi C. Rapoport; *R.* Rev. A. Levin; *Admin.* Ms. H.R. Michaels. (D)

Kenton Synagogue, Shaftesbury Avenue, Kenton, Middx., HA3 0RD. ☎ 020-8907 5959. Fax 020-8909 2677. *R.* Rabbi S. Zneimer, M.A.; *Admin.* Mrs A Primhak; *Youth Dir.* Rabbi S. Miller, ☎ 020-8907 3643.

Kingsbury Synagogue, Kingsbury Green, NW9 8XR. ☎ 020-8204 8089. *M.* Rabbi M. Hool; *R.* ; *Admin.* Mrs N. Hill. (D)

Mill Hill Synagogue, Brockenhurst Gdns., NW7 2JY. ☎ 020-8959 1137. Fax 020-8959 6484. *M.* Rabbi Y.Y. Schochet; *Admin.* Mrs M. Vogel. *Sec.* Mrs R. Polus. (D)

Muswell Hill Synagogue, 31 Tetherdown, N10 1ND. ☎ 020-8883 5925. (Est. 1908.) *M.*; *Admin.* Mrs L. Leighton.

New Synagogue, Victoria Community Centre, Egerton Rd., Stamford Hill, N16 6UB. (Est. in Leadenhall St., 1761.) ☎ 020-8800 6003. *Admin.* Mr. A. Levenson. (D)

New West End Synagogue, St. Petersburgh Place, Bayswater Road, W2 4JT. ☎ 020-7229 2631. Fax 020-7229 2355. (Consec. 1879.) *M.* Rabbi J. Butler; *Admin.* Mrs S. Hayman.

Newbury Park Synagogue, 23 Wessex Close, off Suffolk Road, Newbury Pk., Ilford, Essex, IG3 8JU. ☎ /Fax 020-8597 0958. *M.* Rev. S. Myers, BA; *Admin.* Mrs E.M. Benjamin. (D)

Northwood Synagogue, 21-23 Murray Road, Middx. HA6 2YP. ☎ 01923 820004. Fax 01923-820020. *M.* Rabbi N.Y. Brawer; *Admin.* Mrs E. Granger.

Palmers Green and Southgate Synagogue, Brownlow Road, N11 2BN. ☎ 020-8881 0037. Fax 020-8441 8832. *M.* Rabbi E. Levy B.A.; *R.* B. Segal; *Emer. M.* Rabbi J. Shaw, B.A.; *Admin.* M. Lewis. (D)

Pinner Synagogue, 1 Cecil Park, Pinner, Middx. HA5 5HJ. ☎ 020-8868 7204. Fax: 020-8868 7011. *M.* Rabbi J. Grunewald, B.A. ☎ 020-8868 4377; *Admin.* Mrs C. Lipman; *Youth Leader* Sharon Herman. ☎ 020-8868 7938. (D)

Radlett Synagogue, 22 Watling St., P.O. Box 28, Radlett, Herts. WD7 7PN. ☎ 01923-856878. Fax 01923-856698. *M.* Rabbi G. D. Sylvester. *Admin.* Mrs J. Bower.

Richmond Synagogue, Lichfield Gardens, Richmond-on-Thames, Surrey, TW9 1AP. ☎ 020-8940 3526. (Est. 1916.) *M.* Rabbi D. Rose; *Admin.* Mrs E. Wolf.

St. John's Wood Synagogue, 37/41 Grove End Road, St. John's Wood, NW8 9NG. ☎ 020-7286 3838. Fax 020-7266 2123 (Est. in Abbey Road 1882; present building consecrated 1964.) *M.* Dayan I. Binstock, B.Sc.; *R.* Rev. M. Haschel; *Admin.* Mrs Loraine Young. (D)

South Hampstead Synagogue, 20/22 Eton Villas, Eton Road, NW3 4SP. ☎ 020-7722 1807. Fax 020-7586 3459. *M.* Rabbi S. Levin; *Admin.* Mrs M Spector. (D)

South London Synagogue, 45 Leigham Ct. Road, SW16 2NF. ☎ 020-8677 0234.

Fax 020-8677 5107. *M.* Rabbi P. N. Ginsbury, M.A.; *Admin.* D. Saul.
South Tottenham Synagogue, 111 Crowland Road, N15 6UL. (Call Box; Sun 10.15-11.30am; Wed. 7.00-7.45pm): ☎ 020-8880 2731. (Est. 1938.) *M.; R.* Rev. D. Acoca; *Admin.* Mrs S. Patashnik.
Stanmore and Canons Park Synagogue, London Road, Stanmore Middx., HA7 4NS. ☎ 020-8954 2210. Fax 020-8954 4369. Email stanmore synagogue@cwcom.net. *M.* Rabbi Dr J. M. Cohen, B.A., M.Phil., A.J.C., Ph.D;. *R.* H. Black; *Admin.* Mrs B. S. Dresner. (D)
Watford Synagogue, 16 Nascot Road, Watford, Herts., WD1 3RE. ☎ 01923-222755 (Est. 1946.) *M.* Rabbi J. Rosten; *Admin.* Mrs C. Silverman.
Wembley Synagogue, Forty Avenue, Wembley Park, Middx., HA9 8JW. ☎ 020-8904 6565. Fax 020-8908 2740. *M.* Rabbi M. van den Bergh; *R.* Rev. A. Wolfson, B.Ed., M.A.; *Admin.* Mrs R. Koten. (D)
West Ham and Upton Park Synagogue, 95 Earlham Grove, Forest Gate, E7 9AN. ☎ 020-8522 1917. *M.* Rev. S. Odze; *Admin.* Mrs E. Benjamin.
Willesden and Brondesbury Synagogue, 143 Brondesbury Park NW2 5JL. ☎ 020-8459 1083. (Est. 1934.) *R.; Admin.* Mrs J. Questle. (D)
Woodside Park Synagogue, Woodside Park Road, N12 8RZ. ☎ 020-8445 4236. Fax 020-8445 5515. *M.* Rabbi H. Rader; *R.* Rev. M. L. Plaskow, MBE, A.L.C.M.; *Chairman* Mr H. Kendler, QC; *Admin.* Mrs D. Bruce. (D)

ASSOCIATE SYNAGOGUE
Western Marble Arch, 32 Great Cumberland Place, London, W1H 7DJ. ☎ 020-7723 9333. Fax 020-7224 8065. *M.* ; *Admin.* Malcolm E. Howard.

AFFILIATED SYNAGOGUES
These are syns. belonging to U.S. by means of a scheme for small and newly est. congregations.
Barking and Becontree (Affiliated) Synagogue, 200 Becontree Avenue, Dagenham, Essex RM8 2TR. ☎ 020-8590 2737. *R.; Chairman* M. Leigh; *Hon. Sec.* Mrs B. Berman.
Barnet and District Affiliated Synagogue, Eversleigh Road, New Barnet, Herts. EN5 1NE. ☎ 020-8449 0145. *M.* Rabbi S. Robinson, Email shaul.robinson@which.net; *H. Admin.* Mrs H. Spillman, ☎ 020-8441 2783.
Catford & Bromley Affiliated Synagogue (est. 1937). 6 Crantock Road, SE6 2QS. ☎ 020-8698 9496. *M.* Enq. P.O. Box 4724, London SE6 2YA. *Admin.* Mrs E. Govendir. ☎ 01322-527239.
Chelsea Affiliated Synagogue, Smith Terrace, Smith Street, Chelsea, SW3 4DL. (Reg. Charity No. 242552) ☎ 020-7352 6046. *M.* Rabbi M. Atkins, ☎ 020-8953 3272; *Admin.* F. Joseph.
Enfield & Winchmore Hill Synagogue, 53 Wellington Road, Bush Hill Park, Middx. EN1 2PG ☎ 020-8363 2697. (Est. 1950.) *M.* Rabbi M. Taubman, Rev. D. Levy; *Hon. Sec.* B. Bowman, 204 St Edmunds Road, N9 7PJ, ☎ 020-8292 0229.
Harold Hill and District Affiliated Synagogue, Trowbridge Road, Harold Hill, Essex RM3 8YW. (Est. 1953.) *H. Sec.* Miss D. Meid, 4 Portmadoc House, Broseley Road, Harold Hill, Essex RM3 9BT. ☎ 01708-348904.
Hemel Hempstead and District Affiliated Synagogue, c/o 1 Devreaux Drive, Watford WD1 3DD. *Admin.* H. Nathan. ☎ 01923 232007.
High Wycombe Affiliated Synagogue. *Hon. Sec.* Mrs R. Weiss, 33 Hampden Road, High Wycombe, Bucks. HP13 6SZ. ☎ 01494 529821.
Highams Park and Chingford Affiliated Synagogue, 81a Marlborough Road, Chingford, E4 9AJ. ☎ 020-8527 0937. *M.* Rev. M. Lester; *Admin.* Mrs S.R. Benjamin, 77 Royston Avenue, Chingford E4 9DE. ☎ 020-8527 4750.
Hounslow, Heathrow and District Affiliated Synagogue, 100 Staines Road, Hounslow, Middx. (Est. 1944.) *H. Admin.* L. Gilbert, 9 Park

Ave., Hounslow, Middx. TW3 2NA. ☎ 020-8894 4020.
Kingston, Surbiton and District Affiliated Synagogue, 33-35 Uxbridge Road, Kingston on Thames, Surrey KT1 2LL. (Est. 1947) ☎ 020-8546 9370. Email: rabbicoten@panther.netmania.co.uk. *M.* Rabbi S. Coten. ☎/Fax 020-8399 8689. *H. Admin.* S. Nakar, 85 Alexandra Dr, Surbiton KT5 9AE. ☎ 020-8399 7403.
Peterborough Affiliated Synagogue, 142 Cobden Avenue, Peterborough PEI 2NU. *Admin.* C. Conn. ☎ 01733 571282.
Potters Bar and District Affiliated Synagogue. Meadowcroft, Great North Road, Bell Bar (Nr. Potters Bar), Hatfield, Herts. AL9 6DB. *M.* ☎ 01707 656202; *Sec.* J. Bellman.
Romford and District Affiliated Synagogue, (Reg. Charity No. 242552) 25 Eastern Road, Romford, Essex. (Est. 1929.) *Admin.* J. Rose. ☎ 01708-748199.
Ruislip and District Affiliated Synagogue, Shenley Avenue, Ruislip Manor, Middx., HA4 6BP. ☎ 01895 622059. (Est. 1946.) *M.* Rev D. Wolfson; *Sec.* Mrs S. Green.
St. Albans Affiliated Synagogue, Oswald Road, St. Albans, Herts. AL1 3AQ. ☎ 01727 854872.
Staines and District Affiliated Synagogue, Westbrook Road, South Street, Staines, Middx. TW18 4PR. ☎ 01784-462557. *M.* ; *Hon. Sec.* Mrs P. D. Fellman. ☎ 01784 254604.
Sutton & District Synagogue, 14 Cedar Road, Sutton, Surrey, SM2 5DA. ☎ 020-8642 5419. Rev. Dr Z.H. Amit. ☎ 020-8642 8029; *Admin.* Mrs T. Raphael, 43 Avenue Rd., Belmont, Sutton SM2 6JE. ☎ 020-8642 9285.
Wanstead and Woodford Affiliated Synagogue, 20 Churchfields, South Woodford E18 2QZ. ☎ 020-8504 1990. *M.* Rabbi A. Lewis; *Admin.* Mrs S. Braude. (D)
Welwyn Garden City Affiliated Synagogue, Barn Close, Handside Lane, Welwyn Garden City, Herts. AL8 6ST. ☎ 01438-715686. *M.* Rabbi G. Hyman. *Hon. Admin.* Mrs D. Prag.

BURIAL SOCIETY
Finchley Office: *Man.* Mr M. Wohlman, Finchley Synagogue, P.O. Box 9537, Kinloss Gardens, N3 3DU. ☎ 020-8343 3456. Fax 020-8346 3402 (Bushey & Willesden). Ilford office, Schaller House, Ilford Synagogue, 22, Beehive Lane, Ilford, Essex IG1 3RT. ☎ 020-8518 2868. Fax 020-8518 2926 (Waltham Abbey, East Ham, West Ham, and Plashet). *Man.* A. Harris.

CEMETERIES
Willesden, Beaconsfield Road, NW10 2JE. Opened 1873. ☎ 020-8459 0394. Fax 020-8451 0478; East Ham, Marlow Road, High St. South, E6 3QG. Opened 1919. ☎ 020-8472 0554. Fax 020-8471 2822; Bushey, Little Bushey Lane, Bushey, Herts, WD2 3TP. Opened 1947. ☎ 020-8950 6299. Fax 020-8420 4973; Waltham Abbey, Skillet Hill (Honey Lane), Waltham Abbey, Essex. Opened 1960. ☎ 01992 714492. Fax 01992-650 735. Plashet, High Street North, E12 6PQ. Opened 1896. ☎ 020-8472 0554. West Ham, Buckingham Road, Forest Lane, E15 1SP. Opened 1857. ☎ 020-8472 0554. Alderney Road, E1. Opened for Great Syn. in 1696 (disused). ☎ 020-7790 1445. Brady street, E1. Opened for the New Syn, in 1761; subsequently used also by Great Syn. (disused); Hackney, Lauriston Road, E9. Opened for Hambro' Syn. in 1788 (disused). ☎ 020-8985 1527.

Federation of Synagogues

Constituent and Affiliated Synagogues of the Federation of Synagogues, 65 Watford Way, NW4 3AQ. ☎ 020-8202 2263 Fax 020-8203 0610.

CONSTITUENT SYNAGOGUES
Clapton Federation Synagogue (Sha'are Shomayim), 47 Lea Bridge Road, E5 9QB. ☎ 081-806 4369.(Est. 1919.) *M.* Rev. H. Daviest; *Sec.* W. Jacobs. ☎ 020-8989

5211.
Croydon & District Synagogue, The Almonds, Shirley Oaks, CRO 8YX. *M.* Rabbi H. Vogel; *H. Sec.* Mrs S. Hanover. ☎ 020-8656 0864.
East London Central Synagogue, 30/40 Nelson Street, E1 2DE. ☎ 020-7790 9809. *Sec.* L. Gayer. ☎ 020-8554 5267.
Elstree Beth Hamedrash, 6 Allum Lane, Elstree, Herts WD6 3PH. *M.* Rabbi D. Tugendhaft. *Sec.* M. Slyper. ☎ 020-8953 8444.
Finchley Central Synagogue, Redbourne Avenue, N3 2BS. ☎ 020-8346 1892. *Rab.* Rabbi Z. H. Telsner; *Sec.* M. Moller.
Hendon Beis Hamedrash, 65 Watford Way NW4 3AQ. *M.* Dayan Y.Y Lichtenstein; *H. Sec.* Z. Shenkin ☎ 020-8202 7468.
Ilford Federation Synagogue, 16 Coventry Road, Ilford, Essex IG1 4QR. ☎ 020-8554 5289. (Est. 1927.) *M.*; *R.* Rev. E. Sufrin; *Sec.* Mrs P. Hackner. ☎ 020-8554 5289. (D)
Machzike Hadath Synagogue, 1-4 Highfield Road, NW11 9LU. ☎ 020-8455 9816 (Reg. Charity No. 289999). *M.* Rabbi C. Z. Pearlman; *H. Sec.* R. Shaw. ☎ 020-8204 1887.
Ohel Jacob Beth Hamedrash: (1st Floor) 478 Cranbrook Road, Ilford, Essex IG2 2LE. *M.* Rav R. Godlewsky. ☎ 020-8800 9253; *H. Sec.* Mrs R. Pressman. ☎ 020-8550 4596.
Shomrei Hadath Synagogue, 64 Burrard Road, NW6 1DD. *Sec.* Mrs J. Segal. ☎ 020-7431 0017.
Sinai Synagogue, 54 Woodstock Avenue, NW11 9RJ. (Est. 1935.) *Rab.* Rabbi B. Knopfler; *Sec.* E. Cohen. ☎ 020-8458 8201. (D)
Yeshurun Synagogue, Fernhurst Gdns., Stonegrove, Edgware, Middx. HA8 7PH. ☎ 020-8952 5167. (Est. 1946.) *Rab.* Dayan G. Lopian; *Sec.* D. H. Cohen. ☎ 020-8952 3844 (eves). Fax 020-8905 7439. Email yeshedg@aol.com

AFFILIATED SYNAGOGUES
Congregation of Jacob, 351/355 Commercial Road, E1. (Est. 1904.) *Sec.* P. Da Costa. ☎ 0958 486792.
Fieldgate Street Great Synagogue, 41 Fieldgate Street, E1. ☎ 020-7247 2644. *M.*; *Sec.* Mrs D. Jacobson. (D)
Finchley Road Synagogue, 4 Helenslea Avenue, NW11. (Est. 1941.) *Rab.* Rabbi S. Rubin. ☎ 020-8455 4305.
Greenford & District Synagogue, 39-45 Oldfield Lane South, Greenford, Middx. UB6 9LB. *H. Sec.* R. A. Hyams. ☎ 020-8421 6366.
Leytonstone & Wanstead Synagogue, 2 Fillebrook Road, E11. (Est. 1932.) *Sec.* L. Braham. ☎ 020-8539 0088.
Loughton, Chigwell & District Synagogue, Borders La., Loughton, Essex IG10 1TE. *M.* Rabbi H. Belovski. ☎ 020-8502 1263, Rev. J. Lorraine. ☎ 020-8508 0270. *Hon. Sec.* D. Viniker. ☎ 020-8508 4760. *Admin.* Mrs M. Lewis. ☎ 020-8508 0303.
New Wimbledon & Putney District Synagogue, The Clubroom, Toland Sq., Eastwood Estate, Roehampton Lane, SW15. *H. Sec.* Mrs. R. Diamond. ☎ 020-8788 6669.
Notting Hill Synagogue, 206/8 Kensington Park Road, W11 1NR. (Est. 1900.) *Chairman* P. Fogelman, ☎ 020-8969 8416; *M.*; *Sec.* H. Lamb, ☎ 020-8952 4354.
Springfield Synagogue, 202 Upper Clapton Road, E5 9DH. (Est. 1929.) *Rab.* Dayan I. Gukovitski; *President* and *Hon. Sec.* L. Blackman, 45 Midhurst Avenue, Westcliff on Sea, Essex SS0 0NP. ☎ 01702 340 762.
Stamford Hill Beth Hamedrash, 50 Clapton Common, E5 9AL. *M.* Dayan Grynhaus; *Sec.* M. Chontow. ☎ 020-8800 5465.
Tottenham Hebrew Congregation, 366A High Road, N17 9HT. (Est. 1904.) *M.* Rabbi S. Lewis. ☎ 020-8800 2772; *Sec.* Dr S. S. Cohen. ☎ 020-8245 4243.

Waltham Forest Hebrew Congregation, (Queens Road), 140 Boundary Road, E17 8LA. *Rab.* Rabbi M. Davis; *Sec.* A. Wolpert. ☎ 020-8509 0775.
West End Great Synagogue, 32 Great Cumberland Place, W1H 7DJ. ☎ 020-7724 8121. Fax 020-7723 4413. *M.* Ari Cohen; *Sec.* S. B. Levy.
West Hackney Synagogue & Montague Rd Beth Hamedrash, 233A Amhurst Road, E8 2BS (Est. 1903.) *Chairman* I. Leigh. ☎ 020-8550 9543. *Sec.* Mrs R. Glaser. ☎ 020-7254 8078.

BURIAL SOCIETY
Office: 65 Watford Way, Hendon NW4 3AQ. ☎ 020-8202 3903; Fax 020-8203 0610. *Admin.* M. L. Stuart; *Sexton* Mr. H. Brooks; *Ts.* H. Dony, N. Bruckheimer.

CEMETERIES
Montague Rd., Angel Road, Lower Edmonton, N.18. ☎ 020-8807 2268.
Upminster Road North, Rainham, Essex. Supt. E. Brown. ☎ 017085-52825.

Union of Orthodox Hebrew Congregations
140 Stamford Hill, N16 6QT.
☎ 020-8802 6226 Fax 020-8809 7092.

CONSTITUENTS
Adath Yisroel (Parent) Synagogue, 40 Queen Elizabeth's Walk, N16 0HH. *Rab.* Rabbi J. Dunner; *Sec.* A. Barnett. ☎ 020-8802 6262/3. (D)
Adath Yisroel Tottenham Beth Hamedrash, 55/57 Ravensdale Road, N16. *Rab.* Dayan A. D. Dunner. ☎ 020-8800 3978. (D)
Ahavat Israel Synagogue, D'Chasidey Viznitz, 89 Stamford Hill, N16. ☎ 020-8800 9359. *Rab.* Rabbi F. Schneebalg. (D)
Beit Knesset Chida, Egerton Road, N16.
Beth Abraham Synagogue, 46 The Ridgeway, NW11. *Rab.* Rabbi C. Schmahl. ☎ 020-8455 2848.
Beth Chodosh Synagogue, 51 Queen Elizabeth's Walk, N16. ☎ 020-8800 6754.
Beth Hamedrash Beis Nadvorna, 45 Darenth Road, N16 6ES. ☎ 020-8806 3903. *Rab.* Rabbi M. Leifer. (D)
Beth Hamedrash Cheishev Sofer d' Pressburg, 103 Clapton Common, E5. *Rab.* S. Ludmir. (D)
Beth Hamedrash Chelkas Yehoshua (Biala), 110 Castlewood Road, London N15. *Rab.* Rabbi L Rabbinowitz.
Beth Hamedrash D'Chasidey Belz, 99 Bethune Road, N16. ☎ 020-8802 8233. (D)
Beth Hamedrash D'Chasidey Belz, 96 Clapton Common, E5. *Rab.* Dayan J. D. Babad. (D)
Beth Hamedrash D'Chasidey Gur, 2 Lampard Grove, N16. ☎ 020-8806 4333, and 98 Bridge Lane, NW11. ☎ 020-8458 6243. (D)
Beth Hamedrash D'Chasidey Ryzin, 33 Paget Road, N16. ☎ 020-8800 7979. (D)
Beth Hamedrash D'Chasidey Sanz Klausenburg, 42 Craven Walk, N16. (D)
Beth Hamedrash D'Chassidey Square, 22 Dunsmure Road, N16. ☎ 020-8800 8448.
Beth Hamedrash Divrei Chaim, 71 Bridge La., NW11. ☎ 020-8458 1161. *Rab.* Rabbi Chaim A. Z. Halpern. (D)
Beth Hamedrash Hendon, 3 The Approach, NW4 2HU. *Rab.* Rabbi D. Halpern (D)
Beth Hamedrash Imrey Chaim D'Chasidey Vishnitz-Monsey, 121 Clapton Common, E5. ☎ 020-8800 3741. *Rab.* Rabbi D. Hager (D)
Beth Hamedrash Kehillas Yacov, 35 Highfield Av., NW11 ☎ 020-8455 3066. (D)
Beth Hamedrash Ohel Moshe, 202B Upper Clapton Road, E5. (D)

Beth Hamedrash Ohel Naphtoli (Bobov), 87 Egerton Road, N16. ☎ 020-8802 3979. *Rab.* Dayan B. Blum (D)
Beth Hamedrash of the Agudah Youth Movement, 69 Lordship Road, N.16. Also 95 Stamford Hill, N16. ☎ 020-8800 8873. *Rab.* Rabbi M. J. Kamionka. (D)
Beth Hamedrash Or Yisroel (Sadigur), 269 Golders Green Road, NW11. *Rab.* Y.M. Friedman. (D)
Beth Hamedrash Spinke, 36 Bergholt Cres., N16 5SE. ☎ 020-8809 6903. *Rab.* Rabbi M. Kahana.
Beth Hamedrash Torah Etz Chayim, 69 Lordship Road, N16. ☎ 020-8800 7726. *Rab.* Rabbi Z. Feldman. (D)
Beth Hamedrash Torah Chaim Liege, 145 Up. Clapton Road, E5. *Rab.* Rabbi Y. Meisels. (D)
Beth Hamedrash Toras Chaim, 37 Craven Walk, N16 6BS. ☎ 020-8800 3868. *Rab.* Rabbi J. Meisels. (D)
Beth Hamedrash Vayoel Moshe, 14 Heathland Road, N16.
Beth Hamedrash Yetiv Lev, D'Satmar, 86 Cazenove Road, N16. ☎ 020-8800 2633. (D) Also 26 Clapton Common, E5. ☎ 020-8806 7439. *Rab.* Rabbi C. Wosner. (D)
Beth Shmuel Synagogue, 171 Golders Green Road, NW11. ☎ 020-8458 7511. *Rab.* Rabbi E. Halpern. (D)
Beth Sholom Synagogue, 27 St. Kilda's Road, N16. ☎ 020-8809 6224. *Rab.* Rabbi S. Deutsch. (D)
Beth Talmud Centre, 78 Cazenove Road, N16.
Beth Yisochor Dov Beth Hamedrash, 2-4 Highfield Avenue, NW11. *Rab.* Rabbi G. Hager. (D)
Birkath Yehuda (Halaser) Beth Hamedrash, 47 Moundfield Road, N16 6DT. *Rab.* Rabbi M. Lebovits. ☎ 020-8806 6448. (D)
Bridge Lane Beth Hamedrash, 44 Bridge Lane, NW11 0EG. *Rab.* Rabbi S. Winegarten. (D)
Etz Chaim Yeshiva, 83/85 Bridge Lane, NW11. *Rab.* Z. Rabi. (D)
Finchley Road Synagogue, 4 Helenslea Avenue, NW11. ☎ 020-8455 4305 *Rab.* Rabbi S. Rubin. (D)
Heichal Hatorah, 27 St. Kildas Road, N16. ☎ 020-8809 4331. *R.* L. Rakow.
Hendon Adath Yisroel Synagogue, 11 Brent Street, NW4 2EU. ☎ 020-8202 9183. *Rab.* Rabbi P. Roberts; *Sec.* N. Hammond. (D)
Kehal Chasidim D'Munkatch Synagogue, 85 Cazenove Road, N16.
Kingsley Way Beth Hamedrash (Lubavitch), 3-5 Kingsley Way, London N2. ☎ 020-8458 2312. *Rab.* Rabbi Y. Hertz.
Knightland Road Synagogue of the Law of Truth Talmudical College, 50 Knightland Road, E5 9HS. Corr: 27 Warwick Grove, E5 9HX. ☎ 020-8806 2963. *Rab.* Rabbi S.A. Halpern.
Kol Yaakov, 47 Mowbray Rd., Edgware HA8 8JH. ☎ 020-8959 6131. *M.* Rabbi S. Cutler. (D).
Lubavitch of Edgware, 230 Hall Lane, HA6 9AZ. ☎ 020-8905 4141. *M.* Rabbi L.Y. Sudak.
Lubavitch Synagogue, 107-115 Stamford Hill, N16. ☎ 020-8800 0022. *Rab.* Rabbi N. Sudak. (D)
Machzikei Hadass Edgware Beth Hamedrash, 269 Hale Lane, Edgwarev HA8. *R.* Rabbi E. Schneelbag. ☎ 020-8958 1030. (D)
Mesifta Synagogue, 82-84 Cazenove Road, N16. (D)
North Hendon Adath Yisroel Synagogue, Holders Hill Road, NW4 1NA. *Rab.* Rabbi D. Cooper; *Sec.* A. H. Ehreich. ☎ 020-8203 0797; corr.: 31 Holders Hill Crescent, NW4 1NE. (D)
Ohel Israel (Skoler) Synagogue, 11 Brent Street, NW4. (D)
Shaare Zion, 10 Woodberry Down, N4.
Stanislowa Beth Hamedrash, 93 Lordship Park, N16. ☎ 020-8800 2040. *Rab.* Rabbi E. Aschkenasi. (D)

Yeshiva Horomoh Beth Hamedrash, 100 Fairholt Road, N16 5HH. ☎ 020-8809 3904; 020-8800 4522 (students). *Rab.* Rabbi E. Schlesinger. ☎ 020-8800 2194. (D)
Yeshuath Chaim Synagogue, 45 Heathland Road, N16. ☎ 020-8800 2332. *Rab.* Rabbi S. Pinten; *H. Sec.* I. Kohn. (D)
Yesodey Hatorah Synagogue, 2/4 Amhurst Pk., N16.
Zichron Shlomo Beth Hamedrash, 11 Elm Park Av., N15. ☎ 020-8809 7850. *R.* Rabbi S. Meisels.

The Assembly of Masorti Synagogues

1097 Finchley Road, NW11 0PU.
☎ 020-8201 8772, Fax 020-8201 8917. Email: office@masorti.org.uk; Website: http://www.masorti.org.uk
(Est. 1985. Reg. Charity No. 801846). *Dir.* H. Freedman, *Chairman* P. Shrank.
New London Synagogue, 33 Abbey Road, NW8 0AT. ☎ 020-7328 1026. Fax 020-7372 3142. (Est. 1964) *M.* Rabbi Dr Louis Jacobs, C.B.E.; *Chairman* Anne Cowen; *Sec.* D. Lewis.
New North London Synagogue, The Manor House, 80 East End Road, N3 2SY. ☎ 020-8346 8560. Fax 020-8346 9710. (Est. 1974.) An independent tradition-al com. following the philosophy of Rabbi Dr L. Jacobs. *M.* Rabbi J. Wittenberg;. *Co-Chairpersons* David Halpern, Mrs Gill Caplin; *T.* Martin May; *Sec.* Roger Filer; *Off.* Mrs Barbara Anders; *Community Co-ord.* Mrs Bette Rabie.
Edgware Masorti Synagogue. Synagogue Office/Post/Weekly entrance: Pearl Community Centre, Stream Lane, Edgware, Middx. HA8 7YA. (Reg. Charity No. 291010.) Shabbat entrance: Bakery Path (off Station Road), Edgware, Middx. HA8 7YE. ☎ 020-8905 4096. Fax 020-8905 4333. Email masorti.edg-ware@virgin.net. *M.* Harvey Meirovich, ☎ 020-8952 2633; *Co-Chairpersons* H. Segal, A. Wien; *T.* M. Sobell; *Admin.* Fenella Burman.
Hatch End Masorti, *Co-Chairpersons* M. Reindorp ☎ 020-8866 5484, D. Kosky, ☎ 020-8420 2041.
Hendon Masorti Minyan. *Contact* ☎ 020-8201 8772.
Leeds Masorti, *Contact* A. Selman. ☎ 0113 261700.
New Essex Masorti Congregation, Services: Roding Valley Hall, Station Way, Buckhurst Hill, Essex IG9 6LN. Enqs. ☎ 020-8504 0010/020-8508 6783. *Chairman*; *Sec.* Mrs M. Berger.
New Whetstone Synagogue, Enquiries: 020-8368 3936. *Chairman* E. Slater.
Oxford Masorti (part of Oxford Jewish Congregation – services held last Shabbat each month). *Contact* Mrs W. Fidler ☎ 001865 726959. Email: wendyfidler@compuserve.com
St. Albans Masorti Synagogue, *Co-Chairperson* Dr J. Freedman, L. Harris; *T.* P. Hoffbrand; *Sec.* Mrs K. Phillips. ☎ 01727 860642.

Independent Congregations

Belsize Square Synagogue, 51 Belsize Square, London NW3 4HX. ☎ 020-7794 3949. Fax 020-7431 4559. Email belsqsyn@aol.com. http://www.synagogue. org.uk. (Est. 1939. Reg. Charity No. 233742.) An Independent Synagogue com-bining traditional forms of worship with progressive ideals. *M.* Rabbi Rodney J. Mariner; *Cantor* Rev. Lawrence Fine; *Sec.* Ms. J. Berman; *Chairman* Steven M. Bruck; *H. T.* David Rothenberg; *H. Sec.* Thomas Tausz. Totteridge Branch twice monthly at Badgers Croft.
Commercial Road Talmud Torah Synagogue (formerly 9-11 Christian Street, E1.) 153 Stamford Hill, London N16 5LG. ☎ 020-8800 1618. (est. 1898) *Sec.* A. Becker. Burial Society. Cemeteries: Carterhatch Lane, Enfield. ☎ 020-8363 3384. Silver Street, Cheshunt, Herts. ☎ 01707 874220.
Edgware Adath Yisroel Synagogue, 261 Hale Lane, Edgware HA8 8NX. ☎ 020-

8958 9003. Fax 020-8931 7916. Email: eayc@brijnet.org. *Rab.* Rabbi Zvi Lieberman. (Affiliated to Adath Yisroel Burial Soc. p.12) (D)

Golders Green Beth Hamedrash Congregation, The Riding, Golders Green Road, NW11 8HL. ☎ 020-8455 2974. (Est. 1934.) *Rab.* Rabbi H. I. Feldman; *R.* Rev. N. Gluck.

Ner Yisrael, The Crest (off Brent St.), Hendon, NW4. ☎ 020-8202 6687. Fax 020-8203 5158. *M.* Rabbi A.A. Kimche. ☎ 020-8455 7347. *Admin.* Mrs L. Brayam.

Porat Yosef (est. 1988.) Moroccan Hebrew Congregation. 9 Burroughs Gardens, Hendon, NW4 4AU. ☎ 020-8203 7809. Email neryisrael@londonweb.net. *President* Jacques Onona; *R.* Rabbi Leon Benarroch; *Sec.* B. Benarroch.

Saatchi Synagogue (Est. 1998. Reg. Charity No. 289066), 21 Andover Place, NW6 5ED. ☎ 020-7266 2026. Fax: 020-7289 5957. *Rab.* Rabbi Pini Dunner.

Sandy's Row Synagogue (est. 1854), Sandy's Row, Middlesex Street, E1 7HW. *M.* Rev. Y. Moses; *Sec.* E. Wilder. ☎ 020-7253 8311; 020-7377 5854. (D)

Synagogue Française de Londres (La), 101 Dunsmure Road, N16 5HT. Le Grand Rabbin Henri Brand, 54 Bethune Road, N16 5BD. ☎ 020-8800 8612. *Hon. Tr.* Rabbi C. Pinter; *Hon. Sec.* I. Kraus.

Walford Road Synagogue, 99 Walford Road, Stoke Newington, N16 8EF. *M.* Rabbi H. Gluck; *Sec.* S. Raymond.

Waltham Forest Hebrew Congregation, 140 Boundary Road, E17 8LA. (Est. 1902.) ☎ Off.: 020-8509 0775. Fax 020-8518 8200. *M.* Rabbi Michael Davis; *President* R. Jacobs; *Admin.* A. Wolpert. (D)

West End Great Synagogue, 32 Great Cumberland Place, W1H 7DJ. ☎ 020-7724 8121. Fax 020-7723 4413 (Est. 1880.) *M.* Ari Cohen; *Sec.* S. B. Levy.

Chesed V'Ameth. Cemeteries: Rowan Road, Greyhound Lane, SW16. ☎ 020-8764 1566; Cheshunt Cemetery (Western), Bullscross Ride, Cheshunt, Herts. ☎ 01992 717820.

Affiliated Synagogues: retaining burial rights: *Commercial Road Great Syn., Teesdale Street Syn., *Great Garden Street Syn., *Cong. of Jacob, *Ezras Chaim Syn., *Nelson Street Sephardish Syn., Sandy's Row Syn., *Fieldgate St. Syn.
The synagogues marked * still have a section of members affiliated for burial rights under the Federation of Synagogues.

Western Marble Arch Synagogue, successor to the Western Synagogue (est. 1761) and the Marble Arch Synagogue, 32 Great Cumberland Place, W1H 7DJ. ☎ 020-7723 9333. Fax 020-7224 8065. *M.* ; *Community Admin,* Malcolm E. Howard; Affiliated for burial rights with Western Charitable Foundation in the following Cemeteries: Edmonton, Montague Road, N18, Bullscross Ride, Cheshunt, Herts; *Supt.* M. Clements, Bullscross Ride, Cheshunt, Herts. ☎ 01992 717820.

Affiliated Orgs.: Western Charitable Foundation. *Chairman* S. Jacque, J.P.; *Tr.* W. Ward.

Westminster Synagogue (Est. 1957), Rutland Gdns., Knightsbridge, SW7 1BX. ☎ 020-7584 3953. Fax 020-7581 8012. *M. Emer.* Rabbi A. H. Friedlander, Ph.D., Rabbi T. Salamon; *President* H. I. Connick; *Chairman* E. D. Glover.

Yakar Synagogue, 2 Egerton Gardens, London NW4 4BA. *M.* Rabbi Yehoshua Engelman; *Chair* Sharmaine Selvaratnam. ☎ 020-8202 5551.

Sephardi

Spanish and Portuguese Jews' Congregation (Reg. Charity No. 212517) 2, Ashworth Rd, Maida Vale, W9 1JY. ☎ 020-7289 2573. Fax 020-7289 2709.

SYNAGOGUES
Bevis Marks (1701), EC3A 5DQ. ☎ 020-7626 1274. Fax 020-7283 8825. Rabbi Dr A. Levy B.A. *M.* Rev. H. Benarroch, B.A.
Lauderdale Road Syn. (1896), Maida Vale, W9 1JY.☎ 020-7289 2573. *Rabbi & M.*

Rabbi Dr A. Levy, B.A., Rabbi I. Elia.
Wembley Synagogue, 46 Forty Ave., Wembley, Middx HA9 8LQ. ☎ 020-8904
9912. *Rabbi & M.* Dayan Dr P. Toledano, B.A.
Sir Moses Montefiore Synagogue, Honeysuckle Road, Ramsgate, Kent.

OTHER INSTITUTIONS
Burial Society, 2 Ashworth Road, W9 1JY. ☎ 020-7289 2573.
Welfare Board, 2 Ashworth Road, W9 1JY. ☎ 020-7289 2573. (Est. 1837.)
Sephardi Kashrut Authority, 2 Ashworth Road, W9 1JY. ☎ 020-7289 2573.
Chairman E. H. Silas; *Dir.* Rabbi I. Abraham.
Communal Centre, Montefiore Hall, 2 Ashworth Road, W9 1JY. ☎ 020-7289 2573.
Beth Hamedrash Heshaim, (Instituted 1664.) *T. C.* Sacerdoti. Ad: 2 Ashworth
Road, W9 1JY. ☎ 020-7289 2573.
Montefiore Endowment at Ramsgate (incorporating the **Judith Lady Montefiore
College Trust),** 2 Ashworth Road, W9 1JY. (☎ 020-7289 2573.) Est. by Sir Moses
Montefiore 1866. New scheme est. by the Charity Commission in 1989 'for the
maintenance of the Synagogue, the Mausoleum and the Jewish Cemetery in
Ramsgate', also 'for the promotion of the advanced study of the Holy Law as
revealed on Sinai and expounded by the revered sages of the Mishna and
Talmud' by making grants to charitable institutions for the training of Orthodox
Jewish Teachers, Ministers and Rabbis and by awarding scholarships to such
trainees.
The Mausoleum with the remains of Sir Moses and Lady Montefiore is situated
next to the Synagogue in Ramsgate (see above). Sir Moses's seats in Bevis Marks
and Ramsgate Syns. are still preserved.
Edinburgh House (Beth Holim), 36/44 Forty Avenue, Wembley. (Est. 1747.) Home
for the Aged. *Hd. of Home* C. Gilmour. ☎ 020-8908 4151.

CEMETERIES
253 Mile End Rd., E1. (Disused.) Opened in 1657, the oldest Jewish burial
ground in the United Kingdom. 329 Mile End Road, E1. (Opened 1725.
Disused.) Hoop Lane, Golders Green, NW11. *Keeper* B. H. Calo. ☎ 020-8455
2569. Edgwarebury Lane, Edgware. ☎ 020-8958 3388. *Keeper* B. H. Calo.
Dytchleys, Coxtie Green, Brentwood. (Disused.)

Other Sephardi Synagogues
Aden Jews' Congregation, 117 Clapton Common, E5. *H. Sec.* M. A. Solomon.
☎ 020-8806 1320.
David Ishag Synagogue, Neveh Shalom Community, 352-4 Preston Road, Harrow,
Middx., HA3 0QJ. *H. Sec.* F. Lichaa; *T. J. M.* Sitton. ☎ 020-8904 3009.
Eastern Jewry Community (Est. 1955.) Newbury Park Station, Newbury Park. *M.*
Rabbi C. Tangy; *H. Sec.* D. Elias. ☎ 020-8809 4387.
Ilford Congregation (Ohel David), Newbury Park Station, Ilford. *H. Sec.* ☎ 020-
8809 4387. Fax 020-8809 4441; 020-8458 1468.
Jacob Benjamin Elias Synagogue (Reg. Charity No. 291531), 140 Stamford Hill,
N16 6QT. *M.* Rabbi C. Tangy; *H. Sec.* D. Elias. ☎ 020-8809 4387, 020-8458
8693. Fax 020-8809 4441; 020-8458 1468.
Ohel David Eastern Synagogue, Lincoln Institute, Broadwalk Lane, Golders Green
Road, NW11. (Reg. Charity No. 243901) *M.* Rabbi Abraham Gubbay; ☎ 020-
8455 8125. *H. Sec.* M. Lanyado. ☎ 020-8455 9581.
Persian Hebrew Congregation, 5a East Bank, Stamford Hill, N16. ☎ 020-8800
9261. Corr. *H. Sec.* 17 Arden Road, London N3 3AB. ☎ 020-8446 4321.
Shivtei Israel Hekhal Leah (UHC), 62 Brent Street, NW4 2ES. ☎ 020-8922 3721.
M. Rabbi M. Cohen. (D)
Spanish & Portuguese Synagogue, Holland Park, (Est. 1928 under Deed of

Association with Spanish and Portuguese Jews' Congregation. Reg. Charity No. 248945), 8 St. James's Gdns., W11 4RB. ☎ 020-7603 7961/3232. Fax 020-7603 9471. *Sec.* Mrs R. Lynton.
Manchester, Sha'are Sedek: Sha'are Tefillah: Withington (p.119)

Reform

(Constituents of the Reform Synagogues of Great Britain), The Sternberg Centre for Judaism, 80 East End Road, N3 2SY. *Chief Executive* Rabbi Tony Bayfield. ☎ 020-8349 4731. Fax 020-8343 0901.
West London Synagogue of British Jews (Reg. Charity No. 212143), 34 Upper Berkeley Street, W1. Office, 33 Seymour Place, W1H 6AT. ☎ 020-7723 4404. Fax 020-7224 8258.
The congregation was organised April 15, 1840, to establish a synagogue 'where a revised service may be performed at hours more suited to our habits and in a manner more calculated to inspire feelings of devotion, where religious instruction may be afforded by competent persons, and where, to effect these purposes, Jews generally may form a united congregation under the denomination of British Jews.'
Senior M. Rabbi Mark Winer, Ph.D., D.D.; *M.* Rabbi Helen Freeman; *President* G. D. Leuw; *Chairman* M. Bentata; *Exec. Dir.* M. Ross.
Funerals: ☎ 020-7723 4404. Fax 020-7224 8258.
Cemeteries: Golders Green, Hoop Lane, NW11; Edgwarebury, Edgwarebury Lane, Middx. *Supt.* B. H. Calo. ☎ 020-8958 3388.
Beit Klal Yisrael (North Kensington Reform Syn.) (Reg. Charity No.1034282), P.O. Box 1828, W10 5RT. Services in Notting Hill Gate. *M.* Rabbi Sheila Shulman. *Chairman* L. Urbach. ☎/Fax 020-8969 5080.
Bromley Reform Synagogue (Est. 1964. Reg. Charity No. 1059190). 28 Highland Road, Bromley, Kent BR1 4AD. ☎/Fax 020-8460 5460. *M.* Rabbi Sylvia Rothschild; *H. Sec.* Ms B. Kurtz.
Edgware and District Reform Synagogue, (Reg. Charity No. 1038116). 118 Stonegrove, Edgware HA8 8AB. (Est. 1934.) ☎ 020-8958 9782. Fax 020-8905 4710. *M.* Rabbi A.D. Smith, M.A.; *Assoc. M.* Rabbi M. Michaels, Rabbi Dr M. Leigh, M.A., (Emer); *Admin.* Mrs K. Senitt.
Finchley Reform Synagogue, Fallow Court Avenue, Finchley, N12 0BE. ☎ 020-8446 3244. Fax 020-8446 5980. *M.* Rabbi J. Newman; *Admin.* Jo-Anne Parker.
Hampstead Reform Jewish Community, 37a, Broadhurst Gdns., NW6. *Contact* M. Teper. ☎ 020-7794 8488.
Harlow Jewish Community, Harberts Road, Hare Street, Harlow, Essex CM19 4DT. ☎ 01992-447814. *Sec.* Mrs H. Reeves.
Hendon Reform Synagogue, Danescroft Avenue, NW4 2NA (Est. 1949.) ☎ 020-8203 4168. Fax 020-8203 9385. *M.* Rabbi S. Katz; *Sec.* Mrs R. Bloom.
Cemetery: New Southgate Cemetery, Brunswick Park Road, N11. ☎ 020-8203 4168.
Kol Chai-Hatch End Jewish Community. (Reg. Charity No. 299063). *M.* Rabbi S. Pereira; *Sec.* Floss Slade, Holly Lodge, Holly Grove, Hatch End HA5 4TA. ☎ 020-8421 4802.
Middlesex New Synagogue, 39 Bessborough Road, Harrow, HA1 3BS. ☎/Fax 020-8864 0133/4. (Est. 1959.) *M.* Rabbi S.J. Franses; *Sec.* Mrs A. Simon.
North West Surrey Synagogue, Horvath Close, Rosslyn Pk., Oatlands Dr, Weybridge, Surrey KT13 9QZ. ☎/Fax 01932 855400. *M.* Rabbi Jacqueline Tabick; *H. Sec.* B. Press.
North Western Reform Synagogue, Alyth Gdns., Finchley Road, NW11 7EN. ☎ 020-8455 6763/4. Fax 020-8458 2469 (Est 1933 Reg. Charity No. 247081.) *M.* Rabbi C. Emanuel. (D)

Jewish Joint Burial Society. (Est. 1968.) *H. Sec. P. S.* Michaelis; *Sexton* G. Conway. ☎ 020-8455 8579.

Radlett & Bushey Reform Synagogue, 118 Watling Street, Radlett, Herts WD7 7AA. ☎ 01923 85 6110. *M.* Rabbi Alexandra Wright. *H. Sec.* G. Nathan.

South West Essex and Settlement Reform Synagogue, Oaks Lane, Newbury Park, Ilford IG2 7PL. ☎ 020-8599 0936. (Est.1956.) *M.* Rabbi H. Goldstein; Rabbi L. Rigàl; *Office* Angela Jacobs.

Southgate and District Reform Synagogue (Reg. Charity No. 145 765), 45 High Street, N14 6LD. ☎ 020-8882 6828 Fax 020-8882 7539. *M.* Rabbi C. Eimer; *Chairman* Pamela Sandler.

Sukkat Shalom (Reg. Charity No. 283615). Hermon Hill, London E11. ☎ 020-8530 3345. *M.* Rabbi David Hulbert; *Chair* M. Joseph.

Wimbledon and District Synagogue, 1 Queensmere Rd., Wimbledon Parkside, SW19 5QD. ☎ 020-8946 4836 Fax 020-8944 7790. (Est. 1949. Reg. Charity No. 1040712) *M.* Rabbi W. Wolff; *Admin.* Mrs F. Solomon.

Liberal and Progressive

(Constituents of the Union of Liberal and Progressive Synagogues, The Montagu Centre, 21 Maple St., W1P 6DS.) *Senior V. President* Rabbi Dr Sidney Brichto, M.A., D.D.; *Dir.* Rabbi Dr Charles H. Middleburgh; *Admin. Dir.* Michael Burman. ☎ 020-7580 1663; Fax 020-7436 4184. Email: montagu@ulps.org.

Barkingside Progressive Synagogue (Reg. Charity No. 283547), 129 Perrymans Farm Road, Barkingside, Ilford, Essex IG2 7LX. *Sec.* P. Ordever. ☎ 020-8554 9682; *M.* Rabbi D. Hulbert.

Bedfordshire Progressive Synagogue Rodef Shalom, c/o The ULPS, The Montagu Centre, 21 Maple St., W1P 6DS. ☎ 01234-218387.

Ealing Liberal Synagogue, Lynton Av., Drayton Green, Ealing, W13 0EB. ☎/Fax: 020-8997 0528. (Est. 1944. Reg. Charity No. 1037099) *M.* Rabbi Melinda Carr, M.A.; *Admin.* A. Aarons.

Finchley Progressive Synagogue, 54a Hutton Gro. N12 8Dr (Est. 1953.) ☎ 020-8446 4063. Fax 020-8446 9599. *M.* Rabbi Mark Goldsmith; *Admin.* Mrs R. Lester.

Harrow & Wembley Progressive Synagogue, 326 Preston Road, Harrow, HA3 0QH. (Reg. Charity No. 251172) ☎ 020-8904 8581. Fax 020-8904 6540. Email: info@hwps.win-uk.net. Internet: www.ibmpcug.co.uk./~hwps/ (Est. 1947.) *M.* Rabbi Frank Dabba Smith; *Admin.* Mrs S. Rose.

Hertsmere Progressive Synagogue, High Street, Elstree, Herts. WD6 3BY. ☎ 020-8953 8889. *M.* Rabbi J. Black; *H. Sec.* Estelle Leigh. ☎ 020-8958 9276.

Kingston Liberal Synagogue, Rushett Road, Long Ditton, Surrey, KT7 0UX., Reg. Charity No. 270792. ☎ 020-8398 7400. Email kls@kingstonls.freeserve.co. *M.* Rabbi Danny Rich. ☎/Fax 020-8398 4252; *Chair* P. Levene, ☎ 020-8399 7887.

The Liberal Jewish Synagogue (Reg. Charity No. 235668), 28 St. John's Wood Road, London, NW8 7HA. ☎ 020-7286 5181. Fax 020-7266 3591. Email ljs@netco-muk.co.uk. Est. 1910 by the Jewish Religious Union, now known as the ULPS, the LJS, as it is known, was the first Liberal synagogue in the UK. Syn. rebuilt 1991. Membership. c.1,800 adults. *Chairman* Trevor Moross. *Ms.* Rabbi Emeritus Dr J.D. Rayner, C.B.E.; *Senior Rabbi* Rabbi D.J. Goldberg; *Org. Sec.* D. Rigal.

North London Progressive Synagogue (Est. 1921), 100 Amhurst Pk., N16 5AR. ☎ 020-8800 8931. Fax 020-8800 0416. *M.* Rabbi Marcia Plumb M.A.; *Chair* Ms M. Monnickendam; *H. Sec.* Ms J. Ryam; *Admin.* D. Sylvester.

Northwood and Pinner Liberal Synagogue, Oaklands Gate, Green La., Northwood HA6 3AA. (Est. 1964. Reg. Charity No. 243618) *M.* Rabbi Dr A. Goldstein Rabbi Rachel Benjamin; *H. Sec.* Avril Witte. ☎ 01923 822592. Fax 01923-824454. Email agoldstein@onet.co.uk

South London Liberal Synagogue, (Reg. Charity No. 236771), P.O.Box 14475, Streatham, SW16 1ZW. (Est. 1929.) ☎/Fax 020-8769 4787. Email slls@ulps.org. M. Rabbi N.S. Kraft; Sec. and Admin. Mrs R. Edwards.

Southgate Progressive Synagogue, 75 Chase Road, N14 4QY. (Reg. Charity No. 239096). ☎ 020-8886 0977. Fax. 020-8882 5394. (Est. 1943.) M. Rabbi S. Howard; Sec. Mrs B. Martin.

West Central Liberal Synagogue, The Montagu Centre, 21, Maple St., W1P 6DS. ☎ 020-7636 7627. Fax 020-7436 4184. (Cong. est. 1928; present syn. opened 1954.) M. Rabbi M.L. Solomon B.A., M.A.; Cantor Rev. A. Harman ALCM; Chairman: Dr L. Hepner; H. Sec. H. Berman.

Woodford Progressive Synagogue, Marlborough Road, South Woodford, E18. (Est. 1960.) M.; Sec. D. Gold. ☎ 020-8989 7619. Email woodfordprogressive@synagogue.

CEMETERIES

Funeral-Dir. Martin Board and Son. ☎ 020-8455 2797. Fax 020-8343 9463.

Edgwarebury Lane, Edgware, Middx. ☎ 020-8958 3388. Supt. Mr B. Calo.

Liberal Jewish Cemetery, Pound Lane, Willesden, NW10. Supt. Frank Quinn. ☎ 020-8459 1635. Funeral Dir. Bernard Foreman, ☎ 020-8459 5848.

Religious Organisations

Association of United Synagogue Women. (Est. 1968.) The Association promotes the interests and involvement of women as an integral part of the United Synagogue. It aims to promote and facilitate Jewish cultural and educational schemes that strengthen Orthodox traditional Jewish values. It represents women in Synagogue and communal affairs and also acts in an advisory capacity to Ladies Guilds. President Mrs E. Sacks; Admin. Off. Mrs J. Wayne, c/o United Synagogue, Adler House, 735 High Rd., N12 0US. ☎ 020-8343 8989. Fax 020-8343 6262. Chair Mrs R. Ross; Jt. H. Secs. Mrs S. Mann, Mrs M. Cohen.

London Board for Shechita (Reg. Charity No. 233467), P.O. Box 579, Adastra Suite, 401 Nether Street, N3 1YR. ☎ 020-8349 9160. Fax 020-8346 2209 (Est. 1804.) To administer the affairs of Shechita in London. President Dr M. Segal; V. Presidents A. Magnus, A. J. Kennard; H. T. S. D. Winegarten; Sec. M. T. Kester. ☎ 020-8349 9160. Fax 020-8346 2209.

Sabbath Observance Employment Bureau. (Est. 1909. Reg. Charity No. 209451) Commonwealth House, 1-19 New Oxford St., WC1A 1NF. ☎ 020-7831 6899. To obtain employment for those desirous of observing the Sabbath and Holydays. Man. Mrs E. Statham; Chairman E. F. Kestenbaum; H.T. D. Winter.

Ritual Baths (Mikvaot)

Central Mikvaot Board, 140 Stamford Hill, N16 6QT. ☎ 020-8802 6226/7.

Edgware & District Communal Mikvah, Edgware United Synagogue, Edgware Way, Edgware, Middlesex. (Reg. Charity No. 281586). ☎ 020-8958 3233. Fax 020-8951 5208. Email: estrin4488@aol.com.Gen. enquiries: Mrs Mandy Estrin ☎ 020-8958 4488 (eve), 020-8952 5292 (day).

Ilford Mikvah, 463 Cranbrook Road, Ilford. ☎ 020-8554 5450.

Kingsbury Mikvah, see below. United Synagogue Mikvah.

Lordship Park Mikvah, 55 Lordship Park, N16 (entrance in Queen Elizabeth's Walk). ☎ 020-8800 9621 (day) 020-8800 5801 (evening).

North London Mikvah, adjoining 40 Queen Elizabeth's Walk, N16 (entrance, Grazebrook Road). ☎ 020-8802 2554. Fax 020-8800 8764. H. Sec. A. Barnett.

Northwest London Communal Mikvah, 10a Shirehall Lane, Hendon, NW4. ☎ 020-8202 1427 (day), 020-8202 8517/5706 (evening).

Mikveh of the Reform Synagogues of Great Britain, Sternberg Centre, 80 East End Rd., N3 2SY. Appointments ☎ 020-8349 4731.
Satmar Mikvah, 62 Filey Avenue, N16. ☎ 020-8806 3961.
South London Mikvah, 42 St. George's Rd., Wimbledon SW19 4ED. (Reg. Charity No. 1009208) ☎ 020-8944 7149. Fax 020-8944 7563. *Hon. Sec.* L. Cohen. *Contact:* Mrs S. Dubov.
Stamford Hill Mikvah, 26 Lampard Grove, N16 (entrance in Margaret Road). ☎ 020-8806 3880.
United Synagogue Mikvah, Kingsbury United Synagogue, Kingsbury Green, NW9 8XR. ☎ 020-8204 6390. (See also Friends Group, p.00.)

Memorials

Holocaust Memorial and Garden, Hyde Park, near Hyde Park Corner. Opened in July 1983, on a site given to the Board of Deputies by the British Government.
Holocaust Memorial, Waltham Abbey Cemetery, Skillet Hill, Honey La., Waltham Abbey, Essex. Consecrated 1985 under U.S. auspices.
Holocaust Memorial, Sternberg Centre, 80 East End Road, Finchley N3.
Memorial in Willesden Jewish Cemetery, Beaconsfield Road, NW10, to Jewish Servicemen and Women in the British Armed Forces who died in the two World Wars and have no known graves. Annual service organised by Ajex.
Prisoners' Memorial, Gladstone Park, Dollis Hill Lane, NW2, to those who died in prisoner-of-war camps and concentration camps during the Second World War. Annual service jointly org. by Ajex and the Royal Brit. Legion.
Royal Fusiliers, City of London Regiment Memorial, High Holborn, by City boundary. The names of the 38th, 39th and 40th Battalions are inscribed on the monument, together with all other battalions which served in the First World War. Ajex is represented at the annual service.

Cemeteries

US = United Synagogue. F = Federation of Synagogues. UO = Union of Orthodox Hebrew Congregations. SP = Spanish and Portuguese Synagogue. W = Western Marble Arch Synagogue. WG = West End Great Synagogue. R = Reform. L = Liberal.
Alderney Road Cemetery (disused), E1. ☎ 020-8790 1445. (US).
Brady Street Cemetery, E1. (US).
Bullscross Ride Cemetery, Cheshunt, Herts. ☎ 01992 717820 (W and WG)
Bushey Cemetery, Little Bushey Lane, Bushey, Herts. ☎ 020-8950 6299. (US).
East Ham Cemetery, Marlow Road, High St. South, E6. (US). ☎ 020-8472 0554.
Edgwarebury Cemetery, Edgwarebury Lane, Edgware, Middx. ☎ 020-8958 3388. (SP, R and L.).
Edmonton Federation Cemetery, Montagu Road, Angel Road, Lower Edmonton, N18. ☎ 020-8807 2268. (F).
Enfield Cemetery, Carterhatch Lane, Enfield, Middx. ☎ 020-8363 3384. (UO).
Hackney Cemetery (disused), Lauriston Road, E9. ☎ 020-8985 1527. (US).
Hoop Lane Cemetery, Golders Green, NW11. ☎ 020-8455 2569. (SP and R).
Kingsbury Road Cemetery, Balls Pond Road, N1. (R).
Liberal Jewish Cemetery, Pound Lane and Harlesden Road, NW10. (L).
Mile End Road (disused), E1. (SP).
Plashet Cemetery, High St. North E12. ☎ 020-8472 0554. (US). [Closed except prior to New Year].
Queen's Elm Parade Cemetery (disused), Fulham Road, SW3. (W).
Rainham Cemetery, Upminster Road North, Rainham, Essex. ☎ 017085-52825. (F).
Rowan Road Cemetery, Greyhound Lane, SW16. ☎ 020-8764 1566. (WG).
Silver Street Cemetery, Cheshunt, Herts. ☎ 020-8802 6262. (UO).
Waltham Abbey Cemetery, Skillet Hill (Honey Lane), Waltham Abbey, Essex.

☎ 01992 714492. (US).
West Ham Cemetery, Buckingham Road, Forest Lane, E15. ☎ 020-8472 0554. (US).
Western Synagogue Cemetery, Montagu Road, N18. ☎ 020-8971 7820. (W).
Willesden Cemetery, Beaconsfield Road, NW10. ☎ 020-8459 0394. (US).

EDUCATIONAL ORGANISATIONS
Withdrawal on Friday Afternoons:
When the Sabbath begins at 5 p.m. or earlier, parents of Jewish children attending either State or State-aided schools can request that their children be withdrawn at such time as to reach their homes before the commencement of the Sabbath. Such requests should be submitted to the Head Teacher in writing. Hebrew and Religion Classes are attached to nearly all the syns. listed.

GENERAL
Agency for Jewish Education. (See p.35).
Binoh: The Jewish Special Educational Needs Service, Norwood House, Harmony Way, off Victoria Road, London NW4 2BZ. ☎ 020-8203 3030/954-4555. Fax 020-8203 9605. (Reg. Charity No. 291978). Email binoh@nwrw.org. Binoh is part of Norwood Ravenswood and is a multi-disciplinary Special Education Service for Jewish children. A range of services is provided for children with special educational needs from birth to the end of their school years. Our educational psychologists, therapists, support teachers and other staff aim to help children with special needs to remain within the ordinary school system and to access the best opportunities for developing their potential. *Hd. of Educ. Services* Kathyrn Finlay.
    Training courses and workshops for parents and teachers, Parent Advisory Service and multi-disciplinary services including teaching and therapeutic services. Local teams in Hackney and Redbridge. Part-time Special Needs Units for children with learning difficulties located at Norwood House and Hackney Family and Community Centre.
Jewish Resource Centre (JRC at CREDE), Centre for Religious Education and Development, Roehampton Institute London, Digby Stuart College, Roehampton Lane, SW15 5PH. ☎/Fax 020-8392 3349. JRC at CREDE was set up in 1996 – to serve as a resource for all sections of the Jewish community in South London, as well as for the non-Jewish teaching community. The Centre houses a large stock of books and religious articles for purchase, loan and consultation, and provides a base for educational and cultural activities. Staff are available to visit synagogues, religion schools/chadarim and teachers' centres in the area to run book sales and other events. JRC at CREDE is open on Wednesday afternoons during term-time from 2.00 to 5.00 p.m., and at other times by appointment. *Co-ord.* Anne Clark, B.A. (Hons.), M.A., Dip. Couns.
Schools' J-Link, Bet Meir, 44a Albert Road, Hendon, London NW4 2SJ. ☎ 020-8202 2236. Fax 020-8202 4668. Email: j-link@dircon.co.uk. url: http://www.come.to/j-link (Est. 1993. Reg. Charity No. 1062551) Schools' J-Link is an outreach programme to Jewish children in non-Jewish secondary schools aimed at raising their level of Jewish knowledge, commitment and involvement. Within the school system, it addresses Jewish pupils in Jewish Assemblies and/or Society meetings, as well as at main school assemblies, Religious Studies and history classes, and 6th form general studies, and conducts informal events such as lunch and learn sessions. It provides a broad spectrum of Jewish input by coopting rabbis, youth workers, knowledgeable lay men and women, representatives of various Jewish organisations and visiting speakers from abroad. It also runs training programmes for non-Jewish teachers who are teaching Judaism. Its magazine, *Juicy*, is published each term. Schools' J-Link

currently visits over 70 schools in the London area and meets upwards of 5,000 young Jews in the course of the school year. *Dir.* Rabbi Arye Forta, BA; *Public Relations Off.* Mrs Susan Bolsom.

SCHOOLS

Akiva School, Levy House, The Sternberg Centre, 80 East End Road, N3 2SY. ☎ 020-8349 4980. (Est. 1981.) Primary educ. for pupils, aged 4-11 years, under Reform & Liberal Synagogue auspices. *Head Teacher* Mrs L. Bayfield, B.A. (Hons), PGCE; *Admin.* Mrs V. Chapman.

Avigdor Primary School, 63-67 Lordship Road, N.16. Voluntary-aided school for boys and girls, 3-11. *H.M.* Mrs R. Springer; *Sec.* Mrs Y. Ricketts. ☎ 020-8800 8339.

Clore Shalom School, Hugo Gryn Way, Shenley, Herts WD7 9BL. ☎ 01923 1062730. (Est. 1999) Cross-community, state-aided primary school (4-11), under Liberal, Masorti and Reform auspices. *H.T.* Irene Kay; *Admin.* Angela Peters.

Clore Tikvah School Redbridge, 115 Fullwell Ave., Ilford, Essex IG6 2JN. ☎ 020-8478 3892. (Est. 1999). Cross-community, state-aided primary school (4-11), under Reform, Masorti and Liberal auspices. *H.T.* Michael Jackson, BA, BSc; *Admin.* Mrs Valerie Garnelas.

Gan Aviv Kindergarten, Bushey & District Synagogue, 177–189, Sparrows Herne, Bushey, Herts., WD2 1AJ. ☎ 020-8386 1616. Fax 020-8421 8267. (For children 3-5). *H. Princ.* Rabbi Z. M. Salasnik B.A.; *H. M.* Mrs E. Levine, Cert. Ed.

Hasmonean High School:
Boys, 11/18, Holders Hill Road, NW4 1 NA. ☎ 020-8203 1411. Fax 020-8202 4526.
Girls, 2/4, Page Street, NW7 2EU. ☎ 020-8203 4294. Fax 020-8202 4527.
Recognised by Dept. of Education. Voluntary Aided, London Borough of Barnet. *H. T. Act. Hd.* D. Gilman, B.Ed., Rabbi M. Faculer, Rabbi C. Baddiel, B.A., Mrs B. Perin, B.A.; *Admin.* J. Curzon.

Hasmonean Kindergarten, 8-10 Shirehall Lane, NW4 2PD. ☎ 020-8201 6252. Fax 020-8202 1605 (children 2-4). *Hd.* Mrs M. Knepler.

Hasmonean Primary School, 8-10 Shirehall Lane, NW4 2PD. ☎ 020-8202 7704. Fax 020-8202 1605. (Boys and Girls 4-11.) *Hd.* Mrs J. Rodin, M.Sc. (Ed.Mang.), Cert Ed. Premier Degré (Paris). Rabbi M. Beaton, Rav of the School.

Ilford Jewish Primary School, Carlton Dr, Ilford, Essex IG6 1LZ. ☎ 020-8551 4294. Fax 020-8551 4295. *H. M.*

Immanuel College, (The Charles Kalms, Henry Ronson Immanuel College) 87/91 Elstree Road, Bushey, Herts., WD2 3RH. ☎ 020-8950 0604. Fax: 020-8950 8687. Email: immcoll@rmplc.co.uk (Reg Charity No. 803179) Independent mixed selective school. *H.* Mrs Myrna Jacobs, BA; *Dep. H.* Rabbi D. Radomsky, BA(Hons), MA.; *Sec. Dep. H.* Richard Felsenstein BA(Hons), Cert Ed.

Independent Jewish Day School, 46 Green Lane, NW4 2AH. ☎ 020-8203 2299. Orthodox Primary Sch. & Kindergarten (est. 1979). *Chairman* D. Greenberg. *Princ.* A. A. Kimche, B.A.; *H. T.* Mrs H. Cohen, BA (Hons), PGCE.

Jewish Secondary Schools Movement, Holders Hill Road, NW4. ☎ 020-8203 1411. Fax 020-8202 4526. (Est. 1929.) *Principal.*

J.F.S., 175 Camden Road, NW1 9HD. ☎ 020-7485 9416. Fax 020-7284 3948. (Est. 1958.) *H. T.* Miss R. Robins, B.A., TTHD; *Clerk to Govs.* Mr. N.C.G. Cann, MIM, MInst AM. Goldbloom (Hebrew Studies) Dept.

Kerem House, 18 Kingsley Way, N2 0ER. ☎ 020-8455 7524. (Boys and Girls 3-5.) *H. T.* Mrs D. Rose, Cert. Ed.

Kerem School, Norrice Lea, N2 0RE. ☎ 020-8455 0909. (Boys and Girls 4-11.) *H. Princ.* Rabbi R. Livingstone; *H. T.* Mrs R. Goulden, M. Ed.

King Solomon High School, Forest Road, Barkingside, Ilford Essex IG6 3HB. ☎ 020-8501 2083. Fax 020-8559 9445. *H.M.* A. Falk MA (Cantab), M Ed;

Chairman of Govs. A. Sugar; *H. Corr.* D. Lerner; *Denominational Body:* United Synagogue; *Auth.* London Borough of Redbridge.

Kisharon (Reg. Charity No.: 271519), 1011 Finchley Road, NW11 7HB. ☎ 020-8455 7483. Fax 020-8731 7005. (Est. 1976). *Chairman* S. Greenman; *H. T.* Mrs Ch. Lehman.

Day School: (Mild-Moderate Learning Difficulties, age 3-16). In addition to the subject requirements of the National Curriculum each child has an Individual Educational Programme which focuses on their specific needs. The staff team include a Music Teacher, Music Therapist, Speech Therapist, Consultant Physiotherapist and Occupational Therapist.

Senior Centre 1: Josselson Building, 37 Moss Hall Grove, N12 8PE, 020-8343 9412. Centre 1 offers an independence based programme for young adults with autism aged 16-30. The centre has an on-site established workshop.

Senior Centre 2: Highfield House, 261 Hale Lane, Edgware HA8 8NX, 020-8905 4583. Centre 2 offers further education and vocational opportunities to young adults with mild to moderate learning difficulties. Basic education and religious studies form a basis for the programme, with craft sessions and bookbinding underpinning the students' vocational development. All the students have work experience opportunities in the wider community and attend courses at Barnet College.

Residential Provision: Hannah Schwalbe Home, 48 Leeside Crescent NW11 0LA, offers residential provision for eight young adults with moderate learning difficulties; respite care is available.

Law of Truth Talmudical College (Reg. Charity No.: T31648Z/1), 50 Knightland Road, E5 9HS. *Corr.* 27 Warwick Grove, E5 9HX. ☎ 020-8806 2963. Fax 020-8806 9318. Students: 020-8806 6642. (Est. by Rabbi M. Szneider in Memel, 1911, Frankfurt 1918, London 1938.) *Princ.* Rabbi S. A. Halpern.

Lubavitch Foundation, 107-115 Stamford Hill, N16 5RP. ☎ 020-8800 0022. Fax 020-8809 7324. (Est. 1959.) To further Jewish religious education, identity and commitment. Separate depts. for adult education, summer and day camps, youth clubs and training, univ. counsellors, publications, welfare, and orgs. concerned with Israel. *Princ.* Rabbi N. Sudak; *Dir.* Rabbi S. F. Vogel; *Admin.* Rabbi I. H. Sufrin. Lubavitch House School–Boys' Senior, 133 Clapton Common, E5. ☎ 020-8809 7476. Girls' Senior, 107 Stamford Hill, N16. ☎ 020-8800 0022. *H. M.* Rabbi S. Lew. Boys' Primary, 135 Clapton Common E5. ☎ 020-8800 1044. *H. M.* Rabbi Y. D. Chaiton. Girls' Primary, 113-115 Stamford Hill, N16 5RP. ☎ 020-8800 0022. Fax 020-8809 7324; *Admin.* Mrs S. Sudak. Kindergarten, 107 Stamford Hill, N16. ☎ 020-8800 0022. *H. T.* Mrs F. Sudak. *Librarian* Zvi Rabin, ALA. ☎ 020-8800 5823. Vista Vocational Training, 107 Stamford Hill, N16 5RP. ☎ 020-8802 8772. *Man.* Mrs H. Lew. Women's Centre, 19 Northfield Rd, N16 5RL. ☎ 020-8809 6508. *Admin.* Mrs R. Bernstein. *Publ.* Lubavitch Direct.

Menorah Foundation School, Abbotts Road, Edgware, Middx. HA8 0QS. ☎ 020-8906 9992. Fax 020-8906 9993. *H. T.* Anne Albert Cert.Ed., Dip.Ed.; *Principal* Rabbi H.I. Feldman; *Chairman* Jeremy Kon.

Menorah Grammar School for Boys (Private), Beverley Gdns., NW11 9DG. ☎ 020-8458 8354. Fax 020-8458 1096. *H. M.* Rabbi A. M. Goldblatt.

Menorah Primary School (and Menorah Nursery), Woodstock Avenue, NW11. ☎ 020-8458 1276. Vol. Aided (Lond. Borough of Barnet) for Boys & Girls 3-11. (Est. 1944.) *Princ.* Rabbi H.I. Feldman; *Hd.* Mrs S. Kestenbaum.

Michael Sobell Sinai School, Shakespeare Dr, Kenton, Harrow, Middx HA3 9UD. ☎ 020-8204 1550. (Est. 1981.) Vol. aided primary sch. for boys & girls, aged 3-11. *Chairman Govs.* Mrs C. Hart; *H. T.* Mrs V. Orloff; *H. Corr.* D. Lerner; *Denominational body* Bd. of Rel. Educ.; *Auth.* Lond. Borough of Brent.

MST College (formerly Massoret), 240-242 Hendon Way, NW4 3NL. ☎ 020-8202 2212. ☎/Fax 020-8203 2212. Orthodox women's college providing tertiary education and professional training. Operates within four faculties – Education (Teacher Training); Health and Community Care; Art, Design and Technology; I.T. (Computing) and Business Studies. Full-time and part-time courses combined with essential Torah and Hebrew studies. *Dean* Mrs J. Nemeth; *Exec. Dir.* Mrs O. Joseph.

Naima Jewish Preparatory School, 21 Andover Place, NW6 5ED. ☎ 020-7328 2802. Small caring school for children aged 3-11 years offering a broad secular curriculum together with rich programme of Orthodox Jewish studies. Catering for all children of all abilities through flexible learning programme. *H. Princ.* Rabbi Dr A. Levy; *Hd. T.* Mrs K. Peters.

North-West London Jewish Day School, 180 Willesden Lane, NW6 7PP. ☎ 020-8459 3378. Fax 020-8451 7298. Website: www.nwljds.brent.sch.uk. Email: admin@nwljds.brent.sch.uk. Voluntary Aided. Orthodox Primary sch. and nursery for boys and girls, 3-11 (Est. 1945). *Principal* Dayan J. Binstock; *H. M. D.* Collins, B.Sc., Dip. Ed. Admin., A.C.P.

Pardes House Primary School, Hendon Lane, N3 1SA. ☎ 020-8343 3568. *H. Princ.* Rabbi E. Halpern. *Head* Rabbi Y. Royde. Kindergarten: Golders Grn. Syn., Dunston Rd., NW11. *Matron* Mrs Y. Wilhelm.

Pardes House Grammar School, Hendon Lane, N3 1SA. ☎ 020-8343 3568. *H. Princ.* Rabbi E. Halpern; *Head* M. Rabbi D. Dunner.

Scopus Jewish Educational Trust Schools: (see p.41)
Harry & Abe Sherman Rosh Pinah Jewish Primary School Glengall Road, Edgware, HA8 8TE. ☎ 020-8958 8599. (Est. 1956.) *H. Princ.* Rev. S. Amias, M.B.E.; *H. T.* Mrs. H. Glekin, M.A., PGCE.
Sebba Rosh Pinah Nursery School and Play Group, Mowbray Road, Edgware, Middx., HA8 8JL. ☎ 020-8958 1597. For children aged 2½-5. *H. T.* Mrs B. Mailer, Dip. Ed. (SA).
Mathilda Marks-Kennedy School, 68 Hale Lane, NW7 3RT. ☎ 020-8959 6089. (Est. 1959.) For children between 2½-11, emphasising traditional Jewish education within a Zionist framework. *H. Princ.* Rev. R. Turner; *H. T.* Mrs Jean Shindler, B.Ed., Dip. Ed.
Simon Marks Jewish Primary School & Nursery, 75 Cazenove Road (cnr. Kyverdale Road), N16 6PD. ☎ 020-8806 6048. Fax 020-8442 4722. *H.T.* Mrs L. Last, B.Ed(Hons); *H. Principal* Rev. R. Turner.

Sharon Kindergarten, Finchley Synagogue, Kinloss Gdns., N3 3DU. ☎ 020-8346 2039. (For children 2½-5.) *H. T.* Mrs E. Elek.

Torah Centre Trust, 84 Leadale Road, N15 6BH. ☎ 020-8802 3586. (Est. 1975.) To provide full or part-time facilities for children, in particular those from 'uncommitted' families, to enable them to further their secular and Hebrew educ. *Chairman* Rabbi J. Dunner; *Educ. Dir.* Rabbi M. Bernstein, B.Ed.

Wolfson Hillel Primary School, 154 Chase Road, Southgate, N14 4LG. ☎ 020-8882 6487. Fax 020-8882 7965. (Est. 1992). Vol. aided primary school for boys & girls aged 3-11. *Chairman Govs.* P. Musgrave; *H. T.* Mrs S. Margolis. (United Synagogue Board of Religious Educ.; *Auth.* London Borough of Enfield.)

Yeshiva Gedola, 3/5 Kingsley Way, N2. ☎ 020-8455 3262. *Rosh Yeshiva* Rabbi I. M. Hertz.

Yeshivah Ohel Moshe Etz Chaim, 85 Bridge Lane, NW11.(Reg. Charity No. 312232) ☎ 020-8458 5149. *Princ.* Rabbi Z. Rabi.

Yesodey Hatorah Schools, 2 and 4 Amhurst Park, N16 SAE. ☎ 020-8800 8612. (Est. 1943.) *Princ.* Rabbi A. Pinter; *V. President* Rabbi C. Pinter.
Yesodey Hatorah Nursery, 2 Amhurst Pk., N16 SAE. ☎ 020-8800 9221. *Hd.* Mrs R. Greenberg.
Yesodey Hatorah Kindergarten, 2 Amhurst Pk., N16 5AE. ☎ 020-8800 8612. *Matron* Mrs B. Gottlieb.
Yesodey Hatorah Primary School (Boys), 2 Amhurst Pk., N16 SAE. ☎ 020-8800 8612. *Princ* Rabbi A. Pinter; *Menahel* Rabbi D. Mapper.

Yesodey Hatorah Senior School (Boys), 4 Amhurst Pk., N16 5AE. ☎ 020-8800 8612. *Princ.* Rabbi A. Pinter; *Menahel* Rabbi D. Mapper.
Yesodey Hatorah Primary School (Girls), 153 Stamford Hill, N16 5LG. ☎ 020-8800 8612. *Princ.* Rabbi A. Pinter; *H. M.* Mrs D. Luria; *Dep. H. M.* Mrs C. Berger.
Yesodey Hatorah Senior School (Girls), 153 Stamford Hill, N16 5LG. ☎ 020-8800 8612. *Princ.* Rabbi A. Pinter; *H. M.* Mrs R. Pinter

WELFARE ORGANISATIONS

Abbeyfield (Camden) Society, 178 Walm Lane, London NW2 3AX. ☎ 020-8452 7375. The Abbeyfield Camden Society runs two small residential homes for the able-bodied elderly, with facilities for short-stay visitors. Each resident has his/her own room for which they are responsible, and lunch and supper are provided by the resident housekeeper in the communal dining-room. We aim to preserve independence within a secure and friendly community. *Chairman* Mrs B. Richenberg, 16 Greenacre Walk, Cannon Hill, N14 7DB. *Hon. Sec.* Mrs J. Kessler, 20 Seaforth Gdns., N21 3BS. Branches: Peggy Lang House, 178 Walm Lane, NW2 3AX. Lily Montagu House, 36-38 Orchard Dr, Stanmore, Middx. HA8 7SD.

Agudas Israel Housing Association Ltd., 206 Lordship Rd., N16 5ES. ☎ 020-8802 3819. Fax 020-8809 6206 (Reg. Charity No. 23535.)
Schonfeld Square Development, Fradel Lodge Sheltered Accommodation and Beis Pinchos Residential Home (Reg. Charity No. 1049179). ☎ 020-8802 7477. *Chief Exec.* Mrs Ita Symons, MBE.

Ajex Housing Association Ltd. ☎ 020-8802 3348 Warden. Fax 020-8880 1117. Registered as a Charitable Housing Assoc. (No. 256140). Provides flatlets for elderly and disabled ex-servicemen and women and/or their dependants. *Chairman* H. Newman; *H. Sec.* A. Lawson; *Admin.* Ajex House, East Bank, N16 5RT.

Arbib Lucas Trust (Reg. Charity No. 208666). Provides financial assistance to women in reduced circumstances. *H. Sec.* Mrs Anita Kafton, 16 Sunny Hill, NW4 4LL.

Bnai Brith JBG Housing Association, Harmony Close, Princes Park Ave. NW11 0JJ. ☎ 020-8381 4901. Fax 020-8458 1772. *Chairman* E. Shapiro; *T. L.* Sterling; *Chief Exec.* S. Clarke. The Association owns and/or manages sheltered housing in London, Hertfordshire and Kent. Supported housing for people with special needs is managed on the Association's behalf by Jewish Care and Norwood Ravenswood. Short-term accommodation for young people is located in Golders Green.

Camp Simcha, 19 Ambrose Ave., London NW11 9AP. ☎ 020-8731 6788. Fax 020-8207 0568. (Est. 1994. Reg. Charity No. 1044685) London-based charity to help improve the quality of life for children with cancer. Kosher summer camp in the USA and a full year activity programme. *Chief Exec.* Meir Plancey.

Drugsline Chabad (Reg. Charity No. 1067573), 372 Cranbrook Road, Gants Hill, Ilford, Essex IG2 6HW. Crisis Helpline: Freephone 0800 731 0713 or 020-8518 6470. Office: 020-8554 3220. Fax: 020-8518 2126. Drop in service for those people with drug-related problems, their families and friends. Drug and alcohol education services offered to schools, youth clubs and other organisations. *Dir.* Rabbi Aryeh Sufrin.

Finchley Kosher Lunch Service, (Meals-on-Wheels for the housebound and disabled), Covers Edgware, Finchley, Golders Green, Hampstead Garden Suburb, Hendon, Mill Hill. *H. T.* Mrs Ruth Freed, ☎ 020-8202 8129. Admin. by the League of Jewish Women. (See p.4)

Food for the Jewish Poor, To provide (a) food throughout the year; (b) grocery during Passover; (c) special relief for approved emergency cases. (See Jewish Care).

Friends of the Kingsbury Mikveh − Educational and Support Group, Kingsbury United Synagogue, Kingsbury Green, NW9 8XR. ☎ 020-8204 6390. *Hon.T.*

Janet Rabson, 16 Broadfields Ave., Edgware, HA8 8PG. ☎ 020-8958 9035.
Friends of the Sick (Chevrat Bikkur Cholim), (Reg. Charity No. 91468A), 463a
Finchley Road, NW3 6HN. ☎ 020-7435 0836. (Est. 1947.) To nurse sick and
aged needy persons in their own homes. *President* Peter Gillis; *H. T. M.*
Wechsler; *Gen. Sec.* Mrs E. Weitzman.
Hagadolim Charitable Organisation (Est. 1950.) To provide financial assistance to
Homes and charities in England and Israel, and to visit and provide comforts in
private homes in the Home Counties. *Chairman* L. Dunitz; *Jt. Ts.* B. Wallach,
Mrs R. J. Dunitz; *Sec.* Mrs S. Levy, 4 Edgwarebury Ct., Edgwarebury La.,
Edgware, Middx. HA8 8LP. ☎ 020-8958 8558.
Haven Foundation (Regd. Charity No. 264029), Alfred House, 1 Holly Park,
Crouch Hill, N4 4BN. ☎ 020-7272 1345 (Admin. by Ravenswood Foundation).
Est. 1971. To provide permanent residential care and development training for
Jewish mildly mentally handicapped adults in its hostel, group homes and soc.
development unit. L. *President* Eve Alfred; *Chairman* N. Freeder; *Jt. V. Chairman*
R. Rosenberg, A.C.A.
Hospital Kosher Meals Service (Reg. Charity No.: 1025601), Lanmor House,
370/386 High Road, Wembley, Middx. HA9 6AX. ☎ 020-8795 2058. Fax 020-
8900 2462. Email hkms@compuserve.com. Provides supervised kosher meals to
patients in hospitals throughout Greater London. *Chairman* M.G. Freedman,
M.Sc., F.C.A.; *V. Chairman* H. Glyn, B.Sc., FRICS; *H. T. M.* Blum, F.C.A.
Admin. Mrs E. Stone.
Jewish Aged Needy Pension Society (Est. 1829.) Provides pensions for members of
the Jewish community aged 60 or over, who have known better times and who,
in their old age, find themselves in reduced circumstances. Also supplements
income provided from statutory sources. Services to the middle-class of society
who find themselves in greater financial need and who do not seem to fall with-
in the purview of any other charitable organisations. *President* I. Lewisohnv; *Ts.*
R. W. Gollance, M. E. G. Prince; *H. Sec.* Mrs G. B. Rigal; *Sec./Admin.* Mrs Sheila
A. Taylor, 34 Dalkeith Grove, Stanmore, Middx. ☎ 020-8958 5390.
Jewish Bereavement Counselling Service (Est. 1980. Reg. Charity No. 1047473),
P.O. Box 6748, London N3 3BX. ☎/Fax 020-8349 0839 (24 hour answerphone).
Offers bereavement counselling provided by trained voluntary counsellors under
supervision and support to members of the Jewish community who have been
bereaved. Covers North and NW London. *Chairman* Joy Conway, *Co-ord.* Sandra
Shavick, *Consults.* Roni Goldberg, Jacqueline Toff.
Jewish Blind & Disabled (JBD), the working name of the Jewish Blind & Physically
Handicapped Society, a company limited by guarantee. Reg. Charity No.
259480. Head Office: 118 Seymour Place, London W1H 5DJ. Care &
Campaign Office: 164 East End Road, London N2 0RR. ☎ 020-8883 1000. Fax
020-8444 6729. Email: info@jbd.org. Jewish Blind & Disabled (JBD) provides
caring sheltered housing with communal and welfare services for visually and
physically disabled people, to improve the quality of life, maximise freedom of
choice, respect dignity at all times and help achieve independent living.
    JBD is an independent charity providing independent living. Founded in 1969
by the late Cecil Rosen, who recognised the need for purpose-built, sheltered
housing for blind, partially sighted and disabled people of all ages, within the
community. JBD currently has five modern sheltered projects providing 192 purpose-built apartments able to accommodate up to 300 residents. Resident House
Managers are on site twenty-four hours a day. Jewish Blind & Disabled is the
UK's largest Jewish sheltered housing provider for blind and disabled people.
Chairman John Joseph; *Hon. Chief Exec.* Malcolm J. Ozin; *Housing & Care Dir.*
David A. Brodtman; *Campaign Dir.* Jason J. Ozin; *Trust Dir.* Marilyn Leveson.
JBD Projects: *Sheltered housing schemes:* Fairacres, 164 East End Road, Finchley,
N2; Cherry Tree Court, Roe Green, Kingsbury, NW9; Cecil Rosen Court, 331
East Lane, North Wembley, Middx; Milne Court, 14 Churchfields, South

Woodford, E18; Hilary Dennis Court, 34 Sylvan Road, Wanstead, E11.
Day Centres: Monday Club, Fairacres; Monday Club, Milne Court; Milne Court
Clubbers; Tuesday Club, Hilary Dennis Court; Wednesday Club, Cherry Tree
Court, Kingsbury.
Hostel: Pulham Avenue, Finchley, N2.
Jewish Blind Society (incorporating Jewish Assn. for the Physically Handicapped).
See below: Jewish Care.
Jewish Care, a company limited by guarantee. Reg. in England No.: 2447900, Stuart
Young House, 221 Golders Green Road, London NW11 9DQ. ☎ 020-8922 2000,
Fax. 020-8922 1998. Formed on 1st January 1990 by the merger of the Jewish
Blind Society (est. 1819) and the Jewish Welfare Board (est. 1859, Reg. Charity
No. 802559). Since then the following organisations have also merged their activ-
ities with Jewish Care: The Jewish Home & Hospital at Tottenham; Food for the
Jewish Poor (Soup Kitchen); Jewish Assn. for the Physically Handicapped; Brit.
Tay-Sachs Foundation; Waverley Manor (Friends of the London Jewish Hospital).;
Brighton and Hove Jewish Home: Stepney Jewish (B'nai B'rith) Clubs and
Settlement; Redbridge Jewish Youth and Community Centre.
    Services are provided for over five thousand elderly, mentally ill, visually impaired
and physically disabled people and their families every single day. Resources include
residential and nursing homes, hostels, day centres, sheltered housing, domiciliary
care and social work teams in London and South East England.
    Jewish Care is Anglo-Jewry's largest social services organisation catering for
the needs of the community living in London and south-east England. The
organisation provides a wide and comprehensive range of services employs over
1,500 people and works in partnership with nearly 2,500 volunteers. Jewish
Care relies on funds from generous donations from members of the community,
central and local government, and from The European Union which help Jewish
Care in its mission to provide the highest quality of service and ensure that people who are not in a position to pay can still receive our help. Jewish Care has a
current budget of £34 million. *President* The Lord Levy; *Chairman* Malcolm
Dagul; *Chief Exec.* Melvyn I. Carlowe; *Finance Dir.* Henry Solomon.
Establishments administered by Jewish Care:
    Residential Homes -
    Braemar Royal, Bournemouth; Carlton Dene (holiday home), Bournemouth;
Charles Clore, N10; Brighton & Hove Jewish Home; Ella & Ridley Jacobs, NW4;
Kay Court, NW3; Lady Sarah Cohen House, N11; Morton House, Hemel
Hempstead; Raymond House, Southend-on-Sea; Rela Goldhill Lodge (specialist
for younger people with a physical disablity), NW11; Rubens, N3; Sarah Tankel,
N5; Vi & John Rubens, Redbridge; Waverley Manor, NW4; Wolfson House, N4.
    Day Centres -
    Michael Sobell Community Centre, NW11; Stamford Hill Community
Centre, N16; Redbridge Jewish Day Centre (in conjunction with Redbridge
Jewish Youth & Com. Centre); Stepney Jewish Day Centre (in conjunction with
B'nai B'rith), E1; Southend & Westcliff Jewish Day Centre.
    Special Day Care Units -
    The Dennis Centre, Ilford; Sam Beckman Special Day Care Centre, NW4;
Stanmore & Edgware Special Day Care Centre; Stepney Special Day Care Unit,
E1; Wolfson House Special Day Care Centre, N4.
    Specialist units: Employment Resource Centre, N3; Holocaust Survivors
Centre, NW4; Carers' Centre, NW11.
    Flatlet Schemes (sheltered housing) -
    Shine House (in conjunction with JBG Housing Ltd), N3; Maitland House (in
conjunction with JBG Housing Ltd), Hemel Hempstead; Rosetta House (in con-
junction with JBG Housing Ltd), Hemel Hempstead; Rabbi Pinchas Shebson
Lodge, Southend-on-Sea; Sir John & Lady Cohen Court (Joel Emanual Almshouse
Trust), N.16; Posnansky Court (in conjuction with JBG Housing Ltd), N4.

Mental Health Provision -
Mitkadem, Ilford; The Sholom Centre, NW11; 7A Mapesbury Road (therapeutic hostel), NW2.
   Social Work Teams - c/o Help desk ☎ 020-8922 2222.
Jewish Children's Holidays Fund (Formerly The Jewish Branch of the Children's Country Holidays Fund). (Reg. Charity No.: 295361). (Est. 1888.) *President* Mrs Joyce Kemble, JP; *Chairman* Ian Donoff; *Sec.* Mrs F. Warshawsky, 5 Goodwood Close, Marsh Lane, Stanmore HA7 4HY. ☎ 020-8950 3383.
Jewish Crisis Help Line, Miyad. ☎ 0345 581999. Confidential listening service for those experiencing stress in their lives. Sponsored by the Jewish Marriage Council.
Jewish Deaf Association, Julius Newman House, Woodside Park Rd., London N12 8RP. ☎ 020-8446 0502 (voice and Minicom). Fax 020-8445 7451; Email: jda@dircon.co.uk. (Reg. Charity No. 209892). Provides a welfare and social environment for the profoundly deaf and hearing-impaired. Maintains a Day Centre for deaf people. Runs an Advisory and Resource Room exhibiting aids to daily living for deaf and hard of hearing people of all ages. ☎ 020-8446 0214. *President* G. M. Gee, J.P.; *Chairman* Mrs E. Gee; *Exec. Dir.* Mrs P. Goldring; *H. Chaplain* Rev. M. Plaskow, M.B.E.
Jewish Society for the Mentally Handicapped, now merged with Norwood Ravenswood (see below).
Jewish Welfare Board (incorporating the Jewish Bread, Meat and Coal Society, est. 1779), see Jewish Care, above.
Jews' Temporary Shelter (Reg. Charity no. 212071), 1-2 Endsleigh St., WC1H 0DS. ☎/Fax 020-7387 7447. *Admin.* Mrs R. Lewis.
Lewis Hammerson Memorial Home, Hammerson House, The Bishop's Avenue, N2 OBE. ☎ 020-8458 4523. Fax 020-8458 2537. (Est. 1962, Reg. Charity No. 286002.) *President* Mrs S. Hammerson, O.B.E.; *Chairman* Philip Balcombe. Applications for admission: 020-8458 4523.
MIYAD: Jewish Telephone Crisis Line, ☎ 020-8203 6211, 0345 581999. Sponsored by the Jewish Marriage Council. Confidential telephone line offered to the Jewish community for people needing help in crisis situations.
Necessitous Ladies' Fund, incorporating Delissa Joseph Memorial Fund (both funds founded by Union of Jewish Women). For the relief of Jewish women who are in need, hardship or distress (Reg. Charity No. 266921 A3L1). *Chairman* Mrs Freda Davis; *H. Sec.* Mrs D. Curzon, 14 Blessington Close, SE13 5ED.
Nightingale House (Home for Aged Jews), 105 Nightingale Lane, SW12 8NB. ☎ 020-8673 3495. Fax 020-8675 2258 (Est. 1840, Reg. Charity No. 207316) *Patrons* Lord Rayne, Mrs V. Duffield, C.B.E.; *Chairman* G. Lipton; *Jt Ts.* M. Lawson; L. Green, FCA; K. Goodman, FCA; *Exec. Dir.* Leon Smith. Aid Societies: N.W. London; S.W. London; The Nightingales; Nightingale Ladies' Cttee. Bazaar; The Kentongales. Also manages Rayne House sheltered housing flats.
Norwood Ravenswood, Broadway House, 80/82, The Broadway, Stanmore, HA7 4HB. ☎ 020-8954 4555. Fax 020-8420 6800. Email: Norwood@ort.org. Locally based social service teams are in Hackney (020-8880 2244), North West London (020-8203-3030), Edgware (020-8951 5977), Redbridge (020-8550 6114). Norwood Ravenswood is now the largest Jewish child and family services charity in Europe, working with over 6,000 children, young people, adults, people with learning disabilities and their families every year. We will provide a 'one stop' family service where children can if necessary continue to receive ongoing help throughout their lives. Included are: **Community services** offering a comprehensive range of counselling and support services to children and their families, dealing with problems of child abuse, financial hardship and family breakdown. Extensive community services are also provided to people with learning disabilities and their families, including **Unity** and **Links** providing recreation schemes for children and adults. The Deli and Horticultural Project provide vocational training.

Residential services include an adolescent unit, semi-independent bedsits, a respite care house, a network of community homes and Ravenswood Village. Day services include the **Kennedy Leigh Centre** and **Family Centre** in Hendon and many day opportunity schemes for young people and adults. **Binoh** is our special educational needs service (see p.90), and the Association for Jewish Youth provides training and development services for youth organisations. **Koleinu** is an activity-based service for young Jewish deaf people. **Buckets and Spades Lodge** is Norwood Ravenswood's respite care house. *Patron* HM The Queen; *President* Sir Trevor Chinn; *Chairman* Ronald Gottlieb, OBE; *Exec. Dir.* Norma Brier, MSc.

Raphael Centre (a Jewish Counselling Service) (Reg. Charity No. 278522), c/o Shalvata, Parson St., Hendon, NW1 4EB. ☎ 020-8203 9881 (24 hour). Aims: To provide short- or long-term counselling by professional counsellors and psychotherapists for Jewish people with emotional or psychological problems, such as depression, stress, anxiety, loss or bereavement, relationship or family problems. Counselling supports, and helps with personal growth and the development of personal resources. A contribution is requested within every client's means. *Contact*: Ruth Barnett.

Rishon Multiple Sclerosis Aid Group, 1 Mersham Dr, Kingsbury NW9 9PP. ☎ 020-8204 8622. (Est. 1966. Reg. Charity No. 252359) Affiliated to the Multiple Sclerosis Society of Great Britain. Provides social and cultural activities, help and welfare, for Multiple Sclerosis sufferers and raises funds for this and the encouragement of research into the causes and cure of the disease. *H. Sec.* B. Gold.

Stamford Hill Community Centre, 91-93 Stamford Hill, N16 5TP. ☎ 020-8800 5672. Fax 020-8800 1678 (Reg. Charity No. 802559). Administered by Jewish Care. Community Centre for the elderly and visually handicapped and others with special needs. *Director:* Mrs B. Hart.

Sunridge Housing Association Ltd., 76 The Ridgeway, NW11 8PT. ☎ 020-8458 3389; *Chairman* David Stern; *H. Sec.* Robin Michaelson. *Man.* Mrs M. Lewis.

Westlon and Westmount, 850 Finchley Road, NW111 6BB. ☎ 020-8201 8484. Fax 020-8731 8847. Two separate organisations share this address:
Westlon Housing Association. *H. L. President* His Hon. Alan King-Hamilton, Q.C.; *President* H. Steel; *Chairman* Jennifer Ellis; *Admin.* J.W. Silverman. **Annette White Lodge**, 287/289 High Road, N2 8HB. **Deborah Rayne House**, 33b Sunningfields Road, NW4 4QX. **The Woodville**, Woodville Road, W5 2SE. Applications to 020-8201 8484.
Westmount Charitable Trust (Est. 1978) and **Westmount Housing Association.** *Chairman* Mrs E. Corob; *T. S.* Corob; *Sec.* Mrs S. Berg; *Admin.* J.W. Silverman. Accommodation and amenities for the elderly. **Westmount**, 126 Fortune Green Road, NW6 1DN. Residence for 40 elderly persons. Applications to 020-8201 8484.

Yad Voezer, 80 Queen Elizabeth's Walk, N16 5UQ. ☎/Fax 020-8809 4303. (Est. 1975, Reg. Charity No. 277771) Care for Jewish children and adults with learning disabilities. Services include residential/respite care, Sunday and Holiday Clubs, day care, employment schemes, advice, counselling and family support. Services are managed and run within the N16 area. *Chairman* Rabbi E. Landau; *Ts.* R. Spitzer, S. Singer; *President* Lady A. Jakobovits; *Exec. Dir.* Zelda Landau.

Clubs and Cultural Societies

See also under Synagogues (pp.76–88); Organisations concerned with Jewish Youth (pp.46–54).
London Diary of Jewish Events, 12 Holne Chase, N2 0QN. ☎ 020-8458 2466. Fax 020-8458 5457. (Est. 1995) Monthly publication listing events organised by Jewish institutions for the Jewish community in London. *Ed.* Jazmin Naghar.
London Jewish News (incorporating New Moon), 28 St Albans Lane, NW11 7QE. ☎ 020-8731 8031. Fax 020-8381 4033.

Alyth Choral Society, North Western Reform Synagogue, Alyth Gdns., NW11 7EN. ☎ 020-8455 6763 (Est. 1983.) *Musical Dir.* Vivienne Bellos; *Chairman* R. Goldman; *Sec.* Ms. C. Holmes.

Association of Jewish Friendship Clubs, 26 Enford St., W1H 2DD. ☎ 020-7724 8100. Fax 020-7724 8203 (Head Office). An umbrella organisation for men and women in the 60-plus age group, providing companionship throughout 70 clubs in London and the Provinces. A network of social clubs joining together for activities on a national basis, e.g. group holidays and central London based functions. *Jt Hon. Life Presidents* Lady Jakobovits and Rabbanit Elaine Sacks; *National Chairman* Mrs Anita Daniels; *Hon. Chaplain* Rev. Dr Norman Gale, BA.

Besht Tellers, Maccabi House, 33 Abbey Road, NW8 0AT. ☎/Fax 020-7624 4343. Email: beshttellers@compuserve.com. Professional Jewish Theatre company producing national and international public performances of original Jewish Theatre. Touring community performances, music, and educational workshops available for booking. *Dir.* Rebecca Wolman; *Educ. Dir.* Gabrielle Moss.

Brady-Maccabi, Youth and Community Centre, 4 Manor Pk. Cresc., Edgware, Middx. HA8 7NL. ☎ 020-8952 2948. Fax 020-8952 2393. (Est. 1979.) Open Sun. to Thurs. Snr. Citizens clubs meet Tues. and Thurs. aft. *President* John Cutner J.P., F.C.A.; *Chairman* Stuart Ansher; *Dir.* Miss S. Muscovitch.

Chabad Lubavitch Centre (Reg. Charity No. 227638), 372 Cranbrook Rd., Ilford, Essex IG2 6HW. ☎ 020-8554 1624. Fax 020-8518 2126. (Est. 1986). *Dir.* Rabbi A.M. Sufrin; *Programme Co-ord.* Rabbi M. Muller.

Friends of Jewish Youth, formerly Old Boys' Association. Martin Shaw, c/o A. J. Y., 128 East Lane, Wembley, Middx. ☎ 020-8908 4747. Fax 020-8904 4323.

Friends of Yiddish *Contact* Chaim Neslen, 232 Cranbrook Road, Ilford, Essex IG1 4UT. ☎ 020-8554 6112. We meet every Saturday afternoon at Toynbee Hall, nr Aldgate East Tube Station, from 3 to 4.30pm. Our programme is entirely in Yiddish, and includes readings, live music and some discussion in a friendly and relaxed environment. Special events are advertised in the Jewish press.

The Half-Empty Bookcase, for Progressive Jewish Women's Studies, 80 East End Rd., N3 2SY. ☎ 020-8447 8444. *Co-ord.* Dee Eimer.

Institute for Jewish Music Studies and Performance, 33 Seymour Pl. W1H 6AT. ☎ 020-7723 4404. (Est. 1982) To further the study and knowledge of Jewish music, both liturgical and secular, at the highest academic and performing level. *Dir.* S. Fixman.

Jewish Appreciation Group Tours, 32 Anworth Close, Woodford Green, Essex IG8 0DR ☎ 020-8504 9159. (Est. 1960.) Full history tours of the Jewish East End and the Jews in England from 1066. Historic walks and tours throughout the year. *Tours Org.* Adam Joseph.

Jewish Association of Cultural Societies (J.A.C.S.), Edgware Synagogue, Edgware Way, Edgware Middx. HA8 9YE. ☎ 020-8954 1353. (Est. 1978.) Twenty-eight clubs have been opened throughout the Greater London com., with two in Surrey, one in Bournemouth, one in Brighton, one in Westcliff-on-Sea and one in Cardiff, providing weekly meetings for the 50+, embracing cultural and social programmes. *H. President* Rev. Saul Amias, M.B.E.; *Nat. Chairman* Mrs Annette Pearlman; *H. Sec.* Mrs Lonnie Levey.

Jewish Research Group, c/o 43 Churchill Ct., Ainsley Close, Edmonton, N9 9XJ. ☎ 020-8364 3518. The Jewish Research Group is an autonomous part of the Edmonton Hundred Historical Society and was established in 1978 when the Committee of the 1st Jewish Way of Life Exhibition, held to mark the 50th Anniversary of the Palmers Green and Southgate Synagogue, decided not to disband. The main aim of the J.R.G. is to research Jewish history in the 'Edmonton Hundred', which corresponds approximately to the boundaries of the London Boroughs of Enfield and Haringey, and to publish its findings.

Current membership: 100. Monthly meetings are held at which prominent speakers are invited to address the Group on Jewish historical subjects. Five publications have been printed under the title of 'Heritage'. *President* Mrs Marjorie Glick, BA; *Chairman* Harry Balkin, BA; *V. Chairman* Anita Shapiro; *H. Sec.* Jeffrey Baum; *H. T.* Harold Temerlies.

Kadimah/Victoria Youth Club (Reg. Charity No.: 299323), 127/129 Clapton Common, E5 9AB. ☎ 020-8809 3618. Catering for the traditional and non-traditional Ashkenazi and Sephardi communities. Membership for 5-14 yrs. *Senior Youth Workers* G. Nissim, C. Jackson; *Chairman* Yoel Salem.

L'Chaim Society, Cricklewood Business Centre (Ground Floor), Cricklewood Lane, Cricklewood, NW2 1ET. ☎ 020-88830 5533. Fax 020-8830 5530.

London Jewish Male Choir. *H. Sec.* Bernard Jackson, 62 Rotherwick Rd., NW11 7DB. ☎ 020-8458 6803. Fax 020-8731-8722. (Inland Revenue Number: X 91533). Rehearsals Thurs. evgs., Hendon Synagogue.

Lubavitch of South London (Reg. Charity No. 227638), 42 St. George's Road, Wimbledon, SW19 4ED. ☎ 020-8944 1581. Fax 020-8944 7563. Email lubwdon@aol.com (Est. 1988) Adult Jewish educ., library, food and bookshop, mailings, assemblies, tuition, Mitzva campaigns, youth activities. *Dir.* Rabbi Nissan Dubov.

The Maccabaeans (Est. 1891.) Consisting primarily of those engaged in professional pursuits, its aims being to provide 'social intercourse and co-operation among its members with a view to the promotion of the interests of Jews, including the support of any professional or learned bodies and charities'. *President* Rt. Hon. Sir John Balcombe; *H. T.* D. D. Rosenfelder; *H. Sec.* L. Slowe, 4 Corringway, NW11 7ED.

Manor House Society, Sternberg Centre for Judaism, Manor House, 80 East End Road, N3 2SY. ☎ 020-8346 2288. Fax 020-8343 0901. Jewish cultural soc. providing art exhibitions, concerts and many other activities. *Chairman* L. Hepner; *Admin.* Mrs P. Lewis. Quarterly journal: 'Manna'.

Oxford & St. George's (Reg. Charity No. 207191), 120 Oakleigh Road North, N20 9EZ. ☎ 020-8446 3101. Communal provision and youth clubs.

Redbridge Jewish Community Resource Centre (JPMP), Sinclair House, Woodford Bridge Road, Ilford, Essex, IG5 4LN. ☎ 020-8551 0017. Fax 020-8551 9027. The Resource Centre is a creative dynamic centre for informal Jewish and Zionist education. The Centre has operated in the community for ten years as a resource for educators who require support and advice in this field. The Resource Centre is a focus for leadership training in the community. The Redbridge Jewish Community Resource Centre is a Sinclair House project in association with JPMP (see p.48).

Redbridge Jewish Youth and Community Centre (Reg. Charity No.: 3013185), Sinclair House, Woodford Bridge Road, Ilford, Essex, IG4 5LN. ☎ 020-8551 0017. Fax 020-8551 9027. *Chairman Man. Cttee.* Bernard Sinclair; *Dir.* Neil Taylor. Sinclair House, home of the Redbridge Jewish Youth and Community Centre, meets the social, educational and welfare needs of all sections of the Redbridge and District Jewish Community. More than 3,500 people make use of the centre's facilities each week. The Redbridge Jewish Day Centre provides a high level of essential care for over 450 elderly and disabled people. There are programmes and services for young people, including those with special needs, and social, educational, welfare and active sports programmes for young and adults alike. The Centre is also the base for the Community Shlicha, Clayhall Synagogue, Redbridge Jewish Community Resource Centre (JPMP), the Redbridge Jewish Youth Council and many communal events and activities. The Redbridge Jewish Youth and Community Centre is now part of Jewish Care.

Spec Jewish Youth and Community Centre (Reg. Charity No. 302921), 87 Brookside South, East Barnet, Herts EN4 8LL. ☎ 020-8368 5117. Fax 020-8368 0891. Email spec@ort.org. Est. 1962 to enable Jewish young people to meet in

a secure environment and offer opportunities for personal growth. Activities include youth clubs for 5½-16 age grps. *Chairman* Sharon Lee; *Tr.* J. Hartstone; *H. Sec.* Jeffrey Leifer; *Sec.* Linda Rich.
Stepney Jewish Community Centre, 2-8 Beaumont Grove, E1 4NQ. ☎ 020-7790 6441. Fax 020-7265 8342. (Reg. Charity No. 802559) **Administered by Jewish Care.** Community Centre for the Elderly; Special Care Centre for Physically and Mentally Frail; Kosher Meals on Wheels; and Friendship Clubs. *Centre Man.* Philippa Paine.
Western Charitable Foundation, 32 Gt. Cumberland Place, W1H 7DJ. ☎ 020-7723 7246. *Chairman* Sidney Jaque, J.P.; *V. Chairman* Harold Pasha; *Tr.* W Ward.
Zemel Choir (Reg. Charity No. 252572/ACL), Britain's leading mixed Jewish Choir performing a varied repertoire, with an emphasis on Hebrew, Yiddish, Israeli and liturgical music, and contemporary compositions of Jewish interest. Overseas tours, prestige concerts in London and provinces, recordings, social events. Zemel welcomes enthusiastic and committed singers who read music fairly fluently. Rehearsals most Mondays 8-10.30 p.m. North West London. *Musical Dir.* Vivienne Bellos. *Contact:* Concert Manager Marc Landsman, 26 Larch Close, Friern Barnet, N11 3NN. ☎/Fax 020-8361 3389 (eve.).

Miscellaneous Organisations

ALL ABOARD SHOPS LIMITED
All Aboard operate Charity Shops for the benefit of UK-based Jewish Charities only via their ever-expanding chain of Charity Shops in London and the Provinces. All Aboard welcome donations of clothing, bric-a-brac, etc, and welcome volunteers to assist in the shops and at Head Office. *Exec. Bd.* Stella Lucas, Monique Landau, Jeffrey Pinnick; *Admin.* Carol Marks. ☎ 020-7543 5404/05/15. Fax 020-7973 0130. Shops are located at: **Camden Town**, 59 Camden High Street, London NW1; **Cricklewood**, 14 Cricklewood Broadway, NW2 and 249 Cricklewood Broadway, NW2; **East Finchley**, 124 High Rd., N2; **Edgware**, 1&2 Boot Parade, 88 High St., HA8; **Finchley**, 132 Ballards Lane, N3, 150 Finchley Rd., NW3, 616 Finchley Rd., NW11, 1111, Finchley Rd., NW11; **Golders Green**, 125 Golders Green Road, NW11, 89 Golders Green Road, NW11; **Hendon**, 98 Brent Street, NW4; **Ilford**, 107 Cranbrook Road, Ilford, Essex; **Manchester**, Unit 10, The Longfield Centre, Prestwich, Manchester M25 and 4 Station Bridge, Urmston, Manchester M41; **Paddington**, 12 Spring Street, W2 and 3 Porchester Rd., W2; **Palmers Green**, 321 Green Lanes, N13; **Stamford Hill**, 2a Regent Parade, Amhurst Park, N16; **Streatham**, 83 Streatham High Road, SW16; **Wandsworth**, 107 Wandsworth High St., SW18; **West Hampstead**, 224 West End Lane, NW6; **Westcliff-on-Sea**, 157 Hamlet Court Rd., Westcliff.

LONDON JEWISH MEDICAL SOCIETY
The Medical Society of London, 11 Chandos Street, W1M 0EB. ☎/Fax 020-8383 3162. Fax 020-8383 2029.
(Est. 1928.) A learned society for doctors, senior medical students and members of allied professions. 1999-2000: *President* Dr Bernard Valman; *V. Presidents* Dr Lotte Newman, CBE, Dr John Marks, Dr Adrian Naftalin; *H. Sec.* Dr J. Stern, *H. T.* Dr A. Rinsler.

LONDON SOCIETY OF JEWS AND CHRISTIANS
28 St John's Wood Road, NW8 7HA.
☎ 020-7286 5181. Fax 020-7266 3591.
(Est. 1927.) The oldest interfaith organisation of its kind in the UK, established to give an opportunity to Jews and Christians to confer together on the basis of their common ideals and with mutual respect for differences of religion. *President* The

Rev. Professor Geoffrey Parrinder; *Jt. Chairmen* Rabbi David J. Goldberg, Dr Anthony Harvey; *Memb. Sec.* Margaret Rigal.

VISITATION COMMITTEE
Arranges visits to Jewish patients in hospital in all areas of London. Provides a caring service to Jewish prisoners. Offers a professional counselling service to those who have been bereaved. *Admin.* Josephine Wayne, Adler House, 735 High Road, N12 0US. ☎ 020-8343 8989. Fax 020-8343 6262. *Chairman* Mrs Joy Conway (see also p.8). **Bereavement Counselling Service** (see p.95).

THE REGIONS

Figures in brackets after place names indicate estimated Jewish population (see pp.194-9).

There are Zionist societies in almost every Jewish regional centre, and Women's Zionist societies in most of them.
Details of current burial arrangements have been listed where forthcoming.

Disused cemeteries are maintained by the Board of Deputies of British Jews at a number of towns in the British Isles. General enquiries about these and other locations should be addressed to the Board's Heritage Task Group. **Bath:** Bradford Road, cnr of Greendown Place, abt. 2 miles from town centre. Keys held by City of Bath Probation Office. **Canterbury:** Entrance at end of passageway between 26 and 28 Whitstable Road **Douglas:** Jewish enclosure in municipal cemetery. **Dover:** (maintained by the US) On Old Charlton Road, overlooking the harbour at Copt Hill. **Falmouth:** On main Penryn Road, Ponsharden. Keys from Vospers Garage (adjacent) ☎ 01326-372011. **Ipswich:** In Star Lane, premises of BOCM Pauls Ltd., and Jewish section of municipal cemetery. **King's Lynn:** In Millfleet (pedestrian precinct). Keys from Mr. Colin Drew, West Norfolk District Council, Hardwick Narrows Estate, King's Lynn. **Penzance:** Historic walled Georgian Cemetery; approx. 50 headstones. Passage between 19 and 20 Leskinnick Ter., right at end of arch, cemetery on left. (Access road unsuitable for cars.) Key from Keith Pearce, ☎ 01736-368778. **Sheerness:** Jewish enclosure in municipal cemetery. Another site is behind estate agents at cnr. Hope St./High St. Key from Mr. G. Lancaster, 15 Grange Way, Rochester. **Yarmouth:** On Blackfriars Road, Alma Road, on perimeter of old city walls. Key from Dept. of Technical Services, Gt. Yarmouth Town Hall. (See also **Listed Synagogues and Other Jewish Monuments in the UK**, pp.207-8).

Mikvaoth are maintained in the following centres: Birmingham, Bournemouth, Brighton, Gateshead, Leeds, Leicester, Liverpool, Manchester, Newcastle, Southend, Southport, Sunderland, Cardiff and Glasgow.

Menorah: a magazine for Jewish members of H.M. Forces and Small Jewish Communities is published by the Jewish Committee for H.M. Forces, 25/26 Enford Street, London W1H 2DD.

AMERSHAM (50)
South Bucks. Jewish Community (ULPS).
Services: First Friday each month at 6.30pm at The Friends Meeting House, Whielden St., Amersham. Religion School at Dr Challoner's Grammar School. Enq.: David Sacker, 15 The Willows, HP6 5HT. ☎ 01494 431885. Email sbjc@ulps.org. Elaine Israelson ☎ 01923-721418. **Cemetery:** See Edgwarebury Cemetery (p.89).

BASILDON (Essex) (10)
Services are held in members' homes. *Chairman* M. M. Kochmann, 3 Furlongs, Basildon, Essex SS16 4BW. ☎ 01268 524947. Fax 01268-271358.
Burials arranged through Southend & Westcliff Hebrew Congregation at their cemetery in Southend.

BATH
The last synagogue closed in 1910. Services are currently being revived under the auspices of the Bristol and West Progressive Jewish Congregation (see p.107) at The Friends' Meeting House, York St.

BEDFORD (ca. 30)
In medieval times Bedford was one of the centres of English Jewry. A number of congregations existed at various times from 1803 onwards. The present com. originated during the 1939-45 war.
Hebrew Congregation. *Sec.* R. Berman. ☎ 01234 364723.
See also under Luton for Bedfordshire Progressive Synagogue for Saturday morning services.

BIRMINGHAM (3,000)
This Jewish community is one of the oldest in the provinces, dating from 1730, if not earlier. Birmingham manufacturing attracted early Jewish settlers. In the Anglo-Jewish economy Birmingham's position was similar to a port, a centre from which Jewish pedlars covered the surrounding country week by week, returning to their homes for the Sabbath. The first synagogue of which there is any record was in The Froggery in 1780. But there was a Jewish cemetery in the same neighbourhood in 1730, and Moses Aaron is said to have been born in Birmingham in 1718. The history of the Birmingham community has been investigated by the Birmingham Jewish History Research Group under the leadership of the late Zoë Josephs.
Representative Council of Birmingham and Midland Jewry. (Est. 1937.) *President* R. Diamond, 35 Huntstanton Ave., B17 8SX. ☎ 0121-554 2234; *Chairman* Sir B. Zissman; *H. Sec.* L. Jacobs. ☎ 0121-236 1801; *Admin.* Mrs R. Jacobs, Singers Hill, Blucher St., B1 1QL. ☎ 0121-643 2688. Email: bjrepco@brijnet.org; Website www.brijnet.org//birmingham
Board of Shechita, c/o Hebrew Cong., Singers Hill B1 1HL; *Sec.* B. Gingold.

SYNAGOGUES
Hebrew Congregation, Singers Hill, Ellis Street B1 1HL. ☎ 0121-643 0884. The present syn. was consecrated on September 24, 1856. *M.* Rabbi L. L. Tann; *Admin.* B. Gingold.
Central Synagogue, 133 Pershore Road, B5 7PA. ☎/Fax 0121-440 4044. *M.* Rabbi A. S. Hill; *Sec.* S.Cohen.
Progressive Synagogue (ULPS), 4 Sheepcote Street, B16 8AA. Services Shabat 11.00am. ☎ 0121-643 5640 (9.30 a.m.-1.00 p.m. w/d). *H. Sec.* Mrs S. Conroy, ☎ 0121-449 9300; *M.* Rabbi Dr Margaret Jacobi.

OTHER INSTITUTIONS
Birmingham Jewish Care, 1 Rake Way, Tennant Street, B15 1EG. ☎ 0121-643 2835. Fax 0121-643 5291. *President* R. Jaffa; *Dir.* I. Myers.
Birmingham Jewish Youth Trust, Youth Centre, 19 Sandhurst Road, Birmingham 13. ☎ 0121-442 4459. *Youth Worker* C. Jennings.
Birmingham Rabbinic Board. *Chairman* Rabbi L. Tann ☎ 0121-440 8375.
Birmingham Union of Jewish Students, c/o Hillel House, 26 Somerset Road, Edgbaston, B15 2QD. ☎ 0121-454 5684.
Hillel House, 26 Somerset Road Edgbaston, B15 2QD. ☎ 0121-454 5684. Applications for admission to F. M. Linden, 7 Westbourne Gardens, B15. ☎ 0121-454 5042 or Mrs R. Jacobs ☎ 0121-440 4142/643-2688.
B'nai Brith Joint Lodge. *Jt. Secs.* F. & H. Linden, 7 Westbourne Gardens, Edgbaston, B15 3TJ. ☎ 0121-454 5042.
Home for Aged, Andrew Cohen House, Riverbrook Drive, Stirchley, B30 2SH. ☎ 0121-458 5000.
Jewish Graduates Association. *Sec.* Mrs C. Jacobs, 54 Sir Richards Dr, B17 8SS. ☎ 0121-429 4735.
King David School, 244 Alcester Road, B13 8EY. ☎ 0121-499 3364. *H.T.* Mrs E. Lesser.

Lubavitch Centre & Bookshop, 95 Willows Road, B12 9QF. ☎ 0121-440 6673. Fax 0121-446 4299. *M.* Rabbi S. Arkush. Also at this address: Operation Judaism (see p.64).

Mikva at Central Synagogue, For appointments ☎ 0121-440 5853.

Israel Information Centre, Bookshop and Reference Library, Singers Hill, Blucher St., B1 1QL. *Dir.* Mrs R. Jacobs ☎ 0121-643 2688.

Jewish Education Board. *Chairman* A. Schiller, 33 Greville Drive, B15 2UU. ☎ 0121-440 3418.

CEMETERIES
Brandwood End Cemetery, Kings Heath 14. Enqs. to Hebrew Congregation (☎ 0121-643 0884).

Witton Cemetery, The Ridgeway, College Road, Erdington 23. ☎ 0121-356 4615.

BLACKPOOL (1,500)
United Hebrew Congregation, Leamington Road. (Consecrated 1916.) Services were first held in the 1890s in a private house. Later a syn. was built in Springfield Road. *M.* Rev. D. Braunold. ☎ 01253 392382; *President* F. H. Freeman. ☎ 01253 393767.

Reform Synagogue, 40 Raikes Parade, FY1 4EX. (A constituent of R.S.G.B.) ☎ 01253 23687. *H. T.* Mrs E. R. Ballan, 177 Hornby Road, Blackpool, FY2 4JA. ☎ 01253 25839.

Blackpool Council of Christians and Jews. Rev D. Braunold, 31 Marlborough Road, Blackpool North. ☎ 01253 392382. *H. Sec.* Mrs G. Kay.

Blackpool and Fylde Ajex. *H. Sec.* F. Tomlinson. ☎ 01253 728659.

Blackpool and Fylde Jewish Welfare Society. *President:* Mrs G. Kay; *H. T.* D. Lewis ☎ 01253 295608.

Fylde League of Jewish Women. *H. Sec.* Mrs J. Weinbren, 18 Balmoral Rd., Lytham St Annes, FY8 1ER. ☎ 01253 720597.

BOGNOR REGIS (40)
Hebrew Congregation. *H. Sec.* J. S. Jacobs, Elm Lodge, Sylvan Way. ☎ 01243-823006.

BOURNEMOUTH (3,000)
The Bournemouth Hebrew Cong. was est. in 1905 and met in the Assembly Rooms, where the Bournemouth Pavilion now stands. A syn., built in Wootton Gdns. in 1911, was rebuilt in 1961 to seat some 950 congregants. The Menorah suite was added in 1974, and a mikva in 1976.

Bournemouth Reform Synagogue was started by a small band of enthusiasts in 1947. Ten years later the congregation was large enough to build the present synagogue building at 53 Christchurch Road. It was extended in 1980 and now has a membership of over 700 persons, with a voluntary mixed choir, active Cheder, and many social activities, and is host to the Jewish Day Centre every Monday.

Bournemouth is the religious and social centre for the fast growing community in Dorset, West Hampshire and Wiltshire.

Bournemouth District Jewish Representative Council (incorp. Southampton). *President* Mrs H. Greene, P.O. Box 2287, BH3 7ZD. ☎ 01202-762101; *H. Sec.* Mrs M. Perry.

Wessex Jewish News (community newsletter), P.O. Box 2287, BH3 7ZD.

Hebrew Congregation, Wootton Gdns. BH1 1PW. ☎ 01202 557433. *President* S. White; *M.* Rabbi G. Shisler.

Mikva, Gertrude Preston Hall, Wootton Gdns. ☎ 01202 557433.

Yavneh Kindergarten, Gertrude Preston Hall, Wootton Gdns. BH1 3PW. ☎ 01202 295414. *Princ.* Mrs E. Devine.

Bournemouth Jewish Day School (Scopus), Synagogue Chambers, Wootton Gardens, BH1 1PW. ☎ 01202-553373. *H.T.*

Reform Syngagogue, 53 Christchurch Road, P.O. Box 8, BH1 3PN. (Est. 1947.) (A Constituent of the R.S.G.B.) ☎ 01202-557736. *M.* Rabbi D. Soetendorp; *Chairman* Mrs C. Bradley; *H. Sec.* Mrs J. Gee.

Day Centre, *Co-ordinator* Mrs R. Lesser, 40A East Avenue, BH3 7DA. ☎ 01202 766039.

Bournemouth University Jewish Society, Wallisdown Road, Poole. ☎ 01202 524111.

Friendship Club (over 60s). *H. Sec.* S. Mazin. ☎ 01202 551255.

Home for Aged: Hannah Levy House, 15 Poole Road, Bournemouth. ☎ 01202 765361.

Jewish Care, Braemar Royal, Grand Avenue, Southbourne, Bournemouth. ☎ 01202 423246.

Lubavitch Centre, Chabad House, 8 Gordon Road, Boscombe, Bournemouth. ☎ 01202 396615.

Cemeteries: Kinson Cemetery (used by both Hebrew Cong. and Reform Syn.); Boscombe Cemetery (used by old established mems. Hebrew Cong.).

BRADFORD (170)

Jews of German birth, who began settling in Bradford in the first half of the nineteenth century, were in a large measure responsible for the development of its wool yarns and fabrics exports to all parts of the world. Jewish services, first held in the 1830s in private houses, were held in 1873, on Reform lines, in a public hall. About the same period saw the beginnings of the Orthodox community.

Hebrew Congregation (Orthodox), Springhurst Road, Shipley, West Yorks. BD18 3DN. (Cong. est. 1886, Syn. erected 1970.) *President* A. A. Waxman; *H. Sec.* Mrs A.E. Dye, Brookfield, Hebden Hall Park, Hebden, Grassington, BD26 5DX. ☎ 01756-752012.

Synagogue, Bowland Street, Bradford, BD1 3BW. ☎ 01274 584431. (Est. 1880.) (A constituent of R.S.G.B.) *Chairman* K. Fabian, 26 Thorndale Rise, Poplars Farm, King's Rd., BD2 1NU; *H. Sec.* J. Morris, 9 Beech Ave., Horsforth, Leeds LS18 4PA.

Jewish Benevolent Society. *President* A. A. Waxman; *H. T.* M. Levi.

Cemetery (both Orthodox and Reform), Scholemoor, Necropolis Road, Cemetery Road, Bradford.

BRIGHTON & HOVE (8,000)

There were Jews resident in Brighton in the second half of the eighteenth century, and by the beginning of the nineteenth century there was an organised community. (The earliest syn. was founded in Jew Street in 1792.)

Brighton and Hove Jewish Representative Council. Meetings at Ralli Hall, Denmark Villas, Hove. P.O. Box 2001, Hove, BN3 4HY. ☎ 01273 747722.

Joint Kashrut Board. ☎ 01273 739670.

Sussex Jewish News, P.O. Box 2178, Hove BN1 5NX. ☎ 01273 330550. Fax 01273 504455. Email doris@sussexjewishnews.freeserve.co.uk.

Brighton & Hove Hebrew Congregation (Reg. Charity No. 233221). Synagogues: 31 New Church Road, Hove BN3 4AD and 66 Middle Street, BN1 1AL. *M.* Rabbi P. Efune; *Hon. Sexton* B. Goldberg. ☎ 01273 601088; *Admin.* Rachel Cohen. ☎ 01273 888855. Fax 01273 888810. Email bhhc@breathemail.net.

Mikva, Prince Regent Swimming Complex. ☎ 01273 685692.

Hove Hebrew Congregation, 79 Holland Road, Hove. *M.* Rabbi V. Silverman. ☎ 01273 732035.

Brighton & Hove New Synagogue (Reform, Est. 1955, Constituent of RSGB), Palmeira Avenue, Hove, BN3 3GE. ☎ 01273 735343.

J.A.C.S. meet every Wednesday at 2pm at the Ajex Hall of the New Synagogue.

☎ 01273 774037.
Brighton & Hove Progressive Synagogue (ULPS), (Est. 1935). 6 Lansdowne Road, Hove, BN3 1FF. ☎ 01273 737223. *M.* Rabbi P. Glantz; *H. Sec.* Mandy Randell-Gavin.
Brighton and Hove Jewish Housing Association. ☎ 01273 207328.
Brighton & Hove Jewish Centre (Reg. Charity No. 269474) (incorporating Brighton and Hove Maccabi, B.B.Y.O.; Ralli Hall Amateur Theatrical Society; New Ralli Bridge Club and Jewish Community Art Society), Ralli Hall, 81 Denmark Villas, Hove BN3 3TH. ☎ 01273 202254. *Admin.* Norina Duke; *Chairman* Roger Abrahams. Meeting centre for various senior citizens clubs and youth clubs. Facilities include snooker room, work-out gym, library/reading room, cafeteria, etc. Kosher kitchen (lunch available on Thursdays).
Ajex. *Contact* Aubrey Cole. ☎ 01273 737417.
Ben Gurion University Foundation. *Contact* Godfrey Gould. ☎ 01273 419412.
B&H Arts Society. *Contact* Audrey Davis, 396 Whittingham Gdns, BN1 6PU.
JIA Ladies Committee. Mrs S. Carlton. ☎ 01273 5522821.
Jewish Welfare Board. ☎ 01273 722523. Est. 1846. *H. T.* G.E. Burkeman.
Lubavitch Foundation. ☎ 01273 321919.
Magen David Adom. Mrs E. Hagard, 53a New Church Rd., Hove.
Torah Academy. Mrs S. Granville, 31 New Church Road ☎ 01273 328675.
Brighton and Hove Jewish Home, 20 Burlington Street, BN2 1AU. ☎ 01273 688226.
Hillel House, 18 Harrington Road, Brighton BN1 6RE. *Admin.* Mrs A. Lee. ☎ 01273 503450.
Sussex Jewish Continuity (Reg. Charity No. 1069737). *Contact* Doris Levinson. ☎ 01273 747722.
Sussex ORT. *Contact* Estelle Josephs. ☎ 01903 232932.
Sussex Jewish Golfing Society. *Contact* Ivor Richards. ☎ 01273 720366.
Sussex Tikvah (Home for Jewish adults with severe learning difficulties) ☎ 01273 564021. *Chairman* Peter Senker; *Head of House* Mrs C. Nicholls; *Bursar* Mrs M. Bomzer. ☎ 01273 506665.
Youth Aliyah. *Contact* Mrs E. Posner. ☎ 01273 776671.
Centre for German–Jewish Studies at Sussex University, see p.42.
Cemetery: ☎ 01273 606961.

BRISTOL (375)

Bristol was one of the principal Jewish centres of medieval England. Even after the Expulsion from England in 1290 there were occasional Jewish residents or visitors. A community of Marranos lived here during the Tudor period. There had been a Jewish community in the City before 1754 and the original Synagogue opened in 1786. The present building dates from 1871 and was renovated in 1981-83. Polack's House (Clifton College) was founded in 1878. The Progressive Synagogue was founded in 1961 and their present building was consecrated in 1971.
Bristol Jewish Representative Council, *Chairman* Leonard Glynn, 42 Vicarage Rd., BS3 1PD. ☎ 0117-923 1835. *Sec.* Mrs K. Balint-Kurti, 6 Ashgrove Rd., BS6 6LY. ☎ 0117-973 1150. Email: bjlc@fishpond.demon.co.uk.
Synagogues:
  Bristol Hebrew Congregation, 9 Park Row BS1 5LP, Rabbi Hillel Simon. ☎ 0117-925 5160. Enq. to Mrs H. Barcan. ☎ 0117-942 2610. Services: Sat. 9.45am, Fri. Summer 8.30pm, Winter 7.30 pm;
  Bristol & West Progressive Jewish Cong (ULPS). (Reg. Charity No. 73879), 43-45 Bannerman Road, Easton BS5 0RR. *M.* Rabbi Hadassah Davis. ☎ 0118-954 3768. Enq. to Mrs. J. Belcher. ☎ 0117 968 3524. Fax 0117-904 3454. Email jbelcher@bjcbristol.demon.co.uk. Services: Sat. 11.00am, Fri. 8.00pm Email: bwpjc@fishpond.demon.co.uk.
Bristol University Jewish & Israel Soc., c/o Hillel House.
Hillel House, 45 Oakfield Road, Clifton, BS8 2BA. ☎ 0117-946 6589.

Accommodation enquiries: Mrs S. Tobias, ☎ 01454 412831.

Davar, The Jewish Institute in Bristol, cultural and educational organisation aims to encourage Jewish identity with the widest possible spectrum. ☎ 0117-970 6594. 1-3, Percival Rd., Clifton BS8 3LF. *Admin.* Vena Bunker.

Polack's House, Clifton College, Housemaster, Mr Jo Greenbury. ☎ 0117-973 7634.

Cemetery: Oakdene Avenue, Fishponds, Bristol BS5 6QQ.

CAMBRIDGE (Resident Jewish pop. 500, Students 500 approx.)

Cambridge Traditional Jewish Congregation (Reg. Charity No. 282849). *President* Sharon Blaukopf, 28 Harvey Goodwin Avenue, CB34 3EU. ☎ 01223-352145. During university terms there are services three times a day. During vacations there are regular services on Friday night, Shabbat morning, Sunday morning and other times by arrangement. Shiurim are held throughout the year, including a women's learning group; Cheder; Kosher food is available. ☎ 01223 352145.

The Cambridge University Jewish Society was formed in 1937. It organises services every day during term-time. Kosher meals are served at lunchtime during the week and Shabbat and on Friday nights. There is a resident full-time Student Chaplain. ☎ 01223 354783. *Chaplain* Rabbi S. Robinson ☎ 01223 354783.

Traditional Synagogue, Thompson's Lane, CB5 8AQ. ☎ 01223-515375. Present cong. founded 1888, but there was an organised com. from 1774. Present syn. opened 1937.

Beth Shalom Reform Synagogue. (A Constituent of R.S.G.B.) *Chairman* L. Coppersmith, 3 Cranmer Road, Cambridge CB3 9BL. ☎ 01223 365614.

Cambridge Jewish Residents' Association. ☎ 01223-352963.

L'Chaim Society, 33 Bridge St., CB2 1UW. ☎ 01223-366335. Fax 01223-366338.

Mikvah Committee, *Chairman* D. L. Gilinsky. ☎ 020-8202 1270. Fax 020-7634 2520. (Reg. Charity No. 10670d75). Plans for the opening of a communal mikvah in 1999.

CANTERBURY & DISTRICT (100)

The history of the Canterbury community, 'The Jews of Canterbury, 1760–1931' by Dan Cohn-Sherbok, was published in 1984.

Jewish Community includes members in the whole of East Kent. Regular monthly programme. *Chairman* Prof. G. Rickayzen, 27 Ross Gardens, Rough Common, CT2 9BZ. ☎ 01227 464996; *H. Sec.* Miss P. Brown. There are a number of Jewish students at Kent University.

CHATHAM (ca. 50)

There was an organised Jewish community in Chatham from the first half of the eighteenth century. The present syn., erected in 1869 in memory of Captain Lazarus Simon Magnus, by his father, Simon Magnus, is on the site of its predecessor, erected about 1740. A Centenary Hall and Mid-Kent Jewish Youth Centre was consecrated in 1972. The old cemetery, dating back to about 1790, is behind the syn.

Chatham Memorial Synagogue, 366 High Street, Rochester. Inquiries: Dr C. Harris, Sutton Place, Sutton Road Maidstone, Kent ME15 9DU. ☎ 01622 753040.

CHELMSFORD (145)

Jewish Community (Reg. Charity No. 281498), 11 Haig Court, CM2 0BH. ☎ 01245 266150. The community, est. in 1974, holds regular services, religion classes and social activities. It has burial arrangements through the Joint Jewish Burial Society.

CHELTENHAM (70)

The congregation was est. in 1824 and the present syn. in St. James's Sq. opened in 1839, furnished with fittings from the New Synagogue, Leadenhall Street (1761), which relocated to Great St Helen's in 1837, thus endowing the Cheltenham community with the oldest extant Ashkenazi furniture in the country. 'The History of the Hebrew Community of Cheltenham, Gloucester and Stroud', by Brian Torode, was reprinted in 1999. After two generations, the cong. dwindled and the syn. closed in 1903. Refugees from Central Europe and evacuated children and others from Jewish centres in England, however, formed a new community and a cong. was re-formed in 1939 and the old syn. reopened. The cemetery, dating from 1824, is in Elm St.

Hebrew Congregation, St. James's Sq. (Reg. Charity No. 261470-R). *H. Sec.* H. Bazar, Kynance, 22 Sydenham Road, Cheltenham, GL52 6EA. ☎ 01242 525032.

CHESTER (35)
Hebrew Congregation, Helen & Gordon Viner, 5 Nield Ct., Upton Chester, CH2 1DN. ☎ 01244 383745. Ian & Lesley Daniels, Riverslea, 61 Dee Banks, Chester CH3 5UU. ☎ 01244 313033. Monthly Fri. evg. services.

COLCHESTER (100)
Colchester and District Jewish Community (Reg. Charity No. 237240), Synagogue, Fennings Chase, Priory St., CO1 2QG. Services held on Friday evenings and on all Festivals. The Community has many families with young children and there is a Cheder every Sunday morning. The community has close links with the University of Essex at Colchester which is a popular choice for Israeli students wishing to study for a law degree. For information about services, Cheder and social events please contact the Hon. Secretary, Mrs N. B. Stevenson, ☎ 01206 545992.

COVENTRY (140)
There were Jews settled in Coventry in 1775, if not earlier, and by the beginning of the nineteenth century there was a relatively large community.
Synagogue, Barras Lane. (Consec. 1870) ☎ (02476) 220168. *H. Sec.* L. R. Benjamin, 25 Hathaway Drive, Warwick CV34 5RD. ☎ 01926 499272. Email: lrbenjamin@clara.net
Reform Community, *Chairman* Dr M. Been, 24 Nightingale Lane, Canley Gardens, CV6 6AY. ☎ 02476-672027.

CRAWLEY (ca. 50)
Progressive Jewish Community (ULPS). (Est. 1959.) *H. Sec.* Mrs L. Bloom, 44 Brighton Road, Crawley, West Sussex RH10 6AT. ☎ 01293 534294.

DARLINGTON (40)
Hebrew Congregation (RSGB), Bloomfield Road (Est. 1904.) *Sec.* J. Starr, 2 Desmond Rd., Middleton St. George, DL2 1AN. ☎ 01325 333736; *President* M. Finn, 17 Thornbury Rise, DL3 9NE. ☎ 01325 252234.
Cemetery: Contained in a consecrated section of: The West Cemetery, Carmel Road, Darlington.

EAST GRINSTEAD AND DISTRICT (35)
Jewish Community (Reg. Charity No. 288189). (Est. 1978). *H. M.* Rev. M. Weisman, M.A.; *Warden* E. Godfrey, 7 Jefferies Way, Crowborough, Sussex TN6 2UH. ☎ 01892 653949. Corr: Mrs M. Beevor, 6 Court Close, East Grinstead, West Sussex RH19 3YQ. ☎ 01342 312148.

EASTBOURNE (63)
Hebrew Congregation, 22 Susans Road, BN21 3HA; *H. Sec.* Mrs M. J. Mindell.

☎ 01435 866928. Fax 01435-865783.
Cemetery: Eastbourne Borough Cemetery has a part set aside for the comm. in conjunction with the Brighton Chevra Kedusha.

EXETER (150)
Before the expulsion, Exeter was an important Jewish centre.
The syn. off Mary Arches St. was built in 1763, and the cemetery in Magdalen Road dates from 1757, but Jews are known to have lived in Exeter 30 years earlier and the com. is said to have been founded as early as 1728. The community greatly decreased during the 19th century, but has revived in recent years. Ring for dates of monthly Shabbat services. High Holy-days and Festivals 10am. Synagogue ☎ 01392 251529.
Hebrew Congregation. Synagogue, Synagogue Place, Mary Arches St., EX4 3BA.
☎ 01392 251529. Email: exeshul@eclipse.co.uk Website: www.eclipse.co.uk/exeshul *President* Sonia Fodor. ☎ 01392 254360.

GATESHEAD (1,400)
Synagogue, 180 Bewick Road, 8. ☎ 0191 4770111 (Mikva. ☎ 0191-477 3552).
Rab. Rabbi B. Rakow, 138 Whitehall Road, 8. ☎ 0191-477 3012; *Senior Warden.*
Kolel Synagogue, 22 Claremont Place, Gateshead NE8 1TL. (Constituent of the Union of Orthodox Hebrew Congregations.) *Sec.* Mr Sinason. ☎ 0191-477 2189.
Beis Hatalmud, 1 Ashgrove Tce., Gateshead 8. *Princ.* Rabbi S. Steinhouse. ☎ 0191-478 4352.
Beth Midrash Lemoroth, 50 Bewick Road 8. (Teachers Training College for Girls.) ☎ 0191-477 2620. *Princ.* Rabbi M. Miller. *H. T.* M. Pearlman.
Institute for Higher Rabbinical Studies (Kolel Harabbonim), 22 Claremont Place, Gateshead NE8 ITL. ☎ 0191-477 2189. *Sec.* S. Ehrentreu.
Sunderland Talmudical College and Yeshiva, Prince Consort Road, Gateshead-on-Tyne NE3 4DS. ☎ 0191-490 0195 (Off.); 0191-490 0193 (Students). *Princ.* Rabbi S. Zahn. ☎/Fax 0191-490 1606.
Yeshiva, 88 Windermere Street, 8. ☎ 0191-478 5210 and 477 2616. Students, 179 Bewick Road ☎ 0191-477 1646. *Sec.* S. Esofsky
Yeshive Lezeirim, Gladstone Tce., NE 8. *Princ.* Rabbi E. Jaffe. ☎ 0191-477 0744.
Gateshead Girls High School, 6 Gladstone Tce., NE8. ☎ 0191-477 3471. *Princ.* Rabbi D. Bowden; *H. Sec.* Mrs C. Rabinowitz.
Jewish Boarding School (Boys, aged 10-16), 36-38 Gladstone Terr. (Union of Orthodox Hebrew Congregations.) *Princ.* Rabbi N. Lieberman; *Sec.* J. Salomon. ☎ 0191-477 1431 & 477 2066 (Students).
Jewish Primary School, 18 Gladstone Terr., 8. ☎ 0191-477 2154. *Princ.; H. Sec.* Mrs C. Rabinowitz.
Ohel Rivka Kindergarten, Alexandra Road, NE8. ☎ 0191-478 3723; *H. Sec.* Mrs Esofsky, 13 Grasmere St. ☎ 0191-477 4102.

GRIMSBY (40)
There are records of Jews living here prior to 1290 and a community of sorts existed in the early 1800s. Mass immigration from eastern Europe, when Grimsby, like so many east coast ports, was the first landfall for these 'escapees' from persecution, saw many passing through *en route* for the larger northern cities and even further onward to Canada and the United States but a fair number remained, and a proper community was created. The synagogue and cemetery were consecrated in 1885. The community reached its numerical peak in the 1930s, when it numbered between 450/500, but its gradual decline began in the immediate post-war years. The history of the community has been published: D. and L. Gerlis, 'The Story of the Grimsby Jewish Community', 1986. Regular services are held every Friday evening at 7.00pm, and also on all the major festivals and holidays.
Sir Moses Montefiore Synagogue, Holme Hill, Heneage Road, DN32 9DZ.

President L. Solomon; *T.* H. S. Kalson; *H. Sec.* B. Greenberg, 21 Abbey Park Road, DN32 0HJ. ☎ 01472 351404.
Cemetery: (Chevra Kadisha) First Avenue, Nunsthorpe, Grimsby. *Sec.* B. Greenberg; *T.* H. Kalson, 12A Welholme Avenue, DN32 0HP.

GUILDFORD (100)

Synagogue (1979), York Road, GU1 4DR. The community has grown up since the Second World War. Regular services; Cheder and social activities. *Chairman* Dr S. Cornbleet. ☎ 01483 575787; *Sec.* Mrs B. Gould. ☎ 01483 576470.
University of Surrey Jewish Society, c/o Professor R. Spier. ☎ 01483 259265.
Cemetery: Consecrated section of municipal cemetery.

HARLOW (190)

Jewish Community, Harberts Road, Hare St, CM19 4DT. ☎ 01279-432503. (A Constituent of R.S.G.B.) *President* E. Clayman; *Vice-President* C. Jackson; *Chairman* Mrs C. Peter. ☎ 01992-465482. *Sec.* Mrs H. Reeves.

HARROGATE (150)

'The History of the Harrogate Jewish Community' by Rosalyn Livshin was published in 1995.
Hebrew Congregation, St. Mary's Walk, HG2 0LW. (Est. 1918.) *President* Sandy Royston. ☎ 01423 561188; *Sec.* P.E. Morris. ☎ 01423 871713. *Corr.* L. Fox, 20 Park Parade, HG1 5AF. ☎ 01423 523439.
Zionist Group. *Chairman* Anita Royston. ☎ 01423 561188.

HASTINGS (33)

Hastings and District Jewish Society (Reg. Charity No. 273806). Regular meetings of the Society including a short service are held on the first Friday of the month in Bexhill, at 7 p.m. *H. Sec.* A. Ross, P.O. Box 74, Bexhill-on-Sea, East Sussex TN39 4ZZ. ☎ 01424-848344.

HEMEL HEMPSTEAD (270)

Hebrew Congregation (affiliated to U.S.) Est. 1956. Synagogue, Lady Sarah Cohen Community Centre, Midland Road, Hemel Hempstead, Herts. HD1 1RP. *H. Sec.* H. Nathan. ☎ 01923 32007.

HEREFORD

Hereford Jewish Community (Associate Community of ULPS). Enquiries to Josephine Woolfson. ☎ 01432 271678.

HIGH WYCOMBE (35)

Hebrew Congregation (affiliated to the U.S.). *H. Sec.* Mrs R. Weiss, 33 Hampden Road, High Wycombe, Bucks. HP13 6SZ. ☎ 01494 529821.

HOVE (see Brighton & Hove)

HITCHIN

Yeshivas Toras Chessed, Wellbury House, Great Offley, Hitchin, Herts. *Rab.* A. S. Stern. ☎ 01462 768698.

HULL (650)

In Hull, as in other English ports, a Jewish community was formed earlier than in the neighbouring inland towns. The exact date is unknown, but as a Catholic chapel, damaged in the riots of 1780, was acquired as a syn., the formal constitution of a community was probably about that date. In 1810 a cemetery had been in existence some years. Hull was then the principal port of entry from Northern Europe and most of the Jewish immigrants came through it. In 1851 the Jewish community numbered about 200. Both the old syn. in Osborne St. and the Central

Syn., in Cogan St. were destroyed in air raids during the Second World War.
Jewish Representative Council. *President* Prof. J. Friend, 9 Allanhall Way, Kirkella, HU10 7QU. ☎ 01482 658930; *H. Sec.* Mrs A. Segelman, 251 Beverley Road, Kirkella, HU10 7AG. ☎ 01482 650288.

SYNAGOGUES
Hull Hebrew Congregation, 30 Pryme Street, Anlaby HU10 6SH. *H. Sec.* Mr J. Levine, 104 Beverley Road, Kirkella HU10 7HA. ☎ 01482 657188.
Reform Synagogue (Constituent of R.S.G.B.), Great Gutter Lane, Willerby HU10 7JT. *H. Sec.* Mrs G. Barker, The Cherries, Temple Close, Welton, Brough, East Yorks HU15 1NX. ☎ 01482 665375.

OTHER INSTITUTIONS
Hull Jewish Community Care. (Est. 1880.) *H. Sec.* V. Appleson, 1 Tranby Ride, Anlaby, HU10 7ED. ☎ 01482 653018.
Hillel House, 18 Auckland Avenue HU6 7SG. ☎ 01482 48196. Enquiries to: *H. Sec.* I. Dysch, 1000 Anlaby High Road, HU4 6AT. ☎ 01482 354947.
Talmud Torah, 30 Pryme St., Anlaby, HU10 6SH. *H. Sec.* Mrs. D. Levine, 104 Beverley Rd., Kirkella HU10 7HA. ☎ 01482-657188.
University Jewish Students' Society, c/o Hillel House. ☎ 01482 48196.
Board of Shechita, *H. Sec.* Dr C. Rosen, c/o Hebrew Congregation.

LEAMINGTON & DISTRICT (132)
Progressive Jewish Group. (A branch of the Progressive Synagogue Birmingham, ULPS.) Inq.: Jenny Heilbronn. ☎ 01926 421300.

LEEDS (8,000)
Leeds has the third largest Jewish community in Britain. Jews have lived in Leeds at least from the middle of the eighteenth century, but it was only in 1840 that a Jewish cemetery was acquired. The first so-called synagogue was a converted room in Bridge Street, where services were held up to 1846. Thereafter the place of worship was transferred to the Back Rockingham Street Synagogue, which was replaced by the Belgrave Street Synagogue built in 1860. Another syn. was built in 1877, but this closed in 1983.

The Leeds Jewish community is mainly the product of the persecution of Russian Jewry in the latter half of the nineteenth century. The bulk of immigration settled in Leeds between 1881 and 1905, enhancing the growth of the clothing industry which developed from the woollen and worsted manufacturing in the West Riding of Yorkshire. This industry was made world famous by John Barran, a non-Jew, and his Jewish associate Herman Friend, who was responsible for introducing division of labour into the clothing industry. While the sweating system existed in Leeds, both wages and working conditions were better than in London or Manchester. Trade unionism was successful and the first recorded strike by Jewish industrial workers took place spontaneously in Leeds in 1885.

During the early decades of this century the old Leylands ghetto, where most of the immigrants lived, began to break up. The main move of the Jewish people was to northern districts of Leeds, first to Chapeltown, which flourished in the 1940s, and then to the Moortown and Alwoodley suburbs.

The Leeds Rep. C. republished in 1985 the late Louis Saipe's 'A History of the Jews of Leeds'.

Today this well-organised strong community of approx. 8,500 provides for Leeds Jews with over 100 organisations which are affiliated to the Leeds Jewish Representative Council, the official spokesman of the Leeds Jewish community.

Among the organisations are seven orthodox and one reform synagogue, a vol-

untary Chevra Kadisha, Jewish nursery and day schools, Talmud Torah and adult education. Welfare organisations include the Jewish Welfare Board, The Home for Aged Jews, League of Jewish Women, Kosher meals for hospitals, Day and Leisure Centres.
A Hillel House and Chaplaincy with Campus Chaplain are provided for students. There are also numerous Zionist organisations, Speakers' Panels and A.J.E.X.

GENERAL ORGANISATIONS
Jewish Representative Council, Shadwell La. Synagogue, 151 Shadwell La., LS17 8DW. ☎ 0113 2697520. Fax 0113 2370851. Nearly every syn., charitable org., social and cultural instit. and Zionist Soc. is affiliated to this council and on its exec. cttee. serve ex-officio all local Jewish magistrates, public reps. and BoD members. *President* Dr K. Shenderey, M.B., B.S.; *V. Presidents* Hillary Miller, JP, M.R. Pharm. S., Ian Goldman, LL.B., F.Inst.D.; *T.* Sue Baker, JP; *Exec. Off.* Dr D.A. Friedman; *Hon. Sec.* Mrs S. Dorsey.
A.J.E.X. *Chairman* Stanley Graham; *H. Sec.* Leonard Cohen, 76 The Avenue, LS17 7NZ.
Beth Din, Etz Chaim Synagogue, 411 Harrogate Rd., LS17 7TT. ☎/Fax 0113 2370893. *M.* Dayan Y. Refson; Rev. A. Gilbert, B.A.
Community Shaliach, 411 Harrogate Rd., LS17 7TT. ☎ 0113 2680899. Fax 0113 2668419.
J.N.F. and Zionist Council, 411 Harrogate Rd., LS17 7BY. ☎ 0113 2371951. Fax 0113 2370568. *District org.* S. Cohen.
Kashrut Authority, 151 Shadwell Lane, LS17 8DW. ☎ 0113 2697520. Fax 0113 2370851.
Leeds Emunah Council. *Co-ordinator* Mrs M. Gray, 4 Belvedere Court, LS17 8NF. ☎ 0113 266 1902.
Mikvah, 411 Harrogate Road, LS17 7BY. ☎ 0113 2371096 (answer machine).
U.J.I.A. Office, Balfour House, 399 Street La., LS17 6HQ. ☎ 0113 2693136. Fax 0113 2693961.
Women's Zionist Council (Wizo), 411 Harrogate Rd., LS17 7BY. ☎ 0113 2684773. *Chairman* Mrs L. Jacoby.
Yorkshire Israel Office, 411 Harrogate Rd., LS17 7TT. ☎ 0113 2680899. Fax 0113 2688419.

SYNAGOGUES
Beth Hamedrash Hagadol Synagogue, 399 Street Lane Gdns., LS17 6HQ. (Est. 1874.) *M.*; *R.* D. Apfel; *Exec. Off.* Mrs M. Wilson. ☎ 0113 2692181.
Chassidishe Synagogue (Est. 1897), c/o Donisthorpe Hall, Shadwell Lane, LS17 6AW. All enq. to M. Kent, Flat 8, Sandhill Lawns, Sandhill Lane, LS17 6TT.
Etz Chaim Synagogue, 411 Harrogate Road, LS17 7TT. *Rab.* Rabbi Y. Angyalfi; *M.* Rev. G. Harris; *R.* Rev. A. Gilbert; *Sec.* Sandhill Pde., 584 Harrogate Road, LS17 7DP ☎ 0113 2662214. Fax 0113 2371183.
Masorti, *Contact* A. Selman ☎ 0113 2612700.
Queenshill Synagogue, 26 Queenshill Avenue, LS17 6AX.
Shomrei Hadass Congregation, 368 Harrogate Road, LS17 6QB. ☎ 0113 2681461. *M.* Dayan Y. Refson.
Sinai Synagogue, Roman Avenue, Street Lane, LS8 2AN. ☎ 0113 2665256. (A Constituent of R.S.G.B.) (Est. 1944.) *M.* Rabbi I. Morris; *H. Sec.* Mrs P. Mason. Mon-Fri 9.30am-2pm.
United Hebrew Congregation (Reg. Charity No. 515316) 151 Shadwell La., LS17 8DW. ☎ 0113-269 6141. Fax 0113-237 0851. *M.* Rabbi D. Levy. ☎ 0113-237 0852; *R.* Rev. H. Miller; *Admin.* Mrs A. Silver.
Cemeteries: For information refer to the Representative Council as above.

CULTURAL AND EDUCATIONAL ORGANISATIONS

B'nai B'rith Lodge of Leeds. *President* Mrs Shirley Casdan. ☎ 0113 2264475.

Jewish Education Board (Talmud Torah), 2 Sandhill La., LS17 6AQ. (Est. 1879.) Houses the Talmud Torah classes. Administers Jewish Assemblies for pupils attending State schools. ☎ 0113 2172533.

Jewish Education Bureau, 8 Westcombe Avenue, LS8. ☎ 0113 663613. Provides information and materials on all aspects of Judaism to non-Jewish educationalists and clergy. *Dir.* Rabbi D. S. Charing. ☎ 0870-8008 JEB (532). Fax 0870-800 8533. 'Ask the Rabbi' 0906-690 3042 (premium line). Email jewishedbureau@easicom.com.

Scopus Jewish Educational Trust:
   Brodetsky Jewish Primary School & Nursery, George Lyttleton Centre, Wentworth Avenue, LS17 7TN. *H. M.* Mrs L. Hastings. ☎ 0113 2930578.
   Deborah Taylor Playgroup, George Lyttleton Centre, Primley Park Road, LS17 7HR. *Co-ord.* Mrs S. Saffer. ☎ 0113 2930579.
   Jewish Day Schools' Administrative Office, George Lyttleton Centre, Wentworth Avenue, LS17 7TN. *Admin.* Mrs A. Grant. ☎ 0113 2693176.

Jewish Historical Society (Branch). *President* Judge Arthur Myerson, QC, 20 Sandmoor Lane, LS17 7EA; *H. Sec.* Mrs A. Buxbaum, 17 Pepper Hills, Harrogate Rd., LS17 8EJ. ☎ 0113-266 5641.

Jewish Students' Association, Hillel House, 2 Springfield Mount, LS2 9NE. ☎ 0113 2433211. (Est. 1912.) *Sec.,* c/o Leeds University Union, LS2.

Leeds Council of Christians and Jews (Reg. Charity No. 238005), *Chairman* A.M. Conway, ☎ 0113 2680444; *H. Sec.* L. Collins ☎ 0113 2687556, Mrs S. Crowther ☎ 0113 2561407.

Leeds Jewish Dental Society. *Sec.* Paul H. Leslie, 16 High Ash Ave., LS17 8RG. ☎ 0113-2694510.

Leeds Jewish Youth Service, 2 Sand Hill Lane, LS17 6AQ. ☎ 0113-2172531.

Leeds University Library, Judaica collections (see p.55).

Limelight Drama Group. *Chairman* Harry Venet. ☎ 0113-2250651.

Maccabi Sports and Social Centre, Street Lane Gdns., 393 Street La., LS17 6HQ. ☎ 0113 2693381. *Manager* R.A. Ross.

Makor–Jewish Resource Centre and Israel Information Centre (JPMP), 411 Harrogate Rd., LS17 7TT. ☎ 0113 2680899. *Sec.*

Menorah School, 2 Sandhill Lane, Leeds LS17 6AQW.

Porton Collection, Central Library, LS1 3AB (see p.59). ☎ 0113 2462016

Reform Hebrew Classes, Sinai Synagogue, 22 Roman Avenue, LS8 2AN. ☎ 0113 2665256.

S.E.E.D. Project. Contact: Rabbi Y. Angyalfi, ☎ 0113 2663311.

WELFARE ORGANISATIONS

Chaplaincy Board–Yorkshire & Humberside, 17 Queens Road, LS6 1NY. ☎ 0113 2789597. *Hon. Chairman* M. Sender. ☎ 0113-2680048.

Chevra Kadisha. Leeds *Jt. Chairmen* Dr M. Black, Mrs S. Myerson; *Org.* I. Baum. ☎ 0113 2955748. *Correspondence*: Mrs G. Millward, 60 Primley Park View, LS17 7JZ.

Jewish Day Centre, 26 Queenshill Avenue, LS17 6AX. ☎ 0113 2692018. *Org.* Jackie King.

Jewish Welfare Board, 311 Stonegate Road, LS17 6AZ. ☎ 0113 2684211. Fax 0113 2664754. *President* R. Manning; *Chief Exec.* Ms. S. Saunders.

Miyad Helpline. ☎ 0345-581999.

Residential Nursing Home for the Jewish Elderly, Donisthorpe Hall, Shadwell Lane, LS17 6AW. (Est. 1923.) ☎ 0113 2684248. *Admin.* Judith Ransmdale.

Hospital meals and visitation. Non-residents of Leeds who may be admitted to one of the city's hospitals should contact the Exec. Officer, Leeds Jewish Representative Council, ☎ 0113 2697520.

LEICESTER (670)
There have been Jewish communities in Leicester since the Middle Ages, but the first record of a Jews' Synagogue appears in the 1861 Leicester Directory and the first marriages were consecrated in 1875. The present syn. dates from 1897.
Synagogue, Highfield St. *M.* Rabbi C. Kantrovitz. ☎ 0116 2706622. *H. Sec.* G. J. Louis, 4 Lyndhurst Ct., London Road, LE2 2AP. ☎ 0116 2700997.
Mikva, Synagogue building, Highfield St.
Communal Centre, Highfield St. ☎ 0116 2540477.
Shalom Club for Sr. Citizens. ☎ 0116 2540477.
Jewish Library, Communal Centre, Highfield St.
Ladies' Guild. *Chairman* Mrs H. Reggel, 22 Sackville Gardens, ☎ 0116 270 9687.
Jewish Students' Society, c/o The Union, Leicester University.
Maccabi Association, Communal Centre, Highfield St. ☎ 0116 2540477.
Leicester Progressive Jewish Synagogue (ULPS). (Est. 1950) 24 Avenue Rd. *H. Sec.* J. Kaufman, ☎ 01162-715584. Fax 01162-717571. Services Fri. evgs. and Saturday; Religion Sch., Sundays.
Cemeteries: Leicester Hebrew Cong. uses a section of the Gilroes Cemetery, Groby Road. The Progressive congregation uses a section of the Loughborough Municipal C.

LINCOLN
Lincolnshire Jewish Community (Associate Community of ULPS). Enquiries to the Secretary, Dr Karen Genard ☎ 01469 588951.

LIVERPOOL (3,000)
Liverpool, for centuries an important port, first for Ireland, later also for America, had a natural attraction for Jews looking for a place in which to start their new lives. There is evidence of an organised community before 1750. It appears to have had a burial ground attached. Little is known of this early community. It declined but about 1770 was reinforced by a new wave of settlers chiefly from Europe, who worshipped in a house in Frederick Street, near the river front, with a Mikva and a cemetery. In 1807 a synagogue of some size was built in Seel Street, the parent of the present syn. in Princes Road, one of the handsomest in the country. At this time Liverpool was already one of the four leading regional coms. The site for the Seel St. Synagogue was a gift of the Liverpool Corporation.
Merseyside Jewish Representative Council. (Reg Charity No. 1039809). *President* David A. Coleman; *H. Sec.* Barry Levene, Shifrin House, 433 Smithdown Road, Liverpool L15 3JL. ☎ 0151-733 2292. Fax 0151-734 0212. *Communal Archivist* J.Wolfman, MA.
Liverpool Kashrut Commission, c/o 433 Smithdown Road, Liverpool L15 3JL. ☎ 0151-733 2292. Fax 0151-734 0212. *Rab.* Rabbi L. Cofnas.
Mikva. Childwall Synagogue. *Chairman* Rabbi L. Cofnas. ☎ 0151-722 2079.

SYNAGOGUES
Old Hebrew Congregation, Princes Road, Liverpool L8. ☎ 0151-709 3431 (Congregation founded c. 1740; Synagogue consecrated 1874.) *M.* Rabbi A. Abel; *Sec.* Mrs D. Spratt.
Allerton Hebrew Congregation, Mather Avenue, Liverpool L18. ☎ 0151-427 6848. *Emer. Rabbi* M. Malits, M.A.; *M.* Rabbi D. Golomb; *Admin.* P. Fisher.
Childwall Synagogue, Dunbabin Road, Liverpool L15. ☎ 0151-722 2079. (Est. 1935; consecrated 1938.) Rabbi L. Cofnas; *Admin.* Mrs A. Reuben.
Greenbank Drive Synagogue. (Incorporating Hope Pl. and Sefton Park Hebrew Congregations.) (Est. 1836. Syn. consecrated 1937.) ☎ 0151-733 1417. *Sec.*
Progressive Synagogue (ULPS), 28 Church Road North, Liverpool, L15 6TF. ☎ 0151-733 5871. (Est. 1929. Affiliated to U.L.P.S.) *M.* Rabbi N. Zalud; *H. Sec.* Ruth Stephenson-Tobin. ☎ 0151-733 5871.

Cemeteries: Liverpool Jewish Cemeteries: Springwood; Lowerhouse Lane; Broad Green; Long Lane.

CULTURAL AND EDUCATIONAL ORGANISATIONS
Adult Jewish Education Committee. Mr. E. Rosen. ☎ 0151-475 5671.
Community Centre (Harold House), Dunbabin Road, L15 6XL. ☎ 0151-475 5825.
Crosby Jewish Literary Society. H. Secs. Mrs C. Hoddes, Mrs Y. Mendick. ☎ 0151 924 1795.
Hillel House, 12 Greenbank Dr, L17 1AW. ☎ 0151-735 0793. Applications to: Mrs C. Lewis. ☎ 0151-733-2292; Chaplain Rabbi Y.Y. Rubinstein. ☎ 0161-721 4066.
Jewish Bookshop, Chairman M. Turner. Open at Youth and Community Centre, Sundays 11-1.
Jewish Historical Society (Branch). Chairman A. Lewis, 61 Menlove Ave., L18 2EH.
Jewish Youth Centre, Dunbabin Road, L15 6XL. ☎ 0151-475 5671.
King David Foundation, 433 Smithdown Road, Liverpool L15 3JL. ☎ 0151-733 2292. Fax 0151-734 0212. President J. Max; Clerk Mrs N. Sneeden.
King David High School, Childwall Road, L15 6UZ. ☎ 0151-722 7496. Clerk to Govs. 433 Smithdown Road, L15 3JL. ☎ 0151-733 2292. Fax 0151-734 0212. H. T. J. Smartt, B.Ed., Cert Ed.
King David Kindergarten, Community Centre, Dunbabin Road, L15 6XL. Teachers-in-charge. ☎ 0151-475 5661.
King David Primary School, Beauclair Drive, L15 6XH. ☎ 0151-722 3372. Clerk to Govs. 433 Smithdown Road, L15 3JL. ☎ 0151-733 2292. Fax 0151-734 0212; H. T. Mrs E. Spencer, Cert.Ed.
Liverpool Jewish Resource Centre, Harold House, Dunbabin Road L15 6XL. ☎ 0151-722 3514. Fax 0151-475 2212. Sundays 11-1, Mon.-Thurs. 1-5pm. Admin. Mrs H. Cohen.
Liverpool Yeshivah, Childwall Synagogue, Dunbabin Road, L15. Rosh Yeshiva Rabbi M. L. Cofnas.
Merseyside Amalgamated Talmud Torah, King David Primary School. Chairman Mrs J. Bennett.
Midrasha for Girls, c/o Childwall Synagogue, Dunbabin Road, Liverpool L15.
University Jewish Students' Society, c/o Students' Union, Bedford Street, 7.

WELFARE ORGANISATIONS
Jewish Welfare Council. (Est. 1875.) Chief Exec. 433 Smithdown Road, Liverpool L15 3JL. ☎ 0151-733 2292. Fax 0151-734 0212.
Jewish Women's Aid Society. H. Sec. Mrs S. Gore, 433 Smithdown Road, L15 3JL.
Stapely Residential Home for Aged Jews, North Mossley Hill Road, Liverpool, 18. Admin. ☎ 0151-724 3260 (Adm.), 0151-724 4548 (Hosp. wing).

LUTON & DUNSTABLE & DISTRICT (550)
Luton Hebrew Congregation Synagogue, Postal address: P.O. Box No. 215, LU1 1HW. ☎ 01582 725032.
Ladies' Guild.
Judean Youth Club.
Bedfordshire Progressive Synagogue (ULPS), c/o David Corfan, 39 Broadacres, Bushmead LU2 7FY. ☎ 01234-218387. Sec. Hilary Fox. Services Friday eves; Saturday Luton or Bedford.

MAIDENHEAD (1,240)
Synagogue, 9 Boyn Hill Avenue, SL6 4ET. ☎ 01628 673012. (A Constituent of R.S.G.B.). M. Rabbi Dr J. A. Romain. ☎ 01628 671058.
Cemetery: Braywick Cemetery, Maidenhead.

MAIDSTONE
Kent Liberal Jewish Community. Enquiries to Paul Sinclair. ☎ 01732 364842 or Dinah Binstead ☎ 01732 461994.

MANCHESTER (27,000)
The Manchester community of about 27,000 Jews is the second largest in the U.K. In 1865 there were less than 5,000. The rapid and great increase came between 1883 and 1905, a consequence of the intensified persecution of the Jews in Russia.

Newcomers to England in the eighteenth century were encouraged by their co-religionists in London to go farther afield. This they did, generally financed by their longer-settled fellow-Jews in London, as pedlars along the countryside. As these newcomers prospered they settled in the ports, on their part sending out a wave of later arrivals similarly supplied with small stocks to peddle them in the inland towns and villages. This new wave also ultimately settled down, but for the most part in the interior of the country. Thus was laid the foundation of the Jewish community of Manchester.

Later, a very different class of settler came – merchants and men of substance from Central Europe, some of them political refugees seeking a freer life, others, for instance the first English Rothschild, in the normal course of commercial development. A later influx, a small one, was from North Africa and the Levant, lands closely connected with the cotton business of which Manchester was then the centre. The great immigration came, however, in the last two decades of the nineteenth century, consisting of refugees from Eastern Europe.

Although a few Jews were known to have lived in Manchester in preceding years, a community was not organised until 1780 or a cemetery acquired until 1794. The present Great Synagogue (now amalgamated with the New) claims to be the direct descendant of this earlier community. The leaders of Manchester Jewry in those early days came from the neighbouring Liverpool Jewish community. Bill Williams' 'The Making of Manchester Jewry, 1740–1875' was published in 1976.

GENERAL ORGANISATIONS
Jewish Representative Council of Greater Manchester and Region. The rep. body of the Manchester, Salford and Distr. Jewish com., constituted of reps. from all syns., MPs and MEPs, and other orgs., the local members of the BoD, Magistrates and town councillors. Offices Jewish Cultural Centre, Bury Old Road, Manchester, M8 6FY. ☎/Fax 0161-720 8721. *President* Bella Ansell; *H. Secs.* A. J. Cohen, E. Bolchover. Publ. Yearbook
Joseph Mamlock House, 142 Bury Old Road, M8 4HE. ☎ 0161-740 1825. Organisations at this address include:
  Zionist Central Council of Greater Manchester. *President* A. J. Cohen. ☎ 0161-740 8835
  Jewish Agency Aliyah Dept. ☎ 0161-740 2864.
  WIZO. *Chairman* Beryl Steinberg, Elaine Hamburger. ☎ 0161-740 3367.
Council of Synagogues (Orthodox). *Chairman* S. Goldblatt; *Sec.* M. Green, c/o Central-North Manch. Syn., Leicester Road, Salford M7 4GP. ☎ 0161-740 4830.
Beth Din, 435 Cheetham Hill Road, M8 7PF. ☎ 0161-740 9711. Fax 0161-721 4249. Dayan G. Krausz; Dayan O.Y. Westheim. *Registrar* Y. Brodie, B.A. (Hons.)
Kashrus Authority, 435 Cheetham Hill Road, M8 0PF. ☎ 0161-740 9711. Fax 0161-721 4249. *President* D. Pine; *Admin.* Y. Brodie.
Communal Mikva (under Beth Din authority), Broom Holme, Tetlow La., Salford, M7 0BU. ☎ 0161-792 3970.
Manchester Trades Advisory Council, Jewish Cultural Centre, Bury Old Road, Manchester M8 6FY. ☎/Fax 0161-720 8721. *Chairman* Sir S. C. Hamburger, C.B.E., J.P., D.L., LL.D., M.A.
(Naomi Greenberg) South Manchester Mikva (under Beth Din Authority), Shay Lane, Hale Barns, Altrincham, Cheshire. ☎ 0161-904 8296.

Torah Corps. *President* Rabbi R. Margulies, 24 Hilton Cres., Prestwich M25 8NQ. ☎ 0161-773 1045.
Whitefield Mikveh, Telephone for appointments 0161-796 1054.

SYNAGOGUES
Adass Yeshurun Synagogue, Cheltenham Cres., Salford, M7 4FE. ☎ 0161-792 0795. *M.* Rabbi J. Wreschner; *H. Sec.* M.R. Goldman. ☎/Fax 0161-740 3935.
Adath Israel Synagogue, Up. Park Road, Salford M7 0HL. (Form. Kahal Chassidim Syn., present building opened in 1957). Inq.: 105 Leicester Road, Salford 7. *Sec.* Rev. S. Simon. ☎ 0161-740 3905.
Bury Hebrew Congregation. Sunnybank Road, Bury, BL9 8HE. ☎ 0161-796 5062. *M.* Rabbi B. Singer; *Admin.* Mrs M. Wilson.
Central-North Manchester Synagogue (merged 1978), Leicester Road, Salford M7 4GP. *M.* Rabbi J. Rubinstein. ☎ 0161-740 7762; *Sec.* M. Green. ☎ 0161-740 4830. (Central Syn. est. 1871; N. Manch. Syn. est. 1899).
Cheetham Hebrew Congregation, 453 Cheetham Hill Road, M8 9PA. ☎ 0161-740 7788. *President* B. M. Stone. *M.* Rabbi Y. Abenson.
Cheshire Reform Congregation, (Reg. Charity No. 234762), Menorah Synagogue, 198 Altrincham Road, M22 4RZ. ☎ 0161-428 7746. (Est. 1964.) (A Constituent of R.S.G.B.). *M.*; *H. Sec.* A. Roland. Disabled access. Nursery school.
Damesek Eliezer Synagogue, 74 Kings Road, Prestwich. *M.* Rabbi S. Goldberg. ☎ 0161-740 2486.
Hale and District Hebrew Congregation, Shay Lane, Hale Barns, Cheshire WA15 8PA. ☎ 0161-980 8846. (Est. 1976.) *M.* Rabbi J. Portnoy; *H. Sec.* S. Cantor.
Heaton Park Hebrew Congregation, Ashdown, Middleton Road M8 4JX. *M.* Rev. L. Olsberg, ☎ 0161-740 2767; *Sec.* K.D. Radivan. ☎ 0161-740 4766.
Higher Crumpsall and Higher Broughton Hebrew Congregation, Bury Old Road, Salford, M7 4PX. ☎ 0161-740 1210. *M.* Rabbi A. Saunders, Rev. A. Hillman. ☎ 0161-740 4179; *Sec.* Mrs E. Somers. ☎ 0161-740 8155.
Higher Prestwich Hebrew Congregation, Highbury House, 445 Bury Old Road, Prestwich M25 1QP. ☎ 0161-773 4800. *M.* Rabbi A. Z. Herman; *Sec.* Mrs B. Task.
Hillock Hebrew Congregation, Beverley Close, Ribble Drive, Whitefield, M45. *H. Sec.* R. Walker, 13 Mersey Close, Whitefield, M45 8LB. ☎ 0161-959 5663.
Holy Law South Broughton Congregation, Bury Old Road, Prestwich M25 0EX. ☎ 0161-740 1634. Fax 0161-720 6623. Email office@holylaw.freeserve.co.uk. (Est. 1865, present building opened 1935, merged with South Broughton Syn., 1978). *M.* Rabbi Y. Chazan. ☎ 0161-792 6349 (Study 0161-721 4705); *Admin.* Mrs P. Mann, BSc. Burial Bd. ☎ 0161-740 1289. (D)
Hulme Hebrew Congregation, Hillel House, Greenheys La., Manchester M15 6LR.
Kahal Chassidim Synagogue (Lubavitch), 62 Singleton Road, Salford M7 4LU. ☎ 0161-740 3632. *M.* Rabbi A. Jaffe; *Sec.* D. Lipsidge.
Lubavitch Foundation (Reg. Charity No. X98704), 62 Singleton Road, Salford M7 4LU. ☎/Fax 0161-720 9514. *M.* Rabbi L. Wineberg.
Machzikei Hadass Communities, 17 Northumberland Street, Salford M7 0FE. ☎ 0161-792 1313. *Rav.* Rav. M. Schneebalg. ☎ 0161-792 3063. *Sec.* A. Vogel. ☎ 0161-792 1313.
  Constituent Syn.: Machzikei Hadass. Mikva: Sedgley Park Road, Prestwich. ☎ 0161-773 1537/0161-721 4341.
Manchester Great and New Synagogue (and Community Centre) (Est. 1740), 'Stenecourt', Singleton Road, Holden Road, Salford, M7 4LN. *M.* Rev. G.

Brodie, 43 Stanley Road, Salford M7 0FR. ☎ 0161-740 2506; *H. Sec.* H. Orenstein. ☎ 0161-792 8399 (Sun.-Fri, 9.00am-12.00pm). Email orenstein@ mcmail.com.
Manchester Reform Synagogue, Jackson's Row, M2 5NH. ☎ 0161-834 0415. (Est. 1856). (A Constituent of R.S.G.B.). The former syn. in Park Pl. was destroyed by enemy action in 1941; present premises occupied since 1953. *M.* Rabbi R. Silverman; *Sec.* D. Astbury. ☎ 0161-834 0415. Fax 0161-834 0415.
North Salford Synagogue, 2 Vine St., Kersal, Salford M7 0NX. *M.* Rabbi L. W. Rabinowitz. ☎ 0161-740 7958.
Ohel Torah Congregation, 132 Leicester Road, Salford M7 0ES. (Constituent of the Union of Orthodox Hebrew Congregations.) *M.* Rabbi M. Ellinson; *Sec.* S. Spielman. ☎ 0161-792 2413.
Prestwich Beth Hamedrash, 74 Kings Road, Prestwich M25 8HU. *M.* Rabbi S. Goldberg. ☎ 0161-740 2486.
Prestwich Hebrew Congregation, Bury New Road, Prestwich M25 9WN. ☎ 0161-773 1978. *M.* Rabbi M. Ginsbury; *Sec.* A. Frankel.
Sale and District Hebrew Congregation, Hesketh Road, Sale, Cheshire M33 5AA. ☎ 0161-973 3013. *Sec.* Mrs I. Gould, 32 Kenilworth Rd., Sale, Cheshire M33 5FB.
Sedgley Park Synagogue (Shomrei Hadass), Parkview Road, Prestwich M25 SFA. *Jt.H. Secs.* D. Gordon, S. Baddiel. ☎ 0161-740 0677.
Sephardi Communal Torah Centre, 2 Upper Park Road, Salford M7 0HF. *Dir.* Rabbi Y. Levy. ☎ 0161-740 2050/0321.
Sephardi Congregation of South Manchester, Shaare Hayim (Reg. Charity No. 1067759), 8 Queenston Road, West Didsbury M20 2WZ. ☎ 0161-445 1943. Fax 0161-438 0571. *M.* Rabbi S. Ellituv. ☎ 0161-434 6903. Amalgamated with the former Sha'are Sedek Synagogue.
Sha'arei Shalom, North Manchester Reform Congregation, (Reg. Charity No. 506117), Elms Street, Whitefield, M45 8GQ. (Est. 1977). (A Constituent of R.S.G.B.). ☎ 0161-796 6736.
South Manchester Synagogue, (Reg. Charity No. 231976), Wilbraham Road, M14 6JS. (Est. 1872.) ☎ 0161-224 1366. Fax 0161-225 8033. Steel Memorial Hall. ☎ 0161-224 3744. *M.* Rabbi Y. Rubin; *Admin.* S. L. Rydz, M.A.
Spanish & Portuguese Synagogue, (Est. 1873), 18 Moor La., Salford M7 0WX. ☎ 0161-792 7406. Fax 0161-792 7406. *Hon. Sec.* C. Florentin.
Talmud Torah Chinuch N'orim Synagogue, 11 Wellington Street, East, Salford M7 9AU. ☎ 0161-792 4522. (Constituent of the Union of Orthodox Hebrew Congregations.) *Ms.* Rev. N. Friedman, Rev. P. Koppenheim; *H. Sec.* S. Kornbluh.
United Synagogue, Meade Hill Road, M8 6LS. ☎ 0161-740 9586. *President* Sidney Huller; *Sec.* Reuben Wilner. ☎ 0161-740 9586.
Whitefield Hebrew Congregation, Park Lane, M45 7PB. ☎ 0161-766 3732. Fax: 0161-767 9453. (Est. 1959). *M.* Rabbi J. Guttentag, (B.A. Hons.); *Admin.* Mrs P.M. Deach.
Yeshurun Hebrew Congregation, Coniston Road, Gatley, Cheshire SK8 4AP (Reg. Charity No. XN10469A). ☎ 0161-428 8242. Fax 0161-491 5265 Email yeshurun@btinternet.com. *M.* Rev. Dr A. Unterman, ☎ 0161-490 6050, Rabbi D.S. Kerbel; *R.* M.R. Isdale; *Admin.* L. Kaufmann.
Zerei Agudas Israel Synagogue, 35 Northumberland Street, Salford M7 0DQ. *M.* Dayan O. Westheim.
Zichron Yitzchak (Sephardi Congregation), 2 New Hall Road, Salford 7. *Emer.* Rabbi S. Amor; *Sec.* A. J. Tesciuba. ☎ 0161-795 0822.

CULTURAL ORGANISATIONS
Institute of Contemporary Jewish Studies, ICJS Conference Facility, Abramovitch Wing, Machon Levi Yitschok, Bury Old Road, Manchester. *Youth & Outreach*

Dir. Rabbi Peretz Chein. *Contact* ☎ 0161-795 4000. *Admin.* ☎ 0161-720 9908. Fax 0161-720 9998.

Israel Information Centre, 142 Bury Old Road, M8 6HD. ☎ 0161-721 4344. Fax 0161-740 7407. Email: iicmcr@dircon.co.uk. Information and presentation of Israel's culture. *Dir.* Doreen Gerson. (Est. 1984.)

Jewish Graduates' Association, *Chairman* E. Leigh, Flat 17, Moorfield, Moor La., Salford M7. ☎ 0161-792 4409.

Jewish Historical Society of England (Branch), *Chairman* F. Baigel, 25 Ravensway, Bury Old Road, Prestwich, M25 0EU. ☎ 0161-740 6403. Email frankbaigel@ iname.com

Jewish Library, Central Library. ☎ 0161-236 9422. Stock now absorbed into main Social Sciences Library collection.

Jewish Museum, 190 Cheetham Hill Road, M8 8LW. ☎ 0161-834 9879 and 0161-832 7353. Fax 0161-832 7353. Mon.-Thurs., 10.30 a.m. to 4 p.m. Sun., 10.30 a.m. to 5 p.m. (Reg. Charity No. 508278). Admission charge. Exhibitions, Heritage trails, Demonstration and Talks. Calendar of events available on request. Educational visits for schools and adult groups must be booked in advance with the Administrator. Contact Don Rainger.

Jewish Male Voice Choir. *Cond.* A. Isaacs. ☎ 0161-740 1210.

EDUCATIONAL ORGANISATIONS

Academy for Rabbinical Research (Kolel), (Reg. Charity No. 526665), 134 Leicester Road, Salford M7 4GB. ☎ 0161-740 1960. *Princ.* Rabbi W. Kaufman; *Sec.* Rev. J. Freedman.

Association For Jewish Youth Northern Office, 27 Bury Old Road, Prestwich, M25 0EY. ☎ 0161-740 6168. Fax 0161-740 6169. Email: north.ajy@ort.org. Website: www.ort.org/anjy/ajy (Est. 1899. Reg. Charity No. 305963). *Hd.* Jonny Wineberg.

Bnos Yisroel School, Leicester Road, Salford, M7 0AH. ☎ 0161-792 3896.

Broughton Jewish Cassel Fox Primary School, Legh Road, Salford M7 4RT. ☎ 0161-792 7773 (school), ☎ 0161-792 2588 (nursery), 792 7738 (kindergarten). Fax 0161-792 7768. *Hd.* Rabbi James Kennard.

Bury & Whitefield Jewish Primary School, Parr La., Bury, Lancs. BL9 8JT. ☎/Fax 0161-766 2888. *H. T.* Mrs N. Massel; *Chairman of Govs.* Rabbi A.J. Jaffe. Nursery School, Parr La., Bury, Lancs. ☎ 0161-767 9390. (Children 2 yrs. plus).

Delamere Forest School, Norley, Nr. Frodsham, Cheshire WA6 6NP. (Reg Charity No. 525913). For Jewish children with special needs. Office: Levi House, Bury Old Road, M7 4QX. ☎ 0161-740 5676. *Chairman of Gov.* Mrs B.R. Goodman, MBE; *H.T.* Mrs J. Vegoda.

Hillel House, Greenheys La., M15 6LR. ☎ 0161-226 10161.

Hubert Jewish High School for Girls, 10 Radford Street, Salford, M7 4NT. ☎ 0161-792 2118. Fax 0161-792 1733. *Princ.* Rabbi Y. Goldblat, MA (Oxon), PGCE.

Jerusalem Academy Study Groups. *Chairman* Rev. G. Brodie, 43 Stanley Road, Salford M7 4FR. ☎ 0161-740 2506.

Jewish Senior Boys School - Kesser Torah, Hubert House, 4 New Hall Road, Salford M7 4EL. ☎ 0161-708 9175.

Jewish Education Bureau Resources Centre, Sacred Trinity Centre, Chapel Street, Salford M3 7AJ. ☎ 0161-832 3709. *Dir.* Rabbi D. S. Charing; *Org. Sec.* Mrs G. Abrahams.

Jewish Programme Materials Project (JPMP), 34 Ashley Road, Altrincham, Cheshire WA14 2DW. ☎ 0161-929 5008. Fax 0161-. Email: s.manchester.jyt@ort.org. *Contact* Adam Kaye, B.Soc.Sc. ☎ 0161-941 4358.

King David Schools. (Est. 1838. Reg. Charity No. 526631)

King David High School, Eaton Road, M8 5DY. ☎ 0161-740 7248. Fax 0161-740 0790. *H. of Upper Campus* E.S. Wilson, J.P., B.A., BEd., F.R.S.A.; *Act. H.T.*

B.N. Levy, B.Ed.; *H. of Sixth Form* Mrs J. Bentley, B. Comm, STCSE; *H. of Yavneh* Rabbi S. Rapport, BSc, BEd, MA.

King David Junior School, Wilton Polygon, M8 5DJ. ☎ 0161-740 3343. *H.T.* E.S. Wilson, J.P., B.A., B.Ed., F.R.S.A.

King David Infant School, Wilton Polygon, M8 6DR. ☎ 0161-740 4110. *H.T.* Mrs J. Rich, B.A.

King David Nursery & Crèche, Eaton Road, M8 5DY. ☎ 0161-740 3481. *Nursery Man.* Mrs S. Isaacs; *Crèche Man.* Mrs L. Marks. *Governors' Admin.* Michael D. Epstein. ☎ 0161-740 3181. Fax 0161-740 3182.

Lubavitch Yeshiva, Lubavitch House, 62 Singleton Road, Salford M7 4LU. ☎ 0161-792 7649. *Dean* Rabbi A. Cohen. *Admin.* S. Weiss, ☎ 01161-740 4243.

Manchester Central Board for Hebrew Education and Talmud Torah (Reg. Charity No. 526164), Emanuel Raffles House, 57 Leicester Road, Salford M7 4DA. ☎/Fax 0161-708 9200. *Chairman* S. Pine; *Admin.* Mrs Y. E. Klein & Mrs M. Gaus. Study Centres: Prestwich Shrubberies Synagogue. *H. T.* Mrs Joan Yodaken, B.A. (Hons). North Manchester Jewish Teenage Centre; B. A. Bayit, 72 Singleton Rd., Salford 7. *Coord* Jill Adler. Shaarei Deoh Special Needs Cheder. *H. T.* Mrs M. Gold.

Manchester Jewish Grammar School, (Reg. Charity No. 526607), Beechwood, Charlton Avenue, Prestwich M25 0PH ☎ 0161-773 1789. *Princ.* Rabbi L. W. Rabinowitz; *H. M. P.* Pink, B.Sc.(Econ), Dip.Ed.

Mechinah Leyshiva, 13 Up. Park Road, Salford M7 0HY. ☎ 0161-795 9275.

Moriah Institute for Further Education, Y. Y. Rubinstein, 97 Singleton Road, Salford M7.

North Cheshire Jewish Primary School, St. Anns Road North, Heald Green, Cheadle, Cheshire SK8 4RZ. ☎ 0161-282 4500. Fax 0161-282 4501. (Scopus Jewish Educational Trust). *H. M.* Mrs J. Brown, M.Sc., Cert. Ed.

North Manchester Jewish Teenage Centre (Reg. Charity No. 1009785), at the Bnei Akiva Bayit, 72 Singleton Road, Salford M7 4LU. Open Sunday morning only. Under the auspices of the Manchester Centre Hebrew Board, 57 Leicester Road, Salford M7 4DA. ☎/Fax 0161-708 9200. *Corres.* D. Black.

Project SEED, (Reg. Charity No. 281307), 47 Stanley Rd., Salford M7 4FR. ☎ 0161-740 0906. Rabbi A. Hassan.

Reshet Torah Education Network, Rabbi S.M. Kupetz, 4 Hanover Gdns., Salford M7 4FQ. ☎ 0161-740 5735.

South Manchester Jewish Youth Trust, (Reg. Charity No. 1040648), c/o North Cheshire Jewish Primary School, St Anne's Road North, Heald Green, Cheshire SK8 4RZ. ☎ 0161-428 3623. Fax 0161-491 0140. Email: s.manchester.jyt@ ort.org. *Community Youth Worker* Andy Sollofe; *Chair* David Zucker. Working with young people in the South Manchester community.

Talmud Torah Chinuch N'orim, 11 Wellington Street, East, Salford M7 9AU. ☎ 0161-792 4522. *Chairman, Bd. of Govs.* B. Waldman.

Whitefield Community Kollel, c/o Whitefield Hebrew Congregation, Park Lane, Whitefield, M45 7PB. *Hon. Admin. P.* Struel. ☎ 0161-766 2150.
Academy of Higher Jewish Learning & Rabbinical Training College. *One to One Learning. Contact* Rabbi Malcolm Herman. ☎ 0161-766 6715/8138.
The Kollel also runs informal educational programmes.
J.A.M. (Judaism and Me) Post-Barmitzvah groups through to students, with an associated girls group and discussion groups for teenagers.
C.A.F.E. (Community & Family Education) Lectures and discussions for adults.
Missing Link Adult Education lecture series, particularly refresher courses in Judaism and a Shabbas morning Explanatory Service.

Whitefield Jewish Youth Centre. *Co-ord.* Mrs B. Howard. ☎ 0161-796 8564.

Yeshiva (Talmudical College), Saul Rosenberg House, Seymour Road, Higher Crumpsall, M8 5BQ. (Est. 1911). ☎ 0161-740 0214. *Princ.* Rabbi M. Z. Ehrentreu; *Sec.* Rev. G. Brodie.

Yesoiday HaTorah School, Sedgley Park Rd., off Bury New Rd., Prestwich M25 0JW. ☎ 0161-798 9725. Fax 0161-773 3914. *Princ.* Rabbi Y. Yodaiken; *Clerk* Mrs V. Fagleman.

Yocheved Segal Kindergarten, Sedgley Pk. Road, Prestwich M25 0JW. ☎ 0161-773 8413.

WELFARE ORGANISATIONS

Manchester Jewish Federation (Reg. Charity No. 220165). 12 Holland Road, M8 4NP. ☎ 0161-795 0024. *Chief Exec.* K. Phillips. (Incorporating Jewish Social Services and Manchester Jews' Benevolent Society.)

Aguda Community Services, 35 Northumberland Street, Salford M7 4DQ. (Reg. Charity No. 287367). ☎ 0161-792 6265. Fax 0161-708 9177. Seeks to provide employment for Jewish people wishing to observe the Sabbath and Holy-days. *Sec.* Mrs O. Weissler.

Brookvale, Caring for People with Special Needs (Reg. Charity No. 526086), Simister Lane, Prestwich, M25 2SF. ☎ 0161-653 1767. Fax 0161-655 3635. *Exec. Dir.* Mrs L. Richmond; *Fin. Dir.* M. Walters.

Heathlands Village (Reg. Charity No. 221890), Heathlands Dr., Prestwich, M25 9SB. ☎ 0161-772 4800. Fax 0161-772 4934. *L. President* Sir S.C. Hamburger, CBE, JP, DL, LLD, MA; *President* Mrs J. Cainer. Accommodates 158 residents in self-contained flats and 161 patients in nursing areas.

Jewish Marriage Council, Manchester Branch, Levi House, Bury Old Road, M8 6FX. Appointments: ☎ 0161-740 5764. Offers: Confidential family and mar-riage counselling, assisting couples and individuals with relationship problems whether they are single, married, widowed, divorced or separated.

Jewish Soup Kitchen (Meals-on-Wheels Service), (Reg. Charity No. 226424), Rita Glickman House, Ravensway, Prestwich M25 0EX. ☎ 0161-795 4930. *H. Sec.* Mrs D. Phillips, B.E.M. ☎ 0161-740 1287.

Manchester Jewish Community Care (formerly Manchester Jewish Blind Society), (Reg. Charity No. 257238), Nicky Alliance Day Centre, 85 Middleton Road M8 4JY. ☎ 0161-740 0111. Fax 0161-721 4273. Day Centre and social work ser-vices for visually and physically disabled, isolated elderly and dementia sufferers. *Chief Exec.* M. Galley; *Chairman* G. Nussbaum.

Manchester Jewish Visitation Board. (Est. 1903.) *Convenor* Y. Brodie; *Chairman* Rev. L. Olsberg. ☎ 0161-740 9711.

Morris Feinmann Home (Residential/Nursing Home for the Discerning), 178 Palatine Road, Didsbury, M20 2YW. ☎ 0161-445 3533.

Outreach Community & Residential Services (Reg. Charity No. 509119), 24A Bury New Road, M25 0LD. ☎ 0161-798 0180. Fax 0161-798 5596. Email: out-reach@dial.pipex.com. Website: outreach.co.uk. *Chief Exec.* Mrs S. Bitaye; *Dir. of Care* P. Williamson.

MARGATE (200)

Synagogue, Godwin Road, Cliftonville. (Est. 1904; new syn. consecrated 1929.) *President* D. Coberman. ☎ 01843 228550. *H. Sec.* D. Kaye. ☎ 01843 223219. Outings catered for: contact *H. Sec.*

Thanet and District Reform Synagogue, 293A Margate Road, Ramsgate, Kent CT12 6TE. ☎ 01843 851164. *Enquiries to:* David Mirsky (*President*) ☎ 01843 603241.

Cemetery: For Margate Hebrew Congregation & Thanet Reform at Manston Road, Margate.

MIDDLESBROUGH (65)

(Incorporating Stockton and Hartlepool.) Synagogue reported closed during 1999. **Synagogue,** Park Road South. (Est. 1873.) *H. Sec.* L. Simons. ☎ 01642 819034 (for

details of services and Chevra Kaddisha). J. Bloom. ☎ 01609 8832272.
Cemetery: Ayresome Green Lane, Middlesbrough.

MILTON KEYNES & DISTRICT (182)
Reform Synagogue (Est. 1978). (Affiliated to R.S.G.B) (Reg. Charity No. 1058193) Inq: Len Sharpstone, 214 Grasmere Way, Linslade, Leighton Buzzard, LU7 7QH. ☎ 01525 373010.

NEWARK
Beth Shalom Holocaust Memorial Centre, Laxton, Newark NG22 0PA. ☎ 01623 836627. Fax 01623 836647. *Dirs.* S.D. Smith, J.M. Smith, Mrs M.H. Smith.

NEWCASTLE UPON TYNE (1,110)
The community was est. in the 1820s, when services were held and a Shochet employed. A cemetery was acquired in 1831. Jews, however, had been resident in Newcastle since before 1775. In the Middle Ages Jews are known to have been est. in Newcastle in 1176. The population figure quoted is that of the community's recent census.
Representative Council of North-East Jewry. (Reg. Charity No. 1071515). *President* D. Franks; *V. Presidents* H. Ross, J. Gellert; *H. Sec.* M.A. Levinson, 39 Kenton Road, NE3 4NH. ☎ 0191-284 4647. Fax 01429 274796. Email tilly-law@enterprise.net.
North East Jewish Recorder (communal journal published by the Representative Council), c/o 28 Montagu Court, Gosforth NE3 4JL. ☎/Fax 0191-285 4318. *Edr.*
United Hebrew Congregation (Est. 1973). The Synagogue, Graham Park Road, Gosforth NE3 4BH. ☎ 0191-284 0959. *President* S. D. Pearlman; *M.* Rabbi Y. Black; *Sec.* Mrs P. Ashton. Mikva on premises. **Burial Cttee:** *Chairman* N. Sterrie ☎ 0191-285 2735.
Reform Synagogue, The Croft, off Kenton Road, Gosforth, NE3 4RF. ☎ 0191-284 8621. (Est. 1965.) (A Constituent of R.S.G.B.) *Chairman* Brenda Dinsdale; **Burial Cttee.** Contact ☎ 0191-284 8621.

OTHER ORGANISATIONS
AJEX, *Chairman* C. Topaz. ☎ 01661 824819.
Awakenings (Singles and Young Couples). Contact Susan and Russel Eisen. ☎ 0191 276 7031.
Education and Youth Cttee., c/o United Hebrew Cong. *Chairman* Adrienne Ross.
Jewish Students' Society and Hillel House, 29-31 Hawthorn Road, Gosforth, NE3 4DE. ☎ 0191-284 1407.
Jewish Welfare Society, Lionel Jacobson House, Graham Park Road, Gosforth NE3 4BH. *Sec.* Mrs P. Ashton. ☎ 0191-284 0959.
Joint Israel Appeal. *H. Sec.* J. Mark. ☎ 0191-284 1903.
Kashrus Cttee., c/o United Hebrew Cong. *Chairman* M. Spodick.
Newcastle Jewish Housing Association Ltd., *Chairman* J. Fox, c/o Lionel Jacobson House, Graham Park Road, Gosforth NE3 4BH.
Newcastle Jewish Players. *Co-Chairmen* Marta Josephs ☎ 0191-285 7173, Vanessa Collins ☎ 0191-285 6462.
North East Jewish Community Services. *Chairman* V. Gallant, ☎ 0191-285 7533; *Community Dev. Off.* Bernard Shaffer, Lionel Jacobson House, ☎ 0191-284 1968. **Community Transport** ☎ 0191-284 1968.
North East Jewish Golfing Society. Contact Anthony Josephs. ☎ 0191 285 7173. **The Swingers** (Ladies' Section of Golfing Society). Contact Faga Speker. ☎ 0191 285 3101.
Philip Cussins House (Residential Care for Jewish Aged in the North East), 33/35 Linden Road, NE3 4EY. ☎ 0191 213 5353. Fax 0191 213 5354. Residents 0191 213 5355.

WIZO:
Sharon Group, *Chairmen* Phyllis Leigh, ☎ 0191-285 6227; Audrey Veeder, ☎ 0191-285 8013.
Rosa Wollstein Group, *Chairman* Anne Jacobson, ☎ 0191-285 0650; Faga Speker ☎ 0191-285 3101.
Zelda's (Kosher meats and delicatessen), Unit 7, Kenton Park Shopping Centre, NE3 4RU. ☎ 0191-213 0013.
Cemeteries: Hazelrigg and Heaton, Newcastle upon Tyne; North Shields (Reform).

NORTHAMPTON (185)
The community marked its centenary in 1988. Services, 8 p.m., Fri. evgs., Yom Tovim and occasional morning services.
Hebrew Congregation, Overstone Road, Northampton, NN1 3JW. ☎ 01604 33345. *M.; Sec.* A. Moss, ☎ 01604-633345.
Cemetery: Towcester Road.

NORWICH (170)
The present community was founded in 1813, Jews having been resident in Norwich during the Middle Ages, and connected with the woollen and worsted trade, for which the city was at that time famous. A resettlement of Jews is believed to have been completed by the middle of the eighteenth century. A synagogue was built in 1848 and destroyed in an air raid in 1942. A temporary synagogue opened in 1948 and the present building was consecrated by the Chief Rabbi in 1969. The congregation serves a large area, having members in Ipswich, Gt. Yarmouth, Lowestoft and Cromer.
Norwich Hebrew Congregation Synagogue, 3a Earlham Road, NR2 3RA. ☎ 01603 623948. *M.; President* Mrs E. Imber-Lithman; *H. Sec.* P. Prinsley, FRCS. ☎ 01603 506482. Fax 01603 508131.
Progressive Jewish Community of East Anglia (Norwich). A new community based in Norwich. Affiliated to the ULPS. Regular services at The Old Meeting House, Colegate, Norwich. *Chairman* Dr E. Crasnow; *M.* Rabbi Melinda Carr; Enquiries to: *H. Sec.* Dr J. Lawrence, ☎ 01603 259271. *Publ.* PJCEA Newsletter.
Jewish Ladies' Society, 3a Earlham Road. *President* Mrs F. Cadywould; *H. Sec.* Mrs M. Prinsley.
Chevra Kadisha, 3a Earlham Road, Norwich. *President* B. C. Leveton. ☎ 01603 749706.
Norfolk and Norwich Branch of the Council of Christians and Jews (Est. 1991). *Chairman* Mr B. Leveton.
Norwich Israel Social Society (NISS), *Chairman* Mr P. Stein. ☎ 01692 630086.

NOTTINGHAM (1,050)
A small community has lived in Nottingham since the early 19th century, and in 1890, with a com. increased by immigrants to some 100 families, the Hebrew Congregation built its first synagogue in Chaucer St. During the Second World War, there was a sharp growth in the community, and the congregation acquired its present synagogue in 1954. With the closure of the Derby syn. in 1986, many of its members joined the Nottingham Hebrew Cong. The Progressive Jewish Cong. was est. in 1959.
Nottingham Representative Council, 42 Weardale Rd., Sherwood NG5 1DD. ☎ 0115 9606121. *Chairman* D. Lipman. ☎ 0115 9664690. *Sec.* Mrs A. Lewis.
Hebrew Congregation, Shakespeare Villas, NG1 4FQ. ☎ 0115 472004. *President* David Simmons.
Progressive Jewish Congregation (ULPS), Lloyd Street, NG5 4BP. ☎ 0115 9624761. *Chairman* B. Peters. ☎ 0115 913 2619. *M.* Rabbi Amanda Golby; *H. Sec.* Mrs L. Chapman. ☎ 0115 9281613.
Federation of Women Zionists. *H. Sec.* Mrs S. Flitterman, 11 Priory Road, West Bridgford, NG2 5HU.

Jewish Welfare Board. *Chairman* Dr M. Caplan. ☎ 0115 260245. *Hon. Sec.* P. Seymour, 115 Selby Rd., West Bridgford, NG2 7BB. ☎ 0115 452895.
Miriam Kaplowitch House, Jewish rest home, 470 Mansfield Road, NG5 2DR ☎ 0115 624274 (Residents) and 0115 9622038 (Matron & Admin.) (Est. 1986).
University of Nottingham Jewish and Israel Society, c/o The University of Nottingham, NG7 2RD.
Women's Benevolent Society. *Chairman* Mrs E. Litman, J.P. ☎ 0115 9231102.

OXFORD (Resident Jewish pop. 700 approx.)
An important centre in the medieval period. The modern community was est. in 1842. In 1974 the Oxford Synagogue and Jewish Centre was built on the site of the earlier synagogue. It serves the resident community and a fluctuating number of university students, and is available for all forms of Jewish worship.
Jewish Congregation, The Synagogue, 21 Richmond Road, OX1 2JL. ☎ 01865 53042. *President* Joel Kaye. ☎ 01865 248010.
Oxford Masorti (services held the last Shabbat each month). *Contact* Mrs W. Fidler. ☎ 01565 726959. Email: wendyfidler@compuserve.com.
The Progressive Jewish Group of Oxford (affiliated to ULPS). Inq: Katherine Shock, ☎/Fax 01865 515584, or Ruth Cohen ☎ 01865 765197.
Oxford University L'Chaim Society, Albion House, Albion Place, Little Gate, OX1 1QZ. ☎ 01865 794462.
University Jewish Society. (Est. 1903). *Senior Member* Mike Woodin, Balliol College, ☎ 01865 248073; *Sec.*; *Chaplain* Rev. M. Weisman, M.A. (Oxon.). ☎ 020-8451 3484.

PETERBOROUGH (105)
Hebrew Congregation, 142 Cobden Avenue, PE1 2NU. ☎ 01733 571282. (Congregation est. 1940. Syn. opened 1954. Affiliated to the U.S.) *Admin.* C. Conn. ☎ 01733 571282. Services Kabbalat Shabbat 8pm. Liberal Jewish Community. *Admin.* N. Gordon ☎ 01733 22813; Juliet Vart ☎ 01733 53269. Services first and third Shabbat at 10.30am.
Liberal Jewish Community (ULPS). Enquiries to Elisabeth Walker. ☎ 01733 266188.

PLYMOUTH (100)
The Plymouth cong. was founded in 1745, when a cemetery was opened. Jews lived in the city even earlier. The syn., built in 1762, is the oldest Ashkenazi house of worship still standing in the English-speaking world. Its 225th anniversary in 1987 was marked by a service attended by representatives of the United Synagogue, the Board of Deputies and the Civic Authorities. In the early 19th century, Plymouth was one of the four most important provincial centres of Anglo-Jewry. The history of the community, 'The Plymouth Synagogue 1761–1961' by Doris Black, was published in 1961.
Hebrew Congregation (Reg. Charity 220010), Catherine Street, PL1 2AD. ☎ 01752 301955. (Est. 1761.) *H. Sec.* Dr P. Lee. ☎ 01822 612281.

PORTSMOUTH (385)
The com. was est. in 1746 and opened a syn. in Oyster Row, later to move to a building in White's Row, off Queen St. which was occupied for over 150 years. The present syn. was built in 1936. The cemetery was acquired in 1749 and is the oldest in the Regions still in use. It is situated in Fawcett Road, which has been known for more than 200 years as Jews' Lane. By 1815 Portsmouth was one of the four main Jewish centres outside London, the others being Plymouth, Liverpool and Birmingham. Portsmouth's prosperity declined after the Napoleonic Wars.
See also under Winchester.
Synagogue, The Thicket, Elm Grove, Southsea PO5 2AA. ☎ 02393 821494. *M.* Rev. H. Caplan; *Hon. Sec.* Mrs P. Etherington.

Board of Guardians, The Thicket (Est. 1804)
Chevra Kadisha, The Thicket.
Jewish Ladies' Benevolent Society (Est. 1770.), The Thicket.
Cemeteries: Fawcett Road, Kingston, New Road; Catherington.

POTTERS BAR (205)
Synagogue, (affiliated to the United Synagogue). *M.* Rev. D. Levy. Correspondence
to: P.O. Box 119, Potters Bar, Herts.

PRESTON (25)
Synagogue, est. 1882, now closed. *H. Sec.* Dr C. E. Nelson, 31 Avondale Road,
Southport PR9 0NH. ☎ 01704 538276.

RADLETT (750)
Synagogues:
Radlett (U.S.), 22 Watling St., P.O. Box 28, Herts. WD7 7PN. *M.* Rabbi G.
Sylvester ☎ 01923-856878; *Admin.* Mrs J. Bower.
Radlett & Bushey Reform Synagogue (RSBG), 118 Watling St., Herts. WD7 7AA.
☎ 01923 856110. Email office@r-brs.freeserve.co.uk. *M.* Rabbi Alexandra
Wright. *H. Sec.* G. Nathan.
Hertsmere Progressive Synagogue (ULPS), High St., Elstree. *M.* Rabbi J. Black. *H.
Sec.* Estelle Leigh. ☎ 020-8950 3268.

READING (500)
The community began in 1886 with the settlement of a number of tailors from
London. They attracted the help of such personages as Samuel Montague, Claude
Montefiore, Sir Hermann Gollancz and Lady Lucas to build and support a syna-
gogue in 1900, and the syn. has been in continuous use ever since. This flourishes
today as the centre of the Reading Hebrew Cong., which has a growing member-
ship of 160 families, and is the only Orthodox cong. in Berkshire. The Sir
Hermann Gollancz Hall next to the syn. is the venue of many social groups.
The Progressive Community was founded in 1979 and attracts membership from
across the Thames Valley.
Berkshire Jewish Representative Council (Est. 1998.). *Chairman* J. Foreman, 2b
Tilehurst Rd., RG1 7TN. ☎ 0118-957 1167. Fax 0118-951 0740. *Contact*
Orthodox Synagogue, (Reg. Charity No.: 220098). Goldsmid Road, RG1 7YB.
☎ 0118 9571018. *M.* Rabbi David Lister, ☎ 0118 957 3954; *H. Sec.* Mrs Louise
Creme, ☎ 0118 957 1018. Internet: www. datanet.co.uk/enterprise/rhc/ Email:
Secretary@rhc.datanet.co.uk.
WIZO & Judaica Shop. Mrs Pamela Kay ☎ 0118 9573680.
Food Shop. Kosher meat and provisions. Mrs Carol Kay ☎ 0118 575069.
Thames Valley Progressive Jewish Community. (Est. 1979.) (Constituent of ULPS),
6 Church Street, Reading. For details of services, religious and social events, con-
tact: *Chairman* B. Myer ☎ 01189 882805; *M.* Rabbi Sybil Sheridan
☎ 01628 71058.
University Jewish Society, c/o Reading Hillette, 82 Basingstoke Road, Reading.
☎ 0118 9873282.

REIGATE AND REDHILL (45)
Jewish Community. (Est. 1968.) *Chairman* M. J. Kemper, 59 Gatton Road,
Reigate, Surrey. ☎ 017372 42076.

ST. ALBANS (200)
Hebrew Congregation (Affiliated to the U.S.), Oswald Road, AL1 3AQ. *H. Sec.* H.
Turner, 8 Tudor Court, High Street, London Colney, AL2 1JZ. ☎ 01727 825295.
St. Albans Masorti Synagogue, Inquiries: *Sec.* Mrs K. Phillips. ☎ 01727 860642;
Co-Chair Dr J. Freedman, L. Harris; *T. P.* Hoffbrand.

ST. ANNE'S ON SEA (500)

Hebrew Congregation, Orchard Road, FY8 1PJ. ☎ 01253 721831. *President* P. Davidson. ☎ 01253 723920. *Hon. Secs.* A. Brown & L. Jackson. ☎ 01253-721835. *M.* Rabbi I. Broder. ☎ 01253-781815.
Ladies Guild, *Chairman* Mrs L. Gee. ☎ 01253-726854.
Cemetery: Consecrated section of municipal cemetery at Regents Avenue, Lytham.

SHEFFIELD (ca. 650)

The earliest extant records of the Sheffield Hebrew Congregation date only from 1850, but the congregation had then been in existence for some time, and burial records exist from 1837. There were Jews living in Sheffield at the beginning of the nineteenth century and even earlier. The syn. was at that time in Figtree Lane. Previously there had been one in Holly Lane, and still earlier there had been regular services in private houses. A study of the community, 'Sheffield Jewry: Commentary on a Community' by Armin Krausz, was published in 1980.
Representative Council of Sheffield and District Jews. *President* Selwyn M. Burchhardt; *H. Sec.* Tony Kay, 105 Bents Road, S11 9RH. ☎ 0114 236 0970.
Jewish Congregation & Centre, Wilson Road, S11. ☎ 0114 2662930. *R.* Rabbi Y. Golomb. ☎ 0114 2663567. *President* Eric Kalman; *H. Sec.* Mrs M. Shaw, 67 Bents Rd., S11 9RH. ☎ 0114 2362217.
Sheffield and District Reform Jewish Congregation. (Est. 1989) P.O. Box 675, S11 8SP. Services held alternate Friday nights and every fourth Shabbat. For further information please ring 0114 2308433. *Chairman* Dr J. Kinderlerer. ☎ 0114 2301054.
Hebrew Education Board, Psalter House, Psalter Lane, S11 (Est. 1902.) *President* Dr A. Anderson, 5 Kingscroft Close, Dore, S17 3RE. ☎ 0114 2351041.
Jewish Welfare Board, *H. Sec.* M. Ballin. ☎ 0114 2366800.
Sheffield University Jewish Society, c/o The Sabbatical Office, SUSU, Western Bank, S10 2TN.
Sheffield Israel Society. *Chairman* Mrs F. Wilenski, 62 The Glen, Endcliffe Vale Rd., S10 3FN. ☎ 0114 2662210.
Sheffield Housing Association. *Hon. Sec.* Mrs Joyce Flowers, 44 The Glen, S10 3FN. ☎ 0114 2678744.

SOLIHULL (300)

Solihull & District Hebrew Congregation, Monastery Dr, B91 1DW. *M.* Rabbi Y. Pink; *H. Sec.* P. Fiddler, 14 Abbots Close, Knowle B93 9PP. ☎ 01564 775715.
Solihull Jewish Social & Cultural Society, *H. Sec.* E. Lesser, 43 Vicarage Rd., Yardley, Birmingham B33 8PH. ☎ 0121-783 2464.

SOUTH SHIELDS (9)

Hebrew Congregation, Contact: Mr H. Tavroges. ☎ 0191-285 4834. The synagogue is now closed. Friday evening services at members' homes at 6 p.m. throughout the year.
Cemetery: Consecrated section of the municipal cemetery.

SOUTHAMPTON (105)

The orthodox congregation dates from 1833 when the first synagogue in East Street was founded. The synagogue built in 1864 in Albion Place was demolished in 1963, when the present one was consecrated. There were Jewish residents in Southampton in 1786. Since 1838, when Abraham Abraham was elected to the Town Council, they have shared in civic affairs. The South Hampshire Reform Jewish Community was formed in 1983 (see also Winchester, p.129).
Orthodox Synagogue, Mordaunt Road, Inner Ave. ☎ 02380-220129. *President* S. Ferder. *H. Sec.* C.D. Freeman, 23 Roslin Hall, 6 Manor Rd., Bournemouth BH1 3ES.

South Hampshire Reform (RSGB). Services held at the Unitarian Hall, Bellevue Road, off London Road, on Friday at 7.30pm and Shabbat at 10.30am. *Chairman* Di White. ☎ 02393 480442; *H. Sec.* Sylvia Franks. ☎ 01962 712534.
Hartley Library, University of Southampton, Highfield, houses the Anglo-Jewish Archives and Parkes Library (see p.56).
Hillel House, 5 Brookvale Road. ☎ 02380 557742.
Cemetery: Consecrated section at the municipal Hollybrook cemetery.

SOUTHEND, WESTCLIFF & LEIGH-ON-SEA (4,500)
Jewish families settled in the Southend area in the late 19th century, mainly from London's East End. In 1906 the first temporary synagogue was built in wood in Station Road, Westcliff. In 1912 one of the present synagogues was built in Alexandra Rd, Southend. In continuous use since, it is now one of the historical sights in the area. A breakaway faction built its own syn. in Ceylon Road, Westcliff, in 1928, but the two congs later reunited. A new syn. was built in Finchley Road, Westcliff in 1969 and the Ceylon Road premises were converted into a youth centre. The com. is growing and Jews from different parts of the world now live in the area.
Southend-on-Sea & District Jewish Representative Council. *Chairman* Derek Baum, M.B.E. ☎ 01702 343789; *Sec.* Jeffrey Barcan, 22 Second Ave., Westcliff-on-Sea, Essex SS0 8HY. ☎ 01702-343192.

Southend and Westcliff Hebrew Congregation, Finchley Rd., Westcliff-on-Sea, Essex SS0 8AD. *President* David Gold, 23 Chadacre Road, SS1 3QX. ☎ 01702 586774. *M.* Rabbi M. Lew. ☎ 01702 344900. Fax 01702 391131. *Fin. Sec.* Mrs A. Marx. ☎ 01702 344900; *Admin.* Mrs Janice Steele. Synagogues at: Finchley Road, Westcliff; 99 Alexandra Road, Southend.
Southend and District Reform Synagogue, 851 London Road, Westcliff. ☎ 01702 75809. *Chairman & Sec.* Mr. N. Klass & Mrs A. Klass, 22 Crowstone Ave., Westcliff. ☎ 01702 338460.

Mikva, 44 Genesta Road, Westcliff. ☎ 01702 344900. *Supt.* Rivki Lew. ☎ 01702 344900.
Orthodox Jewish Cemetery, Sutton Road, Southend. (Entr. Stock Road). ☎ 01702 344900.
Reform Jewish Cemetery, Sutton Road, Southend. (Entr. Stock Road).
Myers Communal Hall, Finchley Road, Westcliff. ☎ 01702 344900.
Kashrut Commission, *Chairman* Mrs J. Sheldon. ☎ 01702 344900.
Ladies' Guild (Orthodox). *Chairman* Mrs N. Baum; *H.Sec.* Mrs B. Franks.
Ladies' Guild (Reform). *Sec.* Mrs R. Brenner, 12 The Drive, Westcliff. ☎ 01702 75809.

EDUCATIONAL, CULTURAL AND YOUTH ORGANISATIONS
Coleman & Lilian Levene Talmud Torah (Orthodox), Finchley Road, Westcliff. ☎ 01702 344900. *H.T.* Mrs A. Gilbert.
Emunah Ladies' Society. *Chairman* Mrs F. Sober, 16 Crosby Rd., Westcliff. ☎ 01702-330440. *Sec.* Mrs M. Simons.
Hebrew Education Board. *Chairman* Mrs A. Moss. ☎ 01702 344900.
Herzlia Day School, Finchley Road, Westcliff. ☎ 01702 340986. *H. T.* Mrs M. Hass.
Jewish Lads' & Girls' Brigade. *Chairman* Mrs R. O'Brart, 11 The Drive, Westcliff SS0 8PL. ☎ 01702-714122; *Sec.* Mr R. Rams.
JNF Impact. *Chairman* A. Larholt. *Sec.* L. Barnes, 26 Second Ave., Westcliff, SS0 8HY.
Lecture Board. Mrs S. Greenstein, 62 Chadwick Road, Westcliff SS0 8L. ☎ 01702 343794.

Monday Shalom Club. *Chairman* G. Kalms, 14 Tower Court, Westcliff Parade, Westcliff. ☎ 01702 337152.
Southend District Social Committee (Reform). *Chairman* Mrs S. Kaye.
Talmud Torah (Reform), 851 London Road, Westcliff. *Princ.* Mrs Woods. ☎ 01702 75809.
Thursday Club, *Chairman* Mrs L. Barnes, 26 Second Ave., Westcliff.
UJIA. *Chairman* S. Salt Esq., 100 Grand Parade, Leigh-on-Sea. ☎ 01702 476349.
Women's Zionist Society. *Chairman* Mrs J. Kalms, 6 Leitrim Avenue, Shoeburyness; *H. Sec.* Mrs J. Barnett, 22 Kings Road, Westcliff. ☎ 01702 340731.
Young Marrieds Cultural & Social Group. *Chairman* L. Herlitz Esq., 10 Cliff Road, Leigh-on-Sea, Essex SS9 1JH.
Youth Centre (Orthodox), 38 Ceylon Road, Westcliff. ☎ 01702 346545. *Chairman* A. Witzenfeld; *Sec.* D. Jay, 9 St. Clements Avenue, Leigh-on-Sea.

WELFARE ORGANISATIONS
A.J.E.X. Communal Hall, Finchley Road Synagogue, Westcliff. *Chairman* Mrs R. Plaskow, 8 Crosby Rd., Westcliff-on-Sea. ☎ 01702 340995.
B'nai B'rith. *President* Mrs F. Sober; *Sec.* N. D. Wine, 32 Leasway, Westcliff. ☎ 01702 710607.
Hospital Kosher Meals Service. Rabbi M Lew. ☎ 01702 344900.
Kosher Meals-on-Wheels Service. *H. Sec.* A. Rubin, 14 Drake Rd., Westcliff. ☎ 01702 345568.
Raymond House for Aged, 6 Clifton Terrace, Southend. ☎ 01702 340054 (Residents): 01702 341687 (Matron).
Southend Friends of Ravenswood. J. Freedman, 111 Hampton Gardens, Southend. ☎ 01702-341515.
Southend Aid Society. *Sec.* H. Kanutin, 96 Willingale Way, Thorpe Bay. ☎ 01702 582996.
Southend & District A.J.E.X. *President* Derek Baum, MBE. *Chairman* D. Balch; *H. Sec.* J. Barcan, 22 Second Avenue, Westcliff. ☎ 01702 343192.
Southend & Westcliff Community Centre, Victoria Oppenheim House, 1 Cobham Road, Westcliff. ☎ 01702 334655. *Care Services Man.* Mrs P. Turner.

SOUTHPORT (1,382)
The first Synagogue was consecrated in 1893 and the congregation moved to Arnside Road, in 1924. The New Synagogue (Reform) was est. in 1948. The community grew between and during the First and Second World Wars, but is now decreasing.
Jewish Representative Council. *President* Mrs Sonia Abrahamson, 65 Beach Priory Gardens, PR9 2SA. ☎ 01704 540704; *H. Sec.* Ivor Galkoff, 16, Argyle Court, 3 Argyle Road, Hesketh Park, PR9 9LQ. ☎ 01704 538119.
Synagogue, Arnside Road, PR9 0QX. ☎ 01704 532964. M. Rabbi M. Santhouse; *President* Dr Cyril Nelson; *Sec.* Mrs Maureen Cohen.
Beth Hasepher, Arnside Road. ☎ 01704 532964.
Manchester House, 83 Albert Road. ☎ 01704 534920 (office); 01704 530436 (visitors).
Mikveh, Arnside Road. ☎ 01704 532964.
New Synagogue, Portland St. PR8 1LR. ☎ 01704 535950. M. ; *Emer. Rabbi* Rabbi S. Kay; *H. Sec.* Mrs E. Lippa.
Jewish Convalescent and Aged Home, 81 Albert Road. ☎ 01704 531975 (office); 01704 530207 (visitors.)

STAINES & DISTRICT (390)
(Incorporating Slough & Windsor)

Synagogue (affiliated to the U.S.), Westbrook Road, South Street, Middx. TW18 4PR. *H. Sec.* Mrs P. D. Fellman. ☎ 01784 254604.

STOKE-ON-TRENT (30)
Hebrew Congregation, Birch Terr., Hanley. (Est. 1873. Reg. Charity No. 232104) *President* H. S. Morris, 27 The Avenue, Basford, Newcastle, Staffs. ST5 0ND. ☎ 01782 616417; *T.* H. Slann. ☎ 01782 617700.

SUNDERLAND (60)
The first Jewish settlement was in 1755. The first congregation was est. about 1768; and was the first regional community to be represented at the BoD. A syn. was erected in Moor St. in 1862; rebuilt in 1900; and in 1928 the cong. moved to Ryhope Road, The Beth Hamedrash, which was est. in Villiers St. in 1899, and moved to Mowbray Road in 1938, closed in December 1984. Arnold Levy published a 'History of the Sunderland Jewish Community' in 1956.
Communal Rav. Rabbi S. Zahn, 13 Ashgrove Terrace, Gateshead NE8 1RL. ☎ 0191-490 1606.
Hebrew Congregation, incorporating Sunderland Beth Hamedrash, Ryhope Road, SR2 7EQ. ☎ 0191-5658093. *President* J. Sadlik; *H. Sec.* T. H. Jackson.
Board of Shechita. *President* J. Sadlik; *H. Sec.* Theo Jackson. ☎ 0191-522 7822.
Chevra Kadisha. *President* Dr H. Davis; Contact: Ivor Saville, ☎ 0191-522 9710.
Hebrew Board of Guardians. (Est. 1869).
Mikva, Mowbray Road. Contact Mrs Zahn. ☎ 0191-490 1606.
Talmudical College and Yeshiva. ☎ 0191 490 1606. (See Gateshead p.110.) *Princ.* Rabbi S. Zahn.
Cemetery: Bishopwearmouth Cemetery, Hylton Road, Sunderland.

SWINDON (72)
The community formed by Second World War evacuees has dispersed, but a community was re-formed in 1983.
Jewish Community. (Associated Community of R.S.G.B. Reg. Charity No. 296761). *Acting Chairman* Walter Gainsley; *H. Sec.* Graham Grange, 16 Dowling Street, SN1 5QY. Services: Fri evgs. and Yomtovim. Social evengs on regular basis. *Enq.* Mrs Angie Scott. ☎ 01793-524093 or Martin Vandervelde. ☎ 01793- 521910.

TORQUAY (TORBAY) (20)
Synagogue, Old Town Hall, Abbey Road. Sabbath services 10.30 a.m. on first Sabbath of each month. *Chairman* Dr J. Lyons. ☎ 01803 25511. Inq.: E. Freed, 'Son Bou', 7 Broadstone Park Road, Livermead, Torquay TQ2 6TY. ☎ 01803 607197.
Chevra Kadisha: Cemetery, Colley End Road, Paignton, Torbay. *Chairman* Leon Fredman, JP. ☎ 01803 295130.

WALLASEY (50)
Hebrew Congregation, c/o Hon. Sec. (Est. 1911.) *President* D. Daniels; *T.* D. J. Waldman; *H. Sec.* L. S. Goldman, 28 Grant Road, Wirral, Merseyside, L46 2RY. ☎ 0151-638 6945.

WELWYN GARDEN CITY (290)
Synagogue (Affiliated to U.S.), Handside Lane, Barn Close, Herts AL8 6ST. ☎ 01438-715686. *Admin.* Mrs D. Prag.

WHITLEY BAY (20)
Hebrew Congregation, 2 Oxford Street, Whitley Bay NG26 3TB. *H. Sec.* M. A. Sonn, 2 Grasmere Cres. ☎ 01632 2521367; 01670 367053 (day).

WINCHESTER
South Hampshire Reform Jewish Community. (Reg. Charity No. 1040109. Est.1983). *Chairperson* Deborah White, 25 Havelock Rd., Southsea, Hants. PO5 1RU. *Sec.* Francis Dowty, 61 Newfield Rd., Liss Forest, Hants. GU33 7BW. ☎ 01730 892155. Services every second and fourth Friday at the Synagogue, Mordaunt Rd., The Inner Ave., Southampton. Saturday morning service first and third Saturdays, varying venues. Sunday morning Cheder. Social activities, adult education discussions, etc.

WOLVERHAMPTON (11)
Synagogue, Fryer St. (Est. 1850.) Closure of the synagogue was reported in 1999. Contact Mrs J. Kronheim, 94 Wergs Road, Tettenhall WV6 8TH. ☎ 01902 752474.
Cemetery: Consecrated section at Jeffcock Road Corporation Cemetery, Wolverhampton.

YORK (25)
A memorial stone was consecrated at Clifford's Tower, York Castle, in 1978 in memory of the York Jewish community massacred there in 1190. A small community resettled and continued to live in York until the 1290 expulsion. There is now a small com. in the city and a Jewish Soc. at York Univ.
York Hebrew Congregation. Enq. B. Sugar, 3 Rawcliffe Grove, YO3 4NR. ☎ 01904 624479.
Contact: A. S. Burton. ☎ 01423 330537.

WALES

CARDIFF (1,200)
Jews settled in Cardiff about the year 1787. The present community was founded in 1840.
Jewish Representative Council. *Chairman* Prof. P.D.J. Weitzman; *H. Sec.* Mrs J. R. Cotsen, 71 Cyncoed Road, CF2 6AB. ☎ 02920-484999.
Israel Information Centre Wales & the West of England, P.O.B. 98, Cardiff, CF2 6XN. ☎/Fax 02920-461780. *Dir.* Jean A. Evans.
Orthodox Synagogue, Brandreth Road, Penylan, Cardiff. ☎ 02920-473728/491795. *Sec.* Mrs S. C. Glavin.
New Synagogue, Moira Terrace, CF2 1EJ. (opp. Howard Gdns.). (A Constituent of R.S.G.B.) ☎ 02920-491689. *Sec.* Mrs C. Salmon. ☎ 02920-491689.
Hillel House, 89 Crwys Rd., Cardiff. ☎ 02920-231114. Applications for admission: Mrs P. Freed, 210 Lake Road East, CF2 5NR. ☎ 02920-758614.
Cardiff Jewish Helpline (formerly Cardiff Jewish Board of Guardians). *Chairman* Mr. A. Schwartz, 5 Woodvale Avenue, Cyncoed, Cardiff. ☎ 02920-750990.
Jewish Kindergarten, Penylan Synagogue (as above), Mrs C. Bloom. ☎ 02920-756840.
Kashrus Commission. Rabbi D. Levey at Penylan Synagogue Office. ☎ 02920-473728.
Kosher Butcher & Delicatessen. Visiting butcher A. Gee & Son every Wednesday at Penylan Synagogue. ☎ 02920-491795.
Mikva, .
South Wales Jewish Retirement and Nursing Home, Penylan House, Penylan Road. ☎ 02920-485327. (Est. 1945.) *President* Prof. P.D.J. Weitzman; *Matron* Mrs Varner. *H. Sec.* Mrs M. Cantor.
Union of Jewish Students, c/o Hillel House. ☎ 02920-231114.
Cemeteries: Old Cemetery - High Fields Road, Roath Park; New Cemetery - Greenfarm Road, Ely; Reform: at Cowbridge Road Entrance, Ely Cemetery.

LLANDUDNO AND COLWYN BAY (45)

Hebrew Congregation, 28 Church Walks, Llandudno LL30 2HL. (Est. 1905). Friday night service held from Pesach to Yom Kippur at 8pm. Winter services at 6.15pm. *Sec.* B. Hyman, 9 Glyn Isaf, Llandudno Junction, Gwynedd LL31 9HT. ☎ 01492 572549. Llandudno serves as the centre for the dwindling coms. of North Wales, including Bangor, Rhyl, Colwyn Bay and Caernarvon.

MERTHYR TYDFIL

Synagogue now closed. The com. was est. before 1850. The cemetery is still being maintained. Apply to the Cardiff Jewish Rep. C. (See above).

NEWPORT (Gwent) (10)

Synagogue, (Opened 1871.) 45 St Marks Crescent, NP9 5HE. ☎ 01633 262308. *Chairman* I. Rocker, 2 Stow Park Circle, NP9 4HE.
Burial Society, c/o Cardiff Orthodox Synagogue, Penylan, Cardiff.
Cemetery: Risca Road, Newport.

SWANSEA (245)

The Jewish community dates at the latest from 1768, when the Corporation granted a plot of land for use as a cemetery. In 1780 a syn. was built. Probably its history is even older, for Jews are known to have been living in the town from about 1730. The syn. in Goat St. was destroyed in an air raid in Feb. 1941, but another was erected in the Ffynone district. The former Llanelli cong. is now part of the Swansea com.
Hebrew Congregation. (Est. 1780.) Synagogue, Ffynone. *Chairman* H. M. Sherman, 17 Mayals Green, Mayals, Swansea SA3 5JR. ☎ 01792 401205.
Chevra Kadisha. *Chairman* D. Sandler. ☎ 01792 206285.
Cemeteries at Oystermouth and Townhill.

WELSHPOOL

Welshpool Progressive Jewish Group (Affiliated to ULPS), Elmhurst, Severn Rd., Welshpool, Powys, SY2 7AR. Inq.: dr A. L. Solomon. ☎ 01938 552744.

SCOTLAND

Scottish Council of Jewish Communities, Jewish Community Centre, 222 Fenwick Rd., Giffnock, Glasgow G46 6UE. ☎ 0141-577 8208. Fax 0141-577 8202. Email j-scot@j-scot.org. (Est. 1987 as Standing Committee of Scottish Jewry.) Democratic umbrella body representing the Jewish Community of Scotland. *Convenor* Ephraim Borowski.
The Scottish Jewish Archives Centre. (Est. 1987.) Garnethill Synagogue, 127 Hill Street, Glasgow G3 6UB. ☎/Fax 0141 332 4911. To collect, catalogue, preserve and exhibit records of communal interest. To stimulate study in the history of the Jews of Scotland. To heighten awareness in the Jewish communities of Scotland of their local cultural and religious heritages. *Chairman* Dr Jack E. Miller, O.B.E., J.P.; Dr Kenneth Collins, Ph.D.; *H. T.* Joe Sacharin; *H. Sec.* Mrs Natalie Cohen; *Dir.* Harvey L. Kaplan, M.A.

ABERDEEN (30)

Refurbished synagogue and community centre opened 1983.
Hebrew Congregation, 74 Dee Street, AB1 2DS. ☎ 01224 582135. (Est. 1893.) *H. Sec.* Sandra Shrago. ☎ 01467 642726.

DUNDEE (22)

Hebrew Congregation, 9 St. Mary Place. (Est. 1874. New synagogue opened 1978.) *Chairman* H. Gillis, Sandy Lodge, Carnoustie, Tayside, DD7 6DB. ☎ 01241 853144. Dundee Univ. Jewish Society is centred at the synagogue.

DUNOON
Argyll and Bute Jewish Community. Contact Barry Kaye, Edgemont, 34 Argyll Road, Dunoon, PA23 8ES. ☎/Fax 01369-705 118.

EDINBURGH (500)
The Edinburgh Town Council and Burgess Roll, Minutes of 1691 and 1717, record applications by Jews for permission to reside and trade in Edinburgh. Local directories of the eighteenth century contain Jewish names. There is some reason to believe that there was an organised Jewish community in 1780 but no cemetery, and in 1817 it removed to Richmond Ct. where there was also for a time a rival congregation. In 1795, the Town Council sold a plot of ground on the Calton Hill to Herman Lyon, a Jewish dentist, to provide a burying place for himself and members of his family. In 1816, when a syn. was opened a cemetery was also acquired. The present syn. in Salisbury Road was consecrated in 1932 and renovated in 1980.
Hebrew Congregation, 4 Salisbury Road. ☎ 0131-667 3144. (Est. 1816, New Synagogue built 1932.) M. Rabbi D. Sedley, 67 Newington Road, Edinburgh EH9. ☎ 0131-667 9360; H. Sec. J. Sperber, 20 East Clapperfield, EH16 6TU.
Board of Guardians. H. Sec. I. Shein (as above).
Chevra Kadisha. H. Sec. R. I. Brodie, 60 Telford Road, Edinburgh EH4 2LY. ☎ 0131-332 4386.
Friendship Club. President W. Caplan, 25 Watertoun Road, Edinburgh EH9. ☎ 0131-667 7984.
Jewish Literary Society. President Mrs J. Merrick, 10 Sycamore Gardens EH12 5LA. ☎ 0131-334 0242.
Jewish Old Age Home for Scotland (Edinburgh Cttee). President J. S. Caplan; H. Sec. Miss A. Lurie, 26 South Lauder Road, 9. ☎ 0131-667 5500.
Ladies' Guild. President Mrs H. Rifkind, 37 Cluny Drive, Edinburgh EH10 6DU. ☎ 0131-447 7386.
The Edinburgh Star. Community Journal. Published 3 times a year. Editor, 9 Warrington Crescent, EH3 5LA. ☎ 0131-556 7774.
University Jewish Society. President P. Albert, c/o Societies' Centre, Room 6, 21 Hill Place.

GLASGOW (6,700)
The Glasgow Jewish community was founded in 1823 although there are records of Jewish activity in the city for many years prior to that. The first Jewish cemetery was opened in the prestigious Glasgow Necropolis in 1831 and the community was housed in a variety of synagogues in the city centre for many years. The community grew in the 1870s and the Garnethill Synagogue, the oldest Jewish building in Scotland and home of the Scottish Jewish Archives Centre, was opened in 1879. At the same time Jews began settling in the Gorbals district just south of the River Clyde where there was a substantial Jewish community with many synagogues and Jewish shops and communal institutions until the 1950s. None of these now remains. In more recent years the community has been centred in the southern suburbs such as Giffnock and Newton Mearns where most Jewish institutions are now situated.
Details of Jewish history in Glasgow in the early days (1790–1919) can be found in 'Second City Jewry' and 'Scotland's Jews' by Dr Kenneth Collins, available from the Glasgow Jewish Representative Council.
Jewish Representative Council, 222 Fenwick Rd., Giffnock, G46 6UE. ☎ 0141-577 8200. E-mail: glasgow@ort.org. President Mrs D. Wolfson; H. Sec. S. I. Kliner; Admin. Mrs D. Zellman. Information Desk ☎ 0141-577 8228. Fax 0141-577 8202.
West Scotland Kashrut Commission, Chairman M. Livingstone; H. Sec. H. Tankel. ☎ 0141-423 5830.

Hebrew Burial Society (as Rep. Council), ☎ 0141-577 8226. *Chairman* S. Shenkin. *Enquiries* J. Arthur.

Mikvah, Giffnock & Newlands Syn., Maryville Avenue, Giffnock. *Enquiries*: Mrs C. Fletcher, Dip. Ed. ☎ 0141-620 3156.

United Synagogue Council, Queen's Park Syn., Falloch Road. ☎ 0141-632 1743.

SYNAGOGUES

Garnethill Synagogue, 125/7 Hill Street, G3. ☎ 0141-332 4151. (Est. 1875.) *M. A.* Soudry; *Chairman* G. Levin; *H. Sec.* Mrs V. Livingston.

Queen's Park Synagogue, Falloch Road, G42. ☎ 0141-632 2139. *M.* Rabbi M. Fletcher. *Sec.* Mrs G. Fox. *Chairman* D. Jackson.

Giffnock and Newlands Synagogue, Maryville Avenue, Giffnock G46. ☎ 0141-577 8250. *M.* Rabbi A.M. Rubin; *R.*; *Chairman* Dr K. Collins; *Sec.* Mrs G. Gardner.

Glasgow New Synagogue, 147 Ayr Road, Newton Mearns G77 5ND. *M.* Rabbi P. Tobias; *Sec.* P. Kraven. ☎ 0141-639 1838.

Langside Hebrew Congregation, 125 Niddrie Road, G42. ☎ 0141-423 4062. *M. Chairman* J. Levingstone; *H. Sec.* N. Barnes.

Netherlee and Clarkston Hebrew Congregation, Clarkston Road, Clarkston. *M.* Rabbi A. Jesner; *Chairman* I. Goldman; *Sec.* Mrs P. Livingstone. ☎ 0141-637 8206.

Newton Mearns Synagogue, 14 Larchfield Court, G77 5BH. ☎ 0141-639 4000. *M.* Rev. Philip Copperman; *Chairman* S. Barmack; *Hon. Sec.* H. Hyman. ☎ 0141-639 3399.

EDUCATIONAL AND COMMUNAL ORGANISATIONS

Board of Jewish Education, 28 Calderwood Road, G43 2RU. ☎ 0141-637 7409. *Chairman* M. Clerck; *Jt. H. Sec.* L. Osborne, N. Allon.

Calderwood Lodge Jewish Primary School, 28 Calderwood Road, G43 2RU. ☎ 0141-637 5654. H.M. Mrs R. Levey.

Chaim Bermant Library, 222 Fenwick Rd., Giffnock G46 6UE. ☎ 0141-577 8230. *Admin.* Mrs D. Zolkwer.

Glasgow Israel Committee, 222 Fenwick Rd., Giffnock G46 6UE. ☎ 0141-620 2194. *Chairman* K. Davidson.

Glasgow Kollel. *Dir.* Rabbi M. Bamberger. ☎ 0141-638 6664/0141-577 8260.

Glasgow Maccabi, May Terrace, Giffnock, G46 6DL. ☎ 0141-638 7655. *Chairman* Mrs D. Minster; *Sec.* Mrs J. Statt.

Israel Scottish Information Service, Jewish Community Centre. ☎ 0141-577 8240.

Jewish Choral Society. *Co-Chairmen* Mrs J. Tankel; Mrs D. Mandelstam; *H. Sec.* Mrs A. Sakol. ☎ 0141-639 1756.

Jewish Community Centre. ☎ 0141-577 8222.

Jewish Learning Centre, Jewish Community Centre. Contact Rabbi M. Fletcher. ☎ 0141-577 8245.

Jewish Male Voice Choir. *Chairman* S. Smullen; *Sec.* G. Kitchener. ☎ 0141-638 2982.

Jewish Students' Society. *Contact* ☎ 0141-577 8220.

Jewish Youth Forum, *Contact* Marc Jacobs. ☎ 0141-577 8230.

Lubavitch Foundation, 8 Orchard Dr, Giffnock. ☎ 0141-638 6116. *Dir.* Rabbi Chaim Jacobs.

Maccabi Youth Centre, May Terrace, Giffnock G46. *Chairman* Mrs D. Minster. ☎ 0141-638 7655. *H. Sec.* G. Landa.

Northern Region Chaplaincy Board. *Chairman* D. Kaplan; *H. Sec.* S. Marks. ☎ 0141-639 4497; *Chaplain* Rabbi D. Cohen.

Teenage Centre (Atid), at Jewish Community Centre. *Contact* Rosamund Steinberg ☎ 0141-577 8220.

UJIA (incorporating Glasgow Jewish Continuity), Jewish Community Centre, 222 Fenwick Rd., Giffnock, G46 6UE. ☎ 0141-577 8210. Renewal ☎ 0141-577 8220. Fax 0141-577 8212. *Dir.* Alex Steen; *Renewal Dir.* David Kaplan.

Yeshivah, Giffnock Syn., Maryville Avenue. *Chairman* Dr K. Collins. ☎ 0141-577 8260. *H. M.* Rabbi A.M. Rubin.

WELFARE ORGANISATIONS
Cosgrove Care, May Terrace, Giffnock, G46 6LD. *Chairman* Mr J. Dover; *Dir.* Mrs L. Goldberg; *H. Sec.* Mrs L. Markson. ☎ 0141-620 2500. Fax 0141-620 2501.
Jewish Housing Association, Barrland Court, Barrland Drive, Giffnock, G46 7QD. *Dir.* Mrs Joan Leifer. ☎ 0141-620 1890. Fax 0141-620 3044.
Jewish Blind Society Centre (Reg. Charity No. SCO11789), Walton Community Care Centre, May Terrace, Giffnock, G46 6DL. ☎ 0141-620 3339. Fax 0141-620 2409. *Chairman* D. Strang; *Sec.* Mrs C. Blake.
Jewish Care Scotland (founded 1868), May Terrace Giffnock, G46 6DL. ☎ 0141-620 1800. Fax 0141-620 1088. *Chairman* A. Tankel. *Dir.* Mrs E. Woldman.
Jewish Hospital and Sick Visiting Association. ☎ 0141-638 6048. *Chairman* M. Hartley.
Newark Lodge, Jewish Old Age Home for Scotland, 43 Newark Drive. ☎ 0141-423 8941. *Chairman* A. Jacobson; *Dir.* M. Maddox.
Senior Citizens Club, *Chairman* B. Mann, *Sec.* Mrs V. Mann. ☎ 0141-644 3611.

NORTHERN IRELAND

BELFAST (550)
There was a Jewish community in Belfast about the year 1771, but the present community was founded in 1865.
Hebrew Congregation, 49 Somerton Rd. (Est. 1872; Syn. erected at Carlisle Circus, 1904, present building consecrated, 1964.) *President* Mr. R. Appleton; *Chairman* I. Selig; *H. Sec.* Mrs Norma Simon, 42 Glandore Ave., Belfast, BT15 3FD. ☎ 01232 779491.
Jewish Community Centre, 49 Somerton Rd. ☎ 01232 777974.
Wizo. *Chairperson* Mrs N. Lantin; *H. Sec.* Mrs N. Simon, Mrs M. Black.
Belfast Jewish Record. *H. Sec.* Mrs N. Simon, 42 Glandore Ave., Belfast BT15 3FD.

ISLE OF MAN (ca. 35)

Hebrew Congregation. Contact: Leonard Simons, 118 Slieau Dhoo, Tromode Park, Douglas, I. of M. ☎ 01624 673525. *Visiting M.* Rev. M. Weisman, M.A. (Oxon.). No regular services.
Cemetery: Consecrated section of the Douglas Cemetery, Glencrutchery Rd.

CHANNEL ISLANDS

JERSEY (120)
A syn. existed in St. Helier, the capital of the island, from 1843 until about 1870. The present com. was founded in 1962.
Jersey Jewish Congregation. The syn. is on the corner of Route des Genets and Petite Route des Mielles in the Parish of St. Brelade. Sabbath service at 10.30 a.m. *President* F. E. Cohen; *Sec.* S. J. Regal, 'Armon', rue de la Croix, St. Ouen; *Visiting M.* Rev. M. Weisman,OBE, MA. Nine families of the Jersey Cong. live in Guernsey.

REPUBLIC OF IRELAND (1,300)

Jews lived in Ireland in the Middle Ages, and a Sephardi community was established in Dublin in 1660, four years after the Resettlement in England. In the eighteenth century there was a community also at Cork. The Dublin congregation declined in the reign of George III, and was dissolved in 1791, but was revived in 1822. The

community received its largest influx of members at the turn of the century, the immigrants coming from Eastern Europe, Lithuania in particular. There are now some 1,300 Jews in the country. (See Hyman: The Jews of Ireland, 1972, repr. 1996.)
Chief Rabbi: Rabbi Gavin Broder. Office: Herzog House, Zion Rd., Dublin, 6. ☎ 01-492-3751. *Sec.* N. Caine.
Jewish Community Office, Herzog House, Zion Rd., Dublin, 6. ☎ 492-3751. Fax 492-4680. *Gen. Sec.* N. Caine.
Jewish Representative Council of Ireland, Herzog House, Dublin, 6. *Chairman* A. Benson.
General Board of Shechita & Kashrut Commission. (Est. 1915.) Herzog House, Zion Rd., Dublin, 6.
Irish-Jewish Museum. (Est. 1984.) 3-4 Walworth Rd., off Victoria St., Portobello, Dublin 8. ☎ 453-1797, *Curator* R. Siev. Times: May to September: 11am to 3.30pm on Sundays, Tuesdays and Thursdays; October to April: 10.30am to 2.30pm on Sundays only. The Museum was opened by Irish-born Chaim Herzog, late former President of Israel, on 20th June, 1985 and contains memorabilia of the Irish Jewish Community and a former synagogue is on view.
Jewish Board of Guardians. (Est. 1889.) *H. Sec.* D. Stein, 14 Wasdale Grove, Dublin 6. ☎ 490 5139.
Jewish Home of Ireland, Denmark Hill, Leicester Rd., W6. *Admin.* ☎ 497-2004.
Joint Israel Appeal, Herzog House, Zion Rd., Dublin, 6. ☎ 492-2318. *H. Sec.* L. Bloomfield.
Jewish National Fund, Herzog House, Zion Rd., Dublin, 6. ☎ 492-2318. *H. Sec.* A. Schwartzman.

CORK (30)
Hebrew Congregation, 10 South Terrace. (Est. 1880). *Chairman of Trustees.* F. Rosehill, 7 Beverly, Ovens, Co. Cork. ☎ 870413. Fax 270010. Email rosehill@iol.ie

DUBLIN (1,300)
Chief Rabbi: Rabbi Gavin Broder.

SYNAGOGUES
Dublin Hebrew Congregation, 37 Adelaide Rd. (Est. 1836. Syn. opened 1892; enlarged 1925.) Closed in 1999. Holding services at Terenure. *President* Martin Simmons; *Vice President/H.T.* Don Buchalter; *H. Sec.* Dr Seton Menton, ☎ 2694044.
Terenure Hebrew Congregation, Rathfarnham Rd., Terenure, 6. ☎ 490-8037. *H. Sec.* W. Stein.
Synagogue Machzikei Hadass, 77 Terenure Rd. North, 6. (Est. ca. 1890.) ☎ 493-8991. *H. Sec.* D. Ross.
Jewish Progressive Congregation, 7 Leicester Ave., Rathgar, 6. *Corr:* PO Box 3059, Rathgar, 6. Email finkeljj@indigo.ie (Est. 1945.) *H. Sec.* Mrs J. Finkel. ☎ 490-7605.
Talmud Torah, Stratford Schools, Zion Rd., Rathgar 6. ☎ 492-2315. Fax 492-4680. *H. Sec.* Mrs M. Adler.

Cemeteries: Aughavannagh Rd., Dolphin's Barn, 8. ☎ 454-0806. Inq. to caretaker. The old Jewish cemetery at Ballybough (☎ Ballybough 836-9756) may be visited on application to the caretaker. There is a Progressive cemetery at Woodtown, Co. Dublin.

OTHER COUNTRIES

*Denotes the organisation(s) from which further information about the Jewish community in that country can be obtained. For more detailed information about Jewish communities overseas consult **The Jewish Travel Guide** (Vallentine Mitchell). Population figures taken from 'The Jewish communities handbook 1991' (IJPR and WJC).

AFGHANISTAN (50)

Jews have lived in Afghanistan since antiquity. Just over 100 years ago they reportedly numbered 40,000. Since 1948 there has been a mass emigration to Israel, and only a few families remain in Kabul and Herat.

ALBANIA

After the recent emigration to Israel very few Albanian Jews remain in the country.

ALGERIA (150)

It is believed that there were Jews in Algeria as early as the fourth century, BCE. The fortunes of the community varied under the Turkish regime, which began in 1519. After the French conquered Algeria the community was reorganised and in 1870 most Jews were granted French citizenship. However, there have been anti-Jewish excesses even in the present century. After Algeria's bitter fight for independence, the Jews, like other French nationals, lost their possessions when they left the country. About 120,000 at independence in 1962, they remain less than 150 today: almost all fled to France.

Communal Centre and Synagogue: 6 Rue Hassena Ahmed, Algiers. ☎ (213-2) 62 85 72.

American Joint Distribution Committee, 11 Ali Boumdemdjel, Algiers. ☎ (213-2) 63 29 49.

ANTIGUA (West Indies)

A few Jewish residents live permanently on the island. Corr.: Mrs E. Lygum, Weatherills Estate, P.O.B. 62. ☎ (46)1 0710.

ARGENTINA (240,000)

The early Jewish settlers in Argentina were Marranos, who were gradually absorbed in the general population. The present community grew through immigration (beginning in 1862) from Germany, the Balkans, and North Africa. From Eastern Europe immigrants began to arrive in 1889, many of them going to the agricultural settlements est. by the Jewish Colonization Assn. (see p.72). The com. is est. to number 300,000, incl. 60,000 Sephardim, who have their own separate institutions, according to D.A.I.A., the representative org. of Argentine Jews. The Jewish pop. of Greater Buenos Aires is estimated at 220,000. A survey conducted by the Hebrew Univ. of Jerusalem estimates the Jewish pop. at 240,000, of whom 210,000 are Ashkenazim and 30,000 are Sephardim. This source estimates 180,000 Jews live in Gtr. Buenos Aires.

There are nine other major coms. in Parana, Rosario, Cordoba, Bahia Blanca, Posadas, Resistencia, Tucuman, Mendoza and La Plata. There is a small but very active community in Mar del Plata, south of Buenos Aires. Very few Jewish families remain on the former J.C.A. settlements. There are about 100 syns. (80 Orthodox, one Reform, the rest Conservative or Liberal), and a well-organised network of communal and educ. instits. There are communal offices in **Cordoba** at Alvear 254, and in **Rosario** at Paraguay 1152.

138   ARMENIA

BUENOS AIRES
Congreso Judio Latinoamericano, Larrea 744, 1030. ☎ 961-44532. Fax 963-7056.
Representative Organisation of Argentine Jews: D.A.I.A., Pasteur 633, 5th floor.
Amia Central Ashkenazi Community, Pasteur 633.
Central Sephardi Community: E.C.S.A., Larrea 674.
Latin American Rabbinical Seminary (Conservative), Jose Hernandez 1750.
Argentine Zionist Organisation & Jewish Agency (Sochnut), Cangallo 2471.

ARMENIA (500)

Jews have lived in Armenia for many hundreds of years and the various communities were spread around different parts of the country. There was a synagogue in Yerevan, but in the 1930s it was destroyed. Nowadays, nearly all the Armenian Jews live in Yerevan, with only a few families living in Vanadzor (Kirovakan) and Gjumri (Leninakan), while others are scattered in other small towns and villages. When 'perestroyka' was introduced in 1989, the Jewish community organised itself and in 1991 was registered as a non-formal organisation. Perestroyka opened the doors, so that a large number of the population emigrated to Israel. In 1991 a Jewish Sunday school was opened both for children and adults. In 1992 the Israeli embassy in Moscow financed the school. Over 60 per cent of the population is over 60 years of age and there are about 40 children below the age of 16 years.

President: Mr Willi Weiner, ☎ (7-8852) 525882; Dir. of Education: Dr George Fajvush ☎ (7-8852) 735852; Rabbi: Gersh Bourstein, ☎ (7-8852) 271115.

ARUBA (50)

Beth Israel Synagogue. Dedicated in 1962, this syn. serves the needs of the com. in this island in the Antilles in the Caribbean, of some 35 Jewish families. Jews from Curaçao settled in Aruba early in the nineteenth century, but did not stay there long, and the present com. dates from 1924.

AUSTRALIA (106,000)

The earliest org. of Jews in Australia was in 1817 when 20 Jews in New South Wales formed a burial society. In 1828 a congregation was formed in Sydney and the first specially erected syn. was opened in 1844. The first Jewish service was held in Melbourne in 1839, four years after the beginning of the colonisation on the banks of the River Yarra, and a syn. was opened in 1847. Congregations were est. at Ballarat (1853) and Geelong (1854). In South Australia, a permanent congregation was formed in Adelaide in 1848. A congregation in Brisbane was est. in 1865. In Western Australia the first congregation (now ended) was formed at Fremantle in 1887, and the present Perth congregation est. in 1892, with Kalgoorlie in 1895. In Tasmania a syn. was opened in Hobart in 1845 and another at Launceston in 1846. Organised Jewish coms. were est. in other States a few years later.

In Australia's public life Jews have played a distinguished part, many having risen to high office in the Federal and State Parliaments or on the Judicial bench. Two Governors-General of Australia have been Jews, Sir Zelman Cowen and the late Sir Isaac Isaacs. Sir John Monash, the Commander of the Australian Expeditionary Forces in the First World War, was a Jew. The Executive Council of Australian Jewry represents the central Jewish organisations in each State.

The Australian census has an optional question on religious affiliation. In 1981, 62,127 people declared themselves Jews by religion. If a proportionate number of 'no religion/religion not stated' replies are regarded as Jewish, the number of Jews rises to 79,345. Recent demographic res. indicated that there are probably about 92,000 people in Australia who are religiously or ethnically Jewish. The main Jewish coms. are in Melbourne (50,000); Sydney (35,000); Perth (4,200); Brisbane (1,500); Adelaide (1,250); The Gold Coast, Queensland (1,000); Canberra (500); Hobart (100).

MAIN JEWISH ORGANISATIONS
Executive Council of Australian Jewry,146 Darlinghurst Rd, Darlinghurst NSW 2010. ☎ (02) 9360 5415. Fax (02) 9360 5416.
*N.S.W. Jewish Board of Deputies, 146 Darlinghurst Rd., Darlinghurst, N.S.W., 2010. ☎ 2-360-1600. Fax 2-331-4712. *Exec. Dir.* Mrs M. Gutman.
Jewish Community Council of Victoria, 306 Hawthorn Rd., South Caulfield, Victoria 3162. *President* Mrs N. Bassat; *Communal Affairs Director* Mrs Helen Brustman. ☎ 3-92725566.
Asia Pacific Jewish Association, 306 Hawthorn Rd, South Caulfield, Victoria 3162. ☎ (03) 9272 5585. Fax (03) 9272 5589. E-mail aija@oze-mail.com.au *Chairman* (See p.00.)
Jewish National Fund of Australia, Beth Weizmann, 308 Hawthorn Road, Caulfield, Victoria, 3162. ☎ 3-92725566. Fax 3-92725570. *President* K. Rathner.
Jewish Museum of Australia, 26 Alma Rd., St. Kilda, Victoria 3182. ☎ (03) 9534 0083.
Zionist Federation of Australia, Beth Weizmann, 308 Hawthorn Road, Caulfield, Victoria, 3162. ☎ 3-9272-5644. Fax 3-9272-5640. *President* Mrs A. Zablud.
Association of Rabbis & Ministers of Australia and N.Z., c/o 12 Charnwood Grove, St. Kilda, Victoria, 3182. ☎ 3-9537-1433. Fax 3-9525-3759. *President* Rabbi P. Heilbrunn.
Australian Federation of Sephardim, 40-42 Fletcher St., Bondi Junction, N.S.W., 2022. ☎ 2-389-3355. Fax 2-369-2143. *President*: A. Gubbay.
Australian Institute of Jewish Affairs, 306 Hawthorn Rd, South Caulfield, Victoria 3162. ☎ (03) 9272 5585. Fax (03) 9272 5589.
Australian Union for Progressive Judaism, 78-82 Alma Rd., St. Kilda., Victoria, 3182. ☎ 3-9510-1488. Fax 3-9521-1229.
Federation of Australian Jewish Welfare Societies, 146 Darlinghurst Rd., Darlinghurst, N.S.W., 2010. ☎ 2-331-5184. Fax 2-360-5574. *President* N. Whitmont.
National Council of Jewish Women of Australia, 111-113 Queen St., Woollahra, N.S.W. 2025. ☎ 2-363-0257. Fax 2-362-4092.
Australian Federation of Wizo, 308 Hawthorn Rd., Caulfield, Victoria 3162. ☎ 3-9272-5599. Fax 3-9272-5540.
B'nai B'rith District 21of Australia, N.Z., PO Box 443, Kay's Cross, N.S.W. 2011. ☎ 2-556-1079. Fax 2-597-2755. *President* H. Mueller.
Australasian Union of Jewish Students, Beth Weizmann, 308 Hawthorn Road, Caulfield, Victoria, 3161. ☎ 3-9272-5566. Fax 3-9272-5560; Shalom College, PO Box 1, Kennington, N.S.W. 2033. ☎ 2-931-9660. Fax 2-663-4868.

MAIN SYNAGOGUES AND COMMUNAL CENTRES

SYDNEY
New South Wales Jewish Board of Deputies, 146 Darlinghurst Rd, Darlinghurst, NSW 2010. ☎ 2-9360 1600. Fax 2-9331 4712.
AJWS-Jewish Community Services, Level 3, Leyland House, 332-342 Oxford St, Bondi Junction, NSW 2022. ☎ 2-9369 1400. Fax 2-9369 5455.
The Great Synagogue (Ashk. Orth.), Elizabeth St. (Office: 166 Castlereagh St.), NSW 2000. ☎ 2-267 2477. Fax 2-264 8871.
Central Synagogue (Orth.), 15 Bon Accord Ave, Bondi Junction, NSW 2022 (Temporary: 19 Hollywood Ave., Bondi Junction, NSW 2022). ☎ 2-9389 5622. Fax 2-9389 5418.
North Shore Synagogue (Orth.), 15 Treatts Rd, Lindfield, NSW 2070. ☎ 2-416 3710. Fax 2-9416 7659.
North Shore Temple Emanuel (Lib.), 28 Chatswood Ave., Chatswood, NSW 2067. ☎ 2-9419 7011. Fax 2-9413 1474.

Sephardi Synagogue (Orth.), 40-42 Fletcher St, Bondi Junction, NSW 2025. ☎ 2-9389 3355. Fax 2-9365 3856.
Temple Emanuel (Lib.), 7 Ocean St, Woollahra, NSW 2025. ☎ 2-9328 7833. Fax 2-9327 8715.
Yeshiva Synagogue (Orth.), 36 Flood St, Bondi NSW 2026. ☎2-9387 3822. Fax 2-9389 7652.

MELBOURNE
Melbourne Hebrew Congregation (Ashk. Orth.), One Toorak Rd., South Yarra, Victoria 3141. ☎ 3-9866-2255.
St. Kilda Hebrew Congregation, 12 Charnwood Gr., St. Kilda, Victoria 3182. ☎ 3-9537-1433.
Temple Beth Israel (Lib.), 76 Alma Rd., St. Kilda, Victoria 3182. ☎ 3-9510-1488.
Beth Weizmann, 308 Hawthorn Rd, Caulfield, Victoria 3182. ☎ 3-9272-5566.
Caulfield Hebrew Congregation, 572 Inkerman Rd., Caulfield, Victoria 3161. ☎ 3-9525-9492.

PERTH
Perth Hebrew Congregation, Cnr. Plantation St. and Freedman Rd., Menora, W.A. 6050. ☎ 9-271-0539.
Temple David Congregation (Lib.), 34 Clifton Crescent, Mt. Lawley, 6050. ☎ 9-271-1458.
Jewish Centre, 61, Woodrow Ave., Mt. Yokine, W.A. 6060. ☎ 9-276-8572.

ADELAIDE
Hebrew Congregation, Synagogue Pl., 13 Flemington St., Glenside, S.A. 5065. ☎ 8-338-2922.
South Australian Liberal Jewish Congregation, 41 Hackney Rd., S.A. 5069. ☎ 8-362-8281.
Jewish Community Council, 13 Flemington St. *President* Norman Schueler.

BRISBANE
Brisbane Hebrew Congregation (Orth.), 98 Margaret St., Brisbane, Qld. 4000. ☎ 7-3229-3412.
Temple Shalom (Lib.), 15 Koolatah St., Camp Hill, Qld. 4152. ☎ 7-398-8843.

CANBERRA
National Jewish Memorial Centre (A.C.T. Jewish Community Centre), Canberra Ave. and National Circuit, Forest, P.O. Box 3105, A.C.T. 2603. ☎ (02) 62951052.

AUSTRIA (12,000)
The story of Austrian Jewry is punctuated by accounts of expulsion and re-immigration, of persecution on false accusations of ritual murder and other pretexts and recovery. After the 1848 Revolution the Jews gained equality, and their economic and cultural importance grew. But antisemitism had not ended; it culminated in the violence of the years preceding the Second World War. Austria's Jewish population in 1934 was 191,481 (with 176,034 in Vienna), the number today is about 12,000, almost all of them in Vienna. Other coms. are in Graz, Innsbruck, Linz and Salzburg.
*Jewish Community Centre, Israelitische Kultusgemeinde, Seitenstettengasse 4, 1010 Vienna. ☎ 53 1040. Fax 533 1577. *President* Dr A. Muzicant; *Dir.* Dr A. Hodik.
Chief Syns. Stadttempel, Seitenstettengasse 4, (Trad.); Machsike Hadass, D. Friedmann-Pl.1, 1010, (Orth.); Khal Israel, Tempelgasse 3, 1010. (Orth.); Ohel

Moshe, Lilienbrunnpasse 19, 1020 (Orth.); Misrachi, Judenplatz 8, 1010.
Chief Rabbi: Rabbi Paul Chaim Eisenberg. ☎ 53 104-17.
Jewish Welcome Service, A-1010 Vienna, Stephansplatz 10. ☎ 533 88 91. Fax 533-0323. *Dir.* Dr L. Zelman.

BAHAMAS (200)

Freeport Hebrew Congregation. 20 families. Friday night services held 8.30 pm.
Luis de Torres Synagogue, East Sunrise Highway, P.O. Box F-42515, Freeport.
☎ (242) 373 2008. *President* Geoff Hurst. ☎ (242) 373-4025. Fax (242) 373-2130. Email hurst100@yahoo.com; *V.President* Martin Raft, ☎ (242) 373-6579; *Sec.* Don Nyveen, ☎ (242) 373-7652. Geoff Hurst is happy to make arrangements for tourists, and is the Bahamian Marriage Officer.

BARBADOS (55)

A Jewish com. was formed in Barbados by refugees from Brazil after its reconquest by the Portuguese about the year 1650. In 1802 by Local Govt. Act, all political disabilities of the Jews were removed, but were not confirmed by Westminster until 1820. Barbados was the first British possession to grant full political emancipation to its Jews; Gt. Britain herself doing so more than 50 years later. With the economic decline of the West Indies the fortunes of their Jewish inhabitants also declined. In 1929, only one practising Jew remained, but in 1932 a gp. of Jews settled on the island from Europe. In December, 1987, the Old Synagogue in Bridgetown, one of the two oldest houses of worship in the Western Hemisphere (the other is in Curaçao), reopened for services for the first time in nearly 60 years, following restoration with the island community's support. An appeal fund was launched with Sir Hugh Springer, the Governor-General, as patron. There is a Jewish cemetery by the syn. In 1985, the Barbadian Govt. vested the syn. in the Barbadian Nat. Trust.
   *****Jewish Community Council,** P.O.B. 256, Bridgetown. ☎ 426 4764. Fax 426 4768. *Contact* Benny Gilbert.

BELGIUM (30,000)

Jews have lived in Belgium since Roman times. After the fall of Napoleon the Belgian provinces were annexed by Holland. In 1816 a decree by the Dutch King ordered the erection of two syns. in Maastricht and Brussels. But Belgian Jews had to wait until 1830, when Belgium became independent, to see their status formally recognised. The Constitution accorded freedom of religion in 1831. Before the Second World War the Jewish population was 80,000. Today there are flourishing communities in Antwerp, Brussels, Ostend, Liège, Charleroi and Waterloo totalling (together with the smaller communities) about 30,000 Jews.

ANTWERP

Synagogues and rel. orgs.: Shomre Hadass (Israelitische Gemeente), Terlistr 35, 2018. ☎ 226.05.54. Rabbi D. Lieberman. Syns.: Bouwmeesterstr., Romi Goldmuntz, Van den Nestlei.
Machsike Hadass (Orth.) Jacob Jacobstr. 22. *Rab.* Main syn.: Oostenstr. 42-44.
Sephardi Syn.: Hovenierstr. 31.
Central Jewish Welfare Organisation, Jacob Jacobsstr. 2. ☎ 232 3890.
Home for the Aged and Nursing Home, Marialei 6-8.
Residentie Apfelbaum-Laub., Marialei 2-4. ☎ 218.9399.
Holiday camp, Villa Altol, Coxyde-on-Sea, Damesweg 10. ☎ 058 512661.
Other orgs.: Zionist Fed. Pelikaanstr. 108; Mizrachi, Isabellalei 65; Romi Goldmuntz Centre, Nervierstr. 12; B'nai B'rith–Nervierstr 12AAT 14.

BRUSSELS
*Comité de Coordination des Organisations Juives de Belgique (C.C.O.J.B.). Av. Ducpétiaux 68, 1060 Brussels. ☎ 537 1691.
Consistoire Central Israélite de Belgique, 2 rue Joseph Dupont, 1000 Brussels. ☎ 02 512 21 90.
Cercle Ben-Gurion, 89 Chausée de Vleurgat, 1050 Brussels.
Centre Communautaire Laic Juif, 52 Rue Hotel des Monnaies, 1060 Brussels.
Zionist Offices, 66-68 Avenue Ducpétiaux, 1060 Brussels.
Synagogues: 32 rue de la Régence; 67a rue de la Clinique; 73 rue de Thy; 126 rue Rogier; 11 Ave. Messidor; 47 rue Pavillon (Sephardi); Brussels airport, Zaventem.

MONS
SHAPE International Jewish Community, c/0 SHAPE Chaplains' Office, B-7010 SHAPE, Belgium. ☎/Fax (32) 6572 8769. (Est. 1967) To meet the spiritual, social and educational needs of Jewish military and civilian personnel and their families serving at or temporarily assigned to SHAPE, Mons, Belgium. *Lay Leader* Wing Commander Stephen Griffiths, MBE, RAF.

BERMUDA (125)
Jewish Community of Bermuda, P.O. Box HM 1793, Hamilton, HMHX Bermuda. Contact Diana Lynn, 17 Biological Lane, Ferry Reach, GE01, Bermuda. ☎ 441-297 2267. Fax 809 297 8143. E-mail dlynn@bbsr.edu
The small community drawn from a dozen countries has never had a synagogue or communal building. A lay leader conducts a Friday service each month at the Unity Foundation, 75 Reid Street, Hamilton; a visiting Rabbi conducts High Holy day services and children's classes are held regularly.

BOLIVIA (640)
Although there have been Jews in Latin America for many centuries, they are comparative newcomers to Bolivia, which received its first Jewish immigrants only in 1905. They remained a mere handful until the 1920s, when some Russian Jews made their way to the country. After 1935, German Jewish refugees, began to arrived in Bolivia. Also from Rumania and mostly from Poland. Today some 640 Jews live there, mostly in the capital of La Paz (about 430), Cochambamba (120) and Santa Cruz (85), Tarija and other cities (5).

COCHABAMBA
Syn.: Calle Junin y Calle Colombia, Casilla 349.
Asociación Israelita de Cochabamba, P.O.B. 349, Calle Valdivieso. *President:* René Jacobowitz.

LA PAZ
Syns.: Circulo Israelita de Bolivia, Casilla 1545, Calle Landaeta 346, P.O.B. 1545. Services Sat. morn. only. *President* Ricardo Udler.
Comunidad Israelita Synagogue, Calle Canada Stronguest 1846, P.O.B. 2198, is affiliated to the Circulo. Fri. evening services are held. There is a Jewish sch. at this address. Circulo Israelita, P.O.B. 1545 is the representative body of Bolivian Jewry. All La Paz organisations are affiliated to it.
Two Homes for Aged: Calle Rosendo Gutierrez 307, and Calle Diaz Romero 1765.
Israel Tourist Information Office: Centro Shalom, Calle Canada Stronguest 1846, La Paz Country Club, Quinta J.K.G. Obrajes. Calle 1, esquina calle Hector Ormachea Castilla 1545, La Paz.

SANTA CRUZ
Centro Cruceño P.O.B. 469, WIZO, Casilla 3409. *President* Sra Guicha Schwartz.

BOSNIA HERCEGOVINA (1,100)
Sarajevo Jewish Community, Hamdije Kreševlajkovica 59. ☎ 38771 663 472.
Email la_bene@soros.org.ba

BRAZIL (250,000)
The early history of Brazilian Jewry was affected by the struggles for power
between the Portuguese and Dutch. The Inquisition, revived in Brazil, increased the
number of Marrano Jews. The Dutch, after their victory in 1624, granted full reli-
gious freedom to the Jews, but 30 years afterwards the Portuguese reconquered the
land and reintroduced the Inquisition. In 1822 Brazil declared its independence of
Portugal and liberty of worship was proclaimed. It is believed that about 250,000
Jews are living in Brazil, distributed as follows: Sao Paulo State, 90,000; Rio de
Janeiro State, 80,000; Rio Grande do Sul (Porto Alegre) 25,000; Parana State
(Curitiba) 2,408; Minas Gerais State (Bel Horizonte) 1,656; Pernambuco State
(Recife) 1,276.

RIO DE JANEIRO
*Federacão Israelita, R. Buenos Aires 68, AN15.
Fundo Communitario, R. Buenos Aires 68, AN15.
Orthodox Rabbinate, R. Pompeu Loureiro No.40. ☎/Fax 2360249.
Chevre Kedishe, Rua Barao de Iguatemi 306 (Orthodox).
Congrecão Beth El, Rua Barata Ribeiro 489 (Sephardi).
Associacão Religiosa Israelita, Rua Gen. Severiano 170 (Liberal).
Synagogues: Agudat Israel, Rua Nascimento Silva, 109, Beth Aron, Rua Gado
    Coutinho, 63, Kehilat Yaacov Copacabana, Rua Capelao Alvares da Silva 15;
    Templo Uniao Israel, Rua Jose Higino, 375-381.
Associacão Feminina Israelita, Av. Almte. Barroso, 6/14°.
Organizacão Sionista Unificada, Rua Decio Vilares, 258.
Museu Judaico, Rua Mexico, 90/1° andar-Castelo.

SAO PAULO
Federacao Israelita do Estado de São Paulo, Av. Paulista 726, 2nd floor. ☎ 288
6411.
Synogogues and religious centres: Centro Judaico Religioso de Sao Paulo
    (Orthodox). ☎ 220 5642; Beit Chabad, Rua Chabad 56/60; Communidade
    Israelita Sefaradi, Rua da Abolicao 457; Congregacão Israelita Paulista,
    "Einheitsgemeinde" (Liberal), Rua Antonico Carlos 653.
Zionist Offices, Rua Correa Mello 75.

BULGARIA (6,500)
Bulgarian Jewry dates from the second century C.E. Before the Second World War
there were 50,000 Jews in Bulgaria. From 1948-49 to about 1954/55, 45,000 emi-
grated to Israel. Today the number is about 6,500 of whom about 3,000 live in
Sofia.
Central Jewish Religious Council and Synagogue, 16 Exarch Joseph St., Sofia
    1000. ☎ 359-2/831-273. President Joseph Levy.
Organization of the Jews in Bulgaria "Shalom", 50 Al. Stambolijski St., Sofia 130.
    ☎/Fax 359-2/870-163. President Emile Callo. Publishes newspaper "Evrejski
    Vesti" and research compendium "Annual". Jewish museum in the Synagogue:
    Sofia, 16 Exarch Joseph St. Joseph Caro permanent exhibition in the city
    Museum and a memorial stone in the town of Nikopol. Publishing house
    "Shalom", Jewish Sunday School, Jewish Resource Centre, Memorial stone
    dedicated to the Salvation of the Bulgarian Jews near the Parliament. B'nai Brith,
    Maccabi and other Jewish organizations.

BURMA (Myanmar)

About 25 Burmese Jews live in Rangoon (Yangon), the capital.
Musmeah Yeshua Synagogue (est. 1896), 85 26th St., P.O. Box 45, Rangoon. Man. Tr. J. Samuels. ☎ 951-75062.
Israel Embassy, 49 Pyay Rd. ☎ 951 22290/01. Fax 951-22463.

BYELORUS

GOMMEL
Syn.: 13 Sennaya St.
Jewish Cultural Society, 1A Krasnoarmeyska St., 24600. *Chairman* V. F. Iofedov.

MINSK
Syn.: 22 Kropotkin St. ☎ (017-2) 55-82-70.

ORSHA
Syn.: Nogrin St.

RECHITSA
Syn.: 120 Lunacharsky St.
There are also Jewish communities in Bobruisk, Mozyr, Pinsk, Brest, Grodno, Vitebsk and Borisov.

CANADA (356,300)

Jews were prohibited by law from living in Canada so long as it remained a French possession. Nevertheless, Jews from Bordeaux David Gradis, a wealthy merchant and shipowner, and his son Abraham Gradis, in particular had a large share in the commercial development of the colony.

Jews played some part in the British occupation of Canada. Half a dozen Jewish officers, including Aaron Hart, whose descendants played important roles in Jewish and Canadian life for several generations, were suppliers to the expeditionary force which occupied Quebec.

A number of Jews settled at an early date in Montreal, where the Spanish and Portuguese Synagogue, Shearith Israel (still flourishing), was established in the 1770s and a cong. of 'German, Polish and English' Jews was granted a charter in 1846. A burial society was formed in Toronto in 1849. Montreal Jews were also among the fur traders in the Indian territories. In the 19th century, Jewish immigrants arrived in Canada in some numbers, and in 1832 – a quarter of a century earlier than in Britain the Lower Canada Jews received full civil rights.

A fresh era in the history of Canadian Jewry opened at the close of the century, when emigration on a large scale from Eastern Europe began. Montreal, Toronto, and to a lesser degree, Winnipeg, became the seats of Jewish coms. of some importance.

On the history of the Jews in Canada generally, see A. D. Hart, The Jew in Canada, 1926; L. Rosenberg, Canada's Jews, 1939, and B. G. Sack, The History of the Jews in Canada, 1945. The early colonial period in North America is covered in Sheldon and Judith Godfrey, Search out the land, 1995.

NATIONAL INSTITUTIONS
*Canadian Jewish Congress. (Est. 1919, reorganised 1934.)
National Office: 1590 Docteur Penfield Avenue Montreal, Quebec H3G 1C5. ☎ (514) 931-7531. Fax 931-0548. Website: http://www.cjc.ca. *Nat. President* Moshe Ronen; *Nat. Exec. Dir.* Jack Silverstone.
Atlantic Region: Lord Nelson Hotel, 1515 South Park St., Suite 305, Halifax, Nova

Scotia B3J 2L2. ☎ (902) 422-7491. Fax 425-3722. *Exec. Dir.* Jon Goldberg.
Quebec Region: 1590 Docteur Penfield Ave., Montreal, H3G 1C5. ☎ (514) 931 7531. Fax 931-3281. *Exec. Dir.* David Birnbaum.
Ontario Region: 4600 Bathurst St., Willowdale, M2R 3V2. ☎ (416) 635 2883. Fax 635-1408. *Exec. Dir.* Bernie Farber.
National Capital District: Ottawa Jewish Community Council, 1780 Kerr Ave., Ontario K2A 1RQ. ☎ (613) 789 7306. Fax 789-4593. *Exec. Dir.* Mitchell Bellman.
National Capital Office: Ottawa Jewish Community Council, 100 Sparks St., Suite 650, Ottawa, Ontario K1P 5B7. ☎ (613) 233-8703. Fax 233-8748. *Dir.* Eric Vernon.
Manitoba Region: Winnipeg Jewish Community Council, 123 Doncaster St., Winnipeg, R3N 2B2. ☎ (204) 943-0406. Fax 956-0609. *Exec. V. President* Robert Freedman.
Alberta Region (Calgary): Calgary Jewish Community Council, 1607, 90th Ave. S.W., Calgary, T2V 4V7. ☎ (403) 253-8600. Fax 253-7915. *Exec. Dir.* Joel Miller.
Alberta Region (Edmonton): Jewish Federation of Edmonton, 7200, 156th Street, Edmonton, T5R 1X3. ☎ (403) 487 5120. Fax 481-1854. *Exec. Dir.* Lesley Jacobson.
Saskatchewan Region (Regina): c/o 4715 McTavish St., Regina, S4S 6H2. ☎ (306) 569-8166. Fax (306) 569-8166. *Comm. Dev. Off.* Helene Kesten.
Saskatchewan Region (Saskatoon), c/o 715 McKinnon Ave, S7H 2G2. ☎ (306) 343-7023. Fax (306) 343-1244. *Officer* Linda Shaw.
Pacific Region: 950 West 41st Ave., Vancouver V5Z 2N7. ☎ (604) 257-5101. Fax 257-5131. *Exec. Dir.* Erwin Nest.
Canada-Israel Committee, 130 Slater St., Suite 630, Ottawa K1P 6E2. *Exec. Dir.* Rob Ritter. ☎ (613) 234 8271. Ontario Office: 2221 Yonge St. #502, Toronto M4S 2B4. ☎ (416) 489 8889.
Canadian Association for Labour Israel. (Est. 1939) 7005 Kildare Rd., #14 Côte St. Luc, Quebec H4W 1C1.
Canadian Jewish Historical Society, 7489 Briar Rd., Côte St. Luc, Quebec, H4W 1K9. ☎ (514) 848 2066. *President.* Dr I. Robinson.
Canadian ORT, 3101 Bathurst St #604, Toronto, Ontario M6A 2A6.
Emunah Women of Canada. Nat. *President* R. Schneidman, 7005 Kildare Rd, #18 Montreal H3W 3C3. ☎ (514) 485 2397.
Hadassah-Wizo of Canada, 1310 Greene Av. #650, Montreal H3Z 2B8. (Est. 1917.) *Exec. V. President* Mrs L. Frank. Chapters: 220, in most Jewish centres. Toronto office: 638A Sheppard Ave W, #209, M3H 2S1. ☎(416) 630 8373.
Jewish Immigrant Aid Services of Canada. (Est. 1919.) 4600 Bathurst St., Willowdale, Ont., M2R 3V3. *Exec. Dir.* ☎ (416) 630 9051.
Jewish National Fund. 1980 Sherbrooke St. W., Montreal, H3H 1E8. ☎ (514) 934 0313.
Labour Zionist Movement (Est. 1939), 272 Codsell Ave., Downsview, Ont. M3H 3X2.
Mizrachi Organization of Canada. *Nat. Exec. Dir.* Rabbi M. Gopin, 159 Almore Ave., Downsview, Ont. M3H 2H9. ☎ (416) 630 7575.
National Council of Jewish Women of Canada, 1588 Main St., #118, Winnipeg, Manitoba R2V 1Y3. ☎ (204) 339 9700.
Canadian Zionist Federation (Est. 1967), 5250 Decarie Blvd., #550, Montreal, H3X 2H9. ☎ (514) 486 9526.
United Israel Appeal. *Exec. V. President* S. Ain, 4600 Bathurst St., Willowdale, Ont. M2R 3V3. ☎ (416) 636 7655. Fax (416) 635-5806.

CAYMAN ISLANDS (50)
There are approx. 50 Jewish residents in the 3 Cayman Islands, nearly all living on Grand Cayman. They are joined by about 40 others who are regular visitors. Services in private homes. *Contact:* Harvey De Souza, P.O. Box 72, Grand Cayman, Cayman Islands, British West Indies.

CHILE (25,000)

The number of Jews in Chile is about 25,000. The great majority live in the Santiago area. Communities also in Arica, Chillan, Chuquicamata, Concepción, Iquique, La Serena, Puerto Montt, Punta Arenas, Rancagua, San Fernando, Santa Cruz, Temuco, Valdivia, Vina del Mar/Valparaiso.

SANTIAGO

*Comité Representativo de las Entidades Judias de Chile (CREJ), Miguel Claro 196. ☎ 235 8669. Fax 235 0754.
Comunidad Israelita de Santiago, Tarapaca 870. (Ashkenazi). ☎ 633 1436. Fax 638 2076.
Comunidad Israelita de Santiago Congregacion Jafetz Jayim (Orthodox) Miguel Claro 196. ☎ 2745389.
Comunidad Israelita Sefaradi de Chile, R. Lyon 812. ☎ 209 8086. Fax 204 7382.
Sociedad Cultural, Bne Jisroel, Mar Jónico 8860, Vitacura. ☎/Fax 201 1623 (German).
MAZsE, (Hungarian) Pedro Bannen 0166. ☎ 2742536.
B'nai Brith, Ricardo Lyon 1933. ☎274 2006. Fax 225 2039.
Zionist Federation Offices, Rafael Cañas 246. ☎251 8821. Fax 251 0961.
Estadio Israelita Maccabi, Club, Las Condes 8361. ☎ 235 9096. Fax 251 0105.
Wizo Chile, M. Montt 207. ☎ 235 9096. Fax 251 105.

CHINA (3,100)

In recent years, Jewish tourists from a number of countries, including Britain and the U.S., have visited the ancient city of Kaifeng, 300 miles south of Peking, and met people who claim descent from a sizeable com. which lived there for centuries and dispersed in the 19th century. Some experts believe the Kaifeng Jews to have originated from Persia or Yemen. Few are left of the coms. formed by other immigrants from Asia at the end of the 19th century and by the Russian and German refugees of the First and Second World Wars.

HONG KONG (3,000)

The Hong Kong com. dates from about 1857. The Ohel Leah synagogue, built in 1901, has recently been restored.
The Jewish Community Centre, 1 Robinson Place, 70 Robinson Road, Mid-levels. A new facility with 2 Kosher restaurants and banquet facilities (under Mashgiach supervision), library/function facilities. Meals on the Sabbath. Take-away and Kosher food delivery available. Full programme of activities and classes, Carmel Day School. ☎ (852) 2868-0828. *Information:* ☎ (852) 2801-5440. Fax 2877-0917. *Gen. Man.* Paul W.A. Sprokkreeff.
Synagogues:
Ohel Leah Syn. and Mikvah, 70 Robinson Rd. ☎ (852) 2589-2621. Fax 852 877 0917. *M.* Rabbi Y. Kermaier. Friday night, Saturday and weekday services are held. ☎ (852) 2857-6095. Fax (852) 2548-4200.
Lubavitch in the Far East. 1A Kennedy Heights, Mid-Levels. Holds regular morning services and Shabbat and holiday services in the Furama Hotel. Rabbi M. Avtzon (852) 2523 9770. Fax (852) 2845 2772.
Shuva Israel Beit Medrash and Community Center (Seph), 2/F, Fortune House, 61 Connaught Road Central. ☎ (852) 2851-6218. Fax (852) 2851-7482.
Shuva Israel Synagogue (Seph) (Shabbat and Holidays), 16-18 McDonnel Road, 1-B, Midlevels. ☎ (852) 2851-6128. Fax (852) 2851-7482.
The United Jewish Congregation (Lib/Ref) (Est. 1991). Friday eve. services at the Jewish Community Centre. *M.* Rabbi J.D. Cohen. ☎ (852) 2523-2985. Fax (852) 2523-3961 Email ujc@hk.super.net.
Kehilat Zion (Orth). 4/F, 21 Chatham Road, Tsimshatsui, Kowloon. Rabbi N.

Meoded. ☎ (852) 2366-6364.
Israel Consulate-General, Admiralty Centre, Tower II, Room 701, 18 Harcourt Road. ☎ (852) 25296091. Fax 28550220.
The Jewish Historical Society. Publishes monographs on subjects of Sino-Judaic interest. Information from Mrs J. Green. ☎ (852) 2807-9400. Fax (852) 2887-5235.
The Jewish cemetery is situated in Happy Valley. ☎ (852) 2589-2621. Fax (852) 2548-4200.
The Jewish Women's Assn. is affiliated to WIZO and ICJW. *Chair* Mrs A. Patria. ☎ (852) 2522 8930. Fax (852) 2522 7120.
United Israel Appeal is affiliated to Keren Hayesod. *Information* Mr D. Diestel. ☎ (852) 2408-6330. Fax (852) 2407-6249. Email david@metexhle.com.

SHANGHAI
Notice has been received of a new community established in Shanghai in 1998.
Bnai Yisrael, 1277 Beijing Rd, 19th Floor, Shanghai. *President* Albert Sassoon. ☎ 86-21-6289-9903. Fax 86-21-6289-9957.

COLOMBIA (7,000)
The Jewish population is about 7,000 with the majority living in Bogota. There are also coms. in Barranquilla, Cali and Medellin.
*Centro Comunitario Israelita de Bogotá, Carrera 29 126-31, Apartado 12372 Bogotá. ☎ 274 9069.

COMMONWEALTH OF INDEPENDENT STATES (ie former U.S.S.R)
Before World War I, Russian Jewry was the largest Jewish community in the world. For centuries, until the Revolution of 1917, the Jews were cruelly persecuted under the antisemitic policy of the Tsars. The subsequent Soviet regime virtually destroyed the former religious life and organisation of the Jewish communities. According to the official Soviet 1989 census the Jewish population was 1,449,000 but recent mass emigration will have reduced that total. The break up of the Soviet Union following August 1991 is reflected in the new entries under the separate republics, e.g. Byelorus, Latvia, Moldova, Ukraine, etc. Population figures are difficult to estimate but some 400,000 Jews have left the country since 1989.

RUSSIA (1,450,000) (Russian Federation)

MOSCOW
Synagogues: Central ul. Archipova 8; Marina Roshcha, 2nd Vysheslavtsev per.5-A.

ST. PETERSBURG
Synagogue: 2 Lermontovsky Prospekt. ☎ 216-11-53.
Jewish Association 'LEA', Ryleeva 29-31, 191123. ☎ 812-2756104. Fax 812-2756103.
Jewish Tourist and Research Center HA-IR), Stachek 212-46, 198262. ☎ (812) 184 12 48. Fax (812) 310 61 48.
Other centres of Jewish population include those of Astrakhan, Berdichev, Beregovo, Birobidjan, Irkutsk, Krasnoyarsk, Kuybyshev, Kursk, Malakhavka, Nalchik, Novosibirsk, Ordzhonikidze, Penza Perm, Rostov Saratov, Sverdlovsk, Tula.

COSTA RICA (2,500)
Most of the Jewish population of 2,500 live in San José, the capital, where there

are a synagogue, mikveh and a Jewish primary and secondary school. There is also a country club.

*Centro Israelita Sionista de Costa Rica, Calle 22 y 24. P.O.B. 1473, 1000 San José, Costa Rica. ☎ 233-9222. Fax 233-9321. *President* J. Kierszenson; *Sec.* F.A. Cordero. *Chief Rabbi* Rabbi Gershon Miletski. *Community Dir.* Frida Lang. Email cisdcr@sol.racsa.co.cr

CROATIA (2,500)

(Former constituent republic of Yugoslavia)
There are nine Jewish coms. in Croatia with a total Jewish population of 2,500 affiliated members.

ZAGREB

Jewish Com. and Synagogue. *President* Prof. Dr Ognjen Kraus; *Sec. Gen.* Deon Friedrich; Palmotićeva St. 16., P.O.B. 986; ☎ 434 619; 425 517. Fax 434 638.
The Com. Centre was rebuilt in 1992 after being seriously damaged in an explosion. Services are held on Friday eves and holy days. It houses a Jewish kindergarten, Judaica and Hebraica Library, art gallery, auditorium with daily progammes and other facilities. Here are the headquarters of the Fed. of Jewish Coms. in Croatia, Maccabi Sports Club, Jewish Ladies Assn., the Cultural Society and Union of Jewish Students in Croatia.
The com. publishes an occasional newspaper ha-Kol.
There is an impressive monument to Jewish victims of Holocaust in the Jewish cemetery of Mirogoj and a monument to Jewish soliders fallen in the First World War.
There is a plaque in Praška St. 7 on the site of the pre-war Central Syn. of Zagreb. Before 1941 the com. numbered over 12,000 Jews. Today there are 1,500 members.
Lavoslav Shwartz Old People's Home. *President* Dr Branko Breyer; *Man.* Paula Novak, Bukovacka c. 55; ☎ 210 026; 219 922.

DUBROVNIK

Jewish Com. and Syn., Zudioska St. 3 (Jewish Street).
This is the second oldest syn. in Europe, dating back to the 14th century damaged in the 1991-2 war. There are 47 Jews in the city and services are held on Jewish holidays.

OSIJEK

Jewish Com. and Syn. *President* Ing. Darko Fisher; Braće Radića St. 13; ☎ 24 926.
There are 150 Jews in the city and the com. is quite active. It suffered some damage during the 1991-92 war.

RIJEKA

Jewish Com. and Syn.: *President* Josip Engel; *V. Presidents* Dr Josip Musafia; Ivana Filipovića St. 9; P.O.B. 65. ☎ 425 156.
There are 80 Jews in Rijeka. Services are held on Jewish holidays.

SPLIT

Jewish Com. and Syn.: *President* Eduard Tauber, Zidovski prolaz 1 (Jewish Passage). ☎ 45 672.
There are 200 Jews in Split and the com. is very active one with daily meetings in the com. The syn. is over 350 years old and services are held on Jewish holidays. There is an impressive cemetery dating back to the 16th century.

There are smaller Jewish coms. in Čakovec, Virovitica, Slavonski Brod and

Daruvar. In many towns in north Croatia there are old Jewish cemeteries and former syn. buildings.

CUBA (1,000)

Marranos from Spain settled in Cuba in the sixteenth century, but a real immigration of Jews did not start until the end of the nineteenth century. The majority of the 1,000 Jews live in Havana.
 *Comission Coordinadora de las Sociedades Hebreas de Cuba, Calle Bel Vedado, Havana. ☎ 32-8953.

CURAÇAO (450)

A Sephardi Jewish settlement was est. in 1651, making it one of the oldest coms. in the New World. The Mikve Israel-Emanuel Syn. building, which dates from 1732, is the oldest in continuous use in the western Hemisphere; there is a small Jewish museum in the synagogue compound. About 450 Jews live in Curaçao. The cemetery (Bet Hayim) at Blenheim (est. 1659) is the oldest in the Americas.
 Synagogues: Sephardi-Mikve Israel-Emanuel, Hanchi di Snoa 29, P.O. Box 322. ☎ 4611067. Fax 4654141. *M.*
 Ashkenazi: Shaarei Tsedek, Leliweg 1A, P.O. Box 498. ☎ 375738. *M.*
 Israel Consulate: Dr P. Ackerman, Blauwduifweg 5. ☎ 7365068. Fax 7370707.

CYPRUS (50)

At the beginning of the present era and earlier, Cyprus was an important and large Jewish centre. An unsuccessful revolt against the Romans in 117, however, was followed by a ruthless suppression and the end of the great period of Jewish history in Cyprus. A new period of prosperity and immigration started in the 12th century but came to an end with the coming of the Genoese and later the Venetians as the island's rulers. By 1560 only 25 families remained in Famagusta, mostly physicians. Attempts at agricultural settlement in the 19th century were unsuccessful. The Jewish population now numbers about 50. The cemetery is at Larnaca.
 Jewish Committee has offices in Nicosia c/o S. Ammar, P.O. Box 3807 Nicosia. ☎ 441085.

CZECH REPUBLIC

The break up of Czechoslovakia is reflected by the separate entries here for the Czech lands and for Slovakia on p.180. Records show that Jews were settled in Bohemia in the 11th century and in Moravia as early as the 9th cent. There were flourishing Jewish coms. in the Middle Ages. The Jewish pop. of Czechoslovakia in 1930 was 356,830. The coms. were decimated in the Holocaust.
 Today the Jewish population of the Czech Republic is est. at 10,000. Of these 3,000 are registered as members of the Jewish com., with some 1,400 in Prague. There are today 10 Jewish coms. in Bohemia and Moravia in the regional cities of Prague, Plzen, Usti nad. Labem, Karlovy Vary, Liberec, Teplice, Brno, Ostrava, Olomouc. There are regular Shabbat and holiday services held in all these places. There is a kosher kitchen and restaurant in Prague with rabbinical supervision of the chief rabbi of Prague and Bohemia and Moravia (Rav. K. Sidon).
 Federation of Jewish Communities in the Czech Republic. Maiselova 18, 11001, Prague. ☎ 2481-1090. Fax 2481-0912. E-mail fedzid@vol.cz. *President* Jan Munk; *Exec. Dir.* Dr Thomas Kraus.

PRAGUE
Jewish Community of Prague, Maiselova 18, 11001. Tel/Fax 2318-664. *Chairman* Jiri Danicek.
 B'nai B'rith Lodge, Maiselova 18, 11001.

Society of Jewish Culture, Maiselova 18, 11001. *President* Dr B. Nosek.
Old-New Synagogue (Altneu), Cervena ul. 1, Praha 1 - Stare Mesto.
Jubilee Synagogue, Jeruzalemska 7, Praha 1 - Nove Mesto.

DENMARK (9,000)

The history of the Jews in Denmark goes back to the early years of the seventeenth
century. Nearly all of Denmark's 9,000 Jews today live in Copenhagen. Jews have
had full civic equality since 1814.

COPENHAGEN

Chief Rabbi: Rabbi Bent Lexner, Oestbanegade, 9, DK 2100. ☎ 39 299520. Fax
39 292517.
*Det Mosaiske Troessamfund i Kobenhavn (Jewish Congregation of Copenhagen),
Ny Kongensgade 6, 1472DK. PO Box 2015, 1012 DK. ☎ (33)-128-868. Fax (33)
123-357.
Synagogues: Krystalgade 12, 1172 DK.
Community Centre, Ny Kongensgade 6.

DOMINICAN REPUBLIC

The Jewish community which settled in Santo Domingo in the sixteenth century
has completely disappeared. The present Jewish community, formed shortly before
the Second World War, numbers about 150 in Santo Domingo and Sosua.

SANTO DOMINGO

Synagogue, Avenida Ciudad de Sarasota, 5. ☎ 533-1675.

ECUADOR (1,000)

The Jewish population in Ecuador is about 1,000, mainly resident in Quito and
Guayaquil.
*Asociación Israelita de Quito, Avenida 18 de Septiembre 954, P.O.B. 17-03-800.
☎ 502-734. Fax 502-733 Email aiq@uio.satnet
*Comunidad de Culto Israelita, Cnr. Calle Paradiso and El Bosque, Guayaquil.

EGYPT (240)

The history of the Jewish community in Egypt goes back to Biblical times.
Following the establishment of the State of Israel in 1948 and the subsequent wars,
only about 200 Jews remain, about 150 in Cairo and 50 in Alexandria. Services are
conducted in Shaar Hashamayim Synagogue.

CAIRO

*Jewish Community Headquarters, 13 rue Sebil el Khazendar, Midan el Gueish,
Abbasiya. ☎ 4824613. *President* Mrs Esther Weinstein. ☎ 4824885.
Great Synagogue Shaar Hashamayim, 17 Adly Pasha St. ☎ 3929025.
Ben-Ezra Synagogue, 6 Haret il-Sitt Barbara, Old Cairo.
Heliopolis Synagogue "Vitali Madjar", 5 rue Misalla, Korba, Heliopolis.
Maadi Synagogue Meir Enaim, 55 rue 13, Maadi.

ALEXANDRIA

Great Synagogue Eliahu HaNabi, 69 rue Nebi Daniel, Ramla Station. *President* J.
Harris.

ESTONIA (3,000)
TALLINN
Jewish Community of Estonia. Karu Str. 16. *Contact* Cilja Laud, POB 3576 Tallinn 10507. ☎/Fax 438566.
Syn., 9 Magdaleena St. ☎ 557154.
Jewish Cultural Centre. *EDr* Eugenia Gurin-Loov, POB 3576.
WIZO Estonia. *Contact* Revekka Blumberg, POB 3576, EE0090. ☎ 43-646 1777. Fax 43-8566.

There are Jewish communities in Kohtla-Järve, Narva and Tartu.

ETHIOPIA
The indigenous Jews of Ethiopia, known as Falashas, have probably lived in the country for about 2,000 years. Their origin is obscure but they are believed to be the descendants of members of the Agau tribe who accepted pre-Talmudic Judaism brought into Ethiopia (Abyssinia) from Jewish settlements in Egypt, such as that at Elephantine (Aswan). They were estimated to number half-a-million in the 17th century but by the 1970s the population had shrunk to less than 30,000. In 1975 the Israel Govt. recognised their right to enter under the Law of Return. Towards the end of 1984 the Israel Govt. undertook Operation Moses which entailed transporting about 8,000 Ethiopian Jews from refugee camps in Sudan to Israel. It is estimated that approximately 3,000 died from famine and disease before they could reach Israel. A further dramatic mass emigration to Israel was completed in 1991 and very few remain. A useful book on the subject is David Kessler's The Falashas, the Forgotten Jews of Ethiopia (3rd ed., London 1996), obtainable from Frank Cass Publishers.
Jewish Community, P.O.B. 50 Addis Ababa.

FIJI ISLANDS
Many Jews, mostly from Britain and some from Australia, settled in the islands in the 19th and early 20th centuries. About 12 Jewish families now live in Suva. *Corr.* K. R. Fleischman, G.P.O. Box 905, Suva or Cherry Schneider, P.O.B. 882, Suva.

FINLAND (1,500)
The settlement of Jews in Finland dates from about 1850. The number living there today is about 1,500, with 1,200 in Helsinki, the rest in Turku and other parts of the country.
*Synagogue and Communal Centre: Malminkatu 26, 00100 Helsinki 10. ☎ 6941302, 6941297. Fax 6948916.
Synagogue and Communal Centre: Brahenkatu 17, Turku. ☎ 2312557.

FRANCE (600,000)
The first Jewish settlers in France arrived with the Greek founders of Marseilles some 500 years B.C.E. After the destruction of the Second Temple, Jewish exiles established new communities, or reinforced old ones. Rashi and Rabenu Tam are the best known of hundreds of brilliant medieval French rabbis and scholars. In 1791 the emancipation of French Jewry was the signal for the ghetto walls to crumble throughout Europe. During the Second World War, under the German occupation, 120,000 Jews were deported or massacred; but the post-war influx from Central and Eastern Europe and particularly from North Africa, has increased the numbers of French Jewry to about 600,000 (the fourth largest in the world), of whom 380,000 are in Paris and Greater Paris. There are Jewish coms. in about 150 other towns.

PARIS

*Consistoire Central: Union des Communautés Juives de France. The principal Jewish religious org. in France. It administers the Union des Communautés Juives de France, 19 rue St. Georges, 9°. *President* Jean Kahn; *Dir. Gen.* Leon Masliah. ☎ 49708800. Fax.: 42810366.

Association Consistoriale Israélite de Paris, 17 rue St. Georges, 9°. The principal Jewish religious org. for the Paris area. *President* Moïse Cohen; *V. President* Maitre J. H. Gahnassia. ☎ 40 82 26 26.

Alliance Israélite Universelle, 45 rue La Bruyère, 75009 Paris. This org. works through its network of schools in France, but also in 7 countries, especially in North Africa, Asia and North America. It houses the 'College des Etudes juives' and a library, which includes more than 120,000 books in the field of Hebraica-Judaica. *President* Prof. A. Steg; *Dir.* Jean-Jacques Wahl. ☎ 0153328855. Fax 0148745133.

American Jewish Joint Distribution Committee, Rue De Miromesnil 33, Paris 75008. ☎ 33-14268-05-68. *Dir.* Alberto Senderey.

Association Culturelle Israélite Agudas Hakehilos, 10 rue Pavée, 4°. ☎ 488721 54.

B'nai B'rith Dist. 19-Continental-Europe, 38 rue de Clichy, Paris, 9°. ☎ 40 82 91 11. *President* M. Honigbaum.

Centre de Documentation Juive Contemporaine, 17 Rue Geoffroy l'Asnier, 4°. (Est. 1943.) This org. has gathered and organised data of Jewish life under the Hitler regime in Europe. Founder The late Isaac Schneersohn; *President* Baron Eric de Rothschild.

Communauté Israélite de la Stricte Observance, 10 rue Cadet, 75009. ☎ 42 46 36 47.

*Conseil Représentatif des Institutions Juives de France (Crif), 19 rue de Teheran 8°. (Est. 1943.) The secular mouthpiece of French Jewry linking 64 of the most important Jewish orgs. ☎ 45 61 00 70. Fax 43 59 06 11. *President* Henri Hajdenberg; *Drice* Mme. J. Keller.

Conseil Représentatif du Judaisme Traditionaliste, c/o Eric Schieber, 6 rue Albert Camus, le Montigny 75010 Paris. 16i. Rep. org. of Orthodox Jewry. ☎ 45 04 94 00. *President* I. Frankforter; *Sec. Gen.* E. Schieber.

Fédération des Sociétés Juives de France, 68 rue de la Folie Mericourt 11°. Social, cultural and philanthropic in outlook and links many gps. with East European background. ☎ 48 05 28 60. *President* Mordechai Lerman.

Fédération des Organisations Sionistes de France, 17 bis, rue de Paradis 75010, Paris. ☎ 48 24 03 44. D. M. Kalifa.

Fonds Social Juif Unifié (F.S.J.U.), 19 rue de Tehéran, 8°. French Jewry's central organisation in the cultural, educ. and social fields. ☎ 45 63 17 28. *President* Baron David de Rothschild; *Dir.* David Saada.

Keren Kayemeth Leisrael, 11 rue de 4 Septembre 75002. ☎ 42868888.

Mouvement Juif Libéral de France, 11 rue Gaston-de-Caillavet 15°. ☎ 45 75 38 01. (Affil. to World Union for Prog. Judaism). *President* R. Benarrosh; *Ms.* Rabbi D. Farhi; Rabbi M. Konig.

Mouvement Loubavitch, 8 rue Lemartine 9°. ☎ 45 26 87 60.

Musée d'Art et d'Histoire du Judaisme, Hôtel de St Aignan, 71 rue du Temple, 3ᵉ. ☎ 015302 8653.

ORT, 10 Villa D'Eylau, 16°. ☎ 45 00 74 22.

Renouveau Juif, 18 passage du Chantier 12°. ☎ 43 40 40 55. Est. 1979 by Henri Hajdenberg. Advocates stronger pro-Israel stand.

Siona, 52 rue Richer 9°. ☎ 42 46 01 91. Sephardi Z. movement est. by Roger Pinto.

Union des Juifs pour la Résistance et l'Entr'aide, 14 rue de Paradis, 10°. Social, cultural and political org. of extreme Left-wing political views, founded as an armed Resistance group in 1943 under German occupation. *President* Charles Lederman. ☎ 47 70 62 16.

Union Libérale Israélite, 24 rue Copernic, 75116. Org. of Liberal Judaism. *President* C Bloch. ☎ 47 04 37 27. Fax 47 27 81 02.
Union des Sociétés Mutalistes Juives de France, 58 rue du Chateau d'Eau 10°. ☎ 42 06 62 88. East European background.
Wizo, 54 rue de Paradis, 10°. French women Zionists' centre. ☎ 48 01 97 70. *President* Nora Gailland-Hofman.

SYNAGOGUES
Chief Rabbi of France: Rabbi Joseph Sitruk, Consistoire Central, 19 rue Saint-Georges, 9°. ☎ 49 70 88 00. Fax 40 16 06 11.
Synagogues of the Consistoire de Paris, 44 rue de la Victoire, 9°; 15 rue Notre-Dame-de-Nazareth, 3°; 21 bis rue des Tournelles, 4°; 28 rue Buffault, 9°N Sephardi; 14 rue Chasseloup-Laubat, 15°; 18 rue Sainte-Isaure, 18°; 75 rue Julien Lacroix, 20°; 9 rue Vauquelin, 5°; 70 Avenue Secretan, 19°; 13 rue Fondary, 15°; 6 bis rue Michel Ange, 16°; 14 Place des Vosges, 4°; 84 rue de la Roquette; 120 Boulevard de Belleville 20°; 120 rue des Saule, 18°; 19 Blvd. Poissonniére; 18 rue St. Lazare, 9° (Algerian).
Orthodox Synagogues: 10 rue Cadet, 9°; 31 rue de Montévidéo, 16°; 10 rue Pavee, 4°; 6 rue Ambroise Thomas, 9°; 3 rue Saulnier, 9°; 32 rue Basfroi, H°; 25 rue des Rosiers, 4°; 17 rue des Rosiers, 4°; 24 rue de Bourg Tibourg, 4°; 80 rue Doudeauville, 18°; 5 rue Duc, 18°; 18 rue des Ecouffes, 4°.
Conservative Syn., Adath Shalom, 22 bis, rue des Belles Feuilles, 75116 Paris. ☎ 45 53 84 09.
Liberal Synagogues, 24 rue Copernic, 16°; 11 rue Gaston de Caillavet 15°.
There are also many syns. in the Paris suburbs and in the Provinces.

GERMANY (67,000)

A large Jewish community has existed continuously in Germany since Roman times. Despite recurring periods of persecution, the Jewish communities contributed much of lasting value to culture and civilisation. Hitler and the Nazi regime destroyed the community, which numbered more than half a million before 1933, 160,000 of whom lived in Berlin. Today there are about 67,000 in Germany (incl. 10,700 in Berlin, 6,500 in Frankfurt and 6,300 in Munich). There are 79 other coms. in Germany, and the communities of the former German Democratic Republic have now been integrated in the Zentralrat der Juden in Deutschland. See Hidden Legacy Foundation, p.56.
*Zentralrat der Juden in Deutschland (Central Council of Jews in Germany), Tucholskystr. 9, 10117 Berlin. ☎ 030 284 4560. Fax 030 284 5613.
Central Welfare Org. of Jews in Germany, Hebelstr. 6, 60318 Frankfurt. ☎ 069-944371-0. Fax 069-494817.
Conference of German Rabbis, Landesrabbiner Joel Berger, Hospitalstr. 36, 70174 Stuttgart 1. ☎/Fax 0711-22836.
B'nai B'rith Lodges, Berlin, Cologne, Dusseldorf, Frankfurt, Hamburg, Munich and Saarbrucken.
*Bundesverband Jüd. Studenten, Joachimstaler Str. 13, 10719 Berlin, and at Jewish Student Organisations at Aachen, Cologne, Frankfurt, Stuttgart, Hanover, Hamburg, Heidelberg and Munich.
Hochschule Für Jüdische Studien (University for Jewish Studies), Friedrichstr. 9, 69117 Heidelberg. ☎ 06221-22576. Fax 06221-167696.
Jewish Agency for Israel, Hebelstr. 6, 60318 Frankfurt. ☎ 069-7140225. Fax 069-94333420.
Jewish National Fund, Liebigstr.2, 60323 Frankfurt. ☎ 069-9714020. Fax 069-97140225.
Jewish Women's League (Frauenbund), c/o ZWST, Hebelstr. 6, 60318 Frankfurt.
Jewish Restitution Successor Organisation, Sophienstr. 26, 60481, Frankfurt.

Keren Hayessod, Vereinigte Israel Aktion e.v., Gartenstr. 6, 60594 Frankfurt a.M.
☎ 069-6109380.
Makkabi, Gailenbergstr. 13, 87541 Hindelang. ☎ 08324-8386. Fax 08324-2421.
ORT, Hebelstr. 6, 60318 Frankfurt. ☎ 069-9449081.
Wizo, Joachimstalerstr. 13, 10719 Berlin.
Youth Aliyah, Hebelstr. 6, 60318 Frankfurt.
Zentralarchiv zur Erforschung der Geschichte der Juden in Deutschland, Bienenstr.
5, 69117 Heidelberg. ☎ 06221-164141. Fax 06221-181049.
Zionist Organisation in Germany, Hebelstr. 6, 60318 Frankfurt. ☎ 069-498-0251.
Fax 069-490473.
Zionist Youth, Falkensteiner St. 1, 60322 Frankfurt. ☎ 069-556963.

GIBRALTAR (600)

In 1473 there was a suggestion that the promontory should be reserved for
Marranos (see D. Lamelas, 'The Sale of Gibraltar in 1474', 1992). The present
Jewish community was formed of immigrants from North Africa shortly after the
British annexation in 1704, but Jews had no legal right to settle in the city until
1749, by which year however, the Jewish residents numbered about 600, a third of
the total number of residents, and possessed two syns.

During the siege of 1779 to 1783 the size of the Jewish population was reduced,
a large proportion removing to England. After the siege the numbers rose again,
being at their highest in the middle of the nineteenth century, when they rose above
two thousand. (For the history of the Jews of Gibraltar, see A. B. M. Serfaty, 'The
Jews of Gibraltar under British Rule,' 1933.)
*Managing Board of the Jewish Community, 10 Bomb House Lane. ☎ 72606.
President S. I. Levy. Fax 40487. *Admin.* Mrs E. Benady.
Synagogue Shaar Hashamayim, Engineer Lane. ☎ 78069. Fax 74029. (Est. before
1749; rebuilt 1768.) *H. Sec.* J. de M. Benyunes, P.O. Box 174.
Synagogue Nefusot Yehudah, Line Wall Rd. (Est. 1781.) *H. Sec.* I. Beniso.
☎ 74791. Fax 40907.
Synagogue Es Hayim, Irish Town. (Est. 1759.) *H. M. & Sec.* S. Benaim. ☎ 75563.
Synagogue, Abudarham, Parliament Lane. (Est. 1820.) *H. Sec.* D. J. Abudarham.
☎ 78506. Fax 73249.
Mikveh, Mrs O. Hassan. ☎ 77658.
Joint Israel Appeal. *H. Sec.* E. Benamor. ☎ 77680. Fax 40493.

GREECE (4,800)

There have been Jewish communities in Greece since the days of antiquity. Before
1939, 77,200 Jews lived in Greece (56,000 in Salonika, now known as
Thessaloniki.). Today there are fewer than 5,000, all Sephardim, of these about 2,800
live in Athens; some 1,100 in Thessaloniki; and the rest in some 12 provincial towns.

ATHENS
*Central Board of Jewish Communities, 36 Voulis St., GR 105 57. *Sec. Gen.*
Moissis Constantinis. ☎ (01) 3244315. Fax 3313852. E-mail hhkis@netor.gr
American Joint Distribution Committee, 4 Nikis St., 105 63. Tel/Fax (01) 32-31-
034.
B'nai B'rith, 15 Paparigopoulou St., 105 61. ☎ 323-04-05.
Jewish Community Office, 8 Melidoni St., 105 53. ☎ (01) 3252823. Fax 3220-
761. *Director.*
Synagogue, Beth Shalom, 5 Melidoni St., 105 53. *M.* Rabbi Jakob Arar. ☎ (01) 325
2773.
Jewish Museum of Greece, 39 Nikis St., 105 57. ☎ (01) 32 25 582. Fax 32 31 577.
Communal Centre, 9 Vissarionos St., 106 72. ☎ (01) 36 37 092. Fax 360 8896.

THESSALONIKI
Jewish Community Office, 24 Tsimiski St., 54624. ☎ 031 27 5701. Fax 031-229063.
Monastirioton Synagogue, 35 Sigrou St., 54630. ☎ 524968.
Synagogue Yad Le Zicaron, 24 Vasileos Irakliou St., 54624. ☎ 223231.
Centre of Historical Studies of Thessaloniki Jews, 'Simon Marks', 24 Vasileos Irakliou St., 54624. ☎ 031 223231. Fax 031-229063.

Other communities:
Corfu Jewish Community, 5 Riz. Voulefton St., 49100. *President* Raphael Soussis. ☎ 0661 30591. Fax 0661-31898.
Halkis Jewish Community, *President* M. Maissis. 46 Kriezotou Str. GR 34100. ☎ 0221 27297. Fax 22397.
Ioannina Jewish Community. 18 Joseph Eliyia Str. GR 452 21. ☎ 0651 25195. *President.*
Larissa Jewish Community, Platia Evreon Martiron, GR 412 22. ☎ 041 532965. *President* A. Albelansis.
Rodos Jewish Community, 5 Polidorou Str. GR 85100. ☎ 0241 22364. Fax 0241 73039. *President* M. Soriano.
Trikala Jewish Community, *President* I. Venouziou, Kondili-Philippou, 42100. ☎ 0431 25-834.
Volos Jewish Community, 21B Vassani Str. GR 383 33. *President* R. Frezis. ☎ 0421 23079. Fax 0421-31917.

GUATEMALA (1,500)
Jews have been resident in Guatemala since 1898. The present population is about 1,500, made up of some 300 families all living in the capital.

GUATEMALA CITY
*Comunidad Judia Guatemalteca, 7a. Av. 13-51 Zona 9, Guatemala City, C.A. ☎ (502) 3601509. E-mail Comjugua@guate.net. *President* Jaime Camhi.
Centro Hebreo (East European Jews) 7a. Av. 13-51 Zona 9. ☎ 3311975. *President* Ricardo Rich.
Maguen David (Sephardi), 7a. Avenida 3-80 Zona 2. ☎ 2320932. Fax 360 1589. *President* Saúl Mishaan
Consejo Central Sionista de la Comunidad Judia de Guatemala, Apto. Postal 502, Guatemala, C.A. *President* Mano Permuth.

HAITI (150)
There has been a Jewish community in Haiti for the past 80 years, and it now numbers about 150 people.

HOLLAND (25,000)
From the sixteenth century onwards the Jews of Holland had a distinguished historical record. Since 1792 they have had the same constitutional and civil rights as all other citizens. In 1940 there were approximately 140,000 Jews in the country, but as the result of the Nazi occupation only some 25,000 remain, of whom about half are in Amsterdam. Other small coms. are in Amersfoort, Arnhem, Bussum, Eindhoven, Groningen, Haarlem, The Hague, Rotterdam, Utrecht and Zwolle.
Rabbinate Ashkenazic Community: Rabbi F. J. Lewis, Rabbi I. Vorst (both in Amsterdam); Rabbi J. S. Jacobs (Amersfoort).
Rabbinate Sephardic Community: Rabbi B. Drukarch.
Rabbinate Liberal Jewish Congregations: Rabbi D. Lilienthal (Amsterdam); Rabbi A. Soetendorp (The Hague); Rabbi Dr E. van Voolen (Arnhem).

AMSTERDAM
*Ashkenazi Community Centre and Offices: Van der Boechorststraat 26, 1081 BT.
☎ 646 00 46. Fax 646-4357.
*Sephardi Communal Centre: Mr Visserplein, 3, 1011 RD. ☎ 624 53 51. Fax 625-4680.
Ashkenazi Synagogues: Jacob Obrechtplein; Lekstr 61; Gerard Doustr. 238; Van der Boechorststraat, 26; Straat van Messina 10, Amstelveen.
East European Jew' Synagogue: G. van der Veenstr. 26-28.
Portuguese Synagogue, Mr Visserplein 3.
Liberal Community Centre and Synagogue. J. Soetendorpstraat, 8, 1079. ☎ 6423562. Fax 642-8135. Amsterdam and Dutch Liberal Rabbinate. ☎ 644-2619. Fax 642-8135.
Zionist Offices: Joh. Vermeerstr. 24. Netzer-Kadima at the Liberal Community Centre.
Jewish Historical Museum: Synagogue Bldg., J. D. Meyerplein.
Anne Frank House, Prinsengracht 263. Judith Drake Library at the Liberal Community Centre.

HONDURAS (150)

There has been a Jewish community in Honduras for the past 50 years.
Tegucigalpa Community. *Sec.* H. Seidel.
Israel Embassy S. Cohen, Ambassador; H. Schiftan, Consul. ☎ 32-4232/32-5176. Telex: 1606 Memistra.
San Pedro Sula, Syn. and Com. Centre. *Sec.* M. Weizenblut.

HUNGARY (100,000)

Jews have lived in this part of Europe since Roman times. Tombstones with Hebrew inscription have been found originating from the 3rd century. Before World War II, Hungary's Jewish population was about 800,000, of whom some 250,000 lived in Budapest. Some 600,000 perished in the Holocaust. The estimated Jewish population now is 100,000 and some 80,000 live in Budapest and the remainder in the provincial Jewish communities, all affiliated to the Central Board of the Federation of the Jewish Communities in Hungary.

BUDAPEST
*Federation of the Jewish Communities in Hungary (Magyarországi Zsidó Hitközségek Szövetsége) and the Budapest Jewish Community, 1075 Budapest VII Sip utca 12. ☎ 1-3226-475. Fax 342-1790. *Man. Dir.* Gusztav Zoltai; *Dir. Foreign Rel.* Ernö Lazarovits.
Main Synagogue, Budapest VII Dohany utca 2 (Conservative). Chief Rabbi Robert Frölich.
Central Rabbinate, Budapest VII Sip utca 12. *Dir.* Robert Deutsch, Chief Rabbi.
Orthodox Synagogue, Budapest VII Kazinczy utca 27. *President* Herman Fixler.
Rabbinical Seminary and Jewish University, Budapest VIII, József körut 27. *Dir.* Chief Rabbi Dr Jozsef Schweitzer, Chief Rabbi of Hungary; *Rector* Dr A. Schöner.
There are 20 other syns. and prayer houses in Budapest.
The main provincial coms. are at Debrecen, Miskolc, Szeged, Pécs, Györ.

INDIA (5,600)

The settlement of Jews in India goes back at least to the early centuries of the Christian era. The Indian Jews of today may be divided into four groups: (i) those who arrived in this and the last century mainly from Baghdad, Iran, Afghanistan, etc., known as "Yehudim," forming communities in Bombay, Pune and Calcutta; (ii) Bene Israel, who believe that their ancestors arrived in India after the destruction of the First Temple, and who maintained a distinct religious identity while using local language and dress over the centuries; their main centre is the Bombay area; (iii) the Cochin Jews, in Cochin and the neighbouring centres of the Malabar Coast, in Kerala State in South India, who have records dating back to the fourth century, but who believe that there was a Jewish settlement in Craganore as early as 78 C.E.; (iv) European Jews who came within the last 50 years or so. Since 1948 there has been steady emigration to Israel. According to the 1971 census the Jewish pop. was 6,134. Today, it is estimated at 5,618.

The largest com. is in Maharastra State (4,354), mainly in the Bombay area. Smaller coms. are in Calcutta, Madras, New Delhi and Pune Ahmedabad. In Manipur there are 464 and in Gujarat 217.

*Council of Indian Jewry, c/o The Jewish Club, Jeroo Bldg., Second Fl., 137 Mahatma Gandhi Rd., Bombay, 400023. ☎ 271628. *President* N. Talkar. ☎ 8515195, 861941; *V. Presidents* A. Talegawkar, A. Samson; *Sec.* Mrs J. Bhattacharya. ☎ 6320589.

INDONESIA

Of the 16 Jews living in Indonesia, 15, made up of five families, live in Surabaya where there is provision for prayers. One lives in Jakarta.

IRAN (25,000)

Jews have lived in the country at least since the time of the Persian king, Cyrus, in the sixth century B.C.E. Some 60,000 Iranian Jews emigrated to Israel in the late 1940s and early 1950s, and there has been an increasing trickle of emigration since. The situation of those who remain estimated to be in the region of 25,000 has become precarious under the new revolutionary regime on account of its anti-Israel stance. Most live in Tehran, some thousands in Shiraz, and the rest in Isfahan, Hamedan, Kermanshah and Abadan.

TEHRAN
*Central Jewish Committee of Iran–Tehran, 385 Skeikh-Hadi St. ☎ 372556. Synagogues, Haiim, Ghavamol-Saltaneh St.; Etefagh, Anatole France St.; Yousef-Abad, Yousef-Abad St.; Abrishami, (Kakh-Shomali).

IRAQ (75)

The Jewish community in Iraq (anciently known as Babylonia) is the oldest in the Diaspora. Strong hostility exists towards the Jewish remnant of about 200, mainly elderly, that is now left. They mostly live in Baghdad and a few in Basra.

ISRAEL (4,847,000)

Palestine was administered until May 14, 1948, by Gt. Britain under a Mandate approved by the Council of the League of Nations, the preamble to which incorporated the Balfour Declaration. On November 20, 1947, the Assembly of the United Nations recommended that Palestine should be reorganised as two States, one Jewish, the other Arab, together with an internationalised Jerusalem and district combined in an economic union. On the surrender of the Mandate by Britain on May 14, 1948, the Jewish territory, with a Jewish pop. of 655,000, took the name of Israel and set up a Provisional Govt., with Dr Chaim Weizmann as *President* and David Ben-Gurion as Prime Minister. On July 5, 1950, the 'Law of Return' was proclaimed, conferring on every Jew the right to live in Israel.

The signing of a declaration of a set of principles by Israel and the PLO under the leadership of Yasser Arafat on September 13, 1993, concluded an era of forty-five years of strife between Israel and her Arab neighbours and recognised the aspirations of Palestinian Arabs for territory proposed for them by the UN in 1947. A peace treaty with Jordan was agreed in 1994. Prime Minister Rabin was assassinated in November 1995.

Key events in this history include:
The invasion of the Jewish state by the Arab armies in 1948 concluded by a series of armistices in 1949 and the recognition of Israel by the UN on May 11, 1949; the annexation of Arab Palestine by Jordan in 1950; the absorption by Israel of Jews from Arab lands and the establishment of Palestinian refugee camps in the Arab states; seizure by Egypt of the Suez Canal Zone and the (Franco-British and Israeli) Sinai-Suez campaign of 1956; Egypt's closure of the Straits of Tiran in May 1967 and the Six-Day War of June 1967 which saw the Israeli capture of Jerusalem and occupation of Gaza, Sinai, the Golan and the West Bank and the first National Unity Coalition (1967-70).; the Yom Kippur War of October 1973 and the ensuing negotiations leading to partial Israeli withdrawals in Sinai and the Golan; the Likud election victory of 1977 and the visit to Israel by Egyptian President Anwar Sadat in November 1977 which led to the Camp David Agreement of March 26, 1979, the establishment of diplomatic relations between Egypt and Israel, and the Israeli withdrawal from the whole of Sinai in April 1982; Israel's 'Operation peace for Galilee' in Lebanon in June 1982 and withdrawal in 1985, a war which caused great divisions in Israel; the Intifada of the Palestinians in Gaza and the West Bank starting in 1988; the US-inspired five-point peace plan of 1989 and its failure in 1990; the Gulf War (January 1991) following the Iraqi invasion of Kuwait when the PLO supported Iraq and Israel sustained scud missile attacks without retaliation; the launching of negotiations for a comprehensive Middle East 'peace settlement' between Israel, the Arabs, and representatives of the Palestinians at a meeting in Madrid in October 1991.

It is these negotiations, conducted in public at a series of venues in Europe and the United States, and in secret in Norway since the Labour victory in the elections of June 1992, that came to fruition on the eve of the New Year 5754. Since then, a peace treaty with Jordan has also been signed. Further agreements for the transfer of controls in parts of the West Bank were signed in September 1995. In the interim, the continuing 'peace process' has repeatedly been put under threat by the actions of terrorists intent on destabilising the new situation. Anticipated stages of the process have yet to be achieved and it remains to be seen whether the principles of 'land for peace' on the Israeli side and 'reocgnition of Israel and peace' on the Palestinian can prevail as the basis for long-term accord between Israel and Palestine, and peace in the Middle East.

The assassination of the Prime Minister in November 1995, however, suggests that hostility to the peace process remains the greatest of all dangers to the Israeli polity. The continuing Hamas 'suicide attacks', devastating to Israeli citizens alongside the dispute over Israeli settlements within the occupied territories, and the military conflict in southern Lebanon, resurgent early in 1996 and again in late 1997, interrupted the Peace negotiations which finally reached a new landmark in late 1998.

Government

The Provisional Government of Israel was replaced by a permanent one after the election of the First **Knesset** (Parliament) in January, 1949.

Israel's Basic Law provides that elections must be 'universal, nationwide, equal, secret and proportional'. A general election must be held at least every four years. The Knesset is elected by a form of proportional representation in which members are selected in strict proportion to the votes cast for each party. Any candidate who obtains one per cent of the total votes cast is assured of a Knesset seat.

Mainly as a result of the voting system, no single party has so far been able to form a government on the basis of its own Knesset majority. Until the election in 1977, the dominant political force was a coalition of the Left, which formed governments with the help of various smaller parties, usually those with a religious programme. In the elections of 1977 and 1981 an alliance of the Right was able to form an administration with the help of religious parties. One feature of the political situation has been that the religious parties, in particular, have been able to exercise an influence out of proportion to their members.

Within recent years, however, there has been a marked polarisation of attitudes among sections of Israeli society and this was reflected by the proliferation of small parties which contested the 1984 election. The 1984 election produced an inconclusive result, with only three seats separating the two big party blocs. The two big parties formed Israel's second National Unity Government to cope with the urgent economic and other problems. The office of Prime Minister was held in rotation, first by Mr Shimon Peres, the Labour Alignment leader, and then by Mr Yitzhak Shamir, the Likud leader. The 1988 election was also inconclusive and was followed by another Coalition Government, with Mr Shamir continuing as Prime Minister and Mr Peres as Vice-Premier.The national unity government broke up in March 1990 when the Likud declined to go along with a U.S. plan to promote peace talks. Mr Shamir constructed a centre-right religious government supported by 66% of the 120 members of the Knesset. The elections of 1992 produced a Labour coalition led by Yitzhak Rabin. Demographic changes brought about by the influx of settlers from Eastern Europe and political and economic pressures contributed in large part to this outcome. While political power rests constitutionally in the Knesset, the President of Israel, essentially a symbolic and representational figure, can in certain circumstances exercise a degree of de facto power based on his prestige. In particular, he can emerge as the voice of the Nation's conscience. The President is elected for a five-year period, renewable only once. President Herzog was re-elected in 1988, Ezer Weizman, elected in 1993, was re-elected in 1998.

Elections to the 15th Knesset were held in May 1999. Party votes were as follows:

One Israel (Labour,			United Torah Judaism	5	(4)
Gesher and Meimad)	26	(1996:34)	Third Way		(4)
Likud	19	(32)	United Arabs	5	(4)
Shas	17	(10)	Moledet		(2)
Meretz	10	(9)	Yisrael Beitenu	4	(-)
National			National Union		
Religious	5	(9)	(Haichud Haleumi)	4	(-)
Yisrael ba'Aliyah	6	(7)	Hadash	3	(-)
Shinui	6	(-)	Balad	2	(-)
Centre Party	6	(-)	One Nation	2	(-)

Labour and its allies form the current, 28th, government of Israel.

The Presidents of Israel: Chaim Weizmann 1949-1952; Yitzhak Ben Zvi 1952-1963; Zalman Shazar 1963-1973; Prof. Ephraim Katzir 1973-1978; Yitzhak Navon 1978-1983; Chaim Herzog 1983-1993; **Ezer Weizman** 1993- .
The Prime Ministers of Israel: David Ben-Gurion 1948-1953 and Nov. 1955-1963; Moshe Sharett Dec. 1953–1955; Levi Eshkol 1963–1969; Golda Meir 1969–74; Yitzhak Rabin 1974–1977 and 1992–95; Menachem Begin 1977–1983, Yitzhak Shamir Oct. 1983–Sept. 1984, Oct. 1986–June 1992; Shimon Peres Sept. 1984–Oct. 1986, Nov. 1995–May 1996; Benjamin Netanyahu, May 1996–99; **Ehud Barak,** May 1999-.
Judiciary: The *President* appoints judges on the recommendation of an independent committee.
Defence Forces: Unified command of Army, Navy and Air Force. Small regular

force; compulsory military service for persons aged between 18 and 29 followed by annual service in the Reserve.

Area: Following 1949 armistice agreements – approx. 20,750 sq. km. Following withdrawal from Sinai in April 1982, approx. 28,161 sq. km. (including Golan Heights, West Bank and Gaza Strip).

Neighbouring countries: Egypt, Jordan, Syria, Lebanon.

Population: Sept. 1988: 4,455,000 (incl. 3,653,100 Jews). These figures include 17,000 Druse on the Golan Heights but not the other territories occupied in the Six-Day War (est. at 1,381,000).

Main Towns: Jerusalem (the capital), Tel Aviv, Haifa, Ramat Gan, Petach Tikvah, Netanya, Holon, Bnei Brak, Rehovot, Hadera, Nazareth, Rishon le-Zion, Beersheba, Ashkelon, Ashdod, Bat Yam, Tiberias, Eilat.

Industry: Main products: Cement, fertilisers, metal products, polished diamonds, ceramics, tyres and tubes, plywood, textiles, clothing and footwear, citrus by-products, electrical and electronic applicances, micro-electronics, chemicals, canned fruit, military equipment.

Agricultural Products: Citrus, fruit, vegetables, eggs, milk, wheat, barley, tobacco, groundnuts, cotton, sugarbeet, beef, fish, flowers, wine.

Minerals: Potash and bromine, magnesium, phosphate, petroleum, salt, glass, sand, clay, gypsum, granite, copper, iron, oil, natural gas.

With the exception of Jerusalem and Haifa, the country's largest port, the main centres of population are concentrated in the flat and fertile western coastal plain. Tel Aviv, the centre of Israel's largest metropolitan area, is the chief commercial and industrial centre. Fast-growing Beersheba is the capital of the arid northern Negev, while Eilat, the country's southernmost port, has been transformed from an isolated military outpost into a bustling Red Sea township linked to the northern centres by a modern highway and giving access now to Jordan as well. In the north lie the largely Arab centre of Nazareth, the popular health resort of Tiberias, overlooking the Lake, and Safad. Round Tel Aviv are clustered a number of towns, including Ramat Gan, Holon and Bnei Brak. Throughout the country and along the border areas are dotted kibbutzim and settlements.

President of State Ezer Weizman; *Knesset Speaker* A. Burg.

ISRAELI EMBASSIES AND LEGATIONS
Israel now enjoys diplomatic relations with 160 countries and many of these ties have come into being or have been renewed following the peace agreements of 1993.

Permanent Delegation to U.N. 800 2nd Ave., New York, N.Y. 10017. ☎ (212) 449-5400. Fax (212) 490 9186. Ambassador Gad Yaacobi; *Dep.* Ambassador David Peleg. European H.Q. of U.N. Geneva, 9 Chemin de Bonvent, Geneva; Ambassador N.Y. Lamdan. ☎ 7980500; Vienna, 20 Anton Frankgasse, 1180 Vienna. ☎ 470-4742. Ambassador Yoel Sher.

Embassy to European Communities. 40 Ave. de L'Observatoire, Brussels 1180. ☎ 373-55500. Ambassador E. Halevi.

Permanent Delegation to Council of Europe, 3 Rue Rabelais, 75008 Paris. ☎ 4076-5500. Ambassador A. Gabai.

Albania (see Italy).

Andorra (see Spain).

Angola. Emb. BP 5791, Largo 4 de Fevereire, Hotel Presidente Meridien, Luanda. ☎ 397331. Ambassador Tamar Golan.

Antigua and Barbuda (see Dominican Republic).

Argentina. Emb.: 701 Mayo Ave., Buenos Aires. ☎ 342-1465. Ambassador Itzhak Aviran.

Armenia (see Georgia).

Australia. Emb.: 6 Turrana St., Yarralumla, Canberra, 2600. ☎ 273 2045. Ambassador Shmuel Moyal. ☎ 273 1309.

Austria. Emb.: Anton Frankgasse, 20, Vienna 1180. ☎ 4704377. Ambassador Yoel Sher. ☎ 470 4741.

Azberbaijan. Emb: Stroiteley Prospect 1, Baku. ☎ 385282. Ambassador Eleizer Yotvath.

Bahamas. Consulate, PO Box 7776, Nassau NP. ☎ 3264421. Hon. Consul. Raphael Seligman.

Barbados. Consulate, PO Box 256, Bridgetown. Hon. Consul Bernard Gilbert.

Belarus. Emb.: Partizanski Prospekt 6A, Minsk 220002. ☎ 303479. Ambassador Eliahu Valk.

Belgium. Emb.: 40 Ave. de l'Observatoire, Brussels 180. ☎ 3749080. Ambassador.

Belize (see San Salvador).

Benin (see Côte d'Ivoire).

Bolivia. Emb.: Edificio 'Esperanza', Ave., Mariscal, Santa Cruz; Edificio 'Esperanza', 10 Pizo, Calle 1309, La Paz. ☎ 391126. Ambassador Yair Rekanati.

Botswana (see Zimbabwe).

Brazil. Emb.: Avenida das Nacoes, Lote 38, Brasilia. ☎ 244-7675. Ambassador Yaacov Keinan.

Bulgaria. 1 Bulgaria Sq., NDC Building, 7th Floor. ☎ 5432-01. Ambassador David Cohen.

Burkina Faso (see Côte d'Ivoire).

Burundi (see Zaire).

Kingdom of **Cambodia** (see Thailand).

Cameroon. Emb.: P.O. Box 5934, Yaounde. ☎ 201644. Ambassador.

Canada. Emb.: 50 O'Connor St., Ottawa. ☎ 5676450. Ambassador David Sultan.

Cape Verde (see Senegal).

Central African Republic (see Cameroon).

Chile. Emb.: Av. Bosque, Las Condes San Sebastian 2812, Santiago De Chile. ☎ 246-1570. Ambassador Pinchas Avivi.

China. Emb.: West Wing Offices, 1 Jianguo Menwai Da Ji, Beijing 100004. ☎ 505-2970. Ambassador Ora Namir.

Colombia. Emb.: Edificio Caxdac Calle 35, No. 7-25, Bogota. ☎ 2321067. Ambassador Avraham Hadad.

Congo (see Zaire).

Costa Rica. Emb.: Calle 2 Avendas 2 y 4 San Jose. ☎ 221-0684. Ambassador Shlomo Tal.

Republic of Côte D'Ivoire. O.1. B.P. 1877, Abidjan 01. ☎ 21 31 78. Ambassador Yaakov Revah.

Cyprus. Emb.: 4 Gripari St., P.O.B. 1049, W. Nicosia. ☎ 445195. Ambassador Shemi Tzur.

Czech Republic. 2 Badeniho St., Prague 7. Ambassador Rephael Gvir.

Denmark. Emb.: Lundevangsvej 4, Hellerup, Copenhagen. ☎ 396 26288. Ambassador Avraham Sitton.

Dominica (see Dominican Republic).

Dominican Republic. Emb.: Pedro Henriques Unena 80. ☎ 5418974. Ambassador Pinchas Lavie.

Ecuador. Emb.: Av. Eloy Alfaro 969 Y, Amazonas, PO Box 2138, Quito. ☎ 565509. Ambassador Yaacov Paran.

Egypt. Emb.: 6 Shariah Ibn-el Maleck, Giza, Cairo. ☎ 3610 528. Ambassador David Sultan.

El Salvador. Emb.: 85 Av. Norte 619, Colonia Escalon, Centro de Gobierno, PO Box 1776, San Salvador. ☎ 2985331. Ambassador Yosef Livne.

Eritrea. Emb.: PO Box 55600, 10 Wodejio Ali St., Asmara. ☎ 120137. Ambassador Ariel Kerem.

Estonia (see Latvia).

Ethiopia. P.O. Box 1266, Addis Ababa. ☎ 610 999. Ambassador Avi Abraham Granot.
Fiji (see Australia).
Finland. Emb.: 5a Vironkatu, Helsinki. ☎ 1356177. Ambassador Ali Yihye.
France. Emb.: 3 Rue Rabelais, Paris 8. ☎ 42564747. Ambassador Eliahu Ben Elissar.
Gabon (see Cameroon).
Gambia (see Senegal).
Georgia. Emb.: Achmashenebeli Ave. 61, Tbilisi 380002. ☎ 964 457. Ambassador Lili Hahamy.
Germany. Emb.: 2 Simrock-allee, 5300 Bonn 2. ☎ (228) 8230. Ambassador Avraham Primor.
Ghana (see Côte d'Ivoire).
Gibraltar. Con.: 3 City Mill Lane. ☎ 59555956. Hon. Con. M. E. Benaim.
Grenada. Emb.: (see Jamaica).
Greece. Emb.: Marathonoromu No. 1. Paleo Psychico, Athens. ☎ 6719-530. Ambassador Ran Coriel.
Guatemala. Emb.: 13 Ave 14-07, Zona 10, Guatemala City. ☎ 371-305. Ambassador Shlomo Cohen.
Guinea Bissau (see Senegal).
Guyana (see Venezuela).
Equatorial Guinea (see Cameroon).
Haiti (see Panama).
Honduras (see Guatamala).
Hong Kong. Cons.: Admiralty 701, Tower 2, 18 Harcourt Rd., Central. ☎ 25296091. Con.-Gen. Zohar Raz.
Hungary. Fulank, Utca 8, Budapest. ☎ 1767771. Ambassador Joel Alon.
Iceland. Emb.: (see Norway.) H. Con.-Gen. Pall Arnor Palsson.
India. Emb: 3 Aurangzeb Rd., New Delhi 10011. ☎ 3013238. Ambassador Yehoyada Haim. Cons.: Bombay 400 026, Kailas 50, G. Deshmukh Maro Cumballa Hill. ☎ 386 2793. Consul Walid Mansour.
Ireland. Emb.: Carrisbrook House, 122 Pembroke Rd, Ballsbridge, Dublin 4. ☎ 6680303. Ambassador Mark Sofer.
Italy. Emb.: Via Michele Mercati 12, Rome. ☎ 36198500. Ambassador Yehuda Milo.
Jamaica. Con.: 7-9 Harbour St., Kingston. ☎ 922-5990. Hon. Consul Joseph Mayer-Matalon.
Japan. Emb.: 3 Niban-Cho, Chiyoda-ku, Tokyo. ☎ 3264-0911. Ambassador Moshe Ben Yaakov.
Jordan. Emb.: Forte Grand Hotel, Amman. ☎ 698541. Ambassador Shimon Shamir.
Kazakhstan. Emb: Dgeltoxan St. 87, Almaty. ☎ 507215. Ambassador Israel Mey-Ami.
Kenya. Emb.: Bishop Rd., Fair View Hotel, P.O. Box 30354, Nairobi. ☎ 722182. Ambassador Menashe Zipori.
Kirghizstan (see Kazakhstan).
Kiribati (Republic of) (see Australia).
Korea (South). Emb.: 823-21 Daekong Building, Yoksam-Dong Kangnam-Ku. ☎ 5643448. Ambassador Arie Arazi.
Laos (see Vietnam).
Latvia. Emb.: 2 Elizabetes St., LV 1340 Riga. ☎ 00 371 2 320739/320980. Fax 00 371 830170. Ambassador Oded Ben-Hur.
Lesotho (see Swaziland).
Liberia. Emb.: Gardiner Avenue, Sinkor, POB 2057, Monrovia. ☎ 262073/262861. Fax (977) 4415.
Liechtenstein. Con-Gen. G. Yarden (see Switzerland.)
Lithuania (see Latvia)

Luxembourg (see Belgium).
Macao (see Hong Kong).
Macedonia (see Greece).
Madagascar (see Kenya).
Malawi (see Zimbabwe).
Malta (see Italy).
Marshall Islands (see Australia).
Mauritius (see Kenya).
Mexico. Emb.: Sierra Madre 215, Mexico City 10 D.F. ☎ 540-63-40. Ambassador Moshe Melamed.
Micronesia (see Australia).
Moldova (see Ukraine).
Monaco (see France). Con.-Gen. Joseph Amihoud.
Mongolia (see China).
Morocco. Bureau de Liaison, Souissi, 52 Boulevard Mehdi Ben-Barka, Rabat. ☎ 657680. Head of Liaison Office, David Dadonn.
Mozambique (see Zimbabwe).
The Union of Mayanmar. Emb.: 49 Pyay Rd., Yangon. ☎ 22290. Fax 22463. Ambassador Gad Natan.
Namibia (see Zimbabwe).
Nauro (see Australia).
Nepal. Emb.: Bishramalaya Hse., Lazimpat, Katmandu. ☎ 411811. Ambassador Esther Efrat Smilg.
Netherlands. Emb.: Buitenhof 47, The Hague, 2513 AH. ☎ 3760500. Ambassador Yossi Gal.
Netherlands Antilles. Curaçao Consulate, Blauwduiffweg 5, Willemstad, Curaçao. ☎ 373533. Hon. Consul Paul Ackerman.
New Zealand. Emb.: PO Box 2171, DB Tower, 111 the Terrace, Wellington. ☎ 4722362. Ambassador Nisan Koren-Krupsky.
Nicaragua (see Guatamala).
Nigeria. Emb.: 636 Adeyemo Elakija St., Victoria Island, Lagos. ☎ 2622055. Ambassador Gadi Golan.
Norway. Emb.: Drammensveien 82, Oslo 2. ☎ 2447924. Ambassador Michael Shiloh.
Oman. Israel Trade Representation Office, PO Box 194, Aladhaiba, P.C. 130 Muscat. Hd. of Mission Oded Ben Haim.
Republic of Palau (see Australia).
Panama. Emb.: Edificio Grobman, Calle Manuel Icaza, Quinto Piso, Panama City 5. ☎ 2648022. Ambassador Yaakov Brakha.
Papua, New Guinea (see Australia).
Paraguay. Emb.: Piso 8, Edificion San Rafael, Calle Yergos No. 437 C/25 De Mayo. ☎ 495097. Ambassador Yoav Bar-On.
Peru. Emb.: Sanches 125, 6 Piso Santa Beatriz, Lima. ☎ 4334431. Ambassador Mario Joel Salpak.
Philippines. Emb.: Tratalgar Plaza 23 Floor, 105 H.V. Dela Costa St., Saleeldo Village, Makati, Manila. ☎ 892-5329. Fax 819-0561. Ambassador A. Shetibel.
Poland. Interests Office: Ul. L. Krzywickiego 24, Warsaw. ☎ 250923. Ambassador Gershon Zohar.
Portugal. Emb.: Rua Antonio Enes 16-4°, Lisbon. ☎ 570-251. Ambassador B. Oron.
Qatar. Israel Trade Representation Office, Rm 512 Sheraton Hotel, Doha. ☎ 854-444. Hd. of Mission Shmuel Ravel.
Romania. Emb.: 5 Rue Burghelea, Bucharest. ☎ 6132633. Ambassador A. Millo.
Russia. Emb.:56 Bolshaya Ordinka, Moscow. ☎ 2306700. Ambassador Aliza Shenhar.
Rwanda (see Zaire).

St. Christopher, St. Kitts and St. Nevis (see Dominican Republic).
St. Lucia (see Jamaica).
St. Vincent and the Grenadines (see Jamaica).
San Marino. Con.-Gen. (see Italy).
Sao Tome and Principe (see Cameroon).
Senegal. Emb.: B.P. 296, Dakar. ☎ 231044. Ambassador Arieh Avidor.
Seychelles (see Kenya).
Singapore. Emb.: 58 Dalvey Rd., Singapore 1025. ☎ 235 0966. Ambassador D. Megiddo.
Slovakia (see Austria).
Slovenia (see Austria).
Solomon Islands (see Australia).
South Africa. Emb.: 339 Hilda St., Hatfield, Pretoria. ☎ 3422-693. Ambassador Elazar Granot.
Spain. Emb.: Calle Velazques 150, Madrid 28002. ☎ 4111357. Ambassador Ehud Gol.
Suriname (see Venezuela).
Swaziland. Emb.: Mbabane Hse., Warner St., P.O.B. 146, Mbabane. ☎ 42626. Ambassador.
Sweden. Emb.: Torstenssonsgatan 4, Stockholm. ☎ 6630435. Ambassador Gideon Ben-Ami.
Switzerland. Emb.: Alpenstrasse 32, Berne. ☎ 431042. Ambassador Gavriel Padon.
Tajikistan (see Uzbekistan).
Tanzania (see Kenya).
Thailand. Emb.: 75 Sukumvit Soi 19, Ocean Tower II 25th Floor, Bangkok 10110. ☎ 2604854. Ambassador Mordechai Lewi.
Togo (see Côte d'Ivoire).
Tonga (see Australia).
Trinidad and Tobago (see Venezuela).
Tunisia. Interests Office. ☎ 795-695. Hd. Shalom Cohen.
Turkey. Emb.: Mahatma Gandhi Sok 85, Gaziosmanpasa, Ankara. ☎ 4463605. Ambassador Zvi Elpeleg.
Turkmenistan. Emb.: Ambassador Shmuel Meirom (resident in Jerusalem).
Tuvalu (see Australia).
Uganda (see Kenya).
Ukraine. Emb.: GPE - S, Lesi Ukrainki 34, 252195, Kiev, Ukraine. ☎ 2949753. Ambassador Zvi Magen.
United Kingdom. Emb.: 2 Palace Green, Kensington, W8 4QB. ☎ 0171-957 9500. Opening Hours: Mon.-Thur. 09.00-18.00 and Fri. 09.00-14.00. Ambassador Dror Zeigerman-Eden (see also p.21).
United States of America. Emb.: 3514 International Dr, Washington, D.C., 20008. ☎ 364 5500. Ambassador Zalman Shoval.
Uruguay. Emb.: Bulevar Artigas 1585/89, Montevideo. ☎ 404164. Ambassador Yair Ben Shalom.
Uzbekistan. Emb.: Lachuti Street, No. 16a, Tashkent. ☎ 567823. Ambassador.
Vanuata (see Australia).
Vatican, Rooms 405-8, Via Barnata Onioni 6, Hotel Rivoli, Rome 00197. ☎ 807-6978. Ambassador Samuel Hadas.
Venezuela. Emb.: Avenida Franciso de Miranda, Centro Empresarial, Miranda 4 Piso Oficina 4-D, Los Ruices, Caracas. ☎ 2394-511. Ambassador Yosef Hasseen.
Vietnam. Emb.: PO Box 003, Thai Hoc, 68 Hguyen, Hanoi. ☎ 433140. Ambassador Uri Halfon.
Western Samoa (see Australia).
Zaire. Emb.: 12 Av. des Aviateure, Kinshasa. ☎ 21955. Ambassador S. Avital.
Zambia (see Zimbabwe).

Zimbabwe. Emb.: Three Anchor House, 6th floor, 54 Jason Moyo Ave, PO Box CY3191, Causeway. ☎ 756808. Ambassador Gershon Gan.

Main Political Parties

ISRAEL LABOUR PARTY
Est. 1968 by the merger of Mapai, Achdut Avoda and Rafi. Its programme: 'To attain national, social and pioneering aims, in the spirit of the heritage of the Jewish People, the vision of socialist Zionism and the values of the Labour movement'. *Chairman* Ehud Barak. Ad.: 110 Hayarkon St., Tel Aviv. ☎ 209222.

LIKUD PARTY
Conservative Political Party. Dedicated to the principles of a free-market economy and the attainment of peace with security while preserving Israel's national interests. *Chairman* Binyamin Netanyahu. Ad.: Metsudat Ze'ev, 38 King George St., Tel Aviv. ☎ (03) 621 0666. E-mail webmaster@likud.org.il

MERETZ
Mapam was founded in 1948. Mapam merged with Ratz and members of Shinui into one single party: Meretz Unification Congress 1997. *Chair* Yossi Sarid; *International Sec.* Monica Pollack. Meretz is a member party of the Socialist International and of the Party of European Socialists. Ad.: 2 Homa U'Migdal St., Tel Aviv 61201. ☎ 972-3-6360111. Fax 972-3-5375107. E-mail hasbara@meretz.israel.net

NATIONAL RELIGIOUS PARTY
Created through the merger of Mizrachi and Hapoel Hamizrachi in 1956. Its motto 'The People of Israel in the Land of Israel, according to the Torah of Israel'. Ad.: Sarei Yisrael 12, Jerusalem. ☎ 02-537727. *Sec.* General Zevulun Orlev.

AGUDAT ISRAEL
Founded in 1912 in Katowice, Poland. Its principle is that only the Torah unites the Jewish people. *Political Sec.* M. Porush. Central Off.: Haherut Sq., Jerusalem. (☎ 384357), and 5 Bardechefsky St., Tel Aviv. (☎ 5617844).

HISTADRUT – GENERAL FEDERATION OF LABOUR IN ISRAEL
93 Arlozoroff St., Tel-Aviv. 62098
☎ 972 3 6921513. Fax 972 3 6921512. Email histint@netvision.net.il.
Chairman Amir Peretz, MK.
Histadrut, the largest labour organisation in Israel, is a democratic organisation which strives to ensure the welfare, social security and rights of working people, to protect them and act for their professional advancement, while endeavouring to reduce the gaps in society to achieve a more just society. The executive body of Histadrut is separate from the elected body and the legislative body. The legislative and regulatory body, the Histadrut Assembly, represents the relative strengths of the different political groups of Israel.
    Membership is voluntary and individual, and open to all men and women of 18 years of age and above who live on the earnings of their own labour without exploiting the work of others. Membership totals over 800,000, including workers from all spheres, housewives, the self-employed and professionals as well as the unemployed, students and pensioners. Workers' interests are protected through a number of occupational and professional unions affiliated to the Histadrut. The Histadrut operates courses for trade unionists and new immigrants and apprenticeship classes. It maintains an Institute for Social and Economic Issues and the International Institute, one of the largest centres of leadership training in Israel for students from Africa, Asia, Latin America and Eastern Europe, which includes the Levinson Centre for Adult

Education and the Jewish–Arab Institute for Regional Cooperation. Attached to the Histadrut is a women's organisation, 'Na'amat', which promotes changes in legislation, operates a network of legal service bureaux and vocational training courses, and runs counselling centres for the treatment and prevention of domestic violence, etc.

Selected Educational and Research Institutions

HEBREW UNIVERSITY OF JERUSALEM
Founded in 1918 and opened in 1925 on Mount Scopus. When, contrary to the provisions of the Armistice Agreement after the War of Independence in 1949, access to Mount Scopus was denied by Jordan, the University functioned in scattered temporary quarters until a new campus was built on Givat Ram, and a medical campus in Ein Kerem, both in Jerusalem. After the Six-Day War of June 1967, the Mount Scopus campus was rebuilt and expanded. Today the University serves some 24,000 students in its seven Faculties: Humanities, Social Sciences, Science, Law, Medicine, Dental Medicine and Agricultural and Environmental Quality Sciences (the latter located in Rehovot). There are 12 Schools: Education, Business Administration, Applied Science, Nutritional Sciences, Nursing, Occupational Therapy, Pharmacy, Public Health, Social Work, Veterinary Medicine, Library, Archive and Information Studies, and School for Overseas Students. The Jewish National and University Library is on the Givat Ram campus and there are about 100 research centres. The Magnes Press/Hebrew University publishes scientific and academic works. *Ch. Bd. of Govs.* A. Grass; *President* Prof. Menachem Magidor; *Rector* Prof. Menachem Ben-Sasson. Ad.: Mount Scopus, Jerusalem, 91905. ☎ (02)5 882917. Fax (02) 5883021. Website: www.huji.ac.il

TECHNION-ISRAEL INSTITUTE OF TECHNOLOGY
Established in 1924 as a small technical institute, it now has more than 11,800 students, making it the largest full-service university wholly dedicated to science and technology in Israel. The institute has 19 faculties and departments including: Aerospace, Biomedical, Chemical, Civil, Electrical and Industrial Engineering, and Architecture, Chemistry, Computer Science and Management, Medicine and Physics. The Technion is located on Mount Carmel. The main buildings include the Winston Churchill Auditorium and the Shine Student Union. It also has a graduate school, a school for continuing education and a Research & Development Foundation. *President* Amos Lapidot. Ad.: Technion City, Mount Carmel, Haifa 32000. ☎ (04) 829 2578. Fax (04) 823 5195.

WEIZMANN INSTITUTE OF SCIENCE
The Institute at Rehovot engages in research in Mathematical Sciences, Chemistry, Physics, Biology, Biochemistry and Science Teaching. *President* Prof. H. Harari; *Chancellor* Lord Sieff of Brimpton. Ad.: P.O.B. 26, Rehovot 76100, Israel. ☎ 972-8-9343111. Fax 972-8-9466966.

BAR-ILAN UNIVERSITY
Since its founding in 1955, Bar-Ilan has grown to become Israel's second-largest university, comprising a modern 70-acre campus in Ramat Gan, outside Tel Aviv, with five regional colleges across Israel. Over 6,000 courses are taught in the faculties of exact, life and social sciences, humanities, Jewish studies and law, by 1,300 academic faculty to 25,000 students. Today, Israel's largest schools of education and social work and the premier Jewish studies faculty, operate at Bar-Ilan. Additionally, the university is home to world-class scientific research institutes in physics, medicinal chemistry, mathematics, brain reseach, economics, strategic studies, developmental psychology, musicology, archaeology, bible, Jewish law and philosophy, and more. Some 40 prominent universities around the world maintain academic cooperation agreements with Bar-Ilan. Every day, Israelis of widely varying backgrounds and religious beliefs work and study together in harmony at

Bar Ilan. *Chancellor* Rabbi Prof. Emanuel Rackman; *President* Prof. Moshe Kaveh; *Rector* Prof. Yehuda Friedlander. *Cor.* BIU, Ramat Gan, Israel 52900. ☎ 972-3-531-8111. *Student information:* 972-3-531-8274; Fax 972-3-535-1522. Internet: http//:www.biu.ac.il.

BEN GURION UNIVERSITY OF THE NEGEV, BEERSHEBA
Founded 1965, the university comprises the following faculties: Humanities and Social Sciences, Natural Sciences, Engineering Sciences, Health Sciences and School of Management, and the Kreitman School of Advanced Graduate Studies. *President* Prof. Avishay Braverman. Ad.: P.O. Box 653, Beersheba, 84105. ☎ (07) 6461219.

CENTER FOR JEWISH ART
POB 4262, Jerusalem 91042. ☎ 02-5882281. Fax 02-5882282. E-mail cja@vms.huji.ac.il. www.hum.huji.ac.il/cja *Director* Dr A. Cohen-Mushlin; *Academic Chairman* Prof. Bezalel Narkiss.

DEVELOPMENT STUDY CENTRE
Founded in Rehovot in 1961, its main object is interdisciplinary research & training activities related to regional development in Israel and the developing world, and training new immigrants for better employment. Ad.: P.O.B. 2355 Rehovot, Israel 76122. ☎ 08-9474111. Fax 08-9475884.

UNIVERSITY OF HAIFA
Established in 1963, Haifa is one of the eight accredited research universities in Israel. Academic instruction is conducted in the framework of the Faculty of Humanities, Faculty of Social Sciences and Mathematics, the Faculty of Law, the Faculty of Social Welfare & Health Studies, the Faculty of Education and the School of Education of the Kibbutz Movement, 'Oranim'. Most of the 45 departments and schools offer bachelor's, master's and Ph.D. degrees. Research activity is carried out in the Faculties and Schools and in the framework of research institutes and centres. The Research Authority encourages, initiates, develops and coordinates research at the University. The total student body in the academic year 1998/99 numbered 13,123. *President* Prof. Y. Hayuth; *Rector* Prof. G. Gilbar. Ad.: Mount Carmel, Haifa 31905. Email mtmnh17@uvm.haifa.ac.il; Internet http://www.haifa.ac.il. ☎ 972-4-8240111. Fax 972-4-8342101.

ISRAEL OCEANOGRAPHIC AND LIMNOLOGICAL RESEARCH
(Est. 1967) To develop knowledge and technology for sustainable use of marine and fresh water sources. *Dir.-Gen.* Dr Yuval Cohen. Ad.: Tel Shikmona, P.O.B. 8030, Haifa 31080. ☎ 04-8515202. Fax 04-8511911. Email yuval@ocean.org.il.

JERUSALEM ACADEMY OF JEWISH STUDIES (Yeshivat Dvar Yerushalayim)
53 Katzenellenbogen St., Har Nof, P.O.B. 5454, Jerusalem 91053. ☎ 6522817. Fax 652287. Website www.dvar.org/E-mail dvar@netvision.net.il. Dean Rabbi B. Horovitz, M.A.; UK office (Reg. Charity No. 262716), 1007, Finchley Rd., London NW11 7HB. ☎/Fax 0181-458 8563.

JERUSALEM COLLEGE OF TECHNOLOGY
Est. in 1969 to train engineers and applied scientists within a religious framework. The College has depts. in Electro-Optics and Applied Physics, Electronic Engineering, Computer Sciences, Management Accounting, Technology Management and Marketing, Industrial Engineering Applied Mathematics and Teacher Training. The complex includes a Bet Midrash for Jewish studies; one-year yeshiva academic programme for English-speaking students. The College awards a Bachelor's degree in Technology and Applied Science, Managerial Accounting &

Information Systems. *President* Prof. Y. Bodenheimer; *Rector* Prof. Y. Zeisel. Ad.: 21 Havaad Haleumi St., Jerusalem. ☎ 9722-6751111. Fax 9722-6422075. E-mail pr@avoda.jct.ac.il

THE LOUIS GUTTMAN ISRAEL INSTITUTE OF APPLIED SOCIAL RESEARCH
Founded in 1946 to advise governmental, public and private bodies on research in social psychology, sociology, psychology and related disciplines. *Scientific Dir.* Prof. S. Kugelmass. Ad.: 19 Washington St., Jerusalem, 91070. ☎ 231421.

MIKVEH ISRAEL AGRICULTURAL SCHOOL
The first agricultural school in Israel, it was founded by Charles Netter of the Alliance Isralite Universelle in 1870. The curriculum, in addition to training in agriculture, comprises instruction in the humanities, Jewish subjects, science, etc. Ad.: Mikveh Israel, Doar Holon. ☎ 03-842050. Zip code 58910.

ORT ISRAEL NETWORK
Est. 1948, ORT Israel manages Scientific and Technological Colleges and schools for around 80,000 young and adult students yearly. *Dir. Gen.*: I. Goralnik. Head office: 39, King David Blvd., Tel-Aviv 61160. Tel: 03-5203222.

TEL AVIV UNIVERSITY
The university sponsors studies and research in all the arts and sciences and includes among its faculties a department of space and planetary sciences, its observatory, at Mitzpe Ramon in the Negev, being the first in Israel. A science based industry utilising the university's manpower and equipment has been established. Its Graduate School of Business Administration was the first established in the country. There is a one year course which prepares new immigrants for entry into Israeli universities. *President* Prof. Yoram Dinstein; *Rector* Prof. Dan Amir. Ad.: Ramat Aviv, Tel Aviv. ☎ 5450111.

THE ZINMAN COLLEGE OF PHYSICAL EDUCATION AND SPORTS SCIENCES AT THE WINGATE INSTITUTE
(Est. 1944) Teachers College for Physical Educators. Offers four-year Bachelor of Education course, including Teachers' Diploma. Specializations in early childhood, special education, sports for the disabled, posture cultivation, cardiac rehabilitation, physical activity for the elderly, public health, behaviour analysis, dance and movement, leisure and recreation education, nautical education, scouting education, sports media. Joint M.A. programme with Haifa University.
Faculty of 200, student body of 900 full-time students, 1,500 in part-time in-service courses. Ad.: P.E. College at Wingate Institute, Netanya, Israel 42902. ☎ 972-9-863922. Fax 972-9-8650960. E-mail zinman@wincol.macam98.ac.il. Internet: http://www.zin.macam98.ac.il.

Selected Commercial Organisations

BANK OF ISRAEL
Set up by the Knesset in 1954. Its functions include those usually discharged by central banks. It issues the currency and acts as Government banker, and manages the official gold and foreign reserves. The governor is chief economic adviser to the Government. *Gov.* Ad.: Rechov Eliezer Kaplan, Kiryat Ben-Gurion, Jerusalem, 91007. ☎ (2) 6552211. Fax (2) 6528805. Email webmaster@bankisrael.gov.il

ISRAEL-AMERICA CHAMBER OF COMMERCE AND INDUSTRY
Exec. Dir. Nina Admoni. Ad.: 35 Shaul Hamelech Blvd., Tel Aviv. ☎ (03) 6952341. Fax (03) 6951272. E-mail amcham@amcham.co.il Website http://amcham.co.il

ISRAEL-BRITISH CHAMBER OF COMMERCE
(Est. 1951.) 29 Hamered St., PO Box 50321, Tel Aviv 61502. ☎ (03) 5109424. Fax (03) 5109540. *Exec. Dir.* F. Kipper.

THE ISRAEL PRO BONO ZEDEK FREE LEGAL ADVICE CENTRE and ISRAEL LEGAL REFERRAL SERVICE
PO Box 2828, Jerusalem. ☎ (02)-5820126. Fax (02)-5322094. Email wolfilaw@netvision.net.il. The Israel Pro Bono Zedek Free Legal Advice Centre provides free legal advice and consultations by expert volunteer lawyers who are members of the Israel Bar Association and by volunteer Rabbinical court pleaders, in all legal fields.

MANUFACTURERS' ASSOCIATION OF ISRAEL
Jerusalem: ☎ (02) 252449. Haifa: ☎ (04) 524202. Tel Aviv: ☎ (03) 5198787. *President* D. Propper.

Other Selected Organisations

ASSOCIATION OF JEWISH RELIGIOUS PROFESSIONALS FROM THE SOVIET UNION AND EASTERN EUROPE (SHAMIR)
6 David Yellin St., POB 5749, Jerusalem. ☎ 02-5385384. Fax 02-5385118. *Sec.* Martelle Urivetsky.

ASSOCIATION FOR THE WELLBEING OF ISRAEL'S SOLDIERS
(Ha'aguda Lemaan Hechayal) The Association for the Wellbeing of Israel's Soldiers was founded in 1942, during the Second World War, at a time when the young men of pre-state Israel were being drafted into the allied armies and the Jewish Brigade. The slogan back then was "The Heart of the People is with its Soldiers", and this sentiment continues to guide the Association's activity today. *Head Off.:* P.O. Box 21707, Tel Aviv 61217. *Overseas Dept*: 60 Weizman St., Tel Aviv 62155. ☎ 03 5465135. Fax (03) 5465145. Email awis@inter.net.il

BETH HATEFUTSOTH
The Nahum Goldmann Museum of the Jewish Diaspora, which opened in Tel-Aviv in 1978, tells the story of the Jewish people from the time of their expulsion from the Land of Israel 2,500 years ago to the present. History, tradition and the heritage of Jewish life in all parts of the world are brought to life in murals, reconstructions, dioramas, audio-visual displays, documentary films and interactive multi-media presentation. Ad: Tel-Aviv University Campus, Ramat-Aviv, P.O.B. 39359. Tel-Aviv 61392. ☎ 03-6462020. Fax 03-6462134. E-mail bhmuseum@post.tau.ac.il. Website: http://www.bh.org.il

CHIEF RABBINATE
The Chief Rabbinate consists of two joint Chief Rabbis and a Chief Rabbinical Council of 17. *Chief Rabbis* Rabbi Israel Meir Lau (Ashkenazi) and Rabbi Eliyahu Bakshi Doron (Rishon Lezion, Sephardi). Ad.: Beit Yahav, 80 Yirmiyahu St., POB 7525, Jerusalem. ☎ (02) 531 3192. Fax (02) 259-641. There are District Rabbinical Courts (Batei Din) in Jerusalem, Tel Aviv, Haifa, Petach Tikvah, Rehovot, Tiberias-Safad, Beersheba and Ashkelon.

ISRAEL MOVEMENT FOR PROGRESSIVE JUDAISM
☎ 02-203484. Fax 02-203343.

THE ISRAEL MUSEUM
HaKirya, Jerusalem. ☎ 02-670-8811. Israel's leading cultural institution and a museum of world-class status, its 20-acre campus houses an encyclopaedic collection of art and archaeology, with special emphasis on the culture of the Land of

Israel and the Jewish people. The Museum has the world's most extensive collections of the archaeology of the Holy Land, Judaica and the ethnography of Diaspora Jewish Communities, as well as significant and extensive holdings in the Fine Arts, ranging from Old Masters to Contemporary Art, and including separate departments for Asian Art, the Arts of Africa and Oceania, Prints and Drawings, Photography, and Architecture and Design. The campus also includes the Shrine of the Book, which houses the Dead Sea Scrolls, the Billy Rose Art Garden and a Youth Wing. *Dir.* James Snyder.

ISRAEL NATURE AND NATIONAL PARKS PROTECTION AUTHORITY
The Authority is the result of a merger in 1998 of two bodies, one of which was in charge of the Israeli nature reserves and the other of national parks and heritage sites in Israel. Ad.: 78 Yirmeyahu St., Jerusalem. ☎ (02) 500 5444. Fax (02) 538 3405; 35 Jabotinsky St., Ramat-Gan 52511. ☎ (03) 576 6888. Fax (03) 751 1858.

JEWISH AGENCY FOR ISRAEL
Founded 1929; Reconstituted 1971. Constitutents are the World Zionist Organisation, United Israel Appeal, Inc. (USA), and Keren Hayesod. By reasons of its record and world-wide org. the Jewish Agency has come to be widely regarded as the representative org. of Jews the world over particularly in regard to the development of Israel and immigration to it. The governing bodies of the Jewish Agency are: the Assembly, which lays down basic policy, the Bd. of Governors, which manages its affairs between annual Assembly meetings, and the Executive, responsible for day-to-day operations. Jewish Agency, P.O. Box 92, Jerusalem. ☎ 972 2 6202450. Fax 972 26202303. E-mail ilanr@jaizo.org.il *Ch. Exec.* Avraham Burg; *Ch. Bd.* Charles Goodman; *Dir.-Gen.* Shimshon Shoshani; *Act. Sec.-Gen.* Ilan Rubin.

KEREN KAYEMETH LEISRAEL (Jewish National Fund)
P.O. Box 283, Jerusalem, Israel. *World Chairman* Moshe Rivlin. *Head of Fund Raising* Avinoam Binder. The work of the JNF is to improve the quality of life for Israeli citizens by means of afforestation, ecology, water conservation and site preparation, and development for upbuilding the land to ensure its future.

WOMEN'S INTERNATIONAL ZIONIST ORGANISATION (Wizo)
(Reg. Charity No.: 580057321). 250,000 women, 100,000 of them in Israel, are members of this org. which maintains 800 institutions and services in Israel. World *President* Mrs M. Modai; *V. President and Chairman Exec.* Mrs H. Glaser. Ad.: 38 David Hamelech Blvd., Tel Aviv. 64237. ☎ 03-6923717. Fax 972-3-6958-267.

WORLD ZIONIST ORGANISATION
Founded by Theodor Herzl at the First Zionist Congress in Basle in 1897, it was the moving spirit in the events leading up to the establishment of the State of Israel in 1948. The 'Jerusalem Programme,' adopted by the 27th Zionist Congress in Jerusalem in 1968 reformulates the aims of the Zionist Movement as: The unity of the Jewish people and the centrality of the State of Israel in its life, The ingathering of the exiles in the historic Jewish homeland by aliya; The strengthening of the State of Israel, which is founded on the prophetic ideals of justice and peace; Preserving the uniqueness of the Jewish people by promoting Jewish and Hebr. educ. and upholding Jewish spiritual and cultural values; Defending the rights of Jews wherever they live. The supreme body of the W.Z.O. is the Zionist Congress, to which delegates are elected by members of Z. Federations abroad and by the Z. parties in Israel. The two governing bodies elected by the Congress are: the Executive, and the Zionist General Council to which the Executive is responsible

and which decides Z. policy between Congresses. *Ch. of Executive* Yehiel Leket. P.O. Box 92, Jerusalem 91920. ☎ 202222. Fax 252-353.

YAD VASHEM
Har Hazikaron (Mount of Remembrance), Jerusalem. ☎ 02-6751611. Fax (02) 643 3511. P.O.B. 3477 Jerusalem 91034. Email info@yad-vashem.org.il. Website: www.yad-vashem.org.il.
International centre for Holocaust Studies and International School for Holocaust Studies. The Holocaust memorial and museum includes exhibitions, Hall of Remembrance and children's memorial, also archives and a library.

British Settlements
The following are some of the settlements populated by large groups of immigrants from the United Kingdom and Ireland associated with the JIA Israel (see below), which represents the Israeli Office of the Zionist Federation of Great Britain and Ireland. In some cases groups from Britain themselves established these settlements; in others, they joined existing settlements as 'reinforcement' groups. Several of the entries have been revised extensively for this edition.
Beit Chever (Kfar Daniel) established in 1951 near Ben Shemen by Machal ex-Servicemen, mainly from Britain and South Africa. The 80 settlers there specialise in mixed farming.
Kfar Blum, established in 1943 north of Lake Hula, in Upper Galilee. Named after the late Leon Blum, it was the first kibbutz of British and American Habonim who joined forces with Latvian immigrants. Specialises in mixed farming and fish-breeding. Population over 700.
Kfar Hanassi was founded in 1948 in an abandoned Arab village called Mansura, located near the Jordan River on the Syrian border. The kibbutz was placed there to halt westward advancement by the Syrian Army in any attempt to cut Northern Gallilee in half. Two years later, the kibbutz was moved two kilometres westward to its present site, six kilometers from Rosh Pina. Until the Six Day War the kibbutz had been a border settlement. The kibbutz was named in honour of Israel's first president, Chaim Weizmann ('Kfar Hanassi' means 'Village of the President'). Most of the first settlers came from the Habonim Youth Movement in Britain, where they had spent the war years on training farms and had then joined the illegal immigration by sea to Israel. Many were refugees from Europe, brought over to Britain by the youth transports. There was also a smaller group from France and Australia among the first settlers. In the late 1950s the kibbutz was reinforced by another group from 'Habonim' Britain and it also absorbed individuals from America, South Africa and Israel. Most of the younger members (30-50) are Israelis, born on kibbutzim, and their spouses.
Affilation United Kibbutz Movement: Takam. Kfar Hanassi is a non-Orthodox kibbutz. There are services on high holy days and all Jewish festivals are celebrated communally, based upon old tradition and new kibbutz tradition (especially agricultural festivals).
Population 700, including 450 adults (300 of whom are members, the rest are candidates, volunteers and Ulpan students) and 250 children.
Kibbutz institutions Main decisions in the kibbutz are decided in the general assembly and by polls. On a day-to-day basis, the kibbutz is run by committees, such as those for education, health, transport, housing, culture and finance. Members are usually chosen to serve on a committee for a period of two years.
Agriculture Avocado orchards, citrus groves, field crops (such as corn, cotton or beans), medicinal herb crops, juniper nursery, poultry, sheep.
Industry Foundry for high-quality aluminium casting and stainless-steel ball valves (the kibbutz main branch); guest houses offering bed and breakfast; catamaran trips on the River Jordan; Galilee herbal remedies; hydroelectric plant.

Ad. Kibbutz Kfar Hanassi, Upper Galillee 1, 12305. ☎ 972-6-6914901. Fax 972-6-6914017.

Kfar Mordechai, founded near G'dera in 1950, is named after the late Mordechai Eliash, first Israeli Minister to Britain. Sponsored by the British Zionist Federation, Kfar Mordechai was the first middle-class settlement established for immigrants from Britain. Population about 60 families, half of them from Britain. Sugar is produced from locally grown beet. The moshav holds annual summer camps for local children.

Kibbutz Amiad is located in the southern part of Upper Galilee on the Tiberias–Kiryat Shmona road. It is near the route of the ancient coast road which ran from Syria to Egypt. Amiad was founded in 1946 by a settlement group of Jewish youth who had served together in the Jewish underground defence force (Palmach) which operated during the British Mandate in Palestine. Upon completion of their military service, they received agricultural training in Kibbutz Geva and in 1946 they founded their own community. The site was chosen for its strategic value: it overlooks the main road to Upper Galilee. This strategic importance grew during the War of Independence when the kibbutz housed an Israeli army base. Over the years the founders have been joined by Jewish immigrants from England and Holland. Near the kibbutz are the ruins of a medieval inn which are called 'Joseph's Well'. According the Arab tradition, this is the site of the well into which Joseph was thrown by his brothers. In addition, flint tools from the early Canaanite period have been found near the kibbutz.

Affiliations United Kibbutz Movement; Upper Galilee Regional Council.

Population Approximately 400, including 225 members and 150 children.

Agriculture Admiad farms approximately 15,000 dunams of land (3,750 acres) and has another 20,000 dunams (5,000 acres) of natural pastureland at its disposal. Major branches are orchards, both deciduous and subtropical, bananas, citrus, field crops, chickens and cattle.

Industry The kibbutz factory manufactures plastic and metal irrigation and water-filtering equipment for agriculture, industry and municipalities which is marketed world wide. Other commercial initiatives include a winery, graphic design studio, engineering consultants – plastics, and a bed and breakfast motel.

Ad. Kibbutz Amiad, Mobile Post Galil Elyon 1, 12335. ☎ 972-6-6933550. Fax 972-6-6933866.

Kibbutz Bet Rimon is situated in the hills of Lower Galilee. Established in 1980 by members of British Bnei Akiva. Mixed farming with a large dairy herd. Manufacturers of light agricultural tools and parchment for Torah scrolls, Mezuzot and other religious items. Guest house and seminar centre on the kibbutz. A new community neighbourhood is being established beside the kibbutz for non-kibbutz residents. Population about 100.

Ad. Kibbutz Bet Rimon, D.N. Hamovil Natzeret Illit, 17950. ☎ 972-6-6509611. Fax 972-6-6412583.

Kibbutz Beit Ha'emek, established in 1949, near Nahariya, Western Galilee, is the third kibbutz of British Habonim. The original settlers were Hungarian members of the movement and these were later joined by British and Dutch Habonim. The settlement grows avocado, cotton, citrus fruit and bananas. Its activities include poultry, dairy and sheep farming. It has factories involved in the biochemical industry.

Kibbutz Kadarim, in central Galilee overlooking the Kinneret, is an intimate rural community based on the principles of personal freedom, social justice and communal participation. Established in 1980 with a core population of Israeli, Australian and New Zealand youth movement members, Kadarim today has a population of 50 adults, and 40 young children under the age of ten. Approximately 25 per cent of current members are Olim from Habonim-Dror Australasia. Kadarim is a unique community, a partnership in which members retain their individual freedom: in particular, the right to make independent choices about their work-lives and finances. At the same time, a sophisticated system of communal services are provided to all members – and their children – with particular emphasis on high-quality education and healthcare, communal cultural events and social security. Kadarim is presently absorbing new couples and families, and is currently pursuing the option of home-ownership within the kibbutz framework.

Kadarim's businesses at present include manufacturing (Kapro spirit levels and measuring tools), agriculture (mango and citrus groves, a chicken run and beef cattle), and a newly opened bed and breakfast tourist facility. Many members also pursue their chosen professions outside the kibbutz, in teaching, medicine, alternative therapies, engineering, law, social work and computers. ☎ 06-986222. Fax. 06-986208. E-mail kapro@inter.net.il

Kibbutz Lavi was founded in 1949 by members of 'British Bachad – The Organization of Religious Pioneers' and today is one of the 17 Religious Kibbutzim in Israel. It is located in Lower Galilee, ten minutes west of Tiberias. Over 125 families live in Lavi (total population 650) where they share a communal life based on Torah (Judaism) and Avoda (working and settling the Land of Israel).

Kibbutz Lavi is world famous for its two major businesses: the well-known Kibbutz Hotel Lavi, one of the pioneers of the kibbutz hospitality idea 30 years ago, which hosts tens of thousands of guests each year; and Kibbutz Lavi Furniture Industries, the world's largest manufacturer of synagogue furniture. Kibbutz Lavi is also involved in educational tourism through the Kibbutz Lavi Education Center, which offers programmes and seminars for groups interested in enriching their understanding of Judaism, the kibbutz way of life and the Galilee region. In addition, Kibbutz Lavi has a large dairy and poultry farm, orchards and numerous field crops. E-mail lavi@lavi.co.il

Kibbutz Yassu'r was founded in January 1949 in western Galilee, ten kilometres east of Acco. The first kibbutz of British members of Hashomer Hatzair. Population of about 350. Economy based on mixed farming, 'Tree of Knowledge' (educational assembly kits factory), 'Magi' sock factory and tourist services. *Ad.* D.N., Misgav, 20150. ☎04-9960111. Fax 04-9960113.

Kibbutz Zikim, established in 1949 near the northern border of the Gaza Strip by Romanian members of Hashomer Hatzair. British members of the movement have since joined the settlement. The kibbutz concentrates on arable farming and has large vineyards, in addition to citrus groves and banana plantations. Has foam rubber mattress factory. Population about 250.

Massuoth Yitzhak, near Ashkelon, a Hapoel Hamizrachi moshav shitufi established in 1949. Population nearly 300, including 20 families from Britain. Specialises in mixed farming.

Moshav Habonim (Kfar Lamm) near Atlit, was set up in 1948 by Machal members from Britain and South Africa. Specialises in mixed farming and has factory making building insulating material. Runs summer camp for children. Population about 200.

Kibbutz Mevo Hama. Founded on Golan Heights overlooking Lake Kinneret by British and Australian Habonim after Six-Day War. In addition to beef cattle, ranching and cotton farming, they run a factory, specialising in plastic products.

Kibbutz Mishmar David. Two British Habonim garinim joined to revive this small kibbutz in Jerusalem corridor. Mixed farming and large offset print shop. Originally founded 1948. Population about 140.

Kibbutz Machanayim. Re-established in early 1950s in Upper Galilee near Rosh Pina with members of British Dror movement. Specialises in fruit orchards and mixed farming, particularly flowers. Has a precision tool factory. About 310 members.

Kibbutz Alumim is situated in the north-western Negev, approximately two miles south of Kibbutz Saad; closest towns are Sederot and Netivot. It is an hour's drive from Tel Aviv, one and a half hour's from Jerusalem, and half an hour from both Ashkelon and Beer Sheva. Alumim was established in 1966, by graduates of Bnei Akiva youth movement, and is a member of the Religious Kibbutz Movement (HaKibbutz HaDati). Initially intended as a border settlement, its status changed when Israel captured the Gaza Strip in the 1867 Six Day War.

Alumim's livelihood comes mainly from agriculture: field crops, citrus orchards, avocado plantations, a dairy herd of aproximately 200 milking cows, and rearing chickens for meat. Alumim has no industry but recently opened up several kibbutz branches to outside customers – for example, the garage, carpentry shop, electrical shop and the metalwork shop (now 'Shelah Systems', building computerised automated materials handling systems). There are comfortable, air-conditioned guest rooms and, as a religious kibbutz, all religious facilities are provided.

Alumim has a population of approximately 450, with about 75 families and various temporary groups such as Aliyat HaNoar, Nahal Army groups and youth groups visiting from abroad. Kibbutz Alumim had two large influxes of British Bnei Akiva graduates, in the early 1970s and mid-1980s, and they now comprise about 20 per cent of the population, taking on many of the leading communal roles. Kibbutz Alumim, although past its thirtieth birthday, is young in spirit, financially and socially stable, and set to face the challenges of the twenty-first century. *Ad.* Kibbutz Alumim, D.N. HaNegev 85138. ☎ 07 994 9711. Fax 07 994 9700. Guest Rooms Office 07 994 9805. Correspondence to Shmarya Meller, Kibbutz Secretary.

Kibbutz Adamit. Founded after Yom Kippur War by young members of Hashomer Hatzair from various Western countries. Right on Lebanese border. Farming.

Moshav Sde Nitzan was founded in 1973 by a group of immigrants from English-speaking countries including England, US, Canada, New Zealand, Australia and South Africa. We started with 20 families as a small farming community in the western Negev. We are now celebrating our twenty-fifth anniversary having grown to 74 families, 14 of whom joined us during the last three years. About 50 per cent of original families are still here. The original families were joined over the years by Israeli families. Our main occupation is still agriculture, primarily flowers for export. We also have mango orchards and recently planted 1,600 dunam to citrus. The moshav is, in fact, a small village of independent families. In the future we are planning to open a section of up to 100 lots for non-farming families. Our area of the country is entirely kibbutzim and moshavim and very underpopulated. We have a school complex shared by all the moshavim taking children from 18 months through high school. We also have a regional medical centre, including, in addition to medical doctors and visits from specialists, a pharmacy, a dental clinic and a physical therapy wing. Closest city is Beersheva.

Kibbutz Tuval was established in January 1981 by immigrants from British and South African Habonim-Dror as well as graduates of the Israeli Scout Movement. In the course of its history, the kibbutz has maintained a mix of Anglo-Saxons and Israelis, and this has very much shaped the unique quality of the community. The kibbutz today has 40 members and has recently taken a decision to enlarge its ranks by establishing a 'Community Village' which will run in parallel with the kibbutz. The plan is for 27 families to join the community in the summer of 1998, and an additional 32 families in 1999. The primary sources of income are a dairy herd, chicken houses, a kiwi-fruit plantation and the Tuval Seminar Centre and guest houses, providing educational workshops for both English- and Hebrew-speaking groups. *Ad.* Kibbutz Tuval, D.N. Bikat Bet HaKerem, 25166. ☎ 972-9907-907. Fax 972-4-9907-900.

UJIA Israel (incorporating the British Olim Society). Head Office: 76 Ibn Gvirol St., POB 16266, Tel Aviv 61162. ☎ 03-6965244. Fax 03-6968696. E-mail israel@ujia.org.il. *Man. Dir.* Shifra Levitsky. There are branches in Jerusalem and

Karmel. UJIA Israel is the official representative of the United Jewish Israel Appeal of Great Britain & Northern Ireland. Formerly known as the British Olim Society (est. 1949 in order to assist and support new immigrants from the UK settling in Israel), the merger of BOS and JIA-Israel took place in 1996 under the newly formed UJIA umbrella.

UJIA Israel represents UJIA UK on all campaign-related activities:
Campaign Services The aim of UJIA Israel is to strengthen the ties between British Jewry and Israel. This is achieved by involving British Jewry in projects in Israel, such as Partnership 2000, Project Renewal, study tours and missions.
- provides comprehensive absorption services to new immigrants from the UK, Australia, Scandinavia and Germany.
- operates the 'Israel Experience', the youth volunteer programme, from the UK.
- promotes the absorption needs of various new immigrants in Israel.
During 1990, the BOS Charitable Trust was established as a funding conduit for new immigrant activities and programmes in Israel, essentially aimed at helping the disadvantaged and less fortunate.

English Speaking Residents Association (ESRA). P.O.B 3132, Herzliya 46104. ☎ 972-9-9508371. Fax 972-9-9543781. E-mail esra@trendline. co.il Website www.esra.org.il (non-profit organisation no. 550037451.) A voluntary organisation assisting absorption of English-speaking immigrants, by means of social, cultural, educational and volunteering projects, practical help in finding employment, support, and advice on emotional, social and legal problems. The ESRA Community Fund initiates and supports welfare, educational and professional projects for disadvantaged Israelis, immigrants from distressed countries, the handicapped and victimised women. Tax exemptions on donations in United States, United Kingdom, Canada and Israel. Publ. ESRA Magazine and the ESRA Directory.

Israel, Britain and the Commonwealth Association (IBCA), Industry House, 29 Hamored St., 68125, Tel Aviv. Fax (03) 5104646. Branches in Haifa and Jerusalem. The main aims of the Association are to encourage, develop, and extend social, cultural and economic relations between Israel and the British Commonwealth. *Chairman* L. Harris; *Vice-Chairman* Dr A. Lerner; *Hon. Sec.* Madelaine Mordecai; *Contact* Freida Peled.

ITALY (34,500)

The Jewish community of Italy, whose history goes back to very early times, increased considerably at the time of the Dispersion in C.E. 70. During the Middle Ages and the Renaissance there were newcomers from Spain and Germany. Rich syns. as well as rabbinical schools, yeshivot, and printing houses were set up and became known in many countries. During the first years of fascism Italian Jews did not suffer; only after 1938 (under Nazi pressure) were racial laws introduced and, during the German occupation from 1943 to 1945 nearly 12,000, especially from Rome, were murdered or banished. The number of persons registered as Jews now is around 35,000. The most important communities are those of Rome (15,000), Milan (10,000), and Turin (1,630), followed by Florence, Trieste, Livorno and Venice and other centres.

ROME
*Central organisation: Unione delle Comunità Ebraiche Italiane, 00153 Roma, Lungotevere Sanzio 9. ☎ 5803670. Fax 5899569. *President*.
Community: Lungotevere Cenci, 00186. ☎ 6840061. Fax 68400684. Rabbinical office. Fax 68400655.
Chief Rabbi, Dr Elio Toaff. ☎ 6875051/2/3.
Jewish Agency, Corso Vittorio Emanuele 173, 00185. ☎ 68805290. Fax 6789511.
Synagogues, Lungotevere Cenci; Via Catalana; Via Balbo 33.
Syn. of Libyan refugees-Via Padova 92. ☎ 44233334.

MILAN
Community, Via Sally Mayer, 2, 20146. ☎ (02) 48302806. Fax 02/48304660.
Synagogue, Via Guastalla, 19, 10122. ☎ (02) 5512029. Fax (02) 5512101.
Zionist Fed., Via E de Amicis 49. ☎ (02) 8357558.

JAMAICA (350)

The Jewish settlement here, first composed of fugitives from the Inquisition, goes back before the period of the British occupation in 1655. During the eighteenth century there was an Ashkenazi influx from England. Jewish disabilities were abolished in 1831. There were formerly congregations at Port Royal, Spanish Town (two syns.) and at Montego Bay (1845-1900). The Ashkenazi and Sephardi communities in Kingston merged into one in 1921, the last of eight which once flourished.
*United Congregation of Israelites, Synagogue Shaare Shalom, Duke St. (Syn. built 1885, rebuilt 1911.) *Spiritual Leader* Rev. Dr Ernest H. de Souza,C.D., J.P., DHumL(Hon). ☎ 876-927-7948. Fax 876-978-6240.
Hillel Academy (Est. 1969).
Home for the Aged (Est. 1864).
Managed by the Jewish Ladier Organisation. *Chairman* Mrs Sandra Phillipps.

JAPAN (2,000)

The first Jewish community in Japan (at Yokohama) dates back to 1860 and old Jewish cemeteries exist in Yokohama, Kobe and Nagasaki. Jews were among the early foreign settlers. In 1940, 5,000 Jewish refugees from Germany and Poland arrived in Kobe, subsequently leaving for the U.S.A. and Shanghai. There are now about 2,000 Jews in Japan. About 1,000 live in the Tokyo area. There is a cong. of about 40 families in Kobe.
*Jewish Community of Japan, 8-8 Hiroo 3-chome, Shibuya-Ku, Tokyo (150). ☎ 3400-2559. Fax 03-3400-1827. *M.* Rabbi Eliot Marmon. Kosher meals available on Shabbat and during the week. Advance notification requested.

KENYA (150 families)

Jewish settlement in East Africa dates from 1903, when the British Government offered the Zionist Organisation a territory in the present Kenya for an autonomous Jewish settlement. The offer was refused but not unanimously and shortly afterwards a few Jews settled in the colony. Later, a number of Central European Jewish refugees settled here. The Jewish population in today's independent Kenya is about 150 families, most of whom are Israelis. See 'Jews of Nairobi 1903-1962', by Julius Carlebach.
*Nairobi Hebrew Congregation, P.O. Box 40990, 219703. ☎ 222770. (Est. 1904.) *Chairman* V. Aharoni; *H. T. C.* Szlapak; *H. Sec.* Ms A. Zola.

LATVIA (17,000)

REZHITSA
Syn.: Kaleyu St.

RIGA
Syn.: 6/8 Peitavas St. ☎ (013-2) 22-45-49.
Jewish Library, LOEK, 6 Skolas St., 226050. ☎ (013-2) 28-95-80.

LEBANON (100)

In the civil war which broke out in 1975 most of the 2,000 Jews left the country. About 100 remain in Beirut.

LIBYA (50)
About the time that Libya became an independent State in 1951 there was a mass emigration of most of its 37,000 Jews to Israel, and only very few remain in Tripoli.

LITHUANIA (11,000)
Jewish Community of Lithuania, 4 Pylimo, Vilnius 2001. ☎ 2-613-003. Fax 2-227-915. E-mail root@lzb.vno.osf.lt

KAUNAS
Syn.: 11, Ozheskienes St.
Jewish Community Offices, 26B Gedimino St. ☎ 203-717.

VILNIUS
Syn.: 39 Pylimo St. ☎ (2) 61-25-23.
Vilna Gaon Jewish State Museum, Pamelkalnio Str. 12, Vilnius. ☎ 620730. There are also communities in Druskininkai, Klaipeda, Panevezys and Shiauliai.

LUXEMBOURG (1,000)
There are today about 1,000 Jews in Luxembourg, the majority in Luxembourg City. Since the French Revolution they have enjoyed the same rights as other citizens. Before 1933 there were 1,800 Jews in the country; by 1940 the influx of German and other refugees had brought the Jewish population to about 5,000. The main syn. was destroyed by the Nazis.
Synagogue: 45 Avenue Monterey, Luxembourg City 2163.
Chief Rabbi, Joseph Sayagh, 34 rue Alphonse Munchen, 2172. *Chairman* Aach Guy, 45 Av. Monterey.
Or Chadash Liberal Jewish Community (affiliated to ULPS). *Corr.* 29 rue Leandre Lacoix, 1-1913. Email D1Jaffe@aol.com. *Chair.* Erica Peresman
Esch/Alzette: Synagogue, 52 Rue du Canal. *Chairman* R. Wolf, 19 rue du Nord 4260 Esch/Alzette.

MALTA (50)
There have been Jews in Malta since the period of the Romans, although their number has never been large. During the period of the Knights of St. John and the Spanish Expulsion of 1492, there were few, apart from slaves. A new community, originating from North Africa, arose at the end of the eighteenth century. The synagogue in Spur St., Valetta, opened in 1912, was demolished in 1995 as part of a development scheme. The community has recently launched an appeal for funds to replace it.
Jewish Community of Malta. P.O. Box 42, Birkirkara, Malta. *President* A. Ohayon; *Sec.* S. L. Davis, O.B.E., Melita, Triq Patri Guze Delia, Balzan BZN 07. ☎ 445924. Enquiries: Mrs S. Tayar, ☎ 338663.

MAURITIUS
There is no permanent Jewish community. The Jewish cemetery contains the graves of 125 refugees from Europe. They were part of a group of 1,700 Jews denied entry to Palestine and interned on the island during 1940-1945. *Corr.* P.M. Birger. P.O. Box 209, Port Louis, Mauritius. ☎ 2080821. Fax 2083391.

MEXICO (48,000)
The Jewish presence in Mexico dates back to the Spanish Conquest, although it was not until the final years of the nineteenth century and the beginning of the

twentieth that a mass immigration of Jews from Syria, the Balkanic Countries and eastern Europe, fleeing from persecution and poverty, laid the foundations of the modern Jewish Mexican community. Today's Jewish population is about 40,000, the majority in Mexico City. The cit has eight Jewish day-schools and several Yeshivot attended by up to 75 per cent of Mexican Jewish children. there are communities in Gudalajara, Monterrey and Tijuana.

MEXICO CITY
*Central Committee of the Jewish Community in Mexico, Cofre de Perote 115, Col. Lomas Barrilaco, 11010 Mexico DF. ☎ 540-7376, 520-9393. Fax 540-3050. *Exec. Dir.* Mauricio Lulka.
Synagogues: Askenazi, Acapulco 70, Col. Roma, ☎ 211-0575; Bet El (Conservative) Horacio 1722, Polanco. ☎ 281-2592; Beth Israel (Conservtive, English speaking), Virreyes 1140, Lomas. ☎ 7520-8515; Sephardic, Tehuantepec 188, Col. Roma. ☎ 574-3788; Monte Sinaì (Damascan), Fuente de la Huerta 22, Tecamachalco. ☎ 589-8322; Maguén David (Aleppo), Lafontaine 229, Polanco. ☎ 203-9964.
Jewish Sport Center, Avila Camacho 620, Lomas de Sotelo. ☎ 557-3000.

MOLDOVA (65,000)
CHISINAU
Syn.: Yakimovsky Per, 8, 277000. ☎ (042-2) 22-12-15.
Towns with Jewish populations include: Tiraspol, Baltsy, Bondery, Soroky, Ribnitsa and Orxey.

MOROCCO (7,000)
The Jews of Morocco have a history dating back to the times before it became a Roman province. Under Moslem rule they experienced alternate toleration and persecution. The expulsion from Spain and Portugal brought many newcomers to Morocco. In the nineteenth century many of the oppressed Jews sought the protection of Britain and France. The former French Protectorate removed legal disabilities, but the economic position of most Jews remained very precarious. During the Vichy period of the second World War Sultan Mohamed V protected the community. Before the est. of the independent kingdom of Morocco in 1956 many emigrated to Israel, France, Spain and Canada, and the present Jewish pop. is est. at 7,000 under the protection of King Mohammed VI.

CASABLANCA
*Community Offices, 12 rue Abou Abdallah Al Mahassibi. ☎ 222861.Fax 266953.
Synagogues: Temple Beth El, 61 rue Jaber Ben Hayane. ☎ 267192; Em Habanim, 14, rue Ibn Rochd; Hazan, rue Roger Farache; Tehilla Le David, Blvd. du 11 Janvier; and Benisty rue Ferhat Hachad.
International Organisations: American Joint Distribution Committee, 3 rue Rouget de Lisle. ☎ 274717. Fax 264089; Ittihad-Maroc, 13 rue Addamir Al Kabir. ☎ 2003-72. Fax 2003-09; Ose, 151 bis, blvd. Ziraoui. ☎ 267891. Fax 278924; Lubavitch-Maroc, 174 blvd. Ziraoui. ☎ 269037; Ozar Hatorah (Religious School Organisation), 31 rue Jaber Ben Hayane. ☎ 270920.
There are also coms. in Fez, Kenitra, Marrakech, Meknès, Rabat, Tangier, Tetuan, El Jadida and Agadir.

MOZAMBIQUE
Jewish Community of Mozambique, c/o Natalie Tenzer-Silva. P.O. Box 232, Maputo. ☎ 494413.

NEW ZEALAND (4,000)

The settlement of Jews in New Zealand dates from the establishment of British sovereignty in 1840. In the first emigrant ships were a number of Jews from England. But still earlier a few Jewish wayfarers had settled in the northern part of New Zealand, including John Israel Montefiore, a cousin of Sir Moses Montefiore, who settled at the Bay of Islands in 1831, Joel Samuel Polack, one of the earliest writers on the country, in which he travelled in 1831-37, and David Nathan, who laid the foundations of the Jewish community in Auckland in the early 1840s.

The Wellington Jewish com. was founded by Abraham Hort, under the authority of the Chief Rabbi, on January 7, 1843, when the first Jewish service was held. Communities were later est. in Christchurch and Dunedin and other parts of the South Island. From the earliest times Jewish settlers have helped to lay the foundation of the commercial and industrial prosperity of the country.

The number of Jews in New Zealand is estimated at 3,300. Most live in Auckland and Wellington.

Jews have occupied most important positions in New Zealand including that of Administrator, Prime Minister and Chief Justice. There have been six Jewish mayors of Auckland and two of Wellington. See History of the Jews in New Zealand by L. M. Goldmann 1959. During the last 15 years approximately 400 Soviet Jews have settled in New Zealand, mainly in Wellington and Auckland, but many have since emigrated to Australia.

*United Synagogues of N.Z. *President* S. Goldsmith, 11 Rotherglen Ave., Christchurch.

*New Zealand Jewish Council. *President* Mr D. Zwartz. P.O. Box 4315 Auckland. ☎ 309-9444. Fax 373 2283.

Council of Christians & Jews, PO Box 68-224, Newton, Auckland. ☎ (09) 638-7710.

Council of Jewish Women of N.Z., PO Box 27-156, Wellington. *President*: Mrs S. Payes. ☎ (04) 567-1679.

*Zionist Federation of N.Z. S. Pages, 80 Webb St., Wellington.

Wizo Federation. *President*: Mrs Clements, 80 Webb St., Wellington.

New Zealand Jewish Chronicle (monthly), PO Box 27-211, Wellington. ☎ (04) 385-0720. Fax (04) 384-6542. *Edr.* Anna Veritt.

WELLINGTON (1,000)

Hebrew Congregration. *President* D. Lewis. 80 Webb St. ☎ 4845 081.

Beth-El Synagogue, opened 1870 rebuilt 1929, resited in Jewish Community Centre and opened 1977.

Jewish Community Centre, 80 Webb St., P.O. Box 11-173. Moriah Kindergarten open daily.

Moriah College. (Primary Day Sch.) (Est. 1987.) P.O. Box 27233. ☎ 4842401.

Liberal Jewish Congregation (Temple Sinai). *President* V. Josephs, P.O. Box 27 301. ☎ 4850 720.

Zionist Society. *President* M. Lawrence, 80 Webb Street.

AUCKLAND (1,600)

Hebrew Congregation. *President* R. Max. P.O. Box 68 224. ☎ 372 908.

Beth Israel Synagogue, 108 Greys Ave. P.O. Box 68 224. ☎ 373-2908 (Est. 1841).

Beth Shalom, The Auckland Congregation for Progressive Judaism, 180 Manukau Rd., Epsom. *President* P. Marks. P.O. Box 26052 Epsom.

Kadimah College and Kindergarten, Greys Ave.

Zionist Society, (Est. 1904). P.O. Box 4315.

There are smaller coms. in Christchurch (130), Hamilton (50) and Dunedin (60).

NORTH YEMEN

Since 1948 the vast majority of Yemeni Jews (who then numbered about 50,000) have emigrated to Israel. It is est. about 1,200 remain in Sa'ana.

NORWAY (2,000)

The Jewish population of Norway is estimated to be about 2,000. There are two organised communities, Det Mosaiske Trossamfund Oslo (about 1,000 members) and Det Mosaiske Trossamfund Trondheim (about 100 members).

The community in Oslo is very active, with regular synagogue services (Friday night and Saturday as well as all holidays), a kindergarden, afternoon classes for children of school-going age, regular meetings and seminars for members of different age-groups, a home for the elderly as well as a shop which supplies kosher food.
*Det Mosaiske Trossamfund (Jewish Community): *President* R. Katz, Bergstien 13 0172 Oslo ☎ 22696570. Fax 22466604.
Synagogue and Community Centre, Bergstien 13, Oslo 0172. ☎ 22696570.
Synagogue and Community Centre, Ark. Cristiesgt. 1, Trondheim. ☎ 7352 6568. *President* Julius Paltiel.

PAKISTAN

Two Jewish families remain in Pakistan's port of Karachi. The Magen Shalom Syn. built in 1893, at Jamila St. and Nishta Rd. junction, was reported closed in 1987.

PANAMA (9,250)

The community has been in existence for nearly 150 years and numbers nearly 9,250, with 8,420 in Panama City.
*Consejo Central Comunitario Hebreo de Panama, Apartado 55-0882-Paitilla, Panama, Panama City. ☎ (507) 263-8411. Fax (507) 264-7936. E-mail sion@plazareg.com *Contact* Sion Harari (*President*).
Beth El, (Cons), Apartado 3087, Panama 3, Panama City.
Congregation Shevet Ahim, (Orth.), Apartado 6222, Panama 2, Panama City.
Kol Shearith Israel, (Reform), Apartado 4120, Panama City.
There are smaller coms. in Colon (100) and David (100).

PARAGUAY (900)

The community, which has been in existence since 1912, numbers about 900.
Consejo Representativo Israelita del Paraguay (CRIP), General Diaz 657. Asuncion, P.O.B. 756. ☎ 41744.

PERU (5,000)

Marranos were prominent in the early development of Peru. Many Jews suffered martyrdom during the centuries that the Inquisition prevailed. The present Jewish population is about 5,000 nearly all living in Lima. There are an Ashkenazi community and a Sephardi community.
*Synagogue and Communal Centre, Húsares de Junin 163 (Jesus Maria), Lima. ☎ 241-412, 31-2410.
Sociedad de Beneficencia (Sefaradim), Enrique Villar 581, Lima.
Sociedad de Beneficencia Israelita de 1870, Esq Jose Gálvez 282 Miraflores.

PHILIPPINES (25)

Jewish Association of the Philippines, H.V. de la Costa, crn. Tordesillas, Salcedo Village, Makati, Metro Manila. ☎ 815 0265; 815 0263. Fax 840-2566.
Postal Ad.: MC P.O. Box 1925, Makati, Metro Manila, 1259 Philippines.

POLAND (6,000)

Jews first settled in Poland in the twelfth century. Casimir the Great, the last Polish King of the Piast dynasty (1303-1370), was a staunch protector of the Jews. Periods of Jewish freedom and prosperity have alternated with periods of persecution and sometimes, expulsion. Jewish learning flourished in the land from the sixteenth century onwards.

Mystic Chasidism, based on study of the Cabala, had its wonder rabbis. Famous Talmudic scholars, codifiers of the ritual and other eminent men of learning were produced by Polish Jewry. Of the 3,500,000 Jews in Poland in 1939 about three million were exterminated by Hitler. Many put up an heroic fight, like those of the Warsaw Ghetto in 1943. Under half a million fled to the West and to the Soviet Union. Until 1968 the Jewish population was estimated at about 50,000. Large-scale emigration followed the anti-Jewish policy pursued by the regime from then on under the guise of 'anti-Zionism'. Today's Jewish pop. is estimated at between 6,000 and 8,000.

WARSAW

Synagogue and Religious Organisation: Zwiazek Religijny Wyznania Mojzeszowego (Religious Union of Mosaic Faith),Warsaw 00-105. ul. Twarda 6. ☎ 20-43-24. 20-06-76.

Secular Organisation: Towarzystwo Spoleczno-Kulturalne Zydów w Polsce (Social and Cultural Association of Jews in Poland), Zarzad Glowny (Central Board), Warsaw, 00-104, Plac., Grzybowski 12/16, ☎ 20-05-57, 20-05-54.

CRACOW

Religious Organisation: Zwiazek Religijny Wyznania Mojzeszowego, Kongregacja (Religious Union of Mosaic Faith, Congregation) Cracow, 31-066, ☎ 56-23-49. ul. Skawinska 2.

Secular Organisation: Towarzystwo Spoleczno-Kulturalne Zydów w Polsce (Social and Cultural Association of Jews in Poland), (Cracow Section), Krakow, 31-014, ☎ 22-98-41.ul. Stawkowska 30.

Jewish organisations also exist in the following 16 towns: Bielsko-Biala, Bytom, Chzranów, Dzierzoniów, Gliwice, Katowice, Legnica, Lódz, Lubin, Przyrów, Swindnica, Szczecin Walbrzych, Wroclaw, and Zary.

PORTUGAL (500)

Until the 15th century Jews lived in tranquillity, and were prominent in court circles. In 1496 King Manoel signed an order expelling the Jews from Portugal. But instead of being allowed to leave they were forcibly baptised. Despite the Inquisition Marranos survived in the provinces. A new community was established in Lisbon by British Jews from Gibraltar and others from Morocco during the Napoleonic era. In 1910, after the Revolution, Jews were again granted freedom of worship. The present Jewish population is about 500 centred in Lisbon. There is a synagogue in Oporto built in Moorish style. The Kadoorie family of Hong Kong has been associated with it.

LISBON

*Communal Offices, Rua Alexandre Herculano, 59, Lisbon 1250. ☎ 385 86 04. Fax 388 4304.

Jewish Centre, Rua Rosa Araujo 10. ☎ 357 20 41.

Synagogues: 59 Rua Alexandre Herculano (Sephardi). ☎ 388 15 92. Avenida Elias Garcia 110-1° Lisbon 1050 (Ashkenazi).

PUERTO RICO (1,500)

Some 1,500 Jews live in Puerto Rico, which is an associated Commonwealth of the

USA. A syn. is maintained as well as a pre-school, an afternoon school, adult educ. classes and other organisations.

*Shaare Zedeck Synagogue (Conservative) and Community Centre, 903 Ponce de León Ave. Santurce, P.R. 00907-3390. ☎ (809)724 4110. Fax (809)722 4157 Rabbi A. Winter. ☎ 724 4111.

Temple Beth Shalom (Reform), 101 San Jorge & Loiza St., Santurce, P.R. 00911.

ROMANIA (14,000)

Jews have been resident in the territory that now forms Romania since Roman times. Today they number 14,000, of whom some 5,000 live in Bucharest, and the rest in 68 communities. There are 61 syns., four of them in Bucharest, 18 Talmud Torahs and 11 kosher restaurants. A newspaper in Hebrew, Romanian and English, with a circulation of 6,000, is published fortnightly.

BUCHAREST
Chief Rabbi:
*Federation of Jewish Communities, Mamulari Str., 4, Etaj 1, Apt. 1, Sectorul 3, 4. ☎/Fax 01-336105. *Dir.* Eugen Preda.

SINGAPORE (240)

The Jewish community of Singapore dates from about the year 1840. The street in which Jewish divine service was first held in a house is now known as Synagogue Street. The first building to be erected as a syn. was the Maghain Aboth, opened in 1878. This was rebuilt and enlarged in 1925. A second syn., Chesed El, was built in 1905. The Jewish community consists mainly of Sephardim (of Baghdad origin) but with some Ashkenazim. The affairs of the community are managed by the Jewish Welfare Board, which is elected annually.

*Jewish Welfare Board, 24/26 Waterloo Street, 187950. ☎ 337 2189. Fax 336 2127. *President* Jacob Ballas. *H. Sec.* Mrs M. Whelan.

Synagogue Maghain Aboth, 24 Waterloo Street, 187950. ☎ 337 2189. Fax 336 2127. Email jewishwb@singnet.com.sg. Open daily except Monday mornings. Mikvah available. *Community Rabbi* Mordechai Abergel. ☎ 737-9112. Email mordehai@singnet.com.sg.

Synagogue Chesed El, 2 Oxley Rise, 238693. Open Mon. only.

United Hebrew Congregation (Reform), 65 Chulia St., OCBC Centre #31-00 East Lobby, 049513. *Pres.* K. Lewis. ☎ 536-8300.

SLOVAKIA (6,000)

Written evidence of Jewish settlement in Slovakia goes back to the 13th c. but there may have been Jews in the area as far back as Roman times.

BRATISLAVA
Central Union of Jewish Religious Coms. (UZZNO), *H. Chairman* Prof Pavel Traubner, PhD.; *Exec. Chairman* Fero Alexander. Ad.: Kozia 21/II, 81447 Bratislava, Slovakia. ☎ +421-7-54412167. Fax 421-7-54411106.

Synagogue, Heydukova 11-13, Services: Monday, Thursday, Friday, Saturday.

Bratislava Jewish Com., Kozia 18, 81103 Bratislava. ☎ 421-7-54416949.

Bnai Brith "Tolerance" in Bratislava. *President* Prof. Pavel Trubner, PhD. Ad.: Krizna 32, 81107, Bratislava.

Pension Chez David (Kosher), Accommodation and Restaurant, Mikvah. Fax +42-7-54412642. ☎ +421-7-54413824, 54416943. Mausoleum of Chatham Sopher, Orthodox and Neological Jewish cemeteries.

KOSICE
Jewish Religious Community, Zvonarska 5, 04001 Kosice. Kosher restaurant, Mitvah. *President* DrIvan Kolin. ☎/Fax +421-95-6221047.
Synagogue: Puskinova St.
There are Jewish coms. in Galanta, Dunajska Streda, Presov, Banska Bystrica, Nove Zamky, Komarno, Zilina, Michalovce, Lucenec.

SLOVENIA (78)

LJUBLJANA
Syn.: ☎ 315-884.

SOUTH AFRICA (90,000)

The Jewish Community began as an organised body at Cape Town on the eve of the Day of Atonement, Friday, September 26, 1841. Its first title was 'The Society of the Jewish Community of the Cape of Good Hope', but there had been Jewish residents at the Cape long before the foundation of the Hebrew Congregation. In fact, Jews have been connected with the Cape of Good Hope from the earliest days of South African history.

Jewish pilots accompanied the Portuguese navigators. During the 17th and 18th centuries when the Dutch East India Co. ruled the Cape, there were no professing Jews but it is probable that some individuals were of Jewish origin. After the British occupation in 1806, freedom of religion was extended to all Cape inhabitants and Jews eventually held official positions in the administration.

For further particulars see the 'History of the Jews in South Africa', by Louis Herrman (Victor Gollancz, 1930), The Jews in South Africa: A History, ed. by G. Saron and L. Hotz (Oxford Univ. Press, 1956), The Vision Amazing, by Marcia Gitlin (Johannesburg 1950), South African Jewry, 1976-77, ed. by Leon Feldberg (Alex White, 1977), South African Jewry, ed. by Marcus Arkin (Oxford Univ. Press 1984), Jewish Roots in the S.A. Economy, by Mendel Kaplan (Struik 1986), Chapters from S.A. History, Jewish and General, by Nathan Berger (Kayor, Vol. 1, 1982; Vol. 2, 1986), Jewry and Cape Society, by Milton Shain (Historical Publication Society, 1983), Tiger Tapestry, by Rudy Frankel (Struik, 1988), The Jews of S.A. - What Future? by Hoffman and Fischer (Southern, 1988), Founders and Followers Johannesburg Jewry 1887-1915, Mendel Kaplan (Vlaeberg 1991), The Roots of Antisemitism in South Africa, by M. Shain (Wits U.P. 1994); The Jewish population in South Africa, by A. Dubb (Kaplan Centre, 1994).

The Jews being scattered throughout the territory of the Republic, the organisation of Jewish religious life varies with the density of the Jewish population, which is about 90,000. Over recent years several thousand members of the community have emigrated, especially to Israel, Canada, Australia and the U.S., but the com. has been strengthened by the arrival of some Jews from Zimbabwe and Israel. In all, there are about 50 organised Jewish coms.

The largest coms. are in Johannesburg (58,000), Cape Town (17,500), Durban (3,720) and Pretoria (1,550).

The South African Jewish Board of Deputies is the representative institution of South African Jewry. The B.o.D. for the Transvaal and Natal was founded in 1903, and a similar organisation at the Cape in 1904. The two were united in 1912. The headquarters of the Board is in Johannesburg, and there are provincial committees in Cape Town, Pretoria, Durban, Bloemfontein and Port Elizabeth.

COMMUNAL INSTITUTIONS
*S.A. Jewish Board of Deputies, Anerley Office Park, 7 Anerley Rd., Parktown

2193, PO Box 87557, Houghton 2041. ☎ 486-1434. Fax 646-4940. *National Dir.* S. Kopelowitz.

S.A. Zionist Federation, P.O. Box 29203, Sandringham 2131. ☎ 485-1020. Fax 640-6758. *Dir. General.*

S.A. Board of Jewish Education, P.O. Box 46204, Orange Grove 2119. ☎ 485-1214. *Gen. Dir.*

S.A. Jewish Ex-Service League. See Board of Deputies.

Union of Orthodox Synagogues of South Africa. ☎ 648-9136. Fax 648-4014. Rabbi C. K. Harris, B.A. M.Phil., Chief Rabbi of S. Africa. **S.A. Rabbinical Association.**

S.A. Union for Progressive Judaism, P.O.B. 1190, Houghton 2041. ☎ 728-4796.

Bnai B'rith, P.O. Box 8425 Johannesburg, 2000. ☎ 648-3804.

Jewish Family and Community Council, 5 Becker St., Yeoville 2198. ☎ 648-9124.

Kollel Yad Shaul, 22 Muller St., Yeoville, 2198, Johannesburg. ☎ 648-1175.

Lubavitch Foundation of S.A., 55 Oaklands Rd., Orchards 2192 Johannesburg. ☎ 640-7561.

ORTSA, 93 Iris Rd., Norwood, Johannesburg. ☎ 728-7154.

Union of Jewish Women of S.A., 1 Oak St., Houghton, Johannesburg, 2198. ☎ 648-1053.

Mizrachi Organisation of S.A., P.O. Box 29189, Sandringham 2192. ☎ 640 4420.

Zionist Revisionist Organisation of S.A., 2 Elray St., Raedene, 2192. ☎ 485-1020. Telegrams: Nezorg.

JOHANNESBURG

United Hebrew Congregation (est. 1915.) Beth Din. ☎ 648-9136.

United Progressive Jewish Congregation (est. 1946). ☎ 484-3003.

Adath Jeshurun Congregation, P.O. Box 5128, 41 Hunter St., Yeoville 2198. ☎ 648-6300. Mikva. (Affil. to Union of Orth. Hebr. Congs., London).

Main synagogues. Glenhazel Hebrew Cong., Long Ave., Glenhazel, 2192. Tel: 640-5016 (Orth). Sydenham/Highlands North Heb Cong., 24 Main St., Rouxville, 2192 (Orth) ☎ 640-5021. Temple Emanuel, 38 Oxford Road, Parktown, 2193 (Reform). ☎ 646-6170.

CAPE TOWN

Western Province Zionist Council, 87 Hatfield St., Cape Town, 8001. PO Box 4176, Cape Town 8000. ☎ 021-424-5020. Fax 021-423-2615. Email wpzc@iafrica.com. *Dir. Gen.* I. Wolman.

The Jacob Gitlin Library, Albow Brothers Centre, 88 Hatfield St., Cape Town, 8001, ☎ 021-462-5088. Fax 021-465-8671. Email gitlinlibrary@netactive.co.za.

Union of Orthodox Synagogues of S.A., and Beth Din, 191, Buitenkant St., ☎ 461-6310. Fax 461-8320. *Exec. Dir.* R. Glass.

Main synagogues. Great Syn. Government Ave. (Orth.), Temple Israel, Upper Portswood Rd., Green Point (Reform).

SOUTH KOREA

About 25 Jewish families live in Seoul the capital. Religious services are held on Friday evenings at the 8th U.S. Army Religious Retreat Centre. ☎ 7904-4113.

SPAIN (14,000)

Jews were settled in Spain in Roman times. They made an outstanding contribution to culture and civilisation in medieval times. Persecution by the Church culminated in the Inquisition and the Expulsion in 1492. Today there are about 14,000 Jews in Spain, of whom 3,000 live in Barcelona, 3,500 in Madrid 1,500 in Malaga, and the rest in Valencia, Seville, Alicante, Majorca and the Canary Islands. The Jewish com. in Melilla has 900 members and that in Ceuta 700. Ancient syns. of pre-

Inquisition times (now put to other uses) exist in Cordoba, Seville and Toledo. The Madrid com. was legally recognised in 1965 and the city's first syn. since the Expulsion was consecrated in 1968. Synagogues and Community Centres:
Madrid, 28010-Calle Balmes, No. 3.
Barcelona, 08021-Calle Avenir, No. 24. ☎ 2008513. Fax 2006148
Alicante, Da Lilo Plon-Avda Santander 3, Playa de San Juan.
Ceuta, Calle Sargento, No. 8. Coriat.
Majorca. The first synagogue in 600 years was opened in 1987 in Calle Monserior Palmer, Palma. Fri. evg. and High Holy-day services. *President* J. Segal. ☎ 700243. About 300 Jews live in Majorca.
Malaga, 29001-Calle Duquesa de Parcent, No. 8.
Marbella. Sr Amselem, Jazmines, 21, Urbanización El Real.
Melilla, 29804-Calle General Mola, No.19.
Seville, 41003-Bustos Tavera, 8. ☎ 427-5517.
Valencia. 46026-S. Serfaty, Avda. Ausiás March, 42 Pta. 35.
Tenerife 38001-Jewish Community, P. Abecasis, Ap. de Correos 939, Villalba Hervas, Santa Cruz de Tenerife.
Las Palmas de Gran Canaria, 35006, S. Zrihen, c/Nestor de la Torre, 34.

SRI LANKA

Corr. Mrs A. Ranasinghe, 82 Rosmead Place, Colombo 7. ☎ 695642. Fax 941-446543.

SURINAM (300)

Surinam is one of the oldest permanent Jewish settlements in the Western Hemisphere. The Sephardi Cong. was est. about 1661, but earlier settlements in 1632, 1639 and 1652 have been reported. Some 225 Jews are members of the two synagogues, where Sephardi services are conducted.
Neve Salom Synagogue, Keizerstr. 82, Paramaribo.
Sedek Ve Salom Synagogue, Herenstr. 20, Paramaribo. Temp. not in use due to restoration. *President* René Fernandes, Commewijnestraat 21, Paramaribo. ☎ 400236; P.O. Box 1834, Paramaribo. ☎ 597-411998; Fax 597-471154; 597-402380 (home).

SWEDEN (18,000)

In 1774, the first Jew was granted the right to live in Sweden. In 1782 Jews were admitted to three Swedish towns, Stockholm, Gothenburg and Norrköping, and the Karlskrona com. was founded soon afterwards. After the emancipation of the Jews in Sweden in 1870, coms. were founded in Malmö and several other towns. Today there are some 18,000 Jews in Sweden, 9–10,000 of them in Stockholm. Others are in Gothenburg, Malmö, Borås and Västerås.

STOCKHOLM
*Judiska Församlingen (Jewish community), Wahrendorffsgatan 3, Box 7427 103 91 Stockholm. ☎ 08-679 2900. Fax 08-6112413. Email kansli@jf-stockolm.org.
Jewish Centre, Nybrogatan 19. ☎ 08-6626686.
Synagogues: Wahrendorffsgatan 3 (Great Synagogue, Masorti); Adas Jeshurun, Riddargatan 5 (Orthodox); Adas Jisroel, St. Paulsgatan 13 (Orth).

SWITZERLAND (17,600)

The Jews were expelled from Switzerland in the fifteenth century, and it was not until early in the seventeenth century that they received permission to settle in the Lengnau and Endingen coms. In 1856 immigration increased, most of the immigrants coming from Southern Germany, Alsace and Eastern Europe. The Jewish pop. is now about 17,600 The largest coms. are in Zurich (6,252), Basle (2,005)

and Geneva (3,901). The Swiss Federation of Jewish Communites comprised in 1998 19 coms. with a total membership of 14,000.
Federation of Jewish Communities, PO Box 564, 8027 Zurich. ☎ (01) 201.55.83. Fax (01) 202.16.72. Email sign-fsci@bluewin.ch.
American Joint Distribution Committee, European Headquarters, 75 rue de Lyon, 1211 Geneva 13. ☎ (022) 344.90.00.
OSE, rue du Mont-Blanc 11, 1201 Geneva. ☎ (022) 732.33.01.
World Jewish Congress, rue de Varembé 1, 1211 Geneva. ☎ (022) 734.13.25.
B'nai B'rith, chemin Rieu 10, 1208 Geneva. ☎ (022) 731.69.80.

Basle Communal Centre, Leimenstrasse 24. ☎ (061) 279.98.50; Synagogues: (Orth. Ashk.) Leimenstrasse 24, Rabbi Dr Israel Meir Levinger, Leimenstrasse 45. ☎ (061) 271.60.24; (Orth. Ashk.) Ahornstrasse 14, Rabbi Benzion Snyders, Rudolfstrasse 28. ☎ (061) 302.53.91.
Berne Communal Centre and Synagogue, Kapellenstrasse 2. ☎ (031) 381.49.92.
Fribourg Synagogue, 9 rue Joseph-Philler. ☎ (026) 322.16.70.
Geneva Communal Centre, Rue St Léger 10. ☎ (022) 317.89.00; Synagogues: (Orth. Ashk.) Grande Synagogue Beit Yaakov, Place de la Synagoguge. Chief Rabbi Marc A. Guedj. ☎ (022) 789.07.25; (Orth. Ashk.) Machsike Hadass, 2 Place des Eaux Vives. Rabbi Abraham Schlesinger. ☎ (022) 735.22.98; (Seph.) Hekhal Haness, 54ter, route de Malagnou. ☎ (022) 736.96.32; (Ref.) Liberal Syn., 12 Quai du Seujet. ☎ (022) 732.32.45. Rabbi François Garaï. ☎ (022) 738.19.11.
Lausanne Communal Centre, 3 ave. Georgette. ☎ (021) 341.72.40. Synagogue: 1 Ave. Juste-Oliver (corner Ave. Florimont). Chief Rabbi Hervé Krief. ☎ (021) 311.10.60.
Zürich Communal Centre, Lavaterstrasse 33, ☎ (01) 201.16.59; Synagogues: (Modern Orth. Ashk.) Nüschelerstrasse 36. ☎ (01) 221.01.03. Rabbi Dr Zalman Kossowsky. ☎ (01) 202.52.22; (Orth. Ashk.) Freigutstrasse 37. ☎ (01) 221.01.03. Rabbi Dr Zalman Kossowsky. ☎ (01) 202.52.22; (Orth. Ashk.) Freigutstrasse 37. ☎ (01) 241.80.57. Rabbi Daniel Levy. ☎ (01) 202.48.19; (Orth. Ashk.) Erikastrasse 8. ☎ (01) 463.57.98. Rabbi Schoul Breisch. ☎ (01) 461.30.40; Beth Chabad, Rüdigerstrasse 10. ☎ (01) 289.70.50; Minyan Sikna, Sallenbachstrasse 40. ☎ (01) 455.75.75; Minyan Wollishofen, Etzelstrasse 6. ☎ (01) 482.87.51; (Ref.) Or Chadasch, Fortunagasse 13. ☎ (01) 221.11.52; Rabbi Tovia Ben Chorin. ☎ (01) 342.40.23.

SYRIA (1,500)

The remnants of this historic Jewish community resident in Damascus, Aleppo and Kamishli, have been estimated at 1,500 following recent aliyah.

DAMASCUS
President of Rabbinical Court Rabbi Ibrahim Hamura, Ecole Ben-Maymoun, Kattatib. Al-Ittihad Al-Ahlieh School (Alliance Israélite), rue El Amine.

TAIWAN (180)

More than 30 Jewish families live on the Island, most of them in Taipei, the capital.
Taiwan Jewish Community Centre. Information: F. Chitayat. ☎ 2861-6303.
Mailing address: Donald Shapiro, Trade Winds Company, P.O.Box 7-179, Taipei 10602, Taiwan. ☎ 886-2-23960159. Fax 886-2-23964022. E-mail dshapiro@topz.ficnet. Sunday School. Jewish services at the Ritz Hotel, 155 Minchuan East Road, Taipei, held Friday evenings, Saturday morning, Saturday afternoon. Torah study Saturday afternoons. Holiday services contact Dr F. Einhorn at 2592-2840 or the Ritz Hotel 2597-1234.

THAILAND (250)

The community consists of approx. 250 persons, including citizens of the country and expatriates.

Jewish Association of Thailand, Beth Elisheva Synagogue, Mikveh, Jewish Centre, 121 Soi Sai Nam Thip 2, Sukhumvit 22, Bangkok. ☎ 258-2195. Fax 663-0245. E-mail ykantor@ksc15.th.com

Even-Chen Synagogue, The Bossotel Inn, weekly classes & activities. 55/12-14 Soi Charoengkrung, 42/1 New Road, Bangkok. ☎ 630 6120. Fax 237 3225.

Ohr Menachem-Chabad, 108/1 Ram Buttri Rd., Kaosarn Rd., Banglampoo. Daily services. *M.* Rabbi Y. Kantor. ☎ 282-6388. Fax 629 1153.

TRINIDAD AND TOBAGO

Jewish links go back to 1658 when Portuguese Jews from Livorno and Amsterdam settled there. Most of them left by the end of the 17th century. Portuguese Jews from Venezuela and Curaçao settled in Trinidad in the 19th century. The names of many Catholic families are traceable to 'conversos' of the earlier period. In the mid-1930's some 800 Jews sought temporary refuge in Trinidad and Tobago from Nazi persecution in Germany and Austria and later from other parts of Nazi occupied Europe. Those with German and Austrian passports were subject to internment between 1940 and 1943. Numbers have dropped since with only a few Jews living there now. *Corr* Hans Stecher, c/o The Home Office, Northern Entrance, West Mall, Westmoorings, Port of Spain, Trinidad, W.I. (Caribbean).

TUNISIA (3,000)

The history of the community goes back to antiquity. After Tunisia became a French protectorate in 1881 Jews obtained equal rights with the Moslems, and the continuance of these rights was promised by the authorities of the independent State established in 1957. The Jewish population fell from nearly 100,000 in 1950 to 25,000 in June 1967, and to some 3,000 today. There are coms. in Tunis, Sfax, Sousse and Jerba island, where the ancient El Ghriba synagogue in Hara Sghire village is a listed building.

TUNIS

Grand Rabbinat de Tunisie, 26 Rue Palestine. Communal Offices, 15 Rue du Cap Vert.

Synagogues: 43 Ave. de la Liberté: 3 Rue Eve Nöelle.

American Joint Distribution Committee, 101 Ave. de la Liberté.

TURKEY (25,000)

During the Spanish Inquisition, the Ottoman Empire was one of the principal lands of refuge. With the proclamation of the Turkish Republic, the Jews were granted full citizenship rights. Today their number is estimated at about 25,000 of whom about 23,000 live in Istanbul, 2,000 in Izmir, and 100 each in Ankara, Adana, Bursa, Edirne and Kirklareli.

ISTANBUL

Chief Rabbinate: Rabbi David Asseo, Yemenici Sok. No. 23 Tünel, Beyoğlu. ☎ (212) 2938794-95. Fax (212) 244-1980. *Sec. General.*

Communal Centre, Büyük Hendek Sokak No. 61, Galata. ☎ (212) 2441576. Fax (212) 292 0385.

Synagogues: Neve Shalom, 61 Büyük Hendek Sokak, Galata. ☎ (212) 293-7566; Beth Israel, Efe Sok. 4, Şişli, ☎ (212) 2406599; Etz Ahayim, Muallim Naci Sok. 40/1. ☎ (212) 2601896; (Ashkenazi), 37 Yüksekkaldirim sok, Galata. ☎ 243-6909; (Italian), 29, Şair Ziya Paşa Yokusu, Galata. ☎ (212) 2937784; Hemdat

Israel, Izzettin Sok 65 Kadiköy ☎ (216) 336 5293; Heset Leavraam, Pancur Sok, 15, Büyükada ☎ (216) 382-5788 (summer); Caddebostan, Taş Mektep Sokak Göztepe. ☎ (216) 356-5922.
There are ten charitable and social institutions, six youth clubs, a high school and an elementary school in Istanbul and an elementary school in Izmir. Synagogues also in Izmir, Ankara and Bursa.

UKRAINE (600,000)

KIEV
Syn.: 29 Shchekovichnaya St., 252071. ☎ (044) 463 7085. Fax 463 7088.
Assoc. of Jewish Organisations, Kurskaya ul. 6, ☎ (044) 276-7431.
Jewish Historical Society, Iskrovskaya Str., 3, Apt. 6, 252087. ☎ (044) 242-7944.
Makor Centre for Jewish Youth Activities, 10/1 Gorodeskogo St., Apt. 10, 252001. ☎ 044-229-6141. Fax 044-229-8069.
Other towns with Jewish centres include Bershad, Chernigor, Chernovtsy, Kharkov, Kremenchug, Odessa, Simferopol, Uzhgorod and Zhitomir.

UNITED STATES OF AMERICA (5,800,000)
Though there had been individual Jewish settlers before 1654 in the territory which is now the United States, it was not until that year that Jewish immigrants arrived in a group at New Amsterdam (renamed New York in 1664) 23 of them, who came from Brazil by way of Cuba and Jamaica. The story of the growth of Jewry in the U.S.A. is the story of successive waves of immigration resulting from persecution in Russia, Poland, Romania, Germany and other countries. Today the Jewish population is est. at 5,950,000, of whom 1,720,000 live in the New York Metropolitan Area.
For general information about the American Jewish Community write to: UJA - Federation Resource Line, 130 E 59th St., New York City, 10022.

REPRESENTATIVE ORGANISATIONS
American Jewish Committee, 165 E. 56th St., New York City, 10022.
American Jewish Congress, Stephen Wise Hse., 15 E. 84th St., New York City, 10028.
Anti-Defamation League of B'nai B'rith, 823 United Nations Plaza, New York City, 10017.
B'nai B'rith International, 1640 Rhode Island Av., N.W. Washington, D.C., 20036.
Conference of Presidents of Major Jewish Organizations, 110 E 59th St., NYC 10022.
Consultative Council of Jewish Organizations, 420 Lexington Av., Suite 1733, NYC 10170. ☎ 212-808-5437.
Co-ordinating Board of Jewish Organizations, 1640 Rhode Island Ave., N.W. Washington, D.C., 20036.
Jewish Labour Committee, Atran Centre, 25 E. 21st St., New York City, 10010.
Jewish War Veterans of the United States of America, 1811 R St., N.W. Washington, D.C. 20009.
National Jewish Community Relations Advisory Council, 443 Park Ave. S., I Ith floor, New York City, 10016.
National Council of Jewish Women, 15 E. 26th St., New York City, 10010.
National Conference on Soviet Jewry, 10 E. 40th St., Suite 907, New York City, 10016.
National Council of Young Israel, 3 W. 16th St., New York City, 10011.
North American Jewish Students Network, 501 Madison Ave., 17th Fl., New York City, 10022.
United Jewish Appeal, 99 Park Ave. New York City, 10016.
World Confederation of Jewish Community Centers, 15 E. 26th St. New York City, 10010.

World Jewish Congress, 501 Madison Ave., 17th Fl., New York City, 10022. ☎ 755 5770.

RELIGIOUS ORGANISATIONS
Agudath Israel of America, 84 William St., New York City, 10038.
Agudath Israel World Organization, 84 William St., New York City, 10038.
Association of Orthodox Jewish Scientists, 1373 Coney Island Ave., Brooklyn, New York, 11219.
Central Conference of American Rabbis, 192 Lexington Ave., New York City, 10016 (Reforrn).
Jewish Reconstructionist Federation, 7804 Montgomery Ave., St. No.9, Elkins Park, PA 19027. ☎ 215-782 8500. Fax 215-782 8805. Email info@jrf.org.
Lubavitcher Headquarters, 770 Eastem Parkway, Brooklyn, N.Y. 11213. New York Board of Rabbis, 10 E. 73rd St., New York City, 10021.
Rabbinical Alliance of America, 3 W. 16th St., 4th Fl., New York City, 10011. (Orthodox.)
Rabbinical Assembly (Cons.), 3080 Broadway, New York City, 10027.
Rabbinical Council of America, 275 7th Ave., New York City, 10001. (Modern Orthodox).
Reconstructionist Rabbinical Association, 7804 Montgomery Ave., St. No.9, Elkins Park, PA 19027. ☎ 215-782 8500. Fax 215-782 8805. Email info@jrf.org
Synagogue Council of America, 327 Lexington Ave., New York City 10016.
Union of American Hebrew Congregations, 838 Fifth Ave., New York City, 10021. (Reform).
Union of Orthodox Jewish Congregations, 333 Seventh Ave., New York City, 1000
Union of Orthodox Rabbis, 235 E. Broadway, New York City, 10002.
Union of Sephardic Congregations, 8 W 70th St., New York City, 10023.
United Synagogue of America, 155 Fifth Ave., New York City, 100 10. (Conservative.)
World Union for Progressive Judaism, 838 Fifth Ave., New York City, 10021.

WELFARE AND REFUGEE ORGANISATIONS
American Association for Ethiopian Jews, 2028 P. St., N.W. Washington DC., 20036.
American Federation of Jews from Central Europe, 570 7th Ave., New York City, 10018.
American Jewish Joint Distribution Committee (I.D.C.), 711 Third Ave . New York City, 10017.
American ORT Federation, 817 Broadway, New York City, 10003.
Council of Jewish Federations, 730 Broadway, New York City, 10003.
HIAS, 333 7th Ave., New York City, 1000.
Jewish Conciliation Board, 235 Park Ave. S., New York City, 10003.
JWB, 15 East 26th St., New York City, 10010.
U.J.A. Federation of New York, 130 E. 59th St., New York City, 10022.

ZIONIST ORGANISATIONS and others concerned with Israel
American Associates of Ben-Gurion University of Negev, 342 Madison Ave., Suite 1924, New York City, 10173.
American Committee for Weizmann Institute, 515 Park Ave., New York City, 10022.
American Friends of the Hebrew University, 11 E. 69th St., New York City, 10021.
American Friends of Tel Aviv University, 360 Lexington Ave., New York City, 10017.
American Friends of Haifa University, 41 E. 42nd St., 828, New York City, 10017.
American-Israel Cultural Foundation, 485 Madison Ave., New York City, 10022.
American-Israel Public Affairs Committee, 500 N. Capitol St., N.W. Washington, D.C. 20001.

American Jewish League for Israel, 30 E. 60th St., New York City, 10022.
American Red Magen David for Israel, 888 7th Ave., New York City, 10106.
American Technion Society, 271 Madison Ave., New York City, 10016.
American Zionist Federation, 515 Park Ave., New York City, 10022 from whom information on Zionist organisations and activities can be obtained.
American Zionist Youth Foundation, 515 Park Ave., New York City, 10022.
Americans for Progressive Israel, 150 Fifth Ave., Suite 911, New York City, 10011.
ARZA–Assn. of Reform Zionists of America, 838 5th Ave., New York City, 10021.
Bar-Ilan University in Israel, 853 Seventh Ave., New York City, 10019.
Bnei Akiva of North America, 25 W. 26th St., New York City, 10010.
Betar Zionist Youth Movement, 9 E. 38th St., New York City, 10016.
Dror-Young Kibbutz Movement-Habonim, 27 W. 20th St., New York City, 10011.
Emunah Women of America, 370 7th Ave., New York City, 10001.
Hadassah, Women's Zionist Organization of America, 50 W. 58th St., New York City, 10019.
Hashomer Hatzair, 150 Fifth Ave. Suite 911, New York City, 10011.
Herut–U.S.A., 9 E. 38th St., New York City, 10016.
Theodor Herzl Foundation, 515 Park Ave., New York City, 10022.
Jewish National Fund, 42 E. 69th St., New York City, 10021.
Labor Zionist Alliance (formerly Poale Zion United Labour Org. of America), 275 Seventh Ave., New York City, 10001.
Mercaz, Conservative Zionists, 155 Fifth Ave., New York City, 10010.
Mizrachi-Hapoel Hamizrachi (Religious Zionists of America), 25 W. 26th St., New York City, 10010.
National Committee for Labor Israel–Histadrut, 33 E. 67th St., New York City, 10021.
PEC Israel Economic Corporation, 511 Fifth Ave., New York City, 10017.
Pioneer Women Na'armat, The Women's Labour Zionist Organisation of America, 200 Madison Ave., New York City, 10016.
State of Israel Bonds, 730 Broadway, New York City, 10003
Women's League for Israel, 515 Park Ave., New York City, 10022.
World Confederation of United Zionists, 30 E. 60th St., New York City 10022.
World Zionist Organization, American Section, 515 Park Ave., New York City, 10022.

EDUCATIONAL AND CULTURAL ORGANISATIONS
American Friends of the Alliance Israélite Universelle, 135 William St., New York City, 10038.
American Jewish Historical Society, 2 Thornton Rd., Waltham, Mass., 02154.
Annenberg Research Institute, formerly Dropsie College, 250 N. Highland Ave., Merion. Pa., 19066.
Leo Baeck Institute, 129 E. 73rd St., New York City, 10021. Brandeis University, Waltham Mass., 02254.
Centre for Holocaust Studies, Documentation & Research, 1610 Ave. J., Brooklyn, New York 11230.
Central Yiddish Culture Organization, 25 E. 21st St., New York Clty, 10010.
Gratz College, 10th St., & Tabor Rd., Phila., Pa., 19141.
Theodor Herzl Institute and Foundation, 515 Park Ave., New York City, 10022.
Hebrew Arts School, 129 W. 67th St., New York City, 10023.
Hebrew College, 43 Hawes St., Brookline, Mass., 02146.
Hebrew Union College-Jewish Institute of Religion, 3101 Clifton Ave., Cincinnati, Ohio, 45220; 1 W. 4th St., New York City, 10012, 3077 University Mall, Los Angeles, Calif. 90007; 13 King David St., Jerusalem Israel 94101.
Herzliah Jewish Teachers' Seminary, Touro College, Jewish Peoples, University of the Air, 30 W. 44th St., New York City, 10036.
Histadruth Ivrith of America, 1841 Broadway, New York City, 10023.
JWB Jewish Book Council, 15 E. 26th St., New York City, 10010.

Jewish Education Service of North America, 730 Broadway, New York
Jewish Publication Society, 1930 Chestnut St., Philadelphia, Pa., 19103.
Jewish Museum, 1109 Fifth Ave., New York City, 10028.
Jewish Theological Seminary of America, 3080 Broadway, New York City, 10027.
Memorial Foundation for Jewish Culture, 15 E. 26th St., New York City 10010.
Mesivta Yeshiva Rabbi Chaim Berlin Rabbinical Academy, 1593 Coney Island Ave., Brooklyn, N.Y.
National Foundation for Jewish Culture, 330 7th Ave., 21st. Fl., New York City, 10001.
National Yiddish Book Center, Weinberg Building, Amherst, MH. 01002-3375. ☎ (800) 535-3595; Fax (413) 256-4700.
Reconstructionist Rabbinical College, Church Road and Greenwood Ave., Wyncote, PA, 19095.
Shomrei AdamahÑA Jewish Resource Center for the Environment, Church Road and Greenwood Ave., Wyncote, PA, 19095.
Simon Wiesenthal Centre, 9760 W. Pico Blvd., Los Angeles, Ca., 90035.
Torah Umesorah–National Society for Hebrew Day Schools, 160 Broadway, New York City, 10038.
United Lubavitcher Yeshivoth, 841 Ocean Parkway, Brooklyn, N.Y., 11230.
Yeshiva University, 500 W. 185th St., New York City, 10033; 9760 W. Pico Blvd., Los Angeles, Ca., 90035.
Yivo Institute for Jewish Research, 555 West 57th St., 11th Floor, New York City 10019 (Temporary removal) ☎ (212) 535-6700.

URUGUAY (35,000)

Jewish immigration to Uruguay began in the early 20th century, with a large influx in the 1920s. Some 10,000 European Jews fled to Uruguay with Hitler's rise to power and large numbers came after the Second World War. In the 1940s, 50,000 Jews were est. to be living in the country. At present there are about 35,000, mostly in Montevideo, the capital. Some 12,000 emigrated to Israel before the State was established, during the War of Independence and since.

MONTEVIDEO
*Central and representative org.: Comite Central Israelita del Uruguay, Rio Negro 1308 Piso 5 Esc. 9. ☎ 90 06562. Fax 91 6057.
Communities: Comunidad Israelita del Uruguay, Canelones 1084 Piso 1º; Comunidad Israelita Sefaradi, 21 de Setiembre 3111 (office), Buenos Aires 234 (syn.); Nueva Congregacion Israelita, Wilson Ferreira Aldunate 1168; Comunidad Israelita Hungara, Durazno 972. Each com. maintains its own syns. There are 3 Jewish schs. and an ORT training centre.
Zionist Organisation of Uruguay, H. Gutierrez Ruiz 1278 Piso 4º.
There are also communities at Maldonado and Paysandu.

VENEZUELA (20,000)

The first community was established in the coastal town of Coro by Sephardi Jews early in the 19th century. Today the Jews in Venezuela number some 21,000, most of whom live in Caracas and the rest mainly in Maracaibo.

CARACAS
*Confederación de Asociaciones Israelitas de Venezuela (CAIV), Representative organisation of Venezuelan Jewry, Av. Marqués del Toro No. 9, San Bernardino. ☎ (58-2) 51.03.68; 550.24.54. Fax (58-2) 51.03.77; 550.17.21.
Ashkenazi Synagogue and Centre: Unión Israelita de Caracas, Av. Marqués del Toro, San Bernardino. ☎ (58-2) 51.52.53. Fax (58-2) 552.79.56. M. Rabbi Pynchas Brener.
Sephardic Synagogue and Centre: Asociación Israelita de Venezuela, Tiferet Yisrael, Av. Maripérez, Frente al Paseo Colón, Los Caobos. ☎ (58-2) 574.49.75;

574.82.97. Fax 577.02.59. *M.* Rabbi Isaac Cohén.
B'nai B'rith, 9ª. Transversal entre 7ª. Y Av. Avila, Altarmira. ☎ 261.74.97,
261.40.83. Fax (58-2) 261.40.83.
Zionist Federation **(Federación Sionista de Venezuela),** Edif. Bet Am, Av.
Washington, San Bernardino. ☎ (58-2) 51.25.62; 51.48.52. Fax (58-2) 51.30.89.

VIRGIN ISLANDS (500)

Jews have lived in the Virgin Islands since the seventeenth century and played an
important part under Danish rule. Since 1917 the Virgin Islands have been USA territory. There are some 120 families in the community and the number of affiliated
and non-affiliated Jews is about 350. The 150th anniversary of the rebuilding of
the synagogue, situated in Crystal Gade, St. Thomas, was celebrated in 1983.
Jewish Community, *M.* Rabbi S. T. Relkin.

YUGOSLAVIA (3,500)

(Federal Republic, Serbia and Montenegro)
Jews have lived in this territory since Roman times. In 1941 there were about
34,000 Jews in the territory of present Yugoslavia and some 29,000 perished in the
Holocaust.

BELGRADE (BEOGRAD)
*Federation of Jewish Communities of Yugoslavia,** Ulica Kralja Petra 7la, 111000
Belgrade. P.O.B. 841 Belgrade. ☎ 624-359/621-837. Fax 626 674. *President* Aca
Singer; *Sec.* M. Grinvald.
Jewish Community of Belgrade, Ulica Kralja Petra 71a/II. ☎/Fax 624 289; 622 449.
President Aleksandar Ajzinberg.
Synagogue, Marsala Birjuzova 19.
Jewish Historical Museum, Ulica Kralja Petra 71a/II. ☎ 622 634.
Communities also in Novi Sad, Niš, Pančevo, Priština, Sombor, Subotica, Zemun
and Zrenjanin.

ZAIRE (80)

Before the Congo obtained independence from Belgian rule in 1960, there were
about 2,500 Jews, with eight communities affiliated with the central community in
Elisabethville. Now these are about 65 in Kinshasa (formerly Leopoldville), 2 in
Lubumbashi (formerly Elisabethville), and six others in Likasi, Kannga and
Kisangani. There are also some temporary Israeli residents.
Chief Rabbi of Zaire: Rabbi Moishe Levy. 50, W. Churchill Ave., Box 15, 1180
Brussels, Belgium.

ZAMBIA (35)

(See also Jews of Zambia Project, p.72).
*The Council for Zambia Jewry Ltd.,** P.O. Box 30020, Lusaka 10101. *Chairman*
M. C. Galaun. ☎ 229190. Fax 221428. Email galaun@zamnet.zm.
Lusaka Hebrew Congregation, P.O. Box 30020. (Est. 1941.) *Chairman* M. C.
Galaun.

ZIMBABWE (900)

Jews came to Rhodesia (Zimbabwe) even before the British South Africa Company
received its charter in 1889. Daniel Montague Kisch arrived in the territory in
1869, becoming chief adviser to King Lobengula.
    In the 1880s the number of Jewish pioneers, most of them of East European ori-
gin, gradually increased. Among those who took a leading part in the development

and admin. of the country was Sir Roy Welensky, Prime Minister of the former Central African Federation (1956-1963).

Most of the Jewish settlers came from Russia or Lithuania but others settled from the Aegean Island of Rhodes. Many came up from the South, some through the east coast Portuguese territory of Beira. Joe van Praagh, who became Mayor of Salisbury, walked from Beira. During the 1930s, a small influx of German refugees settled mainly in Salisbury (now Harare) and Bulawayo. Post World War II, others joined them mostly from the United Kingdom and South Africa.

Today, most of Zimbabwe's Jews live in Harare and Bulawayo with a very few residing in the smaller districts around the country about 458 in Harare, 283 in Bulawayo and 4 in other centres. There are two synagogues in Harare and one in Bulawayo and each city has its own Jewish primary day school.

Zimbabwe Jewish Board of Deputies (Head office), 54 Josiah Chinamano Ave., PO Box 1954, Harare. ☎ 702507. Fax 702506. *President* M.C. Ross. *Sec.* Mrs E. Alhadeff, PO Box 783, Ascot, Bulawayo. ☎ 70443. *Sec.* Mrs G. Stidolph.

Central African Zionist Organisation, PO Box 70443, 783 Ascot, Bulawayo. ☎ 67383. *Presidents* A. Leon (North), I. Elkaim (South).

Women's Zionist Council of Central Africa, PO Box 783, Ascot, Bulawayo. ☎ 70443. *President* Mrs Rhebe Tatz.

***Synagogues.** Harare*: Harare Hebr. Cong., Lezard Ave., PO Box 342. (Est. 1895.) ☎ 727576; Sephardi Hebr. Cong., 54 Josiah Chinamano Ave., PO Box 1051. (Est. 1932.) ☎ 722899. *Bulawayo*: Bulawayo Hebr. Cong., Jason Moyo St, PO Box 337. ☎ 67335 (M. Residence). *President* B. Katz.

JEWISH STATISTICS

In view of the large movements of population in recent years and in many countries the difficulty of obtaining exact figures, the compilation of Jewish population statistics can only be based on estimates received from a variety of sources.

The current happily substantial exodus of Russian Jewry has compounded the problem of maintaining reliable figures but for the time being we can only repeat previous figures pending formal revisions from our informants, most notably the IJPR who have furnished the principle figures on Table I (1991), and the World Jewish Congress (1998).

Estimates of the present world Jewish population give a total of about 15,000,000, including 1,450,000 in the former Soviet Union. Some 3,636,490 are in Europe, about 6,888,757 in North and South America, some 4,550,000 in Asia, including 4,500,000 in Israel, about 146,770 in Africa and about 96,320 in Oceania. Based on the 1996 census in Australia, W. D. Rubinstein has provided new figures for the state centres. Figures for the USA have been revised in the light of Kosman & Scheckner (AJYB 1993). The number of Jews in Moslem countries is about 71,600.

The number of Jews in the world before the outbreak of war in 1939 was estimated at a figure slightly under 17,000,000, of whom about 10,000,000 lived in Europe, 5,375,000 in North and South America (which seems to have been an overestimate), 830,000 in Asia, 600,000 in Africa, and less than 33,000 in Oceania. The difference between the pre-war and post-war figures is accounted for principally by the enormous losses suffered by the Jewish people between 1939 and 1945. Although estimates of Jews murdered by the Nazis and their collaborators vary, the number is commonly accepted to be 6,000,000.

From the seizure of power by Hitler until the outbreak of war in 1939, 80,000 refugees from Central Europe were admitted to Britain. During the six years of war, a further 70,000 were admitted and since the end of the war about 70,000 displaced persons as well as refugees from a number of other countries. Probably some 80 per cent of these were Jews. Many of these were, however, only temporary residents.

Table III has been revised in the light of new figures made available in 1998 by the Community Research Unit of the Board of Deputies and the IJPR survey of the community for 1995.

Table I
POPULATION OF THE PRINCIPAL COUNTRIES

Afghanistan	50	Bosnia Hercegovina	1,100
Albania	50	Brazil	250,000
Algeria	150	Bulgaria	6,500
Argentina	250,000	Canada	360,000
Armenia	500	Chile	25,000
Aruba & Curacao	500	China	3,100
Australia	106,000	Colombia	7,000
Austria	12,000	Costa Rica	2,500
Azerbaijan	30,000	Croatia	2,500
Bahamas	200	Cuba	1,000
Barbados	55	Czech Republic	10,000
Belarus	60,000	Denmark	9,000
Belgium	40,000	Dominican Rep.	150
Bermuda	125	Ecuador	1,000
Bolivia	640	Egypt	240

(Table I continued)

El Salvador	100	New Zealand	4,000
Estonia	3,000	New Caledonia	120
Ethiopia	1,000	Norway	2,000
Fiji	40	Panama	9,250
Finland	1,500	Paraguay	900
France	600,000	Peru	5,000
Germany	67,000	Poland	6,000
Gibraltar	600	Portugal	500
* Great Britain and		Puerto Rico	1,500
N. Ireland	285,000	Romania	14,000
Greece	4,800	Singapore	300
Guatemala	1,500	Slovakia	6,000
Haiti	150	South Africa	90,000
Holland	25,000	Spain	14,000
Honduras	150	Surinam	300
Hungary	100,000	Sweden	18,000
India	5,600	Switzerland	17,500
Iran	25,000	Syria	1,500
Iraq	75	Tahiti	130
Ireland	1,300	Taiwan	180
¶ Israel	4,847,000	Thailand	250
Italy	35,000	Trinidad	10
Jamaica	350	Tunisia	3,000
Japan	2,000	Turkey	25,000
Kazakhstan	15,000	U.S.A.	5,800,000
Kenya	330	Uruguay	35,000
Latvia	17,000	†Former U.S.S.R.	1,449,117
Lebanon	100	Uzbekistan	35,000
Libya	50	Venezuela	20,000
Lithuania	11,000	Virgin Islands	500
Luxembourg	1,000	Yemen, North	1,000
Malta	50	Yugoslavia (Serbia)	3,500
Mexico	48,000	Zaire	100
Moldova	65,000	Zambia	35
Morocco	7,000	Zimbabwe	900

¶ Israel Statistical Abstract 1999. Including Eastern Jerusalem and West Bank Settlements. Total Israeli population is 6,145,000.

* According to a report by the Board of Deputies' demographic unit in 1998.

† 1989 census.

Table II
MAJOR CENTRES OF JEWISH POPULATION

EUROPE

Amsterdam	15,000	Malaga	1,500
Antwerp	15,000	Malmo	1,950
Athens	2,800	Marseilles	70,000
Barcelona	3,000	Metz	2,500
Basle	2,000	Milan	10,000
Belgrade	1,627	Minsk	45,000
Berlin	10,000	Moscow	200,000
Bordeaux	6,000	Munich	4,000
Brussels	23,000	Nancy	2,000
Bucharest	11,000	Nice	25,000
Budapest	80,000	Odessa	120,000
Cisinau	50,000	Oslo	900
Cologne	1,260	Paris, Greater	350,000
Copenhagen	8,500	Prague	1,400
Dublin	1,300	Riga	15,000
Dusseldorf	1,710	Rome	15,000
Florence	1,290	Rotterdam	1,500
Frankfurt	5,000	St. Petersburg	100,000
Geneva	3,900	Salonika	1,100
Gothenburg	2,500	Sarajevo	1,090
Grenoble	5,000	Sofia	3,200
Hamburg	1,415	Stockholm	9,500
Helsinki	1,200	Strasbourg	18,000
Istanbul	23,000	Sverdlovsk	20,000
Izmir	1,000	The Hague	2,500
Kaunas	5,500	Toulouse	25,000
Kazan	10,000	Turin	1,630
Kharkov	80,000	Vienna	1,000
Kiev	110,000	Vilnius	4,500
Lille	3,000	Warsaw	2,000
Lisbon	300	Wrocklaw	1,500
Lodz	1,500	Zagreb	1,500
Lvov	25,000	Zhitomir	20,000
Lyons	30,000	Zurich	6,252
Madrid	3,500		

ASIA

Ankara	100	Shiraz	3,000
Bombay	4,354	Tashkent	50,000
Damascus	1,000	Teheran	20,000
Hong Kong	3,000	Tokyo	750
Sa'ana	1,000		

(Table II continued)

ISRAEL

Acco	28,900	Kiryat Gat	27,400
Afula	24,200	Kiryat Motzkin	29,300
Ashdod	72,900	Kiryat Ono	22,000
Askelon	55,700	Kiryat Yam	31,700
Bat Yam	132,800	Lod	33,200
Beersheba	114,600	Nahariya	29,400
Bnei Brak	107,400	Netanya	114,400
Dimona	25,400	Or Yehuda	19,900
Eilat	24,200	Petach Tikva	132,100
Givatayim	45,900	Ramat Gan	115,600
Hadera	43,200	Ramat Hasharon	35,800
Haifa	203,400	Ramle	36,800
Herzlia	70,200	Ra'anana	48,000
Hod Hasharon	23,700	Rehovot	71,900
Holon	143,600	Rishon le Zion	120,100
Jerusalem	346,100	Tel Aviv-Jaffa	308,700
Kfar Saba	52,800	Tiberias	30,800
Kiryat Atta	35,100	Upper Nazareth	21,900
Kiryat Bialik	32,400	West Bank Settlements	140,000

AMERICAS

Alameda (Ca.)	30,000	Miami	535,000
Atlanta	50,000	Middlesex Co. (N.J.)	40,000
Baltimore	94,000	Milwaukee (Wisc.)	29,000
Bergen County (N.J.)	83,700	Minneapolis (Min.)	22,000
Boca Raton-Delray (Florida)	50,000	Montgomery & Prince Georges	105,000
Boston	210,000	Montreal (Que.)	100,000
Buenos Aires	180,000	New Haven (Con.)	26,000
Calgary (Alberta)	5,500	New York (Greater)	1,750,000
Camden (New Jersey)	28,000	Newark & Essex County (N.J.)	79,000
Caracas	18,000	Orange County (Ca.)	75,000
Chicago	248,000	Ottawa (Ont.)	9,000
Cincinnati	22,000	Palm Beach County (Florida)	209,000
Cleveland	70,000	Philadelphia	254,000
Dallas	24,000	Phoenix	50,000
Denver	45,000	Pittsburgh (Pa.)	45,000
Detroit	94,000	Rio de Janeiro	80,000
Edmonton (Alberta)	3,700	Rockland County (N.Y.)	57,000
Elizabeth & Union County (N.J.)	30,000	St. Louis (Mis.)	53,500
Englewood & Bergen Co. (N.J.)	100,000	San Diego	36,400
Fort Lauderdale (Florida)	284,000	San Jose (Ca)	32,000
Halifax (N.S.)	1,500	San Francisco	210,000
Hamilton (Ont.)	4,600	Santiago	21,000
Hartford (Con.)	27,500	Sao Paulo	90,000
Hollywood (Florida)	60,000	Seattle	19,500
Houston	40,000	Toronto (Ont.)	175,000
Kansas City	22,000	Vancouver (B.C.)	18,000
Lima	5,000	Washington (D.C.)	165,000
London (Ont.)	1,900	Windsor (Ont.)	2,500
Los Angeles	490,000	Winnipeg (Man.)	16,000
Mexico City	50,000		

(Table II continued)

AFRICA

Alexandria	100
Bulawayo	350
Cape Town	28,600
Durban	6,420
Fez	1,500
Harare	625
Johannesburg	63,620
Kinshasa	300
Port Elizabeth	2,740
Pretoria	3,750
Rabat	1,500
Tangier	1,000
Tunis	2,200

OCEANIA

Adelaide	1,250
Auckland	1,600
Brisbane	1,500
Canberra	500
Christchurch	60
Dunedin	40
Hamilton	50
Hobart	100
Melbourne	50,000
Noumea (New Caledonia)	100
Perth	4,200
Sydney	35,000
Wellington	1,000

Table III
JEWS IN BRITAIN AND NORTHERN IRELAND

Aberdeen	30
Amersham	50
Basildon	12
Bedford	35
Belfast	550
Birmingham	4,000
Blackpool	1,500
Bognor Regis	40
Bournemouth	3,000
Bradford	170
Brighton & Hove	5,300
Bristol	375
Cambridge	1,000
Canterbury	160
Cardiff	1,500
Chatham & Rochester	50
Chelmsford	145
Cheltenham	70
Chester	35
Colchester	100
Coventry	140
Crawley	50
Darlington	40
Dundee	22
East Grinstead	35
Eastbourne	63
Edinburgh	900
Exeter	150
Gateshead	1,430
Glasgow	5,600
Grimsby (Great)	40
Guildford	100
Harlow	190
Harrogate	150
Hastings	33

Hemel Hempstead	270
High Wycombe	35
Hull	650
Leamington (Warwick)	132
Leeds	8,000
Leicester	670
Liverpool	3,800
Llandudno, Colwyn Bay & Rhyl	45
London (Greater London Area)	196,000
Luton	1,300
Maidenhead (Royal Windsor &)	1,240
Manchester & Salford	26,000
Margate & Thanet	200
Middlesbrough	65
Milton Keynes	182
Newcastle upon Tyne	1,100
Newport	10
Northampton	185
Norwich	170
Nottingham	1,050
Oxford	700
Peterborough	105
Plymouth	100
Portsmouth	385
Radlett	750
Reading	500
Reigate & Banstead	45
St. Albans	200
St. Anne's (Fylde)	500
Sheffield	650
Solihull	300
S. Shields (S. Tyneside)	9
Southampton & Winchester	105
Southend & Westcliff	3,400
Southport (Sefton)	1,100

(Table III continued)

Staines & Slough 390	Welwyn (Hatfield) 290
Stoke-on-Trent 30	Whitley Bay (Blyth Valley) 20
Sunderland 60	Wolverhampton 85
Swansea 245	York 25
Swindon (Thamesdown) 72	
Torquay (Torbay) 20	Isle of Man 35
Wallasey (Wirral) 50	Jersey & Guernsey 150

HISTORICAL NOTE ON BRITISH JEWRY

There were probably individual Jews in England in Roman and (though less likely) in Anglo-Saxon times, but the historical records of any organised settlement here start after the Norman Conquest of 1066. Jewish immigrants arrived early in the reign of William the Conqueror and important settlements came to be established in London (at a site still known as Old Jewry), Lincoln and many other centres. In 1190 massacres of Jews occurred in many cities, most notably in York. This medieval settlement was ended by Edward I's expulsion of the Jews in 1290, after which date, with rare and temporary exceptions, only converts to Christianity or secret adherents of Judaism could live here. The Domus Conversorum, the House for Converted Jews (on the site of the former Public Record Office in Chancery Lane, London) had been established in 1232. Perhaps the most notable Jews in medieval England were the financier, Aaron of Lincoln (d.c. 1186), and Elijah Menahem of London (d. 1284), financier, physician and Talmudist.

After the expulsion of the Jews from Spain in 1492 a secret Marrano community became established in London, but the present Anglo-Jewish community dates in practice from the period of the Commonwealth. In 1650 Menasseh ben Israel, of Amsterdam, began to champion the cause of Jewish readmission to England, and in 1655 he led a mission to London for this purpose. A conference was convened at Whitehall and a petition was presented to Oliver Cromwell. Though no formal decision was then recorded, in 1656 the Spanish and Portuguese Congregation in London was organised. It was followed towards the end of the seventeenth century by the establishment of an Ashkenazi community, which increased rapidly inside London as well as throwing out offshoots before long to a number of provincial centres and seaports. The London community, has, however, always comprised numerically the preponderant part of British Jewry.

Britain has the distinction of being one of the few countries in Europe where during the course of the past three centuries there have been no serious outbreaks of violence against Jews and in which the ghetto system never obtained a footing, though in 1753 the passage through Parliament of a Bill to facilitate the naturalisation of foreign-born Jews caused such an outcry that it was repealed in the following year. A short-lived outbreak of anti-semitism in 1772, associated with the so-called 'Chelsea murders' is also notable for its rarity.

Although Jews in Britain had achieved a virtual economic and social emancipation by the early nineteenth century they had not yet gained 'political emancipation'. Minor Jewish disabilities were progressively removed and Jews were admitted to municipal rights and began to win distinction in the professions. The movement for the removal of Jewish political disabilities became an issue after the final removal of political disabilities from Protestant dissenters and then Roman Catholics (1829), and a Bill with that object was first introduced into the House of Commons in 1830. Among the advocates of Jewish emancipation were Macaulay, Lord John Russell, Gladstone (from 1847) and Disraeli. The latter, who was a Christian of Jewish birth, entered Parliament in 1837. Jewish MPs were repeatedly elected from 1847 onwards, but were prevented from taking their seats by the nature of the various oaths required from all new members. Owing to the opposition in the House of Lords it was not until 1858 that a Jew (Lionel de Rothschild) was formally admitted to Parliament, this being followed in 1885 by the elevation of his son (Sir Nathaniel de Rothschild) to the Peerage. Meanwhile, in 1835, Sir David Salomons was the first Jew to become Sheriff of London, and in 1855 Lord Mayor of London. The first to be a Member of the government was Sir George Jessel, who became Solicitor-General in 1871, and the first Jewish Cabinet Minister was Herbert Samuel in 1909.

During the 19th century British Jews spread out from those callings which had hitherto been regarded as characteristic of the Jews. A further mark of the organisational consolidation of the community can be seen in the growth and strength of many of the communal institutions mentioned elsewhere in this book, such as the Board of Deputies (founded 1760), the Board of Guardians (founded 1859), and the United Synagogue (founded 1870), as well as the development of the office of Chief Rabbi and the longevity of the Jewish Chronicle which marked its 150th anniversary in 1991. Equally significant by the middle of the century was the appearance of a number of newer Jewish communities which had been formed in many of the new industrial centres in the North of England and the Midlands, the intellectual activities and the overseas connections of which received thereby a powerful impetus.

There has always been a steady stream of immigration into Britain from Jewish communities in Europe, originally from the Iberian Penninsula and Northern Italy, later from Western and Central Europe. The community was radically transformed by the large influx of refugees which occurred between 1881 and 1914, the result of the intensified persecution of Jews in the Russian Empire. The Jewish population rose from about 25,000 in the middle of the 19th century to nearly 350,000 by 1914. It also became far more dispersed geographically. The last two decades of the nineteenth century saw a substantial growth in the number of communities both in England and in Scotland, and in consequence the 'provinces' became more significant both in numbers and in the influence upon the community as a whole. The impact of this immigration on the Anglo-Jewish community was intensified because very many of the Jews who left Eastern Europe on their way to North America or South Africa passed through Britain. From 1933 a new emigration of Jews commenced, this time from Nazi persecution, and again many settled in this country. Since the end of the Second World War and notably since 1956, smaller numbers of refugees have come from Iran, Arab countries and Eastern Europe.

One of the main features of the years after 1914 was the gradual transfer of the leadership of the community from the representatives of the older establishment of Anglo-Jewry to the children and grandchildren of the newer wave of immigrants. Another feature was the growth of Zionist movements, firstly the Chovevei Zion (Lovers of Zion) and later, under the inspiration of Theodore Herzl, the English Zionist Federation. Under the leadership of Chaim Weizmann and his colleagues in this country, the Zionist Movement obtained, in 1917, the historic Balfour Declaration from the British Government. In 1920 the first British High Commissioner in Mandate Palestine was Viscount Samuel. It was after the withdrawal of the British Government from the Mandate that the State of Israel was proclaimed in 1948.

A mark of British Jewry's full participation in public life is reflected in the number of Jewish signatories to the proclamation of accession of Queen Elizabeth II in 1952 which included seven Jewish Privy Councillors. In the highest offices of the State, in Parliamentary and municipal life, in the Civil and Armed Services, in the judiciary and the universities, in all professions and occupations, the Jewish subjects of the Crown – both at home and overseas – play their full part as inheritors of the political and civic emancipation that was achieved last century. There were 21 Jewish Members in the House of Commons elected on May 1, 1997.

In its internal life and organisation, British Jewry has constructed the complex fabric of religious, social and philanthropic institutions enumerated in this book. The Jews in Britain are now estimated to number about 285,000 (see the relevant note in the statistical tables) of whom some 196,000 reside in Greater London and the remainder are spread in some 80 regional communities.

UNITED KINGDOM LEGISLATION CONCERNING JEWS

(Prepared (July 1996) by His Honour Judge Aron Owen.)

HISTORICAL BACKGROUND

In the Middle Ages, hostility towards Jews was a common feature in many European countries. In England, during the reign of Edward I (1272–1307), the *Statutum de Judeismo* was passed in 1275. This statute forbade usury and included an order continuing to oblige Jews to wear a distinguishing badge and imposing upon them an annual poll tax.

In 1290, Edward personally decreed the expulsion of Jews from England. During the reign of Charles I (1625–49) the number of Jews in England steadily increased. Menasseh ben Israel (1604–57) of Amsterdam made a direct appeal to Cromwell to authorize readmission. His 'Humble Addresses' presented to the Lord Protector in October 1655 urged the revocation of the edict of 1290 and entreated that the Jews be accorded the right of public worship and the right to trade freely. No formal announcement was ever made of the Jews' 're-admission' but, from about 1657, the edict of 1290 ceased to have effect.

The Religious Disabilities Act 1846 extended to Jews the provisions of the Toleration Act 1688. Under the 1846 Act, British subjects professing the Jewish religion were to be subject to the same laws in respect of their schools, places for religious worship, education and charitable purposes, and the property held with them, as Protestant dissenters from the Church of England.

PRESENT POSITION

Today, English Law does not regard Jews as a separate nationality or as different from any other British citizen. They have no special status except in so far as they constitute a dissenting religious denomination.

Provision for that special religious position of Jews has, from time to time, been made in legislation (see, for example, the 1846 Act mentioned above). A discussion of the subject will be found in Halsbury's *Laws of England*, fourth edition 1975, Volume 14, paragraphs 1423 to 1432.

Some of the various statutory provisions in force today are set out briefly below. Further information and details can be obtained from the Board of Deputies (5th Floor, Commonwealth House, 1-19 New Oxford St., WC1A 1NF. ☎ 0171-543 5400). Legal advice should be sought by those wishing to know the impact of specific legislation upon their own particular circumstances.

1. The *Representation of the People Act 1983* (which is a consolidation of several previous Acts) enables a voter in a parliamentary of local election, 'who declares that he is a Jew' and objects on religious grounds to marking the ballot paper on the Jewish Sabbath, to have, if the poll is taken on a Saturday, his vote recorded by the presiding officer. This right does not apply to Jewish Holy-days other than the Sabbath. A person unable by reason of 'religious observance' to go in person to the polling station may apply to be treated as an absent voter and to be given a postal vote for a particular parliamentary or local election.

2. The *Education Act 1994* permits Jewish parents to have their children attending state or state-aided voluntary schools withdrawn from any period of religious instruction and/or worship where such instruction or worship is not in the Jewish faith. In order to take advantage of these provisions of the Act, a written request must be submitted to the head teacher of the school.

3. The *Oaths Act 1978*. A Jew may take an oath (in England, Wales or Northern Ireland) by holding the Old Testament in his uplifted hand, and saying or repeating after the officer administering the oath the words: 'I swear by Almighty God that ...' followed by the words of the oath prescribed by law. The officer will administer the oath in that form and manner without question, unless the person about to take the oath voluntarily objects thereto or is physically incapable of so taking the oath.

Any person who objects to being sworn (whether in that way or in the form and manner usually administered in Scotland) is at liberty instead to make a *solemn affirmation* which will have the same force and effect as an oath. The form of the affirmation is as follows: 'I ... do solemnly, sincerely and truly declare and affirm that ...' followed by the words of the oath prescribed by law. The form of affirmation omits any words of imprecation or calling to witness.

4. *Marriage Act 1949*. English law expressly recognizes the validity of marriages by Jews in England if the ceremonies of the Jewish religion have been complied with.

The Secretary of a synagogue has statutory powers and duties in regard to keeping the marriage register books, and the due registration of marriages between persons professing the Jewish religion under the provisions of the Marriage Act 1949. He has no authority unless and until he has been certified in writing to be the Secretary of a synagogue in England of persons professing the Jewish religion by the President of the Board of Deputies.

When the West London Synagogue was established, acting on the advice of the Chief Rabbi and other recognized Jewish ecclesiastical authorities, the President of the Board of Deputies refused to certify the secretary of the new congregation. Accordingly, by the Marriage Act 1949, it is enacted that the Secretary of the West London Synagogue of British Jews, if certified in writing to the Registrar-General by twenty householders being members of that synagogue, shall be entitled to the same privileges as if he had been certified by the President of the Board of Deputies. These privileges are also accorded to a person whom the Secretary of the West London Synagogue certifies in writing to be the secretary of some other synagogue of not less than twenty householders professing the Jewish religion, if it is connected with the West London Synagogue and has been established for not less than one year.

The Marriages (Secretaries of Synagogues) Act 1959 gives similar rights to Liberal Jewish synagogues.

5. The *Family Law Act 1996* contains important specific provisions in relation to Jewish religious divorce.

Section 9, subsections (3) and (4) provide as follows:
'(3) if the parties –
   (a) were married to each other with usages of a kind mentioned in Section 26(1) of the Marriage Act 1949 (marriages which may be solemnized on authority of superintendent registrar's certificate), and
   (b) are required to co-operate if the marriage is to be dissolved in accordance with those usages.
the court may, on the application of either party, direct that there must also be produced to the court a declaration by both parties that they have taken such steps as are required to dissolve the marriage in accordance with those usages.
(4) A direction under subsection (3) –

(a) may be given only if the court is satisfied that in all the circumstances of the case it is just and reasonable to give it; and

(b) may be revoked by the court at any time.'

The effect of these provisions is that where parties, who have been married in accordance with the usages of Jewish law (i.e., *Chuppah* and *Kiddushin*), seek a divorce then, before such a Jewish husband and wife would be granted the civil decree of divorce by the English court, they could be required to declare that there has been a *Get*, i.e., the Jewish religious divorce. There would thus be a barrier to such a Jewish husband or wife obtaining a civil divorce and being able to remarry unless and until there has been a prior *Get*.

It is hoped that these new statutory provisions will go some way towards alleviating the plight of an *Agunah*. The usual case of an *Agunah* (literally 'a chained woman') is that of a wife whose husband refuses to give her a *Get* so that she is unable to remarry in accordance with orthodox Jewish law. Under the above provisions of the Family Law Act 1996 such a husband would himself be unable to obtain a civil decree of divorce and remarry.

6. *Shechita*. Animals and birds slaughtered by the Jewish method (*shechita*) for the food of Jews by a Jew duly licensed by the Rabbinical Commission constituted for the purpose do not come within the provision of the Slaughterhouses Act 1974 or the Slaughter of Poultry Act 1967 relating to the methods of slaughter of animals and birds. The right to practice *shechita* is thus preserved.

In March 1995 both Acts (the Slaughterhouses Act 1974 and the Slaughter of Poultry Act 1967) were repealed and replaced by secondary legislation in the form of a Statutory Instrument. This implements the European Community's Directive (93/119/EC) on the protection of animals at the time of slaughter. There is specific provision that the requirement for animals and poultry to be stunned before slaughter or killed instantaneously does not apply in the case of animals subject to particular methods of slaughter required by certain religious rites. *Shechita* is accordingly safeguarded.

7. The *Sunday Trading Act*, which came into operation on 26 August 1994, has removed many of the difficulties caused by the Shops Act 1950. All shops with a selling and display area of less than 280 square metres may be open at any time on Sundays. Shops with a selling and display area of 280 square metres or more are still subject to some restriction, with an opening time limited to a continuous period of six hours between 10 a.m. and 6 p.m.

There is, however, a special exemption for 'persons observing the Jewish Sabbath' who are occupiers of these 'large' shops. Provided such an individual (and there are parallel conditions for partnerships and companies) gives a signed notice to the Local Authority that he is a person of the Jewish religion and intends to keep the shop closed for the serving of customers on the Jewish Sabbath, he may open it as and when he wishes on a Sunday.

The notice given to the Local Authority must be accompanied by a statement from the minister of the shopkeeper's synagogue or the secretary for marriages of that synagogue or a person designated by the President of the Board of Deputies, that the shopkeeper is a person of the Jewish religion. There are severe penalties for any false statements made in connection with this intention to trade.

Large shops which were previously registered under Section 53 of the Shops Act 1950 may continue to trade on Sundays without new notification. But occupiers of food stores and kosher meat shops over 280 square metres who, even if closed on Shabbat, did not previously require exemption, may well have formally to notify their Local Authority that their premises will be closed on Shabbat to enable them to open on Sunday.

Jewish shopkeepers who close their premises for the 25 hours of Shabbat may open after Shabbat.

8. Discrimination against a person on account of his being a Jew is unlawful under the *Race Relations Act 1976.*

9. *Friendly Societies Act 1974.* A Friendly Society may be registered for the purpose, *inter alia*, of ensuring that money is paid to persons of the Jewish persuasion during *Shiva* (referred to in the Act as 'the period of confined mourning').

10. By the *Places of Worship Registration Act 1855*, as amended by the *Charities Act 1960*, the Registrar-General may certify a synagogue. The effect of Certification is freedom from uninvited interference by the Charity Commissioners and, if exclusively appropriate to public worship, from general and special rates.

11. By the *Juries Act 1870*, the minister of a synagogue who has been certified, is free from liability to serve on a jury, provided he follows no secular occupation except that of a schoolmaster.

THE SCOTTISH POSITION

(Prepared by Sheriff G. H. Gordon, Q.C., LL.D.)

Jews do not appear in Scots legislation as a unique group, except in relation to United Kingdom statutes which treat them as such, of which the only one still in force is the Representation of the People Act 1983. European Regulations apply in Scotland as they do in England.

The Education (Scotland) Act 1944 provides by section 9 that every public and grant-aided school shall be open to all denominations, and that any pupil may be withdrawn by his parents from instruction in religious subjects and from any religious observance in any such school.

The oath is administered by the judge in Scots courts, and the witness repeats the words (which begin 'I swear by Almighty God') after him with his right hand upraised. No books are used. A Jewish witness is in practice allowed to cover his head if he wishes to do so. Anyone who indicates a wish to affirm is allowed to do so.

Section 8 of the Marriages (Scotland) Act 1977 provides that a religious marriage may be solemnized by the minister or clergyman of any religious body prescribed by Regulations, or by any person recognized by such a body as entitled to solemnize marriages. The bodies prescribed by the Marriage (Prescription of Religious Bodies) (Scotland) (Regulations) 1977 (S.I.No. 1670) include 'The Hebrew Congregation', whatever that denotes. In practice Orthodox marriages are solemnized by ministers authorized to do so by the Board of Deputies.

The Law Reform (Miscellaneous Provisions) (Scotland) Act 1980 includes regular ministers of any religious denomination among those persons who although eligible for jury service are entitled to be excused therefrom as of right.

The Race Relations Act 1976 applies to Scotland, but the Sunday Trading Act 1994 does not, nor does the Places of Worship Registration Act 1855.

LISTED SYNAGOGUES, FORMER SYNAGOGUES AND OTHER JEWISH SITES IN THE UK

The following list has been compiled by the Working Party on Jewish Monuments in the UK and Ireland and the Survey of the Jewish Built Heritage (see p.5).

LONDON
Grade I
Bevis Marks, EC3 (Joseph Avis 1699–1701)

Grade II*
New West End, St Petersburgh Place, W2 (George Audsley in association with N.S. Joseph 1877–79)
Hampstead, Dennington Park Road, NW6 (Delissa Joseph 1892–1901)

Former synagogues:
Princelet Street, E1 (former synagogue 1870, behind Huguenot house 1719. Hudson 1870. Remodelled by Lewis Solomon 1893. Heritage centre)

Grade II
In use as synagogues:
Sandy's Row, E1 (former chapel 1766. Converted into synagogue 1867. Remodelled by N.S. Joseph 1870)
West London Reform, Upper Berkeley Street, W1 (Davis & Emanuel 1870)
New London, 33 Abbey Road, NW8 (formerly St John's Wood United Synagogue. H.H. Collins 1882)
Spanish & Portuguese, Lauderdale Road, W9 (Davis & Emanuel 1896)

Former synagogues:
Spitalfields Great, 23 Brick Lane/Fournier Street, E1 (former chapel 1743. Converted into synagogue 1897–98. Mosque)
East London, Rectory Square, E1 (Davis & Emanuel 1876–77. Flats)
New, Egerton Road, N16 and attached school (Ernest Joseph 1915. Interior reconstructed from Great St Helen's, Bishopsgate by John Davies 1838)
Dollis Hill, Parkside, NW2 (Sir Owen Williams 1936–38. Torah Temimah Primary School)

Other building types:
Soup Kitchen for the Jewish Poor, Brune Street, E1 (Lewis Solomon 1902. Façade only. Flats)
Stepney Jewish Schools, Stepney Green, E1 (Davis & Emanuel 1906)

Cemeteries:
Velho (Spanish & Portuguese), 253 Mile End Road, E1 (1657)
Alderney Road (Ashkenazi), E1 (1696–97)

ENGLISH REGIONS
Grade II*
Birmingham, Singers Hill, Blucher Street (Yeoville Thomason 1855–56)
Brighton, Middle Street (Thomas Lainson 1874–75)
Exeter, Mary Arches Street (1763–64)
Liverpool, Old Hebrew Congregation, Princes Road (W&G Audsley 1874)
Manchester, Spanish & Portuguese, 190 Cheetham Hill Road, M8 (Edward Salomons 1873–74. Manchester Jewish Museum)
Plymouth, Catherine Street (1762)

Grade II
Blackpool, Leamington Road (R.B. Mather 1916. New listing 1998)
Bradford, Bowland Street Reform (T.H. & F. Healey 1880–81)
Chatham Memorial Synagogue, High Street, Rochester (H.H. Collins 1865–70)

Cheltenham, St James's Square (W.H. Knight 1837–39)
Grimsby, Sir Moses Montefiore Synagogue, Heneage Road – and *mikveh* (B.S. Jacobs 1885–88, *mikveh* 1915–16. New listing 1999)
Liverpool, Greenbank Drive (Alfred Shennan 1936)
Manchester, Higher Crumpsall, Bury Old Road, Salford, M7 (1928–29. New listing 1998)
Manchester, South Manchester, Wilbraham Road, M14 (Joseph Sunlight 1912–13)
Manchester, Withington Spanish & Portuguese, 8 Queenston Road, West Didsbury M20 (Delissa Joseph 1925–27, with Joseph Sunlight 'supervising architect')
Nottingham, Shakespeare Street (built as chapel 1854. Converted to synagogue 1954)
Ramsgate, Montefiore Synagogue and Mausoleum, Honeysuckle Road (David Mocatta 1831–33, 1862)
Reading, Goldsmid Road (W.G. Lewton 1900)
Sunderland, Ryhope Road (Marcus K. Glass 1928. New listing 1999)

Former synagogues:
Brighton, 37–39 Devonshire Place (1824. Remodelled by David Mocatta 1836. Sports club)
Canterbury, King Street – and *mikveh* (H. Marshall 1847–48, *mikveh* 1851. King's School music and rehearsal rooms)
Falmouth, Smithick Hill (1808. Studio)
Hull, The Western, Linneaus Street (B.S. Jacobs 1902. Being converted into flats/offices)
Leeds, New, Louis Street/Chapeltown Road (J. Stanley Wright 1932. Northern School of Contemporary Dance)
Newcastle-upon-Tyne, Leazes Park (J. Johnstone 1879–80. Flats)
Sheffield, Wilson Road – and *succah* (Rawcliffe & Ogden 1929–30. Being converted into church)

Cemeteries:
Exeter, Magdelen Street, Bull Meadows (1757; listed boundary wall 1807?)
Liverpool, Deane Road (1836. Screen wall and railings)
Southampton, The Old Jewish Cemetery, The Common Cemetery, Cemetery Road (1846. *Ohel* listed)

WALES
Grade II
Former synagogues:
Cardiff, Cathedral Road (Delissa Joseph 1896–97. Demolished behind façade. Offices)
Merthyr Tydfil, Bryntirion Road, Thomastown (1877. Fitness centre)

SCOTLAND
B List
Edinburgh, Salisbury Road, Newington (James Miller 1929–32)
Glasgow, Garnethill, 127 Hill Street, G3 (John McLeod in association with N.S. Joseph 1877–79)
Glasgow, Queen's Park, 4 Falloch Road, G42 (Ninian MacWhannel 1927)

Cemeteries:
A List
Glasgow Necropolis, Cathedral Square (opened 1833 – including 'façade of Jews' Enclosure' – column and gateway by John Bryce 1836)

B List
Edinburgh, Sciennes House Place (Braid Place), Causewayside (1820)

PRE-EXPULSION SITES
Bristol, Crypt of St Peter's Church, St Peter's Street
Bury St Edmunds, Moyses Hall (*ca.* 1180)
Leicester, Jewry Wall (Roman)
Lincoln, Aaron the Jews' House (the Norman House), 47 Steep Hill
Lincoln, Jew's House and Jews' Court, 2-3 Steep Hill (*ca.* 1170, Grade I)
Norwich, the Music House or Jurnet's House, Wensum Lodge, King Street (*ca.* 1175)
York, Clifford's Tower (rebuilt)

PRIVY COUNSELLORS, PEERS, MPs, etc.

PRIVY COUNSELLORS

Balcombe, Sir John.
Barnett, Lord.
Brittan, Sir Leon, Q.C.
Clinton-Davis, Lord.
Cowen, Sir Zelman, A.K., G.C.M.G.
  G.C.V.O., Q.C.
Diamond, Lord.
Freeson, Reginald.
Kaufman, Gerald B., M.P.
Lawson, Lord.
Millett, Sir Peter.
Oppenheim-Barnes, Baroness.
Rifkind, Sir Malcolm, Q.C.
Sheldon, Robert, E., M.P.
Woolf, Lord, Master of the Rolls.
Young, Lord.

PEERS

Bearsted of Maidstone, 5th Viscount.
Greenhill of Townhead, 2nd Baron,
  M.D.
Marks of Broughton, 3rd Baron.
Morris of Kenwood, 2nd Baron.
Nathan, 2nd Baron.
Rothschild, 4th Baron, M.A. (Oxon.).
Samuel of Mt. Carmel & Toxteth, 3rd
  Viscount.
Swaythling, 5th Baron.

LIFE PEERS

Barnett of Heywood & Royton, Baron,
  P.C.
Bellwin of Leeds, Baron.
Carlile, Baron.
Clinton-Davis of Hackney, Baron, P.C.
Diamond of Gloucester, Baron, P.C.
Ezra of Horsham, Baron, M.B.E.
Hoffman, Lord Justice, P.C.
Haskel of Higher Broughton, Baron.
Hayman of Dartmouth Park, Baroness
Jacobs of Belgravia, Baron.
Janner of Braunstone, Baron, Q.C.
Lawson of Blaby, Baron, P.C.
Lester of Herne Hill, Baron, Q.C.
Levine of Portsoken, Baron.
Levy of Mill Hill, Baron.
Miller of Hendon, Baroness.
Millett, Baron of St Marylebone, Lord
  Justice.

Mishcon of Lambeth, Baron, D.L.
Oppenheim-Barnes of Gloucester,
  Baroness, P.C.
Peston of Mile End, Baron.
Rayne of Prince's Meadow, Baron.
Saatchi of Staplefield, Baron.
Serota of Hampstead, Baroness, D.B.E.
Sieff of Brimpton, Baron, O.B.E.
Sterling of Plaistow, Baron, C.B.E.
Stern, Baroness.
Stone of Blackheath, Baron.
Weidenfeld of Chelsea, Baron.
Weinstock of Bowden, Baron.
Wigoder of Cheetham, Baron, Q.C.
Winston of Hammersmith, Baron
Wolfson of Marylebone, Baron.
Wolfson of Sunningdale, Baron.
Woolf of Barnes, Lord Justice, P.C.,
  Master of the Rolls.
Young of Graffham, Baron, P.C.

MEMBERS OF PARLIAMENT

Bercow, John (C.), Buckingham.
Bradley, Peter (Lab.), The Wrekin.
Caplin, Ivor (Lab.), Hove.
Cohen, Harry (Lab.), Leyton.
Ellman, Louise (Lab.), Liverpool
  Riverside.
Fabrikant, Michael (C.), Lichfield.
Hamilton, Fabian (Lab), Leeds North
  East.
Harris, Dr Evan (Lib.), Oxford West &
  Abingdon.
Hodge, Margaret (Lab.), Barking.
Howard, Michael, Q.C. (C.), Folkestone
  & Hythe.
Kaufman, Rt. Hon. Gerald, P.C. (Lab.),
  Manchester, Gorton.
King, Oona (Lab.) Bethnal Green and
  Bow.
Letwin, Oliver (C.), Dorset West.
Lewis, Ivor (Lab.), Bury South.
Lewis, Dr Julian (C.), New Forest East.
Merron, Gillian (Lab.), Lincoln.
Roche, Barbara (Lab.), Hornsey &
  Wood Green.
Sheldon, Rt. Hon. Robert, P.C. (Lab.),
  Ashton-under-Lyne.
Steen, Anthony (C.), Totnes.
Steinberg, Gerry (Lab.), Durham City.
Winnick, David (Lab.), Walsall North.

MEMBER OF EUROPEAN PARLIAMENT

Sumberg, David (Cons).

BARONETS

Cahn, Sir Albert Jonas.
Jessel, Sir George, M.C.
Levy, Sir Ewart M.
Richardson, Sir Leslie R.
Tuck, Sir Bruce A. R.
Waley-Cohen, Sir Stephen.

KNIGHTS

Abeles, Sir Peter, A.C.
Alliance, Sir David.
Balcombe, Rt. Hon. Sir John, P.C.
Beecham, Sir Jeremy.
Berman, Sir Franklin.
Blom-Cooper, Sir Louis.
Bondi, Sir Hermann, K.C.B., F.R.S.
Brittan, Rt. Hon. Sir Leon, P.C., Q.C.
Brown, Sir Simon (the Hon. Mr Justice).
Burgen, Sir Arnold, F.R.S.
Burton, Sir Michael (the Hon. Mr Justice).
Calne, Sir Roy, F.R.S.
Caro, Sir Anthony.
Chinn, Sir Trevor, C.V.O.
Cohen, Sir Edward.
Cohen, Sir Ivor Harold.
Cohen, Prof. Sir Philip.
Colman, Sir Anthony (the Hon. Mr Justice).
Copisarow, Sir Alcon.
Cowen, Sir Zelman, A.K., C.G.M.C., G.C.V.O.
Djanogly, Sir Harry.
Dyson, Sir John (the Hon. Mr Justice).
Elton, Sir Arnold.
Elyan, Sir Isadore Victor.
Epstein, Sir Anthony.
Falk, Sir Roger Salis.
Feldman, Sir Basil.
Fox, Sir Paul.
Gainsford, Sir Ian.
Gilbert, Sir Athur.
Gilbert, Sir Martin, C.B.E.
Godfrey, Sir Gerald (the Hon. Mr Justice, Hong Kong Supreme Court).
Gold, Sir Arthur Abraham, C.B.E.
Goldberg, Sir Abraham, F.R.S.E.
Goldberg, Prof. Sir David.

Golding, Sir John.
Goldman, Sir Samuel, K.C.B.
Gombrich, Sir Ernst H.J., O.M., C.B.E.
Green, Sir Allan, K.C.B.
Greengross, Sir Alan.
Grierson, Sir Ronald.
Halpern, Sir Ralph.
Hamburger, Sir Sidney Cyril, C.B.E.
Harris, Sir William Woolf, O.B.E.
Hatter, Sir Maurice.
Hirsch, Sir Peter Bernhard, F.R.S.
Hoffenberg, Prof. Sir Raymond.
Isaacs, Sir Jeremy.
Jacob, Sir Isaac Hai, Q.C.
Jacob, Sir Robin (the Hon. Mr Justice).
Japhet, Ernest I., Hon. K.B.E.
Kalms, Sir Stanley
Katz, Prof. Sir Bernard, F.R.S.
Kingsland, Sir Richard, AO, C.B.E., D.F.C.
Klug, Sir Aaron, P.R.S.
Kornberg, Prof. Sir Hans Leo, F.R.S.
Krusin, Sir Stanley Marks, C.B.
Laddie, Sir Hugh (the Hon. Mr Justice).
Landau, Sir Dennis.
Lauterpacht, Prof. Sir Elihu.
Lawrence, Sir Ivan.
Leigh, Sir Geoffrey.
Levine, Sir Montague.
Lewando, Sir Jan Alfred, C.B.E.
Lightman, Sir Gavin (the Hon. Mr Justice).
Lipworth, Sir Sydney
Lyons, Sir Isidore Jack, C.B.E.
Moser, Sir Claus Adolph, K.C.B., C.B.E., F.B.A.
Ognall, Sir Harry Henry (the Hon. Mr. Justice).
Oppenheim, Sir Alexander, O.B.E.
Phillips, Sir Henry Ellis Isidore C.M.G. M.B.E.
Porter, Sir Leslie.
Rieger, Sir Clarence Oscar, C.B.E.
Rifkind, Sir Malcolm, P.C.
Rix, Sir Bernard (the Hon. Mr Justice).
Robinson, Sir Albert E.P.
Rodley, Prof. Sir Nigel.
Rotblat, Sir Joseph, C.B.E., F.R.S.
Roth, Prof. Sir Martin, F.R.S.
Rothschild, Sir Evelyn de.
Samuelson, Sir Sydney W., C.B.E.
Seligman, Sir Peter Wendel, C.B.E.
Sherman, Sir Alfred.
Sherman, Sir Lou, O.B.E.
Sheilds, Sir Neil Stanley, M.C.
Shock, Sir Maurice.

Sieff, Sir David.
Singer, Sir Hans.
Smith, Sir David, A.K. C.V.O., A.O.
Solomon, Sir Harry.
Sternberg, Sir Sigmund.
Tumim, Judge Sir Stephen.
Turnberg, Sir Leslie.
Weinberg, Sir Mark.
Wolfson, Sir Brian.
Zissman, Sir Bernard.
Zunz, Sir Jack.

DAMES

Heilbron, Dame Rose, D.B.E.
Markova, Dame Alicia, D.B.E.
Porter, Dame Shirley, D.B.E.
Prendergast, Dame Simone, D.B.E.,
    J.P., D.L.
Serota, Baroness, D.B.E.

FELLOWS OF THE ROYAL SOCIETY

Anderson, Prof. Ephraim Saul, C.B.E.
Bondi, Prof. Sir Hermann, K.C.B.
Born, Prof. Gustav Victor Rudolf.
Brenner, Prof. Sydney, C.H.
Burgen, Sir Arnold.
Calne, Sir Roy.
Cohen, Prof. Sydney, C.B.E.
Devons, Prof. Samuel.
Domb, Prof. Cyril.
Dunitz, Prof. Jack David.
Dwek, Raymond
Fersht, Prof. Alan.
Glynn, Prof. Ian Michael.
Goldstone, Prof. Jeffrey.
Hirsch, Prof. Sir Peter Bernhard.
Horn, Prof. Gabriel.
Huppert, Dr. Herbert.
Josephson, Prof. Brian David.
Katz, Prof. Sir Bernard (Vice-President
    1965 and 1968-76).
Kennard, Dr. Olga, O.B.E.
Klug, Sir Aaron (President 1995-),
    O.M.
Kornberg, Prof. Sir Hans Leo.
Mahler, Prof. Kurt.
Mandelstam, Prof. Joel.
Mandelstam, Prof. Stanley.
Mestel, Prof. Leon.
Milstein, Dr. César, C.H.
Nabarro, Prof. F. R. Nunes.
Neumann, Prof. Bernard H.
Orgel, Prof. L. E.

Orowan, Prof. Egon.
Pepper, Dr. Michael.
Perutz, Prof. Max F., O.M.
Roitt, Prof. Ivan.
Rotblat, Sir Joseph, K.C.M.G., C.B.E.
Roth, Sir Martin.
Rothschild, Dr. Miriam, C.B.E.
Sciama, Dr. Denis.
Segal, Dr Anthony Walter.
Shoenberg, Prof. David, M.B.E.
Sondheimer, Prof. Franz.
Tabor, Prof. David.
Weizkrantz, Prof. Lawrence.
Woolfson, Prof. Michael Mark.
Young, Prof. Alec David, O.B.E.

Foreign Members

Calvin, Prof. Melvin.
Feynman, Prof. Richard Phillips.
Katzir, Prof. Ephraim, form. President
    of Israel.
Kornberg, Prof. Arthur.

FELLOWS OF THE BRITISH ACADEMY

Cohen, Prof. Gerald Allan.
Cohen, Laurence Jonathan.
Cohn, Prof. Norman.
Gombrich, Prof. Sir Ernst Hans Josef,
    O.M., C.B.E.
Goodman, Prof. Martin.
Hajnal, Prof. John.
Hobsbawm, Prof. Eric John, C.H.
Israel, Prof. Jonathan Irvine.
Koerner, Prof. Stephan.
Lewis, Prof. Bernard.
Lewis, Prof. Geoffrey, C.M.G.
Lukes, Prof. Steven.
Marks, Prof. Shula.
Moser, Sir Claus A., K.C.B., C.B.E.
Prais, Sigbert J.
Prawer, Prof. Siegbert Salomon.
Schapera, Prof. Isaac.
Segal, Prof. Judah Benzion, M.C.
Steiner, Prof. George.
Supple, Prof. Barry.
Ullendorff, Prof. Edward (Vice-
    President 1980-82).
Vermes, Prof. Geza.
Yamey, Prof. Basil Selig, C.B.E.

Corresponding Fellows

Blau, Prof. J.
Levi-Strauss, Prof. Claude.
Samuelson, Prof. Paul Antony.

VICTORIA CROSS

Lieutenant Frank Alexander De Pass*.
Captain Robert Gee, M.C.*.
Leonard Keysor*.
Acting Corporal Issy Smith*.
Jack White*.
Lieut.-Cmdr. Thomas William Gould R.N.V.R.

GEORGE CROSS

Errington, Harry.
Lewin, Sgt. Raymond M., R.A.F.*.
Latutin, Capt. Simmon*.
Newgass, Lieutenant-Commander Harold Reginald, R.N.V.R.*.

ORDER OF MERIT

Gombrich, Sir Ernst Hans Josef, C.B.E.
Klug, Sir Aaron, P.R.S.
Perutz, Prof. Max F.
Freud, Lucian.

COMPANIONS OF HONOUR

Brenner, Prof. Sydney, F.R.S.
Hobsbawm, Prof. Eric John Ernest, F.B.A.
Milstein, Dr César, F.R.S.

NOBEL PRIZE WINNERS

Peace

Tobias Asser*; Alfred Fried*; Rene Cassin; Henry Kissinger; Menachem Begin*; Elie Wiesel; Yitzhak Rabin*; Shimon Peres; Joseph Rotblat.

Physics

Albert Abraham Michelson*; Gabriel Lippmann*; Albert Einstein*; Niels Bohr*; Enrico Fermi; James Franck*; Gustav Herts*; Otto Stern; Isidor Isaac Rabi; Felix Bloch*; Max Born*; Igor Tamm; Emilio Segre; Donald A. Glaser; Robert Hofstadter*; Lev Davidovic Landau*; Richard Feynman; Julian Schwinger; Hans Bethe; Murray Gell-Mann; Dennis Gabor*; Brian Josephson; Ben R. Mottelson; Aage Bohr; Burton Richter; Arno Penzias; Sheldon Glashow; Steven Weinberg; Leon Lederman; Melvin Schwartz; Jack Steinberger; Georges Charpak.

Chemistry

Adolph Baeyer*; Henri Moissan*; Otto Wallach*; Richard Willstatter*; Fritz Haber*; George de Hevesy*; Melvin Calvin; Max Ferdinand Perutz; William Stein; Herbert Brown; Paul Berg; Walter Gilbert; Roald Hoffmann; Aaron Klug; Dudley Herschebach; Herbert Hauptman; Sidney Altman; Rudolf Marcus; Walter Kohn.

Medicine

Paul Ehrlich*; Elie Metchnikoff; Robert Barany*; Otto Meyerhoff*; Karl Landsteiner*; Otto Warburg*; Otto Lowei*; Joseph Erlanger*; Sir Ernst B. Chain*; Herbert Gasser; Hermann Joseph Muller*; Tadeus Reichstein*; Selman Abraham Waksman*; Sir Hans A. Krebs*; Fritz Albert Lipmann*; Joshua Lederberg; Arthur Kornberg; Konrad Bloch; Francois Jacob-Andre Lwoff; George Wald; Marshall W. Nirenberg; Salvador Luria*; Sir Bernard Katz; Julius Axelrod; Gerald Maurice Edelman; David Baltimore; Howard Martin Temin; Baruch S. Blumberg; Rosalyn Yalow; David Nathans; Baruj Benacerraf; Cesar Milstein; Joseph L. Goldstein; Michael Brown; Rita Levi-Montalcini; Stanley Cohen; Gertrude Aeilion; Harold Vermus; Gary Becker.

Literature

Paul Heyse*; Henri Bergson*; Boris Pasternak*; Shmuel Yosef Agnon*; Nelly Sachs*; Saul Bellow; Isaac Bashevis Singer*; Elias Canetti*; Jaroslav Seifert; Joseph Brodsky*; Nadine Gordimer.

Economics

Paul Samuelson; Simon Kuznets; Kenneth Arrow; Leonid Kantorovich*; Milton Friedman; Herbert Simons; Lawrence Klein; Franco Modigliani; Robert Solow.

* Deceased.

Who's Who

AARON, Martin, M.B.A., F.S.C.A., M.I. Mgt., F.R.S.A.; b. London, Jan. 25, 1937; Fdr. & Chairman, Jewish Assoc. for the Mentally Ill; form. Tr., Ravenswood Foundation; Fdr. and form. Chairman, Jewish Soc. for Mentally Handicapped; Memb. Council of CONCERN for the Mentally Ill; form. Adv.C., Royal Soc. for Mentally Handicapped Children & Adults; Adv. C., Nat. Assn. for Mental Health; Ad. c/o JAMI, 16a North End Rd., London NW11 7PH. ☎ 020-8458 2223.

ABIS, Barrington Gerald, J.P.; b. Ipswich Nov. 28, 1939; Regional Dir. UJIA (1998–); form. Exec. Off, Leeds Jewish Rep. C. (1985-98); Admin. Sec., Leeds Kashrut Authority (1985-98), Beth Din, Admin. Dir., Leeds Judean Club; and S. H. Lyons Tr. (1982-98); Form. Com. Rel. C., Weetwood & Chapeltown North Police Com. Forums; P/Pres. B'nai B'rith Men's Lodge 1055; Ad.: Balfour House, 399 Street Lane, Leeds LS17 6HQ. ☎ 0113-269 3136. Fax 0113-269 3961.

ABRAHAMSON, Hon. Abraham Eliezer, B.A.; b. Bulawayo, Oct. 13, 1922, m. Anita née Rabinovitz; M.P. (Bulawayo East, 1953-64); Min. of Treasury, Local Govt. and Housing (1958), Min. of Labour, Social Welfare and Housing (1958-62); H.L.P. (President 1956-58, 64-79) Central African Jew BoD, Life Member C.A.Z.O. (1989-); Member World Exec. WJC, served on Nat. Exec. S.A. Jewish BoD (1991-); Chairman, S.A.Z. Fed. (1991-94), President (1994-98), Hon. Life P. (1998-); Exec., S.A.Z. Fed (1986); V. Chairman 1988-90. Ad.: 4 Oxford Gdns., 188 Oxford Rd., Illovo 2196, Johannesburg. ☎ 880 1964. Fax 447 2596.

ABRAMSKY, Chimen, B.A. (Jerusalem), M.A. (Oxon); b. Minsk, Mar. 5, 1917; form. President, Jewish Hist. Soc. of England; form. Goldsmid Prof. of Heb. and Jewish Studies; form. Reader in Jewish hist., Univ. Coll., London; Sr. Fel., St. Antony's Coll., Oxford. Publ.: Karl Marx and the Engl. Labour Movement (jt. auth.); Essays in honour of E H. Carr (ed.), two Prague Haggadot (auth.), First Illustrated Grace After Meals, Jews in Poland (jt ed.), many articles and monographs on modern Jewish hist., etc. Ad: 5 Hillway, N6 6QB. ☎ 020-8340 8302.

ABRAMSON, Glenda (née Melzer), BA, MA, PhD (Rand), Hon. DLitt (HUC); b. Johannesburg, Nov. 16, 1940; m. David; Academic; Cowley Lect. Post-Biblical Hebrew, Oxford (1989-); form. Schreiber Fell. Modern Jewish Studies, Oxford Centre for Hebrew and Jewish Studies (1981); form. Sen. Lect., Univ. Witwatersrand (1970–78). Publ.: Modern Hebrew Drama (1979); The Writing of Yehuda Amichai (1989); Hebrew in Three Months (1993, repr. 1998); Drama and Ideology in Modern Israel (1998); Ed.: Essays in Honour of Salo Rappaport (1985); The Blackwell Companion to Jewish Culture (1989); Jewish Education and Learning (1994, with T. Parfitt); Tradition and Trauma (1995, with D. Patterson); The Oxford Book of Hebrew Short Stories (1996); The Experienced Soul: Studies in Amichai (1997). Ad.: Oxford Centre for Hebrew and Jewish Studies, 45 St Giles, Oxford OX1 3LP. ☎ 01865 511869. Fax 01865 311791. Email glenda.abramson@stx.ox.ac.uk

ABSE, Dannie, F.R.S.L., M.R.C.S. L.R.C.P.; b. Cardiff, Sept. 22, 1923; writer (poems and novels) and physician. Ad.: Green Hollows, Craig-yr-Eos Rd., Ogmore by-Sea, Glamorgan.

ABSE, Leo; b. Cardiff, Apr. 22, 1917; Solicitor; V. President Inst. for Study and Treatment of Delinquency (1998-); form. M.P. (Lab.) for Torfaen (1983-87); Pontypool (1958-83). Member, Home Office Adv. Cttees. on the Penal System (1968), on Adoption (1972); first Ch., Select Cttee. on Welsh Affairs (1980); Member, Select Cttee. on Abortion (1975-76), Sec. British-Taiwan Parly Gp

(1983-87). Sponsor or co-sponsor of Private Member's Acts relating to divorce, homosexuality, family planning, legitimacy, widow's damages, industrial injuries, congenital disabilities and relief from forfeiture; sponsored Children's Bill (1973), later taken over by Govt to become Children's Act (1975), sponsored Divorce Bill (1983), later taken over by Govt to become Matrimonial and Family Proceedings Act (1985); initiated first Commons debates on genetic engineering, Windscale, in vitro pregnancies. Led Labour anti-devolution campaign in Wales (1979). Member C. Inst. for Study and Treatment of Delinquency (1964-98); Tr., Winnicott Clinic of Psychotherapy (1980-); P. Nat. C. for the Divorced and Separated (1974-92); V. President, British Assoc. for Counselling (1985-90); Chairman, Parly Friends of WNO (1985-87); Member of C. Univ. of Wales (1981-87); UWIST. Regents' Lectr, Univ. of Calif (1984); Ord. of Brilliant Star (China) (1988); Chairman, Cardiff Poale Zion (1951-54). Publ.: Private Member: a psychoanalytically oriented study of contemporary politics (1973); (contrib.) In Vitro Fertilisation: past, present and future (1986); Margaret, daughter of Beatrice: a psychobiography of Margaret Thatcher (1989); Wotan my enemy (1994) (Awarded JQ Literary prize for non-fiction, etc. 1994); The Man Behind the Smile: Tony Blair and the Perversion of Politics (1996). Ad.: 54 Strand-on-the-Green, W4 3PD. ☎ 020-8994 1166.

ALDERMAN, Geoffrey, M.A., D.Phil. (Oxon.), F.R.Hist.S, FRSA, FICPO, MIQA, MIMgt; b. Hampton Court, Middx., Feb. 10, 1944, m. Marion née Freed; Pro.-V.-C. & Prof. Middlesex University (1994-); form. Prof of Politics & Contemporary History, Royal Holloway Coll. (Lond. Univ.), Senior Associate, Oxford Hebrew Centre; Publ.: British Elections: Myth and Reality, The Railway Interest, The Jewish Vote in Great Britain since 1945, The Jewish Community in British Politics, Pressure Groups and Government in Britain, Modern Britain 1700-1983, The Federation of Synagogues 1887-1987, London Jewry & London Politics, 1889-1986; Modern British Jewry. Ad.: Middlesex University, Trent Park, Bramley Rd., London N14 4YZ. ☎ 020-8362-5963.

ALONY, Dayan Zalman Joseph, b. Penza, Russia, Oct. 10, 1915; Emer.Rosh Beth Din. Fed. of Syns., Lond; form. Dayan, Jewish Coms., Ireland; Chairman, Shechita. Kashrus Cttee., Eire; President, Assn of Jewish Clergy and Teachers. Publ.: Degel Yosef on Law and Ethics (1949), etc.

ALVAREZ, Alfred, M.A. (Oxon), Hon D.Litt.(London); b. London, Aug. 5, 1929; poet, author and critic; poetry critic and editor, The Observer (1956-66), Gauss Seminarian, Princeton Univ. (1958); Vis. Prof., Brandeis Univ. (1960-61), State Univ. of N.Y., Buffalo (1966). Publ.: The Shaping Spirit, The School of Donne, Under Pressure, Beyond All This Fiddle, Beckett, The Savage God (lit.crit.); Life after Marriage, The Biggest Game in Town, Offshore, Feeding the Rat, Rain Forest, Night, Where Did It All Go Right? (non-fiction); Lost, Apparition, Penguin Modern Poets 18, Autumn to Autumn (poems); Hers Hunt, Day of Atonement (novels); The New Poetry, Faber Book of Modern European Poetry (anthologies). Ad.: c/o Aitken & Stone Ltd., 29 Fernshaw Rd., SW10 0TG. ☎ 020-7351 3594. Fax 020-7376 3594.

AMIAS, Rev. Saul, M.B.E.; b. London, Mar. 9, 1907; M. Emer. Edgware Syn.; Fdr., H. Princ., Rosh Pinah Jewish Primary Schs.; Fdr. & President, Jewish Assn. of Cultural Socs.; Life President, Ajex Edgw. Br.: Member, BoD, AJA, JMC, Nat. C. for Soviet Jewry, C.C.J., President, C.C.J. Edgw. Br. V. President Nat. Peace C.; V. President, United Nats. Assn., Edgw. & Stanmore Br.; Emer. Brigade Chaplain, Jewish Lads' & Girls' Bde.; Chaplain, Royal Masonic Hospital; form. Chaplain to Forces, broadcaster; form. President, Union of Anglo-Jewish Preachers. Ad.: 34 Mowbray Rd., Edgware, Middx. HA8 8JQ. ☎ 020-8958 9969.

ANDERSON, Michael John Howard, M.A. (Oxon.), M.Ed.(L'pool), Dip. Soc. Work (B'ham), C.Q.S.W.; b. Sheffield, May 7, 1948; Form. Dir., Manchester Jewish Soc. Services (1986-91); Sec. Regional Jewish Welfare Fed.; Head, Soc.

Work Courses, Manch. Poly. (1985-87); Sr. Lect., Social Work. L'pool Poly. (1977-85). Ad.: 31 Woodland Loop, Edgewater, Western Australia 6027.

APPLE, Rabbi Raymond, A.M., R.F.D., M.Litt., B.A., LL.B.; b. Melbourne, Dec. 27, 1935; Sr. Rabbi, Great Syn., Sydney (1972-); Sr. Rabbi. Australian Defence Force; Member, Sydney Beth Din; H.V. President, New South Wales Bd. of Jewish Educ.; Jt. Hon. M. Mandelbaum House, Sydney Univ.; Lect. in Judaic Studies, Sydney Univ.; Lect., Jewish Law, N.S.W. Univ.; President, Assn. of Rabbis & Mins. of Australia & New Zealand (1980-84; 1988-1992); Jt.P., Australian Council of Christians & Jews (1996-); President, Australian Jewish Hist. Soc.(1985-89); M., Bayswater Syn. (1960-65), Hampstead Syn. (1965-1972); form. Rel. Dir., AJY. Publ.: The Hampstead Syn., 1892-1967; Making Australian Society: The Jews; Francis Lyon Cohen – the Passionate Patriot etc. Ad.: The Great Syn., 166 Castlereagh St., Sydney 2000, N.S.W., Australia. ☎ (02) 9267 2477. Fax (02) 9264 8871. Email: rabbi@greatsynagogue.org.au

ARKUSH, Rabbi Shmuel; b. Birmingham May 5, 1951; Dir. Lubavitch in the Midlands; Dir. Operation Judaism; H.T. B.J.E.B. Talmud Torah; Chaplain of the Midlands Region Chaplaincy Bd. (1980-85). Ad.: 95 Willows Rd., Birmingham B12 9QF. ☎ 0121-440 6673; Fax 0121-446 4199.

AUERBACH, Mrs. Geraldine Yvonne (née Kretzmar), BA(Rand), STC (UCT); b. Kimberly, South Africa, 1940; Founding Festival Dir. Bnai Brith Jewish Music Festival (UK, est. 1984); Founding Chairman The Jewish Music Heritage Trust Ltd. (UK, est. 1989); Founder and MD Jewish Music Heritage Recordings (UK, est. 1984); Founder and former MD (1984-1991) Jewish Music Distribution (UK, est. 1984). Ad.: PO Box 232, Harrow, Middx. HA1 2NN. ☎ 020-8909 2445. Fax 020-8909 1030. Email: geraldine@jmht.org

AVIDAN, Rabbi Hillel, M.A.; b. London, July 16, 1933, m. Ruth; M., Bet David Reform Cong. (1992- (Johannesburg); Chairman Southern African Assoc. Progressive Rabbis (1995–99); F.M., West Central Lib. Syn. (1985-92); M. Ealing Lib. Syn. (1986-92); and Chairman, ULPS Rabbinic Conference (1990-92), form. M., Wimbledon & Distr. Ref Syn. (1974-81), Chairman, RSGB Assembly of Rabbis, (1978-80), Teacher Reali High Sch., Haifa; Libr. Haifa Univ. Publ.: Feasts and Fasts of Israel, (Contrib) Judaism & ecology; Renewing the vision. Ad.: Bet David, PO Box 78189, Sandton, 2146, South Africa. ☎ 783-7117; Fax 883-8991.

BAKER, Adrienne, Ph.D., B.Sc.; b. Manchester, Feb. 15, 1936; Family Therapist & University Lecturer; Senior Lect: School of Psychotherapy, Regent's College, London; Publ.: The Jewish Woman in Contemporary Society: Transitions and Traditions (1993). Ad: 16 Sheldon Ave., Highgate, London N6 4JT. ☎ 020-8340 5970 (home), 020-7487 7406 (college).

BAKER, William, B.A. (Hons.), M.Phil., Ph.D., M.L.S.; b. Shipston-on-Stour, Warwicks., July 6, 1944; Form. Housemaster, Polack's House, Clifton Coll., Lect. in English, Ben-Gurion Univ. (1971-77), Hebrew Univ., Jerusalem (1973-75); Vis. Prof., Pitzer Coll., Claremont, Ca. (1981-82); Sr. Lect., West Midlands Coll. (1978-85); Edr., George Eliot-G. H. Lewes Newsletter; Publ.: George Eliot and Judaism, Harold Pinter (co. auth.), Some George Eliot Notebooks, Vols. I-IV, The George Eliot-G. H. Lewes Library, The libraries of G. Eliot and G. Lewes, Antony & Cleopatra. The Merchant of Venice. Ad:

BALCOMBE, Rt. Hon., Sir (Alfred) John, P.C., M.A. (Oxon.); b. London, Sept. 29, 1925, m. Jacqueline née Cowan; Lord Justice of Appeal (1985-95); High Court Judge (1977-85); Q.C. (1969); Tr. Lincolns Inn (1999-); Pres. The Maccabaeans; Hon. Fel. Hebrew Univ. (1996). Publ.: Exempt Private Companies, (edr.) Title 'Estoppel' - Halsbury's Laws of England (4th ed.) Ad.: 1A Lingfield Rd., SW19 4QA. Fax 020-8944-0527.

BALCOMBE, Andrew David, BA (Com), MBA (Harvard); b. Adlington, Cheshire, Aug. 4, 1942; m. Jean née Steinberg; Chief Executive; Chief Exec. of Armour Trust plc (1970-98); Chairman M@tchnet plc (1998-99); Chairman NetVest.com plc (1999); Chairman, National Council for Soviet Jewry (1980-

82); Founder member of Conscience interdenominational committee for the release of Soviet Jewry (1973-95); Exec. Ctte. Board of Deputies (1980-82); Tr. Metropolitan Charitable Fd. (1975-99); Council Ben Uri Art Society (1999); Steering Group of Jewish Cultural Centre Project. Ad.: 4 Elm Walk, London NW3 7UP. ☎ 020-8455 9974. Fax 020-8209 0416. Email andrew@balcombel. demon.co.uk

BAND, David; b. Lond., April 8, 1931; HM, Michael Sobell Sinai (Primary) Sch. (1981-90); HM, Solomon Wolfson Bayswater Jewish Sch. (1969-81); Educ. Adviser, Provincial Synagogue Hebrew Classes (under Jewish Memorial C. auspices). Ad.: 23 Woodhill Crescent, Kenton, Middx HA3 0LU.

BARD, Basil Joseph Asher, C.B.E., Ph.D., B.Sc., A.R.C.S., D.I.C.; b. London, Aug. 20, 1914; m. Ena née; Scientist; Barrister-at Law; Industrial Consultant (Ret.); V. President (President, 1977-83), AJA; President JMC (1982-90); Gov., and Honorary Fellow Hebrew Univ. (1984-); form. Chairman Admin. Com. (1990-94) (UK Friends); Life Gov. Hebrew University (1994-); various com. offices (since 1944); Consultant to United Nations Development Org. (1972-74); Man. Dir., Nat. Res. Development Corp. (1969-73), form. Member of various Govt. Cttees., Min. of Supply (1941-43); Min. of Aircraft Production (1943-45). Gold Medallist and Life Member Licencing Executives Soc. (1973-). Hon. Member Fdn. for Science and Technology, (1990). Ad.: 23 Mourne House, Maresfield Gdns., Hampstead, NW3 5SL. ☎ 020-7435 5340.

BARNETT, Rt. Hon. Baron of Heywood & Royton, (Life Peer) **(Joel Barnett),** P.C., J.P.; b. Manchester, Oct. 14, 1923, m. Lilian née Goldstone; Accountant and Chairman/Dirs. of Companies; form. V. Chairman B.B.C. Govs.; Mem. European Union Select Cttee.; Chairman European Union Sub. Cttee. on Finance, Trade & Industry; Tr. Victoria & Albert Museum; Chairman Educ. Broadcasting Society Tr.;   Chairman, Public Accounts Cttee.; House of Commons (1979-83); Chief Sec. to H.M. Treasury (1974-79), Member of Cabinet (1977-79), form. Chairman, form. Mem Public Exp. Cttee., M.P (Lab.) for Heywood & Royton (1964-83); Gov., Birkbeck Coll., Lond. Univ., Fel., Centre for Study of Public Pol., Strathclyde Univ., Hon. Doctorate, Strathclyde, Member, Halle Cttee. Publ.: Inside the Treasury. Ad.: 7 Hillingdon Rd., Whitefield, Manchester, M25 7QQ; Flat 92, 24 John Islip St., SW1.

BARON COHEN, Gerald, B.A., F.C.A.; b. Lond., July 13, 1932, m. Daniella née Weiser; Chartered Acct.; President, First Lodge of England, B'nai B'rith, Nat. T., B'nai B'rith, Distr. 15, V. President Hillel Foundation; V. Chairman, U.J.S.; Edr., Mosaic; Dep. Edr., New Middle East, Chairman Bamah-Forum for Jewish Dialogue (Jewish Unity Working Group). Ad.: 70 Wildwood Rd., NW11 6UJ. ☎ 020-8458 1552. Fax 020-8455 1693.

BARRON, Rabbi Moshe, M.A.; b. Manchester Oct. 24, 1946; M. Richmond Synagogue; M. Bayswater and Maida Vale Synagogue (1976-84) M. South Eastern Hebrew Congregation Johannesburg; Founder Lecturer/Tutor Jewish Students University Programme Johannesburg (1972-76) Ad.: 67 Houblon Rd., Richmond, Surrey TW10 6DB. ☎ 020-8948 1977.

BAUM, Derek, M.B.E.; b. Westcliff-on-Sea, Essex, June 9, 1927; Ret. Co. Chairman Estate Agents/Property Developers. M. Consultant & Adv. and Exec. Cttees Chief Rabbinate C.; H. Life-President, Southend & Westcliff Hebrew Cong. (1997-); T. (1968-82); Pres. (1982-97); Pres. Southend & Distr. AJEX. (since 1966); Chairman S. & D. Jewish Rep. Council (since 1997); T. (1986-97); H. Sec. Council of Christians & Jews (1999-); V.Pres. S & D Jewish Youth Centre; V.Pres. & T. Royal British Legion (S. & D.). Chairman Bd. Govs Herzlia Day School. (1984-88); H.Sec. Nat. AJEX (1964-70); Nat. V.Chairman AJEX (1970-74); Found. AJEX Housing Assn.; AJEX Gold Badge (1997); Chairman Southend AJEX (1960-62), (1964-66); Member BoD (1968-80) R.A.F. (1945-48). Ad.: Flat 1, 33 Clifftown Parade, Southend-on-Sea, Essex SS1 1DL. ☎ (01702) 343789.

BAYFIELD, Rabbi Anthony Michael, M.A. (Cantab.); b. Ilford, July 4, 1946;

Chief Exec. Reform Synagogues of Great Britain; Dir. Reform Foundation Trust; Dir., Sternberg Centre for Judaism; Dir. Manor House Trust; form. Chairman, C., Ref & Lib. Rabbis; Tr., Michael Goulston Educ. Fnd., Lect., Leo Baeck Coll.; Edr., 'Manna'; Rabbi, North-West Surrey Syn. (1972-82); Chairman, Assembly of Rabbis, RSGB (1980-81). Publ.: Churban, The Murder of the Jews of Europe (1981); Dialogue with a Difference (Ed. with Marcus Braybrooke) (1992); Sinai, Law & Responsible Autonomy (1993). Ad: The Sternberg Centre for Judaism, 80, East End Road, N3 2SY. ☎ 020-8346 2288. Fax 020-8343 0901. Email: admin@refsyn.org.uk

BEECHAM, Sir Jeremy Hugh, MA, DCL, DL, H. Fellow, Northumbria University; b. Leicester, Nov. 11, 1944; m. Brenda Elizabeth née Wolf; Solicitor; Newcastle City Councillor (1967-); Leader Newcastle City Council (1977-94); Chairman, Assn. Metropolitan Borought Auth. (1991-97); Chairman, Local Govt. Assn. (1997-); Com., English Heritage (1983-87); President, British Urban Regeneration Assn. (1996-). Ad.: 7 Collingwood Street, Newcastle upon Tyne NE1 1JE.

BELLOW, Saul; b. Lachine, Canada, June 10, 1915; novelist; Nobel Prize for Lit. (1976); Prof. in the Cttee. on Social Thought, Chicago Univ. Publ.: Him with His Foot in His Mouth, The Adventures of Augie March, Henderson the Rain King, Herzog, Mr. Sammler's Planet, Humboldt's Gift, To Jerusalem and Back, The Dean's December, The Victim, Mosby's Memoirs and other stories, etc. Ad.: Chicago Univ., 1126 E. 59th St., Chicago, Ill., 60637, USA.

BELLWIN, Baron of Leeds (Life Peer); **Irwin Norman Bellow**, J.P., LL.B., D.L.; b. Leeds, Feb. 7. 1923; form. Min. of State for Local Govt.; form. Parl. Under-Sec., Environment; form. Member, Com. for New Towns; form. V. President, Internat New Towns Assn. (Inta); form Leader, Leeds City C., form. V. Chairman, Assn. Met. Auths., form Member Nat. Sports C.; President, Leeds JBS; Life V. President Leeds Jew Rep. C.; H. President, Moor Allerton Golf Club; President, Soc. of Jewish Past Captains (Golf); form. President, Assn. of Jewish Golf Clubs Socs. of Gt. Britain; form. President, English Basket Ball Assn.; Patron Yorks. Kidney Res. Assn.; Deputy Lieutenant, W. Yorks. Ad.: Woodside Lodge, Ling Lane, Scarcroft, Leeds LS14 3HX. ☎ 0113-2892908. Fax 0113-2892213.

BENADY, S., C.B.E., Q.C., M.A. (Cantab.); b. Gibraltar, May 21, 1905; barrister; Life President (President, 1956-73) Gibraltar Jewish Com.; Fd. & L.President Gibraltar Oxford & Cambridge Assoc.; Leader, Gib. Bar; Sqdn.-Leader; R.A.F., Second World War. Ad.: 124 Main St., Gibraltar. ☎ 78549.

BENEDICTUS, David Henry, B.A. (Oxon.); b. London, Sept. 16, 1938; Author, playwright, theatre dir., Ed. Readings BBC Radio (1989-94) plus Radio 3 Drama from 1992; Commissioning Ed., Channel 4 (1984-86); Judith E. Wilson Vis. Fell., Cambridge Univ. (1981-82); Producer 'Something Understood' (with Mark Tully); Macbeth for BBC Radio 4; Publ.: The Fourth of June, You're a Big Boy Now, This Animal is Mischievous, Hump, or Bone by Bone Alive, The Guru and the Golf Club, A Word of Windows, The Rabbi's Wife, Junk, A Twentieth Century Man, The Antique Collector's Guide, Lloyd George, Whose Life is it Anyway, Who Killed the Prince Consort? Local Hero, The Essential London Guide, Floating Down to Camelot, The Streets of London, The Absolutely Essential London Guide, Little Sir Nicholas, The Odyssey of a Scientist, Sunny Intervals and Showers, The Stamp Collector, The Essential London Entertainment Guide, How to Cope when the Money Runs Out, Poets for Pleasure (audio books). Ad.: The Old Rectory, Wetheringsett-cum-Brockford, Stowmarket, Suffolk IP14 5PP.

BENZIMRA, Maurice; b. Gibraltar, Feb. 21, 1928; Form. Sec., Spanish and Portuguese Jews. Cong., London. Ad.: 119 Poynter House, St. Anne's Rd., W11 4TB. ☎ 020-8603 3255.

BERCOW, John, B.A., M.P.; b. Edgware, Jan. 19, 1963; Public Affairs Consultant; M.P. for Buckingham; Lambeth Councillor (1986-90); Special Adviser to Treasury Ministers (1995), to National Heritage Secretary (1995-96). Ad.:

House of Commons, SW1A 0AA. ☎ 020-7219 3000.

BERENBLUM, Isaac, M.D., M.Sc.; b. Bialystok, Poland, Aug. 26, 1903; Emer. Prof, form. Jack Cotton Prof and Hd. of Dept. of Experimental Biology Weizmann Instit., Rehovot (1950-71); form. Pathologist at Dunn Sch. of Path., Oxford Univ., in charge of Oxford Univ. Research Centre of British Empire Cancer Campaign; Res. Fel., Cancer Dept., Leeds Sch. of Medicine; Beit Memorial Res. Fel., Oxford Univ., Israel Prize for Biology, 1974; Alfred P. Sloan Award & Gold Medal, Gen. Motors Cancer Res. Foundation, Washington D.C. (1980), etc.; Member, Israel Academy of Sciences and Humanities. Publ.: Man Against Cancer, Cancer Research Today, etc. Ad.: 3 Kossover Street, Rehovot 76408, Israel. ☎ 08-9473788

van den BERGH, Rabbi Martin, B.Ed.; b. Hilversum, Holland, Dec. 2, 1952; M. Wembley Synagogue; Senior Hospital Chaplain Visitation Cttee (1995-); Hon. Sec. Rabbinical Council of the U.S.; Memb. Chief Rabbi's Cabinet; form. M., Withington Cong., Span. & Port. Jews, Manchester; Tr., S. Manch. Teenage Centre; Chairman Manchester Jewish Visitation Board, (1990-94); Asst. M., Withington Cong. (1974-77), Sheffield United Hebrew Cong. (1977-78) Fdr. Chairman & H. President, Span. & Port. Cong., Israel (1981-83). Ad.: Wembley Synagogue, Forty Lane, Wembley HA9 8JW. ☎ 020-8904 7407.

BERKOVITCH, Rev. Mordechai, B.A. (Ed.), Dip. Counselling, F.I.B.A.; b. Sunderland, Feb. 15, 1934; Dir., Jewish Studies, Carmel Coll. (1984-92); H. Vis. M., Nightingale House (Home for Aged Jews); M., Kingston, Surbiton & Distr. Syn. (1972-84); Hon. Dir. Welfare Chief Rabbi's Cabinet (1980-1985), Penylan Syn., Cardiff (1968-72), Central Syn., Birmingham (1956-68). Ad.: 2/2 Harosmarin, Gilo, Jerusalem 93758. ☎ 026764 341. Fax 026768 169.

BERKOVITS, Rabbi Berel, LL.B.; b. London, June 3, 1949; (1990-); Dayan of Federation of Synagogues, form. Registrar Lond. Beth Din; Lect., Law Dept., Buckingham Univ. (1977-83). Publ.: Commentary of Ramban on Torah, Vols. 2-4 (Edr. & Translator), Talmud Torah, Oxford Dictionary of Law (Contrib.). Pesach in the Modern Home. Ad.: 65 Watford Way, NW4 3AQ. ☎ 020-8202 2263.

BINSTOCK, Dayan Ivan Alan, B.Sc.; b. London, Oct. 27, 1950; Dayan London Beth Din; Rabbi, St. Johns Wood Syn. (1996-); form. Rabbi, Golders Green Syn.; Princ. North West London Jewish Day School; M. New Syn. (1978-80), Finsbury Pk Syn. (1974-78), R. South-east London Distr. Syn. (1972-74). Ad.: 2 Vale Close, Maida Vale, London W9 1RR. ☎/Fax 020-7289 6229.

BIRAN, Mrs. Jane, J.P., B.A., M.I.P.M. (née Dillon); b. Lond., Sept. 10, 1938, m. Yoav Biran; Dep. Dir, Overseas Dev. Dept., Dir. U.K. Desk Jerusalem Fd.; form. Dir., Bipac; form. Edr., Zionist Year Book; V. President, Brit. Na'amat; Publ.: Anglo-Jewry An Analysis; Effectiveness of Fringe Benefits in Industry, The Violent Society (contrib.). Ad.: The Jerusalem Foundation, 11 Rivka St., Jerusalem 91012. ☎ 02 675 1706.

BIRK, Ellis Samuel, B.A. (Cantab); b. Newcastle upon Tyne, Oct. 30, 1915; Solicitor; V.P. Jewish Care; V. President, Central C. Jewish Communal Services; Gov., Hebrew Univ., Exec., Frs. of Hebrew Univ; Member C., IJPR; Jt. President, Redbridge Jewish Youth and Com. Centre. Ad.: Flat 1, 34 Bryanston Sq., London W1H 7LQ. ☎ 020-7402 4532.

BLACK, Gerald David, L.L.B., Ph.D; b. Montreal, Jan 9, 1928; m. Anita, née Abrahams; Chairman Balfour Society for Children (1964-); Member of Council of Jewish Historical Society (1992-), President (1998-); Tr. of London Museum of Jewish Life and Jewish Museum (1983-). Publ.: Lender to the Lords, Giver to the Poor (1992); Living up West: Jewish Life in London's West End (1994); JFS: The History of the Jews' Free School (1997). Ad.: 54 St. Johns Ct., Finchley Rd., London NW3 6LF. ☎ 020-7624 8320. Fax 020-7372 9015. Email: jhse@dircon.co.uk

BLASHKI, Arnold Roy, O.B.E., A.M.M., B.A., LL.B. (Melb.); b. St. Kilda, May 26

1918; Barrister-at-Law, State P. and Nat. President, Australian Legion of Ex-Servicemen; form. H. Sec., Victorian Jewish BoD, H. Sec. Victorian Branch AJA; President, Mt. Scopus Coll. Assn.; form T. Australian Legion of Ex-Service Men and Women; form. H. Sec., Exec. C. of Australian Jewry; Fed P, Victorian Jew Ex-Service Assn.; Chairman Australian Veterans and Services Assoc. (Victims). Ad.: 44A Clendon Rd., Toorak, Vic. 3181. ☎ 03 98221694.

BLOM-COOPER, Sir Louis, Q.C., Dr. Jur. (Amsterdam), LL.B. (Lond.); Hon. D. Litt. (Loughborough), H.D. Litt. (Ulster); b. London, March 27, 1926; Judge, Courts of Appeal, Jersey & Guernsey (1989-96); Chairman, Mental Health Act Commission (1987-94); Independent Commissioner for the Holding Centres (NI) (1993-99); National Chairman Victim Support (1994-). Ad.: 2 Ripplevale Grove, London Nl 1HU. ☎ 020-7607 8045

BLUE, Rabbi Lionel, O.B.E., B.A., M.A. (Oxon.); b. London, Feb. 6, 1930; Lect., Leo Baeck Coll., form. Convener Beth Din, RSGB; V.-Chairman, Standing Conference Jews, Christians, Moslems in Europe, form. Rel. Dir. (Europe) World Union for Progressive Judaism; Chairman Assembly of Rabbis RSGB, M., St George's Settlement Syn., Middlesex New Syn. Templeton Prize 1993. Publ.: Funeral Service, Forms of Prayer, Vol. I Daily and Sabbath Prayer Book (co-ed.); Vol. III, Days of Awe Prayer Book (co-ed.); Vol.II Shavuoth, Passover & Succoth (co-ed.), To Heaven with Scribes and Pharisees; Bright Blue, A Backdoor to Heaven; Kitchen Blues, Bolts from the Blue, Blue Heaven; The Blue Guide to the Here and Hereafter (co-auth), Blue Horizons; Bedside Manna. How to get up when life gets you down (co-auth.); Tales of body and soul; My affair with Christianity. Ad: c/o Leo Baeck College, Sternberg Centre, 80 East End Rd., London N3 2SY.

BLUMENFELD, Jeffery, B.A. (Hons.); b. London, Dec. 1949; Director, Jewish Marriage C.; Chairman Chief Rabbi's Steering Group on Social and Moral Education (1994-); Act-Chairman JMC Legal Group (1993-); form. Dir. US Youth & Com Services Dept.; Edr., Resources Bulletin, Sch. Assemblies C. (1978-80). Ad.: 23 Ravenshurst Ave., NW4 4EE. ☎ 020-8203 6311. Fax 020-8203 8727.

BLUMENFELD, Simon; b. London, Nov. 25, 1907; author and journalist. Publ.: Jew Boy, Phineas Kahn, Doctor of the Lost, etc. Ad.

BONDI, Sir Hermann, K.C.B., M.A., F.R.S.; b. Vienna Nov. 1, 1919; Master, Churchill Coll., Cambridge (1983-90); Chairman, Natural Environment Res. C. (1980-84), Chief Scientist Dept of Energy (1977-80); Chief Scientific Adv., Min. of Defence (1971-77); form Dir.-Gen. European Space Research Org.; Prof. of Applied Maths, King's Coll., Lond. Univ., form. Chairman, Nat. Cttee for Astronomy; form. Sec., Royal Astronomical Soc., (1956-64); President, I.M.A. (1974-75), President, Brit Humanist Assn. (since 1982); G. D. Birla International Award for Humanism, New Delhi, 1990. Publ.: Scientific works, Science Churchill and Me (autobiography). Ad.: Churchill College, Cambridge CB3 0DS.

BOTEACH, Rabbi Shmuel, b. Miami, Nov. 19, 1966; Rabbi and Director of Oxford, Cambridge and London L'Chaim Societies. Publ.: Dreams (1991); Moses of Oxford: A Jewish Vision of a University and Its Life (1994); The Wolf Shall Lie with the Lamb (1993); Why Me - The Good God and the People Who Suffer (1994); Wrestling with the Divine: a Jewish Response to Suffering (1995); The Jewish Guide to Adultery: How to turn your marriage into an illicit affair (1995), Wisdom, Knowledge and Understanding (1996), Kosher sex (1998), An Intelligent Persons Guide to Judaism (1999), Dating Secrets of the Ten Commandments (1999). Ad.: London L'Chaim Society, Britannia Business Centre, Cricklewood Lane, London NW2 1EZ. ☎ 020-8830 5533. Fax 020-8830 5530.

BOWER, Marcus H., M.A., LL.M. (Cantab.); b. Belfast, Aug. 22, 1918; Barrister; Chairman, Leo Baeck College (1992-96); V. Chairman, European Board of

World Union for Progressive Judaism (1990-96); Chairman RSGB (1987-90); form. Dir., Northern Engineering Industries plc.; Dir., Port of Tyne Auth. Chairman, Northern Counties Inst. of Dirs., Mem. Gov. Body, Newcastle Univ.; Mem. BBC Regional Adv. Council; Ad.: 14 Camelot Cl., SW19 7EA. ☎ 020-8947 5173.

BRAYNIS, Mrs Vera (née Krichefski), M.B.E.; b. Jersey; past Exec. Dir., Children & Youth Aliyah for Gt. Britain; Fdr. and H. President Assn. of Jewish Women's Orgs.: President, League of Jewish Women (1964-67), V. President Intern. C. of Jewish Women (1969-74) and 1st European Chairman. Chief Rabbi's Award for Contribution to Society 1995. Ad: 16 Heathside, Finchley Rd., NW11 7SB.

BRICHTO, Rabbi Sidney, M.A., D.D.; b. Philadelphia, July 21, 1936; Dir.: Joseph Levy Charitable Foundation; Sr. V. President ULPS, Chairman Adv. Com. Israel Diaspora Tr; Bd. Dir. IJPR; Vis. Lect. and Gov. Oxford Centre for Hebrew & Jewish Studies; Hon. Sec. European J. Publ. Soc.; form. Exec. V. President & Dir. ULPS (1964-89); form. Chairman, C. of Ref. and Lib. Rabbis; M., Lib. Jewish Syn. (1961-64). Ad.: The Joseph Levy Charitable Foundation, 37/43 Sackville St., London W1X 2DL. ☎ 020-7333 8111. Fax 020-7333 0660.

BRICKMAN, Rev. Stanley Ivan, b. London, March 29, 1939; Cantor, Hampstead Synagogue (1987-); Chairman Assn. of Ministers (Chazanim); London Regional V. President, Cantorial Council of America (1994-); Cantor: Gt. Synagogue, Sheffield (1960-65); Ilford Synagogue (1966-69); New London Synagogue (1969-71); Singers Hill Synagogue, Birmingham (1971-83); Great Synagogue, Cape Town (1983-86); Publ.: Friday evening service with Zemirot for children (Birmingham 1976); Recording; Synagogue Liturgy Music with Singers Hill Choir, 1981. Ad.: 9 Marlborough Mans., Cannon Hill, Hampstead, London NW6 1JP. ☎ 020-7431 0575.

BRIER, Norma, BA(Hons), MSc, CQSW; b. London, Dec. 23, 1949; Exec. Dir. (Services) Norwood Ravenswood (1996-); Exec. Dir. Ravenswood Foundation (1989-96); Dir. of Com. Services – Ravenswood and Jewish Society for Mental Handicap (1985); Lect. in Soc. and Soc. Work/Counselling (Harrow College) (1982); Psychiatric Soc. Worker (1972); Soc. Worker (Camden) (1968). Ad.: Norwood Ravenswood, Broadway House, 80-82 The Broadway, Stanmore, Middx HA7 4HB. ☎ 020-8954 4555. Fax 020-8420 6800.

BRIER, Sam, M.A.; b. London, July 19, 1946; Chief Exec., KIDS; form. Exec. Dir. (Resources), Norwood Ravenswood. Ad.: KIDS, 80 Waynflete Square, London W10 6UD. ☎ 020-8969 2817. Fax 020-8969 4550.

BRITTAN, Rt. Hon. Sir Leon, P.C., Q.C., MA (Cantab), Hon. D.C.L., Newcastle, Durham, Hon. LL.D., Hull, Edinburgh, Bradford, Bath, D.Econ., Korea; b. London, Sept. 25, 1939; Vice-President Commissioner of the European Communities (1989-); Called to Bar, Inner Temple (1962); Conservative candidate for North Kensington in the Gen. Elections (1966 & 1970); MP (Con) for Cleveland and Whitby (1974-83); MP (Con) for Richmond, North Yorkshire (1983-88); Vice-Chairman, Employment Cttee. of Parl. Conservative Party (1974-76); Opposition Spokesman on Devolution and House of Commons Affairs (1976-78); Opposition Spokesman on Devolution and Employment (1978-79); Minister of State, Home Office (1979-81); Chief Sec. to the T. (1981-83); Home Sec. (1983-85); Sec. of State for Trade and Industry (1985-86); Chairman, Cambridge Univ. Conservative Assn. (1960); President, Cambridge Union (1960); Debating tour of USA for Cambridge Union (1961); Chairman, Bow Group (1964-65); Editor of Crossbow (1966-67); Member, Cttee. of the Brit. Atlantic Group of Young Politicians (1970-78); Vice-Chairman, Nat. Assn. of School Governors and Managers (1970-78); Chairman, Soc. of Conservative Lawyers (1986-89); Distinguished Visiting Fellow at Policy Studies Instit. (1988)'; Bencher of the Inner Temple (1983); Publ.: The Conservative Opportunity (contributions), Millstones for the Sixties (jointly), Rough Justice, Infancy and the Law, How to Save your Schools, A New Deal for

WHO'S WHO 221

Health Care (1988), Defence and Arms Control in a Changing Era (1988), Europe: Our Sort of Community (1989 Granada Guildhall Lecture), Discussions on Policy (1989), Monetary Union: the issues and the impact (1989), Hersch Lauterpacht Memorial Lectures, University of Cambridge (1990), European Competition Policy (1992), Europe: the Europe we need (1994), The 1997 Rede Lecture. Ad.: Commission des Communautés Européens, rue de la Loi 200, 1049 Brussels, Belgium.

BROCH, Mrs. Hazel (née Rubinstein); b. Dublin, Jan. 29, 1936; H. Life V. President (form. P.) Leeds Jewish Rep. C.; H.V. President, Tzfia Goren Emunah; Fdr. Chairman, Leeds Ladies Com. Chevra Kadisha (Chairman 1996/7); H.L.P. Yorkshire and Humberside Chaplaincy Board; Northern Jewish woman of the year 1989. Ad.: 48/8 Shlomo Hamelach, Netanya 42268. ☎ (09) 8342653.

BRODER, Rabbi Gavin, BA (Hons), MA (Lond.); b. Uitenhage, South Africa, April 17, 1963; Chief Rabbi of Ireland (1996-); Form. Newbury Park Syn. (1990-96), Staines Hebrew Cong. (1988-90); Governor Avigdor Primary School. Ad.: Herzog House, 1 Zion Rd., Rathgar, Dublin 6. ☎ 4923751. Fax 4924680.

BRODIE, Rev. Gabriel, b. Bratislava, July 7, 1924; M., Manchester Great & New Syn.; Sec. Manch. Yeshiva; Chairman Jerusalem Academy Study Gps.; Hon Chaplain Jewish Meals on Wheels, 45 Aid Society. Ad.: 43 Stanley Rd., Salford M7 4FR. ☎ 061-740 2506.

BRODIE, Jeffrey, B.A. (Hons.); b. Manchester, Oct. 3, 1950; Admin., Manch Kashrus Authority; Registrar, Manch. Beth Din; Tr., Keren L'David Educ. Tr. Ad.: 56 Stanley Rd., Salford, 7.

BROOKES, Kenneth Joseph Alban, Eur.Ing., B.Sc. (Eng.) Met., C. Eng., F.I.M. F.C.I.J.; b. London, Aug. 5, 1928; Technical Consultant, Author & Journalist; Past-P., Chartered Inst. of Journalists; Chairman CIofJ Int. Division; Vice Chairman, CI of J, Freelance Div.; News Edr., Internat. Journal of Refractory Metals and Hard Materials. Consultant Edr., Metalworking Production; Consultant Edr., Metal Powder Report; UK Edr., Metal Times. Publ.: World Directory and Handbook of Hardmetals and other Hard Materials etc. Ad.: 33 Oakhurst Ave., East Barnet, Herts. EN4 8DN. ☎ 020-8368 4997. Fax 020-8368 4997.

BROWN, Malcolm Denis, M.A.; b. Fulwood, March 24, 1936; m. Barbara née Langford; Research historian; Chairman, Exec. Cttee and V. President JHSE (1999-), President (1996-98); form. Asst. Keeper of Manuscripts, British Museum; Archivist, Anglo-Jewish Archives (1965-66); Asst. ed. Jnl of Warburg and Courtauld Insts (1962-64); Lect. Extra-Mural Dept., Univ. of London (1969-81). Publ.: David Salomons House: Catalogues of Mementoes, Commemorative Medals and Ballooniana (1968, 1969 and 1970). Ad.: c/o The Jewish Historical Society of England, 33 Seymour Place, London W1H 5AP. ☎ 020-7723 5852. Email: jhse@dircon.co.uk

BROWN, Rabbi Dr. Solomon, O.B.E., B.A., Ph.D., H.C.F.; b. London, 1921; Sr M., (Ret.) United Heb Cong., Leeds, M., Hornsey and Wood Green Syn. (1943-47); HM, Redmans Rd. Talmud Torah (1942-47); Sr Jewish Chaplain in Germany, Austria and Trieste (1947-50). Publ.: Waters of Life. Ad.: 21 Sandhill Dr., Leeds LS17 8DU. ☎ 0113 2685320

BULL, John, Cllr., J.P.; D.L., Commandeur de l'Ordre National du Mérite; b. London, Nov. 8, 1927, m. Helen née Baran; Antique Dealer; Lord Mayor, City of Westminster (1984-85); V. President, Chairman, Trades Adv. C.; V. President, North London C.F.I. (1976); B.o.D; Freeman, City of London; Fel., Instit. Dirs.; Gen. C. of Income Tax (1976). Ad.: 85 Mayflower Lodge, Regent's Park Rd., N3 3HX; ☎ 020-8346 6657.

BURMAN, Michael Alfred, B.Sc. (Hons), P.G.C.E., F.R.G.S.; b. Southport Sept. 20, 1944; m. Barbara née Schiltzer; Admin. Dir. ULPS; Chair Gov. Clore Shalom School; Gov. Akiva School; Educ. Consultant, Progressive Jewish Day Schools;

OFSTED Inspector; Memb. Jewish Community Schools Adv. Board. Ad: The Montagu Centre, 21 Maple Street, London W1P 6DS. ☎ 020-7580 1663. Fax 020-7436 4184. Email: m.burman@ulps.org

BURMAN, Rickie Amanda, M.A. (Cantab), M.Phil.; b, Liverpool, July 5, 1955, m. Daniel Miller; Director, Jewish Museum (1995-); Curator London Museum of Jewish Life (1984-95); Res. Fell. in Jewish History; Manchester Polytechnic (1979-84); Museum Co-ord., Manchester Jewish Museum (1981-84). Publ. on history of Jewish women in England, and museum studies. Ad.: The Jewish Museum, Raymond Burton House, 129-131 Albert St., London NW1 7NB. ☎ 020-7284 1997. Fax 020-7267-9008.

BURTON, Raymond Montague, C.B.E., M.A. (Cantab.), F.R.S.A.; b. Leeds, 1917; P. Burton Group, p.l.c. (1978-84), V. President Jewish Museum; V. President, Weizmann Instit Foundation; C., C.C.J.; Master Worshipful Comp. of Loriners (1976); Major, R.A. (1945). Ad.: c/o Trustee Management Ltd., 27 East Parade, Leeds, LS1 5SX.

CALLMAN, His Honour, Judge Clive Vernon, B.Sc. (Econ.); b. June 21, 1927; Circuit Judge, South-Eastern Circuit (1973-), Dep. High Court Judge, Royal Courts of Justice (1975-); Dep. Circuit Judge (1971-73); Senator, London Univ. (1978-94), Gov. Council (1994-); Member Careers Adv. Bd. (1979-92), Gov., Birkbeck Coll. (1982-); Gov. L.S.E. (1990-), C., AJA (1956); BoD (1998-); Gov. Hebrew Univ. of Jerusalem (since 1992); Court City Univ. (1991-), C., West London Syn. (1981-87); Member, Adv. Cttee. for Magistrates' Courses (1979-); Edr. Bd., Media Law & Practice (1980-95); Professional Negligence (1985); Journal of Child Law (1988-94), Child and Family Law Q. (1995-); Exec., Soc. of Labour Lawyers (1958), Chairman, St Marylebone Lab. Party (1960-62). Ad.: 11 Constable Close, NW11 6UA. ☎ 020-8458 3010.

CANNON, Raymond; b. London. Nov. 13, 1933; Solicitor; First Chairman, US Educ. Bd.; form. Chairman, Govs., J.F.S. Comprehensive Sch.; form. T., US Burial Soc.; V.Chairman, Lond. Bd. Jew Rel. Educ., Foundation Chairman, Govs. Michael Sobell Sinai Sch., Chairman, Govs. Solomon Wolfson Jewish Sch; Gov., Ilford Primary Sch. Ad.: 2 Harewood Pl., Hanover Sq. W1R 9HB. ☎ 020-7629 7991. Fax 020-7499 6792.

CANSINO, H. Manuel, M.B.E.; b. Manchester, July 12, 1914; V. President, London Bd. of Shechita; V. P. Bd. Elders, Span. and Port. Cong.; C. AJA, C., Jewish Lads' & Girls' Brigade; C., Adv. Cttee., Jew Eccl. Officers; C., Jew Autistic Soc. Ad.: 117a Hamilton Terr., NW8 9QU. ☎ 020-7624 5050.

CAPLAN, Leonard, Q.C.; b. Merthyr Tydfil, June 28, 1909; Master of Bench, Gray's Inn; T., Gray's Inn (1979); Member, Senate of Inns of Court and Bar (1976-82); Sometime Dep. High Court Judge, President, Medico-Legal Soc. (1979-81); Chairman, Coll Hall (Univ. of London) (1956-67); C., AJA; form. Chairman, Mental Health Review Tribunal, S.E. Region. Publ.: The Great Experiment. Ad.: 1 Pump Court, Temple, E.C.4. ☎ 020-7353 9332.

CAPLAN, The Hon. Lord (Philip Isaac), Q.C., L.L.D. (Hon.) (Glasgow), F.R.P.S., A.F.I.A.P.; b. Glasgow, Feb. 24, 1929, m. Joyce née Stone; Senator of the College of Justice, Scotland (1989); Sheriff Princ., North Strathclyde (1983-1989); Member, Sheriff Courts Rules C. (1983-1989) Memb. Advi. Coun. on Messengers-At-Arms, and Sheriff Officers (1987-88); Com., Northern Lighthouse Bd. (1983-1989); Hon. V. President, Scottish Assn. for Study of Delinquency; Hon. President, Family Mediation Scotland (1994-); Sheriff, Lothian & Borders, Edinburgh (1979-83); V. President, Sheriffs' Assn. (1982-83); Chairman, Plant Variety & Seeds Tribunal (Scotland) (1978-79). Chairman James Powell, U.K. Trust, (1992-); Gov. UK College of Family Mediators (1996). Ad.: Court of Session, Parliament House, Edinburgh.

CAPLAN, Simon, M.A. (Oxon.), P.G.C.E.; b. Hamburg (Brit. Army Hospital), Apr. 28, 1955; Community Consultant; Jerusalem Fellow (1990-93); Dir., Jews' Coll., London 1985-90; Dir., Jewish Educ. Development Tr. 1985-90. Ad.:

Rehov Zeev Bacher 10/9, Jerusalem 93119.

CAPLIN, Ivor Keith, M.P.; b. Brighton, Nov. 8, 1958, m. Maureen née Whelan; M.P. for Hove & Portslade (1997-); PPS (1998); Leader, Hove B.C. (1995-97); Dep. Leader Brighton & Hove UA (1996-98). Ad.: House of Commons, SW1 1AA. ☎ 020-7219 2146, or 01273 292933 (constituency).

CAPLIN, Maxwell, O.B.E., F.R.C.P.; b. Lond., Feb. 6, 1917, m. Nancy née Leverson; Ret. Consultant Physician; Lond Chest Hospital (1983); Consultant in Occupational Health, Royal Brompton Nat. Heart and Lung Hospitals and Nat. Heart & Lung Instit. (1983-1991); Honorary Senior Lecturer, Univ. of Lond. (1979-83); Consultant Member Lond. Medical Appeal Tribunal (1977-89); Medical Referee Dept. of Health (1979-90); Chairman Lond. N E Cttee. for Employment of Disabled People (1980-86); Patron, form. Chairman, later President, Greater Lond. Assn. of Disabled People (1982-89). Other professional and vol. offices. Publs: Medical Writings. Ad: 498 Finchley Rd, NW11 8DE. ☎ 020-8455 3314.

CARLEBACH, Rabbi Felix F., M.A.; b. Lübeck, Apr. 15, 1911; form. M., S. Manchester Syn, (1946-86); Dep. to HM, Jew Secondary Sch, Leipzig (1933-39); Asst. M. Adass Yisroel Syn., Hendon (1939-41); M.& H.M., Palmers Green and Southgate Syn. (1941-46). Ad: 2A Elm Rd., Manchester, 20. ☎ 0161-445 5716.

CARLOWE, Melvyn, B.Soc. Sci.; b. Abingdon Oxon., Apr. 13, 1941; Chief Exec. Jewish Care, form. Exec. Dir. JWB (1972-89) Hon. Sec. Central C. for Jewish Soc. Service (1972-); Tr. Third Sector Trust (L.S.E.); Hon. Vice President, World Conf. of Jewish Com. Services; Exec. N. Lond. Hospice Group; Member London & Quadrant Honorary Cttee, N.E. Thames; Tr. Nat.C. of Voluntary Orgs. Ad.: 221 Golders Green Rd., NW11 9DQ. ☎ 020-8922 2000. Fax 020-8922 1998.

CARTER, Emmanuel, B.Com., F.C.C.A., F.T.I.I., F.C.I.T.; b. London, May 18 1925; Elder US form. V. President, US; Exec., Chief Rabbinate C., Dir. US Trs. Ltd. Fel., Chartered Assn.; Certified Accts., form. Lect., Accounting. Lond. Sch of Econ. Ad.: 37 Deansway, N2 ONF. ☎ 020-8883 7759. Fax 020-7281 2166 (BARWIN).

CASS, Frank, b. London, July 11, 1930, m. Audrey née Steele; Publisher; Chairman, Vallentine Mitchell; Chairman, Frank Cass & Co. Ltd.; Chairman of British Jerusalem Book Fair Committee (1979-); Friends of Jerusalem Award (1989). Ad.: Newbury House, 890–900 Eastern Avenue, Newbury Park, Ilford, Essex IG2 7HH. ☎ 020-8599 8866. Fax 020-8599 0984.

CESARANI, David, D.Phil.; b. London, Nov. 13, 1956; Dr., Inst. of Contemporary History and Wiener Library (1993-95, 1996-); Parkes-Wiener Prof. of 20th Century Jewish History and Culture, University of Southampton (1996-); Alliance Prof. of Modern J. Studies, Univ. Manchester (1995-96); Montague Burton Fel. in Jewish Studies, Univ. of Leeds, (1983-86); Barnett Shine Senior Res. Fel., Queen Mary College, Univ. of London, (1986-89). Publ.: ed. Making of Modern Anglo-Jewry (1990); Justice Delayed (1992); co-ed. The Internment of Aliens in Twentieth Century Britain (1993); ed. The Final Solution (1994); The Jewish Chronicle and Anglo Jewry, 1841-1991 (1994); co-ed. Citizenship, Nationality and Migration in Europe (1996); ed. 'Lest We Forget', CD-ROM Interactive History of the Holocaust; ed. Genocide and Rescue: the Holocaust in Hungary 1944 (1997); Arthur Koestler: the homeless mind (1998). Ad.: Institute of Contemporary History, 4 Devonshire St., London W1N 2BH.

CHARING, Rabbi Douglas Stephen; b. London, Nov. 16, 1945; Dir., Jewish Educ. Bureau, Leeds; Tutor, Geneva Theological Coll., Adv., Theol. & Rel. Studies Bd., Dir. Concord MultiFaith/Multi-Cultural Res. Centre (Leeds), Inter-Euro. Com. on Church & Sch, form. Gov. Centre for Study of Rel. & Educ. (Salford); M., Sinai Syn., Leeds; C. for Nat. Academic Awards; Lect., Leeds Univ., Manchester Police Coll. Member Brd. of Dir. British Friends of the Anne Frank Centre; Exec.

M. Coun. for Religious Freedom; Publ.: Glimpses of Jewish Leeds; Comparative Religions (co-auth.), The Jewish World Visiting a Synagogue, Modern Judaism (audio-visual), Jewish Contrib., The Junior R.E. Handbook, World Faiths in Education, Praying Their Faith (contributor), Religion in Leeds (contributor), A Dictionary of Religious Education In the Beginning (Audiovisual), etc. Ad.: 8 Westcombe Ave., Leeds LS8 2BS. ☎ 0870 787 1876. Fax 0870 787 1875. Email ravdouglascharing@easicom.com

CHERNETT, Jaclyn, A.L.C.M.; b. St. Neots, June 6, 1941; m. Brian Chernett; Dir. Masorti Assoc. (1984-86); Co-chairman, Assembly of Masorti Synagogues (1992-95); Co-Chairman Edgware Masorti Synagogue (1984-92); Hon. Life President, Edgware Masorti Synagogue; V. President, World Council of Synagogues. Publ.: Conference papers, Work in progress on research in the musical development of Biblical cantillation. Ad.: 4 Brockley Close, Stanmore, Middx. HA7 4QL. ☎ 020-8958 5090. Fax 020-8958 7651.

CHEYETTE, Bryan, Ph.D.; b. Leicester, Jan. 15, 1959; m. Susan Cooklin; Prof. Twentieth Century Literature, Univ. Southampton (1999-); form. Reader in English Literature, School of English and Drama, Queen Mary and Westfield College, University of London (1992-99); British Academy Postdoctoral Fellow, School of English, University of Leeds (1989-92); Montague Burton Fellow in Jewish Studies, School of English, University of Leeds (1986-89); editorial board, Jewish Quarterly and Patterns of Prejudice. Publ. Constructions of 'the Jew' in English Literature and Society: Racial Representations, 1875-1945 (1993); (editor), Between 'Race' and Culture: Representations of 'the Jew' in English and American Literature (1996); (editor), H.G. Wells, 'Tono-Bungay' (1997); published widely on British-Jewish Literature. Ad.: Dept of English, Univ. Southampton, Highfield, Southampton SO17 1BJ. ☎ 01703-593409. Fax 01703-592859.

CHINN, Rosser, b. Penrhiwceiber, Wales, May 10, 1906; H. President, JNF for Gt. Britain and Ireland; H. President, Z.F. Ad.: 17 Connaught Pl., W2 2EL. ☎ 020-7705 1212.

CHINN, Sir Trevor, C.V.O.; b. London, July 24, 1935; Chairman, Lex Service PLC; P., UJIA; President Norwood Ravenswood; V.Pres., Jewish Assoc. for Business Ethics; Hon.V. President RSGB; Hon.V. President, Z. Fed.; Dep. Ch., Royal Academy Trust; Tr., Community Security Tr. Ad.: 17 Connaught Pl., London W2 2EL. ☎ 020-7705 1212.

CLINTON-DAVIS, Baron of Hackney (Life Peer), **(Stanley Clinton Clinton-Davis),** P.C., LL.B.; b. London, Dec. 6, 1928; Solicitor; Min. State for Trade (1997-98); Pres. British Airline Pilots' Assoc. (BALPA); J.Pres. of Society of Labour Lawyers; V.Pres. of Chartered Institute of Environmental Health; V.Chairman of the Parliamentary Environment Group; Mem. of the B. of Vice Presidents of The Society for International Trade; Hon. Mem. of The London Criminal Courts Solicitors' Assoc.; H. Fel. of The Chartered Institution of Water and Environmental Management; Opposition Spokesman on Transport and Dep. Opp. Spokesman on Trade & Industry and Spokesman on Foreign Affairs, H. of Lords (1990-97); Member Com. of European Communities (Transport, Environment, Nuclear Safety) (1985-89); Chairman Adv. Cttee. on Protection of the Sea (ACOPS), Consultat. S J Berwin & Co.; M.P. (Lab.), Hackney Central (1970-83); Parl. Under Sec. for Companies, Aviation and Shipping, Dept. of Trade (1974-79); Opposition Spokesman for Trade (1979-81); Dep. Opposition Spokesman for Foreign Affairs (1981-83); Vice-President, Labour Fin. & Industry Cttee.; V. President, Poale Zion; form. B.oD.; Cllr., Hackney Bor (1959-71), Mayor (1968-69); President, Association of the Metropolitan Authorities (1992); President, UK Pilots (Marine) (1991-98); Honorary Member of the Council of Justice (1989-); President, Hackney Multiple Sclerosis Soc.; President, Refugee C.; Tr. Bernt Carlsson Tr.; President of the Panel of Judges of the UNEP-Sasakawa Environmental Prize; Order of Leopold 11 for Services to

EC, 1990; Fel. of Queen Mary and Westfield College and King's College, London Univ.; Honorary Doctorate, Polytechnical Univ. of Bucharest (1993); Fel. of the Royal Society of Arts (1993); Publ., Good Neighbours? Nicaragua, Central America and the United States (jt. auth.). Ad.: House of Lords, London SW1A 1AA. ☎ 020-7533 2222. Fax 020-7533 2000.

COCKS, Lady Valerie (née Davis); b. London, July 10, 1932; Dir., Labour Friends of Israel and Trade Union Friends of Israel (1978-88); Chairman Parliamentary Wives for Soviet Jewry; Hon. Sec. All-Party Friends of Israel Group (H of Lords). Ad.: 162 South Block, County Hall, London SE1 7GE. ☎ 020-7928 4656.

COFNAS, Rabbi Jerachmiel; b. Poland, 1915; M., New Syn., Birmingham, Exec., Initiation Soc., Chairman, Birm. Mikva Cttee. Ad.:

COFNAS, Rabbi Mordechai Leib; b. Birmingham, Dec. 9, 1943; Rabbi, Childwall Syn., Liverpool; Princ. L'pool Yeshiva & Midrasha; Rav, L'pool Kashrut Comm.; form. Sr. M., Cardiff United Syn.; M., Sunderland Hebrew Cong. Ad.: Childwall Synagogue, Dunbabin Rd., Liverpool, L15 6XL. ☎ 0151-722 2079.

COHEN, Arnold Judah, F.C.A., A.T.I.I.; b. London, Dec. 17, 1936; m. Sara née Kaminski; Chartered Accountant; President, Fed. of Synagogues; form. Tr. Fed. of Synagogues. Publ.: An Introduction to Jewish Civil Law (1991). Ad.: 807 Finchley Rd., NW11 8DP.

COHEN, (Bernard) Martin; b. London, Jan. 31, 1933; Administrator, Lobbyist; Chairman, Jewish Defence & Group Relations Cttee., BoD (1991-94); form. Member, United Synagogue Council; Harrow Councillor (1962-68, 1971-80); Chairman, Public Works & Services Cttee. (1971-74); Gen. Sec., Labour Friends of Israel (1972-80); V. Chairman, Jewish Defence & Group Relations Cttee. (1988-91). Ad.: 486 Kenton Road, Kenton, Harrow, Middlesex HA3 9DL. ☎ 020-8204 6300.

COHEN, David Mayer, LL B, CA, MBA; b. Glasgow, April 18, 1949; m. Smadar née Karni; Company Director, Technology Services; Chairman UJIA Bd. (2000-). Ad.: Flat 9, 32 Onslow Square, London SW7 3NS. ☎ 020-7584 9066. Email davidcohen@ps.net

COHEN, Rabbi Isaac, B.A., Ph.D.; b. Llanelli, 1914; Chief Rabbi, Jewish Coms. in Ireland and Ab Beth Din (1958-79) now engaged in research in Talmudic law in Jerusalem; Jt. P. Union of Immigrant Western Rabbis; President, Frs., Hesder Yeshiva, Shiloh, Member of Standing Cttee., Conf of European Rabbis, and Exec. of Israel Assoc. for the Conference; Edr., Irish Jewish Year Book; Rabbi, Edinburgh Hebrew Cong.; M., United Hebrew Cong. Leeds; Harrow & Kenton Cong; and Off. Chaplain to H.M. Forces. Ad.: 1 Epstein St., Kiryat Ha Yovel, Jerusalem, 96664. ☎ 02-6412536.

COHEN, Isaac Norman, M.B.E., B.A., B.Com., B.Sc. (Econ); b. Cardiff, Oct. 30 1924, m. Naomi née Cohen; Tr. Machzike Hadath Comm.; form. Sr. W., Penylan Syn., Cardiff; Member, Chief Rabbinate C.; Gov. Body, Univ. of Wales; form. Chairman, Cardiff JIA Cttee. Ad.: 17 Riverside Drive, 300 Golders Green Rd., London NW11 9PU. ☎ 020-8 381 4305. Fax 020-8381 4302.

COHEN, Rabbi Jeffrey M., B.A., M. Phil., A.J.C., PhD.; b. Manchester, Feb. 19, 1940; M., Stanmore & Canon's Pk. Syn.; Chief Examiner, Mod. Hebrew, Jt. Matric Bd. (1973-1987), Lect., Liturg. Studies, Jews' Coll. (1980-1992), Rabbinical Adv. and Gov., Immanuel College; member, Chief Rabbi's cabinet, Chaplain to Mayor of Harrow (1994-95); Scholar-in-Residence, U.S.A. (1998); form. M. Kenton Syn.; Sr. M., Newton Mearns Syn., Glasgow; Lect. in Hebrew, Glasg. Univ., Princ. Glasg. Heb Coll., Dir. Glasg. Bd. of Jewish Educ.; Dir., Jew Educ., King David Schs., Manchester; Member, Rev. Cttee., Singers Prayer Bk; Publ.: Understanding The Synagogue Service, A Samaritan Chronicle, Festival Adventure, Understanding the High Holyday Services, Yizkor, Horizons of Jewish Prayer, Moments of Insight, Blessed Are You, (Contrib. ed., Judaism section) Penguin Encyclopedia of Religions, Prayer & Penitence, Dear Chief Rabbi (ed.); 1001 Questions on Pesach, Following the Synagogue Service, 1001 Questions and

Answers on Rosh Hashanah and Yom Kippur, Issues of the Day. Ad.: Stanmore & Canon's Pk. Synagogue, London Rd., Stanmore, Middx. HA7 4NS. ☎ 020-8954 2210. Fax 020-8385 7124.

COHEN, Joseph, B.A.; b. London Oct. 1, 1920; Exec. Dir., Brit. Technion Soc. (1957-1986); Chairman Friends of Bikur Cholim Hospital, Jerusalem. Ad.: 10 Leeside Cres., NW11 0DB. ☎ 020-8455 0738.

COHEN, Laurence Jonathan, M.A., D.Litt., F.B.A.; b. London, May 7, 1923; m. Gillian née Slee; Emeritus Fel., form. Fel, and Sr Tutor, Queen's Coll., Oxford; form. Brit. Academy Reader in Humanities, Oxford; form. Vis. Prof., Columbia, Yale, Northwestern Univs.; form. Vis. Lect., Hebrew Univ.; form. Vis. Fel. Australian Nat. Univ.; form. President, Internat. Union of History and Philos. of Science; Sec. General, Int. Council of Scientific Unions (1993-96); form. President, British Soc for Philos. of Science. Publ: Principles of World Citizenship; Diversity of Meaning; The Implications of Induction; The Probable and the Provable; The Dialogue of Reason; Introduction to the Philosophy of Induction and Probability; An Essay on Belief and Acceptance, etc. Ad.: Queen's Coll., Oxford, OX1 4AW. ☎ 01865 279120.

COHEN, The Hon. Leonard Harold Lionel, O.B.E., M.A. (Oxon.); b. London, Jan. 1, 1922; m. Eleanor née Henriques; Barrister-at-Law; Chairman Jewish Chronicle Trust Ltd.; Bencher of Lincoln's Inn; Fell. Royal Free Hospital School of Medicine (1998-); High Sheriff, Berks. (1987-88); Dir.-Gen. Accepting Houses Cttee. (1976-82); Chairman, Community Trust for Berkshire (1988-94); form. President, JWB (1961-66) and J.C.A. Charitable Foundation (1976-92); form. Master, Skinners Company; form. H. Colonel 39th (City of London) Signals Regiment (Volunteers); Chairman, C., Royal Free Hospital Med. Sch. (1982-92). Ad.: Dovecote House, Swallowfield Pk., Reading, RG7 ITG. ☎ 01189-884775.

COHEN, Marion (née Mendelssohn), B.A. (Hons.), M. Phil.; b. Prestwich, Lancs., May 8, 1945; m. David J. Cohen; Chairman, Jewish Book Council. Chairman, Friends of Hillel Lecture Committee (1988-91); Tr. Jewish Literary Trust; Co-admin. Jewish Quarterly/H H Wingate Literary Awards; Instigator and Admin. Porjes Award for Hebrew-English Translation. Ad.: Jewish Book Council, PO Box 20513, London NW8 6ZS. ☎/Fax 020-7483 2092. Email info@jewish bookweek.org.uk

COHEN, Judge Maxwell, O.C., Q.C. LL.D., D.C.L.; b. Winnipeg, March 17, 1910; Emer. Prof of Law McGill Univ. Sch. in Res., Ottawa Univ.; Judge Ad Hoc, Internat. Court of Justice, The Hague; Chairman Canadian-Jewish Cong.; Canadian Z. Fed. Jt. Cttee. on Mid-East Aff. (1952-66); Chairman, Min. of Justice Special Cttee. on Hate Propaganda (1960-95); Chairman For. Aff. Cttee., C.J.C. (1965-67); Chairman, Cong. Select Cttee. on Canadian Constitution (1980-82), Chairman C.J.C. Cttee. Constitutional and Charter Review (1992-); Canadian Co-Ch. (Canadian/US) Internat. Jt. Com. (1974-79); Dean, Law Faculty, McGill Univ. (1964-69); Dir. Instit. of Air & Space Law McGill Univ. (1962-65). Publ.: The Dominion-Prov. Conference, Law and Politics in Space, The Regime of Boundary Waters - Canadian/US Experience; Lawyers and the Nuclear Debate, articles in acad. and other publ.; various Royal Commissions and Task Force reports. Ad.: 200 Rideau Terr., Apt. 1404, Ottawa, Canada, K1M 0Z3 ☎ 741 5891. Fax (613) 741-4645.

COHEN, Michael, B.A., M.Phil., Cert. Ed.; b. Oxford, Nov. 3, 1941; Educ. Consultant to Broughton Jewish Cassel Fox Primary School (Manchester), American Endowment School (Budapest), Prague Jewish Community; form. Exec. Dir. Bd. of Religious Educ. US; form. HM, Mt. Scopus Coll., Melbourne, Dir., Jewish Studies North-West Lond. Jewish Day Sch; Principal of Leibler Yavneh Coll., Melbourne (1993-95). Ad.: 50 Princes Park Ave., NW11 0JT ☎ 020-8458 4537.

COHEN, Lieut-Colonel Mordaunt, T.D., D.L., F.R.S.A.; b. Sunderland, Aug. 6,

1916; Solicitor Reg. Chairman, Industrial Tribunals (1976-89); Chairman (1974-76); Dep. Lieut., Tyne & Wear; Chairman, Provincial Cttee., BoD (1985-91); H. Dir., Central Enquiry Desk (since 1990), BoD; H. Life President, Sunderland Hebrew Cong. (since 1988); form. Member, Chief Rabbinate C., Tr. Ajex Charitable Tr.; V. President, and Nat. Chairman AJEX (1993-95); Chairman Edgware School (1991-96); H. Life President, Sunderland Ajex; Tr. Colwyn Bay Synagogue Trust, Alderman Sunderland Co. Borough C. (1967-74); Cllr., Tyne & Wear County C. (1973-74), Chairman Sund. Educ. Cttee. (1970-72), Ch. Govs., Sund. Polytechnic (1969-72), Court, Newcastle upon Tyne Univ. (1968-72); Chairman, Mental Health Review Tribunal (1967-76); Dep. Chairman, Northern Traffic Coms. (1972-74), President, Sund. Law Soc. (1970); War service, R.A. (1940-46) (dispatches, Burma campaign), T.A. (1947-55), C.O. 463 (M) HAA Regt. (1954-55); Territorial Decoration (1954). Ad.: 1, Peters Lodge, 2 Stonegrove, Edgware, Middlesex HA8 7TY.

COHEN, Judge Myrella, Q.C., LL.B., H. LLD (Sunderland), FRSA, (Mrs. Mordaunt Cohen); b. Manchester, Dec. 16, 1927; Tr., Jewish Law Publ. Fund; Circuit Judge and Dep. High Court Judge (1972-95); Sr. Judge, Harrow Crown Ct. (1989-95); Dep. President (and Chairman UK branch), Int. Assoc. of Jewish Lawyers and Jurists; Member, Parole Bd. (1983-86); V. President North of England Cancer Research Campaign; L.M. the Council of the League of Jewish Women; Exec. Memb. Jewish Marriage Council; Recorder, Kingston upon Hull (1971); Patron, Life M. Emunah; Past President, & H. Member Sunderland Soroptimist International; Patron: Sunderland Family Conciliation Service; Suzy Lampugh Trust; Sunderland C. for Disabled; North of England Distaff Cttee. Ad.: 1, Peters Lodge, 2 Stonegrove, Edgware, Middlesex HA8 7TY.

COHEN, Mrs Ruth (née Goodman); b. London, July 11, 1936; S.V. Pres. World Union for Progressive Judaism; Chairman European Region of WUPJ; V. Pres. (form. chairman) Reform Synagogues of Great Britain. Ad.: 80 East End Rd., London N3 2SY. ☎ 020-8349 4731. Fax 020-8343 0901. Email shalva43@aol.com

COHEN, Shimon David; b. Cardiff, May 24, 1960; Dir. Andrew Lloyd Webber's office; Non-Exec. Dir. Jewish Chronicle Newspaper Ltd; Dir. IJPR; Exec. Memb. AIA; Tr. Jakobovits Charitable Trust; Mem., Inst. of Public Relations; form. Senior Cons. Lowe Bell Communications (1990-96); form. Exec. Dir. The Office of The Chief Rabbi, (1983-90); Youth Officer, Stanmore Syn. (1981-83); Sec. Nat. Chaplaincy Bd. (1983-90); Jewish Youth Leader of the Year 1979. Ad.: 7 Hertford St., London W1Y 8LP. ☎ 020-7495 4044. Fax 020-7629 1279.

COHEN, Sydney, C.B.E., M.D., Ph.D., F.R.C. Path., F.R.S.; b. Johannesburg, S. Africa, Sept. 18, 1921; Emer. Prof, Chemical Pathology, Guy's Hospital Med. Sch.; H. Consultant, Chemical Patholobst, Guy's Hospital; Chairman, Malaria Immunology Cttee., W.H.O. (1978-83); Med. Res. C. (1974-76); Chairman, Tropical Med. Res. Bd. (1974-76). Publ.: Immunology of Parasitic Infections. Ad.: 4 Frognal Rise, London NW3 6RD.

COHEN, Mrs. Zina (née Masie); b. London; form. Chairman Shechita Cttee., BoD (1986-91); Central Enquiry Desk, BoD. (1981-). Ad.: Central Enquiry Desk, Board of Deputies. ☎ 020-7543 5421/2.

COHN, Norman, M.A. (Oxon.), D.Litt. (Glas.), F.B.A. b. London, Jan. 12, 1915; m. Vera Broido; Prof., Sussex Univ., and Dir., Columbus Centre (1966-80), form. Prof of French, Univ. of Durham. Publ.: The Pursuit of the Millennium, Warrant for Genocide, Europe's Inner Demons, Cosmos, chaos and the world to come, Noah's Flood. Ad.: Orchard Cottage, Wood End, Ardeley, Herts. SG2 7AZ. ☎ 01438 869247.

COHN-SHERBOK, Dan, B.A., B.H.L., M.A., M.Litt., Ph.D.(Cantab), D.D.; b. Denver, Col., Feb. 1, 1945; Prof. Judaism, Univ. Wales (Lampeter) (1997-); Form. Rabbi in synagogues in the USA, England, S. Africa, Australia (1971-75); University Lect. in Theology, Univ. of Kent (1975-); Chairman, Dept. of

Theology, Univ. of Kent (1980-2); Vis. Prof., Univ. of Essex (1993-94); Vis. Prof. Univ. Middlesex (1994-), Lampeter (1994-96). Publ.: The Jews of Canterbury (1984); Exploring Reality (ed.) (1986); On Earth as it is in Heaven; Jews, Christians, and Liberation Theology (1987); The Jewish Heritage (1988); Jewish Petitionary Prayer (1989); Holocaust Theology (1989); Rabbinic Perspectives on the New Testament (1990); Issues in Contemporary Judaism (1990); Islam in a World of Diverse Faiths (ed.) (1990); The Salman Rushdie Controversy in Interreligious Perspective (ed.) (1990); The Canterbury Papers: Religious and Modern Society (ed.) (1990); Tradition and Unity: Essays in Honour of Robert Runcie (ed.) (1991); A Traditional Quest: Essays in Honour of Louis Jacobs (ed.) (1991); Dictionary of Judaism and Christianity (1991); The Blackwell Dictionary of Judaica (1992); Israel: The History of an Idea (1992); The Crucified Jew: Twenty Centuries of Christian Anti-Semitism (1992); Many Mansions: Interfaith and Religious Intolerance (ed.); The Jewish Faith (1993); Not a Job for a Nice Jewish Boy (1993); Atlas of Jewish History (1993); Judaism and other Faiths (1994); The Future of Judaism (1994); Jewish and Christian Mysticism (1995); Beyond Death (ed.) (1995); A Short History of Judaism (1995); Jewish Mysticism (1995); A Popular Dictionary of Judaism (1995); Modern Judaism (1996); The Hebrew Bible (1996); God and the Holocaust (1996); Fifty Key Jewish Thinkers (1996); Medieval Jewish Philosophy (1996); After Noah (1997); The Jewish Messiah (1997); A Concise Encyclopaedia of Judaism (1998); Jews, Christians and Religious Pluralism (1999); The Future of Jewish-Christian Dialogue (ed.); Understanding the Holocaust (1999), etc. Ad.: Dept. of Theology and Religious Studies, Univ. Wales, Lampeter SA48 7ED. ☎ 01570 424708.

COLEMAN, Dr Dena, Ph.D., M.A., B.Sc., P.G.C.E.; b. London, Sept., 1952 m. Gordon Coleman; Headteacher of Hasmonean High School. 2-4 Page St., London NW7 2EU. ☎ 020-8203 4294. Fax 020-8202 4527. and Holders Hill Road, London NW4 1NA. ☎ 020-8203 1411. Fax 020-8202 4526.

COLEMAN, Rabbi Dr. Shalom, C.B.E., M.A., B.Litt., Ph.D., J.P., A.M. (Order of Australia); b. Liverpool, Dec. 5, 1918; Rabbi Emer., Perth Hebrew Cong., H. Life President, Assn. of Rabbis & Mins. of Australian & N. Zealand; H. President, Maimonides Coll., Toronto, form. M. South Head Syn., Sydney; United Heb Inst., Bloemfontein. Publ.: Hosea Concepts in Midrash and Talmud, What Every Jew Should Know, What is a Jewish Home? What is a Synagogue? Life is a Corridor (An Autobiography) 1992; etc. Ad.: Unit 1, 72 Spencer Ave., Yokine, Western Australia 6060. ☎ 618-9375 3222; Email shalom@ca.com.au

COLLINS, John Morris, M.A. (Oxon.); b. Leeds, June 25, 1931; Barrister and Head of Chambers; H.L. V. President, Leeds Jewish Rep. C. (form. P., 1986-89); Crown Courts Recorder (1980-98); Dep. Circuit Judge (1970-80); Called to the Bar, Middle Temple (1956), past P. Leeds Lodge, B'nai B'rith; BoD (1971-93); President, Beth Hamedrash Hagadol Syn., Leeds (1992-95). Publ.: Summary Justice (1963). Ad.: 14 Sandhill Oval, Leeds, LS17 8EA. ☎ 0113 2686008.

COLLINS, Kenneth Edward, Dr. MBChB, M.R.C.G.P., M.Phil., Ph.D.; b. Glasgow, Dec. 23, 1947; Co. Chairman: Scottish Jewish Archives Cttee., Chairman: Glasgow Bd., of Jewish Educ. (1989-93), President: Glasgow Jewish Rep. C. (1995-98); Chairman Glasgow Yeshiva. Publ.: Aspects of Scottish Jewry (ed.) (1987), Go and Learn (1988); Second City Jewry, (1990); Glasgow Jewry (1994); Scotland's Jews (1999). Ad.: 3 Glenburn Road, Giffnock, Glasgow G46 6RE. ☎ 0141-638 7462.

CONNICK, (Harold) Ivor, LL.B.; b. London, Jan. 25, 1927; Consultant, Dir., Land Securities plc (1987-98), and A. Beckman plc (1990-98); V. P. Brit. ORT; Chairman, Central Board World ORT Union; Pres. Westminster Syn.; Board JIA (1985-93); Chairman, Professions Div., JIA (1979-83); Dep. Chairman UDS Group PLC (1983), Director (1975-83). Ad.: 54 Fairacres, Roehampton La., SW15 5LY. ☎ 020-8876 7188. Fax 020-8878 6198.

CONWAY, Edward Sidney, M.A. (Liverpool), B.A. (Wales), Ph.D. (Lond.), Dip.

Ed. (Wales); b. Llanelli May 3, 1911; Adv. Head, I.L.E.A (1976-79); Educ. Consultant, Frs. of Z.F. Educ. Tr. J.E.D.T. (1978-84), Inst. Jewish Educ. (1985-87), Friends Hebrew Univ. (1981-84), Spiro Inst. (1982-84); HM, J.F.S. Comprehensive School (1958-76); Princ., Jewish Orphanage (1951-58); HM, Liverpool Hebrew Schools (1944-51). Publ.: The Future of Jewish Day Schools, Going Comprehensive, Comprehending Comprehensives. Ad.: 193 Golders Green Rd., NW11 9BY. ☎ 020-8458 2117.

COOPER, Rabbi Chaim Joshua, M.A., Ph.D.; b. London, Aug. 9, 1912; Rabbi Emet. Hull Hebrew Cong; form. Com. Rabbi, Hull; Chief M., Adelaide Hebrew Cong. (1958-59); M., Kingsbury Distr. Syn. (1951-57). Ad.: 36 Parkfield Dr., Hull, HU3 6TB. ☎ 01482-561180.

COPISAROW, Sir Alcon Charles, D.Sc.; b. St. Annes-on-Sea, Lancs., June 25, 1920; Council IJPR and AJA; Chairman The Eden Trust; Special Adviser Ernst & Young; Form. Lieut. Royal Navy (1943-47); Min. of Defence (1947-54), British Embassy, Paris (1954-60); Chief Scientific Officer, Min. of Technology (1964-66), Senior Partner McKinsey and Co Inc. (1966-76); Subsequently: Chairman Tr., The Prince's Youth Business Trust; Tr., Duke of Edinburgh's Award; C. Royal Jubilee Trusts; Press Council, Gov., Benenden School; Dep. Chairman G. English Speaking Union; Tr. Found. for Manufacturing & Industry; Patron, Conseil National des Ingénieurs et des Scientifiques de France; Chairman & Man. Tr., The Athenaeum; form. Chairman Humanitarian Trust of Hebrew Univ. Ad.: 25 Launceston Place, London W8 5RN.

CORNEY, Hyam, B.A. (Hons.); b. Lond., May 20, 1938; Deputy Edr, Jewish Chronicle; form. Foreign edr. Home News edr. Exec. Dir., Publ. Rel., Israel & Foreign Affairs Cttees., BoD; Lond. Corres 'Jerusalem Post'; Edr., 'Jewish Observer & Middle East Review', Information Dir., JNF Ad.: 25 Furnival St., EC4A 1JT. ☎ 020-7415 1616.

COROB, Sidney, D.Sc. Tech. (h.c.) C.B.E.; b. London, May 2, 1928; Chairman, Corob Holdings Ltd.; H.V. President, Frs. of the Sick; V. President Magen David Adom in Brit.; Chairman, Brit. Technion Soc.; V. President C.C.J.; T., Westmount Housing Assn.; H.T., Westmount Charitable Tr.; V. Chairman Central C for Jewish Soc. Service; Chairman Int. Centre for Learning Potential, Jerusalem. Ad.: 62 Grosvenor St., London W1X 9DA..

CORREN, Asher, M.I.B.M.; b. Warsaw, Nov. 2, 1932; form. Director, Central C. Jewish Community Services; Tr. Richmond, the American International University in London; form. Exec. Dir. Nightingale House; form. Member of Wandsworth Health Authority; form. Member of Exec. Cttee, Alzheimer's Disease Soc.; Member of Adv. Cttee., St Wilfrid's Home for Aged, Chelsea.

COSGROVE, The Honourable Lady, Q.C., LL.D.(Hon), LL.B. (née Hazel Josephine Aronson), b. Glasgow, Jan 12, 1946; m. John A. Cosgrove; Senator of the College of Justice, Scotland; Dep. Chairman of the Boundary Commission for Scotland; Temporary Judge of the Court of Session and the High Court (1992-96); Sheriff of Lothian & Borders at Edinburgh (1983-96); President Scottish Friends of Alyn; Chairman, Mental Welfare Commission for Scotland (1991-96); Mem., Parole Baord for Scotland F(1998-91); Sheriff of Glasgow & Strathkelvin (1979-83); Advocate, Scottish Bar (1968-79); Jr. Counsel, Dept. of Trade (1977-79). Ad.: Parliament House, Edinburgh EH1 1RQ.

COSGROVE, John Allan, BDS (Glasgow); b. Carmarthen, S. Wales, Dec. 5, 1943; m. The Honourable Lady Cosgrove (Hazel Aronson); Dental Surgeon; President Edinburgh Hebrew Congregation (1986-90), currently Hon. V. President; Chairman Edinburgh Hillel Cttee; Co-chairman Council of Christians and Jews, Edinburgh Branch; Chairman Ed. Bd. Edinburgh Star; regular contributor Thought for the Day, BBC Radio Scotland; Scottish representative Chief Rabbinate selection committee (1989-91). Ad.: 14 Gordon Terrace, Edinburgh EH16 5QR. ☎ 0131-667 8955. Fax 0131-667 6684. Email john_cosgrove@csi. com

COWEN, The Rt Hon Sir Zelman, PC, AK, GCMG, GCVO KStJ, GCOMRI
(Italy); QC, BA, LLM (Melbourne), MA, DCL (Oxon), LLD Hon (HK,
Queensland, Melbourne, Australian Nat Univ, West Australia, Tasmania, Turin,
Victoria Univ. Technology), DLitt Hon (New England, Sydney, James Cook Univ
of N Queensland, Oxford); DHL Hon (Hebrew Union Coll, Cincinnati,
Redlands Univ, Calif), D Univ Hon (Newcastle, Griffith Univ), PhD Hon
(Hebrew Univ, Jerusalem, Tel Aviv Univ), Southern Cross, Queensland (1999); b.
Melbourne, Oct. 7, 1919; m. Anna née Wittner; Chairman Australian National
Academy of Music (1995-); Nat. President, Australia-Brit. Assn. (1993-95); P.
Order of Australia Association (1992-95); Chairman (1992-94) and Bd. Member
(1992-96), John Fairfax Holdings Ltd.; Dir., Sir Robert Menzies Memorial
Foundation (Aus.) Ltd. (1991-); Hon. Professor Griffith Univ., Queensland
(1991-); Professorial Assoc., Univ. of Melbourne (1990-); Member Bd. of Gov.
Weizmann Inst. (1990-); Provost, Oriel Coll., Oxford (1982-90); Pro-V.
Chancellor, Univ. of Oxford (1988-90); Chairman, Victoria League for C'wealth
Friendship (1987-89); Tr. Winston Churchill Memorial Tr. (UK) (1987-89); Lee
Kuan Yew Distinguished Visitor Singapore (1987); Sir Robert Menzies Memorial
Tr. (UK) (1984-); Chairman, Press C. (1983-88); Gov.-Gen. of Australia (1977-
82), V. Chancellor Queensland Univ. (1970-77); V. Chancellor, New England
Univ., N.S.W. (1967-70), Professor, Public Law & Dean, Law Faculty, Melbourne
Univ. (1951-66), Emer. Prof (1967); H. Fellowships at New Coll. Oxford, Trinity
Coll., Dublin, Oriel Coll., Oxford, Robb & Wright Coll., Univ. of New England,
St. John's Coll., Univ. Qld, Univ. House, Australian Nat. Univ.; H. Master of
Bench, Gray's Inn; Academic Gov., Bd. of Govs., Hebrew Univ., Tel Aviv Univ.;
Chairman, Van Leer Instit., Jerusalem (1988-95), Hon. Chairman (1995-);
Chairman, Australian V. Chancellors' Cttee. (1977); P. Australian Instit. Urban
Studies (1973-77); Law Reform Com., Australia (1976-77), Chairman,
Australian Studies Centre Cttee., Lond (1982-1990); Menzies Scholar in
Residence, Virginia Univ. (1983), Foreign H. Member, Amer. Academy of Arts &
Sciences (1965); Fel. Royal Soc. of Arts; H. Fel., Australian Nat. Univ. Coll. of
Educ., Academy of Soc. Sciences, Academy of Technolog. Sciences, Academy of
Humanities, Soc. of Accountants, Coll. of Rehabilitation Med., Royal Australian
Instit. of Architects, Royal Australian Coll. of Med. Admin., Royal Australian
Coll. of Obstetricians & Gynaecologists, Instit. of Chartered Accountants in
Australia, Hon. Fel. Australian Coll. of Physicians, Australia for Educational
Admin.; Hon. Fel. Australian Coll. Pathologists; Fel. ANZAAS (1983); Member,
New South Wales Bar Assoc. (life). Knight, Order of Australia; Knight Grand
Cross, Order of St Michael and St. George; Knight Grand Cross, Royal Victorian
Order; Assoc. Knight, Order of St. John; Knight Grand Cross Order of Merit of
Italian Republic, Knight Bachelor. Publ.: (ed. jtly.) Dicey Conflict of Laws; (with
P B. Carter) Essays in the Law of Evidence; (with L. Zines) Federal Jurisdiction
in Australia, (with D. M. da Costa) Matrimonial Causes Jurisdiction; The British
Commonwealth of Nations in a Changing World; Isaac Isaacs; Individual Liberty
and the Law; The Virginia Lectures, Reflections on Medicine, Biotechnology and
the Law; A Touch of Healing, Australia and the United States: Some Legal
Comparisons; American-Australian Private International Law; The Private Man
(ABC Boyer Lectures); etc. Ad.: 4 Treasury Place, East Melbourne, Victoria
3002, Australia. ☎ 61-3-96500299. Fax 61-3-96500301.
CRAFT, Maurice, B.Sc.(Econ.) Ph.D., D.Litt.; b. London, May 4, 1932; Prof. of
Education, Goldsmiths Coll., Univ. London; Res. Prof of Education, Univ.
Greenwich (1993-97). Foundation Dean of Humanities & Social Science, Hong
Kong Univ. of Science and Technology (1989-93); Prof of Educ. Nottingham
Univ. (Dean of Faculty of Education, and Pro-Vice-Chancellor) (1980-89);
Goldsmiths' Prof of Educ., London Univ. (1976-80); Prof of Educ., La Trobe
Univ., Melbourne (1974-75), Sr. Lect. in Educ., Exeter Univ (1967-73); Publ.
include: Teacher Education in Plural Societies (Edr.); Ethnic Relations and

Schooling (Jt. Edr.); Change in Teacher Education (Jt. Edr.); Education and Cultural Pluralism (Edr.); Teaching in a Multicultural Society: the Task for Teacher Education (Edr.); Linking Home and School (Jt. Edr.); Ad.: Dept. of Educational Studies, Goldsmiths College, New Cross, London SE14 6NW. ☎/Fax 020-8852 7611.

CREEGER, Morton. b. Luton, Beds., Sept 22, 1941; Dir. Brit. ORT (1973-85); form. Dir. Ronson Foundation (1985-95); Governor, Charles Kalms Henry Ronson Immanuel College (1990-95); Governor, King Solomon High School, Redbridge (1991-); Dir. King Solomon High School, Redbridge Ltd (1993-97); Vice-Chairman, and Non-Exec. Director, Camden and Islington Community Services NHS Trust (1992-95); Council Member, Association for Research into Stammering in Childhood (1994-97); Fellow, Institute of Charity Fund-raising Managers (1994-). Heron International, 19 Marylebone Road, London NW1 5JL. ☎ 020-7486 4477. Fax 020-7935 7257.

CREWE, Ivor Martin; b. Manchester, Dec. 15, 1945; Univ. teacher; Vice-Chancellor (1995-), Pro V. Chancellor (Academic) (1992-95) Univ. of Essex, Prof. of Government, Univ. of Essex; Hon. Fell. Exeter College, Oxford; Memb. C.CVCP (1997-); Dir. SSRC Data Archive (1974-82); Ed./co-ed. British Journal of Political Science (1977-82, 1984-92); Chairman, Dept. of Government (1985-89). Publ.: Survey of Higher Civil Service (HMSO 1969) (with A. H. Halsey), Decade of Dealignment (CUP 1983) (with Bo Särlvik); SDP: The Birth, Life and Death of the Social Democratic Party (with Tony King). Ad.: Vice Chancellor's Office, Univ. of Essex, Colchester, Essex CO4 3SQ.

CRIVAN, Harry Edward, M.B.E., B.Sc.; F.E.I.S.; b. Edinburgh, Nov. 9, 1907; Member C. Langside College, Glasgow (1991-94), President, Glasgow Jewish Rep. C. (1971-74); Co.-Chairman, C.C.J., Scotland (1979-85); Ex. Comm. Scottish Refugee C.; T., Scottish C. for Racial Equality (since 1982); Exec., Strathclyde Com. Rel. C. (since 1973); President, Scottish Rtd. Teachers' Assn. (since 1979); C., Strathclyde Univ. Graduates Assn. (since 1978). Publ.: Casting of Steel, Iron & Steel for Operatives (Consulting Edr.). Ad.: Flat 5, Homeglen House, Maryville Ave., Giffnock, Glasgow, G46 7NF. ☎ 0141-638 8153.

CUTLER, Rabbi Shlomo, b. Liverpool, Dec. 21, 1927; Rav. Kol Yakov, Edgware; M., Mill Hill Syn. (1959-93); form. M., Luton Syn. Ad.: 38 Selvage Lane, NW7. ☎ 020-8959 6131.

DAICHES, David, C.B.E., M.A. (Edin.), M.A. and D.Phil. (Oxon.), Docteur h.c. (Sorbonne), D.Litt. (Edin., Sussex, Glasgow), D. Univ. (Stirling), Dottore ad honorem (Bologna), etc.; b. Sunderland, Sept. 2, 1912; Dir., Instit. for Advanced Studies in the Humanities, Edinburgh Univ. (1980-86); Prof of Eng., Univ. of Sussex (1961-77); Dean of School of Eng. and Amer. Studies, Univ. of Sussex (1961-68); form. Lect. in English, Univ. of Cambridge, and Fellow of Jesus Coll.; form. Prof of English, Cornell Univ.; form. Fellow of Balliol Coll., Oxford; Second Sec. British Embassy, Washington (1944-46). Publ.: The Authorised Version of the Bible, a study of its origins and sources, A Study of Literature, Robert Burns, Literary Essays, Two Worlds, Milton, A Critical History of English Literature, Was: a Pastime from Time Past, Moses, Glasgow, Edinburgh, God and the Poets, A Weekly Scotsman and other poems, etc. Ad.: 22 Belgrave Crescent, Edinburgh EH4 3AL.

DANGOOR, Naim Eliahou, B.Sc.(London); b. Baghdad, 1914; Company Chairman; editor and publisher – The Scribe, Journal of Babylonian Jewry. Ad.: 4 Carlos Place, London W1Y 5AE.

DAVIDSON, Lionel, b. Hull, Mar. 31, 1922; author. Publ.: The Night of Wenceslas, The Rose of Tibet, A Long Way to Shiloh, Making Good Again, Smith's Gazelle, The Sun Chemist, The Chelsea Murders, Under Plum Lake, Kolymsky Heights. Ad: c/o Curtis Brown Ltd., 28-29 Haymarket, London SW1Y 4SP.

DAVIS, Sydney, O.B.E.; b. London, Nov. 8, 1921; Vice President, Ajex; form. Nat. Chairman, Ajex; form. Gen. Sec., Ajex; form. Gen. Sec. Ajex Charitable Trust;

Management Cttee (form. Admin.) Ajex Housing Assn.; Tr. Ajex 1984 Trust; Nat. Exec, C.C.J. Ad.: Ajex House, East Bank, N16 SRT. ☎ 020-8800 2844.

DEECH, Ruth Lynn (née Fraenkel), M.A. (Oxon), M.A. (Brandeis); Barrister; b. London, April 29, 1943, m. Dr John Deech; Principal, St Anne's College, Oxford; Chairman, UK Human Fertilisation & Embryology Authority; Lecturer in Law, Oxford University (1970–91); Member, Commission on the Representation of the Interests of the British Jewish Community (1998-); Governor, UJIA (1997-); Governor, Oxford Centre for Hebrew and Jewish Studies (1994-); Chairman, Stuart Young Foundation Academic Panel (1991-); Senior Proctor, Oxford University (1985-86); Vice-Principal, St Anne's College (1988-91); Non-executive Director, Oxon Health Authority (1993-94); Governor, Carmel College (1980-90); Member, Committee of Inquiry into Equal Opportunities on the Bar Vocational Course (1993-94); Hon. Bencher, Inner Temple (1996); Rhodes Trustee (1996). Ad.: St Anne's College, Oxford, OX2 6HS. ☎ 01865 274800. Fax 01865 274895.

DEMMY, Lawrence, M.B.E.; b. Manchester, Nov. 7, 1931; Comp. Dir. C. Internat. Skating Union. Ad.: Oak Cottage, 112 Beverley Rd., Kirkella, Hull. ☎ 01482 650232.

DEUTSCH, André, C.B.E.; b. Budapest, Nov. 15, 1917; Publisher, Chairman Aurum Press Ltd. Ad.: 10 Museum St., WC1A 1JS ☎ 020-7379 1252.

DIAMOND, Aubrey Lionel, LL.M., D.C.L., Q.C.; b. London, Dec. 28, 1923; Solicitor, H. Fel., Lond. Sch. of Economics; H. Fel., Queen Mary and Westfield Coll.; Hon. D.C.L., City Univ., Hon. M.R.C.P., Prof. of Law Notre Dame Univ.; Dir., Instit. of Advanced Legal Studies, Lond. Univ. & Prof. of Law (1976-86, now Emer.); Law Com. (1971-76); L.S.E. (1957-66). Publ.: The Consumer, Society and the Law (with Lord Borrie), Introduction to Hire Purchase Law, Instalment Credit (ed.) Sutton and Shannon on Contracts, 7th ed. (co-ed.), Commercial and Consumer Credit, A Review of Security Interests in Property (H.M.S.O.). Ad.: 1 Suffolk St., London SW1Y 4HG. ☎ 020-7484 7800.

DIAMOND, Rt. Hon. Baron of Gloucester (Life Peer), (**John Diamond**), P.C., F.C.A., LL.D. (h.c.); b. Leeds, April 30, 1907; Chartered Accountant Dep. Chairman of Cttees., House of Lords (1974); Chairman, Royal Comm. on the Distrib. of Income and Wealth (1974-79), Chairman, Industry and Parliament Trust (1976-81); Tr. SDP (1981-82); House of Lords, SDP Leader (since 1982); Leader, Parl. Del. to Israel (1984); M.P. for Gloucester (Lab.) (1957-70), Chief Sec., H.M. Treasury (1964-70); Privy Counsellor 1965; Member of Cabinet, (1968-70); form. M.P. for Blackley, Manchester (Lab.) (1945-51); form. Parl. Pte. Sec. to M. of Works; form Member of Gen. Nursing C. and Chairman of its Finance Cttee. (1947-53); form. Chairman, Cambridge and Bethnal Green Boys' Club; form. T., Fabian Soc.; form. Dir., Sadler's Wells Trust. Publ.: Public Expenditure in Practice. Ad.: 'Aynhoe', Doggetts Wood La., Chalfont-St.-Giles, Bucks. HP8 4TH. ☎ 01494 3229.

DOMB, Cyril, M.A., Ph.D. (Cantab.), M.A. (Oxon), F.R.S.; Em. Prof. of Physics. Bar-Ilan Univ. (since 1989); Academic President, Jerusalem Coll. of Tech (1985-94); form. Prof. of Theoretical Physics, King's Coll., Lond. Univ. (1954-81); I.C.I. Fel. Clarendon Lab., Oxford; Univ. Lect. in Maths, Cambridge; President, Assn. of Orthodox Jewish Sci. Professionals. Publ.: Scientific writings, Clerk Maxwell and Modern Science (ed.), Phase Transitions and Critical Phenomena Vols. 1-3, 5, 6 (ed. with M. S. Green), Vols. 7-17 (ed. with J. L. Lebowitz), The Critical Point (1996), Memories of Kopul Rosen (ed.), Challenge, Torah Views on Science and its problems (ed. with A. Carmell), Maaser Kesafim, Giving a Tenth to Charity (ed.). Ad.: Physics Dept., Bar-Ilan Univ., Ramat Gan, 52900, Israel. ☎ (03) 5137928. Fax (03) 5353298.

DOMB, Risa, Ph.D.; b. Israel, Mar. 16, 1937; m. Richard Arnold Domb; University Lecturer; First-ever lecturer in Modern Hebrew at the U. of Cambridge, Director of the Centre for Modern Hebrew Studies, U. of

Cambridge. Publ.: The Arab in Hebrew Prose (1982); Home Thoughts from Abroad (1995); New Women's Writing from Israel (1996). Ad.: Faculty of Oriental Studies, Sidgwick Ave, Cambridge CB3 9DA.

DOVER, Dr. Oskar, M.B., Ch.B., M.R.C.G.P.; b. Danzig, Oct. 31, 1929; form. President, Merseyside Jewish Rep. C.; Tr. (form. Sr. Warden) Liverpool Old Hebrew Cong., Tr., Liverpool Jew Youth & Com. Centre, form. Chairman & Foundation Gov., now Tr. King David High Sch., L'pool; form. Chairman, Harold House C. Ad.: 153 Menlove Ave., Liverpool L18 3EE.

DU PARC BRAHAM, Donald Samuel, F.R.G.S., I.R.R.V., A.C.I.Arb., F.R.S.A.; b. London, June 29, 1928; Lord Mayor, city of Westminster (1980-81); Master of Guild of Freeman of City of London (1989/90); Master of Worshipful Comp. of Horners (1991/1992); President, Regent's Park & Kensington North Conservative Assoc. (1996-); Chairman, London Central European Constituency C. (1988-93); Chairman, Central London Valuation Trib. (1977-); Chairman, Parkinson's Disease Soc. (1990-1991); Pat., Central London Br. Parkinson's Disease Soc. of UK; Member Nat. Exec., C.C.J.; Member, Bd. Man. W. Hampstead Syn.; Member, Jewish Cttee for H.M. Forces; Member, Wiener Library Endowment Appeal Cttee., Member, C. of the Anglo-Jewish Assoc.; Nepalese Order of Gorkha Dakshina Bahu. Ad.: 11 Jerusalem Passage, St. John's Sq., London EC1V 4JP.

DUNITZ, Alfred Abraham, J.P., C.C.; b. London, May 15, 1917; form. Tr. of the Burial Soc. (1978-87); Chairman Burial Soc. (US), (1987-88); Member Exec. Hillel House, Exec. Jewish Memorial Council of AJA; Tr. Jewish Cttee. H.M. Forces; Chairman The Friends of Jewish Servicemen; Worshipful Company of Carmen (Livery Company); The Court of Common Council City of London; Freeman, City of London; Chairman Friends of Ramat Gan (1990-94); Exec. of the JWB (1983-85); restored Exeter Synagogue (fd. 1763) (1980); rest. Aberdeen Syn. (1982); Chairman of the House Committee of the JWB Homes at Hemel Hempstead (1978-85); Eastern Region Council of the C.B.I. (1973-76); restored and maintains disused cemeteries; recipient of Inst. of Waste Management Medal (1999). Ad.: 14 Sherwood Rd., Hendon, NW4 1AD. ☎ 020-8203 0658.

DUNITZ, Prof. Jack David, F.R.S., B.Sc., Ph.D.(Glasgow), Hon. D.Sc. (Technion, Haifa), Hon. D.Sc. (Glasgow), Hon. Ph.D. (Weizmann Instit.), b. Glasgow, March 29, 1923; m. Barbara née Steuer; Scientist and teacher; Prof. Chemical Crystallography at the Swiss Federal Inst of Technology (ETH), Zurich, Switzerland (1957-90); Member Academia Europaea, Foreign Member Royal Netherlands Acad. of Arts and Sciences, Foreign Associate, US National Academy of Science, Member Leopoldina Academy; Member Academia Scientarium Artium Europaea; Foreign Member American Philosophical Society; Foreign Hon. Member American Academy of Arts and Sciences; numerous visiting professorships. Publ.: X-ray Analysis and the Structure of Organic Molecules (1979), Reflections on Symmetry in Chemistry ... and Elsewhere (with E. Heilbronner), (1993). Ad.: Obere Heslibachstr. 77, CH-8700 Küsnacht, Switzerland.

DUNNER, Abraham Moses, MCIJ; b. Konigsberg, Germany, Nov. 13, 1937; m. Miriam née Cohen; Exec. Dir. Community Relations, Conference of European Rabbis; Exec. Dir. Community Centres for Israel Org. (1958-60); Exec. Dir. European Union of Orthodox Hebrew Cong. (1958-60); Dir. Keren Hatorah Education Cttee (1960-71); Sec. Gen. Agudath Israel Org. of Great Britain (1967-71); Ed. Jewish Jewish Tribune (1967-71); Ed. Haderech (1962-70); Hon. Mem. Anglo-Zaire Chamber of Commerce (1987-); Mem. West African Advisory Group to the Foreign Office (1988-90); Tr. Beth Jacobs Schools Israel (1988-); Chairman Lakewood Alumni Assn. (1995-); Bd. of Dirs. Simon Wiesenthal Centre UK (1997-); Special Adviser to the Russian Jews Congress (1998-); Cllr. London Borough of Barnet (1998-). Ad.: 87 Hodford Rd., London NW11 8NH. ☎ 020-8731 9025. Fax 020-8209 1565.

DUNNER, Rabbi Josef Hirsch; b. Cologne, Jan. 4, 1913; Rav., Adath Yisroel Syn.,

Rav Ab Beth Din, Union of Orthodox Hebrew Congs.; Princ., Beth Jacob Teachers' Training Seminary, form Rav., Königsberg Hebrew Cong. Ad.: 69 Allerton Rd., N16 5UF. ☎ 020-8800 3347.

DUNNER, Rabbi Pinchas Eliezer (Pini), B.A. Hons.; b. London, Sept. 25, 1970; m. Sabine née Ackerman; M. 'The Saatchi Synagogue', Maida Vale (1998-); Asst. Rabbi, Moscow Choral Synagogue (1991-92); Rabbi, Notting Hill Synagogue (1992-93); Producer/Presenter, 'Jewish Spectrum', Spectrum Radio (1996-98). Ad.: 21 Andover Place, London NW6 5ED. ☎ 020-7266 2026. Fax: 020-7289 5957.

DUNNETT, Jack, M.A., LL.M. (Cantab.); b. Glasgow, June 24, 1922; Solicitor; M.P. (Lab.) for Nottingham East (1974-83), Central Nottingham (1964-74), form. P.P.S., Min. of Transport and Foreign Office; form. Cllr., M.C.C. and G.L.C., and Ald., Enfield Borough C.; Chairman, Notts. County F.C. (1968-87); Football League Man. Cttee. (1977-89), Football Assn. (1977-89); P. Football League, (1981-86 and 1988-9); V. President Football Assn. (1988-89). Ad.: Whitehall Ct., SW1A 2EP. ☎ 020-7839 6962 .

DWEK, Joseph Claude (Joe), C.B.E., B.Sc., B.A., F.T.I., Hon. D.Sc. UMIST; b. Brussels, May 1, 1940; Chairman, Bodycote Internat. Plc. (1972-98), Penmarric Plc; C.B.I. Council; Director Manchester Federal School of Business & Management; Court of Manchester Univ. and UMIST.; Vice President, Z.F.E.T. Ad.: Suite One, Courthill House, 66 Water Lane, Wilmslow, Cheshire SK9 5AP. ☎ 01625-54908. Fax 01625-530791.

EBAN, Abba, M.A.(Cantab.), Litt.D., LL.D. (Hon.); b. Cape Town, 1915; Chairman Knesset Foreign Affairs & Defence Cttee. (1984-88); Foreign Min., State of Israel (1966-74); Dep. Prime Min. (1963-66), Educ. Min. (1960-63), P. Weizmann Inst. of Science, Rehovot (1958-66); Israeli Amb. to US (1950-59); Perm. Rep. of Israel at United Nations (1949-59); Browne Res. Fel. (Oriental Languages), Pembroke Coll., Cambridge (1938); Vis. Prof, Columbia Univ. (1974); Fel., Instit. Advanced Study, Princeton (1978). Publ.: Maze of Justice, Voice of Israel, My People, My Country; An Autobiography, The New Diplomacy, Heritage: Civilization and the Jews, etc. Ad.: Bet Berl, Kfar Sava, nr. Tel Aviv, Israel.

EHRENTREU, Dayan Chanoch; b. Frankfurt-am-Main, Dec. 27, 1932; Rosh Beth Din, Lond. Beth Din; Av Beth Din, Manchester Beth Din (1979-84); Princ., Sunderland Kolel (1960-79). Ad.: London Beth Din. ☎ 020-8343 6270. Fax 020-8343 6257.

EILON, Samuel, D.Sc. (Eng.), Ph.D., D.I.C., F.I.MeCh.E., F.I.E.E., F.Eng.; b. Tel Aviv, Oct. 13, 1923; Emeritus Prof. and Sr. Res. Fel. at Imperial College, London; form. Chief Ed., Omega, The Int Jl. of Management Science; form. Member, Monopolies and Mergers Comm.; form Prof of Man. Science, and Hd of Dept., Imperial Coll., Lond.; form. Dir. of ARC, Compari Int., Spencer Stuart and Associates; management consultant to many industrial companies; form. Assoc. Prof, Technion, Haifa. Publ.: 300 scientific papers, 15 books. Ad.: Imperial College, Exhibition Rd., SW7 2BX. Fax 020-8455 0561.

EIMER, Rabbi Colin, B.Sc. (Econ.); b. Lond., March 8, 1945; Co. Chair Assembly of Rabbis, RSGB (1999-); M., Southgate & Distr. Reform Syn.; Chairman, Assembly of Rabbis, RSGB (1981-83); Lect., Hebrew and Practical Rabbinics, Leo Baeck Coll., form. M., Bushey Ref. Syn., Lib. Jew Union Syn., Paris. Ad.: 65 Derwent Rd., N13 4QA. ☎ 020-8886 3726. Fax 020-8447 8444.

EISENBERG, Paul Chaim, BHL; b. Vienna, June 26, 1950; m. Annette née Liebman; Chief Rabbi of Vienna and of the Federation of Jewish Communities in Austria. Ad.: A-1010 Vienna, Seitenstetteng. 4. ☎ 43-1-5310416. Fax 43-1-533 15 77.

EKER, Mrs. Rita (née Shapiro), M.B.E.; b. London, Oct. 15, 1938; Co-Chairman, Women's Campaign for Soviet Jewry (the 35s); V. Chairman, Nat. C. for Soviet Jewry; Co-ord. Medical Campaign for Soviet Jewry, Co-Chairman of One to One and organiser of the One to One Treks in Israel, First Cheque 2000 and One to

One Children's Fund. Ad.: Pannell House, 779/781 Finchley Rd., NW11 8DN.
☎ 020-8458 7148/9. Fax 020-8458 9971.
ELLENBOGEN, Gershon, M.A. (Cantab.) F.C.I. Arb.; b. Liverpool, Jan. 7, 1917;
Barrister; V. President & Hon. M. The Maccabaeans; C., Frs. of Hebrew Univ.;
C., AJA; former Deputy Circuit judge. Publ.: Legal Works. Ad.: 9 Montagu Sq.,
W1H 1RB.
**ELLENBOGEN, Myrtle Ruth Franklin (née Sebag-Montefiore, former widow of
David E. Franklin);** b. London, Oct. 18, 1923; form. Chairman, Children's
Central Rescue Fund, Gov. and Hon. Fel. of Hebrew Univ. of Jerusalem,
President, Women Frs. (since 1984), Brit. Frs., Hebrew Univ.; form. Gov., now
Fel. of the Purcell Sch. for Musically Gifted Children (1968-88); Alice Model
Nursery (Chairman 1984-87; 1958-66); Member, ILEA (1967-73); Chairman,
Union of Jewish Women's Loan Fund (1966-72), Chairman, Hampstead & St.
John's Wood Group, form. Chairman, Imp. Cancer R.F. (1987-89); Member,
Exec. Cttee. Anglo-Israel Assn.; V. Chairman, AJA Educ. Cttee. (1990-93). Publ.:
Sir Moses Montefiore 1784 to 1885 (with Michael Bor). Ad.: Flat 83, Apsley
House, 23-29 Finchley Rd., London NW8 0NZ. ☎ 020-7586 0464.
ELLIS, Harold, C.B.E., M.A., D.M., M.Ch., F.R.C.S.; b. London, Jan. 13, 1926;
Emer. Prof. of Surgery, Lond. Univ.; Prof. & Chairman, Surgery Dept. Charing
Cross & Westminster Med. Sch Form. V. President, Royal Coll. of Surgeons;
Consultant Surgeon to the Army, resident surgical posts in Oxford, Sheffield &
Lond. (1948-62). Publ.: Clinical Anatomy (9th ed.), Maingot's Abdominal
Operations, (9th ed.), Famous Operations, etc. Ad.: Dept. of Anatomy, King's
College London (Guy's Campus), London Bridge, SE1 9RT.
ELYAN, Sir (Isadore) Victor, M.A., LL.B.; b. Dublin, Sept. 5, 1909; Barrister, Sr.
Magistrate and Judge; Colonial Legal Service, Gold Coast (1946-54); High
Court Judge and Judge of Appeal; Basutoland, Bechuanaland, Swaziland (1955-
64); Chief Justice of Swaziland (1964-70); Prof of Law, Dean of Law Faculty,
Durban-Westville Univ. (1973-76). Publ.: High Commission Territories Law
Reports 1955-60 (ed.) Ad.: P.O.B. 22001 Fish Hoek, Cape, South Africa.
EMANUEL, Aaron, C.M.G., B.Sc. (Econ.); b. London, Feb. 11, 1912; form. Asst.
Under-Sec. of State Dept of the Environment; Chairman, W. Midlands Econ.
Planning Bd. (1968-72) Consultant, O.E.C.D. (1972-81). Ad.: 119 Salisbury Rd.,
Birmingham, B13 8LA. ☎ 0121-449 5553.
EMANUEL, Rabbi Charles, B.A., M.H.L., D.D. (H.U.C.); b. New York, Dec. 15,
1944; M., North Western Ref. Syn.; form M., Sinai Syn., Leeds. Ad.: North
Western Reform Synagogue, Alyth Gdns., NW11 7EN. ☎ 020-8455 6763. Fax
020-8458 2469.
ENGEL, Ian, M.A., F.C.A.; b. Lond., March 24, 1931; Chartered Accountant; V.
President (1993-) (Life Gov. 1966-), Ravenswood Norwood; Tr. & Exec. the Sir
Georg Solti Music and Arts Fund; Tr. Ian Karten Tr. Ad.: Well Cottage, 22D East
Heath Rd., NW3 1AJ.
EPSTEIN, Arnold Leonard, LL.B., Ph.D; b. Liverpool, Sept. 13, 1924 m. Trude
née Gruenwald; Prof., Emeritus, Social Anthropology, Sussex Univ.; Chairman,
Assn. of Soc. Anthropologists of Brit. Commonwealth (1978-81); V. President,
Royal Anthrop. Instit. (1981-83), form. Prof & Head, Anthrop. Dept.,
Australian Nat. Univ. Canberra; Hon. L.P., Brighton & Hove Ben Gurion Univ.
Foundation, (1991-). Publ.: Politics in an Urban African Community, The Craft
of Social Anthropology (ed.)., Ethos and Identity: Three Studies in Ethnicity;
Urbanization and Kinship, The Experience of Shame in Melanesia; Scenes from
African Urban Life; In the Midst of Life: Affect and Ideation in the World of the
Tolai. Ad.: 5 Viceroy Lodge, Kingsway, Hove BN3 4RA. ☎ 01273
735151/739995. Fax 01273 739995.
EPSTEIN, Trude Scarlett (née Gruenwald), Dip. Economics and Political Science
(Oxon), Dip. Industrial Administration, PhD (Manchester), b. Vienna, July 13,
1922; m. Prof. A. L. Epstein; Social Assessment Consultant; Senior Fel. Research

School of Pacific Studies, ANU Canberra (1966-72); Research Prof., Sussex (1972-84). Publ.: Economic Development and Social Change in S. India (1962); Capitalism, Primitive and Modern (1968); South India: Yesterday, Today and Tomorrow (1973); The Paradox of Poverty (1975); The Feasibility of Fertility Planning (1977); The Endless Day: Some Case Material on Asian Rural Women (1981); Urban Food Marketing and Third World Rural Development (1982); Women, Work and Family (1986); A Manual for Culturally Adapated Market Research in the Development Process (1988); A Manual for Development Market Research Investigators (1991); Village Voices – Forty Years of Rural Transformation in S. India (1998); A Manual for Culturally Adapted Social Marketing (1999). Ad.: 5 Viceroy Lodge, Kingsway, Hove BN3 4RA. ☎ 01273-735151. Fax 01273-739995. Email scarlett-epstein@mail.u-net.com

EZRA, Baron of Horsham (Life Peer), **(Sir Derek Ezra)**, M.B.E.; b. Feb. 23, 1919; Chairman, Nat. Coal Bd. (1971-82). Ad.: House of Lords, SW1.

FAITH, Mrs. Sheila (née Book), J.P.; b. Newcastle upon Tyne, June 3, 1928, m. Dennis Faith; Dental Surgeon; Member Parole Bd., (1991-94); MEP (Conservative) for Cumbria and Lancashire North (1984-89) Memb. Euro Parl. Transport Cttee (1984-87), Energy Res. & Technological Cttee (1987-89); M.P. (C.) for Belper (1979-83) Memb. House of Commons Select Cttee on Health and Social Servs (1979-83), Memb. Exec. Cttee Cons Med. Soc. (1981-84); Sec. Cons Backbench Health and Social Servs Cttee (1982-83); Northumberland C.C. (1970-74); Memb. Health and Social Services Cttees, LEA rep on S. Northumberland Youth Employment Bd; Vice-Ch Jt Consult Cttee on Educ, Newcastle (1973-74); Memb. Newcastle City C. (1975-77), (Memb. Educ Cttee); JP: Northumberland (1972-74), Newcastle (1974-78), Inner London (1978-); President Cumbria and Lancashire N. Cons Euro Constituency C. (1989-95); Memb. Newcastle upon Tyne CAB, served as Chairman of several sch. governing bodies and mangr. of community homes. Ad.: 56 Montagu Ct., Montagu Ave., Gosforth, Newcastle-upon-Tyne NE3 7JL. ☎ 0191-285 4438. Fax 0191-285 4483.

FASS, Richard Andrew, F.C.A.; b. London, Sept. 24, 1945; Chartered Accountant; Man. Dir. Jewish Chronicle Ltd; Member Kessler Fdn.; Non-Exec. Dir. Brent, Kensington, Chelsea & Westminster Mental Health Tr. Ad.: Jewish Chronicle, 25 Furnival St., London EC4A 1JT. ☎ 020-7415 1500. Fax 020-7405 0278.

FEALDMAN, Barry; b. Liverpool, May 3, 1913; form. Art Critic, 'Jewish Chronicle'; Curator & Sec., Ben Uri Art Gallery (1950-76). Ad.: 34 Queens Ave., N3 2NP. ☎ 020-8346 7393.

FEIGENBAUM, Clive Harold, F.B.O.A., F.S.M.C.; b St. Albans, Sept. 6, 1939; Company Dir.; Jt. Chairman, Herut Org., Gt. Brit., BoD. Ad.: St. Margarets, Mount Park Rd., Harrow, Middx. HA1 3JP. ☎ 020-8422 1231.

FEINSTEIN, Mrs. Elaine (née Cooklin), M.A. (Cantab), Hon.D.Litt. (Leic.), F.R.S.L.; b. Bootle, Oct. 24, 1930; m. Dr Arnold Feinstein; Writer; Cholmondley Prize for Poetry (1990). Publ.: The Circle; The Amberstone Exit; The Crystal Garden; Children of the Rose; The Ecstasy of Dr. Miriam Garner; Some Unease and Angels (poems); The Shadow Master; The Silent Areas; Selected Poems of Marina Tsvetayeva; The Survivors; The Border; Bessie Smith (biog.); A Captive Lion: a life of Marina Tsvetayeva; Badlands (poems); Mother's Girl; All you need; Loving Brecht (novel); Lawrence's Women (biog.); Dreamers (novel); Selected poems; Daylight (poems); Pushkin (biography). Ad.: c/o Gill Coleridge & White, 20 Powis Mews, W11. ☎ 020-8221 3717.

FELDMAN, David Maurice, M.A., Ph.D.; b. Lond., Feb. 16, 1957; Historian; Senior Lecturer in History Birkbeck Coll., (1993-); form. Lecturer in Economic & Social History Univ. of Bristol, form. Lect. & Fell., Christ's Coll., Cambridge (1987-90), Junior Res. Fell., Churchill Coll., Cambridge (1983-87); Publ.: Englishmen and Jews, Social relations and political culture 1840-1914 (1993), Metropolis London (ed. with G. Stedman Jones). Ad.: 44 Victoria Park,

Cambridge CB4 3EL. ☎ 01223 312272.
FELDMAN, Rabbi Hyman Israel; b. Llanelli, March 28, 1930; Rav, Golders Green Beth Hamedrash, H. Princ., Menorah Primary Sch. Menoral Foundation Sch.; Edr., Kashrus News; Princ., Gateshead Jewish Boarding Sch. (1960-63). Ad.: 125 The Ridgeway, London NW11 9RX. ☎ 020-8455 5068.
FELSENSTEIN, Denis R., B.A. (Hons), P.G.C.E. (Distinction), Ac. Dip., M.A (Ed); b. London, May 16, 1927; form. Hd. Immanuel Coll., form. Dep. Hd. J.F.S.; Hd.Brooke House, Div. Inspector Camden/Westminster and Senior Staff Inspector (Secondary), ILEA. Publ.: Comprehensive Achievement 1987, part-author Combatting Absenteeism 1986, numerous articles. Ad.: 24, Ossulton Way, London N2 0DS. ☎ 020-8455 2705.
FELSENSTEIN, Frank, B.A. (Hons.), Ph.D.; b. Westminster, July 28, 1944; m. Carole; Director, Honors Program, Yeshiva College, N.Y.; form. Reader in English, Univ. of Leeds; Vis. Prof., Vanderbilt U., U.S.A. (1989-90). Publ.: Anti-Semitic Stereotypes: A Paradigm of Otherness in English Popular Culture, 1660-1830 (1995); The Jew as Other: A Century of English Caricature, 1730-1830, exhibition catalogue (Jewish Theological Seminary, New York, 1995); Hebraica and Judaica from the Cecil Roth Collection, exhibition catalogue (Brotherton Library, 1997). Ad.: 8 Manor Drive, Morristown, N.J. 07960-2611, USA. ☎ 973-889-1323. Fax 973-889-1423. 500 West 185th St., New York, N.Y. 10033.
FERSHT, Alan Roy, M.A., Ph.D., F.R.S.; b. Lond., Apr. 21, 1943; m. Marilyn née; Herchel Smith Prof., Organic Chem., Cambridge; Dir., Cambridge C. for Protein Eng.; Fel., Gonville & Caius Coll.; Prof., Biological Chem., Imperial Coll., Lond. and Wolfson Res. Prof. Royal Soc., (1978-88); Scientific Staff, M.R.C. Lab., Molecular Biology, Cambridge (1969-77). Publ.: Enzyme Structure and Mechanism; Structure and Mechanism in Protein Science. Ad.: University Chemical Laboratory, Lensfield Road, Cambridge, CB2 1EW. ☎ 01223 336341. Fax 01223 336445.
FIERSTONE, Clive A., BA (Hons), MA; b. London, October 5, 1948; Academic Registrar London School of Jewish Studies. Ad.: 44 Albert Road Hendon, NW4 2SJ. ☎ 020-8203 6427. Fax 020-8203 6420.
FINE, Rabbi Yisroel, B.A.; b. Swansea, Nov. 11, 1948; M., Cockfosters and N. Southgate Syn., form. M., Wembley Syn., United Hebrew Cong., Newcastle upon Tyne; Chairman of the Rabbinical C. of the United Synagogue; Hon. Princ. Wolfson Hillel Primary Sch.; Educ. Portfolio, Chief Rabbi's Cabinet. Ad.: 274 Chase Side, N14 4PR. ☎ 020-8449 1750.
FINESTEIN, Israel, Q.C., M.A. Cantab.; Hon. LL.D. Hull; b. Hull, April 29, 1921, m. Marion née Oster; P. BoD (1991-94); V. President (1988-91); Mem (1945-72); form. Crown Court Judge (1972-87) and President, Mental Health Rev. Trib. Member, President of Israel's Standing Conference on Israel and Diaspora (1976-90); Gov. and V-Chairman, Jerusalem Int. Centre to Advance the Study of Jewish Civilisation; Memb. C. IJA; A founder Member of Hillel Fd., P. (1981-94); Chairman of Hillel Union of Jewish Students Educ. Cttee. (1981-91); form. Exec. Cttee. of C.C.J. (1980-95); V. President, Norwood Child Care; President (1983-90); form. Gov. JFS and Exec. Cttee. Jews' College V. President, Central C. for Jewish Soc. Services and lecturer in Council's leadership training courses, Council United Synagogue and Jewish Chaplaincy Bd.; Jewish Memorial Council, Fdr. Member of Yad Vashem Cttee.; Chairman (1992-95) and V.P. UK Branch of Intl. Assoc. Jewish Lawyers; Chairman Jewish Law Publication Fund; V. President, AJY; V. President, Jewish Museum, London and form. Chairman (1989-92) and V. President, Jewish Historical Soc. and form. P. (1973-75, 1993-4); V. President, Conference J. Material Claims Against Germany (1991-94); Member, Exec. Member Fdn. for J. Culture; Ed. Bd. of Christian-Jewish Relations (IJA), V. President, World Jewish Congress (1991-94); V. President, European Jewish Congress, form. President, Cambridge University Jewish Soc. and Chairman, InterUniversity Jewish Federation; Universities Zionist C. and Zionist Youth C.;

V.Chairman, Standing Conference of Jewish Youth, Exec. Cttees. of London Bd. and Central Bd. of Jewish Religious Educ.; Cttee. of British ORT and JWB. Publ.: James Picciotto's Sketches of Anglo-Jewish History (Edr.); Short History of Anglo-Jewry; Jewish Society in Victorian England; Anglo-Jewry in Changing Times: studies in diversity 1840-1914. Ad.: 18 Buttermere Ct., Boundary Rd., NW8.

FINKELSTEIN, Ludwik, O.B.E., M.A., D.Sc., Dr. Univ. h.c., F.R.Eng., F.I.E.E., C. Phys., F.Inst.P., Hon. F.Inst. M.C.; b. Lwow, Dec. 6, 1929; Prof. Emer. of Measurement & Instrumentation, City Univ.; form. Pro-V. Chancellor; form. Prof of Instrument & Control Engineering, City Univ.; form Dean, School of Engineering, City Univ. Scientific Staff N.C.B.; President, Instit. of Measurement & Control (1980), Hartley Medallist; Res. Fel. Jewish History and Thought, Leo Baeck Coll.; Publ.: Works in Mathematical Modelling, Measurement, etc. Ad.: City University, Northampton Sq., EC1V 0HB. ☎ 020-7477-8139. Fax 020-7477 8568.

FINKLESTONE, Joseph, O.B.E.; Author, journalist and radio-television broadcaster; Middle East correspondent of the London Evening Standard and London correspondent of Jerusalem Report; Broadcaster BBC World Service and Television; form. Asst. Editor, Foreign, Home, Diplomatic Editor, Jewish Chronicle; form. Chief Lond. Correspondent, Maariv, Israel; Member, Middle East group, Royal Instit. of Internat. Affairs; Winner, David Holden Award for outstanding internat. journalist of the year in Brit. Press Awards (1981); Chairman, Guild of Jewish Journalists and first recipient of its award for excellence; form. edr. British Z.F. Zionist Review. Publ.: Dangers, Tests and Miracles, the remarkable life story of Chief Rabbi Moses Rosen of Romania (1990), Anwar Sadat: visionary who dared (1996). Ad.: 9 Beulah Close, Edgware, Middlesex HA8 8SP. ☎ 020-8958 5257. Fax 020-8958 5534.

FISHER, Dayan Michael; b. Grodno, Poland, Aug. 11, 1912; Rav Rashi (ret.), Fed. of Syns.; V. President, Mizrachi Fed. Ad.: C/o Federation of Synagogues, 65 Watford Way NW4 3AQ. ☎ 020-8202 2263.

FISHMAN, William J., B.Sc. (Econ.), Dip. Lit.; D.Sc.(Econ.) (London); b. London, April 1, 1921; Barnett Shine Sr. Res. Fel. in Labour Studies, Queen Mary and Westfield Coll, London Univ. (1972-86), & Vis. Prof. (1986); Princ., Tower Hamlets Coll. for Further Educ. (1955-69); Vis. Fel., Balliol Coll., Oxford Univ. (1965), Vis. Prof., Columbia Univ. (1967), Wisc Univ. (1969-70). Publ.: The Insurrectionists, East End Jewish Radicals, Streets of East London, East End 1888, East End and Docklands; Recordings - CDs. Ad.: 42 Willowcourt Ave., Kenton, Harrow, Middx. HA3 8ES. ☎ 020-8907 5166.

FIXMAN, Sydney; b. Manchester, Apr. 5, 1935; Dir., Instit. for Jewish Music Studies & Performance; Music Lect., Lond. Univ. Instit. of Educ.; Fdr., Conductor, Ben Uri Chamber Orchestra, Jewish Youth Orchestra, Music Dir., West Lond. Syn.; form. Guest Conductor, leading orchestras in Brit. & abroad (seasons in Israel: 1976-89); Conductor, B.B.C. (TV & Radio). Publ.: (ed.) Psaume Tehillim (Markevitch); Recordings, CDs. Ad.: 5 Bradby House, Hamilton Tce., NW8 9XE.

FORSTER, Donald, C.B.E.; b. London, Dec. 18, 1920; Chairman Soc. Jewish Golf Captains (1994-); Man. Dir. & Chairman B. Forster & Co. Ltd. (1946-85); Chairman, Merseyside Development Corp. (1984-87); Chairman Warrington/Runcorn Devel. Corp (1981-85), President, Manchester JIA (1981-83); President, Assn. Jewish Golf Clubs & Socs. (1973-83), H.L.P. Whitefield Golf Club; Pilot (Flt.-Lieut.) R.A.F. (1940-45); Rep. England, 1954 Maccabiah (tennis). Ad.: The Dingle, South Downs Drive, Hale, Cheshire WA14 3HR.

FRANKEL, William, C.B.E., LL.B.; b. London, 1917; Barrister-at-Law; Edr., 'Jewish Chronicle' (1958-77); Director Jewish Chronicle Ltd. (1959-94); Emer. Gov., Oxford Centre for Hebrew Studies; Gov. Cambridge Centre for Modern Hebrew Studies; Hon. President New Israel Fund (U.K.); Vice President, IJPR; Tr. Israel Diaspora Trust; London Museum of Jewish Life; New London

Synagogue. Publ.: Friday Nights (Ed.), Israel Observed. Ad.: 30 Montagu Square, W1H 1RJ. Fax 020-7935 3052.
FRANKENBERG Ronald Jonas, B.A. (Cantab), M A. (Econ.), Ph.D. (Manc.); b. London, Oct. 20, 1929; Emer. Prof. of Sociology and Social Anthropology, Dir., Centre for Med. Soc. Anthropology, Keele Univ.; Prof., Assoc., Brunel Univ., Prof., Dean, Zambia Univ. (1966-69); form Manchester Univ. Publ.: Village on the Border, Communities in Britain; Time, Health and Medicine (1992). Ad.: Keele University, Staffs., ST5 2BG; 19 Keele Rd., Newcastle-under-Lyme, Staffs. ST5 2JT. ☎ 01782 628498. Fax 01782 634802. Email: sra@keele.ac.uk
FRANKL, Michael Anthony, B.Sc. (Hons) Chemical Engineering, FCMA; b. London, July 28, 1948; m. Carol Jane née Stechler; Accountant; Chairman, Finchley Reform Synagogue (1994-96); Finance Dir. RSGB (1995-); Dep. Chief Exec. RSGB (1998-). Ad.: 116 Southover, London N12 7HB. ☎ 020 8445 8630. Fax 020 8343 8830. Email franklm@refsyn.org.uk
FRANSES, Rabbi Simon J.; b. Larissa, Greece, May 25, 1943; M., Middlesex New Syn., Chairman of the Assembly of Rabbis RSGB (1989-91); Asst. M., Edgware & Dist. Reform Syn. (1971-74); M., Glasgow New Syn. (1974-87); Member of Children's Panel for Strathclyde Region (1977-87). Ad.: 39 Bessborough Rd., Harrow, Middx. HA1 3BS. ☎ 020-8864 0133.
FREEDLAND, Jonathan; b. London, Feb. 25, 1967; Journalist; Editorial writer and Columnist, The Guardian (1997-); Columnist, The Jewish Chronicle (1998); Washington Correspondent, The Guardian (1993-97). Publ.: Bring Home the Revolution: The Case for a British Republic (1998). Ad.: The Guardian, 119 Farringdon Road, London EC1R 3ER. ☎ 020-7278 2332.
FREEDLAND, Michael Rodney; b. London, Dec. 18, 1934; journalist and broadcaster, contributor to national press; Exec. Ed. & Presenter (BBC and LBC), 'You Don't Have to be Jewish' (1971-94). Publ.: Al Jolson, Irving Berlin, James Cagney, Fred Astaire, Sophie, Jerome Kern, Errol Flynn, Gregory Peck, Maurice Chevalier, Peter O'Toole, The Warner Brothers, Katharine Hepburn, So Let's Hear the Applause-The Story of the Jewish Entertainer, Jack Lemmon, The Secret Life of Danny Kaye, Shirley MacLaine, Leonard Bernstein, The Goldwyn Touch: a Biography of Sam Goldwyn, Jane Fonda, Liza With A Z, Dustin Hoffman, Kenneth Williams, A Biography; Andre Previn; Music man; Sean Connery: a biography; All the Way: a biography of Frank Sinatra; Bob Hope; Bing Crosby; Michael Caine; with Morecambe and Wise, There's No Answer To That; with Walter Scharf, Composed and Conducted by Walter Scharf. Ad.: Bays Hill Lodge, Barnet Lane, Elstree, Herts. WD6 3QU. ☎ 020-8953 3000; 020-8953 7599.
FREEDMAN, Harry, M.A. (London), B.A.; b. London 1950; Dir., Assembly of Masorti Synagogues; Lay minister Exeter Synagogue (1981-87); Dir. & Lecturer Masorti Academy (1994-); Editorial Advisory Committee, Jewish Bible Quarterly, Judaism Today. Ad.: 1097 Finchley Road, London NW11 0PU. ☎ 020-8201 8772. Fax 020-8201 8917. E-mail: office@masorti.org.uk
FREEDMAN, Jeromé David, F.C.A.; b. 1935; Chartered Accountant; Chairperson, Union of Liberal and Progressive Synagogues (ULPS) (1995-); form. Hon. Tr. ULPS (1990-95); Board of Management, Chartered Accountants' Benevolent Association (CABA); Director, CABA Trustees Ltd. Ad.: 5 Thanescroft Gardens, Croydon, Surrey CR0 5JR. ☎ 020-8688 2250. Fax 020-8680 4631. Email jerome@freedman.org
FREESON, Rt. Hon. Reginald, P.C.; b. London, Feb. 24, 1926; Journalist; Urban renewal and housing consultant; Member National Planning & Housing C.; Labour Party (1948-); form. Lab. M.P., Willesden and Brent East (1964-87); Member Town & Country Planning Assn.; Member Labour Finance & Industry Group; Fabian Soc.; Labour Campaign for Electoral Reform; Housing Centre Tr. (1987-99); Centre for Social Policy Studies in Israel UK Advisory Group; Commonwealth Parl. Assoc.; Life Memb. National Tr. & Youth Hostels Assoc.;

Memb. Friends of Kew Gardens, Globe Theatre; Dir. Labour & Trade Union Friends of Israel (1992-94); Pol. Sec. Poale Zion (1987-94); Editor, 'Jewish Vanguard' (1988-); Chairman, DOE inner area studies (1974-77); Journ; M.P. (Lab.) for Brent East (1964-87); Chairman, House of Commons Select Cttee. on the Environment (1981-83); Parl. Assembly C. of Europe (1983-87); form. Min. for Housing Construction & Planning; Parl. Sec., Min. of Housing and Local Govt.; Parl. Sec., Min. of Power, Parl. Private Sec. to M. of Transport, form. Chairman, Brent Borough C.; Leader, Willesden Borough C.; Cllr. and Alderman, Willesden and Brent.; Exec. Member Jewish Welfare Board (1970-74); Dir. JBG Housing Society (1982-83); BoD Inner City Study Gp. (1990); Jewish Orphanage (1931-41); President Norwood Old Scholars Assoc. (1972-). Ad.: 159 Chevening Rd., NW6 6DZ. ☎ 020-8969 7407. Fax 0208 968 7114.

FRIEDLANDER, Rabbi Albert Hoschander, Ph.D., D.D., M.H.L. Ph.B.; b. Berlin, May 10, 1927; M. Emer. Westminster Syn., Dean and Sr. Lect., Leo Baeck Coll.; Vis. Fel. Berlin Institute of Higher Studies; Ed., European Judaism (periodical); f.PEN; International Hon. President, World Conference of Religions for Peace, F. Exec., Leo Baeck Inst.; form. M., Wembley & District Prog. Synagogue; Jewish Chaplain, Columbia Univ. and M., East Hampton and Wilkes-Barre. Publ.: Out of the Whirlwind, Six days of destruction (with E. Wiesel), Five scrolls, Thread of Gold, Riders Towards the Dawn, etc. Ad.: Kent House, Rutland Gardens, SW7 IBX. ☎ 020-7584 2754.

FRIEDLANDER, Evelyn (née Philipp), ARCM, Order of Merit (Germany); b. London, June 22, 1940; m. Albert Hoschander Friedlander; Executive Director, Hidden Legacy Foundation; Publ.: Ich Will nach Hause, aber ich war noch nie da (1996); Mappot ... The Band of Jewish Tradition (1997, co-ed.). Ad.: Kent House, Rutland Gardens, London SW7 1BX. ☎ 020-7584 2754. Fax 020-7584 6896.

FRIEDMAN, Milton, B.A., M.A., Ph.D; b. Brooklyn, July 31, 1912; Economist; Nobel Prize in Economics, (1976); Sr. Res. Fel., Hoover Instit. Stanford Univ.; Paul Snowden Russell Distinguished Service Prof. Emer., Chicago Univ.; many honorary degrees. Publ.: Writings on economics. Ad.: Hoover Institution, Stanford, California 94305-6010 USA. ☎ (650) 723-0580.

FRIEDMAN, Rosemary (née Tibber); b. London, Feb. 5, 1929; m. Dennis Friedman, FRCpsych; Writer. Exec. Cttee Society of Authors (1989-92); Exec. Cttee P.E.N. (1993-). Sole judge, Authors' Club First Novel Award 1989; Judge, Betty Trask Fiction Award 1991; Chair of judges, Jewish Quarterly Literary Prizes 1993 and Macmillan Silver Pen Award 1996. Publ.: Vintage, Golden Boy, An Eligible Man, To Live in Peace, A Second Wife, Rose of Jericho, A Loving Mistress, Proofs of Affection, The Long Hot Summer, The Life Situation, The Ideal Jewish Woman and Contemporary Society (Confrontations with Judaism, Ed. Philip Logworth); Home Truths (play, UK tour 1997); Juvenile: Aristide, Aristide in Paris; Works before 1975 with pen name Robert Tibber: Practice Makes Perfect, The General Practice, The Commonplace Day, The Fraternity, Patients of a Saint, We All Fall Down, Love on My List, No White Coat, The Writing Game (1999). Ad.: 2 St Katherine's Precinct, Regent's Park, NW1 4HH. ☎ 020-7935 6252, Fax 020-7486 2398.

FRIEND, John, BSc, PhD (Liv.), PhD (Cantab), FIBiol; b. Liverpool, May 31, 1931; m. Carol née Loofe; President Hull Jewish Representative Council (1999-); Emer. Prof. of Plant Biology, Hull Univ.; Prof. of Plant Biology, Hull Univ. (1969-97); Pro-V. Chancellor, Hull Univ. (1983-87); Vis. Prof. Hebrew Univ. of Jerusalem (1974); Vis. Fel. Wolfson College, Cambridge (1988). Publ.: Biochemical Aspects of Plant-Parasite Relations (with D.R. Threlfall, 1976); Recent Advances in the Biochemistry of Fruit and Vegetables (with M.J.C. Rhodes, 1983). Ad.: 9 Allanhall Way, Kirkella, Hull HU10 7QU. ☎ 01482-658930. Fax 01482-656394. Email j.friend@biosci.hull.ac.uk.

FROSH, Sidney, J.P.; b. London, Aug. 22, 1923; President, US (1987-92),

Chairman, Beth Hamedrash & Beth Din. Man. Bd., Chairman, Chief Rabbinate C. (1987-92); Chairman, Min. Placement Cttee., Chairman, Singer's Prayer Book Publ. Cttee. (1987-92); V.P. Norwood Ravenswood; V. President, Cen. C. for Jewish Comm. Services; Chief Rabbinate C.; V. Chairman & T., Lond. Bd. of Jewish Rel. Educ. (1968-78), Gov., J.F.S. Ad.: 50 Lodge Close, Edgware, Middx. HA8 7RL. ☎ 020-8952 9097. Fax 020-8951 0823.

GABAY, Isaac, M.B.E.; b. Gibraltar, May 14, 1931; Exec. Head Chef, House of Commons; Head Chef, Hurlingham Club, (1954-62); Head Chef, Army and Navy Club (1962-72). Ad.: 119 Preston Hill, Harrow, Middlesex HA3 9SN. ☎ 020-8204 1943.

GAFFIN, Jean (née Silver), O.B.E., J.P., M.Sc., B.Sc. (Econ.); b. London, Aug. 1, 1936; m. Alexander; Non. Exec. Dir. Harrow & Hillingdon Healthcare NHS Trust (1998-); Memb. Consumer Panel Financial Services Auth. (1999-); Exec. Dir. National Hospice Council (1991-98); Chief Exec. Arthritis Care (1988-91); Exec. Sec., British Paediatric Assoc. (1982-87); Organising Sec., Child Accident Prevention Cttee (1979-82); Lecturer II/Senior Lecturer, Social Policy and Administration, Polytechnic of the South Bank (1973-79); Chairman, OFTEL's Advisory Committee on Telecommunications for Disabled and Elderly People – DIEL (1993-); Open Section, Royal Society of Medicine (Sec. 1988-90, President 1998-); Mem. UK Xeno-Transplantation Interim Regulatory Authority (1997-); Magistrate, Harrow Bench (1981-). Publ. include: (Editor) The Nurse and the Welfare State (1981); with D. Thoms, Caring and Sharing: the Centenary History of the Co-operative Women's Guild (1983, second ed. 1993); Women's Co-operative Guild 1884-1914, in Women in the Labour Movement, ed. L. Middleton (1977). Ad.: 509 Kenton Rd., Harrow, Middx HA3 0UL. ☎ 020-8206 0327.

GAINSFORD, Doreen; b. London, May 9, 1937; Public & Press Relations Off.; form. Chairman, 35's (Women's Campaign for Soviet Jewry). Emigrated to Israel, March, 1978, Coord, JIA Project Renewal, Ashkelon; Founder, 35's Israel Campaign for Soviet Jewry; Dir., TAL Mini Gifts (Israel). Ad.: Yehoshua Ben Nun 2, Herzlia Pituach, Israel 46763. ☎ 09-9507011. Fax 03-9226108.

GALE, Rev. Norman Eric, B.A., Ph.D.; b. Leeds, Nov. 9, 1929; form. M., Hampstead Syn. (1988-95); M., Ealing Syn. (1968-88); M., Harrogate Hebrew Cong. (1958-68); form. Chairman, U.S. Rabbinical C.; Memb. Chief Rabbi's Cabinet (Welfare Portfolio 1990-93); H. Chaplain, Nat. Assn. of Jewish Friendship Clubs; H. Dir., Jewish Prison Chaplaincy; Chaplain, Wormwood Scrubs Prison; Exec. Member JAMI. Ad.: Flat 6, Orford Ct., Marsh Lane, Stanmore, Middx HA7 4TQ. ☎ 020-8954 3843.

GARAI, George, Ph.D. (Lond.); b. Budapest, Aug. 31, 1926; Journalist; Gen. Sec., Z. Fed. of Gt. Brit. & Ireland (1982-92); Dir., Public Rel., Z. Fed. (1975-82); Edr. Staff, 'Jewish Chronicle' (1966-75); Edr., 'Australian Jewish Times' (1960-66). Ad.: Balfour House, 741 High Rd., London N12 0BQ.

GARBACZ, Bernard, F.C.A.; b. Westcliff, Dec. 30, 1932; W., Kingsbury Syn. (1965-72); President, B'nai B'rith First Lodge of England (1976-78); Fdr. Tr, Jewish Education Development Tr. (1980-91); Receiver and Manager, Jewish Secondary Schools Movement (1979-82); Chairman, Bd. of Govs., Hasmonean Boys' Grammar Sch. (1979-82); Chairman, J. Marriage C. (1989-91), T. then V.-Chairman, Brit-Israel Chamber of Commerce (1980-92); T., Jews Coll. (1971-84); V.Chairman, Hillel Foundation (1980-92); H. President, Univ. Jewish Chaplaincy Bd.; Chairman, London Jewish Chaplaincy Bd. (1997-); Dir., Central Middlesex Hospital N.H.S. Tr. (1991-96); Chairman, Black's Leisure Gp. Plc (1986-90), Dmatek Ltd. (1995-96). Publ.: Anglo Jewry Research Project 1985 (Garbacz Report on Communal Funding). Ad.: 1 Chessington Ave., London N3 3DS. ☎ 020-8343 2748. Fax 020-8349 2755.

GASTWIRTH, Rabbi Ephraim Levy, B.A., M.Litt.; b. London, 1920; Ret. Rabbi & Chaplain, Heathlands, Manchester; M., Sale Hebrew Cong. (1979-82),

Blackpool Hebrew Cong. (1976-79); Princ., Judith Lady Montefiore Coll (1968-76); Dir. of Jewish Studies, Carmel Coll. (1964-66); M., Sunderland Hebrew Cong. (1960-64); M., S. Hampstead Syn. (1956-60). Ad.: 3 Falcon Ct., Park St., Salford, M7 4WH. ☎ 0161-792 4239.

GEE, George Maxwell, F.R.S.A., J.P.; b. Gillingham, Jan. 12, 1921; P. U.S. (1981-84), V. President (1973-81), U.S. Jt. T. (1961-73), Elder U.S. (1984-); Chairman, Affil. Syns. Cttee. (1973-77), Member, U.S. Placement Cttee. (and form. Chairman; Member (form. Chairman & Jt. T.) Chief Rabbinate C. (1961-), Member of Chief Rabbinate Conf. (1966 and 1990); C., Jews' Coll. (1971-90); Singer's Prayer Book Publ. Cttee. (since 1983); Chairman, Beth Hamedrash and Beth Din Man. Bd. (1981-84); President, Jewish Deaf Assn. (1979-), V. President, JNF Educ. Tr. (1984-96); President Cttee. for Jewish H.M. Forces (1999-), (Chairman 1971-99); T., Frs., Jewish Servicemen & Women (1971-99); form. Chairman, Dayan Steinberg Member Scholarship Fund (1970-90); Tr., Nathan & Adolph Haendler Char., form. Chairman, U.S. Investment Cttee. (1961-81), Enquiry Cttee. for review of ministers' salaries, status, etc. (1971); U.S. Tr. Affiliated Syns. Cttee.; form. Chairman Building Cttee.; C., World Conf of Syns. & Kehillot (1981-84); Shechita Bd. (1971-77); Kashrus Com. (1971-81); form. Member, Nat. Exec., Ajex; C., AJA; TAC; Lond. Bd. Jewish Rel. Educ.; BoD; Freeman, City of Lond. (1953); Past P & Fdr, Insulating Glazing Assn., Nat. Exec., Fdr. Member, Glass & Glazing Fed.; form. Chairman, Nat. Jt. Indus. C. (London) (Glass Indus.); P.M., Worshipful Comp. Glaziers & Painters of Glass; form. Chairman, Glaziers Tr for preserv. & restor. of glass of hist. interest (1976-84); Chairman of Trustees, London Stained Glass Repository (1989-); L. Member, Royal Engineers O.C.A. Ad.: 23 Denewood Rd., N6 4AQ. ☎ 020-8340 0863. Fax 020-8348 8797.

GILBERT, Sir Martin, C.B.E., D.Litt.; b. London, Oct. 25, 1936; historian; Official Biographer of Winston Churchill (since 1968); Fel., Merton Col., Oxford; Vis. Prof, Hebrew Univ. (1980, 1995-); Vis. Prof, Tel Aviv Univ. (1979); Vis. Prof. UCL (1995-6); Publ.: Winston S. Churchill (6 vols.), Churchill, A Life; The Appeasers (with Richard Gott), Britain and Germany Between the Wars, The European Powers 1900-1945, The Roots of Appeasement, Exile and Return a Study in the Emergence of Jewish Statehood, The Holocaust – the Jewish Tragedy, Churchill a Photographic Portrait, In Search of Churchill, Auschwitz and the Allies, The Jews of Hope, The Plight of Soviet Jewry Today, Shcharansky, Portrait of a Hero; Jerusalem – Rebirth of a City, Jerusalem in the Twentieth Century, First World War, Second World War, The Day the War Ended, The Boys – Triumph over Adversity, Israel, a History; A History of the Twentieth Century (3 vols) and other historical works; 12 history atlases, including the Jewish History Atlas, Jerusalem Illustrated History Atlas and the Atlas of the Holocaust. Ad.: Merton Coll., Oxford.

GINSBURG, Major the Rev. Alec., Hon C.F.; b. Aberavon, Aug. 21, 1920; Chaplain to H.M. Forces; form Sr. M. & Braham Lect., Old Hebrew Cong. Liverpool; form. M., Hove Hebrew Cong., St. Annes, Terenure and Plymouth Syns.; Lect. Classical Hebrew & Semitics Exeter Univ. (1964-74); Lect., Jew Homilies. Irish Sch. Ecumenics, Dublin (1974-76); (perm.) Ecumenical Panel, King Edward VII Hospital, Midhurst, Sussex; Jew Chaplain Hq. CMF (Udine. Italy), CF (J) Hq. British Troops (Klagenfurt) Austria, 1947, Sr. Jewish Chaplain, Hq. Brit. Troops, Egypt & Middle East (1947-50), Jewish Chaplain, Hq. B.A.O.R. (1950-55), UK Hq. Lond. Distr. (1956-62); Mentioned: London Gazette, 8 Jan. 1961 on promotion 3rd Class, 8 June, 1962 as Hon. Chaplain Third Class; Rank: Major on retirement; Chap., Dartmoor, Exeter Prisons (1962-74), H.T., Dublin Univ Jewish Soc. Publ.: Judaism and Freemasonry. Ad.: 15 Courtenay Gate, Kingsway, Hove, E. Sussex, BN3 2WJ. ☎ 01273-739440

GINSBURG David, M.A.; b. Lond., Mar. 18, 1921; Comp. Dir., Economist Market and Marketing Res. Consultant; Broadcaster; Fel., Royal Soc. of Med.;

M.P. (Lab. 1959-81, SDP 1981-83 Dewsbury), Sec., Research Dept. Labour Party(1952-59); Sr. Research Off., Govt. Social Survey (1946-52). Ad.: 3 Bell Moor, East Heath Rd., NW3 1DY. ☎ 020-8435 8700.

GINSBURY, Rabbi Philip Norman, M.A.; b. London, Mar. 26, 1936; M., South London Syn.; form. M., Streatham Distr. Syn., Brixton Syn.; Chairman South London Rabbinical Council. Publ. Jewish Faith in Action (1995). Ad.:146 Downton Ave., SW2 3TT. ☎/Fax 020-8674 7451 .

GLANVILLE, Brian Lester, b. London, Sept. 24, 1931; writer. Publ.: Along the Arno, A Bad Streak, The Bankrupts, Diamond, etc. Ad.: 160 Holland Park Ave.,W11.

GLATTER, Robert, F.C.A.; b. Antwerp, Belgium, Mar. 14, 1937; Chartered Accountant, Non-Exec. Director Bank Leumi (UK) plc.; C P Holdings Ltd.; V.-Chairman, British-Israel Chamber of Commerce; Chairman Bd. Dir. Kfar Maccabiah; V. President B'nai B'rith Hillel Foundation; Exec. Member and Tr., Weizmann Instit. Foundation; form. Tr., Volcani Foundation; Tr., Brady-Maccabi Endowment; Fd., form. Gov., Tr. Carmel Colls.; V. President, Akiva School; President, Maccabi Union of G.B.; Form Chairman, North Western Reform Syn. 1986-88; Chairman, RSGB Cttee. for Educ. and Youth; Chairman, RSGB Israel Action Cttee.; Chairman, V.-Chairman, Tr., V. President Maccabi Union of G.B.; Dep. Chairman, Maccabi Europe; Member, Maccabi World Union; Chairman and Dep. Chairman, Maccabiah Organ. Cttee., Tr. Bd. for Jewish Sport; T., Manor House Tr.; Chairman, Funders Cttee., Assn. Jewish Sixth formers. Ad.: 12 York Gate, NW1 4QS.

GLINERT, Lewis H., B.A. (Oxon), Ph.D.; b. London, June 17, 1950; m. Joan née Abraham; University Lecturer; Prof. of Hebraic Studies and Linguistics, Dartmouth College; form. Prof. of Hebrew, Univ. of London (School of Oriental and African Studies, 1979-97); Dir. Centre for Jewish Studies, S.O.A.S.; Vis. Prof. of Hebrew Studies, Chicago U. (1987/8); Asst. Prof. of Hebrew Linguistics, Haifa U. (1974-77). Publ.: The Grammar of Modern Hebrew (1989); The Joys of Hebrew (1992); Hebrew in Ashkenaz (1993); Modern Hebrew: An Essential Grammar (1994); Mamma Dear (1997). Ad.: Dartmouth College, 6191 Bartlett Hall, Hanover, N.H. 03755, USA. ☎ 603 646 0364. Fax 617 244 4011. E-mail: Lewis.Glinert@Dartmouth.edu

GOLD, Sir Arthur Abraham, C.B.E.; b. Lond., Jan. 10, 1917; Engineer; President, European Athletic Assn.; V.President, Commonwealth Games C. for England; Chairman, Drug Abuse Adv. Group, Sports C.; P. Counties Athletic Union; Life V. President (H.Sec., 1962-77) Brit. Amateur Athletic Bd.; President, Amateur Ath. Assn.; V.President Brit. Olympic Assn.; Member, Sports C.; Exec. Central C. of Physical Recreation; Athletics Team Leader, Olympic Games, Mexico 1968, Munich 1972, Montreal 1976; Commandant, C'wealth Games Team Brisbane 1982, Edinburgh 1986, Auckland 1990; British Olympic Team 1988, 1992; President, Lond. Ath. Club (1962-63); President, Middlesex C.A.A.A. (1963 and 1993). Ad.: 49 Friern Mount Drive, N20 9DJ. ☎ 020-8445 2848.

GOLD, Rev. Sidney, B.A.; b. London Dec. 6, 1919; Emer. M (Chief M., 1960-85) Birmingham Hebrew Cong., form. M., Highgate Syn., Regent's Park & Belsize Park Syn., Bayswater Syn., Member Chief Rabbi's Cabinet (1979-83); P. Union of Anglo-Jewish Preachers (1977-78), form. V.Chairman B'ham C.C.J.; Chairman B'ham Inter-Faith C.; President, B'ham J.I.A Cttee. Publ.: Children's Prayer Book for High Festivals (jt. author). Ad.: 12 Dean Park Mans., 27 Dean Park Rd., Bournemouth BH1 1JA ☎ 01202 551578.

GOLDBERG, Sir Abraham, M.D., D.Sc., F.R.C.P., F.R.S.E.; b. Edinburgh, Dec. 7, 1923; Regius Prof (Materia Med., 1970-78), Emer. Regius Prof. Practice of Med., Glasgow Univ. (1978-89); Chairman, Cttee. on Safety of Medicines (1980-86); Chairman, Biological Res. Cttee., Scottish Home & Health Dept., Glasg. (1978-83); H. Consultant, Western Infirmary, Glasg.; Chairman, Grants Cttee., Med. Res. C. (1972-76), Fdn. P. Faculty of Pharmaceutical Medicine of

Royal Colleges of Physicians (UK), (1989-91); Vis. Prof, Tel Hashomer Hospital, Israel (1966), Henry Cohen Lect., Hebrew Univ. (1973); Lord Provost's Award for Public Service to Glasgow (1989); Chairman Glasgow Friends of Shaare Zedek Hospital, Jerusalem. Publ.: Diseases of Porphyrin Metabolism (jt. auth.), Recent Advances in Haematology (jt. edr.). Ad.: 16 Birnam Cres., Bearsden, Glasgow G61 2AU.

GOLDBERG, Rabbi David J., M.A. (Oxon.); b. London, Feb. 25, 1939; Sr. Rabbi, Liberal Jewish Syn.; Interfaith Gold Medallion (1999); M. Wembley & Dist. Lib. Syn. (1971-75); Associate Rabbi L.J.S. (1975-87); Chairman, ULPS Rabbinic Conference (1981-83, 1996-98). Publ.: The Jewish People: their History and their Religion (with John D. Rayner); The Promised Land: a History of Zionist Thought; On the Vistula Facing East (ed.); Progressive Judaism Today (gen. ed.). Ad.: Liberal Jewish Synagogue, 28 St. John's Wood Rd., NW8 7HA. ☎ 020-7286 5181.

GOLDBERG, David Jonathan, M.A. (Jewish Communal Service) Brandeis; Cert. Youth and Community Studies, London; b. London, June 27, 1961; Dir. Israel Experience UK/UJIA/JAFI (1998-); Exec. Director, Zionist Fed. of Great Britain & Ireland (1992-98); H. Chair, Association of Jewish Communal Professionals (1992-98); H. Sec., Bushey Youth Scene (1996-); Senior Youth and Community Work, Redbridge JYCC (1983-90); Chairman - Redbridge Jewish Youth Council (1980-82); Chairman - National Magen David Adom (1979-81). Ad. 18 Chiltern Avenue, Bushey, Herts WD2 3QA. ☎ 020-8950 0080. Email: dgng@global-net.co.uk

GOLDMAN, William; b. London, April 4, 1910; Novelist. Publ.: A Start in Life, A Tent of Blue, East End My Cradle, In England and in English, A Saint in the Making, The Light in the Dust, Some Blind Hand, The Forgotten Word, etc. Ad.: 12 Quintock House, Broomfield Rd., Kew Gdns., Richmond, Surrey TW9 3HT. ☎ 020-8948 4798.

GOLDREIN, Neville Clive, C.B.E., M.A. (Cantab.); b. Hull; m. Sonia née Sumner; Solicitor; Tr. Southport J. Rep. Council (1999-); form. Dep. Circuit Judge; form. Member (Leader, 1980-81, V. Chairman, 1977-80) Merseyside County C. (1973-86); Leader, Conservative Group (1980-86); Lancashire County Council (1965-74); Crosby Borough C. (1957-71); Mayor of Crosby (1966-67); Dep. Mayor (1967-68); North-West Economic Planning C. (1972-74); Governor Merchant Taylors' Schools, Crosby (1965-74); Chairman, St John Amb. (South Sefton) (1965-87); Area President, St. John Amb., Sefton (1965-87); C., L'pool Univ. (1977-81); Vice-President, Crosby MENCAP (1966-); C. L'pool Chamber of Commerce (1986-); Chairman, Rivers Cttee (1989-93); Chairman, Police Liaison Cttee; Chairman Environment and Energy Cttee (1993-); British Assoc. of Chambers of Commerce, Mem. Local & Regional Aff. Cttee (1994-97); Chairman L'pool Royal Court Theatre (Liverpool) Foundation; Chairman, Crosby Conservative Association (1986-89); Chairman (Appeals), Crosby Hall Educ. Trust (1989-91); Bod (1965-85, and 1992-); Sr.W., L'pool Old Hebrew Cong. (1968-71). Ad.: Torreno, St Andrew's Rd., Blundellsands, Liverpool L23 7UR. ☎/Fax 0151-924 2065. E-mail: goldrein@aol.com

GOLDSCHMIDT, Mrs. Ruth P. (née Lehmann), Dipl. O.A.S., F.L.A.; b. Altona, Germany, Feb. 11, 1930; Libr., Jews' Col. (1955-73); Publ.: Nova Bibliotheca Anglo-Judaica, Anglo-Jewish Bibliography (1937-70, and 1971-1990), Sir Moses Montefiore a bibliography, A Bibliography of Anglo-Jewish Medical Biography, Britain and the Holyland 1800-1914, a select bibliography, etc. Ad.: 6 Tchernichowski St., 92 581, Jerusalem. ☎ 02-5632364.

GOLDSMITH, Walter Kenneth, C.Inst.Man., F.R.S.A.; b. London, Jan. 19, 1938; Chairman, Flying Towers (1990-); Chairman (1987-91), V. President (1992-) Brit Overseas Trade Group for Israel; Dir.-Gen., Inst. of Dirs. (1979-84); Tr., Israel Diaspora Tr. (1982-92); Tr., Leo Baeck Coll. (1987-89); Chairman Wembley & Dist. Lib. Syn. (1974-76); C. and Exec., U.L.P.S. (1956-66); Chairman, Youth

Section, World Union for Progressive Judaism (1960-61). Ad.: c/o Stanley Gibbons, 399 Strand, London WC2R 0LX. ☎ 020-7836 8444. Fax 020-7836 7342.

GOLDSTEIN, Rabbi Andrew, Ph.D.; b. Warwick, Aug. 12, 1943; M., Northwood and Pinner Liberal Syn.; Chairman, ULPS Rabbinic Conf (1979-81); Chairman, ULPS Educ. Cttee. (1970-88); Dir., Kadimah Holiday School, (1970-89); Chairman, ULPS Prayerbook Editorial Cttee, Chairman ULPS Conference Cttee; Consultant Rabbi Bejt Simcha Synagogue, Prague. Publ.: My Very Own Jewish Home, Jerusalem, Tradition Roots, Britain and Israel, Mishnah Kadimah, Exploring the Bible, Parts 1 & 2. Ad.: 10 Hallowell Rd., Northwood, Middx. HA6 1DW. ☎ 01923 822818. Fax 01923 824454. Email agoldstein@onet.co.uk

GOLDSTEIN, Rabbi Henry; b. London, March 10, 1936; M., South-West Essex Reform Syn., M., Finchley Reform Syn. (1967-73); Ch, RSGB Rabbis' Assembly (1973-75). Ad.: 15 Chichester Gardens, Ilford, Essex, IG1 3NB. ☎ 020-8554 2297.

GOLDSTEIN, Michael, M.B.E.; b. London, April 5, 1919; form. Gen. Sec., AJY (1951-77); form. Chairman, Greater Lond. Conf of Vol. Youth Orgs. Ad.: Flat 12, Broadway Close, Woodford Green, Essex, IG8 OHD. ☎ 020-8504 2304.

GOLDWATER, Raymond, LL.B.; b. Hove, Sept. 28, 1918; Solicitor; Elder, US; V. President, AJY; form. Ch, Rel Adv. Cttee., AJY; form Chairman, London Student Counsellor Bd.; form C., Jews' Coll.; form. Lond. Bd., Jewish Rel. Educ.; form. Chairman, Youth & Com. Services Dept. & Jt. T., Bequests & Tr. Funds, US; Chairman, I.U.J.F. & Lond. Jewish Graduates' Assn. Publ.: Jewish Philosophy and Philosophers (Edr.). Ad.: 451 West End Ave., Apt 5E, New York, NY 10024. ☎ 212-873-8221.

GOLOMBOK, Ezra, B.Sc., Ph.D.; b. Glasgow, Aug. 22, 1922; Dir. Israel Information Office, Glasgow; Edr., Jewish Echo; Edr., Scottish Nat. Orchestra Scene; form. Convener, Public Relations Cttee., Glasgow Jewish Rep. C. Ad.: 222 Fenwick Rd., Giffnock, Glasgow G46 6UE. ☎ 0141-577 8240. Fax 0141-577 8241. Email: ezra@isrinfo.demon.co.uk

GOMBRICH, Sir Ernst Hans Josef, O.M., C.B.E., Ph.D. (Vienna), F.B.A., F.S.A.; b. Vienna, March 30, 1909; Dir., Warburg Inst. (1959-1976) and Prof. of the History of the Classical Tradition, Univ. of London; Slade Prof of Fine Art, Univ. of Oxford (1950-53), Univ. of Cambridge (1961-63), and Prof of the Hist. of Art, Univ. Coll., London (1956-59); Premium Erasmianum (1975); Internat. Balzan Prize (1985); Britannica Award 1989, Goethe Preis, (1994); 18 hon. degrees. Publ.: The Story of Art, Art and Illusion, The Sense of Order, Aby Warburg, etc. Ad.: 19 Briardale Gdns., NW3 7PN. ☎ 020-7435 6639.

GOODMAN, Lewis, O.B.E.; b. Breslau, Dec. 9, 1926; V. President, West London Syn.; V.Chairman, Ben Uri Art Soc.; Exec. Anglo-Israel Assoc.; V. President, Brit.Israel Chamber of Commerce; Chairman, Friends of the Jewish Assocation for the Mentally Ill. Ad.: 57 Acacia Rd., NW8 6AG. Fax 020-7586 5906.

GOODMAN, Martin David, M.A., D.Phil. (Oxon.) F.B.A.; b. Aug. 1, 1953; m. Sarah Jane Goodman; Professor of Jewish Studies, University of Oxford; Fellow of the Oxford Centre for Hebrew and Jewish Studies and Wolfson College; Lecturer in Ancient History, University of Birmingham (1977-86); Fellow of Oxford Centre for Hebrew and Jewish Studies (1986-); Senior Research Fellow, St Cross College (1986-91); Reader in Jewish Studies, University of Oxford (1991-96); President, British Association for Jewish Studies (1995); Sec. European Association for Jewish Studies (1995-98); Joint Editor of Journal of Jewish Studies (1995-99). Publ.: State and Society in Roman Galilee, A.D. 132-212 (1983); Johann Reuchlin, On the Art of the Kabbalah (translation with S.J. Goodman) (1983 and 1993); E. Schürer, The History of the Jewish People in the Age of Jesus Christ, rev. ed. (with G. Vermes and F.G.B. Millar), volume 3 (1986 [part 1], 1987 [part 2]); The Ruling Class of Judaea: the origins of the Jewish Revolt against Rome, A.D. 66-70 (1987); The Essenes according to the Classical

Sources (with Geza Vermes) (1989); Mission and Conversion: proselytizing in the religious history of the Roman Empire (1994); The Roman World 44B.C.-A.D.180 (1997); Jews in a Graeco-Roman World (ed. 1998); Apologetics in the Roman Empire (jt. ed. 1999). Ad.: Oriental Institute, Pusey Lane, OX1 2LE. ☎ 01865-278208. Fax 01865-278190. E-mail: martin.goodman@orinst.ox.ac.uk

GOODMAN, Mervyn, M.R.C.S. (Eng.), L,R,C.P. (Lond), F.R.C.G.P., F.R.S.H, D.Obst.R.C.O.G.; b. Liverpool, Jan. 8, 1928; Freeman, City of London; Fel., BMA; Fel. Roy. Soc Med; Past C. L'pool Branch, Jewish Historical Society of England; BoD; Past C. Gov. Norman Pannell Primary School; member, Court of Univ. of L'pool; form. General Medical Practitioner, Clinical Teacher, Dept Gen Pract, Univ of L'pool; President (now Hon. Life V.P.), Merseyside Jewish Rep. C; L'pool Z. Cent C.; L'pool Jewish Med Soc.; L'pool Univ. Jew Students' Soc., Mersey Reg C. BMA; L'pool Div BMA; C. Mersyside Cttee for Adult Jew. Educ.; C. M'side Amalgamated Talmud Torah; C. L'pool Graduates Soc.; Gov. King David Primary School; Liverpool Local Med. Cttee; L'pool Area Med Cttee; V. Ch Cameron Fund; Council, BMA; Tr. & Summer School Dir. IUJF. Publ.: The Jewish Community of Liverpool; From Toxteth to Tel Aviv; A Tiyyul through Toxteth; Medical Epidemiology, Practice Organisation and Therapeutics; Local Jewish Demography. Ad.: 1, Hornby Lane, Liverpool L18 3HH. ☎/Fax 0151-722 7125.

GOODMAN, Mrs. Vera (née Appleberg); b. London, m. Maurice Goodman; BoD (1973-94), Exec. Cttee. (1985-91), form Chairman, Publ. Rel. Cttee.; Bd. of Elders, Span. & Port Jews' Cong. (1977-80; 1990-94); Life V. President (Chairman, 1976-79) Richmond Park Conservative Women's Constit. Cttee.; Nat. C. for Soviet Jewry (1977-80), Greater Lond. Conservative Women's Gen. Purposes Cttee. (1979-85) Conservative Rep., Nat. C. of Women (1974-79); form. Central Lond. C., Conservative Frs. of Israel; Rep., Union of Jewish Women at U.N.A.; Central C., Conservative Party; Conservative Women's Nat. Cttee, Exec.; European Union of Women (Brit. Section); Chairman, Sephardi Women's Guild; Brit. C., World Sephardi Fed., V. Chairman, Govs., Russell Sch., Petersham (1974-82). Ad.: 87 Ashburnham Rd., Ham, Richmond, Surrey, TW10 7NN. ☎ 020-8948 1060.

GORDIMER, Nadine; b. Springs, S. Africa, Nov. 20, 1923; Author; Nobel Prize for Literature (1991); W. H. Smith Literary Award (1961), James Tait Black Member Prize (1972), Booker Prize (1974), Grand Aigle d'Or (1975), Premio Maleparte (1985), Nelly Sachs Prize (1985), Bennett Award, New York (1986). Publ.: Soft Voice of the Serpent, The Lying Days, Six Feet of the Country, A World of Strangers, Friday's Footprint, Occasion for Loving, Not for Publication, The Late Bourgeois World, A Guest of Honour, Livingstone's Companions, The Conservationist, Burger's Daughter, A Soldier's Embrace, July's People, Something Out There, A Sport of Nature (1990), My Son's Story, Jump (1991), None to Accompany Me (1994), The House Gun (1998), The Essential Gesture (1988 non-fiction), Writing and Being (1995, essays), Living in Hope and History (1999, essays), etc. Ad.: c/o A. P. Watt Ltd, 20 John St., London WC1N 2DR. ☎ 020-7405 6774. Fax 020-7831 2154.

GORDON, Gerald Henry, C.B.E., Q.C., M.A., LL.B., Ph.D. (Glasgow), LL.D. (Edinburgh), LL.D. (Hon., Glasgow); b. Glasgow, June 17, 1929; Sheriff of Glasgow and Strathkelvin; Memb. Scottish Criminal Cases Review Cttee. (1978-99); Personal Professor of Criminal Law (1969-72), Professor of Scots Law (1972-76), Dean of Faculty of Law (1970-73), all at University of Edinburgh. Publ. Criminal Law of Scotland (1st ed. 1968; 2nd ed. 1978), with Second Cumulative Supplement, 1992; Renton & Brown's Criminal Procedure (ed.) (4th ed. 1972, 5th ed., 1983, 6th ed. 1996). Ad.: Sheriff Court, PO Box 23, Carlton Place, Glasgow G5 9DA. ☎ 0141-429 8888.

GORDON, Lionel Lawrence, B.Sc. (Econ.); b. London, Aug. 31, 1933; Market Research Dir.; Chairman, Jewish Chronicle Ltd.; Dir. Jewish Chronicle Trust

Ltd.; Ad.: The Hyde, 5 Orchard Gate, Esher, Surrey, KT10 8HY. ☎ 020-8398 5774. Fax 020-8398 1866.

GOULD, Samuel Julius, M.A. (Oxon.); b. Liverpool, Oct. 13, 1924; Prof. of Sociology, Nottingham Univ. (1964-82); form R., Social Instits., Lond. Sch. of Econ. & Pol. Sci.; Chairman, Trs., Social Affairs Unit, Lond. (since 1981); Res. Dir., Instit. for Pol. Res. (1983-85), Bd. of Dirs., Centre for Pol. Studies; Res. Bd. & Pol. Planning Group, IJA; BoD. Publ.: Dictionary of the Social Sciences (jt edr.), Jewish Life in Modern Britain (jt edr.), The Attack on Higher Education Jewish Commitment: A study in London; Ad.: c/o The Reform Club., Pall Mall London SW1.

GOULDEN, Simon Charles, B.Sc. (Eng.), D.M.S., C.Eng., M.I.C.E., M.I.M.; b. London, Mar. 1, 1949; Chief Exec. Agency for Jewish Education; form. Exec. Dir., Jews' College; Acting Chairman, United Synagogue Bd. of Religious Educ.; Member, Ecumenical Standing Conference on Disability; Princ. Engineer London Borough Haringey (1976-1986). Ad.: Bet Meir, 44a Albert Road, London NW14 2SJ. ☎ 020-8457 9700. Fax 020-8457 9707. Email aje@brijnet. org.

GOURGEY, Percy Sassoon, M.B.E., F.R.S.A.; b. Bombay, June 2, 1923; Journalist; Nat. Chairman, Poale Zion; V. Pres. Z Fed.; Chairman Socialist Societies Section of the Labour Party.; Exec. Cttee., BoD, V. Chairman, Erets Israel Cttee., BoD; form. Chairman Jews in Arab Lands Cttee., Z. Fed.; Hon. Fel. WZO (1996); form. ed. Jewish Advocate, Bombay; Co-Fdr. and first ed. The Scribe (London), ex-Lieutenant RINVR; Parl. C.; Member, Royal Instit. of International Affairs, Chatham House, London, Contr. to Encyclopaedia Judaica, etc. Publ.: The Jew and his Mission, Ideals, India, Israel in Asia, Indian Jews and the Indian Freedom Struggle, The Indian Naval Revolt of 1946, etc. Ad.: 4 Poplar Ct., Richmond Rd., E. Twickenham, Middx. TW1 2DS. ☎ 020-8892 8498.

GRADON, Kenneth Jacob; b. Berlin, July 20, 1919; Hon. V. President, Maccabi World Union; P. (Chairman 1967-74), European Maccabi Confed.; Hon. President, Union of Maccabi Assns. in Gt Brit.; Internat. Maccabiah Cttee., form. Chairman Bd. Govs. P. and Tr. of Jew Secondary Schs. Movement; President, B'nai B'rith First Lodge of England (1966-67). Ad.: 4 Meadway Gate, NW11 7LB. ☎ 020-8458 3645.

GRAHAM, Stewart David, Q.C., M.A., B.C.L. (Oxon.). F.R.S.A.; b. Leeds, Feb. 27, 1934; Barrister; form. Chairman, Law, Parl. & Gen. Purposes Cttee., BoD; form. Member, Insolvency Rules Adv. Cttee.; form. Mem., C. & Exec. Cttee. of Justice; Senior Vis. Fellow, Centre for Commercial Law Studies, QMW College; Member C. Insurance Ombudsman Bureau; Assoc. Memb. British & Irish Ombudsman Assoc. Publ.: Works on bankruptcy and insolvency. Ad.: 6 Grosvenor Lodge, Dennis Lane, Stanmore, Middx., HA7 4JE. ☎ 020-8954 3783.

GRAUS, Eric; b. Bratislava, April 22, 1927; President, Likud-Herut Movement of Gt Britain; Vice Chairman, World Likud Movement; Jt. Chairman, Nat. Z. C.; Mem. Bd. Gov. Jewish Agency. Ad.: 143/5 Brondesbury Pk, NW2 5JL. ☎ 020-8451 0002/3.

GREEN, Sir Allan David, K.C.B., Q.C., (K.C.B. 1991); b. March 1, 1935; Form. Dir. of Pub. Prosecutions, First Sr. Treasury Counsel, Central Criminal Court. (1985-87), Sr. Prosecuting Counsel (1979-85), Jr. Prosecuting Counsel (1977-79); Bencher, Inner Temple (1985); Q.C. (1987), Member, Legal Group Tel Aviv Univ. Tr.; Served R.N. (1953-55). Ad.: 1, Hare Court, Temple, EC4Y 7BE.

GREENBAT, Alan, J.P., b. London, April 1929; Hon Consultant, Office of the Chief Rabbi; Sec. Rabbinical Commission for the Licensing of Shochetim; Memb. Inner London Youth Courts (1964-99); Exec. & V.Chairman National Council of Voluntary Youth Services (1981-91); Exec. Dir. Office of the Chief Rabbi (1990-91); Dir. Assoc. for Jewish Youth (1980-89); Dir. Victoria Community Centre (1961-80); V.Pres. AJY (1989-96); V.Pres. London Union of Youth Clubs (1984-94); V.Principal Norwood Home for Jewish Children (1955-

61). Ad.: Adler House, 735 High Road, London N12 0US. ☎ 020-8343 6301. Fax 020-8343 6310.

GREENBERG, Rabbi Philip T., B.A., M.Phil., F.J.C.; b. Liverpool, June 28, 1937; Rabbi, Giffnock & Newlands Syn., Glasgow; Rav. Glasgow Shechita Bd. (1993-); Chairman Va'ad HaRabbonim, Glasgow; H. Chaplain, Calderwood Lodge Jewish Sch., Glasg.; M., Nottingham Syn. (1968-72), Highams Park & Chingford Syn. (1959-68); Head, Mishna Stream, Hasmonean Boys' Sch. (1972-81). Ad.: 20 Ayr Rd., Glasgow, G46 6RY. ☎ 0141-638 0309.

GREENGROSS, Dr. Wendy, M.B., B.S.(Lond.), L.R.C.P., M.R.C.S., D.Obst., R.C.O.G.; Dip. Med. Law & Eth.; b. London, Apr. 29, 1925; Medical Practitioner; Broadcaster; Medical Consultant; Marriage Guidance C.; V. President, AJY Fel., Leo Baeck Coll.; Tr., Leonard Cheshire Foundation; President, Ranulf Assn.; Member Govt. Enquiry into human fertilisation and embryology; Chairman, Ethics Cttee, Wellington Humana Hospital Publ.: Sex in the Middle Years, Sex in Early Marriage; Marriage, Sex and Arthritis; The Health of Women; Entitled to Love; Jewish and Homosexual; Living, Loving and Aging. Ad.: 2 Willifield Way, NW11 7XT. ☎ 020-8455 1153.

GREENWOOD, Jeffrey Michael, M.A., LL.M.; b. London, Apr. 21, 1935; Solicitor; Chairman Wigmore Property Investment Tr. plc; Stow Securities plc; Consultant Nabarro Nathanson; Chairman Central Council for Education and Training in Social Work (1993-98); V. President and Dir. Jewish Care; Exec., Anglo-Israel Assn.; Tr & Exec., English Frs., Jerusalem Coll. of Tech (1980-98); Dir., Bank Leumi (UK) plc; Dep. Chairman Jewish Chronicle Ltd.; M. Council JHSE. Ad.: Lacon House, 2 Theobalds Ct., Theobalds Rd., London WC1X 8SH. ☎ 020-7518 3323. Fax 020-7629 7900.

GROSBERG, Percy, M.Sc., Ph.D.; b. Cape Town, Apr. 5, 1925; Sr. Res. Off, S. African Wool Textile Res. Instit.(1949-55); Res. Prof., Chair of Textile Engineering, Leeds Univ., (1960-90); Member Bd. Gov. and currently Marcus Sieff Prof. Shenkar Coll. of Textile Tech. & Fashion, Ramat Gan; Form. Chairman, Leeds Frs., Bar-Ilan Univ. Publ.: Scientific writings. Ad.: Apt 25, 55 Shlomo Hamelech, Netanya 42267. ☎ 09-8628652.

GROSS, Solomon Joseph, C.M.G.; b. London, Sept. 3, 1920; Ret., Dir., British Steel (1978-90), Plc and other comps.; Dir., Reg. Affairs, B.T.G. (1983-84); Under-Sec., Dept. of Industry (1974-80); Min., Brit. Embassy, Pretoria (1969-73); Brit. Dep. High Com. in Ghana (1966-67). Ad.: 38 Barnes Ct., Station Rd., New Barnet, EN5 1QY.

GRUNEWALD, Rabbi Hans Isaac; b. Frankfurt-am-Main, March 15, 1914; Com. Rabbi of Munich (ret.); Member, Standing Cttee., Conf of European Rab. Union of Orth. Jewish Congs. of Continental Europe, form. Chief Rabbi, Hamburg, Niedersachsen and Schleswig Holstein; President, B'nai B'rith Hebraica Lodge, Munich, President, B'nai B'rith Bialik Lodge, Tel Aviv; President, Z. Org., Munich; Jt. Chairman, C., C.C.J., Munich. Publ.: Die Lehre Israels, (1970); Einblicke, (1989); Ad.: 36 Monarch Ct., Lyttelton Rd., N2 0RA. ☎ and Fax 020-8455 0811.

GRUNEWALD, Rabbi Jacob Ezekiel, B.A.; b. Tel Aviv, Oct. 26, 1945; M., Pinner and Distr. Syn. Ad.: 65 Cecil Park, Pinner, Middx., HA5 5HL. ☎ 020-8723 0654.

GRUNWALD, Henry Cecil, LL.B. (Hons); b. London, Aug. 8, 1949; m. Alison née Appleton; Barrister, Queen's Counsel; V. President BoD (1997-); Warden, The Hampstead Synagogue (1997-); Tr. North London Relate (1995-). Ad.: 2 Tudor Street, London EC4Y 0AA. ☎ 020-7797 7111. Fax 020-7797 7120.

GUBBAY, Lucien Ezra, M.A. (Oxon), MICE; b. Buenos Aires, 1931, m. Joyce née Shammah; Consulting Engineer; President of the Board of Elders, Spanish & Portuguese Jews' Congregation London (1996-); member Exec. Jewish Memorial Council; form. Warden S & P Synagogue; form. Warden Beth Holim; form. Dir. Industrial Dwellings Society (1885) Ltd; Flg. Off. RAF (1952-54).

Publ: Ages of Man (1985), The Jewish Book of Why and What (1987), Origins (1989), Quest for the Messiah (1990), You Can Beat Arthritis (1992), The Sephardim (1992), Sunlight and Shadow: Jewish Experience of Islam (1999). Ad.: 26 Linden Lea, London N2 0RG. ☎ 020-8458 3385.

GUTERMAN, Henry, M.L.I.A. (Dip.), A.M.C.T.; b. Berlin, Jan. 22, 1926; President, Jewish Rep. C. Greater Manchester & Region, (1986-89), Vice-President and Mem. BoD. (1992-98); Chairman, Def. & Publ. Rel. Cttee. (1978-86, 1997-); Exec., Manch. C. for Com. Rel.; Bd., Com. Rel. Housing Assn.; Memb. Coleyhurst Police Community Action Group, North Manchester Crime Prevention Cttee; V. President Disabled Living (1986-); Exec., Manchester Zionist Central Council (1986-); Vice-Chairman CCJ Manchester Branch (1994-); Bd., South-east Lancashire Housing Assoc Ltd. (SELHAL); Exec., Outreach for Jew Youth; Bd., Heathlands Jewish Homes for Aged; Vice-Chairman Manchester Action Cttee. on Health Care for Ethnic Minorities, (M.A.C.H.E.M.) (1984-); Mem. Man. North Manchester Jewish Youth Project (1995-); V.Chairman, Tameside Com. Health C. (1974-77); Chairman, Northwest Cttee. Against Racism (1972-75) C. Nat. League of Hospital Frs. (1968-77) Ad.: 42 Lidgate Grove, Didsbury, Manchester, M20 6TS. ☎ 0161-434 4019; 0161-876 4543 (off.) Fax 0161-877 4340.

HALBAN, Peter Francis, B.A. (Princeton); b. New York, June 1 1946; Book Publisher; Dir., Peter Halban Publishers Ltd. (1986-); C. European Jewish Publication Soc. (1994-); Memb. Exec. Institute for Jewish Policy Research (1994-). Ad.: Peter Halban Publishers, 22 Golden Square, London W1R 3PA. ☎ 020-7437 9300. Fax 020-7437 9512.

HAMBURGER, Sir Sidney Cyril, C.B.E., J.P., D.L., Hon. LL.D. (Manch.), M.A.(Salford); b. Manchester, July 14, 1914; Dep. Lieut, Greater Manch.; Nat. P. (form. Chairman), Trades Adv. C. (1984-); President, Friends of Lithuanian Jewry (1996); V. President, Beth Hatefutsoth; Jt. Life President, JIA (Manchester) 1987; V. President, King David Sch. (1991); President, Citizens Advice Bureaux/Greater Manchester (1990); V. President, British Lung Foundation (North West) 1987; President, Motability North West 1989; Chairman, Citizens' Advice Bureau, Greater Manch. (1985-90); C. Anglo-Israel Assn. (1984); Chairman, Manchester Cttee. For Soviet Jewry (1984-94); Chairman, North Western Reg. Health Auth. (1972-83) Chairman, Age Concern, Salford (1983); Chairman Northeast Manch H.M.C. (1971-74); Cllr. & Alderman, Salford City C. (1946-71); Mayor of Salford (1968-69); L.P Jewish Homes for Aged; Life President, Z. Central C.; V. President, Anglo-Israel Friendship League; form. President, C. of Manch. & Salford Jews; V. President, Magen David Adom; P. J.I.A Manch.; V. President, Mizrachi Fed.; Ch North-West ASH (1975); B'nai B'rith Award (1984); Pro. Ecclesiastical Papal Award (1983); Salvation Army Adv. Bd. (1983); President, Bar-Ilan (Manchester) (1969); Gov., King David School (1969); Supplementary Benefits Com. (1966-75); N.W. Elec. Consumer C. (1953-70); Coun, Manch. Univ. (1974-83); Ch Hillel House, Manch.; Bd. of Govs, H. Fel., Bar-Ilan Univ. (1979); Gov., Ben-Gurion Univ. (1984). Ad.: 26 New Hall Rd., Salford M7 4HQ. ☎ 0161-834 5452. Fax 0161-839 5133.

HAMILTON, Fabian, B.A., M.P.; b. April 12, 1955; m. Rosemary née Ratcliffe; M.P., Leeds North-East (1997-); Leeds City Councillor (1987-97); Chair Edcu. Cttee. (1996-97); Chair Economic Development Cttee (1994-96); Chair Race Equality Cttee (1988-94). Ad.: House of Commons, SW1A 0AA. ☎ 020-7219 3493. Fax 020-7219 4945.

HANDLER, Arieh L.; b. Brun, May 27, 1915; Financial. Consultant; Jewish Agency C. & Member Z. Actions Cttee., P. Mizrachi Fed.; Chairman, Bachad Fellowship (Friends of B'nai Akiva); Chairman, Adv. Body, Torah Dept., Jewish Agency; BoD International Div. (form. Chairman, Israel Cttee.); Exec. Jewish Child's Day, Youth Aliyah, (form Dir., Y.A.); Exec WZO; V.Chairman, Brit Frs.,

Boy's Town, Jerusalem, V. President (form. Chairman) Nat. C. for Soviet Jewry; Montefiore Found.; Jewish Colonial Tr. C.; President, Brit. Frs., Israel Aged, Edr., Jewish Review World Exec. Religious Zionist Movement, T. Mifal Hatorah Aid Foundation; Patron, Jerusalem Institute for the Blind; President, Midreshet Eretz Yisrael; Member, Instit. of Bankers; Fel., Instit. of Dirs.; form. Dir., Hapoel Hamizrachi World Org; form. Man. Dir., Migdal London, Man. Dir. JCB, London. Ad.: c/o Reform Club, SW1.

HARDMAN, Rev. Leslie Henry, M.B.E., M.A, H.C.F.; b. Glynneath, Wales, Feb. 18, 1913; Emer. M., Hendon Syn., V. President, Herut Org.; H. President, N.W. Lond. Jewish Ex-Servicemen's Assn.; Chaplain, Napesbury, Shenley, Hospitals, Edgware Hospital (Medical Section); Publ.: The Survivors. Awards: BBC 'Hearts of Gold', 1993; Simon Wiesenthal Museum of Tolerance, 1995. Ad.: 20 St. Peter's Ct., Queens Rd., NW4 2HG. ☎ 020-8202 6977.

HARMATZ, Joseph; b. Rokishkis, Lithuania, Jan. 23, 1925; Dir.-Gen Emeritus World ORT Union; Dir.-Gen., ORT Israel (1967-79); Comptroller ORT Israel (1960-67).

HARRIS, Rabbi Cyril K., B.A., M.Phil.; b. Glasgow, Sept. 19, 1936; Chief Rabbi of South Africa; H. President S.A. Jewish Board of Educ.; H.V.-P. S.A. Zionist Fed., H. P. Mizrachi Org.; H. President S.A. Rabbinical Assoc.; form. M., Kenton Syn. (1958-72), Edgware Syn. (1975-78), St. John's Wood Syn. (1979-87); Sr. Jewish Chap. to H.M. Forces (1966-71); Nat. Dir. Hillel Foundation (1972-75); Chairman, C., U S Rabbis (1978-82); Jt. Chairman, & V. President; Mizrachi (1983-87). Ad.: c/o Union of Orthodox Synagogues of South Africa, 55 Garden Rd., Orchards 2192, Johannesburg, S. Africa. ☎ 485-4865. Fax 485-1497.

HARRIS, Dr Evan, M.P., B.A., B.M., B.Ch.; b. Sheffield, Oct. 21, 1965; Registrar in Public Health Medicine (1994-97), M.P. (Lib.Dem.) Oxford West and Abingdon (1997-). Publ. Medical papers. Ad.: House of Commons, London SW1 0AA. ☎ 020-72193614; 32a North Hinksey Village, Oxford OX2 8NA. ☎ 01865-250624.

HARRIS, Michael; b. London, Aug. 8, 1928; Public Relations Adviser; Admin. 'Operation Angel'; London repr. Delamere Forest School; form. Dir. United Kingdom Jewish Aid, form. Insurance Manager, Freeman of City of London (1976); AJY: Exec (1953-94), V. Pres (1981-), Chairman (1989-93); AJA: Council (1960-); AJEX: Tr. Sutton AJEX (1990-); BoD: Member (for AJY 1958-73) for Sutton & Cheam (1973-); Central J. Lect.. Comm (1982-94); V.C. (1988-91); Chairman (1991-94), Exec. Comm (1991-94); Educ. Comm (V.C. 1994-97) United Syn. Council (1984-): Israel Comm (1993-) World Confed. JCC's (V.P. (1990-96). Imperial Cancer Research Fund: Life Gov. (1985); Jewish Youth Fund: Adv. Cttee. (1989-95), Nat. Assoc Boys Clubs: C. (1988-); Sutton Synagogue: H. Sec. (1978-84), Warden (1984-88); H. Tr. South London Comm. C. (1990-); North West Jewish Boys Club: H. Sec. (1956-66). Ad.: 40 York Rd., Cheam, Surrey, SM2 6HH. ☎ 020-8643 3228.

HARRIS, Rabbi Michael Jacob, M.A. (Cantab), M.A. (Jerusalem); b. London, Feb. 17, 1964; m. Sara, née Keen; Rabbi, Hampstead Synagogue (1995-); Lecturer in Jewish Law, Jews' College, London (1995-97); Consultant, Limmud; form. Rabbi, Southend and Westcliff Hebrew Cong. (1992-95). Ad.: The Hampstead Synagogue, Dennington Park Rd., London NW6 1AX. ☎/Fax 020-7435 1518. Fax 020-7431 8368.

HASS, Rev. Simon, L.L.C.M.; b. Poland, May 2, 1927; Cantor Central Syn. Gt Portland St., London,W.l. (since 1951); Composer Musical Arranger. Publ.: Many Recordings of Jewish liturgical and classical music. Ad.: "Beit Shirah", 2A Allandale Ave., N3 3PJ.

HAYMAN, Baroness Helene of Dartmouth Park (née Middleweek), M.A. (Cantab); b. Wolverhamp-ton, March 26, 1949; m. Martin Hayman; Parliamentary Under Sec. of State, Dept. of Environment, Transport and the Regions (1997-98); PPS Dept. of Health (1998-); Labour Mem. of Parliament (1974-79);

Chairman, Whittington Hospital (1992-97). Ad.: House of Lords, SW1A 1AA.
HEILBRON, Dame Rose, D.B.E., LL.B., LL.M., Hon. LL.D. (Liverpool), Hon.
LL.D. (Warwick), Hon. LL.D. (Manchester); Hon. LL.D. (C.N.A.A.); b. Liverpool,
Aug. 19, 1914; Judge of the High Court' Family Division (1974-88); Tr., Gray's
lnn (1985); Presiding Judge, Northern Circuit (1979-82); form. Leader, Northern
Circuit Recorder and H. Recorder of Burnley; Bencher, Gray's Inn; H. Fel., Lady
Margaret Hall, Oxford; H.Fel., Manch. Univ. Instit. of Sci. & Tech.
HELFGOTT, Ben; b. Pabianice, Poland, Nov. 22, 1929; Comp. Dir., Chairman,
'45 Aid Soc. (since 1975; 1963-70); Chairman, Yad Vashem Cttee., BoD;
Chairman C., Promotion of Yiddish & Yiddish Culture; C., Jewish Youth Fund;
Exec., Wiener Libr.; Chairman, Polin-Inst. for Polish Jewish Studies; form. Jt. T.,
CBF-WJR; Brit. Weightlifting Champion & Record Holder; competed in
Olympic Games (1956; 1960); Bronze Medal, Commonwealth Games (1958);
Gold Medals, Maccabiah (1950, 1953, 1957). Ad.: 46 Amery Rd., Harrow,
Middx. HA1 3UG. ☎ 020-8422 1512.
HELLNER, Rabbi Frank, B.A., B.H.L., M.A., D.D. (Hon.); b. Philadelphia, Pa.,
Jan. 1, 1935; Emer. Rabbi Finchley Progressive Syn.; Exec., Barnet Com. Rel. C.;
Gov., Akiva Sch.; V. President, Finchley CCJ, Member Leo Baeck Coll. Comp.;
Extra-Mural Lect. Birkbech Coll. (Pt.-time); Chairman, ULPS Rabbinic
Conference (1970-71); Edr., ULPS News (1978-86); Chaplain to Mayor of L. B.
Barnet (1993-94). Publ.: I Promise I Will Try not to Kick My Sister and Other
Sermons. Ad.: Finchley Progressive Synagogue, 54 Hutton Grove, N12 8DR.
Tel/Fax 020-8446 4063.
HENIG, Stanley, M.A., (Oxford); Hon. R.N.C.M., (Royal Northern College of
Music); b. Leicester, July 7, 1939; Prof. (Emeritus) of Politics, University of
Central Lancashire; Leader, Lancaster City Council (1991-); M.P. (Lancaster)
(1966-70) Chairman, R.N.C.M. (1986-89); Secretary Labour Group, Local
Government Association (1997-). Publ.: Uniting of Europe (1997) and other
books on political parties and on European Union. Ad.: 10 Yealand Drive,
Lancaster LA1 4EW. ☎ 01524 69624.
HERMAN, Josef, O.B.E., R.A. Elect; b. Warsaw, Jan. 1, 1911; Artist-Painter;
Exhibitions in many cities in UK and in Geneva, Auckland, Melbourne, Basle,
Frankfurt etc. Gold Medal for services to the Arts in Wales; Works purchased by
public collections in UK, Australia, Canada, Israel, S. Africa. Publ.: Related
Twilights, Notes from a Welsh Diary. Ad.: 120 Edith Rd., W14. ☎ 020-8603 5091.
HERSHON, Cyril P., M.A., Ph.D. (Jewish Ed.) M.I.L.; b. Liverpool March 17,
1937; Writer and Broadcaster; University of the West of England; Associate,
Université de Montpellier. Ret. (as head of M.L.) Clifton Coll.; Housemaster,
Polack's House, Clifton Coll. (1979-86); Court, Bath Univ. Publ.: To Make
Them English, When the Rabbi Laughs, Judaism – a GCSE Resource Book,
Ripples, The Castles of Cary, Judaism - a National Curriculum handbook, Ashes
& Remorse, The Painter and the Poet, Le Breviari d'Amor (co-ed.), Rabbinical
Schools of Medieval Languedoc. Ad.: L.E.S., University of the West of England,
Frenchay Campus, Coldharbour Lane, Bristol BS16 1QY. ☎ 0117- 9656261.
HERTZBERG, Rabbi Arthur, Ph.D.; b. Lubaczow, Poland; Rabbi Emer., Temple
Emanuel of Englewood; form. President, American Jewish Cong.; Hon. V.
President, World Jewish Cong.; V. President, Member Foundation for Jewish
Culture; Prof. of Religion Emer., Dartmouth Coll., Adjunct Prof of Hist.
Columbia Univ, Prof of Hist., Hebrew Univ. (1970-71); Fel. Instit. Advanced
Studies, Hebrew Univ. (1982); Vis. Prof. of the Humanities, New York Univ.
Publ.: The Zionist Idea, Judaism, The French Enlightenment and the Jews, Being
Jewish in America, The Jews in America (1989), Judaism, 2nd ed. (1991), Jewish
Polemics (1992), Jews, the Essence and Character of a People (jt.auth., 1998).
Ad.: 83 Glenwood Rd., Englewood, New Jersey 07631, USA. ☎ 201-568-3259.
HILL, Brad Sabin, A.B., F.R.A.S.; b. New York, Nov. 2, 1953; Librarian and Fel.
in Hebrew Bibliography, Oxford Centre for Hebrew and Jewish Studies; form.

Hd., Hebrew Section, The British Library (1989-96); Curator of Rare Hebraica, National Library of Canada, Ottawa (1979-89). Publ.: Incunabula, Hebraica & Judaica (1981); Hebraica from the Valmadonna Trust (1989); (ed.) Miscellanea Hebraica Bibliographica (1995). Ad.: 119 Banbury Road, Oxford OX2 6LB.

HILTON, Rabbi Michael, M.A., D.Phil., P.G.C.E.; b. London, Feb. 27, 1951; M. North London Progressive Synagogue (1999-); M. Cheshire Reform Congregation (1987-98); Homeless Persons off., L.B. Hammersmith & Fulham (1980-82). Publ.: The Gospels and Rabbinic Judaism (with G. Marshall, 1988.), The Christian Effect on Jewish Life (1994). Ad.: North London Progressive Synagogue, 100 Amhurst Park, London N16 5AR. ☎ 020-8800 8931. Fax 020-8800 0416. Email greystar@zetnet.co.uk

HOBSBAWM, Eric John Ernest, C.H., F.B.A., M.A., Ph.D.; b. Alexandria, Egypt, June 9, 1917; Emer. Prof of Econ. and Soc. Hist., Birkbeck Coll., Lond. Univ.; H. Fel., King's Coll., Cambridge. Publ.: Primitive Rebels, The Jazz Scene, The Age of Revolution, Labouring Men, Industry and Empire, Nations and Nationalism, The Age of Extremes, 1914-1991, Uncommon People, etc. Ad.: Birkbeck College, Malet St., WC1E 7HX. ☎ 020-7631 6000.

HOCHHAUSER, Victor, C.B.E.; b. Kosice, Czechoslovakia, Mar. 27, 1923; Impresario for internat. artists orchestras, ballet companies, etc. Ad.: 4 Oak Hill Way, NW3 7LR. ☎ 020-7794 0987. Fax 020-7431 2531.

HOWARD, Michael, Q.C., M.P.; b. Gorseinon, Wales, July 7, 1941; M.P. (Cons) for Folkestone and Hythe; Shadow Foreign Secretary (1997-99); form. Home Secretary (1993-97); Secretary of State for the Environment (1992-93); Chairman, Conservative Bow Group (1970-71); form. President, Cambridge Union. Ad.: House of Commons, SW1A 0AA.

HUBERT, Walter I., F.R.S.A., F. Inst. Dir.; b. Schluechtern, Germany, Aug. 13, 1932; First Chairman, Gateshead Foundation for Torah, I.J.A.; Patron, Didsbury Jewish Primary Sch.; H. Life V. President, Brit. Cttee., Peylim of Israei; Gov., Global Bd., & H. Fel., Bar-Ilan Univ.; Gov., Ben Gurion Univ.; V. President, Cancer Res. Cttee., Dir. State of Israel Bonds (UK); V.P; British Herut; form. Chairman, Blackburn Rovers F.C.; First Recipient (1981) Bank Hapoalim Silver Rose Award for new Israeli industry; Jerusalem Educ. Medal (1974); Zurich Jewish Secondary Schs.; "Man of Year" Gold Medal (1978); assoc. with many educ. and charitable instit. in Brit., Israel Switzerland, US & Argentina. Ad.: 24 King David Gdns., 27 King David St., Jerusalem, Israel. ☎ 02 241754.

HURST, Alex; b. Liverpool, Jan. 6, 1935; form. Admin., Merseyside Jewish Welfare C.; form. Sec., L'pool Jewish Housing Assn. Ad.: 440 Allerton Rd., Liverpool L18 3JX. ☎ 0151-427 7377.

HYMAN, Barry S., M.I.P.R.; b. Scotland, June 24, 1941, m. Judith; Public Relations and Media Consultant, Broadcaster, Writer; PR consultant and newsletter editor to Reform Synagogues of Great Britain; BoD Public Relations Cttee (1988-97); Member of the Institute of Public Relations (1987-); Head of Corporate Affairs, Media Relations, Community Affairs and Company Archive, Marks and Spencer (1984-94). Publ.: Young in Herts (1996), a history of the Radlett and Bushey Reform Synagogue; (Ed.) Reform Judaism News. Ad.: RSGB, 80 East End Rd., London N3 2SY. ☎ 020-8349 4731. Fax 020-8343 0901. Email: hymanb@refsyn.org.uk

HYMAN, Mrs. Marguerite Grete (née De Jongh); b. London, Mar. 26, 1913; V. President (form. Fin. Sec.) Union of Lib. & Progr. Syns.; Ad.: 14 The Cedars, St. Stephen's Rd., W13 8JF. ☎ 020-8997 8258.

INGRAM, Rabbi Chaim Nota, B.A.(Hons.); b. London, May 14, 1952; Assoc. Rabbi, The Central Synagogue, Sydney; M., Leicester Hebrew Cong. (1986-92); M./R., United Hebrew Cong., Newcastle Upon Tyne (1982-96); R., Cricklewood Syn, London (1979-82). Publ.: Renana Song Book. Ad: 196 Old South Head Road, Bellevue Hill, Sydney, NSW 2023. ☎/Fax 02-9365 5716.

ISRAEL, Jonathan Irvine, M.A., D.Phil., F.R.H.S., F.B.A.; b. London, Jan. 22,

1946; Professor, Dutch Hist. & Instits., Lond. Univ., Univ. Coll.; H. Sec., JHSE (1974-79); Wolfson Hist. Prize (1986); Ed. Littman Library of Jewish Civilization (1990-). Publ.: European Jewry in the Age of Mercantilism, 1550-1750, The Dutch Republic and the Hispanic World, 1606-61, Race, Class and Politics in Colonial Mexico, 1610-70, Dutch Primacy in World Trade (1585-1740), Empires and Entrepots: the Dutch, the Spanish Monarchy and the Jews, 1585-1713, Anglo-Dutch moment: essays on the Glorious Revolution and its world impact, The Dutch Republic, its rise, greatness and fall, 1477-1806 (1995); Conflicts of Empires: Spain, the Low Countries and the Struggle for World Supremacy, 1585-1713 (1997). Ad.: 48 Parkside Dr., Edgware, Middx. HA8 8JX. ☎ 020-8958 6069.

ISSERLIN, Benedict Sigmund Johannes, M.A. (Edin.), M.A., B.Litt., D.Phil. (Oxon.), D.H.L., h.c.; b. Munich, Feb. 25, 1916; form. Reader and Head of Dept. Semitic Studies, Leeds Univ.; form. H. Sec., Anglo-Israel Archaeological Soc.; President, Brit. Assn. for Jewish Studies (1982). Publ.: Writings on Near Eastern Studies, incl. A Hebrew Work Book for Beginners; Ch. on Israelite Art in C. Roth, Jewish Art; Motya, a Phoenician and Carthaginian City in Sicily, I (with J. du Plat Taylor); A Study of Contemporary Dialectal Maltese, I (with J. Aquilina); Contr. Times Atlas of the Bible, The Israelites (1998), and O. Tufnell, Lachish IV. Ad.: c/o Dept. of Arabic and Middle Eastern Studies, Leeds Univ., Leeds, LS2 9JT. ☎ 0113 2751576.

JACKSON, Bernard Stuart, LL.B. (Hons.), D. Phil., LL.D.; b. Liverpool, Nov. 16, 1944; Barrister; Alliance Family Professor of Modern Jewish Studies, Co-Dir. Centre for Jewish Studies, Univ. Manchester (1997-); form. Queen Victoria Prof. of Law, Liverpool Univ. (1989-97); form. Prof. of Law, Kent Univ. (1985-89); Prof. & Head, Law Dept., L'pool Polytechnic (1977-85); Lady Davis Vis. Prof., Hebrew Univ. (1981); Speaker's Lect. in Biblical Studies, Oxford Univ. (1983-86); Gruss Vis. Prof. of Talmudic Legal Studies, Harvard Law School (1992); form. Chairman, Jewish Law Assn.; President BAJS; Edr., The Jewish Law Annual; Sec., J. Law Publ. Fund. Publ.: Theft in Early Jewish Law, Essays in Jewish and Comparative Legal Hist., Semiotics and Legal Theory, Law, Fact and Narrative Coherence, Making Sense in Law, Making Sense in Jurisprudence, (Edr.) Studies in Jewish Legal Hist. in Hon. of David Daube, Modern Research in Jewish Law, Jewish Law in Legal Hist. and the Modern World, Semiotics, Law and Social Science (with D. Carzo), The Touro Conference Volume (Jew Law Assn. Studies I), The Jerusalem Conference Volume (Jewish Law Assn. Studies II), The Boston Conference Volume (Jew Law Assn. Studies IV), The Halakhic Thought of R. Isaac Herzog (Jew. Law Assn. Studies V) The Jerusalem 1990 Conference Volume (Jew. Law Assn. Studies VI) (with S. M. Passamaneck), Legal Visions of the New Europe (with D. McGoldrick), Legal Semiotics and the Sociology of Law, Introduction to the History and Sources of Jewish Law (with N. Hecht & others). Ad.: Centre for Jewish Studies, Dept. of Religions and Theology, Arts Building, Univ. Manchester, Oxford Rd., M13 9PL. Fax 0161-729 0371. Email bernard.jackson@man.ac.uk

JACKSON, Rabbi Edward Leo, B.A.; b. Cork, Oct. 28, 1936; form. M., Hampstead Garden Suburb Syn.; Spec. Adv. to the Chief Rabbi; Rel. Adv., Jewish Marriage C., Member Standing Cttee. Conference of European Rabbis, Co.Chairman, Mizrachi Fed.; form. Chairman, Rabbin C., US; M., Kenton Syn. (1972-80); Kingston Syn. (1961-72) Jewish Chaplain to Pentonville Prison; form. Asst. M., Hampstead Syn; Member, Chief Rabbi Cabinet; Member, Working Party Internat. Year of the Family. Ad.: 8 Norrice Lea, N2 ORE. ☎ 020-8458 3306.

JACOB, Sir (Jack) Isaac Hai, Q.C., LL.B. (Lond.), Hon. LL.D. (Birmingham, London, Staffordshire), Dr. Juris. (Würzburg); b. Shanghai, China, June 5, 1908; Chairman Univ. Lond. Jewish Students Union, 1931; form. Master Queen's Bench Division, 1957-1975, Sr. Master of the Supreme Court and Queen's

Remembrancer (1975-80); H. Bencher, Gray's Inn, form. Dir., Instit. of Advanced Legal Studies (1986-88); Freeman, City of London; Fel.Univ. Coll., Lond., Hon. Fel. Univ. Westminster; Past. Edr. Annual Practice, 1960-66, Gen. Ed. Supreme Court Practice (1967-); Fabric of English Civil Justice (Hamlyn Lectures) (1986); International Perspectives on Civil Justice (1990). Ad.: 31 Totteridge Common, London N20 8LT. ☎ 020-8959 4223.

JACOBI, Rabbi Harry Martin, B.A. Hon.; b. Berlin, Oct. 19, 1925; M. South Bucks Jewish Community; form. M., Zurich Lib. Syn.; M., Wembley Lib. Syn.; Southgate Progressive Syn.; President, Southgate B'nai B'rith Ben-Gurion Lodge (1974-75); Chairman, Frs. of Progressive Judaism in Europe and Israel; Chairman, Rabbinic Bd. ULPS. Ad. 29 Sylvan Court, Holden Rd., London N12 7ED. ☎ 020-8446 1837.

JACOBS, David; b. Manchester, 1951; Dir. Syn. Partnership and Programmes, Reform Synagogues of Great Britain; Vice President, Jewish Genealogical Society of G.B.; Co-fdr. Jewish East End Project (1977); Co-fdr. London Museum of Jewish Life (1983); RSGB Youth Development Off. (1975-79); Dir. Victoria Com. Centre (1988-91). Ad.: RSGB, The Sternberg Centre for Judaism, 80 East End Road, Finchley, N3 2SY.

JACOBS, David Lewis, C.B.E., D.L., Hon. Ph.D, Kingston Univ.; b. London, May 19, 1926; Broadcaster; host and Chairman of BBC radio and television pro-grammes; Dep. Lieutenant for Greater Lond., Rep. Dep. Lieutenant for the R. Borough of Kingston upon Thames; V. President, Stars Org. for Spastics; form. Chairman, Think British, Campaign; V. President, R. Star and Garter Home, Richmond; Past President, Nat. Children's Orchestra; form. V. Chairman, R.S.P.C.A.; President, Kingston Upon Thames Royal British Legion; V. President, Wimbledon Girls Choir; Chairman, Kingston Theatre Trust; Life Governor Imperial Cancer Research Fd.; Jt. Pres. Thames Community Tr.; Pres. S.W. London Area SSAFFA; Chairman Thames FM; Pres. T.S. Steadfast; Patron Age Resource; Patron Kingston Bereavement Tr.; Pres. Kingston Alcohol Service. Publ.: Jacobs', Ladder (autobiog.), Caroline, Any Questions (with Michael Bowen). Ad.: 203 Pavilion Rd., SW1X 0BJ.

JACOBS, David Michael, b. Bristol, June 4, 1930, m. Marion née Davis; Exec. (form. Gen. Sec.), AJA; Exec. Herut-Likud UK; Chairman Jewish Affiliates of the United Nations Assoc.; Vice-P., form. Chairman Guild of Jewish Journalists; H.V. President Chiltern Progressive Syn.; form. Chairman, Beds.-Herts. Progressive Jewish Cong.; form. BoD, Press Officer; Brit. Z. Fed. Publ.: Israel (World in Colour series) 1968, Research & writing for Jewish Communities of the World, (Ed. A. Lerman) 1989. Ad.: 56 Normandy Rd., St. Albans, Herts AL3 5PW. ☎ /Fax 01727-858454.

JACOBS, Rabbi Irving, B.A., Ph.D. (Lond.); b. London, Aug. 2, 1938; Princ. Jews, College (1990-93); Res. Fell, (1966-69), Lect. (1969-84); Dean (1984-90); First Incumbent, Sir Israel Brodie Chair in Bible Studies; Dir., Midrashah Instit. for Israel Studies (1980-82); form. Min., Sutton and District Hebrew Cong. Publ.: The Midrashic Process. Ad.: 28 Elmstead Ave., Wembley, Middx. ☎ 020-8248 5777.

JACOBS, Rabbi Julian Godfrey, M.A.; Ph.D. (Lond.), P.G.C.E.; b. London, March 6, 1934; m. Margaret née; form. M., Ealing Syn.; Chap., Thames Valley Univ.; Chap., Heathrow Airport; M. of Chief Rabbi's Cabinet; Exec. cttee Interfaith Network; form. M., Liverpool Old Hebrew Cong.; M., Blackpool United Hebrew Cong.; Barking & Becontree Syn.; West Hackney Syn.; Richmond Syn. Chap. to Mayor of Ealing (1992-93); Publ.: The Ship has a Captain, From Week to Week, Judaism looks at Modern Issues, A Haftara Companion. Ad.: Rehov Shaulson 30/7, Har Nof, Jerusalem 95400. ☎ 6541859.

JACOBS, June Ruth (née Caller), b. London, June 1, 1930; Professional Volunteer; World President, Int. Council of Jewish Women; Chairman, BOD Standing Conference on Central and Eastern European Jewish Communities; V. Chairman, Jewish Council for Racial Equality and Jewish Black Forum; Co-Chairman, Int. Executive Int. Centre for Peace in Middle East; Life Mem. League of Jewish Women; L. President, Jewish Child's Day; Chairman, Kessler Foundation; Exec. Mem., Council for Jewish Palestinian Dialogue; Exec. Mem., Jewish Youth Fund; Exec. Mem., Board of Deputies; Mem. Intl. Bd. Dir. New Israel Fund; Mem., Inst. of Jewish Policy Research; Sec., Memorial Foundation for Jewish Culture; Exec. European Jewish Congress; Exec. World J. Congress. Ad.: 13 Modbury Gardens, NW5 3QE. ☎ 020-7485 6027. Fax 020-7284 2809.

JACOBS, Rabbi Louis, C.B.E., B.A., Ph.D., H.D.H.L. (Chicago, New York, Cincinnati), H.Li.D. (Lancaster); b. Manchester, July 17, 1920; M., New London Syn. (since 1964); Vis. Prof, Lancaster Univ.; form. H. Dir., Soc. for Study of Jewish Theology; form. Tutor and Lect., Jews, Coll. (1959-62), form. Minister-Preacher, New West End Syn., London (1954-59); and Rab., Manchester Central Syn. Publ: Jewish Prayer, We Have Reason to Believe, Jewish Values, Principles of the Jewish Faith, A Jewish Theology, Teyku, The Talmudic Argument, A Tree of Life, Helping with Enquiries, Holy Living; God, Torah and Israel, Structure and Form of the Babylonian Talmud, Religion and the Individual, The Jewish religion: a companion, Beyond Reasonable Doubt, Ask the Rabbi, Concise Companion to the Jewish Religion, etc. Ad.: 27 Clifton Hill, NW8 0QE ☎ 020-7624 1299.

JACOBS, Myrna, née Appleton; b. London, Aug. 18, 1940; m. Laurance D. Jacobs; Headteacher of Immanuel College; Head of Languages, Anna Head High, Berkeley, California (1962-66); Lecturer, Univ. of California Extension (Berkeley & San Francisco) (1964-66); Head of Language Faculty in Borough of Brent, consecutively Brondesbury & Kilburn, John Kelly Girls, Preston Manor (1973-89); 1st Deputy Head, Immanuel College (1990-95). Ad.: Immanuel College, 87-91 Elstree Rd., Bushey, Herts WD2 3RH. ☎ 020-8950 0604. Fax 020-8950 8687.

JACOBSON, Dan, B.A.; b. Johannesburg, March 7, 1929; Novelist and univ. Prof. Emer., Univ. Coll. London (1994-); Publ.: A Dance in the Sun, The Beginners, The Rape of Tamar, The Story of Stories: the Chosen People and its God, Her Story, Heshel's Kingdom, etc. Ad.: c/o A. M. Heath & Co., 79 St. Martin's La., WC2N 4AA ☎ 020-7836 4271.

JAKOBOVITS, Lady, Amelie (née Munk); b. Ansbach, May 31, 1928; wife of Lord Jakobovits; Fdr. and President, Assoc. of US Women; V. President, Emunah Women's Org.; President, Jewish Marriage C., Dir. of Jewish Care; Fdr. and Patron of Chai Lifeline, L.P. JIA Women's Division; Life V. President, League of Jewish Women; Patron of Dysautonomia Foundation; V. President, Wizo; P. Ladies, Visitation Cttee., US; V. President, Youth Aliyah; Patron 'J' Link; President, 'Chen'. Ad.: 44a Albert Rd., London NW4 2SJ.

JANNER, Baron of Braunstone (Life Peer) (Hon., Greville Ewan), M.A. (Cantab), Hon. Ph.D. (Haifa), Hon. LL.D. (De Montfort), Q.C.; b. Cardiff, July 11, 1928; Barrister-at-law; form. M.P. (Lab.) for Leicester West (1970-97); President Inter Party Council Against Anti-Semitism; Chairman, Select Cttee. on Employment (1993-96); Dir., Ladbroke plc (1986-95); Chairman, JSB Group Ltd., including Effective Presentational Skills (1984-97); President, BoD (1979-85); P. Commonwealth Jewish C.; Chairman, Trs., Commonwealth Jewish Tr.; Hon. V. President, WJC ; Fdr. and V.Chairman, All-Party Parl. Cttee. for Jews from the FSU; V. Chairman, Brit.-Israel Parl. Group, H. Sec., All-Party Parl. War Crimes Group; Chairman, Holocaust Educ. Tr.; President, Maimonides Foundation; Sec., Parl. Cttee. for East European Jewry (1993-97); Chairman, All-Party Parl. Industrial Safety Group (1975-97); P. Ret. Execs. Action Group (REACH); President, Jewish Museum; Bd. Dirs., UJIA; Tr., Elsie & Barnett Janner Tr.; Exec., Lab. Frs. of Israel; V. President, AJY, Ajex; Fel., Inst. of Personnel and Development; Member N.U.J.; H. Member, Nat. Union Mineworkers (Leics. Br.); form. President, WJC (Europe); form. President, Nat. C. for Soviet Jewry; form. Tr., Jewish Chronicle, form. Dir., Jewish Chronicle; President, Camb. Union & Fdr. & Chairman, The Bridge in Britain; Chairman, Camb. Univ. Lab.

Club; form. Chairman, Brady Boys, Club. Lect., contrib. and author 68 books. Ad.: House of Lords, London SW1A 0PW.

JAQUE, Sidney, J.P.; b. Toledo, Ohio, USA, June 23, 1912; Ret. Solicitor; form. Mayor of Holborn (1958), H.L. Patron (form. Chairman), Camden (form. Holborn) Chamber of Commerce; form. Chairman, Camden Commercial Ratepayers Group (since 1979); Past President, now Hon. Life President Western Marble Arch Syn. (form. Western Syn.); Chairman, Western Charitable Foundation; form. Gov., St. Nicholas Montessori Instit.; form. Gov., J.F.S.; form. Dep. Chairman, West Central Magistrates, Div.; V. President (form. President), Holborn & St. Pancras Conservative Assn.; Patron Frs., Royal Lond. Homoeopathic Hospital, Vice-P., London Youth Tr. Publ.: The Western Synagogue, 1961-1991 (1998). Ad.: 56 Sheringham, St. Johns Wood Park, NW8 6RA. ☎ 020-7722 3671. Fax 020-7722 9317.

JOSEPH, Dr Anthony Peter, MB.BChir. (Cantab), MRCGP, FSG; b. Birmingham, April 23, 1937; General Medical Practitioner; Post-graduate tutor in paediatrics, Univ. of Birmingham (1986-91); form. President JHSE (1994-96); President, Jewish Genealogical Society of Gt. Britain (1997-); Chairman, Birmingham Branch of JHSE (1969-); Corresponding member for Great Britain, Australian Jewish Historical Society (1965-); UK rep. of Society of Australian Genealogists (1965-95); Contributor on Jewish Genealogy to Blackwell Companion to Jewish Culture; Author of papers in many different genealogical publications, including JHSE. Ad.: 25 Westbourne Road, Edgbaston, Birmingham B15 3TX. ☎ 0121-454 0408. Fax 0121-454 9758.

JOSEPH, Jack, M.D., D.Sc., F.R.C.O.G., F.C.S.L.T. (Hon); b. Glasgow, Dec. 28, 1913; Emer. Prof., Lond. Univ. Publ.: Textbook of Regional Anatomy, Medical works. Ad.: 17 Greenfield Gdns., NW2 1HT. ☎ 020-8458 4373.

JOSEPH, John Michael; b. London, 11 Feb. 1939; Chairman, GET Plc; Chairman, Jewish Blind & Disabled; Chairman, Cavendish Housing Trust Ltd. Ad.: 24 Rosslyn Hill, London NW3.

JOSIPOVICI, Prof. Gabriel David; b. Nice, France, Oct. 8, 1940; Writer; Univ. Teacher; Prof. of English, School of European Studies, Univ. of Sussex; Asst. Lect. in English, School of European Studies, Univ. of Sussex (1963-5); Lect. in English (1965-73); Reader in English (1973-85); Lord Weidenfeld Vis. Prof., Oxford (1996-97). Publ.: The Inventory, Words, The Present, Migrations, The Air We Breathe, Conversations in Another Room, Contre-Jour, The Big Glass, In a Hotel Garden, Moo Pak, Now, The World and the Book, The Lessons of Modernism, The Book of God, Text and Voice, Touch, On Trust. Ad.: 60 Prince Edward's Rd., Lewes, Sussex BN7 1BH.

JUST, Rabbi Mayer; b. Wignitz, Aug. 15, 1912; President Chief Rabbinate of Holland; Ad.: Frans Van Mierisstraat 77, 107 1 RN Amsterdam.

KALMS, Lady Pamela, M.B.E.; b. London, July 29, 1931; Vol. Services Co-ordinator, Edgware Gen. Hospital; Deputy Chairman, NHS Wellhouse Tr. (Barnet and Edgware Gen. Hospitals); Tr. and Dir., Ravenswood Foundation. Ad.: 29 Farm Street, London W1X 7RD. ☎ 020-7499 3494. Fax 020-7499 3436.

KALMS, Sir Stanley, Hon. F.C.G.I. (1991), Hon. D.Litt. CNAA/ University of London (1991), Hon. D. Univ. North London (1994), Hon. Fellow London Business School (1995), Hon. D. Econ. Richmond (1996); b. London Nov. 21, 1931; m. Pamela née; Chairman Dixons Group plc; Dir. Centre for Policy Studies (1991-); Vis. Prof., Business Sch., Univ. (formerly Poly.) of North London (1991-); Mem. of Bd. of Funding Agency for Schs – Chairman of the Agency's Finance Cttee (1994-97); Gov., Dixons Bradford City Technology Coll. (1988-); Tr. Industry in Educn. Ltd. F(1993-);Gov. of National Institute of Economic & Social Research (1995-); Dir. Business for Sterling (1998-); Tr. – The Economic Education Tr. (1993); F. and Sponsor of Centre for Applied Jewish Ethics in Business and the Professions, Jerusalem; Fd. of Stanley Kalms Foundation; Co-

Fd. and Sponsor of Immanuel College; form. Chairman of The Jewish Educational Development Tr. (1978-89) and Jews' College (1983-89); Non-Exec. Dir., British Gas (1987-97); Chairman King's Healthcare NHS Trust (1993-96). Publ.: A Time for Change (1992). Ad.: 29 Farm Street, London W1X 7RD. ☎ 020-7499 3494. Fax 020-7499 3436.

KARPF, Anne, B.A. Oxon, M.A. Oxon, MSc; b. June 8, 1950; Journalist and writer; Radio critic, the Guardian (1993-); columnist, Jewish Chronicle (1999-). Publ.: Doctoring the Media: The Reporting of Health and Medicine (1988); The War After: Living with the Holocaust (1996). Ad.: c/o The Guardian, 119 Farringdon Road, London EC1R 3ER.

KATTEN, Mrs. Brenda (née Rosenblit), b. London, Sept. 8, 1936; form. Chairman, Bnai Brith Hillel Fd.; Chairman UK National Cttee Jerusalem 3000; H. Vice-Pres. Zionist Fed. of Great Britain & Ireland, (Chairman 1990-94); Jt. H. Pres. British WIZO (Chairman 1981-87); Member JC Tr. Ltd., Ad.: c/o Hillel Foundation, 1/2 Endsleigh St., London WC1H 0DS. ☎ 020-7388 0801. Fax 020-7916 3973.

KATZ, Sir Bernard, M.D., D.Sc., F.R.S.; b. March 26, 1911; Prof. and Head of Biophysics Dept., Univ. Coll., London (1952-78); Nobel Prize for Medicine (1970), V. President, Royal Society (1968-76); Asst. Dir. of Biophysics Res. Lond. Univ.; Res. Fel., Royal Soc. (1946-50) Reader in Physiology (1950-51). Publ.: Scientific writings. Ad.: University Coll., WC1E 8BT. ☎ 020-7387 7050.

KATZ, Dovid, B.A. (Columbia), Ph.D. (Lond.); b. New York, May 9, 1956; Founder of Yiddish Studies at Oxford University; Yiddish linguist and author; form. Dir., Oxford Programme in Yiddish at the Oxford Centre for Postgraduate Hebrew Studies (1978-95); Director, Oxford Institute for Yiddish Studies (1994-97); Founder, Vilnius Programme in Yiddish, Vilnius University (1998); Vis. Prof. in Yiddish Studies, Yale (1998-99); Vis. Prof. and Dir. of the Centre for Stateless Cultures, Vilnius University (1999-2000). Publ.: Grammar of the Yiddish Language (1987); ed. Origins of the Yiddish Language (1987); ed. Dialects of the Yiddish Language (1988); ed. Oxford Yiddish (vol. 1, 1990; vol. 2, 1991; vol. 3, 1995); Klal-takones fun yidishn oysleyg [Code of Yiddish Spelling] (1992); Tikney takones: fragn fun yidisher stilistik [Amended Amendments: Issues in Yiddish Stylistics] (1993); founder and ed. Yiddish Pen (literary and academic monthly) (1994-96); columnist, Yiddish Forward (1993-); Yiddish fiction under pseudonym of Heershadovid Menkes: Edra Don (1992); Der flakher shpits [The Flat Peak] (1993); Misnagdishe mayses fun vilner gubernye [Tales of the Misnagdim of Vilna Province] (1996). Awards: John Marshall Medal in Comparative Philology, University College London (1980). Awards for Yiddish Literature: Israel Marshak, Canada (1979); Sholem Aleichem, Tel Aviv (1988); Hirsh Rosenfeld, Montreal (1994); Chaim Grade, New York (1995); Zhitlovsky, New York (1996); Manger Prize, Tel Aviv (1997); Y.Y. Sigal, Montreal (1999). Ad.: 2 Bryn Aber, Fairy Glen Road, Capelulo, Gwynedd LL34 6YU. ☎ 01492-622944. Fax 01492-622756.

KATZ, Milton, A.B., LL.D.; b. New York City, 1907; Dir. of Internat. Legal Studies and Henry L. Stimson Prof. of Law, Harvard Univ. (since 1954); Emer. Dist. Prof., Suffolk Univ. Law Sch (since 1979); Assoc. Dir., Ford Foundation (1951-54); form. USA Special Rep. in Europe, with rank of Amb. Extraordinary and Plenipotentiary; Chairman, Energy Adv. Crtee., Office of Technology Assessment US Congress (1972-82); Co.-Chairman, Amer. Bar Assn.NAmer. Assn. for Adv. of Science Com. on Science and Law (1978-82); Chairman, Bd. of Tr., Carnegie Endowment for Internat. Peace (197078); Tr., World Peace Foundation P. Citizens, Research Foundation; President, Amer Academy of Arts and Sciences, (1979-82); form. Dir., Nat. Conf of Christians and Jews; Tr., Chairman, Academic Affairs, Brandeis Univ., U.S Legion of Merit; Cmdr.'s Cross West German Order of Merit; Grande Ufficiale Italian Order of Merit. Publ.: Legal, political and foreign policy works. Ad.: 6 Berkeley St., Cambridge, Mass. 02138, USA.

KATZ, Rabbi Steven Anthony, B.A. (Hons.); b. London, Dec. 18, 1948; M., Hendon Ref. Syn., H. Sec. RSGB Assembly of Rabbis; Chaplain, Univ., Coll. Hospital, London. Ad.: Hendon Reform Synagogue, Danescroft Ave., NW4 2NA. ☎ 020-8203 4168.

KATZIR, (Katchalski) Professor Ephraim; b. Kiev, May 16, 1916; Fourth President, State of Israel (1973-78); Chief Scientist, Israel Def. Forces (1966-68); Prof, Weizmann Instit. of Science; Prof Emer., Tel Aviv Univ.; Foreign Member, Royal Society Lond.; Hon. Member, The Royal Institution of Great Britain (1989); Foreign Assoc. Nat. Acad. of Sciences USA; Foreign Hon. Member, Amer Acad. of Arts & Sciences. Many honorary doctorates, honours prizes, medals and awards. Publ.: Papers & reviews in scientific journals & books. Ad.: Weizmann Instit., Rehovot 76100, Israel. ☎ 972-8-9343947. Fax 972-8-9468256.

KAUFMAN, Rt. Hon. Gerald Bernard, M.A., P.C., M.P.; b. Leeds, June 21, 1930; Journalist; Labour Party Parl. Cttee (1980-92); Opposition Spokesman for Foreign Affairs (1987-92); Member, Nat. Exec. Cttee. of the Labour Party (1991-1992), Chairman, House of Commons Nat. Heritage Cttee (1992-); Opp. Spokesman for Home Affairs (1983-87); form. Min. of State, Dept of Industry; Parl. Under-Sec., Industry; Parl. Under-Sec., Environment; M.P. (Lab.) for Ardwick (1970-83) for Gorton, Manchester (since 1983); Parl. Press Liaison Off, Labour Party (1965-70); Pol. Corr., New Statesman, (1964-65); Pol. Staff, Daily Mirror, (1955-64), Asst. Gen. Sec., Fabian Society (1954-55). Publ.: How to be a Minister, To Build the Promised Land, How to live under Labour (co-author), My Life in the Silver Screen, Inside the Promised Land, Meet me in St Louis, The Left (ed.), Renewal (ed). Ad.: 87 Charlbert Ct., Eamont St., NW8 7DA. ☎ 020-7219 5145. Fax 020-7219 6825.

KAUFMANN, Flo (née Israel), J.P., B.A.; b. Berkamsted, Aug. 3, 1942, m. Aubrey Kaufmann; Tr. and Chairman of Finance and Organisation Div. Board of Deputies (1997-); Member of Independent Tribunal Service (1996-); Vice Chairman of BoD Israel Committee (1989-94), Chairman (1994-97). Ad.: Board of Deputies, Commonwealth House, 1-19 New Oxford Street, London WC1A 1NF.

KAUFMANN, Georgia Louise, B.A., M.Sc., D.Phil; b. Edgware, Middx, Jan. 10, 1961; Council Member of Edgware Masorti Synagogue and the Assembly of Masorti Synagogues (AMS) (1998-); Dir. UKJAID (UK Jewish Aid and International Development) (1996-97); Fellow at the Institute of Development Studies (IDS) at the University of Sussex (1992-95); Bell-MacArthur Fellow at the Harvard Center for Population & Development Studies (1994-95). Ad.: 3 Rochester Terrace, London, NW1 9JN. ☎ 020-7485 1689. Email: Georgiak@btinternet.com

KAY, Rabbi Sidney, b. Manchester, Oct. 25, 1920; M., Southport New Syn. (1976-84), Emer. Rabbi (since 1985). Ad.: 4 Westhill, Lord St. West, Southport, PR8 2BJ. ☎ 01704 541344. Fax 01704-514059.

KEDOURIE, Sylvia (née Haim), M.A., Ph.D. (Edin.); b. Baghdad, Iraq; Independent scholar. Publ.: Arab Nationalism: An Anthology (1962, 1967, 1975). Ad.: 75 Lawn Rd., London NW3 2XB. ☎/Fax 020-7722 0901.

KEMPNER GLASMAN, Mrs. Sheila (née Goldstein); b. London, May 22, 1933; Chairman BoD Women's Issues Action Gp. (1995-); Hon. Sec. Int. Council of Jewish Women (1996-); Memb. Thames Customer Service Cttee OFWAT (1993-96); form. President, League of Jewish Women's; V. Chairman, Hillingdon Com. Health C. (1974-82); Member Hillingdon Dist. Health Auth. (1983-87); Member, Women's Nat. Com. (1990-94). Ad.: 10 Ashurst Close, Northwood, Middx. HA6 1EL.

KERSHEN, Anne Jacqueline (née Rothenberg), B.A., M.Phil., Ph.D., F.R.S.A.; b. London, June 8, 1942; Historian; Barnett Shine Res. Fell. Queen Mary &

Westfield Coll. Univ. of London (1990-); Director Centre for the Study of Migration, QMW (1994-); Memb. Faculty Leo Baeck Coll. (1992-); Memb. C. J.H.S.E.; Council Memb Jewish Museum. Publ.: A Question of Identity (1998); London, the Promised Land? (1997); Uniting the Tailors (1995); 150 years progressive Judaism (ed.) (1990); Off-the-peg: Story Women's Wholesale Clothing industry (ed.) (1988); Trade unionism amongst Jewish Tailors in London, 1872-1915 (1988), (with Jonathan Romain) Tradition and Change, the history of Reform Judaism in Britain, 1840-1995 (1995). Ad.: Dept. of Politics, Queen Mary & Westfield College, Mile End Rd., E1 4NS. ☎ 020-7975 5003. Email: a.kershen @qmw.ac.uk

KESSLER, David Francis, O.B.E., B.A.; b. Pretoria, June 6, 1906; Form. Chairman, Jewish Chronicle Ltd.; Fdr. and form. Chairman, Vallentine, Mitchell & Co., Ltd.; C., A.J A., C., Council of Christians and Jews; H. President; CBF-WJR; Hon. Pres. Soc for the Study of Ethiopian Jewry; Major, Royal Artillery, seconded Iraq Levies (1942-44); Political Warfare Exec. (1944-45); Brit. Econ. Mission to Greece (1946). Publ.: The Falashas; The Rothschilds and Disraeli in Buckinghamshire. Ad.: Lovetts, Bragenham Side, Stoke Hammond, Bucks., MK17 9DB. ☎ 01525270/210.

KESTENBAUM, Jonathan, B.A. (Hons.), M.A., M.B.A.; b. Tokyo, Japan, Aug. 5, 1959; Chief Exec., UJIA; form. Ex. Dir. Office of the Chief Rabbi; Mazkir, Bnei Akiva London (1982-83); IDF, Outstanding Soldier Award (1983); Jerusalem Fellows Researcher (1985-87). Ad.: Balfour House, 741 High Rd., Finchley N12 0BQ.

KING, Oona, M.P.; b. Sheffield, Oct. 22, 1967; m. Tiberio Santomarco; M.P. for Bethnal Green & Bow (Lab.) (1997-). Ad.: House of Commons, SW1A 1AA.

KING-HAMILTON, His Honour Myer Alan Barry, Q.C., M.A.; b. London, Dec. 9, 1904; Additional Judge, Central Criminal Court (1964-79); Chairman, Jt. Standing Cttee. of R.S.G.B and ULPS; President, West Lond. Syn. (1977-83 and 1965-72), Hon. Life President (1994-); President, Maccabaeans (1967-75); Leader Oxford Circuit (1961-64); Recorder of Wolverhampton (1961-64), Gloucester (1956-61), Hereford (1955-56); Dep. Chairman. Oxford Qrt. Sessions (1956-64); Bencher, Middle Temple (1961); V. President, World Cong. of Faiths (since 1970); President, Westlon Hsg. Assn. (1970-95), Hon. Life President (1995); London J.; Hsg. Cttee. (1975-); President, Birnbeck Hsg. Assoc. (1995-97), and Hon. Life President (1997-); Chairman, Pornography and Violence Research Trust (form. Mary Whitehouse, etc.) (1986-96); Master, Worshipful Comp. of Needlemakers (1969-70); Freeman of the City of London (1945); form. President, Cambridge Union Soc.; Squadron Leader R.A.F. Publ.: And Nothing But The Truth (autobiog.) Ad.: 33 Seymour Place, W1H 6AP.

KINGSLAND, Sir Richard, A.O., C.B.E., D.F.C.; b. Moree, New South Wales, Australia, Oct. 19, 1916, m. Kathleen J. Adams; President Barnardos Canberra (1995-); Dir. Sir Edward Dunlop Medical Res. Fd. (1995-); Chairman, A.C.T. Health Promotion Fund (1990-94); Tr., Canberra Festival (1988-92); Life Gov. Sir Moses Montefiore Jewish Home, Sydney; Sec., Australian Veterans Affairs Dept. (1970-81); Chairman, Repatriation Com. (1970-81); Sec., Interior Dept. (1963-70); Nat. Dir., Australian Bicentennial Auth. (1983-89); President, Man. Bd., Goodwin Retirement Villages (1984-88); Nat. C., Australian Opera (1983-96); Chairman, Uranium Adv. C. (1982-84); H. Nat. Sec., Nat. Heart Foundation (1976-90); Member at Large since 1990; form. Chairman, Commonwealth Films Review Bd.; First Chairman, C., Canberra Sch. of Art (1975-84); First Chairman, A.C.T. Arts Development Bd. (1981-84); Tr., Australian War Memorial (1966-76); Man. Sydney Airport (1948-49); Dir.-Gen., Org., R.A.A.F. Hq. (1946-48); Dir., R.A.A.F. Intelligence (1944-45); Cdr., R.A.A.F. Base, Rathmines, N.S.W. (1942-43); Cdr., No. 11 Sqdn. R.A.A.F. Papua New Guinea (1941-42); No. 10 Sqdn. R.A.A.F., Brit. (1939-41). Ad.: 36 Vasey Cresc., Campbell, A.C.T. 2612, Australia. ☎ (02) 624 78502.

KLAUSNER, Menny; b. Frankfurt, Sept. 19, 1926; Comp. Dir.; Chairman, Mizrachi–Hapoel Hamizrachi Fed., UK & Ireland; Chairman, Israel Cttee., BoD; CoChairman, Nat. Z.C.; President, Hendon Adath Yisroel Cong.; T., N.W. Lond. Com. Mikva, T., Mifal Hatora Med. Aid Fund; Gov., Hasmonean Prep. Sch., Hendon; Chairman, Frs. of Ariel Instits., Israel; Netiv Meir Sch., Jerusalem; Actions Cttee., WZO, Adv. Bd., Torah Dept. Youth Aff. Com., World Mizrachi Exec.; Chairman, Mizrachi Fed. (1972-76); V. Chairman & T., Jewish Review, (1966-71); V.Chairman, Tora Vavoda (1948-52). Ad.: 1 Edgeworth Ave., NW4 4EX. ☎ 020-8202 9220, 020-7286 9141.

KLUG, Sir Aaron, O.M., Sc.D., P.R.S.; b. Aug. 11, 1926, m. Liebe (née Bobrow); Nobel Prize for chemistry (1982); Med. Res. C. Laboratory of Molecular Biology, Cambridge; Hon. Fel., Peterhouse, Cambridge; form. Nuffield Fel., Birkbeck Col., Lond.; Lect., Cambridge Univ., Cape Town Univ. Publ.: Papers in scientific journals. Ad.: Peterhouse, Cambridge, CB2 1RT.

KNAPP, Alexander Victor, M.A.(Hons.), Mus.B.(Cantab), Hon. A.R.A.M., L.R.A.M., A.R.C.M., Churchill Fellow; b. London, May 13, 1945; m. Caroline; Joe Loss Lecturer in Jewish Music, SOAS (1999-); City Univ. (1992-99); Vis. Scholar Wolfson College, Cambridge (1983-86); Assistant Dir. of Studies, Royal College of Music, London (1977-83). Publ.: Four Sephardi Songs (1993); Anthology of Essays on Jewish Music (in Chinese) (1998). Ad.: Music Department, SOAS, Thornhaugh St., London WC1H 0XG. ☎ 020-7637 6182. Email ak42@soas.ac.uk

KNOBIL, Henry Eric, F.T.I.; b. Vienna, Nov. 27, 1932; V. President British-Israel Chamber of Commerce; Bd. Gov. Immanuel Coll.; Tr., JEDT; Gov., Shenkar Coll.; Bd. Govs., Carmel Coll. (1980-87). Ad.: Apt. 78, Harley House, Marylebone Rd., London NW1 5HN. ☎ 020-7224 4005. Fax 020-7224 0875.

KNORPEL, Henry, C.B., Q.C., B.C.L., M.A. (Oxon).; b. London, Aug. 18, 1924, m. Brenda née Sterling; Barrister; Bencher, Inner Temple; Counsel to the Speaker, House of Commons (1985-95); Solicitor to D.H.S.S. (1978-85); Princ. Asst. Solicitor (1971-78). Ad.: Conway, 32 Sunnybank, Woodcote Grn., Epsom, Surrey KT18 7DX. ☎ 01372 721394

KOCHAN, Lionel, B.A., M.A. (Cantab), Ph.D. (Lond.), F.R. Hist. Soc.; b. London, Aug. 20, 1922; Bearsted Reader in Jewish Hist., Warwick Univ. (1968-87); form. Reader, Mod. Hist., East Anglia Univ.; P, Jew Hist. Soc. (1980-82). Publ.: Russia and Weimar Republic, Pogrom - November 10, 1938, Making of Modern Russia, Struggle for Germany 1914-45, The Jews in Soviet Russia Since 1917 (ed.), The Jew and His History, Jews Idols and Messiahs - The Challenge from History (1990), The Jewish Renaissance and some of its discontents (1992), Beyond the graven image. Ad.: 237 Woodstock Rd., Oxford OX2 7AD. ☎ 01865 558435

KOCHMANN, Max Michael, J.P.; b. Berlin, May 17, 1921; Chairman, Basildon Hebrew Cong.; Chairman, Leo Baeck Housing Association; Chairman, Basildon & District Local Enterprise Agency; Chairman, London Support Group, Centre for German-Jewish Studies, University of Sussex; Chairman, Chevra Kadisha, Belsize Square Synagogue; Life President, British Adhesives & Sealant Association; Chairman, Association of Jewish Refugees (1994-95); Chairman, Otto Schiff Housing Association (1995); President, Bnai Brith Leo Baeck (London) Lodge (1975-77). Ad.: 3 Furlongs, Basildon, Essex, SS16 4BW. ☎ 01268 524947. Fax 01268-271358.

KOPELOWITZ, Lionel, M. A. (Cantab.), M.R.C.S. L.R.C.P., M.R.C.G.P., J.P.; b. Newcastle upon Tyne, Dec. 9, 1926; President, BoD (1985-91); V. President, Trades Adv. C.; V. President, Conf J. Material claims against Germany; Exec. Ctte. Member, Member F. J. Culture; Member, Gen. Med. C. (1984-94); Vice Chairman, North Thames Faculty Bd., Roy. Coll. of General Practitioners (1995-99); Bd. Tr. Clare Wand Fund (BMA); C., BMA (1982-94), Fel. (1980); President, WJC Europe (1988-90), World Exec. WJC (1986); C., AJA; President,

Nat. C., Soviet Jewry (1985-91); President, Rep. C., Newc. Jewry (1967-73); First President, United Hebrew Cong. Newc. (1973-76); Life President, (President 1964-74) Newc. JWB, H.V. President, Tyneside CCJ; Chairman, Newc. Med. Cttee., (1980-86); Family Prac. Cttee. (1979-85); President, Soc. Family Prac. Cttees. (1978-79); President, Cttee., B.M.A Deputising Services; Gen. Optical C. (1979-94); V. President, British Friends Shaare Zedek Hospital Medical Centre; President, Old Cliftonian Soc. (1991-93); Council, United Synagogue (1991-96); Chairman, St. Marylebone Division BMA (1992-) Member Bd. Gov., Clifton College, Bristol; Mem. C., Royal Coll. General Practitioners (1995-99). Ad.: 10 Cumberland House, Clifton Gardens, W9 1DX. ☎ 020-7289 6375; 7 Sea Lane, Middleton-on-Sea, West Sussex PO22 7RJ. ☎ 01243-582167.

KOPS, Bernard; b. London, 1926; Writer; C., Day Lewis Fellowship (1980-83). Pub.: Yes; From No Man's Land, The Dissent of Dominick Shapiro, By the Waters of Whitechapel, The Passionate Past of Gloria Gaye, Settle Down Simon Katz, Partners, On Margate Sands (novels), Collected Plays, The Hamlet of Stepney Green (play), Erica I Want to Read You Something, For the Record (poetry), Barricades In West Hampstead (poetry), The World is a Wedding (auto-biography), Plays One (collection), Shalom Bomb (autobiography continued), Neither Your Honey Nor Your Sting (history), Playing Sinatra (play), Dreams of Anne Frank (play), Green Rabbi (play), Cafe Zeitgeist (play), etc. Ad.: 41B Canfield Gdns., London NW6 3JL. ☎ 020-7624 2940.

KORNBERG, Sir Hans (Leo), M.A., D.Sc. (Oxon) Sc.D. (Cantab), Hon. Sc.D. (Cincinnati), Hon. D.Sc. (Warwick, Leicester, Sheffield, Bath, Strathclyde, Leeds, La Trobe), Hon. D.U. (Essex), Dr. Med., h.c. (Leipzig), Hon. LL.D. (Dundee), Ph.D. (Sheffield), F.R.S., Hon. F.R.C.P. F.l.Biol., F.R.S.A.; b. Herford, Germany, Jan. 14, 1928; Sir W. Dunn Prof of Biochemistry, Cambridge Univ. (1974-95); Master, Christ's Coll. Cambridge (1982-95); H.Fel., Worcester Coll., Brasenose Coll., Oxford, Wolfson Coll., Cambridge; Member, German Acad. Sciences 'Leopoldina', For. Assoc., Nat. Acad. Sci., US; For. H. Member, Amer. Acad. Arts & Sciences; H. Member, Amer. Soc. Biochem. & Mol. Biol.; Japanese Biochem. Soc., German Soc. Biol. Chem. (Warburg Medallist); Fel., Amer. Acad. Microbiol.; Mem. Academia Europea; Accademia Nazionale dei Lincei; American Philosophical Soc.; Hon. Mem. Phi Beta Kappa; Prof. of Biochemistry, Leicester Univ. (1960-75); President, Brit. Assn. Adv. Sci. (1984-85); Academic Gov., Hebr. Univ.; Sci. Gov., Weizmann Inst.; Tr., Nuffield Foundation (1973-93); Gov., Wellcome Trust (1990-95); Gov., Lister Inst. Prev. Med.; Chairman, Royal Comm. on Environmental Pollution (1976-81); Member, (1990-95) Agric. & Food. Res. C. (1981-84); Member Priorities Bd., Res. & Development in Agric. (1984-90); Adv. C., Applied Res. & Development(1982-85), Chairman, Brit. Nat. Cttee. for Problems of Environment (1982-87); P. Internat. Union of Biochem. & Mol. Biol. (1991-1994); President, Biochemical Soc. (1990-95); Ch, Adv. Cttee. on Genetic Modification (1986-95); Dir., UK. Nirex Ltd (1986-95); Chairman, Kurt Hahn Trust (U. of Camb.) (1990-95); Member, Science Res. C. (1967-72) and Chairman, Science Bd. (1969-72). Publ.: Scientific writings. Ad.: The University Professors, Boston University, 745 Commonwealth Ave., Boston, MA 02215. Fax (617) 353-5084.

KOSMIN, Barry A., B.A., M.A., D.Phil.; b. London, Oct. 11, 1946; m. Helen; Professor of Sociology; Exec. Dir. Research Unit, Board of Deputies of British Jews (1974-86); Fellow, Institute for Advanced Studies, Hebrew University (1980-81); Founding Dir., North American Jewish Data Bank, The Graduate School and University Center of The City University of New York (1986-96); Dir. of Research, Council of Jewish Federations, NY (1986-96); Dir. CUNY National Survey of Religious Identification (1989); Dir. CJF 1990 US National Jewish Population Survey (1990). Publ.: Majuta: A History of the Jews in

Zimbabwe (1981); British Jewry in the Eighties: A Statistical and Geographical Guide (1986); Highlights of the CJF 1990 National Jewish Research Population Survey (with S. Goldstein, J. Waksberg, N. Lerer, and A. Keysar) (1991); Contemporary Jewish Philanthropy in America (Jt. Ed. with P. Ritterband (1991); One Nation Under God: Religion in Contemporary American Society (with S. Lachman) (1993). Ad.: Director of Research, IJPR, 79 Wimpole Street, London W1M 7DD. ☎ 020-7935 8266.

KOSSOWSKY, Rabbi Zalman, M.Ed., Ph.D.; b. Teheran, Dec. 15, 1940; Rabbi Israelitische Cultusgemeinde, Zurich; form. Rabbi, Kenton Syn. (1986-91); Chaplain, US Naval Reserve; Rabbi, Sydenham Highlands N. Hebrew Cong., Johannesburg (1978-86); Admin., Colorado Kosher Meats, Colorado Springs, US (1974-78), Rabbi, Young Israel, Greater Miami Florida (1972-74); Assoc. Dean, Talmudic Res. Instit., Colorado (1967-72). Publ.: Prayer Book for Friday Evening and Festivals, Prayer Book for the House of Mourning, The Modern Kosher Home. Ad.: Lavaterstrasse 33, Zürich CH-8002 Zürich, Switzerland. ☎ 201 1659. Fax 202 2287. Email rabbi@icz.org

KRAIS, Anthony, JP; b. Lond., May 3, 1938; Assoc. Ch. Exec., Jewish Care (1990-97); Exec. Dir. Jewish Blind Society (1980-89); Tr., British Frs. Jaffa Inst.; Ch. British Frs. Israel Guide Dog Centre for the Blind; Dep. Ch. Resources for Autism; Member Independent Tribunal Service; General Commissioner of Taxes; Member B'nai B'rith Housing Association. Ad.: 14 Mayflower Lodge, Regents Park Rd., London N3 3HU ☎/Fax 020-8349 0337. Email aik@clara.net

KRAMER, Lotte Karoline (née Wertheimer); b. Mainz, Germany, Oct., 22, 1923; m. Frederic Kramer; Poet. Publ.: Ice Break (1980); Family Arrivals (1981, 1992); A Lifelong House (1983); The Shoemaker's Wife (1987); The Desecration of Trees (1994); Earthquake and Other Poems (1994); Selected and New Poems 1980-1997; Heimweh/Homesick (German/English ed., 1999). Ad.: 4 Apsley Way, Longthorpe, Peterborough PE3 9NE. ☎ 01733-264378.

KRAUSZ, Ernest, M.Sc., Ph.D.; b. Romania, Aug. 13, 1931; Rector, Bar-Ilan Univ. (1986-89), Prof. of Soc. (Dean, Soc. Sci. Faculty (1973-76) Bar-Ilan Univ.; Reader in Sociology, City Univ. Lond. (1971-72); Vis. Prof, Dept. of Social Studies, Newcastle Univ. (1976-77); L.S.E. (1981-82); C., Higher Educ, Israel (1979-81), Planning and Grants Cttee. C. Higher Educ. (1990-96); Mem.C. Israel Science Fd. (1994-); Edr., Studies of Israeli Society (1979-); Dir., Sociological Instit. for Community Studies, Bar-Ilan Univ. Publs.: Leeds Jewry, Sociology in Britain, Jews in a London Suburb, Ethnic Minorities in Britain, Key Variables in Social Research, Social Research Design, On Ethnic and Religious Diversity in Israel, Sociological Research - A Philosophy of Science Perspective, Co-ed. Sociological Papers (1992-). Ad.: Dept. of Sociology Bar-Ilan Univ., Ramat Gan 52900, Israel. ☎ (03) 5344449. Fax (03) 6350995.

KRITZ, Simon Gedaliah, b. Lond., Sept. 17, 1919; Gen. Sec., Mizrachi Fed. Reg., Midrashah Instit. for Israel Studies Asst. Edr., Jewish Review; Sec., Frs. of Mifal Hatorah; Sec., Mizrachi Palestine Fund Charitable Tr., Sec., Brit. Frs. of Ariel; Gen. Sec., Nat. Z. C.; W., Willesden & Brondesbury Syn., Exec. & C., US; form. Fin. Rep., Willesden Syn.; Central Jewish Lect. & Information Cttee., BoD. Ad.:

KUPFERMANN, Jeannette Anne, B.A. (Hons.), M.Phil. Anthropology, (née Weitz); b. Woking, March 28, 1941; Anthropologist, Feature writer for The Sunday Times, Broadcaster Columnist, The Daily Telegraph, TV Critic, Daily Mail, TV writer: The Quest for Beauty (Channel 4); Everyman Film on Edith Stein (B.B.C.). Publ.: The Mistaken Body, When the Crying's Done: A Journey through Widowhood. Ad.: c/o Sunday Times, 1 Pennington St, E1.

KUSHNER, Tony, Ph.D.; b. Manchester, May 30, 1960; University Lecturer; Marcus Sieff Professor, Dept of History, and Director Centre for the Study of Jewish/Non-Jewish Relations Parkes Library University of Southampton; Historian at Manchester Jewish Museum (1985-86); Member of C., JHSE, Convenor, Working Party on Jewish Archives in the UK; Tr., Anne Frank Educ.

Trust, UK; Tr. Searchlight Educ. Trust, UK. Publ.: The Persistence of Prejudice: Antisemitism in British Society During the Second World War (1989); (jt. ed.) Traditions of Intolerance (1989); (jt. ed.) The Politics of Marginality (1990); (ed.) Jewish Heritage in British History: Englishness and Jewishness (1992); (jt. ed.) The Internment of Aliens in Twentieth Century Britain (1993); The Holocaust and the Liberal Imagination (1994); (jt. col.) Belsen in History and Memory (1997); (jt. ed.) Cultures of Ambivalence and Contempt (1998); Refugees in an Age of Genocide (1999). Ad.: Dept. of History, The University, Southampton SO17 1BJ. ☎ 02380-592211.

KUSTOW, Michael David, b. London Nov. 18, 1939; Writer, Theatre Dir.; Literary Dir., Amer. Repertory Theatre (1980-82); Associate Dir., Nat. Theatre (1975-80), Dir., Instit. of Contemporary Arts (1968-71); Publ.: Tank, an Autobiographical Fiction. Ad.: c/o Tim Corrie, The Chambers, Chelsea Harbour, Lots Rd., London SW10 0XF.

LACHS, Judge Henry Lazarus, M.A., LL.B. (Cantab.); b. Lond., Dec. 31, 1927; Circuit Judge; President, L'pool Yeshiva; form. Crown Court Recorder; Regional Chairman, Merseyside Mental Health Review Tribunal. Ad.: 41 Menlove Gdns. West, Liverpool, L18 2ET. ☎ 0151-722 5936.

LAMM, Rabbi Norman, Ph.D.; b. Brooklyn, N.Y., Dec. 19, 1927; President, Yeshiva Univ. & President, Rabbi Isaac Elchanan Theol. Semin., New York (since 1976); Erna and Jakob Michael Prof of Jewish Philosophy, Yeshiva Univ. (since 1966); Fdr. Edr., Tradition; Edr., The Library of Jewish Law and Ethics (14 vols.); Rabbi, Cong. Kodimoh, Springfield, Mass. (1954-58); Rabbi, The Jewish Center, New York (1958-76). Publ. A Hedge of Roses, The Royal Reach; Faith and Doubt, Torah Lishmah, The Good Society, Torah Umadda, Halakhot ve'Halikhot, Shema, The Religious Thought of Hasidism. Ad.: Yeshiva Univ., 500 W. 185th St., New York, N.Y. 10033. ☎ (212) 960 5280.

LANDAU, Frederic Moses, LL.B.; b. London, Jan. 19, 1905, Barrister; Elder, US; Exec., JMC. Publ.: Legal writings. Ad.: 7 Dawson Place, London W2 4TD.

LANGDON, Harold S., B.Com; b. Lond. April 22, 1916; Economist; Chairman, Public Rel. Cttee. (1979-85), BoD; Exec., BoD (1974-91); Life Gov. (Chairman, 1975-78) Leo Baeck Coll.; Chairman, RSGB (1967-70); North Western Reform Syn. (1960-61). Publ.: Contr., A Genuine Search (ed. Dow Marmur). Ad.: 24 Hoop Lane, NW11 8BU.

de LANGE, Rabbi Nicholas, R.M. M.A., D. Phil.; b. Nottingham, Aug. 7, 1944; Reader in Hebrew & Jewish Studies, Cambridge Univ; C., Jewish Hist. Soc. of England; Fel., Wolfson Coll., Cambridge. Publ.: Judaism, Apocrypha Jewish Literature of the Hellenistic Age, Atlas of the Jewish World, Illustrated History of the Jewish People, An Introduction to Judaism, various specialised works and literary translations. Ad.: Faculty of Divinity, St John's Street, Cambridge CB2 1TW. ☎ 01223 332597. Fax 01223 332582.

LAPPIN, Elena, b. Moscow, Dec. 16, 1954; form. Editor, "Jewish Quarterly". Freelance editor & author, New York (1990-94); English (ESL) insutructor, Technion, Haifa, Israel (1986-90). Publ.: Jewish Voices, German Words: Growing up Jewish in Postwar Germany and Austria 1(994), Daylight in Nightclub Inferno: new fiction from the post-Kundera Generation (1997). Ad.:

LAQUEUR, Walter; b. Breslau, May 26, 1921; Co-Dir., Wiener Library (1964-1992); Edr., Journal of Contemporary History; Chairman, Research C., Centre for Strategic and International Studies, Washington, USA.; Several honorary degrees. Publ.: Communism and Nationalism in the Middle East, Young Germany, Russia and Germany, The Road to War - 1967, Europe since Hitler, A History of Zionism. etc. Ad.: CSIS, 1800 K St., Washington D.C. 20006, USA. Fax (202) 686-0048.

LASKY, Melvin J., M.A.; b. New York, Jan. 15, 1920; Co-Edr., Encounter Magazine (Lond.) (since 1958); Edr., Dir., Library Press, New York; Publ., Alcove Press Lond.; Edr. & Publ., Der Monat (Berlin); Dist. Alumnus Award,

New York City Univ. (1978); Michigan Univ. Sesquicentennial Award (1967); US Combat Historian, France & Gemany (1944-45). Publ.: Utopia and Revolution, Festschrift for Raymond Aron, Sprache und Politik, New Paths in American History, The Hungarian Revolution (ed.), Africa for Beginners. Ad.: Encounter, 59 St Martins La., WC2N 4JS. ☎ 020-7836 4194.

LAUTERPACHT, Sir Elihu, C.B.E., Q.C., M.A., LL.B.; b. London, July 13, 1928; Fel., Trinity Coll., Cambridge; Hon. Prof. International Law; Reader, Internat. Law (1980-88); Dir., Res. Centre for Internat. Law, Cambridge Univ. (1983-95); Chairman, East African Common Market Tribunal (1972-75); Dir. of Research, Hague Academy of Internat. Law (1959-60); Legal Adv. to Australian Dept. of Foreign Affairs (1975-77); Consultant, Central Policy Review Staff (1978-80; 1972-74); President, World Bank Admin. Tribunal (1979-98); Chairman, Asian Development Bank Admin. Tribunal(1993-95); Judge ad hoc, Int. Court of Justice (1993-); Chairman, Dispute Settlement Panel, US-Canada NAFTA (1996), US-Mexico (1997-), US-Costa Rica (1997-), US-Ukraine (1998-); Member Institut de Droit International; Bencher, Gray's Inn (1983); H. Fel., Hebrew Univ. of Jerusalem, 1989; H. Member, Amer. Soc. of Internat. Law, (1993). Publ.: Aspects of the Administration of International Justice (1991); Jerusalem and the Holy Places (1968), The Development of the Law of International Organisations; Ed. International Law Reports. Ad.: Lauterpacht Research Centre for Internat. Law, 5 Cranmer Road, Cambridge CB3 9BP. ☎ 01223 335358. Fax 01223-300406.

LAWRENCE, Sir Ivan, M.A. (Oxon.), Q.C.; b. Brighton, Dec. 24, 1936; Barrister and Head of Chambers; Mem. of BoD; Sec. of Holocaust Educational Trust; Mem. of Commonwealth Jewish Council; form. M.P. (C.) for Burton (1974-97); Knighted for political services (1992); Bencher, Inner Temple (1990); Recorder of the Crown Courts (1983); Exec. Mem. Society of Conservative Lawyers; Chairman Conservative Friends of Israel; Mem. of Policy Planning Gp. of IJPR. Ad.: Dunally Cottage, Walton Lane, Shepperton, Middx. TW17 8LH.

LAWTON, Clive Allen, J.P., B.A., M.A., M.Ed., M.Sc., Cert. Ed., A.D.B. (Ed.); b. London, July 14, 1951; Educ. and organisational consultant; Exec. Dir. Limmud; Chair Tzedek; V. Chair Anne Frank Educ. Trust; form. Ch. Exec. Jewish Continuity (1993-96); form. Dep. Dir., Liverpool City Local Educ. Auth.; Member RS Cttee., School's Examination and Assessment Council (SEAC); form. Exec., AJY; Chairman, Shap Working Party on World Rels. in Educ.; Edr., Shap Calendar of World Rel. Festivals; Fdr., Limmud Conf; form. HM, King David High Sch., L'pool; Exec. Dir., Central Jewish Lect. & Information Cttee. & Educ. Off, BoD; Coordinator, Vietnam Working Party; Educ. Off., Yad Vashem Cttee., Exec. C. CCJ; form. V. Chairman, IUJF. Publ.: The Jewish People – Some Questions Answered; The Seder Handbook; I am a Jew; Passport to Israel; Religion Through Festivals; Celebrating Cultures: Islam; Ethics in Six Traditions; The Story of the Holocaust; The Web of Insights. Ad.: 363 Alexandra Rd., London N10 2ET. Email: clive@calawton.demon.co.uk

LEDERBERG, Joshua, B.A., Ph.D., Litt.D., M.D.(h.c.), Sc.D.(h.c.), Sc.D.(h.c.) Tel Aviv Univ. (1991); b. New Jersey, May 23, 1925; Prof., Rockefeller U. (1990-); President, The Rockefeller Univ.; Prof., Stanford U. (1959-78); Nobel Prize for Medicine (1958); US Nat. Medal of Science (1989); Gov. Bd., Weizmann Inst.; Tr., Sackler Med. Sch., Tel Aviv. Publ.: Scientific works. Ad.: The Rockefeller Univ., 1230 York Ave., New York, NY 10021 ☎ (212) 327 7809.

LEE, Arnold, b. London, Aug. 31, 1920; Solicitor; form. Chairman, Jews, Coll. Ad.: 47 Orchard Court, Portman Sq., W1H 9PD. ☎ 020-7486 8918.

LEE, John Robert Louis, b. Manchester, June 2, 1942; MP (Cons.), Pendle, (1983-92) and for Nelson & Colne (1979-83); F.C.A., Fdn. Dir., Chancery Consolidated Ltd., Investment Bankers; Dir., Paterson Zochonis (UK) Ltd., (1975-76); V. Chairman NW Conciliation Cttee., Race Relations Bd. (1976-77); Political Sec. to Rt. Hon. Robert Carr, (1974); Chairman Council, Nat. Youth

Bureau, (1980-83); Jt. Sec., Conservative Back Bench Industry Cttee., (1979-80); PPS to Minister of State for Industry (1981-83); to Sec.of State for Trade & Industry, (1983); Parly. Under Sec. of State MOD, (1983-86); Dept. of Employment, (1986-89); Minister for Tourism, (1987-89); Non-exec.; Chairman, Country Holidays Ltd. (1989); Non-exec. Dir., P. S. Turner (Holdings) Ltd (1989-); Non-exec. Dir., Paterson Zochonis, (1990-); Chairman, A.L.V.A. (1990-). Ad.:

LEGUM, Colin, b. South Africa, Jan. 3, 1919, m. Margaret née Roberts; Journalist, author, broadcaster, lect.; Hon. Life President Royal Africa Soc. (UK); Edr., The Africa Contemporary Record; Assoc. Edr., The Middle East Contemporary Survey; Edr., Third World Reports; Assoc. Edr. and Commonwealth Corresp., The Observer, (1949-81); Gen. Sec., S.A. Lab. Party (1946-48); Edr. The Forward and Illustrated Bulletin (Johannesburg); Political Corr. Sunday Express (Johannesburg); Political Asst S.A. Zionist Fed.; Exec. Memb. Poale Zion (S.A.); S.A. Jewish BoD (1938-47);. Member of Johannesburg City C., (1941-47). Publ.: Books on Africa, Middle East and Third World. Ad.: Kob Cottage, 12 Harris Rd., Kalk Bay, Cape 7975, RSA. ☎/Fax (012) 788 8455.

LEHMAN, Rabbi Israel Otto, M.A. B.Litt., D.Phil., F.R.A.S.; b. 1912; Adjunct Prof. of Jewish Studies, Miami Univ.; Assoc. Oxford Centre for PostGraduate Hebrew Studies; Hon. Fel. of the John F. Kennedy Library; form. Lect., Leo Baeck Coll.; Curator of Manuscripts Emer., Hebrew Union Coll., form. Assist. Keeper, Bodleian Library (1947-56); Fdr., Oxford B.B. Lodge, O.U.J.S. Library. Publ.: Translation of Chief Rabbi's Pentat. into Germ., 'Moses', (ed.), Handbook of Hebrew and Aramaic Manuscripts. etc. Ad.: 3101 Clifton Ave., Cincinnati, Ohio, USA. ☎ 45220-2488.

LEIBLER, Isi Joseph, A.O., C.B.E., B.A. (Hons.); D.Litt. (Hon.), Deakin University; b. Antwerp, Belgium, Oct. 9, 1934; Chairman and Chief Exec. IJL Group Pty. Ltd. (1997-); fnd. Chairman and Chief Exec., Jetset Tours Pty Ltd. (1965-); Chairman, Governing Bd World Jewish Congress (1995-), V.P World Jewish Congress (1988-1991); President, Asia Pacific Region, World Jewish Congress (1981-); Chairman, Asia Pacific Jewish Assoc. (1980-); Chairman, Australian Institute of Jewish Affairs (1983-), President, Exec. Council of Australian Jewry (1978-1980), (1982-1985), (1987-1989), (1992-95); Member Exec. and Gov. Bd., World Jewish Congress (1978-), Bd. of Gov., Memorial Foundation for Jewish Culture (1979-); Board of Gov., Tel Aviv University (1990-); Dir. and Member, Exec. Cttee., Conference on Jewish Claims Against Germany (1979-). Publ.: Soviet Jewry and Human Rights (1963) Soviet Jewry and the Australian Communist Party (1964), The Case for Israel (1972), The Contemporary Condition of World Jewry (1990), Jewish Religious Extremism: a Threat to the Future of the Jewish people. (1991), The Israel-Diaspora Identity Crisis: A looming disaster (1994). Ad.: 116 Kooyong Rd., Caulfield, Victoria, 3161, Australia. ☎ 98288520. Fax 98288555. Email: ileibler@ijlgroup.com.au; 8 Ahad Ha'am St., 92151 Jerusalem. ☎ (02) 561 2241. Fax (02) 561 2243. Email: ileibler@netvision.net.il

LEIGH, Rabbi Michael, M.A., D.D.; b. London, Nov. 12, 1928; M., Emer. Minister Edgware and Dist. Ref. Syn. (Minister 1963-93); form. Assoc. M., West Lond. Syn. (1958-63); Publ.: Jewish Observance in the Home. Ad.: 64 Lansdowne Rd., Stanmore, Middx. HA7 2SA. ☎ 020-8954 3415.

LERMAN, Antony, B.A. Hons.; b. London Mar. 11, 1946; Exec. Dir. Inst. for Jewish Policy Research, Memb. Imperial War Museum Holocaust Exhibition Advisory Cttee; Memb. Runnymede Trust Commission on the Future of Multi-Ethnic Britain; Memb. Jewish Memorial Foundation Think-Tank on the Holocaust; Jt. Ed., Patterns of Prejudice; Ed., JPR Reports; Chairman Jewish Council for Com. Relations (1992-94); Assist Ed., Survey of Jewish Affairs (1982-91); form. Ed., Jewish Quarterly (1985-86). Publ.: Ed., The Jewish Communities of the World (1989), Jt. Gen. Ed. Antisemitism World Report (1992-98) Ad.: 79 Wimpole Street, W1M 7DD. ☎ 020-7935 8266. Fax 020-

7935 3252. Email: lerman.jpr@ort.org
LERNER, Max, A.B. (Yale), M.A., Ph.D.; b. Minsk, Russia, Dec. 20, 1902; author and journalist; form. Prof. of Pol Science, Williams Coll. and Sarah Lawrence Coll., Harvard Univ.; Prof of Amer. Civilisation & World Politics Brandeis Univ.; Welch Prof. of Amer Studies, Notre Dame Univ.; Prof. Graduate Sch. of Human Behaviour, San Diego (since 1974); Publ.: America as a Civilisation (also revised ed.), The Unfinished Country, The Age of Overkill, Education and a Radical Humanism, Ted and the Kennedy Legend: a Study in Character and Destiny, etc. Ad.: 25 East End Ave., New York 10028, USA.
LEVENE, Baron of Portsoken (Life Peer), **(Peter)** KBE; b. Pinner, Middlesex, December 8, 1941; Lord Mayor of London (1998–99); Chairman & Chief Exec. Canary Wharf Ltd; Prime Minister's Adviser on Efficiency & Effectiveness; Deputy Chairman & Managing Dir. Wasserstein Perella & Co. Ltd; Alderman, City of London (Portsoken) (1984-); form. Managing Dir. United Scientific Holdings plc (1968-85); Chairman (1981-85); Chief of Defence Procurement, Ministry of Defence (1985-91); Chairman Docklands Light Railway Ltd. (1991-94). Ad.: One Canada Square, Canary Wharf, London E14 5AB. ☎ 020-7418 2250. Fax 020-7418 2082.
LEVY, Rabbi Abraham, Knight Commander (Encomienda) Order of Civil Merit (Spain), B.A., Ph.D., F.J.C.; b. Gibraltar, July 16, 1939; m. Estelle; Com. Rabbi, Spiritual Head, S. & P. Cong., Lond.; M., Lauderdale Rd. Syn.; Jt. Eccl. Auth. BoD; Dep.P., Jews Coll.; Dir., The Sephardi Centre; form. Dir. Young Jewish Leadership Instit.; H. Princ., Naima Jewish Preparatory Sch.; Gov., Carmel Coll.; President, Union Anglo-Jewish Preachers (1973-75); V. President, AJA. Publ.: The Sephardim – A Problem of Survival; Ages of Man (jt. auth.); The Sephardim (jt. auth.). Ad.: 2 Ashworth Road, W9 1JY. ☎ 020-7289 2573. Fax 020-7285 5957.
LEVY, David, B.A. (Com.), F.C.A., b. Manchester, June 27, 1942; Chart. Accountant; Dir., Brian Forbes Search & Selection; Chief Exec. Brideoak Associates, Financial Arbitration Services; Member, Worshipful Comp. of Chartered Accountants; Freeman, City of London. Ad.: 6, The Mews, Gatley, Cheadle, Cheshire SK8 4PS. ☎ 0161-428 7708/0161-236 8161 (off.).
LEVY, Elkan David, B.A.(Hons.), M.H.L.; b. Preston, Lancs, March 29, 1943; m. Celia, née Fisher; Solicitor; President, United Synagogue (1996-); Chairman, Chief Rabbinate Conference; Chairman, Beth Hamidrash Cttee.; Chairman, Ministerial Placement Cttee.; Chairman, Singers Prayer Book Publication Cttee.; Jt. Chairman, Stanmore Council of Christians and Jews; Mem., BoD (1991-); form. Minister, Belmont Synagogue (1969-73); Warden, Stanmore Synagogue (1980-90); Chairman U.S. Burial Society (1992-96); Mem. United Synagogue Council (1980-92); Mem. London Board of Shechita (1986-96); Mem. Conference to appoint the Chief Rabbi (1989-91). Ad.: United Synagogue, Adler House, 735 Finchley Road, N12 0U. Email elkan.levy@easynet.co.uk
LEVY, Rabbi Emanuel, B.A., b. Manchester, July 31, 1948; M., Palmers Grn. & Southgate Syn.; Vice-Chairman Rabbinical Council of the United Synagogue; Fdn. Gov. JFS School; Memb. Borough of Enfield Educ. Cttee.; Chaplain to Whittington Hospital; Form. Hon. Principal, Herzlia Jewish Day School, Westcliff-on-Sea; form. Rabbi, Southend & Westcliff Hebrew Cong.; Chief Rabbi's Cabinet, Reg. Affairs, to Chief Rabbi's Cabinet Education Portfolio; J. Rep. to Standing Advisory Council for Religious Education (SACRE) for Borough of Enfield: form. Chaplain to Mayor of Southend (1981-82, 1983-84); form. Rabbi, Langside Hebrew Cong., Glasgow; Rabbi, South Broughton Syn., Manchester; Chairman, Rabbinical Council of the Provinces (1986-88); F.P. Southend Community Relations Council, (1986-88). Ad.: 11, Morton Crescent, Southgate, London N14 7AH. ☎ 020-8882-2943.
LEVY, Rev. Isaac, O.B.E., TD., B.A., Ph.D. (Lond.); b. London, Sept. 14, 1910; form. Dir., JNF in Britain; form. M. Hampstead Syn., Hampstead Gdn. Suburb

Syn. and Bayswater Syn.; form. Sr. Jewish Chaplain to H.M. Forces and Middle
East Forces and Brit. Army of the Rhine, V.Pres. CCJ; Emer. Chaplain to Ajex.
Publ.: Daiches Memorial Volume (jt Edr.), Guide to Passover, The Synagogue Its
History and Function, Journeys of the Children of Israel, All About Israel, Now
I Can Tell, Witness to Evil-Belsen 1945. Ad.: 25 Lyndale Ave., NW2 2QB.
☎ 020-7435 6803.
LEVY, Jack Morris, LL.B.; b. Manchester, Aug. 21, 1918; Solicitor; form.
President, C. of Manch. & Salford Jews; BoD Ad.: 11 Cherrington Rd., Cheadle,
Cheshire. ☎ 0161-428 2315.
LEVY, John David Ashley, B.A. (Hon.) Sociology; b. Lond., Sept. 10, 1947; Dir. Frs.
of Israel Educ. Tr.; Dir., F.O.I. Consultants Ltd.; Exec. Dir., Academic Study Group
on Israel & Middle East; Hon. Co-ord. UK Society for the Protection of Nature in
Israel; form. Information Dir., Z. Fed.; Social Worker, Lond. Borough of Lambeth
Ad.: 25 Lyndale Ave., NW2 2QB. ☎ 020-7435 6803. Fax 020-7794 0291. Email
foiasgfree_online.co.uk
LEVY, Baron of Mill Hill (Life Peer) (Michael Abraham), F.C.A., Hon.D. (Middx);
b. London, July 11, 1944; Comp. Chairman; President of Jewish Care (1998-);
Patron of the Ben Uri Art Society (1997-); Trustee of the Holocaust Educational
Trust (1998-); Patron of Friends of Israel Educational Trust (1998-); President of
CSV (Community Service Volunteers) (1998-); Patron of the British Music
Industry Awards (1995-); Member of the Advisory Council to the Foreign Policy
Centre Centre (1997-); Patron of the Prostate Cancer Charitable Trust (1997-);
Member of the International Board of Governors of the Peres Center for Peace
(1997-); Member of the Foreign and Commonwealth Office Panel 2000 (1998);
Hon. V. President UJIA; Chairman Fd. for Education; Chairman, Chief Rabbi's
Awards for Excellence (1992-); Hon. President JFS School (1995-); V. Chairman
Central Council for Jewish Social Services; Member of World Commission on
Israel-Diaspora Relations; recipient of B'nai B'rith First Lodge Award (1994);
Scopus Award Friends of the Hebrew University (1998); form. Member of the
World Board of Gov. of the Jewish Agency - representing Great Britain; form.
Chairman of the Youth Aliyah Cttee. of the Jewish Agency Board of Govs.; form.
V. President, JIA; form. Nat. Campaign Chairman JIA; form. Chairman, JIA Kol
Nidre Appeal; form. V. Chairman British Phonographic Industry; form. V.
Chairman Phonographic Performance Limited. Ad.: Chase House, Nan Clarke's
Lane, Mill Hill, London NW7 4HH. ☎ 020-7487 5394/5174. Fax 020-7486
7919.
LEVY, Peter Lawrence, O.B.E., B.Sc., F.R.I.C.S.; b. Lond., Nov. 10, 1939;
Chartered Surveyor; Chairman, Shaftesbury PLC; Chairman IJPR; President,
Akiva Sch.; Trustee and Tr. Jewish Youth Fund; Vice President Central Council;
Tr., Frs. of Israel Educ. Tr.; V. President Cystic Fibrosis Tr.; V. President, London
Youth; V. Chairman, JIA (1979-81); Chairman, Young Leadership JIA (1973-77);
Professional Div. JIA (1977-79). Ad.: 52 Springfield Rd., NW8 0QN. ☎ 020-
7333 8118. Fax 020-7333 0660.
LEW, Jonathan Michael, B.Com., A.C.M.A.; b. London, Nov. 23, 1937;
Accountant; Hon. Off., United Synagogue (1984-85); Chief Exec., United
Synagogue (1986-). Ad.: Adler House, 735 High Road, N12 0US. ☎ 020-8343
8989.
LEWIN, Mrs. Sylvia Rose (née Goldschmidt), B.A.(Log.), (Rand), R.S.A.
Dip.Sp.L.D.; b. Johannesburg; Speech and Dyslexia Therapist; H. President
(Nat. President 1982-86, 1988) Bnai Brith UK; past Chairman Jewish Music
Heritage Trust; President Bnai Brith First Unity Lodge. Ad.: White Gables, 156
Totteridge Lane, N20 8JJ. ☎ 020-8446 0404. Fax 020-8445 8732. Email:
sylvia_lewin@bigfoot.com
LEWIS, Bernard, B.A. Ph.D., F.B.A., F.R. Hist. S., Hon. Dr. (Hebrew Univ, Tel Aviv
Univ., H.U.C., Univ. Pennsylvania, S.U.N.Y., Univ. Haifa, Yeshiva Univ., Brandeis,
Bar-Ilan Univ.); b. London, May 31, 1916; Cleveland E. Dodge, Prof of Near

Eastern Studies Princeton Univ. (1974-86), now Emer.; Mem. American Philosophical Soc.; American Academy of Arts & Sciences; Corr. Mem. Institut de France, Académie des Inscriptions et Belles-Lettres. Member, Instit. for Advanced Study, Princeton (1974-86); Prof. Near & Middle East Hist., Lond. Univ. (1949-74); Army (1940-41), attached to a Foreign Office dept. (1941-45). Publ.: The Jews of Islam; Semites and Anti-Semites; The Political Language of Islam; books on Turkish and Arabic Studies; Race and Slavery in the Middle East; Islam and the West; Cultures in Conflict; The Middle East: Two Thousand Years of History; The Future of the Middle East; The Multiple Identities of the Middle East (1998). Ad.: Near Eastern Studies Dept., 110 Jones Hall, Princeton University, Princeton, N.J., 08544, USA. ☎ (609) 258 5489. Fax (609) 258 1242.

LEWIS, Ivan, b. Manchester, March 4, 1967; m. Juliette née Fox; M.P. (Lab.), Bury South (1997-); Tr. of Holocaust Educ. Tr. (1998-); V. Chairman, Inter-Parliamentary Council Against Anti-semitism (1998-); V. Chairman, Labour Friends of Israel (1998); member Exec. Cttee of the Commonwealth Jewish Council (1998-); Member Health Select Cttee (1999-); Vice-Chairman All-Party Parliamentary Group for Parenting (1997-); Chief Exec. Jewish Social Services, Greater Manchester (1992-97); Coordinator, Contact Community Care Group (1986-89). Ad.: House of Commons, London SW1A 0AA. ☎ 020-7219 6404.

LEWIS, Dr Julian Murray, b. Swansea, Sept. 26, 1951; M.P. (Con.), New Forest East (1997-); Historian, researcher and campaigner; Jt. Sec. Conservative Backbench Defence Cttee (1997-); Dep. Dir. Conservative Research Dept. (1990-96); Dir., Policy Research Associates (1985-); Research Dir. and Dir., Coalition for Peace Through Security (1981-85). Publ.: Changing Direction: British Military Planning for Post-War Strategic Defence, 1942-1947 (1988); Who's Left? An Index of Labour MPs and Left-wing Causes, 1985-1992 (1992); What's Liberal? Liberal Democrat Quotations and Facts (1996). Ad.: House of Commons, London SW1A 0AA. ☎ 020-7219 3000.

LICHFIELD, Nathaniel, B.Sc., Ph.D., F.R.I.C.S., C.Eng.; b. Lond., Feb. 29, 1916; Emer. Prof. of Economics of Environmental Planning, Lond. Univ.; Fdr. Partner, Nathaniel Lichfield & Part. (1962-92); Partner, Dalia & Nathaniel Associates Urban Planning (1992-); Vis. Prof. Hebrew Univ. (1980-); Nottingham Univ (1989-); Consultant to Mins., internat. orgs., cities in Britain and overseas. Publ.: Israel's New Towns: A strategy for their Future (with A. Berlert and Samuel Shaked), etc. Ad.: 13 Chalcot Gdns., Englands Lane, NW3 4YB. ☎ 020-7586 0461.

LIGHTMAN, Sir Gavin Anthony, b. London, Dec. 20, 1939; Justice of the High Court, Chancery Division; Q.C. (1980-94); Bencher of Lincolns Inn (1987); Deputy President of AJA (1986-92); Chairman of Education Cttee of AJA (1988-94); V. President, AJA (1994-); Chairman Education Cttee of Hillel (1992-94), Vice-President (1994-); Chairman, Legal Friends of Univ. Haifa (1986-); Patron Commonwealth J. Assoc. (1994-); The Hammerson Home (1995-); Chairman, The Bar Adv. Bd. of the College of Law (1996-). Publ.: (with G. Battersby) Cases and Statutes on the Law of Real Property (1965); (with G. Moss) Law of Receivers of Companies (1st ed. 1986, 2nd ed. 1994). Ad.: Royal Courts of Justice, Strand, London WC2 2LL. ☎ 020-7936 6671. Fax 936 6291.

LIGHTMAN, Sidney, F.I.L.; b. Lond. Apr. 5, 1924; journalist, translator; Sec., British & European Machal Assoc.; form. (1981-89) Asst. Foreign Edr., Jewish Chronicle; form. (1966-89) Edr., Jewish Travel Guide. Ad.: 5 West Heath Ct., North End Rd., NW11 7RE. ☎ 020-8455 1673.

LIPMAN, Maureen Diane (Mrs Jack Rosenthal); b. Hull, May 10, 1946; Actress/Writer; Films: 'Captain Jack' and 'Solomon & Gaenor' (1998). TV: 'Eskimo Day' (1996) and 'Cold Enough for Snow' (1997). Theatre: One-woman show 'Live & Kidding' (1997), 'Oklahoma!' National Theatre (1998). Sixth book: You Can Read Me Like a Book. Ad.: c/o Conway Ven Gelder, 18/21 Jermyn Street, SW1Y 6HP. ☎ 020-7287 0077.

LITHMAN-IMBER, Mrs. Ethel; b. London; P. (form. Nat. Chairman), Brit. Olim Relatives Assn.; Hadassah Medal for services to Israel (1967); Staff Off, Brit. Red Cross, Second World War; form. Cttee., Guild Jewish Journs.; form. Member, Norfolk County Council SACRE; President Norwich Hebrew Cong. (1997-); V. President Norwich Hebrew Congregation (1996); form. Act. Chairman, Norwich CCJ. Publ.: The Man Who Wrote Hatikvah. Ad.: c/o BORA, Balfour House, 741 High Road, N12 0BQ. ☎ 01379-674400.

LIVINGSTON, Edward Colin, M.B.E., M.B., B.S. (Lond.), J.P.; b. London, Mar. 22, 1925; Med. Prac.; Barrister; Ombudsman, Central C. for Jewish Community Services; Medical Examiner, Medical Fnd. for Care of Victims of Torture; P/T. Chairman, Soc Sec. Appeal Trib., Harrow; Chairman, Harrow Com. Tr; Liveryman. Soc. of Apothecaries; Freeman, City of Lond.; Flt./Lieut (Med. Br.) R.A.F.V.R. (1948-50); P/T.Chairman, Disability Appeal Tribunal, South East Region. Ad.: Wyck Cottage, Barrow Point La., Pinner, Middx. HA5 3DH. ☎ 020-8868 1973.

LIVINGSTONE, Rabbi Reuben, BA, LLB, MA, LLM, PgDipCPsych, PgDipLaw, JD; b. Johannesburg, South Africa, July 3, 1959; m. Esther née Koenigsberg; Rabbi, Lecturer (barrister/solicitor, non-practising); Rabbi, Hampstead Garden Suburb Synagogue (1999-); Programme Dir., Jewish Cultural Centre, Manchester (1983-85); Rabbi, Sale and District Hebrew Congregation (1985-88); Rabbi, Ilford Federation Synagogue (1988-99); Lecturer in Jewish and Comparative Law, Jews' College, London (1990-98); Corob Lecturer in Jewish Studies, Jews' College, London (1994-95). Publ: Contract in the Law of Obligations: A Comparative Analysis of Jewish Law and English Common Law (1994). Ad.: Hampstead Garden Suburb Synagogue, Norrice Lea, London N2 0RE.

LOBENSTEIN, Josef H., M.B.E.; b. Hanover, Apr. 27, 1927; Mayor, London Borough of Hackney (1997-2000); Hon. Freeman L. B. Hackney; President, Adath Yisroel Syn. and Burial Soc.; Chairman, N. London Jewish Liaison Cttee.; Vice-President; Union of Orth. Hebrew Cong and Chairman External Affairs Cttee; Exec. Kedassia Kashruth Cttee.; Exec., Agudath Israel World Org.; V. Chairman, Agudath Israel of Great Britain; Executive, National Shechita C.; Governor Avigdor Primary School; President Hackney North Conservative Assn.; form. Gen. Sec., Agudath Israel of Great Britain; Member, BoD; Tr. Jewish Secondary School Movement; Conservative Opposition Leader L. B. Hackney (1974-97); Councillor Metropolitan Borough of Stoke Newington (1962-65); Hon. President Hackney and Tower Hamlets Chamber of Commerce. Ad.: 27 Fairholt Rd., N16 5EW. ☎ 020-8800 4746. Fax 020-7502 0985.

LOEWE, Raphael James, M.C., M.A. (Cantab.), F.S.A.; b. Calcutta, Apr. 16, 1919; form. Goldsmid Prof. of Hebrew (form. Dir., Instit. of Jewish Studies), Univ. Coll., Lond.; form. S. A. Cook Fellow, Caius Coll., Cambridge; form. Lect. in Hebrew, Leeds Univ.; Vis. Prof in Judaica, Brown Univ. Providence, R.I. (1963-64); C. (form. P.), JHSE; C., Soc. for Jew Study; C. BAJS (former P.); form. Elder and Warden, Span. & Port. Jews, Cong., London; War service, Suffolk Regt., Royal Armoured Corps. Publ.: Women in Judaism, Omar Khayyam (Hebr.), The Rylands Sephardi Haggadah, Ibn Gabirol, etc. Ad.: 50 Gurney Dr., N2 0DE. ☎ 020-8455 5379.

LUBOFSKY, Rabbi Ronald, AM, BA; b. London, July 7, 1928; m. Shirley née Gold; Rabbi Emer. St. Kilda Hebrew Cong.; Lect. Centre for Jewish Civilisation, Monash Univ.; form. President, Assn. of Rabbis of Australia and N.Z.; Found., Life President, Jewish Museum of Australia; President, CCJ, Australia; past President, Mount Scopus War Memorial Coll., Melbourne; form. M., Great Syn., Sydney, and Cockfosters Syn., London. Ad.: 24 Leaburn Ave., Caulfield, Victoria 3161. ☎ 613 95259405. Fax.: 613 95259921.

LUCAS, Gerald Ephraim, b. London, Oct. 20, 1946; m. Angela née Daltroff; Exec. Dir., B'nai B'rith Hillel Foundation. Ad.: Hillel House, 1/2 Endsleigh Street, London WC1H 0DS. ☎ 020-7388 0801. Fax 020-7916 3973.

LUCAS, Mrs Stella (née Waldman), J.P.; b. London, July 30, 1916; V. President Jewish Care; Chairman, Stepney Girls' Club and Settlement; President, First Women's Lodge B'nai B'rith (1975-77), V. President Assn. of US Women; President, Dollis Hill Ladies, Guild; V. President (Chairman, 1978-84); Frs. of Hebrew Univ. (Women's Group); Exec. Off., Internat. C. of Jewish Women (1963-66); Chairman, Union of Jewish Women (1966-72); Chairman, Women Frs. of Jewis, Coll. (1957-66); Central Council for Jewish Soc. Services; BoD; Chairman, Brodie Instit.; Convenor BoD Central Enquiry Desk; Fdr. 'All Aboard Shops'. Ad.: 51 Wellington Ct., Wellington Rd., NW8 9TB. ☎ 020-7586 3030.

LYONS, Bernard, C.B.E., J.P., D.L., Hon. LL.D. (Leeds); b. Leeds, Mar. 30, 1913, m. Lucy; Chairman 1972-82 U.D.S. Group plc; L.P. Leeds Jewish Rep. C.; Chairman, Yorks. & N.E. Conciliation Cttee.; Race Rel. Bd (1968-70); Community Rel. Com. (1970-72); Dep. Lieutenant Yorks., W. Riding (1971); Leeds City C (1951-65). Publ.: The Thread is Strong; The Narrow Edge; The Adventures of Jimmie Jupiter; Tombola. Ad.: Upton Wood, Black Pack Rd., Fulmer, Bucks. SL3 6JJ. ☎ 01753-662404. Fax 01753-662413.

LYONS, Edward, Q.C., LL.B. (Leeds); b. Glasgow, May 17, 1926, m. Barbara; Recorder (1972-98); M.P. (SDP) Bradford West (1981-83); M.P. (Lab.) Bradford West (1974-81); Bradford East (1966-74); Parl. Pr. Sec. Treasury (1969-70); Bencher, Lincoln's Inn; Nat. Cttee., SDP (1984-89). Ad.: 4 Primley Park Lane, Leeds, LS17 7JR. ☎ 0113 2685351 and 59 Westminster Gardens, Marsham Street, SW1P 4JG. ☎ 020-7834 1960.

LYONS, Sir Isidore Jack, C.B.E., Hon. D.Univ. (York); b. Leeds, Feb. 1, 1916; Life V. President, JIA; Dep. Chairman, Youth Aliyah; Member of Court, York Univ.; H.V. President, Leeds Musical Festival; Ch of Trs., London Symphony Orchestra; Life Tr. Shakespeare Birthplace Trust; Chairman, Henry Wood Rehearsal Hall; H. Fel., Royal Acad. of Music; Chairman, Foreign and Commonwealth Office US Bicentennial sub-cttee.

MACCOBY, Hyam Zoundell, M.A. (Oxon.), D. Univ. (Open U.); b. Sunderland, March 20, 1924; Emer. Fellow Leo Baeck Coll., Lond.; Vis. Prof. Centre for Jewish Studies, Leeds (1998); Edr. Bd., European Judaism; Publ.: Revolution in Judaea, Judaism on Trial, The Sacred Executioner, The Mythmaker, Early Rabbinic Writings, Judas Iscariot and the myth of Jewish evil (awarded Wingate Prize 1992-3), Paul and Hellenism, The Disputation (TV & Stage play), A Pariah People, Ritual and Morality, etc. Ad.: 472 Street Lane West, Leeds LS17 6HA. ☎ 01113-268 1972.

MAGONET, Rabbi Professor Dr Jonathan David, M.B., B.S., Ph.D., (Heid.); b. London, Aug. 2, 1942; Princ., Leo Baeck Coll.; V. President, World Union for Progressive Judaism; Guest Prof. Univ. Oldenburg (1999); Chairman, Yth Section, WUPJ (1964-66); Co-Editor European Judaism (1992-). Publ.: Returning: Exercises in Repentance, Forms of Prayer, Vol. I, Daily and Sabbath (co-ed.); Vol. II, Pilgrim Festivals (co-ed.); Vol. III, Days of Awe Prayerbook (co-ed.); Form and Meaning – Studies in Literary Techniques in the Book of Jonah, Guide to the Here and Hereafter (co-ed.); A Rabbi's Bible (1991); Bible Lives (1992); How To Get Up When Life Gets You Down (1993) (co-ed.); The Little Blue Book Of Prayer (1993) (co-ed.); A Rabbi Reads the Psalms (1994); Kindred Spirits (co-ed. 1995); Jewish Explorations of Sexuality (ed. 1995); The Subversive Bible (1997); The Explorer's Guide to Judaism (1998); Sun, Sand and Soul (co-ed. 1999). Ad.: 18 Wellfield Ave., N10 2EA. ☎ 020-8444 3025.

MAILER, Norman, b. Long Branch, N.J., Jan. 31, 1923; Writer; Pulitzer Prize for non-fiction and Nat. Book Award for Arts and Letters (1969), Ed., Dissent, (1953-69). Publ.: The Naked and the Dead, Barbary Shore, The Deer Park, Advertisements for Myself, Deaths for the Ladies, The Presidential Papers, The armies of the night, Existential Errands, Marilyn, The Fight, The Executioner's Song, Of Women and Their Elegance, Pieces and Pontifications, Ancient Evenings, Tough Guys Don't Dance, Harlot's ghost, Oswald's tale, Portrait of

Picasso as a young man etc. Ad.: c/o Rembar, 19 W. 44th St., New York, NY 10036 USA.

MALITS, Rabbi Malcolm Henry, M.B.E., M.A., D.Litt.; b. Birmingham, Jan. 26, 1919; Emer. R.; M., Allerton Hebrew Cong. Liverpool (1964-90); Chaplain Ajex (Masonry), Past Prov. Grand Chap. for West Lancashire. Ad.: 12 Glenside, Liverpool L18 9UJ. ☎ 0151-724 1967.

MARCUS, Mark Hyman, B.A. (Com.); b. Manchester, Feb. 22, 1933; Bureau Chief London Bureau of Int. Affairs; form. Exec. Dir., B'nai B'rith Distr. 15 (1984-98); Dir. Provincial & London Divisions, IJPR. Ad.: B'nai B'rith Hillel House, 1-2 Endsleigh St., WC1H 0DS. ☎ 020-7383 0442. Fax 020-7387 8014. Email: lbia@ort.org

MARGOLYES, Miriam, B.A. (Cantab.), L.G.S.M&D; b. Oxford, May 18, 1941; Actress. Ad.: c/o Jonathan Altaras Associates Ltd, 2 Goodwins Court, WC2N 4LL ☎ 020-7497 8878 Fax.: 020-7497 8876.

MARINER, Rabbi Rodney John, B.A. (Hons.), Dip. Ed.; b. Melbourne, Australia, May 29, 1941; M., Belsize Sq. Syn.; Convener, Beth Din, RSGB; Assoc. M., Edgware & Distr. Ref. Syn. (1979-82); Asst. M., North Western Ref Syn. (1976-79). Publ.: Prayers For All The Year: Part 1, Shabbat; Part 2, Festivals; Part 3, New Year; Part 4, Atonement. Ad.: 37a Alexandra Gardens, London N10 3RN.

MARKOVA, Dame Alicia, D.B.E., Hon. D.Mus. (Leics. and East Anglia Univs.); b. London, Dec. 1, 1910; Prima Ballerina Assoluta; P.: English National Ballet (since 1989); V. President, Royal Academy of Dancing (since 1958); Dir., Metrop. Opera Ballet, New York (1963-69), Gov., Royal Ballet, Prof. of Ballet and Performing Arts., Univ. of Cincinnati; President, Lond. Ballet Circle (since 1981), President, All England Dance Competition (1983); President, Arts Educ. Schs (1984); Lond. Festival Ballet (1986). Publ.: Giselle and I, Markova Remembers. Ad.: c/o Barclays Bank, P.O. Box 40, SW3 1QB.

MARKS, John Henry, M.D., F.R.C.G.P., D.Obst., R.C.O.G.; b. London, May 30, 1925; m. Shirley, née Nathan; Chairman, C. BMA (1984-90); Chairman, Rep. Body BMA (1981-84); Gen. Med. C. (1979-84, 1989-94); V. President, Lond. Jewish Med. Soc. (1983-84, 1999-). Publ.: The Conference of Local Medical Committees and its Executive: An Historical Review. Ad.: Brown Gables, Barnet La., Elstree, Herts., WD6 3RQ. ☎ 020-8953 7687.

MARKS, Kenneth Anthony, b. London, July 28, 1931; Company Director; Non-Exec. Dir., Bank Leumi (UK) Ltd; Non-Exec. Dir. Cadora plc; Non-Exec. Dir. Focus D.I.Y.; Non-Exec. Dir., Courts plc; Dir., Kenneth Marks Associates Ltd. (Consultants); V. President British-Israel Chamber of Commerce; Gov., Shenkar College, Israel. Ad.: 279 Dover House Rd, Roehampton, SW15 5BP.

MARKS, Shula Eta (née Winokur), O.B.E., F.B.A., B.A.(UCT), Ph.D.(London), Hon. D.Litt.(UCT), Hon. D.Soc.Sci. (Natal); b. Cape Town, Oct. 14, 1936; m. Isaac Meyer Marks; Historian; Prof. History of Southern Africa, SOAS (1993-); Dir. Institute of Commonwealth Studies, Univ. of London (1983-93); Lecturer and Reader, History of Southern Africa, Jointly SOAS and ICS (1963-83); Chair, Society for Protection of Science and Learning (1993-); Chair International Records Management Tr. (1995-). Publ.: Reluctant Rebellion: The 1906-1908 Disturbances in Natal (1970); The Ambiguities of Dependence in South Africa (1986); Not Either an Experimental Doll: The Separate Lives of Three South African Women (1987); Divided Sisterhood: Class, Race and Gender in the South African Nursing Profession (1944). Ad.: Dept. of History, School of Oriental and African Studies, Thornhaugh St., WC1H 0XG. ☎ 020-7637 2388, 020-7323 6046 (Home 020-869936611). Email sm10@soas.ac.uk

MARMUR, Rabbi Dow, b. Sosnowiec, Poland, Feb. 24, 1935; Sr. Rabbi, Holy Blossom Temple, Toronto; form. President, Toronto Board of Rabbis; form. Chairman, C. of Reform and Lib. Rabbis; M., North Western Reform Syn. (1969-83); South-West Essex Reform Syn. (1962-69). Publ.: Beyond Survival; The Star of Return; Walking Toward Elijah; On being a Jew; Reform Judaism (Edr.); A

Genuine Search (Edr.); Choose Life. Ad.: 1950 Bathurst St., Toronto, Ontario, M5P 3K9, Canada. ☎ (416) 789 3291. Fax (416) 789 9697.

MASSEL, Abraham David, B.A. (Admin.); b. Manchester, May 10, 1927; m. Eva; Asst. Dir. Central Enquiry Desk BoD (1995-); Exec. Dir., BoD (1973-95); Sec., C. of Manchester and Salford Jews (1957-59); Sec. Jewish Defence & Group Rel. Cttee. (1959-73); Sec. Jewish Tribunal (Shops Act 1950), (1973-95). Ad.: 43 Green Lane, NW4 2AG. ☎ 020-8203 4467.

MAY, Michael, M.Sc. (econ.); b. Jerusalem, Dec. 16, 1945; Exec. Director, European Council of Jewish Communities; Form. Dir., Institute of Jewish Affairs, London; Dir. Jewish Film Fdn.; form. Assoc. Ed., J. Quarterly; Member BoD Foreign Affairs Cttee.; Member Adv. C., S.T.I.B.A. (Dutch) Foundation for the Fight Against Anti-Semitism; Member Adv. Bd., Intern. Centre for Holocaust Studies, N.Y.; former Dir. Jewish Book Council; Member Gov. Bd., World Jewish Congress (1983-91); Dir., Jewish Literary Trust (1984-91); Co.-Fdr. & Tr. Limmud Conf. (1980-84); Ad.: 74 Gloucester Place, W1H 3HN. ☎ 020-7224 3445. Fax 020-7224 3446. E-mail: ecjc@ort.org.

MAYER, Daniel, b. Paris, April 29, 1909; Member (President, 1983) French Constitutional C.; form. M. of Labour, War-time Member of C.N.R. (Resistance Nat. C.); Deputy for Seine; Sec.-Gen.; Socialist Party, S.F.I.O.; President, Internat. Fedn. of Human Rights; Conseil Supérieur de la Magistrature; President, Ligue des Droits de l'Homme. Ad.: Conseil Constitutionnel, 2 rue de Montpensier, Paris, 1e.

MEHDI, Sion, b. Jerusalem, July 14, 1932; Exec. Dir, Children & Youth Aliyah, Gt. Brit. & Eire (1985-98); Chairman, Exec., Victoria Com Centre; Norwood Child Care Youth & C. Serv. Cttee. (1995-); Chairman, Educ. & Youth Cttee.; BoD (1982-88; 1991-94); Form. H. Sec. Assoc. of Jewish Communal Professionals; Member Council Zionist Fed; Commonwealth Jewish Councils, British Sephardi C.; BoD (1979-); Member Central Jewish Lecture & information Cttee. (1988-91); The Exec. Cttee., AJY (1958-95) and V. President (1990-95); V. Chairman (1990-94), Sec. (1994-), The Herut Movement of G.B.; Member, C. The United Syn. (1989-93), Member, U.S. Bd of Religious Educ. (1989-92); Brent Cross Teenage Centre; Gov., Simon Marks Jewish Primary School (1989-94); Chairman, Cttee. for Welfare of Iranian Jews in Gt. Brit.; H. Sec. Jewish Child's Day, H. Sec., Persian Heb Cong., Frs. of Jewish Youth (1958-97); Sephardi Fed. of Gt. Brit & C'wlth, AJY (1969-95); Exec. Dir., Iranian Jew Centre; Man Bd., Finchley (United) Syn. Ad.: 17 Arden Rd., N3 3AB. ☎ 020-8346 3121. Fax 020-8343 7383.

MELINEK, Rabbi A., B.A., Ph D.; b. London, Sept. 15, 1912; form. Edr., L'Eylah; form. M., Willesden Brondesbury Stoke Newington Syns.; fom. Lect. Jews, Coll., Member, Court of the Univ. of Kent. Publ.: Life and Times of Abarbanel. Ad.: 6 Elm Close, NW4 2PH. ☎ 020-8202 9826.

MICHAELS, Rabbi Maurice Arnold, M.A.; b. Woolmer's Park, Herts., Aug. 31, 1941; Assoc. Rabbi, Edgware and Dist. Reform Syn.; Chairman Govs. Clore Tikva School; Life Gov. of Leo Baeck Coll.; Previous: Chairman and V. President, RSGB; Chairman, Leo Baeck Coll.; Chairman, S. W. Essex Reform Syn.; Chairman, Redbridge Business Educ. Partnership; Gov. of Redbridge Coll.; Gov. of Akiva School; Gov. of Jewish Joint Bur. Soc.; Tr., Redbridge Racial Equality Council; Tr., Limmud; Member, World Union for Progressive Judaism Gov. Body; Member, Redbridge Jewish Cttee; Council Member, Redbridge Campaign Against Racism and Fascism; Dir., Harlow Enterprise Agency; Man. Cttee., West Essex Business Educ. Partnership; V. Chairman, Harlow & Dist. Employers' Group; Member, BoD; Member, Nat. Council Zionist Fed.; Member, Nat. Council Soviet Jewry. Ad.: 18 Exeter Gardens, Ilford, Essex IG1 3LA. ☎ 020-8554 2812.

MIDDLEBURGH, Rabbi Charles H., B.A. Hons., Ph.D.; b. Hove, Oct. 2, 1956. Minister, Kingston Liberal Synagogue (1977-83); Rabbi, Harrow and Wembley

Progressive Synagogue (1983-97); Exec. Dir. Union of Liberal and Progressive Synagogues (1997-); Assoc. Ed. Siddur Lev Chadash (1989-95); Co-Ed., Mahzor Ruach Chadashah (1996-); Chairman, ULPS Rabbinic Conference (1988-90, 1993-95); Lect. and Principal, ULPS Evening Institute (1980-92); Lect. Aramaic, Bible, Practical Rabbinics, Leo Baeck College (1985-). Ad.: The Montagu Centre, 21 Maple St., W1P 6DS. ☎ 020-7580 1663. Fax 020-8436 4184.

MILLER, Arthur, b. New York, Oct. 17, 1915; Novelist and Playwright; President, Internat. P.E.N. Publ.: Focus, All My Sons, Death of a Salesman, After the Fall, A View from the Bridge, The Crucible, Incident at Vichy, The Price, The American Clock Playing for Time, Timebends, The ride down Mount Morgan, etc. Ad.: c/o Kay Brown, I.C.M., 40 West 57th St., New York, N.Y. 10019.

MILLER, Harold, b. London, 1917; Member BoD; form. Chairman, Z.F.; V. President, form. Chairman, Brit Poale Zion; Elected to Fel. of WZO, 1993; Member of Board of Deputies. Ad.: 71 Francklyn Gdns., Edgware, Middlesex. ☎ 020-8958 5418.

MILLER, Rabbi Israel, M.A., D.D. (Yeshiva Univ.); b. Baltimore, Md., April 6, 1918; Sr. V. President Emeritus, Yeshiva Univ.; H. President, Amer. Z. Fed.; President, Conference Jewish Material Claims against Germany; V. President, Amer.-Israel. Publ Affairs Cttee. (1983-90); Sec., Memorial Foundation for Jewish Culture; V.P , Jewish Com. Relations C. of New York; V. President, Nat. Jewish Welfare Bd. (1970-78); Chairmam., Conf of Presidents. of Major Amer. Jewish Orgs. (1974-76); Chairman, Amer. Jewish Conference on Soviet Jewry (1965-67); Chairman, Com. on Jewish Chaplaincy, NJWB (1962-65). Ad.: 2619 Davidson Ave., Bronx, N.Y. 10468. ☎/Fax (718) 561 2496.

MILLER, Dr. Jack Elius, O.B.E., F.R.C.G.P., J.P., O.ST.J.; b. Glasgow, March 7, 1918; form. Treasury Med. Off.; H.V.P (President 1968-71), Glasg. Jewish Rep. C.; H. V. President, Garnethill Syn.; Chairman, Soviet Jewry Com. (1968-78); Chairman, WJC Scotland (1954-63); H. President (Chairman 1950-57, 1960-65), Ajex Scotland (1997); BoD (1979-88), Nat.T. BMA (1972-81); Fel., BMA, Royal Soc. of Med, Royal Coll. of G.Ps.; Gold Medallist, BMA; Freeman of the City of London; Chairman, Scottish Gen. Med. Services Cttee (1969-72); Gen. Med. Services Com.; H. V. President, Scottish Marriage Guidance C. & Glasg. M.G.C.; Race Rel. Bd., Scottish Conciliation Cttee. (1968-75); H. V. President, Prince and Princess of Wales Hospice, Glasg.; Chairman, Epilepsy Assn. of Scotland, Strathclyde Br. (1983-88); Chairman, Working Party on Priorities of the National Health Service; (1985-87); Sharpen, Report (1988); Edr., Glasg. Doctors, Handbook. Ad.: 38 Fruin Ave. Newton Mearns, Glasgow G77 6HJ. ☎ 0141-639 7869.

MILLER, Maurice Solomon, M.B.Ch.B., J.P.; b. Glasgow, Aug. 16, 1920; Med. practitioner; M.P. (Lab.) for East Kilbride (1974-87); M.P. for Kelvingrove (Glasgow) (1964-74), form. H.Sec., Lab. Frs. of Israel, Parl. Br. Publ.: Window on Russia. Ad.:

MILLETT, The Rt. Hon. The Lord Millett, Baron Millett of St. Marylebone, P.C., M.A. (Cantab.); b. London, June 23, 1932; Lord of Appeal in Ordinary (1998-); Judge of the High Court Chancery Div. (1986-94); Q.C. (1973-86), Member, Insolvency Law Review Cttee. (1976-82); Stndg. Jr. Counsel, Trade & Industry Dept. (1967-73); Bencher, Lincoln's lnn, Called to Bar, Middle Temple; form. Chairman, Lewis Hammerson Home (1981-1991); President, West London Syn. (1991-95); Hon. Fel. Trinity Hall (1994). Publ.: (contrib.) Halsbury's Law of England; Ed-in-Chief: Encyclopaedia of Forms and Precedents. Ad.: 18 Portman Cl., W1H 9HJ. ☎ 020-7935 1152.

MIRVIS, Rabbi Ephraim Yitzchak, B.A.; b. Johannesburg, Sept. 7, 1956; Rabbi Finchley Synagogue (1996-); Chairman Rabbinical Council of the U.S.; Member St. Cttee of Conference of European Rabbis; Religious Adv. to the Jewish Marriage Council; M. Western Marble Arch Syn. (1992-96); form. Chief Rabbi, Jewish Coms. of Ireland (1984-92); M. Dublin Hebrew Cong. (1982-84); Lect.

274   WHO'S WHO

Machon Meir, Jerusalem (1980-82). Ad.: 69 Lichfield Grove, London N3 2JJ.
☎ 020-8346 3773.
MISHCON, Baron of Lambeth (Life Peer) (Victor Mishcon), D.L. Q.C.; b. London
Aug. 14, 1915; Solicitor; Official Opposition Spokesman in House of Lords on
Legal Affairs (1983-92); Dep. Lieut. for Greater Lond.; Chairman, L.C.C (1954-
55); form. Chairman, Gen. Purposes Cttee., G.L.C. L.C.C. and various L.C.C.
Cttees., Member, Govt. Com. of Inquiry into Lond. Transport (1953-54),
Member Dept. Cttee. of Inquiry into Homosexual Offences and Prostitution
(1954-57); Member, Nat. Theatre Bd. (1965-90) and South Bank Theatre Bd.;
President Brit. C. of Shaare Zedek Hospital, Jerusalem; H. President, Brit.
Technion Cttee; V. President, (form. P), AJY; Hon. Solicitor, JIA; Patron, and
(1968-88) Chairman, Instit. of Jewish Studies; V. Chairman, CCJ (1977-79);
form. V. President, BoD.; Cdr., Royal Swedish Order of North Star, Star of
Ethiopia; Star of Jordan; LL.D (Hon.) Birmingham Univ. 1991; Hon. Fellow,
U.C.L.; Q.C. (Hon.) 1992. Ad.: House of Lords, SW1A 0PW.
MISHON, Philip, O.B.E., b. London, March 23, 1924; Comp. Dir.; Chairman, Trs.,
UK Frs. for Further Educ. in Israel; V. President (Nat. Chairman, 1966-68) A.J.E.X.
Appointed Tr. 1993; Council, CCJ; J.L.G.B.; President, Ajex Golf Soc. Ad.: 53
Bolsover St., W1P 7HL. ☎ 020-7387 6404. Fax 020-7722 3354.
MITCHELL, Mrs. Eva (née Rose); b. Munster, June 14, 1929; Life V. President,
West Lond. Syn. of Brit. Jews (1994-); Exec. Dir., C.B.F.W.J.R. (1979-89); form.
Chairman, V. President Chairman, RSGB (1973-76); form. Chairman, Assn. of
Jew Women's Orgs. in UK; form. V. Chairman; Nat. C. for Soviet Jewry. Ad.: 15
Avenue Court, Draycott Ave., SW3 3BU. ☎ 020-7584 4746.
MOCKTON, Rev. Leslie, b. Manchester Aug. 5, 1928; form. M., Waltham Forest
Hebrew Cong.; Mayor's Chaplain, Lond. Borough Waltham Forest (1981-82);
Hospital Chaplain Forest. Health Care Trust (1992-96); form. M., Highams Pk.
& Chingford Syn. (1969-87); form. M. Bradford Hebrew Cong. (1965-69);
West End Gt. Syn. (1958-65); Barking & Becontree Hebrew Cong. (1955-58).
Ad.: Waltham Forest Hebrew Con., 140 Boundary Rd., Walthamstow E17 8LA.
☎ 020-8458 1204.
MONTAGU, Iris Rachel (née Solomon), the Hon. Mrs. Ewen Montagu; b.
London, May 9, 1903. Ad.: 24 Montrose Ct., Exhibition Rd., SW7 2OQ.
☎ 020-7458 1204.
MONTAGUE, Lee, b. Bow, London, Oct. 16, 1927; Actor; many leading roles
including Shakespeare and Chekhov, title-role Leon in The Workshop, Raymond
Chandler in Private Dick, O'Connor, in Cause Célèbre (London 1977), Ed, in
Entertaining Mr. Sloane (New York 1965); Court in the Act (London 1987); films
include Moulin Rouge, Mahler, Brass Target, London Affair Silver Dream Racer,
Lady Jane, Madame Sousatzka; television appearances include Holocaust, Thank
You Comrades, Tussy Marx, Parsons Pleasure, The Workshop, Passing Through,
Sharing Time, Kim Dr. Sakharov, Bird of Prey, Much Ado About Nothing,
Countdown to War, Incident in Judaea, House of Elliott; Casualty. Best TV Actor
of the Year 1960. Ad.: c/o Joyce Edwards, 275 Kennington Rd., London SE11
6BY.
MONTEFIORE, Alan Claude Robin Goldsmid, M.A.(Oxon.); b. London Dec. 29,
1926; Emer. Fellow, form. Fellow and Tutor in Philosophy, Balliol College,
Oxford; Vis. Prof. Middlesex Univ.; form. Sr. Lect. in Moral & Political
Philosophy, Keele Univ.; President, Wiener Libr.; Chairman Forum for European
Philosophy. Publ.: A Modern Introduction to Moral Philosophy, British Analytic
Philosophy (co-ed.), Neutrality and Impartiality, The University and Political
Commitment (ed.), French Philosophy Today (ed.), Goals, No-Goals and Own
Goals: A Debate on Goal Directed and Intentional Behaviour (co-ed.), The
Political Responsibility of Intellectuals (co-ed.), Integrity in the Public and Private
Domains (co-ed.), etc. Ad.: 34 Scarsdale Villas, W8 6PR. ☎ 020-7937 7708. Fax

020-7938 4257.
MONTY, Mrs Regina Joy (née Dixon); b. London, Sept. 19, 1935; Hon. President, Fed. Women Zionists (Brit. WIZO); form. Chairman, V. Chairman and Membership Chairman, British WIZO. Ad.: 107 Gloucester Pl., W1H 4BY.
MOONMAN, Eric, O.B.E.; b. Liverpool, Apr. 29, 1929; M.P. (Lab.) for Basildon (1974-79), for Billericay (1966-70); Chair, ERG Group of Radio Stations; V. President, BoD (1994-); Sr. V. President, BoD (1985-91); Chairman, Media Network; Chairman City of Liverpool Continuing Care Cttee (1996-); Prof Health Management, City Univ., London; Chairman, Academic Response to Racism & Antisemitism (1994-); Bd. Memb. IRC, Potomac Inst. for Policy Studies; Consultant, ICRC (Africa) (1992-95); Director Natural History Museum Development Trust (1989-91); (seconded) Chairman, WJC Europe Br. Cttee. on Antisemitism (1985-92, 1998-); Chairman Community Research Unit, (1985-96); Chairman, Z. Fed. (1975-80); President, Friends of Union of Jewish Students; Co.-Chairman, Nat. Jewish Solidarity Cttee. (1975-79); form. Parl. Pte. Sec. to Sec. of State for Educ. and Science; form. Sr. Res. Fel., Manch. Univ.; form. Leader, Stepney Borough C.; Sr. Adv., Brit. Instit. of Management (1956-62); European Adv. WJC (1973-76); Chairman, Nat. Aliyah and Volunteers C.; Chairman, P.R. Cttee., Z.F. (1983-85; 1972-75); Trustee, Balfour Tr.; CRE Award for Multi Racial Service (1996). Publ.: The Alternative Government, The Manager and the Organisation, Reluctant Partnership, European Science and Technology, etc. Ad.: 1 Beacon Hill, N7 9LY.
MORGAN, Rabbi Fred; b. New York City, March 18, 1948, m. Susan Sinclair; M. Temple Beth Israel, Melbourne, Australia; Vice-Chairman C. Progressive Rabbis of Australia & N.Z. (1998-); Hon. Assoc. Rabbi Sim Shalom Jewish Community Budapest; M. North West Surrey Synagogue (1984-97); Lect. in Midrash and Jewish Thought Leo Baeck Rabbinical College (1987-97); V.-Chairman Assembly of Reform Rabbis (1996-97); Lect. in Judaism, Roehampton Institute (1989-92); Lect. in Religious Studies, Univ. of Bristol (1973-79); Vis. Prof. Eotvos Lorand Univ., Budapest (1992-94). Ad.: Temple Beth Israel, 76-82 Alma Road, St Kilda 3182, Victoria, Australia. ☎61-3-9510 1488. Fax 61-3-9521 1229. Email: rav-morgan@starnet.com.au.
MORITZ, Ludwig Alfred, M.A., D.Phil. (Oxon.); b. Munich, May 11, 1921, m. Doris née Rath; retd.; form. V. Princ. (Admin.) and Reg., Univ. Coll., Cardiff (1971-87); Lect., Bedford Coll., Lond. (1950-53), Univ. Coll. Cardiff (1953-60); Prof. of Classics, Univ. Coll. of Ghana (1959-60), Univ Coll., Cardiff (1960-71); Chairman Cardiff New Syn. (1991-95). Publ.: Classical studies. Ad.: 1 Llanedeyrn Rd., Penylan, Cardiff CF23 9DT. ☎/Fax 029 2048 5065.
MORRIS, Henry, b. London Mar. 5, 1921; form. Chairman, Jewish Defence & Group Rel Cttee., BoD; V. President (Nat.Chairman 1979-81) Ajex. Ad.: 94 Randall Ave., NW2 7SU ☎ 020-8452 9805; 020-8636 5361.
MORRIS, Norman Harold, F.R.S.A.; b. London, June 8, 1932; Principal N.M. Consultants; form. Exec. Dir., Balfour Diamond Jubilee Tr. (Consult. 1995-); Exec. Consultant Scopus Jewish Educational Tr. (1995-); Freeman, City of Lond.; form. Exec. Sec. Z. Fed.; Dep. Provincial Dir., Z. Fed.; J.P.A.; Printing & Publ. Cttee., Brit.-Israel Chamber of Commerce; Sec., Eastern Cape Z. C. Ad.: Balfour House, 741 High Rd., N12 0BQ. ☎ 020-83438 8196. Fax 020-8347 7283.
MORRIS OF KENWOOD, Philip Geoffrey, 2nd Baron, J.P.; b. Sheffield, June 18, 1928; form. P. Hotel Caterers and Allied Trades Aid for Israel Cttee.; President, JNF Bridge Tournament. Ad.: 36 Fitzjohn's Ave., London NW3 5JY. ☎ 020-7431 6332.
MORRIS OF KENWOOD, Lady Ruth (née Janner); b. London, Sept. 21, 1932; Solicitor; President, Nat. Cttee., Va'ad Lema'an Habonim; H. Solicitor, various youth orgs.; Dir., W.O.Y.L.; Tr. Jewish Youth Fund; Tr. Brady Maccabi; Memb. Allocations Cttee UJIA; Tr. Elsie & Barnett Janner Charitable Tr.; Dir.

Womankind worldwide; form. Man., Brady Girls' Club; form. exec. Member, Victoria Boys' and Girls' Club; Tr., Rowan Educ.; Tr.; form. Member, Gen. Adv. C., Independent Broadcasting Auth. (I.B.A.). Chairman D.S.S. Appeals Tribunal. Ad.: 36 Fitzjohn's Ave., London NW3 5JY. ☎ 020-7431 6332.

MOSER, Sir Claus, K.C.B., C.B.E., F.B.A., B.Sc. (Econ.) Hon. D. (Southampton, Leeds, Surrey, Sussex, York, Keele, City, Wales, Edinburgh, Liverpool London, Brunel, Brighton, Hull, Heriot-Watt, Northumbria, South Bank Univs); b. Berlin, Nov. 24, 1922; Chancellor, Keele Univ. (1986-); Tr. British Museum (1988-); Chairman British Museum Dev. Trust (1994-); Chancellor Open University Israel (1994-); Warden, Wadham Coll., Oxford (1984-93); Chairman, Harold Holt Ltd. (1990-); Chairman Basic Skills Agency; Dir., V. Chairman, C.B.F.-W.J.R. Publ.: Writings on statistics. Ad.: 3 Regent's Park Tce., NW1 7EE. ☎ 020-7485 1619.

NABARRO, Eric John Nunes, J.P., F.C.A.; b. London, April 5, 1917; m. Cecily née Orenstein; Chartered accountant; P. of Elders, Spanish and Portuguese Jews, Cong., London (1984-88; 1994-96); T., Heshaim (Beth Hamidrash) (1984-94); H. Member, Nat. Shechita C.; Tr., Ravenswood Foundation (1986-92); Chairman, Sephardi Kashrut Auth. (1968-84); President, Sephardi Welfare Bd. (1979-87); T., BoD (1973-79); V. President (T. 1947-72), Victoria Com. Centre; Capt., Jewish Brigade (1945); T., London Bd. for Shechita (1949-63); Chairman, Kosher School Meals Service (1966-73). Ad.: 61 William Ct., 6 Hall Rd., London NW8 9PB. ☎ 020-7266 3787.

NABARRO, Frank Reginald Nunes, M.B.E., M.A., B.Sc. (Oxon.), D.Sc. (Birmingham), D.Sc. (Hon.) (Witwatersrand, Natal, Cape Town), F.R.S., Hon. F.R.S.S.Af.; b. London March 7, 1916; P. Roy. Soc. S. Africa (1988-92); H. Prof Res. Fel., Physics Dept. Witwatersrand Univ., Johannesburg; Fell. S. African CSIR; Dep. V. Chancellor (1978-80), form. Dean, Faculty of Science; Fd. Mem., S.A. Acad. Sci.; Foreign Assoc. U.S. Nat. Acad. Eng. Publ.: Theory of Crystal Dislocations; Physics of Creep (with H. L. de Villiers). Ad.: 32 Cookham Rd., Auckland Park, Johannesburg 2092, S. Africa. ☎ (11) 726 7745. Fax (11) 339 8262.

NADDELL, Alexander Walker, K. St. J., K.M.L.J., ERD., J.P., D.L., F.R.C.S., F.R.F.P.S., F.S.A. (Scot.), F.R.S.A.; b. Glasgow, Dec. 25, 1910; Orthopaedic and Neuro. Surgeon; Queen's Household Surgeon; Fel., Royal Soc. of Med. Col. (T.A. Vol. Res.); Distr. Court Judge; Dir. Glasgow Humane Soc.; V. President, Technion Soc., Glasg. Publ.: The Slipped Disc and the Arching Back of Man, Fight Old Age, Migrain, new method of control and care. Ad. 22 Sandyford Pl., Glasgow, G3 7NG. ☎ 0141-221 7571.

NAGLER, Neville Anthony, M.A. (Cantab); b. London, Jan. 2, 1945; m. Judy née Mordant; Director General BoD; Exec. Cttee, Interfaith Network for the UK; form. Asst. Sec. Home Office (1980-91); UK Representative to UN Narcotics Comm., (1983-88); Chairman, Council of Europe Drug Co-op Group (1984-88); Haldane Essay Prize (1979); Princ. H.M. Treasury; Pte. Sec. Chancellor of Exchequer (1971); Fin. Rep. and Warden, Pinner Syn. (1979-91). Ad.: Board of Deputies ☎ 020-7543 5400. Fax 020-7543 0100. Email bod@ort.org

NATHAN, Clemens Neumann, C.Tex.F.T.I., F.R.A.I., Officers' Cross, Austria; Cavalieri, al Merito della Repub. Italiana; b. Hamburg, Aug. 24, 1933; Comp. Dir., P. (T., 1965-71) Anglo-Jewish Assn.; V. President (President 1983-89); Jt. Chairman Consultant C. of Jewish Orgs. (Non-Govt. Org. at United Nations); Chairman, Centre for Christian–Jewish Studies, Cambridge (1998-); Claims Conf, Memorial Foundation for Jewish Culture; Mem, Jewish Memorial C.; Hon. Fell. Shenkar Coll., Israel; Hon. Fell. SSEES, Univ. London; Director Sephardi Centre; CCJ, Fdr. Member, Internat. Cttee. for Human Rights in Soviet Union (1966); BoD (1979-85); Soc. of Heshaim, Span. & Port. Jews, Cong.,

Lond. (1979-), Bd. of Elders (1977-83); Chairman, Sha'are Tikva Cttee. (1975-81); form. V. President, Textile Instit.; Textile Institute Medal for services to the Industry and Institute. Publ.: Technological and marketing works. Ad.: 2 Ellerdale Cl., NW3 6BE. ☎ 020-7794 6537

NATHAN, David, b. Manchester, Dec. 9, 1926; m. Norma née Ellis; Writer; theatre critic, Jewish Chronicle, theatre critic, Daily Herald - Sun, (1960-69); President, Critics', Circle (1986-88), Deputy Ed., Jewish Chronicle, (1978-91). Publ.: Hancock (biography with Freddie Hancock), The Freeloader; The Laughtermakers, A Quest for Comedy; Glenda Jackson, A Critical Profile; John Hurt, An Actor's Progress; The Story So Far; Contributor to Shaw and Politics, Pennsylvania State Univ. Press. T.V.: That Was The Week That Was, etc.; Plays: A Good Human Story (Granada, 1977); The Belman of London (Radio 3, 1982); The Bohemians (Radio 4, 1983); Royal Television Soc. Writer's Award, Highly Commended 1978. Ad.: 16 Augustus Close, Brentford Dock, Brentford, Middx. TW8 8QE. ☎ 020-8568 8987.

NATHAN, Roger Carol Michael, 2nd Baron; Hon. LL.D. (Sussex); b. London, Dec. 5, 1922; H. President (Chairman 1971-77) C.B.F.-W.J.R (since 1977); President, JWB (1967-71); V. Chairman, Cancer Res. Campaign (Chairman Ex. Cttee. 1970-75); Chairman Cttee. on Energy and the Environment (1974); V. Chairman Cttee. on Charity Law and Practice (1976); Member Royal Com. on Environmental Pollution (1979-89); Memb. House of Lords Select Cttee on Science & Technology (1994-); Member House of Lords Select Cttee. on European Com.; Chairman, Sub-Cttee. (Environment) (1983-87, 1989-92); Chairman, House of Lords Select Cttee. on Murder and Life Imprison-ment (1988-89); Chairman Cttee. on Effectiveness and the Voluntary Sector (1989-90); Sol; V. President (Chairman 1975-77); Royal Society of Arts; Fel., Soc. of Antiquaries; Fel., Royal Geographical Soc.; Chairman, Sussex Downs Conservation Board (1992-97); President Weald & Downland Open Air Museum (1994-97). Master, Worshipful Co. of Gardeners (1964); Capt., 17/21 Lancers (Ment. in Dispatches). Ad.: House of Lords SW1 0PW.

NAVON, Yitzhak, b. Jerusalem, April 9, 1921; Form. Israeli Dep. Prime Min. and Educ & Culture Min.; President, State of Israel (1978-83); Member, Knesset (1965-78; since 1984); form. Chairman, Knesset Foreign Affairs and Defence Cttee.; Dir., Office of Prime Minister (Ben-Gurion) (1952-63). Publ.: Bustan Sephardi, Six Days and Seven Gates. Ad.: 31 Haneviim St., Jerusalem.

NEUBERGER, Rabbi Julia Babette Sarah (née Schwab), M.A. (Cantab.) Hon. Doctorates Univ. Humberside, Ulster, City, Stirling, Oxford Brookes, Teesside, Nottingham, Open U.; b. London, Feb. 27, 1950, m. Anthony; Chancellor Univ. Ulster (1994-); Chief Exec. The King's Fund (1997-); Council Univ. College, London (1994-97); Council Memb. Save the Children Fund (1994-98); Vis. Cttee, Harvard Memorial Church (1994-); Memb. General Medical Council (1993-); Mem. Medical Res. C. (1995-); Chairman, ULPS Rabbinic Conference (1983-85); Lect., Leo Baeck Coll. Nat. Cttee. SDP (1983-85); Harkness Fell Harvard University (1991-92); Memb. Human Fertilisation and Embryology Authority (1990-95); T., Runnymede Trust (1990-97); Visiting Fel., King's Fund Instit. (1989-91); Memb. C. St. George's House, Windsor (1989-96); Chairman, Patients, Assn. (1988-91); Rabbi, S. Lond. Lib. Syn. (1977-89); Assoc., Newnham Coll., Cambridge, Presenter, Choices, BBC-1 (1986-87); Chairman, Camden & Islington Com. Health Services NHS Trust (1993-97). Publ.: 'Women in Judaism'; The Fact and The Fiction in: 'Women's Religious Experience, (ed. Pat Holden), The Story of Judaism (for children), Judaism, in: Spiritual Care in Nursing (ed. McGilloway and Myco), Days of Decision, Vols. I-IV (ed.); Women's Policy, Defence and Disarmament, Bill of Rights and Freedom of Information, Privatisation, Caring for Dying Patients of Different Faiths (Lisa Sainsbury Foundation, 2nd ed. 1994). Ed. (with Canon John White) A Necessary

End (1991); Whatever's happening to women (1991); Ethics and Healthcare: The role of research ethics committees in the UK (Kings's Fund 1992); (ed.) The things that matter (1993); On being Jewish (1995); The best that we can do (1999). Ad.: 28 Regents Park Rd., London Nw1 7TR. ☎ 020-7428 9895. Fax 020-7813 2030.

NEWMAN, Aubrey Norris, M.A. (Glasgow), M.A., D.Phil. (Oxon.), F.R.Hist S.; b. London, Dec. 14, 1927; Prof. of history, Leicester Univ.; President, Jewish Hist. Soc. (1977-79, 1992-93); Scholarship Ctee., JMC. Publ.: The United Synagogue 1870-1970, The Stanhopes of Chevening, Parliamentary Diary of Sir Edward Knatchbull, etc. Ad.: 33 Stanley Rd., Leicester. ☎ 0116 270 4065.

NEWMAN, Eddy, b. Liverpool, May 14, 1953. Manchester City Councillor (1979-85); Labour M.E.P. for Greater Manchester Central (1984-99); Member of the European Parliament's Delegation for Relations with Israel and the Knesset (1994-99); V. Chairman, European Parliament Regional Policy ad Regional Planning Cttee (1984-87); Chairman, European Parliament Cttee on Petitions (1994-97); V. Chairman, Cttee on Petitions (1997-). Publ.: Respect for Human Rights in the European Union', a report of the European Parliament Committee on Civil Liberties, 1994. Ad.: 234 Ryebank Rd., Manchester M21 9LU. ☎ 0161-881 9641.

NEWMAN, Rabbi Isaac, M.Phil. P.G.C.E., Dip. Counselling; b. London, Apr. 3, 1924; Chairman, Rabbis for Human Rights (Israel); M. Retd., Barnet Syn.; Sr. Lect., Judaica, & Chaplain, Middlesex Polytechnic, Trent Park; form. H.Sec., Rabbinical C., United Synagogue; Chaplain to R.A.F. Publ.: Talmudic Discipleship. Ad.: 90 Sderot Herzl, Jerusalem. ☎ 02 6525763.

NEWMAN, Rabbi Jeffrey, M.A.(Oxon.); b. Reading, Dec. 26 1941; m. Bracha; Minister Finchley Reform Synagogue (1973-); form. Chairman Rabbinic In-service training, Leo Baeck Rabbinical College (L.B.C.); form. Chairman, Pastoral Skills and Counselling Department L.B.C.; Chairman of Tr. Israel Palestine Centre for Research and Information; Ed. Living Judaism (1969-73); Lect. in Heimler Training. Contributor to various journals on Judaism, Psychology and Spirituality. Ad.: Finchley Reform Synagogue, Fallowcourt Avenue, N12 0BE. ☎ 020-8446 3244. Fax 020-8446 5980.

NEWMAN, Lotte Therese, CBE, MB, BS, LRCP, MRCS, FRCGP; b. Frankfurt am Main, Jan. 22, 1929; m. Norman Aronsohn; General practitioner; Memb. GMC (1984-); Chairman, Registration Committee, General Medical C. (1997-98); President, London Jewish Medical Society (1998-99); Governor, PPP Medical Trust (1997-); President Royal Coll. General Practitioners (1994-97); Freeman, City of London. Publ.: papers on a wide range of medical, health and training topics. Ad.: The White House, 1 Ardwick Rd., London NW2 2BX. ☎ 020-7435 6630.

OPPENHEIM-BARNES, Baroness of Gloucester (Life Peer) (Sally), P.C.; b. Dublin, July 1930; Min. of State for Consumer Affairs (1979-82); M.P. (Conservative) for Gloucester (1970-87); form. Chairman, Conservative Party Parl. Prices and Consumer Protection Cttee.; form Nat. V. President, Nat. Union of Townswomen's Guilds; form. Nat. V. President, R.O.S.P.A.; Chairman, Nat. Consumer C. (1987-89); Dir. (non-exec.) Robert Fleming (1989-97); Non-Exec. Director. HFC Bank (1989-98). Ad.: House of Lords.

OPPENHEIMER, Peter Morris, M.A.; b. London, Apr 16, 1938; Economics Lect., Oxford Univ., Student (Fel.) Christ Church Oxford; Dir. Jewish Chronicle Ltd.; Delbanco, Meyer & Co. Ltd.; Chief Economist, Shell Internat. Petroleum Co. (1985-86). Ad.: Christ Church, Oxford OX1 1DP. ☎ 01865 558226. Fax 01865-516834.

ORGEL, Leslie Eleazer, D.Phil., F.R.S.; b. London, Jan 12, 1927; m. Hassia Alice née Levinson; Sr. Fellow & Res. Prof., Salk Instit. and Adjunct Prof., Univ. of California, San Diego; Member Nat Acad. Sci., form. Fellow of Peterhouse, Cambridge Univ. Publ.: Scientific work. Ad.: Salk Instit., P.O. Box 85800, San

Diego, California 92186-5800, USA. ☎ (858) 453 4100, ext 1322. Email orgel@salk.edu

ORLINSKY, Harry M., B.A., Ph.D.; b. Owen Sound, Ont., Can, Mar 14, 1908; Prof. of Bible. H.U.C.-J.I.R., New York (since 1943); Ed., Library of Biblical Studies, President, Soc. of Biblical Lit. (1969-70); Centennial Award for Biblical Scholarship; President, Amer. Friends of Israel Exploration Soc. (1951-79); President, Internat. Org. for Masoretic Studies; President, Internat. Org. for Septuagint and Cognate Studies (1969-75), President, Amer. Acad. for Jewish Res.; Fel. Guggenheim Form. Soc. of Scholars, Johns Hopkins Univ. (1982); form. Vis. Prof., Hebrew Univ.; Acad. Cttee., Annenberg Res. Instit. (since 1987). Publ.: Works of Bible, lit. and hist., The Pentateuch A Linear Translation, 5 vols.; Revised Standard Version, Old Testament; The Torah, Edr.-in-chief of J.P.S. trans. (1963); The Prophets; The Writings; The So-called Servant of the Lord and Suffering Servant in Second Isaiah; Ancient Israel; Understanding the Bible; The Bible as Law; Tanakh; Essays in Biblical Culture and Bible Translation, etc. Ad.: 1 West 4th St., New York 10012. ☎ 212-674 5300.

OWEN, His Honour Judge Aron, B.A., Ph.D. (Wales); b. Tredegar, Gwent, Feb. 16, 1919, m. Rose née Fishman; Circuit Judge, South-East Circuit (1980-94); Dep. High Court Judge, Family Division; Freeman, City of Lond; C. JHSE; Patron, Jewish Marriage Co. Publ.: Social History of Jews in Thirteenth-Century Europe, Amos and Hosea, Rashi. Ad.: 44 Brampton Grove, NW4 4AQ. ☎ 020-8202 8151.

OZIN, Malcolm John; b. London, Nov. 14, 1934; Managing Dir., Investment & Securities Trust Ltd.; Hon. Chief Exec. Jewish Blind & Disabled; Tr. Cecil Rosen Found.; Hon. Sec. Cavendish Housing Trust Ltd. Ad.: 118 Seymour Place, W1H 5DJ. ☎ 0207-262 2003. Email: mjo@jblind.org

PADWA, Rabbi Henoch Ber, b. Busk, Poland, Aug. 1908; m. Raisal née Tauber; Principal Rabbinical Authority of the Union of Orthodox Hebrew Congregations (1956-); Rabbi Shomrei Hadass, Vienna (1932-38); Rabbi of Yad Machane Yehuda, Jerusalem (Aidah HaCharedis) (1940-56). Publ.: Responsa Cheshev HaEphod (1963-91), 3 vols. Ad.: 140 Stamford Hill, London N16 6QT. ☎ 0208-802 6226. Fax: 0208-809 2610.

PAISNER, Martin David, M.A. (Oxon), L.L.M. (Ann Arbor, Michigan); b. Windsor, Berkshire, Sept. 1, 1943; m. Susan Sarah née Spence; solicitor; Chairman, The Jerusalem Foundation (1997-); Governor, Weizmann Institute of Science, Ben Gurion Univ., Oxford Centre for Hebrew and Jewish Studies; Dir./Tr., Jewish Care, Weizmann Institute Foundation, EJPS. Ad.: 4 Heath Drive, Hampstead, London NW3 7SY.

PASCAL, Julia, BA (Hons) (Lond.); b. Manchester, Nov. 11, 1949; m. Alain Carpentier; Playwright/Theatre director; Theatre Dir., National Theatre (1978); Assoc. Dir., Orange Tree Theatre (1979); Artistic Dir., Pascal Theatre Co. (1983-2000); Prima Ballerina Assoluta in Virago's 'Truth, Dare or Promise' and Boxtree's 'Memoirs of a Jewish Childhood'. Publ.: The Holocaust Trilogy; Theresa. Ad.: 35 Flaxman Court, Flaxman Terrace, London WC1H 9AR. ☎ 0207-383 0920. Fax 0207-419 9798. Email pascal17038@aol.com

PATTERSON, David, M.A., Ph.D., D.H.L. (Hon.) (Balt.), D.H.L. (Hon.) (H.U.C.); b. Liverpool, June 10, 1922; Cowley Lect. in Post-Biblical Hebrew, Univ. of Oxford (1956-89); Emeritus President & H. Fel., Oxford Centre for Hebrew & Jewish Studies; Emeritus Fel. St. Cross Coll., Oxford; Vis. Prof. (Scholar in Res. 1981) Northwestern Univ. (1983, 1985 & 1993); Fel., Soc. Humanities (Vis. Prof. 1966-71) Cornell Univ. (1983); Fel., Humanities Res. Centre, Canberra (1979); Prof. Jewish Studies, Mt. Holyoke Coll., Mass. (1987-88); Scholar in Res., Vis. Prof. (1993) Hebrew Union Coll. Cincinnati (1982); Vis. Prof., Univ. of Sydney (1993), Vis. Prof. Smith Coll., Mass. (1994-95); Vis. Prof. Hampshire College, Mass. (1996); H.Res. Fel. Centre for J. Studies, Manchester (1998-); form. Lect. in Modern Hebrew, Manchester Univ. (1953-

56); Fel., Jew. Academy of Arts and Sciences, U.S.A.; Brotherhood Award, Nat. Conf., Christians and Jews, USA (1979); Stiller Prize, Baltimore Hebrew Univ (1988); Webber Prize for translation of Hebrew Literature 1989; Member Senate of the Hochschule für Jüdische Studien, Heidelberg (1990-99). Publ.: Abraham Mapu, The Hebrew Novel in Czarist Russia, A Phoenix in Fetters, Tradition and Trauma (with G. Abramson, eds), Random Harvest (transl.), etc. Ad.: 35 Hayward Rd., Oxford, OX2 8LN. ☎/Fax 01865 559003.

PAUL, Geoffrey D., O.B.E.; b. Liverpool, March 26, 1929; Ed. (1977-1990) Jewish Chronicle, American Affairs Ed 'JC' (1991-96). Ad. 1 Carlton Close, West Heath Rd., NW3 7UA. ☎/Fax 020-8458 6948.

PEPPER, Michael, B.Sc., M.A., Ph.D., Sc.D., F.R.S.; b. London, Aug. 10, 1942, m. Jeannette; Physics Prof, Cambridge Univ., Fel.; Trinity Coll.; Warren Res. Fel., Royal Soc. (1978-86); Vis. Prof Bar-Ilan Univ. (1984). Ad.: Cavendish Laboratory, Madingley Rd., Cambridge, CB3 0HE. ☎ 01223 337330.

PERES, Shimon, b. Poland, Aug. 16, 1923; form. Prime Min. (1995-96); Foreign Min. (July 1992-95); Nobel Peace Prize, 1994; Prime Min. (Sept. 1984-Oct. 1986); Vice-Premier & Foreign Min. (Oct. 1986-Dec. 1988); Vice-Premier & Finance Min. (Dec. 1988-March 1990); Chairman, Israel Lab. Party (1977-Feb., 1992); Actg. Prime Min. (1977); Defence Min. (1974-77); Inf. Min. (1974); Communications & Transport Min. (1970-74), Absorption Min. (1969-70); form. Rafi Sec.-Gen.; Dep. Defence Min.; Dir.-Gen. of Defence Min.; went to Palestine 1934. Publ.: From These Men, Tomorrow is Now, The Next Phase, David's Sling. Ad.:.

PERSOFF, Meir, M.A. (Lond), F.R.S.A.; b. Letchworth, Aug. 25, 1941; Judaism Edr., Saleroom corr., form. News Edr. (1974-76), Arts Edr. (1980-85), Features Edr. (1976-90), Jewish Chronicle; President, Israel-Judaica Philatelic Soc.; form. Cttee., Jewish Book C.; form. Publ. Cttee., Jewish Marriage C.; Silver Medallist, internat. philatelic exhibitions, Jerusalem, London, Stockholm, Pretoria, Paris, Madrid. Publ.: The Running Stag: The Stamps and Postal History of Israel, edr., Jewish Living, The Hasmonean, etc. Ad.: 25 Furnival St., EC4A 1JT. ☎ 020-7415 1650.

PILCHIK, Rabbi Ely E., M.H.L., D.D.; b. Baranowicze, Poland, June 12, 1913; President, Central Conf of Amer. Rabbis (1977-79); President, Jewish Book C. of Amer. (1957-58). Publ.: Hillel, From the Beginning, Judaism Outside the Holy Land. Retired, now Senior Scholar-Congregation B'nai Jeshrun, Short Hills, N.J.; Author of 15 miniature books of Jewish content. Ad.: 1025 So. Orange Ave., Short Hills, N.J. 07078, USA. ☎ (201) 379 6275.

PINNER, Hayim, O.B.E., F.R.S.A.; Commander Order of Civil Merit (Spain); b. London, May 25, 1925; Dir., Sternberg Charitable Trust; Hon. Sec. CCJ; form. Sec.-Gen., BoD (1977-1991); H.V. President, Z.F.; V. President, Labour Z. Movt.; form Dir B'nai Brith (1957-77); form Exec., TAC; Lab. Frs. of Israel; Exec., CCJ; Member, Adv. C., World Congress of Faiths, Inter-Faith Network; Central Campaign; Exec., JIA; Chairman, Belsen Commemoration Cttee., Imperial War Museum; Freeman, City of Lond.; Hillel Foundation C.; BoD Defence & Eretz Israel Cttee.; World Zion. "Actions Cttee."; Jewish Agency Assembly; Chairman, Poale Zion; P. Z. Del., Lab. Party Confs.; Edr., Jewish Vanguard, Jewish Labour News, B'nai B'rith Journal. Ad.: 62 Grosvenor St., W1X 9DA. ☎ 020-7485 2538

PINNICK, Jeffrey, F.C.A.; b. London Dec. 6, 1935; T., BoD; Chairman, Fin. Cttee., BoD (V. Chairman, 1982-85); V.Chairman, Frs., Boys Town, Jerusalem, Ad.: Woburn House, Tavistock Sq., WC1H OEP. ☎ 020-7387 3952.

PINTER, Harold, C.B.E.; b. London, Oct. 10, 1930; Playwright. Publ.: The Birthday Party, The Caretaker, The Homecoming, Old Times, No Man's Land, Moonlight, Betrayal, and other plays. Ad.: Judy Daish Associates Ltd., 2 St Charles Place, W10 6EG. ☎ 020-8964 8811. Fax 020-8964 8966.

PLANCEY, Rabbi Alan; b. Edinburgh, Oct. 30, 1941; M., Borehamwood & Elstree Syn.; Chairman, Rabbin. C. U.S. (1987-94); Member Chief Rabbi's

Cabinet; H. V.-President & Rel Adv., Jewish Care; Area Chaplain Met. Police;
Hon. Chaplain Jewish Scouting Adv. Cttee.; Freeman of the City of London; M.,
Luton Syn. (1965-69); Youth M., Hampstead Garden Sub. Syn. (1970-76). Ad.:
98 Anthony Rd., Borehamwood, Herts., WD6 4NB. ☎ 020-8207 3759. Fax
020-8207 0568.

PLASKOW, Rev. Michael Lionel, M.B.E., L.T.S.C., A.L.C.M.; b. Palestine, July 8,
1936; R., Woodside Park Syn. (since 1956); Chaplain to the Mayor of Barnet
(1999-2000); Ch. Central Found. School; Jewish Old Boys Group; Cttee.
Member, and Memb. Reg. Board Initiation Society; form. Chairman, Whetstone
Police Sector Working Group; form. Chairman, Assoc. Ministers (Chazanim);
form. Chap. Barnet General & Finchley Memorial Hospitals; Authorised Mohel;
Vis. M., Kisharon Sr. Sch., Finchley; Chaplain, Jewish Deaf Assn.; Past. Junior
Grand Chaplain in the Grand Lodge of England (Freemasonry); Norman B.
Spencer award 1992 for research into Freemasonry, Freeman City of London
(1994). Publ. The Story of a Community Woodside Park 1937-1987. Ad.: 12
Singleton Scarp, Woodside Park, N12 7AR. ☎ 020-8445 2860.

POLONSKY, Antony, B.A.(Rand), M.A., D.Phil (Oxon); b. Johannesburg, Sept.
23, 1940, m. Arlene née Glickman; Albert Abramson Professor of Holocaust
Studies at the United States Holocaust Memorial Museum and Brandeis
University; Vice-president, Institute for Polish-Jewish Studies, Oxford; Vice-
president, American Association for Polish-Jewish Studies, Cambridge, MA;
Member Exec Ctte, National Polish American-Jewish American Council; Ed.,
Polin: A Journal of Polish-Jewish Studies. Publ. Politics in Idependent Poland
(1972), The Little Dictators (1973), The Great Powers and the Polish Question
(1976), The Beginnings of Communist Rule in Poland (1981), (ed.) The Jews in
Poland (1986), (ed.) A Cup of Tears (1989), (ed.) Recent Polish Debates about
the Holocaust (1990), (ed.) Polish Paradoxes (1990), (ed.) The Jews of Warsaw
(1991), (ed.) The Jews in Old Poland (1992). Ad.: 322 Harvard Street,
Cambridge, MA 02139. ☎ (617) 492 9788, 736 2980, Fax (617) 736 2070.

PORTER, Sir Leslie, Ph.D. (Hon) (Tel Aviv Univ.) O.St.J.; b. July 10, 1920;
President, Tesco p.l.c (1970-1985); Companion, Brit., Instit. of Management; V.
President, Nat. Playing Fields Assn.; Member, Lloyd's; President, Instit., Grocery
Distribution (1977-80); Chancellor, Tel Aviv Univ.; Memb. Coombe Hill Golf
Club; Dyrham Pk. G.C.

PORTER, Dame Shirley (née Cohen), DBE., F.R.S.A., Hon.Ph.D. (Tel Aviv); b.
Nov. 29, 1930; Form. Leader, Westminster City C. (1983-91); Lord Mayor
(1991); V. President London Union of Youth Clubs; Past Master Worshipful Co.
Environmental Cleaners; Freeman of the City of London; form. Dep. Ch.,
London Festival Ballet, Tidy Britain Group. Publ.: A Minister for London,
Efficiency in Local Government. Ad.: PFM Advisory Ltd., 12 Hans Rd., London
SW3 1RT ☎ 020-7584 4277.

POSEN, Felix, B.A. (John Hopkins Univ.), D.Phil. (Hon., Hebrew Univ.); b. Berlin,
Oct. 24, 1928; m. Jane née Levy; Gov. Emer. and Hon. Fellow Oxford Centre
for Hebrew and Jewish Studies; Gov. Hebrew University; Chairman Jerusalem
Fellows; V.-Chairman Mandel Institute, Jerusalem; Tr. Institute of Archaeo-met-
allurgical Studies, University of London; Member of the Bd of Alma Hebrew
College, Tel Aviv; Member of the Bd of the College of Pluralistic Judaism,
Jerusalem; Council member of the JPR; Member Cttee Interfaith Mission for
Christians, Muslims and Jews. Ad.: 24 Kensington Gate, London W8 5NA.
☎ 020-7584 0914. Fax 020-7584 0904. Email: nesop@dircon.co.uk

PRAG, Derek Nathan, M.A. (Cantab.), H.D.Litt. (Univ. Herts), Hon. MEP; b.
Merthyr Tydfil, Aug. 6, 1923; m. Dora née Weiner; MEP (Cons), for
Hertfordshire (1979-94); Dep. Chairman Instit. Cttee. (1989-94); Conservative
Spokesman, Instit. Cttee. (1982-84) and Pol. Cttee. (1984-87); Dep. Chairman,
Cttee. of Enquiry into Racism and Fascism (1984-87); Dep. Chairman European
Parl. Delegation for Relations with ASEAN (1979-87); Member, European Parl.

Delegation for relations with Israel (1989-94); Chairman, All-Party Disablement Group (1980-94); V. Chairman, European Parl.-Israel Intergroup (1990-94); Chairman, Lond. Europe Soc. (1973-); Dir., Lond. Inf. Off., EEC (1965-73); Head Publ. Div., E.E.C. Jt. Inf Service (1959-67); Inf Off., High Auth., Europe Coal & Steel Cttee (1955-59); Journalist with Reuters News Agency (1950-55) in London, Brussels and Madrid, Dep. Chairman, Conservative Group for Europe (1974-77 and 1991-93); H. Dir., Wyndham Place Tr. (1977-79), Mem. Council (1979-); Commander of the Order of Leopold II (Belgium) (1996); Silver Medal of European Merit, Luxembourg (1974); H. Dir., EEC. Com (1974). Publ.: Businessman's Guide to the Common Market (1973), Europe's international strategy (1978), Democracy in the European Union (1998), etc. Ad.: Pine Hill, 47 New Rd., Digswell, Herts., AL6 0AQ. ☎ 01438-715686. Fax 01438-840422.

PRAIS, Sigbert J., M. Com., Ph.D., Sc.D. (Cantab.), Hon. D. Litt. (City), F.B.A.; b. Frankfurt am Main, Dec. 19, 1928; Economist; Sr. Res. Fel., Nat. Instit. of Econ. and Social Res., London; form. Edr. Adv. Bd., Jewish Journal of Soc.; Vis. Prof. of Econometrics, City Univ.; form. H. Consultant, BoD Statistical and Demographic Res. Unit; Economist, Internat. Monetary Fund; Adv. on Statistics, Govt. of Israel; Lect., Cambridge Univ. Publ.: Productivity and Industrial Structure; The Evolution of Giant Firms; Analysis of Family Budgets; Productivity, Education and Training, etc. Ad.: 83 West Heath Rd., NW3 7TN. ☎ 020-8458 4428.

PRAWER, Siegbert Salomon, M.A., D. Litt. (Oxon.), M.A., Litt.D. (Cantab.), Ph.D., Hon.D.Litt. (Birmingham), D. Phil. hc. (Cologne), F.B.A.; b. Cologne, Feb. 15, 1925; Member of the German Academy of Languages and Literature; Taylor Prof of German, Emer., Oxford Univ.; Hon. Fel. Jesus College, Cambridge; Hon. Fel. Queen's Coll.. Oxford; Hon. Fel., form. President, Brit. Comparative Lit. Assn.; H.Fel., form. H. Dir., Lond. Univ. Instit. of Germanic Studies; Hon. Member of the Modern Language Association of America; V. President of the English Goethe Soc. (1994-), President (1991-94); Memb. of the London Bd. of the Leo Baeck Inst. (1969-96); form. Prof of German, Lond. Univ. and Head of German Dept., Westfield Coll.; Sr. Lect. Birmingham Univ.; Vis. Prof, City Coll., New York, Chicago, Harvard, Hamburg, California, Pittsburgh, Otago (New Zealand), Australian Nat. Univ., Canberra, Brandeis; C., Leo Baeck Instit.; Goethe Medal (1973); Isaac Deutscher Prize (1977); Friedrich Gundolf Prize (1986); Gold Medal of the Goethe Gesellschaft 1995. Publ.: Writings on German, English, Jewish and Comparative Literature. Ad.: The Queen's Coll., Oxford OX1 4AW.

PRENDERGAST, Dame Simone Ruth (née Laski), D.B.E., J.P., D.L., O.St. J.; b. Manchester, July 2, 1930;, President C.B.F. World Jewish Relief; Chairman, Jewish Refugees Cttee. (1981-1991); Pt. time Commissioner for Commission for Racial Equality (1996-98); Commandant JLGB (1986-); Co. Patron Fed. Women Zionists; Chairman, Blond McIndoe Centre for Med Res.; Chairman, Westminster Children's Soc. (1980-90); Court of Patrons, Royal Coll. of Surgeons; Chairman, Greater London Area Conservative & Unionist Assns. (1984-87), Solicitors Disciplinary Tribunal (1986-); Lord Chancellors Advisory Cttee. (Inner London) (1981-91); V. Chairman, Age Concern Westminster (1989-); Member East London & Bethnal Green Housing Assoc. (1990); Tr., Camperdown House Trust (1990-). Ad.: 52 Warwick Sq., SW1V 2AJ.

PRESTON, Rosalind (née Morris), O.B.E.; b. London, Dec. 29, 1935; Professional Volunteer; Hon. Vice-President British WIZO (1993-); Jt. Hon. Sec. CCJ (1997-); Co. Vice Chair Interfaith Network, UK; form. V. President, BoD; form. President, The National Council of Women of G.B. (1988-90). Ad.: 7 Woodside Close, Stanmore, Middx. HA7 3AJ. ☎ 020-8954 1411. Fax 020-8954 6898. Email ros.p@dial.pipex.com

PULZER, Peter George Julius, M.A., B.Sc.(Econ.), Ph.D.; b. Vienna, May 20,

1929; Gladstone Prof, Government & Publ. Admin., Fel. All Souls, Oxford (1985-96); Official Student (Fel.) in Politics, Christ Church, Oxford (1962-84). Publ.: The Rise of Political Antisemitism in Germany and Austria, Political Representation and Elections in Britain, Jews and the German State: The Political History of a Minority (1848-1933); German Politics 1945-1995; Germany 1870-1945: Politics, State Formation and War; contr. German Jewish History in Modern Times (ed. M. Meyer). Ad.: All Souls College, Oxford, OX1 4AL. ☎ 01865 279379. Fax 01865 279299.

RABINOVITCH, Rabbi Nachum L., B.Sc., M.A., Ph.D., b. Montreal, Apr 30, 1928; Rosh Yeshiva, Maale Adumim and Res. Prof, Jews, Coll., Lond.; form. Princ., Jews, College; Rab., Clanton Park Syn., Toronto. Publ.: Hadar Itamar, Probability and Statistical Inference in Ancient and Medieval Jewish Literature; Critical Edn. of Rambam's Mishneh Torah with comprehensive commentary, Yad P'shutah, Vols. 1-6. Ad.: 72 Mizpe Nevo St., Maale Adumim, Israel 90610. ☎ (02) 5353655.

RABINOWICZ, Rabbi Harry, B.A., Ph.D.; M., Willesden & Brondesbury Syn.; M., St. Albans Hebrew Cong. (1947-49); M., Ilford and Dist. Syn. (1949-51); Dollis Hill (1951-78), Cricklewood (1978-88). Publ.: The Will and Testament of the Biala Rabbi, The World of Chasidism, Legacy of Polish Jewry, Treasures of Judaica, Guide to Life The Jewish Literary Treasures of England and America, Encyclopedia of Hasidism (ed.), Hasidism and the State of Israel, Guide to Hasidism, Hasidic Story Book, Chasidism: The Movement and its Masters, Chasidic Rebbes, The World Apart: History of Hasidism in England, The Prince who turned into a rooster, Hasidim in the Holy Land (1999), Just Laughter (1999). Ad.: 31 Sherwood Rd., NW4. ☎ 020-8203 2634. Fax 020-8203 2634.

RABINOWITZ, Rabbi Benjamin, B.A., M.Phil., A.J.C.; b. Newcastle upon Tyne June 21, 1945; M., Edgware Syn.; Chaplain, Edgware Hospital (1983-); Tr., Co-Chairman Edgware CCJ (1982-); form. M. Yeshurun Heb Cong., Gatley; Blackpool Hebrew Cong. Ad.: 14 Ashcombe Gdns. Edgware Middx. HA8 8HS. ☎ 020-8958 5320/6126 (Synagogue office).

RABINOWITZ, Rabbi Lippa, b. Manchester, Nov. 15, 1930; Rav, Vine St Syn., Manch.; Princ., Manch. Jewish Grammar Sch., form. Princ. Judith Lady Montefiore Coll., Ramsgate; Lect., Etz Haim Yeshiva, Tangier. Publ.: Eleph Lamateh Chidushim on Sugioth (Israel). Ad.: 57 Waterpark Rd., Salford.

RABSON, Ronald Jeffery, M.A.; Dipl. Arch. F.R.I.B.A.; b. Lond, March 3, 1928; Chartered Architect; form. Chairman & Jt. H. Sec., Lond. Bd. Jewish Rel. Educ.; form. Chairman & Gov., J.F.S. Comp. Sch.; form. Chairman, Instit. of Jewish Educ.; Gov., Michael Sobell Sinai Sch.; Life M., C., US. Ad.: 16 Broadfields Ave., Edgware, Middx, HA8 8PG. ☎ 020-8958 9035. Fax 020-8905 4035.

RADOMSKY, Rabbi David, B.A., M.A.; b. East London, South Africa, Sept. 4, 1956; Deputy H.T. and Head of Jewish Studies at Immanuel Coll.; Lect., Jews, Coll., (1991-); form. M., Wembley Syn.; Com. M. Jewish Com. in Eire (1985-88); Talmud Lect., Midrashiat Noam Yeshiva High Sch. Pardes Hanna, Israel (1982-85). Ad.: 27 Windsor Ave, Edgware, Middx. HA8 8SR. ☎ 020-8958 3879.

RAJAK, Tessa, née Goldsmith, M.A., D.Phil., b. London, Aug. 2, 1946, m. Harry; Scholar and University Teacher; Hd. Dept of Classics, Univ. Reading; Grinfield Lect. in the Septuagint, Oxford (1994-96). Publ.: Josephus, the historian and his society, The Jews among Pagans and Christians in the Roman Empire (jt. ed). Ad.: 64 Talbot Rd., N6 4RA.

RAPHAEL, David Daiches, D.Phil., M.A., Hon. F.I.C.; b. Liverpool, Jan. 25, 1916; Emer. Prof of Philosophy, Lond. Univ.; Chairman, Westminster Syn. (1987-89); form. Head Humanities Dept., Imperial Coll.; Prof. Phil., Reading Univ.; Prof. Pol. & Soc. Phil., Glasgow Univ.; Sr. Lect., Moral Phil., Glasgow Univ.; Prof., Phil., Otago Univ., Dunedin; form. Princ. Off M. of Lab. and Nat. Service. Publ.: The Moral Sense, Richard Price's Review of Morals, Moral

Judgement, The Paradox of Tragedy, Political Theory and the Rights of Man, British Moralists 1650-1800, Problems of Political Philosophy, Adam Smith's Theory of Moral Sentiments (Jt. Edr.), Hobbes: Morals and Politics, Adam Smith's Lectures on Jurisprudence (Jt. Edr.), Adam Smith's Essays on Philosophical Subjects, (Jt. Edr.), Justice and Liberty, Moral Philosophy, Adam Smith, etc. Ad.: Humanities Programme, Imperial College, SW7 2BX.

RAPHAEL, Frederic Michael, M.A. (Cantab.), F.R.S.L.; b. Chicago, Aug. 14, 1931; Writer. Publ.: Novels, Obbligato, The Earlsdon Way, The Limits of Love, The Graduate Wife, The Trouble with England, Lindmann, Darling, Orchestra and Beginners, Who Were You With Last Night?, Like Men Betrayed, April June and November, California Time, The Glittering Prizes, Heaven and Earth, After The War, The Hidden I, A Double Life, Old Scores, Coast to Coast; Short stories, Sleeps Six, Oxbridge Blues, Think of England, The Latin Lover, All His Sons; Non-fiction: Byron, Somerset Maugham, Cracks in the Ice, Of Gods and Men, France: the Four Seasons, The Necessity of Anti-Semitism, Popper: Historicism and its Poverty, Eyes Wide Open; Published Screenplays and Drama: Two for the Road, Darling, Oxbridge Blues, Eyes Wide Shut (with Stanley Kubrick); Translations: (with Kenneth McLeish) The Poems of Catullus, The Oresteia of Aeschylus, Sophocles' Aias, Euripides' Medea, Bacchae and Hippolytus. Ad.: c/o Rogers, Coleridge and White, 20, Powis Mews, W11 1JN.

RASMINSKY, Louis, C.C., C.B.E., LL.D., D.C.L., D.H.L.; b. Montreal, Feb. 1, 1908; Gov., Bank of Canada (1961-73); President, Industrial Development Bank (1961-73); H. Fel., Lond. Sch. of Economics. Ad.: 1006-20 Driveway, Ottawa, Ontario, K2P 1C8, Canada. ☎ 613-594-0150.

RAYNE, Baron, of Prince's Meadow (Life Peer) (Sir Max Rayne), Hon. LL.D. (London); b. Feb. 8, 1918; Dir. of Companies; Chairman, London Merchant Securities, plc.; Chairman, Nat. Theatre Bd. (1971-88); Special Tr., St. Thomas' Hospital; Gen. C., King Edward Vll's Hospital Fund for Lond.; Chairman, Lond. Festival Ballet Tr. (1967-75); Fdr. Patron, The Rayne Fdn.; H.V. President, Jewish Care. H.Fel., Univ. Coll., Lond., Darwin Coll., Cambridge, Univ. Col., Oxford, Lond. Sch. of Economics; Royal Coll. of Psychiatrists; King's Coll. Hospital Med. School; King's College London; Westminster School; Officier, Legion d'Honneur, 1987 (Chevalier, 1973); Hon. Fel., UMDS, 1992; Hon. F.R.C.P. 1992. Ad.: 33 Robert Adam St., W1M 5AH. 020-7935 3555.

RAYNER, Rabbi John D., C.B.E., M.A. D.D.(Hon.); b. Berlin, May 30, 1924; Hon. Life President, Union of Liberal and Progressive Synagogues, M. Emer. (Sr. M. 1961-89), Lib. Jewish Syn.; M., South London Lib. Syn. (1953-57); Chairman, C., Reform and Lib. Rabbis (1969-71, 82-84, 1989-92); V. President and Lect., Leo Baeck Coll.; Co-President, Lond. Soc. of Jews & Christians. Publ.: Guide to Jewish Marriage; Gate of Repentance (co-ed.), Judaism for Today (co-author), Passover Haggadah (ed.), The Jewish People: Their History and Their Religion (co-author), Siddur Lev Chadash (co-ed), An Understanding of Judaism, A Jewish Understanding of the World, Jewish Religious Law: A Progressive Perspective, Principles of Jewish Ethics. Ad.: 37 Walmington Fold, N12 7LD. ☎/Fax 020-8446 6196.

REICHMANN, Eva Gabriele (née Jungmann), Dr. Phil. (Heidelberg), Ph.D. (Lond.); b. Lublinitz, Upper Silesia; Edr., Der Morgen, (Berlin), Bd., Leo Baeck Instit.; C. of Jews from Germany. Publ.: Hostages of Civilisation: A Study of the Social Causes of Antisemitism, Greatness and Doom of German-Jewish Existence (Documents of a Tragic Encounter), etc. Ad.: 2 Strathray Gdns., NW3 4NY. ☎ 020-7794 4343.

REIF, Stefan, B.A., Ph.D. (Lond.), M.A. (Cantab.); b. Edinburgh, Jan. 21, 1944; m. Shulamit; Dir., Taylor-Schechter Genizah Research Unit and Head of Oriental Div., Cambridge Univ. Library; Professor of Medieval Hebrew Studies, Faculty of Oriental Studies, Cambridge Univ.; Fellow St John's College, Cambridge;

President JHSE (1991-92); President Brit. Assoc. for Jewish Studies (1992); T.,
Cambridge Traditional Jewish Cong.; Lect., Hebrew and Semitics, Glasgow Univ.
(1968-72); Princ., Glasgow Hebrew Coll. (1970-72); Asst. Prof., Hebrew
Language and Lit., Dropsie Coll. (1972-73). Publ.: Shabbethai Sofer and His
Prayer Book; Judaism and Hebrew Prayer; Hebrew Manuscripts at Cambridge
University Library; A Jewish Archive from Old Cairo; (ed.) Interpreting the
Hebrew Bible, Genizah Research after Ninety Years, Cambridge Univ. Library
Genizah Series, etc. Ad.: Cambridge University Library, CB3 9DR. ☎ 01223-
333000. Fax 01223-333160.

REISS, Simon, b. Berlin, Dec. 31, 1923; Comp. Dir.; V. President Zionist Fed.;
form. President Western Marble Arch Syn.; Mem. BoD; Chairman, Jt. Cttee.,
Youth Aff; Co-Chairman and Tr. Balfour Diamond Jubilee Trust; Vice-Chairman,
Yad Vashem Cttee., BoD; President, JIA Fur Trade Cttee. Ad.: Third Floor, 25
Enford Street, Marylebone, London W1H 2DD. ☎/Fax 020-7258 0008. Email:
admin@bdjt.win-uk.net

RICHARDSON, Montague, M.A., (Cantab.); b. London, July 4, 1918; Patron
Jewish Museum; form. Welfare & Youth Off., US & Welfare Off., Jewish After-
Care Assn.; form. Chairman, Tower Hamlets Soc.; form. V. Chairman Tower H.
Soc. Service C.; Chaplain: Aldington, Blantyre House, Canterbury, Cookham
Wood Elmley, E. Sutton Park, Maidstone, Rochester, Stanford Hill, Swaleside
Prisons & Dover Youth Custody Centre; V. President (form. Chairman) AJY; Tr.
and form. Chairman, Tower Hamlets Old People's Welfare Trust; form. Tr.,
London Museum of Jewish Life; form. Tr., Children's Aid Cttee. Charitable
Fund; form. Chairman, Brady Boys' Club; form. V. Chairman Tower H. Adult
Educ. Instit.; form. Chairman, Soc. Security Appeal Tribunal; form Exec., Tower
H. Racial Equality C.; Chairman, Zekeinim Club. Ad.: Flat 1, 12 Belsize Sq.,
NW3 4HT. ☎ 020-7794 9684.

RICKAYZEN, Gerald, B.Sc., Ph.D., F.Inst.P., C.Phys.; b. London, Oct. 16, 1929;
m. Gillian Thelma; physicist; Chairman Canterbury Jewish Community (1998-);
Prof. of Theoretical Physics, Univ. of Kent (1965-98), Pro-Vice-Chancellor
(1980-90), Deputy V. Chancellor (1984-90). Publ.: Theory of Superconductivity
(1965); Green's Functions and Condensed Matter Physics (1980). Ad: The
Physics Laboratory, The University, Canterbury CT2 7NR. ☎ 01227 823230.
Email: G.Rickayzen@ukc.ac.uk

RIETTI, Robert, Cavaliere Ufficiale, O.M.R.I., Officer-Knight of the Italian
Republic; b. London, Feb. 8, 1923; Actor, broadcaster, writer, director, editor of
Drama Quarterly GAMBIT; BAFTA nomination for Special Award (1993). Publ.:
English translations of the entire dramatic works of Luigi Pirandello (John
Calder); Look up and dream (1999). Ad.: 40 Old Church Lane, NW9 8TA.
☎ 020-8205 3024. Fax 020-8200 4688.

RIFKIND, Rt. Hon. Sir Malcolm, Q.C., P.C.; b. Edinburgh, June 21, 1946; form.
M.P. for Edinburgh, Pentlands (Con.) (1974-97); Foreign Secretary (1995-97),
Min. of Defence (1992-95), Min. of Transport (1990-92); Sec. of State for
Scotland (1986-90), Min. of State Foreign & Commonwealth Office (1983-86);
Parl. Under-Sec. of State, F.C.O. (1982-83); Parl. Under-Sec. of State, Scottish
Office (1979-82); H. President, Scottish Young Conservatives (1976-77); H.Sec.,
Conservative Frs. of Israel Parl. Group (1974-79); Sec. Conservative Parl.
Foreign & Commonwealth Affairs Group (1977-79); Opposition Spokesman on
Scottish Affairs (1975-76); Select Cttee. on Overseas Development (1978-79);
Edinburgh Town C. (1970-74). Ad.:

RIGAL, Mrs. Margaret H., (née Lazarus); b. London, Nov. 28, 1932; Co.-
Chairman, Women's Campaign for Soviet Jewry (the 35s), H.Sec., Jewish Aged
Needy Pension Soc.; Chairman Jewish Aid Cttee. Ad.: 14 Pembridge Place, W2
4XB. ☎ 020-7229 8845. Fax 020-7221 7302.

ROBERG, Rabbi Meir, B.A. (Hons.), M.Phil., Dip.Ed.; b. Wurzburg Germany,
June 25, 1937; HM, Hasmonean High Sch.; Chairman, Academic Cttee.

Massoret Instit.; Chairman, Assoc. of Head Teachers of Orthodox Jewish Schls.; form. HM Middlesex Reg. Centre; Dep. HM, Yavneh Grammar Sch. Ad.: 34 Green Lane, NW4 2NG. ☎ 020-8203 2632.

ROBINS, Ruth, B.A., TTHD; b. Johannesburg, October 18, 1946; Headteacher JFS. Ad.: 175 Camden Road, London NW1 9HD. ☎ 020-7485 9416. Fax 020-7284 3948.

ROBSON, Jeremy, b. Llandudno, Sept. 5, 1939; Chairman & Man. Dir., Robson Books Ltd. Publ.: 33 Poems, In Focus (poetry), Poetry anthologies, incl. The Young British Poets (ed.), Poems from Poetry and Jazz in Concert (ed.). Ad.: Robson Books, 5/6 Clipstone St., W1P 8LE. ☎ 020-7323 1223. Fax 020-7636-0798.

ROCHE, Barbara Maureen, (née Margolis), B.A. (Oxon.); b. London, April 13, 1954; Barrister; M.P., Hornsey and Wood Green (Lab. 1992-); Parlt. Under-Sec. of State for Small Firms, Trade and Industry (1997-99); Financial Sec. at the Treasury (1999-). Ad.: House of Commons, London SW1. ☎ 020-7219 3000.

ROITT, Ivan Maurice, M.A., D.Sc. (Oxon.), F.R.C.Path., F.R.S., Hon. F.R.C.P.; b. Lond., Sept. 30, 1927; Emer. Prof. Immunology UCL. Publ.: Essential Immunology. Ad.: Windeyer Building, UCL., Cleveland Street, W1P 6DB. ☎ 020-7380 9360. Fax 020-7380 9400.

ROMAIN, Rabbi Jonathan Anidjar, B.A.; Ph.D.; b. Lond., Aug. 24, 1954; m. Sybil Sheridan; M., Maidenhead Syn.; Director, Jewish Information and Media Service; Chairman, Youth Assn. of Syns. in Gt. Brit. (1972-74); form. M., Barkingside Progressive Syn. Publ.: The Open and Closed Paragraphs of the Pentateuch, In a Strange Land, Signs and Wonders, The Jews of England, Faith and Practice, I'm Jewish, My Partner Isn't, Tradition and Change, Till Faith Us Do Part, Renewing the Vision. Ad.: 9 Boyn Hill Ave., Maidenhead, Berks. SL6 4ET. ☎ 01628 671058. Fax 01628 625536.

ROSE, Rabbi Abraham Maurice, M.A.; b. Birmingham, Sept. 7, 1925; Exec. Dir., C. of Young Israel Syn. (Israel) (1975-90); Adm. Dir. & Lect., Jerusalem Academy of Jewish Studies (1973-74); Exec. Dir., Office of the Chief Rabbi (1962-73); Dir., Conf of Europ. Rabbis; form. M., Sutton Syn. (1952-62), Derby Syn. (1948-52). Ad.: Rechov Machal 30/2, Jerusalem 97763. ☎ 5812859. Fax 5810080.

ROSE, Aubrey, C.B.E., F.R.S.A.; b. London, Nov. 1, 1926; Solicitor; Senior V. President, BoD (1991, 1994); Commissioner & Dep. Chairman Commission for Racial Equality (CRE); Tr. Project Fullemploy; Tr. Commonwealth Human Rights Initiative; Member, Working Group Commonwealth Jewish Coun.; form. Chairman, Defence and Group Rel. Cttee. BoD; Chairman, Working Group on Environment BoD, Publ.: Jewish Communities in the Commonwealth (CJT); Judaism and Ecology (1992); Journey into Immortality, the Story of David Rose (1997); Brief Encounters of a Legal Kind (1997). Ad.: Monkenholt, Hadley Green Road, Barnet, Herts. EN5 5PR. ☎ 020-8449 2166. Fax 020-8449 1469.

ROSE, Eliot Joseph Benn, C.B.E., b. London, June 7, 1909; Chairman, Penguin Books (1973-80); Editorial Dir., Westminster Press (1970-73); Dir., Internat. Press Instit. Zurich (1952-62); Dir., Survey of Race Relations in Brit (1963-68); Chairman, Inter-Action Tr. (1968-84), Co. Fdr., Runnymede Tr., (Chairman 1980-91); Tr., Writers & Scholars Educ. Trust; Consultant to Unicef; form. Lit. Edr., 'Observer', Sec., Baldwin Fund for German Jewish Refugees (1939). Publ.: Colour and Citizenship. Ad.: 37 Pembroke Sq., W8 6PE. ☎ 020-7937 3772 .

ROSE, Jeffery Samuel, B.D.S. F.D.S., D.Orth. R.C.S.; b. Harrow, Middx., Dec. 22, 1924; Ret. Consultant Orthodontist, Royal London Hospital (1967-90); Hon. Vice-President RSGB (1999-); Chairman Reform Foundation Tr. (1996-99); President Brit. Orthodontic Soc. (1994-95); V. President World Union Progressive Judaism (1995-99); form. Chairman, Leo Baeck Coll. (1985-88); Life Gov. (1988); Hon. Fellow (1988); Chairman, Euro. Region, World Union Prog Judaism (1990-95); form. V. President & Chairman RSGB; form. V. President & Chairman, North Western Reform Syn.; President, Brit. Paedontic

Soc. (1964-65); President, Brit. Soc. for the Study of Orthodontics (1972-73). President, British Assoc. of Orthodontists (1991-94). Ad.: 9 Meadway Close, NW11 7BA. ☎ 020-8455 5771. Fax 020-8731 9588.

ROSE, Mrs. Joyce Dora Hester (née Woolf), C.B.E., J.P., D.L. (Herts); m. Cyril Rose, b. London, August 14, 1929; Hertfordshire Family Mediation Service (1996-); S.W. Hertfordshire Hospice Charitable Trust (The Peace Hospice) (1996-); Chairman, Nat. Exec. and Council, Magistrate Assn. (1990-93); Mem. Bd. Dir. Apex Tr. (1994-); Herts Care Tr. (1995-); V. President Magistrates Assn. and V. President Hertfordshire Branch; H. D. Laws, Univ. of Hertfordshire (1992); form. P. (1979-80), Chairman (1982-83), Lib. Party; President, S.W. Herts Const. L.D.; form. Chairman, Watford (Herts.) Bench (1990-94); Dep. Chairman, Family Proceedings Panel; P. & Chairman, Women's Liberal Fed. (1972-73); V. Chairman, UK Cttee. for Unicef (1968-70); Ad.: Brindmere, 38 Main Ave., Moor Park, nr Northwood, Middx., HA6 2LQ. ☎ 01923 821385. Fax 01923 840515.

ROSEN, Clive H., F.C.Optom.; b. London Apr. 15, 1938; City Univ. 1963; Dip. Sports Vision, UMIST (1997); Freeman, City of London 1964; Chairman Z. F. Fund-Raising Cttee. (1996-); Hon. Sports Vision Consult. to Leyton Orient FC (1997-); Hon. Tr. East London and the City Health Authority L.O.C. (1994-); Chairman, Menorah J.N.F. Committee (1974-1985); Hon. Off. J.N.F. (1979-81, 1983-90); Memb. Zionist Federation National Council, (1989-); Hon. Tr. Z. F. (1994-96); Founding memb. Israel-Judaica Stamp Club; Chairman, I.-J.S.C. (1990-); Ed. consult., The Israel Judaica Collector Journal; Dir. David Elliott (Opticians) Ltd. (1965-). Ad.: 152 Morton Way, London N14 7AL. ☎ 020-8886 9331. Fax 020-8886 5116. Email: clive@london.web.net

ROSEN, Rabbi Jeremy, M.A. (Cantab.); b. Sept. 11, 1942; Rabbi Western Syn. (1985-1991); Rabbi, Western Marble Arch Syn., (1991-1992); Chief Rabbi's Cabinet advisor Interfaith (1987-90); Prof., Jewish Studies F.V.G. Antwerp. (1991); Tr., Yakar Foundation; Princ., Carmel Coll. (1971-84); Rabbi, Giffnock & Newlands Syn., Glasgow (1968-71). Ad.: c/o Yakar, 2 Egerton Gardens, London NW4 4BA.

ROSENBERG, Mrs. Rosita (née Gould); b. London, Sept. 2, 1933; V. President, form. Dir., ULPS. Ad.: The Montagu Centre, 21, Maple St., W1P 6DS. ☎ 020-7580 1663. Fax 020-7436 4184.

ROSENTHAL, Jack (Morris), C.B.E., B.A., M.A (Hon.), D.Litt. (Hon.); b. Manchester, Sept. 8, 1931; m. Maureen née Lipman; Writer; Brit. Academy of Film and Television Arts Writers Award, 1976; Royal Television Society Writers' Award, 1976, Royal Television Society Hall of Fame (1993). TV plays include: The Evacuees, Ready When You Are, Mr McGill; Barmitzvah Boy (also stage musical); Auntie's Niece; Spend, Spend, Spend; The Knowledge; And A Nightingale Sang; Bag Lady; P'Tang, Yang, Kipperbang, Day to Remember, Wide-Eyed And Legless, London's Burning; Bye, Bye, Baby; Eskimo Day; etc. Feature Films include: Yentl (co. writer), The Chain, Captain Jack. Ad.: c/o Casarotto Ramsay Ltd., 60-66 Wardour St., W1V 4ND.

ROTBLAT, Sir Joseph, K.C.M.G., C.B.E., M.A., D.Sc. (Warsaw), Ph.D. (Liverpool), D.Sc. (Lond.), F.Inst P., F.R.S.; b. Warsaw, Nov. 4, 1908; President Pugwash Conferences on Science and World Affairs (1988-97); Prof. of Physics in the Univ. of London at St. Bartholomew's Hospital Med. Coll. (1950-76), now Emer.; Asst. Dir., Atomic Physics Instit., Free Univ. of Poland (1937-39); Lect., Liverpool Univ. (1940-49); Dir. of Research in Nuclear Physics, Univ. of Liverpool (1945-49); V. President, Atomic Scientists, Assn. (1952-59). Publ.: Scientific works. Ad.: 8 Asmara Rd., NW2 3ST. ☎ 020-7435 1471.

ROTH, Sir Martin, F.R.S.; b. Budapest, Nov. 6, 1917, m. Constance née Heller; Prof. Emer. of Psychiatry Cambridge Univ.; Fel., Trinity Coll. Cambridge; Mems. WHO Steering Cttee for Epidemiological Studies of Alzheimer Disease; form. Prof. of Psychological Medicine, Newcastle Univ.; first P. Royal Coll. of

Psychiatry (1971-75); Member, Medical Research C. (1964-68). Publ.: Clinical Psychiatry (with E. Slater); The Reality of Mental Illness (with J. Kroll, 1986), Handbook of Anxiety, vols. 1-5 (Ed. with R. Noyes & G. Burrows 1990-93), Alzheimer Disease and related disorders (with L. Iversen 1986), Psychiatry, human rights and the law (with R. Bluglass, 1985). Ad.: Trinity College, Cambridge. ☎ 01223-242106. Fax 01223-412193.

ROTHSCHILD, Edmund Leopold de, C.B.E., T.D., Hon. D.Sc., (Salford Univ.); b. London, Jan. 2, 1916; Hon. LL.D. (Univ. of Newfoundland); Hon. V. President, C.B.F., World Jewish Relief; V. President, CCJ; President, Ajex; Bd. Govs., Technical Univ., Nova Scotia; form. Major, Royal Artillery, 1939-46, (Commanded P. Battery, Jewish Field Regt.). Publ.: Window on the World; A gilt-edged life: a memoir. Ad.: New Court, St. Swithin's Lane, EC4P 4DU.

ROTHSCHILD, Sir Evelyn de; b. Aug. 29, 1931; Merchant Banker; Dir., Industrial Dwellings Soc. Ltd.; form. President, JBS Ad.: New Court, St. Swithin's Lane, EC4P 4DU. ☎ 020-7280 5000.

ROTHSCHILD, Leopold David de, C.B.E.; b. London, May 12, 1927; Dir., N. M. Rothschild & Sons; Investment Adv. Cttee., JWB; Ad.: New Court, St. Swithin's Lane, EC4P 4DU. ☎ 020-7280 5000.

ROTHSCHILD, Miriam (Hon. Mrs. Miriam Lane), C.B.E., Defence Medal, F.R.S., Hon. Doc. (Oxford, Hull, Göteburg, North-Western Univ., Chicago Leicester, Essex, Open University); b. Ashton, Peterborough., Aug. 5, 1908; d. of the late Hon. N. Charles Rothschild and aunt of Lord Rothschild; zoologist and farmer; Tr., Brit. Museum; H. Fellow, St. Hugh's Coll., Oxford; Romanes Lect. (1985); Vis. Prof, Lond. Univ.; Wigglesworth Medal, RHS Victorian Medal of Honour; Med. Soc. Chem. Oecology; Linnearc Soc.; Mendel Award. Publ.: Catalogue of Fleas in the Rothschild and British Museum Collection, Fleas, Flukes, and Cuckoos, and 300 other zoolog. works; Biography of 2nd Lord Rothschild The Butterfly Gardener, Atlas of Insect Tissues, Animals and Man, Butterfly Cooing like a Dove, Rothschild Gardens, Rothschild's Reserves. Ad.: Ashton Wold, Peterborough, PE8 5LZ.

ROTHSCHILD, Nathaniel Charles Jacob, Lord, M.A. (Oxon.); b. Cambridge, Apr. 29, 1936; Chairman RIT Capital Partners plc; President St. James's Place Capital plc; Chairman of the J. Rothschild Group; President IJPR (1992-); Chairman of the Tr. of the National Gallery (1985-91); Chairman of the Tr. of the National Heritage Memorial Fund (1992-); C., Weizmann Instit. Foundation; Tr., Jerusalem Foundation. Ad.: 27 St. James's Pl., SW1A INR. ☎ 020-7493 8111. Fax 020-7493 5765.

RUBEN, David-Hillel, B.A., Ph.D.; b. Chicago, July 25, 1943; Director, London School of Jewish Studies (1998-); Professor of Philosophy, London School of Economics (1984-97); University of Glasgow, Lecturer in Philosophy (1970-75); University of Essex, Lecturer in Philosophy (1975-79); The City University, London, Senior Lecturer in Philosophy (1979-84). Publ.: Marxism and Materialism (1979); The Metaphysics of the Social World (1985); Explaining Explanation (1990); Explanation, editor (1993). Ad.: London School of Jewish Studies, 44 Albert Rd., London NW4 2SJ.

RUBENS, Bernice Ruth, Hon. D. Litt. Univ. Wales; b. Cardiff, July 26, 1926; author; film dir.; Fel. Univ. Coll. Cardiff. Publ.: The Elected Member (Booker Prize, 1970), Brothers, Mr. Wakefield's Crusade, Our Father, A Solitary Grief, Mother Russia, Autobiopsy (1993) etc. Ad.: 111 Canfield Gardens, London NW6 3DY. ☎ 020-7625 4845.

RUBENS, Kenneth David, O.B.E., F.R.I.C.S., F.R.S.A.; b. Lond., Oct. 10, 1929; Chartered Surveyor; Chairman, Jewish Museum, London., Chairman, ORT Trust.; L. Elder Span. & Port. Jews, Cong.; Memb. C. World Jewish Relief; Past Master, Worshipful Company, Painter-Stainers.; Hon. Life Mem., Brit. Property Fed. Ad.: 5 Clarke's Mews, London W1N 1RR. ☎ 020-7486 1884.

RUBINSTEIN, William David, B.A., Ph.D., F.A.HA., F.A.S.S.A., F.R.Hist.S.; b.

New York, Aug. 12, 1946; m. Hilary L. Rubinstein; Professor of History, The University of Wales, Aberystwyth (1995-); Prof. of Social and Economic History, Deakin University, Australia (1987-95); Ed., Journal of the Australian Jewish Historical Society (1988-95); President, Australian Association for Jewish Studies (1989-91); Member, Committee of Management, Executive Council of Australian Jewry (1983-95). Publ.: Men of Property: The Very Wealthy in Britain Since the Industrial Revolution (1981); The Jews in Australia: A Thematic History (with Hilary L. Rubinstein) (1991); Capitalism, Culture, and Decline in Britain, 1750-1990 (1993); A History of the Jews in the English-Speaking World: Great Britain (1996); The Myth of Rescue (1997); Britain's Century: A Political and Social History 1815-1905 (1998); Philosemitism: Admiration and Support in the English-speaking World for Jews 1840-1939 (with Hilary Rubinstein, 1999). Ad.: Department of History, University of Wales, Aberystwyth, Penglais, Ceredigion SY23 3DY. ☎ 01970 622661. Fax 01970 622676.

RUDMAN, Michael Edward, M.A. (Oxon.), B.A. (Oberlin Coll.); b. Tyler, Texas, USA, Feb. 14, 1939; Artistic Director, Sheffield Theatres (1992-94); Dir. Chichester Festival Theatre (1989-90); Assoc Dir., Nat. Theatre, (1979-88); Dir. Lyttelton Theatre (1979-81), Bd. Dirs. Art. Dir.; Hampstead Theatre (1973-78); Art. Dir., Traverse Theatre Club (1970-73). Ad.: c/o Peter Murphy, Curtis Brown Group, 4th Floor, 28/29 Haymarket, SW1Y 4SP. ☎ 020-7396 6600. Fax 020-7396 0110.

RUDOLF, Anthony, B.A., (Cantab); b. London, Sept. 6, 1942; Writer, Publisher & Translator; Ad. Ed. Modern Poetry in Translation, Ad. Ed., Jerusalem Review; Adam Lecturer, Kings Coll. London (1990); Ed./Literary Ed. of European Judaism (1970-75). Publ.: The Arithmetic of Memory (1999); Piotr Rawicz and Blood from the Sky (1996); The Diary of Jerzy Urman (1991); Primo Levi's War against Oblivion (1990); After the Dream (1979). Ad.: 8 The Oaks, Woodside Av., N12 8AR. ☎/Fax 020-8446 5571.

RUSSELL, Cllr. Mrs. Theresa Science, O.B.E., J.P., D.C.L. (Hon.) F.R.S.A.; b. Hull; Rotary Intl. Paul Harris Fel. (1989); Lord Mayor (1965-66), form. Lady Mayoress and Sheriff's Lady, Newcastle upon Tyne; Chairman, N. East Emunah; Chairman, Newc. Inf & Publicity Cttee.; Chairman, North-East Diocesan After-Care Cttee.; Brit. President, Internat. Friendship Force; Gov., Royal Grammar Sch.; Reg. Hospital Area Health Auth.; Fdr. President, B'nai B'rith Lodge; B.B.C. Appeals Cttee. Newcastle B.B.C. Radio Cttee.; Vis. Magistrate; Low Newton Prison, Exec., Northumbria Tourist Bd.; Jewish Woman of Distinction Award (1977); Chairman, Newcastle Children in Danger. Ad.:

SABIN, Albert, M.D., D.Sc. (Hon.), Ph.D. (Hon.), Litt.H.D. (Hon.), L.H.D. (Hon.), LL.D. (Hon.); b Bialystok, Aug. 26, 1906; Scientist; form. President, Weizmann Inst., Rehovot, Emer. Dist. Res. Prof., Univ. of Cincinnati Cincinnati, Ohio; Med. Univ. of S Carolina, Charleston, S. Carolina. Publ.: 380 publs. in scientific jnls. Ad.: Sutton Towers, Apt. 1001, 3101 New Mexico Ave. N.W., Washington DC, 200165902 USA. ☎ (202) 363-8066

SACKS, Chief Rabbi Jonathan Henry, M.A. (Cantab.), Ph.D., Hon. DD (Camb.), Hon. DD. (King's Coll., Lond.), Hon. D. Univ. (Middx.); b. London, March 8, 1948; m. Elaine née Taylor; Chief Rabbi of the United Hebrew Congregations of the Commonwealth (1991-); Vis. Prof. Philosophy Hebrew Univ.; Vis. Prof. Theology and Religious Studies, King's College, London; Vis. Prof. Philosophy, Univ. Essex (1989-90); form. Princ., Jews College and holder of the Lord Jakobovits Chair (1984-1990); M. Marble Arch Syn. (1983-1990); M., Golders Green Syn. (1978-1982); BBC Reith Lect. (1990); Ed. L'Eylah (1984-1990); Hon. Fell. Gonville and Caius Coll. Cambridge (1993-). Publ.: Torah Studies (1986); Tradition and Transition (1986); Traditional Alternatives (1989); Tradition in an Untraditional Age (1990); The Persistence of Faith (1991); Arguments for the Sake of Heaven (1991); Orthodoxy Confronts Modernity

(1991); Crisis and Covenant (1992); One People: Tradition Modernity and Jewish Unity (1993); Will We Have Jewish Grandchildren? (1994); Faith in the Future (1995); Community of Faith (1995); The Politics of Hope (1997). Ad.: Office of the Chief Rabbi, 735 High Road, London N12 0US. ☎ 020-8343 6301. Fax 020-8343 6310. Email ocr@brijnet.org

SAFRAN, Rabbi Alexander, Ph.D. (Vienna); b. Bacau, Romania, Sept. 12, 1910; Chief Rabbi of Geneva (1948-); Lect. in Jewish Thought at Univ. of Geneva; form. Chief Rabbi of Romania and Member of Romanian Senate. Publ.: La Cabale, Israel dans le Temps et dans l'Espace, etc. Ad.: 1 rue Crespin, CH 1206 Geneva. ☎ 346-66-97. Fax 346-6739.

SAIDEMAN, Seymour Geoffrey, F.C.A.; b. London, April 5, 1939; Consultant; National President B'nai B'rith; form. President, United Syn. (1992-96); Chairman, Chief Rabbinate Council (1992-96); form. Chairman, Board of Man. of the Beth Hamidrash Cttee.; form. Chairman, Ministerial Placement Cttee.; form. Chairman, Singer's Prayer Book Publications Cttee; form. Chairman, London Board of Jewish Rel. Educ. (1984-87); form. Chairman, Governors JFS Comprehensive Sch. (1984-87). Ad.: Hillel House, 1-2 Endsleigh St., WC1H 0DS. ☎ 020-7387 5278. Fax 020-7387 8014. Email: bnaib@ort.org

SALAMAN, Esther, A.R.A.M., L.R.A.M., (Mrs. Paul Hamburger); b. Barley, Herts; Singing Consultant, Trinity Coll. Music; form. Prof, Guildhall School of Music and Drama; Prof. singer & teacher of Voice, form. Hon. Org., Jewish Inst. Sunday Concerts; Recitals and Talks on B.B.C. Radio 3; form. Consultant Teacher for Nat. Opera Studio. Master Classes and Demonstrations England and Overseas; H. Music Adv., Spiro Instit. Publ.: Unlocking your Voice, freedom to sing (1989; 2nd. 1999). Ad.: 114 Priory Gdns., N6 5QT. ☎ 020-8340 3042.

SALAMON, Rabbi Thomas; b. Kosice, May 10, 1948; Rabbi/Solicitor; m. Renée née Heffes; M., Westminster Syn. (1997-); M., Hampstead Ref. Jewish Com. (1988-90); M., Hertsmere Progressive Syn. (1980-88); Assoc. M., West London Syn. (1972-75); Exec. Dir., Norwood Child Care (1975-80). Ad.: Westminster Synagogue, Kent House, Rutland Gardens, London SW7 1BX. ☎ 020-7584 3953. Fax 020-7581 8012.

SALASNIK, Rabbi Eli; b. Old City of Jerusalem; Rav. in London since 1950 Chairman, Rabbin. C., East Lond. and West Essex; District Rav Lond. Bd. for Shechita. Ad.: 8 The Lindens, Prospect Hill, Waltham Forest, London E17 3EJ.

SALASNIK, Rabbi Zorach Meir, B.A., F.J.C.; b. Lond., July 29, 1951; M., Bushey & Distr. Syn.; V. Chairman Rabbin. C., U.S.; Community Development Programme, U.S.; Central Services Cttee U.S.; Chaplain, Rishon Multiple Sclerosis Aid Gp.; Cttee., Michael Sobell Sinai School; Rabbinical Adv., Agency for Jewish Education; form. M., Notting Hill Syn., Leytonstone & Wanstead Syn. Ad.: 8 Richfield Rd., Bushey Heath, Herts., WD2 3LQ. ☎ 020-8950-6453. Fax 020-8421 8267.

SAMUEL, David Herbert, 3rd Viscount, of Mount Carmel and Toxteth, O.B.E., M.A. (Oxon), Ph.D. (Jerusalem), C.Chem, FRSC (UK); b. Jerusalem, July 8, 1922; m. Eve née Black; Scientist, Prof. Emeritus, Weizmann Inst. of Science, Rehovot; President, Shenkar Coll. of Textile Tech. and Fashion, Ramat Gan (1987-94); Vis. Prof. Dept. of Chemistry, Univ. York (1995-97); Vis. Prof. Dept. of Pharmacology, Yale Univ. Sch. of Med. (1983-84); McLaughlin Prof, McMaster Univ. Sch of Health Sciences, Hamilton, Canada (1984); Royal Society Vis. Prof, M.R.C. Neuroimmunology Unit Zoology Dept., Univ. Coll., London (1974-75); Dir., Centre for Neurosciences and Behavioural Res. (1978-87), Weizmann Inst. of Science; Dean, Faculty of Chemistry (1971-73); Dep. Chairman, Scientific C. (1963-65); Vis. Prof., Sch. of Molecular Sciences, Warwick Univ. (1967); Res. Fel., Laboratory of Chemical Biodynamics (Lawrence Radiation Lab.) Univ. of California, Berkeley (1965-66); Res. Fel., Chemistry Dept., Harvard Univ., Cambridge Mass. (1957-58); Postdoctoral Fel., Chemistry Dept., Univ. Coll., London (1956); Bd. Israel Centre of Psychobiology; Bd. Harry Stern C. for

Alzheimers Disease (Israel); Bd. Tr., Menninger Foundation, Topeka, Kansas USA; Bds. of Bezalel Academy of Arts and Design; Tel Aviv Museum of Art; C., Anglo-Israel Assn., Lond.; form. Chairman, US-Israel Educ. Foundation; Chairman, Isr. Bd. Amer.-Israel Cultural Foundation; Chairman Advisory Bd. Batsheva de Rothschild Foundation; Academic Adv. Cttee., Everyman's (Open) Univ. Cttee on Teaching of Chemistry, Intl. Union of Pure & Appl. Chemistry (1981-89); Served in British Army (UK, India, Burma, Sumatra) (mentioned in Despatches) (1942-46); IDF (1948-49). Publ.: The Aging of the Brain (D. Samuel et al, edrs.); Memory: how we use it, lose it and can improve it (1999), and over 300 scientific articles. Ad.: Weizmann Institute, Rehovot, Israel. ☎ (972)-89344229; 99553242 (home). Fax (972)-99552511.

SAMUEL, Edgar Roy, B.A. (Hons.), M. Phil., F.R.Hist.S., F.C.Optom., D.C.L.P.; b. London, 1928; Chairman Publ. Cttee J.H.S.E.; Past Dir., Jewish Museum (1983-95); Past President, JHSE (1988-90), Records & Treasures Cttee., Span. & Port. Cong., Lond. Publ.: Contribs. to Transactions of Jewish Hist. Soc.; The Portuguese Jewish Community in London, 1656-1830 (1992). Ad.: 4 Garden Court, 63 Holden Rd., N12 7DG. ☎ 020-8445 1327.

SAMUELSON, Sir Sydney Wylie, C.B.E., Hon. D. Sheffield Hallam U.; b. Paddington, London, Dec. 7, 1925, m. Doris née Magen; British Film Commissioner (1991-97); Fel. British Film Institute (1997); Fd., Chairman & Chief Exec., Samuelson Group PLC (1954-1990); Trustee, Chairman Bd. Man. and Fellow, British Academy of Film and Television Arts (1973-); Chairman (1965-85), President (1985-), Israel Association for the Habilitation of the Mentally Handicapped (AKIM) (1965-); Memb., Exec. Cttee, Inter-Parliamentary Council Against Antisemitism; Memb., Beth Hatefutsoth; Patron Comm. for Racial Equality (CRE). Ad.: 31 West Heath Ave., NW11 7QJ. ☎ 020-8455 6696.

SANDELSON, Neville Devonshire, M.A. (Cantab.); b. Leeds, Nov. 27, 1923; Barrister; Dir., Consultancy Comps.; M.P. for Hillingdon, Hayes and Harlington (Lab. 1971-81, SDP 1981-83). Ad.:

SANDLER, Merton, M.D., F.R.C.P., F.R.C.Path; F.R.C.Psych, C.Biol., F.I.Biol.; b. Salford, Mar. 28, 1926; Emeritus Prof. of Chemical Pathology, Royal Postgraduate Med. Sch., Instit. of Obstetrics & Gynaecology, London Univ.; H. Consultant, Chemical Pathologist, Queen Charlotte's and Chelsea Hospital. Publ.: Scientific writings. Ad.: 33 Park Rd., East Twickenham, Middx. TW1 2QD. ☎ 020-8892 9085. Fax 020-8891 5370.

SARAH, Rabbi Elizabeth Tikvah, B.Sc. (Soc.); b. 1955; Semichah Leo Baeck Coll. (1989); Rabbi, Leicester Progressive J. Cong. (1998-); Buckhurst Hill Reform Syn. (1989-94); Pt. time Lect. Leo Baeck College (1997-); Dir., Programmes Division, Reform Synagogues of Great Britain and Dep. Dir. of the Sternberg Centre (1994-97); co-ed., Learning to Lose – Sexism and Education (1980), On the Problem of Men (1982); ed., Reassessments of First Wave Feminism (1982); researcher into Rabbi Regina Jonas, 1902-44 (died in Auschwitz, first woman to receive Semichah); contr. to Hear our voice – women rabbis tell their stories (1994), Jewish Explorations of Sexuality (1995), The Dybbuk of Delight (1995), Renewing the Vision (1996); Chair, Leo Baeck Coll. In-service Training Team; Mem. 'The Half-Empty Bookcase' Co-ord. Group. Ad.: LBC, The Sternberg Centre for Judaism, 80 East End Road, N3 2SY.

SARNA, Nahum Mattathias, M.A., (Lond.), Ph.D.; b. Lond., March 27, 1923; Eminent Scholar of Judaica, Florida Atlantic University (1999-2000), Vis. Prof. (1995-99); Vis. Prof. Columbia Univ. (1992); Vis. Prof., Yale Univ. (1992-94); Prof. Emer. (1985) Bible Studies, Brandeis Univ., USA; Chairman, Nr. Eastern and Judaic Studies Dept., Brandeis (1969-75); President, Assn. for Jewish Studies (1983-85); Departmental Ed., Encyclopaedia Judaica; Ed., translator, Jewish Publ. Soc. Bible; Ed., Proc. of the American Academy for Jewish Research (1990); Gen. Ed., Jewish Publ. Soc. Bible Commentary Series; Ed. Bd. Soc.

Biblical Lit. Monograph Series; Fel., Instit.. Advanced Studies, Hebrew Univ. (1982-83); Academic Adv. C., Nat. Foundation Jewish Culture; Fel., Amer. Academy; Jewish Res. Member, Israel Exploration Soc., Palestine Exploration Soc.; Biblical Colloquium; Minister's diploma, Jews' Coll. Lond.; Ed., Proc. American Acad. Jewish Research. Publ.: Understanding Genesis, Exploring Exodus, Commentary on the Book of Exodus, Commentary on the Book of Genesis, A New Translation of the Book of Psalms (co-auth.), (Contribs.) Encyclopaedia Britannica, Encyclopaedia Judaica, Encyclopaedia Hebraica, Encyclopaedia of Religion, An Introduction to the Book of Psalms, Songs of the heart, Oxford Companion to the Bible, A new translation of the Book of Job (co-author), etc. Ad.: 7886 Chula Vista Crescent, Boca Raton, Fl. 33433. ☎ (561) 395 0486. Fax (561) 395 7289.

SAVITT, Martin F., Inst.S.M., b. London, 1921; form. V. Chairman, Z. Fed. of Brit. & Ireland; Chairman, For. Aff. Cttee. & Chairman (1991-97); form. Org. Cttee. for Warsaw Ghetto Memorial mtgs.; BoD; V. President, BoD (1979-85); form. Chairman Jew Def. & Group Rel. Cttee.; form. Chairman Brit-Isr. Chamber of Commerce; Anti-Boycott Co-ord. Cttee.; Chairman, Euro. Com. on Antisemitism; Mem. Bd. Man. Holocaust Educ. Tr.; Member W.G. Commonwealth Jewish C.; Dir. Material Claims Against Germany; form. Member, Gov. Bd., WJC; V. President, (Ch 1964-66) Ajex; Chairman, Ajex Anti-Defamation Cttee. (1954-58); President, Ajex Housing Assn. Ltd.; Fdr., Jt Cttee. Against Racialism; form. Chairman, All Party & Interfaith Cttee. Racial Justice; form. H. Nat. T., Distr. 15, B'nai B'rith, Com., Anti-Defamation League; Life President, Monash Br., Brit. Legion; Member, Earl Haig Br.; R.A.S.C. Western Desert and M.E. (1941-45), later in charge transport maintenance, Suez Canal zone. Ad.: 18 Laurel View, N12 7DT. ☎ 020-8445 7017. Fax 020-8446 5499.

SCHINDLER, Rabbi Alexander M., B.S.S., B.H.L., M.H.L., D.H.L., C.C.N.Y. and HUC-JIR; b. Munich, Oct. 4, 1925; Immediate Past President, Union of Ameican Hebrew Congs. (Reform); President, Memorial Foundation for Jewish Culture; V. President, World Jewish Congress; Bd. of Directors, American Joint Distribution Cttee; Chairman, Conf. of Presidents of Major Amer. Jewish Orgs. (1976-79); Hon. Doctorates: HUC-JIR, Lafayette, Univesity of South Carolina, Hamilton, Wittenberg, College of the Holy Cross; Townsend Harris Medal, C.C.N.Y.; Bublick Prize, Hebrew University; servied in Ski Troops US Army, won Purple Heart and Bronze Star. Ad: Union of American Hebrew Congregations, 633 Third Ave., New York, N.Y. 10017-6778. ☎ 650-4150. Fax (212) 650 4169.

SCHLESINGER, John Richard, C.B.E., M.A. (Oxon.); b. London, Feb 16, 1926; Film Dir., Princ. Films directed: Terminus, A Kind of Loving, Billy Liar, Darling, Far from the Madding Crowd, Midnight Cowboy, Sunday Bloody Sunday, The Day of the Locust, Marathon Man, Yanks, Honky Tonk Freeway, Separate Tables (HBO & HTV), An Englishman Abroad (BBC), The Falcon and the Snowman, The Believers, Madame Sousatzka, Pacific Heights, Cold Comfort Farm, The Innocent, A Question of Attribution (BBC), Eye for an Eye, Sweeney Todd. Plays: No, Why, Timon of Athens, I and Albert, Heartbreak House, Julius Caesar, True West. Operas: Les Contes d'Hoffmann, Der Rosenkavalier, Un Ballo in Maschera. Ad.: Duncan Heath, ICM, 76 Oxford St., W1R 1RB.

SCIAMA, Dennis William Siahou, M.A., Ph.D., F.R.S.; b. Manchester, Nov. 18, 1926; Prof., Astrophysics, Internat Sch. for Advanced Studies, Trieste; Consultant, Internat. Centre for Theoretical Physics, Trieste; form. Physics Prof, Texas Univ.; Maths. Lect., Cambridge Univ.; Jr. Res. Fel., Trinity Coll., Cambridge; Sr. Res. Fel. All Souls Coll., Oxford; Extraord. Fel., Churchill Coll. Cambridge. Publ.: The Physical Foundations of General Relativity, Modern Cosmology, The Unity of the Universe, Modern cosmology and the dark matter problem. Ad.: 7 Park Town, Oxford OX2 6SN. ☎ 01865 559441.

SEBAG-MONTEFIORE, Harold, M.A. (Cantab.); b. Dec. 5, 1924; m. Harriet née Paley; Barrister at Law, President, AJA (1965-71), Dep. Circuit Judge (1973-83);

Tr., Royal Nat. Theatre Fdn.; Jt. President, Barkingside Jewish Youth Centre (1988-94); Freeman City of London, Chevalier Legion d'Honneur. Ad.: 7B Vicarage Gate, W8 4HH. ☎ 020-7937 1831.

SECHER, Paul, LL.B.; b. Whitehaven, March 1, 1951; Man. Dir., J.S.B. Group (Training Publishing and Consultancy); Chairman, C'wealth Jewish C. Publ.: Co-auth., books & video manual on employment law, health and safety at work, communication skills. Ad.: 37 Fortress Road, NW5 1AD. ☎ 020-7267 7792. Fax 020-7267 6394.

SEGAL, Anthony Walter, M.B., Ch. B., M.D., M.Sc., Ph.D., D.Sc., F.R.C.P., F.R.S.; b. Johannesburg, Feb. 24, 1944; Charles Dent Prof. of Med Lond. Univ., attached Univ. Coll. & Middlesex Hospital Med.; Sch. Ad.: 48B, Regents Park Rd., NW1 7SX. ☎ 020-7586 8745.

SEGAL, Judah Benzion, M.C., M.A. (Cantab.), D.Phil. (Oxon.), F.B.A., b. Newcastle, June 21, 1912; V. President, RSGB (1985-91); Emer. Prof. of Semitic Languages Sch. of Oriental & African Studies, London Univ.; President, form. Princ., Leo Baeck Coll.; President, NorthWestern Reform Syn.; V. President, Anglo-Israel Archaeological Soc; Lect. in Aramaic, Ain Shams Univ., Cairo (1979); form. with Sudan Gov. (1939-41); Intelligence Off, M.E.F. (1942-44); Capt, Brit. Mil. Admin., Tripolitania (1945-46). Publ.: Hebrew Passover, History of the Jews of Cochin and other Orientalist studies Ad. 17 Hillersdon Ave., Edgware, Middx. HA8 7SG. ☎ 020-8958 4993.

SELBY, The Hon. David Mayer, A.M., E.D., Q.C., B.A., LLB., Hon D. Sydney Univ. (1991), Lieut-Col. (R.); b. Melbourne Mar. 13 1906; Justice of the Supreme Court of N.S W. (1962-76); Dep. Chancellor, (1971-87); Fel. Senate, Sydney Univ. (1964-89); President, N.S.W Medico-Legal Soc.; V. President, N.S.W. Marriage Guidance C. (1964-89); form. O.C., Rabaul A/A Battery (1941-42; Chief Legal Off., Eastern Command, Acting Justice Supreme Court, Territory of Papua & New Guinea (1961-62), Life Member, Australian Red Cross Soc. (1990); Hon. Dr. Syd. Univ. 1991. Publ.: Hell and High Fever, Itambu. Ad.: 19 Pibrac Ave., Warrawee N.S.W., 2074.

SHAHAR, Tovia, B.A. (Hebrew Univ.); b. Lond., Sept. 14, 1927; form. Sr. Educ. Officer, London Bd. of Jewish Religious Education; Registrar, Central Exam. Bd., Jews' Coll.; Lect., Hebrew Grammar, Jerusalem Teachers Coll.; HM, Moriah Coll., Sydney; Dir., Jewish Studies, Mt. Scopus Coll., Melbourne. Publ.: Medinatenu. Ad.: 9 Durley Rd., N16 5JW. ☎ 020-8800 2603 .

SHAMIR, Yitzhak; b. Ruzinoy, Poland, 1915; form. Prime Min., State of Israel (June 1990-June 1992; Oct. 1983-Sept 1984; Oct. 1986-Mar. 1990); Vice-Premier (1984-86), Foreign Min. (1980-86); Herut Leader; M. K. (1973-96); Member, Betar in Poland emigrated Palestine 1935; joined Irgun Zvai Leumi (1937); later helped reorganise Central Cttee., Lohamei Herut Yisrael. Publ.: Summing Up (1994). Ad.: Beit Amot Misphat, 8 Shaul HaMelech Blvd., Tel Aviv. ☎ Tel Aviv 695-1166.

SHAW, Rabbi Joseph, B.A.; b. London, July 2, 1922; M. Emer. (M., 1952-87) Palmers Grn. & Southgate Syn.; form. M., Sutton & Distr. Syn. (1948-49); Asst. M., Hampstead Syn. (1949-52); Jt. Chaplain to Mayor of Borough of Southgate (1958-59); Chaplain to Mayor of Borough of Southgate (1964-65); Chaplain to Mayor of Lond. Borough of Enfield (1980-81); Jt. Chaplain, Southgate, Palmers Grn. & Distr. Br., Ajex; H. Chaplain, Nat. Assn. of Jewish Friendship Clubs (1985-93). Ad.: 24 Russell Gdns., NW11 9NL. ☎ 020-8455 5368.

SHAW, Martin, B.A., I.C.F.M.; b. London, Aug. 16, 1949; Ind. Consultant to the Charity and Voluntary Sector (1995-); Exec. Dir. of the Assoc. for Jewish Youth (1989-95), Senior Youth Off., London Borough of Ealing (1986-89); S Youth Off., I.L.E.A. (1983-86), Project Dir. Nat. C. for Voluntary Youth Services (1979-82). Publ.: 'Young People and Decision'. Ad.: 64 The Grove, Edgware, Middx. HA8 9QB. ☎ 020-8958 6885. Email: mshaw@dircon.co.uk

SHAW, Peter; b. Lond., Dec. 17, 1935, m. Leila; Sec., Jewish Youth Fund; Exec.

Dir., Jewish Child's Day; Clerk, Finnart House School Trust; Bd. Memb. (Chief Exec. 1971-77) Redbridge Jewish Youth & Com. Centre; Exec. C., Bernhard Baron St. George's Jewish Settlement (1990-98); Tr., The Duveen Trust Org. (1990-96); Sec., Stamford Hill Assoc. Clubs (1959-71); Dep. Dir., Youth & Hechalutz Dept., WZO (1977-80); Exec. Dir., Norwood Child Care (1980-84); form. Chairman, Jewish Assn. of Professionals in Soc. Work, Chairman, Assn. of Execs. of Jewish Com. Orgs. (1982-84); Chairman, Jewish Programme Materials Project (1980-84). Ad.: 2 Lodge Close, Canons Drive, Edgware, Middx HA8 7RL. ☎ 020-8381 2894. Fax 020-8446 7370.

SHEFF, Mrs. Sylvia Claire (née Glickman), M.B.E., J.P., B.A.; b. Manchester, Nov. 9, 1935; Ret. Teacher; Asst. Nat. Dir. (Nat. Projects Dir., 1974-85), Conservative Frs. of Israel (1985-89); Fdr. & Dir., Friendship with Israel, Group (European Parl.) (1979-90); P. (Fdr. Chairman, 1972-80), Manch. 35 Group Women's Campaign for Soviet Jewry (1980-); H. Sec., Nat. C. for Soviet Jewry (1987-89); Assoc. Dir. Jewish Cultural & Leisure Centre (1990-93); Del. BoD (1987-). Int. Co-ord. Yeled Yafeh Fellowship of Children of Chernobyl (1990-93). Magistrate (1976). Ad.: 6, The Meadows, Old Hall La., Whitefield, Manchester M45 7RZ. ☎/Fax 0161-766 4391.

SHELDON, Rt. Hon. Robert Edward, P.C., M.P.; b. Sept. 13, 1923; M.P. (Lab.) for Ashton-under-Lyne (since 1964); Chairman, Public Accounts Cttee.; form. Fin. Sec., Treasury. Ad.: 27 Darley Ave., West Didsbury, Manchester M20 9ZD.

SHELLEY, Ronald Charles, F.C.A.; b. London, March 27, 1929; T., BoD (1991-97); V. President (Nat. Chairman, 1975-77) Ajex; Chairman, Ajex Housing Assn. (1987-91); Tr., London Museum of Jewish Life. Ad.: Second Floor, 45 Mortimer St., W1M 7TD. ☎ 020-7323 6626. Fax 020-7255 1203.

SHERIDAN, Rabbi Sybil Ann, M.A. (Cantab.); b. Bolton, Lancs., Sept. 27, 1953; m. Jonathan Romain; M., Thames Valley Progressive J. Community, Reading; Lect. Leo Baeck College; form. M., Swindon Jewish Com.; Ealing Lib. Syn. Publ.: Stories from the Jewish World (1987), Creating the Old Testament (contr, 1994), Hear Our Voice (ed) (1994), Christian-Jewish Dialogue (1996, contr.), Renewing the Vision (1996, contr.), Limmud Chavruta Books on Tsedaka (1996), Dorot (1997). Ad. 9 Boyne Hill Ave., Maidenhead, Berks SL6 4ET. ☎ 01628 71058. Fax 01628 625536. Email: sybilsheri@aol.com

SHIELDS, Sir Neil (Stanley) M.C.; b. London, Sept. 7, 1919; Chairman, Com. for New Towns (1982-95); Bd., Lond. Transport (1986-93), Chairman, (1988-89) Dep. Chairman (1989-93); Chairman, Lond. Transport Property Bd. (1986-95); Dep. Leader (1952-61), Hampstead Bor C.; Nat. Exec. Chairman London area (1961-63), Conservative Party; C., AJA. Ad.: 12 London House, Avenue Rd., NW8 7PX.

SHINDLER, Colin, B.Sc., M.Sc. Dip.Ed. (Further Education), Ph.D.; b. Hackney, London, Sept. 3, 1946; Fellow in Hebrew and Israel Studies, SOAS; Lect. in Chemistry; Ed., Judaism Today (1994-); Political Affairs Sec., World Union of Jewish Students (1970-72); Ed., Jews in the USSR, (1972-75). Ed. Jewish Quarterly (1985-94); Dir. European Jewish Publication Soc. (1995-). Publ.: All Party Parl. Exhibition on Soviet Jewry (1974), Exit Visa: Detente, Human Rights and the Jewish Emigration Movement in the USSR (1978), The Raoul Wallenburg Exhibition (1982), Ploughshares into Swords? Israelis and Jews in the Shadow of the Intifada (1991). Israel, Likud and the Zionist Dream (1995). Ad.: 80 Stanhope Ave., London N3 3NA. ☎ 020-8349 1264.

SHINE, Rabbi Cyril, B.A.; b. London, Jan. 24, 1923; M., Central Syn. (1955-90); Domestic Chaplain to Lord Mayor of London (1960-61); Westminster C. Com. Rel. Cttee.; Chairman Central JIA Cttee.; Chaplain, Pentonville Prison; form. M., N. Finchley & Woodside Park Syn., Walthamstow & Leyton Syn. and Peterborough. Ad.: Suite R, 82 Portland Pl., W1N 3DH ☎ 020-7636 3195.

SHIPTON, Sidney Lawrence, LL.B, M.B.A., F.R.S.A., F.I.Mgt.; b. London, Jul. 25, 1929; Solicitor; Freeman of the City of London; Co-ord. The Three Faiths

Forum; Council, JHSE; Exec. Scopus J. Educ. Tr.; Member, Royal Instit. of Internat. Affairs; Mem. of the Praesidium of the WZO Zionist General Council and the Jewish Agency for Israel; V. President Leo Baeck (London) Lodge of Bnai Brith; Hon. V. President Zionist Federation of Great Britain and Chair Constitution Cttee; Hon. V. President Federation of Zionist Youth; Hon. President Hanoar Hazioni; form. Exec. Dir. World Movement for a United Israel (Ta'ali); Exec. Dir., Sephardi Fed. of Brit. & C'wlth; Exec. Dir., WOJAC (British Section); Exec. Member, Council of Christians and Jews; Chairman, Israel Cttee. BoD; form. Chairman, Simon Marks Jewish Day Sch.; Exec. The Network; form. Chairman, Assoc. Execs. of Jewish Com. Orgs.; Gen. Sec., Chairman, H. Sec. and H.T. Z. Fed.; Dir., J.N.F.; Man. Dir., K.K.L. Executor & Tr. Co. Ltd. Ad.: 82 Hurstwood Rd., NW11 0AU. ☎/Fax.: 020-8455 0987.

SHIRE, Michael, B.A. (Hons.), M.A., Ph.D. (Hebrew Union Coll. L.A.); Rabbinic ordination at Leo Baeck Coll. (1996); b. 1957; Dir., Centre for Jewish Education, Reform Synagogues of Great Britain/Union of Liberal and Progressive Synagogues; Gov. Clore Shalom School (1998-); Assoc. Memb. Int. Seminar on Religon and Values; Dir. of Education, Temple Beth Hillel, Hollywood (1983-88); Lect. in Education, Leo Baeck Coll. (1988-); Gov., Akiva School (1990-). Ed. Cons. Illustrated Atlas of Jewish Civilization. The Illuminated Haggadah (1998). Ad.: CJE, The Sternberg Centre for Judaism, 80 East End Road, Finchley N3 2SY.

SHOMBROT, Jeffrey, O.B.E., B.Sc. (Eng.), F.I.C.E.; b. London, Apr. 30, 1915; Ret. Consult, form. Supt. Eng. Admiralty and Environment Dept. Ad. Holly Lodge, 7 Aylmer Dr., Stanmore HA7 3EJ. ☎ 020-8954 4316.

SHORT, Mrs. Renee; b. Apr., 1916; M.P. (Lab.) for Wolverhampton, North-East (1964-87); Member, N.E.C. Lab. Party; form. Chairman, Educ. Cttee.; Chairman, Parl. Select Cttee. for Soc. Services; Patron, Chiropractic Advancement Assn.; President, Nat. Campaign for Nursery Educ; Member, Med. Res. C. (1988) Ethics Cttee. Royal Coll. Physicians; BMA Invitro Fertilisation Ethics Cttee.; P, Action for Newborn; Chairman, CO-ORD; C., N.S.P.C.C.; Hon. Life Member; Inst. Medical Ethics; Working Party on Aids; Hon. Fel., Wolverhampton Polytechnic (1987); Hon. Fel. Royal Coll. Psychiatrists (1988); Hon. MRCP (1989); Ch. Celebrities Guild (1989-92); Member BoD Community Res. Cttee; V. President, Health Visitors Assn.; V. President, Womens National Cancer Control Campaign (WNCCC); V. President, Parl. Scientific Cttee. Publ.: The Care of Long Term Prisoners Ad: 70 Westminster Gdns., Marsham St., SW1P 4JG.

SHUKMAN, Harold, B.A. (Nottingham), M.A., D.Phil. (Oxon.); b. London, March 23, 1931; Emer. Fel., St. Antony's Coll., Oxford; Chairman Edr. Bd., East European Jewish Affairs. Publ.: Lenin and the Russian Revolution, Ed. Blackwell's Encyclopedia of the Russian Revolution, trans. Children of the Arbat, by A. Rybakov; Ed. & trans. Memories by Andrey Gromyko; Ed. & trans. Stalin: Triumph & Tragedy by Dmitri Volkogonov; Ed. Stalin's Generals; trans. Lenin (D. Volkogonov); Ed. & trans. Trotsky, The Rise and Fall of the Soviet Empire; Rasputin; The Russian Revolution; Stalin. Ad.: St. Antony's Coll., Oxford, OX2 6JF. ☎ 01865 284747.

SHULMAN, Milton, B.A., LL.B.; b. Toronto; Writer and critic; Evening Standard, theatre and television critic (1948-97); IPC Critic of the Year Award, 1966; Evening Standard, and Daily Express, film critic (1948-58); Film Critic, Vogue, (1975-87); Regular Member, B.B.C. Radio 4 Stop the Week; Exec. Producer, Granada TV (1958-62); Asst. Controller of Programmes, Rediffusion TV (1962-64); Served in Canada Army (Major, mentioned in dispatches). Publ.: Defeat in the West, How to be a Celebrity, Kill 3, The Ravenous Eye, The Least Worst Television in the World, Marilyn Harlen and Me; Voltaire, Goldberg and Others; Preep; Preep in Paris; Preep and the Queen, etc. Ad.: Flat G, 51 Eaton Sq., SW1. ☎ 020-7235 7162.

SHULMAN, Rabbi Nisson E., B.A., M.A., D.H.L.; Capt. CHC, USNR, Ret.; b.

New York, Dec. 12, 1931; Faculty, IBC, Yeshiva Univ. (1999-); Dir., Dept. of Rabbinic Services, RIETS, Yeshiva Univ. (1994-99); Rabbi St John's Wood Syn., London (1988-94); Rabbi, Central Syn., Sydney, Dayan Sydney Beth Din (1985-88); Rabbi, Fifth Ave. Syn., New York (1978-85); Rabbi Cong. Shaarei Tefila and Dean, Yavneh Hebrew Academy, Los Angeles (1971-77); Rabbi and Educ. Dir., Cong. Sons of Israel, Yonkers, N.Y. (1962-71); Chaplain, US Naval Reserve, Ready (1956-88); Co-Chairman, Com. of Med. Ethics, Fellowship of Jewish Doctors, New South Wales (1985-88); Edr., Proc. of the 1987 Sydney Med. Ethics Conf.; Mem. Med. Ethics Commission, Fed. of Jewish Philanthropies, N.Y. (1971-78); Edr., Yearbook of Med. Ethics, Jews College, London (1993); Proc. Sydney Conf. on Bioethics (1987). Publ.: Authority and Community: 16th Century Polish Jewry (1986); Jewish Answers to Medical Ethics Questions (1988). Ad.: 383 Grand St., Apt. 207, New York City 10002. USA. ☎/Fax 212 505-3432.

SIEFF, Baron of Brimpton (Life Peer) (Sir Marcus Joseph Sieff), O.B.E., M.A., Hon. LL.D. (St. Andrews), Hon. Dr. (Babson Coll., Massachusetts), Hon. Lit.D. (Reading Univ.), Hon. F.R.C.S., Hon. Dr. (Stirling), Hon. DLL. (Leicester), D.Phil (Tel Aviv and Jerusalem); b. July 2, 1913; H. President, Marks & Spencer p.l.c., Hon. P. (1985-); P. (1984-85), Chairman (1972-84), Jt. Man. Dir. (1967-83), joined 1935; Chancellor Weizmann Inst. Science; Hon. President UJIA; Non-Exec. Chairman, The Independent (since 1986); Chairman, First Internat. Bank of Israel Fin. Tr. Ltd. (1983-88); form. Non-Exec. Dir., Wickes plc.; President, Brit.-Israel Chamber of Commerce (since 1975); Member Nat. Export C. (1965-71), (Chairman, Export Cttee. for Israel), (1965-68); V. President (Exec., since 1975), Policy Studies Instit. (form P.E.P.); form. Tr., Nat. Portrait Gallery, Lond.; Hambro Award, Businessman of the Year (1977); Aims Nat. Free Enterprise Award (1978); B'nai B'rith Internat. gold medallion for humanitarianism (1982); Retailer of the Year Award, Nat. Retail Merchants, Assn. (1982); Brit. Instit. of Man. Gold Medal (1983); H. Fel., Corpus Christi Coll., Cambridge (1975); served Royal Artillery (1939-45). Publ.: Memoirs, Don't Ask the Price, Lord Sieff on Management. Ad.: House of Lords, SW1A 0PW.

SILBERG, Rabbi Sidney, M.A.; b. Leeds June 27, 1934; M., Hendon Syn.; form M., Bournemouth Hebrew Cong. Jesmond Hebrew Cong., Newcastle upon Tyne; Ealing & Acton Syn. Ad.: 19 Alderton Cresc , NW4 3XU. ☎ 020-8202 6407.

SILK, Donald, M.A. (Oxon.); b. Lond., 1928; Solicitor; H.V. President, Z. Fed.; C., Hebrew Univ., Ch, Z. Fed. (1967-71); Chairman, Fed. Z. Youth (1953-55), Tr. Chichester Festival Theatre. Ad.: 69 Charlbury Rd., Oxford OX2 6UX. ☎ 01865 513881.

SILVER, Leslie Howard, O.B.E.; b. Lond., Jan. 22, 1925; Chairman Chief Exec. Kalon Group of Comps.; Chairman, Leeds Utd A.F.C.; Yorkshire Businessman of Year (1983); form P , Paintmakers Assn., Paint Res. Assn., Oil & Colour Chemists Assn., Paint Industry Club. Ad.:

SILVERBECK, Michael Harrison, b. Liverpool, Apr. 10, 1940; Chartered Accountant; form. President, Merseyside Jewish Rep C., P. King David Foundation L'pool (1981-87); Chairman, Morris Datnow Hillel Hse (1974-77); T., L'pool Z Central C. (1970-73). Ad.: 7 Queens Dr., Liverpool L18 2DS. ☎ 0151-722 1516.

SILVERMAN, Rabbi Robert Malcolm (Reuven), B.A., Ph.D.; b. Oxford, July 26, 1947; m. Dr Isobel Braidman; M., Manchester Reform Syn.; Hon Fel., Middle Eastern Studies Dept. and Centre for Jewish Studies, Univ. Manchester; Chairman, Assembly of Rabbis, RSGB (1991-93); Anglo-Israel Friendship League, Manch.; Chaplain, Progressive Jew. Students, Manch.; form. Second M., Edgware Reform Syn.; M., Mikve Israel Emanuel, Curacao. Publ: Baruch Spinoza. Ad.: 26 Daylesford Rd., Cheadle, Cheshire, SK8 1LF. Fax 0161-834 0415 or 0161-839 4865.

SINCLAIR, Clive John, B.A., Ph.D. (East Anglia Univ.), F.R.S.L.; b. Lond., Feb 19, 1948; British Library Penguin Writers Fellow (1996); form. Lit. Edr., Jewish Chronicle; Writer-in-Residence Uppsala Univ., 1988; Prizes: Somerset Maugham Award (1981); Jewish Quarterly Award for Fiction (1998); Silver Pen for Fiction (1998). Publ.: The Brothers Singer, Bedbugs, Hearts of Gold, Bibliosexuality, Blood Libels, Diaspora Blues, Cosmetic Effects, Augustus Rex, The Lady with the Laptop, A Soap Opera from Hell. Ad.: 22 Church St., St Albans, Herts. AL3 5NQ.

SINCLAIR, Rabbi Dr Daniel Bernard, LLB, LLM, Dr. Juris, b. London, June 30, 1950; Prof. Jewish Law and Comparative Biomedical Law, Tel Aviv College of Management Law School; Principal, Jews' College (1994-97); Lect. in Jewish Law, Gold College, Jerusalem (1978-84); Research Fellow, Institute for Research in Jewish Law, Hebrew University, Jerusalem (1978-84); Tutor in Jewish Law, Hebrew University, Jerusalem (1980-84); Visiting Research Associate, Centre for Criminology and the Social and Philosophical Study of Law, Edinburgh University (1984-87); M. of the Edinburgh Hebrew Congregation, Edinburgh (1984-87); Tutor in Jurisprudence, Faculty of Law, Edinburgh University, Edinburgh (1985-87); Senior Research Fellow, Institute for Research in Jewish Law, Jerusalem (1987-); Lect. in Jewish Law and Comparative Biomedical Law, Tel Aviv University (1988-); Lect. in Jewish Law and Philosophy of Halakhah, Pardes Institute, Jerusalem (1988-90); Lecturer in Jewish and Comparative Bioethics, Hebrew University, Jerusalem (1991); Jacob Herzog Memorial Prize, 1980; Asst. Ed. Jewish Law Annual (1990). Publ: Tradition and the Biblogical Revolution (1989), Selected Topics in Jewish Law, vols. 4-5 (1994). Ad.: 3/21 Ben Tabbai St., Jerusalem 93591. ☎ (02) 6784268.

SINCLAIR, Dr. Michael J.; b. London, Dec. 20, 1942, m. Penny; Chairman, Sinclair Montrose Trust Ltd.; Partner, Atlantic Medical Partners U.S.A.; Vice Chairman UJIA; Mem. Bd. Gov. Jewish Agency for Israel; Chairman Exec. Bd. World Council of Torah Education; Chairman of Management Cttee, Sidney and Ruza Last Foundation Home; Member of Council The Caldecott Community. Ad.: 5th Floor, Cheapside House, 138 Cheapside, EC2V 6LH. ☎ 020-7776 1500. Fax 020-7776 1592.

SINGER, Rabbi Marcus, B.A.; b. Vienna, Jan. 12, 1926; M., Central Syn., Birmingham. Ad.: 12 Speedwell Rd. Birmingham B5 7PS. ☎ 0121-440 2455.

SINGER, Norbert, C.B.E., B.Sc., Ph.D., Hon. D.Sc (Greenwich), C.Chem., F.R.S.C.; b. Vienna May 3, 1931; Physical Chemist; Fellow Queen Mary & Westfield College; Fellow Nene College; Vis. Prof. Univ. Westminster (1996-); Chairman, Bexley Dist. Health Auth. (1993-94); Chairman Oxleas NHS Tr. (1995-); Chairman Rose Bruford College Gov. Body (1994-); V. Chanc., Univ. Greenwich (1992-93); Dir., Thames Polytechnic (1978-92); Res. Chemist, Morgan Crucibles Co. Ltd. (1954-57); Lect. and eventually Dep. Hd. of Dept. of Chemistry Northern Polytechnic (1958-70); Hd. of Dept. of Life Sciences & Prof., Polytechnic of Central London (1971-1974); Assist. then Dep. Dir., Polytechnic of North London (1974-78); Member of C.N.A.A. & Cttees. (1982-93). Ad.: Croft Lodge, Bayhall Rd.; Tunbridge Wells, Kent TN2 4TP. ☎ 01892 523821.

SITRUK, Rabbi Joseph, b. Tunis, 1944; Chief Rabbi of France; Chief Rabbi Marseilles (1975-87); Rabbi, Strassbourg (1970-75). Ad.: 19 rue St. Georges, 75009 Paris. ☎ 14970 8800.

SKELKER, Philip David, M.A. (Oxon.), F.R.S.A.; b. Sept. 7, 1946; Educational Leadership Dir., UJIA (1998-); English master, Eton College (1997-98); form. HM, Carmel Coll, HM, King David High Sch., Liverpool (1981-84). Ad.: 4 Broadhurst Ave., Edgware, Middx. HA8 8TR.

SKLAN, Alexander, B.Sc., Soc. Sci, M.Sc. Econ., C.Q.S.W.; b. London Jan. 13, 1947; m. Cheryl; Assistant Chief Exec. Jewish Care, Dir. of Quality Assurance; Dir. of Social Services Jewish Care; Dir. of Social Services Jewish Welfare Board (1979-90); Dir. of Social Services Jewish Care (1990-96); Jt. Chairman, Assembly of Masorti Synagogues (1996-).

Ad.: Stuart Young House, 221 Golders Green Rd., NW11 9DW. ☎ 020-8458 3282. Fax 020-8455 7185. Email alex@jewishcare.org

SMITH, Rabbi Amnon Daniel, M.A.; b. Hadera, Israel, Oct. 10, 1949; Sr. M., Edgware & Dist. Reform Syn.; form. Chairman RSGB Assembly of Rabbis; form. M., Wimbledon & Dist. Syn.; form. Assoc. M., West Lond. Syn.; Fdr. Chairman, Raphael Centre - a Jewish counselling service. Ad.: 118 Stonegrove, Edgware, HA8 8AB.

SOBER, Phillip, F.C.A., F.R.S.A.; b. London, April 1, 1931; m. Vivien; Chartered Accountant; Dir. Liberty International plc (form. TransAtlantic Holdings plc) (Member of Chairman's and Remuneration Cttees., Chairman Audit Cttee.) (1983-); Mem. C.Univ. London (1998); Mem. Finance Cttee Univ. London (1999); Dir. Capital & Counties plc (1993-); Dir. Capital Shopping Centres plc (Chairman Audit Cttee.) (1994-); Consultant, BDO Stoy Hayward, Chartered Accountants (1990); Gov. and Chairman of Audit Cttee., London Institute Higher Education Corporation (1994); form. Tr. Jewish Assoc. of Business Ethics; Chairman, Central Council for Jewish Community Services; form. Jt. Tr., Ravenswood; Partner, Stoy Hayward, Chartered Accountants (1958-90); Fell. of the Inst. of Chartered Accountants (1963-); International Partner and Member of Management Cttee., Stoy Hayward, Chartered Accountants (1974-90); Chairman, Accounting Standards Cttee., British Property Federation (1976-83); Member Council, UK Central Council for Nursing, Midwifery and Health Visiting (1980-83); Crown Estate Commissioner (1983-94); Senior Partner, Stoy Hayward, Chatered Accountants (1985-90); Tr., Royal Opera House Tr. (1985-91); President, Norwood Child Care (1989-94); European Regional Dir., Horwath International (1990-94); Consult. Hunting Gate Group Ltd. (1992-95). Publ.: Articles in professional press on various subjects but primarily on property company accounting. Ad.: 4 Horbury Mews, W11 3NL. ☎ 020-7727 2427. Office BDO Stoy Hayward, 8 Baker Street, W1M 1DA. ☎ 020-7486 5888. Fax 020-7487 4585.

SOETENDORP, Rabbi David Menachem Baruch; b. Amsterdam, July 1, 1945; Rabbi, Bournemouth Reform Syn; V. President, B'mouth Br., CCJ; Chairman Exodus 2000; J. Chaplain, Dorchester & Winchester Prison, Bournemouth Univ.; Contrib., local radio, TV; Contr. 'Renewing the Vision', SPC London; Chairman, AFETUK; Rabbi, South Hants Reform Cong. Publ.: Op Weg Naar Het Verleden. Ad.: 25 De Lisle Rd., Bournemouth, BH3 7NF. ☎ 01202 514788.

SOLOMON, Sir Harry, K.B., F.R.C.P. (Hon.); b. Middlesbrough, March 20, 1937; Company Chairman; Hillsdown Holdings plc (1975-1993): Chairman (1987-1993); Non-Exec. Dir. (1993-97); Fel. of the Royal Coll. of Physicians (Hon.). Ad.: Hillsdown House, 32 Hampstead High St., London NW3 1QD. ☎ 020-7431 7739.

SOLOMON, Rabbi Norman, Ph.D (Manc.), M.A. (Cantab.), B.Mus (Lond.); b. Cardiff, May 31, 1933; Fellow, Oxford Centre for Hebrew and Jewish Studies (1995-); Lect. Faculty of Theology, Univ. Oxford; form. Dir., Centre for Study of Judaism & Jewish Christian Relations, Selly Oak Colls.; President BAJS (1994); Edr., Christian Jewish Relations (1986-91); form. M., Birmingham Central Syn., Hampstead Syn., Lond., Greenbank Drive Syn., Liverpool, Whitefield Hebrew Cong., Manchester. Publ: Judaism and World Religion (1991); The Analytic Movement (1993); A Very Short Introduction to Judaism (1996); Historical Dictionary of Judaism (1998). Ad.: 5 Phoebe Court, Bainton Rd., Oxford OX2 7AQ. ☎/Fax 01865-437952.

SPENCER, Charles Samuel, b. Lond. Aug. 26, 1920; Fine Art and Theatre Lect.; Exhibition organiser; Lond. correspondent art publ. in Italy, Germany, Greece, etc.; form. Sec., AJA, Maccabi Union, Brady Clubs, Edr., Art and Artists; Member Jewish Relief Unit (1944-46). Publ.: Erté; The Aesthetic Movement: A Decade of Print Making, Leon Bakst and the Ballets Russes, The World of Serge Diaghilev, Cecil Beaton, Film and Stage Designs. Ad.: 24A Ashworth Rd., W9

1JY. ☎ 020-7286 9396. Fax 020-7286 1759.
SPIRO, Nitza (née Lieberman), M.Phil. (Oxon); b. Jerusalem, Nov. 1937; m.
Robin; Dir. The Spiro Ark, an educational, languages and cultural institute for
adults; Deputy Dir. Ulpan Akiva Netanya, Israel (1959-68); Lector in Hebrew
and Hebrew Literature, Univ. Oxford (1975-83); Dir. Spiro Inst. (1980-88);
teaching of Hebrew on radio. Publ.: Hebrew Correspondence Course (1987);
Hebrew Accelerated Learning Course (Suggestopedia) (co-author). Ad.: The
Spiro Ark, Middlesex University, The Burroughs, London NW4 4HE. ☎ 020-
8201 7173. Fax 020-8201 7173.
SPIRO, Robin Meyer, M.A. (Oxon), M.Phil. (Oxon), F.C.A.; b. London, Feb. 9,
1931; m. Nitza née Lieberman; Company Director, Part-time Lecturer; Fdr.
Spiro Inst. (1978). Publ.: Contributor, Open Univ. Leisure Course; The Jewish
Enigma. Ad.: 43/44 St. John's Wood Court, St. John's Wood Rd., London NW8
8QR.
STEEN, Anthony, M.P.; b. London, July 22, 1939; Barrister, social worker, youth
ldr., law lect; M.P. (Con.) for Totnes (1997-), South Hams (1983-97), for
Liverpool, Wavertree (1974-83); Party Cttees.; Chairman, Urban & Inner City
Cttee., (1987-93); Chairman Deregulation Cttee (1994-); Chairman Sane
Plamony; V. Chairman, Health & Soc. Services (1979-80); Chairman 1974
Conservative M.Ps. Gp; V. Ch, Parl. Brit. Caribbean Gp; Race Rel. (1974-79);
Select Cttee. Environment (1991-); All Party Group Y.M.C.As.; Fdr., First Dir.,
Task Force (1964-68); First Dir., Yng. Vol. Force (1968-74); Bd., Vol. Service
Overseas, Nat. Playing Fields Assn., Com. Transport; Adv., Canadian Govt.
(1970-72) on job creation and economic initiatives; V. Chairman, Task Force Tr.;
V. President Internat. Centre Child Studies. Publ.: New Life for Old Cities,
Tested Ideas for Political Success Public Land Utilisation Management Schemes
(PLUMS) (1988). Ad.: House of Commons, SW1A 0AA. ☎ 020-7219 5045.
STEIN, Cyril, b. London Feb. 20, 1928; V. President, UJIA. Ad.: 94 Wigmore St.,
London W1H 9DR.
STEINBERG, Gerry, M.P.; b. Durham Apr. 20, 1945; M.P. (Lab.) for Durham City;
Member, Parl. Select Ctte. on Educ. Durham Distr. Cllr. (1976-87); form HM,
Spennymoor Special Sch., Durham. Ad.: House of Commons, SW1. ☎ 020-7219
6909.
STEINER, Prof. George, F.B.A., M.A., D.Phil.; Hon. D.Litt: East Anglia, 1976;
Louvain, 1980; Mount Holyoke Coll., USA, 1983; Bristol, 1989; Glasgow,
1990; Liège, 1990; Ulster, 1993; Kenyon College, 1995; Trinity College, Dublin,
1995; b. Apr. 23, 1929; m. Zara née Shakow; Member, staff of the Economist, in
London (1952-56); Extraordinary Fellow, Churchill College, Cambridge (1969);
RA (Hon) Weidenfeld Professor of Comparative Literature, and Hon. Fellow of
Balliol College, Oxford (1995-); Hon. Fellow St. Anne's College, Oxford; Inst.
for Advanced Study, Princeton (1956-58); Gauss Lect., Princeton Univ. (1959-60);
Fellow of Churchill Coll., Cambridge (1961-); Prof. of English and Comparative
Literature, Univ. of Geneva (1974-94). Lectures: Massey (1974); Leslie Stephen,
Cambridge (1986); W. P. Ker (1986), Gifford (1990), Univ. of Glasgow; Page-
Barbour, Univ. of Virginia (1987). Fulbright Professorship (1959-69); Vis. Prof.,
Collège de France (1992). O. Henry Short Story Award (1958); Guggenheim
Fellowship (1971-72); Zabel Award of Nat. Inst. of Arts and Letters of the US
(1970); Faulkner Stipend for Fiction, PEN (1983); Pres., English Assoc., 1975;
Corresp. Mem., (Federal) German Acad. of Literature (1981); Hon. Mem., Amer.
Acad. of Arts and Sciences (1989); FRSL (1964). PEN Macmillan Fiction Prize,
1993. Chevalier de la Légion d'Honneur (1984). Publ: Tolstoy or Dostoevsky,
1958; The Death of Tragedy, 1960; Anno Domini, 1964; Language and Silence,
1967; Extraterritorial, 1971; In Bluebeard's Castle, 1971; The Sporting Scene:
White Knights in Reykjavik, 1973; After Babel, 1975 (adapted for TV as The
Tongues of Men, 1977); Heidegger, 1978; On Difficulty and Other Essays, 1978;
The Portage to San Cristobel of A.H., 1981; Antigones, 1984; George Steiner: a

reader, 1984; Real Presences: is there anything in what we say?, 1989; Proofs and Three Parables, 1992; No Passion Spent, 1996; The Deeps of the Sea, 1996; Homer in English (ed.), 1996; Errata: an Examined Life, 1997. Ad: 32 Barrow Rd., Cambridge CB2 2AS. ☎ 01223 61200.

STEPHENS, Judge Martin, Q.C., M.A. (Oxon.); b. Swansea, June 26, 1939; Circuit Judge (since 1986); Recorder (1979-86); form. Chairman, Cardiff Jewish Rep. C. (1986-95). Member Parole Bd., (1995-); Member Main Bd., Judicial St. Bd. (1997-). Ad.: c/o Central Criminal Court, City of London, London EC4M 7HE.

STERLING, Baron of Plaistow (Life Peer) (Jeffrey Maurice); Kt 1985, CBE; Hon. DBA (Nottingham Trent Univ.); Hon. D.C.L. (Durham), Kt., Order of St John 1998; b. Dec. 27, 1934; m. Dorothy Ann née Smith; Paul Schweder and Co. (Stock Exchange (1955-57); G. Eberstadt & Co. (1957-62); Fin. Dir. Gen. Guarantee Corp. (1962-64); Mng. Dir., Gula Investments Ltd. (1964-69); Chairman Sterling Guarantee Trust plc (1969-) (merging with P&O 1985); The Peninsular and Oriental Steam Navigation Company (1980-, Chairman, 1983-); Chairman, orgn. cttee. World ORT Union (1969-73), Mem. Exec. (1966-), Tech. svcs. (1974-), V. President Brit. ORT (1978-); Dep. Chairman and Hon. Tr. London Celebrations Cttee. Queen's Silver Jubilee (1975-83); Chairman Young Vic Co. (1975-83); V. Chairman and Chairman of the Exec. Motability (1977-); Bd. Dirs. Bitish Airways (1979-82); Spl Adv. Sec. of State for Industry (1982-83) and to Sec. of State for Trade & Industry (1983-90); Chairman Govs. Royal Ballet Sch. (1983); Gov. Royal Ballet (1986-); President of the General Council of British Shipping (1990-91); President, European Community Shipowners' Associations (1992-94); Freeman of the City of London; Hon. Captain Royal Naval Reserve (1991); Elder Brother Trinity House (1991); Hon. Fellow Institute of Marine Engineers (1991); Hon. Fellow Institute of Chartered Shipbrokers (1992); Hon. Member Institute of Chartered Surveyors (1993); Fellow of the ISVA (1995); Hon. Fellow R. Institute of Advanced Architects (1997). Ad. Office: 79 Pall Mall, SW1Y 5EJ. ☎ 020-7930 4343.

STERN, David, J.P., F.R.I.B.A., M.I.P.I.; b. Lond., July 18, 1920; Architect; Dir., Inventerprise; H. President, B.B. Distr. 15. Ad.: 9 Willowdene, View Rd., N6 4DE. ☎ 020-8348 0261. Fax 020-8348 1063.

STERN, Isaac; b. Kreminiecz, Russia, July 21, 1920; Concert Violinist; President, Carnegie Hall; Fd. Mem. Nat. Endowment for the Arts. C., Chairman Emer., Amer.-Israel Cultural Foundation. Ad.: c/o I.C.M. Artists Ltd., 40 West 57th St., New York City, N.Y. 10019, USA.

STERNBERG, Sir Sigmund, Kt (1976), K.C.S.G., J.P.; b. Hungary, June 2, 1921; Chairman Martin Slowe Estates and ISYS plc; Paul Harris Fell., Rotary Internat. Award of Honour; Officer Brother of the Order of St. John; Patron International Council of Christians and Jews; Mem. Board of Deputies of British Jews; Gov. Hebrew Univ. of Jerusalem; Life President Sternberg Centre for Judaism (1996-); Pres. Reform Synagogues of Gt. Britain (1998-); Founder Three Faiths Forum (Christians, Muslims & Jews Dialogue Gp.); Fell. Leo Baeck College; Vis. Prof. Moderna Univ. (Lisbon) (1998); DU Essex (1996); DU Open (1998); Templeton Prize for Progress in Religion (1998); Comdr., Order of Honour (Greece); Commander's Cross Order of Merit (Germany); Cmdr., Royal Order of Polar Star (Sweden) (1997); Wilhelm Leuschner Medal (Wiesbaden) (1998); Order of Commandatore of the Italian Republic (Italy) (1999); The Commander's Cross with a Star of the Order of Merit (Poland) (1999). Ad.: 80 East End Rd., N3 2SY.

SUDAK, Rabbi Nachman; b. Feb. 3, 1936; Princ., Lubavitch Foundation (1959-); Lubavitcher Rebbe's Emissary in Britain. Ad.: 37 Portland Ave., N16 6HD. ☎ H. 020-8800 6432. O. 020-8800 0022.

SUMBERG, David Anthony Gerald, M.E.P.; b. Stoke-on-Trent, June 2, 1941, m. Carolyn née Franks; Solicitor; Dir. Anglo-Israel Association (1997-); form. M.P. (Cons) for Bury South (1983-97); Parl. Pte. Sec., Attorney Gen. (1986-90); Jt.

H.Sec., Parl. Group, Conservative Frs. of Israel, V.Chairman, All-Party Cttee., Release of Soviet Jewry; V. Chairman, All-Party War Crimes Group; Memb. Home Affairs Select Cttee. of the House of Commons, (1991-92); Memb. Foreign Affairs Select Cttee. House of Commons (1992-97); Mem. Lord Chancellor's Adv. Cttee. on Public Records (1992); Tr. Holocaust Educ. Tr. Ad.: 42 Camden Sq., London NW1 9XA. ☎ 020-7267 9590.

SUMRAY, Monty, C.B.E., F.INSTD, F.C.F.I., FRSA; b. London, Oct. 12, 1918; m. Kitty née); Dir. of FIBI Bank (UK) Plc; V.-P., British-Israel Chamber of Commerce; Chairman, British Footwear Manufacturers Federation Project Survival Cttee.; V. President, Jewish Care; V -P., Stamford Hill branch of AJEX; Member of the Anti-Boycott Co-ordination Cttee.; Fel. of the Clothing & Footwear Instit.; Fel. of the Instit. of Dir.; Pres. London Footwear Manufacturers Assoc; Member of the Footwear Industry Study Steering Group, and Chairman of its Home Working Cttee.; President, British Footwear Manufacturers Federation (1976-77); Mem., Footwear Economic Development Cttee. Chairman, British-Israel Chamber of Commerce; Captain Royal Berkshire Regiment (1939-46); Served in Burma. Ad.: 6 Inverforth House, North End Way, London NW3 7EU. ☎ 020-8458 2788.

SUZMAN, Janet; b. Johannesburg, Feb. 9, 1939; Actress/Director; V. Chairman C. of L.A.M.D.A.; Hon. M.A. (Open University); Hon. D.Litt (Warwick Univ., Leicester Univ., QMW, London Univ.); Hon. Assoc. Artist, RSC. Publ.: Acting with Shakespeare (1996); Commentary on Antony and Cleopatra (1999). Ad.: c/o William Morris (UK) Ltd., 1 Stratton St., London W1X 6HB. ☎ 020-7355 8500. Fax 020-7355 8600.

TABACHNIK, Eldred, Q.C., B.A., LL.B. (Cape Town), LL.M. (London); b. Cape Town, Nov. 5, 1943; m. Jennifer; President Board of Deputies (1994–); President European Jewish Congress (1994-98); Hon. Officer (Warden), Richmond Syn. (1980-94); Chairman, British Friends of Boys Town, Jerusalem. Ad.: Board of Deputies, Commonwealth House, 1-19 New Oxford Street, London WC1A 1NF.

TABICK, Rabbi Jacqueline Hazel (née Acker), B.A.(Hons.), Dip. Ed.; b. Dublin, Oct. 8, 1948; Rabbi North West Surrey Syngogue; Past Chairman, Assembly of Rabbis, RSGB; Past Chairman, Central Educ Cttee., R.S.G.B; Council of Reform & Liberal Rabbis. Ad.: 33 Seymour Pl. W1H 6AT. ☎ 020-7723 4404.

TABICK, Rabbi Larry Alan, B.A., M.A.; b. Brooklyn, N.Y., Nov. 24, 1947; Rabbi, Hampstead Ref. Jewish Com. (1990-); Rabbi Leicester Progressive Jewish Community (1994-98); Assoc. Rabbi, Edgware & Dist. Ref. Syn. (1986-90); Asst. Rabbi, Middlesex New Syn. (1981-86), Rabbi Hampstead Ref. Jew Com. (1976-81) Ad.: 1 Ashbourne Grove, Mill Hill, NW7 3RS. ☎ 020-8959 3129

TABOR, David, Sc.D. (Cantab.) Hon. D.Sc. (Bath), F.R.S.; b. London, Oct. 23, 1913; Fellow, Gonville and Caius Coll., Emer. Prof., Dept. of Physics, Cambridge Univ. Publ.: Scientific works. Ad.: 8 Rutherford Rd., Cambridge, CB2 2HH. ☎ 01223-841366.

TANKEL, Henry Isidore, O.B.E., M.D., F.R.C.S.; b. Glasgow, Jan. 14, 1926; surgeon; Non-Exec. Dir., Southern Gen. Hosp. NHS Trust (1993-97); Chairman W. of Scotland Branch CCJ (1998-); Chairman, Glasgow J. Hsng. Assoc. (1996-); H.V. President Glasgow Jew. Rep. C.; Sec. Glasgow and West of Scotland Kashruth Commission; Chairman, Scottish Joint Consultants Cttee. (1989-92); Member Scottish Health Service Advisory Cttee. (1989-92); Jt. Con. Cttee. (UK) (1989-92); Chairman, Youth Liaison Cttee.- Glasgow Hospital Med. Services Cttee; Scottish Hospital Med. Services Cttee. Books: Gastroenterology – an intergrated course (contrib 1983); Cancer in the Elderly (contrib 1990). Ad.: 26 Dalziel Drive, Glasgow, G41 4PI . ☎ 0141-423 5830. Fax 0141-424 3648.

TANN, Rabbi Leonard, B.A.; b. London, Apr. 20, 1945; Chief M., Birmingham Hebrew Cong.; M., Sutton (Surrey) Syn. (1972-82); Hale Syn. (Manch.) (1982-86) . Publ: Books on Philately. Ad.: 61 Wheeleys Rd., Birmingham B15 2LL.

☎ 0121-440 8375.

TANNENBAUM, Mrs. Bernice Salpeter; b. New York City; Chairman Hadassah Magazine; Sec. Jewish Telegraphic Agency; Mem. Bd. Trustees, United Jewish Appeal; form. Chairman, Amer. Section, WZO; form. Nat. Chairman, Hadassah International; Nat. President, Hadassah (1976-80); Exec. Nat. Conference on Soviet Jewry; Life Tr., United Israel Appeal; Exec., WJC Amer. Section; Exec. Bd., Jewish Agency; Hon. President, World Confed., United Zionists; Gov. Bd., Hebrew Univ.; Bd., U.I.A. Publ.: It Takes a Dream, The Story of Hadassah; The Hadassah Idea (co.-ed.). Ad.: Hadassah, 50 W 58 Street, N.Y., 10019. ☎ (212) 303-8081.

TAUSKY, Vilem, C.B.E.; b. Prerov, Czechoslovakia, July 20, 1910; Composer & Conductor; Dir. of Opera, Guildhall Sch. of Music; Freeman, City of Lond.; Czechoslovak M.C. & Order of Merit; form. Conductor, B.B.C.; Mus. Dir. Carl Rosa Opera. Ad.: Ivor Newton House, 10-12 Edward Rd., Sundridge Park, Bromley, Kent BR1 3NQ.

TEMKO, Edward J.; b. Washington, DC, USA, Nov. 5, 1952; Journalist, Ed. Jewish Chronicle (1991-); Foreign Corr. United Press International (1976); Associated Press (1977-78), The Christian Science Monitor (1978-1988); World Monitor Television (1984-90). Publ.: To Win or To Die (Biography of Menachem Begin, 1987). Ad.: 25 Furnival St., EC4A 1JT.

TERRET, Norman Harold, J.P.; Compagnon d'Europe; F.Inst.D., MBA.; b. Ayr, Scotland, Jan. 10, 1951; President, CITS Group Hounslow, Middx.; SITA V. President, Marketing; Tr., British Israel Educ. Tr. Ad.: SITA, Lampton House, Lampton Road, Hounslow, Middx., TW3 4ED.

TIBBER, Judge Anthony Harris; b. London, June 23, 1926; Circuit Judge; Ad: c/o Edmonton County Court, Fore St., N18 2TN. ☎ 020-8807 1666.

TILSON THOMAS, Michael; b. Dec. 21, 1944; Conductor; Musical Director, San Francisco S.; Artistic Director, New World S.; Princ. Guest Conductor, London Symphony Orchestra; Artistic Director, Pacific Music Festival, Sapporo. Ad: c/o Columbia Artists Management Inc., 165 W. 57th Street, New York, NY 10019.

TOLEDANO, Dayan Pinchas, B.A., Ph.D.; b. Meknes, Morocco, Oct. 12, 1939; Ab Beth Din Sephardi Communities of G.B.; Rabbi, Wembley Sephardi Cong.; Eccl. Auth., Lond. Bd. of Shechita; V. President, Mizrachi Fed.; V. President, Herut, Gt. Brit., Patron, Mentally Handicapped Soc., Patron, Massoret; Edr., SRIDIM (Standing Cttee., Conf of European Rabbis). Publ.: Rinah-oo-Tefillah (co-Edr), Fountain of Blessings, Blessings: Code of Jewish Law, Home Ceremonies, Sha'alou - Le Baruch, Rabbinic response (co-edr.) Ad.: 17 Barn Hill, Wembley Park, Middlesex, HA9 9LA. ☎ 020-8904 7658. Fax 020-7289 2709.

TRAVIS, Anthony Selwyn; b. Cardiff, June 9, 1932; Emeritus Prof. of Planning - Univ. of Birmingham; Visiting Prof. in Tourism - Glasgow Caledonian Univ.; Director, East-West Tourism Consultancy; form. Programme Co-ordinator EEC PHARE. Tourism Programme for Poland; Dir. Research, Newcastle City Planning Dept. (1962-62); Prof. of Planning, Heriot Watt Univ., Edinburgh (1967-73); Prof and Dir., Centre for Urban and Regional Studies, Univ. of Birmingham. Publ.: 300, including Recreation Planning for the Clyde (1970), Realising Tourism Potential of the S. Wales Valleys (1985). Ad.: 20 Mead Rise, Birmingham B15 3SD. ☎/Fax 0121-454 1215.

TROPP, Asher, B.Sc.(Econ.), M.A., Ph.D.; b. Johannesburg, Jan. 2, 1925; Prof. of Sociology, University of Surrey (1967-1987). Publ.: The School Teachers (1957); Jews in the Professions in Great Britain 1891-1991 (1991). Ad.: 162 Goldhurst Terrace, NW6 3HP. ☎ 020-7372 6662.

TUCKMAN, Fred, O.B.E.; b. Magdeburg, June 9, 1922; Management Consultant; President, AJA (1989-95); M.E.P (1979-89), Conservative Spokesman, Soc. & Employment Affairs (1985-84); Cllr., Lond. Borough of Camden (1965-71); H.Sec., Conservative Bow Group (1958-9); Commanders Cross of the German Order of Merit 1990. Ad.: 6 Cumberland Rd., London SW13 9LY ☎ 020-8748

2392. Fax 020-8746 3918.
TURNER, Rev. Reuben; b. Karlsruhe, Jan. 8, 1924; H. Princ., Mathilda Marks-Kennedy Sch.; Min., Finsbury Park Syn. (1948-50); Reader, Brixton Syn. (1950-68), Dir. Zion. Fed Syn C. (1967-70); Gen. Sec., Mizrachi-Hapoel Hamizrachi Fed. of Gt. Britain (1970-73). Director JNF Educ. Dept. (1973-91). Publ.: Jewish Living, The Popular Jewish Bible Atlas. Ad.: 13 St. Peter's Court, NW4 2HG. ☎ 020-8202 7023.
ULLENDORFF, Edward, M.A. (Jerusalem), D.Phil. (Oxford), Hon D.Litt. (St. Andrews), Hon. Dr. Phil. (Hamburg); Hon Fell. S.O.A.S., Hon. Fellow Oxford Hebrew Centre, F.B.A.; b. Jan. 25, 1920; Prof Emer., Semitic Languages Lond. Univ. (since 1982); Prof. of Ethiopian Studies (1964-79); form. Prof. of Semitic Languages and Literatures, Manchester Univ. (1959-64); Jt. Edr., Journal of Semitic Studies; V. President, Brit. Academy (1980-82), Schweich Lect. (1967); V. President, Royal Asiatic Soc. (1981-85; 1975-79); Foreign Fell. Accademia Lincei, Rome; served in Brit. Mil. Govt , Eritrea and Ethiopia (1942-46); Asst. Sec. Palestine Govt (1947-48); Res. officer, Inst. Colonial Studies Oxford (1948-49); Reader in Semitic Languages, St. Andrews Univ. (1950-59); Chairman, Assn. of Brit. Orientalists (1963-64); Chairman, Anglo-Ethiopian Soc. (1965-68); Haile Selassie intern. prize for Ethiopian studies (1972). Publ.: The Semitic Languages of Ethiopia, The Ethiopians, Comp. Grammar of the Semitic Languages, Ethiopia and the Bible, Studies in Semitic Languages & Civilizations, The Hebrew Letters of Prester John, The Two Zions, From the Bible to Enrico Cerulli, H. J. Polotsky 1905-91, From Emperor Haile Selassie to H. J. Polotsky, 1995, etc. Ad.: 4 Bladon Close, Oxford, OX2 8AD.
UNTERMAN, Rev. Alan, B.A., B.Phil., Ph.D.; b. Bushey, Herts., May 31, 1942; M., Yeshurun Syn., Gatley, Cheshire; form. Lect., Comparative Rel. & Chaplain to Jewish Students, Manchester Univ.; Lect., Jerusalem Academy of Jewish Studies; Hillel Dir., Victoria, Australia. Publ: Encyclopaedia Judaica (Contribs), Wisdom of the Jewish Mystics, Jews their Religious Beliefs and Practices, Judaism, Penguin Dictionary of Religion (Contribs. on Judaism and Hinduism), Penguin Handbook of Living Religions (Contrib. Judaism), Dictionary of Jewish Lore and Legend. Ad.: 13 South Park Rd., Gatley, Cheshire, SK8 4AL. ☎ 0161-428 8469.
UNTERMAN, Rabbi Maurice Mordecai; b. Mar. 18, 1917; Founding Rabbi and Emer. M. (M., 1961-82) Marble Arch Syn.; V. President and Hon. Chaplain, Ravenswood Foundation for Mental Health; Special Adviser to Chief Rabbi (1984-91), Co-ordinator Centenary Ed. Singer's Prayer Book (1987-91); formerly Jt. Edr. Hamesilah, US journal, Lect., Applied Rabbinics, Jews, Coll., H. Dir., Chief Rabbi's Israel Off; Fdr. member Liaison Cttee. Inter-Community Rels. (1985-95); M., Cardiff United Syn. (1937-46); President, Hove Hebrew Cong. (1953-54); H. Chaplain, Nightingale Hse. (Home for Aged Jews), Dir. Frs. of Bar-Ilan Univ. (1958-61). Ad.: Flat 67, Wellington Ct., Wellington Rd., NW8 9TD. ☎ 020-7722 1331.
URIS, Leon M.; b. Baltimore Aug. 3, 1924; Writer. Publ.: Exodus, Mila 18, and other novels, screenplays and essays. Ad.: c/o Doubleday Publ. Co, 245 Park Ave., New York, 11530, USA.
VEIL, Mme. Simone (née Jacob), b. Nice, July 13, 1927; deported to Auschwitz and Bergen-Bergen Nazi concentration camps (1944-45); m. 1946 Antoine Veil, Inspecteur des Finances. Educ.: Lycée de Nice; Lic. en Droit, dipl. de l'Institut d'Etudes Poliques, Paris; qualified as Magistrate, 1956; Sec. Gen. Superior Coucil of the Magistrature (1970-74); Cons. Adm. ORTF (1972-74); French Health Min. (1974-76), Health and Social Security Min. (1976-79); Member Europ. Parliament (1979-93), President (1979-82); Chairman Liberal Group (1984-89); State Min. Social Affairs, Health and Urban (1993-95); President Haut Conseil à l'Intégration (1997); Memb. Constitutional Council (1998); Chevalier de l'Ordre National du Mérite; Médaille Pénitentiaire; Médaille de

l'Education surveillée. Dr (h.c.) Universities: Princeton, USA; Weizman Institute, Israel; Bar Ilan, Israel; Yale, USA; Cambridge, GB; Edinburgh, GB; Georgetown, USA; Urbino, Italy; Yeshiva Univ., NY, USA; Sussex, GB; Universitié Libre de Bruxelles, Belgium; Brandeis, USA; Glasgow, GB; Pennsylvania, USA. Recipient of honours and prizes from many countries including France, Israel, Germany, Spain, Brazil, Luxembourg, Greece, Ivory Coast, Morocco, Senegal, Venezuela, Sweden, USA, Italy. Publ.: Les Données Psycho-sociologiques de l'Adoption (with Prof. Launay and Dr Soule). Ad : 1 rue Bixio, 75007 Paris. ☎ 01 45 51 09 68.

VERMES, Geza, M.A., D.Litt. (Oxon), Hon. D.D. (Edinburgh, Durham), Hon. D. Litt. (Sheffield), F.B.A., W. Bacher Medallist, Hungarian Academy of Sciences; b. Mako, June 22, 1924; m. Margaret Unarska; Prof. of Jew. Studies, Oxford Univ. (1989-91), now Emeritus; Dir. Forum for Qumran Research, Oxford Centre for Hebrew and Jewish Studies (1991-); R. in Jew. Studies, Oxford (1965-91), Fel. of Wolfson Coll. (1965-91), now Emer.; form. Lect. and Sr. Lect. Divinity, Newcastle Univ. (1957-65); Chairman, Curators of the Oriental Instit. (1971-74); Chairman, Oriental Studies Board (1978-80); President, British Assn. for Jew. Studies (1975, 1988); President, European Assn. for Jew. Studies (1981-84); Edr. Journal of Jew. Studies (1971-); Vis. Prof. Rel. Studies, Brown Univ. (1971); Riddell Memorial Lect., Newcastle Univ. (1981); Dist. Vis. Prof., Judeo-Christian Studies, Tulane Univ., New Orleans (1982); Igor Kaplan Vis. Prof., Toronto Univ. (1985, 1987); Vis. Prof. Judaic Studies, Univ. of Calif. San Diego (1995); Vis. Prof. Hebr. Studies, Peter Pazmany Univ., Budapest (1996); Gunning Lect. Univ. Edinburgh. Publ.: Discovery in the Judean Desert, Scripture and Tradition in Judaism, The Dead Sea Scrolls in English, Jesus the Jew, Postbiblical Jewish Studies, The Dead Sea Scrolls: Qumran in Perspective, The Gospel of Jesus the Jew, Jesus and the World of Judaism, History of the Jewish People in the Age of Jesus Christ by E. Schürer (co-ed. and reviser), The Essenes According to the Classical Sources (co-author), The Religion of Jesus the Jew, The Complete Dead Sea Scrolls in English, Providential Accidents: An Autobiography; Discovery in the Judean Desert XXVI (co-editor): An Introduction to the Complete Dead Sea Scrolls. Ad.: West Wood Cottage, Foxcombe Lane, Boars Hill, Oxford, OX1 5DH. ☎ 01865 735384. Fax 01865 735 034.

VOGEL, Rabbi Shraga Faivish; b. Salford, Lancs, April 22, 1936; Dir., Lubavitch Foundation Ad.: 15 Paget Rd, N16. ☎ 020-8800 7355.

WAGERMAN, Mrs. Josephine Miriam (née Barbanel), O.B.E., B.A. (Hons.), P.G.C.E., Ac. Dip., M.A.(Ed); b. London, Sept. 17, 1933, m. Peter; Inner Cities Religious C. (Dept. of the Environment) (1994-); Mem. Academic Panel, Stuart Young Awards (1990-); Advisor to the Trustees, Pierre and Maniusia Gildesgame Trust (1996-99); Trustee of the Central Foundation Schools London (1996)' Jewish Care Woman of Distinction (1996); Mem. Bd. of Dir. JIA/Continuity (1997-); Chief Exec. Lennox Lewis College (1994-96); Memb.C. Centre for Study of Jewish Christian Relations Selly Oak Colleges (1995-98); form. Headteacher, J.F.S.; Member BoD, V. President (1994-), Senior Vice-President (1997-); President, Lond. A.M.M.A. (1982-83); form. Member, I.L.E.A Standing Jt. Adv. Cttee., Working Party on Teachers Service Conditions, Hist. & Soc. Studies Adv. Cttee; Independent Assessor NHS Non-Exec. Appointments Panel (1998-). Ad.: 38 Crespigny Rd., London NW4 3DX. ☎/Fax 020-8203 7471.

WAGNER, Leslie, M.A. (Econ.); b. Manchester, Feb. 21, 1943, m. Jennifer; Professor, Vice-Chancellor, Leeds Metropolitan Univ. (1994-); V. Chanc. & Chief Exec. University of North London (1987-93); Dep. Sec., Nat. Adv. Body, Publ. Sector Higher Educ. (1982-87); Prof. & Dean, Sch. of Soc. Sciences & Business Studies Central Lond. Poly. (1976-82); Lect. The Open Univ. (1970-76); V. President, United Syn., (1992-93); Member, C., US M. Exec. Comm. of Chief Rabbinate C; C. Cttee of V.Cs and Principals; Chairman, Society for Research into Higher Education (1994-96); Chairman, Higher Education for

Capability; Member Council for Industry & Higher Education; memb. National Skills Task Force; Chairman Jewish Community, Allocation Bd. (1994-96); Chairman UJIA Renewal Strategy Group; Mem. Bd. Gov. UJIA. Publ.: Choosing to Learn: Mature Students in Education (with others), The Economics of Educational Media, Agenda for Institutional Change in Higher Education (Edr.), Readings in Applied Microeconomics (Edr.). Ad.: Leeds Metropolitan University, Calverley Street, Leeds LS1 3HE. ☎ 0113 283 3100.

WALD, George, Ph.D.; b. New York City, Nov. 18, 1906; Emer. Prof. (Higgins Prof of Biology 1968-77), Harvard Univ., Nobel Prize for Medicine (1967). Publ: General Education in a Free Society (co-author), Twenty-Six Afternoons of Biology (Addison Wesley). Ad: 21 Lakeview Ave., Cambridge, Massachusetts, 02138, USA. ☎ (617) 868 7748.

WALSH, David, LLB (Hons); b. Leeds, May 21, 1937; m. Jenny, née Cronin, Solicitor, Director, Peek Plc, Carlisle Group Plc; Mem. Bd. of J.I.A.; form. Chairman, RSGB, now Vice President; form. Chairman, West London Synagogue (1981-85); President, West London Synagogue (1988-91). Ad.: 82 North Gate, Prince Albert Road, London NW8 7EJ. ☎ 020-7586 1118. Fax 020-7483 2598.

WASSERSTEIN, Bernard Mano Julius, M.A., D.Phil., F.R.Hist. S.; b. London, Jan. 22, 1948; President Oxford Centre for Hebrew & Jewish Studies (1996-); President JHSE (2000-); form. Prof. of Hist., Brandeis Univ. (Dean of Graduate Sch. of Arts and Sciences, 1990-92) (1982-96); Lect., Modern Hist., Sheffield Univ. (1976-80); Vis. Lect., Hist. Hebrew Univ. (1979-80); form. Res. Fel., Nuffield Coll., Oxford. Publ.: The British in Palestine, Britain and the Jews of Europe 1939-1945, The Secret Lives of Trebitsch Lincoln, Herbert Samuel, Vanishing Diaspora. Ad.: Oxford Centre for Hebrew and Jewish Studies, Yarnton, Oxon OX5 1PY. ☎ 01865 377946. Fax 01865 375079. Email: bernard.wasserstein@mohist.ox.ac.uk

WEBER, Harry, C.B.E.; b. Nov. 10, 1899; form Princ. Exec. Off , Min. of Educ.; V. President, N W. Lond. Jew. Boys, & Girls, Clubs & V. President Old Boys, Assn. Ad.: Sunridge Ct., 76 The Ridgeway, NW11 8PG ☎ 020-8209 1743

WEBBER, Alan, M.Sc., Ph.D., F.R.I.C.S.; b. London, Sept. 5, 1933; m. Sylvia née Barnett; Managing Director, Brymore Group; Chairman, B'nai B'rith Hillel Foundation (1998-); Chairman of Governors, St. Margaret's School, Hampstead (1990-); Hon. Sec. and Vice-Chairman B'nai B'rith Hillel Foundation (1990-98); President First Lodge, B'nai B'rith (1995-97); Chairman, Jewish Community Information (1994-97); Hon. Officer Hampstead Synagogue (1970-76); Hon. Officer St. John's Wood Synagogue (1990-91); Jt. Ed. (with Sylvia Webber) of Hampstead (1960-70) and St. John's Wood (1986-97) synagogue magazines. Publ.: The B'nai B'rith Hillel Foundation – 1953-1993; B'nai B'rith – 150 years of service to the community. Ad.: c/o Brymore Group, 8 Tavistock Court, Tavistock Rd., Croydon CR9 2ED. ☎ 020-8681 8381. Fax 020-8688 6979. Email AlanWebber@BT.Internet.com

WEIDENFELD, Baron of Chelsea (Life Peer) (Sir George Weidenfeld), Hon. Ph.D., Ben Gurion Univ.; Holder of the Knight Commander's Cross (Badge & Star) of the German Order of Merit; Holder of the Golden Knight's Cross with Star of the Austrian Order of Merit, Chevalier de l'Ordre National de la Légion d'Honneur, France; b. Vienna, Sept. 13, 1919; Publisher; Chairman, Weidenfeld & Nicolson, Lond.; Hon. Fell. St. Peter's College, Oxford (1992), St. Anne's College, Oxford (1993); Member Bd. Gov Institute of Human Science, Vienna; Member of South Bank Bd., Dir. of the Jerusalem Post; Political adv. to President Weizmann of Israel (1950); Member of South Bank Bd., London; Chairman, Bd of Govs., Ben Gurion Univ. of Negev, Gov. V. Chairman, Weizmann Instit. of Science; Gov., Tel Aviv Univ.; Tr., Jerusalem Foundation; Hon. Senator, Univ. Bonn (1996). Publ.: The Goebbels Experiment, Remembering My Good Friends (auto). Ad.: 9, Chelsea Embankment, SW3 4LE. ☎ 020-7351 0042.

WEIL (Brever-Weil), George; b. Vienna July 7, 1938; Sculptor, painter, jeweller, exhibited UK, US, Israel, Tokyo, Switzerland, South Africa etc.; portrait busts Ben-Gurion, Churchill, General de Gaulle, etc., Specialist in Judaica, including Bar-Ilan collection shown in Mann Auditorium, Tel Aviv; collections in Brit. Museum, Antwerp Museum, Royal Museum of Scotland, etc. H. Mem., Japanese Art Carvers Soc. (1986), only Western Artist so honoured. Ad.: 93 Ha Eshel Street, Herzlia Pituach, Israel.

WEINER, Rabbi Chaim, B.A. (Hebrew Univ. of Jerusalem), M.A. (Hebrew Univ. of Jerusalem), Rabbinical Ordination (Seminary of Judaic Studies Jerusalem (Masorti); b. Sydney, Nova Scotia, Nov. 11, 1958; m. Judy; Rabbi of Edgware Masorti Synagogue; National Dir. of Noam, Masorti Youth Movement, Israel (1987-91); Dir. Gesher, Masorti Teenage Centre, London (1991-96). Ad.: Edgware Masorti Synagogue, Stream Lane, Edgware, Middx HA8 7YA. ☎ 020-8905 4096. Email chaim. weiner@ort.org

WEISMAN, Malcolm, O.B.E., M.A. (Oxon.), O.C.F.; Barrister-at-Law; Recorder, S.E. Circuit; Special Adjudicator, Immigration Appeals (1998-); Hon. President Birmingham J. Graduates Assoc. (1995-96); Chief Rabbi's Award for Excellence (1993); B'nai B'rith Award for Community Service (1980); Asst. Com., Parl. Boundaries (1976-85), Rel. Adv. to Small Coms; Member, Chief Rabbi's Cabinet; Chaplain, Oxford Univ. & new univs.; Fell. Centre for the Study of Theology, Univ. of Essex; Hillel Nat. Student Cllr.; Sr. Jew. Chaplain to H.M. Forces; Hon. V. President, Monash Branch of Roy. Brit. Legion; Tr. Jewish Music Heritage Tr.; form. Gov. Carmel College (1996-98); Edr. Menorah, Chairman and Sec.Gen., Sr. Allied Air Force Chaplains (1980-1992) President (1993); Chaplain Award U.S. Airforce Jewish Chaplain Council; Sec. Allied Air Forces Chaplain Cttee.; Member, Council of Selly Oak Coll. Birmingham (1992), Chaplain to Lord Mayor of Westminster (1992-93), Mayor of Barnet (1994-95); Member, Min. of Def. Advisory Cttee on Chaplaincy; Chaplain R.A.F. Univs. Jew Chaplaincy Bd., Progr. Jewish Students Chaplaincy; Nat. Exec., Mizrachi Fed.; Nat. Exec. Council of Christians and Jews; Ct., Lancaster, East Anglia, Kent, Warwick, Sussex and Essex Univs.; Exec. United States Military Chaplains Assoc.; form. JWB, Ajex Exec.; Jewish Youth Fund; President, Univ. Coll. Jew. Soc.; form. H. Sec., I.U.J.F.; form. V. President, Torah V'avodah Org., Provincial Exec., JIA. Ad.: 25 Enford St., W1H 2DD. ☎ 020-7724 7778.

WEITZMAN, Peter David Jacob, M.A., M.Sc., D.Phil. (Oxon), D.Sc. (Bath), FIBiol, F.R.S.A., F.R.S.C.; b. London, Sept. 22, 1935; m. Avis née Galinski; Higher Education consultant; Emer. Prof. Univ. Wales; Dir. of Academic Affairs, Univ. Wales Inst., Cardiff (1988-93); Prof. of Biochemistry, Univ. Bath (1979-88); President, Penylan House Jewish Retirement Home, Cardiff (1991-99); Chairman, South Wales Jewish Representative Council (1997-). Publ.: Scientific writings. Ad.: 41 Hollybush Rd., Cardiff CF23 6SY. ☎ 01222-752277.

WEIZMAN, Ezer; b. Tel Aviv, 1924; President of Israel (1993-); Science and Technology Min., State of Israel, Defence Min. (1977-80); Transport Min. (1969-70); Served as fighter pilot in World War II and Israel War of Independence Commander of Israel Air Force 1958-66; Head of General Staff Branch/GHQ (1966-69). Publ.: On Eagles' Wings (autobiog.), The Battle for Peace. Ad.: Presidential Residence, Jerusalem. ☎ (02) 707211. Fax (02) 660445.

WESKER, Arnold, F.R.S.L., D.Litt (Hon. UEA), D.HL. (Denison Univ.), Hon. Fell. Queen Mary & Westfield Coll., London; b. London, May 24, 1932, m. Dusty Bicker; Co.P., Internat. Playwrights Cttee. (1980-83); Chairman, Brit. Section, Internat. Theatre Instit. (1978-83); Dir. Centre 42 (1960-70). Publ.: Chicken Soup with Barley (1959); I'm Talking about Jerusalem (1960); The Wesker Trilogy (1960); The Kitchen (1961); Chips with Everything (1962); The Four Seasons (1966); Their Very Own and Golden City (1966); The Friends (1970); Fears of Fragmentation (essays) (1971); Six Sundays in January (1971); The Old Ones (1972); The Journalists (1974) (in Dialog; repr. 1975); Love Letters on Blue Paper (stories) (1974), 2nd edn 1990; (with John Allin) Say Goodbye! You May Never See Them Again (1974); Words – as definitions of experience (1976); The Wedding Feast (1977); Journey into Journalism (1977); Said the Old Man to the Young Man (stories) (1978); The Merchant (1978); Fatlips (for young people) (1978); The Journalists, a triptych (with Journey into Journalism and A Diary of the Writing of The Journalists) (1979); Caritas (1981); Shylock (form. The Merchant) (1983); Distinctions (1985); Yardsale (1987); Whatever Happened to Betty Lemon (1987); Little Old Lady (1988); Shoeshine (1989); Collected Plays (vols. 1 and 5, 1989, vols. 2, 3, 4 and 6, 1990, vol. 7), As Much As I Dare (auto-biog.) (1994); Circles of Perception (1996); Denial (1997); Break, My Heart (1997); The Birth of Shylock and the Death of Zero Mostel (1997); The King's Daughters (1998); Letter to a Daughter (1998). Film scripts: Lady Othello (1980); Homage to Catalonia (1990). Television: (first play) Menace (1963); Breakfast (1981); (adapted) Thieves in the Night, by A. Koestler (1984); (adapted) Diary of Jane Somers, by Doris Lessing (1989); Maudie (1995). Radio: Yardsdale (1984); Bluey (Eur. Radio Commn.) (Cologne Radio, 1984, BBC Radio 3, 1985). Ad.: Hay-on-Wye, Hereford HR3 5RJ. Fax.: 01497-821 005.

WHITESON, Adrian Leon, O.B.E., M.B.B.S.(Hons.), M.R.C.S., L.R.C.P.; b. London, Dec. 12, 1934, m. Myrna; Med. Practitioner; President of the Brit. Paralympic Assoc., Chairman, World Boxing Council and European Boxing Union Med. Commission; Chief Med. Off., Brit. Boxing Board of Control; Chairman, The Teenage Cancer Tr.; Member, Govt. Review Body for Sport for People with Disabilities. Ad.: Pender Lodge, 6 Oakleigh Park North, Whetstone, London, N20 9AR. ☎ 020-7580 3637. Fax 020-7487 2504. 58a Wimpole St., W1M 7DE. ☎ 020-7935 3351.

WIEDER, Naphtali, Ph.D.; b. Sziget, Hungary, May 5, 1905; form. Reader in Jewish Studies, Univ. Coll., London; Lect. in Liturgy, Midrash and Talmud, Jews, Coll., Prof. in Talmud, Bar-llan Univ. Publ.: Islamic Influences on Jewish Worship, The Judean Scrolls and Karaism, etc. Ad.: 10 Harav Frank St., Jerusalem.

WIESEL, Elie, D.Lett. (h.c.), D.Hum.Lett. (h.c.), D.Hebrew.Lett. (h.c.), Ph.D. (h.c.), D.L. (h.c.); b. Sighet, Sept. 30, 1928; Survivor of Auschwitz and Buchenwald; Fd. Elie Wiesel Foundation for Humanity; Andrew W. Mellon Prof. in the Humanities, Boston Univ.; Dist. Prof., Judaic Studies, City Univ , N.Y. (1972-76); Chairman, US President's Com. on Holocaust (1979-80); Chairman, US Holocaust Memorial C. (1980-86); Bd. Dirs., Internat. Rescue Cttee., Grand-Officier, Legion of Honour; US Congress Gold Medal (1986); Presidential Medal of Freedom (1992); Nobel Peace Prize (1986); Internat. Peace Prize Royal Belgian Acad. Publ.: Night, Dawn, The Jews of Silence, etc.; Ani Maamin, a can-tata (music by D. Milhaud), Zalmen, or the Madness of God (produced by Habimah, Nouvelle Comedie, etc.), A Jew Today, Messengers of God, Souls on Fire, The Trial of God (play), The Testament (novel), Five Biblical Portraits, Somewhere a Master, Paroles d'Etranger, The Golem, The Fifth Son, Signes D'Exode, Against Silence (3 vols.), Twilight, L'oublié, From the Kingdom of Memory, Reminiscences, The Forgotten, Memoirs: All Rivers Run to the Sea; Vol.II: And the Sea is Never Full (1999), etc. Ad.: Boston University, 745 Commonwealth Ave., Boston, Mass., 02215. ☎ (617) 353 4566.

WIESENBERG, Rabbi Ernest, B.A. Ph.D.; b. Kosice, Czechoslovakia, Mar 11, 1909; Res. Unit, Taylor-Schechter Collection of tbe Cairo Genizah Cambridge; form. Actg. Rav., Lond Machzike Hadath; Reader, Hebrew Dept., Univ. Coll., Lond.; Rab. and M., Great Syn., Sheffield; M.-Preacher, Windsor Place Syn., Cardiff, Hammersmith and W. Kensington Syn. Publ.: Abraham, Maimonides/Æ Commentary on Genesis and Exodus, The Treatise Sanctification of the New Moon, in Moses Maimonides' Code, etc. Ad.: 30 Hillcrest Ave., NW11 0EN.

WIGODER, Baron of Cheetham (Life Peer) (Basil Thomas Wigoder), Q.C., M.A.; b. Manchester, Feb. 12, 1921; Barrister; Recorder, Crown Court. Ad.: House of

Lords, SW1A 0PW.

WINE, Judge Hubert, M.A., LL.B., T.C.D.; b. Dublin, April 3, 1922; Dublin district judge (since 1976), H. President, Jewish Rep. C. of Ireland; Cllr., H.L.P., Dublin Hebrew Cong.; H. President, C. of Ireland for Soviet Jewry; Patron, Criminal Lawyers, Assn., Gt. Brit. & Ireland; Patron, Jewish Adoption Soc., Great Britain & Ireland, H. L. P. Dublin Maccabi Assn., Patron, Irish Frs. of Hebrew Univ.; Patron Israel-Ireland Friendship League; Patron Irish Penal Reform Tr.; Tr. Irish Legal Research and Education Tr.; form. Irish Internat. Table Tennis player & Irish champion; form. Capt., Edmondstown Golf Club. Ad.: 19 Merrion Village, Merrion Rd., Dublin, 4. ☎ Dublin 269 5895.

WINER, Rabbi Dr Mark L., Ph.D, DD; b. Logan, Utah, Dec. 12, 1942; m. Suellen née Mark; Senior Rabbi West London Synagogue (1998-); President National C. of Synagogues (1995-98); V. President, Synagogue C. of America (1993-94); Mem., International Jewish Committee for Interreligious Consultations (1987-). Publ.: Papers for the American Jewish Committee, articles in Reform Judaism, etc. Ad.: West London Synagogue, 33 Seymour Place, London W1H 6AT. ☎ 020-7723 4404. Fax 020-7224 8258.

WINNICK, David, M.P.; b. Brighton, June, 1933; M.P. (Lab.), for Walsall North (1979-), Croydon South (1966-70). Ad.: House of Commons, SW1A 0AA.

WINSTON, Clive Noel, B.A. (Cantab.); b. Lond., April 20, 1925; V. President (form. Chairman) ULPS; form. Tr., European Bd. of WUPJ; form., Dep. Solicitor, Metropolitan Police. Ad.: 2 Bournwell Cl., Cockfosters, Herts. EN4 0JX. ☎ 020-8449 5963.

WINSTON, Baron of Hammersmith (Life Peer) (Robert Maurice Lipson), M.B., B.S., L.R.C.P., M.R.C.S., F.R.C.O.G.; b. London, July 15, 1940; Prof., Fertility Studies, Obstetrics & Gynaecology Instit., Lond. Univ.; Chairman Science & Technology Select Cttee, House of Lords (1999-); Dean, Institute of Obstetrics & Gynaecology (1995-); Consultant Obstetrician & Gynaecologist, Hammersmith Hospital, Lond., Prof. of Gynaecology, Texas Univ. (1980-81); Vis. Prof., Leuven Univ., Belgium (1976-77); Chief Rabbi's Open Award for Contribution to Society (1993). Publ.: Reversibility of Female Sterilization, Tubal Infertility, Infertility: a Sympathetic Approach; Scientific writings on aspects of reproduction. Ad.: 11 Denman Dr., London NW11. ☎ 020-8455 7475.

WINSTON-FOX, Mrs. Ruth (née Lipson), M.B.E., J.P., B.Sc.; b. London, Sept. 12, 1912; form. Mayor & Ald., Lond. Borough of Southgate; V. President, Internat C. of Jewish Women (1974-81); Chairman, Inter-Affilliate Travel Cttee. (1975-81); Chairman, Status of Women Cttee. (since 1984, 1970-78); Chairman, ICJW Cttee., Women in Judaism; form. President, League of Jewish Women; Member Exec. Cttee, Jewish Commonwealth C. (1980-); President, B'nai B'rith First Women's Lodge; Co-Chairman, Women's Nat. Com.; Member BoD (1960-); Member of Exec. BoD (since 1982); Chairman, Educ. Cttee. (1974-80); Fdr., H. Org., Jewish Way of Life Exhibition, sponsored by BoD in many parts of Brit. (1978-); V. President, Southgate Old People's Welfare Cttee., Fdr., Ruth Winston House, Southgate Old People's Centre, the first comprehensive day centre in Brit.; Chairman, Jewish Com. Exhibition Centre; P. Relate (Enfield Marriage Guidance C.) (1985-); Lond. Rent Assessment Panel (1976-83) Herts. Adoptions Consultant (1949-77) Ad.: 4 Morton Cres., London N14 7AH. ☎ 020-8886 5056.

WISTRICH, Robert Solomon, B.A., M.A. (Cantab, 1970), Ph.D. (London, 1974); b. Lenger (USSR), April 7, 1945; Univ Prof.; First Holder of the Jewish Chronicle Chair in Jewish Studies, University Coll., London; Neuberger Chair of Modern Jewish History, Hebrew University of Jerusalem (since 1985). Publ.: Revolutionary Jews from Marx to Trotsky (1976); Trotsky (1979); Socialism and the Jews (1982), Who's Who in Nazi Germany (1982), Hitler's Apocalypse (1985); The Jews of Vienna in the Age of Franz Joseph (1989); Between Redemption and Perdition (1990); Antisemitism: The Longest Hatred (1991); Weekend in Munich (1995); Co-maker, Understanding the Holocaust (film,

1997); Demonizing the Other: Antisemitism, Racism and Xenophobia (1999). Ad.: 63 Woodstock Road, NW11. ☎ 020-8455 6949.

WITTENBERG, Rabbi Jonathan, MA, PGCE; b. Glasgow, Sept. 17, 1957; m. Nicola née Solomon; Rabbi, New North London Masorti Synagogue (1987-); Coord., Multi-faith Chaplaincy of the North London Hospice (1996-); Publ.: The Three Pillars of Judaism: A Search for Faith and Values (1996); The Laws of Life: A Guide to Traditional Jewish Practice in Times of Bereavement (1997); A High Holiday Companion (ed. and co-auth., 1996); A Pesach Companion (ed. and co-auth., 1997). Ad.: 121 Dollis Park, London N3 1BT. ☎ 020-8343 3927. Fax 020-8346 1914. Email wittenberg@masorti.org.uk.

WOLFSON, Dianna (née Sherry), B.A., D.C.E; b. Birmingham, June 29, 1938; Head Teacher (retd.); Head Teacher, Calderwood Lodge Jewish Primary School (1976-98); President, Glasgow Jewish Representative Council (1998-); Chairman, West of Scotland Council of Christians and Jews (1992-95). Ad.: 22 Park Court, Giffnock, Glasgow G46 7PB. ☎/Fax 0141-620 0650.

WOLFSON, Baron of Marylebone in the City of Westminster (Life Peer) (Leonard Gordon Wolfson Kt. 1977), 2nd Bart 1991, Hon. Fel. St. Catherine's Coll. Oxford; Wolfson Coll., Cambridge, Wolfson Coll., Oxford; Worcester Coll.; U.C.L.; L.S.H.T.M., 1985; Queen Mary Coll., 1985; Poly. of Central London, 1991; Imperial CoD., 1985; Patron Royal College of Surgeons, 1976; Hon. F.R.C.P., 1977; Hon. F.R.C.S., 1988; Hon. F.B.A., 1986; Hon. D.C.L., Oxon, 1972; East Anglia, 1986; Hon. L.L.D., Strathclyde, 1972; Dundee, 1979; Cantab, 1982; London, 1982; Hon. D.S.C., Hull, 1977; Wales, 1984; D. Univ. Surrey, 1990; Hon. Dr. Medicine, Birmingham, 1992; Hon. P.H.D., Tel Aviv, 1971; Hebrew Univ., 1978; Weitzmann Inst., 1988, Hon. D.H.L.; Bar-Ilan Univ., 1983; Winston Churchill award British Technion Society 1989; b. London, Nov. 11, 1927; Chairman, since 1972 Wolfson Fodn; Chairman, Great Universal Stores (1981-96) (Man. Dir., 1962, Dir., 1952); Burberrys Ltd. (1978-96); Tr. Imperial War Museum (1988-94); Pr. of Jewish Welfare Bd., (1972-82). Ad.: 8 Queen Anne St., London W1M 9LD.

WOLFSON, Rev. M., b. Liverpool Feb. 22, 1908; Emer. M., Childwall Cong. Ad.: 9 Sinclair Drive, Liverpool, L18 0HN. ☎ 0151-722 5618.

WOOLF, The Lord, The Rt. Hon. Harry, P.C., LL.B., D.L.L. (Hon.), Buckingham 1992, Bristol 1992, Lond. 1993, Anglia 1994, Manchester Metropolitan 1995; b. Newcastle-upon-Tyne, May 2, 1933; Master of the Rolls (1996-); Lord of Appeal in Ordinary (1992-96); Lord Justice (1985-92); High Court Judge (1979-85); Presiding Judge S.E. Circuit (1981-85), Member, Senate Bench & Bar; Master of the Bench, Inner Temple; Pro-Chancellor, Univ. London (1994-); Tr. Jewish Chronicle Trust (1994-); Tr. Jewish Continuity (1994-); Fel. Univ. Coll., Lond.; First Counsel to Treasury (Common Law) (1974-79); Jnr. Counsel to Inland Revenue (1973-74), Recorder of the Crown Court (1972-9); Chairman, Bd. of Man., Instit. of Advanced Legal Studies (1987-94), H. President, Assn. of Law Teachers, (1985-89); Instit. of Jewish Affairs Legal Section; Int. Jewish Lawyers Assoc. (1993-); Anglo-Jewish Archives (1985-89), Tel Aviv Univ. Tr. (Legal Section) (1995); Chairman, Lord Chancellor's Adv. Cttee. on Legal Educ. (1987-90); President, UK Frs., Magen David Adam (since 1987); President, Central C. for Jewish Soc. Services, (since 1987); Gov. of the Oxford Centre for Hebrew & Jewish Studies (1989-93); Chairman, Bar & Bench Cttee., J.P.A. (1974-76); 15/19th Hussars (1954-56) Captain (1955). Publ.: Protecting the Public: the New Challenge (Hamlyn Lectures, 1989), Zamir and Woolf, Declaring Judgement, 2nd Ed. (1993). Appointed to Inquire into Prison Disturbances (1990), Civil Procedure of Access to Justice (1994); Judicial Review of Administrative Action, 5th ed. (1995, ed. jt. with De Smith). Ad.: Royal Courts of Justice, Strand, WC2A 2LL. ☎ 020-7936 6002.

WOOLFSON, Michael Mark, M.A., Ph.D., D.Sc. F.R.S., F.R.A.S., F.Inst P.; b.

London, Jan. 9, 1927; Emer. Prof., Theoretical Physics York Univ., form. Reader in Physics, Manchester Instit. of Sci. & Tech. Publ.: Direct Methods in Crystallography; An Introduction to X-Ray Crystallography; The Origin of the Solar System; Physical and Non-physical Methods of Solving Crystal Structures; An Introduction to Computer Simulation. Ad.: Physic Dept., Univ. York, York, YO10 5DD. ☎ 01904-432230.

WORMS, Fred Simon, O.B.E., F.C.A.; b. Frankfurt, Nov. 21, 1920; President, B'nai B'rith Hillel Foundation; Chairman, B'nai B'rith Foundation; Chairman, European Jewish Publication Society; Chairman, B'nai B'rith Housing Tr.; Hon. President, B'nai B'rith First Lodge of England; Hon. President, B'nai B'rith Gt. Britain & N.I.; Life President, Union of Jewish Students; President, formerly Chairman, Network of Jewish Housing Associations; President, B'nai B'rith JBG Housing Assoc.; Hon. President, formerly President, Maccabi World Union; Gov. Hebrew University; Council, Tel Aviv Museum; Chairman of Tr. B'nai B'rith World Centre; Council, IJPR; Founder Gov., Immanuel College; Tr., Jewish Care Pension Fund; Vice-President, British-Israel Chamber of Commerce; Bd. of Regents, International Cttee for Teaching of Jewish Civilisation; form. Dir. Bank Leumi (UK) PLC and Union Bank of Israel. Awards: B'nai B'rith Award for Communal Services; The Jerusalem Medal (builder of Jerusalem); The Samuel Rothberg Prize in Jewish Education (Hebrew University). Publ.: A Life in Three Cities (1996). Ad.: 23 Highpoint, North Hill, Highgate, N6 4BA. ☎ 020-8458 1181. Fax 020-8458 6045.

WOUK, Herman, B.A., Columbia U., 1934; L.H.D. (Hon.), Yeshiva Univ.; LL.D. (Hon.), Clark U.; D.Lit. (Hon.), American International College; Ph.D. (Hon.), Bart-Ilan Univ., Hebrew Univ.; DST (Hon.) Trinity College; b. New York, May 27, 1915; Writer. Publ.: Non-fiction: This is My God; Novels: Aurora Dawn, Marjorie Morningstar, The Winds of War, War and Remembrance, Youngblood Hawke, Don't Stop the Carnival, The Caine Mutiny, Inside, Outside, City Boy, The Hope (1993), The Glory (1994). Plays: The Caine Mutiny Court-Martial, etc. TV Screenplays: The Winds of War, War and Remembrance. Ad.: c/o B.S.W. Literary Agency, 3255 N. St. N.W., Washington, D.C., 20007, 2845.

WRIGHT, Rabbi Alexandra (née Levitt), B.A., P.G.C.E.; b. London, Dec. 10, 1956; m. Roderick Wright; Rabbi, Radlett and Bushey Reform Synagogue; Co-chair Assembly of Rabbis; Assoc. M. Liberal Jewish Synagogue (1986-89); Lecturer in Classical Hebrew Leo Baeck College (1987-97). Publ.: 'An approach to feminist theology' in Hear Our Voice (1994); 'Judaism' in Women in Religion (1994). Ad.: 90 The Ridgeway, London NW11 9RU. ☎ 020-8455 5305.

WURZBURGER, Rabbi Walter S.; b. Munich Mar. 29, 1920; m. Naomi née Rabinowitz; form. President, Syn. C. of Amer.; form President, Rab. C. of Amer. Rabbi, Emer. Cong. Shaaray Tefila, Lawrence N.Y., Adjunct Prof. of Philosophy Yeshiva Univ.; Edr., Tradition, (1962-87), Co-Edr., A Treasury of Tradition. Publ.: Ethics of responsibility (1994). Ad.: 138 Hards La., Lawrence, New York, N.Y. 11559, USA. ☎ 516-2397181. Fax 516-239 7413.

YAMEY, Basil Selig, C.B.E., B.Com., F.B.A.; b. Cape Town, May 4, 1919, m. Demetra Georgakopoulou; Emer. Prof., Lond. Univ.; form. Economics Prof., Lond. Sch. of Economics; Member, Monopolies and Mergers Com. (1966-78); Tr., National Gallery (1974-81); Tr., Tate Gallery (1978-81); Museums & Galleries Com (1983-85); Tr., Instit. of Econ. Aff (1986-91). Dir., Private Bank & Trust Co. Ltd. (1989-94). Publ.: Economics of Resale Price Maintenance, Economics of Underdeveloped Countries (part auth.), The Restrictive Practices Court (part auth.), Economics of Futures Trading (part auth.), Essays on the History of Accounting, Arte e Contabilità, Art & Accounting. Ad.: London Sch. of Economics, Houghton Street, London WC2A 2AE. ☎ 020-7405 7686.

YOUNG, Rt. Hon. Baron of Graffham (Life Peer) (David Ivor Young), P.C., LL.B. (Hons.); b. London, Feb. 27, 1932; Solicitor; Dep. Chairman, Conservative

Party (1989-90); President, Jewish Care (1990-); Chairman Oxford Centre for Hebrew and Jewish Studies (1989-92); Exec. Chairman, Cable & Wireless plc (1990-); Dir. Salomon Inc. (1990-); Sec. of State for Trade and Industry (1987-89); Sec. of State for Employment (1985-87), Min. without Portfolio, Min. in Cabinet (1984-85); Chairman, Manpower Services Com. (1982-84), Nat. Economic Development Org (1982-89); Chairman, Admin. Cttee., World ORT Union (1980-84), Gov., Oxford Centre for Post-Graduate Heb Studies; form. President, Brit. ORT; Dir., Centre for Policy Studies (1979-82), Chairman Internat. C., Jewish Soc. & Welfare Services (1982-83). Publ.: The Enterprise Years, A Businessman in the Cabinet (1990). Ad.: 88 Brook St., W1A 4NF.

YOUNG, Emanuel, A.R.C.M.; b. Brighton, Feb. 12, 1918; Conductor, Royal Ballet, Royal Opera House Lond. Guest Conductor, concerts, TV recordings, etc.; form. Cond., Royal Opera House, New Lond. Opera Company. Ad.: 16 Selborne Rd., N14 7DH. ☎ 020-8886 1144.

YUDKIN, Leon Israel, b. Northampton, Sept. 8, 1939; m. Meirah (Mickey) née Goss; University Lecturer, Hebrew Dept., UCL (1996-) and Author; Univ. Lect., University of Manchester (1966-96). Publ.: Isaac Lamdan: A Study in Twentieth-Century Hebrew Poetry (1971); Escape into Siege: A Survey of Israeli Literature Today (1974); Jewish Writing and Identity in the Twentieth Century (1982); 1984 and After: Aspects of Israeli Fiction (1984); On the Poetry of Uri Zvi Greenberg (in Hebrew, 1987); Else Lasker-Schueler: A Study in German Jewish Literature (1991); Beyond Sequence: Current Israeli Fiction and its Context (1992); A Home Within: Varieties of Jewish Expression in Modern Fiction (1996); Modern Jewish Writing: Public Crisis and Literary Response (2000); Ed. Modern Hebrew Literature in English Translation (1987); Agnon: Texts and Contexts in English Translation (1988); Hebrew Literature in the Wake of the Holocaust (1993); Israeli Writers Consider the 'Outsider' (1993); Co-edited (with Benjamin Tammuz) Meetings with the Angel: Seven Stories from Israel (1973); Ed. of the monograph series 'Jews in Modern Culture'. Ad.: 51 Hillside Court, 409 Finchley Rd., London NW3 6HQ. ☎ 020-7435 5777. Fax 020-7209 1026. Email l.yudkin@ucl.ac.uk

ZAHN, Rabbi Shamai; b. Nuremberg, Germany, July 6, 1920; Communal Rabbi Sunderland; Princ., Sunderland Talmudical Coll. Publ.: Sepher Beth Shammai (Talmudic Discourses) (Israel)); V'Gam Le-Shemona (Commentary on Rambam's Introduction to Pirkei Aboth). Ad.: 13 Ashgrove Terrace, Gateshead NE8 1RL. (/Fax 0191-490 1606.

ZALUD, Rabbi Norman, A.Ph.S., F.R.S.A.; b. Liverpool, Oct. 5, 1932; M., Liverpool Progressive Syn. Ad.: 265 Woolton Rd., L16 8NB. (0151-722 4389; 0151-733 5871.

ZEIGERMAN, Dror (H.E. Ambassador of Israel), BA, MA (Jerusalem), PhD (Washington); b. May 15, 1948; m. Asi née Sherf; Ambassador (1998-); Consul General, Toronto (1992-95); Gen. Man. Israel School of Tourism (1988-92); MK (1981-84); Hd Students Dept., Jewish Agency (1977-81). Ad.: Israel Embassy, 2 Palace Green, London W8 4QB. (020-7957 9500. Fax 020-7957 9555. Email isr-info@dircon.co.uk

ZELLICK, Graham John., M.A., Ph.D. (Cantab.), C.I Mgt, F.R.S.A., F.R.S.M., F.Inst.D., Hon. F.S.A.L.S., F.I.C.P.D.; b. London, Aug. 12, 1948; Barrister; Assoc. Memb. Chambers (Gray's Inn); Princ., Queen Mary & Westfield Coll., Univ. of London (1991-98); Vice-Chancellor Univ. London (1997-), Dep. V. Chancellor (1994-97); Prof of Law, Univ. of London (1991-98), Emer. Prof. (1998-); Sr. V.-Princ. and Act. Principal QMW (1990-91); Liveryman, Drapers' Co.; Freeman, City of London; Member C. and Chairman Education Cttee, West London Syn. (1990-93); Member, East London and the City Health A. (1995-97); Member, South Thames Reg. Health Authority (1994-95); form. Member C. St. Bartholomew's Hospital Medical College and Governor, The London Hospital

Medical College; Member of Council Cttee. of Vice-Chancellors & Principals (1993-97); Drapers' Prof. of Law (1988-91); Prof. of Public Law (1982-88); Dean of Laws Faculty (1984-88); Hd. of Law Dept., Queen Mary Coll , Lond., (1984-90); Dean of Laws Faculty, Lond. Univ. (1986-88); Member, Lord Chancellor's Adv. Cttee. on Legal Aid (1985-88), Chairman Cttee. of Heads of Univ. Law Schs. (1988-90); Member, Lord Chancellor's Advisory Cttee. on Legal Educ. (1988-90); J.P. (1981-85); Co-Chairman Legal Cttee., All Party Parl. War Crimes Group; Data Protection Tribunal, (1985-96); Academic Adv. Cttee., Jews, Coll. (to 1992); Chairman, Lawyers' Group, Tel Aviv Univ. Tr. (1984-89); Edr., Public Law, (1980-86), European Human Rights Reports (1978-82); Edr. Bd., Brit. Journal of Criminology (1980-90); Howard Journal of Criminal Justice (1984-87), Civil Law Lbr., Ct. of Govs. N. Lond. Poly. (1986-89), Central Lond. Poly. (1973-77); V. Chairman Nat. Adv. Council, Acad. St. Group for Israel & The Middle East. Publ.: (contrib.) Halsbury's Laws of England, 4th edn., etc. Ad.: Senate House, University of London, Malet St., London WC1E 7HU. (020-7862 8004. Fax 020-8862 8008.

ZERMANSKY, Victor David, LL.B. (Hon.); b. Leeds, Dec. 28, 1931, m. Anita née Levison; Solicitor; Past P. Leeds Law Soc. (1988-9), form. Asst. Recorder; H. L. V-P (President, 1974-77), Leeds Jewish Rep. C.; Life President, Leeds Z.C.; Exec., Leeds Kashrut Auth., Beth Din Admin. Cttee., Immigration Appeals Adjudicator (1970-78). Ad.: 52 Alwoodley Lane, Leeds, LS17 7PT. (/Fax 0113 2673523.

ZIPPERSTEIN, Steven J., B.A., M.A., Ph.D. (UCLA); b. Los Angeles, Dec. 11, 1950; m. Sally, née Goodis; Daniel E. Koshland Prof. in Jewish Culture and History, Stanford University; Dir. Programme in Jewish Studies; President, Conference on Jewish Social Studies; Ed. Jewish Social Studies; Prof. Stanford University (1991-); Assoc. Prof. UCLA (1987-91); Frank Green Fellow in Modern Jewish History, Oxford Centre for Postgraduate Hebrew Studies (1981-87); Research Fellow, Wolfson College, Oxford (1983-87). Publ.: Elusive Prophet: Ahad Ha'am and the Origins of Zionism (1993), awarded National Jewish Book Award; Assimilation and Community: The Jews in Nineteenth-Century Europe, jnt. ed. (1992); The Jews of Odessa: A Cultural History (1985), awarded Smilen Prize in Jewish History. Ad.: Dept. of History, Stanford University, 3775 El Centro Palo Alto, CA94306. Fax (650) 725-0597.

ZISSMAN, Sir Bernard Philip, Hon. LL.D. (B'ham), F.R.S.A.; b. Birmingham, Dec. 11, 1934; Chairman, Good Hope Hospital NHS Tr. (1998-); Dir. BRMB (1995-); C. Mem. Birmingham, Chamber of Commerce & Industry; Lord Mayor, City of Birmingham (1990-91); Freeman of the City of London (1991); Leader, Conservative Group, Birmingham City Council (1992-95); Hon. Alderman, City of Birmingham (1995); Tr. City of Birmingham Symphony Orchestra (1992-); Chairman, Representative Council of Birmingham & Midland Jewry (1992-); Chairman, Alexandra Theatre (Birmingham) Ltd (1986-93); Chairman, Cttee to establish Birmingham International Convention Centre/Symphony Hall (1982-86); Mem. Birmingham City Council (1965-95); Chairman, Millennium Point Partnership (1995-); Mem. Council Birmingham Hebrew Congregation (1980-). Ad.: 4 Petersham Place, Richmond Hill Rd., Birmingham B15 3RY. ☎/Fax 0121-454 1751.

Obituaries, November 1998–October 1999

Full obituary notices may be found in the pages of the *Jewish Chronicle*, *The Times* and the *Independent*, and selective journals in music and the arts.

Altman, Manfred, Communal Leader, 20 October 1911–July 1999
Altman, Phyllis, Activist, 1920–1999
Bart, Lionel (né Begleiter), Composer, 1 August 1930–3 April 1999
Baum, John David, Pediatrician, 23 July 1940–5 September 1999
Bellow, Corinne, Arts Administrator, 1 December 1927–3 May 1999
Beloff, Lord, Professor of Politics, 1914–March 1999
Benjamin, Elizabeth, Architect, 7 December 1908–29 March 1999
Bernelle, Agnes (née Bernauer), Actress, 7 March 1923–15 February 1999
Blacker, Harry, Cartoonist and Illustrator, 1 October 1910–27 June 1999
Blech, Harry, Conductor, 2 March 1910–9 May 1999
Bloch, Lionel Herbert, Lawyer, 7 September 1928–5 November 1998
Bor, Walter George (né Bukbinder), Architect, 14 October 1916–4 October 1999
Boyars, Marion (née Asmin), Publisher, 26 October 1927–31 January 1999
Brilliant, Fredda, Sculptress, 7 April 1903–25 May 1999
Bubis, Ignatz, Communal Leader, 12 January 1927–13 August 1999
Burg, Rabbi Yosef, Politician, 31 January 1909–15 October 1999
Burke, Allan, Communal Leader, 7 December 1914–19 October 1999
Cashdan, Rabbi Eli, Scholar, 1 June 1905–14 November 1999
Cohen, Professor Percy, Sociologist, 6 August 1928–15 September 1999
Daube, Professor David, Scholar, 8 February 1909–24 February 1999
Debré, Olivier, Painter, 14 April 1920–1 June 1999
Dimson, Gladys, CBE, Councillor, 23 July 1915–13 March 1999
Englander, David, Historian, 3 June 1949–7 April 1999
Firman, Bert (né Herbert Feuermann), Bandleader, 3 February 1906–April 1999
Gillinson-Shine, Regina Rebecca, Cellist, 30 April 1908–7 April 1999
Godowsky, Frances (née Gershwin), Painter and Singer, 26 December 1906–18 January 1999
Grunfeld, Henry, Merchant Banker, 1 June 1904–10 June 1999
Harris, Stella, Communal Leader, 26 August 1922–26 December 1998
Hartog, Geoffrey, Linguist, 17 January 1916–23 January 1999
Henig, Monty, Communal Leader, 23 March 1915–25 May 1999
Hirshon, Baruch, Activist, 19 December 1921–3 October 1999
Hooker, Rabbi Bernard, 4 February 1922–1 March 1999
Hyman, Joe, Textile Magnate, 14 October 1921–6 July 1999
Indech, Rabbi Jonah, 25 December 1908–22 January 1999
Jakobovits, Baron of Regents Park, Rabbi Sir Immanuel, 8 February 1921–29 October 1999
Jesner, Isaac, Philanthropist, December 1908–4 September 1999
Joel, Sir Asher, Politician, 4 May 1912–9 November 1998
Jouffa, Yves, Lawyer, 28 January 1920–13 January 1999
Kagan, Elie, Photographer, 1928–24 January 1999
Kapp, Yvonne (née Mayer), Biographer, 17 April 1903–22 June 1999
Kaufman, Solomon, Art Historian, Lawyer, 18 May 1908–25 December 1998
Kaye, Sir Emmanuel, CBE, Industrialist, 29 November 1914–28 February 1999
Kleitman, Nathaniel, Scientist, 26 April 1895–13 August 1999
Koenigsberger, Otto Heinrich, Architect, 13 October 1908–3 January 1999
Lawrence, Ruth (née Langer), Sportswoman, 21 May 1921–2 May 1999
Leipman, Flora, Artist, 5 April 1918–24 April 1999

Levi, Jonathan, Physician, 27 July 1933–4 January 1999
Levin, Hanoch, Playwright, 1942–18 August 1999
Levin, Salmond S., Communal Leader, 17 June 1905–25 February 1999
Liebermann, Rolf, Composer, 14 September 1910–2 January 1999
Lipson, Joan, Trades Unionist, 9 December 1916–19 October 1999
Lopian, Rabbi Chaim, 1908–29 November 1998
Lustig, Joseph George, Producer, 21 October 1925–29 May 1999
Malaquais, Jean (né Wladimir Malacki), Writer, 1908–22 December 1998
Menuhin, Lord Yehudi, OM, Musician, 22 April 1916–March 1999
Mosse, George Lachmann, Historian, 18 September 1918–22 January 1999
Nador, George, Bookseller, 23 April 1920–24 January 1999
Peake, Devora Yaffa (née Lubarsky), Fruit Farmer, 28 May 1915–24 March 1999
Phillips, Al, Boxer, 25 January 1920–7 February 1999
Pliatzky, Sir Leo, Civil Servant, 22 August 1919–4 May 1999
Pontecorvo, Guido, Geneticist, 29 November 1907–24 September 1999
Pordes, Henry, Publisher, 19 February 1925–14 November 1998
Rafael, Gideon, Diplomat, 5 March 1913–10 February 1999
Rafael, Yitzhak, Politician, 1914–3 August 1999
Raphael, Adam, Journalist, 11 November 1937–4 May 1999
Razgon, Lev Emmanuilovich, Writer, 1 April 1908–7 September 1999
Rose, Eliot Joseph Ben ('Jim'), Publisher, 7 June 1909–20 May 1999
Rubner, Ben, Trades Union Secretary, 1922–1998
Sallon, Ralph, Cartoonist, December 1899–29 October 1999
Schottlander, Bernard Moritz, Sculptor, 18 September 1924–28 September 1999
Ségal, Marcelle, Journalist, 15 May 1896–28 December 1998
Shilling, Gertrude Ethel T. (née Silberston), Milliner, 3 March 1910–13 October 1999
Singer, Elinor, Doctor, 12 No vember 1903–10 September 1999
Sneh, Simha, Novelist, 15 October 1908–4 April 1999
Steinberg, Saul, Cartoonist, 15 June 1914–12 May 1999
Tinter, Georg, Conductor, 22 May 1917–2 October 1999
Travis, Morris, 29 May 1898–27 June 1999
Vaughan, Frankie (né Abelson), Entertainer, 3 February 1928–17 September 1999
Vergelis, Aron, Poet, 1918–7 April 1999
Wigoder, Geoffrey, Encyclopaedist, 3 August 1922–9 April 1999
Wolf, Ilse, Singer, 7 June 1921–6 September 1999
Wolf, Sir John, Film Producer, 15 March 1913–28 June 1999

Events of 1999

Anniversaries
250th Beth Holim Hospital
160th Cheltenham Synagogue
125th Princes Road Synagogue, Liverpool
125th Middle Street Synagogue, Brighton
125th Leicester Hebrew Congregation
125th Manchester Sephardi community
120th Garnethill Synagogue
Centenary of the AJY
Centenary of *Die Fackel*, edited by Karl Kraus
Centenary of the Fieldgate Street Great Synagogue
Centenary of the Zionist Federation
90th Tel Aviv
80th Jewish Memorial Council
70th Habonim
70th Wilson Road Synagogue, Sheffield
60th Belsize Square Synagogue
60th Warburg Institute in London
50th Hendon Reform Synagogue
50th Mill Hill Synagogue
50th Weidenfeld & Nicolson

January
Opening of the Jewish Museum in Berlin
Opening of Peres Centre for Peace
Shimon Peres delivered the L'Chaim Society Lecture

February
Death of King Hussein
War Crimes (Sowaniuk) trial
Mass demonstration at the Supreme Court in Jerusalem
Death of Kurds at Israel consulate in Berlin
LSJS Degree ceremony held at the Senate House, University of London

March
Fast for Agunot held on International Women's Day
Maimonides Foundation delegation met Yasir Arafat in London
Dispute between JNF and KKL

April
Wallenberg Memorial unveiled in Budapest
Design for Manchester Holocaust Museum approved
Jewish Emergency Aid Committee for Kosova

May
General Elections in Israel
Official naming of James Parkes Building at the University of Southampton
Discovery of the wreck of the Dakar

June
Deconsecration of Adelaide Road Synagogue
Anne Frank Declaration on Racism signed in London
Interfaith football coaching course launched at the Arsenal
Sale of US manuscripts and books at Christie's
Performances of *Perdition* in London

July
Rededication of Exeter Synagogue
Problems at the Hasmonean School
Service at Ramsgate Synagogue
Prime Minister Barak's visit to Washington and London

August
Fighting in Southern Lebanon
Holocaust Centre opened in Cape Town
International Open Day of Jewish Heritage sites in Europe
Death of Mimi Pollack

September
Blue plaque for novelist Italo Svevo unveiled in Charlton, London SE1
Service at Ohel Rachel Synagogue, Shanghai
Machal Volunteers honoured at Israel Embassy

October
Desecration of Berlin cemetery
Reopening of Amia Centre in Buenos Aires
Peter Sheldon elected President of the United Synagogue
Death of Lord Jakobovits

November
Taking Testimonies Forward: conference on the holocaust at the National Sound
    Archive
The Jewish Dickens: Israel Zangwill and the Wanderers of Kilburn, exhibition at
    the Jewish Museum
Jewish Stage and Film Designers Exhibition at the Ben Uri

December
Sale of US silver at Sotheby's

Publications and Booksellers

The following is a list of notable British and Irish publications of 1998–99 with paperback reprints, available from Jewish and general bookshops.

Antisemitism

Cornwall, J.: Hitler's Pope: the secret history of Pius XII, Viking, 1999.
Le Carré, J.: Nervous times, Anglo-Israel Association, 1999.

Biography and Autobiography

Alvarez, A.: Where did it all go right?, Robert Cohen Books, 1999.
Belton, N.: The good listener: Helen Bamber: a life against cruelty, Weidenfeld & Nicolson, 1999.
Bernstein, R.J.: Freud and the legacy of Moses, Cambridge University Press, 1998.
Berger, D.: The Jewish Victorian: genealogical information from the Jewish newspapers, 1871–1880, Robert Boyd Publications, 1999.
Brivati, B.: Lord Goodman, Richard Cohen Books, 1999.
Broido, V.: Daughter of revolution, Constable, 1999.
Browse, L.: Duchess of Cork Street, Giles De La Mare, 1999.
Crown, A., ed.: Noblesse oblige: essays in honour of David Kessler, OBE, Vallentine Mitchell, 1998.
Ferguson, N.: The world's banker: the history of the House of Rothschild, Weidenfeld & Nicolson, 1999.
Fremont, H.: After long silence: a woman's search for her family's secret, Piatkus, 1999.
Frister, R.: The cap, or the pace of a life, Weidenfeld & Nicolson, 1999.
Gitter, B.: The story of my life, Weidenfeld & Nicolson, 1999.
Glanville, B.: Football memories, Virgin, 1999.
Grade, M.: It seemed like a good idea at the time, Macmillan, 1999.
Horstmann, L.: Nothing for tears, Weidenfeld & Nicolson, 1999.
Janner, G.: One hand alone cannot clap, Robson, 1998.
Lichtenstein, R., and Sinclair, I.: Rodinsky's room, Granta, 1999.
Lipman, M.: Lip ready, Robson Books, 1999.
Louvish, S.: Monkey business: the lives of the Marx Brothers, Faber, 1999.
Nadler, S.: Spinoza: a life, Cambridge University Press, 1999.
Raphael, F.: Eyes wide open, Orion, 1999.
Robbins, C.: The test of courage: Michael Thomas, Century, 1999.
Richmond, C., and Smith, P., eds.: The self-fashioning of Disraeli, 1818–1851, Cambridge University Press, 1999.
Rosen, H.: Are you still circumcised? East End memories, Five Leaves Publications, 1999.
Rothschild, M.: Isaiah Berlin, 1998.
Rudolph, A.: The arithmetic of memory, Bellew, 1999.
Smith, P.: Disraeli: a brief life, Cambridge University Press, 1999.
Wheen, F.: Karl Marx, Fourth Estate, 1999.
Williams, B.: Sir Sidney Hamburger and Manchester Jewry: religion, city and community, Vallentine Mitchell, 1999.

Current Affairs

Harris, K., ed.: New voices in Jewish thought – Vol. II, Limmud Publications, 1999.
Kosmin, B., Goldberg, J., Shain, M., and Bruk, S.: Jews of the 'new South

Africa': highlights of the 1998 national survey of South African Jews, IJPR, 1999.
Kushner, T., and Knox, K.: Refugees in an age of genocide, Frank Cass, 1999.

Arts

Arikha, A.: Drawings, Scottish National Gallery of Modern Art, 1999.
Brunstein, S.: The vanished shtetl: paintings, Five Leaves Press, 1999.
Freud Museum: 20 Maresfield Gardens: a guide to the Freud Museum, Serpent's Tail, 1998.
Levy, J.: The Jews: assumptions of identity, Cassell, 1999.
Salys, R.: Leonid Pasternak: the Russian years, 1875–1921: a critical study and catalogue, OUP, 1999.

Bible and Hebrew Studies

Boitani, P.: The Bible and its rewritings, Oxford University Press, 1999.
Douglas, M.: Leviticus as literature, Oxford University Press, 1999.
Feather, R.: The copper scroll decoded, HarperCollins, 1999.
Horbury, W., ed.: Hebrew study from Ezra to Ben Yehuda, T & T Clark, 1999.
Isserlin, B.S.J.: The Israelites, British Museum, 1999.
Miller, J.M., and Hayes, J.H.: A history of ancient Israel and Judah, SCM Press, 1999.
Soggin, J.A.: An introductions to the history of Israel and Judah – 3rd ed., SCM Press, 1999.
Tubb, J.N.: The Canaanites, British Museum, 1999.
Vermes, G.: An introduction to the complete Dead Sea Scrolls, SCM Press, 1999.

History

Aberbach, D., and Aberbach, M.: Roman–Jewish wars and Hebrew cultural nationalism, 66–2000 C.E., Macmillan, 1999.
Alderman, G.: The Jews of England, Oxford University Press, 1998.
Andrews, R.: Blood on the mountain: a history of the Temple Mount, Weidenfeld & Nicolson, 1999.
Beckman, M.: The Jewish brigade, Spellmount, 1999.
Blom, J.C.H., Fuks-Mansfield, G., Schöffer, I.: History of the Jews in the Netherlands, Littman Library, 1999.
Burns, M.: France and the Dreyfus Affair: a documentary history, Macmillan, 1999.
Edmonton Hundred Jewish Research Group: Heritage, No. 5, 1999.
Finestein, I.: Anglo-Jewry in changing times: studies in diversity, 1840–1914, Vallentine Mitchell, 1999.
Grierson, R., and Hay, S.M.: The Ark of the Covenant, Weidenfeld & Nicolson, 1999.
Gubbay, L.: Sunlight and shadow: the Jewish experience of Islam, Sephardi Centre, 1999.
Johnson, M.P.: The Dreyfus Affair, Macmillan, 1999.
Kushner, T., and Valman, N., eds: Remembering Cable Street: fascism and anti-fascism in British society, Vallentine Mitchell, 1999.
Lecker, M.: Jews and Arabs in pre- and early-Islamic Arabia, Ashgate, 1998.
Langermann, Y.Tz.: Jews and the sciences in the middle ages, Ashgate, 1999.
Reif, S.C.: A Jewish archive from old Cairo, Woburn, 1999.
Robertson, R.: The German–Jewish dialogue, Clarendon Press, 1999.
Rozin, M.: The rich and the poor: Jewish philanthropy and social control in

nineteenth century London, Sussex Academic Press, 1999.
Rubinstein, W.D.R., and Rubinstein, H.L.: Philosemitism: admiration and support in the English-speaking world for Jews, 1840–1939, Macmillan, 1999.
Shavit, Y.: Athens in Jerusalem: classical antiquity and hellenism in the making of the modern secular Jew, Littman Library, 1999.
Shulewitz, M.H.: The forgotten millions: the modern Jewish exodus from Arab lands, Cassell, 1999.
Simmons, G., Pearce, K., Fry, H., eds: The lost Jews of Cornwall: from Roman times to the 19th century, Redcliffe Press, 1999.
Sorkin, D.: The Berlin Haskalah and the European enlightenment, Vallentine Mitchell, 1999.
Torode, B.: The Hebrew community of Cheltenham, Gloucester and Stroud, 1999.
Vital, D.: A people apart: the Jews in Europe, 1789–1939, Oxford University Press, 1999.

Holocaust

Abzug, R.H.: America and the holocaust: a brief documentary history, Macmillan, 1999.
Aly, G.: 'Final solution': Nazi population policy and the murder of the European Jews, Arnold, 1999.
Anderson, M.M.: Hitler's exiles: personal stories of the flight from Hitler's Germany to America, I.B. Tauris, 1999.
Bennett, R.: Under the shadow of the swastika: the moral dilemmas of resistance and collaboration in Hitler's Europe, Macmillan, 1999.
Breitman, R.: Official secrets: what the Nazis planned, what the British and Americans knew, Penguin Books, 1999.
Bretholz, L., and Olesker, M.: Leap into darkness: seven years on the run in wartime Europe, Constable, 1999.
Cole, T.: Images of the holocaust: the myth of the 'Shoah business', Duckworth, 1999.
Dean, M.: Collaboration in the holocaust: crimes of the local police in Belorussia and Ukraine, Macmillan, 1999.
Durlacher, G.L.: The search: the Birkenau boys, Serpent's Tail, 1998.
Favez, J.-C.: The Red Cross and the holocaust, Cambridge University Press, 1999.
Hillesum, E.: An interrupted life: the diaries and letters, 1941–1943, Persephone Books, 1999.
Kirby, J.: My mother's diamonds: in search of Holocaust assets, Allen & Unwin, 1999.
Klemperer, V.: To the bitter end: diaries, Vol. II: 1942–1945, Weidenfeld & Nicolson, 1999.
Lee, C.A.: Roses from the earth: the biography of Anne Frank, Viking, 1999.
Muller, M.: Anne Frank: the biography, Bloomsbury, 1999.
Neville, P.: The holocaust, Cambridge University Press, 1999.
Orstein, E.M.: From Anschluss to Albion: memoirs of a refugee girl, 1939–1940, Lutterworth Press, 1998.
Saltzman, L.: Anselm Kiefer and art after Auschwitz, Cambridge University Press, 1999.
Smith, M.: Foley: the man who saved 10,000 lives, Hodder & Stoughton, 1998.
Sompolinsky, M.: The British government and the holocaust: the failure of Anglo-Jewish leadership?, Sussex Academic Press, 1999.

320   PUBLICATIONS

Spielberg, S.: The last days: Steven Speilberg and survivors of the Shoah, Visual History Foundation, Weidenfeld & Nicolson, 1999.
Szpilman, W.: The pianist: surviving the horrors of Warsaw, 1939–45, Gollancz, 1999.

Israel

Goldmann, R., Förg, N., and Kraus, T.: Israel: land of contrasts, I.B. Tauris, 1999.
Goldstein, Y.N.: From fighters to soldiers: how the Israeli defense forces began, Sussex Academic Press, 1999.
Karpin, M., and Friedman, I.: Murder in the name of God: the plot to kill Yitzhak Rabin, Granta, 1999.
Karsh, E.: Fabricating Israeli history: 'the new historians', 2nd ed, Frank Cass, 1999.
Karsh, E.: Israel's transition from community to state, Frank Cass, 1999.
Kumaraswamy, P.R., ed.: Revisiting the Yom Kippur War, Frank Cass, 1999.
Levi-Faur, D., et al.: Israel: the dynamics of change and continuity, Frank Cass, 1999.
Parfitt, T., ed.: The Beta Israel in Ethiopia and Israel: studies in the Ethiopian Jews, Curzon, 1999.
Sofer, S.: Peacemaking in Israel after Rabin, Frank Cass, 1999.
Schwarz, T.: Ethiopian immigrants in Israel, Curzon, 1999.
Summerfield, D.: From Falashas to Ethiopian Jews, Curzon, 1999.
Urian, D., and Karsh, E.: In search of identity: Jewish aspects in Israeli culture, Frank Cass, 1999.

Middle East

Beilin, Y.: Touching peace: from the Oslo Accord to a final agreement, Weidenfeld & Nicolson, 1999.
Gresch, A., and Vital, D.: The new A–Z of the Middle East, I.B. Tauris, 1999.
Hass, A.: Drinking the sea at Gaza: days and nights in a land under seige, Hamish Hamilton, 1999.
Hughes, M.: Allenby and British policy in the Middle East, 1917–1919, Frank Cass, 1999.
Huneidi, S.: A broken trust: Herbert Samuel, Zionism and the Palestinians, I.B. Tauris, 1999.
Papp, I., ed.: The Israel/Palestine question, Routledge, 1999.
Schulze, K.: The Arab–Israeli conflict, Longman, 1999.
Shepherd, N.: Ploughing sand: the British role in Palestine, 1917–1948, John Murray, 1999.

Zionism

Cohen, M., ed.: Habonim in Britain, 1929–1955, Vatikei Habonim, 1999.
Jabotinsky, V.: The political and social philosophy of Ze'ev Jabotinsky, Vallentine Mitchell, 1998.

Judaism

Boteach, Sh.: The intelligent person's guide to Judaism, Duckworth, 1999.
Cohen, J.M.: Issues of the day: a modern orthodox view, Gnesia, 1999.
Goodman, L.E.: Jewish and Islamic philosophy: crosspollinations in the classical age, Edinburgh University Press, 1999.
Jacobs, L.: Beyond reasonable doubt: a sequel to 'We have reason to believe',

Littman Library, 1999.
Kellner, M.: Must a Jew believe anything, Littman Library, 1999.
Maccoby, H.: Ritual and morality: the ritual purity system in Judaism, Cambridge, 1999.
Roth, L.: Is there a Jewish philosophy? Rethinking fundamentals, Littman Library, 1999.
Shapiro, M.B.: Between the Yeshiva world and modern orthodoxy, Littman Library, 1999.

Language and Literature

Abramson, G.: Drama and ideology in modern Israel, Cambridge, 1999.
Alphen, E. van: Caught by history: holocaust effects in contemporary art, literature and theory, Cambridge, 1999.
Barbash, B.: My first sony, Headline, 1999.
Baron, A.: The human kind, Robert Hale, 1999.
Berg, L.: The God stories, Frances Lincoln, 1999.
Berlin, I.: The first and the last, Granta, 1999.
Darke, D.M.: The leaves have lost their trees, The Refugee Council, 1999.
Estraikh, G.: Soviet Yiddish: language-planning and linguistic development, Clarendon Press, 1999.
Fredriksson, M.: Simon and the oaksman, Orion, 1999.
Friedman, P.: No higher game, Headline, 1999.
Friedman, R.: The writing game, Empiricus, 1999.
Gilbert, P.: Laughter in a dark wood, Dewi Lewis, 1999.
Horn, S.: Four mothers, Piatkus, 1999.
Jacobson, H.: The mighty walzer, Jonathan Cape, 1999.
Kerler, D.-B.: The origins of modern literary Yiddish, Clarendon Press, 1999.
McKane, R., ed.: Poet to poet, Hearing Eye, 1999.
Malouf, A.: Ports of call, Collins Harvill, 1999.
Mamet, D.: The old religion, Faber, 1999.
Manguel, A.: Into the looking glass wood, Bloomsbury, 1999.
Michaels, A.: Skin divers, Bloomsbury Publishing, 1999.
Oz, A.: The story begins: essays on literature, Chatto & Windus, 1999.
Paley, G.: The collected stories, Virago, 1999.
Paley, G.: Just as I thought, Virago, 1999.
Patterson, D.: The Hebrew novel in Czarist Russia: a portrait of Jewish life in the 19th century, Rowman & Littlefield, 1999.
Peters, G.: The poet as provocateur: Heinrich Heine and his critics, Boydell & Brewer, 1999.
Rabinyan, D.: Persian brides, Canongate, 1999.
Robertson, R.: The 'Jewish question' in German literature, 1749–1939: emancipation and its discontents, Clarendon, 1999.
Schnitzler, A.: Dream story, Penguin, 1999.
Sherman, M.: Rose, Methuen, 1999.
Singer, I.B.: Shadows on the Hudson, Penguin Books, 1999.
Silkin, J.: Testament without breath, Cargo Press, 1999.
Stavans, I., ed.: The Oxford book of Jewish stories, Oxford University Press, 1999.
Wandor, M.: Gardens of Eden revisited, Five Leaves Press, 1999.
Yehoshua, A.B.: A journey to the end of the millennium, Peter Halban, 1999.
Zangwill, I.: Children of the ghetto, Wayne State University Press, 1998.

Booksellers

The booksellers listed below specialise in Jewish books. Many also supply religious requisites.

GREATER LONDON

J. Aisenthal, 11 Ashbourne Pde., Finchley Rd., NW11. ☎ 0208-455 0501. Fax 0208-455 0501.

Blue & White Shop, 439 Cranbrook Road, Ilford, Essex, IG2 6EW. ☎ 0208-518 1982.

Carmel Gifts, 62 Edgware Way, Middx. ☎ 0208-958 7632. Fax: 0208-958 6226.

Aubrey Goldstein, 7 Windsor Court, Chase Side, N14 5HT. ☎ 0208-886 4075.

R. Golub & Co. Ltd., 305 Eastern Av., Gants Hill, Ilford, Essex IG2 6NT. ☎ 0208-550 6751.

Hebrew Book & Gift Centre, 24 Amhurst Parade, N16 5AA. ☎/Fax 0208-802 0609 (eve. 0208-802 4567).

B. Horwitz–Judaica World, Unit 23, Dollis Hill Estate, 105 Brook Rd., NW2 7BZ. ☎ 07970-018692. Fax 0161-740 5897.

Jerusalem the Golden, 146a Golders Green Rd., NW11 8HE. ☎ 0208-455 4960 or 458 7011. Fax: 0208-203 7808.

Jewish Books & Gifts (Sandra E. Breger), 1 Rosecroft Walk, Pinner, Middlesex HA5 1LJ. ☎ 0208-866 6236.

Jewish Memorial Council Bookshop, 25 Enford St., W1H 2DD. ☎ 0207-724 7778. Fax: 0207-706 1710. Email: jmcbookshop@btinternet.com (Mail order available).

John Trotter Books, 80 East End Rd., N3 2SY. ☎ 0208-349 9484. Fax: 0208-346 7430. Email MHB@jt96.demon.co.uk; www.bibliophile.net/John-Trotter-books.htm

Joseph's Bookstore, 1255-1257 Finchley Rd., NW11 0AD. ☎/Fax 0208-731 7575; Fax 0208-731 6699.

H. Karnac (Books) Limited, 58 Gloucester Road, SW7 4QY.

Kuperard, 311 Ballards Lane, N12 8LY. ☎ 0208-446 2440. Fax 0208-446 2441. Email kuperard@bravo.clara.net. Website www.kuperard.co.uk (publishers and distributors, mail order, educational suppliers, book fairs, book launches).

Manor House Bookshop, see John Trotter above.

Menorah Book Centre, 16 Russell Parade, Golders Green Rd., NW11 9NN. ☎ 0208-458 8289.

Mesorah Bookstore, 61 Old Hill St., N16 6LU. ☎ 0208-809 4310.

Muswell Hill Bookshop, 72 Fortis Green Rd., N10 3HN. ☎ 0208-444 7588.

George & Vera Nador, 63 Cranbourne Rd., Northwood, Middx., HA6 1JZ. ☎ 01923 821152. Hebraica, Judaica, maps. By appointment only.

M. Rogosnitzky, 20 The Drive, NW11 9SR. ☎ 0208-455 7645 or 4112.

Selfridges Departmental Store, Jewish Section of Book Dept., Oxford St., W1A 1AB. ☎ 0207-629 1234.

Stamford Hill Stationers, 153 Clapton Common, E5 9AE. ☎ 0208-802 5222. Fax 0208-802 5224.

Swiss Cottage Books, 4 Canfield Gdns., NW6 3BS. ☎ 0207-625 4632. Fax: 0207-624 9084.

Torah Treasures, 4 Sentinel Sq., NW4 2EL. ☎ 0208-202 3134. Fax 0208-202 3161.

WH Smith, Brent Cross Shopping Centre, NW4. ☎ 0208-202 4226.

Waterstone's, 68 Hampstead High St., NW3 1QP. ☎ 0207-794 1098.

Waterstone's, 82 Gower St., WC1E 6EG. ☎ 0207-636 1577.

The Woburn Book Shop, 10 Woburn Walk, WC1H 0JL (near The Place Theatre), ☎ 0207-388 7278.

REGIONS

BIRMINGHAM Lubavitch Bookshop, 95 Willows Rd., B12 9QF. ☎ 0121-440 6673. Fax: 0121-446 4199.

GATESHEAD J. Lehmann (mail order and wholesale), 20 Cambridge Ter., NE8 1RP. ☎ 0191-490 1692. Fax: 0191-477 5955.

GLASGOW J. & E. Levingstone, 47 & 55 Sinclair Dr., G42 9PT. ☎ 0141-649 2962.

LEICESTER Bookshop: Com. Centre, Highfield St. LE2 0NQ. Inq.: J. Markham, 74 Wakerley Rd., LE5 6AQ. ☎ 0116 273762.

LIVERPOOL Book & Gift Centre, Jewish Youth & Community Centre, Dunbabin Rd., L15 6XL. Sun. only, 11 a.m. to 1 p.m.

MANCHESTER & SALFORD

J. Goldberg, 11 Parkside Ave., Salford, M7 0HB. ☎ 0161-740 0732.
Hasefer, 18 Merrybower Rd., Salford M7 0HE. ☎ 0161-740 3013.
B. Horwitz (Wholesale & retail Judaica), 20 King Edward Bldgs., Bury Old Rd., M8. ☎ 0161-740 5897, & 2 Kings Rd., Prestwich. ☎ 0161-773 4956.
Jewish Book Centre (Mr Klein), 25 Ashbourne Gr., Salford, M7 4DB. ☎ 0161-792 1253.

OXFORD B. H. Blackwell Ltd., 48-51 Broad St., OX1 3BQ. ☎ 01865 792792. Fax 01865 261 355. Email blackwells.extra@blackwell.co.uk. Has a Jewish book section.

SOUTHEND Dorothy Young, 21 Colchester Rd., SS2 6HW. ☎ 01702 331218 for appointment.

PRINCIPAL FESTIVALS AND FASTS 1999–2007 (5760–5767)

Festival or Fast	Hebrew Date	5760 1999-2000	5761 2000-01	5762 2001-02	5763 2002-03	5764 2003-04	5765 2004-05	5766 2005-06	5767 2006-07
New Year	Tishri 1	Sept. 11	Sept. 30	Sept. 18	Sept. 7	Sept. 27	Sept. 16	Oct. 4	Sept. 23
Day of Atonement	Tishri 10	Sept. 20	Oct. 9	Sept. 27	Sept. 16	Oct. 6	Sept. 25	Oct. 13	Oct. 2
Tabernacles, 1st Day	Tishri 15	Sept. 25	Oct. 14	Oct. 2	Sept. 21	Oct. 11	Sept. 30	Oct. 18	Oct. 7
Tabernacles, 8th Day	Tishri 22	Oct. 2	Oct. 21	Oct. 9	Sept. 28	Oct. 18	Oct. 7	Oct. 25	Oct. 14
Rejoicing of the Law	Tishri 23	Oct. 3	Oct. 22	Oct. 10	Sept. 29	Oct. 19	Oct. 8	Oct. 26	Oct. 15
Chanucah	Kislev 25	Dec. 4	Dec. 22	Dec. 10	Nov. 30	Dec. 20	Dec. 8	Dec. 26	Dec. 16
Purim	Adar[1] 14	Mar. 21	Mar. 9	Feb. 26	Mar. 18	Mar. 7	Mar. 25	Mar. 14	Mar. 4
Passover, 1st Day	Nisan 15	Apr. 20	Apr. 8	Mar. 28	Apr. 17	Apr. 6	Apr. 24	Apr. 13	Apr. 3
Passover, 7th Day	Nisan 21	Apr. 26	Apr. 14	Apr. 3	Apr. 23	Apr. 12	Apr. 30	Apr. 19	Apr. 9
Israel Indep. Day	Iyar 5[2]	May 10	Apr. 26	Apr. 17	May 7	Apr. 26	May 12	May 3	Apr. 23
Feast of Weeks	Sivan 6	June 9	May 28	May 17	June 6	May 26	June 13	June 2	May 23
Fast of Ab	Ab 9	Aug. 10	July 29	July 18	Aug. 7	July 27	Aug. 14	Aug. 3	July 24

1. Ve-Adar 14 in Leap Years.
2. When this date occurs on Friday or Sabbath, Israel Independence Day is observed on the previous Thursday.

THE JEWISH CALENDAR

The Jewish Calendar is a lunar one, adapted to the solar year by various expedients. The hour is divided into 1,080 portions or *minims*, and the month between one new moon and the next is reckoned as 29 days, 12 hours, 793 minims. The years are grouped in cycles of 19. The present calendar was fixed by the Palestinian Jewish Patriarch, Hillel II, in 358 C.E. In early Talmudic times the new moons were fixed by the actual observation, and were announced from Jerusalem to the surrounding districts and countries by messenger or beacon.

If the time elapsing between one new moon and another were *exactly* 29½ days, the length of the months could be fixed at alternately 29 and 30 days. But there are three corrections to make which disturb this regularity: (1) The excess of 793 minims over the half day, (2) the adjustment to the solar year, (3) the requirement that the incidence of certain Jewish festivals shall not conflict with the Sabbath. To overcome these difficulties the Jewish Calendar recognises six different classes of years; three of them common and three leap. The leap years, which are the 3rd, 6th, 8th, 11th, 14th, 17th, and 19th of the Metyonic cycle of 19 years, are composed of thirteen months, an additional month being added. It is usually stated that this intercalary month is inserted after the month of Adar which in the ordinary year is of 29 days, but in a leap year has 30 days, but in reality the inserted month precedes the ordinary Adar and always has 30 days. Both the common and the leap years may be either regular, "minimal" , or full. The regular year has an alternation of 30 and 29 days. The "minimal" year gives Kislev only 29 days instead of 30, while in a full year Marcheshvan has 30 instead of 29 days.

Besides the lunar cycle of 19 years there is a solar cycle of 28 years, at the beginning of which the *Tekufah* of Nisan (the vernal equinox) returns to the same day and the same hour.

The chief disturbing influence in the arrangement of the Jewish Calendar is to prevent the Day of Atonement (Tishri 10th) from either immediately preceding or immediately succeeding the Sabbath, and Hoshana Rabba (Tishri 21st) from falling on the Sabbath. Consequently the New Year (Tishri Ist) cannot fall upon Sunday, Wednesday or Friday. A further complication of a purely astronomical character is introduced by the consideration that the Jewish day formally commences six hours before midnight. Hence, if the Molad or lunar conjunction for the month of Tishri occurs at noon or later, the new moon will be seen only after 6 p.m. and the Festival is postponed to the next day. When, after paying regard to these and certain other considerations, the days upon which two successive New Year Festivals fall are determined, the number of days in the intervening year is known and the length of Marcheshvan and Kislev is fixed accordingly.

It is customary to describe the character of a Jewish Year by a "Determinative" consisting of three Hebrew letters. The first of these indicates the day of the week upon which the New Year Festival falls, the second whether the year is regular, "minimal", or full, and the third the day of the week upon which Passover occurs. To this "Determinative" is added the Hebrew word for "ordinary" or "leap".

Authorities differ regarding the manner in which the figure employed for the Jewish Era (this year 5760) is arrived at. It is sufficient to describe it as the "Mundane Era" (dating from the Creation of the World) or the "Adamic Era" (dating from the Creation of Man). The chronology is based on Biblical data.

For the beginning of Sabbaths and Festivals, rules were laid down for the latitude of London by David Nieto, Haham of the Sephardi Community (1702-1728). The hours for nightfall given here are based on those fixed by Nathan Marcus Adler, Chief Rabbi, in accordance with the formula of Michael Friedlander, Principal of Jews' College, but adjusted to take account of the movement of the Jewish population within the Metropolis since their day.

THE JEWISH YEAR

The times in this calendar for the beginning and ending of Sabbaths, Festivals and Fasts are given in Greenwich Mean Time from January 1 to March 25 and October 29 to the end, and in British Summer Time from March 26 to October 28, 2000.

5760

is known as 760 on the short system, and is a full leap year of 13 months, 55 Sabbaths and 385 days. Its first of Tishri is on a Sabbath, and the first day of Passover on a Thursday.

It is the third year of the 304th minor or lunar cycle (of 19 years each) since the Era of Creation, and the twentieth of the 206th major or solar cycle (of 28 years each) since the same epoch.

The year began on Friday evening, September 10, 1999, and concludes on Friday, September 29, 2000.

5761

is known as 761 on the short system, and is a minimal common year of 12 months, 51 Sabbaths and 353 days. Its first of Tishri is on a Sabbath, and the first day of Passover on a Sunday.

It is the fourth year of the 304th minor or lunar cycle (of 19 years each) since the Era of Creation, and the twenty-first of the 206th major or solar cycle (of 28 years each) since the same epoch.

The year begins on Friday evening, September 29, 2000, and concludes on Monday, September 17, 2001.

CALENDAR NOTES

Pent. denotes Pentateuchal readings; **Proph.** denotes Prophetical readings.
Parentheses in either of the above denote Sephardi ritual.
Times for the commencement of the Sabbath during the summer months are, as is the tradition in Britain, given as 20.00. The actual times are given in parentheses.

ABRIDGED JEWISH CALENDAR FOR 2000
(5760-5761)

New Moon Shebat, 5760	Saturday	2000 January 8
New Year for Trees	Saturday	22
New Moon I Adar, 1st day	Sunday	February 6
Minor Purim	Sunday	20
Minor Shushan Purim	Monday	21
New Moon II Adar, 1st day	Tuesday	March 7
Fast of Esther	Monday	20
Purim	Tuesday	21
Shushan Purim	Wednesday	22
New Moon Nisan	Thursday	April 6
Fast of Firstborn	Wednesday	19
First Day Passover	Thursday	20
Second Day Passover	Friday	21
Seventh Day Passover	Wednesday	26
Eighth Day Passover	Thursday	27
Holocaust Memorial Day	Tuesday	May 2
New Moon Iyar, 1st Day	Friday	5
Israel Independence Day	Wednesday	10
Minor Passover	Friday	19
Thirty-third day of the (Lag Ba') Omer	Tuesday	23
Jerusalem Day	Friday	June 2
New Moon Sivan	Sunday	4
First Day Feast of Weeks	Friday	9
Second Day Feast of Weeks	Saturday	10
New Moon Tammuz, 1st day	Monday	July 3
Fast of Tammuz	Thursday	20
New Moon Ab	Wednesday	August 2
Fast of Ab	Thursday	10
Festival of 15th Ab	Wednesday	16
New Moon Elul, 1st day	Thursday	31
First Day New Year, 5761	Saturday	September 30
Second Day New Year	Sunday	October 1
Fast of Gedaliah	Monday	2
Day of Atonement	Monday	9
First Day Tabernacles	Saturday	14
Second Day Tabernacles	Sunday	15
Hoshana Rabba	Friday	20
Eighth Day of Solemn Assembly	Saturday	21
Rejoicing of the Law	Sunday	22
New Moon Marcheshvan, 1st day	Sunday	29
New Moon Kislev	Tuesday	November 28
First Day Chanucah	Friday	December 22
New Moon Tebet	Wednesday	27

ABRIDGED JEWISH CALENDAR FOR 2001
(5761-5762)

Fast of Tebet, 5761	Friday	2001 January 5
New Moon Shebat	Thursday	25
New Year for Trees	Thursday	February 8
New Moon Adar, 1st day	Friday	23
Fast of Esther	Thursday	March 8
Purim	Friday	9
Shushan Purim	Saturday	10
New Moon Nisan	Sunday	25
Fast of Firstborn	Thursday	April 5
First Day Passover	Sunday	8
Second Day Passover	Monday	9
Seventh Day Passover	Saturday	14
Eighth Day Passover	Sunday	15
Holocaust Memorial Day	Thursday	19
New Moon Iyar, 1st Day	Monday	23
Israel Independence Day	Thursday	26
Minor Passover	Monday	May 7
Thirty-third day of the (Lag Ba') Omer	Friday	11
Jerusalem Day	Monday	21
New Moon Sivan	Wednesday	23
First Day Feast of Weeks	Monday	28
Second Day Feast of Weeks	Tuesday	29
New Moon Tammuz, 1st day	Thursday	June 21
Fast of Tammuz	Sunday	July 8
New Moon Ab	Saturday	21
Fast of Ab	Sunday	29
Festival of 15th Ab	Saturday	August 4
New Moon Elul, 1st day	Sunday	19
First Day New Year, 5762	Tuesday	September 18
Second Day New Year	Wednesday	19
Fast of Gedaliah	Thursday	20
Day of Atonement	Thursday	27
First Day Tabernacles	Tuesday	October 2
Second Day Tabernacles	Wednesday	3
Hoshana Rabba	Monday	8
Eighth Day of Solemn Assembly	Tuesday	9
Rejoicing of the Law	Wednesday	10
New Moon Marcheshvan, 1st day	Wednesday	17
New Moon Kislev	Friday	November 16
First Day Chanucah	Monday	December 10
New Moon Tebet, 1st day	Saturday	15
Fast of Tebet	Tuesday	25

JANUARY, 2000
Tekufah Fri Jan 7 04.30

TEBET 23–SHEBAT 24, 5760
Molad Thurs Jan 6 18h 40m 43s

Tebet

1	S	Sabbath ends 16.56. Pent Shemot, Ex 1-6, 1. Proph Is 27, 6-28, 13; 29, 22-23 (Jer 1, 1-2, 3) Benediction of Shebat	23
2	S		24
3	M		25
4	T		26
5	W		27
6	Th	Yom Kippur Katan	28
7	F	Sabbath commences 15.54	29

Shebat

8	S	Rosh Chodesh. Sabbath ends 17.04. Pent Va'era, Ex 6, 2-9 and Num 28, 9-15. Proph Is 66	1
9	S		2
10	M		3
11	T		4
12	W		5
13	Th		6
14	F	Sabbath commences 16.04	7
15	S	Sabbath ends 17.13. Pent Bo, Ex 10, 1-13, 16. Proph Jer 46, 13-28	8
16	S		9
17	M		10
18	T		11
19	W		12
20	Th		13
21	F	Sabbath commences 16.15	14
22	S	New Year for Trees. Sabbath ends 17.23. Pent Beshallach, Shabbat Shirah, Ex 13, 17-17. Proph Judges 4, 4-5 (5, 1-31)	15
23	S		16
24	M		17
25	T		18
26	W		19
27	Th		20
28	F	Sabbath commences 16.27	21
29	S	Sabbath ends 17.34. Pent Yitro, Ex 18-20. Proph Is 6, 1-7, 6 and 9, 5-6 (6, 1-13).	22
30	S		23
31	M		24

Liturgical notes - Jan 8, Half-Hallel; omit Tsidkatcha Tsedek in Minchah.–Jan 22, omit Tsidkatcha Tsedek in Minchah.

FEBRUARY, 2000   SHEBAT 25–ADAR RISHON 23, 5760
Molad Sat Feb 5 7h 24m 47s

Shebat

1	T		25
2	W		26
3	Th	Yom Kippur Katan	27
4	F	Sabbath commences 16.40.	28

5	S	Sabbath ends 17.46. Pent Mishpatim, Ex 21-24. Proph Machar Chodesh I Sam 20, 18-42. Benediction of Adar Rishon.	29

6	S	Rosh Chodesh first day. Pent Num 28, 1-15	30

Adar Rishon

7	M	Rosh Chodesh second day. Pent Num 28, 1-15	1
8	T		2
9	W		3
10	Th		4
11	F	Sabbath commences 16.53	5
12	S	Sabbath ends 17.58. Pent Terumah, Ex 25, 1-27, 19. Proph I Kings 5, 26-6, 13	6

13	S		7
14	M		8
15	T		9
16	W		10
17	Th		11
18	F	Sabbath commences 17.06	12
19	S	Sabbath ends 18.10. Pent Tetsaveh, Ex 27, 20-30, 10. Proph Ezek 43, 10-27	13

20	S	Minor Purim.	14
21	M	Minor Shushan Purim.	15
22	T		16
23	W		17
24	Th		18
25	F	Sabbath commences 17.18	19
26	S	Sabbath ends 18.22. Pent Ki Tissa, Ex 30, 11-34. Proph I Kings 18, 1-39 (20-39).	20

27	S		21
28	M		22
29	T		23

Liturgical notes - Feb 5, omit Tsidkatcha Tsedek in Minchah.–Feb 6 and 7, Half-Hallel.–Feb 19, omit Tsidkatcha Tsedek in Minchah.–Feb 20, omit Tachanun and Lamenatse'ach.–Feb 21, omit Tachanun, El Erech Appayim and Lamenatse'ach.

MARCH, 2000 ADAR RISHON 24–ADAR SHENI 24, 5760
Molad Sun March 5 20h 8m 50s

Adar Rishon

1	W		24
2	Th		25
3	F	Sabbath commences 17.29	26
4	S	Sabbath ends 18.33. Pent Vayakhel. Parshat Shekalim, Ex 35, 1-38, 20 and 30, 11-16. Proph II Kings 12, 1-17 (11, 17-12, 17). Benediction of Adar Sheni.	27

5	S		28
6	M	Yom Kippur Katan	29
7	T	Rosh Chodesh first day. Pent Num 28, 1-15	30
			Adar Sheni
8	W	Rosh Chodesh second day. Pent Num 28, 1-15	1
9	Th		2
10	F	Sabbath commences 17.42	3
11	S	Sabbath ends 18.45. Pent Pekudei, Ex 38, 21 to end of book. Proph I Kings 7, 51-8, 21 (others 7, 40-50)	4

12	S		5
13	M		6
14	T		7
15	W		8
16	Th		9
17	F	Sabbath commences 17.54	10
18	S	Sabbath ends 18.57. Pent Vayikra, Parshat Zachor, Lev 1-5 and Deut 25, 17-19. Proph I Sam 15, 2-34 (15, 1-34)	11

19	S		12
20	M	Fast of Esther ends 18.54. Pent morning and afternoon Ex 32, 11-14 and 34, 1-10. Proph afternoon only Is 55, 6-56, 8 (none)	13
21	T	Purim. Pent Ex 17, 8-16	14
22	W	Shushan Purim	15
23	Th		16
24	F	Sabbath commences 18.06	17
25	S	Sabbath ends 19.09. Pent Tsav, Parshat Parah, Lev 6-8, and Num 19 Proph Ezek 36, 16-38 (16-36)	18

26	S		19
27	M		20
28	T		21
29	W		22
30	Th		23
31	F	Sabbath commences 19.17	24

Liturgical notes - March 6, omit Tachanun in Minchah.-March 7 and 8, Half-Hallel.-March 20, Selichot, Aneinu; omit Tachanun in Minchah; Al Hannissim is said in Maariv; Book of Esther is read; Half-Shekel is given.-March 21, Al Hannissim said; Book of Esther read in morning; omit Tachanun and Lamenatse'ach.-March 22, omit Tachanun and Lamenatse'ach.

APRIL 2000
Tekufah Fri Apr 7 12.00

ADAR SHENI 25–NISAN 25, 5760
Molad Tues Apr 4 8h 52m 53s

			Adar Sheni
1	S	Sabbath ends 20.22. **Pent** Shemini, Parshat Hachodesh. Lev **9-11** and Ex **12**, 1-20. **Proph** Ezek **45**, 16-**46**, 18 (**45**, 18-**46**, 15). Benediction of Nisan	25
2	S		26
3	M		27
4	T		28
5	W	Yom Kippur Katan	29
			Nisan
6	Th	Rosh Chodesh. **Pent** Num **28**, 1-15	1
7	F	Sabbath commences 19.29	2
8	S	Sabbath ends 20.34. **Pent** Tazria, Lev **12-13**. **Proph** II Kings **4**, 42-5, 19	3
9	S		4
10	M		5
11	T		6
12	W		7
13	Th		8
14	F	Sabbath commences 19.41	9
15	S	Sabbath ends 20.47. **Pent** Metsora, Shabbat Haggadol, Lev **14-15**. **Proph** Mal 3, 4-24	10
16	S		11
17	M		12
18	T		13
19	W	**Fast of Firstborn**. Eruv Tavshilin. Festival commences 19.49. **First Seder** in evening	14
20	Th	**Passover first day** ends 20.56. **Second Seder** in evening. **Pent** Ex **12**, 21-51; Num **28**, 16-25. **Proph** Josh 5, 2-6, 1 (and **6**,27).	15

			Omer days	
21	F	**Passover second day**. Sabbath commences 19.53. **Pent** Lev **22**, 26-**23**, 44; Num **28**, 16-25. **Proph** II Kings **23**, 1-9 and 21-25.	1	16
22	S	Sabbath ends 21.00. **Pent** Ex **33**, 12-**34**, 26; Num **28**, 19-25. **Proph** Ezek **37**, 1-14.	2	17
23	S	**Pent** Ex **13**, 1-16; Num **28**, 19-25	3	18
24	M	**Pent** Ex **22**, 24-**23**, 19; Num **28**, 19-25	4	19
25	T	Festival commences 19.59. **Pent** Num **9**, 1-14 and **28**, 19-25	5	20
26	W	**Passover seventh day** ends 21.08. **Pent** Ex **13**, 17-**15**, 26; Num **28**, 19-25; **Proph** II Samuel **22**	6	21
27	Th	**Passover eighth day** ends 21.10. **Pent** Deut **15**, 19-**16**, 17; Num **28**, 19-25. **Proph** Is **10**, 32-**12**, 6	7	22
28	F	Issru Chag. Sabbath commences 20.00 (20.04)	8	23
29	S	Sabbath ends 21.14. **Pent** Acharei Mot, Lev **16-18**. **Proph** Amos **9**, 7-15 (Ezek. **22**, 1-16) Benediction of Iyar. Ethics 1.	9	24
30	S		10	25

Liturgical notes - April 5, omit Tachanun in Minchah.-April 6, Half-Hallel.-April 7 to 19, omit Tachanun.-April 8 and 15, omit Tsidkatcha Tsedek in Minchah.-April 15, read from Haggadah and discontinue Barachi Nafshi in Minchah; omit Vihi Noam in Maariv.-April 18, Bedikat Chamets in evening.-April 19, omit Mizmor Letodah and Lamenatse'ach; abstain from Chamets by 10.39; Biur Chamets; discontinue Tal Umatar after Minchah.-April 20, discontinue Mashiv Haruach in Mussaf; in the evening commence counting the Omer.-April 20 and 21, Whole-Hallel.-April 22 to 27, Half-Hallel.-April 22, read Song of Songs; omit Tsidkatcha Tsedek in Minchah and Vihi Noam in Maariv.-April 23 to 25, omit Mizmor Letodah.-April 28 and 30, omit Tachanun.-April 29, omit Tsidkatcha Tsedek in Minchah.

MAY 2000

NISAN 26–IYAR 26, 5760
Molad Wed May 3 21h 36m 57s

			Omer Nisan days	
1	M		11	26
2	T	Holocaust Memorial Day	12	27
3	W		13	28
4	Th		14	29
5	F	Rosh Chodesh first day. Sabbath commences 20.00 (20.16)	15	30
		Pent Num **28**, 1-15		Iyar
6	S	Rosh Chodesh second day. Sabbath ends 21.27.	16	1
		Pent Kedoshim, Lev **19-20** and Num **28**, 9-15. **Proph** Is **66**. Ethics 2.		
7	S		17	2
8	M		18	3
9	T		19	4
10	W	Yom Ha'atsma'ut – Israel Independence Day	20	5
11	Th		21	6
12	F	Sabbath commences 20.00 (20.27)	22	7
13	S	Sabbath ends 21.40. **Pent** Emor, Lev **21-24**.	23	8
		Proph Ezek **44**, 15-31. Ethics 3		
14	S		24	9
15	M	**First fast day** ends 21.37	25	10
16	T		26	11
17	W		27	12
18	Th	**Second fast day** ends 21.43	28	13
19	F	**Minor Passover**. Sabbath commences 20.00 (20.37)	29	14
20	S	Sabbath ends 21.53. **Pent** Behar, Lev **25-26**, 2. **Proph** Jer **32**, 6-27. Ethics 4	30	15
21	S		31	16
22	M	**Third fast day** ends 21.50	32	17
23	T	**Lag b'Omer–Scholars' festival**	33	18
24	W		34	19
25	Th		35	20
26	F	Sabbath commences 20.00 (20.47)	36	21
27	S	Sabbath ends 22.04. **Pent** Bechukkotai, Lev **26**, 3 to end of book.	37	22
		Proph Jer **16**, 19-17, 14. Ethics 5		
28	S		38	23
29	M		39	24
30	T		40	25
31	W		41	26

Liturgical notes - May 1 to 4, omit Tachanun.-May 5 and 6, Half-Hallel.-May 6, omit Tsidkatcha Tsedek in Minchah.-May 10, see Order of Service and Customs for Israel Independence Day (pubd. Routledge & Kegan Paul, 1964).-May 15, 18 & 22, Selichot are said in some communities and, if there be a Minyan who fast, Vay'chal is read.-May 22, omit Tachanun in Minchah.-May 23, omit Tachanun.

JUNE, 2000

IYAR 27–SIVAN 27, 5760
Molad Fri June 2 10h 21m 0s

			Omer days	Iyar
1	Th	Yom Kippur Katan	42	27
2	F	Sabbath commences 20.00 (20.55). **Yom Yerushalayim– Jerusalem Day**	43	28
3	S	Sabbath ends 22.14. Pent Bemidbar, Num **1-4**, 20. Proph Machar Chodesh, I Sam **20**, 18-42. Benediction of Sivan. Ethics 6.	44	**29**

				Sivan
4	S	Rosh Chodesh. Pent Num 28, 1-15	45	1
5	M		46	2
6	T		47	3
7	W		48	4
8	Th	Festival commences 20.00 (21.01). Eruv Tavshilin	49	5
9	F	**Feast of Weeks** first day. Sabbath commences 20.00 (21.02) Pent Ex **19-20**. Num 28, 26-31. Proph Ezek 1 and 3, 12		**6**
10	S	**Feast of Weeks** second day. Sabbath and Festival end 22.22. Pent Deut 14, 22-16, 17; Num 28, 26-31; Proph Habak 2, 20-3, 19		7

11	S	Issru Chag	8
12	M		9
13	T		10
14	W		11
15	Th		12
16	F	Sabbath commences 20.00 (21.06)	13
17	S	Sabbath ends 22.27. Pent Naso, Num 4, 21-7. Proph Judges 13, 2-25. Ethics 1.	**14**

18	S		15
19	M		16
20	T		17
21	W		18
22	Th		19
23	F	Sabbath commences 20.00 (21.08)	20
24	S	Sabbath ends 22.28. Pent Beha'alotecha, Num **8-12**. Proph Zech 2, 14-4, 7 Ethics 2.	**21**

25	S		22
26	M		23
27	T		24
28	W		25
29	Th		26
30	F	Sabbath commences 20.00 (21.07)	27

Liturgical notes - June 3, say Av Harachamim in morning service; omit Tsidkatcha Tsedek in Minchah and Vihi Noam in Maariv.-June 4, Half-Hallel.-June 5 to 8, omit Tachanun.-June 9 and 10, Whole-Hallel.-June 10, Book of Ruth is read.-June 11, omit Tachanun.

JULY, 2000

Tekufah Fri July 7 19.30

SIVAN 28–TAMMUZ 28, 5760

Molad Tammuz Sat July 1 23h 5m 3s
Molad Ab Mon July 31 11h 49m 7s

			Sivan
1	S	Sabbath ends 22.26. **Pent** Shelach Lecha, Num **13-15**. **Proph** Joshua 2 Benediction of Tammuz. Ethics 3.	**28**
2	S	Yom Kippur Katan	29
3	M	Rosh Chodesh first day. **Pent** Num **28**, 1-15	30
			Tammuz
4	T	Rosh Chodesh second day. **Pent** Num **28**, 1-15	1
5	W		2
6	Th		3
7	F	Sabbath commences 20.00 (21.04)	4
8	S	Sabbath ends 22.21. **Pent** Korach, Num **16-18**. **Proph** I Sam **11**, 14-12, 22. Ethics 4.	**5**
9	S		6
10	M		7
11	T		8
12	W		9
13	Th		10
14	F	Sabbath commences 20.00 (20.58)	11
15	S	Sabbath ends 22.15. **Pent** Chukkat-Balak, Num **19-25**, 9. **Proph** Micah 5, 6-6,8. Ethics 5	**12**
16	S		13
17	M		14
18	T		15
19	W		16
20	Th	**Fast of Tammuz** ends 22.00. **Pent** Morning and afternoon. Ex **32**, 11-14 and **34**, 1-10. **Proph** Afternoon only Is. **55**, 6-56, 8 (none)	**17**
21	F	Sabbath commences 20.00 (20.51)	18
22	S	Sabbath ends 22.03. **Pent** Pinchas, Num **25**, 10-30, 1. **Proph** Jer **1-2**, 3. Ethics 6	**19**
23	S		20
24	M		21
25	T		22
26	W		23
27	Th		24
28	F	Sabbath commences 20.00 (20.41)	25
29	S	Sabbath ends 21.51. **Pent** Mattot-Massei, Num **30**, 2-end of book. **Proph** Jer 2, 4-28; 3, 4 (Jer 2, 4-28; **4**, 1-2) Benediction of Ab. Ethics 1	**26**
30	S		27
31	M		28

Liturgical notes - July 2, omit Tachanun in Minchah.-July 3 and 4, Half-Hallel.-July 20, Selichot, Aneinu.

AUGUST, 2000

TAMMUZ 29–AB 30, 5760

Molad Elul Wed Aug 30 0h 33m 10s

			Tammuz
1	T	Yom Kippur Katan	29
			Ab
2	W	Rosh Chodesh. Pent Num **28**, 1-15	1
3	Th		2
4	F	Sabbath commences 20.00 (20.29)	3
5	S	Sabbath ends 21.37. Pent Devarim, Shabbat Chazon, Deut **1**, 1-**3**, 22. **Proph** Is **1**, 1-27. Ethics 2	**4**

6	S		5
7	M		6
8	T		7
9	W	Fast commences 20.34	8
10	**Th**	**Fast of Ab** ends 21.21. Pent Morning Deut **4**, 25-40; afternoon: Ex **32**, 11-14 and **34**, 1-10. **Proph** Morning Jer **8**, 13-**9**, 23; afternoon Is **55**, 6-**56**, 8 (Hosea **14**, 2-10 and Micah **7**, 18-20)	9
11	F	Sabbath commences 20.00 (20.17)	10
12	S	Sabbath ends 21.22. Pent Va'etchanan, Shabbat Nachamu, Deut **3**, 23-**7**, 11. **Proph** Is **40**, 1-26. Ethics 3	**11**

13	S		12
14	M		13
15	T		14
16	W	**Festival of Ab**	15
17	Th		16
18	F	Sabbath commences 20.00 (20.03)	17
19	S	Sabbath ends 21.07. Pent Ekev, Deut **7**, 12-**11**, 25. **Proph** Is **49**, 14-**51**, 3. Ethics 4.	**18**

20	S		19
21	M		20
22	T		21
23	W		22
24	Th		23
25	F	Sabbath commences 19.48	24
26	S	Sabbath ends 20.50. Pent Re'eh, Deut **11**, 26-**16**, 17. **Proph** Is **54**, 11-**55**, 5 Benediction of Elul. Ethics 5	**25**

27	S		26
28	M		27
29	T		28
30	W	Yom Kippur Katan	29
31	Th	Rosh Chodesh first day. Pent Num **28**, 1-15	30

Liturgical notes - Aug 1, omit Tachanun in Minchah.-Aug 2, Half-Hallel.-Aug 5, say Av Harachamim in morning service.-Aug 9, omit Tachanun in Minchah; Book of Lamentations is read in Maariv.-Aug 10, read Kinot; omit Tachanun, El Erech Appayim and Lamenatse'ach; say Aneinu and insert Nachem in Minchah.-Aug 15, omit Tachanun in Minchah.-Aug 16, omit Tachanun.-Aug 30, omit Tachanun in Minchah.-Aug 31, Half-Hallel.

SEPTEMBER, 2000   ELUL 1, 5760–TISHRI 1, 5761
Molad Tishri Thurs Sept 28 13h 17m 13s

Elul

1	F	Rosh Chodesh second day. Sabbath commences 19.33.	1
		Pent Num **28**, 1-15	
2	S	Sabbath ends 20.34. Pent Shof'tim, Deut **16**, 18-**21**, 9. Proph Is **51**, 12-**52**, 12.	2
		Ethics 6	

3	S		3
4	M		4
5	T		5
6	W		6
7	Th		7
8	F	Sabbath commences 19.17	8
9	S	Sabbath ends 20.17. Pent Ki-Tetsei, Deut **21**, 10-**25**. Proph Is **54**, 1-10. Ethics 1 and 2	9

10	S		10
11	M		11
12	T		12
13	W		13
14	Th		14
15	F	Sabbath commences 19.01	15
16	S	Sabbath ends 20.00. Pent Ki-Tavo, Deut **26-29**, 8. Proph Is **60**. Ethics 3 and 4	16

17	S		17
18	M		18
19	T		19
20	W		20
21	Th		21
22	F	Sabbath commences 18.45	22
23	S	Sabbath ends 19.44. Pent Nitsavim-Vayelech. Deut **29**, 9-**31**. Proph Is **61**, 10-**63**, 9.	23
		Ethics 5 and 6	

24	S		24
25	M		25
26	T		26
27	W		27
28	Th		28
29	F	Sabbath and Festival commence 18.29	29

Tishri

| 30 | S | **New Year 5761 first day**. Sabbath ends 19.27. | 1 |
| | | Pent Gen 21; Num **29**, 1-6. Proph I Sam **1**, 1-2, 10 | |

Liturgical notes - Sept 1, Half-Hallel.-Sept 1 to 28, the Shofar is blown on weekdays.-Sept 24 to 29, Selichot.-Sept 29, omit Tachanun.

OCTOBER, 2000   TISHRI 2–MARCHESHVAN 2, 5761
Tekufah Sat Oct 7 03.00   Molad Cheshvan Sat Oct 28 2h 1m 17s

Tishri

1	S	**New Year second day** ends 19.25. Pent Gen **22**; Num **29**, 1-6. **Proph** Jer **31**, 2-20	**2**
2	M	**Fast of Gedaliah** ends 19.17. Pent Morning and afternoon Ex **32**, 11-14; **34**, 1-10. **Proph** Afternoon only Is **55**, 6-**56**, 8 (none)	**3**
3	T		4
4	W		5
5	Th		6
6	F	Sabbath commences 18.13	7
7	S	Sabbath ends 19.12. Pent Ha'azinu, Shabbat Shuvah, Deut **32**. **Proph** Hosea **14**, 2-10; Joel **2**, 15-27 (Hosea **14**, 2-10 and Micah **7**, 18-20)	**8**

8	S	**Fast of Atonement** commences 18.08; service at 18.20	9
9	M	**Day of Atonement** ends 19.07. Pent Morning Lev **16**; Num **29**, 7-11. Afternoon **10** Lev **18**. **Proph** Morning Is **57**, 14-**58**, 14; Afternoon Book of Jonah and Micah **7**, 18-20	
10	T		11
11	W		12
12	Th		13
13	F	Sabbath and Festival commence 17.57	14
14	S	**Tabernacles first day**. Sabbath ends 18.57. Pent Lev **22**, 26-**23**, 44; Num **29**, 12-16. **Proph** Zech **14**	**15**

15	S	**Tabernacles second day** ends 18.55. Pent Lev **22**, 26-**23**, 44; Num **29**, 12-16. **16** **Proph** I Kings **8**, 2-21.	
16	M	Pent Num **29**, 17-25	17
17	T	Pent Num **29**, 20-28	18
18	W	Pent Num **29**, 23-31	19
19	Th	Pent Num **29**, 26-34	20
20	F	**Hoshana Rabba**, Sabbath and Festival commence 17.42 Pent Num **29**, 26-34	21
21	S	**Eighth day of Solemn Assembly**. Sabbath ends 18.42 Pent Deut **14**, 22-**16**, 17; Num **29**, 35-**30**, 1. **Proph** I Kings **8**, 54-66	**22**

22	S	**Rejoicing of the Law** ends 18.40. Pent Deut **33-34**; Gen **1-2**, 3; Num **29**, 35-**30**, 1. **Proph** Joshua **1** (1, 1-9)	**23**
23	M	Issru Chag	24
24	T		25
25	W		26
26	Th		27
27	F	Sabbath commences 17.28	28
28	S	Sabbath ends 18.29. Pent Bereshit, Gen **1-6**, 8. **Proph** Machar Chodesh, I Sam **20**, 18-42. Benediction of Marcheshvan	**29**

29	S	Rosh Chodesh first day. Pent Num **28**, 1-15	30
			Marcheshvan
30	M	Rosh Chodesh second day. Pent Num **28**, 1-15	1
31	T		2

Liturgical notes - Oct 1, Tashlich.-Oct 2 to 8, Selichot said on weekdays.-Oct 2, Aneinu.-Oct 7, omit Vihi Noam in Maariv.-Oct 8, omit Mizmor Letodah, Tachanun and Lamenatse'ach; Vidduy said in Minchah.-Oct 10 to 13, omit Tachanun.-Oct 14 to 22, Whole Hallel.-Hoshanot: Oct 14, Om Netsurah; Oct 15, Lema'an Amitach; Oct 16, E'eroch Shu'i; Oct 17, Even Shetiyah; Oct 18, El Lemoshaot; Oct 19, Adon Hammoshia.-Oct 21, Ecclesiastes is read and Mashiv Haruach commenced in Mussaf.-Oct 23, omit Tachanun.-Oct 28, Barachi Nafshi commenced in Minchah and Tsidkatcha Tsedek omitted therein.-Oct 29 and 30, Half-Hallel.

NOVEMBER, 2000   MARCHESHVAN 3–KISLEV 3, 5761

Molad Sun Nov 26 14h 45m 20s

Marcheshvan

1	W		3
2	Th		4
3	F	Sabbath commences 16.15	5
4	S	Sabbath ends 17.17. Pent Noach, Gen 6, 9-11. Proph Is 54, 1-55, 5 (54, 1-10)	6
5	S		7
6	M		8
7	T		9
8	W		10
9	Th		11
10	F	Sabbath commences 16.04	12
11	S	Sabbath ends 17.07. Pent Lech Lecha, Gen 12-17. Proph Is 40, 27-41, 16	13
12	S		14
13	M		15
14	T		16
15	W		17
16	Th		18
17	F	Sabbath commences 15.54	19
18	S	Sabbath ends 16.58. Pent Vayera, Gen 18-22. Proph II Kings 4, 1-37 (4, 1-23)	20
19	S		21
20	M	**First Fast Day** ends 16.50	22
21	T		23
22	W		24
23	Th	**Second Fast Day** ends 16.48	25
24	F	Sabbath commences 15.46	26
25	S	Sabbath ends 16.52. Pent Chayei Sarah, Gen 23-25, 18. Proph I Kings 1, 1-31 Benediction of Kislev	27
26	S		28
27	M	**Third Fast Day** ends 16.45. Yom Kippur Katan	29
			Kislev
28	T	Rosh Chodesh. Pent Num 28, 1-15	1
29	W		2
30	Th		3

Liturgical notes - Nov 20, 23 & 27, Selichot are said in some communities and, if there be a Minyan who fast, Vay'chal is read.–Nov 27, omit Tachanun in Minchah.–Nov 28, Half-Hallel.

DECEMBER, 2000

KISLEV 4–TEBET 5, 5761

Molad Tues Dec 26 3h 29m 23s

			Kislev
1	F	Sabbath commences 15.40	4
2	S	Sabbath ends 16.48. Pent Tol'dot. Gen 25, 19-28, 9. Proph Malachi 1, 1-2, 7	5

3	S		6
4	M		7
5	T		8
6	W		9
7	Th		10
8	F	Sabbath commences 15.37	11
9	S	Sabbath ends 16.46. Pent Vayetsei, Gen 28, 10-32, 3. Proph Hosea 12, 13-14, 10 (11, 7-12, 12)	12

10	S		13
11	M		14
12	T		15
13	W		16
14	Th		17
15	F	Sabbath commences 15.36	18
16	S	Sabbath ends 16.46. Pent Vayishlach, Gen 32, 4-36. Proph Hosea 11, 7-12, 12 (Others, Book of Obadiah)	19

17	S		20
18	M		21
19	T		22
20	W		23
21	Th	First Chanucah Light.	24
22	F	**Chanucah first day**. Sabbath commences 15.39. Pent Num 7, 1-17	25
23	S	**Chanucah second day**. Sabbath ends 16.49. Pent Vayeshev, Gen 37-40; Num 7, 18-23. Proph Zech 2, 14-4, 7. Benediction of Tebet	26

24	S	**Chanucah third day**. Pent Num 7, 24-35	27
25	M	**Chanucah fourth day**. Pent Num 7, 30-41	28
26	T	**Chanucah fifth day**. Pent Num 7, 36-47	29
			Tebet
27	W	Rosh Chodesh. **Chanucah sixth day**. Pent Num 28, 1-15 and 7, 42-47	1
28	Th	**Chanucah seventh day**. Pent Num 7, 48-59	2
29	F	**Chanucah eighth day**. Sabbath commences 15.44. Pent Num 7, 54-8, 4	3
30	S	Sabbath ends 16.54. Pent Mikkets, Gen 41-44, 17; Proph I Kings 3, 15-4, 1	4

31	S		5

Liturgical notes - Dec 4, Tal Umatar commenced in Maariv.–Dec 21, omit Tachanun in Minchah.–During Chanucah say Al Hannissim and Whole-Hallel; omit Tachanun, El Erech Appayim and Lamenatse'ach, and on Sabbath Tsidkatcha Tsedek in Minchah.

JANUARY, 2001
Tekufah Sat Jan 6 10.30

TEBET 6–SHEBAT 7, 5761
Molad Wed Jan 24 16h 13m 27s

Tebet

1	M		6
2	T		7
3	W		8
4	Th		9
5	F	Sabbath commences 15.51 **Fast of Tebet** ends 16.54. Pent Morning and afternoon Ex **32**, 11-14 and **34**, 1-10. **Proph** Afternoon only Is **55**, 6-56, 8 (none)	10
6	S	Sabbath ends 17.01. **Pent** Vayiggash, Gen **44**, 18-47, 27. **Proph** Ezek **37**, 15-28	**11**
7	S		12
8	M		13
9	T		14
10	W		15
11	Th		16
12	F	Sabbath commences 16.01	17
13	S	Sabbath ends 17.10. **Pent** Vay'chi, Gen **47**, 28 to end of Book. **Proph** I Kings **2**, 1-12	**18**
14	S		19
15	M		20
16	T		21
17	W		22
18	Th		23
19	F	Sabbath commences 16.12	24
20	S	Sabbath ends 17.20. **Pent** Shemot, Ex **1-6**, 1. **Proph** Is **27**, 6-28, 13; **29**, 22-23 (Jer **1**, 1-**2**, 3) Benediction of Shebat	**25**
21	S		26
22	M		27
23	T		28
24	W	Yom Kippur Katan	29
			Shebat
25	Th	Rosh Chodesh. **Pent** Num **28**, 1-15	1
26	F	Sabbath commences 16.24	2
27	S	Sabbath ends 17.31. **Pent** Va'era, Ex **6**, 2-9. **Proph** Ezek **28**, 25-29, 21	**3**
28	S		4
29	M		5
30	T		6
31	W		7

Liturgical notes - Jan 5, Selichot, Aneinu.-Jan 24, omit Tachanun in Minchah.-Jan 25, Half-Hallel.

FEBRUARY, 2001

SHEBAT 8–ADAR 5, 5761

Molad Fri Feb 23 4h 57m 30s

Shebat

1	Th		8
2	F	Sabbath commences 16.36	9
3	S	Sabbath ends 17.43. Pent Bo, Ex 10, 1-13, 16. Proph Jer 46, 13-28	10

4	S		11
5	M		12
6	T		13
7	W		14
8	Th	New Year for Trees.	15
9	F	Sabbath commences 16.49	16
10	S	Sabbath ends 17.55. Pent Beshallach, Shabbat Shirah, Ex 13, 17-17. Proph Judges 4, 4-5 (5, 1-31)	17

11	S		18
12	M		19
13	T		20
14	W		21
15	Th		22
16	F	Sabbath commences 17.02	23
17	S	Sabbath ends 18.07. Pent Yitro, Ex 18-20. Proph Is 6, 1-7, 6 and 9, 5-6 (6, 1-13). Benediction of Adar.	24

18	S		25
19	M		26
20	T		27
21	W		28
22	Th	Yom Kippur Katan	29
23	F	Sabbath commences 17.15. Rosh Chodesh first day. Pent Num 28, 1-15	30

Adar

24	S	Sabbath ends 18.19. Rosh Chodesh second day. Pent Mishpatim. Parshat Shekalim. Ex 21-24; Num 28, 9-15 and Ex 30, 11-16. Proph II Kings 12, 1-17 (11, 17-12, 17; Is 66, 1 and 23)	1

25	S		2
26	M		3
27	T		4
28	W		5

Liturgical notes - Feb 7, omit Tachanun in Minchah.-Feb 8, omit Tachanun.-Feb 22, omit Tachanun in Minchah.-Feb 23 and 24, Half-Hallel.-Feb 24 omit Tsidkatcha Tsedek in Minchah.

EVENING TWILIGHT VARIATION FOR REGIONS

This table shows the number of minutes required to be added to, or substracted from, the times for London, in order to determine the time of the termination of Sabbath, Festival, or Fast. For dates between those indicated here, an approximate calculation must be made. Acknowledgement is made to the Royal Greenwich Observatory for valued co-operation in the compilation of this table.

		BIRMINGHAM	BOURNEMOUTH	GLASGOW	LEEDS	LIVERPOOL	MANCHESTER	NEWCASTLE
Jan.	1	+ 9	+15	0	+ 4	+11	+ 8	0
	11	+ 9	+14	+ 1	+ 4	+11	+ 8	0
	21	+ 9	+14	+ 3	+ 5	+12	+ 9	+ 2
	31	+ 9	+13	+ 6	+ 6	+12	+ 9	+ 3
Feb.	10	+ 9	+12	+ 9	+ 7	+13	+10	+ 5
	20	+ 9	+11	+12	+ 8	+14	+11	+ 7
Mar.	2	+10	+10	+16	+10	+16	+13	+10
	12	+10	+ 9	+20	+12	+18	+15	+13
	22	+10	+ 7	+22	+12	+18	+15	+14
Apr.	1	+11	+ 7	+27	+15	+20	+17	+18
	11	+12	+ 7	+31	+17	+22	+19	+22
	21	+13	+ 7	+35	+20	+24	+21	+26
May	1	+16	+ 7	+40	+23	+27	+24	+30
	11	+18	+ 7	+46	+26	+30	+27	+35
	21	+20	+ 7	+52	+30	+34	+31	+42
	31	+23	+ 7	+57	+34	+37	+34	+48
June	10	+25	+ 7	+63	+38	+40	+38	+55
	20	+26	+ 7	+64	+40	+41	+39	+58
	30	+26	+ 7	+62	+38	+40	+38	+55
July	10	+23	+ 7	+57	+35	+38	+35	+50
	20	+21	+ 7	+51	+31	+34	+31	+43
	30	+19	+ 8	+46	+27	+30	+27	+38
Aug.	9	+17	+ 8	+40	+24	+27	+24	+32
	19	+16	+ 8	+35	+20	+25	+22	+27
	29	+16	+ 8	+30	+18	+23	+20	+23
Sept.	8	+14	+ 8	+26	+15	+20	+17	+18
	18	+13	+ 8	+23	+12	+18	+15	+15
	28	+13	+10	+20	+12	+18	+15	+14
Oct.	8	+12	+10	+16	+10	+16	+13	+10
	18	+11	+12	+13	+ 9	+15	+12	+9
	28	+11	+12	+10	+ 8	+14	+11	+6
Nov.	7	+10	+13	+ 7	+ 6	+13	+10	+4
	17	+10	+14	+ 4	+ 5	+12	+ 9	+3
	27	+10	+14	+ 2	+ 4	+11	+ 8	+1
Dec.	7	+10	+15	0	+ 4	+11	+ 8	0
	17	+ 9	+15	0	+ 3	+11	+ 7	- 1
	27	+ 9	+15	0	+ 3	+11	+ 8	- 1
	31	+ 9	+15	0	+ 4	+11	+ 8	0

SIDROT AND HAFTAROT FOR 2001
(5761-5762)

Haftara parentheses indicate Sephardi ritual.

2001	5761	HAFTARA	SIDRA
Jan. 6	Tebet 11	Ezekiel 37, 15-28	*Vayiggash*
13	18	I Kings 2, 1-12	*Vay'chi*
20	25	Isaiah 27, 6-28, 13; and 29, 22-23 (Jer 1, 1-2, 3)	*Shemot*
27	Shebat 3	Ezekiel 28, 25-29, 21	*Va'era*
Feb. 3	10	Jeremiah 46, 13-28	*Bo*
10	17	Judges 4, 4-5, 31 (5, 1-31)	*Beshallach (Shirah)*
17	24	Isaiah 6, 1-7, 6; 9, 5-6 (6, 1-13) ..	*Yitro*
24	Adar 1	II Kings 12, 1-17 (11, 17-12, 17 and Isaiah 66, 1 and 23)	*Mishpatim (Shekalim)*
Mar. 3	8	I Samuel 15, 2-34 (15, 1-34)	*Terumah (Zachor)*
10	15	Ezekiel 43, 10-27	*Tetsaveh*
17	22	Ezekiel 36, 16-38 (16-36)	*Ki Tissa (Parah)*
24	29	Ezek 45, 16-46, 18 (45, 18-46, 15 and I Sam 20, 18 and 42)	*Vayakhel-Pekudei (Hachodesh)*
31	Nisan 7	Isaiah 43, 21-44, 23	*Vayikra*
Apr. 7	14	Malachi 3, 4-24	*Tsav (Haggadol)*
14	21	II Samuel 22, 1-51	*Pesach (7th day)*
21	28	II Samuel 6, 1-7, 17 (6, 1-19)	*Shemini*
28	Iyar 5	II Kings 7, 3-20	*Tazria-Metsora*
May 5	12	Amos 9, 7-15 (Ezek 20, 2-20) ...	*Acharei Mot-Kedoshim*
12	19	Ezekiel 44, 15-31	*Emor*
19	26	Jeremiah 16, 19-17, 14	*Behar-Bechukkotai*
26	Sivan 4	Hosea 2, 1-22	*Bemidbar*
June 2	11	Judges 13, 2-25	*Naso*
9	18	Zechariah 2, 14-4, 7	*Beha'alotecha*
16	25	Joshua 2, 1-24	*Shelach Lecha*
23	Tammuz 2	I Samuel 11, 14-12, 22	*Korach*
30	9	Judges 11, 1-33	*Chukkat*

Sidrot and Haftarot

2001		5761	HAFTARA	SIDRA
July 7	Tammuz	16	Micah 5, 6-6, 8	*Balak*
14		23	Jeremiah 1, 1-2, 3	*Pinchas*
21	Ab	1	Jeremiah 2, 4-28 and 3, 4 (2, 4-28; 4, 1-2 and Isaiah 66, 1 and 23)	*Mattot-Massei**
28		8	Isaiah 1, 1-27	*Devarim (Chazon)*
Aug. 4		15	Isaiah 40, 1-26	*Va'etchanan (Nachamu)*
11		22	Isaiah 49, 14-51, 3	*Ekev*
18		29	Isaiah 54, 11-55, 5 (and I Samuel 20, 18 and 42)	*Re'eh***
25	Elul	6	Isaiah 51, 12-52, 12	*Shof'tim*
Sept. 1		13	Isaiah 54, 1-10	*Ki Tetsei*
8		20	Isaiah 60, 1-22	*Ki Tavo*
15		27	Isaiah 61, 10-63, 9	*Nitsavim*
		5762		
22	Tishri	5	Hosea 14, 2-10 and Joel 2, 15-27 (Hosea 14, 2-10 and Micah 7, 18-20)	*Vayelech (Shuvah)*
29		12	II Samuel 22, 1-51	*Ha'azinu*
Oct. 6		19	Ezekiel 38, 18-39, 16	*Chol Hamoed Succot*
13		26	Isaiah 42, 5-43, 10 (42, 5-21)	*Bereshit*
20	Cheshvan	3	Isaiah 54, 1-55, 5 (54-1-10)	*Noach*
27		10	Isaiah 40, 27-41, 16	*Lech Lecha*
Nov. 3		17	II Kings 4, 1-37 (4, 1-23)	*Vayera*
10		24	I Kings 1, 1-31	*Chayei Sarah*
17	Kislev	2	Malachi 1, 1-2, 7	*Tol'dot*
24		9	Hosea 12, 13-14, 10 (11, 7-12, 12)	*Vayetsei*
Dec. 1		16	Hosea 11, 7-12, 12 (Obadiah)	*Vayishlach*
8		23	Amos 2, 6-3, 8	*Vayeshev*
15		30	Zechariah 2, 14-4, 7 (and Isaiah 66, 1 and 23; I Sam 20, 18 and 42)	*Mikkets (Chanucah)*
22	Tebet	7	Ezekiel 37, 15-28	*Vayiggash*
29		14	I Kings 2, 1-12	*Vay'chi*

* The Haftara is that of Massei, not of Rosh Chodesh.
**The Haftara is that of Re'eh, not of Machar Chodesh.

MARRIAGE REGULATIONS (General)

Marriages may be contracted according to the usage of the Jews between persons *both* professing the Jewish religion, provided that due notice has been given to the Superintendent Registrar and that his certificate (or licence and certificate) has been obtained. There is no restriction regarding the hours within which the marriage may be solemnised, nor the place of marriage, which may be a synagogue, private house, or any other building.

The date and place of the intended marriage having been decided, the parties should consult the Minister or Secretary for Marriages of the synagogue through which the marriage is to be solemnised. He will advise of the necessary preliminary steps and the suitability of the proposed date.

Notice of the intended marriage must be given to the local Superintendent Registrar, and the document or documents obtained from him must be handed to the Synagogue Marriage Secretary in advance of the date appointed. In the case of a marriage in a building other than a synagogue, care should be taken that these documents contain the words *"both parties being of the Jewish persuasion"* following the description of the building.

If the marriage is to be solemnised at or through a synagogue under the jurisdiction of the Chief Rabbi, his Authorisation of Marriage must be presented. The minister of the synagogue will explain how this may be obtained.

No marriage is valid if solemnised between persons who are within the degrees of kindred of affinity (e.g., between uncle and niece) prohibited by English law, even though such a marriage is permissible by Jewish law.

A marriage between Jews must be registered immediately after the ceremony by the Secretary of Marriages of the synagogue of which the husband is a member. If he is not already a member he may become one by paying a membership fee in addition to the marriage charges.

The belief that marriage by licence may be solemnised only by civil ceremony at a Registry Office is erroneous. It may take place in a synagogue, or any other building, provided that the place of solemnisation is stated to the Superintendent Registrar when application is made for his licence.

No marriage between Jews should take place without due notice being given to the Superintendent Registrar, and without being registered in the Marriage Register of a synagogue. Marriages in such circumstances are not necessarily valid in English law. (Outside England and Wales other regulations apply and the Minister of the synagogue should be consulted.)

According to the regulations valid among Orthodox Jews, marriages may not be solemnised on the following dates:

2000		2001
–	Fast of Tebet	5 January
20 March	Fast of Esther	8 March
21 March	Purim	9 March
19 April	Day before Pesach	7 April
20-27 April	Pesach	8-15 April
7-22 May	Sephirah	25 April-10 May
24 May-2 June	Sephirah	13-22 May
8 June	Day before Shavuot	27 May
9-10 June	Shavuot	28-29 May
20 July-10 August	Three Weeks	8-29 July
29 September	Day before Rosh Hashana	17 September
30 Sept.-1 October	Rosh Hashana	18-19 September
2 October	Fast of Gedaliah	20 September
8 October	Day before Yom Kippur	26 September
9 October	Yom Kippur	27 September
13 October	Day before Succot	1 October
14-22 October	Succot	2-10 October
–	Fast of Tebet	25 December

Nor on any Sabbath

Among Reform Jews, marriages are solemnised during the Sephirah, from the Fast of Tammuz until the Fast of Ab (but not on the Fast of Ab itself), on the days that precede Festivals, on the Second days of Festivals, and on Purim, but not on the other prohibited days mentioned above.

JEWISH CALENDAR FOR THIRTY YEARS

5745–5774

(1984–2014)

INSTRUCTIONS FOR USE

The following Table shows on one line the civil date and the day of the week on which every date of the Jewish year falls during the thirty years which it covers; those dates which occur on Sabbath are printed in *heavier* type. Thus, Tishri 10, 5752, coincided with September 18, 1991, and this was a Wednesday, since September 14 is marked as being Sabbath. The civil dates on which the festivals and fasts (or any other occasion of the Jewish Calendar) occur in any particular year may be ascertained in the same manner. The Table is arranged according to the months of the Hebrew Year, the day of the month being shown in the left-hand column.

YAHRZEIT. – This is always observed on the Jewish date on which the parent died. It has never been customary under the jurisdiction of the Chief Rabbi of the United Hebrew Congregations of the British Commonwealth to observe the Yahrzeit after the death on the anniversary of the burial as is enjoined, in certain circumstances, by some authorities. If the death took place after dark, it must be dated from the next civil day, as the day is reckoned among Jews from sunset to sunset. This date must be located in the Table, according to the month and day, and the civil date of the Yahrzeit in any particular year will be found on the same line in the column beneath the year in question. It should be noted, however, that if a parent died during Adar in an ordinary year, the Yahrzeit is observed in a leap year in the First Adar. (Some people observe it in both Adars.) If the death took place in a leap year the Yahrzeit is observed in a leap year in the same Adar (whether First or Second) during which the death happened. The Yahrzeit begins and the memorial light is kindled on the evening before the civil date thus ascertained.

BARMITZVAH. – A boy attains his Barmitzvah (religious majority) when he reaches his thirteenth birthday, i.e., on the first day of his fourteenth year, this being computed according to the Jewish date on which he was born. The date and year of birth being located in the Table, the corresponding civil date of the first day of his fourteenth year will be found on the same line in the 13th column. If this be a Sabbath, he reads his *Parsha* on that day; if a week-day, he reads it on the following Sabbath. By consulting the Calendar the scriptural portion of the week may be ascertained. It should be noted, however, that if a boy be born in Adar of an ordinary year and become Barmitzvah in a leap year, the celebration falls in the Second Adar. If he were born in a leap year and becomes Barmitzvah in a leap year it is celebrated in that Adar (whether First or Second) during which his birth occurred. If he were born in a leap year and the Barmitzvah is in an ordinary year, it is observed in Adar.

TISHRI (30 days)

Tish	5745 1984 Sept-Oct	46 85 Sept-Oct	47 86 Oct-Nov	48 87 Sept-Oct	49 88 Sept-Oct	50 89 Sept-Oct	51 90 Sept-Oct	52 91 Sept-Oct	53 92 Sept-Oct	54 93 Sept-Oct	55 94 Sept-Oct	56 95 Sept-Oct	57 96 Sept-Oct	58 97 October	59 98 Sept-Oct	60 99 Sept-Oct	61 2000 Sept-Oct	62 01 Sept-Oct	63 02 Sept-Oct	64 03 Sept-Oct	65 04 Sept-Oct	66 05 Oct-Nov	67 06 Sept-Oct	68 07 Sept-Oct	69 08 Sept-Oct	70 09 Sept-Oct	71 10 Sept-Oct	72 11 Sept-Oct	73 12 Sept-Oct	74 13 Sept-Oct
1	27	16	4	24	12	30	20	9	28	16	6	25	14	2	21	11	30	18	7	27	16	4	23	13	30	19	9	29	17	5
2	28	17	5	25	13	1	21	10	29	17	7	26	15	3	22	12	1	19	8	28	17	5	24	14	1	20	10	30	18	6
3	29	18	6	26	14	2	22	11	30	18	8	27	16	4	23	13	2	20	9	29	18	6	25	15	2	21	11	1	19	7
4	30	19	7	27	15	3	23	12	1	19	9	28	17	5	24	14	3	21	10	30	19	7	26	16	3	22	12	2	20	8
5	1	20	8	28	16	4	24	13	2	20	10	29	18	6	25	15	4	22	11	1	20	8	27	17	4	23	13	3	21	9
6	2	21	9	29	17	5	25	14	3	21	11	30	19	7	26	16	5	23	12	2	21	9	28	18	5	24	14	4	22	10
7	3	22	10	30	18	6	26	15	4	22	12	1	20	8	27	17	6	24	13	3	22	10	29	19	6	25	15	5	23	11
8	4	23	11	1	19	7	27	16	5	23	13	2	21	9	28	18	7	25	14	4	23	11	30	20	7	26	16	6	24	12
9	5	24	12	2	20	8	28	17	6	24	14	3	22	10	29	19	8	26	15	5	24	12	1	21	8	27	17	7	25	13
10	6	25	13	3	21	9	29	18	7	25	15	4	23	11	30	20	9	27	16	6	25	13	2	22	9	28	18	8	26	14
11	7	26	14	4	22	10	30	19	8	26	16	5	24	12	1	21	10	28	17	7	26	14	3	23	10	29	19	9	27	15
12	8	27	15	5	23	11	1	20	9	27	17	6	25	13	2	22	11	29	18	8	27	15	4	24	11	30	20	10	28	16
13	9	28	16	6	24	12	2	21	10	28	18	7	26	14	3	23	12	30	19	9	28	16	5	25	12	1	21	11	29	17
14	10	29	17	7	25	13	3	22	11	29	19	8	27	15	4	24	13	1	20	10	29	17	6	26	13	2	22	12	30	18
15	11	30	18	8	26	14	4	23	12	30	20	9	28	16	5	25	14	2	21	11	30	18	7	27	14	3	23	13	1	19
16	12	1	19	9	27	15	5	24	13	1	21	10	29	17	6	26	15	3	22	12	1	19	8	28	15	4	24	14	2	20
17	13	2	20	10	28	16	6	25	14	2	22	11	30	18	7	27	16	4	23	13	2	20	9	29	16	5	25	15	3	21
18	14	3	21	11	29	17	7	26	15	3	23	12	1	19	8	28	17	5	24	14	3	21	10	30	17	6	26	16	4	22
19	15	4	22	12	30	18	8	27	16	4	24	13	2	20	9	29	18	6	25	15	4	22	11	1	18	7	27	17	5	23
20	16	5	23	13	1	19	9	28	17	5	25	14	3	21	10	30	19	7	26	16	5	23	12	2	19	8	28	18	6	24
21	17	6	24	14	2	20	10	29	18	6	26	15	4	22	11	1	20	8	27	17	6	24	13	3	20	9	29	19	7	25
22	18	7	25	15	3	21	11	30	19	7	27	16	5	23	12	2	21	9	28	18	7	25	14	4	21	10	30	20	8	26
23	19	8	26	16	4	22	12	1	20	8	28	17	6	24	13	3	22	10	29	19	8	26	15	5	22	11	1	21	9	27
24	20	9	27	17	5	23	13	2	21	9	29	18	7	25	14	4	23	11	30	20	9	27	16	6	23	12	2	22	10	28
25	21	10	28	18	6	24	14	3	22	10	30	19	8	26	15	5	24	12	1	21	10	28	17	7	24	13	3	23	11	29
26	22	11	29	19	7	25	15	4	23	11	1	20	9	27	16	6	25	13	2	22	11	29	18	8	25	14	4	24	12	30
27	23	12	30	20	8	26	16	5	24	12	2	21	10	28	17	7	26	14	3	23	12	30	19	9	26	15	5	25	13	1
28	24	13	31	21	9	27	17	6	25	13	3	22	11	29	18	8	27	15	4	24	13	31	20	10	27	16	6	26	14	2
29	25	14	1	22	10	28	18	7	26	14	4	23	12	30	19	9	28	16	5	25	14	1	21	11	28	17	7	27	15	3
30	26	15	2	23	11	29	19	8	27	15	5	24	13	31	20	10	29	17	6	26	15	2	22	12	29	18	8	28	16	4

In the left-hand margin figures in **black type** denote major Holy-days; elsewhere they denote Sabbaths. 1st and 2nd, New Year; 3rd, Fast of Gedaliah (if on Sabbath, postponed to Sunday); 10th, Day of Atonement; 15th to 23rd, Tabernacles, etc.; 30th, First day of New Moon of Marcheshvan.

CHESHVAN or MARCHESHVAN (29 or 30 days)

Chesh	74 / 13	73 / 12	72 / 11	71 / 10	70 / 09	69 / 08	68 / 07	67 / 06	66 / 05	65 / 04	64 / 03	63 / 02	62 / 01	61 / 2000	60 / 99	59 / 98	58 / 97	57 / 96	56 / 95	55 / 94	54 / 93	53 / 92	52 / 91	51 / 90	50 / 89	49 / 88	48 / 87	47 / 86	46 / 85	5745 / 1984
	Oct-Nov	Oct-Nov	Oct-Nov	Oct-Nov	Oct-Nov	Oct-Nov	Oct-Nov	Oct-Nov	Nov-Dec	Oct-Nov	Oct-Nov	Oct-Nov	Oct-Nov	Oct-Nov	Oct-Nov	Oct-Nov	November	Oct-Nov	Oct-Nov	Oct-Nov	Oct-Nov	Oct-Nov	Oct-Nov	Oct-Nov	Oct-Nov	Oct-Nov	Oct-Nov	Nov-Dec	Oct-Nov	Oct-Nov
1	5	17	29	9	19	30	13	23	3	16	27	7	18	30	11	21	1	14	25	6	16	28	9	20	30	12	24	3	16	27
2	6	18	30	10	20	31	14	24	4	17	28	8	19	31	12	22	2	15	26	7	17	29	10	21	31	13	25	4	17	28
3	7	19	31	11	21	1	15	25	5	18	29	9	20	1	13	23	3	16	27	8	18	30	11	22	1	14	26	5	18	29
4	8	20	1	12	22	2	16	26	6	19	30	10	21	2	14	24	4	17	28	9	19	31	12	23	2	15	27	6	19	30
5	9	21	2	13	23	3	17	27	7	20	31	11	22	3	15	25	5	18	29	10	20	1	13	24	3	16	28	7	20	31
6	10	22	3	14	24	4	18	28	8	21	1	12	23	4	16	26	6	19	30	11	21	2	14	25	4	17	29	8	21	1
7	11	23	4	15	25	5	19	29	9	22	2	13	24	5	17	27	7	20	31	12	22	3	15	26	5	18	30	9	22	2
8	12	24	5	16	26	6	20	30	10	23	3	14	25	6	18	28	8	21	1	13	23	4	16	27	6	19	31	10	23	3
9	13	25	6	17	27	7	21	31	11	24	4	15	26	7	19	29	9	22	2	14	24	5	17	28	7	20	1	11	24	4
10	14	26	7	18	28	8	22	1	12	25	5	16	27	8	20	30	10	23	3	15	25	6	18	29	8	21	2	12	25	5
11	15	27	8	19	29	9	23	2	13	26	6	17	28	9	21	31	11	24	4	16	26	7	19	30	9	22	3	13	26	6
12	16	28	9	20	30	10	24	3	14	27	7	18	29	10	22	1	12	25	5	17	27	8	20	31	10	23	4	14	27	7
13	17	29	10	21	31	11	25	4	15	28	8	19	30	11	23	2	13	26	6	18	28	9	21	1	11	24	5	15	28	8
14	18	30	11	22	1	12	26	5	16	29	9	20	31	12	24	3	14	27	7	19	29	10	22	2	12	25	6	16	29	9
15	19	31	12	23	2	13	27	6	17	30	10	21	1	13	25	4	15	28	8	20	30	11	23	3	13	26	7	17	30	10
16	20	1	13	24	3	14	28	7	18	31	11	22	2	14	26	5	16	29	9	21	31	12	24	4	14	27	8	18	31	11
17	21	2	14	25	4	15	29	8	19	1	12	23	3	15	27	6	17	30	10	22	1	13	25	5	15	28	9	19	1	12
18	22	3	15	26	5	16	30	9	20	2	13	24	4	16	28	7	18	31	11	23	2	14	26	6	16	29	10	20	2	13
19	23	4	16	27	6	17	31	10	21	3	14	25	5	17	29	8	19	1	12	24	3	15	27	7	17	30	11	21	3	14
20	24	5	17	28	7	18	1	11	22	4	15	26	6	18	30	9	20	2	13	25	4	16	28	8	18	31	12	22	4	15
21	25	6	18	29	8	19	2	12	23	5	16	27	7	19	31	10	21	3	14	26	5	17	29	9	19	1	13	23	5	16
22	26	7	19	30	9	20	3	13	24	6	17	28	8	20	1	11	22	4	15	27	6	18	30	10	20	2	14	24	6	17
23	27	8	20	31	10	21	4	14	25	7	18	29	9	21	2	12	23	5	16	28	7	19	31	11	21	3	15	25	7	18
24	28	9	21	1	11	22	5	15	26	8	19	30	10	22	3	13	24	6	17	29	8	20	1	12	22	4	16	26	8	19
25	29	10	22	2	12	23	6	16	27	9	20	31	11	23	4	14	25	7	18	30	9	21	2	13	23	5	17	27	9	20
26	30	11	23	3	13	24	7	17	28	10	21	1	12	24	5	15	26	8	19	31	10	22	3	14	24	6	18	28	10	21
27	31	12	24	4	14	25	8	18	29	11	22	2	13	25	6	16	27	9	20	1	11	23	4	15	25	7	19	29	11	22
28	1	13	25	5	15	26	9	19	30	12	23	3	14	26	7	17	28	10	21	2	12	24	5	16	26	8	20	30	12	23
29	2	14	26	6	16	27	10	20	1	13	24	4	15	27	8	18	29	11	22	3	13	25	6	17	27	9	21	1	13	24
30	3	—	—	7	17	—	—	21	—	—	25	5	—	—	9	19	—	—	23	—	14	—	7	—	28	—	—	2	—	—

Figures in **black type** denote Sabbaths.
30th, First day of New Moon of Kislev.

KISLEV (29 or 30 days)

Kis	74	73	72	71	70	69	68	67	66	65	64	63	62	61	60	59	58	57	56	55	54	53	52	51	50	49	48	47	46	5745
	13	12	11	10	09	08	07	06	05	04	03	02	01	2000	99	98	97	96	95	94	93	92	91	90	89	88	87	86 87	85	1984
	Nov-Dec	Nov-Dec	Nov-Dec	Nov-Dec	Nov-Dec	Nov-Dec	Nov-Dec	Nov-Dec	Dec	Nov-Dec	Nov-Dec	Nov-Dec	Nov-Dec	Nov-Dec	Nov-Dec	Nov-Dec	Nov-Dec	Nov-Dec	Nov-Dec	Nov-Dec	Nov-Dec	Nov-Dec	Nov-Dec	Nov-Dec	Nov-Dec	Nov-Dec	Nov-Dec	Dec-Jan	Nov-Dec	Nov-Dec
1	4	15	27	8	18	28	11	22	2	14	26	6	16	28	10	20	30	12	24	4	15	26	8	18	29	10	22	3	14	25
2	5	16	28	9	19	29	12	23	3	15	27	7	17	29	11	21	1	13	25	5	16	27	9	19	30	11	23	4	15	26
3	6	17	29	10	20	30	13	24	4	16	28	8	18	30	12	22	2	14	26	6	17	28	10	20	1	12	24	5	16	27
4	7	18	30	11	21	1	14	25	5	17	29	9	19	1	13	23	3	15	27	7	18	29	11	21	2	13	25	6	17	28
5	8	19	1	12	22	2	15	26	6	18	30	10	20	2	14	24	4	16	28	8	19	30	12	22	3	14	26	7	18	29
6	9	20	2	13	23	3	16	27	7	19	1	11	21	3	15	25	5	17	29	9	20	1	13	23	4	15	27	8	19	30
7	10	21	3	14	24	4	17	28	8	20	2	12	22	4	16	26	6	18	30	10	21	2	14	24	5	16	28	9	20	1
8	11	22	4	15	25	5	18	29	9	21	3	13	23	5	17	27	7	19	1	11	22	3	15	25	6	17	29	10	21	2
9	12	23	5	16	26	6	19	30	10	22	4	14	24	6	18	28	8	20	2	12	23	4	16	26	7	18	30	11	22	3
10	13	24	6	17	27	7	20	1	11	23	5	15	25	7	19	29	9	21	3	13	24	5	17	27	8	19	1	12	23	4
11	14	25	7	18	28	8	21	2	12	24	6	16	26	8	20	30	10	22	4	14	25	6	18	28	9	20	2	13	24	5
12	15	26	8	19	29	9	22	3	13	25	7	17	27	9	21	1	11	23	5	15	26	7	19	29	10	21	3	14	25	6
13	16	27	9	20	30	10	23	4	14	26	8	18	28	10	22	2	12	24	6	16	27	8	20	30	11	22	4	15	26	7
14	17	28	10	21	1	11	24	5	15	27	9	19	29	11	23	3	13	25	7	17	28	9	21	1	12	23	5	16	27	8
15	18	29	11	22	2	12	25	6	16	28	10	20	30	12	24	4	14	26	8	18	29	10	22	2	13	24	6	17	28	9
16	19	30	12	23	3	13	26	7	17	29	11	21	1	13	25	5	15	27	9	19	30	11	23	3	14	25	7	18	29	10
17	20	1	13	24	4	14	27	8	18	30	12	22	2	14	26	6	16	28	10	20	1	12	24	4	15	26	8	19	30	11
18	21	2	14	25	5	15	28	9	19	1	13	23	3	15	27	7	17	29	11	21	2	13	25	5	16	27	9	20	1	12
19	22	3	15	26	6	16	29	10	20	2	14	24	4	16	28	8	18	30	12	22	3	14	26	6	17	28	10	21	2	13
20	23	4	16	27	7	17	30	11	21	3	15	25	5	17	29	9	19	1	13	23	4	15	27	7	18	29	11	22	3	14
21	24	5	17	28	8	18	1	12	22	4	16	26	6	18	30	10	20	2	14	24	5	16	28	8	19	30	12	23	4	15
22	25	6	18	29	9	19	2	13	23	5	17	27	7	19	1	11	21	3	15	25	6	17	29	9	20	1	13	24	5	16
23	26	7	19	30	10	20	3	14	24	6	18	28	8	20	2	12	22	4	16	26	7	18	30	10	21	2	14	25	6	17
24	27	8	20	1	11	21	4	15	25	7	19	29	9	21	3	13	23	5	17	27	8	19	1	11	22	3	15	26	7	18
25	28	9	21	2	12	22	5	16	26	8	20	30	10	22	4	14	24	6	18	28	9	20	2	12	23	4	16	27	8	19
26	29	10	22	3	13	23	6	17	27	9	21	1	11	23	5	15	25	7	19	29	10	21	3	13	24	5	17	28	9	20
27	30	11	23	4	14	24	7	18	28	10	22	2	12	24	6	16	26	8	20	30	11	22	4	14	25	6	18	29	10	21
28	1	12	24	5	15	25	8	19	29	11	23	3	13	25	7	17	27	9	21	1	12	23	5	15	26	7	19	30	11	22
29	2	13	25	6	16	26	9	20	30	12	24	4	14	26	8	18	28	10	22	2	13	24	6	16	27	8	20	31	12	23
30	3	—	26	7	17	27	—	21	31	—	25	5	15	—	9	19	29	—	23	3	14	—	7	17	28	—	21	1	—	24

Figures in **black type** denote Sabbaths.

25th to 29th or 30th, Chanucah (opening days); 30th, First day of New Moon of Tebet.

TEBET (29 days)

Year	74	73	72	71	70	69	68	67	66	65	64	63	62	61	60	59	58	57	56	55	54	53	52	51	50	49	48	47	46	5745
	13/14	12/13	11/12	10/11	09/10	08/09	07/08	06/07	06	04/05	03/04	02/03	01/02	2000/01	99/2000	98/99	97/98	96/97	95/96	94/95	93/94	92/93	91/92	90/91	89/90	88/89	87/88	87	85	1984/1985
Teb	Dec-Jan	Dec-Jan	Dec-Jan	Dec-Jan	Dec-Jan	Dec-Jan	Dec-Jan	Dec-Jan	January	Dec-Jan	Dec-Jan	Dec-Jan	Dec-Jan	Dec-Jan	Dec-Jan	Dec-Jan	Dec-Jan	Dec-Jan	Dec-Jan	Dec-Jan	Dec-Jan	Dec-Jan	Dec-Jan	Dec-Jan	Dec-Jan	Dec-Jan	Dec-Jan	January	Dec-Jan	Dec-Jan
1	4	14	27	8	18	28	10	22	1	13	26	6	16	27	10	20	30	11	24	4	15	25	8	18	29	9	22	2	13	25
2	5	15	28	9	19	29	11	23	2	14	27	7	17	28	11	21	31	12	25	5	16	26	9	19	30	10	23	3	14	26
3	6	16	29	10	20	30	12	24	3	15	28	8	18	29	12	22	1	13	26	6	17	27	10	20	31	11	24	4	15	27
4	7	17	30	11	21	31	13	25	4	16	29	9	19	30	13	23	2	14	27	7	18	28	11	21	1	12	25	5	16	28
5	8	18	31	12	22	1	14	26	5	17	30	10	20	31	14	24	3	15	28	8	19	29	12	22	2	13	26	6	17	29
6	9	19	1	13	23	2	15	27	6	18	31	11	21	1	15	25	4	16	29	9	20	30	13	23	3	14	27	7	18	30
7	10	20	2	14	24	3	16	28	7	19	1	12	22	2	16	26	5	17	30	10	21	31	14	24	4	15	28	8	19	31
8	11	21	3	15	25	4	17	29	8	20	2	13	23	3	17	27	6	18	31	11	22	1	15	25	5	16	29	9	20	1
9	12	22	4	16	26	5	18	30	9	21	3	14	24	4	18	28	7	19	1	12	23	2	16	26	6	17	30	10	21	2
10	13	23	5	17	27	6	19	31	10	22	4	15	25	5	19	29	8	20	2	13	24	3	17	27	7	18	31	11	22	3
11	14	24	6	18	28	7	20	1	11	23	5	16	26	6	20	30	9	21	3	14	25	4	18	28	8	19	1	12	23	4
12	15	25	7	19	29	8	21	2	12	24	6	17	27	7	21	31	10	22	4	15	26	5	19	29	9	20	2	13	24	5
13	16	26	8	20	30	9	22	3	13	25	7	18	28	8	22	1	11	23	5	16	27	6	20	30	10	21	3	14	25	6
14	17	27	9	21	31	10	23	4	14	26	8	19	29	9	23	2	12	24	6	17	28	7	21	31	11	22	4	15	26	7
15	18	28	10	22	1	11	24	5	15	27	9	20	30	10	24	3	13	25	7	18	29	8	22	1	12	23	5	16	27	8
16	19	29	11	23	2	12	25	6	16	28	10	21	31	11	25	4	14	26	8	19	30	9	23	2	13	24	6	17	28	9
17	20	30	12	24	3	13	26	7	17	29	11	22	1	12	26	5	15	27	9	20	31	10	24	3	14	25	7	18	29	10
18	21	31	13	25	4	14	27	8	18	30	12	23	2	13	27	6	16	28	10	21	1	11	25	4	15	26	8	19	30	11
19	22	1	14	26	5	15	28	9	19	31	13	24	3	14	28	7	17	29	11	22	2	12	26	5	16	27	9	20	31	12
20	23	2	15	27	6	16	29	10	20	1	14	25	4	15	29	8	18	30	12	23	3	13	27	6	17	28	10	21	1	13
21	24	3	16	28	7	17	30	11	21	2	15	26	5	16	30	9	19	31	13	24	4	14	28	7	18	29	11	22	2	14
22	25	4	17	29	8	18	31	12	22	3	16	27	6	17	31	10	20	1	14	25	5	15	29	8	19	30	12	23	3	15
23	26	5	18	30	9	19	1	13	23	4	17	28	7	18	1	11	21	2	15	26	6	16	30	9	20	31	13	24	4	16
24	27	6	19	31	10	20	2	14	24	5	18	29	8	19	2	12	22	3	16	27	7	17	31	10	21	1	14	25	5	17
25	28	7	20	1	11	21	3	15	25	6	19	30	9	20	3	13	23	4	17	28	8	18	1	11	22	2	15	26	6	18
26	29	8	21	2	12	22	4	16	26	7	20	31	10	21	4	14	24	5	18	29	9	19	2	12	23	3	16	27	7	19
27	30	9	22	3	13	23	5	17	27	8	21	1	11	22	5	15	25	6	19	30	10	20	3	13	24	4	17	28	8	20
28	31	10	23	4	14	24	6	18	28	9	22	2	12	23	6	16	26	7	20	31	11	21	4	14	25	5	18	29	9	21
29	1	11	24	5	15	25	7	19	29	10	23	3	13	24	7	17	27	8	21	1	12	22	5	15	26	6	19	30	10	22

Figures in **black type** denote Sabbaths.
1st to 2nd or 3rd, Chanucah (final days); 10th, Fast of Tebet.

SHEBAT (30 days)

Sheb	74	73	72	71	70	69	68	67	66	65	64	63	62	61	60	59	58	57	56	55	54	53	52	51	50	49	48	47	46	5745
	14	13	12	11	10	09	08	07	06	05	04	03	02	01	2000	99	98	97	96	95	94	93	92	91	90	89	88	87	86	1985
	January	Jan-Feb	Jan-Feb	Jan-Feb	Jan-Feb	Jan-Feb	Jan-Feb	Jan-Feb	Jan-Feb	Jan-Feb	Jan-Feb	Jan-Feb	Jan-Feb	Jan-Feb	Jan-Feb	Jan-Feb	Jan-Feb	Jan-Feb	Jan-Feb	January	Jan-Feb	Jan-Feb	Jan-Feb	Jan-Feb	Jan-Feb	Jan-Feb	Jan-Feb	Ja-Fe-Ma	Jan-Feb	Jan-Feb
1	2	12	25	6	16	26	8	20	30	11	24	4	14	25	8	18	28	9	22	2	13	23	6	16	27	7	20	31	11	23
2	3	13	26	7	17	27	9	21	31	12	25	5	15	26	9	19	29	10	23	3	14	24	7	17	28	8	21	1	12	24
3	4	14	27	8	18	28	10	22	1	13	26	6	16	27	10	20	30	11	24	4	15	25	8	18	29	9	22	2	13	25
4	5	15	28	9	19	29	11	23	2	14	27	7	17	28	11	21	31	12	25	5	16	26	9	19	30	10	23	3	14	26
5	6	16	29	10	20	30	12	24	3	15	28	8	18	29	12	22	1	13	26	6	17	27	10	20	31	11	24	4	15	27
6	7	17	30	11	21	31	13	25	4	16	29	9	19	30	13	23	2	14	27	7	18	28	11	21	1	12	25	5	16	28
7	8	18	31	12	22	1	14	26	5	17	30	10	20	31	14	24	3	15	28	8	19	29	12	22	2	13	26	6	17	29
8	9	19	1	13	23	2	15	27	6	18	31	11	21	1	15	25	4	16	29	9	20	30	13	23	3	14	27	7	18	30
9	10	20	2	14	24	3	16	28	7	19	1	12	22	2	16	26	5	17	30	10	21	31	14	24	4	15	28	8	19	31
10	11	21	3	15	25	4	17	29	8	20	2	13	23	3	17	27	6	18	31	11	22	1	15	25	5	16	29	9	20	1
11	12	22	4	16	26	5	18	30	9	21	3	14	24	4	18	28	7	19	1	12	23	2	16	26	6	17	30	10	21	2
12	13	23	5	17	27	6	19	31	10	22	4	15	25	5	19	29	8	20	2	13	24	3	17	27	7	18	31	11	22	3
13	14	24	6	18	28	7	20	1	11	23	5	16	26	6	20	30	9	21	3	14	25	4	18	28	8	19	1	12	23	4
14	15	25	7	19	29	8	21	2	12	24	6	17	27	7	21	31	10	22	4	15	26	5	19	29	9	20	2	13	24	5
15	16	26	8	20	30	9	22	3	13	25	7	18	28	8	22	1	11	23	5	16	27	6	20	30	10	21	3	14	25	6
16	17	27	9	21	31	10	23	4	14	26	8	19	29	9	23	2	12	24	6	17	28	7	21	31	11	22	4	15	26	7
17	18	28	10	22	1	11	24	5	15	27	9	20	30	10	24	3	13	25	7	18	29	8	22	1	12	23	5	16	27	8
18	19	29	11	23	2	12	25	6	16	28	10	21	31	11	25	4	14	26	8	19	30	9	23	2	13	24	6	17	28	9
19	20	30	12	24	3	13	26	7	17	29	11	22	1	12	26	5	15	27	9	20	31	10	24	3	14	25	7	18	29	10
20	21	31	13	25	4	14	27	8	18	30	12	23	2	13	27	6	16	28	10	21	1	11	25	4	15	26	8	19	30	11
21	22	1	14	26	5	15	28	9	19	31	13	24	3	14	28	7	17	29	11	22	2	12	26	5	16	27	9	20	31	12
22	23	2	15	27	6	16	29	10	20	1	14	25	4	15	29	8	18	30	12	23	3	13	27	6	17	28	10	21	1	13
23	24	3	16	28	7	17	30	11	21	2	15	26	5	16	30	9	19	31	13	24	4	14	28	7	18	29	11	22	2	14
24	25	4	17	29	8	18	31	12	22	3	16	27	6	17	31	10	20	1	14	25	5	15	29	8	19	30	12	23	3	15
25	26	5	18	30	9	19	1	13	23	4	17	28	7	18	1	11	21	2	15	26	6	16	30	9	20	31	13	24	4	16
26	27	6	19	31	10	20	2	14	24	5	18	29	8	19	2	12	22	3	16	27	7	17	31	10	21	1	14	25	5	17
27	28	7	20	1	11	21	3	15	25	6	19	30	9	20	3	13	23	4	17	28	8	18	1	11	22	2	15	26	6	18
28	29	8	21	2	12	22	4	16	26	7	20	31	10	21	4	14	24	5	18	29	9	19	2	12	23	3	16	27	7	19
29	30	9	22	3	13	23	5	17	27	8	21	1	11	22	5	15	25	6	19	30	10	20	3	13	24	4	17	28	8	20
30	31	10	23	4	14	24	6	18	28	9	22	2	12	23	6	16	26	7	20	31	11	21	4	14	25	5	18	1	9	21

Figures in **black type** denote Sabbaths.

15th, New Year for Trees; 30th, First day of New Moon of Adar.

ADAR (29 days); in Leap Year, known as ADAR RISHON — 1st ADAR (30 days)

Adar	74	73	72	71	70	69	68	67	66	65	64	63	62	61	60	59	58	57	56	55	54	53	52	51	50	49	48	47	46	5745
year	14	13	12	11	10	09	08	07	06	05	04	03	02	01	2000	99	98	97	96	95	94	93	92	91	90	89	88	87	86	1985
month	Feb-Mar	Feb-Mar	Feb-Mar	Feb-Mar	Feb-Mar	Feb-Mar	Feb-Mar	Feb-Mar	March	Feb-Mar	Feb-Mar	Feb-Mar	Feb-Mar	Feb-Mar	Feb-Mar	Feb-Mar	Feb-Mar	Feb-Mar	Feb-Mar	Feb-Mar	Feb-Mar	Feb-Mar	Feb-Mar	Feb-Mar	Feb-Mar	Feb-Mar	Feb-Mar	March	Feb-Mar	Feb-Mar
1	1	11	24	5	15	25	7	19	1	10	23	3	13	24	7	17	27	8	21	1	12	22	5	15	26	6	19	2	10	22
2	2	12	25	6	16	26	8	20	2	11	24	4	14	25	8	18	28	9	22	2	13	23	6	16	27	7	20	3	11	23
3	3	13	26	7	17	27	9	21	3	12	25	5	15	26	9	19	1	10	23	3	14	24	7	17	28	8	21	4	12	24
4	4	14	27	8	18	28	10	22	4	13	26	6	16	27	10	20	2	11	24	4	15	25	8	18	1	9	22	5	13	25
5	5	15	28	9	19	1	11	23	5	14	27	7	17	28	11	21	3	12	25	5	16	26	9	19	2	10	23	6	14	26
6	6	16	29	10	20	2	12	24	6	15	28	8	18	1	12	22	4	13	26	6	17	27	10	20	3	11	24	7	15	27
7	7	17	1	11	21	3	13	25	7	16	29	9	19	2	13	23	5	14	27	7	18	28	11	21	4	12	25	8	16	28
8	8	18	2	12	22	4	14	26	8	17	1	10	20	3	14	24	6	15	28	8	19	1	12	22	5	13	26	9	17	1
9	9	19	3	13	23	5	15	27	9	18	2	11	21	4	15	25	7	16	29	9	20	2	13	23	6	14	27	10	18	2
10	10	20	4	14	24	6	16	28	10	19	3	12	22	5	16	26	8	17	1	10	21	3	14	24	7	15	28	11	19	3
11	11	21	5	15	25	7	17	1	11	20	4	13	23	6	17	27	9	18	2	11	22	4	15	25	8	16	29	12	20	4
12	12	22	6	16	26	8	18	2	12	21	5	14	24	7	18	28	10	19	3	12	23	5	16	26	9	17	1	13	21	5
13	13	23	7	17	27	9	19	3	13	22	6	15	25	8	19	1	11	20	4	13	24	6	17	27	10	18	2	14	22	6
14	14	24	8	18	28	10	20	4	14	23	7	16	26	9	20	2	12	21	5	14	25	7	18	28	11	19	3	15	23	7
15	15	25	9	19	1	11	21	5	15	24	8	17	27	10	21	3	13	22	6	15	26	8	19	1	12	20	4	16	24	8
16	16	26	10	20	2	12	22	6	16	25	9	18	28	11	22	4	14	23	7	16	27	9	20	2	13	21	5	17	25	9
17	17	27	11	21	3	13	23	7	17	26	10	19	1	12	23	5	15	24	8	17	28	10	21	3	14	22	6	18	26	10
18	18	28	12	22	4	14	24	8	18	27	11	20	2	13	24	6	16	25	9	18	1	11	22	4	15	23	7	19	27	11
19	19	1	13	23	5	15	25	9	19	28	12	21	3	14	25	7	17	26	10	19	2	12	23	5	16	24	8	20	28	12
20	20	2	14	24	6	16	26	10	20	1	13	22	4	15	26	8	18	27	11	20	3	13	24	6	17	25	9	21	1	13
21	21	3	15	25	7	17	27	11	21	2	14	23	5	16	27	9	19	28	12	21	4	14	25	7	18	26	10	22	2	14
22	22	4	16	26	8	18	28	12	22	3	15	24	6	17	28	10	20	1	13	22	5	15	26	8	19	27	11	23	3	15
23	23	5	17	27	9	19	29	13	23	4	16	25	7	18	29	11	21	2	14	23	6	16	27	9	20	28	12	24	4	16
24	24	6	18	28	10	20	1	14	24	5	17	26	8	19	1	12	22	3	15	24	7	17	28	10	21	1	13	25	5	17
25	25	7	19	1	11	21	2	15	25	6	18	27	9	20	2	13	23	4	16	25	8	18	29	11	22	2	14	26	6	18
26	26	8	20	2	12	22	3	16	26	7	19	28	10	21	3	14	24	5	17	26	9	19	1	12	23	3	15	27	7	19
27	27	9	21	3	13	23	4	17	27	8	20	1	11	22	4	15	25	6	18	27	10	20	2	13	24	4	16	28	8	20
28	28	10	22	4	14	24	5	18	28	9	21	2	12	23	5	16	26	7	19	28	11	21	3	14	25	5	17	29	9	21
29	1	11	23	5	15	25	6	19	29	10	22	3	13	24	6	17	27	8	20	1	12	22	4	15	26	6	18	30	10	22
30	2	—	—	6	—	—	7	—	—	11	—	4	—	—	7	—	—	9	—	2	—	—	5	—	—	7	—	—	11	—
	R			R			R			R		R			R			R		R			R			R			R	

Figures in **black type** denote Sabbaths.

13th, Fast of Esther (if on Sabbath, observed the preceding Thursday); 14th, Purim; 15th, Shushan Purim.

NOTE. — In a Jewish leap year, indicated by the letter **R** (for Adar Rishon) at the foot of a column, the above days are observed in 2nd Adar.

In a leap year, 30th day is First day of New Moon of the 2nd Adar.

2nd ADAR — ADAR SHENI, also known as VE-ADAR (29 days)

2nd Adar	5745	46	47	48	49	50	51	52	53	54	55	56	57	58	59	60	61	62	63	64	65	66	67	68	69	70	71	72	73	74
	1985	86	87	88	89	90	91	92	93	94	95	96	97	98	99	2000	01	02	03	04	05	06	07	08	09	10	11	12	13	14
		Mar-Apr			Mar-Apr			Mar-Apr			March		Mar-Apr			Mar-Apr			Mar-Apr		Mar-Apr			Mar-Apr			Mar-Apr			March
1		12			8			6			3		10			8			5		**12**			**8**			7			3
2		13			9			**7**			**4**		11			9			6		13			9			8			4
3		14			10			8			5		12			10			7		14			10			9			5
4		**15**			**11**			9			6		13			**11**			**8**		15			11			10			6
5		16			12			10			7		14			12			9		16			12			11			7
6		17			13			11			8		**15**			13			10		17			13			**12**			**8**
7		18			14			12			9		16			14			11		18			14			13			9
8		19			15			13			10		17			15			12		**19**			**15**			14			10
9		20			16			**14**			**11**		18			16			13		20			16			15			11
10		21			17			15			12		19			17			14		21			17			16			12
11		**22**			**18**			16			13		20			**18**			**15**		22			18			17			13
12		23			19			17			14		21			19			16		23			19			18			14
13		24			20			18			15		**22**			20			17		24			20			**19**			**15**
14		25			21			19			16		23			21			18		25			21			20			16
15		26			22			20			17		24			22			19		**26**			**22**			21			17
16		27			23			**21**			**18**		25			23			20		27			23			22			18
17		28			24			22			19		26			24			21		28			24			23			19
18		**29**			**25**			23			20		27			**25**			**22**		29			25			24			20
19		30			26			24			21		28			26			23		30			26			25			21
20		31			27			25			22		**29**			27			24		31			27			**26**			**22**
21		1			28			26			23		30			28			25		1			28			27			23
22		2			29			27			24		31			29			26		**2**			**29**			28			24
23		3			30			**28**			**25**		1			30			27		3			30			29			25
24		4			31			29			26		2			31			28		4			31			30			26
25		**5**			**1**			30			27		3			**1**			**29**		5			1			31			27
26		6			2			31			28		4			2			30		6			2			1			28
27		7			3			1			29		**5**			3			31		7			3			**2**			**29**
28		8			4			2			30		6			4			1		8			4			3			30
29		9			5			3			31		7			5			2		**9**			**5**			4			31

Figures in **black type** denote Sabbaths.

13th, Fast of Esther (if on Sabbath, observed on the preceding Thursday); 14th, Purim; 15th Shushan Purim.

NISAN (30 days)

Nis	74 / 14 / April	73 / 13 / Mar-Apr	72 / 12 / Mar-Apr	71 / 11 / Apr-May	70 / 10 / Mar-Apr	69 / 09 / Mar-Apr	68 / 08 / Apr-May	67 / 07 / Mar-Apr	66 / 06 / Mar-Apr	65 / 05 / Apr-May	64 / 04 / Mar-Apr	63 / 03 / Apr-May	62 / 02 / Mar-Apr	61 / 01 / Mar-Apr	60 / 2000 / Apr-May	59 / 99 / Mar-Apr	58 / 98 / Mar-Apr	57 / 97 / Apr-May	56 / 96 / Mar-Apr	55 / 95 / April	54 / 94 / Mar-Apr	53 / 93 / Mar-Apr	52 / 92 / Apr-May	51 / 91 / Mar-Apr	50 / 90 / Mar-Apr	49 / 89 / Apr-May	48 / 88 / Mar-Apr	47 / 87 / Mar-Apr	46 / 86 / Apr-May	5745 / 1985 / Mar-Apr
1	1	12	24	5	16	26	6	20	30	10	23	3	14	25	6	18	28	8	21	1	13	23	4	16	27	6	19	31	10	23
2	2	13	25	6	17	27	7	21	31	11	24	4	15	26	7	19	29	9	22	2	14	24	5	17	28	7	20	1	11	24
3	3	14	26	7	18	28	8	22	1	12	25	5	16	27	8	20	30	10	23	3	15	25	6	18	29	8	21	2	12	25
4	4	15	27	8	19	29	9	23	2	13	26	6	17	28	9	21	31	11	24	4	16	26	7	19	30	9	22	3	13	26
5	5	16	28	9	20	30	10	24	3	14	27	7	18	29	10	22	1	12	25	5	17	27	8	20	31	10	23	4	14	27
6	6	17	29	10	21	31	11	25	4	15	28	8	19	30	11	23	2	13	26	6	18	28	9	21	1	11	24	5	15	28
7	7	18	30	11	22	1	12	26	5	16	29	9	20	31	12	24	3	14	27	7	19	29	10	22	2	12	25	6	16	29
8	8	19	31	12	23	2	13	27	6	17	30	10	21	1	13	25	4	15	28	8	20	30	11	23	3	13	26	7	17	30
9	9	20	1	13	24	3	14	28	7	18	31	11	22	2	14	26	5	16	29	9	21	31	12	24	4	14	27	8	18	31
10	10	21	2	14	25	4	15	29	8	19	1	12	23	3	15	27	6	17	30	10	22	1	13	25	5	15	28	9	19	1
11	11	22	3	15	26	5	16	30	9	20	2	13	24	4	16	28	7	18	31	11	23	2	14	26	6	16	29	10	20	2
12	12	23	4	16	27	6	17	31	10	21	3	14	25	5	17	29	8	19	1	12	24	3	15	27	7	17	30	11	21	3
13	13	24	5	17	28	7	18	1	11	22	4	15	26	6	18	30	9	20	2	13	25	4	16	28	8	18	31	12	22	4
14	14	25	6	18	29	8	19	2	12	23	5	16	27	7	19	31	10	21	3	14	26	5	17	29	9	19	1	13	23	5
15	15	26	7	19	30	9	20	3	13	24	6	17	28	8	20	1	11	22	4	15	27	6	18	30	10	20	2	14	24	6
16	16	27	8	20	31	10	21	4	14	25	7	18	29	9	21	2	12	23	5	16	28	7	19	31	11	21	3	15	25	7
17	17	28	9	21	1	11	22	5	15	26	8	19	30	10	22	3	13	24	6	17	29	8	20	1	12	22	4	16	26	8
18	18	29	10	22	2	12	23	6	16	27	9	20	31	11	23	4	14	25	7	18	30	9	21	2	13	23	5	17	27	9
19	19	30	11	23	3	13	24	7	17	28	10	21	1	12	24	5	15	26	8	19	31	10	22	3	14	24	6	18	28	10
20	20	31	12	24	4	14	25	8	18	29	11	22	2	13	25	6	16	27	9	20	1	11	23	4	15	25	7	19	29	11
21	21	1	13	25	5	15	26	9	19	30	12	23	3	14	26	7	17	28	10	21	2	12	24	5	16	26	8	20	30	12
22	22	2	14	26	6	16	27	10	20	1	13	24	4	15	27	8	18	29	11	22	3	13	25	6	17	27	9	21	1	13
23	23	3	15	27	7	17	28	11	21	2	14	25	5	16	28	9	19	30	12	23	4	14	26	7	18	28	10	22	2	14
24	24	4	16	28	8	18	29	12	22	3	15	26	6	17	29	10	20	1	13	24	5	15	27	8	19	29	11	23	3	15
25	25	5	17	29	9	19	30	13	23	4	16	27	7	18	30	11	21	2	14	25	6	16	28	9	20	30	12	24	4	16
26	26	6	18	30	10	20	1	14	24	5	17	28	8	19	1	12	22	3	15	26	7	17	29	10	21	1	13	25	5	17
27	27	7	19	1	11	21	2	15	25	6	18	29	9	20	2	13	23	4	16	27	8	18	30	11	22	2	14	26	6	18
28	28	8	20	2	12	22	3	16	26	7	19	30	10	21	3	14	24	5	17	28	9	19	31	12	23	3	15	27	7	19
29	29	9	21	3	13	23	4	17	27	8	20	1	11	22	4	15	25	6	18	29	10	20	1	13	24	4	16	28	8	20
30	30	10	22	4	14	24	5	18	28	9	21	2	12	23	5	16	26	7	19	30	11	21	2	14	25	5	17	29	9	21

In the left-hand margin figures in **black type** denote major Holy-days; elsewhere they denote Sabbaths. 14th, Fast of the Firstborn (if on Sabbath, observed on the preceding Thursday); 15th to 22nd, Passover; 30th, First day of New Moon of Iyar.

IYAR (29 days)

Year	Civil	Month	1	2	3	4	5	6	7	8	9	10	11	12	13	14	15	16	17	18	19	20	21	22	23	24	25	26	27	28	29
74	14	May	1	2	3	4	5	6	7	8	9	10	11	12	13	14	15	16	17	18	19	20	21	22	23	24	25	26	27	28	29
73	13	Apr-May	11	12	13	14	15	16	17	18	19	20	21	22	23	24	25	26	27	28	29	30	1	2	3	4	5	6	7	8	9
72	12	Apr-May	23	24	25	26	27	28	29	30	1	2	3	4	5	6	7	8	9	10	11	12	13	14	15	16	17	18	19	20	21
71	11	May-Jn	5	6	7	8	9	10	11	12	13	14	15	16	17	18	19	20	21	22	23	24	25	26	27	28	29	30	31	1	2
70	10	Apr-May	15	16	17	18	19	20	21	22	23	24	25	26	27	28	29	30	1	2	3	4	5	6	7	8	9	10	11	12	13
69	09	Apr-May	25	26	27	28	29	30	1	2	3	4	5	6	7	8	9	10	11	12	13	14	15	16	17	18	19	20	21	22	23
68	08	May-Jn	6	7	8	9	10	11	12	13	14	15	16	17	18	19	20	21	22	23	24	25	26	27	28	29	30	31	1	2	3
67	07	Apr-May	19	20	21	22	23	24	25	26	27	28	29	30	1	2	3	4	5	6	7	8	9	10	11	12	13	14	15	16	17
66	06	Apr-May	29	30	1	2	3	4	5	6	7	8	9	10	11	12	13	14	15	16	17	18	19	20	21	22	23	24	25	26	27
65	05	May-Jn	10	11	12	13	14	15	16	17	18	19	20	21	22	23	24	25	26	27	28	29	30	31	1	2	3	4	5	6	7
64	04	Apr-May	22	23	24	25	26	27	28	29	30	1	2	3	4	5	6	7	8	9	10	11	12	13	14	15	16	17	18	19	20
63	03	May	3	4	5	6	7	8	9	10	11	12	13	14	15	16	17	18	19	20	21	22	23	24	25	26	27	28	29	30	31
62	02	Apr-May	13	14	15	16	17	18	19	20	21	22	23	24	25	26	27	28	29	30	1	2	3	4	5	6	7	8	9	10	11
61	01	Apr-May	24	25	26	27	28	29	30	1	2	3	4	5	6	7	8	9	10	11	12	13	14	15	16	17	18	19	20	21	22
60	2000	May-Jn	6	7	8	9	10	11	12	13	14	15	16	17	18	19	20	21	22	23	24	25	26	27	28	29	30	31	1	2	3
59	99	Apr-May	17	18	19	20	21	22	23	24	25	26	27	28	29	30	1	2	3	4	5	6	7	8	9	10	11	12	13	14	15
58	98	Apr-May	27	28	29	30	1	2	3	4	5	6	7	8	9	10	11	12	13	14	15	16	17	18	19	20	21	22	23	24	25
57	97	May-Jn	8	9	10	11	12	13	14	15	16	17	18	19	20	21	22	23	24	25	26	27	28	29	30	31	1	2	3	4	5
56	96	Apr-May	20	21	22	23	24	25	26	27	28	29	30	1	2	3	4	5	6	7	8	9	10	11	12	13	14	15	16	17	18
55	95	May	1	2	3	4	5	6	7	8	9	10	11	12	13	14	15	16	17	18	19	20	21	22	23	24	25	26	27	28	29
54	94	Apr-May	12	13	14	15	16	17	18	19	20	21	22	23	24	25	26	27	28	29	30	1	2	3	4	5	6	7	8	9	10
53	93	Apr-May	22	23	24	25	26	27	28	29	30	1	2	3	4	5	6	7	8	9	10	11	12	13	14	15	16	17	18	19	20
52	92	May-Jn	4	5	6	7	8	9	10	11	12	13	14	15	16	17	18	19	20	21	22	23	24	25	26	27	28	29	30	31	1
51	91	Apr-May	15	16	17	18	19	20	21	22	23	24	25	26	27	28	29	30	1	2	3	4	5	6	7	8	9	10	11	12	13
50	90	Apr-May	26	27	28	29	30	1	2	3	4	5	6	7	8	9	10	11	12	13	14	15	16	17	18	19	20	21	22	23	24
49	89	May-Jn	6	7	8	9	10	11	12	13	14	15	16	17	18	19	20	21	22	23	24	25	26	27	28	29	30	31	1	2	3
48	88	Apr-May	18	19	20	21	22	23	24	25	26	27	28	29	30	1	2	3	4	5	6	7	8	9	10	11	12	13	14	15	16
47	87	Apr-May	30	1	2	3	4	5	6	7	8	9	10	11	12	13	14	15	16	17	18	19	20	21	22	23	24	25	26	27	28
46	86	May-Jn	10	11	12	13	14	15	16	17	18	19	20	21	22	23	24	25	26	27	28	29	30	31	1	2	3	4	5	6	7
5745	1985	Apr-May	22	23	24	25	26	27	28	29	30	1	2	3	4	5	6	7	8	9	10	11	12	13	14	15	16	17	18	19	20

Figures in **black type** denote Sabbaths.
18th, 33rd Day Omer, Scholars' Festival.

SIVAN (30 days)

Sivan	74	73	72	71	70	69	68	67	66	65	64	63	62	61	60	59	58	57	56	55	54	53	52	51	50	49	48	47	46	5745
	14	13	12	11	10	09	08	07	06	05	04	03	02	01	2000	99	98	97	96	95	94	93	92	91	90	89	88	87	86	1985
	May-Jn	May-Jn	May-Jn	Jn-July	May-Jn	May-Jn	Jn-July	May-Jn	May-Jn	Jn-July	May-Jn	June	May-Jn	May-Jn	Jn-July	May-Jn	May-Jn	Jn-July	May-Jn	May-Jn	May-Jn	May-Jn	Jn-July	May-Jn	May-Jn	Jn-July	May-Jn	May-Jn	Jn-July	May-Jn
1	30	10	22	3	14	24	4	18	28	8	21	1	12	23	4	16	26	6	19	30	11	21	2	14	25	4	17	29	8	21
2	31	11	23	4	15	25	5	19	29	9	22	2	13	24	5	17	27	7	20	31	12	22	3	15	26	5	18	30	9	22
3	1	12	24	5	16	26	6	20	30	10	23	3	14	25	6	18	28	8	21	1	13	23	4	16	27	6	19	31	10	23
4	2	13	25	6	17	27	7	21	31	11	24	4	15	26	7	19	29	9	22	2	14	24	5	17	28	7	20	1	11	24
5	3	14	26	7	18	28	8	22	1	12	25	5	16	27	8	20	30	10	23	3	15	25	6	18	29	8	21	2	12	25
6	4	15	27	8	19	29	9	23	2	13	26	6	17	28	9	21	31	11	24	4	16	26	7	19	30	9	22	3	13	26
7	5	16	28	9	20	30	10	24	3	14	27	7	18	29	10	22	1	12	25	5	17	27	8	20	31	10	23	4	14	27
8	6	17	29	10	21	31	11	25	4	15	28	8	19	30	11	23	2	13	26	6	18	28	9	21	1	11	24	5	15	28
9	7	18	30	11	22	1	12	26	5	16	29	9	20	31	12	24	3	14	27	7	19	29	10	22	2	12	25	6	16	29
10	8	19	31	12	23	2	13	27	6	17	30	10	21	1	13	25	4	15	28	8	20	30	11	23	3	13	26	7	17	30
11	9	20	1	13	24	3	14	28	7	18	31	11	22	2	14	26	5	16	29	9	21	31	12	24	4	14	27	8	18	31
12	10	21	2	14	25	4	15	29	8	19	1	12	23	3	15	27	6	17	30	10	22	1	13	25	5	15	28	9	19	1
13	11	22	3	15	26	5	16	30	9	20	2	13	24	4	16	28	7	18	31	11	23	2	14	26	6	16	29	10	20	2
14	12	23	4	16	27	6	17	31	10	21	3	14	25	5	17	29	8	19	1	12	24	3	15	27	7	17	30	11	21	3
15	13	24	5	17	28	7	18	1	11	22	4	15	26	6	18	30	9	20	2	13	25	4	16	28	8	18	31	12	22	4
16	14	25	6	18	29	8	19	2	12	23	5	16	27	7	19	31	10	21	3	14	26	5	17	29	9	19	1	13	23	5
17	15	26	7	19	30	9	20	3	13	24	6	17	28	8	20	1	11	22	4	15	27	6	18	30	10	20	2	14	24	6
18	16	27	8	20	31	10	21	4	14	25	7	18	29	9	21	2	12	23	5	16	28	7	19	31	11	21	3	15	25	7
19	17	28	9	21	1	11	22	5	15	26	8	19	30	10	22	3	13	24	6	17	29	8	20	1	12	22	4	16	26	8
20	18	29	10	22	2	12	23	6	16	27	9	20	31	11	23	4	14	25	7	18	30	9	21	2	13	23	5	17	27	9
21	19	30	11	23	3	13	24	7	17	28	10	21	1	12	24	5	15	26	8	19	31	10	22	3	14	24	6	18	28	10
22	20	31	12	24	4	14	25	8	18	29	11	22	2	13	25	6	16	27	9	20	1	11	23	4	15	25	7	19	29	11
23	21	1	13	25	5	15	26	9	19	30	12	23	3	14	26	7	17	28	10	21	2	12	24	5	16	26	8	20	30	12
24	22	2	14	26	6	16	27	10	20	1	13	24	4	15	27	8	18	29	11	22	3	13	25	6	17	27	9	21	1	13
25	23	3	15	27	7	17	28	11	21	2	14	25	5	16	28	9	19	30	12	23	4	14	26	7	18	28	10	22	2	14
26	24	4	16	28	8	18	29	12	22	3	15	26	6	17	29	10	20	1	13	24	5	15	27	8	19	29	11	23	3	15
27	25	5	17	29	9	19	30	13	23	4	16	27	7	18	30	11	21	2	14	25	6	16	28	9	20	30	12	24	4	16
28	26	6	18	30	10	20	1	14	24	5	17	28	8	19	1	12	22	3	15	26	7	17	29	10	21	1	13	25	5	17
29	27	7	19	1	11	21	2	15	25	6	18	29	9	20	2	13	23	4	16	27	8	18	30	11	22	2	14	26	6	18
30	28	8	20	2	12	22	3	16	26	7	19	30	10	21	3	14	24	5	17	28	9	19	1	12	23	3	15	27	7	19

In the left-hand margin figures in **black type** denote major Holy-days; elsewhere they denote Sabbaths. 6th and 7th, Pentecost; 30th, First day of New Moon of Tammuz.

TAMMUZ (29 days)

Year	Greg.	Month	1	2	3	4	5	6	7	8	9	10	11	12	13	14	15	16	17	18	19	20	21	22	23	24	25	26	27	28	29
74	14	Jn-July	29	30	1	2	3	4	**5**	6	7	8	9	10	11	**12**	13	14	15	16	17	18	**19**	20	21	22	23	24	25	**26**	27
73	13	Jn-July	9	10	11	12	13	14	**15**	16	17	18	19	20	21	**22**	23	24	25	26	27	28	**29**	30	1	2	3	4	5	**6**	7
72	12	Jn-July	21	22	**23**	24	25	26	27	28	29	**30**	1	2	3	4	5	6	**7**	8	9	10	11	12	13	**14**	15	16	17	18	19
71	11	July	3	4	5	6	7	8	**9**	10	11	12	13	14	15	**16**	17	18	19	20	21	22	**23**	24	25	26	27	28	29	**30**	31
70	10	Jn-July	13	14	15	16	17	18	**19**	20	21	22	23	24	25	**26**	27	28	29	30	1	2	**3**	4	5	6	7	8	9	**10**	11
69	09	Jn-July	23	24	25	26	**27**	28	29	30	1	2	3	**4**	5	6	7	8	9	10	11	12	13	14	15	16	17	**18**	19	20	21
68	08	July-Au	4	**5**	6	7	8	9	10	11	**12**	13	14	15	16	17	18	**19**	20	21	22	23	24	25	**26**	27	28	29	30	31	1
67	07	Jn-July	17	18	19	20	21	22	**23**	24	25	26	27	28	29	**30**	1	2	3	4	5	6	**7**	8	9	10	11	12	13	**14**	15
66	06	Jn-July	27	28	29	30	**1**	2	3	4	5	6	7	**8**	9	10	11	12	13	14	**15**	16	17	18	19	20	21	**22**	23	24	25
65	05	July-Au	8	9	10	11	12	13	14	15	**16**	17	18	19	20	21	22	**23**	24	25	26	27	28	29	**30**	31	1	2	3	4	5
64	04	Jn-July	20	21	22	23	24	25	**26**	27	28	29	30	1	2	**3**	4	5	6	7	8	9	**10**	11	12	13	14	15	16	**17**	18
63	03	July	1	2	3	4	**5**	6	7	8	9	10	11	**12**	13	14	15	16	17	18	**19**	20	21	22	23	24	25	**26**	27	28	29
62	02	Jn-July	11	12	13	14	**15**	16	17	18	19	20	21	**22**	23	24	25	26	27	28	**29**	30	1	2	3	4	5	**6**	7	8	9
61	01	Jn-July	22	**23**	24	25	26	27	28	29	30	1	2	3	4	5	6	**7**	8	9	10	11	12	13	14	**15**	16	17	18	19	20
60	2000	July-Au	4	5	6	7	**8**	9	10	11	12	13	14	**15**	16	17	18	19	20	21	**22**	23	24	25	26	27	28	**29**	30	31	1
59	99	Jn-July	15	16	17	18	**19**	20	21	22	23	24	25	**26**	27	28	29	30	1	2	**3**	4	5	6	7	8	9	**10**	11	12	13
58	98	Jn-July	25	26	**27**	28	29	30	1	2	3	4	5	6	7	8	9	10	**11**	12	13	14	15	16	17	**18**	19	20	21	22	23
57	97	July-Au	6	7	8	9	10	11	**12**	13	14	15	16	17	18	**19**	20	21	22	23	24	25	**26**	27	28	29	30	31	1	**2**	3
56	96	Jn-July	18	19	20	21	**22**	23	24	25	26	27	28	**29**	30	1	2	3	4	5	**6**	7	8	9	10	11	12	**13**	14	15	16
55	95	Jn-July	29	30	**1**	2	3	4	5	**6**	7	**8**	9	10	11	12	13	14	**15**	16	17	18	19	20	21	**22**	23	24	25	26	27
54	94	Jn-July	10	**11**	12	13	14	15	16	17	**18**	19	20	21	22	23	24	**25**	26	27	28	29	30	1	2	3	4	5	6	7	8
53	93	Jn-July	20	21	22	23	24	25	**26**	27	28	29	30	1	2	**3**	4	5	6	7	8	9	**10**	11	12	13	14	15	16	**17**	18
52	92	July	2	3	4	5	6	7	8	9	10	**11**	12	13	14	15	16	17	**18**	19	20	21	22	23	24	25	26	27	28	29	30
51	91	Jn-July	13	14	**15**	16	17	18	19	20	21	**22**	23	24	25	26	27	28	**29**	30	1	2	3	4	5	6	7	8	9	10	11
50	90	Jn-July	24	25	26	27	28	29	**30**	1	2	3	4	5	6	7	8	9	10	11	12	13	**14**	15	16	17	18	19	20	**21**	22
49	89	July-Au	4	5	6	7	**8**	9	10	11	12	13	14	**15**	16	17	18	19	20	21	**22**	23	24	25	26	27	28	**29**	30	31	1
48	88	Jn-July	16	17	**18**	19	20	21	22	23	24	**25**	26	27	28	29	30	1	**2**	3	4	5	6	7	8	**9**	10	11	12	13	14
47	87	Jn-July	28	29	30	1	2	3	**4**	5	6	7	8	9	10	**11**	12	13	14	15	16	17	**18**	19	20	21	22	23	24	**25**	26
46	86	July-Au	8	9	10	11	**12**	13	14	15	16	17	18	**19**	20	21	22	23	24	25	**26**	27	28	29	30	31	1	**2**	3	4	5
5745	1985	Jn-July	20	21	**22**	23	24	25	26	27	28	**29**	30	1	2	3	4	5	**6**	7	8	9	10	11	12	**13**	14	15	16	17	18

Figures in **black type** denote Sabbaths.
17th, Fast of Tammuz (if on Sabbath, postponed to Sunday).

AB (30 days)

Jewish Yr	Greg Yr	Month	1	2	3	4	5	6	7	8	9	10	11	12	13	14	15	16	17	18	19	20	21	22	23	24	25	26	27	28	29	30
74	14	July-Au	28	29	30	31	1	2	3	4	5	6	7	8	9	10	11	12	13	14	15	16	17	18	19	20	21	22	23	24	25	26
73	13	July-Au	8	9	10	11	12	13	14	15	16	17	18	19	20	21	22	23	24	25	26	27	28	29	30	31	1	2	3	4	5	6
72	12	July-Au	20	21	22	23	24	25	26	27	28	29	30	31	1	2	3	4	5	6	7	8	9	10	11	12	13	14	15	16	17	18
71	11	August	1	2	3	4	5	6	7	8	9	10	11	12	13	14	15	16	17	18	19	20	21	22	23	24	25	26	27	28	29	30
70	10	July-Au	12	13	14	15	16	17	18	19	20	21	22	23	24	25	26	27	28	29	30	31	1	2	3	4	5	6	7	8	9	10
69	09	July-Au	22	23	24	25	26	27	28	29	30	31	1	2	3	4	5	6	7	8	9	10	11	12	13	14	15	16	17	18	19	20
68	08	August	2	3	4	5	6	7	8	9	10	11	12	13	14	15	16	17	18	19	20	21	22	23	24	25	26	27	28	29	30	31
67	07	July-Au	16	17	18	19	20	21	22	23	24	25	26	27	28	29	30	31	1	2	3	4	5	6	7	8	9	10	11	12	13	14
66	06	July-Au	26	27	28	29	30	31	1	2	3	4	5	6	7	8	9	10	11	12	13	14	15	16	17	18	19	20	21	22	23	24
65	05	Au-Sep	6	7	8	9	10	11	12	13	14	15	16	17	18	19	20	21	22	23	24	25	26	27	28	29	30	31	1	2	3	4
64	04	July-Au	19	20	21	22	23	24	25	26	27	28	29	30	31	1	2	3	4	5	6	7	8	9	10	11	12	13	14	15	16	17
63	03	July-Au	30	31	1	2	3	4	5	6	7	8	9	10	11	12	13	14	15	16	17	18	19	20	21	22	23	24	25	26	27	28
62	02	July-Au	10	11	12	13	14	15	16	17	18	19	20	21	22	23	24	25	26	27	28	29	30	31	1	2	3	4	5	6	7	8
61	01	July-Au	21	22	23	24	25	26	27	28	29	30	31	1	2	3	4	5	6	7	8	9	10	11	12	13	14	15	16	17	18	19
60	2000	August	2	3	4	5	6	7	8	9	10	11	12	13	14	15	16	17	18	19	20	21	22	23	24	25	26	27	28	29	30	31
59	99	July-Au	14	15	16	17	18	19	20	21	22	23	24	25	26	27	28	29	30	31	1	2	3	4	5	6	7	8	9	10	11	12
58	98	July-Au	24	25	26	27	28	29	30	31	1	2	3	4	5	6	7	8	9	10	11	12	13	14	15	16	17	18	19	20	21	22
57	97	Au-Sep	4	5	6	7	8	9	10	11	12	13	14	15	16	17	18	19	20	21	22	23	24	25	26	27	28	29	30	31	1	2
56	96	July-Au	17	18	19	20	21	22	23	24	25	26	27	28	29	30	31	1	2	3	4	5	6	7	8	9	10	11	12	13	14	15
55	95	July-Au	28	29	30	31	1	2	3	4	5	6	7	8	9	10	11	12	13	14	15	16	17	18	19	20	21	22	23	24	25	26
54	94	July-Au	9	10	11	12	13	14	15	16	17	18	19	20	21	22	23	24	25	26	27	28	29	30	31	1	2	3	4	5	6	7
53	93	July-Au	19	20	21	22	23	24	25	26	27	28	29	30	31	1	2	3	4	5	6	7	8	9	10	11	12	13	14	15	16	17
52	92	July-Au	31	1	2	3	4	5	6	7	8	9	10	11	12	13	14	15	16	17	18	19	20	21	22	23	24	25	26	27	28	29
51	91	July-Au	12	13	14	15	16	17	18	19	20	21	22	23	24	25	26	27	28	29	30	31	1	2	3	4	5	6	7	8	9	10
50	90	July-Au	23	24	25	26	27	28	29	30	31	1	2	3	4	5	6	7	8	9	10	11	12	13	14	15	16	17	18	19	20	21
49	89	August	2	3	4	5	6	7	8	9	10	11	12	13	14	15	16	17	18	19	20	21	22	23	24	25	26	27	28	29	30	31
48	88	July-Au	15	16	17	18	19	20	21	22	23	24	25	26	27	28	29	30	31	1	2	3	4	5	6	7	8	9	10	11	12	13
47	87	July-Au	27	28	29	30	31	1	2	3	4	5	6	7	8	9	10	11	12	13	14	15	16	17	18	19	20	21	22	23	24	25
46	86	Au-Sep	6	7	8	9	10	11	12	13	14	15	16	17	18	19	20	21	22	23	24	25	26	27	28	29	30	31	1	2	3	4
5745	1985	July-Au	19	20	21	22	23	24	25	26	27	28	29	30	31	1	2	3	4	5	6	7	8	9	10	11	12	13	14	15	16	17

Figures in **black type** denote Sabbaths.

9th, Fast of Ab (if on Sabbath, postponed to Sunday); 30th, First Day of New Moon of Elul.

ELUL (29 days)

Elul	74/14	73/13	72/12	71/11	70/10	69/09	68/08	67/07	66/06	65/05	64/04	63/03	62/02	61/01	60/2000	59/99	58/98	57/97	56/96	55/95	54/94	53/93	52/92	51/91	50/90	49/89	48/88	47/87	46/86	5745/1985
	Au-Sep	Au-Sep	Au-Sep	Au-Sep	Au-Sep	Au-Sep	Sept	Au-Sep	Au-Sep	Sep-Oct	Au-Sep	Au-Sep	Au-Sep	Au-Sep	Sept	Au-Sep	Au-Sep	Sep-Oct	Au-Sep	Au-Sep	Au-Sep	Au-Sep	Au-Sep	Au-Sep	Au-Sep	Sept	Au-Sep	Au-Sep	Sep-Oct	Au-Sep
1	27	7	19	31	11	21	1	15	25	5	18	29	9	20	1	13	23	3	16	27	8	18	30	11	22	1	14	26	5	18
2	28	8	20	1	12	22	2	16	26	6	19	30	10	21	2	14	24	4	17	28	9	19	31	12	23	2	15	27	6	19
3	29	9	21	2	13	23	3	17	27	7	20	31	11	22	3	15	25	5	18	29	10	20	1	13	24	3	16	28	7	20
4	30	10	22	3	14	24	4	18	28	8	21	1	12	23	4	16	26	6	19	30	11	21	2	14	25	4	17	29	8	21
5	31	11	23	4	15	25	5	19	29	9	22	2	13	24	5	17	27	7	20	31	12	22	3	15	26	5	18	30	9	22
6	1	12	24	5	16	26	6	20	30	10	23	3	14	25	6	18	28	8	21	1	13	23	4	16	27	6	19	31	10	23
7	2	13	25	6	17	27	7	21	31	11	24	4	15	26	7	19	29	9	22	2	14	24	5	17	28	7	20	1	11	24
8	3	14	26	7	18	28	8	22	1	12	25	5	16	27	8	20	30	10	23	3	15	25	6	18	29	8	21	2	12	25
9	4	15	27	8	19	29	9	23	2	13	26	6	17	28	9	21	31	11	24	4	16	26	7	19	30	9	22	3	13	26
10	5	16	28	9	20	30	10	24	3	14	27	7	18	29	10	22	1	12	25	5	17	27	8	20	31	10	23	4	14	27
11	6	17	29	10	21	31	11	25	4	15	28	8	19	30	11	23	2	13	26	6	18	28	9	21	1	11	24	5	15	28
12	7	18	30	11	22	1	12	26	5	16	29	9	20	31	12	24	3	14	27	7	19	29	10	22	2	12	25	6	16	29
13	8	19	31	12	23	2	13	27	6	17	30	10	21	1	13	25	4	15	28	8	20	30	11	23	3	13	26	7	17	30
14	9	20	1	13	24	3	14	28	7	18	31	11	22	2	14	26	5	16	29	9	21	31	12	24	4	14	27	8	18	31
15	10	21	2	14	25	4	15	29	8	19	1	12	23	3	15	27	6	17	30	10	22	1	13	25	5	15	28	9	19	1
16	11	22	3	15	26	5	16	30	9	20	2	13	24	4	16	28	7	18	31	11	23	2	14	26	6	16	29	10	20	2
17	12	23	4	16	27	6	17	31	10	21	3	14	25	5	17	29	8	19	1	12	24	3	15	27	7	17	30	11	21	3
18	13	24	5	17	28	7	18	1	11	22	4	15	26	6	18	30	9	20	2	13	25	4	16	28	8	18	31	12	22	4
19	14	25	6	18	29	8	19	2	12	23	5	16	27	7	19	31	10	21	3	14	26	5	17	29	9	19	1	13	23	5
20	15	26	7	19	30	9	20	3	13	24	6	17	28	8	20	1	11	22	4	15	27	6	18	30	10	20	2	14	24	6
21	16	27	8	20	31	10	21	4	14	25	7	18	29	9	21	2	12	23	5	16	28	7	19	31	11	21	3	15	25	7
22	17	28	9	21	1	11	22	5	15	26	8	19	30	10	22	3	13	24	6	17	29	8	20	1	12	22	4	16	26	8
23	18	29	10	22	2	12	23	6	16	27	9	20	31	11	23	4	14	25	7	18	30	9	21	2	13	23	5	17	27	9
24	19	30	11	23	3	13	24	7	17	28	10	21	1	12	24	5	15	26	8	19	31	10	22	3	14	24	6	18	28	10
25	20	31	12	24	4	14	25	8	18	29	11	22	2	13	25	6	16	27	9	20	1	11	23	4	15	25	7	19	29	11
26	21	1	13	25	5	15	26	9	19	30	12	23	3	14	26	7	17	28	10	21	2	12	24	5	16	26	8	20	30	12
27	22	2	14	26	6	16	27	10	20	1	13	24	4	15	27	8	18	29	11	22	3	13	25	6	17	27	9	21	1	13
28	23	3	15	27	7	17	28	11	21	2	14	25	5	16	28	9	19	30	12	23	4	14	26	7	18	28	10	22	2	14
29	24	4	16	28	8	18	29	12	22	3	15	26	6	17	29	10	20	1	13	24	5	15	27	8	19	29	11	23	3	15

Figures in **black type** denote Sabbaths.

INDEX

A

Abbeyfield (Camden)
Society 94
Aberdeen (Scotland) . . .132
Abridged Calendar
2000 327
Abridged Calendar
2001 328
Academic Study Group on
Israel & Middle East . .24
ACJR 17
Adath Yisroel Burial
Society 12
Adath Yisroel Synagogue .81
Adath Yisroel Tottenham
Beth Hamedrash 81
Aden Jews'
Congregation 85
Adelaide (Australia) 140
Admission of Jewish
Ecclesiastical Officers,
Advisory Committee
for 61
Affiliated Synagogues,
US 78
Federation 80
Afghanistan 137
Aged Needy Pension
Society, Jewish 94
Agency for Jewish
Education 35, 48
Agudas Harabbonim 60
Agudas Hashochtim
v'Hashomrim 60
Agudas Israel 66
Agudas Israel Community
Services 66
Agudus Israel Housing
Assoc. 94
Ahavat Israel Synagogue .81
Ajex 62
Housing Association . . .94
Military Museum 54
AJR Charitable Trust 17
AJY 46
Akim 24
Akiva School 91
Albania 137
Alderney Road
Cemetery 89
Alexandria 150
Algeria 137
Aliyah Department of
Jewish Agency 21
Alyn, Friends of 29
All Aboard Shops . . .2, 101
Alliance Israelite
Universelle 67, 152
Altmann Library 57

Alyth 86
Choral Society 99
American Jewish
Committee 188
American Joint Distribution
Committee 137, 189
Amersham 103
Amsterdam 156
Anglo-German
Cultural Forum 17
Anglo-Israel Archaeological
Society 24
Anglo-Israel Association .25
Anglo-Jewish
Archives 54, 56
Anglo-Jewish Association .3
Anne Frank Educational
Trust 18
Antigua 137
Anti-Tuberculosis
League, Friends of 30
Antwerp 141
Arbib Lucas Trust 94
Argentina 137
Argyle & Bute.
See Dunoon
Armenia 138
Art Museums of Israel,
Friends of 26
Aruba 138
Asia-Pacific Jewish
Association 67, 139
Assaf Harofeh Medical
Centre, Friends 26
Assembly of Masorti
Synagogues 12, 83
Assembly of Rabbis
(Reform) 12
Association for Jewish
Youth 46
Association for Soldiers'
Welfare 169
Association of Adath
Yisroel Synagogues 11
Association of British
Settlers 175
Association of Children
of Jewish Refugees 17
Association of Jewish
Communal
Professionals 60
Association of Jewish
Ex-Berliners 18
Association of Jewish
Ex-Service Men &
Women 61
Association of Jewish
Friendship Clubs . . .3, 99
Association of Jewish Golf
Clubs & Societies 62

Association of Jewish
Humanists 62
Association of Jewish
Refugees 18
Association of Jewish
Sixth-Formers 52
Association of Jewish
Teachers 35
Association of Jewish
Women's
Organisations 3
Association of Ministers
(Chazanim) of Great
Britain 60
Association of Orthodox
Jewish Professionals . . .36
Association of Reform
and Liberal
Mohalim 13
Association of United
Synagogue Women 88
Athens 154
Auckland
(New Zealand) 179
Australia 138-40
Austria 140
Authorisation of
marriage - Office of
Chief Rabbi 7
Avigdor Primary School . .91

B

Bachad Fellowship 49
Bahamas 141
Balfour Diamond Jubilee
Trust 25
Bank Leumi (U.K.) 25
Bank of Israel 168
Bar-Ilan University 166
Friends of 29
Barbados 141
Barcelona 185
Barking & Becontree
Synagogue 78
Barkingside Progressive
Synagogue 87
Barmitzvah Dates . . .348-61
Barnet Synagogue 78
Baronets 210
Basle 186
Basildon 103
Bath 103
Baths, Ritual. See Mikvaot
Bedford 104
Beit Klai Yisrael 86
Belfast 135
Belgium 141
Belgrade 192
Belmont Synagogue 76

Belsize Square Synagogue 83
Ben Gurion University . . 167
  Foundation 25
Ben Uri Arts Society 54
Bereavement Counselling 95
Bermuda 142
Berne 186
Besht Tellers 99
Betar-Tagar 50
Beth Abraham
  Synagogue 81
Beth Chodos Synagogue .81
Beth Din (U.S.) 7
Beth Din (Federation) . . .11
Beth Din (Reform) 12
Beth Din (Sephardi) 10
Beth Hamedrash
  Beis Nadvorna 81
Beth Hamedrash
  D'Chasidey Belz 81
Beth Hamedrash
  D'Chasidey Gur 81
Beth Hamedrash
  D'Chasidey Ryzin 81
Beth Hamedrash D'Chasidey
  Sans-Klausenburg 81
Beth Hamedrash
  D'Chasidey Square 81
Beth Hamedrash
  Divrei Chaim 81
Beth Hamedrash
  Hendon 81
Beth Hamedrash
  Heshaim 85
Beth Hamedrash Imrey
  Chaim D'Chasidey
  Vishnitz-Monsey 81
Beth Hamedrash
  Ohel Naphtoli 82
Beth Hamedrash
  Torah Etz Chaim 82
Beth Hamedrash
  Torah Chaim Liege 82
Beth Hamedrash
  Yetiv Lev 82
Beth Hatefutsoth 169
Beth Holim 85
Beth Israel (Trisker)
  Synagogue 82
Beth Shalom Holocaust
  Memorial 35, 123
Beth Shmuel Synagogue .82
Beth Sholom Synagogue .82
Beth Talmud Centre 82
Beth Yisochor Dov Beth
  Hamedrash 82
Bevis Marks 84
Bikur Cholim Hospital,
  Jerusalem, British
  Committee for 29
Binoh Centre for Special
  Jewish Education 90

Bipac, Britain-Israel
  Public Affairs Centre . . .26
Birkath Yehuda Beth
  Hamedrash 82
Birmingham 104
Blackpool 105
Blind, Jewish Homes for .94
Blind Society, Jewish 95
Bloomsbury Advertising
  Agency 21
B'nai B'rith 67
B'nai B'rith Hillel
  Foundation 52
B'nai B'rith JBG Housing
  Association 94
B'nai B'rith Jewish
  Music Festival 39
B'nai B'rith Youth
  Organisation 46
Bnei Akiva 50
Bnei Brak Hospital,
  British Committee of . .26
Board for Shechita
  (London) 88
Board of Deputies 1-2
Bodleian Library 54
Bognor Regis 105
Bolivia 142
Bonds, State of Israel 34
Bonn (Sir Max) Memorial
  Youth Centre 49
Booksellers 322-3
Borehamwood &
  Elstree Synagogue 76
Bosnia Hercegovina . .143
Botgi, British Overseas
  Trade Group of Israel . .28
Bournemouth 105
Boys' Town Jerusalem,
  Friends of 29
Bradford 106
Brady-Maccabi Centre . . .99
Brady Street Cemetery . .89
Bratislava 182
Brazil 143
Bridge Lane Beth
  Hamedrash 81
Brighton & Hove 106
Brijnet 7
Brisbane 140
Bristol 107
Britain-Israel Public
  Affairs Centre 26
British Academy,
  Fellows of 211
British Aliya Movement . .20
British Association for
  Jewish Studies 42
British Council for Jews
  in Eastern Europe 19
British Emunah 20
British & European
  Machal 26

British-Israel Arts
  Foundation 28
British-Israel Chamber of
  Commerce 28
British-Israel Forum 28
British-Israel
  Parliamentary Group . .28
British Jewry, historical
  note 200
British Library (Hebrew
  Department) 54
British Olim Relatives
  Association (Bora) 20
British Olim Society . . .175
British ORT 14
British Overseas
  Trade Group 28
British Settlements in
  Israel 171-4
British Tay-Sachs
  Foundation 14
British Technion
  Society 28
British Video Archive . . .37
British Wizo 21
Bromley Reform
  Synagogue 86
Brotherton Library,
  Leeds 55
Brussels 142
Bucharest 182
Budapest 156
Buenos Aires 138
Bulawayo 193
Bulgaria 143
Bullscross Ride
  Cemetery 83, 89
Burial Societies:
  Adath Yisroel 12
  Federation 10, 81
  Liberal & Reform 88
  Sephardi 85
  United Synagogue, . .8, 79
  West End Great 84
Burma 144
Bushey Cemetery 89
Bushey & District
  Synagogue 76
Byelorus 144

C

Cairo 150
Calendar 325
Calendar for 2000 327
Calendar for 2001 328
Calendar for 30
  years 348-61
Cambridge 108
Cambridge University
  Library 55
Camp Simcha 94

Campaign for the
Protection of Shechita . .62
Canada 144-5
Canberra 140
Canterbury 108
Cape Town 184
Cardiff 131
Casablanca 178
Catford and Bromley
Synagogue 78
Cayman Islands 145
Celebrities Guild of
Great Britain 62
Cemeteries (London) .89-90
Federation 81
Liberal 87
Reform 85
Sephardi 85
United 79
West End Great 83
Western 84
Cemeteries, Disused,
The Regions 103
Central Council for
Jewish Community
Services 14
Central Enquiry Desk
and Communal Diary . . .2
Central Mikvaoth Board .88
Central Synagogue 76
Centre for German-Jewish
Studies 42
Centre for Jewish Art . .167
Centre for Jewish-
Christian Relations 42
Centre for Jewish
Education (CJE) 36
Centre for Jewish Studies
(Leeds) 42
(Univ. London) 42
Centre for Modern
Hebrew Studies 43
Ceuta 184-5
Chabad Lubavitch
Centre 99
Chai-Lifeline 14
Chamber of Commerce:
British-Israel 27
Israel-British 169
Channel Islands 135
Chaplain to the
Forces 9, 306
Chatham 108
Chelmsford 108
Chelsea Synagogue 78
Cheltenham 108
Chester 109
Chief Rabbinate
(British) 7
(Israel) 169
Chief Rabbinate
Council 8

Chief Rabbi's Office (and
for the authorisation of
marriages) 8
Chigwell & Hainault
Synagogue 76
Child Resettlement Fund:
Emunah 20
Children and Youth
Aliyah Committee 21
Children's Aid Committee
Charitable Fund 14
Children's Country
Holidays Fund
(Jewish Branch) 96
Chile 146
Chiltern Progressive
Synagogue 87
China 146
Chingford. See Highams
Park & Chingford
Christians and Jews,
Council of 3
International
Council of 71
Christians, London
Society of Jews and . . .101
Circumcision 9, 13
City of London
Regiment Memorial . . .88
CJE 36
Clapton Synagogue 79
Clayhall Synagogue 76
Clifton College,
Polack's House 41
Clore Shalom School 91
Clore Tikvah School 91
Club 1943 18
Clubs and Cultural
Societies (London) 98
Cockfosters and North
Southgate Synagogue . .76
Cohen Scholarship Trust
Fund, Alfred Louis 9
Colchester 109
Colombia 147
Committee for the
Preservation of Jewish
Cemeteries in Europe . .68
Commonwealth of
Independent States . . .147
Commonwealth Jewish
Council 68
Trust 68
Communal Diary 2
Community Research
Unit, Board of
Deputies 1
Companions of Honour 212
Conference of European
Rabbis 69
Conference on Jewish
Material Claims
against Germany 69

Congregation of Jacob . .80
Conjoint Passover Flour
Committee 8, 9
Connect: Jewish
Marriage Bureau 62
Conservative Friends of
Israel 29
Constituent Synagogues,
Federation 79
Constituent Synagogues,
U.S. 76
Consultative Council of
Jewish Organisations . .69
Copenhagen 150
Cordoba (Argentina) . . .137
Cork 136
Costa Rica 147
Council of Reform &
Liberal Rabbis 13
Council of Christians &
Jews 3
Council of Jews from
Germany 18
Counselling Services: See
Welfare Organisations;
See also:
Bereavement 95
Chai-Lifeline 14
Get Advisory Service . .14
Jewish AIDS Trust 14
Jewish Bereavement
Counselling 95
Jewish Care 95
Jewish Crisis Helpline . .96
Jewish Emergency
Support Services 14
Jewish Information
Services 2, 7
Jewish Lesbian & Gay
Helpline 15
Jewish Marriage
Council 15
Jewish Women's Aid . . .16
Miyad 97
Operation Judaism 64
Raphael Centre 97
Tay Sachs Screening
Centre 17
Court of the Chief
Rabbi (Beth Din) 7
Coventry 109
Cracow 181
Crawley 109
Cricklewood Synagogue .76
Croatia 148
Croydon Synagogue 79
Cuba 149
Cultural Societies
(London) 98
Cultural Societies, Jewish
Association of 99
Curaçao 149
Cyprus 149

Czech Memorial Scrolls
Centre 55
Czech Republic 149

D

Damascus 186
Darlington 109
Dames 211
Davar 36
David Ishag Synagogue ..85
Deaf Association Jewish .96
Defence Committee (of
Board of Deputies) 1
Delissa Joseph Memorial
Fund. See Necessitous
Ladies Fund
Denmark 150
Deputies, Board of 1-2
Discount Bank Ltd 32
Discount Bank of New
York 32
Dollis Hill Synagogue ...76
Dominican Republic ...150
Dror 51
Drugsline 94
Dublin 136
Dundee 132
Dunoon 133
Dunstable. See Luton
Dvar Yerushalayim 36

E

Ealing Liberal
Synagogue 87
Ealing Synagogue 76
East Grinstead 109
East Ham Cemetery 89
East London Central
Synagogue 79
East European Jewish
Heritage Project 19
Eastbourne 109
Eastern Jewry Community
(London) 85
Ecuador 150
Edgware Adath Yisroel
Synagogue 83
Edgware Masorti
Synagogue 83
Edgware Reform
Synagogue 86
Edgware Synagogue 76
Edgwarebury Cemeteries .89
Edinburgh 133
Edinburgh House 85
Edmonton Cemetery 89
Education and Youth
Committee, Board of
Deputies 1

Education and Youth
Department, Reform
Synagogues of Great
Britain 49
Educational
Organisations 35-46
Educational Organisations
(London) 90-4
Egypt 150
Elstree. See Borehamwood
Emunah 20
Enfield & Winchmore
Hill Synagogue 78
Enfield Cemetery 89
English Speaking Residents
Assoc. (ESRA) 174
Enquiry Desk, Central 3
Estonia 151
Ethiopia 151
European Association for
Jewish Studies 69
European Community,
Israeli representation
with 160
European Council of
Jewish Communities ...69
European Israeli Forum ..70
European Jewish
Congress 70
European Jewish
Publication Society 70
European Parliament,
Members of 210
European Rabbis,
Conference of 68
European Union of
Jewish Students 70
Evening Institute of
ULPS 36
Evening Twilight
Variation Table 343
Exeter 110
Exhibition Centre,
Jewish Community 57
Exhibitions, Museums
& Libraries 54-9
Exodus 2000 19
Ex-Service Men & Women,
Association of Jewish ..62
Ezra Youth Movement ...50
Ezrath Nashim Hospital .28

F

Federation of Jewish
Relief Organisations ...29
Federation of
Synagogues 11, 79-81
Federation of Women
Zionists 20
Federation of Zionist
Youth 50
Festivals & Fasts 324

Fieldgate Street
Synagogue 80
Fiji Islands 151
Finchley Central
Synagogue 79
Finchley Kosher Lunch
Service 94
Finchley Progressive
Synagogue 87
Finchley Reform
Synagogue 86
Finchley Road
Synagogue 80, 82
Finchley Synagogue 76
Finland 151
Finsbury Park
Synagogue 76
Finnart House School
Trust 14
Food for the Jewish
Poor 94
45 Aid Society 17
France 151-3
French Synagogue
(London) 83
Friendly Societies/
Jewish 63
Friends of Assaf Harofeh
Medical Centre 26
Friends of Israel:
Conservative 29
Labour 33
Liberal Democrat 33
Friends of the Hebrew
University 29
Friends of the Kingsbury
Mikveh 94
Friends of Israel Aged
(Re'uth) 30
Friends of Israel Cancer
Association 30
Friends of Israel
Educational Trust 30
Friends of Israel Free
Loan Association 26
Friends of Jewish Youth ..99
Friends of Progressive
Judaism 31
Friends of the Sick 95
Friends of Yiddish 99
Friendship Clubs
Association of Jewish ...3
Friendship with Israel
(European Parliament) ..70

G

Gan Aviv Kindergarten ..91
Garden Suburb Beth
Hamedrash 82
Gateshead 110
General Federation of
Jewish Labour 165

General Zionist
 Organisation 21
Geneva 186
Genizah Research Unit ..55
George Crosses, Jewish .212
Germany 153
Germany, Council of
 Jews from 17
Get Advisory Service 14
Gibraltar 154
Glasgow 133-5
Goldbloom (Hebrew Studies
 Department) J.F.S.
 Comprehensive School .91
Golders Green Beth
 Hamedrash
 Congregation 83
Golders Green
 Synagogue 76
Grand Order of Israel &
 Shield of David 64
Greater London Radio ...6
Greece 154
Greenford Synagogue ...80
Grimsby 110
Group Relations
 Committee (of Board of
 Deputies) 1
Guatemala 155
Guernsey
 (Channel Islands) 135
Guild of Jewish
 Journalists 60
Guildford 111

H

Habonim-Dror 51
Hackney Cemetery 89
Hackney & East
 London Synagogue 76
Hadassah Medical Relief
 Association United
 Kingdom 31
Haendler (Nathan &
 Adolphe) charity 16
Haftarot and Sidrot for
 2001 344-5
Hagadolim Charitable
 Organisation 95
Haifa University 167
 Friends of 27
Haiti 155
Half-Empty Bookcase ...99
Hamashbir Hamerkazi ..31
Hammersmith & West
 Kensington Synagogue .76
Hammerson, Lewis, Home
 for Elderly People 97
Hampstead Garden
 Suburb Synagogue 77
Hampstead Reform
 Synagogue 86

Hampstead Synagogue ..77
Hanoar Hatzioni 51
Harare 193
Harlow 111
Harold Hill Synagogue ..78
Harold House
 (Liverpool) 116
Harrogate 111
Harrow Progressive
 Synagogue 87
Harry & Abe Sherman Rosh
 Pinah Primary School ..92
Harry Rosencweig
 Collection (of Jewish
 Music) 55
Hartley Library,
 Southampton 55
Hashomer Hatzair 51
Hasmonean Schools 91
Hastings 111
Hatch End Jewish
 Community 86
Haven Foundation 95
Hebraica Libraries
 Group 54
Hebrew University 166
 Friends of 29
Hebreware User Group ..71
Heimler International ...71
Helen Lucas Fund. See Arbib
 Lucas Fund
Help Lines: See Counselling
 Services; Welfare
 Organisations
Hemel Hempstead
 Synagogue 78, 111
Hendon Adath Yisroel
 Synagogue 82
Hendon Reform
 Synagogue 86
Hendon Synagogue 77
H.M. Forces Jewish
 Committee for 9
Hereford 111
Hertsmere Progressive
 Congregation 87
Herut Movement
 (Great Britain) 21
Hias 71
Hidden Legacy
 Foundation 56
High Seas Sailing Club ..63
High Wycombe 78, 111
Highams Park and
 Chingford Synagogue ..78
Highgate Synagogue 77
Hillel Foundation 52
Historical note on
 British Jewry 200
Hitchin 111
Holland 155
Holland Park
 Synagogue 85

Holocaust
 Beth Shalom 36
 Education Trust 36
 Imperial War Museum .56
 Memorials ...36, 88, 123
 Stanley Burton Centre .46
 Survivors' Centre 18
Holyland Philatelic
 Society 31
Home for Aged Jews 97
Homes (Jewish Care) ..96-7
Homes for Jewish
 Children, Norwood ...97
Homes for the Blind,
 Jewish 94
Homes for Handicapped
 Jewish Children 97
Honduras 156
Hong Kong 146
Hoop Lane Cemetery ...89
Hospital Kosher Meals
 Service 95
Hospital Visitors Branch,
 Visitation Committee .102
Hounslow Synagogue ...78
Hove. See Brighton
Hull 111
Hungary 156

I

IJPR 71
Ilford Congregation
 (Sephardi) 85
Ilford Federation
 Synagogue 80
Ilford Jewish Schools 91
Ilford Synagogue 77
Immanuel College 91
Imperial War Museum
 Holocaust Exhibition ..56
Independent
 Congregations
 (London) 83
Independent Jewish Day
 School 91
India 156
Indonesia 157
Information Committee,
 Board of Deputies 1
Information Services 7
Initiation Society 9
Institute for Jewish Music
 Studies and Performance.99
Institute for Jewish Policy
 Research (IJPR) 71
 Research Library 56
Institute of Community
 Relations 63
Institute of Contemporary
 History 56
Institute of Jewish
 Studies 43

International Association
of Jewish Lawyers
& Jurists 71
International Council
of Christians & Jews . .72
International Council
of Jewish Women 72
International Council
on Jewish Social and
Welfare Services 72
International Jewish
Genealogical
Resources 72
International Jewish
Vegetarian Society 72
International
Organisations 66-75
Iran 157
Iranian Jewish Centre . . .73
Iranian Jews in Great
Britain, Committee for .18
Iraq 157
Ireland, Northern 135
Ireland, Republic of . .135-6
Isle of Man 135
Israel 157-75
British Immigrant
Offices 175
British Settlements . .171-4
Chief Rabbinate 169
Commercial
Organisations 168
Educational and Research
Institutions 166
Embassies and
Legations 160-5
London 21
Government 158
Knesset 159
Political Parties 165
President 159
Israel Action 34
Israel Aged, Friends of . . .30
Israel Britain and the
Commonwealth Assoc.
(IBCA) 175
Israel-British Chamber
of Commerce 169
Israel Cancer Association,
Friends of 30
Israel Discount Bank Ltd. 32
Israel Discount Bank of
New York 32
Israel Educational Trust,
Friends of 30
Israel Embassy (London) . .21
Israel Folk Dance
Institute 37
Israel Free Loan
Association, British
Friends of 27
Israel Government Tourist
Office 32

Israel Information 21
Israel Institute of
Technology 166
Israel-Judaica Stamp
Club 32
Israel Labour Party 165
Israel Museum 169
Israel, Organisations
concerned with 24-35
Israel Philharmonic
Orchestra, British
Friends of 27
Israel War Disabled,
British Friends of 27
Israel Zangwill
Memorial Fund 37
Israeli Embassies and
Legations 21, 160-5
Istanbul 187
Italy 175
"It's Kosher" 7

J

Jacob Benjamin Elias
Synagogue 85
J.A.C.S. 99
Jamaica 176
Japan 176
JBD 95
J.C.A. Charitable
Foundation 73
JCi 7
Jersey 135
Jerusalem College of
Technology 168
Friends of 30
Jerusalem Foundation . . .32
Jerusalem Rubin Academy
of Music, Friends of . . .30
Jewish Aged Needy
Pension Society 95
Jewish Agency for
Israel 21, 170
Jewish AIDS Trust 14
Jewish Appreciation
Group Tours 99
Jewish Association for
Business Ethics 63
Jewish Association for
the Mentally Ill 15
Jewish Association for
the Physically
Handicapped 94
Jewish Association of
Cultural Societies 99
Jewish Association of
Spiritual Healers 63
Jewish Bereavement
Counselling Service . . .95
Jewish Blind and
Disabled 95-6
Jewish Blind Society 96

Jewish Blind in Israel
Association 32
Jewish Book Council 37
Jewish Book List . . .317-21
Jewish Calendar 324
Jewish Calendar for 30
years 348
Jewish Care 96-7
Jewish Children's
Holiday Fund 97
Jewish Child's Day 15
Jewish Chronicle
Newspaper 6, 37
Jewish Colonization
Association 72
Jewish Committee for
H.M. Forces 9
Jewish Communal
Marriage Bureau 62
Jewish Communal
Professionals
Association 59
Jewish Community Day
School Advisory Board .37
Jewish Community
Exhibition Centre 56
Jewish Community
Information (JCi) 7
Jewish Community
Services,
Central Council for . . .13
Jewish Community
Theatre 37
Jewish Council for
Racial Equality 63
Jewish Crisis Helpline . . .97
Jewish Deaf Association .97
Jewish Defence and
Group Relations
Committee 1
Jewish Documentation
Centre (Paris) 152
Jewish Education Aid
Society 38
Jewish Educational
Development Trust 38
Jewish Emergency
Support Service 14
Jewish Ex-Service Men
and Women,
Association of 62
Jewish Feminist Group . .64
Jewish Film Foundation .38
Jewish Friendly
Societies 64
Jewish Friendship Clubs,
Association of 3
Jewish Gay and Lesbian
Group 64
Jewish Genealogical
Society 38
Jewish Guide Advisory
Council 46

Jewish Historical
  Society of England 38
Jewish Homes for the
  Blind 94
Jewish Information
  Services 5
  Central Enquiry Desk . . .3
Jewish Journalists,
  Guild of 59
Jewish Lads' and Girls'
  Brigade 47
Jewish Learning
  Exchange 47
Jewish Lesbian and Gay
  Helpline 15
Jewish Marriage Council .15
Jewish Medical Society,
  London 101
Jewish Memorial
  Council 9
Jewish Museum 57
Jewish Music Festival . . .38
Jewish Music Heritage
  Trust 38
Jewish Music Institute . . .38
Jewish National Fund . . .21
  Charitable Trust 21
  Education Dept. . . .21, 48
  Younger J.N.F. 21, 53
Jewish Nurses & Midwives
  Association 60
Jewish Press (United
  Kingdom) 5-6
Jewish Radio
  Programmes 6
Jewish Reconstructionist
  Federation 73, 189
Jewish Relief and
  Education Trust
  (JRET) 20
Jewish Representative
  Councils (United
  Kingdom) 2-3
Jewish Research Group . .99
Jewish Resource Centre . .90
Jewish Scout Advisory
  Council 48
Jewish Secondary
  Schools' Movement . . .91
Jewish Socialists' Group .64
Jewish Society for the
  Mentally
  Handicapped 97
Jewish Statistics 194-9
Jewish Students,
  Union of 54
Jewish Students, World
  Union of 74
Jewish Studies Library,
  UCL 57
Jewish Telephone Crisis
  Line (Miyad) 97

Jewish Vegetarian
  Society 72
Jewish Welfare Board . . .97
Jewish Women,
  International
  Council of 71
Jewish Women,
  League of 4
Jewish Women's Aid
  (JWA) 15
Jewish Women's
  Organisations,
  Association of 3
Jewish Youth, Association
  for 46
Jewish Youth Fund 47
Jewish Youth Orchestra . .47
Jewish Youth,
  Organisations concerned
  with 46-53
Jewish Youth Study
  Groups 47
Jews & Christians, London
  Society of 101
Jews' College, See London
  School of Jewish Studies
Jews' Free School 91
Jews of Zambia Project . .73
Jews' Temporary Shelter .97
J.F.S. (Comprehensive
  School) 91
JMC Bookshop 10
JNF Future 52
Joe Loss Research
  Fellowship 39, 43
Johannesburg 184
John Rylands University of
  Manchester Library . . .57
Joint Kashrus Committee . .12
Joseph Mamlock House
  (Manchester) 117
Journalists,
  Guild of Jewish 59
JPMP 48
Judaica Philatelic Society .32
Judith Lady Montefiore
  College 84

K

Kadimah-Victoria Youth
  Club 99
Kehal Chasidim
  Synagogue 82
Kedassia: see Joint
  Kashrus Committee
Kenton Synagogue 77
Kenya 176
Kerem Schools 91
Keren Hatorah Library . . . 58
Keren Kayemeth Le
  Israel 170

Keren Yaldenu, British
  Committee of 26
Kesher 39
Kibbutzim, British 171-4
Kibbutz Representatives .52
Kidmah 52
King Solomon School . . .91
Kingsbury Road
  Cemetery 89
Kingsbury Synagogue . . .77
Kingston Liberal
  Synagogue 87
Kingston & Surbiton
  Synagogue 78
Kisharon 92
K.K.L. Executor &
  Trustee Co. 22
Knesset 159
Knightland Road
  Synagogue 82
Knights 210
Kol-Chai – Hatch End
  Jewish Community 86
Kosher Meals Services . . .94
Kressel Collection
  Oxford (Archive and
  Library) 58

L

Labour Friends of Israel .33
Labour Zionist
  Movement 22
Latvia 176
Lauderdale Road
  Synagogue 84
Lausanne 186
Law of Truth
  Talmudical College 92
L'Chaim Society
  Cambridge 108
  London 100
  Oxford 125
League of Jewish
  Women 4
Leamington 112
Lebanon 176
Leeds 55, 112-14
Legislation, United Kingdom,
  concerning Jews 203-6
Leicester 115
Leo Baeck College 43
  Library 58
Leo Baeck Institute 44
Leopold Muller Memorial
  Library 58
Leytonstone & Wanstead
  Synagogue 80
Liberal Democrat
  Friends of Israel 33
Liberal Jewish Cemetery .89
Liberal Jewish
  Synagogue 87

Liberal & Progressive
Synagogues,
Union of 12, 86-7
Libraries, Museums &
Exhibitions 54-9
Libya 177
Licensing of Shochetim,
Rabbinical
Commission for 10
Life Peers 209
Lifeline for the Old 33
Likud (Alliance) Bloc . . .165
Likud-Herut Movement .22
Limmud 39
Lincoln 115
Lisbon 181
Listed Buildings
(UK) 207-8
Lithuania 177
Littman Library 39
Liverpool 115-16
Living Memory of the
Jewish Community 59
Llandudno 132
London 76-102
London Academy of
Jewish Studies 39
London Beth Din - See
Beth Din (U.S.)
London Board for
Shechita 88
London Bureau of Int.
Affairs 68
London Diary of Jewish
Events 98
London Jewish Academy .36
London Jewish Housing
Committee 93
London Jewish
Male Choir 100
London Jewish Medical
Society 101
London Jewish Music
Centre 39, 99
London Jewish News .6, 98
London Metropolitan
Archives 58
London Museum of
Jewish Life 57
London School of Jewish
Studies 44
Library 58
London Society of Jews
& Christians 102
Loughton and Chigwell
Synagogue 80
Lubavitch Foundation . . .92
Lubavitch Lending
Library 59
Lubavitch of South
London 100
Lubavitch Synagogue 82

Lucas Trust. See Arbib Lucas
Trust
Lusaka 192
Luton 116
Luxembourg 177

M

Maccabeans, The 100
Maccabi, Brady, Centre . .99
Maccabi Associations,
Union of 49
Maccabi World Union . . .73
Machal Association 25
Machzikei Hadath
Synagogue 80
Madrid 185
Magen David Adom,
Friends of 31
Maidenhead 116
Maidstone 117
Maimonides Foundation .64
Majorca 185
Makor 48
Malaga 185
Malta 177
Mamlock House 117
Manchester 117-22
Manor House Centre for
Psychotherapy &
Counselling 16
Manor House Media 39
Manor House Society . .100
Manor House Sternberg
Centre for Judaism 13
Manufacturers'
Association of Israel . .169
Mapam (United
Kingdom) 22
Young 52
Marble Arch Synagogue .78
Margate 122
Margulies Library 57
Marriage Bureau, Jewish
Communal 62
Marriage Regulations . .346
Marriage, Authorisation
of 7
Masorti
Academy 40
Assembly of
Synagogues . . .12, 82-3
Massoret see MST
Mathilda Marks-
Kennedy School 92
Mauritius 177
Mazal Tov 16
Medical Aid
Committee for Israel . .33
Medical Society,
London Jewish 101
Melbourne 140
Melilla 185

Member of European
Parliament 210
Members of Parliament .209
Memorial Foundation
for Jewish Culture 73
Memorial to Jewish
Servicemen & Women .88
Memorials 88
Menorah 6, 103
Menorah Foundation
School 92
Menorah Grammar
School for Boys 92
Menorah Primary
School 92
Mentally Handicapped,
Jewish Society for 96
Merthyr Tydfil 132
Mesifta Synagogue 82
Mexico 177
Michael Goulston
Educational Foundation . .40
Michael Sobell House . . .96
Michael Sobell Sinai
School 92
Middlesbrough 122
Middlesex New
Synagogue (Reform) . . .86
Midrashia, Friends of . . .31
Mikvaot 88, 103
Milan 176
Mile End Road
Cemetery 89
Mill Hill Synagogue 77
Milton Keynes 123
Minsk 144
Mishcon Library 58
Miyad 97
Mizrachi-Hapoel
Hamizrachi Federation . .22
Mocatta Library &
Museum 57
Mohelim 9, 13
Moldova 178
Monash Branch, Royal
British Legion 64
Mons 142
Montagu Jewish
Community Trust 64
Montefiore (Sir Moses)
Synagogue 85, 110
Montefiore Endowment
Committee 85
Montevideo 191
Morocco 178
Moscow 147
Mozambique 178
MST 92
Multiple Sclerosis Aid
Group 97
Museum of Jewish
East End 57

Museums, Libraries &
  Exhibitions 54-9
Muswell Hill Synagogue .77

N

Nairobi 176
Naima Jewish Preparatory
  School 93
Nathan & Adolphe
  Haendler Charity 16
National Council for
  Soviet Jewry 20
National Council of
  Shechita Boards 10
National Jewish Chaplaincy
  Board 53
National Life Story
  Collection 59
National Network of
  Jewish Social Housing .16
National Religious Party 165
National Tay Sachs
  Centre 16
National Zionist Council .22
Necessitous Ladies' Fund .97
Ner Yisrael Synagogue . . .83
Netherlands. See Holland
Netzer/Reform Synagogues
  of Great Britain 49
Neveh Shalom
  Community 85
New Essex Masorti
  Congregation 83
New Israel Fund of
  Great Britain 33
New London Synagogue .82
New North London
  Synagogue 83
New Synagogue 77
New West End
  Synagogue 77
New Whetstone
  Synagogue 83
New Wimbledon and
  Putney Synagogue 80
New York 188
New Zealand 179
New Zealand, Zionist
  Federation 175, 179
Newark 123
Newbury Park
  Synagogue 77
Newcastle upon Tyne ..123
Newport (Gwent) 132
Nightingale House 97
Noah Project..........64
Noam (Noar Masorti) . . .48
Nobel Prize Winners . . .212
North Finchley Synagogue.
  See Woodside Park
  Synagogue

North Hendon Adath
  Synagogue 82
North London Progressive
  Synagogue 87
North-West London
  Jewish Day School 93
North-West Surrey
  Synagogue (Reform) . . .86
North-Western Reform
  Synagogue 86
North Yemen 180
Northampton 124
Northern Ireland 135
Northwood and Pinner
  Liberal Synagogue 87
Northwood Synagogue ..77
Norway 180
Norwich 124
Norwood Child Care . . .97
Norwood Ravenswood ..97
Notting Hill Synagogue ..80
Nottingham 124

O

Obituary 313-14
Ohel David Synagogue ..85
Ohel Israel Synagogue ...82
Ohel Jacob Beth
  Hamedrash 80
Ombudsman 13
Operation Judaism 65
Operation Wheelchairs
  Committee 33
Organisations Concerned
  with Soviet Jewry ..19-20
Order of Merit 212
ORT 13, 74, 168
ORT House Conference
  Centre 4
Orthodox Hebrew
  Congregations, Union of .11
Otto Schiff Housing
  Association 16
Oxford 125
Oxford Centre for Hebrew
  & Jewish Studies 44
Oxford Institute for
  Yiddish Studies 45
Oxford & St. George's
  Jewish Centre 100

P

Pakistan 180
Palmers Green &
  Southgate Synagogue ..77
Panama 180
Paraguay 180
Pardes House Schools . . .93
Paris 152
Parkes Library 55
Parliament, Members of 209

Passover Flour,
  Conjoint Committee 8
Peers 209
Pensions Fund, Jewish
  Memorial Council 9
Persian Synagogue
  (London) 85
Perth (Australia) 140
Peru 180
Peterborough 79, 125
Philippines 179
Physically Handicapped,
  Jewish Association for
  the 94
Pinner Synagogue 77
Plashet Cemetery 89
Plymouth 125
Poale Agudat Israel 34
Poale Zion 22
Polack's House, Clifton
  College 40, 108
Poland 181
Polish-Jewish Ex-
  Servicemen's
  Association 19
Polish Jewish Refugee
  Fund 19
Populations, Jewish ..194-9
Porath Yosef Synagogue ..83
Porton Library 59
Portsmouth 125
Portugal 181
Potters Bar
  Synagogue 79, 126
Prague 149
Press 5
Preston 126
Prisoners' Memorial 89
Privy Counsellors 209
Pro-Zion: Progressive
  Religious Zionists 23
Professional
  Organisations 59-60
Progressive Jewish Marriage
  Bureau 16
Progressive Jews for
  Israel 31
Progressive Judaism
  World Union for 74
Progressive Judaism in
  Israel & in Europe,
  Friends of 31
Progressive Synagogues,
  Union of Liberal and ..12
Project SEED Europe . . .40
Provincial Hebrew
  Classes Committee 9
Provincial Jewish
  Ministers' Fund 60
Public Schools'
  Committee 9
Puerto Rico 181

Q

QMW Programme for
Yiddish & Ashkenazic
Studies 45
Queen's Elm Parade
Cemetery 89
Quito 150

R

Rabbinic Conference
(Liberal) 13, 61
Rabbinical Commission
for the Licensing of
Shochetim 10
Rabbinical Council of
East London and West
Essex 61
Rabbinical Council of
the Provinces 61
Rabbinical Council of
United Synagogue 61
Rabbinical Court
(Reform) 12
Radio Programmes
(U.K.) 7
Radlett 77, 87, 126
Rainham Cemetery 89
Rambam Medical Centre,
British Friends of 27
Ramsgate 85
Raphael Centre 98
Rav Rashi (Federation) . .10
Ravenswood Foundation.
See Norwood
Ravenswood
Reading 126
Redbridge Jewish
Programme &
Materials Project 100
Redbridge Jewish Youth &
Community Centre . . .100
Redhill (see Reigate)
Reform Foundation 12
Reform & Liberal
Association of
Mohalim 13
Reform Students 53
Reform Synagogues of
Great Britain . . . 12, 85-7
Reform Synagogue
Youth/Netzer 49
Refugee
Organisations 17-19
Refugees, Association of
Jewish 17
Reigate & Redhill 127
Religious Instruction at
Schools 43
Religious Organisations
(U.K.) 7-13

Religious Organisations,
London 87
Representative Councils . .2
Representative
Organisations 1-4
Research Unit, Board of
Deputies 1
Richmond Synagogue . . .77
Riga 176
Rio de Janeiro 143
Rishon Multiple
Sclerosis Aid Group . . .98
Ritual Baths 88
Romania 182
Rome 175
Romford Synagogue 79
Rosario (Argentina) 137
Rosh Pina Jewish
Schools 92
Roth Collection 55
Rowan Road Cemetery . .89
Royal British Legion
Monash Branch 65
Royal Fusiliers
Memorial 89
Royal Society, Fellows . .211
R.S.G.B. 12
RSGB Israel Action 34
RSY-Netzer 48
Ruislip Synagogue 79
Russia 147

S

Saatchi Synagogue 84
Sabbath Observance
Employment Bureau . . .88
St. Albans 79, 83, 126
St. Anne's-on-Sea 127
St. John's Wood
Synagogue 77
St. Petersburg 147
Salford. See Manchester
San Jose 147
Sandy's Row Synagogue .84
Santiago (Chile) 146
Santo Domingo 150
Sao Paulo 143
Sarah Herzog Memorial
Hospital, British
Friends 27
Sarajevo 143
Scandinavian Zionist
Federation 175
Scholarships, Jewish
Memorial Council 9
Schonfeld Square
Development 94
School of Oriental &
African Studies 45
Library 59
Schools & Colleges. See
Educational Organisations

Schools' J-Link 90
Schools, Sabbath
Observance in 90
Scopus Jewish Educational
Trust 40, 93, 114, 116
Scotland 132-5
Legislation 206
Scottish Council of Jewish
Communities 132
Scottish Jewish Archives 132
Sebba Rosh Pina
Nursery School 93
Sephardi Burial Society . .85
Sephardi Centre 41
Library 60
Sephardi Communal
Centre 85
Sephardi Kashrut
Authority 85
Sephardi Synagogues 84
Sephardi Welfare Board . .85
Settlement Synagogue . . .87
Shaare Zedek Medical
Centre, Jerusalem,
British Council of 26
Shamir Organisation . . .167
Shanghai 147
SHAPE International
Jewish Community . . .142
Sharon Kindergarten 93
Shasha Library 60
Shatnez Centre Trust 65
Shechita Board, London .88
Shechita Boards,
National Council of . . .10
Shechita Committee,
Board of Deputies 1
Sheffield 127
Shelter,
Jews' Temporary 97
Sherman, Harry & Abe,
Rosh Pinah Jewish
Primary School 92
Shochetim, Rabbinical
Commission for the
Licensing of 9
Shomerim,
Association of 59
Shomrei Hadath
Synagogue 80
Sidrot and Haftarot for
2001 344-5
Silver Street Cemetery . . .89
Simon Marks Jewish
Primary School 92
Simon Wiesenthal Centre,
European Office 73
Sinai Synagogue 80
Sinclair House 100
Singapore 182
Singer's Prayer Book
Publication
Committee 10

Sir Max Bonn Memorial
Centre 49
Sir Moses Montefiore
Synagogue 85, 110
Sixth-Formers,
Association of Jewish . .53
Slovakia 182
Slovenia 183
Small Communities
Committee of Jewish
Memorial Council 10
SOAS 45
Library 59
Society for Jewish Study .41
Society of Friends of
Jewish Refugees 19
Society of Friends of the
Torah 66
Solihull 127
South Africa 183-4
South Bucks Liberal
Jewish Community . . .103
South Hampshire Reform
Jewish Community . . .130
South Hampstead
Synagogue 77
South Korea 184
South London
Communal Council . . .61
South London Liberal
Synagogue 88
South London
Synagogue 77
South Shields 127
South Tottenham
Synagogue 77
South-West Essex
Reform Synagogue 87
Southampton 127
Southend &
Westcliff 128-9
Southgate Progressive
Synagogue 88
Southgate Reform
Synagogue 87
Southgate Synagogue,
Palmers Green and 77
Southport 129
Southsea. See Portsmouth
Soviet Jewry, National
Council for 19
Spain 184
Spanish & Portuguese Jews'
Congregation . . .10, 84-5
Archive 59
Spec Jewish Youth &
Community Centre . . .101
Spectrum (Radio) 6
Spiro Ark 41
Spiro Institute 41
Springboard Education
Trust 41

Springfield Synagogue . . .80
Sri Lanka 185
Staines 79, 129
Stamford Hill Beth
Hamedrash 80
Stamford Hill
Community Centre 98
Stanislowa Beth
Hamedrash 82
Stanley Burton Centre
for Holocaust Studies . .45
Stanmore & Canons
Park Synagogue 78
State of Israel Bonds 34
Statistical & Demographic
Research Unit, Board
of Deputies 1
Statistics, Jewish 194-9
Stepney Jewish B'nai
B'rith Clubs and
Settlement 101
Sternberg Centre for
Judaism 13
Other organisations
located at this address:
Council of Reform &
Liberal Rabbis 13
Israel Action 32
Leo Baeck College .40, 58
London Museum of
Jewish Life 57
Manor House Centre for
Psychotherapy &
Counselling 15
Manor House Media . .41
Manor House Society . .99
Michael Goulston
Educational
Foundation 41
Pro-Zion: Progressive
Religious Zionists . . .23
Reform & Liberal
Association of
Mohalim 13
Reform Synagogues of
Great Britain 12, 85
Reform Synagogue
Youth/Netzer 49
Stockholm 185
Stoke-on-Trent 130
Students Jewish,
organisations
concerned with 53-4
Students,
Union of Jewish 54
Students, World Union
of Jewish 74
Sukkath Shalom Reform
Synagogue 86
Sunderland 130
Sunridge Housing
Association 98

Support Group for Parents
of Jewish Gays and
Lesbians 65
Surinam 185
Survey of the Jewish Built
Heritage 5
Sutton Synagogue 79
Swansea 132
Sweden 185
Swindon 130
Switzerland 185
Sydney, Australia 139
Synagogue Française de
Londres 84
Synagogue Secretaries'
Association 61
Syria 186

T

Taiwan 186
Tay-Sachs Screening
Centre 17
Taylor-Schechter
Geniza Collection.
See Cambridge
Technion 166
Technion Society, British. .28
Tehilla 34
Tehran 157
Tel Aviv University 168
Trust 34
Temporary Shelter, Jews .97
Thailand 187
Thames Valley Progressive
Jewish Community
(Reading) 126
Thanet & District Reform
Jewish Community
(Margate) 122
The 35s 20
Three Faiths Forum 4
Torah Centre Trust 93
Torquay (Torbay) 130
Tottenham Congregation
and Talmud Torah 80
Trade Union Friends of
Israel 34
Trades Advisory Council . .2
Trinidad 187
Tunisia 187
Turkey 187
Tzedek 65

U

UJIA 23, 174
UK Society for the
Protection of Nature
in Israel 34
Ukraine 188
ULPS 13, 87-8
Evening Institute 36

Youth Dept. 49
Union of Jewish
  Students 53
Progressive Synagogues
  (ULPS) 13
Union of Maccabi
  Associations 49
Union of Orthodox
  Hebrew
  Congregations . . .11, 81-2
United Kingdom Jewish
  Aid and International
  Development
  (UKJAID) 65
United Kingdom
  Legislation
  Concerning Jews . . .203-6
United Mizrahi Bank
  Ltd. 35
United Nations
  (Jewish Organisations
  with consultative
  status) 66
United Nations, Israel
  Representations at . . .159
United States of
  America 188-91
United Synagogue . .8, 76-9
United Synagogue
  Secretaries'
  Association 61
United Synagogue
  Women, Association of .87
United Zionists of Great
  Britain 23
University Centres &
  Orgs. 42-6
University College
  London 46
University Jewish
  Chaplaincy Board 54
University Scholarships . . .9
Uruguay 191

V

Venezuela 191
Victoria Community
  Centre 99
Victoria Crosses, Jewish 212
Vienna 140
Vilnius 177
Virgin Islands 192
Visitation Committee 8, 102
  Hospital Visitors
  Branch 102

W

Wales 131
Waley Cohen Memorial
  Scholarship, Sir Robert . .9

Walford Road
  Synagogue 83
Wallasey 130
Waltham Abbey
  Cemetery 89
Waltham Forest
  Synagogue 81, 84
Wanstead & Woodford
  Synagogue 79
Warsaw 181
Watford Synagogue 78
Waverley Manor 95
Weizmann Institute,
  Rehovot 166
  Foundation 35
Welfare Organisations
  (London) 94-8
  (U.K.) 13-17
Wellington
  (New Zealand) 179
Welshpool 132
Welwyn Garden
  City 79, 130
Wembley Sephardi
  Synagogue 85
Wembley Synagogue 78
West Central Liberal
  Jewish Synagogue 88
West End Great
  Synagogue 81, 83
West Hackney
  Synagogue 81
West Ham Cemetery 90
West Ham & Upton Park
  Synagogue 78
West London
  Synagogue 85
Westcliff. See Southend
Western Charitable
  Foundation 101
Western Marble Arch
  Synagogue 78, 84
Western Synagogue
  Cemetery 90
Westlon Housing
  Association 98
Westlon Trust 98
Westminster Synagogue . .84
Westmount Charitable
  Trust 98
Westmount Housing
  Association 98
Whitley Bay 130
Who's Who 213-312
Wiener Library 56
Willesden & Brondesbury
  Synagogue 78
Willesden Cemetery 90
Wimbledon Synagogue
  (Reform) 87
Wimbledon, New
  Synagogue
  (Federation) 80

Winchester 131
Windsor 129
Wingate Institute 168
Wingate Youth Trust 54
WIZO 21
Wolfson Hillel Primary
  School 93
Wolverhampton 131
Women, International
  Council of Jewish 70
Women,
  League of Jewish 4
Women Zionists,
  Federation of 21
Women's Campaign for
  Soviet Jewry (The 35s) .20
Women's International
  Zionist
  Organisation 21, 170
Women's Organisations
  (UK)
Association of Jewish
  Ex-Service Men &
  Women 62
Association of
  Jewish Women's
  Organisations 3
Association of
  United Synagogue
  Women 88
Ezrath Nashim
  Hospital 27
Federation of Women
  Zionists 21
Half-Empty Bookcase . .99
Jewish Feminist Group . .64
Jewish Nurses & Midwives
  Association 60
Jewish Women's Aid . . .16
League of Jewish
  Women 4
The 35s 20
Women Zionists,
  Federation of 21
Women's Organisations,
  Association of Jewish . . .3
Woodford Progressive
  Synagogue 88
Woodside Park
  Synagogue 78
Working Party on
  Jewish Archives in
  the United Kingdom &
  Ireland 5
Working Party on Jewish
  Monuments in the UK
  & Ireland 5
World Council of
  Conservative/Masorti
  Synagogues 74
World Jewish Congress . .74
World Jewish Relief 17
World ORT Union 74

World Union for
Progressive Judaism . . .75
World Union of Jewish
Students 75
World Zionist
Organisation 23, 170

Y

Yad Sarah, Friends of 31
Yad Vashem 171
Committee, Board of
Deputies 1
Yad Voezer 98
Yahrzeit Dates 348-61
Yakar
Study Centre 42
Synagogue 84
Yarnton Manor 44
Yavneh Synagogue 80
Year, The Jewish 326
Yeshiva Etz Chaim 93
Yeshiva Gedola 93
Yeshiva Horomoh Beth
Hamedrash 83
Yeshivat Dvar
Yerushalayim, Friends
of, ...31

Yeshuath Chaim
Synagogue 82
Yeshurun Synagogue 80
Yesodey Hatorah Schools . .93
Yesodey Hatorah
Synagogue 82
Yiddish, Friends of 99
Yiddish Studies:
Oxford 45
QMW 46
SOAS 46
UCL 44, 57
York 131
Young Jewish
National Fund 21, 53
Young Mapam 52
Youth Aliyah, Child
Rescue 35
Youth & Hechalutz
Department, World
Zionist Organisation . . .24
Youth, Organisations
concerned with
Jewish 46-53
Yugoslavia (Serbia) 192

Z

Zaire 192
Zagreb 148
Zambia 192
Zangwill (Israel)
Memorial Fund 37
Zemel Choir 101
Zimbabwe 192
Zinman College of
Physical Education . . .168
Zionist Council of
Europe 75
Zionist Federation of
Great Britain &
Ireland 24
Zionist Organisation,
World 170
Zionist Organisations . . .20-4
Zionist Youth Groups
. 50-3
Zionist Youth,
Federation of 50
Zurich 186

JEWISH
CARE

ALL OF THE FOLLOWING ORGANISATIONS AND AGENCIES NOW
COME UNDER THE UMBRELLA OF JEWISH CARE:

- JEWISH WELFARE BOARD -
- JEWISH BLIND SOCIETY -
- JEWISH HOME AND HOSPITAL AT TOTTENHAM -
- FOOD FOR THE JEWISH POOR (SOUP KITCHEN) -
- BRITISH TAY-SACHS FOUNDATION -
- WAVERLEY MANOR
(FRIENDS OF THE LONDON JEWISH HOSPITAL) -
- BRIGHTON & HOVE JEWISH HOME -
- STEPNEY JEWISH (B'NAI B'RITH) CLUBS & SETTLEMENTS -
- SINCLAIR HOUSE - REDBRIDGE JEWISH
YOUTH & COMMUNITY CENTRE -

FOR MORE INFORMATION CALL 0181 922 2000

Jewish Care: one big family.

JEWISH CARE REGISTERED OFFICE: STUART YOUNG HOUSE, 221 GOLDERS GREEN ROAD, LONDON NW11 9DQ TELEPHONE: 0181 922 2000. FAX: 0181 922 1998 CHARITY REGISTRATION NUMBER 802559 JEWISH CARE IS A COMPANY LIMITED BY GUARANTEE REGISTERED IN ENGLAND NUMBER 2447900